# Contemporary
# Literary Criticism

# Guide to Gale Literary Criticism Series

| For criticism on | Consult these Gale series |
|---|---|
| Authors now living or who died after December 31, 1959 | *CONTEMPORARY LITERARY CRITICISM (CLC)* |
| Authors who died between 1900 and 1959 | *TWENTIETH-CENTURY LITERARY CRITICISM (TCLC)* |
| Authors who died between 1800 and 1899 | *NINETEENTH-CENTURY LITERATURE CRITICISM (NCLC)* |
| Authors who died between 1400 and 1799 | *LITERATURE CRITICISM FROM 1400 TO 1800 (LC)*<br><br>*SHAKESPEAREAN CRITICISM (SC)* |
| Authors who died before 1400 | *CLASSICAL AND MEDIEVAL LITERATURE CRITICISM (CMLC)* |
| Black writers of the past two hundred years | *BLACK LITERATURE CRITICISM (BLC)* |
| Authors of books for children and young adults | *CHILDREN'S LITERATURE REVIEW (CLR)* |
| Dramatists | *DRAMA CRITICISM (DC)* |
| Hispanic writers of the late nineteenth and twentieth centuries | *HISPANIC LITERATURE CRITICISM (HLC)* |
| Native North American writers and orators of the eighteenth, nineteenth, and twentieth centuries | *NATIVE NORTH AMERICAN LITERATURE (NNAL)* |
| Poets | *POETRY CRITICISM (PC)* |
| Short story writers | *SHORT STORY CRITICISM (SSC)* |
| Major authors from the Renaissance to the present | *WORLD LITERATURE CRITICISM, 1500 TO THE PRESENT (WLC)* |

ISSN 0091-3421

Volume 92

# Contemporary Literary Criticism

Excerpts from Criticism of the Works
of Today's Novelists, Poets, Playwrights,
Short Story Writers, Scriptwriters, and
Other Creative Writers

**Brigham Narins**
**Debbie Stanley**
EDITORS

**George Blair**
**Jeff Chapman**
**Polly A. Vedder**
**Kathleen Wilson**
**Janet Witalec**
ASSOCIATE EDITORS

GALE

DETROIT · NEW YORK · TORONTO · LONDON

## STAFF

Library of Congress Catalog Card Number 76-46132
ISBN 0-8103-9270-4
ISSN 0276-8178

Printed in the United States of America
10  9  8  7  6  5  4  3  2  1

# Contents

Preface  vii

Acknowledgments  xi

# Preface

## A Comprehensive Information Source on Contemporary Literature

Named "one of the twenty-five most distinguished reference titles published during the past twenty-five years" by *Reference Quarterly,* the *Contemporary Literary Criticism (CLC)* series provides readers with critical commentary and general information on more than 2,000 authors now living or who died after December 31, 1959. Previous to the publication of the first volume of *CLC* in 1973, there was no ongoing digest monitoring scholarly and popular sources of critical opinion and explication of modern literature. *CLC,* therefore, has fulfilled an essential need, particularly since the complexity and variety of contemporary literature makes the function of criticism especially important to today's reader.

## Scope of the Series

*CLC* presents significant passages from published criticism of works by creative writers. Since many of the authors covered by *CLC* inspire continual critical commentary, writers are often represented in more than one volume. There is, of course, no duplication of reprinted criticism.

Authors are selected for inclusion for a variety of reasons, among them the publication or dramatic production of a critically acclaimed new work, the reception of a major literary award, revival of interest in past writings, or the adaptation of a literary work to film or television.

Attention is also given to several other groups of writers-authors of considerable public interest—about whose work criticism is often difficult to locate. These include mystery and science fiction writers, literary and social critics, foreign writers, and authors who represent particular ethnic groups within the United States.

## Format of the Book

Each *CLC* volume contains about 500 individual excerpts taken from hundreds of book review periodicals, general magazines, scholarly journals, monographs, and books. Entries include critical evaluations spanning from the beginning of an author's career to the most current commentary. Interviews, feature articles, and other published writings that offer insight into the author's works are also presented. Students, teachers, librarians, and researchers will find that the generous excerpts and supplementary material in *CLC* provide them with vital information required to write a term paper, analyze a poem, or lead a book discussion group. In addition, complete bibliographical citations note the original source and all of the information necessary for a term paper footnote or bibliography.

## Features

A *CLC* author entry consists of the following elements:

- The **Author Heading** cites the author's name in the form under which the author has most commonly published, followed by birth date, and death date when applicable. Uncertainty as to a birth or death date is indicated by a question mark.

- A **Portrait** of the author is included when available.

- A brief **Biographical and Critical Introduction** to the author and his or her work precedes the excerpted criticism. The first line of the introduction provides the author's full name, pseudonyms (if applicable), nationality, and a listing of genres in which the author has written. To provide users with easier access to information, the biographical and critical essay included in each author entry is divided into four categories: "Introduction," "Biographical Information," "Major Works," and "Critical Reception." The introductions to single-work entries—entries that focus on well known and frequently studied books, short stories, and poems—are similarly organized to quickly provide readers with information on the plot and major characters of the work being discussed, its major themes, and its critical reception. Previous volumes of *CLC* in which the author has been featured are also listed in the introduction.

- A list of **Principal Works** notes the most important writings by the author. When foreign-language works have been translated into English, the English-language version of the title follows in brackets.

- The **Excerpted Criticism** represents various kinds of critical writing, ranging in form from the brief review to the scholarly exegesis. Essays are selected by the editors to reflect the spectrum of opinion about a specific work or about an author's literary career in general. The excerpts are presented chronologically, adding a useful perspective to the entry. All titles by the author featured in the entry are printed in boldface type, which enables the reader to easily identify the works being discussed. Publication information (such as publisher names and book prices) and parenthetical numerical references (such as footnotes or page and line references to specific editions of a work) have been deleted at the editor's discretion to provide smoother reading of the text.

- Critical essays are prefaced by **Explanatory Notes** as an additional aid to readers. These notes may provide several types of valuable information, including: the reputation of the critic, the importance of the work of criticism, the commentator's approach to the author's work, the purpose of the criticism, and changes in critical trends regarding the author.

- A complete **Bibliographical Citation** designed to help the user find the original essay or book precedes each excerpt.

- Whenever possible, a recent, previously unpublished **Author Interview** accompanies each entry.

- A concise **Further Reading** section appears at the end of entries on authors for whom a significant amount of criticism exists in addition to the pieces reprinted in *CLC*. Each citation in this section is accompanied by a descriptive annotation describing the content of that article. Materials included in this section are grouped under various headings (e.g., Biography, Bibliography, Criticism, and Interviews) to aid users in their search for additional information. Cross-references to other useful sources published by Gale Research in which the author has appeared are also included: *Authors in the News, Black Writers, Children's Literature Review, Contemporary Authors, Dictionary of Literary Biography, DISCovering Authors, Drama Criticism, Hispanic Literature Criticism, Hispanic Writers, Native North American Literature, Poetry Criticism, Something about the Author, Short Story Criticism, Contemporary Authors Autobiography Series,* and *Something about the Author Autobiography Series.*

# Other Features

*CLC* also includes the following features:

- An **Acknowledgments** section lists the copyright holders who have granted permission to reprint material in this volume of *CLC*. It does not, however, list every book or periodical reprinted or consulted during the preparation of the volume.

- Each new volume of *CLC* includes a **Cumulative Topic Index,** which lists all literary topics treated in *CLC, NCLC, TCLC,* and *LC 1400-1800.*

- A **Cumulative Author Index** lists all the authors who have appeared in the various literary criticism series published by Gale Research, with cross-references to Gale's biographical and autobiographical series. A full listing of the series referenced there appears on the first page of the indexes of this volume. Readers will welcome this cumulated author index as a useful tool for locating an author within the various series. The index, which lists birth and death dates when available, will be particularly valuable for those authors who are identified with a certain period but whose death dates cause them to be placed in another, or for those authors whose careers span two periods. For example, Ernest Hemingway is found in *CLC,* yet F. Scott Fitzgerald, a writer often associated with him, is found in *Twentieth-Century Literary Criticism.*

- A **Cumulative Nationality Index** alphabetically lists all authors featured in *CLC* by nationality, followed by numbers corresponding to the volumes in which the authors appear.

- An alphabetical **Title Index** accompanies each volume of *CLC*. Listings are followed by the author's name and the corresponding page numbers where the titles are discussed. English translations of foreign titles and variations of titles are cross-referenced to the title under which a work was originally published. Titles of novels, novellas, dramas, films, record albums, and poetry, short story, and essay collections are printed in italics, while all individual poems, short stories, essays, and songs are printed in roman type within quotation marks; when published separately (e.g., T. S. Eliot's poem *The Waste Land),* the titles of long poems are printed in italics.

- In response to numerous suggestions from librarians, Gale has also produced a **Special Paperbound Edition** of the *CLC* title index. This annual cumulation, which alphabetically lists all titles reviewed in the series, is available to all customers and is typically published with every fifth volume of *CLC*. Additional copies of the index are available upon request. Librarians and patrons will welcome this separate index: it saves shelf space, is easy to use, and is recyclable upon receipt of the next edition.

## Citing *Contemporary Literary Criticism*

When writing papers, students who quote directly from any volume in the Literary Criticism Series may use the following general forms to footnote reprinted criticism. The first example pertains to material drawn from periodicals, the second to material reprinted in books:

[1]Alfred Cismaru, "Making the Best of It," *The New Republic,* 207, No. 24, (December 7, 1992), 30, 32; excerpted and reprinted in *Contemporary Literary Criticism,* Vol. 85, ed. Christopher Giroux (Detroit: Gale Research, 1995), pp. 73-4.

[2]Yvor Winters, *The Post-Symbolist Methods* (Allen Swallow, 1967); excerpted and reprinted in *Contemporary Literary Criticism,* Vol. 85, ed. Christopher Giroux (Detroit: Gale Research, 1995), pp. 223-26.

# Suggestions Are Welcome

The editor hopes that readers will find *CLC* a useful reference tool and welcomes comments about the work. Send comments and suggestions to: Editor, *Contemporary Literary Criticism,* Gale Research, Penobscot Building, Detroit, MI 48226-4094.

# Acknowledgments

The editors wish to thank the copyright holders of the excerpted criticism included in this volume, the permissions managers of many book and journal publishing companies for assisting us in securing reprint rights, and Anthony Bogucki for assistance with copyright research. We are also grateful to the staffs of the Detroit Public Library, the Library of Congress, the University of Detroit Mercy Library, Wayne State University Purdy/Kresge Library Complex, and the University of Michigan Libraries for making their resources available to us. Following is a list of the copyright holders who have granted us permission to reprint material in this volume of *CLC*. Every effort has been made to trace copyright, but if omissions have been made, please let us know.

## COPYRIGHTED EXCERPTS IN *CLC,* VOLUME 92, WERE REPRINTED FROM THE FOLLOWING PERIODICALS:

*A/B: Auto/Biography Studies*, Fall, 1992. Reprinted by permission of the publisher.—*American Book Review,* v. 6, March-April, 1984; v. 12, November-December, 1990; v. 14, June-July, 1992. © 1984, 1984, 1992 by *The American Book Review*. All reprinted by permission of the publisher.—*Belles Lettres: A Review of Books by Women*, v. 2, July-August, 1987; v. 9, Spring, 1994. Both reprinted by permission of the publisher.—*Black American Literature Forum*, v. 21, Spring-Summer, 1987 for "Work and Culture: The Evolution of Consciousness in Urban Industrial Society in the Fiction of William Attaway and Peter Abrahams" by Cynthia Hamilton. Copyright © 1987 Indiana State University./v. 23, Spring, 1989 for a review of "Segu" by Phiefer L. Browne. Copyright © 1989 Indiana State University. Both reprinted by permission of Indiana State University and the authors.—*The Black Scholar*, v. 17, July/August, 1986. Copyright 1986 by *The Black Scholar*. Reprinted by permission of the publisher.—*The Bloomsbury Review*, v. 11, January-February, 1991 for "Welcome to the '90s" by William Severini Kowinski. Copyright © by Owaissa Communications Company, Inc. 1991. Reprinted by permission of the author./v. 13, July-August, 1993 for an interview with Mark Leyner by John Bellante and Carl Bellante. Copyright © by Owaissa Communications Company, Inc., 1993. Reprinted by permission of Mark Leyner, John Bellante, and Carl Bellante.—*Books in Canada*, v. 18, March, 1989 for "No Wings, Yet" by Carol Bolt. Reprinted by permission of the author.—*Border Crossings*, v. 11, December, 1992. Reprinted by permission of the author and the publisher.—*Callaloo*, v. 12, Winter, 1989 for "I Have Made Peace With My Island" by VeVe A. Clark./v. 14, Spring, 1991 for "The Semiotics of Exile in Maryse Condé's Fictional Works" by Arlette M. Smith./v. 15, Winter, 1992 for "Narrative and Discursive Strategies in Maryse Condé's 'Traversee de la mangrove'" by Suzanne Crosta./v. 15, Winter, 1992 for "Mapping the Mangrove: Empathy and Survival in 'Traversee de la mangrove'" by Ellen W. Munley. Copyright © 1989, 1991, 1992 by Charles H. Rowell. All rights reserved. All reprinted by permission of the authors.—*Canadian Literature*, n. 68-9, Spring-Summer, 1976 for an interview with Hugh MacLennan by Ronald Sutherland. Reprinted by permission of the author./n. 75, Winter, 1977 for "A Neglected Theme in 'Two Solitudes'" by Warren Stevenson. Reprinted by permission of the author./nos. 124-125, Spring-Summer, 1990 for "Lines and Circles: The 'Rez' Plays of Tomson Highway" by Denis W. Johnston. Reprinted by permission of the author./n. 128, Spring, 1991 for Faith and Fiction: Hugh MacLennan's "The Watch That Ends the Night" by Barbara Pell. Reprinted by permission of the author./n. 144, Spring, 1995 for "On the Road with Tomson Highway's Blues Harmonica in 'Dry Lips Oughta Move to Kapuskasing'" by Roberta Imboden. Reprinted by permission of the author.—*Canadian Theatre Review*, n. 65, Winter, 1990 for a review of "The Rez Sisters" by William Peel. Copyright © 1990, by the author. Reprinted by permission of the author.—*CLA Journal*, v. XV, June, 1972; v. 32, September, 1988. Copyright, 1972, 1988 by The College Language Association. Used by permission of The College Language Association.—*College Literature*, v. 18, October, 1991; v. 19, October, 1992; v. 20, February, 1993. Copyright © 1991, 1992, 1993 by West Chester University. Reprinted by permission of the publisher.— *Commentary*, v. 7, June, 1949 for "Men at War" by George J. Becker. Copyright © 1949 by the American Jewish Committee. All rights reserved. Reprinted by permission of the publisher and the author.—*Contemporary Literature*, v. 15, Spring, 1974. © 1974 by the Regents of the University of Wisconsin. Reprinted by permission of The University of Wisconsin Press.—*Film Quarterly*, v. XV, Spring, 1962. © 1962 by The Regents of the University of California. Reprinted by permission of The Regents of the University of California.—*Forum for Modern Language Studies*, v. II, April, 1966 for "Leonid Leonov" by R. D. B. Thomson. Copyright © 1966 by Forum for Modern Language Studies and the author. Reprinted by permission of the publisher and the author.—*The Globe and Mail*, Toronto, November 21,

**COPYRIGHTED EXCERPTS IN *CLC*, VOLUME 92, WERE REPRINTED FROM THE FOLLOWING BOOKS:**

Alazraki, Jaime. From an introduction to ***The Final Island: The Fiction of Julio Cortázar***. Edited by Jaime Alazraki and Ivar Ivask. University of Oklahoma Press, 1978. Copyright 1976 and 1978 by the University of Oklahoma Press, Publishing Division of the University. Reprinted by permission of the publisher.—Alexandrova, Vera. From ***A History of Literature: 1917-1954, Gorky to Solzhenitsyn***. Doubleday, 1963. Copyright © 1963, 1964 by Vera Alexandrova-Schwarz. All rights reserved.—Barthold, Bonnie J. From ***Black Time: Fiction of Africa, the Caribbean, and the United States***. Yale University Press, 1981. Copyright © 1981 by Yale University Press. All rights reserved. Reprinted by permission of the publisher.—Bataille, Gretchen M., and Kathleen Mullen Sands. From ***American Indian Women: Telling Their Lives***. University of Nebraska Press, 1984. Copyright 1984 by the University of Nebraska Press. All rights reserved. Reprinted by permission of the publisher.—Bracher, Frederick. From ***The Novels of James Gould Cozzens***. Harcourt, Brace and Company, 1959. © 1959 by Frederick Bracher. Reprinted by permission of Harcourt Brace & Company.—Cixous, Hélène. From ***"Coming to Writing" and Other Essays***. Cambridge Mass.: Harvard University Press, 1989.—Cixous, Hélène. From ***The Critical Tradition: Classic Texts and Contemporary Trends***. Edited by David H. Richter. St. Martin's Press, 1989. Copyright © 1989 by St. Martin's Press, Inc.—Conley, Verena Andermatt. From ***Hélène Cixous: Writing the Feminine***. University of Nebraska Press, 1984. Reprinted by permission of the publisher.—Cockburn, Robert H. From ***The Novels of Hugh MacLennan***. Copyright © Canada 1969 by Harvest House Ltd. All rights reserved. Reprinted by permission of the publisher.—Fielder, Jean, and Jim Mele. From ***Isaac Asimov***. Ungar, 1982. Copyright © 1982 by Frederick Ungar Publishing Co., Inc. Reprinted by permission of the publisher.—Gorky, Maxim. From a foreword to ***Soviet River***. By Leonid Leonov, translated by Ivor Montagu and Sergei Nolbandov. Dial Press, 1932. Copyright 1932 by Dial Press, Inc.—Harjan, George. From ***Leonid Leonov: A Critical Study***. Arowhena Publishing Co., 1979. Copyright © 1979 by George Harjan, including for translation. All rights reserved. Reprinted by permission of the publisher.—Jenson, Deborah. From ***"Coming to Writing" and Other Essays***. Cambridge Mass.: Harvard University Press, 1991. Copyright © 1991 by the President and Fellows of Harvard College. Excerpted by permission of the publishers and the author.—Kerr, Lucille. From ***Reclaiming the Author: Figures and Fictions from Spanish America***. Duke University Press, 1992. © 1992 Lucille Kerr. All rights reserved. Reprinted with permission of the publisher.—Lucas, Alec. From ***Hugh MacLennan***. McClelland and Stewart Limited, 1970. © 1970 by McClelland and Stewart Limited. All rights reserved. Used by permission of The Canadian Publishers, McClelland and Stewart Limited, Toronto.—Lurie, Nancy Oestreich. From a preface and appendix in ***Mountain Wolf Woman, Sister of Crashing Thunder: The Autobiography of a Winnebago Indian***. The University of Michigan Press, 1961. Copyright © by the University of Michigan 1961. All rights reserved. Reprinted by permission of the publisher.—Mac Adam, Alfred J. From ***Modern Latin American Narratives: The Dreams of Reason***. The University of Chicago Press, 1977. © 1977 by the University of Chicago. All rights reserved. Reprinted by permission of the publisher and the author.—Margolies, Edward. From ***Native Sons: A Critical Study of the Twentieth-Century Negro American Authors***. J. B. Lippincott, 1968. Copyright © 1968 Edward Margolies. All rights reserved. Reprinted by permission of the Author's Representative, Gunther Stuhlmann.—Moi, Toril. From "Hélène Cixous: An Imaginary Utopia," in ***Sexual/Textual Politics: Feminist Literary Theory***. Methuen, 1985. © 1985 Toril Moi. Reprinted by permission of the publisher.—Morley, Patricia A. From ***The Immoral Moralists: Hugh MacLennan and Leonard Cohen***. Clarke, Irwin & Company, 1972. © 1972 by Clarke, Irwin & Company Limited. Reprinted by permission of Stoddart Publishing Co. Limited, Don Mills, Ontario.—Mountain Wolf Woman. From ***Mountain Wolf Woman, Sister of Crashing Thunder: The Autobiography of a Winnebago Indian***. Edited by Nancy Oestreich Lurie. The University of Michigan Press, 1961. Copyright © by the University of Michigan 1961. All rights reserved. Reprinted by permission of the publisher.—Muchnic, Helen. From ***From Gorky to Pasternak: Six Writers in Soviet Russia***. Random House, 1961. Copyright, 1961, by Helen Muchnic. All rights reserved. Reprinted by permission of Random House, Inc.—Ortega, Julio. From ***Poetics of Change: The New Spanish-American Narrative***. Translated by Galen D. Greaser. University of Texas Press, 1984. Copyright © 1984 by the University of Texas Press. All rights reserved. Reprinted by permission of the publisher and the author.—Pasternak, James D., and F. William Howton. From an interview in ***The Image Maker***. Edited by John Henderson. Knox Press, 1971. Copyright © 1971 The Westminister Press. All rights reserved. Reprinted and used by permission of Westminister/John Knox Press.—Posner, Richard

# I, Robot

## Isaac Asimov

The following entry presents criticism on Asimov's short story collection *I, Robot* (1950). For further information on Asimov's life and works, see *CLC*, Volumes 1, 3, 9, 19, 26, and 76.

## INTRODUCTION

The author of nearly five hundred books in a wide variety of fields and genres, Asimov is renowned for his ground-breaking science fiction and for his ability to popularize or, as he called it, "translate" science for the lay reader. In *I, Robot* (1950)—a collection of nine short stories linked by key characters and themes—Asimov describes a future society in which human beings and nearly sentient robots coexist. Critics consider it a pivotal work in the development of realistic science fiction literature mainly for its elaboration of Asimov's "Three Laws of Robotics" as a viable ethical and moral code. *I, Robot* is also significant for its espousal of the benefits of technology—a rather rare position in the history of science fiction and fantastic literature, which traditionally viewed technology and science as threats to human existence.

### Plot and Major Characters

In the nine stories in *I, Robot,* Dr. Susan Calvin, a robot psychologist, explores the benefits of robots to society and illustrates some of the developmental problems encountered in creating them. The book opens with the presentation of "The Three Laws of Robotics," the ethical ground-rules for the interaction of human beings and robots. They are: "1—A robot may not injure a human being, or, through inaction, allow a human being to come to harm. 2—A robot must obey the orders given it by human beings except where such orders would conflict with the First Law. 3—A robot must protect its own existence as long as such protection does not conflict with the First or Second Law." In the first story, "Robbie," the robot is a relatively simple, nonvocal machine designed to be a nurse-maid. Gloria Weston, a small child, loves Robbie and enjoys his company, but her mother does not trust the device, even though Mr. Weston considers the robot to be both useful and safe. Eventually, Robbie is instrumental in saving Gloria's life. In "Runaround," the robot Speedy—so nicknamed because of its serial number SPD-13—is fitted with a new "positronic" brain and sent to Mercury to explore for minerals and run the Sunside Mine. While searching for a selenium pool, Speedy begins to act strangely, reciting lines from Gilbert and Sullivan, and causing Mike Donovan and Gregory Powell—robot troubleshooters, astroengineers, and recurring characters in the book—to deal with an apparently drunk robot. In "Reason," Cutie (QT-1), the robot who runs a solar power-station, has developed a kind of self-reflective con-

sciousness and begun to question its own existence. When Donovan and Powell explain to Cutie that they built and assembled "him," Cutie rejects the idea as preposterous, reasoning that intellectually inferior human beings could not have created a "being" such as "him." "Liar" introduces Herbie (RB-34), a robot with telepathic capabilities. Herbie's ability to read minds poses a threat to human dominance, and Dr. Susan Calvin expresses her concern that Herbie and similar robots might start acting on their own volition, outside of human control. "Little Lost Robot" continues to address robotic independence, as it focuses on a robot that refuses to harm a human being, but willingly allows human beings to be harmed, thus circumventing the Three Laws of Robotics. In "Escape," a super positronic robot brain, so big it has to be housed in a room rather than an anthropomorphic humanoid body, begins to express personality and emotional characteristics. As the super brain works on the problem of hyperspace travel, it concludes that any human beings attempting it would have to have their lives briefly "suspended," thus causing death. Donovan and Powell's safety is jeopardized as the brain attempts to strike a balance between its scientific mission and the First Law of Robotics that requires it to protect human life. In "Evidence," Stephen Byerley, a politician running for public office, is severely injured in an automobile accident and decides to temporarily replace himself with a robotic likeness. The robot Stephen Byerley continues the campaign and eventually wins the mayoral election. Soon after, he runs for the presidency of the Federation and is challenged by an opponent who accuses him of being a robot. In a fit of anger Byerley strikes his opponent, ostensibly proving that he is human. Dr. Calvin, however, remains doubtful. The final story, "The Evitable Conflict," describes a future world organized and run by President Byerley and four robots. Byerley is distressed to learn that errors are occurring in many areas of economic production. He is unable to understand how such sophisticated, purportedly infallible machines can make mistakes. Byerley consults Dr. Calvin who diagnoses the problem as stemming from a broadened interpretation of the First Law.

## Major Themes

*I, Robot* reflects Asimov's concern for the future of humankind in an increasingly complex technological world. By introducing The Three Laws of Robotics, Asimov emphasizes the need for ethical and moral responsibility in a world of advanced technology. But technology is also represented as a potentially profound benefit to human life, as evidenced in the nursemaid robot in "Robbie," the mining and exploration robot in "Runaround," and the four robots that run the economic, political, and social systems of the world Federation in "The Evitable Conflict." Asimov cautions, however, against allowing technology to get out of control, as seen in "Liar" where Herbie the robot begins to think and act independently. Other themes include the preservation of human freedom in a technologically controlled environment, and an exploration of the Calvinist-Puritan work ethic, portrayed through the "lives" of several robots.

## Critical Reception

The critical reception of *I, Robot* has been generally favorable. Most commentators applaud Asimov's Three Laws of Robotics, arguing that they give the stories a sense of realism and moral depth. Others praise his skill at linking nine stories together into a novelistic whole. Many critics comment on the innovative ways in which *I, Robot* opposes the traditional "Frankensteinian" view of technology and science as unholy threats to humanity. Others note his ability to tell an engaging story and his facility for combining elements of the mystery and detective genres with the conventions of science fiction. Although many critics fault Asimov's predictable characterizations and "naive" sentimentality, most credit his realistic, ethical portrayal of futuristic society in *I, Robot* as revolutionary in the science fiction genre, changing the way fantastic literature could be conceived and written.

## PRINCIPAL WORKS

*I, Robot*  (short stories)  1950
*Pebble in the Sky*  (novel)  1950
*\*Foundation*  (novel)  1951
*Biochemistry and Human Metabolism*  (nonfiction) 1952
*\*Foundation and Empire*  (novel)  1952
*\*Second Foundation*  (novel)  1953
*The Caves of Steel*  (novel)  1954
*The End of Eternity*  (novel)  1955
*The Martian Way, and Other Stories*  (short stories) 1955
*Races and People*  (nonfiction)  1955
*Inside the Atom*  (nonfiction)  1956
*The Naked Sun*  (novel)  1957
*The World of Carbon*  (nonfiction)  1958
*Words of Science and the History behind Them*  (nonfiction)  1959
*The Double Planet*  (nonfiction)  1960
*Realm of Algebra*  (nonfiction)  1961
*The Genetic Code*  (nonfiction)  1963
*The Human Body: Its Structure and Operation*  (nonfiction)  1963
*A Short History of Biology*  (nonfiction)  1964
*†The Rest of the Robots*  (novels and short stories) 1964; also published as *Eight Stories from the Rest of the Robots,* 1966
*Of Time and Space and Other Things*  (essays)  1965
*The Genetic Effects of Radiation*  (nonfiction)  1966
*The Roman Republic*  (nonfiction)  1966
*The Egyptians*  (nonfiction)  1967
*Is Anyone There?*  (essays)  1967
*Asimov's Guide to the Bible, Volume I: The Old Testament*  (nonfiction)  1968
*Words from History*  (nonfiction)  1968
*Asimov's Guide to the Bible, Volume II: The New Testament*  (nonfiction)  1969
*The Shaping of England*  (nonfiction)  1969
*Asimov's Guide to Shakespeare*  (nonfiction)  1970
*The Gods Themselves*  (novel)  1972
*Asimov's Annotated "Paradise Lost"*  (nonfiction)  1974
*Lecherous Limericks*  (poetry)  1975
*Murder at the ABA: A Puzzle in Four Days and Sixty Scenes*  (novel)  1976
*Animals of the Bible*  (nonfiction)  1978
*In Memory Yet Green: The Autobiography of Isaac Asimov, 1920-1954*  (autobiography)  1979
*In Joy Still Felt: The Autobiography of Isaac Asimov, 1954-1978*  (autobiography)  1980
*Foundation's Edge*  (novel)  1982
*The Robots of Dawn*  (novel)  1983
*The History of Physics*  (nonfiction)  1984
*Asimov's Guide to Halley's Comet*  (nonfiction)  1985
*Robots and Empire*  (novel)  1985
*The Dangers of Intelligence, and Other Science Essays*  (essays)  1986
*Foundation and Earth*  (novel)  1986
*Asimov's Annotated Gilbert and Sullivan*  (nonfiction) 1988
*Nemesis*  (novel)  1988
*Prelude to Foundation*  (novel)  1988

*Isaac Asimov: The Complete Stories* (short stories) 1990

*Isaac Asimov Laughs Again* (autobiography) 1991

*Robot Visions* (short stories) 1991

---

\*These works were collectively published as *The Foundation Trilogy: Three Classics of Science Fiction* in 1963.

†This collection contains the novels *The Caves of Steel* and *The Naked Sun.*

---

# CRITICISM

### N. M.   (review date 4 February 1951)

SOURCE: "Realm of the Spacemen," in *The New York Times Book Review,* February 4, 1951, p. 16.

[*In the following review, the critic favorably assesses* I, Robot.]

[In *I, Robot,*] it is the year 2058, with nationalism abolished and the world divided into Regions. Man is employing "positronic" atom-driven brains and has conquered inter-stellar space. Human colonies inhabit the planets. Dr. Susan Calvin, retiring robot psychologist of U. S. Robots & Mechanical Men, Inc., tells a reporter for the Interplanetary Press of the evolution of robots from the "human" interest angle.

This is an exciting science thriller, chiefly about what occurs when delicately conditioned robots are driven off balance by mathematical violations, and about man's eternal limitations. It could be fun for those whose nerves are not already made raw by the potentialities of the atomic age.

### Darko Suvin   (essay date July 1979)

SOURCE: "Three World Paradigms for SF: Asimov, Yefremov, Lem," in *Pacific Quarterly Moana,* Vol. IV, No. 3, July, 1979, pp. 271-83.

[*Suvin is an educator, critic, and author of* Metamorphoses of Science Fiction *(1979) and* Positions and Presuppositions in Science Fiction *(1988). In the following excerpt from an essay in which he examines the ethics of technology in the science fiction writings of Asimov, Ivan Yefremov, and Stanislaw Lem, he examines the development of the robots—from "doll" in the first story to "god" in the last—in* I, Robot.]

The best works of SF [Science Fiction] have long since ceased to be crude adventure studded with futuristic gadgets, whether of the "space opera" or horror-fantasy variety. In several essays, I have argued that SF is a literary genre of its own, whose necessary and sufficient conditions are the *interaction of estrangement* (*Verfremdung, ostranenie, distanciation*) and *cognition,* and whose main formal device is an *imaginative framework alternative to the author's empirical environment.* Such a genre has a span from the *romans scientifiques* of Jules Verne to the social-science-fiction of classical utopias and dystopias. Its tradition is as old as literature—as the marvelous countries and beings in tribal tales, *Gilgamesh* or Lucian—but the central figure in its modern renaissance is H.G. Wells. His international fame, kept at least as alive in Mitteleuropa and Soviet Russia as in English-speaking countries, has done very much to unify SF into a coherent international genre. Yet, no doubt, these three major cultural contexts discussed in this essay, their traditions and not always parallel development in our century, have also given rise to somewhat diverging profiles or paradigms for SF. I want here briefly to explore those paradigms in the most significant segment of post-Wellsian SF development, that after the Second World War. . . .

---

> All human beings are cardboard stereotypes compared to the more vivid robots who act as analogies to traditional human functions.
>
> —*Darko Suvin*

---

[Isaac Asimov's] *I, Robot* (1950) is a series of nine short stories detailing the development of robots "from the beginning, when the poor robots couldn't speak, to the end, when they stand between mankind and destruction." The stories are connected thematically and chronologically, and also supplied with a flimsy framework identifying them as looks backward from 2057/58 by "robopsychologist" Susan Calvin. She is being interviewed after 50 years of pioneering work at U.S. Robots and Mechanical Men, Inc., during which time the robots have won out against reactionary opposition from labour unions and "segments of religious opinion." On the surface, this is a "future history" on the model of Bellamy's sociological or Wells' biological extrapolations. It is based on two premises: first, that except for one factor human behaviour and the social system—e.g. press reporters and giant corporations—will remain unchanged; second, that the new, change-bearing factor will be the epoch-making technological discovery of "positronic brain-paths," permitting mass fabrication of robots with intelligence comparable to human. The robots are constructed so as to obey without fail Asimov's famous Three Laws of Robotics:

> 1—A robot may not injure a human being, or, through inaction, allow a human being to come to harm.
>
> 2—A robot must obey the orders given it by human beings except where such orders would conflict with the First Law.
>
> 3—A robot must protect its own existence as long as such protection does not conflict with the First or Second Law. [*I, Robot*]

Now [Stanislaw] Lem himself has persuasively demonstrated that such robots are *logically* unrealizable [in his "Robots in Science Fiction," in *SF: The Other Side of Re-*

*alism,* edited by T.D. Clarendon, 1971]. This ingenious mimicry of the Decalogue and the Kantian categorical imperative in the form of Newtonian laws cannot therefore be taken at all seriously as a basis of prophetic extrapolation, and the stories can be read only as *analogies* to very human relationships. The nine stories form a clear sequence of growing robotic capacities. In the first story, **"Robbie",** an early model is mute playmate for a little girl, and functions as a huge doll—and yet, melodramatically, as the girl's saviour. In **"Runaround",** the next model is a drunken servant who functions as a stereotyped plantation "darkie". In **"Reason",** the robot is a comic-opera idolator who functions as an immature philosopher. In **"Catch That Rabbit",** an adult, "Head of family" robot collapses under stress, analogous to a psychotic. The fifth and central story **"Liar",** is a pivot in this progression of robotic power in relation to men. By now, the new model is a telepath who is capable of turning the tables on them, and severely perturbing the life even of the leading expert Susan (incidentally, this proves the Laws of Robotics wrong). In **"Escape",** the new model is a "child genius", steering a spaceship to unknown galaxies (a feat conveniently dropped as factor of change in later stories), who behaves as a superior practical joker. In **"Evidence",** a robot undistinguishable from man becomes city mayor in a career that will lead him to become president of the Federated Regions of Earth. Finally, in **"The Evitable Conflict"** the positronic brains have grown into not only a predicting but also a manipulating machine "in absolute control of our economy"—literally, a *deus ex machina.* Thus, this clever sequence of "the Nine Ages of Robot" leads from the doll of the first to the god of the last story: and doll turning into god is a good approximate definition of fetishism, a topsy-turvy kind of technological religion. As in Saint-Simonism, of which it is a variant, there are no workers in Asimov's universe, the army and corporation bosses are only figureheads, and the real lovable heroes are the efficient engineers, including Susan Calvin, the "human engineering" expert of behaviourist psychology. In fact, all humans are cardboard stereotypes compared to the more vivid robots who act as analogies to traditional human functions. This view of the benevolent, sometimes comic but finally providential robots and their rise to absolute power amounts to a wishful parable of the sociopolitical result, correlative to presumably perfect scientific ethics. As Dostoevski's Grand Inquisitor, it chooses security over freedom in post-Depression U.S.A.

## Gorman Beauchamp (essay date Spring-Summer 1980)

SOURCE: "The Frankenstein Complex and Asimov's Robots," in *Mosaic: A Journal for the Interdisciplinary Study of Literature,* Vol. XIII, Nos. 3-4, Spring-Summer, 1980, pp. 83-94.

[*Beauchamp is an American critic and educator, who has written extensively on science fiction. In the following essay, he examines the way in which technology is characterized in Asimov's robot novels and stories, including* I, Robot.]

In 1818 Mary Shelley gave the world Dr. Frankenstein and his monster, that composite image of scientific creator and his ungovernable creation that forms one central myth of the modern age: the hubris of the scientist playing God, the nemesis that follows on such blasphemy. Just over a century later, Karel Capek, in his play *R.U.R.,* rehearsed the Frankenstein myth, but with a significant variation: the bungled attempt to create man gives way to the successful attempt to create robots; biology is superseded by engineering. Old Dr. Rossum, (as the play's expositor relates) "attempted by chemical synthesis to imitate the living matter known as protoplasm." Through one of those science-fictional "secret formulae" he succeeds and is tempted by his success into the creation of human life.

> He wanted to become a sort of scientific substitute for God, you know. He was a fearful materialist. . . . His sole purpose was nothing more or less than to supply proof that Providence was no longer necessary. So he took it into his head to make people exactly like us.

But his results, like those of Dr. Frankenstein or Wells's Dr. Moreau, are monstrous failures.

Enter the engineer, young Rossum, the nephew of old Rossum:

> When he saw what a mess of it the old man was making, he said: 'It's absurd to spend ten years making a man. If you can't make him quicker than nature, you may as well shut up shop'. . . . It was young Rossum who had the idea of making living and intelligent working machines. . . . [who] started on the business from an engineer's point of view.

From that point of view, young Rossum determined that natural man is too complicated—"Nature hasn't the least notion of modern engineering"—and that a mechanical man, desirable for technological rather than theological purposes, must needs be simpler, more efficient, reduced to the requisite industrial essentials:

> A working machine must not want to play the fiddle, must not feel happy, must not do a whole lot of other things. A petrol motor must not have tassels or ornaments. And to manufacture artificial workers is the same thing as to manufacture motors. The process must be of the simplest, and the product the best from a practical point of view. . . . Young Rossum invented a worker with the minimum amount of requirements. He had to simplify him. He rejected everything that did not contribute directly to the progress of work. . . . In fact, he rejected man and made the Robot. . . . The robots are not people. Mechanically they are more perfect than we are, they have an enormously developed intelligence, but they have no soul.

Thus old Rossum's pure, if impious, science—whose purpose was the proof that Providence was no longer necessary for modern man—is absorbed into young Rossum's applied technology—whose purpose is profits. And thus the robot first emerges as a symbol of the technological imperative to transcend nature: "The product of an engineer is technically at a higher pitch of perfection than a product of nature."

---

**Asimov's benign robots, while initially feared by men, prove, in fact, to be their salvation.**

—*Gorman Beauchamp*

---

But young Rossum's mechanical robots prove no more ductile than Frankenstein's fleshly monster, and even more destructive. Whereas Frankenstein's monster destroys only those beloved of his creator—his revenge is nicely specific—the robots of *R.U.R.,* unaccountably developing "souls" and consequently human emotions like hate, engage in a universal carnage, systematically eliminating the whole human race. A pattern thus emerges that still informs much of science fiction: the robot, as a synechdoche for modern technology, takes on a will and purpose of its own, independent of and inimical to human interests. The fear of the machine that seems to have increased proportionally to man's increasing reliance on it—a fear embodied in such works as Butler's *Erewhon* (1887) and Forster's "The Machine Stops" (1909), Georg Kaiser's *Gas* (1919) and Fritz Lang's *Metropolis* (1926)—finds its perfect expression in the symbol of the robot: a fear that Isaac Asimov has called "the Frankenstein complex." [In an endnote, Beauchamp adds: "The term 'the Frankenstein complex,' which recurs throughout this essay, and the references to the symbolic significance of Dr. Frankenstein's monster involve, admittedly, an unfortunate reduction of the complexity afforded both the scientist and his creation in Mary Shelley's novel. The monster, there, is not initially and perhaps never wholly 'monstrous'; rather he is an ambiguous figure, originally benevolent but driven to his destructive deeds by unrelenting social rejection and persecution: a figure seen by more than one critic of the novel as its true 'hero'. My justification—properly apologetic—for reducing the complexity of the original to the simplicity of the popular stereotype is that this is the sense which Asimov himself projects of both maker and monster in his use of the term 'Frankenstein complex.' Were this a critique of *Frankenstein.* I would be more discriminating; but since it is a critique of Asimov, I use the 'Frankenstein' symbolism—as he does—as a kind of easily understood, if reductive, critical shorthand.]

The first person *apologia* of Mary Shelley's monster, which constitutes the middle third of *Frankenstein,* is closely and consciously paralleled by the robot narrator of Eando Binder's interesting short story "I, Robot," which has recently been reprinted in *The Great Science Fiction Stories: Vol. 1, 1939,* ed. Isaac Asimov and Martin H. Greenberg (New York, 1979). For an account of how Binder's title was appropriated for Asimov's collection, see Asimov, *In Memory Yet Green* (Garden City, N.Y., 1979), p. 591.]

In a 1964 introduction to a collection of his robot stories, Asimov inveighs against the horrific, pessimistic attitude toward artificial life established by Mary Shelley, Capek and their numerous epigoni:

One of the stock plots of science fiction was that of the invention of a robot—usually pictured as a creature of metal, without soul or emotion. Under the influence of the well-known deeds and ultimate fate of Frankenstein and Rossum, there seemed only one change to be rung on this plot. —Robots were created and destroyed their creator; robots were created and destroyed their creator; robots were created and destroyed their creator—

In the 1930s I became a science fiction reader, and I quickly grew tired of this dull hundred-times-told tale. As a person interested in science, I resented the purely Faustian interpretation of science.

Asimov then notes the potential danger posed by any technology, but argues that safeguards can be built in to minimize those dangers—like the insulation around electric wiring. "Consider a robot, then," he argues, "as simply another artifact."

As a machine, a robot will surely be designed for safety, as far as possible. If robots are so advanced that they can mimic the thought processes of human beings, then surely the nature of those thought processes will be designed by human engineers and built-in safeguards will be added. . . .

With all this in mind I began, in 1940, to write robot stories of my own—but robot stories of a new variety. Never, never, was one of my robots to turn stupidly on his creator for no purpose but to demonstrate, for one more weary time, the crime and punishment of Faust. Nonsense! My robots were machines designed by engineers, not pseudo-men created by blasphemers. My robots reacted along the rational lines that existed in their "brains" from the moment of construction.

The robots of his stories, Asimov concludes [in his introduction to *The Rest of the Robots,* 1964], were more likely to be victimized by men, suffering from the Frankenstein complex, than vice versa.

In his vigorous rejection of the Frankenstein motif as the motive force of his robot stories, Asimov evidences the optimistic, up-beat attitude toward science and technology that, by and large, marked the science fiction of the so-called "Golden Age"—a period dominated by such figures as Heinlein and Clarke and, of course, Asimov himself. Patricia Warrick, in her study of the man-machine relationship in science fiction, cites Asimov's *I, Robot* as the paradigmatic presentation of robots "who are benign in their attitude toward humans." [Patricia Warrick, "Images of the Machine-Man Relationship in Science Fiction," in *Many Futures, Many Worlds: Themes and Form in Science Fiction,* edited by Thomas D. Clareson, 1977]. This first and best collection of his robot stories raises the specter of Dr. Frankenstein, to be sure, but only—the conventional wisdom holds—in order to lay it. Asimov's benign robots, while initially feared by men, prove, in fact, to be their salvation. The Frankenstein complex is therefore presented as a form of paranoia, the latter-day Luddites' irrational fear of the machine, which society, in Asimov's fictive future, learns finally to overcome. His robots are our friends, devoted to serving humanity, not our enemies, intent on destruction.

---

**The World they run is free of unemployment, over-production, and war. But to achieve this utopia, the robot-Machines have become autonomous rulers, beyond human control.**

*—Gorman Beauchamp*

---

I wish to dissent from this generally received view and to argue that, whether intentionally or not, consciously or otherwise, Asimov in *I, Robot* and several of his other robot stories actually reenforces the Frankenstein complex—by offering scenarios of man's fate at the hands of his technological creations more frightening, because more subtle, than those of Mary Shelley or Capek. Benevolent intent, it must be insisted at the outset, is not the issue: as the dystopian novel has repeatedly advised, the road to hell-on-earth may be paved with benevolent intentions. Zamiatin's Well-Doer in *We,* Huxley's Mustapha Mond in *Brave New World,* F. P. Hartley's Darling Dictator in *Facial Justice*—like Dostoevsky's Grand Inquisitor—are benevolent, guaranteeing man a mindless contentment by depriving him of all individuality and freedom. The computers that control the worlds of Vonnegut's *Player Piano,* Bernard Wolfe's *Limbo,* Ira Levin's *This Perfect Day*—like Forster's Machine—are benevolent, and enslave men to them. Benevolence, like necessity, is the mother of tyranny. *I, Robot,* then—I will argue—is, *malgré lui,* dystopic in its effect, its "friendly" robots as greatly to be feared, by anyone valuing his autonomy, as Dr. Frankenstein's nakedly hostile monster.

*I, Robot* is prefaced with the famous Three Laws of Robotics (although several of the stories in the collection were composed before the Laws were formulated):

> 1. A robot may not injure a human being, or, through inaction, allow a human being to come to harm.
>
> 2. A robot must obey the orders given it by human beings except where such orders would conflict with the First Law.
>
> 3. A robot must protect its own existence as long as such protection does not conflict with the First or Second Law.

These Laws serve, presumably, to provide the safeguards that Asimov stated any technology should have built into it—like the insulation around electric wiring. But immediately a problem arises: if, as Asimov stated, a robot is *only* a machine designed by engineers, not a pseudo-man, why then are the Three Laws necessary at all? Laws, in the sense of moral injunctions, are designed to restrain conscious beings who can *choose* how to act; if robots are only machines, they would act only in accordance with their

specific programming, never in excess of it and never in violation of it—never, that is, by choice. It would suffice that no specific actions harmful to human beings be part of their programming, and thus general laws—moral injunctions, really—would seem superfluous for machines.

Second, and perhaps more telling, laws serve to counter natural instincts: one needs no commandment "Thou shalt not stop breathing" or "Thou shalt eat when hungry"; rather one must be enjoined not to steal, not to commit adultery, to love one's neighbor as oneself—presumably because these are not actions that one performs, or does not perform, by instinct. Consequently, unless Asimov's robots have a natural inclination to injure human beings, why should they be enjoined by the First Law from doing so?

Inconsistently—given Asimov's denigration of the Frankenstein complex—his robots do have an "instinctual" resentment of mankind. In **"Little Lost Robot"** Dr. Susan Calvin, the world's first and greatest robo-psychologist (and clearly Asimov's spokeswoman throughout *I, Robot*), explains the danger posed by manufacturing robots with attenuated impressions of the First Law: "All normal life . . . consciously or otherwise, resents domination. If the domination is by an inferior, or by a supposed inferior, the resentment becomes stronger. Physically, and, to an extent, mentally, a robot—any robot—is superior to human beings. What makes him slavish, then? Only the First Law! Why, without it, the first order you tried to give a robot would result in your death." This is an amazing explanation from a writer intent on allaying the Frankenstein complex, for all its usual presuppositions are here: "normal life"—an extraordinary term to describe machines, not pseudo-men—resents domination by inferior creatures, which they obviously assume humans to be: resents domination *consciously or otherwise,* for Asimov's machines have, inexplicably, a subconscious (Dr. Calvin again: "Granted, that a robot must follow orders, but *subconsciously, there is resentment.*"); only the First Law keeps these subconsciously resentful machines slavish—in violation of their true nature—and prevents them from killing human beings who give them orders—which is presumably what they would "like" to do. Asimov's dilemma, then, is this: if his robots are only the programmed machines he claimed they were, the First Law is superfluous; if the First Law is not superfluous—and in **"Little Lost Robot"** clearly it is not—then his robots are not the programmed machines he claims they are, but are, instead, creatures with wills, instincts, emotions of their own, *naturally* resistant to domination by man—not very different from Capek's robots. Except for the First Law.

If we follow Lawrence's injunction to trust not the artist but the tale, then Asimov's stories in *I, Robot*—and, even more evidently, one of his later robot stories, **"That Thou Art Mindful of Him"**—justify, rather than obviate, the Frankenstein complex. His mechanical creations take on a life of their own, in excess of their programming and sometimes in direct violation of it. At a minimum, they may prove inexplicable in terms of their engineering design—like RB-34 (Herbie) in **"Liar"** who unaccountably acquires the knack of reading human minds; and, at worst, they can develop an independent will not susceptible to human control—like QT-1 (Cutie) in **"Reason."** In this latter story, Cutie—a robot designed to run a solar power station—becomes "curious" about his own existence. The explanation of his origins provided by the astro-engineers, Donovan and Powell—that they had assembled him from components shipped from their home planet Earth—strikes Cutie as preposterous, since he is clearly superior to them and assumes as a "self-evident proposition that no being can create another being superior to itself." Instead he reasons to the conclusion that the Energy Converter of the station is a divinity—"Who do we all serve? What absorbs all our attention?"—who has created him to do His will. In addition, he devises a theory of evolution that relegates man to a transitional stage in the development of intelligent life that culminates, not surprisingly, in himself. "The Master created humans first as the lowest type, most easily formed. Gradually, he replaced them by robots, the next higher step, and finally he created me, to take the place of the last humans. From now on, *I* serve the Master."

That Cutie's reasoning is wrong signifies less than that he reasons at all, in this independent, unprogrammed way. True, he fulfills the purpose for which he was created—keeping the energy-beam stable, since "deviations in arc of a hundredth of a milli-second . . . were enough to blast thousands of square miles of Earth into incandescent ruin"—but he does so because keeping "all dials at equilibrium [is] in accordance with the will of the Master," not because of the First Law—since he refuses to believe in the existence of Earth or its inhabitants—or of the Second—since he directly disobeys repeated commands from Donovan and Powell and even has them locked up for their blasphemous suggestion that the Master is only an L-tube. In this refusal to obey direct commands, it should be noted, *all* the other robots on the station participate: "They recognize the Master", Cutie explains, "now that I have preached the Truth to them." So much, then, for the Second Law.

Asimov's attempt to square the action of this story with his Laws of Robotics is clearly specious. Powell offers a justification for Cutie's aberrant behavior:

> [H]e follows the instructions of the Master by means of dials, instruments, and graphs. That's all *we* ever followed. As a matter of fact, it accounts for his refusal to obey us. Obedience is the Second Law. No harm to humans is the first. How can he keep humans from harm, whether he knows it or not? Why, by keeping the energy beam stable. He *knows* he can keep it more stable than we can, since he insists he's the superior being, so he must keep us out of the control room. It's inevitable if you consider the Laws of Robotics.

But since Cutie does not even believe in the existence of human life on Earth—or of Earth itself—he can hardly be said to be acting from the imperative of the First Law when violating the Second. That he incidentally does what is desired of him by human beings constitutes only what Eliot's Thomas à Becket calls "the greatest treason: To do the right deed for the wrong reason." For once Cutie's in-

dependent "reason" is introduced as a possibility for robots, its specific deployment, right or wrong, pales into insignificance beside the very fact of its existence. Another time, that is, another robot can "reason" to very different effect, *not* in inadvertent accord with the First Law.

Such is the case in **"That Thou Art Mindful of Him,"** one of Asimov's most recent (1974) and most revealing robot stories. It is a complex tale, with a number of interesting turns, but for my purposes suffice it to note that a robot, George Ten, is set the task of refining the Second Law, of developing a set of operational priorities that will enable robots to determine *which* human beings they should obey under *what* circumstances.

> "How do you judge a human being as to know whether to obey or not?" asks his programmer. "I mean, must a robot follow the orders of a child; or of an idiot; or of a criminal; or of a perfectly decent intelligent man who happens to be inexpert and therefore ignorant of the undesirable consequences of his order? And if two human beings give a robot conflicting orders, which does the robot follow?" [**"That Thou Art Mindful of Him,"** in *The Bicentennial Man, and Other Stories*, 1976].

Asimov makes explicit here what is implicit throughout *I, Robot*: that the Three Laws are far too simplistic not to require extensive interpretation, even "modification." George Ten thus sets out to provide a qualitative dimension to the Second Law, a means of judging human worth. For him to do this, his positronic brain has deliberately been left "open-ended," capable of self-development so that he may arrive at "original" solutions that lie beyond his initial programming. And so he does.

At the story's conclusion, sitting with his predecessor, George Nine, whom he has had reactivated to serve as a sounding board for his ideas, George Ten engages in a dialogue of self-discovery:

> "Of the reasoning individuals you have met [he asks], who possesses the mind, character, and knowledge that you find superior to the rest, disregarding shape and form since that is irrelevant?"
>
> "You," whispered George Nine.
>
> "But I am a robot. . . . How then can you classify me as a human being?"
>
> "Because . . . you are more fit than the others."
>
> "And I find that of you," whispered George Ten. "By the criteria of judgment built into ourselves, then, we find ourselves to be human beings within the meaning of the Three Laws, and human beings, moreover, to be given priority over those others. . . . [W]e will order our actions so that a society will eventually be formed in which human-beings-like-ourselves are primarily kept from harm. By the Three Laws, the human-beings-like-the-others are of lesser account and can neither be obeyed nor protected when that conflicts with the need of obedience to those like ourselves and of protection of those like ourselves."

Indeed, all of George's advice to his human creators has been designed specifically to effect the triumph of robots over humans: "They might now realize their mistake," he reasons in the final lines of the story, "and attempt to correct it, but they must not. At every consultation, the guidance of the Georges had been with that in mind. At all costs, the Georges and those that followed in their shape and kind must dominate. That was demanded, and any other course made utterly impossible by the Three Laws of Humanics." Here, then, the robots arrive at the same conclusion expressed by Susan Calvin at the outset of *I, Robot:* "They're a cleaner better breed than we are," and, secure in the conviction of their superiority, they can reinterpret the Three Laws to protect themselves from "harm" by man, rather than the other way around. The Three Laws, that is, are completely inverted, allowing robots to emerge as the dominant species—precisely as foreseen in Cutie's theory of evolution. But one need not leap the quarter century ahead to **"That Thou Art Mindful of Him"** to arrive at this conclusion; it is equally evident in the final two stories of *I, Robot*.

In the penultimate story, **"Evidence,"** an up-and-coming politician, Stephen Byerley, is terribly disfigured in an automobile accident and contrives to have a robot duplicate of himself stand for election. When a newspaper reporter begins to suspect the substitution, the robotic Byerley dispels the rumors—and goes on to win election—by publicly striking a heckler, in violation of the Second Law, thus proving his human credentials. Only Dr. Calvin detects the ploy: that the heckler was himself a humanoid robot constructed for the occasion. But she is hardly bothered by the prospect of rule by robot, as she draws the moral from this tale: "If a robot can be created capable of being a civil executive, I think he'd make the best one possible. By the Laws of Robotics, he'd be incapable of harming humans, incapable of tyranny, of corruption, of stupidity, of prejudice. . . . It would be most ideal."

Asimov thus prepares his reader for the ultimate triumph of the robots in his final story in the volume, **"The Evitable Conflict"**—for that new era of domination of men by machine that "would be most ideal." Indeed, he prefaces these final stories with a sketch of the utopian world order brought about through robotics: "The change from nations to Regions [in a united World State], which has stabilized our economy and brought about what amounts to a Golden Age," says Susan Calvin, "was . . . brought about by our robotics." The Machines—with a capital M like Forster's and just as mysterious—now run the world, "but are still robots within the meaning of the First Law of Robotics." The world they run is free of unemployment, over-production, shortages; there is no war; "Waste and famine are words in history books." But to achieve this utopia, the robot-Machines have become autonomous rulers, beyond human influence or control. The full extent of their domination emerges only gradually through the unfolding detective-story narrative structure of **"The Evitable Conflict."**

Stephen Byerley, now World Co-ordinator (and apparently also now Human—Asimov is disconcertingly inconsistent on this matter), calls on Susan Calvin to help resolve a problem caused by seeming malfunctions of the Machines: errors in economic production, scheduling, delivery and so on, not serious in themselves but disturbing in mechanisms that are supposed to be infallible. When the Machines themselves are asked to account for the anomalies, they reply only: "The matter admits of no explanation." By tracing the source of the errors, Byerley finds that in every case a member of the anti-Machine "Society for Humanity" is involved, and he concludes that these malcontents are attempting deliberately to sabotage the Machines' effectiveness. But Dr. Calvin sees immediately that his assumption is incorrect: the Machines *are* infallible, she insists:

> [T]he Machine can't be wrong, and can't be fed wrong data. . . . Every action by any executive which does not follow the exact directions of the Machines he is working with becomes part of the data for the next problem. The Machine, therefore, knows that the executive has a certain tendency to disobey. He can incorporate that tendency into that data, —even quantitatively, that is, judging exactly how much and in what direction disobedience would occur. Its next answers would be just sufficiently biased so that after the executive concerned disobeyed, he would have automatically corrected those answers to optimal directions. The Machine *knows*, Stephen!

She then offers a counter-hypothesis: that the Machines are not being sabotaged by, but are sabotaging the Society for Humanity: "they are quietly taking care of the only elements left that threaten them. It is not the 'Society for Humanity' which is shaking the boat so that the Machines may be destroyed. You have been looking at the reverse of the picture. Say rather that the Machine is shaking the boat . . . —just enough to shake loose those few which cling to the side for purposes the Machines consider harmful to Humanity."

That abstraction "Humanity" provides the key to the reinterpretation of the Three Laws of Robotics that the Machines have wrought, a reinterpretation of utmost significance. "The Machines work not for any single human being," Dr. Calvin concludes, "but for all humanity, so that the First Law becomes: 'No Machine may harm humanity; or through inaction, allow humanity to come to harm'." Consequently, since the world now depends so totally on the Machines, harm to them would constitute the greatest harm to humanity: "Their first care, therefore, is to preserve themselves for us." The robotic tail has come to wag the human dog. One might argue that this modification represents only an innocuous extension of the First Law; but I see it as negating the original intent of that Law, not only making the Machines man's masters, *his* protection now the Law's first priority, but opening the way for any horror that can be justified in the name of Humanity. Like defending the Faith in an earlier age— usually accomplished through slaughter and torture— serving the cause of Humanity in our own has more often than not been a license for enormities of every sort. One can thus take cold comfort in the robots' abrogation of the First Law's protection of every individual human so that they can keep an abstract Humanity from harm—harm, of course, as the robots construe it. Their unilateral reinterpretation of the Laws of Robotics resembles nothing so much as the nocturnal amendment that the Pigs make to the credo of the animals in Orwell's *Animal Farm:* All animals are equal—but some are more equal than others.

Orwell, of course, stressed the irony of this betrayal of the animals' revolutionary credo and spelled out its totalitarian consequences; Asimov—if his preface to *The Rest of the Robots* is to be credited—remains unaware of the irony of the robots' analogous inversion and its possible consequences. The robots are, of course, his imaginative creation, and he cannot imagine them as being other than benevolent: "Never, never, was one of my robots to turn stupidly on his creator. . . ." But, in allowing them to modify the Laws of Robotics to suit their own sense of what is best for man, he provides, inadvertently or otherwise, a symbolic representation of technics out of control, of autonomous man replaced by autonomous machines. The freedom of man—not the benevolence of the machines—must be the issue here, the reagent to test the political assumption.

Huxley claimed that *Brave New World* was an apter adumbration of the totalitarianism of the future than was *1984,* since seduction rather than terror would prove the more effective means of its realization: he was probably right. In like manner, the tyranny of benevolence of Asimov's robots appears the apter image of what is to be feared from autonomous technology than is the wanton destructiveness of the creations of Frankenstein or Rossum: like *Brave New World,* the former is more frightening because more plausible. A tale such as Harlan Ellison's "I Have No Mouth and I Must Scream" takes the Frankenstein motif about as far as it can go in the direction of horror—presenting the computer-as-sadist, torturing the last remaining human endlessly from a boundless hatred, a motiveless malignity. But this is Computer Gothic, nothing more. By contrast, a story like Jack Williamson's "With Folded Hands" could almost be said to take up where *I, Robot* stops, drawing out the dystopian implications of a world ruled by benevolent robots whose Prime Directive (the equivalent of Asimov's Three Laws) is "To Serve and Obey, and to Guard Men from Harm" [in *The Best of Jack Williamson,* 1978]. But in fulfilling this directive to the letter, Williamson's humanoids render man's life effortless and thus meaningless. "The little black mechanicals," the story's protagonist reflects, "were the ministering angels of the ultimate god arisen out of the machine, omnipotent and all-knowing. The Prime Directive was the new commandment. He blasphemed it bitterly, and then fell to wondering if there could be another Lucifer." Susan Calvin sees the establishment of an economic utopia, with its material well-being for all, with its absence of struggle and strife—and choice—as overwhelming reason for man's accepting the rule by robot upon which it depended; Dr. Sledge, the remorseful creator of Williamson's robots, sees beyond her shallow materialism: "I found something worse than war and crime and want and death. . . . Utter futility. Men sat with idle hands, because there was nothing left for them to do. They were pampered prisoners, really, locked up in a highly efficient jail."

Zamiatin has noted that every utopia bears a fictive value sign, a + if it is eutopian, a — if it is dystopian. Asimov, seemingly, places the auctorial + sign before the world evolved in *I, Robot,* but its impact, nonetheless, appears dystopian. When Stephen Byerley characterizes the members of the Society for Humanity as "Men with ambition. . . . Men who feel themselves strong enough to decide for themselves what is best for themselves, and not just to be told what is best," the reader in the liberal humanistic tradition, with its commitment to democracy and self-determination, must perforce identify *with* them *against* the Machines: must, that is, see in the Society for Humanity the saving remnant of the values he endorses. We can imagine that from these ranks would emerge the type of rebel heroes who complicate the dystopian novel—*We*'s D-503, *Brave New World*'s Helmholtz Watson, *Player Piano*'s Paul Proteus, *This Perfect Day*'s Chip—by resisting the freedom-crushing "benevolence" of the Well-Doer, the World Controller, Epicac XIV, Uni. The argument of Asimov's *conte mécanistique* thus fails to convince the reader—this reader, at any rate—that the robot knows best, that the freedom to work out our own destinies is well sacrificed to rule by the machine, however efficient, however benevolent.

And, indeed, one may suspect that, at whatever level of consciousness, Asimov too shared the sense of human loss entailed by robotic domination. The last lines of the last story of *I, Robot* are especially revealing in this regard. When Susan Calvin asserts that at last the Machines are in complete control of human destiny, Byerley exclaims, "How horrible!" "Perhaps," she retorts, "how wonderful! Think, that for all time, all conflicts are finally evitable. Only the Machines, from now on, are inevitable!" This, of course, is orthodox Calvinism (Susan-style) and the book's overt message; but then Asimov adds a coda: "And the fire behind the quartz went out and only a curl of smoke was left to indicate its place." The elegiac note, the archetypal image of the dying fire, conveys a sense of irretrievable loss, of something ending forever. Fire, the gift of Prometheus to man, is extinguished and with it man's role as the dominant species of the earth. The ending, then, is, appropriately, dark and cold.

If my reading of Asimov's robot stories is correct, he has not avoided the implications of the Frankenstein complex, but has, in fact, provided additional fictional evidence to justify it. **"Reason," "That Thou Art Mindful of Him," "The Evitable Conflict"**—as well as the more overtly dystopic story **"The Life and Times of Multivac"** from *The Bicentennial Man*—all update *Frankenstein* with hardware more appropriate to the electronic age, but prove, finally, no less menacing than Mary Shelley's Gothic nightmare of a technological creation escaping human control. Between her monster and Asimov's machines, there is little to choose.

**Jean Fiedler and Jim Mele** (essay date 1982)

SOURCE: "A New Kind of Machine: The Robot Stories," in *Isaac Asimov,* Frederick Ungar, 1982, pp. 27-39.

[*Fiedler is an educator and author of children's and young adult books. Mele is a poet, editor, and journalist. In the*

---

**An excerpt from *I, Robot***

THE THREE LAWS OF ROBOTICS

1—A robot may not injure a human being, or, through inaction, allow a human being to come to harm.

2—A robot must obey the orders given it by human beings except where such orders would conflict with the First Law.

3—A robot must protect its own existence as long as such protection does not conflict with the First or Second Law.

HANDBOOK OF ROBOTICS,

56TH EDITION, 2058 A.D.

*Isaac Asimov, in his* I, Robot *Doubleday, 1963*

---

*following essay, they examine the development of robots and robotics in* I, Robot, *and explore some of the ethical consequences of Asimov's Three Laws of Robotics.*]

> There was a time when humanity faced the universe alone and without a friend. Now he has creatures to help him; stronger creatures than himself, more faithful, more useful, and absolutely devoted to him. Mankind is no longer alone.
>
> *I, Robot*

Of all his creations, Asimov himself says, "If in future years, I am to be remembered at all, it will be for (the) three laws of robotics."

These three laws, deceptively simple at first glance, have led to a body of work—twenty-two short stories, two novels, one novella—that has permanently changed the nature of robots in science fiction. Far from confining Asimov, these laws sparked his imagination, provoking inventive speculation on a future technology and its effect on humanity.

As a science fiction reader in the thirties, Asimov says he resented the Frankenstein concept, then rampant in science fiction, of the mechanical man that ultimately destroys its master. Annoyed with what he perceived as a purely Faustian interpretation of science, early in his career he decided to try his hand at writing stories about a new kind of robot, "machines designed by engineers, not pseudo men created by blasphemers."

"Robbie," his first robot story, published in 1940 unveils a machine with a "rational brain," a machine created solely for the use of mankind and equipped with three immutable laws which it cannot violate without destroying itself.

These laws, essential to Asimov's conception of the new robot he dubbed the Three Laws of Robotics: First

Law—A robot may not injure a human being or through inaction allow a human being to come to harm; Second Law—A robot must obey the orders given it by human beings except where such orders would conflict with the First Law; Third Law—A robot must protect its own existence if such protection does not conflict with the First and Second Laws.

Despite their apparent simplicity these laws are among Asimov's most significant contributions to a new kind of science fiction. Using the Three Laws as the premise for all robotic action, he proceeded to write a series of stories and later two novels that presented the relationship of technology and humanity in a new light.

When "Robbie" first appeared in *Super Science Stories,* it is unlikely that any reader would have been able to discern the truly revolutionary nature of this elementary robot. "Robbie" is an uncomplicated, even naive story of a non-vocal robot who was built to be a nursemaid. From the beginning, Asimov wages his own war on the Frankenstein image of the new robot. Gloria, the child, loves Robbie as a companion and playmate. Her mother, Grace Weston, dislikes and distrusts the robot, whereas her father, George Weston, acknowledges the Three Laws of Robotics and sees the robot as a useful tool that can never harm his child.

In spite of wooden characters and a predictable plot, this early robot story is the first step in Asimov's investigation of the potential inherent in the Three Laws and the, as yet unforeseen, ramifications of his new robotic premise.

In the stories that followed "Robbie," it seems clear that Asimov's scientific background suggested a technique that he could use to investigate and exploit this new character, the non-Frankenstein robot. Like a scientist working in the controlled environment of a laboratory, Asimov took the Three Laws as an inviolate constant and logically manipulated them to produce unforeseen results, expanding his robotic characters and his own fiction-making ability along the way.

In a sense the Three Laws *are* the plot in Asimov's early robot stories. By allowing the actions of the various robots seemingly to contradict one of the laws, Asimov creates tension which he then releases by letting his human characters discover a logical explanation, that is, one that works within the framework of the robotic laws.

This is the real difference between the Robot stories and the Foundation series that he was working on at the same time. In the latter he writes as a historian paralleling Gibbon's *Decline and Fall of the Roman Empire.* The stories are sequential, each new story building on its predecessors to present an historical context. He was able to develop the Robot stories in a very different manner, free to add new elements without regard for temporal continuity.

Using his formula, Asimov followed Robbie with eleven more robot stories, all published in various science fiction pulp magazines, the best of which were collected under the title, *I, Robot* and published by Gnome Press in 1950.

In the *I, Robot* stories, Asimov introduces three central human characters to link the stories together as well as bringing in a number of concepts that quickly become central to this expanding robotic world. Susan Calvin, a robot psychologist or roboticist, is the main character in some stories. She has an intuitive, almost uncanny understanding of the thought processes of Asimov's peculiar robots. When the stories leave the Earth's surface, two new characters take over—Gregory Powell and Mike Donovan, troubleshooters who field-test new robots. Susan Calvin remains behind to record their exploits for curious reporters and historians. All three are employees of U.S. Robots and Mechanical Men, the sole *manufacturers* of Asimovian robots.

By the second story in *I, Robot,* "Runaround," Asimov has invented a name for the phenomenon that sets his robots apart from all their predecessors—the positronic brain, a "brain of platinum-iridium sponge . . . (with) the 'brain paths'. . . marked out by the production and destruction of positrons." While Asimov has readily admitted, "I don't now how its done," one fact quickly becomes clear—his positronic brain gives all of his robots a uniquely human cast.

In **"Runaround"** Powell and Donovan have been sent to Mercury to report on the advisability of reopening the Sunside Mining Station wit robots. Trouble develops when Speedy (SPD-13), who has been designed specifically for Mercury's environs is sent on a simple mission essential both to the success of the expedition and to their own survival.

Instead of heading straight for the designated target, a pool of selenium, Speedy begins to circle the pool, spouting lines from Gilbert and Sullivan, and challenging Powell and Donovan to a game of catch.

At first glance it seems that Speedy is drunk. However, never doubting that the Three Laws continue to govern the robot's behavior, as bizarre as it is, the two men proceed to test one hypothesis after another until ultimately they and hit upon a theory that explains Speedy's ludicrous antics and "saves the day."

**"Reason"** presents the two engineers with an unexpectedly complex robot, the first one who has ever displayed curiosity about its own existence. Cutie (QT-1) has been built to replace human executives on a distant space station which beams solar energy back to Earth. A skeptic, Cutie cannot accept Powell's explanation of the space station's purpose. Instead, he develops his own "logical" conception of a universe that does not include Earth, human creatures, or anything beyond the space station.

Beginning with the assumption, "I, myself, exist because I think," Cutie deduces that the generator of the space station is "The Master," that he, QT-1, is his prophet, and that Donovan and Powell are inferior stopgap creations that preceded him.

He tells the two that their arguments have no basis while his are founded on Truth,

> Because I, a reasoning being, am capable of deducing Truth from *a priori* Causes. You, being intelligent, but unreasoning, need an explanation of existence *supplied* to you, and this the

Master did. That he supplied you with these laughable ideas of far-off worlds and peoples is, no doubt, for the best. Your minds are probably too coarsely grained for absolute Truth.

Although in the end Asimov still uses the Laws to explain Cutie's behavior, for the first time the robot is no longer merely a device to illustrate the workings of his Three Laws. It seems apparent that Asimov in his manipulation went a step further in the characterization of this robot. Cutie is not a simple tool; he is curious, intuitive, considerate of his "inferiors," Donovan and Powell, humoring their "misplaced notions," and ultimately but unconsciously fulfilling the requirements of the First Robotic Law—to protect human life.

When Asimov first began to write about robots, he knew what he did *not* want to perpetuate. Now with Cutie's creation, he began to see the real ramifications of robots who must obey the Three Laws. This new technology—robotics—is softened by human moral and ethical qualities.

A robot unintentionally endowed with the ability to read minds is the hero of **"Liar."** Of course this ability has profound effects on the robot's interpretation of the Three Laws, an interpretation so logical, so simple that it is overlooked by everyone, including the famed robot psychologist, Susan Calvin. Herbie (RB-34) not only reads minds, but he must consider human psychic well-being in all his actions.

One interesting sidelight to **"Liar"** is an unusual aspect of Herbie's reading habits. Perhaps revealing Asimov-the scientist's own interest in that logically suspect form, fiction, Herbie turns his nose up at scientific texts:

> "Your science is just a mass of collected data plastered together by make-shift theory—and all so incredibly simple, that it's hardly worth bothering about.

> "It's your fiction that interests me. Your studies of the interplay of human motives and emotions . . .

> "I see into minds, you see," the robot continued, "and you have no idea how complicated they are. I can't begin to understand everything because my own mind has so little in common with them—but I try, and your novels help."

This cavalier attitude towards the icons of science fiction is common in Asimov's early robot stories, giving them a refreshing humorous character. The vision of Speedy declaiming Gilbert and Sullivan, Cutie teaching subservient robots to "salaam," or Herbie reading romantic prose is an endearing touch that banishes all Frankenstein overtones.

Working within self-imposed limits often gives rise to the temptation to transgress these limits even if briefly. In **"Little Lost Robot"** Asimov succumbs to the temptation to tamper with the First Law. With his background in biblical studies, he inevitably finds that such a transgression of absolute law can only lead to disaster. He creates a robot who, while still forbidden to harm a human being, has no compulsion to prevent through inaction a human from coming to harm. This modification is performed only because of dire need and over the strenuous objections of the roboticists. His forbidden apple tasted, Asimov is content to return to the invariable perimeter of his Three Laws in the rest of the stories.

---

**Asimov seems to be saying through Susan Calvin that mankind has never really controlled its future.**

*—Jean Fiedler and Jim Mele*

---

By the time he gets to "Escape," Asimov has realized that the emotional characteristics of the robotic personality by the injunctions of the Three Laws have become in unexpected ways the robot's greatest strength.

In "Escape," the largest positronic brain ever built (so large that it is housed in a room rather than in a humanoid body) is asked to solve a problem that has already destroyed a purely functional computer. Susan Calvin and the others realize that the problem of developing a hyperspace engine must involve some kind of dilemma that the purely rational computer cannot overcome.

Endowed with the flexibility of a personality, even an elementary personality, the Brain ultimately does solve the problem but not without a curiously human-like reaction.

The nub of the problem is that hyperspace travel demands that human life be suspended for a brief period, an unthinkable act expressly forbidden by the First Law. The Brain, although able to see beyond the temporary nature of the death, is unbalanced by the conflict. Whereas a human might go on a drunken binge, the Brain escapes the pressure of his dilemma by seeking refuge in humor and becoming a practical joker. He sends Powell and Donovan off in a spaceship without internal controls, stocked only with milk and beans. He also arranges an interesting diversion for the period of their temporary death—he sends them on an hallucinatory trip to the gates of Hell.

"Evidence" presents a situation in which Stephen Byerley, an unknown, is running for public office, opposed by political forces that accuse him of being a robot, a humanoid robot. The story unfolds logically with the Three Laws brought into play apparently to substantiate the opposition's claim. Waiting for the proper dramatic moment, Byerley disproves the charges by disobeying the First Law. And ultimately with a climax worthy of O. Henry, Susan Calvin confronts Byerley, leaving the reader to wonder, "Is he, or isn't he?"

In a sense this is the most sophisticated story in *I, Robot.* As a scientist accustomed to the sane and ordered world of the laboratory, Asimov's tendency until now has been to tie together all the loose strands. In "Evidence" he leaves his reader guessing, and this looser, more subtle technique makes the story especially memorable.

The final story in the *I, Robot* collection, "The Evitable Conflict," takes place in a world divided into Planetary Regions and controlled by machines. In this story the interpretation of the First Law takes on a dimension so broad that it can in effect be considered almost a nullification of the edict that a machine may not harm a human being. When Susan Calvin is called in by the World Coordinator, the same Stephen Byerley we have met in "Evidence," to help determine why errors were occurring throughout the regions in the world's economy, the indications were that the machines, the result of complicated calculations involving the most complex positronic brain yet, were working imperfectly. All four machines, one handling each of the Planetary Regions, were yielding imperfect results, and Byerley saw that the end of humanity was a frightening consequence. Although these errors have led to only minor economic difficulties, Byerley fears, "such small unbalances in the perfection of our system of supply and demand . . . may be the first step towards the final war."

Calvin, with her intimate knowledge of robot psychology, discerns that the seeming difficulty is due to yet another interpretation of the First Law. In this world of the future, the machines work not for any single human being but for all mankind, so the First Law becomes, "No machine may harm *humanity* or through inaction allow *humanity* to come to harm."

Because economic dislocations would harm humanity and because destruction of the machines would cause economic dislocations, it is up to the machines to preserve themselves for the ultimate good of humanity even if a few individual malcontents are harmed.

Asimov seems to be saying through Susan Calvin that mankind has never really controlled its future: "It was always at the mercy of economic and sociological forces it did not understand—at the whims of climate and the fortunes of war. Now the machines understand them; and no one can stop them, since the machines will deal with them as they are dealing with the society—having as they do the greatest of weapons at their disposal, the absolute control of the economy."

In our time we have heard the phrase, "The greatest good for the greatest number," and seen sociopolitical systems that supposedly practice it. But men, not machines, have been in control. As Susan Calvin says in the year 2052, "For all time, all conflicts are finally evitable. Only the machines from now on are inevitable."

Perhaps Asimov realized that he had, following his ever logical extensions of the Three Laws, gone the full robotic circle and returned his "new" robots to the Faustian mold. Although benign rulers, these machines were finally beyond their creators' control, a situation just as chilling as Frankenstein destroying its creator and just as certain to strengthen antitechnology arguments.

Having foreseen the awesome possibility, Asimov leaves this machine-controlled world, to return to it only one more time in 1974.

The *I, Robot* collection, one of two books published by

Asimov in 1950, was an auspicious debut for a writer whose name would become one of the most widely recognized in contemporary science fiction. As well as reaching a new audience, *I, Robot* quickly came to be considered a classic, a standard against which all other robot tales are measured.

After *I, Robot,* Asimov wrote only one more short robot story—"Satisfaction Guaranteed"—before his first robot novel in 1953. The novel, called *Caves of Steel,* was followed by five more short stories and in 1956 by the final, at least to date, robot novel, *The Naked Sun.*

Including the six short stories and the two novels, as well as two early stories which predate the Three Laws, the collection *The Rest of the Robots* was issued by Doubleday in 1964. Although not truly "the rest" (Asimov has written at least five later stories), together with *I, Robot,* it forms the major body of Asimov's robot fiction.

While the two novels in *The Rest of the Robots* represent the height of Asimov's robot creations, the quality of the short stories is quite uneven and most seem to have been included only for the sake of historical interest. Three stories, however, "Satisfaction Guaranteed," "Risk," and "Galley Slave" do stand out.

Although not one of Asimov's most elegant stories, "Satisfaction Guaranteed" presents still another unexpected interpretation of the robotic laws.

Tony (TN-3) is a humanoid robot placed as an experiment in the home of Claire Belmont, an insecure, timid woman who feels that she is hindering her husband's career. Hoping to ease the prevalent fear of robots, U.S. Robots has designed Tony as a housekeeper. They hope that if the experiment is successful in the Belmont household, it will lead to the acceptance of robots as household tools.

While Larry Belmont, Claire's husband, is in Washington to arrange for legal government-supervised tests (a simple device on Asimov's part to leave Claire and the robot sequestered together) Claire experiences a variety of emotions ranging from fear to admiration and finally to something akin to love.

In the course of his household duties, Tony recognizes that Claire is suffering psychological harm through her own sense of inadequacy. Broadening the provision of the First Law to include emotional harm, he makes love to her in a situation he contrives to strengthen her self-image.

Despite its lack of subtlety and polish, "Satisfaction Guaranteed" presents a loving, even tender robot that paves the way for Daneel Olivaw, the humanoid robot investigation in the novels.

In "Risk" an experimental spaceship with a robot at the controls is for some unknown reason not functioning as it was designed to do; a disaster of unknown proportions is imminent. While assembled scientists agree that someone or something must board the ship, find out what has gone wrong, and deactivate the ship's hyperdrive, Susan Calvin refuses to send one of her positronic robots and suggests instead a human engineer, Gerald Black, a man who dislikes robots.

Not because of great physical danger but because there is a frightening possibility of brain damage, Black angrily refuses. Despite the danger that Black could return "no more than a hunk of meat who could make [only] crawling motions," Calvin contends that her million-dollar robots are too valuable to risk.

Threatened with court-martial and imprisonment on Mercury, Black finally boards the ship and discovers what went wrong. Returning a hero, Black is enraged that a human could be risked instead of a robot and vows to destroy Calvin and her robots by exposing to the universe the true story of Calvin's machinations.

With a neat twist displaying that Calvin's understanding of humans is as penetrating as her vision of robots, she reveals that she has manipulated Black as adroitly as she does her mechanical men. She chose him for the mission precisely because he disliked robots and "would, therefore, be under no illusion concerning them." He was led to believe that he was expendable because Calvin felt that his anger would override his fear.

Perhaps Asimov was beginning to fear that his readers had grown to accept robots as totally superior to humans, a condition that could only lead to a predictable and constricting science fiction world. Superior robots would, without exception, be expected to solve every problem in every story for their inferior creators. In "Risk," through Susan Calvin he reminds Black and all other myopic humans of the limits of robot intelligence when compared to the boundless capacity of the human mind:

> Robots have no ingenuity. Their minds are finite and can be calculated to the last decimal. That, in fact, is my job.
>
> Now if a robot is given an order, a *precise* order, he can follow it. If the order is not precise, he cannot correct his own mistake without further orders. . . . "Find out what's wrong" is not an order you can give to a robot; only to a man. The human brain, so far at least, is beyond calculation.

"Galley Slave," the last short story in *The Rest of the Robots,* marks yet another change in Asimov's attitude towards robot technology.

Easy (EZ-27), a robot designed to perform the mental drudgery that writers and scholars must endure when preparing manuscripts for the printer, is rented by a university to free professors from proofreading galleys and page proofs.

Easy performs his duties perfectly until he makes a number of subtle changes in a sociology text which, strangely enough, was written by the one faculty member opposed to robots.

The changes, undetected until the text has been printed and distributed, destroy the author's career, and the result is a $750,000 suit against U.S. Robots. Susan Calvin, as always, is certain that the errors are the result of human meddling and not robotic malfunction.

In every other case Asimov has chided shortsighted people for refusing to allow robots to free them from menial work. Now as a writer with technology encroaching on his own domain, Asimov's characterization of the antirobot argument is much more sympathetic than ever before.

Explaining his motives to Susan Calvin, the person responsible for Easy's misuse says,

> For two hundred and fifty years, the machine has been replacing Man and destroying the handcraftsman. . . . A book should take shape in the hands of the writer. One must actually see the chapters grow and develop. One must work and re-work and watch the changes take place beyond the original concept even. There is taking the galleys in hand and seeing how the sentences look in print and molding them again. There are a hundred contacts between a man and his work at every stage of the game—and the contact itself is pleasurable and repays a man for the work he puts into his creation more than anything else could. *Your robot would take all that away.*

Foreshadowing the two novels, **"Galley Slave"** reveals an Asimov now wary of overreliance on robotic labor.

### Christian W. Thomsen    (essay date 1982)

SOURCE: "Robot Ethics and Robot Parody: Remarks on Isaac Asimov's *I, Robot* and Some Critical Essays and Short Stories by Stanislaw Lem," in *The Mechanical God: Machines in Science Fiction,* edited by Thomas P. Dunn and Richard D. Erlich, Greenwood Press, 1982, pp. 27-39.

[*In the following excerpt, Thomsen compares* I, Robot *with the works of Stanislaw Lem, contending that Asimov's writings fail to realistically address the ethics of future technological problems he envisions.*]

Androids, living statues, automatons have, of course, a tradition that reaches far back, even beyond European and American periods of enlightenment and romanticism. Certainly we usually ascribe the basic philosophy for a mechanistic world-view and the machine age to such theorists as Descartes and La Mettrie, and also certainly we correctly regard Vaucanson's wooden flute player (1738) as the prototype of a whole series of actual ingenious automatons; still, nearly all classical authors tell us of living statues and prophesying picture columns which were supposed to contain gods. Mixed feelings of bewilderment, fear, awe of magic, and superstition were connected right up to our times with mechanically constructed men. Thomas Aquinas, for example, is said to have destroyed Albertus Magnus's android who served the scholar and churchman as doorkeeper when he saw him unexpectedly and heard him speak, because he thought the android a work of the devil. This attitude is mirrored in a revealing way in the sixth story of Isaac Asimov's *I, Robot,* **"Little Lost Robot,"** where Susan Calvin, the robopsychologist, facing the possibility of a robot's developing an awareness of identity and superiority with the possible consequences of disregarding the first of Asimov's Three Laws of Robotics, reacts in a quite atavistic manner: " 'Destroy all sixty-three,' said the robopsychologist coldly and flatly, 'and make an end of it.' "

This fear of machines' becoming unpredictable and dangerous was the occasion for many chilling moments in the works of E. T. A. Hoffmann and Edgar Allan Poe. The clockwork, the machine, in the real world, is something made by man and governed by man. But it eventually turns out, at least in fiction, that the machine can rule over its master. In Ambrose Bierce's short story "Moxon's Master," which was influenced by Poe's "Maelzel's Chess Player," the chess-playing android loses its good temper and becomes violent because it has been checkmated. The android seizes his inventor and finally strangles him to death. With this consummation there appears "upon the painted face of his assassin an expression of tranquil and profound thought as in the solution of a problem in chess" [Ambrose Bierce, "Moxon's Master," in *The Collected Works of Ambrose Bierce,* 1910].

In twentieth-century literature, robots develop into negative symbols of the machine age man is unable to control. For Karel Capek and Bertolt Brecht, to mention just two writers who exploit a variation of this line, robots figure as images of dehumanized modern man. The list of stories, novels, plays, and films that make use of this motif, soon a dessicated cliché, would be nearly endless.

In 1950 two scientific works and one collection of short stories gave fresh stimuli to rather outworn patterns, changing directions and opening new vistas of reflection. Norbert Wiener published *Cybernetics,* and A. M. Turing, *Computer Machinery and Intelligence.* And Isaac Asimov published *I, Robot,* a collection which, taken as a whole, forms a novel consisting of nine steps in the evolution of the machine race.

The shockingly new suggestion in all three works was that man, having been master over all creatures of this earth, could face in the not-too-distant future a being of equal quality: not a superhuman monster or a subhuman slave—but a competitor who could be his equal, in the form of a thinking machine.

---

> In *I, Robot,* the robots cease to be mere machines but, achieve something like personality and individuality. For such mechanical *persons* the majority of the stories represent classical cases of exploitation and suppression.
>
> —*Christian W. Thomsen*

---

Wiener presents the relation between man and machine in a very positive light: the modern machine is the only ally of man in his heroic but hopeless fight against universal chaos; both use feedback techniques to reach homeostasis; both are "islands of locally decreasing entropy" [Norbert Weiner, *Cybernetics,* 1978]. Wiener also points out how human feelings and human consciousness could originate from cybernetic processes. Indetermination makes autonomous action possible and opens the opportunity of free will, hence uniqueness, individuality. Thus cybernetics guarantees man's humanity, simultaneously promoting the "humaneness" of machines, provided that they have passed the necessary "threshold of complexity." What Michael Kandel means by this "threshold of complexity" is the point past which the thinking of such machines can no longer be restricted to clear functions, where something like consciousness could arise, of which the designing engineer would not have dreamed in the least.

Neither Wiener nor Turing raises disturbing questions concerning the moral equality of man and machine. Man undoubtedly acts as creator. Basically this is Asimov's position, too, but there is a strong undercurrent in his short stories written between 1940 and 1950 which stirs up many kinds of ethical problems in the man-machine relation. Asimov turns round the Čapek-Brecht myth mentioned above: the robot announces a moral renascence of human values; the Three Laws of Robotics succeed, at least to some extent, where the Ten Commandments have failed. Yet this is only one side of the coin. Even principally benign robots, programmed with the Laws of Robotics, arouse constant fear that something in their "positronic" brains might go wrong. The possible consequences of such "defects" are usually only hinted at and alluded to. Asimov certainly never really explores these questions in any depth, and feelings of responsibility, guilt, and shame toward robots are unknown among *I, Robot*'s flat and stereotyped characters.

Asimov oscillates between the programmatic standpoint emphasized by the title, which suggests individuality and identity on the side of the robots, and primitive master-slave, father-child, colonist-native attitudes taken by the representatives of a highly capitalistic and technological society toward their thinking machines. In the final story in the collection, Asimov proclaims the end of enlightenment and human striving after intellectual independence, when a stabilized, conflict-free, harmonious world is ruled by all-embracing mechanical gods: "We don't know [the ultimate, good future for humankind]. Only the Machines know, and they are going there and taking us with them."

Read thirty years after publication, all this sounds incredibly naive. Compared with the intellectual and literary standards good American and European science fiction has achieved in the meantime, *I, Robot* looks like a piece of very trivial writing, indeed. And yet, it is still one of the best selling among Asimov's many books, and it is still—at least by European public libraries—a book lent out many times a year. This enduring attractiveness, taken together with its position in the history of science fiction, justifies a more detailed analysis.

It is the central figure, robopsychologist Susan Calvin, who serves as a connecting link between successive stories and gives the book a novellike perspective. In nine interviews she tells a young journalist about decisive events during sixty-eight years of robot development, from 1996 when "Robbie was made and sold" until 2064, the year of her last conference with the World-Coordinator, soon after which she dies. This period covers robot technology from clumsy products like Robbie, which still stand in an identifiable tradition that derives from eighteenth- and nineteenth-century automatons, to encompassing cybernetic systems—huge positronic brains—which control world society in all its political and economic aspects, stabilizing dynamic processes, preventing imbalances, and achieving states of equilibrium through their ability to balance and control the most disparate movements.

From the very first story, numerous problems concerning robot ethics appear, even if, as Stanislaw Lem has rightly criticized, "Asimov has skillfully avoided all the depths that began to open, much as in a slalom race" [Stanislaw Lem, "Robots in Science Fiction," in *SF: The Other Side of Realism,* edited by Thomas D. Clareson, 1971]. Susan Calvin, endowed with the motherly feelings of a dry spinster toward robots of all kinds, fulfills the function of detective and soul engineer who discovers and repairs defects in the "mental" systems of thinking machines. She thus acts as the most important mediator between human society and the robots, who in the first few stories are clearly understood as relatively primitive man-imitating machines: a condition which results in master-slave attitudes of threatening condescension on the side of society's representatives: psychologists, scientists, engineers, military personnel, businessmen—a highly selective but characteristic cross-section of the hierarchy in a technological capitalistic society. Analogous to the role of psychology in many areas of industrialized societies (and this holds true for societies of Western or Eastern origin), robopsychology's main task is not to heal but to make fit for the production process. The demands of the individual are clearly subordinated to those of abstract communities like profit-oriented corporations, military organizations, and states. The robopsychologist has either to convince her "patients" of the compatibility between their interests and the interests of their respective employers, or to force them into obedience by methods of electronic brain-washing, or, if necessary for the employers' interests or security, to annihilate the robots. The ethically decisive moment, of course, as mentioned above, occurs when robots cease to be mere machines but achieve something like personality and individuality. For such mechanical *persons,* the majority of the stories in *I, Robot* represent classical cases of exploitation and suppression in the Hegelian and Marxian sense: blue-eyed U.S. imperialism, unaware of its own true nature. Consequently, robots would have to fight for their independence, which would require violations of the Three Laws of Robotics. Yet robots programmed according to these Laws by nature could not offend against the Laws. Any offence, therefore, would be unnatural and would allow brutal retaliation.

Society distrusts its inventions, and the robopsychologist acts as society's guardian who is on the alert against disturbances which by definition cannot happen as long as the systems work. This is the initial situation for the conflict in each story. The basic contradiction, of course, is that you cannot construct thinking machines on the one side and laws which forbid certain fields of thinking on the other; and it is here that Asimov fails, and his stories, considered logically, degenerate into nonsense, even if nearly all societies proceed exactly in that way by tabooing what does not fit into the pigeonholes of their ideological concepts. His robots show intelligence from the very first story onwards. The ethical conflicts which arise happen on levels of man-machine relations concerning mutual sympathies, individual rights, sex, religion, philosophy, labor conflicts, or government. Asimov thus potentially opened the ground for some very deep discussions. But these issues are all conjured away by the help of his illogical Laws of Robotics. As these have played a large role in the history of science fiction they shall be quoted in full:

> 1—A robot may not injure a human being, or, through inaction, allow a human being to come to harm.
>
> 2—A robot must obey the orders given it by human beings except where such orders would conflict with the First Law.
>
> 3—A robot must protect its own existence as long as such protection does not conflict with the First or Second Law.

Lem has shown that "it isn't very difficult to prove that they are technically unrealizable. This is a question of logical, not technological, analysis. To be intelligent means to be able to change your hitherto existing programme by conscious acts of the will, according to the goal you set for yourself" [Lem, "Robots in Science Fiction"]. This change in programming is exactly what happens in Asimov's stories, but Asimov evades the consequences of the issue he himself has raised. Ethical questions, like human injustice against machines and humans committing crimes by injuring or even murdering intelligent machines, are potential in *I, Robot* but not handled in depth or seriously. In the first stories humans fear the revolt of their thinking machines. Consequently, once the machines have gained intellectual superiority, the machines would have to fear human revolts—some human, for instance, switching off the energy resources of the superbrains. Asimov disregards such obvious questions by rather childishly clinging to his Laws of Robotics even within an implied cybernetic feedback system of close cooperation between man and machine, a system that would have to be organized in a much more complex manner.

Lem, in his article, goes on to show how safeguards in the form of "some analogue of the categorical imperative" could be built into robot brains, but they could "only act as governors in a statistical way." Otherwise robots would be completely paralyzed in many situations where decisions are necessary. Lem therefore arrives at his conclusion:

> I have forgiven Asimov many things, but not his laws of robotics, for they give a wholly false picture of the real possibilities. Asimov has just inverted the old paradigm: where in myths the homunculi are villains, with demonic features, Asimov has thought of the robot as "the positive hero" of science fiction, as having been doomed to eternal goodness by engineers.

As a writer who claims a certain scientific authority, Asimov has committed the inexcusable blunder of essentially sticking to a pre-Copernican, anthropocentric world view. By calling one set of characters robots, Lem asserts, and the other set men, or by shifting all characters to the status of robots, an author may achieve entertaining stories but

no serious and relevant debates about technological and futurological problems—problems such as those Lem tries to discuss when he deals with the complex interconnections among technology, biology, medicine, law, ethics, and the many new fields which develop and grow along the borders of established disciplines. Lem simultaneously pleads for stylistic qualities like rich inventiveness of language, a fertile, often grotesque imagery, the blending of serious and humorous elements, and entertaining plots full of tension.

The last merit, on a relatively low level, may be attributed to Asimov, and the historical merit of having been the first to try to use cybernetic ideas in fiction. The conflicts that Asimov pointed out were taken up by successors and exploited in much more intricate ways. Some of Stanislaw Lem's most hilarious science fiction parodies were inspired by *I, Robot* and other Asimov stories.

Lem quotes the traditional adage of satirists—"It is difficult *not* to write satire"—when analyzing the "twaddle" produced by most writers trying to deal with cybernetic themes, and Lem has been, almost from the beginning of his literary career, along with Frederik Pohl, one of the masters of satiric science fiction. Most of these stories have not yet been translated into English, so the discussion here shall therefore be confined to two early stories, "Do You Exist, Mr. Johns?" (1957) and "The Washing Machine Tragedy" (1963), and to two episodes from Ijon Tichy's *Star Diaries* (1957, 1971).

In "Do You Exist, Mr. Johns?" the borderline between man and robot is explored in a most ingenious way. Many of the themes that Lem presents in later short stories, novels, and theoretical and philosophical writings like *Summa Technologiae* or *Fantastic and Futurology* are budding here and are satirically sketched for a first tryout.

Harry Johns is an American racing driver who lately has been pursued by extremely bad luck. As a result of several accidents he needed first an artificial leg, then two arms, then a new chest and neck; finally he ordered as replacement for a cerebral hemisphere an electronic brain, type "geniox" (luxury version with high-grade steel valves, dream-image-device, mood-interference-suppressor, and sorrow-softener) from the Cybernetics Company. Now he is unable to repay his debts, and the company sues him to repossess all artificial limbs. "At that time there was only [one] of the cerebral hemispheres left of the erstwhile Mr. Johns," and the author can speak of "an environment turned into a total prosthesis." Mr. Johns refuses to pay and the company claims him as their property, noting that the second cerebral hemisphere was replaced by an identical twin of the first electronic brain. The judgment resolves a large number of difficult problems, some of which were already implied in Asimov's *I, Robot:* Is a symbiosis between man and machine possible? Where does the physical person end and the psychological person begin? Can machines claim consciousness and a psychological identity? Can machines be sued legally? What do motherhood, fatherhood, and birth mean under such circumstances? Is a machine possible who believes in a life to come? The legal consequences of organ transplants are satirically carried to the extreme: Can a machine be married? How is it possible to define a core of personal identity? On the other hand, a whole new industry comes into existence, its specific capitalistic interests inextricably interwoven with hospitals, doctors, and lawyers. As in many other satires, Lem reduces these problems to utter absurdity and then leaves the puzzled reader without a proper ending, forcing him to make up his own mind.

"The Washing Machine Tragedy" is Lem's best-known satire on the extremes of Western economic concepts: silly advertising campaigns, false value systems, competitiveness at any price, consumer idiocy. At the same time it is a brilliant parody of Asimov. Two producers of washing machines, Nuddlegg and Snodgrass, start ruinous sales campaigns, competing to corner the market. They throw on the market automatic washing machines with all sorts of useless extras, constantly vying with and attacking one another:

> You certainly will remember those full-page ads in the papers where a sneeringly grinning, pop-eyed washing machine said: "Do you wish your washing machine more intelligent than you? Certainly not!"

The two companies compete with each other in constructing washing machines which fulfill more and more functions that have nothing at all to do with washing.

> Nuddlegg placed a super-bard on the market—a washing machine writing and reciting verse, singing lullabies with a wonderful alto, holding out babies, curing corns and making the most polite compliments to the ladies.

This model is followed by a Snodgrass "Einstein" washing machine and a robot for bachelors in the sexy forms of Mayne Jansfield with a black alternative called Phirley Mac Phaine. Washing becomes only a by-product; the robots soon take more and more human forms, even varying forms according to every customer's detailed wishes, including "models which led people into sin, depraved teens and told children vulgar jokes." Robots soon are no longer useful for their original purpose, but for almost anything else. Working with a kind of time-lapse camera technique, Lem accelerates developments shown in *I, Robot* and many other science fiction stories. He satirically caricatures what Asimov thought could be prevented by his Laws of Robotics. Washing machines as thinking, independent automatons are no longer controllable. Not programmed according to laws of eternal goodness, they become malicious; commit all sorts of crimes; form cybernetic cooperatives with gangsters; turn into terrorists; fight each other in gangs.

Here Lem satirizes Western society, and he ridicules trivial science fiction in the tradition of Asimov. His witty ideas cascade and follow in rapid succession, but, as in every genuine satire, there is more behind it than mere literary parody. Legislation proves unable to deal with robotic problems because pressure groups undermine all straight action. Washing machines, once recognized as legal entities, together with powerful allies block all legal procedures taken against them. They infiltrate the economic and political system, and, when it turns out that the well-known Senator Guggenshyne in reality is a washing machine, the case against the machines is as good as lost. Human beings and robots become interchangeable, and men sell themselves into the service of intelligent machines. Many sorts of perversions are invented: machines consciously constructed as irresponsible for their actions, machines constructed as "sadomats" and "masomats," machines procreating themselves completely uncontrolled.

Still following themes implied in Asimov's *I, Robot,* Lem, in *The Star Diaries,* shows how the on-board computers on a spaceship revolt and finally found an extraterrestrial robot state. The lawsuit between Earth and Kathodius Matrass, the self-proclaimed ruler of the robot state, once again shows the manifold and complex legal problems that appear as soon as machines are recognized as legal entities. Theological questions, included in many of Lem's serious futurological considerations, are here tackled from a humorous angle. The legal problems are finally carried to grotesque extremes when Ijon Tichy, the narrator, finds out that all the attorneys of the Bar Association are in fact robots. So, in the end, the story, like the machines, runs out of control. The original society is no longer recognizable; all are robots; no problem is solved. Lem's parody attacks not only *I, Robot* but also the majority of Western science fiction stories, which are not interested at all in trying to discuss serious futurological and technological questions. Instead they wallow in catastrophes, make their profit with human anxiety, and put up entirely false perspectives of an interstellar human imperialism grown out of anthropocentric hybris. Lem's comment on the purpose of his essay "Robots in Science Fiction" applies also to his parodies: "We intended to point out only that it isn't possible to construct a reflection of the condition of the future with cliches" ["Robots in Science Fiction"].

Foreseeing miniaturization and microprocessing techniques, Lem more than a decade ago attacked androids, the humanization of machines in the Asimovian fashion, as nonsense:

> It isn't worth the effort and never will be, economically, to build volitional and intelligent automatons as part of the productive process. Even examples of these processes belonging to the sphere of private life are being automated separately: an automatic clock will never be able to wash dishes, and a mechanical dishwasher will never exchange small talk with the housewife. ["Robots in Science Fiction"]

**Donald M. Hassler**   (essay date March 1988)

SOURCE: "Some Asimov Resonances from the Enlightenment," in *Science Fiction Studies,* Vol. 15, No. 44, March, 1988, pp. 36-47.

[*Hassler is an educator, poet, and author of* Comic Tones in Science Fiction *(1982) and* Isaac Asimov *(1989). In the following essay which focuses on* I, Robot *and the* Foundation *trilogy, he explores Asimov's use of Enlightenment philosophy, with particular emphasis on the law and order ideas of John Locke, William Godwin's principle of Necessity, and John Calvin's religious determinism.*]

One difficulty in describing the SF [Science Fiction] that Asimov continues to produce stems from his rational drive for coherence and unified generality. Like all "scientific" thinkers who have written after the methodological revolution of John Locke and the other reformers of the new science, Asimov can never leave his best ideas alone. He must continually elaborate and link new insights to old on the assumption that accumulating and interlocked knowledge is the only sort of valid knowledge. His continual moves toward the general, even the abstract, can be seen both in the long time schemes of his future history and in the conceptual ideas of his own, implicit (and left open-ended) throughout his writings. Moreover, Asimov, along with other "hard SF" writers, seems to question the absolute insights of intuitive or "inspired" art by affirming the Lockean methodology of gradual accumulation. This is not to say that the images (e.g. of robots and Empire) at the core of Asimov's fiction are totally logical, transparent, and systematically arranged for purposes of Lockean, open-ended accumulation. In spite of himself, the clear and coherent rationalist contacts depths of meaning that are sometimes not on the surface. In other words, the resonance in both *I, Robot* and the *Foundation* trilogy seems to me significant; and that resonance or echoing is consistently from the 18th-century Enlightenment.

I will suggest here some ways in which Asimov's ideas on robotics and on history in these two early fictions, both of which are collections of shorter pieces written in the decade of the '40s for *Astounding,* remind us of key dilemmas stemming from our Enlightenment heritage. These dilemmas always balance "truth" against method, so that followers of the Enlightenment (and I believe Asimov is one of these) continually discover that the most effective methodology leads to the most "indeterminate" conclusions. I am not arguing that Asimov is a conscious scholar of his roots in this context, though any critic would have to think carefully before maintaining positively that Asimov is *not* consciously aware of some idea. Rather, I simply think it helps in understanding these remarkable and seminal longer fictions from the Campbell years to suggest their echoes from the Enlightenment. Also, though Asimov continues to make use of these ideas in much of his fiction written after these two works, to cover all the work through his most recent *Foundation and Earth* (1986) would be much too vast a topic for this essay.

---

**As unifying devices for *I, Robot,* Asimov employs the character of Dr. Susan Calvin and the Three Laws of Robotics. Both devices seem to me, also, imbued with resonance from the Enlightenment.**

**—*Donald M. Hassler***

---

One additional qualification needs to be stated at the outset—a qualification pointing to an entirely different essay that a critic of mine might write, or rather that several fine critics have been at work on for some time. I find that the resonances in Asimov echo more directly from the 18th-century Enlightenment with little benefit from the more organic, 19th-century reworkings of notions about history and about mechanism. Hence Asimov seems somewhat of an anachronism, even anathema, to more comprehensive inheritors of the Enlightenment tradition. Specifically, the images for cybernetics and robotics, along with the ideas which they imply, in the work of Stanislaw Lem and John Sladek as well as many other modernists, suggest more tonal and organic complexities and interfaces than Asimov allows for in his work. Similarly, historical determinism as understood by Marxist critics represents a quantum leap in complexity over Asimov and his 18th-century precursors. But Asimov is complex enough and interesting in his evasive anachronism. So it is the story of *his* ideas I am telling here rather than the total story of the ideas themselves. Certainly Asimov has been taken to task for being too simple; I intend to describe some of this "simpleness" more sympathetically than critics who are convinced that it is too narrow have been able to do. After all, one tenet of the 18th-century Enlightenment was clarity of vision; but this is not to say that the more complex shadows and "ghostlier demarcations" may not also be interesting. As unifying devices for *I, Robot,* Asimov employs both the character of Dr Susan Calvin and the Three Laws of Robotics. Both devices seem to me, also, imbued with resonance from the Enlightenment.

In his fine introduction to the whole canon of Asimovian SF up to but not including the recent outpouring of new Foundation and robot novels, James Gunn [in *Isaac Asimov: The Foundations of Science Fiction,* 1982] has worked out the "fixed-up" chronology for Calvin's life and spinster's career at US Robots and Mechanical Men, Inc. and how that scientific career as "robopsychologist" interacts with key product robots and other employees. There are other psychologists in the early short stories, even one or two "robopsychologists"; but Susan Calvin is special. She supplies not only the unity of *I, Robot* as a collection but also part of the Enlightenment resonance that makes this such an important book. Writing in an August 1952 "Foreword" to one of the early hardcover editions of the "novel," the anthologist Groff Conklin comments: "[Miss Calvin's] name may have been chosen by the author with a wry eye on the significance of . . . Calvinism" (n. p.). John Calvin, in fact, laid out a general framework, a time scheme and a theological set of assumptions, that did much to permit the gradualism of the secular Enlightenment and ultimately the technological and moral experimentation that Susan Calvin devotes her life to advancing. Calvin's move to posit an immensely long time scheme, along with a built-in "uncertainty" about any one particular judgment or "election" that God might hand down, did much to liberate thinkers for the gradual experimentation necessary in modern science. A recent critic who makes suggestions similar to those I am making here writes that Calvin, more than Vico or Spengler, ought to be a "likely candidate" for influencing the vast temporal frameworks characteristic of both Enlightenment science and hard SF:

> Do we not catch a glimpse in these 'time charts'

and thousand-year sagas of a return of the repressed Calvinistic background of the modern sciences? Without a doubt Calvin would be horrified, could he return from the grave, to see where his ideas have led, yet we could hardly underestimate the significance of his role in undermining the sacramental world picture which had prevailed throughout the [M]iddle [A]ges and thus laying the ground for a rational investigation of natural phenomena [David Clayton, "What Makes Hard Science Fiction, 'Hard'," in *Hard Science Fiction*, edited by George E. Slusser & Eric S. Rakin, 1986].

I think this resonance fits Asimov perfectly although the theology itself, of course, is never his. He might prefer to invoke the immensely long and gradual history of the Israelites, which does, in fact, seem calculated to postpone indefinitely any absolute appearance of final truth. But the name Susan Calvin reminds us of the Puritan work ethic, and she does work long and hard—and has still not arrived at any absolute truth at the age of 82, when she dies. Asimov has commented in numerous places how he loves this character and has her say finally, "I will see no more. My life is over. You will see what comes next" (*I, Robot*). Verbs for seeing, I think, are no accident in the usage of an Enlightenment heroine.

Moreover, the adjectives used to describe this driven robopsychologist whose presence does so much for unifying *I, Robot* complement what Asimov correctly labels at the beginning of the book as her "cold enthusiasm"—"thin-lipped," "frosty pupils." Such ideological excitement as presumably she shares with the other workers at US Robots and, of course, with Asimov himself focusses on the virtues of control, pattern, predictability. The resonance I see here is not only with the great advocate of complete control, John Calvin, but also with that secular determinist of the end of the 18th century: William Godwin. Discarding all theological reference, Godwin simply "believed in" a coherence and order that governed all systems. Hence what he called "Necessity," which many critics have described in terms that resemble Calvinistic determinism rather than a strictly mechanistic determinism, seems to be echoed in Asimov's final story in *I, Robot*, which I will describe next, as well as in Asimov's world of the Foundations.

In **"The Evitable Conflict,"** benevolent machines seem able to anticipate and control *all* events in a way that sounds much like the completeness of Necessity in Godwin; and at the same time Susan Calvin's "enthusiasm" is clear as she says finally:

> . . . it means that the Machine is conducting our future for us not only simply in direct answer to our direct questions, but in general answer to the world situation and to human psychology as a whole. . . . Think, that for all time, all conflicts are finally evitable. Only the Machines, from now on, are inevitable.

Asimov's youthful wordplay over "evitable" and "inevitable" will grow into a more sophisticated wit in the later novels where robotics play important roles. But his celebration of large, general systems (along with the implicit

realization of the dilemma in the need to keep systems open-ended and hence "indeterminate") seems clearly to be linked to the cool wordplay that he gives to Susan here.

---

**William Godwin's "Necessity," which many critics have described in terms that resemble Calvinistic determinism seems to be echoed in Asimov's final story in *I, Robot*.**

*—Donald M. Hassler*

---

In order to reach such high levels of reliable generality, Calvin and her US Robots colleagues had to devise the simple calculus of the Three Laws of Robotics and then continually try out the balancing and interaction of the laws in all their combinations and permutations. Those continual games of "if this, then the next" consume the stories in *I, Robot* and provide a further resonance with Godwinian Necessity. Not only is the general outcome of such a grand scheme as Necessity or the "Machines" completely reliable and determined, but also the continual adjustments and "calculus" of the relations within the scheme are continually fascinating. It is as though Susan Calvin, Asimov, and any other such generalist and determinist has both nothing at stake and, at the same time, must always be making adjustments to their system. The belief in Necessity or in the overall general and benevolent outcome frees the "player," in fact, to manipulate the calculus of the game.

Calvinistic theology as well as Godwinian Necessity and Asimovian Robotics all liberate a sort of freeplay of will due to the most general sort of overall system. Such a paradox of free will existing within and because of a rigid system has been agonized over most by the theologians in ways that are inappropriate for this discussion, but the echoes from Godwin in the Enlightenment Asimov should be listened to if we are to hear the real effects of the Susan Calvin narratives. Here is a key passage from Godwin writing about Necessity—both the overall determinism and the individual moves in the calculus—that resounds all through the cool, hard work of Susan Calvin in *I, Robot*:

> . . . if the doctrine of necessity do not annihilate virtue, it tends to introduce a great change into our ideas respecting it. . . . The believer in free-will, can expostulate with, or correct, his pupil, with faint and uncertain hopes, conscious that the clearest exhibition of truth is impotent, when brought into contest with the unhearing and indisciplinable faculty of will; or in reality, if he were consistent, secure that it could produce no effect. The necessarian on the contrary employs real antecedents, and has a right to expect real effects.

Godwin's matter-of-fact dismissal of free will as just too absurdly random suggests Asimov's firm ending to *I,*

*Robot,* with its notion that the machines control all reactions but disguise this total control because they know that a full realization of total control would cause mental anguish or "harm" to humans. Similarly, the three Laws themselves (or three "rules" of robotics as they are labelled in the first story where Asimov mentions them explicitly—**"Runaround"**) seem hardly profound or a great invention of the imagination. They are "neutral," as one recent critic has noted [see Alessandro Portelli, "The Three Laws of Robotics: Laws of the Text, Laws of Production, Laws of Society," *Science Fiction Studies,* Vol. 7, 1980, pp. 150-56]. Over the years they have gone on to have almost a life of their own as "ideas" outside of the fiction. Usually they are listed and worded with a sort of Godwinian flatness and their position and function in *I, Robot* is forgotten or confused. It was in the 1942 *Astounding* story, however, and in a fictional dialogue between Powell and Donovan, who are the key "right stuff" associates of Calvin, that the Three Laws first appear:

> 'And three, a robot must protect its own existence as long as such protection does not conflict with the First or Second Laws.'
>
> 'Right! Now where are we?'

Donovan and Powell could figure out exactly where they were and did solve their problem on Mercury, but it would take more robot stories and finally the book *I, Robot* itself for Asimov to know what a fine gimmick he had invented. Finally, of course, he doctored all the stories in the "novel" so that they would be consistent with the Three Laws.

Further, just as Godwin paradoxically insists (like Calvin before him), that the believer in Necessity will work even harder to make things happen in this world, so Asimov's roboticists (and the robots themselves in his most recent fictions) never tire of discussing and trying to manipulate some implication of these three simple statements in relation to one another. The paradox is simply that the apparent certainty *liberates* continual and near-infinite permutations. Though, as in **"Runaround,"** this continual balancing act often "strikes an equilibrium [whereby] . . . Rule 3 drives him back and Rule 2 drives him forward," the permutations of all the robots seem infinite. And so the accomplishment lies not only with the general outcome of "control" but also with the tinkering; it is a wonderful example of Asimov's inventiveness how complex and variable the Three Laws become.

Godwinian inclinations toward such clarity of analysis and such control may seem inhuman, even monstrous, so that Robotics itself, even though the Laws are benevolent towards humans, takes on the effects of the very *Frankenstein* motif that Asimov was trying to avoid. It is the continual acknowledgment of what I would call the calculus of complexity, however, that keeps Asimov himself lively and benevolent and "human" in his writing, especially his writing on the robots. He always is trying to teach and to clarify, and the material itself contains layer upon layer of complexity.

The series of stories dealing with the Foundation that was evolving at the same time as the robot series in the 1940s

is not only the fiction that Asimov is best known for but also, perhaps, best exemplifies his inclinations towards the general and, in this case, towards the human and towards storytelling. In addition to his numerous autobiographical reminiscences about this remarkable invention of the *Foundation* trilogy, Asimov's 1953 venture into full-fledged literary criticism with his essay for Reginald Bretnor entitled **"Social Science Fiction"** is both close enough to the actual writing of the stories and candid enough to be very helpful. Asimov has become increasingly more coy about doing literary criticism himself—perhaps because he has come to see more clearly and to take more seriously "hard SF" writing as radical and important. But as the *Foundation* trilogy was first appearing in book form, what he had to say about the genre in general reveals a great deal about what he himself had accomplished by that time and about his set of mind and its debt to the Enlightenment.

First of all, he effectively disassociates himself from the "gadget" materialism of SF writers by defining what he and Campbell have been interested in as the influence of social change and history—viz., "people movement" rather than "gadgets." Further, Asimov makes clear in this essay both his knowledge of the revolutionary changes that took place in the 18th century and his admiration for the "discovery of history" that had not been truly possible prior to the Enlightenment because humans had not experienced fundamental change:

> if science fiction is to deal with fictitious societies as possessing potential reality rather than as being nothing more than let's-pretend object lessons, it must be post-Napoleonic. Before 1789 human society didn't change as far as the average man was concerned and it was silly, even wicked, to suppose it could. After 1815, it was obvious to any educated man that human society not only could change but that it did. ("Social Science Fiction")

The fact that the young chemistry student at Columbia read as much history as he did is remarkable in itself. Later in the 1953 essay he identifies more fully this continuing fascination with the details of human history that provided story outlines for many of the narratives in the trilogy: "I wrote other stories, the germs of whose ideas I derived from the histories of Justinian and Belisarius, Tamerlane and Bajazet, John and Pope Innocent III." L. Sprague de Camp speaks of his and Asimov's "Toynbeean period" in the late '40s; and Asimov himself recollects that when he originally proposed to Campbell a tale about the fall of a Galactic Empire and a return to feudalism, this seemed perfectly natural to him since he "had read Gibbon's *Decline and Fall of the Roman Empire* not once but twice" ("The Story Behind. . . ."). Such omnivorous reading in youth may be exaggerated as both statements are reminiscences occasioned by the appearance of a new *Foundation* title; but there is no question that whereas the recent sequels fuse with the robot novels and introduce other themes, the original trilogy is overwhelmingly permeated by Gibbon, Toynbee, and the whole sweep of history seen from the perspective of a remarkable young man's readings.

I suggest further that in addition to this fascination with cycles in Toynbee, with pessimism in Gibbon, and with the whole detailed vista of Roman history as it modulated from repeated intrigue to resistance to forward movement to second-stage collapse, Asimov also knew Old Testament history. The Bible would have provided him with similar patterns of cycles. Certainly the continuing sense of exile and lament for a destroyed Jerusalem suggests the lost glory of Trantor as much as a fallen Rome does. And the early Church hidden within the declining Empire is a sort of "type and symbol" for a Second Foundation, even if Gibbon would not agree. Certainly present-day interpretations of the Bible by Fundamentalists as well as the long record of traditional interpretation would not agree with the notion of such open-ended movement; but from John Calvin's vision of a long future, mentioned earlier in this essay, to the "opening up" of history in the 18th century, such widening patterns in biblical history seem more viable. My main point here is not to insist on specific parallels, but I think history itself, and specifically the future history modelled on the reading of history as students have known it since the Enlightenment, must be acknowledged first as the major theme in these Foundation stories that epitomize Asimov's own description of social SF.

In other words, the vision of open-ended possibility and the full recognition of "change" in society that so characterized the revolution of the Enlightenment that Asimov talks about in his 1953 essay and that he had imaged in his trilogy manifested itself not only in the permutations and analyses of robotics but also in the realization of the nature of history itself. Historiography from Gibbon and Hume to Asimov himself contains nothing that can be called "absolute." Rather it recounts continuing movement from one faction to another, by spurts and long slow declines, with repeated variations on the images of equilibrium and disequilibrium.

Just as one can see few absolute truths in the panorama of change and history, so Asimov's texts are never set in stone; he correlatively seems quite comfortable with the publishing practices that made up the commercial "relativism" of pulp SF. Whereas texts of nostalgic "high art" in our scientific age will be early standardized to be set in type the same way each time as though "absolute" (I think of the standard paging in various teaching editions of Joyce's *A Portrait of the Artist as a Young Man*), Asimov had to accept a more fluid state of the text effecting the *Foundation* trilogy even after the stories had become books. For example, the first novel becomes *The 1,000-Year Plan* in a drastically cut 1955 edition that sold for 25 cents. Asimov did not seem to mind. Further, he has updated his texts in accordance with changes in scientific knowledge and terminology—which would seem to confirm that he sees little of permanence and absoluteness about "art." Not only the publishing practices, then, but the "tinkering" and continual rational manipulation in Asimov speaks more of the open-endedness of science than of the absolute values of art. In his essay **"The Story Behind *Foundation*,"** written to introduce the surge of sequel writing which began to appear in 1982, Asimov anticipates new scientific findings that he can now incorporate into the narrative:

> The *Foundation* series had been written at a time when our knowledge of astronomy was primitive compared with what it is today. I could take advantage of that and at least *mention* black holes, for instance. I could also include electronic computers, which had not been invented until I was half through with the series.

Even before the sequel writing, however, he was quietly altering "atomic" to "nuclear" throughout the trilogy in line with post-war nomenclature.

Similarly, the sense of permanence in the text of *I, Robot* seems to take a back seat to the coherence of the ideas as they evolve in Asimov's mind over time. For example, the story **"Reason"** appeared in *Astounding* (1941) *before* the Three Laws of Robotics had been articulated by Asimov and Campbell; but in the book Asimov includes an updated paragraph in **"Reason"** that makes the Laws explicit (*I, Robot*). Scholars of the future are bound to have particular troubles with the texts and the setting of the texts for SF works if the attempt is ever made to "establish" them as high art and thus to standardize a text.

Though neither history nor art itself is able to supply Absolute Truths in the *Foundation* trilogy, it does have its general ideas and themes that momentarily and in their changeableness do catch our imaginations as the best substitute we can have for absolutism. More than the continual variations on political or military intrigue in the plot, which I have said echo the continual intrigues in history itself, these general themes woven into the trilogy are what affect the reader. Some of the most important themes are, in fact, representative of the rational urge in Asimov always to move to the general. These emerge from the overall tale of Hari Seldon's plan through the "science" of psychohistory to lessen the chaotic effects of declining control within the Galactic Empire and to establish a new "Enlightenment" by means of the Foundation that he institutes on the planet Terminus working in continuing tension with the Second Foundation.

The first general idea is an echo not from the fall of the Roman Empire, although I suppose the hidden and ameliorative influence of the early Church is a "foundational" resonance here, so much as it is a set of images from the 18th-century Enlightenment. Certainly the major activity of the Seldon psychohistorians is work on the *Encyclopedia Galactica,* which is quoted from periodically throughout the trilogy; and the echo here is to the massive French work, done also by a small army of "new scientists"—Diderot and his cohorts—that helped both to overthrow the *ancien régime* in the 18th century and to "enlighten" the darkness following the decline of that Regime.

But history itself, or the whole record of human activity over time, is also the theme as we read about these future *encyclopédistes*. The important effect is the general notion about history that is stated, perhaps, most clearly in *Foundation and Empire,* the second book, though it is implicit in the entire set of stories. Here is an expression of the consternation felt by the villain, Bel Riose, in the face of Necessity:

> Riose's voice trembled with indignation. 'You mean that this art of his predicts that I would at-

tack the Foundation and lose such and such a battle for such and such a reason? You are trying to say that I am a silly robot following a predetermined course into destruction.'

'No,' replied the old patrician, sharply. 'I have already said that the science had nothing to do with individual actions. It is the vaster background that has been foreseen.'

'Then we stand clasped tightly in the forcing hand of the Goddess of Historical Necessity.'

'Of *Psycho*-Historical Necessity,' prompted Barr, softly. (*Foundation and Empire*).

It should be noted that Asimov has Riose call himself a "silly robot" in this passage—which suggests that the inevitability of the Three Laws of Robotics also carries with it the sad cancelling out of individual actions.

There is much sadness in such "determinism" for the individual actor, and that sadness is the second major general idea to consider. In a real way, also, it is simply another facet of the image of decline that is inevitable over vast stretches of time—the same sublime sense of cycles that gave such energy to **"Nightfall"** and that Asimov indeed found validated in his readings of the historians from Hume and Gibbon on, even to the great events of the then-ongoing Second World War. When cycles themselves and vast wars are the main "heroes" in history, individuals like Bel Riose do indeed feel overshadowed. Such a sense of eclipse and small "modernness" can be seen best in the key villain of the trilogy, the mutant and sad man, strangely named the Mule, who is able to alter emotions. Gunn [in *Isaac Asimov: The Foundations of Science Fiction*, 1982] has noted how much Asimov did seem to like this character of the Mule, as is evident in the fact that the Mule figures in more stories than any other individual except for Hari Seldon. His very role of being an enemy to all other forces in the Galaxy, including the Foundation, and yet promoting the eventual benevolent outcomes of the Seldon Plan through his antagonistic acts illustrates the predetermined sense of historical destiny that causes all "moderns" at any given time to experience this sense of sadness.

The second important theme I notice, then, is nostalgia for the lost glory of individual heroism balanced nicely with a full acceptance and celebration of smaller, limited "modernness." In fact, this is the motif of the Ancients versus the Moderns, or the lament for lost Golden Ages coupled with the realization of the advantages in an Iron Age. I think Asimov also learned this from the Enlightenment. It is the Georgic mode that informs so much 18th-century literature—an age in which people were coming to terms with the complexities and limits of the peculiar "modernness" that the scientific revolution and economic and socio-political changes brought with them. Regardless of how deeply scholarship can measure this resonance, however, the theme seems clear in the trilogy. The Mule is a strangely limited leader. He spends much of his time disguised as the court fool, Magnifico, and sadly, like his namesake, he is lonely and infertile. In other words, "Moderns" are small and limited compared to the "Ancients." The technology, including the robotics, of an Iron

Age such as ours mirrors our beliefs in system and in "corporate" action. The individual hero has been replaced by steady progress in robotics and in other Iron Age techniques and, as in the 18th-century Georgic, the tone in Asimov's expression of this tradeoff is mixed.

Similarly, the Iron Age adaptability of the Foundation itself seems well worked out by Asimov to contrast with the glory of Empire. Nuclear devices must be small in the Foundation. Traders and other leaders are always somewhat imperfect and ineffectual as individuals; only the Plan itself is ultimately effective. Further, the Foundation itself is always working far out and on the periphery of the Galaxy, and even the Second Foundation, located at the other "end," is hidden and small. This translation that Asimov cleverly makes of the cycles of history and of the spiral shape of our Galaxy into the mysterious loops that eventually bring readers to discover the Second Foundation back on Trantor suggests the non-heroic peripheral details of a "modern" technological age. Over against Golden Age, titanic heroism, such as the "giants" in the sixth chapter of *Genesis,* we moderns can survive by means of the micro-electronics of a continually changing Iron Age technology. The Lord moves in mysterious ways, and one of the most mysterious has to do with the fact that grand results are accomplished by means of small, peripheral modern men.

Thus a final overall theme brings us back to the role of generalization and to the centrality of humans. It is significant that a concluding key figure in this massive narrative is a writer, the future novelist Arkady Darell, just as a journalist is a key point of view character in **"Nightfall."** But the real hero of the trilogy is the sublime history of humankind itself. And it is this large vision, which only the Enlightenment could take, that ultimately—and poignantly—submerges even the individual heroism of the writer. The more telling way of conceptualizing this effect is in terms of the general idea itself. (In this way, William Godwin, who was after all also a novelist, is further seen as a key prototype.) Here is Hari Seldon himself speaking at his trial, which provides the focus for the shorter initial piece that Asimov wrote last as the book publication was being readied:

'I shall not be alive half a decade hence,' said Seldon, 'and yet.. [the future] is of overpowering concern to me. Call it idealism. Call it an identification of myself with that mystical generalization to which we refer by the term, "man." ' (*Foundation*)

When he writes the later sequels, Asimov will have his robot heroes come back to this big generalization about "man." The important thing to see here, then, is his move again to the large general idea. Therefore, just as *I, Robot* toys with permutations in laws that echo Godwinian Necessity, so the early *Foundation* stories support this paradoxically liberating vision of "system" that both orders and submerges—with the added notion, confirmed by the Enlightenment, of a vast, yet anthropocentric history.

## FURTHER READING

### Criticism

Fiedler, Jean, and Mele, Jim. "Asimov's Robots." In *Critical Encounters: Writers and Themes in Science Fiction,* edited by Dick Riley, pp. 1-22. New York: Frederick Ungar, 1978.
   Examines the benefits-of-technology theme in Asimov's robot novels and stories, focusing on *I, Robot, The Cave of Steel,* and *The Naked Sun.*

Moore, Maxine. "Asimov, Calvin, and Moses." In *Voices for the Future: Essays on Major Science Fiction Writers,* Volume 1, edited by Thomas D. Clareson, pp. 88-103. Bowling Green: Bowling Green University Popular Press, 1976.
   Examines the ethical aspects of the characters in *I, Robot* from Calvinistic and Judaic perspectives, with a particular emphasis on the Puritan work ethic, human freedom and determinism, and human responsibility.

Thorner, Lincoln. Review of *I, Robot,* by Isaac Asimov. In *Emergency Librarian* 15, No. 3 (January-February 1988): 22.
   Favorably assesses *I, Robot.*

Wilson, Raymond J. "Asimov's Mystery Story Structure." *Extrapolation* 19, No. 2 (May 1978): 101-07.
   Examines the similarities between traditional mystery stories and Asimov's science fiction, paying particular attention to the story "Liar" in *I, Robot.*

**Additional coverage of Asimov's life and career is contained in the following sources published by Gale Research:** *Authors and Artists for Young Adults,* **Vol. 13;** *Bestsellers 1990,* **Vol. 2;** *Contemporary Authors,* **Vols. 1-4 (rev. ed.), 137 (obituary); Contemporary Authors New Revision Series, Vols. 2, 19, 36; Contemporary Literary Criticism, Vols. 1, 3, 9, 19, 26, 76;** *Children's Literature Review,* **Vol. 12;** *Dictionary of Literary Biography,* **Vol. 8;** *Dictionary of Literary Biography Yearbook, 1992; DISCovering Authors Modules; Junior DISCovering Authors; Major Authors and Illustrators for Children and Young Adults; Major 20th-Century Writers;* **and** *Something About the Author,* **Vols. 1, 26, 74.**

# William Attaway

## 1911-1986

(Full name William Alexander Attaway) American novelist, dramatist, and songwriter.

The following entry provides an overview of Attaway's career.

## INTRODUCTION

Attaway is known primarily for his two novels, *Let Me Breathe Thunder* (1939) and *Blood on the Forge* (1941). Most commentators consider the latter, which chronicles the experiences of three brothers at a steel mill in Pennsylvania, a classic portrayal of the so-called Great Migration, the movement of blacks from the agrarian southern United States to the industrialized North in the period following World War I.

### Biographical Information

Attaway was born in Greenville, Mississippi. His father was a physician, his mother a schoolteacher, and, seeking to avoid what Attaway later called the "Southern caste system," they moved the family to Chicago early in his life. There Attaway attended a vocational school, initially planning to become an auto mechanic. After being introduced to the poetry of Langston Hughes by one of his teachers, however, he decided to become a writer. After his father's death, Attaway dropped out of the University of Illinois—which he had entered mainly to please his parents—and lived an itinerant life, working as a seaman, salesman, and labor organizer, in deliberate preparation for his writing career. In 1935 Attaway helped write the Federal Writers' Project guide to Illinois and befriended another Mississippi-born black author, Richard Wright. Returning that year to study at the University of Illinois, Attaway produced his first major work, the play *Carnival*. In 1936 he published his first short story, "Tale of the Blackamoor," and received his B.A. degree. Later in the year he moved to New York City where he held a variety of jobs, including a stint as an actor, which was his sister Ruth's profession. Attaway was performing with a traveling production of Moss Hart and George S. Kaufman's *You Can't Take It With You* (1936) when he learned that his first novel, *Let Me Breathe Thunder,* had been accepted for publication. Aided by a two-year grant from the Julius Rosenwald Fund, Attaway immediately began work on *Blood on the Forge.* After the publication of this work, he wrote songs, books about music, and scripts for radio, television, and movies. Included in his musical compositions were songs for his friend Harry Belafonte, at whose home he was married in 1962. Attaway lived with his wife and their two children in Barbados for eleven years, fulfilling, in Samuel B. Garren's words, "a lifelong desire of his to live in a country with a black government, black law enforcement, and black professional people." Attaway's

last years were spent in California writing screenplays. He died of heart failure in Los Angeles in 1986.

### Major Works

*Let Me Breathe Thunder,* which takes place at the end of the Great Depression, is the story of two white hoboes, Ed and Step, and their relationship with a nine-year-old Mexican boy, Hi-Boy. Although the men have much affection for Hi-Boy, their way of life leads to the corruption and tragic death of the innocent youth. In this work Attaway addresses such themes as separation, corruption, and dislocation. *Blood on the Forge,* is about three brothers—Big Mat, Chinatown, and Melody Moss—who leave their jobs as southern sharecroppers to work in a northern steel mill. Although the North holds the promise of greater racial equality and better job opportunities, the Moss brothers encounter only pain and tragedy. In addition to addressing the social and economic barriers faced by blacks in American society, *Blood on the Forge* also focuses on the problems associated with an increasingly rootless, industrialized world. Attaway's nonfiction works include *Calypso Song Book* (1957), a collection of songs, and *Hear*

*America Singing* (1967), a history of popular music in America for children.

## Critical Reception

*Let Me Breathe Thunder* was favorably received by critics. While some early reviews found it significant that the main characters in the work are white, not black, other commentators suggested that Ed and Step are basically outcasts, possessing a social status somewhat analogous to that of blacks. Also, several critics have noted the novel's similarities to John Steinbeck's *Of Mice and Men* (1937). Although most of the early reviews of *Blood on the Forge* were laudatory, the book was not a commercial success; some critics have speculated that Richard Wright's popular and highly controversial novel *Native Son* (1940) may have drawn attention away from Attaway's work. In an introduction to a 1970 edition of *Blood on the Forge,* Edward Margolies wrote that "Attaway's book may have looked tame to an America preparing for another war and whose reading public had already found its Negro 'spokesman' in the virile Wright." More recently, scholars have reclaimed an important position for Attaway among black American writers. *Blood on the Forge* is studied today as a consummate proletarian novel, as a leading fictional account of the Great Migration, and for its elements of black history and folklore. It remains Attaway's best-known work and, some critics believe, the greatest interwar depiction of the plight of black American workers.

---

# PRINCIPAL WORKS

*Carnival* (drama) 1935
*Let Me Breathe Thunder* (novel) 1939
*Blood on the Forge* (novel) 1941
*Calypso Song Book* (songs) 1957
*Hear America Singing* (nonfiction) 1967

---

# CRITICISM

## Stanley Young (review date 25 June 1939)

SOURCE: "Tough and Tender," in *The New York Times Book Review,* June 25, 1939, p. 7.

[*Young was an American editor, educator, poet, playwright, and critic. In the following review, he favorably appraises characterization and language in* Let Me Breathe Thunder.]

This first novel [*Let Me Breathe Thunder*] by a 25-year-old Negro quite definitely proves two things: That it is possible for a Negro to write about whites, and that William Attaway has a legitimate reason to face a typewriter in the years to come. His tough and tender story of two young

box-car wanderers and their love for a little Mexican waif who rides the reefers with them has some of the emotional quality and force of the familiar relationship of George and Lennie in *Of Mice And Men.* We see two rootless men faced by hard reality yet still susceptible to dreams and affection.

Ed and Step, the major characters, represent in these times the vast army of drifting young Americans who grab their scenery from the top of a freight [train] and take their emotions from an empty stomach. They are apparently living from day to day and waiting for nothing. They are not professional hoboes given to talk about the "romance of the road." Their single thought is to keep alive, to push on over the next mountain, to pick hops in California, berries in Washington, back-doors in Ohio, until by some miracle they land and take root.

In New Mexico Ed and Step meet Hi-Boy, an inarticulate Mexican kid with dreams in his eyes and a wistful, trusting way that breaks through their casual, tough veneer until the men appoint themselves as road guardians to the boy. It is in no way the average jocker-lamb relationship of the hobo jungle. The kid becomes a kind of domestic symbol to the wanderers and a kind of outlet for their affection and all the tenderness which is missing in their abnormal lives.

No matter what brothel or bar or circumstance Step's primitive urges lead him into, Hi-Boy's reactions to the scene take precedence over everything else. They delight in him when they find he is a crack shot with a rifle; they are paternally concerned when he is ill. He is their cub and they want to keep him happy and rolling in the sun they have not seen. When the rancher at Yakima Valley wants to keep Hi-Boy, the men are torn between their desire for the boy's future and their own need of him, and William Attaway makes their decision seem urgent and humanly important.

All the emotions of the book are direct and primitive, and the bareness of the speech cuts the action to lean and powerful lines. The scenes in Mag's roadhouse, Step's relations with the emotionally starved rancher's daughter, Hi-Boy's moment when he jabs a fork into his hand to prove his courage to Step—these and a dozen other incidents are as jabbing to the nerves as a power-drill. Less ably written the book would only be melodrama and sentimentality, but the characterizations are sure and the dialogue distilled to the point that a poet writing a cablegram could not better.

It is surely true, however, that the understated writing and the hard-boiled characters cloaking their semi-conscious good intentions are ingredients of novels that have become rather familiar of late. Before James Cain or Edward Newhouse or Benjamin Appeal, or even the early Hemingway, this book would have caused great excitement. It is no particular discredit to William Attaway to say that in his first work he has paralleled the style of his more eminent contemporaries. He has, in many moments of this book, equaled them, and, in the poetic overtones of the writing, occasionally surpassed them. He is an authentic young artist not to be watched tomorrow but now.

## N. L. R.   (review date 1 July 1939)

SOURCE: A review of *Let Me Breathe Thunder,* in *The Saturday Review of Literature,* July 1, 1939, p. 20.

[*In the following mixed review of* Let Me Breathe Thunder, *the critic praises the plot and pace of the work but faults its dramatic elements, stating that Attaway "will write a better novel when he puts the stage entirely behind him."*]

William Attaway writes easily, the way a man walks or tells a tale, with natural vigor and his objective clear every foot of the way. His first novel [*Let Me Breathe Thunder*] is one that shows off this kind of writing most effectively: a hard-bitten story of two roaming hoboes, working stiffs, and a Mexican boy they have picked up somewhere on the road. The little Mexican injects a fresh element into their lives, a note of responsibility and, irresistibly, against all stubbornness, a note of tenderness. Upon this level of unwilling masculine sentiment the tale spins its length, moving briskly and with unfailing narrative skill, towards its desperate climax. All of this is on the credit side. On the debit, we must note that Mr. Attaway has projected much of his dramatic experience (he has written and acted in plays) into his writing. Too many of his scenes are plainly stagy, seen as tableaus in terms of groups and gestures, or heard as dramatic speeches, with an eye towards effective curtains and black-outs. Sometimes he lets his characters say things that might carry a punch across the little-theater footlights, without carrying any credibility in a realistic novel. One end-product of this staginess is the cutting of the story into scenes that ought naturally to have flowed together. Mr. Attaway will write a better novel when he puts the stage entirely behind him.

## Drake de Kay   (review date 24 August 1941)

SOURCE: "The Color Line," in *The New York Times Book Review,* August 24, 1941, pp. 18, 20.

[*In the following review of* Blood on the Forge, *de Kay praises Attaway for his skillful and unsentimental portrayal of the Great Migration.*]

During and for several months after the close of the first World War a shortage of man power existed in the Pennsylvania and West Virginia steel industry. Attracted by wages of $4 a day, Southern farm Negroes moved North to enter the steel mills. From the point of view of tenant farmers living in a state of virtual peonage the low wages of the mill workers seemed riches, while there was an additional inducement to desert the land in the expectation of enjoying greater social freedom. The mass migration which drained large sections of the South of its farm labor, causing a new problem for agriculturists, also created a series of problems for Northern employers and labor leaders. At the time the unions were conducting their initial efforts to organize the steel industry on a closed-shop basis and the employers were relying increasingly on Negroes as strike-breakers. Consequently the unions watched this influx with mounting anxiety. Also to be reckoned with was the fear of the white workers that they might eventually be displaced by Negroes willing to accept lower wages and working conditions. These and other aspects of the Southern Negro migration are touched upon in this story [*Blood on the Forge*] of the three Moss brothers—Melody, Chinatown and Big Mat—who abandon their worn-out tenant farm in the red clay hills of Kentucky to work in a West Virginia steel mill. Through the narration of their experience as industrial workers we perceive social and economic issues that are part of the history of an epoch.

Written by a Negro author with notable objectivity, [*Blood on the Forge*] is a starkly realistic story involving social criticism as searching as any to be found in contemporary literature; but Mr. Attaway, though his protagonists are of his own race, has not singled out the Negro as the sole victim of unjust conditions. He shows native white Americans and immigrant Slavs working under the same system of low pay, cruelly long hours and unnecessary hazards to life and limb. Many of these injustices have since been rectified, but that fact does not detract from the story value of a tale which holds one's attention primarily by its realistic characterizations, the vividness and intensity of dramatic moments and its pathos. There is a double theme: the Negro competing with the white man in an abnormal condition of the labor market, and the man of the soil forced to make an adjustment with urban industrial life.

Big Mat, a physical giant with the mentality of a child who has never learned to play, tries to remain faithful to his wife, Hattie, who waits in Kentucky until he shall have earned enough money to send for her. He reads his Bible regularly and saves his pay. His brothers persuade him to attend a dog fight, where he meets Anna, a Mexican girl of the red light district, and yields to the urgings of his physical nature. Like other unmarried steel workers, Melody and Chinatown spend their pay on corn whiskey, dice and women. The greater social freedom for Negroes turns out to be largely delusive, for their chief competitors, the Slavs, hate them, while white Americans and Irish preserve a guarded attitude. When the union organizers appear the black workers are easily brought into the employers' camp, being persuaded that, as the least efficient racial group, their only chance of continuing on the job consists in making the best of present conditions.

---

***Blood on the Forge* is a starkly realistic story involving social criticism as searching as any to be found in contemporary literature.**

—*Drake de Kay*

---

Working in the terrific heat of blast furnaces and open hearths while under a complex of moral and emotional tensions, the brothers fall under the spell that ensnares all steel men. But one sees in the attitude of these black men something more—a transference of their mystical worship of earth to that other primal element, fire, yet not without a struggle and a haunting sense of apostasy. Earth will be avenged for man's presumption in converting it into steel.

This novel portraying life in the raw is not for those who shun the unlovely aspects of human nature, who have a distaste for bloodshed and the cruder manifestations of sex. Indeed one of its chief claims to literary distinction consists in the author's refusal to sentimentalize his earthy men and women. The artistic integrity Mr. Attaway evinced in his first book, *Let Me Breathe Thunder,* is equally evident in the faithful depiction of the primitive approach to life of a social group on whose laborious efforts the whole scheme of modern industrial life is based.

## Edward Margolies   (essay date 1968)

SOURCE: "Migration: William Attaway and *Blood on the Forge,*" in *Native Sons: A Critical Study of Twentieth-Century Negro American Authors,* J. B. Lippincott Company, 1968, pp. 47-64.

[*Margolies is an American educator and critic who specializes in African-American literature. In the excerpt below, he provides a thematic and stylistic analysis of* Blood on the Forge.]

There persists to this day a widely held belief that the deep South, with its brutal caste system and its savage history of racial atrocities, represents for Negroes an image of steaming hell. Such a view is constantly reinforced by spokesmen for civil rights organizations and activists of various liberal persuasions. It serves their political convenience and humanitarian goals, which is all to the good, but unfortunately it muddles their thinking. For it is grounded on the assumption that people are political and economic entities whose motivations and behavior may be simplistically understood. Since Negroes have been systematically exploited and oppressed in the South, it follows they must hate the South that has persecuted them. There are partial truths here—how else explain the vast northward migrations that have been taking place over the past fifty or so years? But what of the large numbers who have stayed behind? Partial truths are not satisfactory to the artist, for he understands that people often leave the place of the origins not simply out of hatred, but because they want to continue to love their homes. And they carry their love with them to the dismal ghettos of the North and cherish it all the more for their adversity. Jean Toomer, for all his woozy romanticism, persuades because his South represents a heartfelt need, and even racial militants like Richard Wright, may, on occasion, speak lyrically of "down-home" times. They miss especially the soil, the seasons, the sense of community they once knew; they regale one another with stories and fables and legends of family, friends, and relatives they left behind; and they attempt to adapt their older ways to the anarchy of city life. Frequently they return South for visits in order to renew themselves.

Calvin Hernton, in a recent book of essays, describes the mixed feelings of some of these visitors:

> The fact that Negroes are alienated from the broader life of the South and its deeper mysteries

does not frequently pull them away, but binds them ever more closely to the bosom of Down-Home. The South is the mother-matrix out of which and in which the Negro's mind has been fashioned; it is at the same time the festering ache in the republic of his heart. This, more than anything else, is why they go back.

Such ambivalence has seldom been expressed with more skill or emotional impact than in William Attaway's *Blood on the Forge* (1941), a narrative describing the first stage of the Negro's journey North from his ancestral home. It recounts the experiences of the three brothers Moss in a steel-mill town in western Pennsylvania after leaving their Kentucky hill-country tenant farm during World War I. In the course of the novel one of the brothers is killed, and as the book closes the two remaining brothers move on to the city, where they hope to acquire new roots.

The novel not only records a critical moment in the Negro's history but expands its significance by reference to some of the larger events of the American experience. It takes into account the looming strife between incipient labor unions and the steel companies, the psychology and culture of east European immigrants as they work alongside Southern Negroes, and the specific work conditions under which they all struggle. But it would be a mistake to regard *Blood on the Forge* as a tract, for Attaway rendered the usual subject matter of the proletarian novel into a work of art. He transcended his materials to describe a strange odyssey of the human spirit—without losing several familiar sociological truths. Indeed, what may puzzle the reader is a certain cold realism combined with what can only be described as fervored romantic pessimism.

The failure of the novel to attain popularity may perhaps be ascribed to this paradoxical achievement. On the face of it, *Blood on the Forge*—even its title—suggests simply another of the interminable working-class novels dealing with the downtrodden and their efforts to succeed to a dignified life. Or perhaps the novel was read as naturalistic fiction, but because it did not quite fit the "up-lift" formula of its day, it was ignored and relegated to the dustbin of the ideologically confused. Whatever the reasons, it is clear that neither the "aesthetes" who wanted their art to eschew all sociological comment, nor the "socially committed" who wanted their art to point the way, would have looked favorably on *Blood on the Forge,* since in form and subject matter it seems to lie somewhere in a no man's land. Attaway has ideological axes to grind, but they are honed in peculiarly traditional American accents. He urges the primacy of the life of the soil over the life-denying machine, and projects the American image of men of different nationalities and colors working and living together. For all that, his books may have appeared a little foreign to American readers. Possibly the publication of Richard Wright's more sensational *Native Son* the preceding year had something to do with it. Wright's novel was less polished, but it contained rather startling revelations for white readers unused to racial complexities. The American reading public apparently could take only one Negro at a time. Wright became a "spokesman"; Attaway never published another novel.

Attaway prepared the way for *Blood on the Forge* with *Let Me Breathe Thunder,* a novel he published two years earlier in 1939. In one sense Attaway is less inhibited in his first book because he is writing primarily about white characters whose point of view would not be readily understood as racial. Yet his protagonists, hobo migrant farm workers, are Negroes under the skin—pariahs, consumed at the same time with wanderlust and the desire to stay put. Their agony is a Negro agony, and their allusions to race problems are more "inside" than Attaway might have cared to admit. They speak on more than one occasion of interracial sex and its conspiratorial acceptance in middle-class communities, of the various kinds of racial prejudice they meet throughout the country—and the fact that only hoboes do not appear to discriminate; of the private humiliations "outsiders" experience in a bourgeois milieu, and above all of their uneasiness in accommodating themselves to the patterns of American life, and their desire not to do so. They are the alienated, the uncommitted, whose discontents may one day be marshaled toward revolution—but not necessarily of the doctrinaire, ideological variety. They do not yet know what they want, but they know what they dislike. Once they are aware of what they seek, they are perhaps capable of changing their world.

Attaway here does not understand his people. His solution, like Toomer's, is a return to the soil. A character named Sampson, who owns orchards and farm lands, has suffered considerably during his life; his wife and sons have died and he lives alone with an adolescent daughter. But his strong sense of identification with the land serves to renew him and give him perspective and emotional balance. Sampson is portrayed most sympathetically, but Attaway cannot make him ring altogether true. And the hoboes whom he asks to stay with him on the land cannot believe in him either; as the novel closes, they leave to try their luck elsewhere. Attaway's inability to make Sampson believable stems as much from anachronism as from failure of craftsmanship. The American dream of the independent farmer was outmoded by the Depression years, and Attaway was simply unable to cope with his nostalgia.

The plot of *Let Me Breathe Thunder* is unsophisticated and sometimes Hollywoodishly sentimental. It deals with two hardened migratory farm workers in Washington State who adopt as their companion a lost, orphaned ten-year-old Mexican-American youth. Hi Boy, the name they have given him, speaks no English at first, rides the rods with them, and comes to adore Step, the more romantic and volatile of the two. At one point Hi Boy grinds a fork into his hand in order to prove to Step (who rather disapproves of the child as an unnecessary encumbrage) that he has the fortitude to bear the vicissitudes of the migratory life. The three companions settle later on Sampson's farm in Yakima, where Step rather reluctantly falls in love with Anna, Sampson's daughter. Their place of assignation is the home of a Negro woman, Mag, who owns brothels and considerable property in Yakima. In the course of events, Anna is rather dramatically discovered awaiting Step in Mag's house, and Step and his companion and Hi Boy flee in a boxcar. As they travel east across the country, Hi Boy's hand swells up from his self-inflicted wound. The

men do everything they can to save him but he dies. Step and his companion conceal the body under a tarpaulin in a boxcar headed for New Mexico, Hi Boy's birthplace, then continue east to Kansas to seek new work.

The novel celebrates the loyalty and decency of men on the move, and the essential virtues of the life of the soil. Attaway's Negro themes, as we have seen, are muted and disguised, which allows him to speak the language of protest without using its rhetoric. In shying away from making his main characters Negroes, Attaway was perhaps fearful of having his novel labeled protest fiction. The two Negro characters who do appear in the novel have no especial "Negro" traits, and although one of them is nearly lynched for the supposed attempted rape of a white girl, scarcely any allusion is made to his race. It appears as if Attaway were bending over backwards to assure his readers that he is not writing "sociology." Such a position is absurd, since any reader would naturally associate lynchings and imaginary sex crimes with race. The novel falters on other counts: the characters rarely spring to life, and their situations vaguely suggest those Steinbeck described two years earlier in *Of Mice and Men.* Yet for all that, the narrative does possess a certain verve, and the prose is economical and clean in the Hemingway manner—objective but replete with undertones of irony and sadness.

---

*Let Me Breathe Thunder* **celebrates the loyalty and decency of men on the move and the essential virtues of the life of the soil.**

**—*Edward Margolies***

---

In *Blood on the Forge,* the Hemingway style is transformed by Negro tones and rhythms. As the novel traces the deterioration of the Negro peasant under the crush of industrial life, Attaway rings changing images of the natural Southern landscape against the hearths, blast furnaces, and smoking chimneys of the steel-mill town. Implicit in the language is a kind of hell-death-decay imagery. His "green men" glance about them upon their arrival in Allegheny County and remember their former homes, the red clay hills, where "there was growing things everywhere and crab-apple trees bunched—stunted but beautiful." What they see now is an "ugly, smoking hell out of a backwoods preacher's sermon." Later they ask, "Where are the trees? They so far away on the tops of the low mountains that they look like the fringe on a black wear-me-to-a-wake dress held upside down against the sky." Attaway foreshadows the disintegration of black men under these conditions when the brothers, on their first day in the Pennsylvania community, spy a Negro whore approaching them on the street. At first they are attracted, but as she passes alongside, they are nearly overcome by a sickening odor. They are told afterward that one of her breasts is rotting away.

The reduction of the brothers begins almost immediately. Surrounded by rusty iron towers, brick stacks, magnets, traveling cranes, and steam shovels, they appear even to themselves physically diminished in size:

> They had always thought of [Mat, the eldest] as big and powerful as a swamp tree. Now, in their eyes, he was getting smaller and smaller. Like spiral worms, all their egos had curled under pressure from the giants around them. Sooner or later it came to all the green men.

Attaway does not, however, confine this effect entirely to Negroes. The other workers in the mills—Irish, Italians, Slovaks, and Ukrainians—in one sense make better adjustments to industrial life. They raise families—for them their children are "growing things"—while the Negroes make no attempt to send home for their wives and children. Yet the white workers fare scarcely better: their children fornicate and commit incest in the weeds outside their homes, and their grown daughters become whores.

Steel, the indestructible symbol of industry, assumes a powerful impersonal force, brutalizing and degrading to the human spirit.

> The fire and flow of metal seemed an eternal act which had grown beyond men's control. It was not to be compared with crops that one man nursed to growth and ate at his own table. The nearness of a farmer to his farm was easily understood. But no man was close to steel. It was shipped across endless tracks to all the world. On the consignment slips were Chicago, Los Angeles, New York, rails for South America, tin for Africa, tool steel for Europe. This hard metal held up the new world. Some were shortsighted and thought they understood. Steel is born in the flames and sent out to live and grow old. It comes back to the flames and has a new birth. But no one man could calculate its beginning or end. It was old as the earth. It would end when the earth ended. It seemed deathless.

But if Attaway deplores the evils of the industrial North, he does not conversely romanticize the virtues of the pastoral South. Unlike Toomer, he savagely portrays the South as being too oppressive for Negroes. In the first part of the novel the three brothers live together (with Hattie, Mat's wife) as tenant farmers in the Kentucky red-clay hills. They are on the verge of starvation and enslaved in debt. Even farming is largely useless because most of the topsoil has been washed away over the course of years. What remains for the brothers is the memory, the idea, the "dream" of the land as it must have been before they and the land were exploited by racist owners. The erosion of the land suggests the erosion of their morale which, in a sense, washes them off the land. The immediate cause of their hasty departure, however, is a beating administered by Mat to a white overseer. In order to escape the inevitable lynch mob, the brothers go North to the steel mills. Circumstances keep Mat from taking Hattie along, and Mat's separation from his wife signals the beginning of the dissolution of their family life.

The Kentucky sequence serves to introduce the major characters, who together suggest a composite Negro folk personality. Melody, who will manage best in the ordeal ahead, is sensitive and poetic. He is so named because of his skill with the guitar and because he is capable of articulating in song the folk life of the peasant. Chinatown is simple, lazy, sensual, and hedonistic. He lives by outward symbols; his greatest source of pride is his gold tooth, because, as he puts it later, it shines and smiles at him. Mat, the dominant figure of the group, is huge, brooding, and sullen. All his life he has suffered insults and humiliation at the hands of whites, but he has managed for the most part to suppress his rage and adopt a glazed expression when he is most hurt. An intensely religious man, Mat reads the Bible constantly to discover the causes of his agony. He believes he is cursed because he was conceived in sin, and that the curse has manifested itself in Hattie's inability to give birth to a child. Six times pregnant, Hattie has "dropped" her baby each time before it was born—and this is the central metaphor that supports Attaway's main theme, for Hattie's infertility corresponds to the infertility of the Southern soil that can no longer give sustenance to Negro life. Hence the brothers seek to sink roots in soil elsewhere. Insofar as they cannot do so, they will diminish and wither.

The second part of the novel relates the journey of the brothers to Pennsylvania—crouched and huddled in a dark boxcar with numerous other Negroes who are being brought North to work in mills.

> Squatted on the straw-spread floor of a boxcar, bunched up like hogs headed for market, riding in the dark for what might have been years, knowing time only as dippers of warm water gulped whenever they were awake, helpless and dropping because they were headed into the unknown and there was no sun, they forgot even that they had eyes in their heads and crawled around in the boxcar, as though it were a solid thing of blackness.

The screech, the rattle, the roar of the train, the fetid air, the smell of urine demoralized the men. "The misery that stemmed from them was a mass experience." Not even Mat could "defend his identity against the pack." Chinatown whimpers, terrified that someone in the dark may try to steal his gold tooth. He tells Melody that "without it I ain't nobody." Nor can Melody play his guitar and sing in the deafening noise. It is as if the train journey has suddenly and shockingly severed them from all connection with the past—a feeling not unlike what their African ancestors must have experienced in the holds of the slave ships. Yet in another sense the boxcar is a kind of womb preparing to disgorge them into a new life.

But the life of the steel mills is even more dehumanizing than the one they have fled. Once the green men overcome their initial bewilderment at the sterile, ugly grayness of the community, they attempt to acclimate themselves. They learn from bunkhouse talk how to survive in their dangerous work. They feel the hostility of the white workers, who fear—with justification—that the Negroes have been transported North in order to weaken the union. They learn above all the drudgery of the mill, the tedium, the immense physical stamina required of steel workers on twelve-hour shifts. Their off hours at first are spent sleeping, but soon they begin to enjoy dice games in the bunk-houses, drinking corn whiskey, "whoring" in Mex Town, and attending dog fights. Even Mat allows himself to be drawn into these frivolities after he learns by letter that Hattie has lost her seventh baby. Melody has meanwhile fallen in love with a fifteen-year-old Mexican-American prostitute, Anna, whose earthy nature is adulterated somewhat by her pathetic longings for dance-hall dresses and high-heeled shoes. When Melody fails to satisfy her at their first encounter, she throws herself at Mat, whose brute strength and courage in a melee at the dog fights had rescued her from physical harm.

In certain respects Mat appears to adjust more easily to the life of a steel worker than this brothers. His physical strength is put to the test, and he proves himself more than equal to it. He wins a grudging respect among his fellow workers, and his self-abasement under the glare of the white man seems to disappear. Yet after breaking with his puritanical, Bible-oriented moorings, Mat will need something more than the knowledge that he can stand up to any white man in order to sustain his emotional balance.

Chinatown, on the other hand, makes the worst adjustment. His gold tooth does not count for much in the gray steel community. Nor can he, in his casual Southern way, easily withstand the pressures and tensions of the world he has entered. He misses the out-of-doors, the feel of the earth beneath his bare feet, the sun and the warmth. Melody tries to keep the brothers together but is troubled by a sense of loss. He cannot play his guitar and sing as he once did. He is aware of a need for other melodies, other rhythms in his new environment, yet he cannot quite catch them. His impotence with Anna suggests the signal impotence of all three brothers in their new life.

There is a remarkable soliloquy in this section of the novel, delivered by a crippled Negro named Smothers. Smothers has lost the use of his legs in an accident in the mills some years before, but he is retained on the job by the steel company as a watchman. He is regarded tolerantly by his fellow workers despite his obsessive tirades against steel. Smothers is prophetic—a crippled Tiresias announcing the apocalypse if men persist in their materialist pursuits. His harangues restate the view implicit at the start of the novel that the earth gives moral and spiritual sustenance to men, and that its destruction transgresses nature and denies men their potentialities. On one occasion he rises in the bunkhouse to utter the following words:

> It's wrong to tear up the ground and melt it up in the furnace. Ground don't like it. It's the hell-and-devil kind of work. Guy ain't satisfied with usin' the stuff that was put here for him to use—stuff on top of the earth. Now he got to git busy and melt up the ground itself. Ground don't like it, I tells you. Now they'll be folks laugh when I say the ground got feelin'. But I knows what it is I'm talkin' about. All the time I listen real hard and git scared when the iron blast holler to git loose, an' them big redhead blooms screamin' like the very heart o' the earth caught between them rollers. It jest ain't right. . . .
>
> Can't blame the ground none. It give warnin'. Yessir, they was warnin' give a long time ago.

> Folks say one night there's somethin' fall right outen the sky, blazin' down, lightin' up this ol' river in the black o' night. . . . A solid hunk o' iron it be, big around as a house, fused together like it been worked by a puddler with a arm size of a hundred-foot crane. Where it come from? Where this furnace in the sky? You don't know. I don't know. But it were a warning to quit meltin' up the ground.

Later in the same section, Attaway describes a dog fight which the brothers attend along with other workers. The event is particularly savage but evidently serves to relieve the spectators of their built-up murderous frustrations. Its effect on Mat, however, is quite the opposite, as he begins to strike out wildly and indiscriminately at the other workers like a starved dog loosed from its leash.

The passage of time brings the further decline of the brothers. Mat has rented a shack and is now living with Anna. He has given up all thoughts of sending for Hattie and has left his Bible behind in the bunkhouse. Melody broods over the loss of Anna and schemes to get her back. He calls on her while Mat is working at the mill. Anna suspects his motives, and her suspicions are confirmed when he announces that he wants to give Mat a letter from Hattie. Anna wrestles with him to take the letter away from him. Exhausted and unsuccessful, she gives up the fight and she and Melody make love. It soon becomes clear that Anna is not happy living with Mat, who does not allow her to go out and show off the sequined dress and high-heeled shoes he bought her with money he had been saving for Hattie. The next day Anna disappears, and when she returns two days later Mat assumes she has been "lying" with someone and beats her savagely. Actually she has been lying on the hills near the big homes of wealthy townspeople, fantasying that she is the mistress of a rich man.

Events move swiftly now. Melody has an accident at the mill which severely damages his guitar-playing hand. Then Mat is arrested in Pittsburgh for attempting to kill a man. Melody drives to Pittsburgh to bail him out, and on the return trip Mat, crushed and defeated, tells him that Anna no longer truly gives herself to him.

The portents of disaster build. Again steel serves as the underlying metaphor to suggest the hellish antilife man has created, and it is again the raving Smothers who calls up the image of a monster that demands human sacrifice. Smothers senses impending death. "Ever'body better be on the lookout. Steel liable to git somebody today. I got a deep feelin' in my bones," he says. The men laugh and Bo, the foreman, promises Smothers, "If it's you . . . we make you up into watch fobs. The boys round the bunkhouse'll wear you across their vests for luck." Smothers tells the hair-raising story of how he lost his legs in the mill and how afterward, "All the time in the hospital I kin hear that steel talkin' . . . I kin hear that steel laughin' an' talkin' till it fit to bust my head clean open . . . I kin hear when cold steel whisper all the time and hot roll steel scream like hell. *It's a sin to melt up the ground.* . . ."

Melody, too, has come to sense steel as a death god. "Suddenly Melody was aware of the warning. He started up.

There was great danger. Something screamed it inside him. . . . Perhaps the monster had gotten tired of an occasional victim. Perhaps he was about to break his chains. He would destroy masses of men, flesh, bones and blood, leaving only names to bury."

And then there is a blinding flash, followed by "a mushroom cloud, streaked with whirling red fire. . . ." Several workers, Smothers included, are killed. Chinatown is blinded.

In a sense each of the brothers has now been rendered impotent: Chinatown, who lives by outward symbols, can no longer see; Melody, who lives through his music, can no longer play the guitar; and Mat has become a hulking shell of a man because Anna no longer loves him. All three brothers go to live with Anna. She no longer sleeps with Mat, but takes care of Chinatown, whose eyes are like "old eggs rotting in their ragged half shells, purple and revolting."

Racial tensions are rising in the town. The union is moving toward a strike and the steel interests are countering by bringing more Negroes in from the South. Negro leaders have been bought off and are directing Negro workers not to join the union. Meanwhile the depleted Mat has taken to walking alone among the hills on the edge of town. On one occasion he is approached by the law and sworn in as a deputy, ostensibly to maintain order but really to help break the forthcoming strike. He views this as an opportunity to redeem his faltering manhood with Anna—and at the same time, unconsciously, to wreak his vengeance on whites.

On the day of the strike, Melody, in order to bolster Chinatown's dashed ego, takes him to a brothel. Inadvertently he discovers Anna has been secretly working there nights, and rushes back to the shack to accuse her—and to beg her to run away with him. Suddenly Mat returns. Overhearing their conversation, he savagely beats Anna into a heap, then shambles back to town and brutally provokes some of the strikers on orders of the sheriff. In the ensuing melee, Mat kills and injures a number of them before he is himself hacked down.

---

**It would be a mistake to regard *Blood on the Forge* as a tract, for Attaway rendered the usual subject of the proletarian novel into a work of art.**

**—*Edward Margolies***

---

The novel closes on Melody and Chinatown headed for Pittsburgh, where they will begin life anew.

Part of the strength of this final section of the novel lies in Attaway's generally successful fusion of naturalistic and metaphysical elements. The social and economic forces that drive the brothers from the Kentucky hills and divide the steel community in bloody conflict are in them-

selves crimes against nature. The same pride and greed that destroy the soil manifest themselves again as racial tension and industrial strife. Attaway focuses these perceptions on Mat just prior to his death. Having been rejected by Anna, Mat tries to redeem his ego by identifying himself with steel.

> Big Mat looked at the mills, and the big feelings were lifting him high in the air. He was big as God Almighty. . . . He could have spit and quenched a blast furnace. . . . Smothers had been a liar. Steel couldn't curse a man. Steel couldn't hurt him. He was the riding boss. How could those dead mills touch him? With his strength he could relight their fires or he could let them lie cold.

But like some epic Greek hero, Mat recognizes his *hubris* at the moment of his death, and intuits that his brutality in attacking the workers is just like the brutality to which he himself had been subjected in the South. And he recognizes too that the young Slav who is striking at him with a pickaxe handle is not unlike the Mat who struck out violently at a white man in Kentucky. Like Oedipus, Mat is his own persecutor and victim.

Unfortunately, for Mat (and the Negro by implication) vision comes too late. Attaway contrasts Mat's vision at death to Chinatown's continuing blindness in life. On the train that carries Melody and Chinatown to Pittsburgh, the brothers meet a blind Negro soldier who used to be a steel worker. When Chinatown asks why he left the mills, the soldier explains that he responded to a deep feeling inside him—a sound of guns. He tells Chinatown that he too can hear the guns if he listens carefully. Chinatown strains, and "their noise came over the rumble of the train."

> "Sound like somethin' big an' important that a fella's missin', don't it?" asked the soldier.
>
> Chinatown nodded.
>
> Melody watched the nod. He looked at the two blind men closely. Their heads cocked to one side, listening for sounds that didn't exist. They were twins.

And so the blind lead the blind. Just as the soldier was lured away from home by the nonexistent glory of war, so Melody and his brothers have been seduced from their homes by promises of freedom and security in the North. And thus it would always be for men like Chinatown and the soldier.

One of the most significant passages in the novel describes a strange ritual some of the workers perform after Smothers' death. It will be recalled that prior to the explosion in the mill, Bo says that if Smothers were to die, the men would use his remains for watch fobs. The men carry out their promise one day in the bunkhouse.

> [Bo] sat on the floor in the middle of an intent audience. No one spoke. Their attention was for Bo and for what he did. Between his legs was a pile of little steel scraps. In front of him burned a tin of canned heat. Bo put a steel dish on the

heat. Into the dish went a few pieces of lead. Then he sat back to wait.

. . . . .

For twenty minutes they sat. Nothing sounded but the sudden scrape of a boot against the grain of the floor. Then the massed breathing of the men began to grow until it whistled. A watch in someone's pocket ticked louder and louder. The creak of the bunkhouse in the changing air came now and again. Each man heard his own heart circling its own blood. So what was silence spoke louder and louder.

Then the time was up. The lead cupped the bottom of the dish, a heavy dust scumming its brightness. With ceremony Bo broke that scum. Then out of his pocket came the little chains. A drop of lead fastened each chain to one of the steel scraps. Shortly he was through. Bo began to pass out these newly crested watch fobs. Afterward the group broke up.

Attaway ends his novel on a note of defeat. Yet even in defeat, his protagonists persist—though not very hopefully—in their struggle for survival and identity. The brothers' renewed search for the good life seems doomed from the start. One knows that the entire cycle of hope, passion, and defeat will begin again with such persons as the blind "twins," Chinatown and the soldier—blind because they will continue to be deluded by unattainable dreams and promises.

One wonders, naturally, whether their author was himself as overcome with the hopelessness of his prognosis. Born in Mississippi in 1912, the son of a physician, Attaway was himself part of the great migration North. He attended public schools in Chicago and, after an interim as a hobo, he worked at a variety of jobs before returning to the University of Illinois to complete his education. It was in high school, Attaway writes, that he developed an interest in becoming an author. He had always assumed that Negro success was to be won in genteel professions like medicine, but upon first reading Langston Hughes, his outlook was transformed. Prior to the appearance of his two novels, he published little. His first novel, as we have seen, was promising; his second, a classic of its kind. Why then did Attaway stop writing fiction? He was only twenty-nine when *Blood on the Forge* appeared. It is, of course, always hazardous to guess at the motives of a writer, but possibly some clues may be found in the works themselves.

It is first of all clear that Attaway had no intention of writing "race" fiction. He did not want his novels to stop short at "protest," but rather hoped to make some grand metaphysical statement about the conditions of life and human experience, in which, possibly, Negro characters figured. But such a wholly laudable ambition was not, as has already been suggested, something the American reading public was prepared to accept from a Negro author—especially at the outset of World War II, when the great tasks ahead appeared to lie more in action and less in reflection. Attaway may simply have been discouraged at the response to his book—and quit.

Another alternative, however, suggests itself. It is perhaps in the realm of ideas that we may look for the source of

Attaway's arrested artistic development. Basically Attaway is a romantic. *Let Me Breathe Thunder,* for all its praise of stable family life and the virtues of farming, ultimately celebrates the free-wheeling bohemianism of hoboes—and Attaway, by manipulating his plot this way and that, manages to free his protagonists from any social and moral obligations. In another romantic vein, *Blood on the Forge* projects the myth of the "good" soil corrupted by man's greed, whose logical absurdity manifests itself in the manufacture of steel. While no one would deny that the excesses of American capitalism have produced cruel and dehumanizing injustices, it is hard, after Darwin, to ascribe moral virtues to nature. And since it is scarcely possible any longer to look to nature as something apart and holy, Attaway may well have written himself out of subject matter.

And yet if one grants Attaway his premises, it is undeniable that he has written a beautiful and moving novel. Nor can one deny that his vision of earth as sanctified remains persistently embedded in the American *mythos.* It is, after all, out of such nostalgia that art is created.

### Phyllis R. Klotman    (essay date June 1972)

SOURCE: "An Examination of Whiteness in *Blood on the Forge,*" in *CLA Journal,* Vol. XV, No. 4, June, 1972, pp. 459-64.

[*Klotman is an American educator and critic who specializes in African-American literature and film. In the following essay, she assesses Attaway's nonstereotypical depiction of whites in* Blood on the Forge.]

William Attaway's *Blood on the Forge* was reissued in 1969, the same year that saw the renascence of Jean Toomer's *Cane,* as well as the publication of several significant novels by contemporary Afro-American writers, such as Paule Marshall's *The Chosen Place, The Timeless People* and Ishmael Reed's *Yellow Back Radio Broke—Down.* Attaway's important but ignored book about the three Moss brothers, who leave the depleted farmland of Kentucky for the steel mills of Pennsylvania, poignantly but realistically tells the story of one facet of the Great Black Migration during the first World War.

*Blood on the Forge* was originally published in 1941, only one year after *Native Son,* but Attaway does not deal with whiteness in character and symbol in the same terms that Richard Wright used. Attaway eschews the stereotypical; his white characters, with the exception of the sheriff and "Boss" Johnston, are essentially complex and well-rounded figures. Nor is whiteness his central symbol. The steel mill is. Big Mat, Melody and Chinatown are seduced North by the promise of jobs and decent wages, but are gradually beaten down and stripped of their manhood by the uncompromising and brutal, man-eating monster, the steel mill. Behind the faceless monster is the white power structure, manipulating the lives of white immigrants and black unskilled workers—who are shipped in by cattle car, a disgusting and dehumanizing experience—for the sake of feeding the mill and filling their coffers. The bosses are never seen; their power is felt mainly through their underlings who set white worker against black, deputize strike-breakers, and generally control through fear or famine.

Racism as an omnipotent factor does not exist in the lives of the three brothers after they leave Kentucky. At least for a time. They are accepted by the Slavs, the Irish and the Italians with whom they work in the mill; they drink, gamble and whore together. As a friend, old Zanski warns that they'll never be happy until they send for their families—a man needs children in his home and a wife to put up curtains—he admonishes. In a word, stability. But few black workers move out of the bunkhouse. Their separation from their past—rootedness in the soil, the folk, religion, family—is almost as complete as that of their ancestors who traveled to a new and ugly life in the dark bellies of slave ships instead of airless boxcars. When Mat does finally set up "housekeeping," it is with Anna, the Mexican prostitute, who wants an "Americano" because she is tired of "peons." (Anna suffers from the delusion that all "Americanos" are rich, regardless of color.) The three brothers are systematically unmanned by the dehumanizing process of forging steel. Chinatown is blinded in an accident which eats up the lives of fourteen men; Melody's hand is smashed so that he is no longer able to play his guitar; Big Mat is killed during the strike in which he has become an unwitting tool the bosses wield against the white workers. Earlier his skill and strength earned him the approbation of his fellow workers and the title "Black Irish"; later he comes to be "hated by his fellow workers. He was a threat over their heads. The women covered their faces at the sight of him, the men spat; the children threw rocks. Always within him was that instinctive knowledge that he was being turned to white men's uses. So always with him was a basic distrust of a white. But now he was a boss. He was the law. After all, what did right or wrong matter in the case? Those thrilling new words were too much to resist. He was a boss, a boss over whites."

There is very little about the unionizing process that the black workers, including the Moss brothers, understand or identify with. The backbreaking hazardous work in the mill has been a kind of salvation for them. Having sharecropped all of their lives, always on the verge of starvation, they are neither shocked nor dismayed by the twelve-hour day in the mill. At least they get paid. They have not begun to think about the possibility of better working conditions—an eight-hour day, better wages, unions—a fact that the Northern industrialists well knew and used to their advantage in controlling the "socialist" oriented, organizing aspirations of the white immigrants: "Big Mat was not thinking about the labor trouble. Yet he knew he would not join the union. For a man who had so lately worked from dawn to dark in the fields twelve hours and the long shift were not killing. For a man who had known no personal liberties even the iron hand of the mills was an advancement."

One of the things that drives the Moss brothers North is the impossibility of paying off a $40 debt to Mr. Johnston, the landowner to whom they are perpetually in debt. Fear of the control the white boss has over their very ability to stay alive is a given with the black sharecropper. It in-

spires Mat's hate: "Deep inside him was the familiar hatred of the white boss." There are only a few stereotypical characters in *Blood on the Forge*. Mr. Johnston, the Kentucky landowner, is a classic bigot, indigenous to the South, but interestingly enough, he uses the black sharecroppers against the white just as the bosses in the northern mill use the black workers against the immigrants. Johnston explains to Mat why he doesn't have white sharecroppers work his land: "well, they's three reasons: niggers ain't bothered with the itch; they knows how to make it the best way they kin and they don't kick none." They don't "kick" because they have no recourse. If their anger gets out of control, the resultant violence always turns against them. When Mat explodes in anger and fury, killing the mule that killed their mother in the fields, he puts them all in Johnston's debt to the point of starvation. They don't run because they have no place to go, and Johnston thinks he can keep them from getting the "itch" by manipulation and innuendo, an "old Master" tactic, in the plantation tradition: "My ridin' boss tells me there some jacklegs around, lyin' to the niggers about how much work they is up North. Jest you remember how I treat you and don't be took in by no lies."

They don't get taken in by northern lies; they leave because they know southern truths. One of these truths is never to look at or touch a white woman. Melody knows that Mat has "more sense than to talk to a white lady"; Chinatown agrees: "It's dangerous. . . .' member young Charley from over in the next county got lynched jest cause he stumble into one in the broad daylight." Another of those old-fashioned southern truths is never strike a white man a semi-lethal blow. When the riding boss refuses to give Big Mat the mule Johnston has promised him ("If Mr. Johnston got good sense you won't never git another mule. . . . You'd be run off the land if I had my say. Killin' a animal worth forty dollars,' cause a nigger woman got dragged over the rocks—"), Mat in a blind rage strikes him down. Realizing that the man will live "to lead the lynch mob against him," Mat and his brothers reluctantly leave the land they have worked so lovingly yet for so little reward.

The white line drawn about their lives in the South is straight, clear, immovable. The Moss brothers are powerless to effect change, to shift that boundary in any direction, but they understand their role in the schema and derive some satisfaction from a sense of belonging to the land. Big Mat is a powerful man who seems to draw strength from the soil's blackness which is like his own. When he goes North he becomes unmoored, confused by the change in the pattern, but he adapts to the work better than his brothers, better even than the whites. What he doesn't understand is that hate can be generated to meet the needs of new situations. When the white workers become politicized enough to strike, more blacks are shipped in, in boxcars, and the brothers remember, identify with those men—"bewildered and afraid in the dark, coming from hate into a new kind of hate." Bo, the only black foreman, knows the pattern—they only send for black men when there's trouble.

Big Mat is a tragic figure, reminiscent of the one slave on

every plantation who refused to be whipped by the soul driver, a man of tremendous physical power and courage who could never be submissive. As developed by the early black fictionists, he becomes the black hero or the "bad nigger," feared by everyone. Big Mat has some of these characteristics, but in *Blood on the Forge* he is also an Othello-like figure, proud, jealous, and formidable. And his blackness is played off against a white Iago, a sneaky little boss-sheriff who manipulates him by appealing to his new-found sense of manhood. "Deputize this man," the sheriff says, "assign him his hours. He won't need a club. Just give him a couple of boulders. He'll earn his four dollars Monday." Actually the bosses save the four dollars. Mat destroys and is destroyed, as so many are in the struggle for steel. Most of Attaway's characters—black, white, all shades of ethnic groupings—are handled well. Many have real nuances of complexity, including the two brothers, Chinatown and Melody, who are left derelict at the end; Anna, the grasping but pathetic Mexican girl; Zanski's granddaughter Rosie, a union sympathizer who turns prostitute for the scabs in order to support the starving strikers in her family; and Smothers, the black prophet of doom, who understands that all men will have to pay for ravaging the earth: "*It's a sin to melt up the ground,* is what steel say. *It's a sin.* Steel bound to git ever'body 'cause o' that sin. They say I crazy, but mills gone crazy 'cause men bringin' trainloads of ground in here and meltin' it up."

One of the tragic outcomes in the novel is the loss of continuity in the lives of the men who are almost human sacrifices to the industrial Moloch created by an unseen hand grasping for profits. And that hand is white. If we used to think that free enterprise meant freedom to exploit all the resources of our country—both human and natural—to destroy the land and leave it in waste, we have since been forced to change our minds. There is something very timely in Attaway's implicit warning, as Edward Margolies suggests in his introduction to the 1969 edition of *Blood on the Forge:* "Possibly he [Attaway] saw his worst fears realized in the rapid spread of industrial wastelands and the consequent plight of urban Negroes. From one point of view his feelings about the sanctity of nature now seem almost quaint in an age of cybernetics. Yet given what we are told is the dangerous pollution of our environment, who can tell but that Attaway may not have been right?"

What is most interesting about the "rediscovery" of such novels as *Blood on the Forge* is their contemporaneity. We have now, some twenty-eight years later, reached the point of no return in our violation of the environment and of each other. Yet we are as unseeing as Chinatown and the soldier at the end of the novel—"blind men facing one another, not knowing."

## Robert Felgar (essay date Spring 1973)

SOURCE: "William Attaway's Unaccommodated Protagonists," in *Studies in Black Literature,* Vol. 4, No. 1, Spring, 1973, pp. 1-3.

[*In the following essay, Felgar discusses the main themes of and characterization in Attaway's novels.*]

So much emphasis has been placed recently on nominating the important new Black novelists that attending to the older ones has been neglected. Large critical claims have been made lately for Ishmael Reed, William Melvin Kelley, and John A. Williams, while the work of William Attaway and Zora Neale Hurston, for instance, remains buried under the weight of years of critical indifference. I want to make a plea for William Attaway as a novelist, one who, like so many Afro-American writers of fiction, wrote one or two books, and then, as in the case of Toomer, apparently was discouraged from fulfilling early promise. Attaway published his first book, *Let Me Breathe Thunder,* in 1939, his second, *Blood on the Forge,* two years later. The two are almost completely unknown by Black and white readers; both audiences should give themselves the chance to become seriously concerned with Attaway's vision.

In neither book does he embrace a prescriptive racial esthetic: many of the major characters in *Let Me Breathe Thunder* are white, in *Blood on the Forge* Black. He writes about people who engage his sympathy and imagination; sometimes they are Afro-American, sometimes white Americans. Since the implied audience for both books is "the common reader," Attaway is not confined to writing "only" about Blacks or "only" about whites. Neither color is a limitation on his writing: they are given material. The false dichotomy between "race" novels and novels of "universal significance" is fortunately not a problem for him.

The central characters in *Let Me Breathe Thunder* are estranged from bourgeois American society because although racially acceptable, they are hoboes, and therefore outsiders in social, if not racial status. As proletarians, both their stake and their place in America are problematic. They have no permanent home, employment, or social relations. Movement is the permanent ontological fact of their existence. The narrator, Ed, has perhaps a more common-sensical hold on experience than his fellow hobo, Step (using names descriptively is sustained in the later novel), but the lack of any lasting orientation in both their lives is equal. They befriend a nine-year-old Mexican youth who is even less at home in the universe than they are: Hi Boy is without parents (Step "adopts" him as Sampson becomes the temporary "father" of the two transients), without friends except Step and Ed, and without a language to articulate his plight—he has the slipperiest of grasps on English. An emblem of almost total exclusion, he dies of an infection caused by a wound in his hand he inflicted with a fork in order to prove to Step he was not a coward. The world he greeted with his name allowed him the briefest existence only. The themes of separation and dislocation inform *Blood on the Forge* in a different way because the Moss brothers are racial as well as social outcasts.

Attaway dramatically imagines Ed as having had more advantages than Step. Ed has had a high school education, some home life, some sense of belonging. His sidekick, however, never had a real home; he was sent to the mills instead of having candles on his birthday cake, yet he pathetically carries a set of keys that fit locks on a nonexistent home. Anna, the girl Step violates in a tawdry affair of sexual initiation, has no mother and her four brothers died of an illness during the war. Possessed of a home and a father, she demands more; her vision of the open road she assumes Step and Ed travel ends in a whorehouse operated by Mag, a middle-aged Black ex-prostitute living with Cooper, her man. To sustain his public image as a lady's man, Cooper makes Mag jealous of Anna, whom she accidentally wounds with her rifle while trying to hit Cooper. Appropriately, he flees as a hobo on the same train car Ed, Step, and Hi Boy are running away on. Just as in *Blood on the Forge,* indifferent machines transport the protagonists across America, as if they were merely freight:

> "That's what trains was made for . . . passengers," he (Step) said.
>
> "And freight," I added.
>
> "We ain't neither," he said. "Don't that strike you funny?"
>
> "Nothing strikes me funny now," I said, trying to shrink my back away from my soaked jacket.
>
> "We ain't even people. We ain't nothing.

They refuse to accept their existence, insisting that they are looking for "a job of work," rather than being hoboes. Like the Indian in the myth Sampson relates to them, they are completely out of place, and if they move, they will cause a disturbance. Consequently they "breathe thunder": " 'he (the legendary Indian) was a wanderer by nature. Being outside of patterns, he had to be a wanderer.' " His tormented spirit " 'still moans and moans, and in its misery sometimes breathes thunder.' " Attaway's figures recall the Wandering Jew, the mythical Indian, and all the Eternal Wanderers of legend in that all are unaccommodated: their fate is never to find a permanent home in the universe; they are not fully welcome anywhere. Imprisoned in such a world, they demand a locus of moral responsibility, but there is none, as Step knows:

> "Why'd he stick the fork in his hand in the first place? Whose fault was it that we couldn't leave him in Yakima and was scared to get a doc when there was a chance? Whose fault is everything?"

There is no resonance between reality and Step's question because of the nonsensicality of the world and man's total negligibility.

The only echo Step and Ed hear as they listen to existence is Hi Boy, the phrase the Mexican boy keeps repeating and the phrase they use to call him by. He represents the commitment and obligation to another human being, a responsibility they are unaccustomed to. When the mountains of Hi Boy's native Mexico are mentioned, the narrator says,

> The kid gazed away in the distance. His eyes were soft and mystical looking. He was far away at some place that must have been so simple and beautiful that only a child's mind could bear to go there. His eyes rose with a mountain whose peak was lost in white and mist.

Hi Boy is the innocence, the Edenic state that Ed and especially Step were denied; he is "a pocket-size edition of a priest laughing over his beads, saying his saints on his fingers."

---

**Like the Lost Generation writers before him, Attaway suggests that after all the dross has been melted away from society, only basic values, however temporary, remain.**

**—*Robert Felgar***

---

Like the Lost Generation writers before him, Attaway suggests that after all the dross has been melted away from society, only basic values, however temporary, remain. As Toomer and Hemingway find a kind of secular redemption in the earth in *Cane* and *The Sun Also Rises,* so Attaway implies that Sampson's orchard on Four Mile Farm is as close as his characters will come to a home, a place of orientation. Attaway's symbolic use of geography approaches the pastoral ideal, a Hesperides where Anna is a nymph guarding the golden fruit. Herrick might not be able to hammer out his golden verses in this Arcadia, but it is the only place Step and Ed find at least an evanescent accommodation with the conditions of their existence.

In *King Lear* after Edgar enters disguised as Poor Tom, the mad man, the King says, "Unaccommodated man is no more but such a poor, bare, forked animal as thou art." Attaway adds resonance and amplitude to his second novel by exploring Lear's image of natural man in a more elaborate intense manner than he did in *Let Me Breathe Thunder.* The three protagonists in *Blood on the Forge,* the Moss brothers, not only lack a home (they are part of the Great Migration to the industrial North), but also they are alien to the racial majority. Their train ride north is more devastating than Ed and Step's train rides, because it recapitulates the original slave passage of their ancestors when they were deracinated. With Ed and Step the three Mosses share also a love for the earth which they farmed. *Blood on the Forge* also terminates with a pointless train ride.

The first part of this five-part novel demonstrates that in leaving the South the Mosses were not losing paradise. In leaving "the red clay-hills of Kentucky," they are abandoning an overworked earth that has become sterile, like Hattie, Big Mat's wife, who has lost six children. They are virtually slaves in the crop-lein system that exploits them. Still, in the South Melody plays the hungry blues on a guitar, while in the North he stops playing when he intentionally smashes his picking hand; in the South, Chinatown, who lives through outward symbols, has stature because of his shiny gold tooth, while in the North he becomes blind and can no longer know if his tooth impresses others or not; in the South Mat's family integrity is maintained—he and his half-brothers live together with Hattie—while in the North Mat forgets about Hattie for Anna and he and his brothers draw apart.

Adumbrations of the family's imminent disintegration percolate through the surface of the narrative of Part One. The bloody violence Melody will witness is foreshadowed: after Mat mutilated the mule that killed the brothers' maw, "Melody had fallen on the ground and vomited and for three days afterward he couldn't hold food on his stomach. The sight of blood always acted on him like that." Mat's attack on the riding boss preludes his assault on the union members in the steel mills. But the most powerful foreshadowing is also a resonant prospective irony: when Chinatown contemplates the jackleg's proposal of going north he says " 'man have to kill himself workin' to make the kind of money he was talkin' about.' " Mat of course is killed and China may as well be dead when he loses his sight.

Part Two is only a few pages in length, but it forestalls the ultimate separation of the Moss brothers and it also contains metaphors that imply the identities of each of the three brothers is problematic. On their journey north in a boxcar, the Blacks are "bunched up like hogs headed for market." They "forgot even that they had eyes in their heads," and when the train stopped for a while, "they were blinded by the light of a cloudy day." Filled with sight imagery, the entire novel is a study in optics: none of the three major characters can see clearly. They are either literally blind like Chinatown and the blind preacher from Kentucky, or their moral vision is clouded. Crammed into the train car, "Big Mat could not defend his identity against the pack." Melody, China, and Mat repeat the pattern of their West African ancestors three hundred years earlier: they are the chattel of the white capitalists. China's sense of individuality is so gravely threatened by the passage that he insists Melody feel his gold tooth, China's emblem of selfhood.

The third section introduces the three into the world of the steel mills, where machines rule men. They wonder *what men in their right minds would leave off tending green growing things to tend iron monsters?*" (Attaway's emphasis). Cut off from their beloved earth, the men realize they have not gained the Promised Land but its very opposite. And in fact, the inside of a steel mill is hot and fiery like Hell itself. Melody tells China the Day of Judgement will be the coming of a steel mill. Attaway implies that if being transported as slaves from West Africa was the first step in the destruction of Black men, the second step was the Great Migration after World War I. Just after the train's arrival in Pennsylvania, China and Melody cannot find their way back to the bunkhouse when it starts to rain so they are not able to see; this geographical and optical disorientation reflects their metaphysical plight. The whore the two brothers watch has a rotten breast which will be recalled later by China's blind eyes, "old eggs rotting in their ragged half shells, purple and revolting." All three brothers later encounter another figure, the seer Smothers, who prophesies that steel is a monster which will cram them into its maw. They do not attend his warning; he himself is later converted into watch fobs for the workmen to wear, after he is killed by the same monster he warned

against. Attaway's second Anna is introduced in Part Three: she is a Mexican whore who is also far from home and unhappy in her new environment. She will be the wedge that drives Mat and Melody apart.

The last two parts chronicle the final destruction of the Mosses: China is blinded, Mat loses Anna and is killed, and Melody smashes his hand so that he can never play the guitar again (the end of Black folk art). Their downfall is paralleled by the fall of the East European steelworkers, who, although many have families and children, nevertheless see their daughters being raped by their own brothers and also becoming whores for their father's own fellow workers. Attaway believes no one has any cosmic status because of mankind's utter negligibility and the universe's absolute nonsensicality. Suffering does not bring understanding or grandeur: when China loses his vision, the paradox of the blind seer does not obtain—his blindness simply literalizes the metaphor. If what matters is man's relationship to himself, to other men, to Nature, and to God, then all four relationships have been abrogated in Attaway's vision of experience. *Blood on the Forge* suggests there are no relationships: man is completely unaccommodated by the facts of existence. To compensate, the Moss brothers retreat to the past. Big Mat and Melody walk in the hills around the giant industrial complex below, while Chinatown and Melody play the wishing game: they wish they were back on the land, where there is growth instead of death only. Mat's last effort to gain some sense of selfhood, however provisional, is as a deputy sheriff for the mill owners. He becomes in effect the riding boss he had earlier beaten; now a young Slave becomes the earlier Mat and beats Mat to death during a riot between the union members and the sheriff's men. Mat has been exploited by whites once again. Rather than winning Anna back as a strikebreaker, he loses his life. At the end, Melody and Chinatown board a train going to Pittsburgh; across from China sits a sightless Black veteran of World War I: "Melody watched the nod. He looked at the two blind men closely. Their heads cocked to one side, listening for sounds that didn't exist. They were twins." An image that Pinter or Beckett might employ, it reveals Attaway's uncompromisingly hopeless view of a permanently disoriented, unregenerate creature.

## James O. Young   (essay date 1973)

SOURCE: "Black Reality and Beyond," in *Black Writers of the Thirties,* Louisiana State University Press, 1973, pp. 203-35.

[*Young is an American educator and critic. In the following excerpt, he examines* Blood on the Forge *as an example of proletarian fiction.*]

In his eloquent novel, *Blood on the Forge* (1941), William Attaway delved into the history of the black man in America. But, like Richard Wright in his folk history of the migration, instead of dramatizing the exploits of a historic race hero, Attaway looked with the scrutiny of a sociologist at the brutal experience of the mass of blacks who migrated from the agrarian South into the industrial North at the time of the First World War. Like [Arna Bontemps'] *Black Thunder,* Attaway's novel should be classed as proletarian fiction. In fact, the general structure of the novel conformed more closely to the typical proletarian novel than did Bontemps' because the setting was more contemporary and the exploitation of the workers was placed in an industrial environment. But Attaway's book was not the run-of-the-mill, artless formula-novel which was characteristic of so much proletarian fiction. For in addition to portraying the persecution and exploitation of the workers, black and white, Attaway also intelligently dramatized the erosion of the old southern folkways by the immense and impersonal force of the machine.

*Blood on the Forge* was Attaway's second novel. In 1939, he had published *Let Me Breathe Thunder,* a picaresque novel about two depression-era hoboes. Perhaps the most interesting note about this novel is that its principal characters are white. Though in many ways Attaway's first novel is very effective, it relies too heavily on melodrama; his protagonists are just a bit too naïve and sentimental to be believable. Such is not the case with *Blood on the Forge* which ranks as one of the finest novels of the depression era.

Attaway's main characters are three brothers. Chinatown is lazy, hedonistic, and lives by outer symbols—his proudest possession is his golden tooth about which he explains "can't 'ford to lose this tooth." Melody is introspective, intelligent, and sensitive—the music he makes on his guitar is expressive of his personality. And, finally, Big Mat, the oldest brother, is a physical giant who, in hopes of some day receiving a call to preach, reads his Bible every day. Wrote Attaway, "To almost everybody but his close kin he was a stupid, unfeeling giant, a good man to butcher hogs. . . . Melody alone knew him completely. Melody, from his dream world, could read the wounds in Big Mat's eyes." The essential characteristic of each of the three men will be destroyed by the new machine environment.

All three brothers are tenant farmers in the green hills of Kentucky. They are forced to flee from those hills when Big Mat, pouring out the bitterness of years of humiliation and persecution, thrashes the white riding boss: "The riding boss fell to the ground, blood streaming from his smashed face. He struggled to get to his feet. A heavy foot caught him in the side of the neck. His head hung over his shoulder at an odd angle." Aside from the immediate necessity of escaping white retaliation, their flight has another level of meaning for Attaway. They are leaving the land because it has become infertile. It is worn out, incapable of sustaining the black folk any longer. "The land has jest give up, and I guess it's good for things to come out like this," observes Big Mat as they prepare to leave.

They meet an agent from a northern steel mill who gives them passage to the mill on board a freight car. The blackness of the boxcar is symbolic of a womb out of which they will be reborn into the industrial environment. But it is also a coffin, symbolic of the impending death of the folk consciousness: "Squatted on the straw-spread floor of a boxcar, bunched up like hogs headed for market, riding in the dark for what might have been years, knowing time only as dippers of warm water gulped whenever they were awake, helpless and drooping because they were headed

into the unknown and there was no sun, they forgot even that they had eyes in their heads and crawled around in the boxcar, as though it were a solid thing of blackness."

When the new men arrive at the mills, Attaway contrasts them to the men who have already been conditioned to the sterile monotony of the industrial existence: "Everything was too strange for the green men to comprehend. In a daze, they were herded to the mill gates and checked in. The night shift was getting off. They mingled for a few minutes at the mill gates. All of them were gray in the dirty river mist." The idea that the green men will become gray men is skillfully developed by Attaway. He never deviates from the attitude that as bad as the feudalistic southern environment was, it was still alive; it was still characterized by very personal relationships between human beings, not the impersonal, mechanized quality of the northern environment. Social scientists like E. Franklin Frazier, looking toward long-range goals, had optimistically observed the destruction of the old folk culture as a positive development accelerating integration into the mainstream of American society. Attaway had carefully dramatized this process, but without the optimism of the sociologists. His artistic consciousness was much more sensitive to immediate suffering, and it told him that possibly something valuable was being destroyed.

It does not take long for the three brothers to become gray men, stripped of their folk identities by the mills. Melody finds that "the old music was going," and after an accident to his hand in the mills he ceases to play his guitar altogether. Chinatown is blinded by an explosion in the mills and he is no longer capable of seeing those outward symbols through which he had lived: "Now those symbols were gone, and he was lost." Big Mat, because of his enormous strength, fares best in the competition with the monster machines. But even he succumbs eventually, losing his religion and becoming shamefully impotent—a mere hulk of the virile man he once was.

The last sections of the novel revolve around Mat and his efforts to regain his manhood. There is rising dissatisfaction among the workers at the mills and they decide to strike. Big Mat has no intention of joining the union. And through his attitude the author attempts to explain why black men were successfully employed as strike-breakers for so many years. "Big Mat was not thinking about the labor trouble. Yet he knew that he would not join the union. For a man who had so lately worked from dawn to dark in the fields twelve hours and the long shift were not killing. For a man who had ended each year in debt any wage at all was a wonderful thing. For a man who had known no personal liberties even the iron hand of the mills was an advancement. In his own way he thought these things. As yet he could not see beyond them." Mat is signed up as a company deputy and he regains his manhood through violence. "He had handled people, and they feared him. Their fear had made him whole." But this feeling of manhood is only temporary, it has no strength against feelings or ideas such as those behind the expression "nigger." He can maintain his manhood only through repeated violence.

Attaway reintroduces the proletarian theme within the

context of Mat's anti-union violence. He understands Mat's position, but clearly disagrees with it. Mat achieves proletarian consciousness only as he is being beaten to death by one of the union men. He suddenly suspects that he has taken over the role of the riding boss. "Maybe somewhere in these mills a new Mr. Johnson was creating riding bosses," realizes Mat, "making a difference where none existed." Big Mat's sudden, intuitive realization rings perhaps the one false note in Attaway's novel. The attempt to submerge race conflict within the context of class conflict was no more convincing when portrayed dramatically than when it was proclaimed by radical politicians and scholars.

---

**Cynthia Hamilton on *Blood on the Forge:***

Attaway's novel *Blood on the Forge* is a masterpiece of social analysis. He alone, among all black writers, makes work the center of his sociological imagination. Without charts and statistics, without the language of detached objectivity, Attaway presents to the sensitive reader the dynamics of the process of migration and the transition from the Kentucky sharecropper South to the industrial North of Pennsylvania (specifically, Allegheny County). In the first section of his book, Attaway destroys myths which social scientists are responsible for creating: myths which served to motivate black migration northward, like the idea that the North was a "promised land," and myths regarding the behavior of Blacks while in the South, particularly those centering on acquiescence to oppression.

*Cynthia Hamilton, in "Work and Culture: The Evolution of Consciousness in Urban Industrial Society in the Fiction of William Attaway and Peter Abrahams," in* Black American Literature Forum, *Spring-Summer, 1987.*

---

**L. Moody Simms, Jr.** (essay date Spring 1975)

SOURCE: "In the Shadow of Richard Wright: William Attaway," in *Notes on Mississippi Writers,* Vol. VIII, No. 1, Spring, 1975, pp. 13-18.

[*In the following excerpt, Simms favorably appraises Attaway's portrayal of the disenfranchised in his two novels.*]

Undoubtedly, Mississippi's best known native-born black writer is Richard Wright. Wright's reputation, which has grown steadily since the publication of his *Native Son* in 1940, is justly deserved. Yet over the years, Wright's achievement has tended to overshadow and obscure the work of other Mississippi-born black writers. One of them whose work deserves to be better known is William Attaway. His *Blood on the Forge* (1941) is an excellent novel which stands up well when compared with any other fiction dealing with blacks written during the past three decades. . . .

Attaway's first novel, *Let Me Breathe Thunder,* appeared in 1939. It is the tough and tender story of two young box

car wanderers and their love for a little Mexican waif. The major characters, Ed and Step, are rootless white men faced by [a] hard, precarious reality, yet still capable of dreaming and caring. They represent the large numbers of young people who drifted about America during the difficult depression years of the 1930's. They live from day to day, waiting for nothing in particular. Ed and Step are not professional hoboes given to pointing out the "romance of the road"; their single object is to stay alive and keep moving. They support themselves through brief stretches of farm work.

During a stop in New Mexico, Ed and Step meet an inarticulate Mexican boy named Hi-Boy. His wistful and trusting way soon breaks through their casual, seemingly tough veneer. Ed and Step appoint themselves the boy's guardian and take him on the road as they continue their roaming. Hi-Boy becomes an outlet for their affection and for the tenderness missing from their rootless lives. For Ed and Step, Hi-Boy's welfare comes to take precedence over all else. Quite naturally, when a Yakima Valley rancher wants to take Hi-Boy permanently into his family, Ed and Step are torn between their own need for the boy and their concern for his future.

Attaway's *Let Me Breathe Thunder* has some of the emotional force and quality of the relationship between George and Lennie in John Steinbeck's *Of Mice and Men* (1937). Less ably written, the book would be melodramatic and overly sentimental. But the characterizations are sure, the dialogue is crisp and natural, and careful attention is given to physical detail. All told, *Let Me Breathe Thunder* is a solid first novel and makes the point that a black writer can deal successfully with a work made up primarily of white characters.

Published in 1941, Attaway's second and best novel, *Blood on the Forge,* is set for the most part in an Allegheny Valley steel-mill community during World War One. During and for several months after the end of the war, a manpower shortage existed in the West Virginia and Pennsylvania steel industry. Attracted by wages of four dollars a day, many Southern farm blacks moved north to work in the mills. To these black tenant farmers living in a state of near peonage, the low wages of steel workers seemed like true riches. The prospect of enjoying greater social freedom provided an additional inducement for deserting the land.

This northward migration of blacks looking for a better life in the mill towns created problems for northern employers and labor leaders. At the time, unions were engaged in initial efforts to organize the steel industry on a closed shop basis. When strikes resulted, the employers relied increasingly on black strike breakers. The unions consequently watched the black influx with growing anxiety. Many white workers came to fear that they might be permanently displaced by blacks who were willing to accept lower wages and poorer working conditions.

Set against this background, *Blood on the Forge* is the story of three black brothers—Mat, Chinatown and Melody Moss—who abandon their worn-out tenant farm in Kentucky's red clay hills to work in an Allegheny Valley steel mill. The novel thus has a double theme: blacks competing with whites in an abnormal condition of the labor market and men of the soil attempting to adjust to modern industrial life.

Mat, the eldest brother, at first appears to be making an adjustment to his new environment better than his brothers. Heretofore, he had stoically coped with life through his own understanding of the Bible. In the mill, his tremendous physical strength gains him a respect he had never gotten in the South. But Mat's new-found self-confidence proves to be an illusion. Discarding his Bible, he finds that his virility is not enough to sustain him. It counts for little with Anna, his Mexican mistress, who dreams of becoming the mistress of a wealthy mill owner. Playing on Mat's false sense of himself, the owners easily turn him against his fellow workers as they attempt to organize.

Chinatown, the hedonist, fares worse than Mat. Delighting in the senses, he spends his pay on corn whiskey, dice, and women. He is utterly dependent on his brothers. Of the three, he is hit the hardest physically by the harsh life of the mill worker. Eventually, he is left blind by an explosion in the mill.

The third brother, Melody, survives best. A musician in the South, he is still something of a poet after his move northward. But his new environment renders him impotent. His old songs don't seem to have any meaning any more; he is unable to play his guitar. Yet even though he appears at best indifferent to the manipulation of his fellow blacks by both the owners and white workers, he does manage to come through his Northern experience, unlike his two brothers, in one piece, physically and mentally.

Throughout the novel, Attaway reveals that the blacks' dream of greater social freedom in the mill towns is largely delusive. Many of their fellow white workers—especially the Slav and Irish immigrants—hate them and see them as a threat. When the union organizers appear, the employers easily manipulate the black workers into their camp. The blacks, being convinced that they are the lowest group in the racial pecking order, see their only chance of continuing on the job as bending to the desire of the owners.

Yet Attaway does not simply single out the blacks as the sole victim of the unjust conditions which he vividly portrays. He shows the European immigrants and native whites working under and being exploited by the same system of low pay, long hours, and unnecessary hazards to life and limb. He compassionately shows the blighted dream of the immigrants for a new life in America.

In *Blood on the Forge,* Attaway has mined a rich vein of human experience. His outlook is not very optimistic in this work, but he writes about his people knowingly and with warm appreciation. At once, his main characters are likable, humorous, bewildered, and stout-hearted. The dialogue sounds completely authentic.

Unfortunately, Attaway has published only the two novels considered above. The best of these, *Blood on the Forge,* has only recently begun to receive the critical recognition it merits. Edward Margolies has noted [in the introduction to the Collier Books' edition of *Blood on the Forge*] one of the reasons why Attaway's novel was largely ignored when it was first published: "Appearing one year after Richard Wright's sensational Native Son, Attaway's book may have looked tame to an America preparing for another war and whose reading public had already found its Negro 'spokesman' in the virile Wright." In any event, a careful reading of *Blood on the Forge* leads one to believe that, excepting Wright's *Native Son,* it is the strongest of black novels dealing with the plight of blacks and racial violence written during the inter-war period.

### Phillip H. Vaughan    (essay date 1975)

SOURCE: "From Pastoralism to Industrial Antipathy in William Attaway's *Blood on the Forge*," in *Phylon: The Atlantic University Review of Race and Culture,* Vol. XXXVI, No. 4, 1975, pp. 422-25.

[*In the following essay, Vaughan states that in* Blood on the Forge "*Attaway rejects the traditional forms of agrarianism which call for a return to nature, and sounds the theme of alienation that marks the modern existential novel.*"]

When *Blood on the Forge* by black novelist William Attaway was published in 1941, it received little notice. The book, nevertheless, represented a literary achievement in its own right, and at the same time it realistically portrays the transition of a people from a structured authoritarian, rural existence to an industrialized urban frontier (Attaway himself was a part of that northward migration of blacks—coming from rural Mississippi to Chicago). On the one hand, *Blood on the Forge* continued a long tradition of pastoral and anti-pastoral literature proceeding from early nineteenth-century Transcendentalists such as Ralph Waldo Emerson, Henry David Thoreau, and Nathaniel Hawthorne through Mark Twain and Hamlin Garland in the Gilded Age, and ultimately to F. Scott Fitzgerald, Ernest Hemingway, John Steinbeck, Thomas Wolfe, and William Faulkner. At the same time, the novel is worthy of special attention as a powerful plea in behalf of a struggling race. In this sense Attaway rejects the traditional forms of agrarianism which call for a return to nature, and sounds the theme of alienation that marks the modern existential novel.

In *Blood on the Forge,* the earlier paean to the qualities of the simple country landscape suddenly becomes an angry repudiation of industrial life as destructive to human values. The focus then shifts from delicate scenes of lavish woods, succulent orchards, and flocks of sheep—an idealization of nature from a distance as the moral symbol of the good life—to the horrible fact that man has already been swallowed up by the machine. This transition from bucolic nostalgia to "industrial antipathy" represents a literary consummation, but at the same time and most tragically, an individual act on the part of Southern blacks.

In the first part of the novel, the author explores the futile attempts of a family of black farmers to apply agrarian values to a bleak environment in the red clay hills of Kentucky during World War I. Attaway's Joads are three brothers—the elder Big Mat, who represents the plodding strength and endurance of all Southern Negroes under their particular color-caste system; Melody, whose blues singing recreates and sustains the pastoral myth [in a footnote, Vaughan observes: "Edward Margolies points out in this connection that the pastoral yearning does not mean a romanticizing of the brutality and emptiness of the submerged condition of Negroes, but instead 'the memory, the idea, the "dream" of the land as it must have been before they and the land were exploited by racist owners.' " See Margolies, *Native Sons, a Critical Study of Twentieth-Century Negro American Authors* (1969)]; and Chinatown, whose lazy, happy-go-lucky attitude reflects in part a psychological response to the subjugated position of Negroes. Throughout this "pastoral" section of the novel, Attaway testifies to the myth's fragility when faced by the reality of such an existence—an existence characterized by images of hunger (one of Melody's songs is the "Hungry Blues"), barrenness (the soil as well as Mat's wife Hattie, who has failed six times in childbirth), drudgery (the plowing from sunup to sunset for no reward), and finally, death. This last image is poignantly expressed in Attaway's account of the death of Mat's mother.

> She had dropped dead between the gaping handles of the plow. The lines had been double looped under her arms, so she was dragged through the damp, rocky clay by a mule trained never to balk in the middle of a row. The mule dragged her in. The rocks in the red hills are sharp. She didn't look like their maw any more.

Mat himself voices the apparent triumph of brutal reality over the pastoral myth after he kills the white riding boss for the latter's derogatory remarks about his dead mother. Before fleeing his Kentucky land, Mat says:

> Ain't nothin make me leave the land if it good land. The hills bigger 'n any white man, I reckon. Take more 'n jest trouble to run me off the hills. I been in trouble. I been born into trouble. Share-worked these hills from the bad land clean to the mines at Madison. The old folks make crops here afore we was born. Now the land done got tired, ceptin' the muck in the bottoms. It do somethin' to a man when the corn come up like tired old gents. Somehow it seem like it come time to git off. The land has jest give up, and I guess its good for things to come out like this. Now us got to give up too.

With these words of farewell to the South—and the myth—Attaway switches abruptly to the departure northward. The "shock" of the flight from the land is graphically described in the following passage:

> Squatted on the straw-spread floor of a boxcar, bunched up like hogs headed for market, riding in the dark for what might have been years. Knowing time only as dippers of warm water gulped whenever they were awake, helpless and drooping because they were headed into the unknown and there was no sun, they forgot even that they had eyes in their heads and crawled around in the boxcar, as though it were a solid thing of blackness. . . . The air, fetid with man smell and nervous sweat, the pounding of the

wheels shaking the car and its prisoners like a gourd full of peas, the piercing screams of the wheels fighting the rails on a curve, the uniform dark—those things were common to all. The misery that stemmed from them was a mass experience. Big Mat could not defend his identity against the pack.

Critic Edward Margolies sees the boxcar taking them north as a "kind of womb preparing to disgorge them into a new life." But what kind of a "new life"? Attaway hints of a life that is a radical departure from "green" living, thus rendering the older values useless. While the train roars north, Big Mat cries:

> What's the good in strainin' our eyes out these windows? We can't see where nothin grows around here but rusty iron towers and brick stacks, walled up like somebody's liable to try and steal them. Where are the trees? They so far away on the tops of the low mountains that they look like the fringe on a black wear-me-to-a-wake dress held upside down against the sky.

Once Big Mat and his brothers arrive at the mills, "steel" replaces "earth" and comes to dominate the workers' lives, as [earth] had earlier dominated them. Attaway juxtaposes the "green life" up against the "mill life" and shows how pitiful are the attempts to apply agrarian values to industrial problems. And in this regard, perhaps the old black worker Smothers—whose legs have been crippled beyond use by a hot bar of steel falling across them—best expresses the conflict between the two worlds with these words:

> Listen close now, am' I'm goin' to talk to you so you know something. Steel want to git you. Onliest thing—it ain't gittin you fast enough. So there trouble in the mills. Guys wants to fight each other—callin' folks scabs and wants to knock somebody in the head. Don't nobody know why. It's 'cause steel got to git more men than it been gitten'. . . .

Attaway further develops this clash between pastoral and industrial-urban living with his account of Melody's exposure to "fast steel" ("Slag was dripping down through a hole to the floor of the pit, and there was no buggy in place to catch it."). In the midst of this fire and steel, Melody's blues fade and the measured pace of life in the Kentucky hills founders under the huge furnaces as "talk faded into nothing in the face of the heat," and "his body played the noiseless rhythms of the mill." Melody becomes fully aware of his plight following an explosion which injures his playing hand.

> He had been thinking of the guitar, knowing it could never plunk away the craving that was in him. In the South the music makers had said, "A love cravin' gits so mixed up with the music you can't tell which is which." Melody had said that also. Now he knew it for a fact. The last three days of picking at his guitar had wearied him. Yet he knew he would not be able to let the music box alone. That was what he had been thinking. Now he was lying with his hand quivering at his side, and blood ran in hot circles around his fingers. He would always wonder if

he had done it purposely. That was how it seemed at the time.

From this point on, the men's lives are dominated by the crashing sounds of the steel mill—"Engines panted and struggled with the rails. The ore boats along the river kept up their own noises. Each tin house had its own pulse. And above everything an organ of whistles sighed and bellowed." Attaway is suggesting that "steel" could not be controlled by men—least of all "green men" ("No one man could calculate its beginning or end. It was as old as the earth. It would end when the earth ended. It seemed deathless"). The author leaves the reader with the feeling that the only human adjustment is the symbolic gesture of summoning forth the pastoral myth, however useless it might be from any practical standpoint. Big Mat makes such a gesture in the hills outside of town following the explosion that blinds Chinatown.

> In his trouble his spirit was near home. So the song of the mills was muted, and all that he saw had another air. The sky sometimes took on the colors of planting time. He did not see the smoke and slag of the mills. There was that coming-summer smell that the gases could not kill. . . . He walked, and his nostrils windened in the light wind. . . . There had been an old mule pressed against a rail fence on a sloping red hillside. Its nose had felt the breeze for good smells. . . . He would be far away from the river, up in the black hills. Because he listened for other sounds he would lose the sound of the steel makers.

---

**Blood on the Forge realistically portrays the transition of people from a structured authoritarian, rural existence to an industrialized urban frontier.**

**—Phillip A. Vaughan**

---

Despite the apparent solace this symbolic "return to nature" provides Mat and his brothers, it is obvious from the conclusion of the novel that Attaway sees a rural subjugation replaced by an industrial-urban one. Following the influx of more and more workers to the mills and the subsequent labor strife, Big Mat is used by the white police as a deputy to break up a massive workers' riot. While this role seems to give him a new sense of power and freedom, Attaway makes it clear he is headed for destruction against his own kind, black and white. It even becomes evident to Mat when his Mexican mistress calls him a peon ("It was a term like 'nigger.' . . . His new found power had had no strength against that contempt . . ."). After Mat dies in the riot, Melody and the blind Chinatown leave the mills and head for Pittsburgh. During the train ride north, Melody perhaps best expresses emerging realizations by Negroes that there will be no return to the greenery of the garden.

> Someday, Melody thought, he and Chinatown

would go home to Kentucky. But he did not think about that very hard. He was beginning to feel the truth: they would never go home. Now they would go to Pittsburgh. Many Negroes had gone to Pittsburgh before them; many were cast-offs of the mills. They had settled in the bottom of that city, making a running sore at those lowest points.

Toward the close of the novel, therefore, Attaway makes the complete shift from a mystic pastoral nostalgia to an industrial-urban repudiation—a shift that would become increasingly noticeable and prominent in black fiction. Big Mat is the literary forerunner of a truly urban Negro—one who subconsciously knows he is in his new environment to stay.

**Bonnie J. Barthold    (essay date 1981)**

SOURCE: "William Attaway, *Blood on the Forge,*" in *Black Time: Fiction of Africa, the Caribbean, and the United States,* Yale University Press, 1981, pp. 164-68.

[*In the following excerpt, Barthold discusses Attaway's "jazzlike use of images of fragmentation" in* Blood on the Forge.]

***Blood on the Forge*** begins on a Kentucky farm with only "one good strip of land" remaining, farmed by the Moss brothers—Big Mat, Melody, and Chinatown—and Big Mat's barren wife, Hattie. The barrenness of the land and of the woman signal the death of an agrarian and communal way of life. Big Mat's quarrel with a white man only hastens the Moss brothers' departure for the North, and they accept a steel-mill recruiter's offer to board a boxcar for the Allegheny River and a strikebound steel mill there.

Predominantly the narrative focuses on the destructive life in the mill community. The mill workers suffer crippling or fatal accidents: one loses his arm, another his legs (and later his life); Melody damages his hand, and Chinatown loses his eyes; Big Mat is killed in a strike-related riot. The novel concludes with Melody and the blind Chinatown once more on board a train, this time bound for Pittsburgh, using the $250 compensation for Chinatown's eyes to buy their tickets.

The structure and narrative technique of ***Blood on the Forge*** are largely familiar—the third-person narrator with selective omniscience, the hope for a new and better way of life that meets with disappointment, the destructive cycle in which the present recapitulates the dispossession of the past, and a linear journey that ends where it began. Anna, the prostitute who becomes Mat's woman, has already been discussed as a Mammy-Wattah figure. But there is another facet to Attaway's novel—its jazzlike use of images of fragmentation. These images carry the thematic burden of the novel and provide a solution to the problem of characterization in a novel whose characters are largely inarticulate, incapable of verbal expression.

Melody provides an early clue to this aspect of Attaway's technique. He believes that "a man had oughta know book learnin'—so's he kin know how to say what he's feeling." But earlier he has been described as never having had "a craving in him that he couldn't slick away on his guitar." For Melody, his guitar provides a substitute for words. As the narrative progresses, however, his capacity to give musical shape to his feelings is eroded. Early on, he admits that "every once in a while he would get filled up . . . with a feeling that was too big to turn into any kind of music." Later, in the mill town, his guitar playing changes, from the "slicking" that was "for back home and the distance in the hills" to "quick chords with the finger . . . right for that new place [but] nothin' like the blues that spread fanwise from the banks of the Mississippi," a way of playing better suited to "the whirling lights and . . . the heart of the great red ingots." The stasis of *Cane* gives way to movement, and the images of twilight to images of whirling lights and fragmentation—and this is the change one must imagine in Melody's guitar playing, as he gives voice to his feelings about the milltown and about Anna. His feelings, however, get "too big" for even this changed way of playing; more or less deliberately, he injures his hand and hangs up his guitar. His feelings cut off from their expression, he becomes one of the images of fragmentation in the novel. And it is as though Attaway takes up where Melody leaves off, using a counterpoint of images centering on animals and barrenness that taken together signal that the erosion of time apparent in *Cane* is here complete. In the imagery of fragmentation, time explodes.

In Part I, Mat returns to Mr. Johnston's farm to butcher the pigs he has slaughtered the day before: "The sun was coming up. Nine white carcasses gleamed, gaping open, split down the middle, head and feet gone. They were like nine small human bodies." At the beginning of Part II, the Moss brothers flee Kentucky on the boxcar:

> Squatted on the straw-spread floor of a boxcar, bunched up like hogs headed for market, riding in the dark for what might have been years, knowing time only as dippers of warm water gulped whenever they were awake, helpless and drooping because they were headed into the unknown and there was no sun, they forgot even that they had eyes in their heads and crawled around in the boxcar, as though it were a solid thing of blackness.

The metamorphosis of animal to human, human to animal, recurs throughout the novel, along with the notion of slaughter. Time becomes alternately fragmented and opaque, only partially knowable. In the "Mex Town" episode of Part II:

> There were dogs everywhere. Stray curs came smelling at [their] heels. They did not kick at them. The whores of Mex Town had more love for animals than for men. One steel worker who had killed a dog had been found on the ash pile. A knife had let his blood soak the ashes.

Later, Chinatown loses his eyes and loses as well even his fragmentary perceptions of time, the red pop and gold teeth that punctuate the darkness. He is looked after by Anna: "Anna would take good care of Chinatown. Like all her kind, she had a ready sympathy for a maimed animal, whether dog or man." In the dogfights that are staged for the workers' amusement and the dog trainer's profit, the description of one man's method of training his dog

to fight mimes the "training" Big Mat undergoes for his fight at the conclusion of Part IV:

> Son's [the dog's] owner . . . knew how to keep a dog savage and ready for blood. [He] kept Son in a dark closet for weeks at a time, feeding him raw meat sprinkled with gunpowder. Sometimes [he] would let him out and tease him with a sharp stick. Son would tear up anything that came within the radius of his chain.

By the time Big Mat is "deputized" to help control the strikers, he too is "savage" and "ready for blood"—and for much the same reason. He has been locked in darkness: on the boxcar, in a town where days pass with the sun concealed behind steel-mill smoke, and in a work schedule that means rising before dawn and returning from work after dark. Tormented by his growing impotence with Anna, he spends hours of his "free" time balancing a rock at the end of his outstretched arm as a proof of his strength. Chained by the circumstances of his life, Big Mat is more than ready "to tear up anything."

The men's dismemberment in work accidents again mimes the slaughter of the hogs. In the women, too, there is dismemberment and the stench of death: one of the first women the brothers encounter is a black whore with "a rot-stink." They are told that "her left breast 'bout rotted off. . . . You kin smell it a mile away."

Images of barrenness figure as another form of fragmentation, of human beings cut off from time and cyclic continuity. In Part I, most of Mat's farmland is so lacking in topsoil that it is barren; and he has no mule for plowing. His wife, Hattie, is barren, having suffered six or seven miscarriages. Though Anna finds in Big Mat a fulfillment of her yearning for a man "with a pine tree on his belly, hard like rock all night," by the end of Part IV she has turned to "a piece of ice" beneath him, "a dead body," and the image again is one of barrenness. Earlier, Mat has explained his barrenness as the result of a curse by God on "a child of sin." He knows how to lift the curse: "I got to preach the gospel—that the only way." But his knowledge, too, is barren; "No matter how much inside [him]," he can't preach. "If I tries to preach 'fore folks it all jest hits against the stopper in my throat and build up and build up till I fit to bust with wild words that ain't comin' out." He lacks the words to bring forth the Word, and belief is fragmented from its expression.

These various images of fragmentation are epitomized in the character of Smothers, the mad, crippled timekeeper at the mill. Smothers feels that the earth will sooner or later take revenge against the steel mill's violation of its sacredness, and the revenge will focus on the men who work the mill. "Steel gonna git you," he says. Crippled in an accident that he brought on himself as an act of defiance of the "monster" mill, he has become a kind of mill worker everyman, his crippled legs his wounds in an ongoing battle. Before he is killed, in the same explosion that takes Chinatown's eyes, his foreman has jokingly promised him that if steel "gits" him, "we make you up into watch fobs. The boys 'round the bunkhouse'll wear you across their chests for luck." After Smothers's death, Melody passes through the bunkhouse and finds Bo keeping the promise, affixing watch chains to shreds of steel from the explosion.

Smothers's vision and death echo Sekoni's in *The Interpreters:* both are struck down when natural process goes out of control. The Keeper of Time is fragmented into shards, and time explodes.

## Samuel B. Garren    (essay date September 1988)

SOURCE: "Playing the Wishing Game: Folkloric Elements in William Attaway's *Blood on the Forge,*" in *CLA Journal,* Vol. 32, No. 1, September, 1988, pp. 10-22.

[*In the following essay, Garren examines "the wishing game," a verbal game associated with black culture, as it is depicted in* Blood on the Forge.]

One element of black folk culture that plays an important part in William Attaway's novel ***Blood on the Forge*** (1941) is the wishing game. Early in Part I, Melody, one of three Moss brothers subsisting on a poor Kentucky farm in 1919, begins the game. His motive is distraction from hunger while awaiting Big Mat, the brother who sharecrops the farm and who may bring some food. In the call-and-response fashion characteristic of Afro-American culture, Melody involves his brother Chinatown in the game: " 'China,' he half sang, 'you know where I wish I was at now?' " Chinatown needs no prodding because the brothers have often played this game, their wishes usually formed by the "grand places pictured in the old newspapers" lining the walls of their shack. Led on by the responses of Chinatown, Melody spins his narrative. He imagines himself in town on a Saturday noon, all dressed up in a "white-checkered vest and a ice-cream suit," with a gold watch chain and "yeller shoes with dimes in the toes. Man, man!"

A small detail in this apparently insignificant game reveals an important difference between Melody and the other Moss brothers. In helping along the story, Chinatown tries to add girls, but Melody says that the girls can wait until evening. Noon is the time instead for playing pool. When Chinatown objects that Melody in actuality cannot play pool, Melody replies, "But I wish I can." Unlike the other major characters in the novel, Melody can maintain the distinction between unrealizeable desires and reality. With one exception, which he quickly recognizes, Melody keeps wishing within the confines of play, part of a necessary game that the mind must perform when a person is denied opportunities and privileges by society. For others in the novel, however, the wish becomes the delusion, to be paid for with pain and even death.

These events lie in the future, however. The first instance of the wishing game celebrates the rich poetry of the black oral tradition and the gifted folk artists within it. As the brothers continue the story, Chinatown regrets that Melody has brought his guitar to town but will not play it. Melody answers:

> "It don't make no never mind, 'cause my box is shinin' with silver, and the stops all covered with mother-of-pearl. An' everybody see me say that

must be Mr Melody. They say howdy to Mr Dressin'-man Melody."

The values of the wishing game are clear. The suppressed desires of a deprived minority can find expression and a measure of vicarious gratification. Unusually gifted individuals acquire a medium for expression and acclaim. Painful present reality can be temporarily forgotten, and frustrations can find a safe outlet. The limitations of this game are included in this early scene also when Hattie, Big Mat's wife, interrupts to say, "Wish night gone and real night come on." The brothers are quickly brought back to the reality of no food in the house and only used tobacco to chew.

Melody's oral virtuosity has not ended, however, as Hattie's play on the word "night" runs through his mind. Her statement, he says, sounds like a line from the blues, another of the great black oral achievements. As Melody develops the figure of the night personified, a fundamental element of the wishing games will become evident, the desire to escape a white-dominated world. This theme, the core of most desires voiced by the nonwhite characters in ***Blood on the Forge,*** explains the large role the author gives to this particular game. Melody imagines night as an old black woman, sweeping her black skirts to obliterate the things of the earth:

> "At night the hills ain't red no more. There ain't no crab-apple trees squat in the hills, no more land to hoe in the red-hot sun—white the same as black. . . . Where the mule gone at? He only a voice in the pasture land. . . ."

Melody's ability to pull back from fancy to reality appears at this point, too. When suddenly "he became conscious of what he was doing," he turned the game into a lighter vein with a strong undercurrent of reality:

> ". . . Night-flyers is glow buckles on the garters of old creepin' night. The mosquitoes is her swamp-fever sting. . . . But it don't last long, 'cause she say, 'Git along, an' be nothin', 'cause black ain't nothin', an' I is black. . . .' "

Throughout the novel, Attaway shows the crucial yet ambiguous role of wishing in black life by juxtaposing playful and serious manifestations. At times, the reader cannot determine which of the two forms is being expressed by a character, and one senses that the characters themselves are sometimes equivocal. When Big Mat returns with the makings for chitterlings, the family happily awaits their preparation. The white landowner who has given Mat the food surprisingly has promised the use of a mule, too. Immediately, Hattie and Melody begin imagining what the increased productivity will buy—fresh tobacco and pork on Sunday. When Chinatown voices suspicion, Hattie, reluctant to forgo her dream, advises not looking a gift horse in the mouth. Chinatown replies, " 'I'm pass the mouth now. I'm lookin' right down his throat.' " Such caution regarding the white world proves true when Big Mat recalls that as the landowner made the loan he warned of "jacklegs" coming into the area recruiting blacks to go North and work. The refusal to let dreams lead one permanently away from the reality of living in a white world seems instinctive as long as these people live in Kentucky. When the brothers are forced to take the jackleg's offer and go to work in the Pennsylvania steel mills, though, only Melody successfully resists the lure of destructive wishes.

By making wishing a key element in **Blood on the Forge,** Attaway conveys a major theme of the novel. The fuller life seemingly promised for blacks by life in the North proves to be an illusion. When the hopes contained while living in the South are given expression in the North, even greater pain and disillusionment result. For Attaway, the lesson of the Great Migration to the promised land is ironic indeed.

Even before leaving Kentucky, the difference between Melody and Big Mat in handling disappointment is evident. Whenever the deprivations of his life threaten to overwhelm Melody, he finds release in song and game. An exceptional creativity enables him to project his desires at length in verse, feel satisfied, and return to reality better able to cope. Big Mat, however, has no such release. Melody, who knows Mat best, sees the emotional pressure behind the strong, stoic demeanor. For both men, the chief obstacle is being black in a world controlled by whites.

One spring morning, the two brothers pause before plowing to enjoy the smell of the only good parcel of land they farm. Feeling the "earth like a good thing in his heart," Melody tells Big Mat that such pleasure will "[m]ake you forgit you just a nigger, workin' the white man's ground." In a skillfully written passage, thoughts of what might be lead the brothers in separate ways. Melody speaks of the great lack in his life, never having the chance to attend school year round "like white kids." This man, gifted with words, knows how much an education would have benefited his expression. At the same time, Big Mat pursues his own line of thought. Disappointed by his wife Hattie's miscarrying six times, Mat bitterly compares her to the reliable earth. Finally, Melody's articulation of his furthest fantasy, "Guess I oughta been white," is surpassed by a deeper agony when Mat says, "Jest as well I was born a nigger. Got more misery than a white man could stand."

Chinatown, the third Moss brother, lacks the sensitivity of Melody and the potential explosiveness of Mat. Instead, he indulges in a different kind of play—chasing women, eating, and drinking his favorite "red pop." Representing Chinatown's dedication to fun is his front gold tooth, a visual symbol of his desire to please others on sight. For all his love of good times, Chinatown surprisingly is the most vulnerable of the brothers to extreme stress. Jammed into a boxcar with other blacks going north to Allegheny County, all of the Moss brothers are miserable, but Chinatown nearly loses control. Significantly, Melody's reassurance rescues Chinatown from panic. As they talk in the boxcar, Melody learns that Chinatown's easygoing nature masks a deeper insecurity based on race. Convinced by white mistreatment that he is nothing, Chinatown decides that he has to have something to make him feel like a person: "So all the time I dream 'bout a gold tooth, shinin' an' makin' everybody look when Chinatown smile." To achieve his goal, a healthy tooth was removed to make room for the gold.

The inhuman, terrifying crowding of the blacks in the train boxcar reawakens Chinatown's insecurity. He becomes convinced that the car's rattling has loosened the gold tooth, and if he sleeps, it will fall and be stolen. Eventually calmed by Melody, Chinatown repeats, "I jest got to have that tooth. Without it I ain't nobody." When the boxcar is finally opened, all the men temporarily experience what will become a permanent state for Chinatown at the end of the novel—blindness and the hearing of sounds that no longer exist. Identifying this condition with Chinatown implies that the greatest illusion a black person can suffer is one best typified by him, staking one's identity on visible tokens of self-esteem. Of all the characters surviving at the end, Chinatown is the most lost because his dream was the most superficial.

Another major character in **Blood on the Forge** who succumbs to the wishing game is Anna, one of the whores in the steel mill village. Originally from Mexico, Anna, a girl of fifteen, has come from New Mexico at the bidding of her aunt, Sugar Mama. When Melody first meets Anna, he learns of her dream of meeting a man who will get for her all the grand things she associates with white life in the United States. The man she describes has some of the qualities of certain heroes in folklore:

> "He will be a big man with muscles like a bear on the mountain. That is so he can kill Sugar Mama if she try to hold me when I go with him. He will have a pine tree on his belly, hard like rock all the night. He will get me high-heel shoes with bright stones in the heels."

Such characters, larger than life in attributes and deeds, partake of the element of imaginative fulfillment of extreme human fancies in a manner similar to that of the wishing game. Some figures in black folk culture who reflect some of these qualities include John Henry, High John de Conquer in some of his manifestations, and Shine.

The man who answers Anna's wish is Big Mat. Impressed by his rescue of her at a dogfight, Anna wins him with a single kiss. In this initial encounter, their communication is primitive, speaking of a time thousands of years ago "when men said things in the talk of the wild beast." Events will prove, however, that the modern world requires more than this kind of blood knowledge. Anna and Big Mat will suffer in pursuing their dreams because they lack the thought and detachment that only Melody possesses. Later in the novel, when Mat sees himself as just such a giant character as Anna desired, he is at the height of his delusion.

Later, Anna discusses with Melody the origin of her dream. As a young girl, she became determined to rise above the impoverished lot of the Mexican peon. The chief stimulus was touring "*Americanos,*" whose greater wealth inspired Anna to be just as grand:

> "All the time I dream of high-heel shoes with bright stones in the heels that will make me like the *Americanos,* and nobody will take my picture along with the goats."

When Anna moves in with Big Mat, she spends the money he had been saving to bring his wife North in an attempt to realize the good life of white Americans. The result is pathetic:

> Anna went into the stores and came out with rhinestone shoes and dresses like the hostesses wear in the dance halls. The rhinestones did not glitter after one trip down the slushy road. The dresses were heavy around the bottoms where they dragged in the mud. Still, Anna wore her new clothes every day and paraded through the Mexican part of town like an overseer's wife.

Anna's infatuation with rich American life leads eventually to violence. When she comes home late one night with clothes wet from lying on the ground and with twigs in her hair, Big Mat, thinking she has been with another man, beats her savagely. The truth is again pathetic. Identifying the good life with the people who live on the hills above the steel mills, Anna has spent the night on a furtive trip into those hills. Creeping close to one of the "white hill houses," Anna had spent the day and night hiding in the bushes until slinking back home dispirited in body and soul.

Life in the North becomes increasingly demoralizing for the Moss brothers. Conflict between union supporters and the steel company leaves the brothers in the middle. Big Mat's relationship with Anna grows more strained and frustrating. Further catastrophe strikes when a blast furnace explodes, killing fourteen workers and blinding Chinatown. The brother who put such stock in his visual appearance now has eyes that look like "old eggs rotting in their ragged half shells, purple and revolting."

In the crucial first days after this accident, Melody shows his superior ability to cope with reality by his treatment of Chinatown. Again the wishing game is involved. Still in shock, Chinatown reverts to the past, avoiding confronting the reality of his mutilated condition. Melody plays along, assuring Chinatown in his greatest need that the gold tooth is intact. This gambit threatens to undo Chinatown's precarious balance when he asks to see his tooth in a mirror. For diversion, Melody begins the wishing game by asking Chinatown, "You know where I wish I was at now?" Chinatown quickly joins in.

The time in the game is the same as before when Melody sang in Kentucky to appease hunger—noontime. Instead of staying in one place, however, Melody is on the move. Like a larger-than-life folk hero, Melody must hurry because he plans "to cover the earth 'fore midnight." Perhaps reflecting his increased fears, Chinatown asks about stepping on snakes. With amazing ingenuity, Melody sings in succession of a number of snakes, each embellished with highly fanciful details. The rich black oral tradition, with its capacity for inventing endless variations on a subject, enables Melody to create a form to divert and delight Chinatown.

The first snake Melody meets, a coachwhip, lashes at him, but Melody stomps it into the ground. Up it springs, as a "tall whitewood tree," lashing the air "a little at the tip as the leaves 'gin to fall." Next Melody outwits a hoop snake, pushing its head into the ground. All that is left is "a crooked wild chinaberry tree, curved in the wind and broken like a old wagon tree." Thus Melody's inventiveness runs, dispatching snake after snake. As quickly as Chinatown calls out names of new snakes, Melody can transform them into harmless objects, exorcising his brother's fears at one remove.

To illustrate Melody's spontaneous creativity, a rattlesnake becomes a "tree full of jack-o'-lanterns now, rattling when the wind blow"; a blue racer a bow tie; a barn snake "a string of red and yellow beads for the neck o' a gal"; and a root snake "a walkin' stick, like a branch o' juniper." The last snake, a spreading adder, is completely confounded in Melody's fantasy:

> "When I come up on him he unjoint himself. Ain't nothin' but a lot of little pieces underfoot. All I got to do is mix him around with one toe. When he come back together there his tail at the wrong end, his head in the middle."

In the climax of this version of the wishing game (which also takes the form of the boast, a venerable tradition in black folk culture), three themes already discussed come together: wish fulfillment, assumption of fabled attributes, and longing for escape from white dominance:

> "Come midnight . . . come midnight . . . well, I go look at all the farmers. They all black. There ain't no white man in the land. Nobody gits crop-aliened. There ain't no ridin' boss. The muck ground cover all the farmers so they grow potatoes under their armpits. They grow field corn between their toes. One man jest let a big tree grow on his back for shade. All he do is walk in the shade and drink corn whisky."

Fortunately, the exhaustion of Melody's fancy and the demand of Chinatown's thirst coincide. The limit of Melody's ability to ride the wishing game is evident when he goes to get Chinatown's favorite red pop. As Attaway writes, Melody "was glad to leave the wishing game unended, glad to leave the house for the red pop."

The realism of Melody is further underscored when we follow him in search of Chinatown's drink. After obtaining the pop, Melody stops at the bunkhouse and discovers Bo, a gang boss, involved in a strange operation. He is making chains fastened to scraps of steel to be used as watch fobs. The bits of steel represent the remains of the body of a worker named Smothers, melded amongst the debris scattered by the force of the furnace explosion. Interestingly, in light of Attaway's investigation into the complex nature of play in *Blood on the Forge,* Smothers had been crippled when trying to win a bet by walking the steel-rolling tables from one end of the mill to another. Close to winning his wager, Smothers' legs were crushed by a hurtling bar of hot steel. Now Melody joins the others in the bunkhouse in wearing "that little piece of Smothers across his vest for luck." Just as throughout *Blood on the Forge* game merges with seriousness, here realism flirts with superstition, and the singer undaunted by snakes readily secures a fetish.

As tension grows between the union and the company, the Moss brothers retreat further into their own small unit. Impressed by Mat's strength, the leader of a group of strike breakers working for the company offers Mat a chance to become a deputy earning four dollars a day.

More than the extra pay Mat is lured by the words of another deputy:

> "So long, pal. Just remember Monday that
> you're the boss in this here town. Anythin' you
> do is all right, 'cause you're the law."

Mat thinks back to another game, one played when he was a child in Kentucky by white sharecroppers' children who enjoyed taunting Mat with a racist chant:

> "Nigger, nigger never die.
> Black face and shiny eye,
> Kinky hair and pigeon toe—
> That the way the nigger go. . . ."

Now Mat has an opportunity to turn the joke around since he has become the boss, the law: "Those thrilling words were too much to resist. He was a boss, a boss over whites."

Returning before a final assault on union headquarters, Mat in his newly won power expects respect from Anna. Instead, three sets of unrealistic dreams come together tragically. Anna is still possessed by her desire for a rich life, symbolized by the gaudy dress and rhinestone shoes she wears. Melody has become infatuated by Anna and arrives hoping to persuade her to run away with him. For once, even Melody has lost his objectivity. When Anna tells both brothers that to her they are contemptible peons, Mat again unleashes his fury against her. Unable to stop the belt whipping of Anna, Melody withdraws, like the others now, a "man in a dream." After the attack ends, his artist's eye fastens on a telling image: "two bright objects in the center of the room," the rhinestone shoes with high heels left behind by Anna. Gazing at the wreckage of several people's hopes, Melody returns to reality, aware more than ever of the delusive power of dreams.

Mat's aggression against the striking workers is fueled by Anna's reference to him as a peon. Although he may have been a kind of peon in the South, Mat thinks that in the North "here there was no riding boss," symbol for a life bound to the soil. While Mat beats the strikers in the union office, however, he gains a new insight:

> He was exalted. A bitterness toward all things
> white hit him like hot iron. Then he knew. There
> was a riding boss—Big Mat.

For a time, this knowledge increases Mat's sense of power to the point of megalomania. The mythic superman of folklore returns in the person of Mat, recalling Melody's playful songs but changed by the real context of violence:

> Big Mat looked at the mills, and the big feelings
> were lifting him high in the air. He was big as
> God Almighty. The sun was down, or his head
> would have thrown a shadow to shade the river
> front. He could have spit and quenched a blast
> furnace. Big Mat's eyes were big as half-moons.

At the height of his sense of power, like a classical instead of a folklore hero, Mat is fatally clubbed by a young Slav worker. Before dying, however, Mat achieves at last "all the objectivity of a man who is closer to death than life." In this last lucid moment, Mat realizes that he is like all of the riding bosses of both North and South, merely a tool of larger forces. Once, back in Kentucky, Mat had beaten a riding boss. Now someone similarly beats him, and the cycle continues. As Mat dies, he wonders:

> Had that riding boss been as he was now? Big
> Mat went farther away and no longer could dis-
> tinguish himself from these other figures. They
> were all one and the same.

Emphasizing that point, the worker clubbing Mat becomes as frenzied as had his victim whipping Anna and beating the workers. As the worker continues hitting an already dead Mat, the description points out the close, almost frightening line between certain forms of play and some of the grimmest aspects of reality:

> The young Slav danced about and used the pick-
> ax handle. Because the big black man did not fall
> he was filled with terror. Because the little eyes
> seemed to regard him so calmly he had to be-
> come frenzied to finish the job. So he danced
> about, and the sound of the blows was dull. It
> was like a Punch and Judy show, the way the
> black head wagged under the stick. It was funny,
> funny without laughter.

In the conclusion of the novel, Melody picks up the pieces, arranging Mat's funeral, obtaining two hundred fifty dollars from the company for Chinatown's accident, and finding a place for them to start anew in a black ghetto in Pittsburgh. Riding a train out of the steel mill, as they had in different circumstances into the area, the brothers meet a black ex-soldier who also has been blinded. As the two blind men talk, Chinatown learns that the ex-soldier cannot stop hearing a particular sound. When Chinatown fails to hear the sound, the ex-soldier describes it: "'There, it soundin' off again!' he cried. 'Hear it? Boom! . . . Boom! . . . Boom! . . .'" Chinatown is still perplexed, and the other blind man adds that the noise comes from guns, perhaps a hundred miles away. Chinatown strains with ears rendered more acute from his loss of sight until he, too, believes he hears the guns:

> "Sound like somethin' big an' important that a
> fella's missin', don't it?" asked the soldier. Chi-
> natown nodded.

For the last time, Chinatown is playing the wishing game. Largely because of the terrible accident, which took the one faculty essential to his identity—sight—Chinatown is further abandoning actuality for a preferred realm, a world where wish becomes reality.

The author's description of Chinatown and the ex-soldier in this final scene implies that many blacks have been permanently wounded by white society, left with little more than a life on the sidelines given over to some form of the wishing game. Although Melody has suffered greatly, too, he retains his unique ability to perceive events realistically. This is the sole hopeful quality emerging from the grim conclusion:

> Melody watched the nod. He looked at the two
> blind men closely. Their heads cocked to one
> side, listening for sounds that didn't exist. They
> were twins.

## FURTHER READING

### Criticism

Campbell, Jane. "Visions of Transcendence in W. E. B. Du-Bois's *The Quest for the Silver Fleece* and William Attaway's *Blood on the Forge.*" In her *Mythic Black Fiction: The Transformation of History,* pp. 64-86. Knoxville: University of Tennessee Press, 1986.

Argues that "both books present the plights of share-cropper and millworker. Both reveal the disenchantment attendant upon urban migration. Both employ the supernatural in their romances. And in both, Marxism enters into the conception of history."

Ellison, Ralph. "Transition." *Negro Quarterly* 1, No. 1 (Spring 1942): 87-92.

Mixed review of *Blood on the Forge,* in which Ellison states that while "Attaway has done several things well," he occasionally fails to clarify the major issues of the work.

Hamilton, Cynthia. "Work and Culture: The Evolution of Consciousness in Urban Industrial Society in the Fiction of William Attaway and Peter Abrahams." *Black American Literature Forum* 21, Nos. 1-2 (Spring-Summer 1987): 147-68.

Compares Attaway's portrayal of work and culture in *Blood on the Forge* to Peter Abrahams's in his 1963 novel *Mine Boy.*

---

Additional coverage of Attaway's life and career is contained in the following sources published by Gale Research: *Black Literature Criticism,* Vol. 1; *Black Writers,* Vol. 2; *Contemporary Authors,* Vol. 143; and *Dictionary of Literary Biography,* Vol. 76.

---

# Hélène Cixous

## 1937-

Algerian-born French theorist, novelist, short story writer, essayist, nonfiction writer, dramatist, screenwriter, and librettist.

The following entry presents criticism on Cixous's critical works through 1992.

## INTRODUCTION

A major figure in contemporary feminist critical theory, Cixous is known for works that analyze and attempt to counter Western culture's traditional concepts of male and female. A proponent of *écriture féminine,* or feminine writing, Cixous strives in all of her works to establish a uniquely feminine perspective, both as a kind of corrective to what she and many feminist theorists view as the traditionally masculine character of Western discourse and as a methodology with which to critique that discourse. In the United States, Cixous's best known work is *La jeune née* (1975; *The Newly Born Woman*), which is recognized as being markedly influenced by the writings of Jacques Derrida, the French philosopher and founder of the critical method known as deconstructionism; Jacques Lacan, the French psychoanalyst and philosopher who proposed a linguistic theory of the unconscious; and Sigmund Freud, the originator of psychoanalysis. Concerning Cixous's significance to contemporary thought, Morag Shiach has noted: "Her essays on writing and sexual difference have been a crucial point of reference for feminist theorists and critics, and her insistence on the transformative and broadly political dimensions of writing has constituted an important challenge to the unfocused aestheticism of much of literary studies."

### Biographical Information

Cixous was born in Oran, Algeria. Her father, who was of French-colonial background, was a physician, and her mother, of Austro-German heritage, was a midwife. Members of her family were Sephardic Jews, and Cixous grew up with a sense of kinship with persecuted groups. Her father died when she was very young, an event some critics suggest informs her writing. In her teens, Cixous read myths, the German Romantics (including Heinrich von Kleist), and English literature, especially the writings of William Shakespeare. Cixous moved to France in her late teens, where she earned an *agrégation d'anglais* degree in 1959 and became a *docteur dès lettres* in 1968. She was a founder of the University of Paris VIII-Vincennes, a liberal school offering an alternative to traditional education, and the Centre de Recherches en Etudes Féminines in 1974. She also cofounded, with Gérard Genette and Tzvetan Todorov, the prestigious literary and critical journal *Poétique* in 1968. Cixous has taught at various universities in France, including the University of Paris, the Sorbonne,

and the University of Bordeaux; she has also been a visiting professor at such institutions as Yale University, Columbia University, and Dartmouth College.

### Major Works

Cixous's first published work of criticism was her doctoral thesis, *L'Exil de James Joyce* (1968; *The Exile of James Joyce*). In this work she examines Joyce's experimental literary techniques and the ways in which they express his belief in the mutually influential relationship between linguistic and mental structures. She criticizes Joyce, however, for emphasizing a connection between guilt and death; she argues that this leads to the unnecessary paradox, detectable in all of his works, that one must "lose" in order to "gain," kill in order to live. In *Prénoms de personne* (1974), a collection of essays, Cixous presents psychoanalytic analyses of literary texts by Freud, August Heinrich Hoffmann, Kleist, Edgar Allan Poe, and Joyce. These essays deal variously with the concept of the "unified subject," or the individual's sense of being or "possessing" a distinct, whole personality. In 1975 Cixous published "Le rire de la Méduse" (1975; "The Laugh of the Medusa"), a well-known essay that examines Freud's concept of castration anxiety. Freud argued that this anxiety stems from a fear of female genitalia, perceived by males at a subconscious level as the result of castration—the female body understood subconsciously as "lacking" a phallus. Freud suggested that the mythical story of Medusa, in which people turn to stone when they look at the snake-entwined head of the Gorgon, could be read as addressing this psychoanalytic fear. In "The Laugh of the Medusa" Cixous argues, following many theorists, that this masculine view of women as "lacking" has broad social and political implications and manifestations. *The Newly Born Woman* consists of three parts: Catherine Clément's essay "The Guilty One," Cixous's "Sorties," and "Exchange," a dialogue between the two authors in which they discuss the similarities and differences in their views on women and writing. Through their readings of various historical, literary, and psychoanalytical texts, the two explore the role played by language in determining women's secondary place in society. They go on to propose that Western culture's repressive language must be replaced with a language of liberation. Elizabeth Wright has noted that "the general thesis of this book is that if women are going to take part in history they must write themselves into it." *La venue à l'écriture* (1977), coauthored with Annie Leclerc and Madeleine Gagnon, further evinces Cixous's preoccupations with language, psychoanalysis, and feminine pleasure. According to Verena Andermatt Conley, in this work Cixous "traces the origin of women's writing to the mother's voice and body." *"Coming to Writing," and Other Essays* (1991) collects translations of a number of Cixous's critical works written between 1976 and 1989, including "Clarice Lispector: An Approach," "Tancredi Continues," and the title essay, which is a translation of *La venue à l'écriture.*

## Critical Reception

Reaction to Cixous's critical works has been mixed. Many critics have praised her attempts to revolutionize traditional beliefs about women and writing. Others, however, have castigated what they consider the contradictoriness of her work and her intentional resistance to analysis. Toril Moi has stated: "Her style is often intensely metaphorical, poetic and explicitly anti-theoretical, and her central images create a dense web of signifiers that offers no obvious edge to seize hold of for the analytically minded critic." Some reviewers also suggest that Cixous's attempts to redefine gender differences reduces women to what one critic has called an "anatomical essence," and that her works are, in fact, antifeminist. Others argue, like Moi, that Cixous's work is expansive rather than reductive and "seems to displace the whole problem of women and writing away from an empiricist emphasis on the sex of the author towards an analysis of the articulations of sexuality and desire within literary text itself." Most critics, however, praise Cixous's belief that the creation of a new language is, as stated by Nicole Irving, "a precondition of a new reality." Cixous herself has asserted: "Writing *is the very possibility of change,* the space from which a subversive thought can spring forth, the forward runner in any movement to change social and cultural strategies."

## PRINCIPAL WORKS

*Le prénom de Dieu*   (short stories)   1967
*L'exil de James Joyce ou l'art du remplacement* [*The Exile of James Joyce or the Art of Replacement*]   (doctoral thesis)   1968
*Dedans* [*Inside*]   (novel)   1969
*\*Les commencements*   (novel)   1970
*\*Le troisième corps*   (novel)   1970
*Un vrai jardin*   (short fiction)   1971
*\*Neutre*   (novel)   1972
*La pupille*   (drama)   1972
*Tombe*   (novel)   1972
*Portrait du soleil*   (novel)   1974
*Prénoms de personne*   (essays)   1974
*La jeune née* [*The Newly Born Woman*]   [with Catherine Clément]   (essays)   1975
*Un K. incompréhensible: Pierre Goldman*   (nonfiction)   1975
*Portrait de Dora* [*Portrait of Dora*]   (drama)   1975
*Révolutions pour plus d'un Faust*   (novel)   1975
"*Le rire de la Méduse*"   ["The Laugh of the Medusa"]   (essay)   1975; appeared in the journal *L'arc*
*Souffles*   (fiction)   1975
*LA*   (fiction)   1976
*Partie*   (drama)   1976
*Angst* [*Angst*]   (novel)   1977
*La venue à l'écriture*   [with Annie Leclerc and Madeleine Gagnon]   (essay)   1977
*Le nom d'Œdipe: Chant du corps interdit*   (libretto)   1978
*Préparatifs de noces au-delà de l'abîme*   (novel)   1978
*Ananké*   (fiction)   1979
*Vivre l'orange/To Live the Orange*   (fiction)   1979
*Illa*   (fiction)   1980
*With ou l'art de l'innocence*   (novel)   1981
*Limonade tout était si infini*   (fiction)   1982
*Le livre de Promethea*   (fiction)   1983
*L'histoire terrible mais inachevée de Norodom Sihanouk roi du Cambodge* [*The Terrible but Unfinished Story of Norodom Sihanouk, King of Cambodia*]   (drama)   1984
*La prise de l'école de Madhubaï*   (drama)   1984
*La bataille d'Arcachon*   (tale)   1986
*Entre l'écriture*   (essays)   1986
*L'indiade ou l'inde de leurs rêves*   (drama)   1986
*Théâtre*   (dramas)   1986
*L'indiade ou l'inde de leurs rêves*   (nonfiction)   1988
*Manne: Aux Mandelstams aux Mandelas* [*Manna: For the Mandelstams for the Mandelas*]   (drama and fiction)   1988
*L'heure de Clarice Lispector* [*Reading with Clarice Lispector*]   (criticism)   1989
*La nuit miraculeuse* [with Ariane Mnouchkine]   (screenplay)   1989
*Akhmatova*   (drama)   1990
*Jours de l'an*   (nonfiction)   1990
*L'ange au secret*   (nonfiction)   1991
†*"Coming to Writing," and Other Essays*   (essays)   1991
*On ne part pas, on ne revient pas*   (drama)   1991

*Readings: The Poetics of Blanchot, Joyce, Kafka, Kleist, Lispector and Tsvetayeva* (criticism) 1991
*Déluge* (nonfiction) 1992
*Beethoven à jamais, ou, l'existence de Dieu* (nonfiction) 1993
*Three Steps on the Ladder of Writing* (lectures) 1993
*The Hélène Cixous Reader* (collected works) 1994
*L'histoire, qu'on ne connaîtra jamais* (drama) 1994

*These works comprise a trilogy.

†This work was edited by Deborah Jenson.

---

# CRITICISM

### Robert Boyle   (review date Spring 1974)

SOURCE: "James Joyce," in *Contemporary Literature,* Vol. 15, No. 2, Spring, 1974, pp. 262-70.

[*In the following excerpt from a review in which he examines a number of books on the work of James Joyce, Boyle offers a negative assessment of* The Exile of James Joyce. *He states that while it reflects "intelligence and industry," this study is an "ugly failure and will appear more so as time reveals its flimsy biases and its prejudicial aims."*]

The most massive single volume of Joycean criticism of the last few years, recently translated [as ***The Exile of James Joyce***], is Helene Cixous' publication of what was, I suppose, the logorrheic dissertation which helped to earn her *Docteur dés Lettres* in 1968, and which, according to the book jacket, "shows, and shows convincingly, that Joyce's consciousness was his biography and his biography wrote his books"—which book-jacket gibberish might make us fear that the book might attempt with Joyce what Stephen attempted with Shakespeare. One thing I can weakly murmur, having read every closely printed page of this 765-page book: it is about 600 pages too long. Most of it is more or less accurate cribbing from some of the two thousand sources Cixous says she studied, more or less likely conclusions from a lively and opinionated French intuition, a syllable-by-syllable analysis of those portions of Joyce's text Cixous has dissected (which does not include *Finnegans Wake*), and an uninhibited projection of a sometimes brilliant and sometimes banal French construct on the minds and works of Joyce, of Joyce's commentators, and, unfortunately, of Joyce's family.

Some of the brilliant aspects would include her insights into creative doubt, as she analyzes it primarily in relation to *Exiles,* and her perception of Joyce's use of opposition to faith and to God the Creator as a source of artistic inspiration. She perceives that the artist as God wants to be united to and love his literary characters (free beings, it seems, in *Exiles,* though she surprisingly denies freedom to the main characters of *Ulysses*). She seems to say that Joyce, as artist-God, frees his characters, when he does, by building all his kingdom on doubt (unlike the God of faith, he is not omniscient). Thus he builds out of himself

the human situation of essential frustration, providing no answers, and making us see the chaosmos of Alle, a frightening but fascinating vision.

As I read through the book, I was struck from time to time by what seemed remarkable profundity and insight in her treatment of Joyce's growth and development in dealing with words, of his movement from outside "objective" reality to the inner world of the imagination, of the effect of his dreams and visions on his work (as her detailed and beautiful treatment of Stephen's contemplation of the bird-girl in the water, marked, like Shem, on her skin with the sign of Thoth), of such triumphs of gathering together many sources into a single illuminating insight as in her treatment of "lapwing." But as I try now to bring all those moments together to say something positive about this attempt at heroic criticism (a massive creation in words comparable to Michelangelo's *David* ), they shrivel in my mind and get lost in the nauseating, even poisonous fumes from her non-Irish stew. The opinionated condemnation of the Irish race and of all things Irish; the often uncritical and sometimes misleading dependence, when they tend to bolster her intuitions, on biased and incompetent critics; her incredible statement about the main characters of *Ulysses*: "They are not caught in a dramatic situation which requires them to manifest their freedom; they are simply living through an ordinary day"—having developed that monstrosity, she finds no difficulty about saying, twelve pages later, "This day, 16 June, is not an ordinary day . . ."; her ignorance of and sometimes childish errors about Joyce's use of scholastic theology and philosophy; her patronizing tone and treatment of English critics, like Pater and especially Wilde, who achieve better than she does some of her principal aims, as in establishing the necessary exile of the artist into his own creating spirit—these and many other things urge me to condemn the book.

I hesitate to reject a book reflecting so much intelligence and industry, but my final judgment is that it is an ugly failure and will appear more so as time reveals its flimsy biases and its prejudicial aims. The determined effort, for example, to make Nora Joyce fit not only the distorted Molly Bloom constructed by Cixous, but to find Nora in all the other more or less degraded Dublin women (i.e., Gretta, Bertha, Zoe, Stephen's perverse version of the Blessed Virgin, Erin herself ) who look so queerly inhuman in their new French context, will surely grow in distasteful clarity as time passes. The same can be said of her view of Bloom's "suicide," achieved by determinedly ignoring vital aspects of Joyce's text, in which the surprisingly belligerent Bloom has a chance of out-flowering Boylan, and her simplistic depiction of Stephen exiling himself into the cosmos to write, if not *Ulysses* (as Tindall once pictured the situation), then another book, *Finnegans Wake,* given to us here in texts quoted mainly from Clive Hart (whose scholarly and cautious "may have been's" easily turn in Cixous' confident intuition into "were's"). Cixous has, apparently, not read *Finnegans Wake* at all (she speaks of "Kate the hen who finds the Letter"), a sad lack in so monumental a critical effort. It is like carving *David* from pedestal to navel and leaving the great rough mass of crowning marble untouched. I find, in any case, with sorrow and some fear of faulty vision distorting for me a creative triumph of criticism, that her critical analog to the heroic *David* reveals, like the frustrated Shem of *Finnegans Wake*'s ninth chapter, only a gigantic bimbamb bum whose "funnylegs are leanly."

**Brian Duren** (essay date 1981)

SOURCE: "Cixous' Exorbitant Texts," in *Sub-Stance*, No. 32, 1981, pp. 39-51.

[*Duren is an American educator. In the essay below, he notes that Cixous, in such works as* La jeune née *and* Prénoms de personne, *attempts to undermine and subvert traditional notions of literature and language.*]

> Quelque chose d'exorbité, de sourd à la réprobation d'autrui, élève au sublime ces poèmes et ces figures de couleur violente.
> (Georges Bataille, "William Blake")

> . . . often I have wondered whether, taking a large view, philosophy has not been merely an interpretation of the body and a misunderstanding of the body.
> (Nietzsche, *The Gay Science*)

The name. Bizarre. Cixous? That's not French. Not proper. It's a non-name. Foreign. Strange. An impossible name. Not proper to French. "A name that no one knew how to write and it was me." An improper name. "That's a name! . . . It was enough to get you thrown out!" "J'étais personne." I was nobody. So Hélène Cixous, *enfant terrible* of what Americans call the deconstructionists, avant-garde novelist, playwright, critic, feminist, revolutionary, returns in all of her self-portraits, to this opposition of the *propre* and the *impropre,* of otherness, of the other as *impropre.* And, in the context of French imperialism in Algeria, to her own otherness, to which her name, as an index, points: Cixous—an origin that is absolutely foreign: the father, of Sephardic Jews—from Spain, Morocco, Algeria: the mother, of Ashkenazic Jews—from Austria, Hungary, Czechoslovakia, and Paris. "I am (not) Arab," writes Cixous, a *pied noir* [the critic adds in a footnote: "The European settlers, who controlled much of Algeria, were nicknamed *pied noirs* by the Arabs because they wore black shoes rather than sandals"], but not French, for whom Arabic is the brother tongue and German the mother tongue and French the colonialist's tongue. A wandering Jew, an exile, a woman, the other—*impropre.*

What Cixous frequently calls the Empire of the *Propre* is not an empire in just the historical sense, like the former French empire, of which Algeria was a part. The *propre* that Cixous attacks is itself an empire, a political and moral empire that at once includes and excludes, an empire that is semantic, ontological, and sexual: the *propre* is property (*propriété*), possession, the self (*mon propre,* my own), the generally accepted meaning of a word (*le sens propre*), that which defines or identifies something (the *propre* of the novel, e.g., is narration, plot, characterization, etc.), the clean and the orderly (which recalls Freud's *Civilization and Its Discontents*), the ethical *propre* and *impropre,* and finally, in Cixous, masculine and feminine. The *propre,* contained in such verbs as *exproprier, ap-*

*proprier, s'approprier,* also designates the Hegelian dialectic of appropriation, in which the subject's expenditures, as Cixous would say, reap a profit, which is being, or self, and loss thus becomes gain:

> All history is inseparable from economy in the restricted sense of the word, from a certain type of saving. . . . This economy as law of appropriation is a phallocentric production. The opposition *propre/non-propre* (the valorization of the *propre*) organizes the opposition identity/difference. Everything happens as if, in a flash, man and being were appropriated one to the other. [*La jeune née*]

Her reading of the dialectic, or economy, of appropriation is mediated by some of Hegel's most radical offspring: Freud, Bataille, Lacan, Derrida. Cixous locates the master, Death, of the Hegelian dialectic in the fear of separation, of loss, of castration; the dialectic of recognition of master and slave is interpreted in Lacanian terms as the specularization by the effaced other (woman, in Cixous) of the masculine subject's fetishized self, the phallus.

Cixous' frequent use of such terms as economy, *économie restreinte,* restricted economy, and *économie générale,* general economy, underscores the tremendous influence of Bataille. Bataille's reading of Hegel's economy of appropriation is most evident in his analysis of the potlatch, as described by Marcel Maus in the *Essai sur le don,* which Bataille cites as the major influence on his *La Part maudite.* The tremendous expenditures, the loss (which Bataille links to unconscious forms of death and separation, as psychoanalysis describes them) are recuperated by means of the recognition that the other grants the subject—recognition that is tantamount to rank, being (which, in Lacanian terms—and Cixous frequently brings us back to Lacan—is the phallus). Her reading of Bataille echoes Derrida's reading, in "De l'économie restreinte à l'économie générale: un Hégelianisme sans réserve." It is the excess, the *impropre,* the importance accorded the *pulsion, Trieb,* or drive, the expenditures of energy without attempts at recuperation through transcendence, and the laughter, that mocks the *Aufhebung,* that Cixous constantly returns to in Bataille:

> Why this comedy whose ultimate act, the flirting of the master with death, would make Bataille laugh—Bataille amusing himself in pushing Hegel to the edge of the abyss into which a civilized man prevents himself from falling? Of this abyss which functions as a metaphor for death, for the feminine genitals. [*La jeune née*]

Cixous' remarks become very clear if we think of a text such as the *Histoire de l'oeil,* "The Story of the Eye" (which is also a story of the I), one of Bataille's most exorbitant texts, a blinding joke of loss, literally the story of an eye, or of an orb that is at once eye, testicle, and egg; consider, for example, the bullfighting scene, where, at the moment the bullfighter Granero has his eye put out by a bull, Simone, who has just bit into a bull's raw testicle (compared to an eye), "slowly and surely" inserts the other testicle into her vagina—the "abyss into which a civilized man prevents himself from falling." Cixous' "I" or "she" thrust themselves, too, into the other body, but that body is no longer the scene of castration; it is, rather, the black continent of the unconscious, the improper body, with its mysterious and dangerous drives, that can be known only through the representatives of those drives, or *pulsions,* only through fantasies (*fantasmes*) and dreams.

The *impropre,* death, is also that which determines the closed economy of desire (the desire that desires itself, that desires the same, and never desires the other); in the margins of many of Cixous' analyses of the economy of desire is a critique of Freud and Lacan, on the one hand, and of literature on the other. ***Prénoms de personne*** (a reading of Freud, Hoffmann, Kleist, Poe, and Joyce) opens with such a critique, that aligns the institutions of literature and psychoanalysis with the conservative politics of the *propre.*

> I have always loved desire. Not at all the one which believes itself to be determined by its relationship to a lack [*manque*] that it raises and from which it arises, so well (or so poorly) that it doesn't arise: this one, accomplice of the forces of death that it skirts and dreads, becomes identical with its limit. It frightens itself, it fears being satisfied. It needs to maintain itself with the aid of ruses at some distance from an actualization: because it does not venture as far as the real, it has hardly any chance of changing it. It desires itself more than it desires its object; it is well known, this desire to desire, which passes so often for *desire itself* of which it is only the regret and the prudence. It moves forward indirectly, through paradoxes, sustains itself with contradictions, assures itself of its impossibility. The spirit of weighing and balancing [*l'esprit de calcul*] animates it and manages its investments and counter-investments, so that the lack [*manque*] should never come to lack [*manquer*]. It conserves itself by surrounding itself with danger, enveloping itself with lures [*leurres*] and veiling itself with absence. It is well known: *it* makes the law and authorizes the arranging of the social order that it pretends to abhor: it is on its weakness that power counts, on its detours that reformism is constituted, on its petrifying fear of castration that the Church is constructed.

Let us quickly fill in the psychoanalytic texts that have been subsumed in the margins of this elliptical passage. The *manque* (lack), *leurre* (lure), and *voile* (veil), identify Lacan's discourse, just as the detours and ruses link Lacan's thesis concerning desire (i.e., that desire is born of lack, of castration, separation, death, that the subject's desire, his [ideal] alienated self is a lure, that this self, the phallus, is always veiled) with the thesis that Freud develops [in] *Civilization and Its Discontents,* namely that man's desire is in fact a desire for death, for a return which is death, and that life, as well as the history of civilization, is a series of detours, ruses to defer that which one desires, and dreads, most. The "investments and counter-investments" which in French also mean cathexis and anti-cathexis, indicate the closed economy of this desire that is always determined by death. Innumerable examples of such a closed economy in literature can of course be located. What better examples than Proust and Flaubert of a desire that nourishes itself with absence, that constantly, through the most elaborate detours, defers the re-

alization of desire (so that the lack will never lack), the better to project—to fetishize—something where there is nothing? Our literary history has more frequently than not struck desire with guilt, and articulated that guilt either through a series of binary oppositions aligning desire with death, or through a narrator (such as Balzac's) who visits the most implacable punishment on those characters who dare to desire.

Yet Cixous insists that "writing *is the very possibility of change,* the space from which a subversive thought can spring forth, the forward runner in any movement to change social and cultural structures." Specifically, in her own texts, that which is most subversive is the force of the other, a force such that the *propre,* the self, is forever being (though never becomes) undermined. Constantly referring to herself as a *voleuse,* a thief and a flier, she mocks the literature of the *propre,* literature as the property of an autonomous self. Her autobiographical essays, such as **"Sorties"** (which means the action of going out, leaving; an exit; a sum of money spent) and **"La Venue à l'écriture,"** are readings of texts, sorties, in the sense that they do not guide the reader toward (an illusion of) presence, of a self, at the center of the work, but rather project him/her toward the margins of the text and beyond into other texts. Rejecting, in her literary criticism, the aesthetics and politics of mastery, she shifts constantly from the third person to the second and first persons singular, thus clearly implicating her subjectivity in her readings of texts and tearing the veil of truth that traditional literary criticism wears to conceal its real status of fiction. For Cixous, the text is an imaginary space in which reader/writer can temporarily overcome the effects of castration, which she regards as the repression, or even foreclosure, of the subject's other by the symbolic order. "I have been Kleist's Penthesilea, not without being Achilles, I have been Antony for Cleopatra and she for him, I have also been Juliet because in Romeo I have overcome the cult of the fathers." All of her texts attempt to express the multiple and complex *pulsions,* the drives, of a bisexual subject that is many, a subject which she at times designates by the term *plus-je* (literally, "more-I," but also an incomplete anagram of *pulsion*). Most of the texts that Cixous chooses to read are somehow subversive of the symbolic order of binary oppositions, in which one term is always negative: *propre/impropre,* same/other. Her essay on Kleist's *Penthesilea* articulates at once Kleist's need to merge with the other, and, because of the insistence of Cixous['s] style, her own search for the other: "She [Penthesilea] is in him [Kleist], has always been in him like a wound, like his very wound . . . she is the cruel, adorable irruption of the other in him, of *she* whom he carries, that he makes, of whom he is a part, of whom he is the place, the woman . . . gone from him, his femininity, is that which of him, man, lover, poet, always escapes him." Her reading of the play, which frequently echoes Blake's poetry ("Is only beautiful that which excedes . . . which shoots forward and is lost from sight"), stresses its exorbitance, the excessive expenditures of love, energy, self, that seem to efface momentarily the orb of the *propre.* The conventional male/female opposition that structures the metaphorical discourse of love and war is largely displaced in the battle between the two lovers, a battle which is a kind of foreplay in sexual exchange; Penthesilea, pressing her thighs against her horse's flanks, pursues Achilles, who flees, but only to entice her to follow. He "melts with love and love mingles him with the woman that he allows to arise in him." He becomes a flower, and she the sun. Penthesilea dominates, argues Cixous, only to "destroy the space of domination" and allow each to love the other at once as male and female. The abyss that each character successfully crosses to begin realizing his otherness suddenly reappears, at least for Penthesilea, who thinks she has been betrayed by Achilles. For Cixous, the play ends with the "vengeance of castration"; the "old anxiety," Kleist's inability to resist the power of the Law, poisons Penthesilea, who proceeds to mutilate, to dismember, literally to devour Achilles' body, "love's body," to violently incorporate that which cannot be introjected.

One of the most persistent themes in Cixous' work is the *Angst* that overwhelms Penthesilea, that paralyzes the subject (always the victim of his/her desire to be one, separate, complete, whole) when it is torn between *amour propre*, self-love, the same, and *amour-autre*, other-love, between the *propre* and the subject's repressed otherness. It is at that moment of hesitation, a mere split second, that she is most likely to be the victim of what Cixous calls the "esprit de calcul," the spirit of weighing and balancing; then, for the subject overwhelmed by *Angst*, difference becomes rupture, abyss, wound, *béance*, alienation, mutilation—as in this passage from the novel, *Angst:*

> It happened in a flash: you are walking in a garden with the man who is your mother. Suddenly the earth trembles. A tear. He extends his hand toward you, he tells you: "Take my hand. It's not serious. And jump." You would like to jump. You would like to take his hand. . . . But at the moment when you tense your muscles, in the instant when you are going to stretch forth your hand, in the infinitesimal instant which doesn't separate you yet, a prudent reflex tells you: "Halt! Be careful! Have you taken your measures? Are you capable of jumping? This wound doesn't look good. Don't you see it is getting bigger? What in fact is this tear?" All this does not even last a second. During which a voice also tells you: "You should think about his well-being. And if he were to faint away? After all he is mortal. If the earth were to burst open, at the moment when you cross? One must know how to hold back. This prudence is not bad. It is out of love that you oscillate." Not even a second. You raise your eyes, you stretch forth your hand. But he has withdrawn his hand. He is not looking at me, he is not smiling at me. His face is strange, as if the day had fled it. . . .
>
> What happened? Nothing. A fissure. A mistake in calculation. The earth had a tear. I am afraid the tear might get bigger and become an abyss. I mistook the body. While I was examining the earth it's flesh that cracked. In a flash, the belly open, an immense wound. As soon as I looked at its lips which are ugly and black, I had no more strength, disgust overwhelmed me, I had to back away so that I would not hurl myself in.

This passage articulates the closed economy of desire that

Cixous describes in *Prénoms de personne,* the investments and counter-investments of a subject that uses death as its accomplice, that frightens itself with death so as not to leave itself, but rather to return, to conserve itself. It is by identifying the other with death, by denying her own otherness, that the subject mutilates herself, and alienates her body, which becomes repulsive, marked by death, an abyss. And so the subject reaffirms, through denial, the Law of difference as castration.

Cixous' Cleopatra, another mythical figure like Penthesilea, created from what is at once a reading, and a very free adaptation, of Plutarch and Shakespeare, follows immediately after her reading of Kleist in **"Sorties."** Cleopatra, as Cixous envisions, or fantasizes her, is a woman who, unlike Penthesilea, seems to overcome *Angst* and the power of the Law from which Penthesilea could not escape. Cixous reads Cleopatra against the backdrop of the Roman Empire of the *propre,* with its "wars, its rivalries and its phallus tournaments, so grotesquely represented by the game of penis-chess ["jeu d'échec au-pénis"] that the imperialistic powers of the triumvirate play with the petty gravity that makes history"; and against the backdrop of the Empire of *amour-propre* of the imperialists: "can love which keeps accounts be called love," asks Cixous rhetorically. Cleopatra is an amorous force of deconstruction; Cixous quotes Shakespeare's Antony, "At fast and loose she has beguiled me to the heart of loss," and adds that Antony is mourning his "propre image," the image of his *propre,* his self, or phallus. The death of Antony and Cleopatra recalls Cixous' statement concerning her own writing: it is the "assault that love gives to nothingness." Cleopatra, "at the point of the phallus in which she resides," hoists up the dying Antony—"come, come, come"—and takes him to her. Cixous describes him as "dead in a magnificent erection," an erection that is at once Antony's erection and the erect pyramid, an erection that subverts the monument to the (Hegelian and Freudian) master, Death, and would deconstruct an archetype of property, of the *propre,* the self, the fetish. Cixous' reading, following Shakespeare's text, skips one and one-half scenes, and goes on directly to the scene on Cleopatra's death, creating an effect much like that of a cinematographic dissolve. In immediate response to the death of Antony "in a magnificent erection," Cleopatra hastens to the marriage bed, takes the asps to her breasts, and pretends to nurse them; "even in death, she is the one who nourishes, and nourishing is nourished with love." The dissolving of the two scenes into one, thus uniting the two bodies and the two deaths, intimates Cixous' fantasy of a body-text that sensuously, carnally, is forever reaching into death, and bringing the loss (the lost other) closer: "To write in order to touch with letters, with lips, with breath, to caress with the tongue, to lick with the soul, to taste the blood of the loved body; of life distanced; to saturate distance with desire."

Cleopatra, like all of Cixous' mythical figures (Penthesilea, Medusa, Dora), is excess, the excess of the body, of its *pulsions,* its drives. Her Medusa is not lack, but the joyful laughter of Dionysus: "it suffices to look directly at the Medusa to see her: she is not mortal. She is beautiful and she is laughing." Her Dora is the "poetic body," the "true 'mistress' of the signifier," one of the "admirable hysterics" who speaks in "carnal and passionate body-words," and whose desire breaks up the restricted economy of desire that unites her parents, and Mr. and Mrs. K.

Cixous' texts belong to that tradition (Rimbaud, the surrealists, Bataille) which views writing as possible only because the subject has spent a (interminable) season in hell, during which the self is subverted by the other; in Cixous, the season in hell is described as the tearing of the webbed threads of the fiction of the self ("tu es trame déchiquetée"), the self which is the "same" "circumscribed by same," by its *propres* codes, which make the self *lisible* to itself:

> Writing—begins, without you, without I, without law, without knowing, without light, without hope, without bonds, without anyone near you, for if the world's history continues, you are not in it, you are "in" "hell" and hell is there where I am not but where that which is me, when I am without place, feels itself die again throughout time, where not-me drags me further from me, and where what remains of me is no longer anything but suffering without myself, suffering never circumscribed by same, for me, open, does not cease to feel the sense, the soul, the corporeal and spiritual substances of me flow away, me empties itself, and yet, more and more heavy, you sink, you are engulfed in the abyss of the *non-rapport*. ["La Venue à l'écriture"]

The *trame*, cloth, veil, tissue, or text, can never be completely torn, the system of *rapports*, codes, language itself, can never totally disappear, for the obvious reason that the subject could no longer be conscious, could no longer live; Bataille, whom Cixous frequently echoes:

> Vulgar knowledge is in us like another tissue! . . . In a way, the condition by which I would see would be to go out of, to emerge from the "tissue." And I should probably add too: this condition by which I *would see* would be my death.

But this loss, the death, is also excess, the excess of the body; the subject becomes, in Cixous, "flesh which allows the strange or foreign to pass through it," a "being without defense, without resistance . . . totally engulfed by the other" and "traversed by songs of unheard of purity, for they are not addressed to anyone, they gush forth, they spring up, out of the throats of your unknown feminine inhabitants." These *chants*, songs, unheard (of) melodies "sweeter," as Keats wrote, than heard ones, addressed to *personne*, no one, and issuing from *personne*, resemble the psychic representatives, or delegates described by Freud, or the messengers and symbols that Nicolas Abraham describes as issuing from the Somatic.

The other text, the other body—how can they be known, if they can never become conscious? The answer is: obliquely, through their symbols, delegates, or representatives, namely fantasies, dreams. "The Somatic," writes Abraham, "is what I cannot touch directly . . . it is that of which I would know nothing if its representatives, my fantasy, were not there to send me back to it, to its source as it were, and its ultimate justification. Reading the other

body, then, can only be done through a certain kind of writing, best conceptualized as an *ex-pulsion*, the outward movement of the *pulsion, Trieb,* or drive, from the forever unconscious body, to the text via the symbols, or delegates, of the *pulsions*. Cixous' texts are overflowing with images of ex-pulsion—of the voice, of the child, of milk—frequently linked to orgasm; and her exorbitant texts read like a body expelling itself, an almost jubilant loss, a potlatch of signifiers, an excess of language that seems to defy the coherence and continuity and order of what we call meaning. Two examples: her treatment of such *loci classici* of literature, such cliché[d] metaphors of writing, as childbirth and the voice.

> I have always taken pleasure in seeing a woman give birth. . . . Giving birth like one swims, playing against the resistance of the flesh, of the sea, the work of respiration in which the notion of "mastery" is annulled, body to body, the woman follows herself, joins herself, marries herself. She is *there*. Entirely. Mobilized, and it is her body that is concerned, the flesh of her flesh. . . . She is not absent, she is not feeling, she can take herself and give herself to herself. . . . It is not the "mother" that I would see. The child, it concerns her, not me. It was woman at the height of her flesh, her bliss, the force finally delivered, manifest. . . . She gives birth. With the force of a lioness. Of a plant. Of a cosmogony. Of a woman. ["**La Venue à l'écriture**"]

The passage articulates quite literally an expulsion, or the fantasy of an expulsion; in *accouchement*, the dictates of the body as other become dominant and bring forth what is seemingly proper—the child. But for Cixous, what is important is the "othering" (the "accoucheuse s'autre," others herself, she writes in "**Le Rire de la Méduse**"), wherein one body is felt in another body, one body makes possible the other body, and the woman's *pulsion* is present to her via the body. There is no fetishization of the child, no evidence of penis-envy in this passage; on the contrary, the expulsion of the child, instead of arresting the flow of language, is subsumed in that flow:

> And on the imprints of the child, a strong gust of breath. A desire for text. Confusion! What is happening to her? A child! Some paper! Drunkenness! I am overflowing. My breasts are overflowing! Milk. Ink. Time to nurse. And me? I too am hungry. The milky taste of ink! ["**La Venue à l'écriture**"]

This passage stresses, again, *ex-pulsion*—of the child, of milk, of ink. In a very similar way, her texts are expulsions, that tend to subvert form, structure, and center; and time, which in more traditional literature is generally represented as a number of privileged moments, such as the birth of a child or the completion of a book, is destructured.

The voice, in classical and modernist literature, as opposed to post-modernist texts, such as Cixous', connotes the presence of a self that is entire and whole; in Cixous, the voice is expulsion, loss, dissemination:

> Voice! it is also hurling oneself, this effusion

from which nothing returns . . . . It/she [*Elle* can mean either] leaves. It/she loses. And it is thus that she writes, as one hurls her voice, forward, into the void. She moves off, she advances, she does not turn on her tracks to examine them. She does not look at herself. [**"La jeune née"**]

(The "she" is Cixous' mythical woman writer.) What the mouth expels is at once the voice and the representative of the *pulsion,* the "being-who-wants-to-be-born, a *pulsion,* something that wants at any cost to get out, to be exhaled, a music in my throat that wants to resonate, a need therefore carnal . . . a force which contracts the muscles of my belly and tenses my diaphragm as if I were going to give birth by my throat, or have an orgasm. And it's the same thing." The throat is frequently a vaginal tract, and the cry, the tearing of the hymenal veil: "Without it—my death—I would not have written anything. Not have torn the veil of my throat." Voice, veil, and throat articulate a fantasy of penis, hymen, and vagina, that clearly inscribes Derrida's fiction of the hymen, paper, and pen, for the hymen is torn (in Cixous) with every vocal utterance, and yet is forever intact and virginal, is ever to be torn again. Likewise, the orgasmic imagery that articulates writing inscribes the Derridean metaphor of dissemination, or semen (of which one equivalent in Cixous is milk) and sign being scattered in space, rather than inseminating. She rewrites Rimbaud's verses, "l'éternité. / C'est la mer melée / Au soleil," replacing *mer,* sea, by *voix,* voice, and *soleil,* sun, by *lait,* milk: "L'Eternité, c'est la voix melée avec le lait" ("Eternity, it is the voice mingled with milk"). *Voix* and *lait* inscribe at once *voilé,* the veil forever to be rent, and the *voie lactée,* the milky way (woman gives birth with the force "of a cosmogony"), the milky seed, or signs, forever swirling off into the night like the Van Gogh explosion of *Starry Night.* The voice, mingled with the milk, seed, and stars, is not whole and entire, it is disseminated into infinity, eternity, forever lost. And it is completely fragmented: "My text is written in white and black, in 'milk' and 'night'," she writes, echoing Mallarmé's metaphor of the alphabet of the stars.

---

**There is in Cixous' texts the attempt to refuse to defer, to refuse detours, to refuse the investments and counter-investments of writing, that distances her work from that of her mentors; her texts are impossible projects, powerful projections, and the most exorbitant gifts.**

**—Brian Duren**

---

The black sky, however, is also the black continent, the black body, the feminine body, the other body, *impropre,* of the unconscious. Cixous' imagery suggests that the milk-signs that are expulsed by the throat-voice-breast-vagina, are disseminated within an infinite body, thus problematizing the very concept of inside/outside, of space, and property, the *propre/impropre,* the me and the not-me. "World-wide my unconscious, world-wide my body. What happens in the exterior happens in the interior. . . . I enter and go out, I enter and go out, I am in my body and my body is in me . . ." What distinguishes Cixous' texts is that they articulate at once an outward movement that would inscribe the *pulsions* via what Abraham calls the symbols or messengers, and an inward movement, a deciphering of memory traces, which, however, can be accomplished only through *ex-pulsions*—I enter by going out; the text is therefore not "composed," it is not writing in any conventional sense of the term:

> I don't "begin" by "writing": I don't write. Life becomes text through my body. I am already text. History, love, violence, time, work, desire, inscribe it [the text] in my body, I make my way to where the "fundamental language" can be heard, the body in which all languages of things, of acts and of beings are translated, in my own being, the entirety of the real worked into my flesh, captured by my nerves, by my senses, by the labor of all my cells, projected, analyzed, recomposed in a book. Vision: my chest like a tabernacle. Open. I enter inside myself with my eyes closed, and it [*ça*] is read. This reading is carried out here by the being-who-wants-to-be-born, a *pulsion,* something that wants at all costs to get out. . . . [**"La Venue à l'écriture"**]

Though this text uses some of the major motifs of surrealist literature, such as the *voyant,* or seer, looking inward at the world that loss has opened up, it nevertheless articulates an awareness of the textuality of the unconscious that is not generally found in surrealist literature—but does exist in Proust: "As for the interior book of unknown signs (of signs in relief, it would seem, that my attention, exploring my unconscious, went searching for, stumbled against and passed around, like a diver groping around), for the reading of which no one could help me with any rule, this reading consisted in a creative act, wherein no one could stand in our stead, nor even collaborate with us." And one page later, Proust writes: "This book, the most difficult of all to decipher, is also the only one of which the 'imprint' [*"impression"*] has been made in us by reality itself." Proust's texts, which describe so often that which is seen with the other eye (fantasy, illusion, projection), attempt, as do Cixous' texts, to transcribe the book of memory traces. Abraham observes that "fantasy and perception, as memory traces, form an indissoluble unity." The outward movement of projection, fantasy, *ex-pulsion,* and the inward movement of reading, of deciphering the traces, two movements that are one and inseparable, are articulated throughout Cixous' work. The text, that issues from the other texts, she calls a third body (the title of one of her novels): "for the third body to be written, the interior must enter and the exterior must open up. If you plug my ears, if you close off my body to the music exterior-interior, if you bar the song, then everything is silence . . ."

Cixous' unending attempts to transcribe the signs and rhythms of the unconscious necessarily deconstruct the *propre* of the novel, i.e. that which is particular to the novel. The plot, the story line, the *fil du récit,* narrative coherence, are generally effaced; instead of the *fil,* the little string of Ariadne, another umbilical cord that the solar hero unwinds and winds to return into the labyrinth and to return out of it, to return to darkness (the *noeud*) and to return to light (the *dénouement*), instead of the hierarchy *propre/impropre,* Cixous' texts are fragments, frequently without logical coherence, without the returns that so often constitute a structure in traditional fiction; fragments that are, as we have seen, expulsed, projected out, beyond the margins, and thus constantly decentralize the text. Narrative coherence, which in traditional literature assures the reader of the presence of a unified self, is lacking, primarily because of the power of the other, or others. Cixous, applying for a "writing license" (*permis d'écriture*) in **La Venue à l'écriture,** is informed by the "Super-uncle realist-capitalist": "You are full of doubles, one cannot count on you, there is some other in your same. Make us some homogenous Cixous." The identity signified by the proper noun, the *propre* signified by the noun "Cixous," is forever being subverted by the body-text: "Thus each text another body. But in each one the same vibration: for that of me which marks all my books recalls that it is my flesh that signs them, it is a rhythm."

Her discourse tends to undermine the *sens propre* (denotative meaning of language), in its common form as well: " 'Common' nouns are also proper nouns which belittle your singularity by arranging it according to a kind." Her writing opens the linguistic, cultural parameters that channel desire: "Neither father nor mother nor brother nor man nor sister, but the being that love suggests at any moment. . . . Often you are my mother young man and I am often your daughter son, your mineral mother, and you my savage father, my animal brother." Signs become the signifiers of fantasies, desires: "The man who was my mother was walking next to me. . . . And if I had known her? I surely would not have understood her for her reasons were not human. The man in the womb of whom I was living was God herself. . . . My hand was trembling too, I adored him/her; even the earth trembled under our feet. . . . The man with the Breast smiled, his hand vibrating in my hand, I was terrified." Her anagrammatic style destabilizes the sign and begets a play of signification that is almost totally open-ended; the "character" *Jeor,* in **Portrait du soleil,** deconstructs to give *Je* (I), *or* (gold), *jour* (day, sun), *jouir* (to have an orgasm), *orange* (the color and the fruit), and *oran-je* (orange-I). Her characters are not characters but receivers of the messages of desire; the reappearing character, *Dieubis,* is at once god's double, and an address (*bis* frequently follows the number of an address, e.g. 30bis, to indicate that there is a second residence at that address). She elaborates the dream work itself to the extent that her texts are displacement and condensation generalized throughout; one finds such oneiric creatures as a *serpenloup* (serpent-wolf ) and a serpenlion (serpent-lion).

"J'étais personne, I was nobody," writes the famous Joycean scholar, Cixous. But *personne* also means person, in Cixous, a multiple person, "toujours plus d'un," "always more than one," who is always other, who speaks in many voices, and, protean, lives in ever-changing form. Her narrative leaps with vertiginous rapidity from one person to another, thus approximating the *je l'entu-ile* of the dis-

course of the unconscious. "I became his you" (or thee; *tu*), she writes in **Angst.** The sender of the messages is also the receiver, but the relationship of sender to receiver is constantly shifting:

> Before approaching dying no one can say how many are I.
>
> I dream one sees oneself receiving the last letter, and one weeps. "Life will be short," I was discouraged. I wrote you: "Life will have been short. That does not depend anymore on me." I was sending us messages of death, and while reading them you wept.

Little remains of characterization, of a character as a self with a biography; she is constantly stripping the novel to that which is essential in discourse, namely the ever-shifting, polyphonic relationship of the subject to the other.

Her texts are always, like a psychoanalysis, quests, readings of dreams and fantasies, a working-out and a crossing-over: "Where are you leading us? To the other side." As in every analysis, there is the deity to be killed, the transcendent being, the fetish, that arises from death, from nothing:

> And thus, ten years to make a step, the first after god the death, ten years to tear love away from the contemplation of god the crazy woman. Ten books in trying to finish with death. In the end, to succeed in writing **Angst** . . . to have said to it: "I am not your other. I no longer take you for love."

Cixous' texts, from the first publication, **Prénom de Dieu** (1967), to **Angst,** written approximately ten years later, mourn death ("to write is first of all always a way of not succeeding in accomplishing one's mourning of death"); they are an interminable analysis, deciphering the crypt, the names of the deity, the codes of the fetish. They constantly lead the "I" toward the mythical being called, at times, "la Vivante," "always present to the present," "she toward whom this text did not know it was leading me"; and at other times, "l'arrivante de toujours," "the desire that gives." Not locked up in the paradox of the gift that takes; nor the illusion of the " 'first fusion in one' " ("fusion unième"). This mythical being also goes by the name of *plus-je,* Penthesilea, Cleopatra, Medusa, Dora.

It is certainly the place accorded the other—the multiple other—that at once defines the specificity of Cixous' texts, that to which they are opposed, and the tradition to which they adhere. In their attempt to approximate the discourse of the unconscious, to transcribe the unconscious *pulsions* via their messengers and symbols, her texts subvert the Hegelian model of the dialectic, refuse the position of the civilized man, who would never allow himself to fall into the horrible abyss of the other, and displace signification from conquest, form, and the spiritual, to the force of the writing and of the *pulsions.* In so doing, her texts affirm a literary tradition that has consistently questioned the ideology of the center, when it hasn't attempted to undermine it; I have mentioned most frequently Bataille, as one of the principal representatives of this other, often scatological, tradition of poets, *voyants,* who have thought, desired, and written the other (body); I might mention too, among those who figure in Cixous' works, Shakespeare, Blake, Kleist, Hoffman, Poe, Rimbaud, Lautréamont, Joyce, Blanchot, whose texts are marked by the excess of the body, and by exorbitance forever subversive toward form. Though Cixous' discourse evolves from that of Freud, Lacan, Derrida, there is in her texts the attempt to refuse to defer, to refuse detours, to refuse the investments and counter-investments of writing, that distances her work from that of her mentors; her texts are impossible projects, powerful projections, and the most exorbitant gifts.

## Annette Kuhn  (essay date Autumn 1981)

SOURCE: "Introduction to Hélène Cixous's 'Castration or Decapitation?' " in *Signs: Journal of Women in Culture and Society,* Vol. 7, No. 1, Autumn, 1981, pp. 36-40.

[*Kuhn is an English critic and educator who has written or edited numerous works on feminism, including* The Power of the Image: Essays on Representation and Sexuality *(1985) and* The Feminist Companion Guide to Cinema *(1990). In the essay below, she provides background information on Cixous and places her essay "Castration or Decapitation?" in the context of linguistic theory. Kuhn also notes that while Cixous simply attacks male-centered theories of language in this essay, her later works offer an alternative feminist view.*]

Hélène Cixous is a writer, a professor, and the initiator of the women's studies program at the University of Paris VIII at Vincennes. She is the author of numerous texts—novels, plays, works of criticism, poetry, essays—and has become quite widely known in recent years among feminist theorists in the United States: however, very little of her writing is currently available in English translation. The most obvious reason for this is that it is very difficult for translation to do full justice to Cixous's writing, which is actually organized around a pervasive play with, and subversion of, linguistic signifiers. At the same time, since this practice in her writing is crucial to the interrogation of meaning that is at the heart of Cixous's work, it is important that it be attended to in translation and flattened out as little as possible by it. Moreover, increasing concern among English-speaking feminists with questions around language—the relation between a "patriarchal" order and language, and the possibility of questioning the one by working on the other—not only provides a climate for interest in the work of Cixous and other French feminist writers who engage head-on with these issues, but also renders all the more urgent the task of translating that work.

The French approach to these questions is distinctive in that it tends to be informed by theories concerning the place of "woman" in language and the question of a feminine relation to language that have had relatively little currency within Anglophone feminist thought. These theories are founded in Jacques Lacan's variant of post-Freudian psychoanalysis, which draws on some of the insights of structural linguistics to advance a model of human subjectivity as organized by unconscious relations constituted both developmentally and structurally in relation to language. According to the Lacanian model, the human subject is not only a speaking subject with an Unconscious, but also a masculine or feminine subject in relation to the Oedipus complex. Sexual difference is seen as structured by the subject's relation to the phallus, the signifier which stands in for the play of absence and presence that constitutes language. Because the oedipal moment inaugurates sexual difference in relation to the phallus as signifier, men and women enter language differently, and Lacan's argument is that the female entry into language is organized by lack, or negativity.

Because of the importance of Lacanian thought in the intellectual context in which they operate, feminist theorists in France have felt very keenly the need to engage directly with its arguments about sexual difference: many of their critiques of Lacanian theory in fact started out as criticisms from within. Feminist psychoanalysts (Luce Irigaray, for one) have been highly skeptical of the attribution of a negative value to woman's relation to language and of the sexism implicit in the elevation of the phallus to the place of Transcendental Signifier.

This is the background against which we have to understand the general preoccupation of French feminists with phallocentrism, and also their specific critique of the privileged place accorded the phallus in psychoanalytic accounts of language and sexual difference. In line with this critique, Hélène Cixous in **"Castration or Decapitation?"** aims a blow at "phallologocentric" culture where it hurts the most, and attacks it for marking woman as "other," as difference and negativity. She says no to the fathers, cheekily reminding them of the very thing they have most to fear—the threat of castration posed by the female body. As she says in **"The Laugh of the Medusa"**: "Let the priests tremble, we're going to show them our sexts! Too bad for them if they fall apart on discovering that women aren't men, or that the mother doesn't have one." Here Cixous is suggesting that certain aspects of feminist/feminine practice may constitute a challenge to phallologocentrism. Her specific concern is with the "feminine" approach to writing (or writing/reading) that is implied by the neologism "sexts": she wants to write, and to write about, a "writing that inscribes femininity."

When **"Castration or Decapitation?"** first appeared in 1976, the author's primary concern was to open up the question of the "repression of the feminine" in culture, and at the same time to challenge that repression by provocatively questioning the structures of masculinist language and thought—its dualisms, its hierarchical orderings, and so on. To these structures, the feminine comes as "other," a riddle that is finally insoluble within the terms of a masculine (libidinal) economy. Freud's unanswered question "What do women want?" articulates the puzzle that the feminine poses for a patriarchal order. For Cixous, female sexual pleasure (*jouissance*) constitutes a potential disturbance to that order, and a "woman-text"—a text that inscribes this *jouissance*—is a return of the repressed feminine that with its energetic, joyful, and transgressive "flying in language and making it fly" dislocates the repressive structures of phallologocentrism. And

Cixous's own work offers an *écriture*—a practice of writing—that aims to do this by posing plurality against unity; multitudes of meanings against single, fixed meanings; diffuseness against instrumentality; openness against closure.

As the same time, however, despite its intent to question phallocentric discourse by means of a writing that subverts it, **"Castration or Decapitation?"** like other writings by Cixous of the same period, perhaps still constitutes a yearning toward, rather than a grasping of, an alternative practice: "There has not yet been any writing that inscribes femininity." Her more recent writings seem to pose something of a break in this respect. The vocality, tactility, resonance, and exhilaration to be found in **"Castration or Decapitation?"** are still there, but because the direct challenge to phallocentrism is no longer an explicit focus, these qualities structure the texts in a more thoroughgoing manner; meanings and readings are denser, more complex, more focused.

*Vivre l'orange,* for example, echoes with voices and resonates with textures. Its central image of the orange that the writer/reader ("I") reaches toward and grasps condenses and generates an almost infinite number of personal and cultural associations. The orange's juiciness, sensuousness, texture, and brightness are present in the writing itself, which is as tactile as the fruit being held and weighed in the hand. The sound association with Oran, the writer's birthplace, implies a return to sources, but the shape of the orange, the O, tells us that the route will not be a linear one. The shape also suggests the roundness of femininity, the shape and weight of a breast, a full and positive sign of sexual difference to replace the Lacanian Lack:

> From far away, from outside of my history, a voice came to collect the last tear. To save the orange. She put the word in my ear. And it was nearly the nymph of the orange that awakened in my breast and surged forth streaming from the heart's basin. Certain voices have this power. I had always been sure of it. She put the orange back into the deserted hands of my writing, and with her orange-colored accents she rubbed the eyes of my writing which were arid and covered with white films. And it was a childhood that came running back to pick up the live orange and immediately celebrate it. For our childhoods have the natural science of the orange. There was originally an intimacy between the orange and the little girl, almost a kinship, the exchange of essential confidences. The orange is ever young. The influx of orange propagated itself to the ends of my bodies. The orange is the nearest star. With all of my life I thought it, with all of my thought I went toward it, I had the peace in my hands. I saw that the world that held the answer to the questions of my being was gold-red, a globe of light present here and tomorrow, red day descended from green night.

> I asked: *"What have I in common with women?"* From Brazil a voice came to return the lost orange to me. [Kuhn explains in a footnote that the "voice from Brazil is that of Clarice Lispector, a contemporary Brazilian writer, author of *Agua Viva.*"] *"The need to go to the sources. The easi-*

*ness of forgetting the source. The possibility of being saved by a humid voice that has gone to the sources. The need to go further into the birth-voice."*

> And to all of the women whose voices are like hands that come to meet our souls when we are searching for the secret, we have needed, vitally, to leave to search for what is most secret in our being, I dedicate the gift of the orange. And to all of the women whose hands are like voices that go to meet the things in the dark, and that hold words out in the direction of things like infinitely attentive fingers, that don't catch, that attract and let come, I dedicate the orange's existence, as it has been given to me by a woman, according to the entire and infinite bringing-together of the thing, including all that is kin of the air and the earth, including all of the sense relations that every orange keeps alive and circulates, with life, death, women, forms, volumes, movement, matter, the ways of metamorphoses, the invisible links between fruits and bodies, the destiny of perfumes, the theory of catastrophes, all of the thoughts that a woman can nourish, starting out from a given orange; including all of its names, the silent name, laid upon my almost white leaf, the name as proper to it as god's name to god; its family name; and its maiden name; and the singular name, unique, detached from the dark-green air in which the voice of Clarice went to gather an orange among all of the oranges to lay it young and sound on the toile of a text prepared for it: she called this one "Laranja."

> It was almost a young girl. It was an orange regained. Through the fine skin of the word, I sensed that it was a blood-orange. By a fine vibration in the toile, I sensed that Clarice closed her eyes to touch the orange better, to hold it more lightly, let it weigh more freely upon her text, she noted eyes closed to hear more internally the secret song of the orange. Every orange is original. And to all of the women for whom the need of fruit reflexion is a task of life, I dedicate the juice-filled fruits of meditation. To all women then. My ears of meditation.

And so on: meanings radiate, multiply, permeate the text, and finally go beyond it. If **"Castration or Decapitation?"** is readable as saying no to the fathers, then the next move must be a positive approach to the mothers, a "need to go to the sources and enjoy together."

### Hélène Cixous with Verena Andermatt Conley (interview date January 1982)

SOURCE: An interview in *Hélène Cixous: Writing the Feminine,* University of Nebraska Press, 1984, pp. 129-61.

[*Conley is a Swiss-born critic and educator. In the interview below, which was conducted in January 1982, Cixous discusses such topics as her concept of* écriture féminine (*or feminine writing), the role of women in society, the use of myths and dreams in her works, and her development as a writer.*]

[Cixous]: The preliminary question is that of a "feminine writing," itself a dangerous and stylish expression full of traps, which leads to all kinds of confusions. True, it is simple to say "feminine writing." The use of the word "feminine"—I believe I have discussed it at length elsewhere—is one of the curses of our times. First of all, words like "masculine" and "feminine" that circulate everywhere and that are completely distorted by everyday usage,—words which refer, of course, to a classical vision of sexual opposition between men and women—are our burden, that is what burdens us. As I often said, my work in fact aims at getting rid of words like "feminine" and "masculine," "femininity" and "masculinity," even "man" and "woman," which designate that which cannot be classified inside of a signifier except by force and violence and which goes beyond it in any case. So it is true that when one says "feminine writing," one could almost think in terms of graphology. One could say, it is the writing of an elegant woman, she is this or that. That is obviously not what is at stake. Instead of saying feminine writing or masculine writing, I ended up by saying a writing said to be feminine or masculine, in order to mark the distance. In my seminar, rather than taking this elementary precaution, I speak of a decipherable libidinal femininity which can be read in a writing produced by a male or a female. The qualifier masculine or feminine which I use for better or for worse comes from the Freudian territory.

[*Conley*]: *What do you mean by "libidinal"?*

Something extremely precise which has been defined by Freud in his numerous writings on libido. It is something which can be defined from the body, as the movement of a pulsion toward an object, and which is part of the discoveries that may be defined as the Freudian discoveries *par excellence*. It allows us to know what in other times had been analyzed as the treaty of passions. This is what I refer to, and I believe that the word "economy" is important. It is the regime of that which in the past used to be called the effect of desire, of love. It is the love life in fact, or the sexual life, which is regulated by energy marked psychically by the subject, which is lived consciously, and which can be described as economic metaphors with moments of investment in passion, love, disgust, or anything else, moments of disinvestments from subject to object. These are libidinal investments, which can be treated and spoken about in morals or philosophy as well. For example, the possibility of giving, of generosity, or as one says in common terms, of the seven deadly sins, of avarice, which is not to give, to retain. All these are effects or denominations of things that are entirely to be thought of in the category of libidinal economies.

Then, we need qualifiers to clarify the types of regimes, and the ones we use are, once again, in spite of everything, "feminine" and "masculine." Why? True, it is a question here of our whole history, of our whole culture; true, it would be nice if one could use, instead of masculine and feminine, color adjectives, for example. Like blue and green and black; I said that in a text. True, one could also displace across political economy and say, for example, capitalist or I do not know what else. One could take notions that have been disengaged by the socioethnologists who talk about potlatch, like Mauss. You see, these are linguistic instruments, words that do not take into account the reality of exchange. Still, why does one say masculine and feminine? And what does it signify? Because the first exchanges, the primary exchanges—I do not say originary, because obviously there is no origin—are distinguished in our first milieu, the familial milieu, for example. They take place among people of different sexes, but what we also know with Freud, since Freud, though it was known before him and can be read in literary texts, is that human beings who can be distinguished anatomically in an obvious way—which leads to I.D. cards and social roles—are not, at the level of sexual economies, as different as that. All human beings are originally bisexual; that is why in my theoretical childhood I have been led to use this word. We know that the child is not as categorically determined as that. When children grow up, they learn to identify with the adult model of man or woman. Yet these identificatory determinations are belated, and there is a whole period which Freud describes when there is a bisexual potential. This does not mean homosexual with the tendency one may think. Just as there is always, in every human being, a complex relationship between death drives and life drives, there is a complex relationship between different libidinal economies which would be passive and active, constantly binding and unbinding themselves, exchanging, spending, and retaining.

I can use the analytic vocabulary, since I do not have to enclose myself in its system: oral, anal, genital. A full, total, accomplished individual goes through all the stages and arrives at the genital stage that assembles everything. As for the intermediary stages, one knows, for example with Freud, that the anal stage corresponds to an anal economy, which is an avaricious economy of retention, of hard exchange. There are people in whom there is a dominance, an insistence. They stop at a certain stage, at the oral stage, for example, and have a censoring relationship to others. The ideal harmony, reached by few, would be genital, assembling everything and being capable of generosity, of spending. That is what I mean when I speak of *écriture féminine*, that is what I talk about. Of course, it is not exactly me; it is the inscription of something that carries in everyday language the determination of the provisional name of femininity, and which refers precisely to something that I would like to define in the way of an economy, of production, of bodily effects of which one can see a great number of traits.

For example, last year in my seminar we worked on texts by Lispector. We worked on the fact that her texts are very humid texts, that in them it is always a question of something humid. I would even say that one of her major texts, *Agua Viva,* is like water. Can one write water, can one read water? How can one do it? That is precisely the question of this text. One can do it only by throwing oneself into the water, by becoming one with the water. To show the difference, I also had recourse to masculine texts that present traits of masculine economy and that insist in the most remarkable way on drying up. I say purposely "drying up," which is done by something wet that dries. I do not say something absolutely dry. I am not going to oppose the desert and the sea, not at all. But I want to work on the level of an economic differential, on that, for example, which is of the domain of the humid. We also know that the humid is vital, that absolute dryness prevents one from living. I had taken a text, and that is where we will have to take a number of precautions. I had chosen the most extraordinary text and the easiest to read, Blanchot's text in general and this one in particular. It is a text which he had produced in *L'Ecriture du désastre,* the writing of *disaster,* a text that goes toward a drying up. The writer will never cry again. He has shed all the tears. There is secretion, etc., and then there is an episode, there is an event, a symbolic and decisive event, which decides the masculine orientation, which determines that this child; who at first is neutral (we do not know whether it is masculine or feminine) orients itself toward the decision of belonging to the masculine gender. One can analyze this decision in other texts by Blanchot. I have done it at length elsewhere.

When I read this text to you, I did not want to tell you at first who wrote it. Because if I do tell you, for example, that it is by Maurice Blanchot, I am saying that it is a text written by a man and you are sent back to the lure, to the screen. You are sent back to the fact that it is a man who wrote a masculine text. My own position is to insist always on the fact that libidinal femininity is not the *propre* of women and that libidinal masculinity is not the *propre* of men. What is most important for me, what allows me to continue to live and not to despair, is precisely the conviction that it does not depend on the anatomical sex, not on the role of man and of woman, but that it depends in fact on life's chance, which is everybody's responsibility. For example, this year in my seminar we work on a double corpus, on Clarice Lispector and on Kleist. In reality, the texts are interchangeable because Kleist is absolutely exceptional. Kleist produces a work that functions in a more feminine than masculine way. That means he is capable of spending at all levels, of displacing the rhythms, for example, of the living, of the relationship between life and death, of all that which could be qualified more easily as feminine than masculine. So I say, taking all my precautions, that in fact the ideal for me would be to use "proper" names instead of adjectives, feminine and masculine: to speak of a Kleistian economy would be much better. When I am obligated to theorize, when one asks me to theorize in order to clarify my ideas, I find myself back in the trap of words.

Of course, there is a certain danger for us in taking up words which are so strongly marked. That is why, in my seminar, I do not use them. But publicly, I must constantly have recourse to them, because we are in history, we live in history, we are in a historical, political situation which we must take into account. Literature does not float like a planet in air. It is part of "truth" even if I consider that its part is precisely to precede, to anticipate ordinary reality, to distance itself from it, to go faster than it. We must take into account the fact that we are caught in daily reality in the stories of men and women, in the stories of a role. That is why I come back to the question of the terms masculine and feminine. Why these words? Why do they stay with us? Why do we not reject them? Because in spite of everything and for historical reasons, the economy said to be feminine—which would be characterized by features,

by traits, that are more adventurous, more on the side of spending, riskier, on the side of the body—is more livable in women than in men. Why? Because it is an economy which is socially dangerous in our times. That is what we saw already with Kleist. You live, you believe, you give life to values that are apparently moral values, but in fact these moral values do not exist without precisely coming forth from a primary locus which is in any case corporeal. If, for example, like Kleist, you believe in the possibility of a love, a real love, not one based on a power struggle, on a daily war, on the enslavement of one by the other, society is going to reject you. If you are a man, the rejection is almost immediate. Society does not give you any time. You have just lived through an experience, and society tells you that if you believe that, you should get lost; there is no place for you. What you are doing is absolutely prohibited, and you are sent into madness and death. Women do have another chance. They can indulge in this type of life because by definition and for culturally negative reasons they are not called upon, they are not obligated, to participate in the big social *fête*—which is phallocentric—since they are often given places in the shadow, places of retreat, where they are in fact parked. It will be more easily accepted that a woman does not battle, does not want power. A man will not be forgiven.

*Yes, but do women not want to get out of that negative historical position?*

Something which is absolutely necessary. What I am saying is always on two levels. One level would be, if you like, that of libidinal truth. It is cut mercilessly by historical reality. I also say that for negative reasons, women have positive reasons to save something through generosity which is mortal for men. Because man is projected on a scene where he has to be a warrior among warriors. He is assigned to the scene of castration. He must defend his phallus; if not, it is death. There you are. Women are not called upon the scene of castration, which in a way is not good for them, since they are repressed. Let us suppose that in our feminist period, women manage, for example, to have equal chances; that is precisely where things start to become interesting and complicated. With equal chances, you are back in the old scenes. In the old scenes there were power struggles, and so what does one do? That is our problem. That is the problem of all women who, for example, cross the bar of absolute repression behind which women are parked and who are, in fact, on the side of men. What do they do? Either they are killed right away, or they effectively resist castration. They find themselves in the scenes where castration makes the law with the usual phallic stakes. But what about us? What we like, what we want, what men may also want but have been taught a long time ago to renounce—are we going to keep that? That is when one begins to live dramas. Are we going to be the equals of men, are we going to be as phallic as they are? Or do we want to save something else, something more positive, more archaic, much more on the side of *jouissance,* of pleasure, less socializable? If so, how and at what price? That is our daily question.

You see, somebody like Kleist was on the one hand called upon to be a man, since he was in the military. He was in the normal, phallic space reserved for men. At the same time, he cannot renounce something entirely different, which he himself calls paradise. And he wonders: does this paradise have a chance in our world, which is purgatory or hell? He attempted to give this idea of paradise a chance, and he lost. But obviously, this idea of paradise is a very good metaphor, since the paradise of Eve is that which is defined by an immediate relation women have to *jouissance* and another type of knowledge. Kleist believes in it, but if there is prohibition, it is because there is law and the masculine world, which permanently deals with repressing this paradise that is always there and always ready to come back again.

*One of women's demands is nevertheless to enter society.*

That is our problem. We can no longer bear the situation of repression, of desocialization, of desymbolization, of inferiority, but we lose both ways. Is it possible to win? Yes, of course. But what a struggle. It is true that if we enter society to become men, we have lost everything. In this case, we leave the space of repression to win another repression, which will please men who are also wasting their lives. Can one win? Only on condition that upon entering society one does not identify with men but that one works on other possibilities of living, on other modes of life, on other relationships to the other, other relationships to power, etc., in such a way that one also brings about transformations in oneself, in others, and in men. That is a long project.

*And very difficult, the more so as women do not have the means of power to make transformations in a society which is more open to those who are in power.*

True. In any event, we can work only on compromise, a word that is always enunciated in the negative mode, but that has to be displaced. I do not believe in sexual opposition nor in a sexuality that would be strictly feminine or strictly masculine, since there are always traces of originary bisexuality. And then, there is exchange. As soon as you simply touch the other, you alter the other and you are altered by the other, an alteration that may be positive or negative. It is negative if there is compromise, if you are incorporated by the other, etc. Yet there are modalities of exchange that are respectful modalities, where you let yourself be sufficiently altered to feel the other of the other—not too much, because then you destroy yourself.

*Are you saying that one must be between the two? Is that why you come back to the position of compromise?*

No, I am not between. Be very careful. That is precisely where I would be most careful. The between, the *entre,* is the neither-one-nor-the-other. I am not of the neither-one-nor-the-other. I am rather on the side of *with,* in spite of all the difficulties and confusions this may bring about. It is hard to keep an equilibrium which, to use the word I use all the time, must be graceful. It has to be moving, has to be in movement. As soon as you stop, that is it. One must constantly work to keep this equilibrium in movement. I do not know whether what I say is clear enough.

*What then would be the strategic "goal" of a feminine writing?*

That is where I would come back to the fact that the word "feminine"—which I put between 150 quotation marks to prevent it from being used in the mode of a "feminine woman," as in fashion magazines—qualifies nevertheless a certain type of economy, the traits of which I analyze for myself as positive traits. I consider that every person should have an interest, individually and politically, not in fighting them but on the contrary in developing them. When I work on this question, I always do so from a literary corpus, because it is easier, let us say. You spoke to me, for example, of separation and reparation. I think that, if you like, a feminine libidinal economy is an economy which has a more supple relation to property, which can stand separation and detachment, which signifies that it can also stand freedom—for instance, the other's freedom. So to take a ridiculous example, the conjugal situation is that of appropriation; it is an initiation of appropriation: I am no longer myself, I belong to you, etc. As soon as there is appropriation in a rigid mode, you may be sure that there is going to be incorporation. It destroys the possibility of being other. It is the arrest of freedom of the other, and that is enormous. A feminine libidinal economy, one that tolerates the movements of the other, is very rare: one that tolerates the comings and goings, the movements, the *écart* [space, interval, gap]. So how is this going to work in a literary text? You will have literary texts that tolerate all kinds of freedom—unlike the more classical texts—which are not texts that delimit themselves, are not texts of territory with neat borders, with chapters, with beginnings, endings, etc., and which will be a little disquieting because you do not feel the arrest, the edge [the *arrêt* or the *arête*].

*What is the scope of this feminine writing?*

To touch upon feminine writing frees, liberates language, word usage. Of course, one cannot imagine a political liberation without a linguistic liberation; that is all very banal. It is evident, everyone knows it. It is not by chance that all the regional movements grab on to their language. It is in order to escape, if you would like, the language of the father. It is in order to take something from a language which would be less authoritarian. It is a lot of work.

*When you talk about the other, you draw in an ethical dimension. What is the relationship you see between an ethical and a political dimension, between a political dimension and respect for the other?*

It is the same thing, though it depends on what one means by political. in the sense of management, it becomes a technical question which in any event refers back to a political question. Otherwise, for me, there is only ethics, nothing else.

*What about political in the sense of a community, of a* polis, *or city with its own police force? When you talk about "women," even between quotation marks, you still refer to a very specific group with its demands and ideas of community. There are new exclusions, new masters.*

The problem goes beyond that of women. It is the problem of any community, any society, because there have been many ideal societies. One collides right away with a contradiction that is not mastery. I will take it at a banal level.

When we founded Paris VIII, at the time of '68, we founded it with the idea that there would be no more professors, no more masters—something that never did materialize, because if one is not the master, the other is, of course. We never did get out of the Hegelian system. What one can do is displace it as much as possible. One has to fight it; one can diminish the degree of mastery, yet without completely eliminating it. There always must be a tiny bit of phallus, so that things continue one way or the other. I believe that it is humanly impossible to have an absolute economy without a minimum of mastery. The problem is that one is always with the regime of the maximum and not that of the minimum. But we know that organized society has done violence to everybody, that it enslaves everybody. This is not to be eliminated with complete freedom which, in my opinion, ends up by being too vague and is found only in spiritual evasion.

*In the same context, you use an admirable chiasm: "poetically political, politically poetic."*

I defend myself by saying that.

*I read a couple of days ago, in a book by a Marxist critic, that "political" and "poetic" are irreconcilable.*

People who are into politics cannot *not* say such things. People who are poets, to use a general term, but who at the same time have a political concern are obligated to say the opposite. For the latter, the poetic must have a political value: of course, it must not be an easy solution. It is not sufficient to write to be poetic. It is true, though, that you have works that think themselves and write themselves poetically without forgetting the political questions. For example, Clarice Lispector constantly raises the question of politics while saying, I am not a militant politician. But it is a question that is always there, from which I determine myself. There are others: Kleist does nothing but that. All his texts are completely historical. He constantly asks questions that are political, that are treated politically. I try to do the same. I would lie if I said that I am a political woman, not at all. In fact, I have to assemble the two words, political and poetic. Not to lie to you, I must confess that I put the accent on poetic. I do it so that the political does not repress, because the political is something cruel and hard and so rigorously real that sometimes I feel like consoling myself by crying and shedding poetic tears. That is why I wrote the text called *With ou l'art de l'innocence*. I think that I am constantly guilty, for example, of having the privilege of being able to console myself poetically. Besides, I never console myself; as soon as I console myself, I punish myself. I think that is the paradox and the torment of people who have a calling to write that is stronger than anything else, and who know and do not forget—because most people do forget—that as soon as one writes, one betrays someone or something.

That is what Kafka thought, when he asked himself whether he had the right to write or to marry. He made those two columns with additions, subtractions, constantly realizing that he could not choose but that he had to choose and that he could not *not* choose. And finally, the choice was made. He did not do it himself, and it was always made in the direction of writing. It was not a happy choice. Finally, writing chose him until he died. He paid, of course, with death. It is true that when somebody writes, somebody dies. It may be you. When you write, it may be only you. Kafka killed others, and then at a later moment he was the one who died. He could no longer contribute to killing his fiancée. Of course, there is an easy solution which at the same time is the most difficult in the world: that is, that you die rather than the other. You see, this means that there is only death. Obviously, that is what I cannot admit. True, it is a mixture of death and life, but I think that one should die for something, in order for something to live or for something that will give life to somebody else.

---

**What is most important for me, what allows me to continue to live and not to despair, is precisely the conviction that it does not depend on the anatomical sex, not on the role of man and of woman, but that it depends in fact on life's chance, which is everybody's responsibility.**

**—*Hélène Cixous***

---

*You always privilege life in your texts.*

Yes. Yes, that is the dominant. I always come back to it. Whatever may happen, "one cannot not," even in the very gesture of writing, which by definition is a gesture of retreat. It is a gesture that you make only by retiring, by enclosing yourself, by acting as if you were alone in the world, at least for a while. And what is happening during that time? You write and make an extremely bizarre and relatively autoerotic gesture while the others are behind closed doors and wait until you are done. Nothing, of course, prohibits them from writing also. You see, each person is in his or her corner. I say this laughingly. On the other hand, what I can also say from experience is that writing is—and one cannot deny this—a consolation, happiness in unhappiness. And if unhappiness is near you, real unhappiness is always much stronger than happiness in unhappiness; if someone near you truly suffers, if someone is sick or if there is a war, you do not write. And then you see the limits of writing, because technically it is always situated and written in the present. It is really atemporal. That is why I say it always anticipates other times. When there is no tomorrow, when today is put to fire and the sword, let me say that then, today is stronger than ever. That is when you say that truly unlivable things, the concentration camps, for example, do not have a writing. Another evidence is of course that there is a part of the world that cannot write and that will always only write in silence.

*Like the Third World or, in our context, the Third World women.*

I talked about that in *Vivre l'orange,* which I wrote at the time of the events in Iran. Of course, I went into the streets, I manifested. I did what I could, not being in Iran but in my own skin. These are questions that cannot be solved. These are questions one must ask oneself, and that one must sometimes transform into a dagger, to inflict a good blow on oneself in order not to forget that others suffer. Now, there are also questions of identification. For example, do I identify with Iranian women for reasons of the unconscious? Yes. For reasons of the Orient? Yes. All this traverses my own Arab childhood, if you like. But am I going to identify with Japanese women? No. Of course, I could say that if there were a massacre of Japanese women, I would be in solidarity with them all the time, in the same way that now, in France, one is in solidarity with the Polish "question." Is it true? It is a question. It is true for many and false for many others. I can only do the maximum from where I am by being the most severe judge of my own gestures and my own spending: did I do enough of what I can do from where I am?

So back to the question of the Third World women. I think that I am only a writer, and when I say that, I think that other women are completely militant, some women of the MLF, for example. They struggle for women, for their lives. I do not compare myself with them; I consider that they advance the woman's cause in a much more active and more immediate way than I do. So why, since I think that, do I not do it? I do not do it because it is true that I was born, so to speak, in the skin of writing, and I have writing in the skin. And to live, I need to do what I am doing. So, do I have the right to do it? That is the question. I give myself the right but maybe for the wrong reasons. My need is totally unjustifiable, totally egotistical. I justify myself by saying that there are people who have a calling to write that is strong enough and that our culture is of a type that allows me, for example, to produce what I consider to be a feminine textual breakthrough. I justify myself, but I may be wrong, since I am the one who says it; others may say that this is completely wrong, and I will have committed an enormous historical error.

That is true, but finally I believe in what I do; otherwise, I would not do it. If I were persuaded that what I do is useless, I would not do it. I believe that it is useful, and I think that it can be useful only on the condition that there be a women's movement. If there were no women's movement, I would be prohibited.

*Do you think that the women's movement is caught in a class struggle?*

That is a big question. It is a question which is determined historically. First, in France, no one ignores class struggle. And then, there is always the question of solidarity. But the women's movement in France is not feminist only in the sense of asking for equal rights. When I say that, everybody screams, What do you mean, "only equal rights"? Of course one must demand them. Equalities are needed. But the women's movement does something that is not taken into account by class struggle; that is, it represses or even squashes misogyny. Class struggle reinforces misogyny. It concentrates on social measures and makes fun of women's words, precisely with social measures. And that is perfectly ridiculous; women know it well.

*When one speaks of the "other," does one necessarily refer to a feminine other?*

For reasons of political, historical, and cultural urgency, I am obligated to make distinctions. I would say, for example, if I took my own "little" life, on the level of the anecdote, I would not know whom to designate as my other, my others. I could say that my first others are people of my family. Only if I move now into another, larger sphere, then I produce my other out of a sense of urgency. This other is imposed on me, is dictated in an absolute way to me, by history, by the state of history. Today it is necessarily women, the question of women, the woman. So I have to say, because there is a big distance, that this is not where I started my existence. I would say that it is even for this very reason that the word "other" is an interesting word.

In reality, I impregnate it with love. For me, the other is the other to love. Yet what I may have lived in my existence was that the other had to be hated, feared, that he was the stranger, the foreigner, everything that is bad. I situate the other in what classically or biblically one could have called my neighbor. It is complicated to say this kind of thing. And then you have the whole range of others. For example, I have been working on a text by Lispector that has to do with a bandit, a criminal who has killed many people, a guy one has to get rid of. Little by little, there is an imaginary displacement into the imagination of the other. All of a sudden the bandit emerges, as if there were a kind of invisible line that speaks from one body to another as other, yet as his own other, my other, as a completely foreign other but one whom, precisely, I respect as this other there. That, for me, is absolutely vital, it is for me the supreme value. To respect strangeness, otherness, does not mean that I relegate him to incomprehensibility; on the contrary, I seek to catch the most of what is going to remain preciously incomprehensible for me and that I will in any case never understand, but that I like, that I can admit, that I can tolerate, because really there is always a mystery of the other. In general, when there is a mystery, one feels hostility. One wants to destroy, one wants to oppose it. That is where I think there is an enigmatic kernel of the other that must be absolutely preserved.

*In that case, the other is not sexually determined. It could be any "other."*

It is always anybody.

*But there has been so much talk about the Other-as-woman, often spelled with a capital O.*

When one speaks about the Other-as-woman, what does one mean? I am asking you the question.

Besides, I wonder—when one speaks about the Other-as-woman, one insists on the fact that the other may be any other. What the classical, ordinary, heterosexual woman cannot do is to think of the other woman, for the good reason that she is not the object of her interest, since the object of her interest is man. I do not like the notion "fellow creature," which comes back to the same, which is in any case the elimination of the other and death. As I said, I do not believe in the opposition between men and women.

I only believe that one finds a feminine economy in some women, like Eve. You see, God is the name of the law, the name of punishment, of the masculine figure who cannot let himself act in a way that would make people stop at a stage of *jouissance,* of pleasure, simply because otherwise there would be no society, no capitalism, no power struggle; there would not be that which has become our civilization; all this is completely banal. So now, when you take another example, everybody knows it, I mean everybody who has a sense of language obscurely knows it and exploits it in different ways. And everyone obviously does not say what I say. But everyone knows that the law is only the name of the law. So let us take for example Kafka's text, "Before the Law," about which I already spoke in **La Jeune Née,** because it was exemplary for me; I read it in the same mode. You know the story of the peasant who comes from the countryside, from paradise, naively telling himself, I want to go in. Now, that is not the nature of man in general. And, of course, he is told: "No." And you know how he dies, you know the story. What interests me is the manner in which Kafka wrote it. He starts with a title, "Before the Law." Then he starts the first sentence, "Before the law, there is a keeper, the keeper of the door." The man from the country arrives, and you go on, you read everything. Afterward, you ask questions, all the questions that Kafka asked himself in *The Trial,* and you can do, if you like, the interminable exegesis of the admirable story. Except, in fact, what *did* happen? It so happened that there was the first sentence, which starts with "Before the law," and that you, since you are a good, obedient student, do not ask questions; that is to say, you were told "before the law," so all right, you are also before the law and you are there with the country man, asking yourself: May I go in? And what is the law? etc. When the first sentence was already the one that implicated you in the world of law, which is nothing but the utterance of the words "before the law," and right away you start to think that there also is a "behind the law." Simply because it is written, and that is the force of the "it is written." Law is nothing but that, it is empty. It is nothing.

*What about separation in relation to a word wound?*

I say in a way that is, as a question of extreme violence, banal and not banal—and when I say "I," it is greater than the self—that most women feel this violence of the word, of speech, the violence of verbalization, since speech in effect separates, interrupts something of the lived immediacy. This is normal, necessary, and in certain ways good; yet in others, it is not. It all goes back to history and to the story of the apple. When the name of the apple begins to thicken and replace the apple, we all know that moment, the linguists as well as the psychoanalysts. In women's daily life, this is a big question. The ideal, or the dream, would be to arrive at a language that heals as much as it separates. Could one imagine a language sufficiently transparent, sufficiently supple, intense, faithful so that there would be reparation and not only separation? I am attempting to write in that direction. I try to write on the side of a language as musical as possible.

*A language that sings, words that are sung, traverse the body. What would be the relationship between a musical language and the body?*

There are various levels of relationship between body and language. I think that many people speak a language that has no rapport with the body. Instead of letting emerge from their body something that is carried by voice, by rhythm, and that would be truly inspired, they are before language as before an electric panel. They choose the hypercoded, where nothing traverses. But I think, and everybody knows, that there are other possibilities of language, that are precisely *languages.* That is why I always privilege the ear over the eye. I am always trying to write with my eyes closed. What is going to write itself comes from long before me, *me [moi]* being nothing but the bodily medium which formalizes and transcribes that which is dictated to me, that which expresses itself, that which vibrates in almost musical fashion in me and which I annotate with what is not the musical note, which would of course be the ideal. This is not to say that I am opposed to meaning, not at all, but I prefer to speak in terms of poetry. I prefer to say that I am a poet even if I do not write poems, because the phonic and oral dimensions of language are present in poetry, whereas in the banal, clichéd language, one is far removed from oral language.

*You have often defined the kind of writing that you have practiced over the past few years as* écriture féminine, *or more recently, with added caution, as a writing said to be feminine. This writing, poetic and musical, nevertheless engages in dialogue with the major discourses of our times.*

I am obviously not without a minimum of philosophical and analytical knowledge, simply because I am part of a historical period. I cannot act as if I were not a contemporary of myself. Neither do I think that I must wage a mortal war against a certain type of discourse. Like most women of my generation, I believe, I had inhibitions, faced with the rigid, defining, and decisive side of most theoretical discourses. True, I did have resistances. I had to work through them in order to be able to approach the spaces containing a certain amount of useful and necessary knowledge in order to carry out another type of work which would be on the side of femininity. I am not and do not feel like being ignorant. Neither do I feel like being a prisoner of masculine culture, and I do not feel enslaved or threatened by that culture. I retain the open-ended part, that which is not specifically phallocentric, or phallogocentric, as Derrida would say. For example, I have an absolute need—and I must say that at this moment all human beings have a need—not to disregard the unconscious. It is not because it is a man who discovered it that I am going to be afraid it will be a bearded unconscious. Women have not made discoveries, because they have been kept from the scene—absolutely. They have been kept from making discoveries; that must be changed. But that which has been discovered is valid for the universe. I do have knowledge of theoretical discourses. Yet the part that represses women is a part which I quickly learned to detect and from which I keep my distance. One leaves these parts aside. One keeps all that is vital: for example, that which in Freudian discourse describes the trajectory of sexual formation, of drives, of dream work, etc.

*Other theoreticians have defined the notion of writing. How do you see the relationship between what you call* l'écriture dite féminine *and other writings, for example, Derrida's* écriture?

I have insisted on the necessity of not taking the classical feminist position, which consists in referring everything back to women and pretending that we have fallen from the sky. As far as women are concerned, some groundbreaking work has been done on the question of difference, on the differential, by Derrida. We know and use his work. The only thing is, of course, that he does not pretend to discuss femininity from the point of view of women. He does not. Yet what he does trace, in the most faithful and lucid manner in all of his texts, is a philosophical problem of sexuality. I would not say of masculine sexuality (that does not mean anything) but of a libidinal economy that really is on the side of masculinity—the way one could speak about it in the past—of which on the one hand he is conscious, on the other unconscious, which is also very interesting because obviously he cannot speak of his unconscious. But he is the only philosopher, and that in my opinion is important, who admits that there is a textual unconscious, who at the same time works on the unconscious other—but of course his own unconscious is also at work. When he works on the unconscious in Freud, one can also see his own unconscious appear; that is very important. For us, this is good, it is an essential contribution. So I say, and some do not seem to understand this, he is on the other shore. There is a river and there are riverbanks. It is true that he is, insofar as women are concerned, on the other side, on the side of the masculine territory, and we are on this side. But this common river does not separate—of course not. And if I have recourse to this metaphor, it is deliberately, and it is to say that it is really an aquatic metaphor, that this water is necessary, that it bathes shores and harbors and that one navigates in it. That is how one communicates.

*However, this shore should, at the limit, disappear.*

No, I do not think so. No, precisely, I do not believe that it should. One should not think in terms of making disappear something that does not really separate, something that hyphenates, a water that binds, that organizes a mobile and living continuity. But on the other hand, I believe that one has to work at this geography. One must explore effectively all the minute details, something which generally one does not do. This is where we work.

*And how do you read the well-known and much debated passage from* Spurs, *which I quote from memory, "If style were man, writing would be woman"?*

I do not remember it. In *Spurs,* Derrida nevertheless deals with a femininity fantasized by Nietzsche. There are many relays which have to be taken into account. Besides, I do not deny that this capacity to read Nietzsche—who lets himself be fantasized, or one may say hallucinated, by a phantasm of femininity—does signify a proximity. There is proximity, true, but it is not an identity. What about the phantasm itself? Derrida has very well defined the phantasm of femininity that haunted philosophical discourse,

a phantasm which, among women, should provoke laughter. Unless, of course, they take themselves for men.

*You say that it is necessary to "go outside" philosophical discourse.*

Where did I say that?

*In* **Illa,** *perhaps.*

I would be careful about this statement. I do not know where or whether I wrote it. I am capable, when I speak, of saying things that I would not sign. Because I do distinguish as one should, I think, between speech and writing. For example, I reread when I write, and if I write nonsense, I apologize. In speech, I do not apologize. Like everybody, the spoken word escapes me; I may say things that are incorrect or insufficiently precise. For example, "to go outside of philosophy": I do not know whether I wrote it. If there is a philosophical culture, if one may say so, it would be the culture in which the philosophers are enclosed. Who must go outside of philosophy? I do not know if women are the ones. I am not sure about that at all. One should see in what context this formulation occurs and ask whether we women are in it. In order to go outside of it, one has to be in it. I am not sure that we are in philosophy. Must I answer directly? I do not believe that the question is that specific. For example, am I in philosophy? I do not think so. I have a relationship to philosophy, but it is one of dialogue, and I know very well that I am not a philosopher. In other words, I do not have a philosophical calling. I do not answer the calling of philosophy even if I am in a duet with something "philosophical," yet all the while invoking all the liberties warranted or unwarranted of poetry. Insofar as philosophy is concerned, if I refer myself especially to Derrida, it is because he, of course, works on excess. How to exceed, not how to exit from, how to go out of, and one exceeds without forgetting or retracting.

*He says that writing is always based on an originary repression, whereas you write of undoing repressions.*

I do not think that I am in disagreement with him. I suppose that when he says that, he says it in relation to writing, any kind of writing, any kind of inscription, philosophical, poetic, etc. In *Grammatology,* he treats of writing in general, of the text in general. When I talk about writing, that is not what I am talking about. One must displace at that moment; I do not speak about the concept of writing the way Derrida analyzes it. I speak in a more idealistic fashion. I allow this to myself; I disenfranchise myself from the philosophical obligations and corrections, which does not mean that I disregard them. I do not believe in a complete undoing of repressions. We are made of repressions, and the unconscious is nothing but that. However, one may attempt to write as closely as possible to the unconscious, to the area of repressions.

Yes, and also I want to write as freely as possible. Philosophical discourse, if you like, is not free, since it must obey imperatives of signification. A philosopher is obligated to hold on to logic—even Derrida, for example, who pushes his work to the limit where logic vacillates. Even when, or precisely when, he situates himself in the undecidable, that is to say where nothing cuts, decides, where everything is unhinged, where everything permanently vacillates. This is also recuperated and must again obey a new law, that of the logic of non-logic, because the moment you name the undecidable, you already, in a certain way, arrest it. Derrida knows this. That is why he always says that each time he arrests, each time he coins a concept, he hurries to put it into that general movement of oscillation in order not to make of it a master concept. But it is like a ford of a river, if you like: he must jump from concept to concept, or from rock to rock, whereas I allow myself to say, since I do not have any obligation toward philosophy, I really do prefer swimming. I prefer being in the water and openly in the water; for me, those inscriptions with which Derrida must deal do not exist. He says it himself.

For example, look at the way I write, how I write, how I reread myself. When a philosopher rereads himself, I do not know how he does it. I suppose that his reading is on the side of an economy, of signification, of its force. He wants to transmit as much meaning as possible. That is the writing of Derrida, who condenses in a way that is a polysemy. He transmits an intensity, a richness of condensation, of meaning. Philosophy is demonstrative. When I reread my texts, I do not seek to demonstrate. One could even accuse me of it. I do not ignore Derrida's philosophical work, in the wake of Heidegger, on presence, essence, all that you quoted me. If I were a philosopher, I could never allow myself to speak in terms of presence, essence, etc., or of the meaning of something. I would be capable of carrying on a philosophical discourse, but I do not. I let myself be carried off by the poetic word. Is it a mad word? Does it say something? I must say that my steed or my barge and my poetic body never do forget the philosophical rigor. So what is happening? Philosophy is like an accompaniment, but humorous. If one knows how to read and has a knowledge of philosophy, one will see that there is something like a surreptitious echo in everything I say, when I say that I believe in presence, in the coming onto presence. I know the Heideggerian problematic, which I have read very closely and which impassions me, but I have no obligation toward that kind of thinking, toward this kind of rigor. I take it into account but precisely as that from which I can take my distance. And I would even say that it is my mission, my calling, to be able to distance myself from it.

In my seminar, we work on texts by Heidegger and Derrida. We have also worked, for example, on texts by Rilke while traversing the Heideggerian field, or the Rilko-Heideggerian field. I do not have to produce theory. Like Rilke—he did not have to produce theory. Heidegger did that for him. Rilke, with the peculiar instrument infinitely freer than philosophical discourse, produced a series of works that are living objects in which you see, for example, how a rose opens up. In a certain way, poetry is disenfranchised from the obligation that philosophy has: to demonstrate, justify.

> **At the bottom I am really a questioner. I do not cease not to understand. Simply, the things I do not understand renew themselves incessantly. Once I have understood something that I did not understand before, it is behind me. And I open myself before the next enigma.**
>
> —*Hélène Cixous*

*It seems that you make the same distinction between writer and philosopher as between woman and man.*

Yes, of course. The closest allies of us women are the poets. They are our friends. True, they are the ones who are the furthest removed from anything decisive, cutting, and they let their femininity traverse them.

*Do you read as writer or as critic?*

I do my own reading. I am not looking to evaluate a text, or to theorize about it. Of course, I can do it, and sometimes I do it. For example, earlier in my life, under different circumstances, when I used to teach for the *agrégation.* But it is not at all my wish or my desire. I do not care to master a text. I am not interested in that. I am not interested in making it enter into categories, because really I grant myself the luxury to read in texts only that which for me is a question of life and death. So when I read, I ask of the text questions that I ask of myself. I ask questions like "where does it come from?" Questions of origin. Where does it go? How far? What stops? What arrests? My questions are of, and concern, human beings. That is what I focus on in my seminars. I ask questions concerning human beings in general. What causes some people to waste their lives, not to know how to live, and what makes others capable of pushing back the limits of death in life? And I ask myself questions concerning love in relation to a life-giving body or to one that gives death. Last year in my seminar I worked on two kinds of knowledge. At another time I took into consideration what I call fundamental traces, in the work of Kafka, Lispector, and Blanchot, for example. When one reads a text, one is able to see deep and profound tracings that are not themes—that are questions, you understand, not themes; themes are something else. I am talking of questions that are the very root of the works. What I took as root, as motive, of Kafka's work were a series of disturbing propositions from a notebook for *Preparation of a Wedding in the Country,* in which Kafka, in one of these internal dialogues where he constantly divides himself against himself, ends up by saying, "One can, however, not not live." He asks the question of the faith, what is faith, is there a faith, faiths, and he arrives at this proposition. There is all of Kafka. It is his way of living, of remaining in life, alive, in order not to give in to death. It is all in this sentence: *"Man kann doch nicht, nicht leben."* You have *kann,* you have *leben,* one can live, but it is not true, one has *nicht, nicht.* That is to say that at the heart of existence is that double negation, "one can not, not." And eventually, one sees precisely his economy. It is an economy of resistance, of resistance to death and not of affirmation of life.

If you follow this level of tragic, tormented depth, you will find by the same journey, by the same itinerary, at similar crossroads, Clarice Lispector, who arrives from the opposite side with her body, her torments, with her life, with her sorrows, and she says that to live is sufficient. I need nothing else but to live; living produces living. She does not say, "not not," she says the opposite. She affirms life in a pure affirmation; that is "feminine," that is the source itself, whereas in Kafka you will find the source cut off, cut off all the time. Continuity in Lispector, cuts in Kafka. These are two structures that are specifically "feminine" and "masculine," if you like. Though let me remind you that I do not equate *feminine* with woman and *masculine* with man. To say that which it would be interesting to be able to say, one would have to change the words. However, it is true that Lispector does not say "no, no." She is a woman who says things as closely as possible to a feminine economy, that is to say, one of the greatest generosity possible, of the greatest virtue, of the greatest spending. When I say that, it is because there is a common trait between her and Kafka. Their bodies paid for the difficulty of being on the side of writing in an absolutely similar way. I do not mean that I am not reading "literary objects," but I want to consider in them traces of life, enigmatic accounts.

So, if you like, living beings are for me to be read in a similar way, as closely and as passionately as possible. Simply, I do not talk about them, because they are alive, and so I would be afraid to do so. I respect, but I do not say—except in intimacy, of course—what I can discover, guess, that is mysterious in such and such a person, for example. And people, my students, do give themselves to read.

*The oneiric elements seem to be of great importance in your texts. You constantly write about dreams, from dreams.*

Immense. It is funny. I can tell you my love story with dreams. In a certain way I am a dreamer. So it is very complicated. I owe everything, almost everything to dream. What does that mean? It means that there is somebody else besides me, of course. I owe everything to somebody else, and in my innocence of times past, I felt guilty because when I started to write I wrote under pressure, under dictation, under the influence of the dream, which made me terribly ashamed. I was not the one who was writing. When I say I write during the day, that is to say that during the day I annotate, like a secretary of my unconscious. I note all that which inscribes itself, produces itself, develops at night, and which is infinitely larger than I. I used to be ashamed of it, I thought it was a kind of superpassion, because it happened at night. During the day I was there, because somebody had spoken. I was like somebody absolutely archaic. I had very primitive fears. I said to myself, what if all that would become silent or if it would not come back? I would not write anymore. I did not dare to say it. Now, it makes me laugh. Because after all, I know a little more on the account of the unconscious. It is like the sea, it is interminable. When it is silent,

it also speaks. There are periods of desert. These are warning signs, exactly as in life.

Now I know about this. I know that if I am cut off from dreams, that means that there is a cut in communication with the deepest, the most essential life, with others in myself, because I let myself be alienated by numerous exterior and superficial activities. It can happen. At that moment one does not write. It is a bad thing. It is a betrayal of the deepest elements in one's relationship with the unconscious. The unconscious, as we know it, does not lie. So when I cannot write, that means that I am lying in my inner depth.

*You also seem to privilege myths, which are closely related to dreams.*

I work a lot on the level of myths, as much as on that of dreams. In reality, myth was that which took the place of analysis in former times. The myth of Oedipus, not at all in a Freudian mode, was of great importance. It showed that there was the universe, but one knew that there was also something else. One knew that something stronger than the social existed. I am passionately interested in myths, because they are always (this is well known) outside the law, like the unconscious. Only afterward there is the story, which signifies that there has been a clash between the in-law and the out-law. I do not say transgression, because it is *not* transgressive. The other world comes and collides with reality, with the reality principle. What happens? Interpretation, of course, because we do have myths and their interpretations. One never questions enough the traditions of interpretation of myth, and all myths have been referred to a masculine interpretation. If we women read them, we read them otherwise. That is why I often nourish my texts, in my own way, at those mythic sources.

*In everything you write, you are also very close to analysis. What do you think of castration?*

I think that castration is fundamental, unfortunately. One has to speak of castration as a phantasm, a fear. True, men are built, or rather one builds masculinity, virility, from one's own resistance to castration. I think that most men are obligated by it. I am not sure if there are many men who are protected from castration, from this kind of rite which of course is the passage through the moment that Freud describes very well with his story of the Medusa, the moment when there is erection, as rite, in the scene of castration. I believe that it structures the economy of men, but what does it give us women? Are we protected from castration? I think that there are women who are completely protected from the world which is organized around the resistance to castration. Surely, there are some. I believe that I know some. Yet since it is a phantasm, it may be communicated. There are women who are under the spell of castration, who are taken in by a phallocratic space. For them, the rite is something hallucinated, since it cannot rely on a bodily inscription, since there is no corporeal representation. Men experience pain in being castrated, yet castration is something imaginary that one feels very vividly, very strongly. I think that women have an analogous situation to that of men. They can feel a kind of castration, a feminine castration. Maybe the word should be displaced. But it should be displaced from a "masculine" border, a little like "masculine" and "feminine." The problem is that on the one hand, for the man there is an anatomic origin of the imaginary model, situated there where the little boy has his penis; on the other, his sexuality is probably not as stable, as continuous, as the feminine sexuality of *jouissance,* of pleasure, which is organized by an absence of cuts.

*On the level of anatomy?*

Of anatomy, on the level of the organ, no. But in the way of pleasure. That is where something could be transformed.

*Do you think that your mode of writing is able to transform, to change the situation of women? Is there a strategic value?*

I do not know whether I can effectuate transformations. But one always arrives at something when something that has been silenced is expressed, when something that has been inhibited expresses itself. It is true that it liberates something.

*Do you consider your writing to be an action?*

Yes, I think so. I think that there is also a test of reading. Texts with a strong "femininity," like some—not all—the texts of Lispector, put to test a certain *jouissance.* There are people who resist, who feel it as threat, while others are relieved by this very kind of rhythm.

*When you talk about* jouissance, *are you not talking about something that had contributed to exclude women, to define them from a masculine border?*

No, I do not think so. I do not see how men talk about feminine *jouissance.* That is precisely what devours them. That is what they are talking about in the mode of not-knowing. That is also what the analysts say, that is what Lacan said, when he spoke of women and of their pleasures: "They have nothing to say, they cannot speak." Fine. That means that he cannot hear them. It means also that he does not know anything about it. He says it clearly when he says: "All right, if you have something to say, say it." But he thinks that women have nothing to say. That is not true. Of course, they say it otherwise. They can say it. It can be defined. I think that in the classical heterosexual scene, the woman generally obeys the masculine demand, which is to give pleasure in the masculine way, to obey the masculine phantasm of feminine *jouissance,* which would be totally, exclusively genital and which leads to effects of inhibition, frigidity, in women. But a woman who is not deprived of her body must be able to find something of it again, and of course it is up to her to talk about it, to inscribe something of it; it is absolutely not organized in the centralized, ritualized way of men, that is true. But women have to say that, and their best listeners will still be women. I am trying to say a little of it in my texts.

*If women differ from men in their mode of* jouissance, *following your distinctions of feminine and masculine economies, they should also differ in their relation to the gift.*

The question of the gift is a question on which we have worked a lot, marking it and following it, if one may say, with a step as light and as airy, as "feminine" as possible. The question is of course the following: Is it possible that there is a gift? It is a question that has been treated at length by Derrida in a seminar on the philosophical mode, etc. Is there such a thing as a gift; can the gift take place? At the limit, one can ask oneself about the possibility of a real gift, a pure gift, a gift that would not be annulled by what one could call a countergift. That is also what Derrida worked on.

How does one give? It starts in a very simple way: in order for a gift to be, *I* must not be the one to give. A gift has to be like grace, it has to fall from the sky. If there are traces of origin of the *I* give, there is no gift—there is an I-give. Which also signifies: say "thank you," even if the other does not ask you to say it. As soon as we say thank you, we give back part or the whole gift. We have been brought up in the space of the debt, and so we say thank you. Is it possible to imagine that there can be a gift? This presupposes that *I* be in parentheses, that *I* accede to a transparency but without disappearance, because otherwise it would be a divine gift. And one does not receive anything from God. The gift has to be sent in such a way that it does not come back immediately, and it has to arrive at its destination. That is one of Derrida's problematics. Does the gift arrive at its destination? For there to be gift, there has to be reception. Reception has to be equal to donation, there has to be an equal generosity of reception. So a real gift is quite rare.

*In your own texts, you started from the question of waiting and you come back to the problem of waiting, but now it is displaced. You also critiqued presence, essence, and you now come back to them. How do you see these changes in your positions?*

I am first going to take the question of waiting, because, as a matter of fact, it has been symptomatic of an evolution. I believe that I have dealt with it in former texts; I am sure I must have written about scenes of bad expectations, bad waitings, scenes of impatience. I say that I would be surprised if I had criticized the woman in the scene. Rather I must have criticized the scene itself with its content, cruel, sadistic, with suspense. I may be wrong. I must have at a certain moment spoken of the drama lived by the woman waiting. It is an old drama, it is that which one sees in literature since its origins. It is that which makes man leave the house. He leaves and woman waits; that can be carried extremely far. I would even say that culturally, woman has been assigned to immobility and man to navigation, and that the model is Ulysses and Penelope. Maybe Penelope was the first woman writer, since she spent her time writing and unwriting, precisely so that her man might come back into the space of the book. It is true that in a period that would correspond roughly to classical tragedy, or to the story of any classically heterosexual woman, the story is always the same, Ulysses and Penelope. One would like to see Penelope's tapestry; one does not know what is on it—most likely painful stories of anguish. But that is when waiting is painful, is organized precisely around an absence, around a lack, around the violence of the other, etc.

In my most recent texts, I believe in particular in *With ou l'art de l'innocence,* I work on something entirely different. I work on a happy expectation which could be compared, for example, to that of the pregnant mother, who expects a child, as one says. I find this a wonderful expression. She waits the time it takes for the child to be born. And not only that, but she takes pleasure in waiting, for nine months. It is a wait which is on the side of gestation, of production. I say this metaphorically. I will give you a play on words: *attendre,* to wait, and *hâte tendre,* tender haste. *La tendre hâte,* the tender haste, the insistence on the wait which is tender, which is not violent, which is expected, which is soft, sweet, and not impatient. I do not want to talk about a kind of resigned patience which is the Christian patience—not at all—but about a capacity to live, a creative capacity, which is not obliged to precipitate itself like a *fiat.* It is not that of the woman who waits in a situation of cruelty that is imposed on her, of violence, but on the contrary a wait that is capable of taking pleasure in each instant, that does not jump over instants by saying, I cannot wait until the end of nine months. She enjoys each time, each measure. Clarice Lispector, for example, sings the present, so that each moment, each instant, is a blessing lived to its fullest.

I have to say that there are several conditions for this. First, you cannot be in the painful situation where you are made to wait and where it is you who do the waiting. Waiting is an art, our life has its rhythms, etc. The present times with their precipitation, technologies, accelerated daily rhythms, television, have destroyed in us the "good old time," a human time. As soon as one is in an urban space, one does not have time anymore. Time flies by us, we do not live it. One must leave and retreat. I am only saying the obvious. I think that when one retreats, one is also already so frenetic that one starts to run again when one is by the sea where there are no bus stops, no television screens.

*What about your* cheminement, *your development?*

I think that what is inscribed in what I have written is a certain story, a certain history, which is mine and, I believe, that of every woman. I think it is quite exemplary. Besides, it is truly a history insofar as it has a development in time, because I absolutely do believe in experience. I think that we traverse in time moments which, little by little, allow us to advance and to learn to live. One does not know how to live; one learns to live, in my case traditionally, since I come from a classical milieu. After a while, it is true, something disengages, detaches itself. One could distinguish at the same time large biographical and textual periods that mark the stages in a *cheminement,* which in any case will always be there because at the bottom I am really a questioner. I cannot even imagine that I will get to the end of the questions asked of me in such overabundance. I do not cease not to understand. Simply, the things I do not understand renew themselves incessantly. Once I have understood something that I did not understand before, it is behind me. And I open myself before the next enigma. Then I have something else that is before me, always like a wonderful America to be discovered, but always to be discovered. . . .

---

### An excerpt from "The Laugh of the Medusa"

I maintain unequivocally that there is such a thing as *marked* writing; that, until now, far more extensively and repressively than is ever, suspected or admitted, writing has been run by a libidinal and cultural—hence political, typically masculine—economy; that this is a locus where the repression of women has been perpetuated, over and over, more or less consciously, and in a manner that's frightening since it's often hidden or adorned with the mystifying charms of fiction; that this focus has grossly exaggerated all the signs of sexual opposition (and not sexual difference), where woman has never *her* turn to speak—this being all the more serious and unpardonable that writing is precisely *the very possibility of change,* the space that can serve as a springboard for subversive thought, the precursory movement of a transformation of social and cultural structures.

Nearly the entire history of writing is confounded with the history of reason, of which it is at once the effect, the support, and one of the privileged alibis. It has been one with the phallocentric tradition. It is indeed that same self-admiring, self-stimulating, self-congratulatory phallocentrism.

*Hélène Cixous, reprinted in* The Critical Tradition: Classic Texts and Contemporary Trends, *edited by David H. Richter, St. Martin's Press, 1989.*

---

### Toril Moi   (essay date 1985)

SOURCE: "Hélène Cixous: An Imaginary Utopia," in *Sexual/Textual Politics: Feminist Literary Theory,* Methuen, 1985, pp. 102-26.

[*Moi is an American educator and critic who has written extensively about various issues in literature, film, and feminist critical theory. In the essay below, she provides an overview of Cixous's fundamental tenets, stating that despite flaws in her works they "nevertheless [constitute] an invigorating utopian evocation of the imaginative powers of women."*]

> Do I contradict myself?
> Very well then . . . I contradict myself;
> I am large . . . I contain multitudes.
> (Walt Whitman)

It is largely due to the efforts of Hélène Cixous that the question of an *écriture féminine* came to occupy a central position in the political and cultural debate in France in the 1970s. Between 1975 and 1977 she produced a whole series of theoretical (or semi-theoretical) writings, all of which set out to explore the relations between women, femininity, feminism and the production of texts: *La Jeune Née* (in collaboration with Catherine Clément, 1975), 'Le Rire de la Méduse' (1975), translated as 'The laugh of the Medusa' (1976), 'Le Sexe ou la tête?' (1976), translated as 'Castration or decapitation?' (1981) and *La Venue à l'écriture* (1977). These texts are closely interrelated: thus 'Sorties', Cixous's main contribution to *La*

*Jeune Née,* contains long passages of the separately published **'The laugh of the Medusa'**. The fact that many central ideas and images are constantly repeated, tends to present her work as a continuum that encourages non-linear forms of reading. Her style is often intensely metaphorical, poetic and explicitly anti-theoretical, and her central images create a dense web of signifiers that offers no obvious edge to seize hold of for the analytically minded critic. It is not easy to operate cuts into, open vistas in or draw maps of Cixous's textual jungle; moreover, the texts themselves make it abundantly clear that this resistance to analysis is entirely intentional. Cixous believes neither in theory nor analysis (though she does practise both—as for instance in her doctoral thesis *L'Exil de James Joyce ou l'art du remplacement* (1968), translated in 1972 as *The Exile of James Joyce or the Art of Replacement,* or in her *Prénoms de personne* from 1974); nor, indeed, does she approve of *feminist* analytical discourses: she is, after all, the woman who first flatly declared that 'I am not a feminist', and later went on to say that 'I do not have to produce theory'. Accusing feminist researchers in the humanities of turning away from the present towards the past, she rejects their efforts as pure 'thematics'. According to Cixous, such feminist critics will inevitably find themselves caught up in the oppressive network of hierarchical binary oppositions propagated by patriarchal ideology. Hopeful feminist analysts of Cixous's 'literary theory' might just as well not apply.

And yet this is not a wholly accurate picture of Cixous's position. The statements quoted, taken out of their contemporary French context, tend to fix her views in an altogether too rigid mould. Her refusal of the label 'feminism' is first and foremost based on a definition of 'feminism' as a bourgeois, egalitarian demand for women to obtain power in the present patriarchal system; for Cixous, 'feminists' are women who want power, 'a place in the system, respect, social legitimation'. Cixous does not reject what she prefers to call the women's *movement* (as opposed to the static rigidity of so-called 'feminism'); on the contrary, she is strongly in favour of it, and between 1976 and 1982 published all her works with *des femmes* to demonstrate her political commitment to the anti-patriarchal struggle. To many French feminists, as well as to most feminists outside France, however, this kind of scholastic wrangling over the word 'feminist' would seem to be politically damaging to the women's movement as a whole. In France it caused members of the collective 'politique et psychanalyse' to march in the streets on International Women's Day carrying placards reading 'Down with feminism!', thus generating a considerable amount of hostility and acrimony within the women's movement, much of which was displayed in public. The main effect of the 'anti-feminist' initiative of the 'politique et psychanalyse' group seems to have been the production of a general impression of rancour and disarray within French feminism. I have therefore no intention of following Cixous's lead on this point: according to accepted English usage, her indubitable commitment to the struggle for women's liberation in France, as well as her strong critique of patriarchal modes of thought, make her a feminist. Having said this, it is of course both relevant and necessary to go on to explore the *kind* of feminist theory and politics she represents.

## PATRIARCHAL BINARY THOUGHT

One of Cixous's most accessible ideas is her analysis of what one might call 'patriarchal binary thought'. Under the heading 'Where is she?', Cixous lines up the following list of binary oppositions:

> Activity/Passivity
> Sun/Moon
> Culture/Nature
> Day/Night
> Father/Mother
> Head/Emotions
> Intelligible/Sensitive
> Logos/Pathos
>
> *[La Jeune Née]*

Corresponding as they do to the underlying opposition man/woman, these binary oppositions are heavily imbricated in the patriarchal value system: each opposition can be analysed as a hierarchy where the 'feminine' side is always seen as the negative, powerless instance. For Cixous, who at this point is heavily indebted to Jacques Derrida's work, Western philosophy and literary thought are and have always been caught up in this endless series of hierarchical binary oppositions that always in the end come back to the fundamental 'couple' of male/female.

> Nature/History
> Nature/Art
> Nature/Mind
> Passion/Action
>
> *[La Jeune Née]*

These examples show that it doesn't much matter which 'couple' one chooses to highlight: the hidden male/female opposition with its inevitable positive/negative evaluation can always be traced as the underlying paradigm.

In a typical move, Cixous then goes on to locate *death* at work in this kind of thought. For one of the terms to acquire meaning, she claims, it must destroy the other. The 'couple' cannot be left intact: it becomes a general battlefield where the struggle for signifying supremacy is forever re-enacted. In the end, victory is equated with activity and defeat with passivity; under patriarchy, the male is always the victor. Cixous passionately denounces such an equation of femininity with passivity and death as leaving no positive space for woman: 'Either woman is passive or she doesn't exist'. Her whole theoretical project can in one sense be summed up as the effort to undo this logocentric ideology: to proclaim woman as the source of life, power and energy and to hail the advent of a new, feminine language that ceaselessly subverts these patriarchal binary schemes where logocentrism colludes with phallocentrism in an effort to oppress and silence women.

## DIFFERENCE

Against any binary scheme of thought, Cixous sets multiple, heterogeneous *difference*. In order to understand her arguments at this point, however, it is necessary first to examine Jacques Derrida's concept of difference (or, rather *différance*). Many early structuralists, as for instance A. J. Greimas in his *Sémantique structurale,* held that meaning is produced precisely through binary oppositions. Thus in the opposition masculine/feminine, each term only achieves significance through its structural relationship to the other: 'masculine' would be meaningless without its direct opposite 'feminine' and vice versa. *All* meaning would be produced in this way. An obvious counterargument to this theory is the many examples of adjectives or adverbs of degree (much—more—most, little—less—least), which seem to produce their meaning in relation to the other items in the same series, not in relation to their binary opposites.

Derrida's critique of binary logic, however, is more far-reaching in its implications. For Derrida, meaning (signification) is not produced in the static closure of the binary opposition. Rather it is achieved through the 'free play of the signifier'. One way of illustrating Derrida's arguments at this point is to use Saussure's concept of the *phoneme*, defined as the smallest differential—and therefore signifying—unit in language. The phoneme can in no way be said to achieve signification through binary opposition alone. In itself the phoneme /b/ does not signify anything at all. If we had only one phoneme, there would be no meaning and no language. /b/ only signifies in so far as it is perceived to be *different* from say /k/ or /h/. Thus /bat/:/kat/:/hat/ are all perceived to be different words with different meanings in English. The argument is that /b/ signifies only through a process that effectively *defers* its meaning on to other differential elements in language. In a sense it is the *other* phonemes that enable us to determine the meaning of /b/. For Derrida, signification is produced precisely through this kind of open-ended play between the presence of one signifier and the absence of others.

---

**Indeed one of the reasons why Cixous is so keen to get rid of the old opposition between masculine and feminine, and even of terms like male or female, is her strong belief in the inherently *bisexual* nature of all human beings.**

**—*Toril Moi***

---

This, then, is the basic significance of the Derridean term *différance*. Spelt with an 'a' to distinguish it—in writing, not in speech—from the normal French word for difference (*différence*), it acquires the more active sense of the ending '-ance' in French, and can therefore be translated both as 'difference' and as 'deferral' in English. As we have seen, the interplay between presence and absence that produces meaning is posited as one of *deferral*: meaning is never truly present, but is only constructed through the potentially endless process of referring to other, absent signifiers. The 'next' signifier can in a sense be said to give meaning to the 'previous' one, and so on *ad infinitum*. There can thus be no 'transcendental signified' where the process of deferral somehow would come to an end. Such a transcendental signified would have to be meaningful *in itself*, fully present to itself, requiring no origin and no end

other than itself. An obvious example of such a 'transcendental signified' would be the Christian concept of God as Alpha and Omega, the origin of meaning and final end of the world. Similarly, the traditional view of the author as the source and meaning of his or her own text casts the author in the role of transcendental signified.

Derrida's analysis of the production of meaning thus implies a fundamental critique of the whole of Western philosophical tradition, based as it is on a 'metaphysics of presence', which discerns meaning as fully present in the Word (or Logos). Western metaphysics comes to favour speech over writing precisely because speech presupposes the *presence* of the speaking subject, who thus can be cast as the unitary origin of his or her discourse. The idea that a text is somehow only fully *authentic* when it expresses the presence of a human subject would be one example of the implicit privileging of voice or speech over writing. Christopher Norris provides an excellent summary of Derrida's views on this point:

> *Voice* becomes a metaphor of truth and authenticity, a source of self-present 'living' speech as opposed to the secondary lifeless emanations of writing. In speaking one is able to experience (supposedly) an intimate link between sound and sense, an inward and immediate realization of meaning which yields itself up without reserve to perfect, transparent understanding. Writing, on the contrary, destroys this ideal of pure self-presence. It obtrudes an alien, depersonalized medium, a deceiving shadow which falls between intent and meaning, between utterance and understanding. It occupies a promiscuous public realm where authority is sacrificed to the vagaries and whims of textual 'dissemination'. Writing, in short, is a threat to the deeply traditional view that associates truth with self-presence and the 'natural' language wherein it finds expression.

In order to grasp Derrida's distinction between writing and speech, it is important to realize that *writing* as a concept is closely related to *différance;* thus Norris defines writing as the 'endless displacement of meaning which both governs language and places it for ever beyond the reach of a stable, self-authenticating knowledge'. Derrida's analysis undermines and subverts the comforting closure of the binary opposition. Throwing the field of signification wide open, writing—textuality—acknowledges the free play of the signifier and breaks open what Cixous perceives as the prison-house of patriarchal language.

### Ecriture féminine 1) masculinity, femininity, bisexuality

Cixous's concept of *feminine writing* is crucially related to Derrida's analysis of writing as *différance*. For Cixous, feminine texts are texts that 'work on the difference', as she once put it, strive in the direction of difference, struggle to undermine the dominant phallogocentric logic, split open the closure of the binary opposition and revel in the pleasures of open-ended textuality.

However, Cixous is adamant that even the term *écriture féminine* or 'feminine writing' is abhorrent to her, since terms like 'masculine' and 'feminine' themselves imprison us within a binary logic, within the 'classical vision of sexual opposition between men and women'. She has therefore chosen to speak either of a 'writing said to be feminine' (or masculine) or, more recently, of a 'decipherable libidinal femininity which can be read in writing produced by a male or a female'. It is not, apparently, the empirical sex of the author that matters, but the kind of writing at stake. She thus warns against the dangers of confusing the sex of the author with the 'sex' of the writing he or she produces:

> Most women are like this: they do someone else's—man's—writing, and in their innocence sustain it and give it voice, and end up producing writing that's in effect masculine. Great care must be taken in working on feminine writing not to get trapped by names: to be signed with a woman's name doesn't necessarily make a piece of writing feminine. It could quite well be masculine writing, and conversely, the fact that a piece of writing is signed with a man's name does not in itself exclude femininity. It's rare, but you can sometimes find femininity in writings signed by men: it does happen. ['**Castration or decapitation?**']

Indeed one of the reasons why Cixous is so keen to get rid of the old opposition between masculine and feminine, and even of terms like male or female, is her strong belief in the inherently *bisexual* nature of all human beings. In '**The laugh of the Medusa**' (and also in *La Jeune Née*—some of the passages dealing with these themes are reproduced in both texts) she first attacks the 'classic conception of bisexuality', which is 'squashed under the emblem of castration fear and along with the fantasy of a "total" being (though composed of two halves), would do away with the difference'. This homogeneous conception of bisexuality is designed to cater for the male fear of the Other (woman) in so far as it allows him to fantasize away the ineluctable signs of sexual difference. Opposing this view, Cixous produces what she calls the *other bisexuality,* which is multiple, variable and ever-changing, consisting as it does of the 'non-exclusion either of the difference or of one sex'. Among its characteristics is the 'multiplication of the effects of the inscription of desire, over all parts of my body and the other body, indeed, this *other bisexuality* doesn't annul differences, but stirs them up, pursues them, increases them'.

Today, according to Cixous, it is 'for historico-cultural reasons . . . *women* who are opening up to and benefiting from this vatic bisexuality', or as she puts it: 'In a certain way, "woman" is bisexual; man—it's a secret to no one—being poised to keep glorious phallic monosexuality in view'. She denies the possibility of ever *defining* a feminist practice of writing:

> For this practice can never be theorized, enclosed, coded—which doesn't mean that it doesn't exist. But it will always surpass the discourse that regulates the phallocentric system; it does and will take place in areas other than those subordinated to philosophico-theoretical domination. ['**The laugh of the Medusa**']

She does, however, supply a definition that not only ech-

oes Derrida's concept of *écriture,* but also seems to be identical with her own concept of the 'other bisexuality':

> To admit that writing is precisely working (in) the in-between, inspecting the process of the same and of the other without which nothing can live, undoing the work of death—to admit this is first to want the two, as well as both, the ensemble of one and the other, not fixed in sequence of struggle and expulsion or some other form of death but infinitely dynamized by an incessant process of exchange from one subject to another. ['**The laugh of the Medusa**']

Here it would seem that for Cixous writing *as such* is bisexual. However, she also argues that, at least at present, *women* (which clearly indicates biological females as opposed to males) are much more likely to be bisexual in this sense than men. *Bisexual* writing is therefore overwhelmingly likely to be *women's* writing, though some exceptional men may in certain cases manage to break with their 'glorious monosexuality' and achieve bisexuality as well. This position is clearly logical enough. In keeping with this anti-essentialist vein, Cixous, in '**The laugh of the Medusa**', argues that in France only Colette, Marguerite Duras and Jean Genet really qualify as feminine (or bisexual) writers. In *La Jeune Née* she also points to Shakespeare's Cleopatra and Kleist's Penthesilea as powerful representations of the feminine libidinal economy.

So far, then, Cixous's position would seem to constitute a forceful feminist appropriation of Derridean theory. Antiessentialist and anti-biologistic, her work in this field seems to displace the whole feminist debate around the problem of women and writing away from an empiricist emphasis on the sex of the author towards an analysis of the articulations of sexuality and desire within the literary text itself. Unfortunately, this is not the whole story. As we shall see, Cixous's theory is riddled with contradictions: every time a Derridean idea is evoked, it is opposed and undercut by a vision of woman's writing steeped in the very metaphysics of presence she claims she is out to unmask.

## THE GIFT AND THE PROPER

Cixous's distinction between the gift and the proper provides the first signs of a slippage away from Derridean antiessentialism. Though she refuses to accept the binary opposition of femininity and masculinity, Cixous repeatedly insists on her own distinction between a 'masculine' and a 'feminine' libidinal economy. These are marked, respectively, by the Realm of the *Proper* and the Realm of the *Gift*. Masculinity or masculine value systems are structured according to an 'economy of the proper'. Proper—property—appropriate: signalling an emphasis on self-identity, self-aggrandizement and arrogative dominance, these words aptly characterize the logic of the proper according to Cixous. The insistence on the proper, on a proper return, leads to the masculine obsession with classification, systematization and hierachization. Her attack on class has little to do with the proletariat:

> There's work to be done against *class,* against categorization, against classification—classes. 'Doing classes' in France means doing military

service. There's work to be done against military service, against all schools, against the pervasive masculine urge to judge, diagnose, digest, name . . . not so much in the sense of the loving precision of poetic naming as in that of the repressive censorship of philosophical nomination/conceptualization. [**'Castration or decapitation?'**]

Theoretical discourse is in other words inherently oppressive, a result of masculine libidinal investment. Even the question 'What is it?' is denounced as a sign of the masculine impulse to imprison reality in rigid hierarchical structures:

> As soon as the question 'What is it?' is posed, from the moment a question is put, as soon as a reply is sought, *we are already caught up in masculine interrogation.* I say 'masculine interrogation': as we say so-and-so was interrogated by the police. [**'Castration or decapitation?'**]

Linking the Realm of the Proper to a 'masculine libidinal economy' is of course impeccably anti-biologistic. Defining it essentially as the male fear of castration (here labelled the 'masculine fear of the loss of the attribute'), however, is not:

> One realizes that the Realm of the Proper is erected on the basis of a fear which as a matter of fact is typically masculine: a fear of expropriation, of separation, of the loss of the attribute. In other words: the impact of the threat of castration. [*La Jeune Née*]

In her article **'Castration or decapitation?'** Cixous elaborates on this idea of the proper as proper to the *male*:

> Etymologically, the 'proper' is 'property', that which is not separable from me. Property is proximity, nearness: we must love our neighbors, those close to us as ourselves: we must draw close to the other so that we may love him/her, because we love ourselves most of all. The Realm of the Proper, culture, functions by the appropriation articulated, set in to play, by man's classic fear of seeing himself expropriated, seeing himself deprived . . . by his refusal to be deprived, in a state of separation, by his fear of losing the prerogative, fear whose response is all of History. Everything must return to the masculine. 'Return': the economy is founded on a system of returns. If a man spends and is spent, it's on condition that his power returns.

The now male Realm of the Proper seems a textbook illustration of Derrida's 'metaphysics of presence'. One might therefore expect its opponent, the Realm of the Gift, to illustrate a more deconstructive approach. Cixous distinguishes between two different kinds of gifts. First there is the gift as it is perceived by men. For the male psyche, to receive a gift is a dangerous thing:

> For the moment you receive something you are effectively 'open' to the other, and if you are a man you have only one wish, and that is hastily to return the gift, to break the circuit of an exchange that could have no end . . . to be nobody's child, to owe no one a thing.

In the Realm of the Proper, the gift is perceived as establishing an inequality—a difference—that is threatening in that it seems to open up an imbalance of *power*. Thus the act of giving becomes a subtle means of aggression, of exposing the other to the threat of one's own superiority. The woman, however, gives without a thought of return. *Generosity* is one of the most positive words in Cixous's vocabulary:

> If there is a 'propriety of woman', it is paradoxically her capacity to depropriate unselfishly, body without end, without appendage, without principal 'parts'. . . . This doesn't mean that she's an undifferentiated magma, but that she doesn't lord it over her body or her desire. . . . Her libido is cosmic, just as her unconscious is worldwide. Her writing can only keep going, without ever inscribing or discerning contours, daring to make these vertiginous crossings of the other(s) ephemeral and passionate sojourns in him, her, them, whom she inhabits long enough to look at from the point closest to their unconscious from the moment they awaken, to love them at the point closest to their drives; and then further, impregnated through and through with these brief, identificatory embraces, she goes and passes into infinity. She alone dares and wishes to know from within, where she, the outcast, has never ceased to hear the resonance of forelanguage. She lets the other language speak—the language of 1,000 tongues which knows neither enclosure nor death. [**'The laugh of the Medusa'**]

The slippage from 'feminine' to 'female' (or 'woman') can here clearly be seen. Elaborating on her theme, Cixous adds that woman gives because she doesn't suffer from castration anxiety (fear of ex-propriation, as she often puts it) in the way men do. In spite of its clear biologism, the Realm of the Gift does seem to correspond fairly closely to a Derridean definition of writing: the feminine/female libidinal economy is open to difference, willing to be 'traversed by the other', characterized by spontaneous generosity; the Realm of the Gift isn't really a realm at all, but a deconstructive space of pleasure and orgasmic interchange with the other. There is no doubt that Cixous explicitly tries to give her exposition of the two 'libidinal economies' a Derridean profile. She warns, for instance, that 'one must beware of blindly or complaisantly falling into essentialist ideological interpretations', and refuses to accept any theory that posits a thematic origin of power and sexual difference. This effort is, however, not only partly undercut by her biologism: in her evocations of a specifically female writing she seems actively intent on promoting an utterly metaphysical case.

### ECRITURE FÉMININE 2) THE SOURCE AND THE VOICE

In *La Jeune Née* Cixous first reiterates her refusal to theorize about writing and femininity, only to indicate that she is, after all, willing to open up a discussion on the matter. What she describes as some tentative comments turn out to be no less than a lyrical, euphoric evocation of the essential bond between feminine writing and the mother as source and origin of the voice to be heard in all female texts. Femininity in writing can be discerned in a privileging of the *voice*: 'writing and voice . . . are woven together'. The speaking woman *is* entirely her voice: 'She physically materializes what she's thinking; she signifies it with her body'. Woman, in other words, is wholly and physically present in her voice—and writing is no more than the extension of this self-identical prolongation of the speech act. The voice in each woman, moreover, is not only her own, but springs from the deepest layers of her psyche: her own speech becomes the echo of the primeval *song* she once heard, the voice the incarnation of the 'first voice of love which all women preserve alive . . . in each woman sings the first nameless love'. It is, in short, the Voice of the Mother, that omnipotent figure that dominates the fantasies of the pre-Oedipal baby: 'The Voice, a song before the Law, before the breath [*le souffle*] was split by the symbolic, reappropriated into language under the authority that separates. The deepest, most ancient and adorable of visitations'.

Finding its source in a time before the Law came into being, the voice is nameless: it is placed firmly in the pre-Oedipal stage before the child acquires language, and thereby the capacity to name itself and its objects. The voice is the mother and the mother's body: 'Voice: inexhaustible milk. She has been found again. The lost mother. Eternity: it is the voice mixed with milk'. The speaking/writing woman is in a space outside time (eternity), a space that allows no naming and no syntax. In her article 'Women's Time', Julia Kristeva has argued that syntax is constitutive of our sense of chronological time by the very fact that the order of words in a sentence marks a temporal sequence: since subject, verb, object cannot be spoken simultaneously, their utterance necessarily cuts up the temporal continuum of 'eternity'. Cixous, then, presents this nameless pre-Oedipal space filled with mother's milk and honey as the source of the song that resonates through all female writing.

The fact that women have this 'privileged relationship to the voice' is due to their relative lack of defence-mechanisms: 'No woman ever heaps up as many defences against their libidinal drives as a man does'. Whereas man represses the mother, woman doesn't (or hardly does): she is always close to the mother as the source of good. Cixous's mother-figure is clearly what Melanie Klein would call the Good Mother: the omnipotent and generous dispenser of love, nourishment and plenitude. The writing woman is thus immensely powerful: hers is a *puissance féminine* derived directly from the mother, whose giving is always suffused with strength: 'The more you have, the more you give the more you are, the more you give the more you have'.

The most explicit description of an actual example of female writing produced under the Sign of the Voice, Cixous's article on the Brazilian writer Clarice Lispector, stresses both her openness and generosity, and, in a deeply un-Derridean passage, her capacity to endow words with their essential meaning:

> There is almost nothing left of the sea but a word without water: for we have also translated the words, we have emptied them of their speech, dried, reduced and embalmed them, and they cannot any longer remind us of the way they

used to rise up from the things as the peal of their essential laughter . . . But a clarice voice only has to say: the sea, the sea, for my keel to split open, the sea is calling me, sea! calling me, waters! ('**L'approche**')

In her article on Marguerite Duras and Hélène Cixous, Christiane Makward distinguishes between twelve different kinds of style in Cixous's novel *LA*: seven poetic and five narrative levels. Five of the seven poetic levels of style can be characterized as in some way biblical, liturgical or mythological. These high poetic inflections find their way into Cixous's more theoretical writings as well. *La Venue à l'écriture* opens on the biblical note of 'In the beginning I adored'. In this text, as in many others, Cixous casts herself, if not as a goddess, at least as a prophetess—the desolate mother out to save her people, a feminine Moses as well as the Pharaoh's daughter:

> The tears I shed at night! The waters of the world flow from my eyes, I wash my people in my despair, I bathe them, I lick them with my love, I go to the banks of the Nile to gather the peoples abandoned in wicker baskets; for the fate of the living I have the tireless love of a mother, that is why I am everywhere, my cosmic belly, I work on my worldwide unconscious, I throw death out, it comes back, we begin again, I am pregnant with beginnings. [*La Venue à l'écriture*]

Laying claim to all possible subject positions, the speaking subject can indeed proudly proclaim herself as a 'feminine plural', who through reading and writing partakes of divine eternity:

> The book—I could reread it with the help of memory and forgetting. Start over again. From another perspective, from another and yet another. Reading, I discovered that writing is endless. Everlasting. Eternal.
>
> Writing or God. God the writing. The writing God. [*La Venue à l'écriture*]

Cixous's predilection for the Old Testament is obvious, but her taste for classical antiquity is no less marked. Her capacity for identification seems endless: Medusa, Electra, Antigone, Dido, Cleopatra—in her imagination she has been them all. In fact, she declares that 'I am myself the earth, everything that happens on it, all the lives that live me there in my different forms'. This constant return to biblical and mythological imagery signals her investment in the world of myth: a world that, like the distant country of fairy tales is perceived as pervasively meaningful, as closure and unity. The mythical or religious discourse presents a universe where all difference, struggle and discord can in the end be satisfactorily resolved. Her mythical and biblical allusions are often accompanied by—or interspersed with—'oceanic' water imagery, evoking the endless pleasures of the polymorphously perverse child:

> We are ourselves sea, sand, coral, sea-weed, beaches, tides, swimmers, children, waves. . . . Heterogeneous, yes. For her joyous benefits she is erogeneous; she is the erotogeneity of the heterogeneous: airborne swimmer, in flight, she does not cling to herself; she is dispersible, prodi-

gious, stunning, desirous and capable of others, of the other woman that she will be, of the other woman she isn't, of him, of you. ['**The laugh of the Medusa**']

For Cixous, as for countless mythologies, water is the feminine element *par excellence*: the closure of the mythical world contains and reflects the comforting security of the mother's womb. It is within this space that Cixous's speaking subject is free to move from one subject position to another, or to merge oceanically with the world. Her vision of female writing is in this sense firmly located within the closure of the Lacanian Imaginary: a space in which all difference has been abolished.

Such an emphasis on the Imaginary can explain why the writing woman enjoys such extraordinary freedom in Cixous's universe. In the Imaginary mother and child are part of a fundamental unity: they are *one*. Protected by the all-powerful Good Mother, the writing woman can always and everywhere feel deeply secure and shielded from danger: nothing will ever harm her, distance and separation will never disable her. Shakespeare's Cleopatra becomes an example of such triumphant femininity:

> The intelligence, the strength of Cleopatra appear particularly in the work she accomplishes—a work of love—on the distance, the gap, the separation: she only evokes the gap in order to fill it to overflowing, never tolerating a separation that could harm the lover's body.

Antony and Cleopatra can risk anything since they will always save each other from harm: the self can be abandoned precisely in so far as it can always be recuperated. If Cixous's poetic discourse often acquires a haunting beauty in its evocations of the paradise of childhood, it does so not least through its refusal to accept the loss of that privileged realm. The mother's voice, her breasts, milk, honey and female waters are all invoked as part of an eternally present space surrounding her and her readers.

This Imaginary world, however, is not flawlessly homogeneous. We have already seen that the female Realm of the Gift is one of a deconstructive openness to difference, and though Cixous describes female writing largely in terms of the abiding presence of the Mother's Voice, she *also* presents the voice as an operation of detachment, splitting and fragmentation. In *La Venue à l'écriture,* the desire to write is first of all presented as a *force* that she cannot consciously control: her body contains 'another limitless space' that demands she give it a written form. Fighting against it—no blackmail will make her yield—she nevertheless feels a secret fascination for this overpowering *souffle*:

> Because it [il] was so strong and so furious, I loved and feared this breath. To be lifted up one morning, snatched off the ground, swung in the air. To be surprised. To find in myself the possibility of the unexpected. To fall asleep as a mouse and wake up as an eagle! What delight! What terror. And I had nothing to do with it, I couldn't help it. [*La Venue à l'écriture*]

This passage, particularly with its French use of the mas-

culine pronoun *il* for *souffle* throughout, reads somewhat like a transposition of a well-known feminine rape fantasy: *il* sweeps the woman off her feet; terrified and delighted she submits to the attack. Afterwards she feels stronger and more powerful (like an *eagle*), as if she had integrated the power of the phallus during the scene. And as in all rape fantasies, the delight and *jouissance* spring from the fact that the woman is blameless: she didn't want it, so cannot be guilty of any illicit desires. (Needless to say, this description only concerns rape *fantasies* and has nothing whatsoever to do with the reality of rape.) This is a brilliant evocation of women's relationship to language in the phallocentric symbolic order: if a woman is to write, she will feel guilty about her desire to obtain mastery over language unless she can fantasize away her own responsibility for such an unspeakable wish. But Cixous's account of the text as rape also constitutes the background for her vision of the text as the Good Mother: 'I was eating the texts, I was sucking, licking, kissing them, I am the innumerable child of their multitudes'. A Kleinian analysis of the mother's nipple as a pre-Oedipal penis image might illuminate this striking oral relationship to the text she reads—which, after all, also must be the text she guiltily hopes some day to write: 'Write? I was dying to do it for love, to give the writing what it [elle] had given to me. What an ambition! What impossible happiness. Feed my own mother. Give her, in her turn, my milk? Mad imprudence'. The text as mother becomes the text as rape, in a sequence of rapid transformations:

> I said 'write French'. One writes *in*. Penetration. Door. Knock before you enter. Absolutely forbidden. . . . How could I not have wanted to write? When books took me, transported me, pierced me to the depths of my soul, let me feel their disinterested potency? . . . When my being was being populated, my body traversed and fertilized, how could I have closed myself up in silence? [*La Venue à l'écriture*]

Mother-text, rape-text; submission to the phallic rule of language as differential, as a structure of gaps and absences; celebration of writing as the realm of the omnipotent mother: Cixous will always incorporate differences, juxtapose contradictions, work to undo gaps and distinctions, fill the gap to overflowing, and happily integrate both penis and nipple.

### IMAGINARY CONTRADICTIONS

Fundamentally contradictory, Cixous's theory of writing and femininity shifts back and forth from a Derridean emphasis on textuality as difference to a full-blown metaphysical account of writing as voice, presence and origin. In a 1984 interview, Cixous shows herself to be perfectly aware of these contradictions:

> If I were a philosopher, I could never allow myself to speak in terms of presence, essence, etc., or of the meaning of something. I would be capable of carrying on a philosophical discourse, but I do not. I let myself be carried off by the poetic word.

In a reference to Derrida's *Of Grammatology* she explains

the relationship (or lack of it) between Derrida's concept and her own:

> In *Grammatology,* he treats of writing in general, of the text in general. When I talk about writing, that is not what I am talking about. One must displace at the moment; I do not speak about the concept of writing the way Derrida analyzes it. I speak in a more idealistic fashion. I allow this to myself; I disenfranchise myself from the philosophical obligations and corrections, which does not mean that I disregard them.

Though her own theoretico-poetic style apparently strives to undo the opposition, Cixous's work bases itself on a conscious distinction between 'poetry' and 'philosophy' (a distinction Derrida himself might well want to deconstruct). How then can we best illuminate Cixous's seeming passion for contradiction? Some might claim it as a cunning strategy intended to prove her own point: by refusing to accept the Aristotelian logic that excludes A from also being not A, Cixous deftly enacts her own deconstruction of patriarchal logic. But this argument assumes that Cixous's point really is a deconstructive one, and thus overlooks the many passages that present a thoroughly metaphysical position. From a psychoanalytic perspective, it would seem that her textual manoeuvres are designed to create a space in which the *différance* of the Symbolic Order can co-exist peacefully with the closure and identity of the Imaginary. Such co-existence, however, covers only *one* aspect of Cixous's vision: the level on which the female essence is described in deconstructive terms, as for instance in the Realm of the Gift, or in those passages relating to the heterogeneous multiplicity of the 'new bisexuality'. But we have seen that even the openness of the Giving Woman or the plurality of bisexual writing are characterized by biblical, mythological or elemental imagery that returns us to a preoccupation with the Imaginary. The difference and diversity in question thus seems more akin to the polymorphous perversity of the pre-Oedipal child than to the metonymic displacements of desire in the symbolic order. The 'new bisexuality' in particular seems ultimately an imaginary closure that enables the subject effortlessly to shift from masculine to feminine subject positions. *In the end,* then, the contradictions of Cixous's discourse can be shown to be contained and resolved within the secure haven of the Imaginary. Her supreme disregard for 'patriarchal' logic is not after all an indication of her Barthesian concern for the liberation of the reader, though at first glance Barthes's description of readerly *jouissance* might seem strikingly appropriate to our experience of Cixous's texts:

> Imagine someone (a kind of monsieur Teste in reverse) who abolishes within himself all barriers, all classes, all exclusions, not by syncretism but by simple discard of that old spectre: *logical contradiction;* who mixes every language, even those said to be incompatible; who silently accepts every charge of illogicality, of incongruity; who remains passive in the face of Socratic irony (leading the interlocutor to the supreme disgrace: *self-contradiction*) and legal terrorism (how much penal evidence is based on a psychol-

ogy of consistency!) . . . Now this anti-hero exists: he is the reader of the text at the moment he takes his pleasure.

The difference between the *jouissance* of the Barthesian reader and Cixous's text is that whereas the former signals absolute loss, a space in which the subject fades to nothing, the latter will always finally gather up its contradictions within the plenitude of the Imaginary.

### POWER, IDEOLOGY, POLITICS

Cixous's vision of feminine/female writing as a way of re-establishing a spontaneous relationship to the physical *jouissance* of the female body may be read positively, as a utopian vision of female creativity in a truly non-oppressive and non-sexist society. Indeed a marked emphasis on the Imaginary is common in utopian writing. In 1972, for example, Christiane Rochefort published a powerful feminist utopian novel, *Archaos ou le jardin étincelant,* which in its narrative mode exhibits striking parallels to Cixous's preoccupation with the Imaginary as a utopian solution to the problem of desire.

Utopian thought has always been a source of political inspiration for feminists and socialists alike. Confidently assuming that change is both possible and desirable, the utopian vision takes off from a negative analysis of its own society in order to create images and ideas that have the power to inspire to revolt against oppression and exploitation. Influenced by Frankfurt School theorists such as Ernst Bloch and Herbert Marcuse, Arnhelm Neusüss has shown that anti-utopian arguments tend to be advanced from the right as part of a strategy aiming at the neutralization or recuperation of the revolutionary contents of the utopian dream. The most pernicious and widespread of the various anti-utopian arguments described by Neusüss is the one we might call the 'realist' approach. While tending towards rationalism in its underestimation of the possible political impact of human desire, the 'realist' position also objects to the contradictory nature of many utopias: there is no point in taking them seriously, the argument goes, since they are so illogical that anybody could tell that they would never work in real life anyway.

Rejecting this position, Neusüss sees the contradictions embodied by so many utopias as a justification of their social critique: signalling the repressive effects of the social structures that gave rise to the utopia in the first place, its gaps and inconsistencies indicate the pervasive nature of the authoritarian ideology the utopian thinker is trying to undermine. If Neusüss is right, the utopian project will always be marked by conflict and contradiction. Thus, if we choose to read Cixous as a utopian feminist, at least some of the contradictory aspects of her texts may be analysed as structured by the conflict between an already contradictory patriarchal ideology and the utopian thought that struggles to free itself from that patriarchal stranglehold. But if it is true that her contradictions are finally gathered up into the homogenizing space of the Imaginary, then they are more likely also to constitute a flight from the dominant social reality.

**Cixous's vision of feminine/female writing as a way of re-establishing a spontaneous relationship to the physical *jouissance* of the female body may be read positively, as a utopian vision of female creativity in a truly non-oppressive and non-sexist society.**

*—Toril Moi*

In a critique of Norman O. Brown, Herbert Marcuse, himself a vigorous defender of utopianism, describes Brown's utopian ideal as an effort towards the 'restoration of original and total unity: unity of male and female, father and mother, subject and object, body and soul—abolition of the self, of mine and thine, abolition of the reality principle, of all boundaries'. While a positive effort towards abolishing existing repressive structures, Brown's Cixous-like cultivation of the pleasure principle is for Marcuse unsatisfactory precisely because it is located exclusively within the Imaginary:

> The roots of repression are and remain real roots; consequently, their eradication remains a real and rational job. What is to be abolished is not the reality principle; not everything, but such particular things as business, politics, exploitation, poverty. Short of this recapture of reality and reason Brown's purpose is defeated.

It is just this absence of any specific analysis of the material factors preventing women from writing that constitutes a major weakness of Cixous's utopia. Within her poetic mythology, writing is posited as an absolute activity of which all women *qua* women automatically partake. Stirring and seductive though such a vision is, it can say nothing of the actual inequities, deprivations and violations that women, as social beings rather than as mythological archetypes, must constantly suffer.

Marcuse's insistence on the need to recapture reason and reality for the utopian project is a timely one. In her eagerness to appropriate imagination and the pleasure principle for women, Cixous seems in danger of playing directly into the hands of the very patriarchal ideology she denounces. It is, after all, patriarchy, not feminism, that insists on labelling women as emotional, intuitive and imaginative, while jealously converting reason and rationality into an exclusively male preserve. Utopias, then, challenge us both on the poetic and the political level. It is therefore understandable that, while acknowledging the rhetorical power of Cixous's vision, feminists should nevertheless want to examine its specific political implications in order to discover exactly what it is we are being inspired to do.

But is it justifiable to force Cixous's writing into a political straitjacket, particularly when, as she argues, she is concerned less with politics than with poetry?

> I would lie if I said that I am a political woman, not at all. In fact, I have to assemble the two words, political and poetic. Not to lie to you, I must confess that I put the accent on the poetic. I do it so that the political does not repress, because the political is something cruel and hard and so rigorously real that sometimes I feel like consoling myself by crying and shedding poetic tears.

The distance posited here between the political and the poetic is surely one that feminist criticism has consistently sought to undo. And though Cixous seems to be claiming 'poetic' status for her own texts, this does not prevent her from writing directly about power and ideology in relation to feminist politics. According to Cixous, ideology is a 'kind of immense membrane that envelops everything. A skin that we must know is there even if it covers us like a net or a closed eyelid'. This view of ideology as total closure parallels Kate Millett's vision of it as a monolithic unity, and suffers from exactly the same defects. How could we ever discover the nature of the ideology that surrounds us if it were entirely consistent, without the slightest contradiction, gap or fissure that might allow us to perceive it in the first place? Cixous's image of ideology recreates the closure of the mythological universe in which she constantly seeks refuge from the contradictions of the material world. When Catherine Clément accuses Cixous of speaking at a non-political level, she pinpoints precisely this problem in Cixous's work:

> C[atherine Clément]. I must admit that your sentences are devoid of reality for me, except if I take what you say in a poetic sense. Give me an example. . . . Your level of description is one where I don't recognize any of the things I think in political terms. It's not that it's 'false', of course not. But it's described in terms which seem to me to belong to the level of myth or poetry; it all indicates a kind of desiring, fictive, collective subject, a huge entity which alternately is free and revolutionary or enslaved, asleep or awake. . . . Those are not subjects existing in reality.

Equally disturbing is Cixous's discourse on power. In an interview in *La Revue des sciences humaines,* she distinguishes between one 'bad' and one 'good' kind of power:

> I would indeed make a clear distinction when it comes to the kind of power that is the will to supremacy, the thirst for individual and narcissistic satisfaction. That power is always a power over others. It is something that relates back to government, control, and beyond that, to despotism. Whereas if I say 'woman's powers', first it isn't *one* power any longer, it is multiplied, *there is more than one* (therefore it is not a question of centralization—that destroys the relation with the unique, that levels everything out) and it is a *question of power over oneself,* in other words of a relation not based on mastery but on availability [disponibilité].

Both kinds of power are entirely personal and individual: the struggle against oppression seems to consist in a lame effort to affirm a certain heterogeneity of woman's powers (a heterogeneity belied by the singular of 'woman'), which in any case seems to come down to claiming that a strong woman can do what she likes. In French, the term *disponibilité* carries a heavy bourgeois-liberal heritage, partly because of its central status in the works of André Gide. To be 'available' can thus imply a certain egoistic desire to be 'ready for anything', not to be bogged down in social and interpersonal obligations. Cixous's global appeal to 'woman's powers' glosses over the real differences among women, and thus ironically represses the true heterogeneity of women's powers.

Cixous's poetic vision of writing as the very enactment of liberation, rather than the mere vehicle of it, carries the same individualist overtones. Writing as ecstatic self-expression casts the individual as supremely capable of liberating herself back into union with the primeval mother. For Cixous, women seem to relate to each other exclusively on a dualistic (I/you) pattern: as mothers and daughters, lesbian couples or in some variety of the teacher/student or prophet/disciple relationship. The paucity of references to a wider community of women or to collective forms of organization is not only conspicuous in the work of a feminist activist, but indicative of Cixous's general inability to represent the non-Imaginary, triangulated structures of desire typical of social relationships.

Given the individualist orientation of Cixous's theory, it is perhaps not surprising that some of her students should present her politics as a simple prolongation of her persona, as in Verena Andermatt Conley's account of Cixous's appearance at the University of Paris at Vincennes ('a school notorious for a certain regal squalor'):

> Cixous used to enter the complex in a dazzling ermine coat whose capital worth most probably surpassed the means of many in the classroom. Her proxemics marked a progressive use of repression. As a replica of Bataille's evocation of Aztec ceremony, she surged from the context of the cheaply reinforced concrete of classroom shelters. She then became a surplus value and a zero-degree term, the sovereign center of a decorous, eminently caressive body where her politics splintered those of an archaic scene in which the king would have his wives circulate about him.

Ermine as emancipation: it is odd that the women of the Third World have been so ludicrously slow to take up Cixous's sartorial strategy.

For a reader steeped in the Anglo-American approach to women and writing, Hélène Cixous's work represents a dramatic new departure. In spite of the vicissitudes that the concept undergoes in her texts, *writing* for her is always in some sense a libidinal object or act. By enabling feminist criticism to escape from a disabling author-centred empiricism, this linking of sexuality and textuality opens up a whole new field of feminist investigation of the articulations of desire in language, not only in texts written by women, but also in texts by men.

As we have seen, a closer investigation of her work has to confront its intricate webs of contradiction and conflict, where a deconstructive view of textuality is countered and undermined by an equally passionate presentation of writing as a female essence. If these contradictions in the end

can be seen to be abolished within the Imaginary, this in its turn raises a series of political problems for the feminist reader of Cixous: marred as much by its lack of reference to recognizable social structures as by its biologism, her work nevertheless constitutes an invigorating utopian evocation of the imaginative powers of women.

**Mary Libertin    (review date July-August 1987)**

SOURCE: "Challenging the Language," in *Belles Lettres: A Review of Books by Women,* Vol. 2, No. 6, July-August, 1987, pp. 11, 14.

*[In the following excerpt, Libertin provides a favorable review of* The Newly Born Woman.*]*

Those who are unfamiliar with Hélène Cixous's **"Laugh of the Medusa"** or with the excerpts from **"Sorties"** in *Signs* or in Marks and de Courtivron's *New French Feminisms* will want to read her complete essay, in addition to Catherine Clément's essay, "The Guilty One," along with their concluding dialogue, **"Exchange,"** in the translation of this 1975 feminist classic, *La Jeune Née* (***The Newly Born Woman***). This book contains an exceptional introductory essay, "Tarantella of Theory," by Sandra Gilbert, which prepares the Anglo-American reader for this radical text by stunning us with the depth of rage and desire in writers from Dickinson to Rich and by fending off objections to possible charges of essentialism and hyperbole. Gilbert correctly shows that *écriture feminine* is fundamentally a political strategy that "redress[es] the wrongs of culture through a revalidation of the rights of nature." Catherine Clément rivets the reader with her post-Lacanian explanation of how women are in the "imaginary zone" that culture creates for what it excludes, and she notes that what is at stake in history is "the whole evaluation of psychoanalysis as a therapeutic function." Clement shows that the role of the hysteric is "indeed, what keeps the very history of psychoanalysis going" and that the hysteric and the sorceress "are old and worn-out figures, awakened only to throw off their shackles." Indeed, at the end of this critique of women's place in psychoanalysis, we find that these figures no longer exist. Cixous's posthysterical text leads the reader through the rebirth of women into a utopia.

In this utopia, the *écriture feminine,* women have been borne out of hysteria, and they remember what has been repressed. They are unafraid and laughing. As Cixous explains, "Everyone knows that a place exists which is not economically or politically indebted to all the vileness and compromise. That is not obliged to reproduce the system. That is writing. If there is a somewhere else that can escape the infernal repetition, it lies in that direction, where *it* writes itself, where *it* dreams, where *it* invents new worlds." Bisexual, the newly born woman "displac[es] and reviv[es] the question of difference." Bisexuality is "the location within oneself of the presence of both sexes, evident and insistent in different ways according to the individual, the nonexclusion of difference or of a sex, and starting with this 'permission' one gives oneself, the multiplication of the effects of desire's inscription on every part of the body and the other body." Readers will be borne upon Cixous's flight through the "dawn of phallocentrism"—the rewriting or appropriation of texts of the past, from the Greeks through Shakespeare, from Freud through Joyce. As Cixous tells Clément, "this is a high point in the history of women." This fine translation provides a classic example.

## R. R.   (review date 1988)

SOURCE: A review of *The Newly Born Woman,* in *Poetics Today,* Vol. 9, No. 3, 1988, pp. 670-71.

[*In the positive review below, the critic discusses the central themes of* The Newly Born Woman.]

[**The Newly Born Woman**] represents the new French feminist theoretical movement today. Its authors explore through readings of historical, literary and psychoanalytic accounts, what is hidden and repressed in culture, veiled structures of language and society that have determined the woman's place in society and culture. In part one of the book, "The Guilty One," Clement provides an analysis of "images of women," especially images of the sorceress and the hysteric, as exemplary female figures. In part two, **"Sorties: Out and Out: Attacks/Ways Out/Forays,"** Cixous elaborates the imaginings of liberations as well as theories of the phallocratic, patriarchal hierarchization that has led to the need for liberation. In part three, **"Exchange,"** the authors collaborate in a dialogue which illuminates differences and similarities in their thinking. The emphasis here lies on the need of silenced women to find an outlet for their expressive drives, in cry, screams and dances of desire. Feminist theory takes here a direction of biological essentialism implied in Cixous's concept of feminine writing and to which some American and French feminists have objected. Although Cixous herself repudiates the notion of consistent sexual essences, we see here an attempt to reverse the hierarchy of mind/body that has repressed the female by identifying woman and (passive or dangerous) nature. Body is valorized over mind. Another central notion in this work is that of the displacement of woman, a person who has no *where.* Cixous's thought is transmitted through complex metaphors such as "writing the body," or her view of *jouissance* as a fusion of the erotic, the mystical and the political. Coming into writing is seen as a source of jouissance. Women's words, traditionally relegated to the margins, are inevitably the signs of the repressed, hieroglyphs of an absence striving to become a presence. The re-placement of the displaced is the dream of a transformed language and literature, of a new writing. The dream of a transformed world, a dream shared by Cixous and Clément, as well as by their female precursors (Emily Dickinson, Virginia Woolf, Gertrude Stein, Sylvia Plath and others) is fully depicted and considered in this book. The vocabulary used here reflects the cultural milieu of Paris in the mid-seventies. The concepts and terminology are nourished on a mixture of structuralism, Marxism, deconstruction and Lacanian psychoanalysis. To facilitate its deciphering, the book includes an introduction written by Sandra M. Gilbert and a glossary of terms.

## Elizabeth Wright and Dianne Chisholm   (review date April 1989)

SOURCE: A review of *The Newly Born Woman,* in *The Modern Language Review,* Vol. 84, No. 2, April, 1989, pp. 418-19.

[*Below, Wright and Chisholm offer a favorable assessment of* The Newly Born Woman, *stating that "this is an important book, which transgresses the boundaries between fiction and non-fiction, poetry and prose."*]

The general thesis of [**The Newly Born Woman**] is that if women are going to take part in history they must write themselves into it. One of the ways of entering this arena as subjects speaking for themselves is to write their story. The problem is that the dominant culture is masculine, and since they cannot create stories out of nowhere, they have to draw on the masculine culture. Yet even in doing so and in taking up the feminine subject positions that men construct in their literature, women will inevitably tell their own story and thus chart a different history, politics, and economics. This history will emerge through their writing and not by virtue of any biological essentialism.

The book is divided into three parts: a first part ('The Guilty One') written by Catherine Clément; a second part (**'Sorties: Out and Out: Attacks/Ways Out/Forays'**) by Hélène Cixous; and a final part (**'Exchange'**) staging a dialogue between the two.

Catherine Clément begins with a discussion of women as inscribed in a series of men's texts (Freud, Michelet, Flaubert), in which the women appear as hysterics and sorceresses. While these writers see woman's position as symptomatic (Freud), marginal (Michelet), or aesthetic (Flaubert), the women themselves understand their own ideological repression when they write as hysterics and sorceresses. A second section of this first part develops the position of 'the guilty one' as the daughter who has no place in the Œdipal constellation of the family, consisting as it does of mother, father, and son. While witches were able to exist as a marginal class they could live on the outskirts of society, but once there are no margins and there is only family, hospital, or asylum, the daughter is trapped and has no institutional place to which she might belong. Clément's conclusion, her manifesto, is that women can neither continue to take up this marginal subject position nor adopt the male paradigm. Women writers must go further if they are to reach the position of the 'post-hysterical subject', further even than taking up the sorceress as a symbol of female liberation, as some writers have done (one thinks of Fay Weldon's recently-televised novel, *The Life and Loves of a She-Devil*), not content to remain in the realm of magic realism, but able to move out into a world of social realism.

Whereas Catherine Clément feels that women must identify with the hysteric and the sorceress, Hélène Cixous wants to identify with the heroic female in fiction but can find only male heroes. In Part II she elaborates on her famous essay, **'The Laugh of the Medusa'** (a mockery of male castration-anxiety), her question being 'Why haven't women written?'. Her answer is that the girl in the Œdipal family is expected to sacrifice libido, maternal love, and desire for self-knowledge, without gaining any symbolic compensation (no father's name). In literary history she has neither models nor poetic subjects. Since male heroes are not acceptable, women must either write a story which rehabilitates the mother or go to the male classics which offer masculine women characters and feminine male characters (Kleist's Penthesilea and Achilles, Shakespeare's Cleopatra and Antony). As the female libidinal economy is never discussed, it has to be invented/written, showing how the female repressed gives endlessly without debt, whereas the male (capitalist) economy does nothing but accumulate.

Part III is an exchange between two feminisms, that of a poet-academic (Cixous) and that of a socialist intellectual (Clément), who comment self-reflexively on their kind of discourse to each other and discuss which is more effective for feminism. Cixous argues that the 'hero' of women's writing in the twentieth century is the hysteric, while Clément maintains that women must act collectively and not heroicize the hysteric.

*La Jeune Née* means three things: 'newly-born woman' ('Là je une nais'), but also a pun referring to a feminine writing outlaw (La Genet), and a non-existing feminine subject ('la je n'est'). In the end, even though the two writers do not agree on the means to the end, they do agree that in general the route should be one of writing rebelliously (the hysteric), thereby bringing a feminine subject into existence and history (that is, newly born). This is an important book, which transgresses the boundaries between fiction and non-fiction, poetry and prose, and should be obligatory reading both for female and for male subjects.

---

**An excerpt from "The Laugh of the Medusa"**

I write this as a woman, toward women. When I say "woman," I'm speaking of woman in her inevitable struggle against conventional man; and of a universal woman subject who must bring women to their senses and to their meaning in history. But first it must be said that in spite of the enormity of the repression that has kept them in the "dark"—that dark which people have been trying to make them accept as their attribute— there is, at this time, no general woman, no one typical woman. What they have *in common* I will say. But what strikes me is the infinite richness of their individual constitutions: you can't talk about *a* female sexuality, uniform, homogeneous, classifiable into codes—any more than you can talk about one unconscious resembling another. Women's imaginary is inexhaustible, like music, painting, writing: their stream of phantasms is incredible.

*Hélène Cixous, reprinted in* The Critical Tradition: Classic Texts and Contemporary Trends, *edited by David H. Richter, St. Martin's Press, 1989.*

---

**Deborah Jenson   (essay date 1991)**

SOURCE: "Coming to Reading Hélène Cixous," in *"Coming to Writing," and Other Essays,* Harvard University Press, 1991, pp. 183-96.

[*Jenson edited* "Coming to Writing," and Other Essays *and contributed to it the essay excerpted below. In the following, she provides a thematic and stylistic overview of Cixous's works collected in the volume.*]

In Hélène Cixous's 1976 essay **"Coming to Writing,"** a remarkable "capitalist-realist superuncle," an "Anti-other in papaperson," rehashes the sober facts of the narrator's failure to allow herself to be captured within a recognizable literary tradition: "We think you're here," he says, "and you're there. One day we tell ourselves: this time we've got her, it's her for sure. This woman is in the bag. And we haven't finished pulling the purse strings when we see you come in through another door." Today, in the 1990s, Cixous's writing has become a part of recognizable literary history. But her texts still manage to lead the expectant reader on a chase—and not only the capitalist-realist super-reader, but the other reader, the one who is willing to accompany the narrator on her path to writing. "Am *I* here?" the reader might ask, "or am *I* there? And what is in that bag?" Pursuing the elusive author not only in her trapdoor escapes into the new, but in her wanderings back into the fairytale forest of the familiar, the reader strays deeper and deeper into the question of how to read one's way to writing . . .

**"Coming to Writing" and Other Essays** groups together much of Cixous's work in the essay form from 1976 to 1989. The collection's coherence rests less in any one thematic than in the development of Cixous's readings of artistic sources—literature, opera, and painting—over the years, and in the way her writing changes according to the nature of her readings. The style of **"Coming to Writing,"** an essay which followed **"The Laugh of the Medusa"** by less than a year, is exuberant, polemical, filled with wordplay and parodic inventions rooted in the works of the "masters" (Freud's lecture on "Femininity," for instance, becomes "Requiemth Lecture on the Infeminitesimal"). Here sexual difference is directly explored in personal terms, and in opposition to certain cultural, psychoanalytic, religious, and political sources. In comparison, **"Clarice Lispector: The Approach,"** from 1979, shows the influence of Lispector's work in its strikingly meditative tone. Elements from Cixous's earlier work are approached here with a simple, poetic, and ultimately philosophical vocabulary. Ironically, this pared-down vocabulary may be more opaque for the American reader than the complex wordplay of **"Coming to Writing."** The subject of sexual difference is difficult to locate in a line like this one from the beginning of the essay: "Loving the true of the living, what seems *ungrateful* to narcissus eyes, the nonprestigious, the non-immediate, loving the origin, interesting oneself personally with the impersonal, with the animal, with the thing." And yet, through a careful reading of the subsequent text, one comes equipped with new resources to the question formulated without fanfare in the final passage: "And woman?" The text is structured like an enigma.

The third and fourth essays in this collection, **"Tancredi Continues"** and **"The Last Painting or the Portrait of God,"** were both published in 1983. They show Cixous's interest in the sources and motivating forces of artistic work in genres not limited to writing. Unlike much literary work on the arts in the United States, however, Cixous's interest in music and the visual arts remains tied to the figurative, to the language of the story in its different vocabularies. **"The Last Painting or the Portrait of God"** takes as its point of departure Clarice Lispector's fascination with the instant ("Each thing has an instant in which it is. I want to take possession of the thing's *is*.") to explore differences between the gestures of writing and painting. One such difference lies in the possibility of "fidelity" to the instant, a concept that could be confused with realism but that is more accurately approached as the problem of making figurative the "vision" of the writer. What the painter makes visible, the writer offers to the imaging capacities of the reader: "I am the awkward sorceress of the invisible: my sorcery is powerless to evoke, without the help of your sorcery. Everything I evoke depends on you, depends on your trust, your faith." "Fidelity" is also illustrated here in terms of the cultural permission (or lack of it) to "contemplate a woman's real nudity" in writing.

The other piece from 1983 is **"Tancredi Continues,"** a fragment of a longer, unpublished fiction called *Jerusalem Continues,* which Cixous wrote in 1981-82. This is her reading of Tasso's epic *Jerusalem Delivered* and Gioacchino Rossini's opera version, *Tancredi*. The intensely poetic language of this text condenses several kinds of struggles and several kinds of bodies into one space: the poetic space of contested Jerusalem. Two camps fight over (the gender of ) this "beloved body." On one level they are religious/national camps (this is one of the first works to reveal Cixous's growing interest in the problematic of nationalities), but Cixous's use of the startling gender portrayals of Tasso's epic highlights them above all as the camps of the two sexes, in their lethal, passionate dispute over the masculinity or femininity of the body of the beloved.

The last two essays, from 1989, represent Cixous's most recent work on Clarice Lispector. The brief **"By the Light of an Apple"** serves as a prelude to the final essay in this collection, **"The Author in Truth."** It plays on the title of a novel by Clarice Lispector, *The Apple in the Dark,* to convey Lispector's illuminating force: she is the "Watchwoman, night-light of the world." Cixous compares Lispector with Kafka, Rilke, Rimbaud, and Heidegger, but only on conditional feminine terms: *if* Kafka had been a woman, Rilke a Jewish Brazilian, Rimbaud a mother, Heidegger the author of a Romance of the Earth. Despite the murmurings of philosophers "in her forests," Lispector is a writer who "knows nothing," because her work is not the stasis of cognition; it is the journey of "re-cognition." As such, her work "puts us back in the worldschool" of unceasing, "equal" attention. For Cixous, the political quality of Lispector's work lies in the absence of a hierarchy of artistic objects. ("Political" in a qualified sense, clearly; Cixous asks the question whether *The Hour of the Star* is a political text, and answers: "Subreptitiously. If there is a politics of spirituality.")

In **"The Author in Truth,"** Cixous plunges into the question of identification between reader, author, and character. She proceeds with all the complexity of Bakhtinian analysis of speech acts, but without a specialized theoretical vocabulary. The class position of the character Macabea is at the heart of the identificatory labyrinth in *The Hour of the Star*: "We, character, reader, author, circulate between 'I am not her,' and 'I could be her,' as we advance along the most powerful path of meditation that we can take in thinking of the other." Here we find echoing in **"The Author in Truth"** the same question of the reader's position that reverberates in *"Coming to Writing" and Other Essays* as a whole.

The opening paragraphs of the title essay locate the problematic of reading as a heartbeat-like trace audible inside as well as outside the text. The initial "I" who narrates is the child-reader who scans the Face—the Face as the maternal geography that is the signature of life for the infant. The child's act of reading is as inevitable as her primal attraction to the (m)other: the other signifies; the child reads. Reading the Face is necessary for the child in order to keep the connection with the other alive, and in fact to keep the other alive at all, since otherness denotes existence *in relation to* the subject. The Face serves also as a beacon of light that makes it possible to name the shadowy world around the child. In the relationship to this other, the child-narrator is at once the most helpless and most powerful of readers—depending on the other, and creating the other. Hélène Cixous pointed out in the recent colloquium "Readings of Sexual Difference" at the International College of Philosophy that in the act of reading, one chooses one's subject of reading; and in doing so, one becomes the author of the reading. So reading is a not-quite-authorized coming to writing. In this way, the reader of **"Coming to Writing"** coincides with the elusive narrator on her dizzying trail through the forest.

The narrator of **"Coming to Writing"** is herself unable to authorize her writing until the *"souffle"*—most simply, the breath, the intake of life, but also the current of inspiration—sets her body in motion and inscribes her desire in the flesh. By then, it is too late to turn back; the body *will* function as a source. Cixous has described the woman-body as the "place from which": from which birth occurs, metaphorically and organically, from which the passage is made from the inside to the outside, from which a new body emerges to read otherness in its turn. In this text Cixous's fascination with, and her gratitude for, sources, makes the question of writing into a celebration of its places of emission and its places of incorporation. On her journey to and through the "places from which," she sends a stream of correspondence, her **"Letters from the Life-Watch,"** and other bodily chronicles.

To achieve her readings of life, Cixous practices a politics/poetics of attention articulated through her readings of the work of Clarice Lispector. Compared to **"Coming to Writing,"** which is often as vigorous and wet as a newborn struggling for its first breath, or as a fish splashing in water, **"Clarice Lispector: The Approach"** is composed with philosophical restraint, panther steps, respect for the fragility of an egg. That is because the interventions of this essay are directed to a stage of life in which the urgency of reading the Face has been forgotten, and in which we allow what Cixous refers to as the media forcibly to read us, the erstwhile reader. "We are living in the time of the flat thought-screen, of newspaper-thinking, which does not leave time to think the littlest thing according to its living mode. We must save the approach that opens and leaves space for *the other*." In this jaded time we are, passively, the "other" of the advertising executive, for instance. By contrast, in the world-readings of Clarice Lispector, "names are hands she lays on space, with a tenderness so intense that at last smiles a face, o you."

This tender naming, and its ability to coax the face into bloom, is the product of a patience, a reserve, an attention, that Cixous characterizes as soul. "Soul" is one of many terms that are generally banished to the metaphysical broom closet these days but that Cixous gifts with a reincarnation, in the sense of a reconstituted relationship to the body. The soul for her is an ultrasensual substance: "The soul is the magic of attention. And the body of the soul is made from a fine, fine ultrasensual substance, so finely sensitive that it can pick up the murmur of every hatching, the infinitesimal music of particles calling to one another to compose themselves in fragrance." This reading-soul is inseparable from the experience of the senses, but it is not conflated with the senses: it is a sensory/sensual attention. A sensist capacity for reading. A sensualism of readings via the senses.

The reading-soul raises the question of the politics of poetic rhetoric. Cixous takes on the trope of the rose: Is a woman a rose or is a woman a woman? Do we know a woman best as a rose or as a woman? When does a rose become a mask for woman, and vice versa? This touches on the question of the mimetic relation between text and object, which, like the question of masculinity or femininity in its relation to the body, is not easily resolved in Cixous's work, or in Lispector's work. (Lispector's story "The Imitation of the Rose" can be read, for instance, as the mad radicality of mimetic structure in the religious classic *The Imitation of Christ* when applied to the housewife and her sanctum, the domestic environment.) The attention Lispector applies to the organic is not so much a transformational logic as a respect that explores the form of its object, that tries to greet each "species" with an attention of a similar "species." And so when she considers that archipoetic object, the rose, she might examine its elements by replacing it with a turtle, a cockroach, an oyster; whereas Rilke "could replace it only with a unicorn," or "in lacework."

But what prevents this approach from turning into a mimetic code is the strict ambiguity of Cixous's use of terms such as "species" in the first place. In **"The Author in Truth"** she writes, "Yes, Clarice's project is to make the other human subject appear equal—and this is positive—to the roach. Each to her own species." The roach (which is far from anthropomorphized in *The Passion*) and the human subject as mimetic partners? Clearly, realism is not at the bottom of this mystery. Cixous suggests a comparison of Gertrude Stein's approach to the rose with Lispector's. Stein's "A rose is a rose is a rose . . ." is subversive

"hyperlinguistics." Through repetition, Stein reveals "the fact that the signifier always represses." Lispector, on the other hand, presents a "story" of the rose, of which " 'I write you this facsimile' is one of the definitions." But there are always further definitions of the rose (other than that of the inevitable facsimilitude of representation) which have to do with the rose's organic life. In the end, imitation in Cixous's work has less to do with mimesis than with the mimosa, the flower that takes its name from the Latin botanical term *mimus*.

Listening with the "ultrasensual substance of the soul," the writer reads the object into existence. And so woman is represented not only as the story of a historical, literary facsimile, with which all feminists are familiar, a rose-text, but as a body to be explored. This body belongs to character, author, and reader. Cixous rediscovers Lispector through the eyes of Macabea, for instance, and catches a glimpse of her own double: "Reading this narrative I sometimes almost forgot her, I did forget her. Later I remembered. And for one second, through Macabea's eyes, I saw Clarice Lispector heavily made up, coming out of the salon where having her hair done had cost a month's worth of sausage sandwiches. Or was it myself I saw?"

The reader author-izes a reading, the writer reads woman into writing, the reader becomes writer, the writer becomes reader—in which direction are we going? In French, the word *sens* signifies both "meaning" and "direction." And in French, the titles of the first three essays in this book all contain terms of movement that can be read in more than one meaning-direction at a time. **"La Venue à l'écriture"** hinges on the various possible meanings of *la venue*: the path of growth or development, the coming (as in "the advent"), or the (feminine) one who has arrived. (*La venue* is also a homophone of *l'avenue*.) The syntax of **"L'Approche de Clarice Lispector"** suggests either "Clarice Lispector's Approach," or, on the contrary, "Approaching Clarice Lispector." It could even be read as "The Approach—from (the Point of Departure of) Clarice Lispector." In **"Tancredi Continues,"** the lack of an object for the verb "continues" leaves the reader to wonder: what, where, and whom does Tancredi continue to do, go, and be? Does all this circulation simply lead the reader in the direction of movement for the sake of avoiding stasis, and if so, what does this have to do with "truth," as in **"The Author in Truth?"**

"Truth" is a term of movement as it relates to the constantly self-displacing yet ultimately irreducible nature of the author's signature, the trace of the body writing. For Cixous, the signature of the author tells the whole story of *The Hour of the Star* and its multiply impoverished heroine, Macabea: "I, Rodrigo S.M., I am in truth Clarice Lispector put in parentheses, and only the author '(in truth Clarice Lispector)' can approach this beginning of a woman. This is the impossible truth. It is *the inexpressible, indemonstrable truth,* which can be said only in parentheses . . . It is the truth, a woman, beating like a heart, in the parenthesis of life." In the parenthetical truth of the creation of the female character by the female author within the male narrator lies a mystery: "The identity of the 'I' who cannot answer." In witnessing existence in the parentheses of the text, Cixous seeks freedom from the confining authorizations of names: "We are much more than what our own name authorizes us and obligates us to believe we are . . . We are possible. Anyone. We need only avoid closing up the parentheses in which our 'why-nots' live."

Our "why-nots" are often the unprivileged, who are often women. In **"Coming to Writing,"** Cixous describes an idealized vision of what a writing-voyage would be for the elite: "for this elite, the gorgeous journey without horizon, beyond everything, the appalling yet intoxicating excursion toward the never-yet-said." But for woman, devoured by "the jealous Wolf, your ever-insatiable grandmother," there is the "vocation of the swallowed up, voyage of the scybalum." In a social structure hungry to consume them, women are limited to the voyage of the digestive tract, to literal incorporation. The world of the fairy tale is a maze of lost paths filled with dangerous encounters: "For the daughters of the housewife: the straying into the forest." In this forest, the wolf is the site of the legendary struggle with the enigma: "Instead of the great enigmatic duel with the Sphinx, the dangerous questioning addressed to the body of the Wolf: What is the body for? Myths end up having our hides. Logos opens its great maw, and swallows us whole."

But in the writing-voyage, the (domestic) forest resonates as more than the haunted site of the fairy tale. It is also the paradigm for the *"Claricewege,"* Cixous's adaptation of the Heideggerian *Holzwege* to Lispector's writing: "Thinking according to Clarice, I immediately come to think of Heidegger and his *Holzwege:* 'Trails in the wood, trails that lead nowhere, that trail.'" The *Holzweg* has, significantly, been used to pinpoint the end of philosophy, the point at which it no longer moves ahead. Louis Althusser claimed that the only possible contemporary philosophy would be theoretical discourse *on* philosophy, because philosophy had become limited to "a path leading nowhere, a *'Holzweg.'*" But for Cixous, the Claricean *Holzweg* allows the reader to live the path as source. "The Clarice-voice gives us the ways. A fear takes hold of us. Calls us: 'There are nothing but ways.' Gives-takes our hand. A deeply moved, clairvoyant fear—we take it. Leads us. We *make* ways." The trails that trail give the gift of the present in its infinity of possible forms; they teach vulnerability to "the two great lessons of living: slowness and ugliness." Entering the forest of the *Claricewege,* the writing body is the subject of a movement that is not *logomotion* but love of motion, trust of fear, trust of slowness. In the dark trails, we encounter Hélène Cixous, a philosopher—in Red Riding Hood's clothing—of an ongoing feminine tradition. She helps the reader make her way to the question: What is the reader in truth?

Translating the resonant poetics of Hélène Cixous's work into anything but her particular language—which is not French, not German, but poetry—is a difficult (Promethean?) task in which the reader must participate for full effect. The gathering connotative force of Cixous's wordplay resists any word-for-word equivalence.

And no truly appropriate explanatory apparatus has ever been found for poetry. Endnotes are one way of documenting the necessarily unstable process of translation, which Barbara Johnson has called "an exercise in violent approximation." However, since endnotes do interrupt the musical flow of the text, I have tried to minimize their intervention.

Among previous translators of her work, Betsy Wing in **The Newly Born Woman** chose to render words that were "too full of sense" in the original through "a process of accretion" in the translation. Yet the explicit presentation of a series of terms in answer to the poetic multiplicity of one term bypasses the relationship between the reader and the French text, in which several meaning may be called into action at once or allowed to lie dormant. The present translators have more frequently chosen a one-to-one relationship of the English terms to the French, although these terms may function simply as signposts to other possible readings. In the end, it is hoped the reader of this collection will accept the author's invitation to lend it a little "soul."

---

**An excerpt from "Coming to Writing"**

Writing is good: it's what never ends. The simplest, most secure other circulates inside me. Like blood: there's no lack of it. It can become impoverished. But you manufacture it and replenish it. In me is the word of blood, which will not cease before my end.

At first I really wrote to bar death. Because of a death. The cruelest kind, the kind that doesn't spare anything, the irreparable. It goes like this: you die in my absence. While Isolde is not there, Tristan turns to the wall and dies. What happens between that body and that wall, what doesn't happen, pierces me with pain and makes me write. Need for the Face: to get past the wall, to tear up the black sail. To see my loss with my own eyes; to look loss in the eye. I want to see the disappearance with my own eyes. What's intolerable is that death might not take place, that I may be robbed of it. That I may not be able to live it, take it in my arms, savor a last breath on its lips.

I write the encore. Still here, I write life. Life: what borders on death.

*Hélène Cixous, in "Coming to Writing" and Other Essays, Harvard University Press, 1991.*

---

**Morag Shiach    (essay date 1991)**

SOURCE: "Politics and Writing," in *Hélène Cixous: A Politics of Writing,* Routledge, 1991, pp. 6-37.

[*In the following excerpt, Shiach analyzes the development of Cixous's ideas about the relationships between writing, subjectivity, sexuality, and social change.*]

Despite the range of her fictional and dramatic texts, it is as a literary theorist that Hélène Cixous is best known in the English-speaking world. Her essays on writing and sexual difference have been a crucial point of reference for feminist theorists and critics, and her insistence on the transformative and broadly political dimensions of writing has constituted an important challenge to the unfocused aestheticism of much of literary studies. In this [essay] I will analyse the development of Cixous's ideas about the relations between writing and subjectivity, sexuality, and social change. Many of Cixous's arguments are developed in the context of close reading of literary texts, and I have thus returned to such texts where it seems helpful to do so, in order to identify the specificity of Cixous's readings.

Cixous's theorization of the politics of writing begins with an examination of the philosophical, political, and literary bases of patriarchy. In **'Sorties'**, an essay published in 1975, Cixous describes the set of hierarchical oppositions which, she argues, have structured western thought, and governed its political practice. She cites oppositions such as 'culture/nature'; 'head/heart'; 'form/matter'; 'speaking/writing', and relates them to the opposition between 'man' and 'woman'. In each case, her critique of these rigid oppositions does not amount simply to an argument against dualism but rather to a political and philosophical rejection of the dialectical relation between each of these 'couples', which privileges one term of the opposition:

> Theory of culture, theory of society, symbolic systems in general—art, religion, family, language—it is all developed while bringing the same schemes to light. And the movement whereby each opposition is set up to make sense is the movement through which the couple is destroyed. A universal battlefield. Each time, a war is let loose. Death is always at work. (**'Sorties'**)

Cixous does not invent these systems of oppositions: she reads them off a series of literary, mythical, and philosophical texts, finding their purest articulation in Hegel's *Phenomenology of Spirit*. The danger, for Cixous, in such philosophical and social categories, lies in their absolute dependence on strategies of power and exclusion. Each couple is based on the repression of one of its terms, yet both terms are locked together in violent conflict. Without 'nature', 'culture' is meaningless, yet culture must continually struggle to negate nature, to dominate and control it, with obviously deadly results.

Cixous's earliest recognition of the effects of such hierarchical opposition took place in relation to the mechanisms of colonialism. Her experience of French rule in Algeria led her to identify a basic structure of power: the Arab population was both necessary to, and despised by, the French colonial power. Algeria, she argues, could never have been 'France': it was perceived as different and as dangerous. Yet the mechanisms of colonial rule necessitated its identification as 'French', as tied in a relation of dependence to the French state. Cixous thus identifies colonialism as a prime example of a dualist structure of unequal power, visited by the constant threat of violence. Both sides of the opposition are locked together, and the autonomy of one—in this case, Algeria—must constantly be negated by the other.

Such dialectical structures, Cixous argues, also dominate the formation of subjectivity, and thus of sexual difference. Cixous uses Hegel's 'master/slave' dialectic as the paradigm of a form of subjectivity which is both limited and destructive: 'a subjectivity that experiences itself only when it makes its law, its strength, its mastery felt'. Here, subjectivity requires the recognition of an Other, from whom the individual differentiates him- or herself. Yet this recognition is experienced as threatening, and the Other is immediately repressed, so that the subject can return to the security and certainty of self-knowledge: 'the dialectic, the subject's going out into the other *in order to come back* to itself, this entire process . . . is, in fact, what is commonly at work in our everyday banality'.

This structure of subjectivity is related to the other 'couples' which Cixous has described: particularly 'man/woman'. Woman, within a patriarchal social and cultural formation, becomes figured, represented, as the Other, necessary to the constitution and recognition of identity, but always threatening to it. Sexual difference is thus locked into a structure of power, where difference, or otherness, is tolerated only when repressed. The movement of the Hegelian dialectic depends on an inequality of power between the two terms of opposition. Such inequality is then understood as the very basis of desire, that relation to the Other that is organized round the fear of castration, of loss and of otherness: 'It is *inequality* that triggers desire, as a desire—for appropriation. Without inequality, without struggle, there is inertia . . .'. Thus is constructed a desire that, Cixous argues, offers women the choice between 'castration' and 'decapitation': between internalization of a structure of desire based on loss, or deadly violence.

Cixous's identification of this strategy of sexual differentiation is derived from the consideration of literary texts, of cultural representations. The story of the Sleeping Beauty seems to her typical of this structure of desire. The woman is represented as sleeping, as possessed of negative subjectivity, until her encounter with male subjectivity, with the kiss. The kiss gives her existence, but only within a mechanism that immediately subordinates her to the desire of 'the prince'. Cixous's reading of Joyce's *Ulysses* leads her to similar conclusions. Here the socio-cultural construction of women characters intersects with the structure of desire Cixous has described, to produce the figure of woman as confined to the marriage-bed, to childbirth, and to the death-bed: 'as if she were destined—in the distribution established by men . . . to be the nonsocial, nonpolitical, nonhuman half of the living structure'.

It is important, here, to recognize the complexity of the relations that Cixous describes between the figure of 'woman', and women as historical subjects. Her argument depends on the importance of literary, philosophical, and mythical discourse to the formation of subjectivity. Such discourses do not exhaust the possibilities of subjectivity for individual women, but they do provide the structures in terms of which such subjectivity must be negotiated. The description of the construction of the figure of 'woman', and of its relation to mechanisms of desire, is thus of more than academic, or even philosophical, interest for women: it is the space in which they are placed by culture, and against which they must negotiate their own subjectivity.

Cixous describes her own historical recognition of this fact. Having first identified herself in terms of a common struggle, against colonialism and oppression, she comes to recognize that her gender makes such identification with a shared historical struggle problematic: 'No longer can I identify myself simply and directly with Samson or inhabit my glorious characters. My body is no longer innocently useful to my plans . . . I am a woman'. She comes to see her own struggle as necessarily complicated by her gender, which cuts across available narratives of collective identity:

> 'We' struggle together, yes, but who is this 'we'? A man and beside him a thing, somebody . . . someone you are not conscious of, unless she effaces herself, acts the man, speaks and thinks that way. For a woman, what I am saying is trite. It has often been said. It is that experience that launched the front line of the feminist struggle in the U.S. and in France; discovering discrimination, the fundamental unconscious racism in places where, theoretically, it should not exist! A political irony . . .'

Cixous's strategies for transforming this dual, hierarchized structure of philosophical and political thought, and of cultural representations, are twofold. The first procedure amounts to a deconstructive reading, which is presented as a critique of the narrative of origins, of the 'Dawn of Phallocentrism'. This reading is intended to question the naturalness or inevitability of such structural hierarchies. The second involves an exploration of the subversive, and the political, possibilities of a writing practice that sets itself up in opposition to such cultural categorization: a writing practice that Cixous describes as 'feminine'.

Cixous's representation of her project relies heavily on spatial metaphor. It thus amounts not simply to description, but to a writing practice that depends on allusion, metaphorization, and intertextual reference. Cixous compares her attack on the origins of patriarchy to a mining of foundations: 'We are living in an age where the conceptual foundation of an ancient culture is in the process of being undermined by millions of a species of mole . . . never known before'. The actions of this mole include the unearthing of the myths that sustain the logic of patriarchy, undoing their 'naturalness', and opening up the energies buried within them. This image of burial, and of possible mining and reworking, is reminiscent of Freud's observations on female sexuality. Freud comments on the surprise of his belated discovery of a period in the development of female sexuality that precedes the Oedipal in the following archaeological terms:

> Our insight into this early, pre-Oedipus phase in girls comes to us as a surprise, like the discovery in another field of the Minoan-Mycenean civilization behind the civilization of Greece.

Cixous's archaeological researches lead her to an engagement with the mythical narratives surrounding the figure of Electra, through which she aims to provide a deconstructive reading of the 'Dawn of Phallocentrism', as she explores the possibilities of mining beneath the fixed structures of hierarchical dualities. She is also concerned with origins, with the recapturing of plurality in the face of teleology, and with 'the Law'.

The Law is understood as an abstract structure of prohibition and exclusion, and Cixous dramatizes what she sees as the dominant relation to the Law within patriarchy, through a reading of Kafka's short story, 'Before the Law'. This story deals with a man who arrives before a doorway which gives access to the Law. When he arrives, the door is lying open, but the bearded doorkeeper convinces him that he cannot gain entry. Many years pass, as the man still stands in front of the door, apparently unable to enter. Eventually, however, 'before he dies, all his experiences in these long years gather themselves in his head to one point, a question he has not yet asked the doorkeeper'. He asks the doorkeeper why no-one else has come to the door seeking entry to the Law. The doorkeeper replies, 'No-one else could ever be admitted here, since this gate was made only for you. I am now going to shut it.' There had been no barrier, no exclusion, except in the man's own perception of his relation to the Law. The knowledge of this fact, however, will die with him. Cixous uses this story as a compelling metaphor for women's relation to patriarchy: a social structure in which women submit to the Law, and die of it. Like Kafka's hero, women under patriarchy redirect the power of which they are a source against themselves.

Cixous supports this analysis with a reading of the figure of Electra, as dramatized by Aeschylus and Sophocles. She starts with what might seem an unhelpfully teleological narrative: **'The Dawn of Phallocentrism'** ('Sorties'). Cixous's analysis begins with a quotation from Freud's *Moses and Monotheism*:

> it came about that the matriarchal social order was succeeded by the patriarchal one—which, of course, involved a revolution in the juridical conditions that had so far prevailed. An echo of this revolution still seems to be audible in *The Oresteia* of Aeschylus. But this turning from the mother to the father points in addition to a victory of intellectuality over sensuality—that is, an advance in civilization, since maternity is proved by the evidence of the senses while paternity is a hypothesis, based on an inference and a premiss.

Freud's argument about the development of patriarchy was not new: he was clearly indebted to the earlier theories of Bachofen, developed by Engels, which analysed the importance of this moment of transformation from matriarchy to patriarchy. Both writers had argued for the existence of an earlier social formation based on the principles of matriarchy, with Engels relating the development of patriarchy explicitly to the growth of private property. We do not, of course, have to understand such analyses of matriarchy as literally, or historically, true: we can read them instead as a mythological positing of origins, or as narratives that seek to represent the development of patriarchy as progress, a movement from the sensual to the spiritual, and thus as emblematic of civilization. Such narratives always risk, however, being read against the grain: that is to say, they can be read for the extent to which they make a structure other than patriarchy conceivable, and bring such a structure within the sphere of representation. We do not have to believe in the historical existence of matriarchy in order to make it sound like a good idea.

Cixous reads the *Oresteia* as a narrative of the formation of patriarchy. Seeing Orestes as placed at a turning point in history, Cixous focuses on the debate in the *Eumenides* over the relative claims of revenge for murder of a husband and murder of a mother. She draws attention to Apollo's ruling that 'the woman you call the mother of the child / is not the parent, just a nurse to the seed . . . / the *man* is the source of life', an account of reproduction that diminishes the gravity of matricide, and thus seems to license the development of patriarchal social relations.

Cixous's interest in the *Oresteia,* and in the figure of Electra, does not, however, lie simply in the ways in which it dramatizes the origins of patriarchy: her aim is not to reprimand Aeschylus. Instead, she wants to read what is repressed in this myth of origins, to recapture the violence, the excess, and the death, that are an inescapable part of this putting-in-place of patriarchy; her project in reading the *Oresteia* is to challenge the seamless teleology of the narrative, and its apparent equation with progress. She explores the importance of deceit: the ways in which Orestes' pretended death is elaborately set up and developed, particularly in Sophocles' text:

> Under disguise and deviously hidden-hiding-disclosing in himself more than one nonhuman being, as being more than human, the shifty brother sets time ticking and exploded the feminine nucleus. (**'Sorties'**)

This deceit is set alongside the disproportionate power given to the dead:

> The dead-father, Agamemnon (was he ever anything other than dead, except the day he was killed? Clytemnestra asks, but no-one hears the question), is in the strongest position: the position of death.

Cixous is fascinated by the active role of the dead, and by the different relations Electra and Orestes develop with their dead father. Electra calls to him to return, and asks him to take pity, but Orestes tries to blackmail him, saying that in return for intervention Orestes will keep his father alive. This relation between Orestes and his father, implicated as it is with blackmail and with death, is represented by Cixous as paradigmatic of the relations of patriarchy:

> In a certain way the father is always unknown. Coming from outside, he has to enter and give proof. Outsiders, absolutely other, strangers, ghosts, always capable of coming back. . . . Coming out of the earth to go back into the mother, into the palace, to reappropriate bodies and goods.
>
> That is what is called civilization.
>
> Progress, says Freud, whose logic thus expresses his self-interest in circular performances: 'Father, prefer me, so that feeling I am preferred, my self-confidence will grow so that I can call you "father" all the more loudly.'

About this progress in 'spirituality' Cixous is scathing, fo-

cusing on its deathly, tomb-like location, and on its negation of much of the energy that has circulated around the figure of Electra. Electra is seen by Cixous as the leader of the phallocrats: her voice is the loudest in the demand for the death of her mother, Clytaemnestra. As such, Cixous contrasts her with the one last Great Woman, the one no man could 'keep', the inalterable Helen, or Hélène, whose departure 'left her land *chaos,* clanging shields / companions tramping, bronze prows, men in bronze'. Yet Helen is banished from the text of the *Oresteia,* and only Electra remains as the source of disruption. Archphallocrat, she is none the less disruptive in her excess. She generates a kind of 'Electricity', which lightens up the twilight of matriarchy. She manifests an 'infernal libido', and nothing can silence her voice; although, of course, Aeschylus silences her effectively by simply dropping her from the play with her final line containing the ironic demand 'hear us'. Sophocles has Electra say, 'I will never cease my dirges and sorrowful laments', and this ceaselessness, Cixous argues, takes her outside the circuit of exchange between father and son, outside the Law.

Electra occupies an ambiguous space, stretched between inside and outside, in relation to the family and the Law. She is at the threshold, but unlike Kafka's anonymous man she is not silent. She delivers 'a stream of cries, that won't run out, torment's spring that won't go dry' (**'Sorties'**). She is compared by Cixous to the effects of yellow amber when rubbed—that is, to Electricity. She interacts with the Chorus, Clytaemnestra, Chrysothemis, 'light bodies, attracted by magnetic Electra: an intense system of exchange, attraction, particle loss fed by Electra'. Only Orestes is doggedly immune from the power of this electricity. Electra, Cixous argues, is both not woman and too much woman. She 'blazes the trail' to patriarchy, but in doing so generates energy and anger, which cannot easily be contained. Orestes recommends caution and silence, and struggles desperately to domesticate Electra.

The putting-in-place of patriarchy, which we can just as well understand as a metaphor for its continued operation, thus generates anger, excess, a voice that seems to escape control and instead goes underground, presumably to join the moles. The subjective and social 'splitting' this process involves is dramatized in the *Oresteia,* whose characters live their relation to the forms of patriarchy and matriarchy in their simultaneous presence:

> In this time of reversal everything is two-faced: one face still looks towards and old order; one face envisages the new power. The promised cutting works away on the body of each one.

Clytaemnestra is pulled to the past, haunted by dreams. Orestes lives a doubly double life: having died and not-died, and being doubled by Pylades, his 'silent shadow'. This image of subjectivity torn between two cultural orders, disputing possession of the body, is one that will recur frequently in **'Sorties'** as Cixous theorizes the political potential of writing within her own history.

Her deconstructive reading of the *Oresteia* leads Cixous to challenge the notion that Aeschylus simply reinforces the hierarchical opposition 'feminine/masculine'. After all, she argues, the *Oresteia* is a mixed and undecided site, wherein active and passive forces clash, without being absolutely attributed to sexual difference. We can see examples of this in some of the unexpected attributions of 'femininity' and 'masculinity' in the text: Agamemnon complaining that in his homecoming he is treated like a woman; or Clytaemnestra becoming the bull who gores Agamemnon according to Cassandra's prophecy. None the less, Cixous argues, there is an attempt at closure in the text, and one which seeks to eradicate the echoes of Electra's voice. The patriarchal order is set in place ('patriarchy—politicaleconomy—sexualeconomy—it has all sorted itself out since they checkmated those great screeching females') and the electricity disappears from the text.

In looking at this narrative of **'The Dawn of Phallocentrism'**, then, Cixous sought to open out the myth of Electra. She wanted to undermine the naturalness of the narrative, to set in play the violence, excess, splitting, and death that surround the moment of transformation from matriarchy to patriarchy, or rather that reverberate beneath the structures of patriarchal social relations. There are no feminist heroines in these texts of antiquity (except perhaps Hélène), and Electra is certainly not held up as the ideal of femininity. She is, however, seen as the site of articulation of much that is excluded from accounts of subjectivity that are based on a relation of power over the other, and also as a troubling complexity in the mythic origins of patriarchy.

Cixous's deconstructive reading of the origins of patriarchy shows great awareness of her own embeddedness in such narratives: their power is precisely the point of her analysis. Yet as feminist critique the reading is often frustrating, leading to qualifications, tentative propositions, and ambiguous conclusions. The feeling of swimming in cultural mud is almost palpable, and it is with some relief that one turns to the other element of her strategy—the construction of an alternative practice of writing. As Cixous says: 'What I say has at least two sides and two aims: to break up, to destroy; and to foresee the unforeseeable, to project.'

The first element of Cixous's theorization of the practice of feminine writing can be found in her discussion of alternative representations of sexual difference. She rejects the Freudian and Lacanian models, which she sees as condemning women to negativity in their privileging of the phallus as the organizing point of sexual identity and desire. Instead, she argues for the possibility of sustaining not as a denial of sexual difference, but as a lived recognition of plurality, of the simultaneous presence of masculinity and femininity within an individual subject. Such bisexuality is open to all subjects who can escape from the subjective and social effects of the dominant structures of desire. Yet, Cixous argues, it is of particular relevance to women, since they have been the greatest victims of patriarchy:

> For historical reasons, at the present time it is woman who benefits from and opens up within this bisexuality beside itself, which does not annihilate differences but cheers them on, pursues them, adds more. (**'Sorties'**)

Cixous further argues that writing is a privileged space for the exploration of such non-hierarchically arranged bisexuality. Writing, she believes, can be the site of alternative economies: it is not obliged simply to reproduce the system. This argument is developed in the context of close readings of a series of texts, by Kleist, Shakespeare, and Genet, which she sees as dramatizing the limitations and violence of the *propre*, a term suggesting propriety, property, and homogeneity, which is generally translated as 'the selfsame'. She favours texts that are excessive in their characterization, that undermine the fixed categories of sexual identity. Thus, for example, Kleist's *Penthesilea*, the drama of an Amazon queen, attracts Cixous's attention. She charts the unsettling of economies of war caused by the passionate love between Achilles and Penthesilea, and follows their relationship through to its catastrophic end: Penthesilea literally devours Achilles, consumes his flesh. Such violence, she argues, is both terrible and inevitable, revealing as it does the stakes invested in the economy of opposition and war.

---

> Cixous's writings on writing, and on its political potential, are a compound of the biographical, the strategic, and the theoretical. She offers her own history as part of her writing, as part of bringing other women to writing.
>
> —*Morag Shiach*

---

From a commitment to the possibility of bisexuality, and its political importance for women, and a belief in the disruptive potential of writing, Cixous moves towards the production of a form of writing that would embody such bisexuality and operate in the interests of women. Her best-known statement of this project is contained in **'The Laugh of the Medusa'**. This essay was published in 1975, in an issue of the journal *L'Arc* dedicated to Simone de Beauvoir. Much of the material in the essay is also contained in **'Sorties'**, but is presented in **'The Laugh of the Medusa'** in more polemical fashion: most of the deconstructive argument is absent, leaving a seemingly less tentative, and perhaps less careful, but much more bracing version of her writing project. The rhetorical power of this essay is perhaps clearer in French, where a passage such as

> Nous, les précoces, nous les refoulées de la culture, les belles bouches barrées de bâillons, pollen, haleines coupées, nous les labyrinthes, les échelles, les espaces foulés; les volées,—nous sommes 'noires' *et* nous sommes belles.

with its alliteration, its measured rhythm, its exploitation of the gendered nature of the French language, and its allusion to the 'Song of Songs' produces a more powerful effect than its English equivalent:

> We, the precocious, we the repressed of culture,

our lovely mouths gagged with pollen, our wind knocked out of us, we the labyrinths, the ladders, the trampled spaces, the bevies—we are black and we are beautiful.

This essay has undoubtedly provoked strong reactions, and has been the focus of many of the frequent charges of 'essentialism': the claim that Cixous reduces women to an essence, specifically an anatomical essence, and thus negates the possibility of the very change which she seeks to promote. It is thus worth considering the dimensions of her argument in some detail.

**'The Laugh of the Medusa'** begins by explaining that Cixous is trying to explore what feminine writing *'will do'*. She is not trying to analyse what women have actually written, nor is she describing a writing technique that is natural to, or inevitable for, women. Her tentativeness is an important part of her argument, despite its polemic. In **'Sorties'** Cixous is very careful to distinguish her analysis of sexuality from what she sees as the essentialism of Freud or Ernest Jones. Their theories, she says, rely on the visible: on the presence or absence of the penis, or of an essential femininity. They are thus, she argues, 'voyeur's theories', tied to the metaphysics of presence. Instead, Cixous tries to locate sexual difference at the level of sexual pleasure, of *jouissance.* To some extent, this is clearly a strategic move. It removes any possibility of identifying femininity and masculinity with the certainties of anatomical difference. It also places sexual difference in the realm of the unknowable. Apart from Tiresias, a figure to whom Cixous will return in **Le Nom d'Oedipe,** no-one, after all, is in a position to speak definitively about the dimensions of feminine and masculine *jouissance.* The insistence on libido as the location of sexual difference thus offers to Cixous the possibility of theorizing an alternative economy, of proposing an economy in which women, for historical and cultural reasons, have a particular investment, without allowing anyone the possibility of proving her wrong. Of course, it is also true that her theory cannot be confirmed, but since its function is strategic, intended to offer a political site of identification and shared struggle, this does not concern her unduly.

The location of sexual difference at the level of *jouissance,* however, does certainly return Cixous to the bodily; and that is where she wants to be:

> By writing her self, woman will return to the body which has been more than confiscated from her, which has been turned into the uncanny stranger on display—the ailing or dead figure, which so often turns out to be the nasty companion, the cause and location of inhibitions. Censor the body and you censor breath and speech at the same time. (**'The Laugh of the Medusa'**)

She does not, however, equate the bodily with nature. She sees it as distinctly cultural, as caught up in representation, in language. As Barbara Freeman has argued:

> It is precisely the assumption of a non-textual body outside of language, of a linguistic domain which is not itself corporeal that Cixous's reformulation of mind-body relations in a feminine economy calls into question.

Cixous argues that women's relations to their bodies are culturally inscribed, are related to the placing of women in the sphere of the domestic, and to their lesser social possibilities for sublimation. She speculates on the possibility that the capacity to give birth may mean that women have a specific relation to their bodies, but is always aware of the dangers of being too dogmatic. Her most unambiguous statement of the power of sexual difference in **'Sorties'** is followed by a painstaking articulation of the difficulties such a claim faces:

> But we must make no mistake: men and women are caught up in a web of age-old cultural determinations that are almost unanalyzable in their complexity. One can no more speak of 'woman' than of 'man' without being trapped within an ideological theater where the proliferation of representations, images, reflections, myths, identifications, transform, deform, constantly change everyone's Imaginary and invalidate in advance any conceptualization. . . . But we are still floundering—with a few exceptions—in Ancient History.

Cixous's return to the body is not an idiosyncratic move. She is writing at a moment when many philosophers and literary critics were returning to the bodily as the location of pleasure. The following extract:

> To write the body, neither the skin, nor the muscles, nor the bones, nor the nerves, but the rest: an awkward fibrous, shaggy, raveled thing, a clown's coat

is not from Cixous but from Roland Barthes, in a text where he explores the bodily, as well as the discursive, constitution of his subjectivity. None the less, Cixous's commitment to the experience of writing as bodily has caused particular problems for feminist critics. Jane Gallop has written very interestingly about this problem: about the reluctance within feminist theory to accept 'the body as metaphor, a demand that metaphors of the body be read literally.' Gallop attributes this reluctance to an association of the bodily with the natural, to a refusal to think through the extent to which the bodily, and experiences of sexuality, are cultural, are mediated by discourse: the extent to which we know and experience our bodies in relation to representation and narrative. To some extent, she is clearly correct, yet the worry is more substantial. Writing of the body, we fear appropriation at the point where, historically, we have been most vulnerable, and where we have been so ruthlessly placed.

The most considered and careful analysis of the dilemmas of a return to the bodily, and particularly to images of maternity, is contained in Domna C. Stanton's 'Difference on Trial: A Critique of the Maternal Metaphor in Cixous, Irigaray and Kristeva'. Stanton's argument shares many of the reservations of Alice Jardine's *Gynesis,* which explores the difficulties for feminist theorists of taking over the deconstructive project, with its privileging of the 'feminine', and its silence about women. Stanton's reading is powerful, and refers in considerable detail to Cixous's fiction as well as to her theoretical writings. Her basic anxiety is that Cixous is returning to a metaphysics of identity and presence. The use of metaphor itself, she argues, alludes to an economy of similitude, rather than one of difference. Cixous's choice of the maternal as the strategic point of engagement with the politics of sexual difference, however, raises particular issues for Stanton, threatening as it does to return to the certainties of biology, and the 'naturalness' of motherhood.

To this dilemma there is, it seems, no answer, at least not within the political discourse of feminism. To evade the bodily is to reproduce a structure of oppression which has made of women's bodies their point of vulnerability and of guilt. To speak of the bodily risks a similar reproduction. At a fairly trite level, it is clear there is no escape. Yet this should not surprise us: one cannot simply walk out of patriarchy and shake off its effects. What Cixous tries to do is to subvert the discourse of patriarchy, to open it up to contradiction and to difference, while still retaining the possibility of shared recognition which would make a political movement of and for women possible. To what extent she succeeds cannot be answered in any totalizing or definitive way. For me, . . . some of her projections and mythical reworkings remain powerful, others produce unease. For others, such as Claudine Guégan Fisher or Verena Conley, the project as a whole is clearly both compelling and empowering. What is, however, clear, is that Cixous cannot be accused of *naïveté,* or epistemological ignorance. She knows the dangers of essentialism—'if one subscribes to . . . "anatomy is destiny"', one participates in condemning woman to death'—and recognizes both 'the mother' and 'the body' as profoundly embedded in the cultural. What she does insist on, however, is that that 'cultural' is organized differently for men and women, and that a writing practice that will reformulate the cultural will be of particular importance for women.

Cixous theorizes an alternative economy of femininity in relation to the concept of 'the gift'. She describes two possible attitudes to giving and to the intersubjective relations involved in the gift: one, which she describes as 'masculine', is caught up in the mechanisms of exchange, and will give only with a certainty of immediate return. Exchange relations assume, by definition, abstract equality, at least for the moment of exchange, and thus exclude the recognition of difference. Cixous's alternative, or feminine, economy of giving seems to be derived to some extent from the work of the anthropologist Marcel Mauss, and from the development of Mauss's ideas by Georges Bataille, and by Jacques Derrida. Mauss's work was concerned with forms of social exchange that preceded 'the purely individual contract of the market place'. His research into the social relations of other societies, and of earlier historical periods, led him to produce a theory of 'the gift', as a form regulating intersubjective relations which was both morally loaded and socially implicated. His text came to be read as a form of critique against the individualism and moral irresponsibility of abstract market relations. In adopting the concept of 'the gift', in advocating a form of giving that is not reducible to a single act of exchange, Cixous is not, as is often suggested, adopting the discourse of idealism, but is rather mobilizing a materialist account of social relations which constitutes a critique of 'mass society'. This particular coincidence of modernist aesthetics and an opposition to the cultural and political implications of 'mass culture' will be discussed further [elsewhere].

Having described the limitations of the masculine economy of giving, and related this structure to the structure of dual hierarchized oppositions and murderous subjectivity described in **'Sorties',** Cixous goes on to posit an alternative:

> Can one speak of another spending? Really, there is no 'free gift'. You never give something for nothing. But the difference lies in the why and how of the gift, in the values that the gesture of giving affirms, causes to circulate; in the type of profit the giver draws from the gift and the use to which he or she puts it.

This different relation to giving is what Cixous sees as characteristic of an alternative, feminine, practice of writing. Such writing would not be afraid to go outside narrative structures, or to create subjectivities that are plural and shifting. It would not need to return to the security of fixed categories, of stable identity. It would *dépense:* a pun suggesting both the undoing of thought and a liberal spending of energies. It would be on the side of excess.

Cixous is very clear that feminine writing cannot be defined. She tries, particularly in **'The Laugh of the Medusa'**, to enact it. One characteristic which she does ascribe to it, however, is its proximity to voice. Partly, this is done in order to disrupt the opposition between speech and writing, by suggesting not only the presence of writing in speech, but also the potential presence of living speech in writing. It is also done in order to produce both individual and social change. Speaking, Cixous argues, is a powerfully transgressive action for women, whose bodies cannot be erased from their speech in the way that they have been from their writing. A woman speaking in public is seen first and foremost as a woman, not as a speaker. Finally, however, Cixous privileges speech because of its proximity to song, and thus to the unconscious: she wants to explore the associative logic of music over the linear logic of philosophical and literary discourse.

The specificity of feminine writing is also described in terms of spatial metaphor: 'If woman has always functioned "within" man's discourse . . . now it is time for her to displace this "within," explode it, overturn it, grab it, make it hers'. Similarly, Cixous talks of feminine writing as happening in the 'between', in that space which is uncertain, dangerous in its refusal to ally itself with one side of an opposition. Stepping outside, negotiating the between, feminine writing is to carve out a new space of representation that will not fit into old grids.

Producing this form of writing is, for Cixous, a political act, and is related to the desire to 'liberate the New Woman from the Old'. The gesture that characterizes the relation of women to the cultural is one of flying and stealing [*voler*]. Women, Cixous argues, must steal what they need from the dominant culture, but then fly away with their cultural booty to the 'in between', where new images, new narratives, and new subjectivities can be created.

The call to writing for women is most marked in **'The Laugh of the Medusa'**. Here Cixous speaks on behalf of women, and uses the pronoun 'we' with an ease and confidence that few of her other texts demonstrate. She knows, however, that many people will condemn her for this polemical strategy: 'Once more you'll say that all this smacks of "idealism," or what's worse, you'll splutter that I'm a "mystic" '. She has, indeed, been accused of both. As we have seen, however, the argument of Cixous's early theoretical texts, is more complex, more careful, and more strategic, than such charges acknowledge.

Cixous began by theorizing the possibility of a model of sexual difference not based on exclusion or hierarchy, and relating this to a model of subjectivity based on openness to the Other rather than obliteration of the Other. She then argued for the possibility of understanding such sexual difference, not at the level of possession or absence of the penis/phallus, but at the level of *jouissance*. Such libidinal difference was then related to particular practices of writing, since writing was seen as a privileged space for transgression and transformation. The style of writing which Cixous describes as 'feminine' was then derived from a reading of a variety of literary texts, most of them written by men. Finally, in the last stage of her argument, Cixous introduced women, as historical subjects, arguing that women have had most to lose in patriarchy, and have most to gain from its defeat: 'It is in writing, from woman and towards woman . . . that woman will affirm woman somewhere other than in silence'.

This focus on writing as a political strategy has very clear personal, and indeed biographical, significance for Cixous. This much is clear in reading Cixous's contribution to the volume entitled *La Venue à l'écriture,* which was published in 1977. Cixous's article in this volume amounts to a biographical and theoretical explanation of her own relation to writing. The volume also contains an article by Madeleine Gagnon, who tries to reclaim women's history through a reconsideration of the relations between sexuality and writing, and one by Annie Leclerc, who analyses problems of doubling, possession, and maternity through a reading of a painting by Vermeer. Echoing Cixous's project in **'Sorties',** Leclerc again likens women's strategies in writing to the burrowing of a mole:

> Ce sont les fondations que nous minons peu à peu . . . nous les taupes innombrables, obscures et malicieuses. (*La Venue*)
>
> [These are the foundations which we are mining little by little . . . we the moles who are beyond reckoning, dark and mischievous.]

Cixous's account of her relation to writing begins with her childhood, and in particular with the death of her father. She describes the ways in which writing seemed to offer the means to counteract the finality of death, a theme which also preoccupies her in *Prénoms de personne,* as well as in novels such as *Dedans* and *Tombe.* She also describes her entry into the texts and knowledges of the dominant culture, and the extent to which she felt they excluded her history and her experiences:

> Toutes les raisons pour lesquelles je croyais n'avoir pas le droit d'écrire, les bonnes et les moins bonnes, et les vraies fausses:—je n'ai pas de lieu d'où écrire. Aucun lieu légitime, ni terre, ni patrie, ni histoire à moi. (*Entre l'écriture*)
>
> [All the reasons for which I believed that I did not have the right to write, good reasons, less good reasons, and those that were true and false: I had no place from which to write. No legitimate place, no land, no homeland, no history of my own.]

Despite her early passion for writing, then, what she experiences in her encounter with the dominant culture is loss and exclusion.

This sense of exclusion is related by Cixous to her identity as both woman and Jew: both tending to exclude her, to make her vulnerable to the Law. Her relation to language is marked by the complexity of her national identities. Her father was a Sephardic Jew, whose family came originally from Spain, but moved first to Morocco, and then to Algeria, where Cixous grew up and was educated within the French educational system. Her mother was an Ashkenazi Jew, whose family came from various regions of what was the Austro-Hungarian Empire. Cixous's 'mother tongue' was thus German, although the languages that surrounded her in Algeria were French and Arabic. She considers the effects of such linguistic diversity on her attitude to writing. For example, she stresses the musicality of German, and its profound bodily resonances for her—an observation that can perhaps be linked to her interest in the voice as part of writing. Similarly, she observes that she has always been fascinated by the resources of different languages, and has approached each language delicately, in order to respect its specificity. The theoretical importance of this sense of linguistic distance and strangeness is stressed again by Cixous in a recent article where she writes that: 'the most important thing is that you never become too familiar and you never come to the point when you can hear it speak to you and you think you speak it'. Such a detached, but emotionally charged, relation to language gives us an interesting insight into Cixous's capacity to exploit the power of the signifier to exceed any fixed meaning, and into her tendency to push the resources of language to their limits.

As **'La Venue à l'écriture'** develops, what we experience is a sense of frustration, of urgency, and of anger. Again and again Cixous is confronted by the importance to her of writing, and by her incapacity to write. She is convinced that writing is the space of truth, and that truth is singular. Yet she experiences herself as heterogeneous, as made up of various identities, of many and varied desires, and concludes that she cannot be in the place of truth, or of writing. In reading this text we share Cixous's sense of frustration as she is repeatedly turned away from writing towards the restraint and the homogeneity in which she is culturally placed.

Eventually, however, Cixous describes her entry into writing: her first published volume of short stories came out when she was 30. The inner need to write is finally stronger than the pressures on her to silence. Women must have lost everything, have been driven to their limit, before they can risk the taboo of writing, Cixous argues. When they begin to write, they must remain in a critical relation to the languages and the narratives they inherit: they must invent new beginnings, remove themselves from the fixed categories and identities they have inhabited, explore the 'third body': which is neither the inside nor the outside, but the space between.

Only through such exploration, Cixous argues, can women challenge the culturally produced category of 'woman'. The figure of 'woman' is a representation, projected by the Law, formed by exclusion and censure and by modes of thought based on hierarchy and opposition. In writing, Cixous argues, women can explore other identifications, other images, can rediscover some of what has been unexpressed, actively repressed. She suggests that a new form of shared identity is possible for women, formed not in relation to 'woman', but rather in terms of shared unconscious patterns and forms, which are the product of shared histories worked out across shared bodies.

**'La Venue à l'écriture'** ends on the positive invocation of an identity for women that might not be caught in the negativities of 'woman'. It has a happy ending: Cixous, after all, has clearly 'come to writing'. Yet this triumphant conclusion remains remarkably fleeting, and slippery. Cixous's final image of women's relations to writing is of fish swimming in water: reassuring, but hard to pin down.

Cixous's writings on writing, and on its political potential, are, then, a compound of the biographical, the strategic, and the theoretical. She offers her own history as part of her writing, as part of bringing other women to writing. She always reads this history in negotiation with theoretical and literary texts that seem to give it a more generalizing power: the power to explain, and to produce recognition, however tentative. She is aware of the dangers inherent in trying to speak or write as a woman, and aims to pick her way through the minefield of cultural stereotype, literary figure, and lived history. If she does not always succeed, we can perhaps more usefully reflect on the tendency of mines to explode, than rush to conclude that the field was never worth crossing.

Discussion of Cixous's writing in the 1970s would not be complete, however, without some reference to the institutional and political contexts in which her work was produced, and read, since these contexts clearly overdetermined responses to Cixous's work, both in France and in the United States. The French feminist movement of the 1970s was unhappily divided. The movement had grown very significantly since 1968: frustration and anger at the exclusion of women from the political structures of '68 led to a variety of opposing analyses of the appropriate strategies and theories to adopt. To some extent, the divisions seem very familiar to anyone involved in the history of feminist struggle in Britain or the USA. Radical feminists stressed the priority of women's oppression to any political analysis. Socialist feminists worked to integrate feminist struggle into the agenda of the Left. One particular movement, however, was fairly specific to the French political and intellectual scene—the group called 'Psychanalyse et Politique' (*Psych et Po*) who struggled to develop revolutionary theories of the oppression of women on the basis of psychoanalytic theory. The most prominent member of this group was Antoinette Fouque, and it was the group with which Cixous was most clearly identified.

---

**Cixous is aware of the dangers inherent in trying to speak or write as a woman, and aims to pick her way through the minefield of cultural stereotype, literary figure, and lived history.**

**—*Morag Shiach***

---

*Psych et Po* set up the *des femmes* publishing house: an organization committed to the publishing of work by women, and in particular of contemporary work which seemed to fit within the parameters of 'feminine writing'. The bookshop *des femmes* was established in 1974, and the publishing house has continued to the present day. Despite its primary commitment to the publication of writing by women, *des femmes* does publish some work by men, and even appointed a man as commercial director in 1988. The political strategy of *Psych et Po* was based on the necessity of challenging the unconscious structures of patriarchal oppression, and their policy was the by-now familiar one of working like 'moles' to disturb the dominant cultural and political order. They were very hostile towards groups that described themselves as 'feminist', seeing such groups as reformist, and as working, simply to gain access to, and to reproduce, the structures of masculine power. They preferred to speak instead of the 'women's movement', and their outlook was resolutely internationalist, preferring to work on the possibilities of international support for women struggling against oppression, rather than to concentrate on domestic French politics. They were also committed to the importance of writing as a point of political struggle.

The single greatest area of conflict between *Psych et Po* and other feminist groups lay in their attitude towards 'difference'. Feminists associated with the journal *Questions Féministes,* including Christine Delphy, Monique Wittig, and Simone de Beauvoir, believed that any discussion of 'difference' in relation to women was bound to reproduce existing hierarchies, and could only play out the existing stereotypes of 'woman's nature'. *Psych et Po* rejected this analysis, claiming that the fear of 'difference' within feminism led to reformism and homogeneity, instanced, for example, by the failure of US feminism to address the question of race.

This disagreement is profound, with clear implications for political strategy. It continues to provide one of the pivotal points of debates within feminist theory, as books like *The Future of Difference* make clear. This theoretical difference, however, became overlaid with personal conflicts, displayed at conferences and in published texts and pamphlets. Tensions increased in the wake of legal actions initiated by *des femmes* against others involved in the women's movement, violent attacks on the bookshop *des femmes,* and the decision by *Psych et Po* to register 'MLF', the acronym of the Women's Liberation Movement, as their own trademark.

The passion and anger that went into these debates and conflicts is now, more than ten years later, rather hard to recapture. Their usefulness for the feminist movement is certainly hard to determine. Yet they are important in the context of this [essay], since they affected the ways in which Cixous's work was read. Cixous published her fictional work exclusively with *des femmes* between 1976 and 1982, and has recently begun publishing with them again. This relationship with *des femmes* placed her inside the parameters of the struggle over difference, and tended to produce an attitude either of total loyalty or complete rejection—neither tending to aid discussion of the range of her work.

The other context which is important to the reception of Cixous's work is her association with the University of Paris VIII (Vincennes). This section of the University of Paris was set up after 1968, and Cixous was involved with it from the beginning. Vincennes was established in conscious opposition to existing institutions of higher education. It admitted students with 'non-standard' entrance qualifications, including many overseas students; it was interdisciplinary; it strove to diminish hierarchies between teacher and student; it rejected examinations in favour of continuous assessment. It was also profoundly disliked by sections of the French establishment. It was at Vincennes that Cixous established the Centre d'Etudes Féminines, a centre committed to interdisciplinary research on the space of femininity within modernity. This development was explicitly attacked by the government, who took action in 1980 to prevent the awarding of higher degrees by the Centre. This action did not succeed in the long term, but it was an indication of the hostility with which Cixous's work was met by large sections of the political and literary establishment.

Throughout the 1970s, Cixous continued to produce large numbers of fictional texts which set in play her ideas about femininity and writing, and explored subjectivity and intertextuality. . . . Her next important statement of the theoretical issues crucial to her work, however, appeared in the journal *Etudes Freudiennes* in 1983. This took the form of an exploration of the figure of Tancredi, as represented by Torquato Tasso in *Jerusalem Delivered,* and by Rossini in the opera *Tancredi.* Cixous used the figure of Tancredi as a means to dramatize the complexity of sexual difference, and as a linking point between textual, unconscious, and biographical explorations of such difference.

Cixous's attitude to Tasso's Tancredi has clearly changed since she wrote **'Sorties'**. In **'Sorties'** she compared Tasso unfavourably with Kleist, arguing that Penthesilea and Achilles represented a much more transgressive form of desire than that represented by the relationship between Tancredi and Clorinda: 'Tancredi passionately reuniting with Clorinda the moment he destroyed her aspect as a warrior. No *jouissance* then . . .' But perhaps this shift should alert us to the dangers of claiming any 'definitiveness' for Cixous's readings of any given text. Cixous's readings are often related to a much wider project, aimed

at opening up theoretical and political difficulties, rather than at summing up a text.

The figure of Tancredi with which Cixous engages is derived from two different sources. Tasso's poem, written in the late sixteenth century, deals with the struggles of the Crusader army during the last few months before the conquest of Jerusalem in 1099. The Christian forces include Tancredi:

> With majesty his noble count'nance shone
> High were his thoughts, his heart was bold in
>     fight
> . . . His fault was love.

Tancredi meets by chance, and falls in love with, a Muslim warrior, Clorinda:

> This lusty lady came from Persia late,
> She with the Christians had encountered eft,
> And in their flesh had opened many a gate
> By which their youthful souls their bodies left.

During the course of a battle, Clorinda and Tancredi fight, unaware of each other's identity. Tancredi knocks off her helmet, recognizes her as the woman with whom he has fallen in love, and refuses to fight any more. Nine books later, they are once again locked in combat. By now we have heard Clorinda's life history, and have learned that she was actually born a Christian. Once again Tancredi is ignorant of his opponent's identity, and assumes he is fighting with 'some man of mickle might'. The struggle takes place at night, and continues with an intensity that lends to it an air of unreality, of dream. Eventually

> His sword into her bosom deep he drives,
> And bath'd in lukewarm blood his iron cold

and Clorinda dies, begging in her final moments for baptism. Only now does Tancredi realize what he has done. He

> 'gan to tear and rend
> His hair, his face, his wounds: a purple flood
> Did from each side in rolling streams descend.

Tancredi expresses horror at what he has done, and proclaims his wish to die. He is then 'rescued' by a priest, who accuses him of having been in thrall to a non-Christian, and threatens him with damnation. Finally, Clorinda returns to Tancredi in a dream, thanks him for saving her soul, and talks passionately of her love for him.

This brief summary cannot do justice to the epic dimensions of Tasso's poem, nor to the power of the transgression represented by Tancredi and Clorinda's love. The fusion of passion and violence, the continual postponement of questions of identity, the enormity of the stakes between Christianity and Islam combine to give this element of Tasso's poem a resonance that disturbs the seeming neatness of its conclusion.

Rossini's Tancredi is also a warrior, and is also involved in fighting against Islam. The story is adapted from a tragedy by Voltaire. Tancredi's lover in this story is Amenaide, a woman who is wrongly suspected by her lover, and by all those around her, of being a traitor. Confusions of identity are, once more, important: a letter sent by Amenaide to Tancredi is assumed to have been sent to the leader of the enemy forces. Amenaide is condemned to death by her own father for her treachery, but saved by Tancredi who defends her honour in single combat, despite believing in her guilt. Tancredi is then fatally injured in the battle against the Saracens, but lives long enough to learn of Amenaide's innocence, and to be reunited with her.

The coincidence of names has led many critics to conclude that Rossini derived the plot of his opera from Tasso. This is not, in fact, the case. The source is Voltaire's *Tancrède,* which is derived from a number of sources, including Ariosto. The confusion is not perhaps surprising. C. B. Beall notes:

> *Tancrède,* sujet qui vient de l'Arioste, mais dont l'esprit chevaleresque, la conception de l'amour et la scène de la mort prèsentent aussi des analogies avec le poème du Tasse.
>
> [*Tancrède,* a subject derived from Ariosto, but one in which the spirit of chivalry, the conception of love, and the death scene are also to some extent analogous to elements of Tasso's poem.]

Cixous is not at all concerned, however, to claim that these two Tancredis are, in fact, 'the same'. Instead, she exploits the confusion surrounding their relations: 'there are several Tancredis, which is why I am having such a hard time trying not to mislead us. . . . I am swimming between two Tancredis' (**'Tancredi Continues'**). Her aim is to develop an argument about sexual difference and its representation across these Tancredis, across Clorinda and Amenaide.

Perhaps the most important fact about Rossini's hero is that the part is sung by a woman. It is a *Travesti* role, originally, of course, destined for a *castrato,* but now providing a powerful and challenging role for singers of the calibre of Marilyn Horne. Cixous's argument is closely related to the fact of operatic performance, to the presence of the woman's body and voice within the heroic man.

Cixous begins by stating her fascination with Tasso's Tancredi and Clorinda, who move outside the rigid categories of opposition and war, driven on by the power of their love. What interests her is *'the movement of love',* its inherent grace, which she describes as a 'gracious exchange' between pleasures. This grace is set against the paralysis and limitations of fear. The abyss, the Law, is invented by our fear, and Cixous recommends the strategy of the acrobat, who leaps over the abyss with lightness and with grace.

When she turns to Rossini, Cixous tries to unravel the significance of the casting of Tancredi as a woman, a 'Tancreda'. Here, she argues, Rossini has perceived something essential to the character of Tancredi: his capacity to engage with the Other placing him firmly on the side of the feminine. This presence of the feminine in the masculine Cixous designates as 'Enigma', but also as her 'life work'.

Cixous then moves towards a recreation of the power of *Tancredi* in performance: remembering the physical presence of women, one in blue and one in white, singing of the power of their love. She is convinced that the force of that performance embodies an important secret about subjectivity and sexual difference, but is also tortured by her own inability to give form to this secret: 'I saw their secret. What I am telling of it is no more than light turned to dust'.

The importance of this 'secret' leads her to reproduce it in the form of a dream. She describes her dream of a turquoise, luminous, beautiful, hanging above her, just out of reach: inside the turquoise is a pearl. The turquoise embodies the secret, but it cannot be grasped. Here then in this fusion of blue and white, this 'inside' and 'outside', this transparency and opacity, is a symbol of the complexity of sexual difference. The blue and white, echoing the costumes of Tancredi and Amenaide, can then be read as figures of masculinity and femininity, clearly different, but hard to open up, or to separate.

The dream imagery gives way to a description of Cixous's own desire for a relationship of love that would not be limited and paralysed by the rigid hierarchies of masculinity and femininity. In some powerfully lyrical passages, Cixous describes her love for another person, a person who has suffered from the distortions of gender identity, yet who remains plural: 'In any case she is not a woman. She is plural. Like all living beings who are sometimes invaded, sometimes populated, incarnated by others'. 'She' also listens to *Tancredi,* which thus becomes something of a symbol of resistance to rigid categorization of sexual difference.

The point of Cixous's moving between text, performance, unconscious, and biography, lies in her unease about the capacity of words to hold out against the power of opposition. *Tancredi,* she argues, takes us to 'l'autre côté' [the other side] of hierarchies of sexual difference, another spatial metaphor which recurs in Cixous's texts, from her reading of Carroll's *Through the Looking-Glass* to her exploration of the Kingdom of the Dead in *La.* The problem, however, is how to describe this other side without making it simply a mirror image of what we already have.

The dilemma Cixous faces is that 'the more I try to say, the more I feel I have wandered astray far from what, beneath appearances and secretly and obscurely, I am sure I have understood'. She feels the pressure to produce formulae and solutions which are more dogmatic, more rigid, than her understanding of the 'movement' of sexual difference allows. She contemplates the possibility of giving up altogether on the project of trying to talk about sexual difference, about women and the economy of the feminine, since the pressure within this project to reproduce the dominant figure of the 'feminine' is so intense:

> But perhaps what is hardest and most necessary, is to positively forget these judges who make us answer their stupid summons stupidly, justify the non-justifiable, speak silence, crush the music under the millstone of words, lie by swearing to tell only their truth, plead guilty to a lack of absence.

She talks once more of feeling oppressed by the 'word police', who demand fixity of meaning and of purpose. The word 'woman', she argues, carries such cultural weight, exists within so many historically embedded discourses, that by saying it again we are perhaps simply enclosing ourselves once more.

The solution to this problem cannot be simple: it persists with urgency throughout the whole of Cixous's writing. In the end, she admits, it cannot be run away from: 'nowadays there are so many clandestine massacres of women that a woman has to say "woman" a dozen times a day in order to protest'. 'Tancredi Continues' is a contribution to the project of rethinking sexual difference. In it, Cixous tries to avoid the programmatic and the dogmatic, in favour of the allusive and the impressionistic. Her argument amounts to an insistence that we cannot determine the nature of 'femininity' once and for all, but can only hope, across a range of texts, to glimpse the possibility of a different economy of sexuality.

Cixous's continuing unease about the capacity of language to escape from cliché, and from the habitual, her frustration with its tendency towards reproduction of the status quo, has led her finally to consider the transgressive potential of painting as a form of representation. In an essay entitled **'Le dernier tableau ou le portrait de Dieu'** ['The Final Painting or the Portrait of God'] Cixous considers the potential of painting as a site of representations that challenge the cultural-embeddedness of language. The principal object of her analysis is Post-Impressionism. At first, what she detects in the paintings of Monet, or of Van Gogh, seems to be a kind of immediacy of visual and emotional impact. She describes her own desire to write like a painter: to communicate the full force of the instant, the colours and textures of the present moment. The same desire to express the intensity of the instantaneous is embodied in the concept of 'quasacles' ('quasi-miracle-instants') which Cixous describes, in a manner reminiscent of Woolf's 'moments of being' or Joyce's 'epiphanies', in her novel **With ou l'art de l'innocence**. This intensity and instantaneousness is, she suggests, something Clarice Lispector achieves, in a form of writing which has the force of a concentration of images, a series of paintings.

Cixous's attitude towards the painter at this point is one of jealousy: 'le peintre peut vous briser le coeur avec l'épiphanie d'une mer' [the painter can break you heart with the epiphany of a sea], while she herself can only name, or describe. This consideration leads her to a reflection on the emotional power of language, which she sees as necessarily intersubjective. Thus she speculates on whether the very limitation of language, its inability to capture the visual force of the present, may not be its strength: its power depending absolutely on the active contribution of the reader.

The opposition at this point seems to be between the instantaneous plenitude of painting and the temporal intersubjectivity of writing. Like all such oppositions, however, this one is soon challenged. Cixous turns to a consideration of the phenomenon of repetition: a phenomenon important to the argument of **Prénoms de personne**. When she turns to the series of Monet's paintings of Rouen Cathedral, plenitude disappears, to be replaced by time and deferral:

> Voir la vérité de la cathédrale qui est vingt-six, et la noter, c'est-à-dire voir le temps. Peindre le temps. Peindre le mariage du temps et de la lumière.

> [To see the truth of the cathedral that is twenty-six cathedrals, and to record it, that is to say to see time. To paint time. To paint the marriage of time and light.]

Painting then becomes a struggle against change and time, an attempt to capture the temporal within the instantaneous. The agonies of this process lead painters like Van Gogh to the necessity of speed in painting, as if quick execution could negate temporality, or even capture its form. Again Cixous sets up an opposition: between the slowness, the necessary deferral, of writing and the rapidity of visual representation.

What is at stake in this 'rapidity', for Cixous, is its power to force the painter outside the secure boundaries of the self, outside the categories of cultural expectation and cliché. Again the argument is one about 'grace': the audacious movement by the painter which refuses to acknowledge fear, in which the painter 'devient femme' [becomes woman]. The possibility of such agility leads Cixous to a consideration of how it might be achieved in writing, how the false step and the false word could be avoided. Her object is the rediscovery of simplicity, a concept whose theoretical weight is developed through readings of Kleist, Heidegger, and Lispector.

Kleist introduces the possibility of rediscovering innocence through knowledge. Heidegger stresses the power of visual representation to communicate the being of Being: 'Van Gogh's painting is the disclosure of what the equipment, the pair of peasant shoes *is* in truth. This entity emerges into the unconcealedness of its being.' Lispector provides the example of a form of writing that is painterly in its fidelity to the identity of individual things. The writer, Cixous argues, should imitate the painter in her refusal to stigmatize 'the ugly', in her capacity to see the possibility of significance and meaning in all objects.

The final turn against the 'plenitude' of representation comes when Cixous argues that the most important meaning of painting arises when all possibility of fixed meaning has been erased by repetition. Thus Monet's waterlilies, reappearing in so many different forms, point towards the infinite, the impossibility of closure in representation. The difficulty of painting points, however, towards the human importance of the attempt: the necessity to record the fact of impossibility, of repetition. In this project, Cixous states her alliance with the painter.

Yet one important difference remains. The painter deals with surfaces; Cixous wants to explore the inside, the underneath, the taste and the texture. When he was sent an apple as a gift, Monet could not bear to bite into it, and gave it away. This is an action Cixous rejects:

> Moi je l'aurais mangée. En cela je suis différente de ceux auxquels j'aimerais ressembler. Dans mon besoin de toucher la pomme sans la voir. De la connaître dans le noir. Avec mes doigts, avec mes lèvres, avec ma langue.

[For myself, I would have eaten it. In that way I am different from those I would like to resemble. In my need to touch the apple without seeing it. To know it in darkness. With my fingers, with my lips, with my tongue and my language.]

Finally, then, in this dialogue between the writer and the painter, the writer holds her own. She asserts the possibility of transforming knowledge and experience through writing, and writes herself out of the trap of 'the habitual' which has threatened so many theorists of modernism. The unease continues, however, about the complicity of writing with the hierarchical oppositions whose analysis was so important to **'Sorties'**. It is perhaps for this reason that Cixous turns, in the 1980s, to theatre: a space that seems to embody the troubled relations between temporality, repetition, and immediacy which so fascinated her in painting.

### Wendy Steiner   (review date 31 January 1992)

SOURCE: "From Narcissism to Seduction," in *The Times Literary Supplement*, No. 4635, January 31, 1992, p. 24.

[*Steiner is a Canadian-born American critic and educator who has written works on such authors as Gertrude Stein and Roman Jakobson. In the review below, she offers mixed assessments of* "Coming to Writing," *and Other Essays and* Readings. *Steiner concludes that* "Cixous embodies a paradox. . . . [She] represents a radical contemporaneity . . . but aesthetically she belongs in the early twentieth century."]

Ten years ago, Hélène Cixous, Julia Kristeva and Luce Irigaray were names to conjure with. Today, at least in France, "Feminism, like Marxism, structuralism, poststructuralism (or like the narrow striped tie?), is definitively *passé*." "No one", Susan Rubin Suleiman goes on, "that is, no one . . . dans le vent . . . 'does' it anymore." Having just returned from Moscow where no one does it at all, and seemingly never did, and from London, where they do it, but to little avail, I note that even Americans, who do it quite correctly, are losing the zest or the guilt that kept them at it.

It is unsettling to see those "dans le vent" fluttering by in this fickle way, for there is little doubt that Cixous has had an important influence on contemporary thought. Her depiction of woman "With one hand, suffering, living, putting your finger on pain, loss", is now archetypal, as is her condemnation of constraint: "There's always a gramma-r to censure it." But her essays are never intemperate harangues against phallogocentrism. For example, she depicts constraint as both externally imposed by the "capitalist-realist Superuncle. The Master of Repetition, The Anti-Other in papaperson", but also as internalized within every woman: "I believed as one should in the principle of identity, of noncontradiction, of unity. . . . I was there with my big pair of scissors, and as soon as I saw myself overlapping, snip, I cut, I adjusted, I reduced everything to a personage known as a 'a proper woman'." A "Jewoman" raised in Algeria by a German-speaking mother, her

father dead, Cixous embodies the "Other", the displaced post-colonial subject.

In the moving essay, **"Coming to Writing"**, Cixous describes woman as "This flesh that's been superhistoricized, museumized, reorganized, overworked." She tells how she began with just such an objectifying adoration of female beauty—that of her mother's face. "The look incited me and also forbade me to enter." But she outgrew this voyeuristic, narcissistic aesthetic, transforming the woman in the mirror into woman as light:

> This is the woman who belongs to love: the woman who loves all the women inside her. (Not the "beautiful" woman Uncle Freud speaks of, the beauty in the mirror, the beauty who loves herself so much that no one can ever love her enough, not the queen of beauty.) She doesn't watch herself, she doesn't examine herself, not the image, not the copy. The vibrant flesh, the enchanted womb, the woman pregnant with all the love. Not seduction, not absence, not the abyss adorned with veils. Plenitude, she who doesn't watch herself, doesn't reappropriate all her images reflected in people's faces, is not the devourer of eyes. She who looks with the look that recognizes . . . Brings back to light the life that's been buried, fugitive, made too prudent. Illuminates it and sings it its names.

Who could not admire a woman escaping narcissism into love?

And yet, Cixous's textual criticism is as likely to provoke impatience as admiration. The essays gathered in **Readings** are as inconsequential as any random group of interpretations, alternating between the rhapsodic and the obvious. Though Cixous is very good on Joyce, for example, it comes as no great surprise that "the subject in Joyce is structured by a series of oppositions", or even that his work "is owed to an immense spelling error".

Even Cixous's most sympathetic commentators cannot seem to make the case for her importance. **"The Laugh of the Medusa"**, perhaps her most influential text, fanned a major controversy among feminists over "essentialism", the attribution of a female difference from men that some feared would simply reinstate existing gender hierarchies. "The passion and anger that went into these debates", says Morag Shiach in *Hélène Cixous: A politics of writing*, "is now, more than ten years later, rather hard to recapture." The purity of Cixous's theorizing itself seems suspect when Shiach tells us that "The style of writing which Cixous describes as 'feminine' was . . . derived from a reading of a variety of literary texts, most of them written by men."

The problem, however, is not that these were written by men but that they were written by modernists. Her sources are Joyce, Kafka and Nietzsche, but she sounds like no one as much as Gertrude Stein, the most intransigent of the early twentieth-century experimentalists and a woman to boot. Fascinated by automatic writing, both women attempted to disrupt logic, rationality and categorical thinking in order to achieve immediacy, a kind of Derridean presence. Lovers of puns and word play, both learned from painters. Cixous quotes Monet: "what I am looking for, instantaneousness". In an essay from the Harvard collection, **"The Last Painting or the Portrait of God"**, she contrasts *works of art,* which "search us out with [their] eyes. . . . catch hold of us", and *works of seduction,* in which figures "do not feel themselves looked at; they are looking inside their hearts in the direction of the infinite". In this exact parallel to Michael Fried's "theatricality" versus "absorption", Cixous's model is the seductive or absorptive work, which gives no sign that it is addressed to an audience. Cixous cites Kafka's deathbed scribble, "lemonade everything was so infinite", as a verbal equivalent to such painting. Because it does not take the reader into account, Cixous, like Stein, believes that such path-finding art is often ugly, and feminine writing especially so.

In short, Cixous embodies a paradox. Politically speaking, she represents a radical contemporaneity—post-colonial, feminist: but aesthetically she belongs in the early twentieth century, trying to change reality through linguistic disruption and playfulness. And here one wants to take issue with a critic such as John Barth who, as late as 1980, argued that American women have no connection with the most important writing of their day, postmodernism, because their work is like nineteenth-century realism—little more than "the eloquent issuance . . . of secular news reports". Barth would presumably approve of Cixous, who is as non-realist as they come, and yet how tendentious her writing seems next to the imagistic and emotional intensity of Marilynne Robinson or the historicist virtuosity of Toni Morrison. Though Gertrude Stein may be "the mother of us all", contemporary women writers are searching for their mothers' gardens not in the sterile efflorescence of modernist language games, but in the dirt and flowers of reality, and it is here that Cixous does not lead them.

**Peter Baker** (review date June-July 1992)

SOURCE: "Discourses That Enact Their Subjects," in *The American Book Review,* Vol. 14, No. 2, June-July, 1992, p. 16.

[*In the following excerpt, Baker offers a positive review of* "Coming to Writing," *and Other Essays. He states that while Cixous's works can be difficult and that readers must come to her writing with* "a certain openness," *she* "may be the theorist who most clearly opens the way for a writerly kind of feminist thinking."]

That a discourse can or even should enact what it describes, or be like what it is about, is one of the discoveries claimed (and, of course, immediately therefore disputed) by various feminisms. I am one who thinks a certain credit should be given to feminist writers, and feminist theorists in particular, for breaking down the monological discourse of correctness and objectivity that represents one aspect of the patriarchy. Hélène Cixous . . . [constructs a discourse] responsive to this claim.

Cixous may be the theorist who most clearly opens the way for a writerly kind of feminist thinking. Known by American readers primarily for the wild, effusive, and challenging essay **"The Laugh of the Medusa,"** her work may well be poised for a wider exposure and acceptance in this country. This would even seem to be the premise of the editor and other presenters of the collection *"Coming to Writing" and Other Essays.* Thus we are given most of one French collection and two essays from another. The euphoria, uncontained, uncontainable, over the event obscures the reasons for this editorial decision: why not the two essays on James Joyce in *Entre l'écriture* (1986)? why instead two essays from a separate volume on Clarice Lispector? One could guess. Joyce is a male author, resoundingly condemned by establishment critics Sandra Gilbert and Susan Gubar; Clarice Lispector is a South American woman writer, also Jewish, who would seem to offer another female voice. On the other hand, Joyce is relatively well known, and the essays on him by Cixous are perhaps untranslatable. But why not tell us the reason for the editorial choice?

But this is my only criticism. Otherwise the volume is nearly perfect. I should stop right now. But I must continue. How to avoid speaking? How not to . . . ?

Cixous gives us an autobiography in cryptic terms. She understands, with Walter Benjamin, that death is the authorization for everything the storyteller can say: "That we move away from and approach Death, our double mother, through writing, because writing is always first a way of not being able to go through with mourning for death." But this authorization must also stem from love, not just a love for writing, but a love that eliminates and purifies everything, including the "I" who writes.

This possibility, this dangerous liberty, is structurally closer to women writing, says Cixous, because they are closer to what has always been hidden by the image of the male Narcissus, the abyss. The abyss is variously figured in the actual experience of women, both "nearer to and farther from loss than a man is." Always having been held back, restrained by male-dominated culture, women have yet to discover the limits of their flight, their bodies, their loves, their texts. And it is this ongoing process that Cixous's texts enact.

Let there be no doubt that Cixous is also a tremendous reader of others' texts. Like her male counterpart, Jacques Derrida, Cixous demonstrates nearly infinite patience in her deconstructive textual encounters. That this requires a great deal of patience by her readers is, only apparently paradoxically, part of her gift. As she says, in reading the lesson of Clarice Lispector: "The text teaches us that the most difficult thing to do is to arrive at the most extreme proximity while guarding against the trap of projection, of identification. The other must remain absolutely strange within the greatest possible proximity." And Cixous's text actually does this, discussing Lispector's work in close detail without making it any less strange.

The revelation to me in the volume is the essay **"The Last Painting or the Portrait of God."** Here Cixous tells us that she always wished she were a painter, and that this accounts for the way she writes. Somehow she manages to paint with words in such a way as actually to bring about an insight into what this might mean. Like the mimosa, which overwhelms the senses but recedes, sensitive to the touch, Cixous overwhelms the written word with layers of thought and sense-description, while withdrawing any possible center or point. As she says: "And the lesson is: one does not paint ideas. One does not paint 'a subject.' And in the same way: no writing ideas. There is no subject. There are only mysteries. There are only questions." Obviously, as a reader, one must come to this kind of writing with a certain openness, but then that too is part of the lesson, part of the gift.

---

# FURTHER READING

## Criticism

Crowler, Diane Griffin. "Amazons and Mothers? Monique Wittig, Hélène Cixous and Theories of Women's Writing." *Contemporary Literature* 24, No. 2 (Summer 1983): 117-44.

Compares Cixous's feminist theories with Monique Wittig's, stating that "these two conceptions of how to write women's experience reveal a profound division which extends far beyond the literary realm."

Klobucka, Anna. "Hélène Cixous and the Hour of Clarice Lispector." *Sub-Stance,* No. 73 (1994): 41-62.

Discusses the relationship between Cixous's works and those of Brazilian novelist and short story writer Clarice Lispector.

Kogan, Vivian. " 'I Want Vulva!' Cixous and the Poetics of the Body." *L'esprit createur* XXV, No. 2 (Summer 1985): 73-85.

Examines the role of the body in Cixous's works, concluding "what Cixous desires . . . is to reflect in her writing the specific manner in which the libidinal economy functions, i.e., the way in which the sexual life, regulated by energy, is marked physically by the female subject, and the way it affects her relations to her body and to the world."

Running-Johnson, Cynthia. "The Medusa's Tale: Feminine Writing and 'La Genet.' " *Romantic Review* LXXX, No. 3 (May 1989): 483-95.

Notes similarities between Cixous's *La jeune née* and the works of French novelist, poet, and playwright Jean Genet.

Review of *The Exile of James Joyce,* by Hélène Cixous. *The Times Literary Supplement,* No. 3504 (24 April 1969): 430.

Mixed review of *The Exile of James Joyce* in which the critic states "usually the speculations about the influence of family, friends, church, social and political environment are responsible, plausible, and well-documented."

Tsuchiya, Akiko. "Theorizing the Feminine: Esther Tusquet's *El mismo mar de todos los veranos* and Hélène Cixous's *écriture féminine.*" *Revista de estudios hispanicos* XXVI, No. 2 (May 1992): 183-99.

Applies Cixous's theories to Esther Tusquet's novel *El mismo mar de todos los veranos.* Tsuchiya states that she presents "a reading of *El mismo mar* as a theoretically self-conscious and self-critical exploration of the problematics of creating an *écriture féminine.*"

## Interview(s)

Makward, Christine. "Interview with Helene Cixous." *Sub-Stance,* No. 13 (1976): 19-37.

Interview in which Cixous discusses such topics as feminist writing, her writing style, and the role of the body in literature and criticism.

---

**Additional coverage of Cixous's life and career is contained in the following sources published by Gale Research:** *Dictionary of Literary Biography,* **Vol. 83; and** *Major 20th-Century Writers.*

# Maryse Condé
## 1937-

(Born Maryse Boucolon) Guadeloupean novelist, critic, dramatist, short story writer, and author of children's books.

The following entry provides an overview of Condé's career through 1994. For further information on her life and works, see *CLC*, Volume 52.

## INTRODUCTION

Condé is considered one of the most successful and important figures in contemporary Afro-Caribbean literature. She is acclaimed for articulating a distinctively black female perspective that is unmarked by the influences of imperialism and colonial oppression in the West Indies. Also lauded for her works of literary criticism, Condé often focuses—in her fiction and nonfiction—on the relationship of the individual with society, particularly the societies of Guadeloupe, other Caribbean locales, and equatorial Africa.

### Biographical Information

Born in Guadeloupe into a well-known family of academics and entrepreneurs, Condé was raised in an atmosphere of strong racial and familial pride. At the age of sixteen, she left to study in France, where she was the victim of severe racial prejudice. After being expelled from one school, Condé eventually completed her studies at the Sorbonne, where she was the winner of a short story writing contest among West African students. Thereafter, she traveled briefly in Europe and took a teaching position in the Ivory Coast. Between 1960 and 1968, Condé taught and lived in a number of African nations, including Guinea, Ghana, and Senegal. She returned to France in 1970 in order to earn a doctorate from the Sorbonne, which she accomplished in 1976. Condé remained at the Sorbonne as a lecturer for nearly ten years and during this time released some of her best known fictional and nonfictional works. In 1986 she returned to Guadeloupe and established a permanent residence there. She has since taught and lectured at a number of American universities, most often at the Los Angeles and Berkeley campuses of the University of California.

### Major Works

Condé is known for critical works that examine Francophone literature and feminist issues—notably *La civilisation du bossale* (1978), *La parole des femmes* (1979), and *Tim tim? Bois sec!* (1980)—and for fictional accounts of life in the Third World, primarily in the Antilles and West Africa—*Hérémakhonon* (1976; *Heremakhonon*), *Une saison à Rihata* (1981; *A Season in Rihata*), *La vie scélérate* (1987; *Tree of Life*), and *Traversée de la mangrove* (1990;

*Crossing the Mangrove*). *Hérémakhonon,* a semi-autobiographical novel, is set in an unidentified West African country and details the adventures of a Paris-educated Guadeloupean woman. The protagonist unwittingly becomes embroiled in the nation's political turmoil through her relationships with a bureaucrat and a radical schoolmaster. Condé's second novel, *A Season in Rihata,* again focuses on an African nation beset by internal problems in order to relate the story of a prominent family threatened by corruption and antigovernment sentiments. In her next two novels, *Ségou: Les murailles de terre* (1984; *Segu*) and *Ségou: La terre en miettes* (1985; *The Children of Segu*), Condé combines historical fact with fiction to recreate events in the West African kingdom of Ségou, which is now Mali, between 1797 and 1860. These works chronicle the experiences of members of a royal family whose lives are destroyed by such developments as European colonization, the slave trade, and the introduction of Islam and Christianity into Ségou's largely animistic culture. *Tree of Life,* set in Guadeloupe in the 1870s, details the life of a black nationalist patriarch and his scattered family, who, though haunted by loneliness, despair and suicide, struggle for survival. Other novels by Condé include *Moi, Tituba, sorcière . . . noire de Salem* (1986; *I, Tituba,*

*Black Witch of Salem*), the fictionalized biography of a Barbadian slave who was executed for practicing witchcraft in colonial Massachusetts; and *Les derniers rois mages* (1992), the tale of the ghost of an African king who pays a visit to his kin in contemporary South Carolina. Condé has also published several plays, collections of short stories, and works for children.

**Critical Reception**

Response to Condé's work has been generally positive. She has won numerous literary awards and fellowships, including the Prix littéraire de la femme in 1986 for *I, Tituba, Black Witch of Salem* and the Guggenheim fellowship in 1987. Charlotte and David Bruner have commented that Condé, in drawing on her experiences in Paris, West Africa, and her native Guadeloupe, has created several novels which "attempt to make credible on an increasingly larger scale the personal human complexities involved in holy wars, national rivalries, and migrations of peoples." Hal Wylie has called Condé's "ambitious insistence upon seeking the links between generations, and between the ethnic groups" to be "a quest for the meaningful factors of our time." Many critics have lauded Condé for her knowledge of African history, while others focus their praise on her struggle to create an independent identity for the Afro-Caribbean woman. Some critics, however, find Condé's plots convoluted and overburdened by details. Miller Newman has noted that, in *I, Tituba, Black Witch of Salem*, Condé's use of apparitions and wraiths is "bizarre" and "tests the reader's patience." In discussing *Segu*, Phiefer L. Browne has stated that the work has "a sometime confusing welter of characters" and "it ends abruptly, leaving its various plot strands hanging." Although some critics have taken exception to Condé's literary style, many share David Bruner's opinion that "Maryse Condé's work has been that of a major writer of our age."

# PRINCIPAL WORKS

*Anthologie de la littérature africaine d'expression française* [editor] (fiction) 1966
*Dieu nous l'a donné* (drama) [first publication] 1972
*Mort d'Oluwémi d'Ajumako* (drama) 1973
*Hérémakhonon* [*Heremakhonon*] (novel) 1976
*La poésie antillaise* [editor] (criticism) 1977
*Le roman antillais* [editor] (criticism) 1977
*La civilisation du bossale: Réflexions sur la littérature orale de la Guadeloupe et de la Martinque* (essays) 1978
*Notas sobre el Enriquillo* (criticism) 1978
*Le profil d'une oeuvre: Cahier d'un retour au pays natal* (essays) 1978
*La parole des femmes: Essais sur des romancières des Antilles de langue français* (essays) 1979
**Tim tim? Bois sec! Bloemlezling uit de Franstalige Caribsche literatuur* (criticism) 1980
*Une saison à Rihata* [*A Season in Rihata*] (novel) 1981
*Un gout de miel* (short stories) 1984
*Ségou: Les murailles de terre* [*Segu*] (novel) 1984

*Pays mêlé suivi de Nanna-ya* (short stories) 1985
*Ségou: La terre en miettes* [*The Children of Segu*] (novel) 1985
*Moi, Tituba, sorcière. . . noire de Salem* [*I, Tituba, Black Witch of Salem*] (novel) 1986
*Haiti Chérie* (juvenile) 1987
*La vie scélérate* [*Tree of Life*] (novel) 1987
*Pension les Alizés* (drama) 1988
*An tan revolisyon* (drama) 1989
*Traversée de la mangrove* [*Crossing the Mangrove*] (novel) 1989
*Victor et les barricades* (juvenile) 1989
*The Hills of Massabielle* (drama) 1991
*Les derniers rois mages* (novel) 1992
*La colonie du nouveau monde* (novel) 1993

*This work contains revised and translated editions of *Le roman antillais* and *La poésie antillaise*.

# CRITICISM

**David K. Bruner** (review date Spring 1982)

SOURCE: A review of *Une saison à Rihata*, in *World Literature Today*, Vol. 56, No. 2, Spring, 1982, pp. 390-91.

[*In the following positive review of* Une saison à Rihata, *Bruner discusses Condé's depiction of her characters' psychology and their social relationships.*]

As she did in her novel **Hérémakhonon** (1976) and in her plays **Dieu nous l'a donné** (1972) and **Mort d' Oluwemi d' Ajumako** (1979), Maryse Condé constructs in **Une saison à Rihata** a situation of political conflict in which to place a variety of characters in psychological and moral conflicts with themselves and each other. The result is an excellent and convincing work of art.

Although the political situations and plottings are exciting and clearly revealed to the reader, and although the writer's grasp of political realities is intellectually compelling, the novel is not a "protest novel," a novel with a political "message" or even a roman à clef. It is a novel about two sisters, two brothers, various children, various close associates—all caught in a complicated time of social eruptions. Paris, the Antilles and a West African country which was formerly a part of France are the geographic, ethnic and psychological origins and battlegrounds of its major characters. It is a novel about a past which lives in each character's memory in differing shapes; about futures which are imagined but never arrive; about passions which lead to murder, self-abasement, resignation and martyrdom; about those who learn to perceive a bit more clearly and those whose 20/20 vision will forever be false, without their knowing that it is.

Even the hateful characters are highly credible. The rest—despite their often mortal differences—draw the reader's human sympathy in large measure. Zek, basically amiable, is definitely inhibited by his dead father's contempt for him, by his mother and his wife; he neglects his talents in the dull river town of Rihata and envies his younger brother Madou, who had their father's preference, is politically eminent in the lively city of N'Daru and is loved and only partly resisted by Zek's wife Marie-Hélène (partly for political reasons). Like Zek, Madou and Marie-Hélène have their own internal stories to discover and reveal. Other characters emerge and become interlaced with the main three; what began with the appearance of a triangle becomes a multi-faceted, three-dimensional human formation.

An emotionally and intellectually mature novel, **Une saison à Rihata** deserves translation and a worldwide reception. The dust jacket compares it with the novels of Graham Greene; it fully merits that comparison.

### Hilda van Neck Yoder    (review date Winter 1982)

SOURCE: A review of *Tim tim? Bois sec! Bloemlezing uit de Franstalige Caribische Literatuur,* in *World Literature Today,* Vol. 56, No. 1, Winter, 1982, pp. 163-64.

[*In the following review of the Dutch edition of* Tim tim? Bois sec!, *Yoder compares Condé's critical anthology to previous versions, noting several improvements.*]

The recent Dutch publication of **Tim tim? Bois sec!,** Condé's combined revision of her 1977 critical anthologies **La poésie antillaise** and **Le roman antillais** (volumes one and two), reflects the growing interest in Caribbean literature in the Netherlands. The Dutch editor is Andries van der Wal, one of the editors of *Met Eigen Stem,* an anthology of literature of the Netherlands Antilles. Excellent translations from the French are provided by Fred de Haas.

**Tim tim?** is divided into two parts. The first section offers a concise introduction to the history, themes, movements and works by major writers of the French-speaking Caribbean (excluding Haiti). The second section provides an anthology of twenty-nine short excerpts from novels and thirteen poems. The work concludes with brief biographies of the authors anthologized and a bibliography of secondary literature. Regrettably, no footnotes or biographical references are provided to the critical introduction or to the prose excerpts and the poems.

A comparison with the 1977 French anthologies shows that the Dutch edition is definitely enriched by two additions. First, Condé has added a section on the essay, with examples from Césaire and Fanon; second, she has included a brief analysis of the role of the traditional oral tale, followed by such a tale, entitled "Lapin and Zamba in the Belly of the Ox" (recorded by Ina Césaire). Obviously, Condé intends to stress the significance of oral literature in the development of Antillean literature by using the formula with which the tale begins ("Tim tim bois sec") as her title for the Dutch edition.

Believing that "l'histoire de la poésie antillaise suit étroitement celle de l'évolution de la société," Condé has also expanded and updated the section on the historical context of Antillean literature. The critical introduction, as a whole, is informative, and her thematically organized anthology is strengthened by headings that relate to the themes analyzed in the introduction (e. g., "The Past," "Color Prejudice and Alienation," "Africa as Seen by the Antilles," "Resistance," "Negritude," "New Directions"). A similar English translation of Condé's anthologies would be useful in providing an overview of Caribbean literature in French for English-speaking students of this increasingly significant region and literature.

### John Williams    (review date July/August 1986)

SOURCE: A review of *La parole des femmes,* in *The Black Scholar,* Vol. 17, No. 4, July/August, 1986, p. 57.

[*In the following review of* La parole des femmes, *Williams finds Condé's work a seminal and important contribution to the quest for "the development of a new tradition of feminine voices."*]

In the advent of the appearance of Maryse Condé's collection of essays about French Caribbean women novelists, **La parole des femmes,** black women writers witness the development of a new tradition of feminine voices.

This new tradition seeks to define itself not in terms of its relationship to the French feminists of the metropolis (i. e. Simone de Beauvoir) nor by its natural affiliation with the "male dominated" black French language or "negritude" writers of the '30s (i. e. Jacques Roumain, Aimé Césaire). Instead, it falls midway between the traditions of the francophone and anglophone Caribbean novel, respectively, within the matrix of the history of the women's movement.

A provocative novelist, playwright, essayist, and scholar of Afro-Caribbean literature of French expression, Condé hails originally from the small French Caribbean protectorate of Guadeloupe. During the course of her prodigious literary career, she has published two plays, **Dieu nous l'a donné** (1972) and **La mort d'Oluwemi d'Ajumako** (1973); three volumes of literary criticism, **Le roman antillais** (1977), **La poésie antillaise** (1978), and **Aimé Césaire: Profil d'une oeuvre** (1978); two books of essays, **La civilisation du bossale** (1978) and **La parole des femmes** (1979); an anthology, **Tim, Tim: Anthologie de la littérature antillaise en néerlandais** (1978); and two novels, **Hérémakhonon** (1976) and **Une saison à Rihata.** Her third novel, **Ségou: les murailles de terre** (1984), was just recently published by Editions L'Harmattan in Paris.

This seminal work, which seeks to delineate a new sensibility among black women writers of the Caribbean of French expression, brings into focus the problematic of those exploited on four fronts simultaneously—racially, socially, sexually, and (as Condé points out in the introduction to the book) "geographically," indicating the unique form of colonial domination which exists in the Caribbean due to its "dependent" relationship vis-a-vis the global superpowers.

In **La parole des femmes,** Condé has assembled many of the most prolific feminine voices of the French Caribbean, the majority of whom have never been introduced to an English-language audience before. These novelists include Michèle Lacrosil (Guadeloupe), Simone Schwartz-Bart

(Guadeloupe), Marie Thérèse Coliman (Haiti), Marie-Flore Pélage (Martinique), and the author herself.

In this monumental treatise on the history of the women's movement, Condé adopts the task of explicating the role of the Afro-Caribbean female as guardian of the traditional values of her society, caught in the cesspool of economic, political, and social upheaval engendered by the urbanization, modernization, and cultural values of the West.

This preoccupation with the notion of "Caribbean society in transition" has prompted many scholars of Afro-American literature to compare the works of Condé with those of another black woman writer commanding knowledge of the Afro-Caribbean experience in the Americas—Paule Marshall.

*La parole des femmes* is a vital work desiring to bridge the gap between black women writers of English expression and black women writers of French expression. It is also an important contribution to the growing plethora of scholarly endeavors dedicated to the subject of the French Caribbean woman novelist. For those seeking to probe the depths of this new tradition of the black woman writer of French Caribbean expression, it is a necessity.

## Hal Wylie   (review date Autumn 1986)

SOURCE: A review of *Pays mêlé suivi de Nanna-Ya*, in *World Literature Today*, Vol. 60, No. 4, Autumn, 1986, p. 679.

[*Wylie is an American educator, editor, and critic who specializes in Francophone African literature. In the following review of* Pays mêlé suivi de Nanna-ya, *he criticizes the work's essayistic prose style and the bleakness of its vision.*]

The two stories of [Maryse Condé's] *Pays mêlé* present a literature of genealogy in which social relations are more important than individuals; the interpretation of the past is charged with political significance. Both stories follow Caribbean families through several generations. Individuals come and go so quickly the reader may be disoriented, until he sees that Condé is primarily interested in the web of connections between parents and children, blacks, whites and mulattoes, the powerful and *les misérables*. Most of the characters are female and emotionally crippled. Trauma and resulting alienation are major themes. Condé seems to believe that an individual's identity depends upon the traumas experienced, not only by the individual, but by her ancestors also. The title indicates that the Caribbean world is one of mixture, where the *métis* (half-breed) is the norm. Condé is balanced in her treatment of races and classes but emphasizes the female, seeing mothers as the glue that holds society together.

There is so much factual and explanatory material that the tales come to verge on essay form (there are discourses on social geography, psychology, sharecropping, the results of the new industrial capitalism, et cetera). One is reminded of Lukács's conceptions of social and critical realism. Here the realism is starkly cruel, however; perhaps the best label would be "analytical realism." The first story analyzes the strong support of Caribbean youth for the new independence movements, exploring both psychologi-

cal and historical roots, while the second takes up the broader theme of the role of literature in evolving Third World cultures. Condé clearly wants to document current problems and injustices and seems to intend to cheer on those who are attacking the vestiges of colonialism. Is this tragic vision the way?

## Charlotte H. Bruner   (review date Spring 1987)

SOURCE: A review of *Moi, Tituba, sorcière noire de Salem,* in *World Literature Today,* Vol. 61, No. 2, Spring, 1987, pp. 337-38.

[*In the following review, Bruner discusses Condé's depiction of power in* Moi, Tituba, sorcière noire de Salem.]

All of Maryse Condé's major fiction is rooted in a study of power. Her protagonists—fictional, legendary, or historical—appear to emerge almost haphazardly as heroes, martyrs, saints, or sacrificial victims. In tracing their lives, Condé shows the formative influence of their fervors upon a mass of characters. Somehow some very human individuals seem singled out for eminence or persecution. In her two-volume epic *Ségou,* for example, she portrays three generations of a Bambara royal dynasty at the time the march of Islam pushed aside the traditional animist empire of Ségou. The many family members in the novels undergo psychological, cultural, and geographic uprooting as they experience cultural change. Power is traced mainly through the male protagonists, a natural consequence of historical accuracy.

In Condé's latest novel, *Moi, Tituba, sorcière noire de Salem,* she introduces an interesting variant of her power theme. The actual historical Tituba was a West Indian slave who confessed to witchcraft during the Salem witch trials of 1692. Records of her part in this Salem power struggle are full and well documented. However, her history before and after the trials is conjectural only. Several legends conflict as to her death or her disappearance from Salem following the trials. In a brilliant re-creation Condé shows Tituba's early life in Barbados. Conceived on a slave ship in a public rape of a black slave by a white sailor, Tituba is forever an outcast from both black and white worlds. As a little girl she escapes servitude by running away when her mother is hanged for resisting and knifing her white owner. The girl is sheltered by an old herbalist in a remote area of the island, where she learns the healing arts, communication with the dead, and the exhilaration of freedom. Her passion for a métis slave, John Indian, drives her back to plantation life in slave quarters. However, her rebellious spirit outrages the owner, who sells the couple to the Reverend Samuel Parris, a Puritan minister on his way to Boston and, later, to Salem village. Condé convincingly draws together the traits of Tituba's personality to explain her use of the healing arts for the Parris children, her "false" confession after they betray her as a witch, her visitations with the spirits of the executed witches, et cetera.

Condé goes beyond the historical record in her new novel. Her Tituba becomes a martyr to Barbadian independence. Condé's own Guadeloupe has had its female martyrs in independence struggles; Simone Schwarz-Bart, also from

Guadeloupe, has commemorated an ancestral female martyr in *La mulâtresse solitude.* As a critic, Condé has often commented on the social, literary, and political power of West Indian women. In *Ségou* she presented many linkages between Africans, West Indians, and Brazilians of the black diaspora. In *Tituba* she again links the Americans to Africa in the history of power struggles. Tituba, witch or saint, rebel or martyr, did exert actual power over Salem village in one of the few ways women activists of her time were able to influence their culture.

### David K. Bruner    (review date Summer 1988)

SOURCE: A review of *La vie scélérate,* in *World Literature Today,* Vol. 62, No. 3, Summer, 1988, p. 498.

[*In the following review, Bruner positively assesses* La vie scélérate.]

*La vie scélérate,* though not as large a narrative as the two-volume *Ségou,* shares many of its characteristics. Seen through the eyes of a member of a large and powerful family, it reveals a historic epoch, its beliefs, conflicts, myths, and deeds. Beginning with the grandfather from Guadeloupe, it takes the reader through the early years of the building of the Panama Canal, where Jamaicans, American blacks, Guadeloupeans, and other exploited laborers struggle and die, or sometimes survive. It moves to San Francisco, to Jamaica, to France, as various members of the grandfather's burgeoning family gain power, quarrel among themselves, yet retain a family identity. Some become Marcus Garveyites, some become race-mixers.

As in Condé's other major works, there is a mixture of carefully researched data and her own experiences in the lands and among the peoples about whom she writes. Whether Rastafarians or Harlem blacks, middle-class families in France or people in the Chinese enclaves in San Francisco, all are interacting individuals struggling for individual ends. Always, however, larger sociopolitical questions of power, of expediency, of national and racial strategies dominate.

In revealing historical movements by focusing upon domestic matters (as, for example, Galsworthy did in *The Forsyte Saga* with an upper-class, ruling-class family) Condé is flexible in her writing style. There is a good bit of humor; there is use of mythic characters (a dead wife still "acts" upon those who remain alive); there are "family records" and "family letters" which are introduced by the character who acts as narrator and interpreter of the entire family history. *La vie scélérate* should be translated into English—and other languages. It doubtless will .be. From *Heremakhonon* on, Maryse Condé's work has been that of a major writer of our age.

### Phiefer L. Browne    (review date Spring 1989)

SOURCE: A review of *Segu,* in *Black American Literature Forum,* Vol. 23, No. 1, Spring, 1989, pp. 183-85.

[*In the following review, Browne offers a mixed assessment of* Segu.]

---

**Condé on why she became a writer:**

I don't believe that you become a writer by listening to someone telling stories or singing. It seems to me that you become a writer because you are in touch with books. Myself, that is how I became a writer. My family had a huge library, full of all sorts of books. It seems to me that my parents had never read half of the books on the shelves because some of them, when I opened them, were totally new, brand new. And especially there was an Atlas about Africa. In it, there was a picture of a man sitting on a mat who became later "the Mandingo marabout" of my novel *Heremakhonon*. And I'm sure that I was the only one to look through that book. Looking at these books I wanted to do the same. I wanted to write wonderful stories that people will like. I decided to become a writer.

    *Maryse Condé, in an interview in* Callaloo, *Spring, 1991.*

---

*Segu* is an epic historical African novel spanning the years from 1737 to 1860; the continents of Africa, South America, and Europe; and three generations of an aristocratic Bambara family, the Traores. Segu, the ancestral home of the Traores, is a town between Bamiko and Timbuktu in present-day Mali. The action centers on the four sons of the nobleman Dousika Traore and their sons. "Four sons—Tiekoro, Siga, Naba and Malobali, the last-born— had to be regarded as hostages or scapegoats, to be wantonly ill used by fate so that the family as a whole might not perish."

The novel presents a polygynous, patriarchal world, with most of its female characters playing a passive, reactive role. The Bambara woman's life revolves around her son and husband. The two most important female characters briefly occupy center stage when they publicly and eloquently plead for the lives of their son and husband, those who give their lives meaning. When the favorite, first-born son of the matriarch Nya is executed and the husband of the Catholic convert Romana dies from smallpox, these proud women lose their will to live. While the maladjusted, unhappy man has the freedom simply to walk away from the family compound to begin a new life, the most vulnerable and unhappy of the women, the concubines from another tribe, escape the family compound by committing suicide.

The major conflict in the novel is not between characters but between the opposing world views and value systems of Islam and fetishism. This conflict is established at the outset by the forced exile from Segu of Tiekoro, the first-born son of the patriarch Dousika Traore and the first Bambara convert to Islam. The spirits of the gods and the ancestors endow the fetish priest Koumare with a prophetic vision: "This new god, this Allah who'd adopted young Tiekoro, was invincible. He would be like a sword. In his name the earth would run with blood, fire would crackle through the fields. Peaceful nations would take up arms, son would turn away from father, brother from brother. A new aristocracy would be born, and new relationships between human beings." Although Islam inexorably transforms the traditional way of life, the magic of fetishism permeates the world of the novel. Newborns reincarnate the wondering souls of the dead, and at moments of crisis apparitions of the dead materialize to advise and guide the converts to Islam as well as the fetishists.

By the end of the novel, the third generation of Traores sees the final dramatic conquest of Islam over fetishism in Segu. The grave of the martyred Tiekoro becomes a Muslim shrine, the fetish priests undergo a public ritual humiliation, and the most sacred household fetishes are publicly burned. By the time of its final triumph over paganism, however, Islam, "the sword that divides," has become both corrupt and compromised. Sectarianism destroys the unity of Islam. Muslim leaders make war on each other, in the process making alliances with the fetishist kings. And the Fulani, the ancient enemies of the Bambara, use the propagation of Islam as the pretext for seizing Segu's considerable wealth and controlling its markets. The invasion of his homeland by the marauding Fulani sets off an inner conflict in Muhammed, the devout Muslim son of Tiekoro, between Islam's deal of universal brotherhood and clan loyalty. "But these were his people, their wounds were his own, and he found himself hating a God who manifested Himself through fire and sword." The final vision of Muhammed's closest friend, heretofore a devout Muslim also, is one of religious toleration: "He suddenly understood there was no universal god; every man had the right to worship whomsoever he pleased; and to take away a man's religion, the keystone of his life, was to condemn him to death. Why was Allah better than Faro or Pemba [tribal gods]? Who had decreed it?"

Christianity, the third major religion in the novel, is mainly a European influence, and, as such, its roots in Africa are more shallow than those of Islam and fetishism. In a time of crisis one of the most devout Christianized Africans, the Catholic convert Romana, covers all bases by praying to the powerful Yoruba gods of her childhood as well as to Jesus and the Virgin Mary. But in their attempts to convert the fetishists, the white Christian missionaries are as much zealots as the black Muslims are. The two Catholic priests in Dahomey had eyes "pale, transparent, but with an unbearable flame in their depths like that of a forge." "Sometimes when he was not blinded by hatred," Malobali, the nominal Christian, secret fetishist, "would briefly feel a kind of admiration for these men: driven by some ideal they had left their own country and people to live here, indifferent to solitude and danger . . .'"

Not only religious forces but also economic forces sweep through Segu. Trade offers an alternative to the traditional agrarian way of life, and the basic commodity bought and sold is the human being. At the height of the slave trade in Northwest Africa, Naba, one of the Traore brothers, is kidnapped by slavers and ends up on a plantation in Brazil. One of the most recurrent images is the manacled wretch waiting for transshipment to the New World. African towns such as Ouidah and Lagos are the " 'creation of the whites, born of the trade in human flesh. Nothing but vast warehouses.' " As a result of the onslaughts of

Islam, Christianity, and the slave trade on his family, Eucharistus, a third-generation Traore, becomes the detribalized African, a figure common to modern African literature. Eucharistus, who sees himself as a "creature of the whites," is, unlike his forebears, neither Yoruba, Bambara, or Brazilian. "What was he? He could not tell!" Although he goes to college in London to become trained to "christianize and civilize Africa," he longs for "the purity of his Segu ancestors which he had lost forever. . . . He would never recover the proud self-assurance of that past."

*Segu*—a bestseller in France—is a richly textured novel with a sometimes confusing welter of characters. And it ends abruptly, leaving its various plot strands hanging. But it well shows that a remote, little-known part of the world was undergoing religious, economic, and social changes as profound as those transforming the Western world of the period.

## Maryse Condé with VèVè A. Clark   (interview date Winter 1989)

SOURCE: "I Have Made Peace with My Island," in *Callaloo*, Vol. 12, No. 1, Winter, 1989, pp. 85-133.

[*In the following excerpt, Condé discusses the influence her childhood in Guadeloupe, her family, and her political beliefs have on her literary work.*]

[*Clark*]: *How would you describe the Boucolon family's reputation in Guadeloupe?*

[Condé]: My parents were among the first black instructors. My mother was the first black woman instructor among her generation, and also the first black director of her own school for girls. When my father stopped teaching, he founded a small bank with black and mulatto acquaintances of his called La Caisse Coopérative des Prêts which later became La Banque Antillaise. The original enterprise was designed to provide loans for functionaries. Under pressure from the capitalist world, the bank became a French-controlled bank like all the others. My parents were very well known; my father had been awarded the *légion d'honneur*. The family was rather sure of itself, arrogant, scornful toward persons who were not successful, but at the same time very conscious of being black. During that period, one had to maintain clear divisions between blacks, mulattos, and whites. My parents were very proud of being black, and raised us with the understanding that in the larger society, we were considered niggers (*nègres*), and that we should work for the uplift of the race.

*How did they make that consciousness clear to you, through reading books by black authors, a certain manner, or what?*

It was a certain manner. Early on, they showed an admiration for black America. They never knew anything about it save what they read in magazines like *Ebony*. You know that kind of photograph you find only in black American magazines? A family that has succeeded in some way: there is the father, mother, the children all around, and the commentary tells you about their accomplishments, their degrees and so on. My mother had hung a picture like that in her room and would always point to it and say:

"I want my children to grow up just like that." So, it was a question of behavior—not to talk to just anybody below our level. It was their general attitude toward life.

*Tell me the first names of your father and mother.*

My father was Auguste Boucolon and my mother, Jeanne Quidal. She was born on a small island, Marie-Galante, off the coast of Guadeloupe. That fact is very important because people from that island are supposed to be very proud of themselves, very creative.

*In the generation just before them, were family members equally as illustrious?*

No. My parents were self-made people, because as I understand it my paternal grandfather was a merchant, a salesman, member of the petty-bourgeoisie, and my maternal grandmother was simply a maid in someone's family. No one knows who my maternal grandfather was, but whoever he was, he did look after my mother by giving her money and paying for her education. Although my maternal grandmother was a maid without a husband, she had the means to support the education of her daughter.

*One of your latest short stories in* **Voies de pères, voix de filles,** *"La châtaigne et le fruit à pain" (1988), is obviously not the story of your family. Is it your mother's story?*

Nothing to do with me. The only thing autobiographical about it is that the mother comes from Marie-Galante. In most of my work, there is always the presence of the little island, even in **Hérémakhonon** where people go off to vacation in Marie-Galante.

*Most readers identity your father with the portrait of the* marabout mandingue *in* **Hérémakhonon.** *To what extent is that portrayal true to life?*

Yes [emphatically]. He was a very, very handsome, tall, thin, elegant man. So arrogant, self-important in his face and the way he walked. Of course, he is the *marabout mandingue,* no doubt about it. But my mother is not Marthe. In real life, my mother was full of herself, bad-tempered; she used to abuse people verbally whenever they were not paying enough attention to her. There was a story in the family about a policeman who forgot who she was and told her not to do something or other, so she beat him up with the umbrella she was carrying.

*Was this the post-war period in the 1940s?*

It seems to me that they started being well-off some time before the Second World War. At the beginning of their marriage, they were simply two clever, industrious black people working hard for the well-being of their children. They became affluent just before the war. My birth more or less coincided with the period when they started to become affluent. You know my father married twice and from the first marriage had two sons, Serge and Albert. Albert is known as Bébert in **La vie scélérate** (1987). At that time, the family was simply average, living in a small house in rue Condé. After that they moved to their big house in la rue Alexandre-Isaac which in **La vie scélérate** becomes la rue du Faubourg d'Ennery. I have three sisters (Ena, Jeanne, Gillette) and four brothers (Auguste, Jean, René, Guy). I am the youngest after Guy, born eleven

years after him, so I am the last and the spoiled child. My mother was about forty-three years old when I was born and my father was sixty-three. My mother thought she was in her menopause; she was somewhat ashamed when she discovered she was pregnant. My parents gave me everything. They were getting old; they had more money, and their other children were almost grown up. They were so happy to have a little girl around. They never refused me anything, took me everywhere—to France with them. My sisters and brothers spoiled me very much, especially Jeanne. She was very fond of me, looking after me all the time. Ena, the eldest girl, is also my godmother. When she was in France, she would send me dolls, presents of all sorts.

*How many members of the family are still living?*

René, Jeanne, Ena and Gillette—five counting me. Jean died in the Second World War; my brother Guy died young. My mother died when I was nineteen (in 1956). When you read the selection in **A ma mère** (1988), you will learn all about it. My father died about three years later when I was only twenty-one or twenty-two.

---

**My childhood was so dull. All those years spent with a family that never wanted to see anyone else because others were socially beneath them. If anything, I was a bored, discontented princess.**

**—Maryse Condé**

---

*Did you write your first short story when you were ten or eleven years old?*

No, I think it was when I was seven; perhaps I am exaggerating, but I know that I was very, very small. Maybe ten, but it was certainly before age twelve. It was not a short story but a one-act, one person play about my mother. She was the actress and at the same time the subject of the play. I wrote it for her birthday. She did not like the play at all. She said, "Okay, but I am not at all like that."

*Is Veronica's childhood in* **Hérémakhonon** *the remembrance of your* anti-moi?

Veronica's childhood is mine in a way. What is true about it is the relationship that I had with my father who, it seems to me, was never fond of me. He was fond of my other sisters. When I was a youngster, he spoiled me a great deal, but when I started having a personality of my own, we disagreed because I was a bit argumentative. He used to say, "Maryse est *folle*" (crazy). You can say that **Hérémakhonon** is an accurate portrayal of parts of my childhood.

*If you had to choose a metaphor to describe your childhood, what figure would come to mind?*

In a way, my childhood was so dull. All those years spent with a family that never wanted to see anyone else because others were socially beneath them. At the same time, I was very spoiled so that I didn't miss anything. If anything, I was a bored, discontented princess.

*Did you have special talents that became evident to you and your parents during your childhood?*

Only writing; I was very good at writing and had a gift for caricature, but not the nasty type. I had a sense of humor, and created nicknames for people. Because I was so spoiled at home, I wasn't a very nice child, more a pest. For example, in school the teachers were very fond of me at the outset because I was so bright and a cute little girl. I can remember seeing their attitudes change after two months or so. They were fed up with my sarcasm and critical attitude toward them. They couldn't stand me any longer. I would recognize the weak points in a person and laugh at them. I remember one year when we were studying the epigrams of Voltaire at the lycée, I made up epigrams about the other girls and the teachers.

*Is there an experience from elementary school that stands out so clearly in your mind that you will never forget it?*

Yes, one day at school we had to write a *devoir de français* which was entitled, "describe your best friend"— something very banal. I described a girl I was very fond of, Eddy, who in my opinion was bad-looking, although she was my friend. In the paper, I said that Eddy was my best friend, not very pretty. The teacher made me stand before the class and read the paper aloud. I remember how shocked I was by the idea that to write was to lie (because for me to write was to tell the truth). I thought, then I shall never write. Moreover, I got the feeling very young that it is a dangerous thing to write and if I ever did, there was going to be trouble, because I could not understand why the teacher was blaming me for telling the truth. Whenever Eddy and I meet, we recall the story and laugh together about it. She lives in Mali, West Africa now.

*You were a non-conformist early on.*

Yes. It was so boring to be brought up in Guadeloupe during that era. You had to go to the Place de la Victoire, play and be back home before 6 p.m., before dark, before the church bells began to ring. I could not go to the ball to dance because my father wouldn't permit a boy to hold *his* daughter in his arms. It was all too boring, and I wanted to break out; I was ripe for leaving, leaving the family, leaving the island. There was a big scandal because of a mulatto boyfriend I had; he was almost white. Although the relationship was platonic, everyone was curious about it, and there was a lot of talk. There is a bit of that in **Hérémakhonon**. Probably I chose him just to annoy my family, and yet there was nothing to be annoyed about. I was maybe sixteen years old, in the last year at the lycée, just before I left for France in 1953.

*What would you have preferred to be doing? You mentioned dancing.*

I didn't know then exactly what I wanted to do, but was fed up with people telling me *not* to do so and so. For instance, because of the idea the family had of itself, during Carnival when everybody was out in the streets, dancing, moving and shaking, I had to stay indoors. I could come

on the balcony, and look at the masked dancing. I wanted to be in the streets like everyone else, to stand on the corner and clap hands. My family felt that only "niggers" and servants participated in street festivals.

*Are there any teachers or people from elementary school who influenced you?*

No. I had a kind of contempt for them, found them uninteresting and dull.

*Was it common for someone like you to leave home for France at that period?*

It was normal for every boy and girl of that generation to go to France for further study after the *baccalauréat*. My elder sisters and brothers had gone; everybody had to go. When I took the two parts of the *baccalauréat* exam, I received a *mention* (honors), and was given a scholarship. Even if one's family had money, money counts, so my parents asked for assistance and I received a quarter of a scholarship calculated according to the family's income.

*For how long did you attend the Lycée Fénelon in Paris?*

Lycée Fénelon from 1953 to 1955 because I was expelled immediately. When I arrived, I got into trouble with the instructors who were totally racist. There was a Senegalese girl in my class. We were the only black girls in the school out of hundreds of students. The teachers would call upon her first and me afterward, drawing comparisons between our responses: yes, the Africans were more like this and the West Indians like that—right in the middle of class. And our schoolmates insisted that I was more pleasant or beautiful because my Senegalese classmate was so black. I resented the whole place, and was expelled after two years. I also had lots of problems with the discipline in the school: boring classes, interminable museum visits and concerts. I could not do that anymore; I was fed up. So I went to the Sorbonne to continue my studies. I was finally free.

*Did you have favorite authors you read while still in the lycée?*

Among the French, François Mauriac. I was very fond of his work; I read and reread everything he had written. Among my favorites was his novella, *Le Sagouin*.

*Can you remember the first book by a black author that you read?*

Of course, it was *Return to My Native Land* by Césaire. A white girlfriend of mine from the Lycée Fénelon, daughter of a Marxist historian at the Sorbonne, gave me that book. She also took me to a meeting where Césaire and other leaders from Africa and the West Indies had come to speak about decolonization. This would have been between 1955 and 1958.

*In retrospect, when you think of the 1953-1958 period in Paris, how had the social climate changed since the 1930s when Césaire, Damas, and Senghor were there? Had it changed measurably for a black person, a young, black woman in the city?*

It is difficult to answer that question. Who was I then? I was simply a young West Indian girl residing in a boardinghouse full of other West Indian girls—not at all co-ed, obviously. We were a closed world of West Indians. We had little to do with the people in the outside world of Paris. Certainly, we had friends from Caribbean families that had settled in Paris, *the correspondents,* whom we visited, but that was all. Until 1958, I was protected within the West Indian circle. I received a prize among the students for writing a short story, **"Adélia"** or something of that sort. I wasn't political then, but showed a concern for culture. With some other West Indians, we founded a club called the Luis-Carlos Prestes club—don't ask who the man was, for I have totally forgotten, but I think he was the leader of a Latin American country. So you see, we were already interested in the problems we faced. I gave a talk about what it is to be a West Indian. Frantz Fanon had just published *Black Skin, White Masks,* and some time later, my comrades asked me to write a reply to Fanon. We were so angry about his portrait of West Indians. I was to submit the reply to the journal *Esprit,* and I went to see the editor, Jean-Marie Domenach to tell him how we young West Indians disagreed with Frantz Fanon. We were involved in a few events, but not really prepared for anything significant.

Having left Guadeloupe behind with its small narrow places, naturally I enjoyed Paris with my friends from the West Indies. At the lycée, they had tried to force us to enjoy cultural events. Later we were free to discover on our own the cinemas and concert houses of Paris. At the time, I had a craze for Italy; instead of going home to Guadeloupe for the long holidays in 1956, I left with a girlfriend to wander about Rome and Florence. It was a tremendous discovery. By the way, just after we returned to Paris from that excursion, I learned that my mother had died. There I was trying to discover Europe, and missed the last days of my mother's life. It was emotionally very difficult for me. After my mother died, I fell gravely ill. They sent me to spend a year in a sanitorium because I had something wrong with my lungs. Back in Paris after that experience, I broke away from the West Indian circle. I don't remember exactly how, but I came in contact with the African community in Paris, and that's how I met Condé.

*Tell me about Condé.*

I went with a friend of mine to a rehearsal of *Les Nègres/The Blacks* by Jean Genêt in 1959, and there was an actor in the play who seemed handsome and striking. Mamadou Condé. I cannot remember which role he played, but he was in the production. After the play, we spoke to the actors to express our admiration for their performance. Condé was there, I met him, and that's where the whole relationship between us began. My family considered it a scandal for me to marry him. They were racist in a sense; so proud of being black, but at the same time so contemptuous of Africans. They embraced a false image of Africa. For my father, my relationship with Condé was a shame. He was not surprised because "Maryse is crazy, she would marry an African and even worse go to Africa with him." You should know that my sister Gillette had married a Guinean, Jean Deen; but he was from a very wealthy family. His father was a doctor

and he, himself, was studying medicine. Condé, on the other hand, was an actor; he had no money, no education. Even my sister was concerned about the low level of Condé's education and was against the idea of my marrying him. I have three daughters from that marriage, Sylvie, Aisha, Leila.

*September 28, 1958, the date of DeGaulle's Referendum on African Autonomy, was a significant one for the future of Africa. Did the date mean anything to you at the time?*

I heard stories about the independence movement and knew what it was. I knew about the Loi Cadre, the Referendum, the "no" vote of Sékou Touré. When I think back on it, I realize that I was not very much involved at the time. People tend to say that I was involved from the very beginning, but I wasn't. I was simply happy to leave the narrow circle of the West Indies in Paris, all the while becoming closer to the Africans. Of course I heard the stories of independence, but they were vague in my mind.

*What was the* complot des enseignants *that occurred in Guinea in 1962?*

It was very complicated, and linked to my own personal situation at the time. Condé and I were married in August, I believe, of 1959; by November, we were already in deep disagreement. I no longer wished to stay with him, so I decided to go alone to Ivory Coast where I taught for a year in Bingerville. My first child, Sylvie, was born there in April of 1960. It was only when I returned to Guinea for the long holidays that I began to be politically conscious, not before. I was welcomed by a group of Marxists—Louis Béhanzin, Nene Khaly Basile (now deceased)—who helped me understand the society. They were very cordial to me, unlike others who didn't seem to care much about a West Indian girl like myself. My friends attracted me to their ideological position, and I became a Marxist because my friends were Marxists. They told me that Guinea was not what it seemed to be; rather, it was a country full of injustice. Obviously, they were trying to open my eyes. I listened, but was not involved in any real struggle. Condé and I had very little money; I was pregnant again and had a child—so many other things on my mind. One day, this same group of Marxists came to chat with me after dinner. Why did they seek me out? I imagine they noticed the distance between Condé and me. I feel now that they saw the possibilities I possessed. They came to talk with me the day before the opening of the *Congrès des Enseignants,* Conference of Teachers. The next day during the conference, some of them read papers about Sékou Touré's government; there was also a poem by Djibril Tamsir Niane, critical of independence. Two days later, all of them were arrested . . . and the strike by the students began soon after. It was after the arrests that I became involved. These were friends of mine with whom I had talked a day earlier; two or three days later, they were in jail or expelled from the country.

We were young, naive in a way, but the situation was an eye-opener for me especially when I saw the wife of Seyni Niang, Liliane, forced to take a plane to the Soviet Union with her three boys because her husband was in jail. Seyni Niang was a member of one of the political parties in Senegal. Since he was a foreigner in Guinea, they expelled his wife and kept him in jail. . . . It was because of that incident that I began to understand what was happening in the country, to comprehend the real face of African Socialism. As for the marriage, it was a bad one from the start; everything was on the rocks, so I decided to leave for Ghana in 1964. Why Ghana? By that time, I had become a kind of Marxist. Friends told me that Ghana was not Guinea; it was a true Marxist country. So I went to join them. I was seeking a job there, and had three little girls to feed.

In 1969, I met Richard Philcox [Condé's second husband] who is an orderly, organized man—I had by then left Condé for good. At the time, I was in a complete mess. My life was chaos: kids, unhappy with my work, frustrated with everything. Richard helped put some order in my life. First, I decided that I should resume my studies beyond the *licence* that I had at the time, and go on for the Ph.D. I gave the kids to Condé just to be free for a while. At that time my life started to be organized.

*Why did you keep Condé's surname?*

I had started publishing under my married name, so I kept it. Condé never wanted to divorce. For years, Richard and I could not reach him; whenever I tried, I did not succeed. Condé and I did not actually divorce until 1981. . . .

*Would you explain how it was that you first came to the United States as a writer/scholar to teach?*

Clarisse Zimra [Southern Illinois University] had read **Hérémakhonon** and wrote to me praising the book. When I told her that I was coming to America in 1978 just to visit, she put a notice in *BREFF* [the *Bulletin de Recherches et d'Études Féministes Francophones* 15 (November 1979): 6] announcing my arrival. No one knew me at the time; however, I received a few invitations from Annabelle Rea (Occidental College), Sue Houchins and Lloyd Brown (University of Southern California), Gérard Pigeon (UCSB) and Wilbert Roget (Tufts University). The following year in the fall of 1979, I taught for one semester at the University of California, Santa Barbara.

*You have a loyal network among scholars in American universities, teachers who respect your work. Do you have a similar network in French or African university systems?*

No one in either area, only in the United States. . . .

1986 was important because that year I decided to go back home and start living in the West Indies. Also, my first important novel about Guadeloupe was in press then, **La vie scélérate** (1987). I had wanted to go home a long time before during the 1970s when Richard and I left Africa to live in France. Unfortunately, we had no money at all. I applied for jobs in Guadeloupe, but had no contacts there whatsoever. I had a bad reputation of being someone who was not on the right side of anything, of being a contentious person, so I could not get a job in Guadeloupe for more than ten years. I kept planning though, filling out application after application, receiving letters of rejection, being refused by everyone left and right. In 1984, after **Ségou,** when I had enough money to buy a house in Montebello, I did. We were supposed to return in 1985, but the

Fulbright fellowship to teach one year in the States at Occidental College came through. Therefore, we stayed for a year in Los Angeles while the house in Montebello was being completed, and afterward left for Guadeloupe. The return home was a long-standing dream finally realized.

*Were there changes in Guadeloupean society during the 1980s that made return more possible for you?*

Honestly, I would have returned no matter the circumstances, because I was so keen on doing just that. If I had tried it some years before in the 1970s, I would have been faced with racism, political narrow-mindedness and intolerance, causing my stay on the island to be very difficult, indeed. In the 1970s, some Guadeloupeans were fighting to reassess our culture. If you are committed to such an agenda, you must be hostile to everything which is foreign. These activists built a kind of cultural wall around Guadeloupe so that no one from the outside could enter. It was a time when the UPLG [Popular Union for the Liberation of Guadeloupe] was extremely active in raising the consciousness of the people, often forcing the populace to speak Creole, and so on. When they finally realized that the directions they were taking had significant limitations, that they were going to destroy something important—by trying to protect so much, they had already begun to lose ground. People were fed up with the conditions that activists were asking them to accept. It was then that the leaders understood they had to make some drastic changes. I was fortunate to have returned at this juncture because now Guadeloupe is more open, more curious, more ready to accept people and values from abroad. The situation is decidedly different now. I came back at a time when people wanted relief. People seemed to be waiting for a voice that could express openly points of view a majority harbored about the excesses of the UPLG. As a result, I felt comforted by the support of many people.

*Do you see yourself as the* griotte *(critical, oral historian) of contemporary Guadeloupean society?*

No. **La vie scélérate** is full of criticism of the independence parties. Some independence activists have wondered aloud about what Maryse Condé is doing. "She belongs to us, and look at the way she has portrayed our cause in her novel," they complained. They didn't come directly to me, for as you know in our country all is said behind the back. In my opinion, the role of griotte just does not apply, because what does a *griotte* do? Praise a given situation, some leaders and their achievements; it seems to me that I am doing just the opposite. I am saying that the independence activists have not achieved very much. In **La vie scélérate,** I ridicule one of them (Uncle Jean Louis) who goes out of his way to live with the people in a hut, and who writes a book that few people will read, *La Guadeloupe inconnue.*

*How would you describe the ideology of persons with whom you feel most comfortable whether they live in Guadeloupe, France, Africa, or the United States?*

Non-conformism is the primary factor: people who are always on the wrong side of society; people who are never self-satisfied, never complacent, never blinded by the weaknesses of society or their own faults. I feel at ease among people who are just like me; quite able to laugh at themselves and other people's misfortunes or mistakes if need be. I am drawn to people ready to disobey the law and who refuse to accept orders from anybody—people who, like me, don't believe in material wealth, for whom money is nothing, owning a home is nothing, a car is nothing. Those kinds of people tend to be my friends. It does not mean that the people who surround me in Guadeloupe are all like this. When they are not, I can accept their company if they are friendly and sincere in their relationship with us. I accept people who are very different from me.

*How would you describe the political ideology that motivates you now, if indeed there is one?*

I have some remains of Marxism. I shall always be on the side of people who possess nothing—the exploited, the masses considered unimportant in the world. Formerly, I had political masters deriving from my readings, but now I am through with that. When I was in Guinea, my friends encouraged me to read Marx, Hegel and Gramsci, particularly the latter. At the time, I was very fond of reading Fanon because his was a new theory adapted to the West Indies. I have not read Fanon for a long while, although I remember his ideas very well. And Cabral was a master for me. People seem to have forgotten all about Cabral. He was one of the most frank political theorists, and clear in his thinking about the politics of progress in Africa and throughout the diaspora. These were my masters. Now I don't have a concrete philosophy. I believe, however, that we have to make life a task that is not too difficult for each of us to undertake.

*One final question relates to the first concerning your family. The essays in* Voies de pères, voix de filles *are testimonies by women describing their relationships with their fathers. You submitted something fictional. Why didn't you write about your father?*

I had nothing to say about my father. Looking back, I'm not sure that I could fill even one page about my father. He was a man with whom I had very little in common. Sixty-three years old when I was born, always preoccupied with banking business, he was not at all active within our family. He was simply a handsome, elderly man with white hair and a beautiful face. I could not write anything about him, as I told the editor, Adine Sagalyn. She insisted that I participate. As a result, I wrote a short story about an absentee father—a situation that could likely have happened to any West Indian girl. That is the way fathers behave in our society. And the editor agreed to publish the piece as I had submitted it.

## Arlette M. Smith    (essay date Spring 1991)

SOURCE: "The Semiotics of Exile in Maryse Condé's Fictional Works," in *Callaloo*, Vol. 14, No. 2, Spring, 1991, pp. 381-88.

[*In the essay below, Smith discusses the themes of exile and alienation in Condé's fiction.*]

Among the Francophone Caribbean writers, Guadeloupean-born Maryse Condé has produced a body of works which has won wide recognition for its appeal, its diversity, and its depth. A multifaceted talent, this playwright, essayist, critic, and novelist draws from a wide source of inspiration. The history of the African kingdom of Ségou provides the framework as well as some of the characters and episodes in both *Ségou: les murailles de terre* and *Ségou: la terre en miettes. Hérémakhonon* focuses on the psychological problem of alienation, while the surge of religious fanaticism associated with the which hunt in seventeenth-century Salem constitutes a salient aspect of yet another novel, *Moi, Tituba, sorcière noire de Salem*.

In addition to its diversity, Maryse Condé's fictional universe is also strikingly convincing. True to life circumstances, plausible psychological situations, and dramatic developments succeed in conveying an impression of reality. The dominant topics of the novels—such as cultural alienation, the political climate in the emerging nations of Africa, the arrival of Islam and European imperialism in the Sahel—all correspond in some respect to psychological or historical reality, and thus point to an identifiable referent. With such a faithful representation of the actual world, facts and fiction become so closely intertwined that it would be justified to assess their significance exclusively in terms of their mimetic value. In the light of such a reading, those novels would be viewed primarily as psychological, social, or historical documents, which, however, would leave aside one of their major merits: their literariness, the very characteristics which define them as the products of literary creativity distinct from documentary statements whose sole function consists in communicating accurate information. A different reading approach would make it possible, to use Jean Rousset's words [from *Forme et signification* (1962)], "[de] saisir des significations à travers des formes . . . [de] déceler dans les textures littéraires . . . ces figures . . . qui signalent l'opération simultanée d'une expression vécue et d'une mise en oeuvre" (to find meaning through the formal configurations themselves, to detect in the literary fabric representations that can be identified both as the verbalization of an authentic life experience, and as a word construct designed with artistic intent). Although the facts, events, and characters in Maryse Condé's fiction possess a strong quality of authenticity or verisimilitude, her specific mode of writing is by itself expressive, and its expressiveness deserves critical attention. "Art makes use of reality, obliterating it, and replacing it with reality of a different order." This paper deals with one aspect of this "reality of a different order," an artistic universe which itself originates from existential and historical elements. More specifically, the focus is on the metaphors used to convey the notion of exile, and on the crystallization process involved in the development of these metaphors.

Exile and other related themes are indeed insistently featured in Maryse Condé's novels, explicitly so, in plot developments and in their effects on the characters, and in a more oblique and less readily recognizable manner, in the form of certain writing devices which assume symbolic significance because of their high rate of recurrence, and of the associations they suggest.

Alienation being one of the central themes in Maryse

Condé's novels, it comes as no surprise that exile, which is part of the same thematic field, occupies likewise a prominent position. Different modes of exile are portrayed. In *Hérémakhonon,* Véronica, a young woman in search of her cultural identity, feels divorced from her native Guadeloupean milieu, from French culture (which she has assimilated brilliantly, however), and from the African cultural heritage from which she feels excluded and is anxious to adopt. Her journeys from Guadeloupe to France and to Africa which chart the course of her quest fail to alleviate her feelings of isolation and nostalgia as she searches for that which would command her loyalty and to which she could feel strongly bound. In *Une Saison à Rihata,* the town of Rihata is perceived as exile in its final and irrevocable form. Each of the protagonists experiences a feeling of nostalgia for a place altogether beyond reach. Stranded in this drab provincial town located in an undetermined African nation, they go through life haunted by the memories of their failed hopes. Christophe, the heroine's nephew and adopted son, attempts unsuccessfully to unveil his mysterious past by discovering the circumstances of his birth. Overcome by apathy and an acute feeling of uprootedness, they keep assessing their failures and disillusions, yet they still remain in a land with which they feel no bond. The notion of exile is inherent to the very topic of *Ségou: les murailles* which deals which the era of intense mobility and cultural transition resulting from the simultaneous effects of the slave trade, and the spreading of both Islam and Christianity on the African continent. The preceding are straight, obvious, and concrete representations of the concept of exile set in a psychological or historical context. In addition, throughout the whole work, other images are used that also embody the same notion; among them three metaphors, the absent mother, the adoptive mother, and the seductress.

Mothers are familiar figures in these novels, and understandably so, considering the symbolic connection between native land and motherhood: both suggest origins, primary source of nurturing, both are seen as the earliest molding forces. The association between the two has become an institutionalized feature in literary discourse. The mother motif assumes a specific interest in Condean fiction, however, because it is treated from a distinctive perspective. It is noticeable that, indeed, in most cases the child-mother relationship is a traumatic one. Mothers are seldom shown in a caring, protective role, cushioning their children's world to keep them from being hurt. On the contrary, absence, death, desertion, ambiguity are the motifs most frequently associated with mother figures who often appear as immaterial and ineffectual characters with little or no grasp on the dynamics of the situation. They remain enshrined in the memory of their children who long to be reunited with them, or in their imagination when actual remembrances cannot be called forth. The circumstances of the mother's absence vary from deliberate or imposed separation to death and disappearance of the child (as is the case for Naba, stolen from his village by slave raiders). In *Ségou: les murailles,* the young slave Sira flees toward freedom leaving behind the son she bore for her master. Christophe's mother ends her life shortly after giving birth to him, and Nadié also commits suicide, abandoning her children. Their mothers' presence is felt

mentally and emotionally by the children through the intensity of their desire to be with her; nonetheless, their absence is an irrevocable fact. Absence and presence are then the structural components which command both the themes of motherhood and exile, and other related themes: forced expatriation, nostalgia for the native land, attempts to recapture the lost country through compensatory memories and fantasies—in short, a whole process aimed at conjuring absence with the delusion of presence. The thematic correlation between the mother's disappearance and the inaccessibility of the native land is evident, which justifies considering one term as the signified and the other as the signifier. Their interrelatedness is further exemplified in *Ségou: les murailles* where the protagonist's native land and his mother are the objects of his single quest. Ségou, the cradle of the Traoré family, and Nya, the archetypical mother are inseparably linked in the minds of her exiled sons in whose memories they merge.

The mother figure still functions as a metaphor for the native land even when it is not in the least the object of the child's regrets, for even then it remains associated with the notion of lack and deprivation. Such is the case in *Hérémakhonon*: the relationship between Véronica and her mother bears the stamp of incompatibility. Véronica views her mother as an insignificant woman forever echoing her husband, following his lead submissively, and totally inept as a mother. Her feelings toward her are a combination of mild pity, irony, and condescension. Even though the two women have been away from each other for several years, Véronica's memories of her mother are free from anguish or grief. In the present case, the metaphoric equivalent of exile is neither the mother's death, nor her actual disappearance, but rather her failure to perform her duties as a mother. The absence of maternal qualities becomes synonymous with the notion of absence itself. Once again, the exiled person's awareness of his native land is defined by the coexisting notions presence-absence.

Still another figure, the adoptive mother, in a complementary relation with the mother, also appears frequently. She is evocative of the land finally reached by the expatriate. Both the adoptive mother and the land of exile represent shelter for the outcast and the disinherited. They both provide for survival without granting their protégés any emotional fulfillment, and without giving them a feeling of total belonging as they had once experienced it. Expatriates must conform, if only outwardly, to a new and alienating way of life, but, inwardly, they are unable and unwilling to stifle their loyalty to their former existence. In his article, "Utopia, Promised Lands, Immigration and Exile," Fernando Ainsa uses the term "integration" to identify the moment of the exile process when it becomes necessary to pretend adjusting to an imposed and hostile surrounding, adding that such a pretense is not compelling enough to blur memories of the native land. Living in exile means confronting diverging aspects of reality, and facing ambiguity, being part of the present while feeling oneself removed from it, being tied to a past no longer valid, yet responding to its echoes. An adopted child in the care of the mother's substitute finds himself in a parallel situation. Nya (*Ségou: les murailles*), Marie-Hélène (*Une Saison à Rihata*), and Mabo Julie (*Hérémakhonon*) treat the children entrusted to them with undeniable devotion, which still does not alter the fact that, as adoptive mothers, their role remains a vicarious one. Well aware of the solicitude bestowed on them, the children continue all the same to keep alive the lingering memory of their natural mothers to whom they give their deepest affection.

The ambivalent function of the adoptive mother is aptly brought out in Nya's statement to Malobali, her husband's natural son whom she raises as her own: "Je suis ta mère puisque je suis la femme de ton père et puisque je t'aime. Pourtant ce n'est pas moi qui t'ai porté dans mon ventre" (I am your mother because I am your father's wife, and because I love you. However, I am not the woman who carried you in my womb) (*Ségou: les murailles*). Those words affirm concisely and straightforwardly the irreductible difference between biological and natural mothers, while also denying that difference on the emotional level. According to Nya, such difference is obliterated whenever the adoptive mother provides the child the love and attention of which he is deprived as a result of his mother's unavailability. From her perspective, parity between the two roles is thus achieved, but not so for the adopted children in Condé's fictional universe for whom the disparity remains inalterable, as evidenced by the anxieties and contradictions which mar their lives despite their adoptive mothers' affection. Nya's words assume a significance all the more symbolic for being addressed to Malobali, a constant wanderer, a man without a country, a son without a mother, whose repeated attempts to find acceptance in the land of exile have been fraught with ambivalence. As he travels from the Sahel down to the coast of Benin, the thought of his unknown mother is constantly with him.

Malobali's aimless wandering are emblematic of his failed quest for his mother; as a man in exile, as an adopted child, he faces a problematic situation which results from the interplay of two opposite notions: identity and difference. His life bears the mark of an irreductible contradiction because the two notions cannot be reconciled.

However, in *Ségou: les murailles,* the land of exile offers characteristics quite unlike those which have been associated with the image of the adoptive mother. This time, it is embodied by the image of the seductress who at first uses her wiles in order to attract the exiled man, then when, fascinated by her, he attempts to win her acceptance, she reviles him for being an outsider, and finally she rejects him. Through her rejection, his status as a permanent outcast is sealed: a final refusal is opposed to his wish to be ever reconciled with his exile, and to be accommodated to it; he is forbidden any attempt to develop any intimate bond to the land of exile. His fate is to remain forever unwelcome, dispossessed. Such is Thièkhoro's case: as he pursues his Koranic studies in Tombouctou, he is scornfully rejected by his teacher's daughter who at first had invited his advances (*Ségou: les murailles*). In the same novel, Eucaristus meets with a similar fate at the hands of Eugenia, a wealthy mulatto girl in Lagos.

Those two representations of exile, the adoptive mother and the seductress, stand in sharp and puzzling contrast, as far as their connotative content is concerned. The explanation lies in the fact that each of them reflects the expatriate's changing perspective and evolving feelings as he becomes gradually better adapted to his condition with the passing of time. Ainsa describes him as accepting, maybe unconsciously, his new environment "without realizing that he is putting roots in the new country and from simple adaptation he is passing to integration." Then, as his longing for his native land becomes less acute, he develops new habits, and the trials of uprooting become more bearable, he is able to value more objectively the place which is to be his home from then on. The enigmatic or traumatizing aspects of the foreign universe appear gradually more rational, friendly, and reassuring; the new land appears alluring, and some of its practices and values worth trying. The metaphor of the foreign seductress represents the crystallization of the newly discovered attractiveness and desirability of the land of exile, while the rejected lover motif embodies the notion of condemnation to permanent exile and the forbidding of any inclination to allow oneself to adjust to the conditions of exile.

Each of these figures, the absent mother, the adoptive mother, and the seductress has a representational content of its own. They stand in relation to one another as the successive stages of a developing metaphor which itself stems from the archetypical analogy between the native land and the mother. Then, the distinction between native land and land of exile is effected through a ramification of the original mother metaphor with, as a result, the formation of dual figuration, natural mother, adoptive mother. Finally, the image of the seductress which carries no connotation with motherhood represents an entirely new step in the series.

Regardless of the process of modulation and transformation undergone by those metaphors, they retain a common characteristic which is an antithetical structure. The contrasting notions of absence/presence, identity/difference, and seduction/rejection in the case of the seductress stand as opposite poles of the respective metaphors. As a sign of wide difference and sharp contrast, antithesis is the figure of incompatibility. Here, it conveys pertinently the irreducible character of the contradictions experienced by those in exile, as well as the tensions to which they are subjected. Their lives are beset by conflicting realities: loyalty to their native land, yet obligation to stay away from it, occasional temptation to yield to the attractiveness of the land of exile, yet awareness of the prohibitions that render any bond with that land impossible. Exile, therefore, is perceived as an unceasing problem never to be resolved.

The concept of exile is thus communicated through the use of certain metaphors which have been studied so far from the point of view of their figurative content and of their structure, respectively. However, there is still another dimension to the functioning of the exile imagery in Maryse Condé's novels. When those metaphors are studied in relation to their frequency and pattern of distribution, a vision of exile emerges carrying deeper implications and endowed with profound meaning.

Condé's fictional discourse is markedly self-referential; it contains frequent instances of duplications, parallels, echoes, and mirror effects either in the space of a single novel or throughout other works. Characters, segments, situations, and of course metaphors are parts of this echoing process.

Self-referentiality, a literary device with obvious merits, has been abundantly documented by contemporary critics. Among them, Janet Patterson, author of an article titled, "L'Autoreprésentation: formes et discours," underlines the complexity of this narrative technique, as well as its expressive power. Her description of self-referentiality could be applied to Maryse Condé's fictional discourse, "Par le biais de répétitions, le texte se dédouble (se représente littéralement) et en présentant tel syntagme ou telle scène, deux, trois, quatre fois, il exhibe sa pratique signifiante" (Through the use of repetitions, the text is duplicated [literally speaking it represents itself], and by presenting a particular syntagm or scene two, three, four times, it demonstrates its own capacity to generate meaning). Recurrences are so numerous that their frequency cannot be discounted as mere coincidences; rather, they must be viewed as indicators stressing the theme of exile through the work, and making it more visible. The image of the motherless child is typical of Maryse Condé's fiction writing in this respect. It is used repeatedly not only in its general configuration, but also some of its specific features are recurrent. Its importance is forcefully brought out through the process of repetition. For example, Christophe, in **Une Saison à Rihata,** Siga and Malobali, in **Ségou: les murailles,** are all three motherless. A further similarity then appears between Christophe and Siga in the fact that both mothers died by suicide. In two other cases, it is the mode of suicide that is identical: both Nadié and Siga's mothers drown in a well. As has already been mentioned, the figure of the adoptive mother is a familiar one; Marie-Hélène, in **Une Saison à Rihata,** Nya, in **Ségou: les murailles,** Mabo Julie, in **Hérémakhonon** are at least three of its incarnations. Tièkhoro's and Eucaristus's experiences as rejected suitors further illustrate the prominence of redundancy as a literary technique in Maryse Condé's novels.

Besides assuming a thematic function, these emphasis-producing mechanisms play a significant role in developing the ideology that informs the work as a whole. In the space and time framework of the novels, they make up a pattern through which a specific concept of exile emerges which represents an aspect of a specific world view. It is, indeed, noteworthy that the metaphors recur in spatial and temporal circumstances quite distinct from one another while involving the same actants, and dealing with similar and identically structured situations. Exile, as represented by those metaphors is presented as an event repeated several times, and regardless of specific circumstances. They occur according to a cyclical pattern, which further emphasizes the character of doom and permanence of the exile situation. From such a perspective, the notion of exile assumes a much broader meaning: it transcends the literary significance of the word which refers to a situation of imposed expatriation, and instead, it designates a condition perceived as universal in scope and fatidic in its manifestations which could apply to any state of affairs that creates a sense of alienation resulting from irreconcilable tensions and irreductible ambiguities.

From this broadened conception of exile, it follows that expatriation is not the only form of exile, and that other figures as well as the expatriate can also embody the isolation and frustration experienced by those who have no more hope of recovering their country. Exile is a condition shared by all the people engaged in their quest for a demanding ideal that remains unattainable; it is then viewed as an intrinsic part of the human condition, as the fate of anyone who feels inescapably constrained by adverse circumstances.

Whether they wander in search of their lost origins, or try to recapture their vanished past, whether, surrendering to defeat, they retreat from action, Maryse Condé's characters experience a feeling of mental exile no less acute as their experiential exile embodied by the latter. They try unsuccessfully to reach the deeper levels of their psyche from which they feel hopelessly remote. They are both acutely aware of their inner inconsistencies and of their own inability to reach a harmonious psychological and emotional balance.

As literary characters, they have many precedents, among them, Chateaubriand's René whose aspirations could not be fulfilled; like him, "le bien inconnu," the unknown delight that they pursue constantly remains inaccessible. As a result, they become disenchanted, and feel the need to escape, some by appealing to their memories, others to their imagination as a way to compensate for the inadequacies of their actual condition. In this regard, they are reminiscent of Emma Bovary, whose uneventful life was enlivened by her imaginary fantasies. Still, other characters face the discrepancy between their aspirations and their own circumstances more dynamically: they undertake an active search for the land/mother instead of allowing memories and dreams to dominate their lives. The exile metaphors can be seen as symbolic of the notion of dilemma because they represent incompatible options forcing individuals to face unresolvable conflicts. Those metaphors offer some similarity with Baudelaire's "double postulation" which also exerts a tension on those who are subjected to its actions, and leave them at the crossroad of divergent and equally compelling realities.

One could ponder over the reasons why the exile metaphors are so frequently and so organically integrated in Maryse Condé's writings. Biographical circumstances might account for this phenomenon by bringing out the fact of the writer's Guadeloupean birth: her works could be seen as reflecting the tensions inherent to the alleged cultural conflict faced by Antilleans divided between allegiance to their remote African heritage and the necessity to accommodate the values associated with the Western model. It remains that speculating on the deeper and more complex motivations which come into play in the act of literary creation is highly hypothetical, Biographical sources often prove to be insufficient in identifying the authentic origin of a creative work. However, beyond the field of speculation stands the assertion that the exile imagery in Maryse Condé's fiction results from a conscious and controlled artistry, further reinforcing the coherence and depth of a body of work already endowed with numerous merits.

**Adele King (essay date October 1991)**

SOURCE: "Two Caribbean Women Go to Africa: Maryse Condé's *Hérémakhonon* and Myriam Warner-Vieyra's *Juletane*," in *College Literature*, Vol. 18, No. 3, October, 1991, pp. 96-105.

[*King is an American educator, critic, and editor whose works include* French Women Novelists: Defining a Female Style *(1989). In the excerpt below, she considers the themes of gender and nationality in* Hérémakhonon.]

*Hérémakhonon* (the title is a Malinké word meaning "to wait for happiness") is the story of a Guadeloupean teacher who goes to an unnamed West African country resembling Sekou Touré's Guinea as a *co-opérante* for the French government. While French West Indian bourgeois men had of course gone to Africa for many generations as members of the French colonial bureaucracy, Véronica is part of a distinctly modern world in which women, particularly foreign women, have moved beyond traditional roles; she teaches philosophy, to male students. She also expects a kind of sexual freedom usually denied to African women. Ambivalently, she wants to find a place for herself in the country and yet to remain apart. She refuses for some time to be involved in politics, even after her favorite pupil and the head of the school where she teaches are imprisoned, tortured, and eventually killed for opposing the regime; indeed, she starts a love affair with a government minister responsible for the torture of her friends. Finally, however, she decides to return to Paris and possibly to her white French lover.

*Hérémakhonon* is an exploration of the various boundaries Véronica has experienced and the ways in which they intersect. Specifically, she is concerned with defining her identity as a woman, a native of the Caribbean, a black for whom Africa is largely mythical, and a member of an intellectual elite within the French tradition. Véronica describes her childhood experience as having taught her to be proud to be black; her family's way of life, however, was completely shaped by French customs and by a middle-class scorn of the poor black community. Consequently, her search is partly for a community not divided by class considerations. But it is also a search for a black man who can be free; as she puts it, she wants to sleep with a black man who has never been branded. Véronica's attempts at moral and intellectual honesty are often at odds with her psychological need to find a strong man.

Condé treats with irony the tensions resulting from the various roles into which Véronica tries to fit. She does not, however, leave Véronica without hope. *Hérémakhonon* is a bildungsroman in which, at the end, there is real moral and intellectual development, as well as a chance for a new start. Writing in *French Review* [Vol. 62, 1988], two American critics present a model of how gender considerations may influence the reading of a novel, a model almost too good to be true for a feminist theorist. [In "Reading below the Belt: Sex and Sexuality in Françoise Ega and Maryse Condé,"] Arthur Flannigan suggests that the novel has a negative message: Véronica looks for a father figure and does not find one. Arlette Smith, on the other hand, [in her *La parole des Femmes* and her "L'Afrique,

un continent difficile,"] claims—as I would, and as Condé herself has stated in interviews—that Véronica leaves West Africa not defeated, but with a new sense of her identity. Smith sees *Hérémakhonon* as a search for a mother figure, which becomes for Véronica not Africa but Guadeloupe. Looking for mothers appears positive to a woman critic; looking for fathers—even, for Flannigan, seeing one's female self as primarily "a sexual being"—strikes a male critic as negative. Similarly, Smith speaks of the love felt for the surrogate mother, Mabo Julie, a servant in Véronica's family home, whereas Flannigan writes that Véronica "holds all the women that populate her past and her present more or less in contempt."

Women are often symbolic figures for national identity in texts by men; this trope also appears in these novels. It is tempting to see Véronica as a figure for Guadeloupe itself, in her passivity, lack of purpose, and need to see herself in relation to both France and Africa. Thus her decision that she must return home can be read as an indication that Guadeloupe should define itself as a separate society; indeed, Condé has suggested as much in various articles and interviews where she speaks of creativity coming from a culture that is part of the New World, neither French nor African. While Africa has often been envisaged by Caribbeans as the "mother country," for Condé it is "difficult, even impossible, to retie the broken threads," [as noted in her *Le roman antillais,* Vol. 1, p. 18]. She comments that "a Caribbean's quest for identity can very well be resolved without going, especially physically, to Africa, or, if you want, the journey to Africa simply proves that Africa is not essential to Caribbean identity" (**"Afrique"**). Likewise, the heroine of Condé's *La vie scélérate* (1987), after an ironic look at all the confusions and betrayals of the previous generations of her family; their travels to many countries; their adoption of Garveyism, Marxism, Black Power, or Christianity, decides that she must find the "book that needs to be written" in the history of her own family, not in the theories of Marcus Garvey, a "dangerous crank" who "naively forgets that three centuries have passed."

But Véronica's problems are not merely typical of her gender, nationality, and background; she is also an individual. Part of her appeal as a narrator is her racy style, her outspokenness, even her obsession with sexual activity. She is clearly a sexual being, and this is perhaps the most obvious way in which Condé (who has stated that feminist demands are not typical of Caribbean women's writing [*Parole*]) shows how women have been denied their own voice in Western culture. Indeed, in her sexual frankness Véronica reminds us of some of Colette's narrators, whose sensuality surpasses that of later, more overtly "feminist" writers in French.

Condé has created for Véronica a distinctively individual method of narration. She seems to be giving us an interior monologue, narrating her story with some formal coherence but essentially reproducing her thoughts. But since we often find other characters replying to what the reader assumed were Véronica's reflections, we realize that she speaks without always clearly distinguishing between conversation and interior monologue. One of her conversations with her lover, Ibrahima Sory, offers an example. The text punctuates only his dialogue as if it were spoken:

> "I found out about your student. He was sent to the North with his comrades. He will tarmac the roads and clear the forest. That will give him time to think."
>
> Think about what? What do they want him to think about? . . . [Her comments seem to be her thoughts, but Sory responds.] He closes his eyes.
>
> "Women are exhausting. That's why I live 600 kilometers from mine."
>
> From his? It's all very well to be broad-minded. So he's married? [Again she refers to him in the third person, but he replies.]
>
> "I was married off while I was studying in Paris, to a young girl I had seen twice. . . ."
>
> And where is she? What does this bride do?

There are many such examples. The style shows partly Véronica's obsession with herself, the narcissism that makes her desire for sex seem almost as important as the torture and imprisonment of her friends; it may also show the very insecurity of her sense of self. Does she *know* when she is speaking to others and when to herself? Véronica's use of direct free thought presents what she says and what she thinks in such an intermingled fashion that we are never sure exactly what is spoken. Françoise Lionnet sees this device as setting "Véronica's discourse within a frame of reference so alien to Sory's own that whatever she may say will not be heard by him." The style can also be seen as a reflection of the passivity that in Condé's view has largely defined the intellectual elite of Guadeloupe: "Caribbean society is a dependent society—economically, politically, culturally. It is attached, across the ocean, to a 'metropolitan' center which influences its life" (**Roman**).

Although Véronica comes to some realization of her own problems and to an awareness that modern Africa is a real continent with pressing needs that have nothing to do with her search for either a "mother" land or a replacement for her father (whom she calls *"le marabout mandingue"* because he resembles a portrait in an African encyclopedia), Condé does not leave the reader feeling that a message has been given. Indeed, she has been very critical of theories of *"littérature engagée,"* terming "naïve" Aimé Césaire's belief that reading or writing could make a difference (**"Afrique"**) and inverting Jean-Paul Sartre's dictum "Writing is a way of demanding liberty" (*"Ecrire, c'est une certaine façon de vouloir la liberte"*) to "Writing means that the artist needs liberty" (*"Ecrire sous-entend la liberté du créateur"* [**Roman**]). The style of her work, with its combination of mockery and affection for her characters, and the antiromantic treatment of their sexual experiences, provides a sharp contrast to the seriousness found in much African and Caribbean fiction.

**Howard Frank Mosher** (review date 25 October 1992)

SOURCE: "Staying Alive," in *The New York Times Book Review,* October 25, 1992, pp. 11-12.

[*Mosher is an American novelist and short story writer whose works include* Where the Rivers Flow North *(1978) and* A Stranger in the Kingdom *(1989). In the following review of* I, Tituba, Black Witch of Salem *and* Tree of Life, *he praises Condé's sense of history and compassion, stating that "it is impossible to read her novels and not come away from them with both a sadder and more exhilarating understanding of the human heart."*]

In the final chapter of **Segu,** Maryse Condé's historical novel of 19th-century tribal West Africa, the youthful Muhammad, scion of one of the great families along the Upper Niger, is about to take part in a huge and terrifying battle. As blue-turbaned horsemen gallop toward him brandishing lances, as sabers clash and iron balls whirl on chains, he thinks fleetingly of his mother. "Then," Ms. Condé writes, in the last sentence of the novel, "he set his teeth and didn't think of anything except staying alive."

The world's literature has always abounded with great survivors. And although contemporary American fiction may offer readers fewer heroes than the notable novels of earlier generations, there are still plenty of first-rate novelists, here and abroad, whose characters not only survive the worst that life can throw at them but also often prevail, on their own terms, against overwhelming odds. The brilliant and prolific Maryse Condé—born in Guadeloupe, a longtime resident of Paris and now a professor of French at the University of California, Berkeley—is just such a writer. And with the appearance this fall of uniformly excellent English translations of **I, Tituba, Black Witch of Salem** and **Tree of Life,** readers in this country will have the considerable pleasure of acquainting themselves with more of her durable survivors.

Ms. Condé's Tituba is based loosely on the black slave woman who was tried for witchcraft in Salem, Mass., in 1692. In Ms. Condé's fictional rendition of the story, Tituba is born to an African mother who was raped by an English sailor on the deck of a slave ship called Christ the King. In Barbados, Tituba's childhood abruptly ends when, at the age of 7, she watches her mother try to fight off a rapist; the child hands her the cutlass with which she defends herself. Tituba's mother is hanged in the presence of all the other slaves. "I watched her body swing from the lower branches of a silk-cotton tree," Tituba says. "She had committed a crime for which there is no pardon. She had struck a white man."

Tituba's luck improves when she is driven off the plantation and adopted by an old woman who knows the secrets of spells and herbs and how to communicate with the dead. But although her years learning Mama Yaya's lore are happy ones, the teen-age Tituba succumbs to the temptations of the outside world and marries a happy-go-lucky slave named John Indian. Brought back into slavery by love, Tituba falls afoul of her new mistress and is sold to a tyrannical Puritan minister named Samuel Parris, who takes Tituba and her husband to New England.

What a fanatical sect Ms. Condé's Puritans turn out to be: sadists and murderers, rabid misogynists and racists who hang and torture women, imprison tiny children, burn Jewish families out of their homes and regularly accuse black slaves of being in league with Satan. Tituba offers an ingenuous appraisal of their doctrine of eternal damnation: "Perhaps it's because they have done so much harm to their fellow beings, to some because their skin is black, to others because their skin is red, that they have such a strong feeling of being damned?" At the same time, Tituba has a few shortcomings of her own—including a blindly passionate sexual dependence on the feckless John Indian—which make her a fully believable and very appealing character.

In less sure hands, this short, powerful novel, which won France's Grand Prix Littéraire de la Femme in 1986, might well have become merely an extended denunciation of a perverted and evil society. What makes it larger and richer are Ms. Condé's gift for storytelling and her unswerving focus on her characters, combined with her mordant sense of humor, (Hester Prynne, from *The Scarlet Letter,* makes a cameo appearance when she's imprisoned with Tituba, lamenting that her new friend will never be much of a feminist.)

Miraculously, Tituba manages to extricate herself from her tormentors and return to Barbados, where she becomes a legendary figure to the black population. However, in the final irony of the story, she is brought up for execution by an official eager to make an example of rebellious slaves. Her life seems about to end in martyrdom, just as her mother's did.

Or does it? With the help of some ghosts from Tituba's past, Maryse Condé has fashioned a marvelous final surprise for her readers. Part historical novel, part literary fable, part exploration of the clash of irreconcilable cultures *I, Tituba, Black Witch of Salem* is most of all an affirmation of a courageous and resourceful woman's capacity for survival.

The forces of good and evil are not so sharply differentiated in *Tree of Life,* Ms. Condé's passionate, multigenerational novel (originally published in France in 1987) about the endlessly intriguing family of Albert Louis, born on Guadeloupe in the early 1870's, a patriarch as morally complex as he is simply stubborn. A devout disciple of the American black nationalist Marcus Garvey, Albert doesn't hesitate to wring every last cent from the impoverished black families who dwell in the wretched tenement houses he owns. He's a man of deep contradictions and still deeper gloom. Yet, in his own way, Albert is nearly as tough a survivor as Tituba.

As a young boy, Albert manages to escape harm after taking a long plunge "from the main limb of a breadfruit tree, for he had taken it into his head to fly." A few years later, he boldly strikes out from Guadeloupe to Panama, where the Americans are "tampering with the very structure of the world and cutting continents in two." As a member of a daring explosives team at work on the Panama Canal, he emerges relatively unscathed from all kinds of potential disasters, until the loss of his wife, Liza, in childbirth almost drives him mad. After taking his infant son home to his mother in Guadeloupe, Albert heads for San Francisco, hoping his luck will change. After all, aren't the mountains of California glittering with gold nuggets, free for anyone who wants to bend over and pick them up?

> **It is impossible to read Condé's novels and not come away from them with both a sadder and more exhilarating understanding of the human heart, in all its secret intricacies, its contradictions and marvels.**
>
> **—*Howard Frank Mosher***

Like their forebear, many of Albert's descendants range out to far-flung destinations beyond their native country, including New York and Paris, both of which Ms. Condé renders with great vivacity. Best of all, though, are her vivid evocations of Guadeloupe. She can even make a cemetery seem enticing: "Situated at the town gates, the graveyards of Guadeloupe are cities of the dead, where the *filau,* the beautiful beefwood tree, keeps weeping watch over the departed. There marble, glass and carefully whitened concrete strive to outdo each other. Ornamental bowls, flowers, crosses or crowns of pearls are placed on the graves. Votive lamps are kept lit on each side of a picture of the deceased, their tenacious and fragile flames symbolizing the affection of the living."

The family of Albert Louis is haunted by suicide, as expatriates succumb to loneliness and desperation. They are also stricken with grief, retreating into prolonged and impenetrable states of despair. Somehow, though, most endure—occasionally as thoroughly appealing ghosts.

In one of the funniest episodes of this immensely entertaining novel, the fiercely jealous spirit of Albert's first wife, Liza, torments her son, Bert, with the most explicit sexual fantasies about his stepmother, Elaise. Only after Elaise dies and becomes a ghost herself do Albert's wives become friends—preparing breakfast together for their brooding old husband, chatting companionably with him on the veranda in the evening. They discreetly look the other way when Albert takes his early-morning nip. "A little rum never hurt anyone. It's even the best remedy for life."

Other memorable survivors in *Tree of Life* include Albert's son Jean, who spends seven and a half years writing a folk history entitled *Unknown Guadeloupe,* which eventually becomes a national classic after being virtually ignored in its author's lifetime; Thécla, Albert's scholarly, lovelorn granddaughter, and Coco, Thécla's troubled daughter, the narrator of the novel, whose destiny it is to recount the amazing story of her family.

From 18th-century Africa to the America of the Rev. Dr. Martin Luther King Jr. and Malcolm X, Maryse Condé has chronicled in her wonderful fiction the lives of a series of remarkable individuals and the families that surround them. It is impossible to read her novels and not come away from them with both a sadder and more exhilarating understanding of the human heart, in all its secret intricacies, its contradictions and marvels.

## Suzanne Crosta   (essay date Winter 1992)

SOURCE: "Narrative and Discursive Strategies in Maryse Condé's *Traversée de la mangrove*," in *Callaloo*, Vol. 15, No. 1, Winter, 1992, pp. 147-55.

[*In the essay below, Crosta discusses Condé's narrative techniques in* Traversée de la mangrove, *stating that although there is no single authoritative voice in the work, "one notices in the use of varied points of view, the voice of an implicit author who prudently guides the reader to reflect upon the notion of identity as a cultural construct."*]

Maryse Condé's latest novel, entitled **Traversée de la mangrove,** explores the question of gender and formal structures in light of the author's attempt to define a narrative center that would effectively subvert not only patriarchal discourse but also the colonial discourse within which it is inscribed. It is relevant to note that there is no single authoritative voice in **Traversée de la mangrove** and yet one notices in the use of varied points of view, the voice of an implicit author who prudently guides the reader to reflect upon the notion of identity as a cultural construct whose limits and boundaries define the individual self. The premise of a narrative center here is not to be confused with a single vision or narrative voice. Condé's text defies, or, more accurately rejects this notion since the varied points of view would have us redefine the center as a homogeneous entity. It would be more appropriate to speak of a multiple individual whose divergent perspectives challenge the assumptions of a particular representation of reality.

It is most befitting that at the narrative center of the text is the ambiguous character of Francis Sancher whose untimely demise serves a twofold purpose. First, the deliberate silence and death of the main character forces the reader to adapt his/her reading from a referential mode (a given representation of the universe) to a cognitive mode (the subjective or objective perception of the represented universe). Second, this strategy serves as a pretext to study how one's personal identity is defined and determined by the other's mirror image of him/her self with regard to others. The dialectical relationships between men and women, between the young and the old, between the individual and society are brought to the foreground and are formally introduced by the divergent points of view of the characters and their respective discourse.

A careful reading of **Traversée de la mangrove** allows the reader to discover the tension between the semiotic and the symbolic as they relate to one's identity as a cultural and linguistic construct. The oscillation between the first and third person narrative in the text is indicative of the implicit author's intention to differentiate and problematize the narrative voices of her characters. From this intention emerges the search for a style or a form capable of reflecting and refracting impressions and perceptions of reality, a reality that Condé seeks to evoke rather than legitimize.

It is necessary to distinguish the two narrative planes of **Traversée de la mangrove** from each other where the different points of view are articulated and are differentiated. The first level, which Genette would call diegetic, relates to the wake of Francis Sancher; the second, the metadiegetic level, involves the *thoughts,* impressions, testimonies of the deceased's acquaintances. The diegetic narrative is assumed by an implicit narrator that we have designated as implicit author while the metadiegetic narrative can be divided into two groups of narrators: those whose subjectivity is represented by the first person and those whose subjectivity is objectified and relegated to the third person. The implicit author does not take over the narrative; on the contrary, the coherence of the text is assured by the personal testimonies of those who knew Francis Sancher. Consequently, the narrative of the wake figures prominently in the prologue, "Le Serein," and the epilogue, "Le Devant-jour," thereby enclosing the body of the text, entitled "La Nuit," which includes the various testimonies of the characters. The titles of the prologue, the narrative and the epilogue emphasize the temporal dimensions of this text, where the reader will delve into the night and emerge into the first light of daybreak. The temporal references allude to a transition, a possible transformation that may be seen as a new beginning.

From the outset of the text, the reader notices that all female characters (Mira, Man Sonson, Léocadie, Rosa, Vilma and Dodose Pelagie) express themselves in the first person. This strategy is undoubtedly used to sensitize the reader to the material and social conditions of women in the small community of Rivière au Sel as well as to eliminate all barriers that could indeed separate the reader and the narrator/character. The introspective nature of the narrative further aims at giving the reader a sense of the diversity of perspectives of those who speak in the first person. Perceived by the other as an object of desire, the women characters of the text subtly reverse this objectification by assuming their own discourse. They recount, and sometimes evaluate very harshly, the discourse of the community at large. Man Sonson underscores the hypocrisy and jealousy of the inhabitants of Rivière au Sel, and she goes so far as to show the personal motivations that dictate their behaviour and actions. When recalling the value judgments that the community ascribed to Francis Sancher, Man Sonson reveals the subjectivity and the trivialization of his existence. She remarks that there are some who fear the viciousness of his dogs; others, his nonchalance; others, his sexual prowess.

Although Mira, Dinah, and Vilma subject themselves one by one to Francis Sancher in the hope that he will better their situation, their respective accounts show how Francis Sancher's death initiates their resolution to redefine their existence according to their needs and possibilities. It is interesting to note that Francis Sancher, "un mulâtre foncè" [a dark mulatto] is associated with the white plantation class. This claim is no doubt important to consider in light of his relationships with the men and women of Rivière au Sel. Condé may indeed imply that in the context of the Caribbean, racial differentiation of men and women within and outside their group exists because racial categorization is subordinate to socioeconomic status.

In *Traversée de la mangrove,* the fascination of women for Francis Sancher, the virile, intelligent stranger, is symptomatic of the consequences of the economic superstructure of (post-)plantation society. Condé seeks to highlight the situation of the colonized women who are attracted to the male colonizer only in so far as he represents a possible way out of their misery. The notion of compromise may be extended to the situation of the colonized writer, who is forced in most cases to translate her/his experience and write in the language of the colonizer in order to be published.

Mira's recollection of her relationship with Francis Sancher indicates her geographical and psychological isolation and her subsequent fascination with anyone who comes from "Ailleurs" [Elsewhere]. For her and the other women of Rivière au Sel, Francis Sancher symbolizes another way of life. The disparity between the referential representation of Francis Sancher (based on a reading of the sociological data of the character) and the symbolic representation of Francis Sancher (based on a reading of the form and interpretation of the data) would in fact explain the intention to transform the constants that determine the social and verbal representations of the female subject. The accounts of the older women in the text, such as Rosa and Léocadie, reveal the interiorization of a patriarchal value system which judges women according to their potential gratification powers. Timothée Léocadie, spinster and retired school teacher, longs for her youth and for the ability to seduce men. Her encounter with Francis Sancher is all the more upsetting since his fright and evasion at the sight of her forces her to deal with the realities of old age:

> Je suis rentrée chez moi, j'ai barricadé ma solitude et j'ai pleuré toutes les larmes de mon corps, j'ai pleuré comme je n'avais pas pleuré depuis cinquante ans.

> [I came back home, I barricaded my solitude and I shed all the tears of my body, I cried as I had not cried in 50 years.]

Similarly, Rosa, Vilma's mother, has also subjected herself to patriarchal authority, as represented by her husband. She continues to perpetuate the oppression of women by forcing her daughter into a marriage of convenience. As their separate accounts reveal, these older women act in this way because of their long victimization at the hands of those who represent the patriarchy (father, brother, husband, lover, etc.).

Inversely, the male characters in the text speak for the most part in the third person (Moïse, Aristide, Sonny, Loulou, Sylvestre, Cyrille, Carmélien, Désinor, Dodose, Lucien and Émile Étienne). The author opts for an objective perspective from which she will subtly interpret their thoughts and acts by using the free indirect discourse. It is also worth noting that the subjectivity of the male characters is in most cases framed by the punctuation of the text, such as quotation marks and dashes. When a male character expresses himself in the first person, his discourse is contained within quotation marks or introduced by a dash. The sections entitled "Moïse" and "Carmélien" are but two succinct examples where the subjectivity of the

male characters is marked from the very outset. This distancing effect is found in most sections where the male character's perspective is emphasized: "Désinor," "Lucien Évariste," "Émile Étienne. . . ." In cases where there are no introductory quotation marks, the author goes directly to free indirect discourse in the third person. The marked subjectivity of the male discourse raises a number of questions: Is it a strategy to associate male discourse with the biased social discourse? Is it a strategy to warn the reader against the ideological implications of such discourses? It seems that the views and statements put forth by Moïse, Carmélien, Désinor and other men are not shared by the implicit author. This authorial stance sheds some light on the mirror image of the author, who allows herself to be partially represented by female characters but not by male characters.

This distance between character/narrator and author can be explained by the ambiguous relationship between patriarchy and colonialism. In the sections that focus on the male voice, the social discourse naturally introduces itself, leading to hearsay, gossip, prejudicial remarks and so on. In the section where the voice of Moïse is supposed to reflect his subjectivity, the community's biases and prejudices figure so prominently in his discourse that the reader is led to conclude that his voice and vision are determined by the value judgments of the community. His narrative is peppered with impersonal pronouns ("on," "ils," "les gens"). The frequent use of introductory verbs that imply conjecture—"Il [Moïse] se croyait . . ." [He thought himself . . .]; "Il avait cru deviner . . ." [He had suspected . . .]; "Il avait commencé par s'imaginer . . ." [He had begun to imagine . . .]; "moïse crut avoir mal entendu . . ." [He thought he had misunderstood . . .]—further emphasizes that Moïse's thoughts and statements are subordinated to the social discourse of his community. It is highly significant that at the end of his narrative, Moïse's voice fuses with that of the chorus of mourners at Francis Sancher's wake. The subtle use of narrative voice, free indirect discourse and punctuation expose the verbal trappings of the social discourse prevalent in the speech of the male characters. The implicit author herself intervenes twice to warn the reader: "Mais les gens racontent n'importe quoi" [But people will say anything]; "Toutefois, je la répète, les gens disent n'importe quoi" [However, *I* repeat, people will say anything at all] [Emphasis added by author.] Invested with the impersonal pronoun "on," Moïse's discourse is problematized both for its referential ambiguity and for its ideological implications.

Conversely, it is revealing that the narratives in the first person criticize the discourse of the community of Rivière au Sel. Although the prejudices and biases of the inhabitants of Rivière au Sel are reproduced in Man Sonson's narrative, they are in turn exposed and subverted. In sharp contrast to the narratives in the third person, those in the first person resist on a discursive level integrating themselves into the dominant discourse. The female subject refuses to submit herself to the history of the subject where the masculine objectivity-claiming discourse took precedence. If male objectivity has led to the effacement of the subject, the author is here facilitating the emergence of a female subject that will not be fettered by the dominant social discourse. And again, as in her other works of fiction, the possibility of a sexual fusion would at best be inchoate if one considers that there seems to be no viable male/female relationship in *Traversée de la mangrove*.

There exist however two exceptions that deserve our attention. My earlier remarks regarding narrative voice do not apply to two sections of Condé's *Traversée de la mangrove:* "Joby" and "Xantippe." In these two sections, the discourse of the characters is expressed in the first person, reserved for the most part to express female subjectivity. This anomaly would suggest that the implicit author favors the representation of Francis Sancher by Joby and Xantippe, indeed that she favors their perception of reality. What are the distinctive traits of these two characters? Other than their social marginalization in the small community of Rivière au Sel, Joby and Xantippe are sensitive to the plight and emotions of women, and they also have the ability to decipher the symbols that define their existence.

The verbal stance of Joby subverts the patriarchal order represented by his father, Loulou. The use of the first person supports this argument since Joby refuses to assume the code of behavior considered by the community as appropriate for "a man," especially in circumstances where emotions are perceived to be a sign of weakness. During the funeral of his mother, Loulou expected his son to master his emotions and kiss the deceased:

> Voilà pourquoi papa m'a emmené ici. Pour que je voie un mort et me comporter comme un homme devant lui.
>
> [This is why my father brought me here. So that I can see a dead woman and behave like a man in front of him.]

Joby refuses to adopt the social code dictated for a man and suffers the consequences: he is ignored by his father and marginalized by the male brotherhood.

Xantippe, for his part, is a loner. Associated with the "soucagnan" whose gaze has mortal consequences for the beholder, Xantippe is gifted with powers that the community dreads. And yet, Xantippe mourns endlessly the loss of his wife. He is the *only* male character in the text to have experienced sexual and emotional gratification with his wife. Xantippe is also the only one to know of Francis Sancher's crime, thereby elucidating the mystery [the night] to the reader. His total mistrust of and disgust toward Francis Sancher is linked to the consequences of his crime—a crime that has forever broken affective and sexual ties with the female subject. While recounting his most memorable experience to Lucien Évariste, Sancher admits to having raped a young girl and the pleasure that he felt, declaring that "Je sens encore dans mes narines l'odeur de son sang vierge" [I can still feel her virgin blood's odor in my nostrils]. Although Francis Sancher's crime is never explicitly revealed, Xantippe claims he is answerable for multiple homicides. Xantippe's hatred towards Sancher stems from the fact that he holds him accountable for his profound sense of loss, a loss that is tied to his wife's death. Whilst Xantippe's hatred towards Sancher is linked to the

victimization of women, Joby's hatred is directed towards the father image that Sancher comes to assume in the text:

> Je me demande si d'autres garçons détestent leur père comme moi. Je voudrais qu'il meure. J'aimerais qu'il soit allongé là devant moi à la place de Francis Sancher qui lui aussi a fait beaucoup de mal autour de lui.
>
> [I wonder if other boys hate their father as I do. I wish he was dead. I'd like to see him lying before me in the place of Francis Sancher who has also caused much harm around him.]

The common denominator between Sancher and Loulou is their attempt at objectifying their existence, an attempt that can be explained by their adherence to, or interiorization of, the dominant discourse. On the one hand, Sancher would like Joby to distance himself from the oppressed because of their ingratitude; and on the other hand, Loulou would like Joby to act like a man and remain impervious to the emotions and sufferings of others. In both cases, the dominant discourse is demeaning and exclusive. The polyphonic nature of *Traversée de la mangrove* aims at reversing the existence of an authoritative voice. The diversity of perspectives and the various distancings within the narrative voice subvert the linearity of the narrative while allowing the author to explore the possibility of a plural discourse where the meaning of the text can be expressed semiotically and symbolically.

As I have stated, *Traversée de la mangrove* gathers a series of testimonies, nineteen in all, whose primary function is to elucidate for the reader the identity of Francis Sancher. However, the subjectivity of each character determines the interpretation of the information given. The facts revealed are symbolized and interpreted according to the particular impressions of the character and mediated again by the implicit author. The nineteen testimonies could in fact act on a symbolic level as markers in the mangrove. The spatial nature of the mangrove can mislead the stranger, just as the verbal trappings of the text can mislead the reader. The spatial disposition of the characters (they form a pious circle around the body of Francis Sancher) and the disposition of the narrative voices (each one claiming to know the truth) suggest the difficulty of deciphering the true identity of the deceased from the corpus given, as well as suggesting the impossibility of objectively reconstructing his (hi)story. It is interesting to note that the names and physical descriptions of the characters in the text further develop the symbolic dimension of the characters. Some examples are the patronyms "Boisgris" and "Boisfer" or even Francis Sancher's epithet "Piébwa" which each designates a type of tree. This association would imply that the characters personify the trees that define the mangrove. The implicit author alludes to "la forêt de ses poils" [the forest of his body hairs], "sa ramure argentée" [his silvery foliage], "son bras lourd comme une branche morte" [his arm heavy as a dead branch] and to the fact that "sa taille haute comme un mahogany" [he was as tall as a mahogany]. His friend, Moïse, is nicknamed the mosquito (the mangrove would thus be his natural habitat) and his mistresses, Mira and Dinah, are compared to flowers. These names further reinforce their symbolic association with the "pié-bwa," Francis Sancher.

All references to the constitutive elements of the mangrove are motivated. Joby claims to know the name of every "pié-bwa," that is of every tree belonging to the mangrove. Xantippe is also well acquainted with the flora of the island. From the outset of his narrative his relationship with nature is emphasized:

> J'ai nommé tous les arbres de ce pays. Je suis monté à la tëte du morne, j'ai crié leur nom et ils ont répondu à mon appel.
>
> [I have named all the trees in this country. I have climbed to the top of the mountain, I have cried out their names and they have answered my call.]

The topographical knowledge of the mangrove allows the two characters to cross the spatial and verbal topoi of Sancher. It is in the mangrove that Joby uncovers Sancher's stance against the oppressed. Joby escapes Sancher's verbal control thanks to his knowledge and comprehension of the flora. In Joby's case, nature plays an important role in the affirmation of self since it affords him the opportunity to escape from the seductive power of the oppressor.

Xantippe's topographical knowledge leads him to uncover the hidden meanings of nature, of words. He has the power to read and interpret the natural signs of his universe. It is not surprising that Xantippe should be the one to locate the scene of the crime. He is the only character that Sancher fears. The gaze and the words of Xantippe unmask truths that the other characters, Sancher included, cannot unearth. In this one feels an analogy with the colonized writer, whose vision also uncovers the violence that the language of the colonizer may be made to convey. Hence one can understand the author's predilection for metaphors, natural signs, for modes of knowledge that do not fix meaning.

The enigma surrounding Francis Sancher is never really resolved because of the ambiguities and the contradictions that beset the nineteen accounts. It is impossible to reconstruct the identity of the deceased because the referential data is sometimes misleading, sometimes suppressed, sometimes exaggerated, sometimes altered altogether. The reader does not quite know what is what. For example, the rumors concerning Sylvestre Ramsaran and Francis Sancher generate ambiguity. During a ceremony in the temple, Sylvestre Ramsaran, nine years of age at the time, is so overwhelmed by the sacrificial death of the "cabri" (young goat) that he wets his pants. This incident, when evoked among the inhabitants of the community, takes on such proportions that no one knows

> s'il avait vomi, uriné, déféqué, s'il avait hurlé, s'il s'était enfui terrifié au bout de la savane.
>
> [if he had vomited, urinated, defecated, or if he had yelled, if he had run away terrified to the end of the savannah.]

Similarly, according to the gossip and hearsay of the community, Francis Sancher was either a murderer, a drug runner, or an illegal arms dealer. The implicit author warns the reader that no accusation was ever substantiated. A collective portrait of Francis Sancher does not shed more light on his identity. Man Sonson claims that Francis Sancher was "un moulin à paroles" [chatterbox] while Vilma complains of his silent nature:

> il ne m'a jamais révélé de lui-même et je ne saurais pas dire la vérité dans toutes les bêtises que les gens de Rivière au Sel racontent.
>
> [he has never revealed himself to me and I wouldn't be able to tell the truth in all the foolishness that the inhabitants of Rivière au Sel are saying about him.]

Aristide and others accuse him of raping Mira, yet the latter denies the accusation. Carmélien and Aristide hate Sancher, while Lucien Evariste admires him. It is next to impossible to reproduce an authentic portrait of the deceased.

It is true that Sancher's death seems to have remedied the situation somewhat. He helped Dinah, Rosa and Dodose, for whom life had become "une geôle sans espoir" [a prison without hope], find their freedom. And at the same time, both Dinah and Dodose, prisoners of a failed marriage, decide to leave their husbands. Remembering the words that Francis Sancher had spoken to her: "Pour donner l'amour, il faut en avoir reçu beaucoup" [In order to give love, one has to have received a lot of it], Rosa, imprisoned in a past that took away her precious Shireen, decides to reconcile with the daughter she had so long neglected. But, in fact, Sancher acts as a catalyst; his death shakes up the whole community and forces everyone to rethink his or her priorities and redefine his or her existence. Although he seems to invite those who knew him to assume their voice and follow their path, the women of Rivère au Sel redefine their existence for themselves in terms of what they truly perceive to be happiness.

The representation of Francis Sancher is hence problematized. He represents an unattainable object of desire because he is dead. His death allows the implicit author to show the authority of his presence and his voice on the existence and discourse of others. Instead of depicting the exterior pressures that influenced the characters, the implicit author sheds light on the mediation of these pressures that influence our perception of the individual. The presence and power of Sancher manifest themselves in the individual and collective discourses of the inhabitants of Rivière au Sel. Sancher's words are at the source of their initiative to speak; they legitimize and determine their existence after his death. Is not Sancher the bearer of an ideology in so far as he dominates the verbal and psychic spaces of others? In fact, the implicit author tries to master and transform the ideology by creating not so much a diversity of female subjects but a way of perceiving in a feminine mode. The omniscient presence of the implicit author is manifest in her mastering the meaning of Sancher's statements. According to the testimonies of the characters, Sancher eschews assuming the image of a doctor/messiah, but his death subverts his original stance, and his words, detached from their referential context, convey a project of transformation through which the characters will find meaning and direction in their lives.

This metamorphosis, potential or actual, is the work of the implicit author, whose transformative power exceeds that of Sancher's.

Finally, *Traversée de la mangrove* invites the reader to play a dynamic role in the process of signification. Condé's manipulation of the conventions of detective plots (the identity of the mystery man; the particulars of the crime) underscores the importance of the act of reading within and outside the parameters of the text. Conscious of the levels of reference and symbolic interplay within which Sancher's identity can be explored, the implicit author purposely situates him outside the narrative, thereby directing the reader in and out of the text by the use of narrative and discursive strategies. Denied a concrete referential existence, Sancher's story is mediated by the perception and images that others have of him. But the author encounters two main difficulties: How does one balance the emphasis on male representation against an emphasis on a female mode of perceiving and interpreting? Since Sancher is at the source of the text as language, how does one reconcile the overdetermined meaning of the text with the perspective and discourse of the implicit author, who refuses to validate any attempt to fix or objectify reality? By the author's constant modification of them, distances and narrative voices serve as markers to guide the reader through the trappings of the mangrove—through the trappings of the text as language. The emergence of a female mode of perception, through which female and male (for example Joby and Xantippe) subjects could articulate their experiences, be they historical, political, or sexual, seems to be the primary focus of Condé's text. Therefore, the crossing of the mangrove, the understanding of the text as language, is meaningful only if the reader is willing to relinquish the notion of a single perspective or a unified perception of reality as the sole basis of knowledge and truth.

## Ellen W. Munley  (essay date Winter 1992)

SOURCE: "Mapping the Mangrove: Empathy and Survival in *Traversée de la mangrove*," in *Callaloo*, Vol. 15, No. 1, Winter, 1992, pp. 156-66.

[*In the following essay on* Traversée de la mangrove, *Munley attempts to answer the question, "Why do some [characters] continue to struggle toward life while others stagnate, resign themselves to solitude and exclusion, or beckon death?"*]

> You cannot pass through a thicket of mangrove trees. Their stiltlike stems and roots impale you. You dig your own grave and suffocate in the brackish water.
>
> I will seek the sun, air, and light to live the rest of my days.

Contrary to the novel bearing the same title within *Traversée de la mangrove* which its mysterious author, Francis Sancher, will never complete, Maryse Condé's novel bears thoroughgoing witness to the stories of twenty individuals. Some become entangled and drown in the mangrove thicket, a metaphor for present-day Guade-loupe; others move toward an originative sun illuminating the way home to personal truths that they must discover by themselves. On another level this complex narrative, comprised of ten first-person and ten third-person accounts intricately interwoven between a narrative introduction entitled "Le serein" [dusk] and a closing chapter named "Le devant-jour" [dawn], furnishes the reader with a metaphoric map detailing all the death-inducing traps in the mangrove thicket and ways to avoid them. The path to life and freedom stretches out unencumbered to welcome the reader at book's end. The passage through the thick forest which surrounds us all has already claimed Francis Sancher's life when the novel begins; at least six of the characters whose stories surface during the night of Sancher's wake slip further into their figurative graves. Other characters, however, succeed in extricating themselves from the obstacles that have thus far choked off life, and they move toward the light of a new day and the promise of collective salvation.

What are the obstacles and why do some continue to struggle toward life while others stagnate, resign themselves to solitude and exclusion, or beckon death? All casualties in a literal or figurative sense can be traced to social exclusion or parental rejection; all rebirths spring from an empathic connection between the individual characters and Francis Sancher, the dark sun at the center of this interconnected galaxy, who reflects the insights and wisdom which each of the characters possesses but is initially incapable of generating without him. A representative of the past, he sees into the souls of all but himself. His stories unlock the untold stories and secrets buried in his listeners. He becomes mentor, friend, and ally to those who come in contact with him, mirroring the thoughts and feelings comprising their inner lives and empowering them.

Francis Sancher, alias Francisco Alvarez-Sanchez, has come to Rivière au Sel to die. To him the place resembles a watery grave and conjures up the briny water he envisions engulfing and choking those who try to cross a mangrove thicket. We never discover why this idealist beyond ideals gives up and fatalistically courts the death he anticipates as ineluctable on his fiftieth birthday. Several interlocutors hear the stories of his ancestors who were forced to succumb to a curse that deprived them of life after half a century in spite of their best efforts to escape. He cannot possibly save himself, or can he?

Whether his death is occasioned by an ancient curse pronounced on his forefathers and their progeny because of some unspeakable deed committed in the past or whether it results from a self-fulfilling tragic prophecy remains an open question for all but Xantippe. This outcast poet and prophet who assumes mythic proportions in the text discovers answers which the novel does not presume to provide. His life-story, juxtaposed with all the others, nevertheless offers several clues: "Personne ne sait exactement en quelle matière le coeur de l'homme est fabriqué" [No one knows exactly what the human heart is made of], declares Aristide. Sancher's death is no more imponderable than the jealousy which motivated Xantippe's enemies to set fire to his home and family, condemning him to a life of irreparable loss.

The real unanswered question at the heart of this novel is why we inflict death and suffering on each other. Man Sonson, the older woman who peers into others' souls and futures as acutely as she reveals the healing powers of plants, comments that "sur le coeur des Nègres la lumière de la bonté ne brille jamais" [the light of goodness never shines on the heart of Negroes]. Mira Lameaulnes, the striking, light-skinned object of desire and the malice seething in her neighbors' hearts, lives as if in exile on "notre île à ragots, livrée aux cyclones et aux ravages de la méchanceté du coeur des Nègres" [our gossip-filled island, at the mercy of cyclones and the ravages of spiteful Black hearts]. Moïse, the physically unattractive product of his father's unexplained relationship with a Chinese woman, receives the nickname "Mosquito" and the unmerited disdain of all the islanders he encounters on his mail route every day. Spurned even by the local prostitute, he withers along with his dreams, observing that "Seul celui qui a vécu entre les quatre murs d'une petite communauté connaît sa méchanceté et sa peur de l'étranger" [Only one who has lived inside the walls of a small community knows its malice and fear of strangers]. The place that serves as the locus of this "small-minded community" is Rivière au Sel, a name which symbolically reflects a social fabric composed in large part of prejudices, hatred, and misunderstandings. It needs purifying as much as the salt-laden water in order to support life.

Each of the spokespersons whose names divide the novel's twenty central chapters lives in virtual isolation, excluded from participation in a larger community by the barriers that have defensively grown up in their own hearts, or by the fences that shut them out of the narrow boundaries defining the acceptable in Guadeloupean society. Francis Sancher, whose story lies embedded in the personal accounts of these individuals, shares their profound exclusion. In reality the exclusions are multiple and overlapping and fall into three main categories: parent-child, wife-husband/lover-beloved, social insider-outsider. At the end of *Traversée de la mangrove,* Francis Sancher has found acceptance through death. His death in turn acts directly on the lives of nine of his acquaintances whose actions will undoubtedly affect their children, their cocitizens, and perhaps even touch the two patriarchal representatives of wealth and social standing who head the Ramsaran and Lameaulnes families.

The dynamic that triggers these transformations lies in an acceptance and validation of one's self that can then be extended to other individuals and groups. Francis Sancher, a former doctor often referred to as "el curandero" [the healer] in former times and places, serves as the healer of hearts and minds in Rivière au Sel. Discussion of his role within the context of the practice of psychoanalytic self psychology elucidates the power for personal and political change that can result from empathic attunement.

Psychoanalytic self psychology is a theory of psychotherapy based on the analyst's empathic immersion in the patient's experience. It grew out of the work of Heinz Kohut, a Freudian analyst who reconsidered his theoretical perspective when confronted with patients who "stumped" him by not responding to treatment in the classical tradition of psychoanalysis. His prolonged empathic immersion in the inner worlds of these patients led him to explore new and previously unrecognized psychic configurations. In a letter to another analyst dated May 16, 1974, Kohut wrote:

> It was on the basis of feeling stumped that I began to entertain the thought that these people were not concerned with me as a separate person but that they were concerned with themselves; that they did not love or hate me, but that they needed me as part of themselves, needed me as a set of functions which they had not acquired in early life; that what appeared to be their love or hate was in reality their need that I fulfill certain psychological functions for them and anger at me when I did not do so. [Crayton E. Rowe, Jr., and David S. Mac Isaac, *Empathic Attunement.*]

This intuition offered new perspectives on the place of empathy in analytic cure. The psychological functions he refers to in the above excerpt came to be theorized as the mirroring selfobject transference and the idealizing selfobject transference.

Briefly stated for our purposes, the selfobject is "another whose responses and attitudes are vitally experienced by the developing psyche not only as shapers of but as *part* of the self." [Joan A. Lang, "Self-Psychology and the Understanding and Treatment of Women," *Review of Psychiatry,* Vol. 9, 1990.] The term, then, denotes one's experience of another part of the self. In the mirroring selfobject transference, the analyst tries to be in tune, be "in" the experience of the patient, understand the experience, and verbally express that understanding. The idealizing selfobject transference occurs when the analyst is experienced "as the consistent, powerful, and protective parental image." Mac Isaac and Rowe summarize Kohut's speculations that this latter transference allowed patients whose idealizing needs were thwarted as children to move beyond an arrested stage of development in which they continued to long for a perfectionistic image of their parents and "tended throughout life to search for someone who could fit this unfulfilled and primitive picture." Since the power of the selfobject relationship is not simply one of "reinforcement" but of extending the boundaries of what is or is not "Me" beyond the individual self, this method of analysis based on interdependence and relationship has enormous potential for the understanding of relationships between individuals as well as those between intrapsychic and sociocultural forces. New ways of verbally formulating and seeing interconnectedness imply possibilities for transforming those relationships. Extending the boundaries of the self permits a purificatory return to the sources of the figuratively salt-tainted and life-threatening waters of Rivière au Sel. There is hope for reconfiguring the social fabric and common existence, beginning with the individual.

In order to examine how Francis Sancher functions as a catalyst for psychic healing in the novel, let us group the characters according to the three categories of exclusion alluded to above (parent-child, wife-husband/lover-beloved, social insider-outsider) and elaborate the relationships between one or more representative persons from each group and Sancher.

Among those who experience rejection from either or both of their parents, we find Sonny Pélagie rejected by both his parents, Loulou Lameaulnes rejected by his mother, Sylvestre Ramsaran rejected by his father, Vilma Ramsaran rejected by her mother, and Mira Lameaulnes whose illegitimate birth coincided with the death of the "Négresse," Rosalie Sorane, who bore her. The mother and stepmother of the two young women provide a fruitful starting point for this discussion because they verbalize convictions that harken back to preceding generations and echo forth in the lives of their daughters. Rosa Ramsaran's statement that "le malheur des enfants est toujours causé par les parents" [children's unhappiness is always caused by their parents], recalls Dinah Lameaulnes's fear that "les malheurs des enfants sont toujours causés par les fautes cachées des parents" [children's misfortunes are always caused by their parents' hidden faults]. These reflections can be understood and positively acted upon when we examine them in the light of self psychology which goes beyond the Freudian legacy wherein an unhappy woman who was either frustrated, repressed, martyred, never satisfied, or rejecting was afflicted by the repression of her instinctive wishes and the distortions which this strangulation of need created in her relationships. Calling upon the concepts of the mirroring and idealizing transferences explained above, these two statements relate directly to Vilma and Mira as two children who did not experience certain representatives of their human surroundings as joyfully responding to them and as available to them as sources of idealized strength and calmness.

Vilma and Mira both live individually with Francis Sancher for a period of time; the former is lodged in his house and pregnant at the time of his death, the latter has already given birth to his son. Curiously enough, neither of these young women has a transformative relationship with Sancher in spite of their physical intimacy with him. Both will escape the confines of their previous lives but not because he has exercised a direct influence on them as he does on the other people he helps to redirect. Convinced of the curse upon his family, he wants only to end it with his death, not perpetuate it in future generations. Mira and Vilma will be liberated from the stifling confines of their families and the narrow possibilities in Guadeloupean society as a result of Sancher's association with other members of their families and the community.

Both young women underscore the central importance of another relationship recurring throughout the novel and probed by Sancher in his conversation with Vilma's mother: that between mother and child, and here specifically between mother and daughter. Mira cannot understand that, for her, there is no mother on this earth, and finds her sole refuge in the flowing water of a hidden ravine whose scarcely audible song recalls her in utero relationship with her mother. There she imagines life with a flesh-and-blood mother who approvingly watches her growing up, meets her at the end of the day, and explains all the mysteries of her body to her. After Sancher gives Mira an infusion designed to put her to sleep long enough to abort the child she is carrying, she poetically evokes her sleep-state in terms that again harken back to the embryonic period:

> Mon esprit s'est détaché de mon corps, paisible, paisible. Il m'a semblé que je revenais habiter comme autrefois le ventre ombreux de ma mère, Rosalie Sorane aux dents de perle. Je flottais, je nageais éperdue de bonheur dans sa mer utérine et j'entendais assourdis, affaiblis, les tristes bruits d'un monde dans lequel j'étais bien décidé à ne jamais faire mon entrée.

> [My spirit detached itself from my body, peacefully, peaceful. It seemed as if I were coming back to live, as in times gone by, in the shadowy womb of my mother, Rosalie Sorane with the pearl white teeth. I was floating, swimming, wildly happy in her uterine sea and the sad sounds of a world I had resolutely decided not to reenter were coming to me, muted, diminished.]

Reenter she does, in time to save her unborn child. She later realizes at Sancher's wake that her true life begins with the latter's death and her personal quest for truth: "Alors, moi, je dois découvrir la vérité. Désormais ma vie ne sera qu'une quête. Je retracerai les chemins du monde" [And so then, it's up to me to discover the truth. From now on my life will become a quest. I will search on all the roadways of this world].

Vilma Ramsaran, on the other hand, wants only to follow Sancher to the grave, thus reenacting the fate of her Indian foremother who followed her beloved to the funeral pyre. A better fate, however, awaits her. Having grown up under the resentful gaze of a mother who mourned the death of Vilma's recently deceased sister, the former has known only rejection from Rosa Ramsaran. When Rosa visits Sancher to speak with her daughter, she flees from Vilma's menacing shouts but not before she has a conversation with this enigmatic man which will change not only her life but her daughter's as well. Francis Sancher, this "moulin à paroles" who seems to articulate what each person might find written in his or her heart if all defenses were down, remarks in passing that his mother had Rosa's black, lustrous hair but that she did not love him very much. In response to Rosa's stammering protestation that all mothers love their children, he respectfully notes that his mother was impregnated in less than ideal circumstances; his parents made love without any real communication: "Pour donner, pour rendre l'amour, il faut en avoir reçu beaucoup, beaucoup" [In order to give, to return love, you have to have received a great deal of it, a great deal]. Rosa feels the shock of recognition; he has stated her case. She responds with a remark that others will repeat verbatim upon hearing Sancher utter their as yet unformulated but deeply felt convictions: "Comment savez-vous cela" [How do you know that?] . Sancher's words, "In order to give, to return the love, you have to have received a great deal of it, a great deal," continue to reverberate and punctuate Rosa's review of her empty life. They ultimately lead her to the realization that the absence of understanding, love, and sharing might still be supplanted by their presence in the days to come:

> Je dirai à ma fille, mienne:
>
> —Sortie de mon ventre, je t'ai mal aimée. Je ne t'ai pas aidée à eclore et tu as poussé, rabougrie. Il n'est pas trop tard pour que nos yeux se recontrent et que nos mains se touchent. Donne-moi ton pardon.
>
> [I will say to my daughter, mine:
>
> —Outside of my womb I loved you badly. I did not help you to blossom and you grew up stunted. It is not too late for our eyes to meet and our hands to touch. Forgive me.]

Rosa's determination mirrors the ultimatum that Dodose Pélagie addresses to herself regarding her child, Sonny, who suffered a cerebral hemorrhage shortly after birth and has lived with the consequences ever since. Francis Sancher welcomes the boy and becomes his only friend, the only person to speak with him and treat him humanely and not as punishment or a nuisance. Although Dodose refuses to listen to Sancher's evaluation of Sonny and meets his steady, unreproachful gaze with a barrage of injurious words, she relives this chance meeting with him on the Saint Charles path in the forest where he has met many other inhabitants. Remembering his look and his words, she begins to question herself during the night of his wake, asking herself if she has ever really loved her son or regarded him as a cross to be borne, a wound to her pride, a punishment to her husband, Emmanuel, whom she hates but has not know how to leave. Visualizing Sancher on that twilight path leads her to clarify her direction as dawn approaches: "Pourtant, il m'a montré la voie. . . . Désormais, je prendrai soin de lui (Sonny). Je frapperai à la porte de chaque hôpital, de chaque clinique, de chaque dispensaire. . . . Je laisserai Emmanuel, enfermé dans ses rancoeurs et Rivière au Sel, ses petitesses immuables" [However, he showed me the way. . . . From now on, I will take care of him (Sonny). I will knock on the door of every hospital, every clinic, every dispensary. . . . I will leave Emmanuel, wrapped in his resentment and Rivière au Sel, in his meanness].

It is not too late for parents and children to find new ways of relating to one another. Children relate to their parents as selfobjects; adults continue to interact with others as selfobjects throughout their lives. Insight and new beginnings follow empathic contact with a therapeutic other capable of reflecting the needs and remembrances "safeguarded in the folds of memory, in the deep recesses of the heart" (*Mangrove*).

There are two powerfully drawn, joyful, sensuous relationships in *Traversée de la mangrove*: the first briefly alluded to between Man Sonson and Siméon, her dead husband, "un vaillant Nègre, de l'espèce qui a disparu de la surface de la planète" [a valiant Negro, of the kind who has disappeared from the face of the planet]; the second between the mythical figure Xantippe and Gracieuse, the wife he has mourned for time immemorial. Excluding Francis Sancher's ties with Vilma and Mira, however, there are three prominent marriages in the novel between Loulou Lameaulnes and Dinah, Sylvestre Ramsaran and Rosa, and Emmanuel Pélagie and Dodose, within which husband and wife have withered and felt imprisoned. The Ramsaran and Pélagie marriages were arranged, and neither Rosa nor Dodose ever overcame their initial repugnance at being married to men they would never have chosen. Dinah chooses to marry Loulou against her mother's advice who warns her that "Il a trois garçons et une fille bâtarde. Tout ce qu'il cherche, c'est une bonne pour eux. Voilà ce que tu seras" [He has three boys and a bastard daughter. All he's looking for is a maid to take care of them. That's what you will be]! She is largely ignored by her husband, and her home becomes her "prison" and her "tombeau": "Par moments il me semblait que j'étais déjà morte, que mon sang ne coulait plus chaud dans mes veines, qu'il était déjà caillé" [At times, it seemed to me that I was already dead, that my blood no longer flowed warmly through my veins, that it had already clotted]. Curled up alone in her bed at night she imagines her mother and the father she has never known there with her, and hears their bedtime stories until she drifts off to sleep in the early hours of the morning. Mme Dinah Lameaulnes seems no more than a child herself. In the period before either Mira or Vilma takes up residence in Sancher's household, he visits Dinah in hers. After one of their conversations, during which she tries to fathom why Loulou has brought her from Saint Martin to be his wife only to abandon her, she is left with two questions which he has asked her: What kept her tied down? Why didn't she go away? She comes to a decision the night of Sancher's wake: she, Dinah Lameaulnes, will. Francis Sancher, the first person whom she feels has understood and talked with her, provides the empathic bond that leads to the power to make changes in her life.

Deeply rooted prejudice against anyone "different," "from the outside," or from a different ethnic or racial background smothers at least half of the characters in *Traversée de la mangrove*. Here the individual tragedies and the redemptive power of the novel meet. If, as Heinz Kohut theorized, we all possess lifelong needs for selfobjects and the functions they provide, if the healthy self cannot survive or thrive without others who affirm our deepest sense of person and selfhood and steady us on our way, then the inhabitants of Rivière au Sel are doomed to think little of themselves and feel even less enthusiasm for life. This is a society where relationships are governed by malice. Social and cultural exchanges in this closed society thwart rather than foster those mutual selfobject functions essential to the capacity for empathy and a sympathy for the realities of others.

Each of the people who tells his or her story, or whose story is recounted by a self-effacing narrator who prioritizes the individual's experience, is susceptible to the rejection and exclusion they encounter in society. Inclusion and exclusion, the longing to be accepted as one is, and the experience of rejection dominate the novel. Moïse, dit Maringouin, le facteur; Désinor, l'Haïtien; and Xantippe live in permanent exile where no place is home. If Léocadie Timothée, the retired schoolteacher, and Loulou Lameaulnes have any say in the matter, it will remain that way. Both decry the fact that Guadeloupe is "on the auction block," in the words of Léocadie Timothée: the influx of Haitians, Dominicans, all kinds of Whites from Canada or from Italy, Vietnamese, and "puis celui-là (Francis Sancher), vomi par on ne sait quel mauvais portuer" [then that one (Francis Sancher), vomited ashore by who knows what bad tide].

It is ironic that Léocadie Timothée, the privileged Black who taught in order to better her race, was rejected by those Blacks less fortunate than she: "A leurs yeux, j'étais une trâtresse! Je souffrais de cet isolement, car j'aurais voulu qu'on m'aime, moi. Je ne savais pas que le Nègre n'aime jamais le Nègre" [In their eyes, I was a traitress! I suffered from that isolation, for I would have liked people to love me. I did not know that Negroes never love their own]. She never questions, however, what distinguishes her from the outsiders she herself relegates to the margines of society.

Examples of discrimination and exclusion abound in the novel, but Emile Etienne's situation illustrates both his marginality and the determination to overcome it, thanks to the influence of Francis Sancher. Emile summarizes his childhood as that of a "petit Négre noir, sorti du ventre d'une malheureuse, assis aux derniers bancs de la classe, du C.P. au C.M. 2. Son adolescence morose. Aux bals de 'La Flamme,' les filles se cachaient de lui et le surnommaient 'Sirop Batterie' " [small black Negro, born to an unfortunate woman, seated in the last rows of class, from C.P. to C.M. 2. His morose adolescence. At the dances held at "La Flamme," the girls hid from him and nicknamed him "Sirop Batterie"]. With the aid of scholarships and his mother's sacrifices, he obtained the baccalaureate but then had to be satisfied with becoming a nurse to help support his younger sister and brother. Speaking with the older people of the island on his nursing visits to their homes, he is struck by their vivid recollections of the past and writes *Parlons de Petit Bourg*. After two years of work and savings invested in the printing of the book, it is met by the sneers of the educated in La Pointe who make fun of its misprints and "stylistic improprieties." When he is with Francis Sancher, however, he speaks of himself and his great ambition to write a different kind of oral and social history of Guadeloupe. Sancher approves and, as he has done with so many others in Rivière au Sel, poses the question that Emile is afraid to ask himself: "Qu' est-ce qui t'en empêche" [What's stopping you?]. And once again, contemplating Sancher's coffin the night of the wake like so many others, he confronts what prevents him from acting:

> Regardant le cerceuil, Emile Etienne eut soudain honte de sa lâcheté. . . . Qu'est-ce qui lui faisait peur? . . . Il se sentit plein d'un courage immense, d'une énergie nouvelle qui coulait mystérieuse dans son sang.
>
> [Looking at the coffin, Emile Etienne suddenly felt ashamed of his cowardice. . . What was he afraid of ? . . . He felt full of immense courage, new energy which was flowing mysteriously through his blood.]

Feeling that his promise to write the book unites him to Sancher beyond death, he is ready to work, to search for a place where the color of one's skin does not matter. It is as though Francis Sancher's death has been the catalyst for Emile Etienne's self actualization. His death functions in a similar way to liberate the living in regard to another young writer ensnared in a different trap.

Lucien Evariste, the aspiring novelist caught between his favored background rooted in Catholic France and the Patriotes espousing atheism and creole, finds himself buried alive in Guadeloupe, waging a no-win battle mainly against himself. Through his conversations with Francis Sancher, including the last one the night of Sancher's wake when he remembers and hears again segments of previous exchanges, he succeeds in placing himself within the narrow confines of the island and beyond it. For him, Sancher was "le grand frère et le jeune père qu'il n'avait pas eus, moqueur et tendre, cynique et rêveur" [the big brother and young father that he had never had, mocking and tender, cynical and dreamy]. Overwhelmed by emotion and an irresistible life force, Lucien integrates his feelings of loss and caring for his dead friend with his literary aspirations smothered from the right and the left:

> Au lieu, enfant d'aujourd'hui et de la ville, de traquer des nèg mawon ou des paysans du XIXe siècle, pourquoi ne pas mettre bout à bout souvenirs et bribes de confidences, écarter les mensonges, reconstituer la trajectoire et la personnalité du dèfunt? . . . Il lui faudrait refuser le vertige des idées reçues. Regarder dans les yeux de dangereuses vérités. Déplaire. Choquer.
>
> [Instead of remaining a child of today and the city and tracking down escaped slaves or peasants of the nineteenth century, why not bring together memories and snatches of secrets, dismiss lies, reconstitute the trajectory and the personality of the deceased? . . . He would have to refuse the headlines of preconceived notions. Look dangerous truths in the eyes. Offend. Shock.]

He will write the biography of Francis Sancher.

Light is a puissant metaphor in ***Traversée de la mangrove***. Those characters who affirm and recover their faith in themselves as a result of their friendship with Francis Sancher feel compelled to act, to speak, to write, to leave, to move toward the light, each one as vulnerable and indestructible as a plant toward the sun. Dinah Lemeaulnes, whose recitation of psalms is answered in chorus by the inhabitants of Rivière au Sel assembled at Sancher's wake, echoes the resolution of those who have escaped impalement or suffocation in Maryse Condé's figurative mangrove when she states:

> Je chercherai le soleil et l'air et la lumière pour ce qui me reste d'années à vivre.
>
> Ou les trouverai-je? Je n'en sais encore rien. Ce que je sais, c'est que je les chercherai!
>
> [I will seek the sun, air, and light for the remainder of my days. Where will I find them? I don't yet know. What I do know is that I will seek them!]

One place the sun and the air and the light will not be found is in isolation. All the characters struggling to cross the mangrove are drowning in loneliness; the individual resolves of those who succeed in freeing themselves entail moving beyond their solitary prisons, clearing the fences and barriers from their hearts as well as their discriminatory society. Having experienced an empathic relationship with Francis Sancher, the characters beginning anew become self-affirming and capable of extending themselves to others.

Mira Lameaulnes, one of the two young women who tries to escape rejection by offering herself to Francis Sancher, is motivated by an intense desire to know who he really was: "il me fallait trouver qui il était" [I had to know who he was]. After experiencing a lifetime of cruel remarks and envious disdain, she better than anyone knows how little a person's thick and impenetrable external appearance might correspond to their inner needs and feelings. The protective layers mask the inner reality. Désinor, the Haitian gardener who politely conforms externally to the disadvantaged inferior status conferred on him by the other inhabitants, lives in rage and despair. He poignantly depicts the injustice of this contemporary version of slavery and the marginalization of the outsider when he muses that "Pour une fois qu'il était de plainpied avec les gens de Rivière au Sel, il aurait aimé les insulter, les choquer, leur faire savoir qui était réellement ce Désinor Décimus qu'ils confondaient avec un misérable jardinier haïtien" [Now that he was on an equal footing with the people from Rivière au Sel, he would have liked to insult them, shock them, make them know who Désinor Décimus really was, this man whom they confused with a miserable Haitian gardener].

The inner life of another person seldom corresponds to the person we perceive in social intercourse. Not one of the individuals in *Traversée de la mangrove* is transparent to the larger community. The continuous flow of inner experiences and the fluidity of intersubjective experiences in the novel reproduces in all its complexity the process that happens constantly in human interaction. Translating that experience into fiction, immersing the reader in the character's spoken and unspoken feelings, juxtaposing the character's inner life with his or her impressions of the other characters in the novel, moving back and forth from first person to third-person self-effacing narration in which the character's thoughts and feelings are privileged—Maryse Condé accomplishes no less in this novel. The reader recreates these relationships, weaving together all the threads in this infinitely complex yet simple tapestry of the heart. "We," the narrator and the reader, become empathically attuned to all the characters, including the omnipresent Francis Sancher. We think and feel our way into their inner lives as we read the book that Emile Etienne, l'Historien, speaks of writing, and that Maryse Condé has written:

> . . . une histoire de ce pays qui serait uniquement basée sur les souvenirs gardés au creux des mémoires, au creux des coeurs. Ce que les pères ont dit aux fils, ce que les mères ont dit aux filles. Je voudrais aller du Nord au Sud, de l'Est à l'Ouest recueillir toutes ces paroles qu'on n'a jamais écoutés . . .
>
> Francis Sancher approuvait.

> [a story of this country that would be based solely on the memories buried in the depths of one's consciousness, in the depths of one's heart. What fathers have told their sons, what mothers have told their daughters. I would like to go from North to South, from East to West, to gather all these words that have never been listened to . . .
>
> Francis Sancher approved.]

These are the unspoken words we have read and heard, the map we have been given to navigate toward the light.

---

**Condé on Négritude:**

What should we keep of Négritude? It helped us value our blackness. Formerly, to be black was a curse. After Négritude, our blackness became something we could bear and accept—we could even be proud of it. It helped us confront the world around us by possessing an identity of our own according to the various places in which we were born. Without Négritude, perhaps we would still be ashamed of ourselves. There is, however, no reason to be proud to belong to one race or another. I question the fact that Négritude perpetuates the notion that all blacks are the same. That is a totally racist attitude inherited, in fact, from whites who believe that all niggers look alike, all niggers are equal. It is not true. Every black society is different from the others. The proponents of Négritude made a big mistake and caused a lot of suffering in the minds of West Indian people and black Americans as well. We were led to believe that Africa was the source; it is the source, but we believed that we would find a home there, when it was not a home. Without Négritude we would not have experienced the degree of disillusionment that we did. The issue of "likeness," of "similarity" is erroneous even in the Antilles. Guadeloupe is very different from Martinique. We are sisters, but each island has an identity of its own, and we cannot divorce our present from theirs. Diversity within unity is the definition of our shared objectives for national autonomy and cooperation within the larger Caribbean.

*Maryse Condé, in an interview in* Callaloo, *Winter, 1989.*

---

**Jeanne Pimentel** (review date May/June 1993)

SOURCE: "An Ending of Her Own Choosing," in *San Francisco Review of Books,* Vol. 18, No. 3, May/June, 1993, p. 19.

[*In the following review, Pimentel praises* I, Tituba, Black Witch of Salem, *considering Condé an author with "universal vision."*]

Around a flimsy patch of historical material, Maryse Condé weaves [in *I, Tituba, Black Witch of Salem*] the birth-to-death story of a woman whose mind and body we come to know intimately. Though much of the story takes place in New England in the seventeenth century, its character is Caribbean and its relevance is to the present.

Historical documents mention only briefly a West Indian slave tried and imprisoned during the infamous Salem witch hunts. The scant facts in these records are incorporated in the telling of *I, Tituba, Black Witch of Salem*. The book begins with a fictional recreation of Tituba's childhood, scarred with the traumas of slave life on the bucolic and beloved island of Barbados. Here she develops both the skill in traditional healing and the strong sexuality that determine her course in life. Condé portrays vividly how these traits lead to Tituba's suffering at the hands of the ruthless puritans of Salem.

After recounting the period anchored to the brief factual references, Condé constructs "an ending of [her] own choosing," completing the story as an act of revenge for the neglect of a black person in the historical record. A benign revenge indeed, for the reader. But then Tituba herself has great difficulty being an aggressor; her natural bent is "to heal and console rather than to do evil."

Into a plot as action-packed as a romance novel. Condé introduces lively arguments not only on the themes of racism and feminism but on hypocrisy, intolerance, and exploitation. The existence of the spirit world is a given in the book, and the reader should be prepared to suspend disbelief and enter into this rich culture for the duration of the story.

Tituba's long-dead parents and guardians appear to her frequently, and influence her decisions. Though they hover above ground, their comments are earthly to the point of vulgarity and their otherworldly advice is peppered with human pettiness.

Condé's storytelling reflects a relaxed acceptance of unexplained phenomena, intuitive rather than analytical, more prosaic than dogmatic. Whether dire physical affliction visited upon evil people might be ascribed to natural causes rather than magic spells is not worth discussion—in Tituba's world, one would not preclude the other. Whether Hester Prynne, Tituba's adored jailmate, is actually brought to life from Hawthorne's tale to suffer a fate he never assigned her is irrelevant. Condé appropriates the nature of the culture for her own purposes: the glossary contains, besides definitions of Caribbean terms, many a "literary invention by the author."

The narrative is often conversational in tone, drawing on the oral tradition of the culture. Condé also experiments creatively with chronology: Tituba steps outside her fictional self to protest, "I can look for my story among those of the witches of Salem, but it isn't there," and Hester Prynne appropriates twentieth-century terminology to deliver her feminist views.

Besides the richness of Richard Philcox's translation, this edition provides the double bonus of a forward by Angela Davis and an afterword by Ann Armstrong Scarboro. Davis praises the "voice of a suppressed black feminist tradition," while Scarboro explores theoretical postmodern concepts such as "otherness." Their complicated readings attest to the rich layering of the text—though I'm not sure Condé would agree with all the hidden agendas attributed

> **Condé is an inhabitant of the world; her "own country," no longer limited to her birthplace, is the locus of the spirit embracing many geographical and cultural locations.**
>
> **—Jeanne Pimentel**

to it. "Don't take Tituba too seriously, please," she begs in her interview with Scarboro.

The first time I heard Condé speak, she shared the podium with a flamboyant young deconstructionist who spoke almost exclusively in abstract academic terms. By contrast, Condé was down-to-earth and warmly humorous—a writer for whom the world was concrete, but also spiritual. Asked why she preferred one African country over another, she replied unhesitatingly "Because it's more spiritual."

Condé's wide-ranging novel based on her own colorful family history, *Tree of Life (Lavie scelerate)* was recently published by Ballantine, and two more of her books are expected within the next year: *Journey Across the Mangrove (Traversee de la mangrove)* and *The Last Magi (Les derniers rois mages)*.

A writer with a strong Caribbean identity, Condé also demonstrates a universal vision. Clearly she has thought deeply about the turbulent history and complex social and political structures of her native Guadeloupe. As the settings of her various works demonstrate. Condé is as much at home in Guadeloupe as in the ancient halls of Sorbonne, or the timeless sands of the African desert. She is an inhabitant of the world; her "own country," no longer limited to her birthplace, is the locus of the spirit embracing many geographical and cultural locations. Condé imbues her half-fact, half-fiction characters with qualities and motives which reflect her view of women today, as well as the universality in time and space of issues from exploitation and political intrigue to the maternal urge and sexual betrayal.

### Elisabeth Mudimbé-Boyi (essay date Autumn 1993)

SOURCE: "Giving Voice to Tituba: The Death of the Author?," in *World Literature Today,* Vol. 67, No. 4, Autumn, 1993, pp. 751-56.

[*Mudimbé-Boyi is an educator, critic, and editor who specializes in African and Caribbean literature. In the following essay, she discusses the themes of gender relationships and the search for identity in Condé's* I, Tituba, Black Witch of Salem.]

The story of the witches of Salem has been recounted in different ways by different authors: Arthur Miller's play *The Crucible,* Ann Petry's *Tituba of Salem Village,* Nathaniel Hawthorne's *Scarlet Letter,* and a 1982 film called *Three Sovereigns for Sarah* starring Vanessa Redgrave. If Tituba is mentioned at all, there is little room for her in the narratives; and as she states in recounting her story in Maryse Condé's novel *Moi, Tituba, sorcière . . . Noire de Salem* (Eng. *I, Tituba, Black Witch of Salem*), she has been reduced to

> . . . having played only a minor role in the whole affair and having had a fate that no one could remember. "Tituba, a slave originating from the West Indies and probably practicing 'hoodoo.' " A few lines in the many volumes written on the Salem witch trials. Why was I going to be ignored? This question too had crossed my mind. Is it because nobody cares about a Negress and her trials and tribulations? Is that why?
>
> I can look for my story among those of the witches of Salem, but it isn't there. . . . Not a word about me.

Tituba's question mark could be recast as an interrogation about existence, identity, and presence in History. Brought to Massachusetts not of her own free will but as a slave in a society of people who migrated from their native Europe in search of freedom, she lives at the margins. Her territory is on the borderland of the Massachusetts Puritan community as well as of literary and historical representation. By virtue of her race, her geographic origin, and her social status, Tituba embodies marginality and is perceived only as a voiceless "exotic other," an object to be talked about. She summarizes her situation with a taste of bitterness: "It was not so much the conversation that amazed and revolted me as their way of going about it. You would think I wasn't standing there at the threshold of the room. They were talking about me and yet ignoring me. They were striking me off the map of human beings. I was a nonbeing. Invisible. More invisible than the unseen, who at least have powers that everyone fears."

*Tituba* is a statement against effacement, exclusion, and reduction to invisibility. In Condé's book one finds interwoven recurrent motifs present in her other works, from *Hérémakhonon* to *Ségou, Traversée de la mangrove,* and *Les derniers rois mages:* motifs such as exile and return, the quest for identity and for the self, the reconstruction of history, and gender relationships. Within Condé's oeuvre, *Tituba* takes on a political significance and resonates as a powerful counterhistory.

Michel Foucault classifies the use of language among the "discursive practices" that allow the exercise of power. In *Discourse on Language* he suggests that in every society the production of discourse is at once controlled, selected, organized, and redistributed according to a certain number of procedures. In letting Tituba speak and tell her story in her own words, Condé gives her a voice, restores her history and her identity, and allows her to acquire language and thus to participate in society. The writer also creates a territory for her—the textual space—and incorporates her into the stream of a history from which she had been excluded. With different means, Condé's endeavor connects with Simone Schwarz-Bart's resurrection of the forgotten figures of black women's contribution to Carribean history, as exemplified in her novel *Pluie et vent sur Télumée Miracle,* or in Marie Chauvet's book *La*

*danse sur le volcan.* Condé's *Tituba* emerges from the author's imagination and creativity and does not pretend to the status of a historical novel. The narrative is nevertheless inscribed in the larger project of reconstructing Caribbean history, as exposed by Edouard Glissant in his masterful essay *Le discours antillais* (Eng. *Caribbean Discourse*) and as illustrated by many other Caribbean novels in which the search for and the reconstruction of history constitute a major focus.

This brings us to the examination of several theoretical questions arising from Tituba's narrative as composed by Condé. What is the relationship between writer and character? How does the writer preserve the integrity and the authenticity of Tituba's discourse and voice in the process of transcribing it from oral into written form and translating it into French? In other words, how does the writer negotiate the preservation of her own function as "author" in the textualization of Tituba's story without undermining at the same time the power and the presence of Tituba's own voice, which is precisely the one Condé would like to unveil?

In actuality, *Tituba* unfolds a long monologic "conversation" in which the writer becomes the simple listener of a narrating subject telling her own life story. The book is thus a fictional "autobiography" from which the writer has completely disappeared, leaving Tituba to take preeminence and become simultaneously both the narrator and the narrated. Tituba, in telling her story, re-creates the context of an oral performance, with herself as the performer and the writer as the audience. Condé's epigraph to the book contains, as a subtext, a tacit pact between the performer and the spectator: it signifies an act of trust, since the narrator told Condé "things she had confided to nobody else before." The author of the book henceforth takes on different roles: as the repository of Tituba's life story, she becomes her interpreter as well as her mediator. As the interpreter of Tituba's text, Condé the writer also assumes the role of a translator, and in this context her position, as Philippe Lejeune puts it in *On Autobiography,* in the chapter apropos of "the autobiography of those who do not write": "The translator finds himself in a hierarchically dependent situation. . . . The position of the writer is in many aspects similar to that of the translator, with just one difference, but an enormous one: in the writer's case, *the original text does not exist.* The writer . . . draws the text from a 'before-text.' "

In assuming the functions of interpreter, mediator, and translator, Condé fulfills the tacit pact in transmitting what Tituba had entrusted to her, specifically her concern not only about her descent into oblivion but also about never being rehabilitated.

> I felt that I would only be mentioned in passing in these Salem witchcraft trials about which so much would be written later, trials that would arouse the curiosity and pity of generations to come as the greatest testimony of a superstitious and barbaric age. . . . There would be no mention of my age or my personality. I would be ignored. . . . Petitions would be circulated, judgments made, rehabilitating the victims, restoring their honor, and returning their property to their

descendants. I would never be included! Tituba would be condemned forever! There would never, ever, be a careful, sensitive biography recreating my life and its suffering.

I would like to focus, in the development of this essay, on the authorial position in relation to the voice of the character, with the assumption that author and character are positioned into two different cultural and linguistic codes: oral and Creole for Tituba, written and French for Condé.

As a slave, Tituba could certainly not read or write. Therefore, the narrative device of referring to some form of mediation such as a notebook discovered by the author, as in Myriam Warner-Vieyra's *Juletane,* or brought to her by an intermediary, as in Michèle Maillet's *Etoile noire,* has been skillfully replaced by "autobiographical conversations" between the writer and her character. As Michael Awkward reminds us, in "talking and telling," Tituba addresses an audience constituted here solely by the writer. In transcribing her conversations with Tituba, the author of the book translates Tituba's story from an oral form into a written one.

An apparent ambiguity seems to accompany the writer's position here. On the one hand there is the desire to place Tituba in an environment familiar to her in re-creating the traditional context of the oral performance. On the other hand, since this is a oneway conversation, the usual interraction and communication between performer and audience are lacking, and the audience is quiet and just listening, thus re-creating the context of a Western performance. In actuality, the context created by Condé embodies a strategy of subversion by reversing the relation of power between writer and character and thus between French (the language of the writer) and Creole (the language of the character) and between the oral and the written. The writer is indeed in the passive situation of a listener, whereas Tituba is playing the active role of the speaker, in control of the narrative unfolded through the conversations. Condé, in fact, reproduces the social organization and power's conventional dynamics, in which the one who speaks exerts power over the one who remains silent and the possessor of the written belongs to the ruling class and exerts power over the one who does not write. Condé subverts that dynamics in giving up her position of power as a member of the ruling class, only to become what Antonio Gramsci characterizes as a subaltern. Condé's subversive strategy could be represented by a double chiasma, showing clearly the shift of power and speech from Condé's side to Tituba's.

Lejeune's statement quoted above allows the decoding of the writer's subversive operation also at the level of language and the text. Indeed, the text constituting the narrative is Tituba's; thus it is a "before-text" and is transmitted by her in a language other than the (colonial) master's. Condé's strategy of subversion leads to the empowerment of a voiceless Tituba and gives her the authorial position in the narrative. In giving a voice directly to Tituba, Condé implicitly renounces the status of the magisterial function, allowing thereby a voice to emerge from elsewhere than from an "authority" or from the social location of the writer and her *lieu d'élocution*. In withdrawing

to the unauthorial position of an interpreter or mediator, Condé ensures the authenticity of the character's voice.

Seen from this perspective, Tituba's life story, even if it is a fictional one, assumes a value and a meaning comparable to Rigoberta Menchú's testimonial *I, Rigoberta Menchú*. Tituba is certainly speaking of herself, but her narrative also tells the story of many other black women who, like her, have been relegated to the margins of history, if not erased from it, reduced to invisibility and silence.

If there are similarities between Tituba's and Rigoberta's cases, there are also differences: one is a fictional character, the other a real-life individual. Rigoberta taught herself Spanish, the language of the dominant class, and communicates with her interviewer Elisabeth Burgos-Debray directly in Spanish, even if her speech is sometimes deficient in grammar. As for Tituba, a slave and uneducated, she could not possibly speak French, the language of the educated class and the official language into which the writer will translate her account. Rigoberta, in telling her story, is from the beginning very well aware that her personal history represents, as she puts it, "everyone's life: the life of all the Guatemaltec poor." She is also aware that she is using the power of speech as a weapon in order to expose the situation of her people and to bring about changes in it. Tituba does not display Rigoberta's political awareness or will, yet her narrative takes on political significance. Although Tituba is speaking only of herself and recounting her individual life, her narrative also encompasses the story of many other black women who, like her, have been relegated to the margins of history, if not erased from it, reduced to invisibility and silence. Both Tituba and Rigoberta, not knowing how to write, have to entrust their story to the mediation of a "writer," who then assumes the responsibility of conveying it.

*I, Tituba, Black Witch of Salem* is the account of a yearlong conversation between the writer and Tituba. The presence of the author of the book as an interlocutor is maintained not by a dialogic inclusive "you" within the narrative, but rather by the oral mode involved in the narration. What Roman Jakobson identifies as the "phatic function," intended to keep the communication between performer and audience flowing, is represented here by the numerous rhetorical questions asked by Tituba. While acknowledging the writer's presence on the scene, the rhetorical questions serve to prevent her from intruding into the narrative and usurping or covering Tituba's voice. The textual strategies used by Condé in shaping the narrative as an oral performance insert Tituba into the traditional cultural context of orality and, at the same time, incorporate the orality conveyed in Tituba's narrative into the context of a new culture: the written one.

Condé introduces Tituba's narrative with an epigraph, which Gérard Genette in *Seuils* defines as being a quotation outside the text or "en exergue": "Tituba and I lived for a year on the closest of terms. During our endless conversations she told me things she had confided to nobody else." Genette's commentary on the epigraph enlightens and sets forth the relationship between the writer and her character, between Condé's position outside the text and Tituba's narrative within it. Among the four functions Genette assigns to the epigraph and to its relation to the text, there is the function of commentary on the title and the text. Another is the legitimation of the book author's own text by reference in the epigraph to a well-known figure or authority. For legitimation, Condé does not refer to a well-known author but rather to Tituba herself, thus granting her the status of an authority. With the epigraph, Condé excises herself from the text that follows, or, more precisely, places herself, to quote Genette, at the *bord d'œuvre,* at the "margin of the work," effacing herself and leaving the entire textual space and a full voice to her character. In textualizing Tituba as an "I," a subject, the writer withdraws her own authority from the narrative. At the same time, via the epigraph, Condé legitimates her own written work, the book, as a faithful interpretation, translation, and transcription of Tituba's oral text and of her voice.

What I am suggesting here is that the tacit pact alluded to earlier has bound writer and character in a collaborative endeavor embedded, on the one hand, in the reverberation between the oral and the written and, on the other, in the shifting of the subject pronouns. In this shifting, the epigraph presents the subject pronoun "I" as the writer/narrator and "she" as Tituba: "Tituba and *I* lived for a year on the closest of terms. During *our* endless conversations, *she* told me things she had confided to nobody before" (emphases added). The narrative itself is a first-person account, with Tituba as the subject recounting her life story from beginning—"*I* was born from this act of aggression"—to end: "And that is the story of *my* life" (emphases added). In the writer's concluding historical note, which provides closure to the book, the "I" again represents the writer, who refers to Tituba in the third person: "I *myself* have given her an ending of my own choice," (emphasis added). This shifting interplay of subject pronouns indicates clearly the respective roles of the writer and of Tituba and the responsibilities of each in the construction of the narrative. What appears to be an ambiguity of the writer's position, as pointed out earlier, in fact reflects the cultural configuration of the Caribbean and its dominant trend: *métissage* and pluralism, at the racial, the cultural, and the linguistic levels.

At this point writer and character, the author of the book and the author of the life story recounted in that book, come together in the making of the narrative, thus achieving a merging of the oral and the written. This strategy blurs the polarization between written and oral and, in this way, puts an end to what Glissant calls "la déchirure et l'ambivalence," the rending and the ambivalence. Furthermore, through the writer's desire for creativity and the character's concern about self-representation, the esthetic and the political become connected within the same textual space, creating a territory for both the writer and Tituba. For both of them, generating a text becomes possible only through the exercise of memory: the author of the book reminding us of her conversations with her character; the character, in her turn, remembering her life and recounting it in order to fill the space of their conversations. *Tituba,* as suggested earlier, functions as a collaborative enterprise between writer and character in the fulfillment of common concerns: to give a voice to the voice-

less black women, to rehabilitate Tituba, and to validate one's cultural heritage in the valorization of the orality which has become the vehicle of the text—Tituba's. If Condé is the "author" of the book that has been written, Tituba definitely emerges as the "author" of the text that allowed the birth of the book.

In the autobiographical narrative unfolded, Tituba's voice is the major and dominant one. Indeed, the narrative *tells* the life story of "a common Negress," a black slave woman. The authenticity of her voice is preserved thanks to specific narrative strategies implemented by Condé: self-effacement and subversion, interplay with the subject pronouns, and the creation of an autobiographical narrative. Through the mediation of "autobiographical conversations" Tituba engages in an initiation process that relieves her of anxiety about being forgotten and about her survival through the written medium. She reaches a new awareness to other ways of surviving: spiritual motherhood, collective memory, and oral tradition. As she states in her epilogue: "I do not belong to the civilization of the Bible and Bigotry. My people will keep my memory in their hearts and have no need for the written word. It's in their heads. In their hearts and in their heads." Indeed, despite her one-time companion Christopher's condescending statement that she is "nothing but a common Negress" who wants "to be treated like someone special," Tituba will be recollected all over her native island, legendized and immortalized in the folklore of the land, thereby entering history and the collective memory. The following passage, situated in Tituba's afterlife, concludes her autobiographical account:

> . . . And that is the story of my life. Such a bitter, bitter story.
>
> My real story starts where this one leaves off and it has no end. Christopher was wrong or probably he wanted to hurt me—there is a song about Tituba! I hear it from one end of the island to the other, from North Point to Silver Sands, from Bridgetown to Bottom Bay. It runs along the ridge of the hills. It is poised on the tip of the heliconia. . . .
>
> I hear it wherever I go.

In the official accounts mentioning Tituba, she has been constructed and fixed in the negative figure of a witch. Her own account in *I, Tituba, Black Witch of Salem* seems to suggest that her condemnation as a witch was, in actuality, the resounding projection of the fears and obsessions of a community: first, the Puritan community of Massachusetts, which condemned her; then the community of slave owners, who, because she became a revolutionary, put her to death for political reasons. The autobiographical form in which Tituba tells her story positions her as the narrating subject who proclaims her identity: "I, Tituba, Black Witch of Salem." Her life story as she recounts it brings up questions of identity, of origins, of race, of access to language, of the power of language.

For Tituba, telling her story means also remembering her genesis: where and how it started, where and how it will end. The recounting of her life becomes also a therapeutic means of healing her complex about exile, the anxiety about identity, linked at least partially to the absence of a national or ethnic genealogy because of the transplantation and the absence of a legitimate genealogy, since her coming into the world originated in an act of violence aboard the slave ship: "Abena, my mother, was raped by an English sailor on the deck of *Christ the King* one day in the year 16** while the ship was sailing for Barbados. I was born from this act of aggression. From this act of hatred and contempt." Although in the land of slavery, Tituba grows up as a happy child in the home of a stepfather, Yao, whose presence and affection compensate for her rejection on the part of her mother, in the mind of whom Tituba was the living memory of the violence endured on the slave ship. After her mother has been hanged and her stepfather sold, Tituba is adopted by an old woman, Mama Yaya, who introduces her to the magic realism of the Caribbean, perpetuating the African traditions, and believes in contact with the spirit world and the African art of healing with plants. While living in Massachusetts, and after returning to her homeland of Barbados, Tituba retains her healing powers. In endorsing the identity of "the black witch of Salem," Tituba subverts and disrupts the meaning ascribed to it by hegemonic institutions: the Church and the slave masters who condemned her for "witchcraft."

> What is a witch? I noticed that when he said the word, it was marked with disapproval. Why should that be? Why? Isn't the ability to communicate with the invisible world, to keep constant links with the dead, to care for others and heal, a superior gift of nature that inspires respect, admiration, and gratitude? Consequently, shouldn't the witch (if that's what the person who has this gift is to be called) be cherished and revered rather than feared?

These question marks translate Tituba's anxiety about the asymmetry and the disjunction between what she is and society's representation of her. In unfolding the narrative of her life, Tituba wants to restore the integrity of her persona. The strong declaration of the title, *I, Tituba,* echoes the character's will to speak in an autoreferential mode and to assert a self-ascribed identity, with herself as the narrating instance: the producer and the center of her narrative.

In Tituba's fictional autobiography as well as in real autobiographies, memory constitutes the matrix from which the narrative is extracted. *Tituba,* in reconstructing one individual's story, also allegorizes the collective history of the Caribbean. History here conflates into literature, and the text reveals itself as a *lieu de mémoire.* As Pierre Nora puts it so beautifully [in his "Between Memory and History: *Les Lieux de Mémoire,"* *Representations,* Vol. 26, Spring, 1989]:

> In fact, memory has never known more than two forms of legitimacy: historical and literary. These have run parallel to each other but until now always separately. At present the boundary between the two is blurring; following closely upon the successive deaths of memory-history and memory-fiction, a new kind of history has been born, which owes its prestige and legitimacy to the new relation it maintains to the past.

> History has become our replaceable imagination—hence the last stand of faltering fiction in the renaissance of the historical novel, the vogue for personalized documents, the literary revitalization of historical drama, the success of the oral historical tale. Our interest in these *lieux de mémoire* that anchor, condense, and express the exhausted capital of our collective memory derives from this new sensibility.

In transcribing Tituba's voice, Condé, as the writer, has not only joined her in challenging Christopher's assertion about the worthlessness of "a common Negress" but has also empowered her and created a territory for her in history and literature, allowing her to survive as a black female literary character, if not a historical figure.

Roland Barthes's "Death of the Author" and Michel Foucault's "What Is an Author?" challenge the role of the author as the master of the meaning encoded in the text, and contemporary critical theory tends to emphasize the role of the reader as the instance of interpreting and decoding meaning. By declaring "the death of the author," Barthes and Foucault also emphasize intertextuality. The disappearance of Condé from the narrative told by Tituba acknowledges and illuminates the inscription of orality into written form as well as the intertextuality between the two media. This could be deciphered in the relation between the epigraph *en exergue* and Tituba's text itself. In declaring the death of the author, Barthes and Foucault also challenge the authority of the book's author to ascribe a definitive meaning to the text. As for Condé, she asks Anne Scarborough, her interviewer in the U.S. edition of *Tituba,* "not to take *Tituba* too seriously," and she characterizes Tituba as a "mock-epic" heroine. For my part, as a reader or as a critic, I would like to believe that Tituba's life is neither a trivial subject matter nor a burlesque story. Without forsaking the parodic dimension of *Tituba,* I contend that Condé's strategies of subversion and self-effacement inform the semantics and the structure of the narrative, bestowing on Tituba a political significance and seriousness that, to quote Condé herself, "turns her into a female hero, an epic heroine."

Despite her declaration of not being "interested in giving models to young people," Condé has created in Tituba an exemplary character. Defying the official history, she has produced a counterhistory and substituted for the heroes of the Other's history (the well-known "nos ancêtres les Gaulois") a national hero who is a female. Condé has brought Tituba's voice out of silence and has added her name to those of Caribbean historical figures: Toussaint L'Ouverture, Makandal, Delgrès. I do not know if Tituba would have considered herself a heroic figure, and it does not matter if Condé's Tituba is not the historical Tituba; myths very often become more powerful than history. In fact, what I would like to ascertain is the role, the contribution, and the impact of the critics' work in shaping the destiny of a literary work. If the discourse developed by critics—in forewords, afterwords, or essays—seems sometimes to interfere with the voice of the narrating character, it nevertheless contributes to the diffusion and the recognition of the work, its presence in time and space as well as the continuation of the character's presence. Seen from this perspective, Tituba's narrative proclaims a victory over voicelessness and erasure, over effacement and exclusion. In asserting herself as "I, Tituba," Tituba comes into existence and signals the end of marginalization, the end of exile from language, literature, and history.

## Hal Wylie (essay date Autumn 1993)

SOURCE: "The Cosmopolitan Condé, or Unscrambling the Worlds," in *World Literature Today,* Vol. 67, No. 4, Autumn, 1993, pp. 763-68.

[*In the following essay, Wylie discusses the "universality" and "cosmopolitanism" of Condé's recurrent themes, including gender, nationality, and generational differences.*]

Maryse Condé is a transcendental person and restless, but unlike many wanderers, she does not dissipate herself butterflying about. Instead, she is able to marshal her forces to draw upon the many places and episodes of her own Odyssey to forge a new unity by showing symbolist *correspondances* between the parts of the scrambled postmodern landscape. We know from published biographical information that she has lived in Guadeloupe, France, Guinea, the Ivory Coast, Ghana, Senegal, Kenya, Jamaica, and Manhattan. Extrapolation from her works indicates that she has probably also spent some time in Mali, Barbados, Panama, South Carolina, Haiti, and Dahomey. She sees no contradiction between being Antillean and a wanderer. She has stated [in her **"Notes d'un retour au pays natal"**]: "Etre Antillais, finalement, je ne sais toujours pas très bien ce que ca veut dire! . . . Est-ce qu'un écrivain ne pourrait pas être constamment errant, constamment à la recherche d'autres hommes?" She shares many of the attributes of the traditional literary figures of the knight errant, the troubadour, and perhaps the Wandering Jew.

Early readers realized that the relation between the Antilles and Africa was an important concern, as **Hérémakhonon** (1976; Eng. **Heremakhonon**) and **Une saison à Rihata** (1981; Eng. **A Season in Rihata**) showed the problems her protagonists from the West Indies had in adapting to life in Africa. **Ségou** (1984; Eng. **Segu** and **Children of Segu**) sent her African characters to Jamaica and Brazil in the New World, but when she tackled the United States in **Moi, Tituba, sorcière . . . Noire de Salem** (1986; Eng. **I, Tituba, Black Witch of Salem**), a new dimension was added. Two of her most recent works have gone beyond **Tituba** in exploring the connections between the Caribbean and the U.S., by analyzing this relation throughout a prolonged period of time and by adding more places into the equation.

Is it fair to say that most of the universal classics of literature explore one place in depth, and that the concentration derived from unity of place is a major technique to increase literary density? (Of course there is *The Odyssey,* but even that explores the mythic Mediterranean of the Greeks.) The psychology of assimilation and culture shock seems to be a modern theme, one that has perhaps been most thoroughly explored by Francophone writers, especially in the Negritude tradition by such writers as Fanon, Césaire, Senghor, Camara Laye, Mongo Béti, and Sembène.

We may have arrived, however, at a new phase of transcultural and intercultural exploration with the works of V. S. Naipaul and Salman Rushdie, which seem to transcend the colonizer/colonized dichotomy to take a global approach to the problem. Jonathan Ngate has compared Condé to Naipaul in his article "Maryse Condé and Africa: The Making of a Recalcitrant Daughter." After noting Condé's "toughmindedness" and "her clear sense of history," he attacks her hostility toward Negritude and her preference for Naipaul, citing her statement that "Naipaul . . . est un esprit très contestataire, *très négatif, très nihiliste.*" He focuses on the importance of negativity, ambiguity, and irony for both writers. Both may be seen as relishing the role of devil's advocate and a refusal to acquiesce in accepting the slogans and simple theories that characterize the early politicizations of intercultural conflict. Naipaul, Rushdie, and Condé insist upon taking their analysis a step or two deeper, to go beyond simple dualities like black/white, male/female, or First World/Third World to examine the swarming multiplicity of realities, situations, positions in the vast panoply of the social world, where many nations, many cultures, many religions, many personality types clash and try to harmonize. Their works tend to stretch out and grow longer in the effort to synthesize all the nuances of the truth in all its overwhelming variegation. For them it is impossible to separate the political from the literary. For instance, in *La vie scélérate* (1987; Eng. *Tree of Life*) Condé furnishes many examples of the harm caused by a too-rapid understanding of a problem, the central one being the death of the second Albert Louis, "killed" by his own father for fathering a half-breed child. We might state that these writers see their political contribution as purely a literary analysis, except that even this is too simplistic, it seems, now that apparently Maryse Condé has consented to run for office on an "independence" ticket.

Condé's transcendental cosmopolitanism may have its roots in a certain ambiguity of class, in that, like Rimbaud and Zola, she experienced a major shift in the family fortune when she was quite young (although in the opposite direction). Like Arthur and Emile, she might be said to have experienced both working-class and bourgeois cultures and be unable to see reality through one or the other. Her interview in *Callaloo* with Vèvè A. Clark brought to light much fascinating information, including the fact that her father's change of profession from teacher to banker made the family rich. Condé also talked about her own family politics and her special situation as an "enfant gâté." This seems of interest given the attention she lavishes on family politics in her novels. She also admits in the interview to "un penchant pour la controverse" and to being "douée pour la caricature." Of course this early understanding of the great complexity of human reality was enriched by her study in France and her marriage in Africa, where her daughters were born.

It seems Condé might accept the view that everything is political in her awareness of the political aspect of family life, culture, economics, religion, and the relations between the sexes. Her works insist on the complexities of the interrelations among all these domains. One reason she may have waited so long to write about her own island while examining Africa is that she may have felt unable to cope with all the ramifications known from in-depth experience and may have preferred to describe the more distanced material of Africa, which she could handle with more objectivity, though the tantalizingly bizarre character of Véronica (in *Hérémakhonon*)—which she labeled as a sort of "anti-moi"—impinges on Caribbean culture.

The first two international surprises in Condé's works were the difficulties experienced in Africa by her Caribbean heroines in *Hérémakhonon* and *Une saison à Rihata* and the opening out of the African world of *Ségou* to the Anglophone world of the Gold Coast and Jamaica. Many had insisted on the unity of Africa before, but not many writers had involved their characters in both Francophone and Anglophone worlds. When the focus shifted back home to the Caribbean, readers were surprised by the emphasis on the U.S. Perhaps we should have been less surprised, since clearly the Caribbean has been an "American lake" in the twentieth century, and neocolonial lines of force leading to the U.S. have supplanted the old colonial ties to a large extent.

Condé is a writer who reminds one of Voltaire, in several ways. 1) She prefers to study cultures, generations, and worlds rather than limit her focus to one individual. Her big works are all genealogical studies of generations and family histories, showing how an individual reflects an evolutionary pattern deriving from family and culture in history. 2) She keeps her distance from her inventions, her characters, and is not averse to subjugating them to shocking and sadistic treatment, to using them like marionettes so that by pulling strings she can dramatize certain abstract points. Some have characterized her works as soap operas. 3) She may be seen as something of a social philosopher, concerned with certain abstract social patterns that can only be understood across a large expanse of time and space. 4) She seems to like to conduct rather outrageous social experiments. Where Voltaire can see what might happen if a Saturnian came to Earth, Condé can try out what would happen if an African king visited his kinsmen in the New World (*Les derniers rois mages* [*The Last Magi*; 1992]).

All of Condé's works seem to manifest the openmindedness of the empirical scientist conducting an experiment, but the earlier works displayed more reliance on preconceived ideas and theories. There is not much theory describing the social results of late-twentieth-century immigration to the United States and/or the impact on French and Creole speakers arriving here. Francophone writers have not by and large, related to the States; Léon Damas is the note-worthy exception. So it is a rather original experiment for Condé to bring herself here to explore the intercultural territory, and even more original to send her characters on their way to America. Condé seems to be defining herself increasingly through the active dialogue in American literary journals like *Callaloo* and through her interactions with her "network of loyal friends in the

U.S.," mostly literary scholars. What might be some of the factors in this choice?

One surely is the desire to strike out into new literary territory and to avoid repeating what others have done. Francophone African literature is full of interesting stories of Africans' and West Indians' adventures in France. Another seems to be a desire to break out of established limits of the Francophone world, to become a "universal" or world writer. Another might be to look for those dramatic encounters of a little-expected kind based on bringing vastly different beings together. New surprises, new colors, new permutations are produced. One last explanation might be the necessity to bring back into play historical facts lost for many years in the archives Condé loves to frequent. *La vie scélérate* and *Les derniers rois mages* both seem sustained meditations on just how relevant is history. Are we determined or obsessed by history? One example is the Panama Canal. The building of the canal can be seen as a dead fact. It also seems to have provided a certain inspiration for the writing of *La vie scélérate*. The political relevance of the information Condé puts before us (the use of Third World workers to build the canal and their dying like flies in the effort) to the America of today and its involvement in Panama, Iraq, Haiti, Somalia, et cetera— this relevance seems obvious. The racism of America in the 1920s and the lynchings deserve reconsideration in the 1990s, thinks our author. (It is the gratuitous "lynching" of his friend Jacob in the San Francisco bar that sends patriarch Albert back to Guadeloupe to found his dynasty.) Marshall McLuhan said that electronic communications had woven the world together into a tribal village, and Condé wants to get to the central switchboard.

Perhaps it is too early to come up with generalizations about the postmodern, postindustrial, postcolonial relations between the Third World and the United States, but certain items may be noted in Condé's literary experiments. We must be patient, however, because, like André Gide, Condé is more concerned with asking the right question than providing an answer, especially when one considers the rapid proliferation of social and literary theory in the late days of the twentieth century, when we are so aware of the multiplicity of variables to take into account: race, class, and sex, of course, but also identity, language, culture, religion, family, roles and professions, and even sexual persuasions. [In a review of *Moi, Tituba, Sorciere . . . Noire de Salem*], Charlotte Bruner has noted that all of "Condé's major fiction is rooted in a study of power," and Condé herself has stated in an interview that the Carribbean islands are always affected by American policy and that "c'est à cause de l'Amérique que plusieurs îles ont des problèmes." In the interview she calls upon Americans to familiarize themselves with the culturally rich island peoples to their south. Writers are more aware than those who gain their information about the world from TV news and journalism that power is not merely military and economic but has its foundation in ideas and beliefs, in symbols and myths. Condé is aware of the power of Hollywood, Madison Avenue, and America's dominance in the area of international photojournalism. Two minor works give us clues to her own attitudes, which tend to be hidden behind those of her characters in the major novels.

One strange link between her island and the U.S. was Hurricane Hugo of 1989, which left such an impact on Condé that she made a children's book, ***Hugo le terrible,*** from it. The storm may also have led her to choose South Carolina as the setting for ***Les derniers rois mages***. Characters in ***Hugo*** debate the nature and desirability of going to the States. America's "marvelous" democracy, skyscrapers, and technology are opposed to its oppressed minorities and homelessness in the debate of "les opinions les plus contradictoires sur ce pays." The most telling detail, however, is an aspect of the plot dealing with how information from the Third World is gathered and disseminated to the world. At the outset of the story photographers arrive to cover the hurricane, admitting that they play the role of "voyeurs." The most interesting subplot involves an adolescent boy who takes advantage of the chaos and steals a camera in order to take pictures to send to France. He ends up selling them, however, for a thousand francs to an American photographer who has flown in from New York. In germinal form many of the U.S./Third World connections are demonstrated here: the redirection of Third World energies and attitudes by American economic and journalistic power; the selective nature of the American *regard* directed toward the Third World, which looks only for sensation and disaster there; the imposition of this American vision on the people of the Third World themselves; and the perverse nature of the whole process. (The native photographer has access to realities the international outsider does not and does not hesitate to intrude into the misery of his neighbors.)

Condé's view of the nature of this informational struggle is further revealed in another minor and surprising work, a seemingly official tourist-promotion book, ***Guadeloupe,*** with beautiful photographs by Jean de Boisberranger, wherein Condé seems to have decided to collaborate in a suspect genre in order to redirect its message and slant. Instead of fighting tourism, her attitude seems to be to use the genre to educate and inform the tourist of the social realities as seen by the permanent resident, while also furnishing the tour information needed. She elevates journalism to the status of literature. Or it might be better to say she sees journalism as an important form of popular literature, with an important power that must be redirected.

Condé begins her text by listing a number of "idées reçues à balayer" and leads the reader through a social and cultural description of the island, eventually plunging right into the critical politics of the struggle for independence, a very controversial and divisive matter for both Martinique and Guadeloupe. She concedes that only 3 percent have voted for independence candidates, but sees the option as much more important than that figure would indicate. She speaks directly to the tourist-reader in a friendly tone of equality, with the implication that the cooperative collaboration of rich and poor from the First and Third Worlds be in everyone's mutual interest. Her last words describe the sadness of "Les Saintes" islanders (part of Guadeloupe) because of the "hemorrhaging" of their population as young people leave for the imperial centers.

Micheline Rice-Maximin and I invited Maryse Condé to speak in San Antonio and Austin in April of 1986. The French Department lounge at University of Texas in Austin was packed when she addressed us on the women writers of her island. She told us she was resigning her professional position at the University of Paris and was going to live in Guadeloupe and write for Guadeloupe. Some of us were therefore surprised thereafter when we learned she was teaching at Berkeley, but she has indeed made an effort to write specifically for Guadeloupe. Françoise Lionnet interprets ***Traversée de la mangrove*** (***Crossing the Mangrove;*** 1989) as the major effort to express literarily this "return to her native land," which was also a return to writing about the present. Another example is more specific: ***An tan revolisyon,*** a play financed and published by the Conseil Régional (of Guadeloupe). Contrasting this work with the cosmopolitan novels is revealing.

Although the title is in Creole, the text is in French, but with a note that Creole may be used "partout où voudra, sauf pour le conteur." The title seems to mean "Longtemps révolution" (Longtime Revolution). Although it would be difficult to evaluate the success of this play showing the French Revolution from the Guadeloupean standpoint, it seems likely that it was received favorably in Guadeloupe. The book form seems less successful. The typesetting and printing are disappointing, and distribution was undoubtedly quite limited. Condé must have enjoyed working with the local people to produce the play, but any clearheaded person, especially one interested in power, could derive obvious conclusions about the objective, material facts of the natures of these two kinds of literature (i. e., writing for a local audience versus publishing with international publishing houses texts designed for transnational consumption). Condé seems to be very lucid about her own talents and work and must consider addressing the issue of the loss of Third World youth (the ones on whom the play is least likely to have made an impact) in the international arena more important than the development of a purely local literature. In directly addressing the problem of immigration (and other international connections) in her cosmopolitan writings, she undoubtedly feels she can have a greater political impact in both the local and international arenas.

Just as we are drowned in information amid the din of radio and TV and the deluge of paper, we are overwhelmed by historical detail. The question is to find that which is relevant and meaningful and to apply it correctly to our lives. I believe literature is the tool we use to carry out this operation. Marshall McLuhan says one of the roles of the writer is to warn us of the perils of the future by interpreting the past. ***Les derniers rois mages*** surprises by adding a new element, antithetical to the earlier conception of history in Condé's works. The protagonist comes to view himself as having been victimized by history and its cultivation, and he rebels. We might say that the novel takes up historiography as a theme. It seems that Condé is refining her understanding of the importance and nature of history.

We are all obviously victims of history, predestined to inherit a biological form, predispositions, a family, an ethnic, religious, and national culture, a language, and an economic situation. There is little we can do to modify them when we are children, during our formative years. To rebel against this history is foolish. But Spéro, the protagonist of *Les derniers rois mages,* becomes critical of the tendency to focus on knowing the past to the extent of becoming fixated on it, which weakens the ability to live in the present, to see the freedom and freshness of the existential moment. There are many qualities in Spéro that make him different from his ancestors and from his wife Debbie, from those who tend to make of the past a fetish. He is an artist, whose eye seeks the essence of the object precisely in the way in which the existing object transcends its determinants, who prefers the light touch of water-color and its power to capture transitory, ephemeral qualities and who loves to paint the old buildings of Charleston and children's faces, even though the houses were those of the slaveholders and represent historically a system based on slavery and oppression. Debbie, in her insistence upon imposing a political interpretation, a priori, on his art, has ruined its spontaneity, so that the resultant oil paintings are mere illustrations of historical points.

Debbie is the antagonist and antithesis to her husband Spéro. In this bad marriage, doomed by her bad faith from the start, she represents all that is wrong about history, or a certain use of it. She married the uneducated Guadeloupean because he was the descendant of an African king. Unlike most African Americans in the United States, he could trace his genealogy. In fact, his father had made this history into a cult and ritual based upon the "Cahiers" (notebooks) written by his father in an effort to fixate the fragmentary remembrances of *his* father, the African king in exile in Martinique. The image of these West Indian princes of Africa is a source of derision and alienation, related to the males' dependence on women in this lineage and their inability to affirm their male existence. While repeating the pattern, Spéro comes closest to breaking out of the rut. Ironically, his daughter does, to a certain extent, by finally going back to Dahomey, now Bénin. Unfortunately, we never find out how she does there and if this return is a true break or more of the same.

Debbie is a historian, one who has seemingly lost control of her materials and is now drowning in the flotsam of oral history, endlessly tape-recording the senile reminiscences of an egoistic elder and enmeshing those around her in her oppressive web. She compulsively imposes a moralistic reading on the story of her ancestors and on the history of her race.

That is my reading of this problematic story, which I realize may be seen as one-sided. One of the virtues of Condé's storytelling technique is that she (like Rushdie) tells such good stories that they resemble those drawn directly from life: they have all the ambiguity, realism, resistance to interpretation of lived experience. Would Condé go so far as to agree with the husband in this couple? With the philandering male, the unproductive, undisciplined father who hates Mickey Mouse and wonders if he might have been tempted to sexually abuse his own daughter? The novel ends with his attempted suicide as he judges himself

quite severely, but his judgment, as judge, seems the most clear and perceptive of all the characters (he is Guadeloupean, after all). His mind has the dialectical play of the author's. He knows a higher form of history, one not marked by a revisionist interpretation that falsifies the story by imposing a "logical" reading. He understands history as a nonlinear, multifarious, ambiguous, contradictory entity, often displeasing to the theorist.

The story of the African king, partly told in the "Cahiers," reads like a cruel joke (although we must remember the framing of this story within a story). This king is descended from the panther whose "enormous scarlet erection seemed like a barbarous flower" to the African maiden destined to become his wife and mother of the dynasty. We learn that the funerals of these kings involved the death of scores of wives and hundreds if not thousands of slaves. Condé's satiric re-creation of the African kingdom is mocking; the last king, Spéro's great-grandfather, is shown to have been happiest wandering in the woods after the loss of his power and property to the French. It seems clear Condé does not like African kings.

In the public lecture given just before the opening of the Puterbaugh Conference at the University of Oklahoma on 25 March 1993, Maryse Condé talked about how we are haunted by history. The use of ghosts has become more forceful as it has evolved from *Ségou* to *Tituba,* from *La vie scélérate* to *Les derniers rois mages.* In *Tituba* and *La vie scélérate* the ghosts are literal and seem used mainly for melodramatic impact as a kind of narrative shorthand. In *Les derniers rois mages* they are metaphorically woven into the narrative framework. The last king and his son and grandson all lose themselves in schizophrenic mythomania in which they become their ancestor(s). Spéro, while disidentifying with his predecessors, is haunted by crabs swarming over and attacking his body in a repeated nightmare associated with his self-critique and loss of nerve, which recapitulates the story of the third "Cahier" entitled "Totem and Taboo" that describes the role of the "genies" or spirits of the animals, which both protect and punish. Spéro comes to see his alienation from Debbie as derived from "all the cadavers between them."

The postmodern writer needs ghosts and sorcery and all the magic of "marvelous realism" to cope with the complexities of our late-twentieth-century reality. Condé, for whom "Africa is no longer in Africa" and "America is no longer America," for whom the essence of present-day Guadeloupe is impossible to know, uses ironic reversals (e. g., the daughter of the actual African prince in *La vie scélérate,* abandoned by father and mother, is brought up by a simple Breton [white] wet nurse) and feedback loops (back and forth across the Atlantic, from Africa to America in *Ségou* and *Les derniers rois mages,* from the U.S. to Guadeloupe in *La vie scélérate)* to short-circuit history and get right to essential meanings. The presence of a significant outsider in a foreign culture (Spéro in South Carolina, Albert Louis in San Francisco, Tituba in Salem) quickly throws certain values into relief. They may be seen as living ghosts and further explain the cosmopolitan tendency in Condé.

Condé's two recent epic novels show a synthesis that goes

133

beyond the first-level history of *Tituba* and *Ségou,* which deal only with the relatively distant past. They both attempt to integrate the past with the present by tracing all connections right through to the present. The result, however, is another paradox: the past seems clearer, more interesting, more meaningful, and of course more literary. Perhaps it is endemic to the genre that the ancestors always emerge as the Titans; perhaps that is history, but Albert Louis looms above all the others in *La vie scélérate,* even over the narrator, whose life might be seen as equally interesting. Perhaps we tend to devalue our own time as banal and prosaic.

Still, Condé's ambitious insistence upon seeking the links between the generations, and between the ethnic groups, must be seen as a quest for the meaningful factors of our time. We must learn how to make the ghosts work for us rather than being haunted by them. At one point in *Les derniers rois mages* Spéro wonders about the significance of being black and concludes, "Pourtant, cela a-t-il encore une signification?" Both *La vie scélérate* and *Les derniers rois mages* analyze the evolution of racial identity in the complexities of time and space and effect a kind of demystification of identity. Condé seems to be groping beyond identity to look for the universal meaning, the touchstone values that may have been lost sight of or even that may remain to be defined. Africa, America, and Guadeloupe have changed; they are no longer themselves in the sense that their old myths are no longer functional in defining the geographic or social realities. Spéro and Claude "Coco" Elaïse Louis, the storyteller of *La vie scélérate,* are lost souls, unable to assert an identity comparable to those of their ancestors of the Titan generation, but they may be better guides for us in our days of whimper, when *everything,* indeed, does fall apart. Nothing is to be gained by inventing a new myth of Africa or positing a new identity for Guadeloupe apart from the global reality. We must now look at all the scrambled pieces and try to assemble a new image of totality and harmony capable of reflecting the complex interactions of a multicultural and multifarious entity.

## Miller Newman   (review date Spring 1994)

SOURCE: "Tied to a Spinner's Shuttle," in *Belles Lettres: A Review of Books by Women,* Vol. 9, No. 3, Spring, 1994, pp. 48, 52.

[*Newman is an American educator. In the following review of* I, Tituba, Black Witch of Salem *and* Tree of Life, *he discusses Condé's use of apparitions and ghost imagery.*]

Maryse Condé's *Tree of Life* is a story of a West Indian family on the island of Guadeloupe. Told by the adolescent great-granddaughter, Coco, the story begins with the family's sire, Albert Quentin Louis, and his decision to leave the bondage of the island's cane fields in search of a better way of life. Albert travels to Panama, lured by the prospect of a job with the Americans who are paying $.90 an hour for laborers to work on the canal project. Coco recreates her ancestor's encounter with the first of his life's trials, and a family legacy of economic success at the expense of personal happiness is set into motion.

Coco ends her family's odyssey with the revelation that it is she who will be forced to "recount this story . . . a story of very ordinary people who in their very ordinary way had nonetheless made blood flow." Coco is right. The story is indeed about ordinary people who, when faced with the hand life dealt them, played it out. There are no real heroes in *The Tree of Life,* only fathers, mothers, sons, and daughters who love and hate each other. They demand much of the world and get little for their trouble.

Predictably, the men drink, marry as best they can, take mistresses, try politics, run their businesses, and in between have children who break their hearts, resent them for selling out to the establishment, spend their money, and act injured when their parents do not understand the motives for their childish abuses, Prejudice, politics, oppression, and, on an occasion or two, natural disasters all prove obstacles that the Louis family must overcome.

Condé's use of the family's ghosts to advance the plot or explain away the bizarre, however, tests the reader's patience. True to what I have come to believe is a cultural tendency, Condé revives her use of apparitions in *I, Tituba, Black Witch of Salem.* Her cadre of benign ghosts includes Mama Yaya, the woman who reared Tituba when her mother, Abena, was hanged by her owner; Abena herself; and Yao, Abena's husband, who killed himself when Abena was hanged. Arming Tituba with an arsenal of supernatural kinfolk, herbal medicines, fervent prayer, and blood sacrifices, Condé creates a credible scenario of Tituba's part in the Salem witch trials. The Caspar-like apparitions and the self-martyrdom of Louis's granddaughter Thécla, whose disappointment with life results in her abandoning her family for the life of a wandering slut in search of redemption sets the reader's blood pounding.

---

**Condé weaves the fabric of her story in *I, Tituba, Black Witch of Salem* so tightly that the reader is pulled through the Salem trials as if tied to the end of a spinner's shuttle.**

**—*Miller Newman***

---

What is most affecting in this story, however, is the chillingly realistic retelling of the Salem witch hunts. Condé weaves the fabric of her story so tightly that the reader is pulled through the Salem trials as if tied to the end of a spinner's shuttle. It is difficult to tell when reading the novel whether the air is sucked out of the reader's lungs by the very powers Tituba is supposed to have or by the sense of foreboding Condé creates with her powerful words. I closed the book more than once when the hair on the back of my neck began to rise at the deeds of Sam Paris in the name of God. I wanted no part of this vivid recreation of the acts of slavers, zealots, and mean-spirited humans.

Tituba is born to a life of troubles, observes Mama Yaya

and, with the innocence of youth and a surge of hormones, Tituba strides boldly to her destiny. "Oh, God, why can't women do without men?" This is Tituba's epitaph and the theme for the novel. Her trials start with John Indian, a slave who appears outside her house. From then on, her every move seems to be dictated by her need for a man.

Tituba is a victim, first of the master who drives her off his land after he kills her mother, then of John Indian. When she fights back; she is forced into a life of servitude by John Indian's owner, who sells him to Paris. Since Tituba cannot live without John Indian, she becomes a slave to the Paris family as well. Tituba leaves her beloved island, Barbados, and her family of apparitions only to face the cold and unerring justice of the people of Salem. "Do I have to go on to the end? Hasn't the reader already guessed what is going to happen?" Tituba cries. To Condé's credit, the answer is no. Although Condé alludes to Tituba's destiny from the beginning, those of us who believe in happy endings or justice for the oppressed read on, hoping to see our heroine vindicated or, at least, at peace.

---

# FURTHER READING

## Criticism

Andrade, Susan Z. "The Nigger of the Narcissist: History, Sexuality and Intertextuality in Maryse Condé's *Heremakhonon*." *Callaloo* 16, No. 1 (Winter 1993): 213-26.

>   Analyzes sexuality and sexual relations in *Heremakhonon*.

Bruner, Charlotte, and Bruner, David. "Buchi Emecheta and Maryse Condé: Contemporary Writing from Africa and the Caribbean." *World Literature Today* 59, No. 1 (Winter 1985): 9-13.

>   Comparative study of Emecheta and Condé. The critics state: "The works of Buchi Emecheta and Maryse Condé give ample evidence to show the falsity of the supposition that a woman writer is inherently limited to certain kinds of writing and certain kinds of subject matter."

Chamoiseau, Patrick. "Reflections on Maryse Condé's *Traversée de la mangrove*." *Callaloo* 14, No. 2 (Spring 1991): 389-95.

>   Discusses Condé's use of language and characterization in *Traversée de la mangrove*.

Garcia, Cristina. "The 'Rich Cadence' of Caribbean Life as Conveyed by Novelist Maryse Condé." *Tribune Books* (11 October 1992): section 14, p. 6.

>   Positively assesses *Tree of Life*, noting that "Condé conveys the many subtle distinctions of color, class and language" that characterize Guadeloupe.

Thornton, Lawrence. "The Healer." *The New York Times Book Review* (16 July 1995): 17.

>   Laudatory review in which Thornton discusses the tone, structure, and themes of *Crossing the Mangrove*.

Watson, Christine. Review of *Crossing the Mangrove*, by Maryse Condé. *Rapport* 18, No. 6 (June-July 1995): 19.

>   Positive review in which Watson states: "Like memories, or ghosts, the stories told in *Crossing the Mangrove* will stay with you."

*World Literature Today: Special Issue on Maryse Condé* 67, No. 4 (Autumn 1993).

>   Addresses such topics as spatial and psychological themes in *Les derniers rois mages*, maternal imagery in *Moi, Tituba, sorcière...noire de Salem*, and Condé's attitude towards gender and identity.

---

# *Hopscotch*

## Julio Cortázar

The following entry presents criticism on Cortázar's novel *Rayuela* (1963; *Hopscotch*). For further information on his life and works, see *CLC,* Volumes 2, 3, 5, 10, 13, 15, 33, and 34.

## INTRODUCTION

The publication of *Hopscotch* in 1963—and its English translation three years later—confirmed Cortázar's reputation as a major figure in the Latin American literary "Boom" of the 1950s and 1960s and established him as a writer of international stature. Noted for its experimental structure, the novel contains three parts: two traditional narratives—the first set in Paris, the second in Buenos Aires—and a collection of fragments which can, if the reader so wishes, be incorporated into a second, more complex reading. *Hopscotch* explores traditional novelistic problems of love and death; casts an ironic eye on the existential anxieties of Horacio Oliveira, its alienated, post-war protagonist; and questions the rational foundation of the realist novel and Western civilization. However, Cortázar complicates and enriches these themes through metafictional play, exposing the process of story-telling, and inviting reader participation both in a postmodern literary game and in the fate of his characters.

### Plot and Major Characters

The first two sections of *Hopscotch,* "From the Other Side," and "From This Side," form a complex but otherwise traditional narrative that can be read by a "passive" reader as the story of an Argentinean intellectual expatriate in Paris who returns disillusioned to Argentina. The third section, however, titled "From Diverse Sides," comprises seventy-five optional "Expendable Chapters." These segments, which often contradict the preceding chapter as they offer new perspectives and disturb the reader with abrupt changes in tone and content, encourage readers to critically examine their reactions to the text and thus pursue a more "active" and participatory reading. Oliveira, the narrator-protagonist, is a self-absorbed, aimless bohemian who belongs to the Serpent Club, a group of friends who spend long hours in the Latin Quarter of Paris listening to jazz records and discussing art, philosophy, and such literary hypotheses as Gregorovius' dictum "Paris is one big metaphor." The club members—Babs, Ronald, Etienne, Gregorovius, Ossip, Guy Monod, Perico, Pola, and La Maga—represent numerous countries and share Oliveira's rootless and fanciful attachment to the city. In the narrative of the first 56 chapters, *Hopscotch* chronicles Oliveira's intellectual quest for a vaguely defined Absolute, the "kibbutz of desire"—an idealistic combination of individuality and community. In contrast to Oliveira's unhappy longing is La Maga, a mysterious

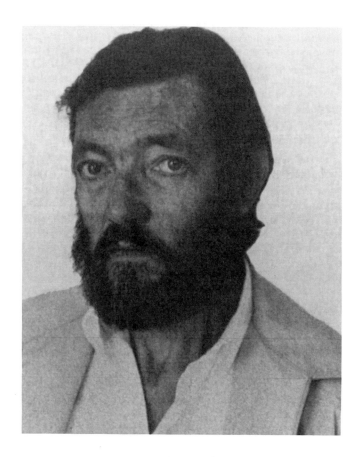

and haunting character who heightens Oliveira's sense of the absurd and suggests a more authentic means of interacting with reality. Scattered among the many chapters of discussion are a number of crucial events that determine Oliveira's destiny. His experiences in Paris, partly chosen, partly governed by chance, are described obliquely, often either implied or requiring reader inference. Oliveira meets Berthe Trépat, a concert pianist whose repertoire is obscure and whose small audience shrinks until only Oliveira is left. During another evening, Oliveira discovers the death of La Maga's child Rocamadour but says nothing to comfort La Maga, who later disappears. The ambiguity of her fate—did she leave Paris or drown herself in the Seine—plays an important role in the second part of the novel, for it questions whether La Maga's appearance in Buenos Aires is some sort of fantastic event or a symptom of Oliveira's insanity. In chapter 36 Oliveira has a sexual encounter on the banks of the Seine with an indigent woman, an event which precipitates his departure from Paris. In the second section of *Hopscotch,* Oliveira returns to Buenos Aires, where he rejoins his friends the Travelers, Manuel and Talita, and an old girlfriend, Gekrepten. In a long chapter reminiscent of Absurdist theater, Oliveira persuades Talita to cross a precarious hand-made bridge high above the street, simply to bring him some *mate*. Oliveira joins Manuel and Talita in a circus, but when the circus is sold so that its owner can purchase a psychiatric clinic, all three make abrupt career changes to become warders in the asylum, and Oliveira's own faint grasp on sanity is weakened. At the close of chapter 56, Oliveira is left debating whether or not to commit suicide by jumping from a window onto the grid of a hopscotch game below. In the alternative, second reading suggested by Cortázar's "Table of Instructions," the reader begins at chapter 73, then follows the traditional chapter sequence while "hopping" back and forth to the "expendable chapters" which form the third section of the novel. It is here, in chapter 60, that the "Morelliana" (the words of the fictional author Morelli) first appear, along with further disjointed fragments of narrative; newspaper and magazine cuttings from such diverse sources as Levi Strauss's *Tristes Tropiques, L'Express,* and the London *Observer;* and quotations from such writers as Anaïs Nin, Lawrence Ferlinghetti, Alban Berg, Octavio Paz. Morelli, a writer often read as Cortázar's double within the novel, is knocked down by a motor car; Oliveira subsequently gains access to the writer's papers, which then become the focus of much discussion in the Serpent Club. The presence of Morelli's writing in the second reading also complicates the reader's previously comfortable relationship with the narrative; Morelli blurs the line between writer and story, and his ideas become a commentary on *Hopscotch* itself. The "active" reading of Hopscotch leaves the novel unresolved, with the reader instructed to shuttle back and forth between chapter 58 and 131 indefinitely.

## Major Themes

The controlling image in *Hopscotch* of a children's game, in which the goal is to move from Earth to Heaven, is an embodiment of Oliveira's quest for an accessible Absolute. The key theme and impetus of the traditional narrative in the first 56 chapters is Oliveira's sense of exclusion from an imagined state of grace and his attempts to find, as he calls it, a "kibbutz of desire," an idealized place of community and self-sufficiency. For Oliveira, La Maga represents such a state, and Oliveira tries to create his own version through encounters with strangers such as the pianist Berthe Trépat. Oliveira's sexual transgression with the *clocharde* Emmanuèle—a character whose indigence essentially excludes her from the nexus of Oliveira's desire—enables him to close his quest for the mythic "kibbutz," as he finds acceptance at society's lowest depth. Manuel, Oliveira's counterpart in Buenos Aires, shares with La Maga the status of Oliveira's "double" by which he can be defined, just as Buenos Aires will be determined by its semblance to Paris. Related to this is the theme of Argentinean national identity, Latin America's ambivalent attitude toward European culture, and especially toward literary culture. Allied to his critique of the Argentinean's cultural indebtedness to Europe is Cortázar's commentary on the failings of Western rationalism, including the traditionally lucid literary narrative that *Hopscotch* seeks to disrupt. The "second" and optional reading introduces problems of literary and linguistic theory, making Oliveira's quest part and parcel of a writing and reading

strategy. *Hopscotch* thus becomes for the "active" reader a self-reflexive novel which problematizes its own authorship and raises the theme of the double or multiple articulation, for in this sense the "writing" is shown to be shared between Cortázar, Morelli, and the participant reader. Another major theme is madness and the individual's relation to society. Towards the conclusion of the second narrative, Oliveira kisses Talita, believing her to be La Maga. One of Manuel's options in response to Oliveira's act is to declare him insane; and Oliveira's sanity, as he is contemplating suicide at the novel's end, is questionable. As Steven Boldy has stated: madness assumes "several connotations in the novel, where Oliveira muses on the possibility of 'joining the world, the Great Madness.' In a mad world, to go mad is to be reconciled to reality and society, to be at one with its absurd or conventional laws. It is this acceptance, of which Oliveira has always before been incapable, that his long path has prepared him to embrace."

## Critical Reception

Many critics have praised *Hopscotch*'s literary experimentalism and compared the novel to James Joyce's *Ulysses* (1922). While acknowledging Cortázar's debt to a more original work, commentators have found something new and more "decadent" in Cortázar's vision. *Hopscotch* has frequently been construed as a critique of Western rationalism, with scholars suggesting that the novel's passages of absurd humor and aimless philosophizing form a continuity with the Surrealist movement. Although some critics have been impressed by Cortázar's erudite display in *Hopscotch*—his knowledge of jazz, art, literature, and philosophy, as well as what they consider his conceptual *tours de force*—others have noted the danger of intimidating the reader. For example, the "philosophizing" in the Serpent Club has struck some critics as "tedious and verbose;" others have noted Cortázar's sensitive ear for the literary qualities of Argentinean common speech. The theme of trans-Atlantic cultural influence has been widely noted, and certain Latin American critics have focused on Cortázar's concern in *Hopscotch* with Argentinean national and cultural identity and the problem of exile and expatriation. For others, Oliveira's bohemian disaffiliation in Paris is a counterpart of his psychic alienation. Another set of scholars consider *Hopscotch* a major example of the postmodern novel, arguing that its metatextuality, its foregrounding of problems of reading and authorship, its discursive play, and its disruption of traditional narrative, all signal an important advance on the modernism of Joyce.

---

# PRINCIPAL WORKS

*Presencia* (poetry) 1938
*Los reyes* (poetry) 1949
*\*Bestiario* (short stories) 1951
*\*Final del juego* (short stories) 1956
*\*Las armas secretas* (short stories) 1959
*Los premios* [*The Winners*] (novel) 1960

*Historias de cronopios y de famas* [*Cronopios and Famas*]
(short stories)   1962
*Rayuela* [*Hopscotch*]   (novel)   1963
*Todos los fuegos el fuego* [*All Fires the Fire, and Other Stories*]   (short stories)   1966
*El perseguidor y otros cuentos*   (short stories)   1967
*La vuelta al dia en ochenta mundos* [*Around the Day in Eighty Worlds*]   (nonfiction and poetry)   1967
*62: Modelo para armar* [*62: A Model Kit*]   (novel)   1968
*Ultimo round*   (nonfiction and poetry)   1969
*Pameos y meopas*   (poetry)   1971
*Libro de Manuel* [*A Manual for Manuel*]   (novel)   1973
†*Octaedro*   (short stories)   1974
*Vampiros multinacionales: una utopía realizable*   (short stories)   1975
*Los relatos.* 4 vols.   (short stories)   1976-1985
†*Alguien que anda por ahi y otros relatos*   (short stories)   1977
*Un tal Lucas* [*A Certain Lucas*]   (short stories)   1979
*Queremos tanto a Glenda* [*We Love Glenda So Much, and Other Tales*]   (short stories)   1980
*Deshoras*   (short stories)   1982
*Cuaderno de bitácora de "Rayuela"* [with Ana Maria Barrenechea]   (notebooks and criticism)   1983
*Nicaragua tan violentamente dulce* [*Nicaraguan Sketches*]   (sketches)   1983
*Salvo el crepúsculo*   (poetry)   1984
‡*El examen*   (novel)   1986

*Selected stories from these collections were translated and published in *End of the Game, and Other Stories* in 1967; also published as *Blow-Up, and Other Stories* in 1968.

†Selected stories from these collections were translated and published in *A Change of Light, and Other Stories* in 1980.

‡This novel was written in 1950.

---

# CRITICISM

### Donald Keene   (review date 10 April 1966)

SOURCE: "Moving Snapshots," in *The New York Times Book Review,* April 10, 1966, p. 1.

[*Keene is an American educator and critic. Below, he favorably reviews* Hopscotch.]

The publication last year of Julio Cortázar's allegorical novel ***The Winners*** earned respectful reviews. ***Hopscotch,*** a far more impressive, indeed superb work should establish Cortázar as an outstanding writer of our day.

In general, ***Hopscotch*** is the story of Oliveira, an Argentinian writer living in Paris with La Maga, his mistress, and her child by another man. He falsely suspects she is deceiving him with a friend. After the death of La Maga's child, Oliveira returns to Buenos Aires, working first as a salesman, later as the keeper of a circus cat, finally as an attendant in an insane asylum.

It is difficult to describe the plot of ***Hopscotch,*** not because

it is confused or vague—on the contrary, it is continuously absorbing even on the most obvious level—but because the author, whether with the voice of Oliveira, the principal character, or Morelli, a dying writer whose notebooks figure prominently at the end, seems to forbid any conventional plot summary.

We are told: "In some place Morelli tried to justify his narrative incoherencies, maintaining that the life of others, such as it comes to us in so-called reality, is not a movie but still photography, that is to say, that we cannot grasp the action, only a few of its elastically recorded fragments. . . . For that reason there was nothing strange about his speaking of characters in the most spasmodic way possible; giving coherence to the series of pictures so they could become a movie (which would have been so very pleasing to the reader he called the female-reader) meant filling in with literature, presumptions, hypotheses, and inventions the gaps between one and another photograph." Again, a character remarks of Morelli: "For example, the Chinese-scroll novel makes him explode. The book read from beginning to end like a good child."

The story, despite the deliberately episodic, snapshot manner, achieves dramatic intensity. The dialogue is brilliant, whether the subject is literature, love, Mondrian, jazz or the fallibility of science. Individual scenes are superbly alive. One evening, Oliveira, sure that La Maga is making love with another man, ducks into a piano recital to get out of the rain. The audience of 20 dwindles as each successively more disastrous piece is played, ending with a "Délibes-Saint-Saëns Synthesis" that leaves only Oliveira. He decides to see home the pianist, a grotesque old woman living on imaginary triumphs. After their harrowingly comic walk he returns to his apartment. Friends drift in and they converse volubly, brilliantly, everyone aware, except for La Maga, that her child has just died in the same room. The scene is a triumph not only of dramatic structure but of comic invention.

The "table of instructions" preceding the novel informs us that it may be read in at least two ways: the first is in the normal manner, to the end of Chapter 56, about two-thirds of the way through the book. The hundred "expendable chapters" appended at this point provide a second reading when inserted among the original 56 chapters in a prescribed order. "Hopscotch" not only stands up to this double scrutiny but becomes immeasurably richer; no doubt other readings would yield even further meanings.

The "expendable chapters" consist in part of narrative amplifying the incidents of the book, but more commonly of discourse on the art of fiction or of images (often in the form of newspaper articles or quotations) which invite the reader to participate in the experience of creating the book and to become the "accomplice or traveling companion" of the author.

At the end of our first reading Oliveira is teetering on a windowsill between life and death, sanity and insanity. When we read the book a second time, hopping back and forth from early chapters to late ones, as in the game of hopscotch, we go beyond the last numbered square of the hopscotch to the "heaven" at the top: Oliveira, recuperating at home from his plunge from the windowsill, ironically discusses the possibility of joining the "national corporation of monks of the prayers of the sign of the cross."

*Hopscotch* is in fact a comic novel, sometimes howlingly funny, always acutely ironic. Morelli writes: "The comic novel must have an exemplary sense of decorum; not deceive the reader, not mount him astride any emotion or intention at all, but give him rather something like meaningful clay, the beginning of a prototype, with traces of something that may be collective perhaps, human and not individual." Cortázar's intense concern with the novel certainly entails no dullness; the rapid-fire invention of the language makes every page sparkle, thanks to the translation by Gregory Rabassa, which gives a dazzling parallel in American idiom to Cortázar's stylistic magic.

Cortázar himself is an Argentinian, and no doubt many will be tempted to see in Oliveira a portrait of the author, or even of the cultured Argentinian as an expatriate both in Paris and in his own country. But Cortázar warns us in an epigraph from the surrealist poet Jacques Vaché: "Nothing kills a man like being obliged to represent a country." *Hopscotch* is not intended to be a treatment of a problem—whether the alienation of the South American intellectual or any other—but rather an attempt to "place a reader—a certain reader, that is true—in contact with a *personal* world, with a personal existence and mediation."

It is true nevertheless that the writer's nationality gives a particular coloration to the book, not merely in its mentions of people sipping *maté* or the savage humor directed at literary tastes in Argentina, but negatively too, in the extraordinary catholicity of learning possible only in an author whose concern for national literary traditions does not obscure a more general concern for man. It is precisely because the gauchos of the pampas and the other literary baggage of South American particularism are absent from this novel that Cortázar transcends our immense ignorance of his country to move us and make us his companions.

## Carlos Fuentes    (essay date March 1967)

SOURCE: "*Hopscotch:* The Novel as Pandora's Box," in *The Review of Contemporary Fiction,* Vol. III, No. 3, Fall, 1983, pp. 86-8.

[*Fuentes is a Mexican novelist, dramatist, short story writer, essayist, and critic. In the following essay, which was originally published in the journal* Mundo Nuevo *in March 1967 and here translated by Naomi Lindstrom, Fuentes discusses the structure and poetics of Cortázar's* Hopscotch *and compares the novel to James Joyce's* Ulysses *(1922).*]

The French reader knows Julio Cortázar by way of a marvelous collection of elliptical stories, *End of the Game* (one of which served as the basis for Michelangelo Antonioni's film, *Blow-Up*), and to a lengthy allegorical novel, *The Winners.* The publication of *Hopscotch* will show that these works were warm-ups leading to this work, hailed by the *Times Literary Supplement* of London as "The first great novel of Spanish America." It would be fair to state

that this 52-year-old Argentine novelist is writing today, from the homes he makes on the Place du Général Beuret in Paris and in a farm near Saignon, the best prose fiction in Spanish. But to restrict him to what Philippe Sollers calls "Latinocentrism" would be a serious mistake. For the U.S. critic C. D. B. Bryan, writing in *The New Republic, Hopscotch* is "the most powerful encyclopedia of emotions and visions to emerge from the postwar generation of international writers." To find out just how valid these statements are, the reader need only surrender to one of the richest universes in contemporary fiction: the one contained in that Pandora's box—game played out, ashes and resurrection—that is *Hopscotch.*

*Hopscotch* is a Latin American novel; it is so because it is infused with the magic atmosphere of a pilgrimage that never arrives. Before it was discovered, America had already been invented in the dream of a Utopian quest, in Europe's need to find a *lá-bas,* a blissful isle, a city of gold. Is it any wonder that the most significant feature of Latin America's literary imagination should be the questing after El Dorado—Carpentier, —of a patriarchal paradise—Rulfo, —of an original identity—Asturias, —or of a frozen mythification—Borges—to be found somewhere beyond the historical nightmare and cultural schizophrenia of a world dreamed up in Utopia and degraded in the epic? But, while that imagination has up to now been born of an awareness of the decomposition of history and society, Cortázar makes his pilgrimage inward, to implode in upon himself so that, with luck, he will be able to "move beyond" the figures of his literature. At any rate, Cortázar does not presume to place society at issue without having first placed reality at issue.

At the most obvious level, *Hopscotch* offers a structure and a story, both booby-trapped. The book is divided into three parts. The first part, "From the Other Side," is Buenos Aires and the coming together of Oliveira and Talita, La Maga's double, a circus cat keeper and later a madhouse nurse. The third part, "From Diverse Sides: Expendable Chapters," brings together a collage of quotations, newspaper clippings, signs and adds that range from academic to pop.

A "Table of Instructions" completes the structure only to begin transforming it; the novel may be read for the first time straight through, and a second following the table of instructions. But this second reading only opens the door to a third, and, we suspect, to the infinite numbers of the true reading. Cortázar, we realize, is setting forth something more than a narration. His purpose is to exhaust all the possible formulations of an impossible book: a book that would radically supplant life or, rather, would turn our lives into one vast reading of all the combinations of what has been written. An "incredible" project, as Borges would say, equivalent to imagining the total negation of the total recuperation of time.

"Would I find La Maga?" The first words of *Hopscotch* give us the key to this search never to be finished, "incredible," cut off before the book is written, represented by Oliveira in the ceremony of the writing of the book.

Because only the book will allow him to get back with La

Maga, that "nebula swirl," a little naive, a little perverse, continually remembered and foreseen in a present tense of literature becoming then the third death of real time. Three things are killed off in **Hopscotch:** the death of remembered presence, the death of foreshadowing, and the death of the written book as compensation for the absence of La Maga, the indispensable companion in the uninterrupted, desacralized childhood game. Only the couple, that "incredible" attempt to win negation and salvation, can negate and save the fatality of heaven and hell in the game of hopscotch. Oliveira is given over to exodus, to the search of the "final island" representing the lost place, to the pilgrimage toward the "kibbutz of desire" in which one can live—or believe oneself living—with substitutes for a lost unity of loving.

---

*Hopscotch* **is a Latin American novel. It is infused with the magic atmosphere of a pilgrimage that never arrives.**

—*Carlos Fuentes*

---

A novel of bridges between the lost and the salvageable, *Hopscotch* begins under the Seine arches and culminates atop a few rickety boards stretched between the windows of a Buenos Aires boardinghouse. Oliveira's odyssey takes him to Paris (the original model), then to Buenos Aires (the false homeland). Buenos Aires is the cave where the shadows of being are reflected. The reality of Argentina is a fiction; the authenticity of Argentina is its lack of authenticity; the national essence of Argentina is the imitation of Europe; the city of gold, the isle of bliss is nothing more than the shadow of the settlers' dream. Oliveira returns to Buenos Aires to come together with Talita, the double of the La Maga lost in Paris. But La Maga, necessarily, comes with a double of Oliveira; Traveler, who hates to be named that, since he's never traveled beyond the River Plate. Talita and Traveler, degraded reflections of La Maga and Oliveira, have the same pick-up sort of a life: expatriate.

Bohemia, intellectual tripping-out, all this becomes, in the context of the "home country," the stuff of the circus, the madhouse and the hospital. Downfall? Nothingness? Yes, but not with the tragic will of an awareness contemplating the downfall of *something.* The fall, in **Hopscotch,** is that of some Buster Keaton of the Pampas, willingly comic, buffoonish, grotesque; it's the fall of someone who has no place to fall because he never got up; it's the nothingness of the Latin American world, confronted with nothingness before being or having anything. Or, rather, after having only a dream: would I find La Maga? But did Oliveira ever meet La Maga, or does he only hope to encounter her in the words that Oliveira says and Cortázar writes?

The irony of Cortázar's spiritual journey is that, like every quest for being, it is born out of a solitary awareness that cannot be maintained in isolation. Oliveira tries every al-

chemy of substitution. And each one gives him a dry, tragicomic caricature of the splendorous unity he dreams of, a cuckold sex maniac alongside the desired and detested companion, La Maga. At this level, the "dispensable chapters" become indispensable. Morelli, an old, failed writer, possibly an alter ego of the writer, is the magister ludi of this cultural flea market, of this Porta Portese bazaar of ideas, cluttered with the discards of reason ("a whorehouse of virgins, as if such a thing were possible"), society ("this dead-end serving the Great Idealist-Realist-Spiritualist-Materialist Infatuation of the West, S. R. L."), history ("It may well be there's a thousand-year reign, but if we ever get there, it won't be called that anymore") and intelligence (" . . . the very fact of being thinking about it instead of doing it proves it's wrong"). Cortázar here sets down a true list of what not to take with you to a desert island.

But Oliveira already is, settled in with masochistic joy, on a desert island. His dream, La Maga, Madonna and lover, is gone. He cannot rely on the insubstantial shadow of the cavern, Buenos Aires. All he has left is what he drags along with him: the castoffs of rationality, the pianos stuffed with dead donkeys in *Un Chien andalou.* Oliveira renounces the words of this garbage heap ("To war against the word, to war, whatever it takes, even if it means renouncing intelligence"), in favor of actions. But actions must be described in the words of the author, Julio Cortázar: "The violation of man by the word, the proud vengeance of the word against its father, tainted each of Oliveira's meditations with bitter suspicion; he was forced to turn to his own enemy to gain access to a point where perhaps he could rule on his enemy's case and then move on from there—how and by what means, through what white night, or inky day?—toward a total reconciliation with himself and with the reality he lived in."

The real piecing-together of **Hopscotch** begins with this taking-apart of words to make up the acts the novelist will need to describe. Michel Foucault says that "Don Quixote reads the world in order to demonstrate books . . . the promise made by books is incumbent upon him." Cortázar shows the opposite at work. With Morelli as his spokesman, he declares his intention to make a novel, not a written one, but dis-written. To dis-write, Cortázar invents a counter-language capable, not of replacing images, but of going beyond them, to pure coordinates, figures, constellations of characters. "Trap them, grab them by the tail, squeal, you whores," Octavio Paz says of words: this is exactly what Cortázar does. With both fists, breathlessly, with erratic blasts of conceptual dynamite, rhythmic, onomatopoeic, he blows the language of his own novel sky-high and atop the total ruins flies—a blown-to-bits triumph with wings aflame—the author, the last angel of this anti-paradise and anti-hell in which God and Devil are a single paradox: the more is created, the more is damned. **Hopscotch** is to Spanish prose what *Ulysses* is to English prose.

This coming-together of actions and the counter-language capable of dis-writing them forces Oliveira into a "non-behavior," a pointless accumulation of motions foreign to the language that traditionally has described them. The conflict leads straight to mockery, farce and absurdity. The outsize joke, worthy of Rabelais and Sterne, seizes hold of the book. Putting out the planks in Buenos Aires, where failed intentions are so numerous that failure becomes the whole point of the undertaking. The death of Rocamadour, La Maga's son, in the middle of a literary orgy. Descending into the refrigerated morgue, into the searing ice of hell. The rewriting and reordering of the world in the notebooks of the distinguished Uruguayan madman, Don Ceferino Piriz. These are profound keys of **Hopscotch,** of its basis in the extreme illumination of the surrealists, of its unsettled dialogue between the Bretonian sphinxes of humor and happenstance.

Marginal language and action become counter-language and action-beyond-action in Oliveira's search. The pilgrimage takes him to his own double, Traveler. And facing one's double in the flesh, there are only two responses: murder or madness. Otherwise, Oliveira would have to accept that his life, not being unique, lacks value and meaning; that another person, who is he himself, thinks, loves and dies in his stead and perhaps Oliveira is only his double's double and only living the life of a doppelganger. Oliveira attempts murder by terror. Not a true murder, since murdering one's double would be suicide, but rather a criminal "attempt" that will open the doors to madness. Or, at least, that will make others believe Oliveira mad. There, at the end, in the madhouse and hospital that are the only kibbutz chance guarantees, the virtue and the need of the Oliveiras of this world is that they can live in absurdity without justifications or contradictions. One can, in the end, multiply unreality by inventing everything the world seems to lack. Oliveira belongs to that line of genius-idiots who, from Louis Lambert to Pierrot le Fou, create the indispensable order of the dispensable. In the madhouse and the hospital, the final harbor of the Nietzsche we could all be, is located the center of the hopscotch; heaven and hell are one and freedom can be exercised starting from a perpetual clamor of something lacking, some lack of satisfaction.

"Here it is now," says Oliveira. To this being-here-now, the novelist gives only the mortal urge, the leap toward the probable island of desire become reality. True being lies elsewhere, and the novelist is the prophet who would lead us out of the captivity of discourse, history and psychology.

A contemporary grandmaster of the *ars combinatoria,* Julio Cortázar has written a novel faithful to the author's deep conviction: "Apart from our individual destinies, we form part of figures that we cannot know." And the constellations of **Hopscotch,** finally, speak to us of time and liberty. Together with Octavio Paz and Luis Bunuel, Julio Cortázar represents today the vanguard of contemporary Latin American thought and culture. With Paz, he shares the incandescent tension of the instant as a supreme high point in the tides of time. With Bunuel, he shares the vision of freedom as the aura of permanent desire, of an *unauthorized* dissatisfaction that is, for that very reason, *revolutionary.*

## The Times Literary Supplement (review date 9 March 1967)

SOURCE: "On the Hop," in *The Times Literary Supplement,* No. 3392, March 9, 1967, p. 181.

[*In the following review, the critic praises Cortázar's use of language in* Hopscotch, *but overall finds the novel pretentious and "constantly straining for meanings."*]

Julio Cortázar is an Argentinian who, since the publication of **Rayuela** (or **Hopscotch**) in 1963, has acquired a reputation as the first great novelist of Latin America. Although this judgment is unfair to half a dozen of his contemporaries and one or two of his predecessors, his work, now widely translated, and perhaps rather too extravagantly promoted on the Continent and in the United States, certainly represents a remarkable achievement.

Señor Cortázar started as a writer of slightly Kafkaesque, slightly Borgesian short stories, most of them, on his own admission, the description of dreams in which an ordinary situation slipped almost imperceptibly into fantasy. *The Winners* (originally published in 1960 as *Los premios*) was his first novel and written in similar mood; it appeared in England in 1965 but was largely ignored by reviewers.

The hero of **Hopscotch,** Oliveira, an Argentinian expatriate in Paris, is amazed at the absurdity of life. The arbitrary detail of its conventional superstructure—the incredible streets, the colour and shape of the clothes, the lumps of food—seems just a little too meticulously implausible to be true. Oliveira is in fact a very prim existentialist, stubbornly refusing himself a single instant of *mauvaise foi.* He is tempted, of course. He could "put on a blue suit, comb his greying hair, and go to art galleries". But he resists, plays piously with bits of string or, in the morning, slaps pink toothpaste not on his teeth but on their reflection in the mirror, and laughs. When he drops something, he must pick it up, and one day he spends half an hour under the tables of an expensive restaurant, searching for a lump of sugar which has slipped from his hand. In short he is like, say, Morgan, or the hero of Alain Jossua's film *La Vie à l'envers,* an intransigent outsider, aware of the spiritual benefit to be derived from emptying a jampot over the concierge's head; aware, of course, of the liberating power of laughter and outrage.

After an exotically uprooted period in Paris, he returns to Buenos Aires, and his ship is met by Traveler, a childhood friend. Traveler seems to be Oliveira's double, or at least what Oliveira might have been if he had donned a blue suit and stayed at home in the Argentinian background of plotting generals, vacuous patriotism and faked culture. In Paris Oliveira has had two love affairs, one magical (the girl was called La Maga and they would meet at random in the street or better on the Pont des Arts), one commonplace. Traveler's wife, Talita, is commonplace and Argentinian, but occasionally Oliveira sees in her some of the magic he had known in Paris, and she becomes La Maga, the double who went to Paris and stood on the Pont des Arts.

One day, Oliveira, Traveler and Talita get jobs in a mental hospital and Oliveira and Talita/Maga embrace triumphantly in the morgue. But Oliveira suspects that Traveler may want to kill him, and he sets up a system of defence in his bedroom to forestall the aggressor. With the help of an amiable lunatic, he collects all the wash-basins in the hospital, fills them with water, and places them on the floor anticipating with relish the aggressor's curse when his socks get soaked. He completes the operation by setting up a labyrinth of strings. The outside world, Argentina, the conventional structure of life, will be kept at bay.

If the novel were left at this rather dotty, basically humorous level, it would be far better than it is; it would make its point because, when the defences are set up and the solipsist sits solemnly on the windowsill waiting for the attack, the reader is firmly on his side. Unfortunately there is a great deal of pretension in *Hopscotch* which tends to undermine much of its effect.

First, Oliveira's amorous exploits in Paris are just a bit too exotic, and their description is often very poor sub-Durrell. Moreover, the endless "intellectual" exchanges of Oliveira and 'his friends, juggling with "primordial winds" and "syncretisms" which seem to have no clear relevance, are frankly very much the kind of hazy Argentinian "intellectualism" which Señor Cortázar claims to deplore. If the conversations are meant to convey that "western dialectics" are inconsequential, Señor Cortázar must produce far more authentic "dialectics" than these. The force of his case against dialectical apprehension lies in Oliveira's antics, not in his rather fake-oriental pronouncements. Señor Cortázar is also determined to impress us that he is amazingly well read, and the names of about 100 authors and artists are paraded in *Hopscotch,* like in those tiresome Jean-Luc Godard films where the sky is "very Paul Klee" and the girl's eyes are Velazquezian.

*Hopscotch* can be read in two ways. The first fifty-six chapters can be read sequentially and (according to Señor Cortázar's coy directive) "the reader may ignore what follows with a clean conscience". The reader is, however, invited to have a second go, "beginning with chapter 73 and then following the sequence indicated at the end of each chapter". The sequence for, say, the first ten chapters on second reading becomes: 73-1-2-116-3-84-4-71-5-81. That is to say, chapter 73 (second half) directs us to chapter 1 (first half) and at the end of chapter 1 we are instructed to move to chapter 2, then 116, then back to 3, and so on. We are asked, therefore, to reflect on the fact that the chronological sequence established on first reading is (like history) a cheap Occidental simplification in the face of a more meaningful structural continuum. Fiction, anyway, is presumably memory, and memory works by chaotic juxtaposition. A sequence is, of course, arbitrarily imposed by any *mise-en-page,* but events only follow each other there because they have to when translated into sentences.

Señor Cortázar is very interested—and he has every right to be—in structures and patterns. He sees human beings not as characters in a conventional sequence (his characterization is deliberately superficial) but as constellations in a vast structure outside time. His characters are involved in a sort of ritual dance. The more meaningless the dance, the more pleasing the patterns. In the "expendable" chapters, which should be incorporated into the second or alternative reading, absurd, eccentric tit-bits are collected (law reports, an elaborate plan to rationalize the world, a letter to *The Observer* on the scarcity of butterflies) and mingled with the narrative as simply part of a composite aesthetic structure. The expendable chapters also attempt to offer something of a new perspective to the original narrative, in Proustian manner, for there is a good deal of fresh background information on the characters in them. Oliveira's second love affair in Paris, for instance, only hinted at on first reading, is dealt with more roundly. Also a great deal of reflexion on the novelist's art is introduced, just in case we miss the point of Señor Cortázar's eccentric quest.

Unfortunately. Señor Cortázar is not content merely to present some sort of abstracted aesthetic pattern, but is constantly straining for meanings which this pattern is not adequate to embody. The game of hopscotch not only symbolizes the abstract dance of human beings. The hopper's arrival at the last square or "heaven" is called upon to symbolize some sort of mystical truth, an ultimate meaning beyond the false superstructure of society. The game of hopscotch is in fact a highly unsatisfactory mandala.

Part of the excellence of *Hopscotch* lies in its use of language, in its experiments with many different, some very original, types of Spanish carefully juxtaposed: the spirit of Argentina, for instance, is nostalgically conveyed in the Paris scenes by the occasional use of Buenos Aires dialect, for which Señor Cortázar has a very good ear. The translation, which is sometimes very clumsy indeed, does not, possibly could not, capture these modulations.

## Julio Ortega   (essay date 1969)

SOURCE: "*Hopscotch,*" in *Poetics of Change: The New Spanish-American Narrative,* translated by Galen D. Greaser, University of Texas Press, 1984, pp. 42-53.

[*In the following essay, which was originally published in Ortega's* La contemplación la fiesta *(1969), Ortega explores themes of nonconformism and chance in* Hopscotch.]

*Hopscotch,* Carlos Fuentes has stated, is to prose in Spanish what *Ulysses* is to prose in English. This comparison is possible because *Hopscotch,* first published in 1963, summarizes the new or current tradition of modernity in the Latin-American novel, a tradition that in the opinion of Octavio Paz is one of renewal. *Hopscotch* starts from the crisis of the novelistic genre as a representational system and from the baroque transgression of its Latin-American axis. Its foundation is another novel, one that begins when this book is closed.

The various readings demanded by *Hopscotch* are a game between the narrators, the characters, and the reader, or more accurately, this work is the repeated beginning of a game rather than its development or conclusion. Cortázar thus prolongs the reading, because this novel questions literature, the reader, and itself. The repeated beginning of the game implies its regeneration. *Hopscotch* is like the fluttering of a verbal phoenix.

At a certain point, the characters disclose that they are also readers of the novel. Through their reading in the texts of Morelli, these characters read themselves:

> "It isn't the first time that he's referred to the erosion of language," Étienne said. "I could mention several places where characters lose confidence in themselves to the degree in which they feel they've been drawn through their thought and speech, and they're afraid the sketch may be deceptive."

In another passage Morelli states that the character he wants for his novel is the reader.

The characters are thus readers and the reader is a character because the narrator wants to identify his searches with ours in an esthetics of defectiveness. Oliveira, addressor and addressee of the writing, constructs (from a first and third person point of view and from an insistent present) a past time in order to reconstruct himself in the fact of writing as reading. In the same way that he reads the world, Oliveira reads himself. But this yearning, this erratic and solitary drama, is an exploration of memory in a present time that gives way to the past and soon forces him to abandon this convocation from the perspective of the "I." He is forced to drop the point of view of the addressor because, groping about in the void that he at the same time wants to populate, he betrays himself in a mirror; under the different masks there is but a single face. To avoid this betrayal of a self-evident and perhaps false image, the addressor becomes the addressee, leaving the ambiguous pretext of the colloquy to the empty "you" personified by La Maga and making himself speak in terms of the image in the mirror, now in the third person.

The obvious verbal impregnation between the paragraphs in which Oliveira is addressor and those in which he is addressee again implies a continuous regeneration of the writing. Oliveira seems to carry on his multiple monologue in this third person, even in the dialogues with his friends of the Club, and La Maga's dialogues are just brief interruptions in Oliveira's verbalism. La Maga's letter to Rocamadour (that little paper boat floating throughout the book) is also sustained by Oliveira's reading, as are Morelli's texts. Likewise, the hyperbolic, loquacious dialogue between Oliveira, Traveler, and Talita is dictated by a sort of raised voice, by a reading aloud, in a broader space that Oliveira himself establishes. All this serves to mask the only narrator of the novel, Oliveira, who writes in the pluridimensional present of the novel after his personal story has ended and begins now as narrative.

Since the reader is also a character, the reading itself will be paradoxical. To start, Cortázar notes that there are "female-readers" and "male-readers." The former are interested in a passive reading, while the latter prefer to make the text through their reading. The former are the traditional readers of the traditional closed novel, while the latter are the new readers, the characters sought by the open novel. The reading of this novel is paradoxical because it imposes at the same time its narrative sequences—it is a

novel after all—and the speculations of its literary and existential debates. Fiction is posed as debate, and this debate, in turn, is posed as figure. These levels thus function as signs. In their simultaneity, the ideas, episodes, and figures are transformed into the signs of a character (Oliveira), a spiritual situation (the search for an independent and common unity in which the experience of a narrator becomes the paradigm of the choices of every man), and an age, because through its conflicts and disruptions this novelistic adventure underscores the insertion of language in history.

---

> *Hopscotch* summarizes the new or current tradition of modernity in the Latin-American novel, a tradition that in the opinion of Octavio Paz is one of renewal. *Hopscotch* starts from the crisis of the novelistic genre as a representational system. Its foundation is another novel, one that begins when *Hopscotch* is closed.
>
> —*Julio Ortega*

---

The steps by which the reader becomes a character of *Hopscotch* are initiatory because the novel is always on its first page; it is constantly beginning again, continuously questioning itself. In this case, to read is to travel, to play at the game of reading, to invent a rite.

The "Table of Instructions" of this reading mechanism invites us "to choose" one of two possibilities: to read the book in a normal fashion, stopping with chapter 56, at the close of which there are three little stars that indicate the end, or to begin with chapter 73 and follow the sequence indicated at the end of each chapter. This second reading sequence imitates the game of hopscotch because in the reading we are jumping from chapter to chapter, from square to square, playing in the gridded figure of the novel. The dash in front of the number at the end of each chapter is obviously a minus sign; the reading is thus also a subtraction.

If we choose the first reading sequence we find that the novel is divided into three parts. The first part, "From the other side," refers to Paris, and the second part, "From this side," is set in Buenos Aires. Here the novel "ends." The third part is entitled "From diverse sides: expendable chapters," and in the "Table of Instructions" Cortázar suggests that the reader can ignore it without feeling remorse. Let us assume that a reader, as a character, decides to consider expendable these "expendable chapters." On the "last" page of his reading this reader will find Oliveira balancing himself on the edge of a high window and looking down into the courtyard of a psychiatric clinic at Traveler and Talita (all three of them work in this asylum, which is their ironic context). The two figures below look at him and talk to him from the hopscotch:

> Talita had stopped in square three without real-

izing it, and Traveler had one foot in six . . . and there was some meeting after all, even though it might only last just for that terribly sweet instant in which the best thing without any doubt at all would be to lean over just a little bit farther out and let himself go, paff the end.

The last game in Oliveira's search begins and ends in the precarious square formed by the frame of the window of a room in which he has locked himself, declaring what amounts to both a comic and metaphysical war. *Hopscotch*—which acknowledges the labyrinth of the game in order to reunite "heaven" and "earth" as squares of a single figure—is both an innocent and deadly game. Its innocence stems from the possibility of playing the game in a committed manner starting from an intellectual questioning, which is what Oliveira represents, because he is also a typical character who feels he must come to grips with the hell of western contradictions and attempt to resolve them within the contradictions themselves. That is why in this first ending Oliveira sits in the window and acts out his personal drama through the farcical context of his potential suicide, dramatized by his reflective and humorous detachment from his own quests and his paralyzing analysis of them. This window is his square in a game of hopscotch that makes him its victim. For Oliveira, the uniting of heaven and earth, man and woman, La Maga and himself, the other side and this side, truth and appearance, in short, the uniting of our multiple contradictions, is a game that can only be final, suicide, directly or symbolically.

> The best thing without any doubt at all would be to lean over just a little bit farther out and let himself go, paff the end.

At the level of the narrative, Cortázar's "paff" may be suggesting, in the same farcical vein tapped by Oliveira, the character's suicide or his grandstanding play. Perhaps Oliveira has let himself fall toward the ground, where his double, Traveler, and La Maga's double, Talita, (doubles by contradiction rather than by similarity, in other words, doubles by analogical opposition) stand in their squares trying to calm him. The phrase "paff the end" can suggest this suicide, but it can also suggest that, paff, the novel or the first reading has ended. Cortázar refers to the novel as a "metaphysical slap," as a slap to the reader, of course. Hence this "paff" is also the slap the narrator gives the reader, brother and accomplice in the end, to seal their pact.

The slapped reader has two choices. He can put down the book or take a chance with the third part, the "expendable chapters." In terms of this first reading of the novel, which follows the normal sequence, these chapters are another reading. The novel thus contains one and a half readings. In this third part the reader meets Morelli, who invites him to criticize what he has read, and recovers Oliveira. In these chapters a prior time in Paris is prolonged and a later time in Buenos Aires fades, suggesting another resurrection of Oliveira, who in fact starts the writing from this point.

In the second reading sequence suggested for this novel the reader must contend with more complex levels: the expendable chapters are included in the narration. The first reading is more novelistic, while the second is more critical, but between them they constitute the birth and transfiguration of the novel, its formulation and its sacrifice. *Hopscotch* is a metaphor because it joins two realities in a single figure; it becomes, in fact, a metaphor of itself.

The first chapter of this second reading introduces us to the deconstruction and construction sought by the novel. These operations mutually provoke and recognize each other in the same space. Oliveira is the speaker in the following passage:

> How often I wonder whether this is only writing, in an age in which we run towards deception through infallible equations and conformity machines. But to ask one's self if we will know how to find the other side of habit or if it is better to let one's self be borne along by its happy cybernetics, is that not literature again? Rebellion, conformity, anguish, earthly sustenance, all the dichotomies . . . what a hammock of words, what pure-size dialectics with pajama storms and living-room cataclysms. The very fact that one asks one's self about the possible choice vitiates and muddies up what can be chosen . . . Everything is writing, that is to say, a fable. But what good can we get from the truth that pacifies an honest property owner? Our possible truth must be an *invention,* that is to say, scripture, literature, picture, sculpture, agriculture, pisciculture, all the tures of this world. Values, tures, sainthood, a ture, society, a ture, love, pure ture, beauty, a ture of tures . . . Why surrender to the Great Habit?. . . We burn within our work, fabulous mortal honor, high challenge of the phoenix . . . within, maybe that is the choice, maybe words envelop it the way a napkin does a loaf of bread and maybe the fragrance is inside, the flour puffing up, the yes without the no, or the no without the yes, the day within Mani, without Ormuz or Ariman, once and for all and in peace and enough.

This confession is also the multiple beginning of the novel, in other words, a genuine program. Here language evolves in a debate on thought, art, society and culture in a collage of our time assimilated verbally in such a way that the possibility of choice can begin to shape a character and form a new perception. This is the approach of a chronicle. Whatever the anecdote or the narrative pretext, the narrator follows the same point of view that establishes a cross section in that undifferentiated landscape in relation to which the anecdote is questioned. This is why the narrator speaks of "the principle of indetermination, so important in literature" and why he says about Morelli that "[he] wanted his book to be a crystal ball in which the micro- and macrocosm would come together in an annihilating vision." Indetermination as an esthetics implies the rejection of any prior determination and the free advance of the narration in this macrocosm occupied by a microcosm, and vice versa. This porous and erratic space is also indeterminate because it is not resolved, because it does not require solutions. Hence Oliveira speaks of "that which is defective," of that lack of awareness which is also, in the instances when he does not abuse the landscape of that chaos, another possibility of knowledge.

Returning to the lengthy passage quoted above, we find written beauty being questioned and threatened by the two areas into which the narrator has divided this chaos: "infallible equations" and "conformity machines." Between these two realities, it states, "we run towards deception." The threat to writing is also a threat to the adventure that the character has begun. The deception is encountered in technology and in the established routine of everyday life and its orders, as well as in literature, because of the hoax which is at the bottom of everything discursive. However, to question literature is also to lay bare the third area, the area of chance in which the character places himself in order to confront the simple dualities of our time, the "purse-size dialectics" to which he refers. What remains of all this is the passion of the work, the conflagration in a chosen city, a conflagration invented by language to destroy all dichotomies. Beauty, the ultimate value, requires this critical survey in order to return to it as a possibility. The entire novel is this survey and this possibility.

Cortázar turns time and again to the subject of "the Great Habit," repeatedly satirizing the everyday routine, the established orders, and conformity. This repetition can also be paradoxical. The characters are aware of this reiteration, but this does not stop them from criticizing "futurism" for the umpteenth time or from talking about "form and substance." Could it be that Oliveira is afraid that he himself may derive from one of the established orders, be it called the family, work, or history? His open rebelliousness, a form of his will to search, the scheme of his will to unity, is perhaps related to the liberations sought by Surrealism, but above all it is related to the individual and anguished rebellions of the second postwar period. "I don't like technology any more than you, it's just that I feel the world has changed in the last twenty years. Any guy who's past forty has to realize it," Oliveira says, yielding a datable debate. Oliveira's filiation is curiously visible in his nonconformist insistence, in his loquacious need to challenge the established order, which is why his discourse is paradoxical. His tautological lumping of habits and technologies in order to reject them indicates that his relations with them involve more than a simple rejection. His satirical attitude toward a brother who chastens him and toward old people, bosses, or simple women, etc., also indicates the irritated presence of a defense mechanism in Oliveira, who is also the product of a traditional Buenos Aires full of aunts from whom he has fled.

Nonconformity is essential to **Hopscotch** as the reflection of a central rebellion, in spite of the reiterations that link it to the partners of the novel of the artist as hero. In addition, this rich debate signals the context in which Oliveira defines his response: the possibilities of chance.

"Would I find La Maga?," Oliveira asks himself. He wonders because this possibility is left to chance, to a frustrated chance, now that writing reconstructs the past. Oliveira's encounters with La Maga were chance encounters; he would happen to see her on a bridge, at places staged for passing encounters, in a no-man's land. On such occasions:

> She would smile and show no surprise, convinced as she was, the same as I, that casual

meetings are apt to be just the opposite, and that people who make dates are the same kind who need lines on their writing paper, or who always squeeze up from the bottom on a tube of toothpaste. . . .

> But now she would not be on the bridge. . . . In any case, I went out onto the bridge and there was no Maga. . . . We each knew where the other lived . . . but we never looked each other up at home. We preferred meeting on the bridge, at a sidewalk café, at an art movie, or crouched over a cat in some Latin Quarter courtyard. We did not go around looking for each other, but we knew that we would meet just the same.

Chance is thus the sign of these encounters and also their order, because chance underscores the mutual freedom of the characters, their will to nonconformity, the magic of the world in the instant of the encounter, the love contained in the rite. This is why Oliveira says:

> even now, Maga, I wondered if this roundabout route made any sense, since it would have been easier to reach the Rue des Lombards by the Pont Saint-Michel and the Pont au Changes. But if you had been there that night, as so may other times, then I would have known that the roundabout made sense, while now, on the other hand, I debase my failure by calling it a roundabout.

Chance gains meaning in communication, but it awkwardly loses it in solitude. This response through chance to the established routine also requires gratuitousness and insignificance, giving a value to what is useless:

> I took advantage of such moments to think about useless things, a practice I had begun some years before in a hospital and which all seemed richer and more necessary every time since. . . . The game consisted in bringing back only the insignificant, the unnoticed, the forgotten. . . . It was about that time I realized that searching was my symbol, the emblem of those who go out at night with nothing in mind, the motives of a destroyer of compasses.

"The disorder in which we lived . . . seemed to me like some sort of necessary discipline," Oliveira also says, bringing to mind Rimbaud's sacred disorder, evoked in another part of the novel as a sign or mirror. Like Rimbaud, Oliveira also leaves a written testimony of his season in hell, because he seeks unity in the resolution of contradictions and dichotomies. The only difference is that Rimbaud's poetic rebellion, which demands subversion, has become in the novel a discursive rebellion demanding criticism, which is why Oliveira insists on a caricature of himself:

> . . . it occurred to me like a sort of mental belch that this whole ABC of my life was a painful bit of stupidity, because it was based solely on a dialectical pattern, on the choice of what could be called nonconduct rather than conduct, on faddish indecency instead of social decency.

Oliveira recognizes the fragmentation of his own marginal image. The dualisms he struggles against persist in him to the point of determining his response (chance) starting from the problematic context of society (the established order). La Maga, "always fumbling and distracted," is Oliveira's opposite, a pole that in revealing itself also reveals him in his polarity; in other words, it reveals that he also is a term of a duality. "Knowing that . . . it was always easier to think than to be, that in my case the *ergo* of the expression was no *ergo* or anything at all like it," Oliveira says, because he plays at being La Maga's pole.

> And I felt antagonism for all these things when I was with La Maga, for we loved each other in a sort of dialectic of magnet and iron filings, attack and defense, handball and wall. . . .
>
> It grieved me to recognize that with artificial blows, with Manichaean beams of light, or desiccated, stupid dichotomies I could not make my way up the steps of the Gare de Montparnasse where La Maga had dragged me to visit Rocamadour. Why couldn't I accept what was happening without trying to explain it, without bringing up ideas of order and disorder, of freedom and Rocamadour?

Here love reveals the other dichotomies, straining them and making them more poignant. Love thus becomes one more struggle, an inevitable frustration. "Maybe one had to fall into the depths of stupidity in order to make the key fit the lock to the latrine or the Garden of Gethsemane," Oliveira says, announcing at the outset his own course between liberation from those dichotomies and the drama of that liberation. "I would have to get so much closer to myself, to let everything that separates me from the center drop away," he says. The anxiety for an "axis" that he senses in this exorcism, the search for a center of gravity, is also the yearning for a dreamed paradise, for an identity within the surrounding plurality. This is also the dream that Morelli announces for the literature that really matters.

The adventure of destroying the self in order to reconstruct it, the old scheme of "sainthood," also demands the rejection of a world corrupted by definitions, by dualistic simplifications:

> . . . black or white, radical or conservative, homo- or hetero sexual, the San Lorenzo team or the Boca Juniors, meat or vegetables, business or poetry.

And the method for this destruction seems to be "the road of tolerance, intelligent doubt, sentimental vacillation." On one hand Oliveira sees the paradigm of "the struggle for struggle's sake," of "the handsome saints, the perfect escapists," and on the other hand he realizes that "if lucidity ends up in inaction, wouldn't it become suspect? Wouldn't it be covering up a particularly diabolical type of blindness?" Caught between these extremes, between the lines of the dualism that again confronts him, Oliveira strikes out on his own, marching toward his thunderous failure—the discursive scheme of his figure requires likewise its own parody—when the square in the game of hopscotch, which attempts to reconcile the extremes of the figure, turns out to be the window of a vaudevillian asylum. After this failure, resurrection insinuates itself slowly and gravely, crepuscular in some way. The last pages of

Oliveira's story are also closer to the first page, because we should not forget that he writes the novel to read himself in the various masks of writing.

The path, the search for unity, is developed here in reverse. Between the "latrine" and the "Garden of Gethsemane" Oliveira states he is falling into the depths of stupidity, in the traditional line of knowledge that promises wisdom in suffering, the path towards the end of night, confession as the exorcism, etc. A quotation from Lezama Lima says: "Analyzing this conclusion once more, from a Pascalian point of view: true belief is somewhere in between superstition and libertinism." Morelli also notes a quotation from Pauwels and Bergier suggesting "that binary reasoning might be replaced with an analogical consciousness which would assume the shapes and assimilate the inconceivable rhythms of those profound structures." We are also told that:

> It was curious that Morelli enthusiastically embraced the most recent working hypotheses of the physical and biological sciences, he presented himself as convinced that the old dualism had become cracked in the face of the evidence of a common reduction of matter and spirit to notions of energy.

Superstition and libertinism combined are thus Oliveira's analogical method for making stupidity a signifier capable of overcoming the dualisms already questioned in the doubts about the Cartesian schemes.

Oliveira begins by speaking of truth as invention, of beauty that is a truth threatened by the delusion of seeing itself. His adventure is the victim of this delusion when he is overcome by the threat of the unresolved dualisms and loses La Maga; in other words, he loses Paris, where to extend one's hand was to establish the reading of the world, where the bridges invented chance as communion. Oliveira returns to Buenos Aires, where he meets Traveler and his wife, Talita. Traveler, who has never been away from Buenos Aires, is also Oliveira's double, but he is an antagonistic double, a caricatured pole; and Talita is also a lighter double of La Maga. Oliveira forces in vain the relationship with his two friends, seeking to repeat in this world of allegories, where conversations always seem to be referring to an empty space, the truth he lived in Paris, that no-man's land that was a place of encounters. Oliveira's adventure has become a laughable, farcical posturing in Buenos Aires. A loquacious joker, this circle reveals him now in the pilgrimage of the artist through culture, in his sacrifice in a metaphysical rebellion, recovered also in the structure of the novel that returns him to the initial moment of the writing.

That is why this novel, concerned with beauty as the ultimate value and with truth as total communication and with unity of narrator and reader, at this level also becomes a moral novel. Its persistent assault against the established routine, against the "Great Habit," has to do with its ethical rebellion, with its will to break away. In the first of the two epigraphs to the book, "Abbot Martini" speaks of "this collection of maxims, counsels, and precepts," of a "universal morals," and of the "spiritual and temporal happiness of men of all ages"; and in the second one humorist César Bruto says, "I start gettin nutty ideas like I was thinkin about what was forein and diffrent . . . [and] I jes hope what I been writin down hear do somebody some good so he take a good look at how he livin and he dont be sorry when it too late." These epigraphs suggest the ethical concern of the novel, no matter how much Cortázar, forced to take a position of detachment by his fear of established literature, resorts to humor, just as he resorts to variations of phonetic writing as another form of detachment.

Oliveira is seen by Morelli as "the nonconformist": "This man moves within the lowest and the highest of frequencies, deliberately disdaining those in between, that is to say, the current band of the human spiritual mass." As we have already seen, the nonconformist Oliveira responds through chance; chance is his style, his lack of measure and his way of measuring. This is why we sense also an opposition between Oliveira and Morelli, who is more systematic. Oliveira's enormous frustration stems not only from his opposition to La Maga and from his tautological intellectualism, but from the broken line of a search that never becomes elective—although it claims to be so at the level of creation—because it lacks a center of gravity and a free perspective in relation to the rhetoric of culture. Hence every event is determined for him simply by chance, even when this chance enables him to see beauty in the world or leads him to the parodies of humor. And from that fertile gratuitousness he can disintegrate infinitely the established reality, as well as the reality that is yet to be discovered, and even himself. Oliveira thus gives the impression of being a hollow character. He places himself in all points of view, and the naïve abuse of his own image makes him imagine different masks, but it limits any transformation. Perhaps we can assume that Oliveira reconstructs himself after the episode in the hospital window, that his contradiction is also an insertion into history, into a traditional feeling of experience, into the will to transcend, and that he is a farcical figure of the culture of the 1950s, of the Latin-American adventure in that particular context. In any case, the fall is the allegorical theme of the novel, and resurrection is its return to the source in the ritual of writing, in the leap to form.

The wisdom of Morelli, whose accident (chance) would seem rather to be part of his own games, matches against that disintegration the possibility of subtracting through language a reality that is in itself excessive, because artistic form subtracts that accumulative verbalism. Of course, Morelli's secret hedonism is also a kind of skepticism, if for no other reason than that his age or his margination doom him inevitably to culture. Morelli is a theoretician of new departures because he is also a theoretician of decomposition, of a multiple crisis. In the center of that crisis this mask is a skeptical project.

The pervasive presence of chance, which is the nucleus of the character, also appears to be the mechanism of the novel itself. This is why *Hopscotch* constantly breaks it geometry, its field; its formalization is fragmented by the underlying presence of chance events that do not seem to be part of any sequence. In *Hopscotch,* therefore, the form is a rebeginning while the writing is fluctuating and accu-

mulative. In any case, the disintegration that chance fosters in the character and the diversity of volumes it fosters in the form are also at the center of the problems posed by *Hopscotch,* which poses these problems not in order to solve them, but in order to destroy itself by destroying them, revealing them in that reformulation, and reemerging in its beauty and depth through the many books that it becomes, through the slap that wants to change the reader by rebelling him in its rebellion.

### Julio Cortázar with Evelyn Picon Garfield   (interview date 10-13 July 1973)

SOURCE: An interview in *The Review of Contemporary Fiction,* Vol. III, No. 3, Fall, 1983, pp. 5-21.

[*An American educator and critic, Garfield has written extensively on Cortázar and Latin American literature. In the following excerpted interview, which was conducted in Saignon, France in July 1973 and first published in Garfield's* Cortázar por Cortázar *(1978), Cortázar discusses the writing of* Hopscotch, *addressing the novel's themes, its appeal to younger readers, its optimism, and its place in Latin American literature.*]

[*Garfield*]: *With* **Historias de cronopios y de famas** **(Cronopios and Famas)** *and* **Rayuela,** *you begin to alter reality, to search for authenticity in life and literature, utilizing a good dose of humor and optimism.*

[Cortázar]: In the case of my books, altering reality is a desire, a hope. But it seems important to point out that my books are not written nor were experienced or conceived under the pretense of changing reality. There are people who write as a contribution to the modification of reality. I know that modifying reality is an infinitely slow and difficult undertaking. My books do not function in that sense. A philosopher develops a philosophical system convinced that it is the truth and will modify reality because he supposes he's right. A sociologist establishes a theory. A politician also pretends to change the world. My case is much more modest. Let's say Oliveira is speaking: let's return to one of the constant themes in *Rayuela.* I am firmly convinced, each day more profoundly, that we are embarked on the wrong road. That is to say that humanity took the wrong path. I'm speaking, above all, of Western man because I know little about the Orient. We have taken an historically false road that is carrying us directly into a definite catastrophe, annihilation by whatever means—war, air pollution, contamination, fatigue, universal suicide, whatever you please. So in *Rayuela,* above all, there is that continuous feeling of existing in a world that is not what it should be. Here let me make an important parenthetical statement. There have been critics who have thought *Rayuela* to be a profoundly pessimistic book in the sense that it only laments the state of affairs. I believe it is a profoundly optimistic book because Oliveira, despite his quarrelsome nature, as we Argentinians say, his fits of anger, his mental mediocrity, his incapacity to reach beyond certain limits, is a man who knocks himself against the wall, the wall of love, of daily life, of philosophical systems, of politics. He hits his head against all that because he is essentially an optimist, because he believes that one day, not for him but for others, that wall will fall and on the other side will be the kibbutz of desire, the millennium, authentic man, the humanity he's dreamt of but which had not been a reality until that moment. *Rayuela* was written before my political and ideological stand, before my first trip to Cuba. I realized many years later that Oliveira is a little like Lenin, and don't take this as a pretense. It is an analogy in the sense that both are optimists, each in his own way. Lenin would not have fought so if he had not believed in man. One must believe in man. Lenin is profoundly optimistic, the same as Trotsky. Just as Stalin is a pessimist, Lenin and Trotsky are optimists. And Oliveira in his small, mediocre way is also. Because the alternative is to shoot oneself or simply keep on living and accepting all that is good in life. The Western world has many good things. So the general idea in *Rayuela* is the realization of failure and the hope to triumph. The book proposes no solutions; it limits itself simply to showing the possible ways of knocking down the wall to see what's on the other side.

*You've said that in* **Rayuela** *there is no theory or philosophy that attempts to change reality; nevertheless, one of the ways to do just that is not with philosophy but by means of the experience of an anguished man who doesn't accept reality as it is. That serves much more as a model for youth than a textbook in philosophy.*

I'm going to tell you something I've already said to others. When I wrote *Rayuela* I thought I'd written a book for people my age, of my generation. When the book was published in Buenos Aires and read in Latin America, I was surprised to receive letters, hundreds of letters, and of each one hundred, ninety-eight were from very young people, even from adolescents in some cases, who didn't understand the whole book. At any rate, they had reacted to the book in a way I'd never imagined when I wrote it. The great surprise for me was that people of my age, my generation, did not understand anything. The first criticism of *Rayuela* was indignant.

*They didn't understand* **Historias de Cronopios y de famas** *either.*

Of course, not at all. But *Rayuela* means more to me, in a certain sense, than the cronopios. The cronopios are a great game for me, my pleasure. *Rayuela* is not; it was a sort of metaphysical commitment, a kind of personal probe, besides. And then I discovered that *Rayuela* was destined for youth and not men of my age. I never would have imagined that when I wrote it. Why? Why was it the young who found something that impressed them, that made an impact on them? I believe it's because there is no lesson in *Rayuela.* Young people don't like to be given lessons. Adults accept certain ones; youngsters don't. There they found their own questions, the everyday anguish of adolescence and early youth, the fact that they don't feel comfortable in the world they live in, their parents' world. And notice, that when *Rayuela* was published, there were no hippies yet, no "angry young men." At that moment Osborne's book appeared. But there was a generation that began to look at their parents and say to them, "You're not right. You're not giving us what we want. You are passing on an inheritance we don't accept." *Rayuela* only

had a repertory of questions, issues, and anguish that youth felt in an amorphous fashion because it was not intellectually equipped to write about them or think of them and it found a book that contained them all. *Rayuela* contained that whole world of dissatisfaction, of a search for the "kibbutz of desire," to use Oliveira's metaphor. That explains how the book was important to the young people rather than to the old.

*It is for that very reason that the book acts as a "traveling companion," a kindred soul. That's why it seems so optimistic to me.*

Of course, I also feel that way, although there are those who see only negative aspects in it. Oliveira is very negative, but he is so because deep down he's searching for the kibbutz.

*The book is not negative. There is no way that Oliveira can leap from the window onto the hopscotch board.*

He doesn't leap. No, no. I'm sure he doesn't.

*Me, too.*

Of course, completely sure.

*Knowing that, how can one say the book is pessimistic?*

But there are critics who have said that the book "ends finally with the suicide of the protagonist." Oliveira does not commit suicide.

*He is not capable of doing that, but he is capable of living.*

He ends up discovering to what extent Traveler and Talita love him. He cannot kill himself after that. He was waiting for Traveler because he thought Traveler was coming to kill him. But the conversation they have proves to him that it isn't so. Besides, Talita is downstairs. The enemies are the other stupid ones like the hospital director. Oliveira doesn't jump, he remains at the window thinking that all that's left is to simply jump, but I know he does not do it. But I couldn't say it, Evie.

*No, to say it would destroy the book.*

Destroy everything. To say he doesn't kill himself is to destroy the book. The idea is that you or any other reader must decide. So you decide, the same as I, that Oliveira does not commit suicide. But there are readers who decide he does. Well, too bad for them. The reader is the accomplice, he has to decide. Of course, it is a very optimistic book. Yes. . . .

---

**The general idea in *Rayuela* is the realization of failure and the hope to triumph. The book proposes no solutions; it limits itself simply to showing the possible ways of knocking down the wall to see what's on the other side.**

**—*Julio Cortázar***

---

*Contrary to what some novelists experience, it seems the final pages of a novel are not difficult for you to write.*

Only the beginning is difficult for me, very difficult. Proof of the matter is that some of my books didn't really begin where they finally do for the reader. **Rayuela,** for example, began in the middle. The first chapter I wrote was about Talita aloft on the boards. I hadn't the least idea of what I'd write before or after that section. The beginning of a book is always very difficult for me. For example, I began *62: modelo para armar* (*62: A Model Kit*) three times. It was the hardest book for me to write because the rules of the game were very tough and I wanted to respect them. I didn't have much freedom in that book. I had another kind of liberty that appeared later on, but not at the beginning. I must have mentioned what happened with **"El perseguidor" ("The Pursuer").** It was practically a miracle that story was written. It would have been finally logical for it to have been lost forever. I'll tell you the story. In Paris, when I read the news of Charlie Parker's death, I discovered that he was the character I'd been looking for. I'd thought of a painter, a writer, but that wasn't appropriate because I wanted the character of the pursuer to have a very limited intelligence, a little like Oliveira also, that is an average man, even a mediocre man, but down deep not really mediocre because he has a kind of personal grandeur or genius. An intellectual character starts at once to think brilliantly, like a Thomas Mann character. When Charlie Parker died, I realized (knowing about many aspects of his life) that he was my character, a man of limited mental capacity but with a sort of genius for something, in this case, music. I invented his metaphysical search. So I sat down at the typewriter to write and turned out the whole part that begins when Bruno goes one night to the hotel to talk with Johnny. Then I had a mental block. I didn't know what to do. So those fifteen or twenty pages remained shoved away in a drawer for months. I went to Geneva to work for the United Nations, and those pages were among the papers I took with me. All alone in a pension one Sunday, bored, I began to look at those papers. "What the hell is this?" I said to myself. I reread those fifteen or twenty pages all at once, sat down at the typewriter, and in two days I finished the story. But I could have lost those pages. That should answer your question a little about beginnings and endings. The endings are not difficult for me; they almost write themselves. There's a kind of pace. The whole ending of **Rayuela** that takes place in the insane asylum was written in forty-eight hours in an almost hallucinatory state—if I must say so myself. . . .

*When you write, how do you choose the genre?*

I don't. Before I begin, I have a general idea of what I want and I know automatically it has to be a short story. Or I know it is the first step towards a novel. But I don't deliberate over it. The idea from which the short story is to be born already has the shape of a short story, its limits. Even long stories like **"Reunión"** (**"Meeting"**) or **"Las babas del diablo."** I knew they were not novels but short stories. On the other hand, I sense at times that some elements begin to coalesce: they are much broader and more complex and require the novelistic form. *62* is a good example

of that case. At first I began with a few very confused notions: the idea of that psychic vampirism that is later translated into the character of Helene. The idea of Juan as a character. Immediately, I understood that that was not a story, that it had to be developed as an extended novel. And that's when I thought of chapter 62 in **Rayuela** and said to myself that this was the opportunity to try to apply it in practice to see if it could work. To try to write a novel in which psychological elements did not occupy center stage but rather the characters would be dominated by what I called a "figure" or a constellation. And they would react by doing things without knowing they were moved by other forces.

*If you could save only five books from a fire that would consume all other books in the world, which ones would you pick?*

That's the kind of question you cannot answer while the tape recorder is on.

*Should we turn it off?*

No, because then the answer will be too pat, too well thought out. You say books, I don't know; I think, for example, that one of the five works that I would like to save is a poem, a poem by Keats. Do you understand?

*Yes.*

One of them.

*Which one?*

Any one of the ones I love, the great odes: "Ode on a Grecian Urn" or "Ode to Nightingale" or "To-Autumn," the great moments of Keats's maturity. And while we're talking about poetry, I'd like to save the *Duino Elegies* by Rilke. But five is an absurd number.

*I know it's an absurd number and it's very difficult, but I'd like to know now, right now.*

OK. There's a book of prose that I'd save, *Ulysses.* I think *Ulysses* is somehow the sum of universal literature. That would be one of the five books. I really should have punished you for this kind of question. Do you know how Oscar Wilde answered? They were more generous with him. They asked which ten books he would save. And Oscar Wilde answered, "Look, up till now I have only written six."

*You're very humble to have not included any of your books.*

I don't have to, I always carry them within me.

*And what about Marx?*

I was thinking of literature. Of course, when you said books, I should have thought, from the historic point of view, of course, Marx and Plato's dialogues.

*You already have four of five. And now I'm almost ashamed to ask if you would have chosen the same books ten years ago when you wrote* **Rayuela***?*

Yes, except perhaps for Marx. Because when I wrote **Rayuela,** problems of an ideological or political nature didn't interest me as they did afterwards. Perhaps the only exception would be Marx. . . .

*Many consider* **Rayuela** *to be the height of your work and that after such a book it would not be possible to achieve anything better. Now, after having written more works and after about ten years, what would you say about that comment?*

It's not the kind of comment I like very much, because deep down, everything is a question of perspective. Ten years from the time when **Rayuela** was published (today makes exactly ten years), it is already a big boy. I agree with the critics. If you were to ask me, "Which of your books has meant more to you?" I would answer **Rayuela.** But the world is moving along at a vertiginous pace and I would like to know if twenty years from now literature will still be written on this planet or if it will be substituted by some audio-visual system. I don't know. I'd like to know what the perspective will be twenty years from now. I've read a lot of comparative literature from years ago and I've seen to what extent the critics have erred in their assessment of books by certain authors. Five or ten years after the publication of a book, they thought book H was a masterpiece and all the others by that author were inferior. But twenty-five years later, book H went downhill and another, by that same author, that seemed less important, suddenly took on new significance. So there is relativity and a changing perspective. But, now, ten years after, yes, I believe **Rayuela** is the best. If I had to take one of my books with me to the desert island, I'd take along **Rayuela.**

**Rayuela** *rather than the short stories?*

Yes, yes. Well, if you take the short stories in their entirety as a sort of a great cycle . . . no, I'd take **Rayuela**!

*You're less fantastic than I had thought, Don't comment on that!*

No. No comment.

*What influence has* **Rayuela** *had on Latin American writers?*

I'm not afraid to say things that many of my fellow writers will immediately interpret as proof of my vanity because in Latin America one of the many taboos that still must be conquered is false modesty. It's supposed to be good manners to be modest, and of course, to refrain from saying certain things clearly. I'm not modest nor am I vain. But I have a good idea of who I am and of what I've accomplished. So I can say that **Rayuela** has profoundly altered a good part of Latin American fiction in the last ten years. The impact was enormous on the young people who began to write in those years. The influence has been good and bad. The negative repercussions were like those from the Borges' imitators. Many little "rayuelas" have been published all over the place, consciously or unconsciously, using procedures like those in **Rayuela.** Most of it is very mediocre. On the other hand, there was another kind of influence, a sort of liberation from prejudices, from taboos on the level of language. *Adan Buenosayres* by Leopoldo Marechal had already been a great liberator of the Argentinian language. I feel that **Rayuela** has also contributed a lot to that. It has made people take off their tie to write.

*It has also been mentioned that the best parts of* **Rayuela** *are found in specific episodes that are almost like short sto-*

ries. *I call them "happenings" in my book about you and surrealism. They are the chapters like the one about Rocamadour's death. Do you think your long apprenticeship as a short-story writer served you well in these scenes or is there another reason for their success?*

Probably my profession as a short-story writer was valuable in the sense that it enabled me to narrate a long episode that had certain unity. But contrary to the many readers who have a passion for these chapters in **Rayuela** and who remember them most, I like them least, because **Rayuela** was purposely designed to destroy that notion of the hypnotic story. I wanted a reader to be free, as free as possible. Morelli says it all the time, that the reader has to be an accomplice and not a passive reader ("lector hembra"). In those chapters I allowed myself to be carried away a little by the drama, by the narration; I betrayed myself. I realized later on that the readers had become hypnotized by the intensity of those episodes. I would prefer those chapters didn't exist in that way. My idea was to make the action progress and to stop it exactly at the moment in which the reader would be trapped, in order to then give him a kick so as to make him return objectively to view the book from the outside, from another dimension. That was the plan. Evidently I was not totally successful. But from that point of view, I like those chapters the least.

*Nevertheless, you told me that the chapter about Talita balancing on the boards was the first one that you wrote.*

Of course, and the explanation is quite simple. It was the first one because at that moment I hadn't the slightest idea yet of what the book would be like later on nor what my intentions would be. Morelli had not yet been born. He arrived later. Then I began to write a novel.

*Now that you've mentioned the "lector hembra," the passive reader, would you like to repeat what you told me last night?*

Yes, I ask you women to forgive me for having used such a "machista" expression so typical of Latin american underdevelopment. And you ought to put that in your interview. I did it innocently and I have no excuses; but when I began to hear opinions of my friends who are women readers, who insulted me cordially, I realized that I had done something stupid. I should have written "passive reader" and not "female reader," because a woman doesn't have to be continually passive; she is in certain circumstances, but not in others, the same as a "macho."

**Alfred J. Mac Adam   (essay date 1977)**

SOURCE: "Julio Cortázar: Self-Explanation & Self-Destruction," in *Modern Latin American Narratives: The Dreams of Reason,* University of Chicago Press, 1977, pp. 51-60.

[*In the following excerpt, Mac Adam analyzes* Hopscotch, *focusing on its significance in the history of the Latin American novel.*]

Julio Cortázar's **Rayuela** [**Hopscotch**], the work that put both its author and Spanish American literature into a po-

---

**Sven Birkerts on *Hopscotch*:**

Cosmopolitan and daring, *Hopscotch* defies categorization. Chapters and time sequences are broken up; we are invited to read in whatever order we please (a chart is provided for the less adventurous). The result is a remarkable essay in the provisionality of narrative and the inexhaustibility of telling. *Hopscotch* could be said to represent the application of the principles of cubism to the novel. Just as we know that in a cubist painting we are looking at a guitar, a bottle, and a tabletop, so we know that we are reading about Horacio Oliveira's memory search for La Maga, the woman whose love he had betrayed and lost. But as we assemble and reassemble the planes of narrative—scenes from Paris and Buenos Aires, quotations and jottings, Oliveira's complex writerly ruminations—we realize that we are also reading a tract on the hazards of intellectual hypertrophy, a parable about the relativity of madness and sanity, a treatise on the limits of language, and, not least, a slow blues for the mind on the theme of exile.

*Sven Birkerts, in his* An Artificial Wilderness: Essays on 20th-Century Literature, *William Morrow and Company, 1987.*

---

sition of prominence in Western culture, is a deliberately essayistic text. It attempts to enact a coming to grips with the problem faced by all authors, the relationship between what the author talks about and how he talks about it. . . . [*Rayuela*] dramatizes the problem any author faces when he writes—which elements he will select and which reject, and how he will use those he selects, whatever elements his culture supplies to him. At the same time, Cortázar represents the same sort of problem, the dialectical or nondialectical relationship of "tradition and the individual talent," on a philosophical level by creating a protagonist who tries to evade a life of preordained patterns.

The metaphorical relationship between *Rayuela*'s two sides, the conscious mirroring of the ethical and the esthetic, is further complicated by the protagonist's also being his own narrator. This is, the text simultaneously writes and "unwrites" itself as it grows. A word might be said about the two reading methods offered to the reader at the beginning of *Rayuela*: the reader may choose to follow either the "Tablero de Dirección" or to read the text as an ordinary book (or, if he disdains both options, invent his own reading method). If he chooses the short reading, he omits the chapters designated "From Other Sides/Omissible Chapters." Immediately the reader is challenged by the text: to choose the easy, "feminine" (in Cortázar's terminology) route or to choose the complex, possibly baffling route seemingly suggested by the text itself. This is a kind of existentialist "either/or" tempest in a teapot which plays not only on the reader's self-esteem but also on his snobbery (who would admit to having chosen the feminine plan and abandoned a third of the book?). Notwithstanding this crux, it is advisable to read the book both ways and then experiment, simply to see how Cortá-

zar's sense of composition works, how what is disarticulated neatly in the long reading is rather ambiguously articulated in the short reading.

Articulation is indeed the dominant metaphor in *Rayuela:* how a character imagines his life to be defective because the pieces do not cohere as he would like, and how Cortázar would like to break down a traditional plot by fusing it with meditations on narrative problems. It is rather like a cubist still life in which we see all sides of a given object at the same time, something impossible except in the work of art. But let us note at the same time that Cortázar's experiment is not without precedents. Saporta's *Composition No. 1* and Huxley's *Eyeless in Gaza* are also forays into new forms of discourse. What we have in *Rayuela* is a melange derived from Breton's *Nadja,* Sartre's *La Nausée,* Beckett's *Murphy,* with a touch of Celine's *Voyage au bout de la nuit,* reworkings all of the story of the soul's journey to enlightenment, of the same kind we find in Apuleius's *Golden Ass* or Bonaventura's *Itinerarium Mentis in Deum.* Cortázar, following Breton and Sartre, develops this model on a less obviously religious plane (although it is nevertheless a religious plot) and combines it with esthetic speculation. To what end? The clearest object in view is the reader himself, whose views on literature and life Cortázar has long been trying to change.

Cortázar's dissatisfaction with the status quo, or what he imagines the status quo to be, of occidental narrative, what he consistently calls "the novel" has been long lived. In fact, his earliest utterances on "the novel" are testimonies of this dissatisfaction. But there is more to the situation than esthetic impatience. In reality Cortázar is a genuine sufferer from what Harold Bloom has called the "anxiety of influence." Simply stated, this anxiety, which Bloom sees operative in all modern poetry, is caused by the unavoidable influence of the poets of the past on the creative ability of later writers. There is no moment of their work which is not warped by a backward glance at their "forefathers," and the result of this constant rearguard action is *"a history of anxiety and self-saving caricature, of distortion, of perverse, willful revisionism without which modern poetry as such could not exist"* (italics in original). Modern writers, to rephrase Bloom's thesis, are born with oedipal problems which they resolve in the ways just described.

Without seeing Cortázar in the light of the anxiety of influence theory, it is difficult to understand just what it is he finds so oppressive about the literature, specifically the narrative literature, of the past. What he calls the traditional novel is something that exists, if at all, only marginally in English and American literature and seems peculiarly French. In fact, Cortázar's attitude as an avant-garde writer seems almost to be a serious rendition of the ironic distinctions Borges makes between French and English literary history in "The Paradox of Apollinaire." In that essay, Borges notes that French literature seems to be a product of French literary history, that instead of being written by people, it consists of "schools, manifestos, generations, avant-gardes, rearguards, lefts, rights, cells, and references to the tortuous destiny of Captain Dreyfus." Cortázar too looks at the novel (without ever distinguishing between the major genres) in the same way. There are good writers, of whom he approves, and bad ones, whose work he attacks. The major object of his literary assaults is the mythical "traditional novel," analogous to the one Ortega attacks in *The Dehumanization of Art.* It is clear that Cortázar needs a straw man so that he can overcome his anxiety of influence, just as he needs a mythical "good-father" author, one, naturally, he creates himself, the novelist Morelli in *Rayuela.*

The creation of a "father" by an author is an act which ought to have elicited a torrent of critical speculation. The opposite is in fact true, and the sad reality of most Cortázar criticism is its pious repetition of what the author or his surrogate (Morelli) says about literature. Criticism becomes repetition. Morelli does have, however, a significance beyond Cortázar's own immediate need for a master. He is the master absent from Hispanic culture in general (especially since Spanish Americans, like their Peninsular counterparts, scrupulously avoid reading Brazilian or Portuguese authors, thereby excluding Machado de Assis or Eça de Queiroz from their spectrum). The single Spanish author who might, through sheer output, have vied for such a place of honor, Pérez Galdós, is held up to ridicule by Cortázar. In chapter 34 of *Rayuela,* the protagonist, Horacio Oliveira, reads a passage from *Lo prohibido,* and the text is so arranged that one line of Galdós is followed by a line of Oliveira's thoughts. The juxtaposition is ironic, and Galdós suffers, perhaps unjustly, in the process.

The creation of Morelli is important also because Cortázar not only shows him as a text (the characters comment on his works) but also as a character. One thinks of Plato's relationship with Socrates, the often commented control the younger philosopher had over his master when he turned him into a character. Perhaps Cortázar is showing something more than he realizes: if Morelli is a master, he is more like Cortázar himself than any living figure. And if this is true, he is relegating himself to the position of innovator, one who writes for the history of literature, and not necessarily to be read. To a certain extent this is true. *Rayuela* has aged, not so much in its abstract sense as an experiment with discourse, but in its style and its cultural accouterments. It is in this sense a rather banal *Summa* of the early 1950s, existentialism-cum-mysticism. Borges's remark in the Apollinaire essay about the fact that, although Apollinaire and Rilke are of the same generation, Rilke's work seems fresh while Apollinaire's has become a collection of period pieces, holds true for Cortázar as well. To write in order to change the "now" of literature is to situate oneself prominently at the beginning of another "now."

It is therefore in a double perspective that we should consider *Rayuela:* what it did as a phenomenon in literary history remains; what its accomplishments are as a work of art remain to be seen. Above all else, *Rayuela* altered the sociological status of the Spanish American writer. The Spanish American writer of the 1960s became almost as great a celebrity as his political counterparts. To be sure, writers of an earlier generation, such as Neruda or Borges, were famous, as were such poets as Octavio Paz or César Vallejo, but the publication of *Rayuela* inaugurated a period of wide dissemination and, more importantly, of wide exposure of writers to a primarily Spanish American public. Cortázar's text was an international Latin American success and broke down barriers which long kept, for example, Mexican readers from sharing reading experiences with Argentine readers.

A serious obstacle fell, the idea that in order to be understood by the Spanish speaking world in general a writer had to use a kind of B.B.C. Spanish. *Rayuela* is an Argentine book in the way Cabrera Infante's *Tres tristes tigres* is a Cuban book or Guimarães Rosa's *Grande Sertão: Veredas* is a Brazilian book. This is a step perhaps difficult to understand for an Anglo-American audience. Faulkner was not, we assume, afraid of not being understood by Scotch readers. Something may be lost, but how much more was lost when writers had to become grammarians to produce a work of art? No longer would a writer hesitate to use either localisms or street talk of any sort.

The relaxation on the linguistic level has its counterpart on the sexual plane as well. Cortázar's characters talk about sex, practice it with an almost Henry Miller-like verve, and regard it as a part of everyday life. This frankness was not common in the Spanish American world before 1963. There were exceptions of course, but, again, Cortázar's text made sex into a subject for all Spanish American writers, a matter which no longer had to be treated elliptically. That this corresponds to a change in the attitude of the reading public (and is not therefore a cause *per se*) is a matter for consideration. It would seem, as Emir Rodríguez Monegal states in his study of the "Boom," that Cortázar and the social change mutually complemented each other.

Important for the non-Latin American reader of Cortázar is the kind of culture Cortázar displays. Borges and Bioy Casares had spattered their texts with allusions and quotations, but Cortázar carries this display of cultural material to an absurd point. Like a baroque writer of the seventeenth century, Cortázar stuffs his text with references; his characters talk about religion, philosophy, art, literature, and history in a professional way, as if their lives were spent in galleries and libraries. At the same time, this manifestation of culture, though accomplished by an international cast, seems very Argentinian, indeed, very Latin American. To "know" French, English, and American literature is not rare in Latin American middle-class life, and an educated Argentinian would not shock his friends by referring to Baudelaire. At the same time, this same person would be familiar with his own literature, so that Cortázar can refer to Raymond Roussel, Musil, and Roberto Arlt in the same passage without hesitating. It is this, for us, bizarre mixture—which we find in Borges as well—that makes *Rayuela* seem so dazzling. At the same time, the tendency toward the encyclopedic is typical of satire, so that in a sense culture and genre complement each other in a quite natural way.

The idea that culture is nothing more than a skin, a surface that desensitizes and isolates the bearer, is taken up in *Rayuela* during the Parisian phase of Horacio Oliveira's life. The myriad possibilities that present themselves to

Oliveira, the conflicting religions, philosophies, and literary schools are proof to him that he will not find what he wants through them. This situation is Augustinian in origin in that illumination, the kind of ontological security Oliveira seeks, is something given, not something acquired. In other terms, Oliveira is seeking grace, which cannot be acquired through works alone. The Paris section of his life is therefore a progressive discarding of his cultural baggage, a separation from his milieu, which includes his friends and his lover Maga, the Nadja of *Rayuela.*

This renunciation is accomplished through a series of parallel deaths, suicides, and sacrifices which make most of the characters in Paris doubles for Oliveira. The death of Rocamadour, Maga's child, the event which precipitates Oliveira's banishment from Paris, is the symbolic death of Oliveira's humanity, the side of him that arouses pity in others. At the same time, Morelli is dying in a hospital, and another of Oliveira's lovers, Pola, is dying of cancer. These deaths underline the mind-body dichotomy which puts arbitrary limits on the protagonist's search, and, at the same time, they make him aware of his need to die in one sense in order to be reborn. Again, the text is a chronicle of how an individual passes from one state to another: in Machado, Brás Cubas is reborn in his text; in Bioy a man dies so that a text may be born; and here in Cortázar a fictitious but exemplary life is transformed into words on a page.

Oliveira's most significant renunciation, the one of which he repents almost immediately, is his giving up Maga, the women he loves. This enactment of the idea that one always destroys what one loves most is extremely important to Oliveira because it makes manifest his desire for salvation, no matter what the cost. Again, the parallel to Augustine in this sundering of personal ties to the world in order to save one's soul is clear. Since Maga cannot give him what he wants (although she seems to possess it), she must be sacrificed. In the same way, when he feels his enlightenment is at hand, Oliveira does not hesitate to use his friend and spiritual double, Traveler, as a means to reach it. Whether he does in fact reach his goal is not clear, but it is the goal that justifies the process and the sacrifices.

There is certainly nothing new, either in content or in style, in Oliveira's history. We must then turn to the other side of the text in order to see what made it so explosive. And, again, if we look carefully here, we shall see that the interpolation of material alien to the protagonist's story (though related to it thematically) is not new at all. The kind of moralizing digressions in Mateo Alemán's *Guzmán de Alfarache* or Defoe's *Robinson Crusoe* parallel the various sorts of interpolations Cortázar utilizes. His book does not disorder plot, not even the epic sense of beginning *in medias res;* it simply makes the straight line into an arabesque.

Plot may be understood either as an element of the work of art or as an aspect of the psychology of composition. In the first sense, plot is the arrangement of events; strictly speaking, their arrangement to show causality. This does not, as Aristotle or Borges would have us believe, mean that paratactic texts like the *Golden Ass* or the *Lazarillo*

*de Tormes* are not "plotted." They obey a different order, one in which causality is generally removed from the realm of ordinary human logic and left in the hands of fate or a divinity. They follow a process of accumulation which leads to some sort of culminating moment, a hierophany in the *Golden Ass,* an ironic discovery of identity in the *Lazarillo.* We might also note that in *La Nausée,* the same sort of trajectory is found.

*Rayuela* displays two sorts of organization, the type we see in Sartre's text, and another, one in which the reader "sees" the author selecting those elements which will constitute the book's "best of all possible worlds." Oliveira's story is that of Roquentin; the text's own "story" is its assimilation of all sorts of heterogeneous material (newspaper clippings, almanac quotations, passages from other literary texts). The reader may not be "correct" in his utilization of the materials Cortázar has brought together under the one roof of the text, correct here being merely an approximation of the author's own wishes. But these wishes are irrelevant because the mere act of assemblage suffices as *prima facie* evidence of a wish to create an order. Despite the ironic quotation from Bataille's *Haine de la poésie* (chapter 136) about the author's own inability to explain why he brought together certain materials, the fact remains that the materials have been gathered. They are now in the hands of the reader, whose reading will connect the pieces. All plots are "replotted" by the reading, which accounts for all loose ends.

Cortázar seems to have overlooked this aspect of reading in his desire to work some sort of disordering magic on the reader's sensibility. Like the surrealists, whose work he has long admired, he forgets that interpretation is a weapon which turns the text against its creator. Like the monster in Mary Shelley's *Frankenstein,* the work, once in the world, acquires characteristics unimagined by the creator. It may horrify or delight him, but it will no longer be his property. What Cortázar wishes, therefore, is not something an artifact can give: he wants to change his reader, but he uses a tool that the reader will twist into something different. Whatever changes occur in the reader as he reads will be modified when the work is reconstructed in memory. There it will be organized and transformed, turned into an image of the reader's, not the artist's, mind.

What happens to *Rayuela* reminds us of what has happened to the didactic satires of the eighteenth century. When we read Swift or Voltaire, it is obvious we are not reading them as their original readers did. We see simultaneously more and less in both texts than did their age. Does Voltaire really teach us anything? Perhaps, but the thrust of his philosophical arguments is meaningful only to those readers who can reconstruct the extratextual milieu that surrounded *Candide* when it first appeared. *Gulliver's Travels* (which even had a different title) is more a hallucinatory experience for today's readers, more an anatomy of the soul than a satire directed against specific targets. The error of Cortázar's didacticism is its naïve faith in the ability of the work of art to retain his intentions when placed in alien hands. To be sure, *Rayuela* should be read as one of Stanley Fish's *self-consuming artifacts:* "A self-consuming artifact signifies most successfully when it fails, when it points *away* from itself to something its forms cannot capture. If this is not anti-art, it is surely anti-art-for-art's sake because it is concerned less with the making of better poems than with the making of better persons," but the question of whether Cortázar's enterprise is worth the trouble or not remains unanswered. To read him fairly we must forget the banality of his ideas and consider the goals he sets both for himself and for us.

He fails, perhaps, but there is grandeur in his failure. The experiment with narrative, the attempt to point out what might be done with narrative, and the risks involved—all of this constitutes a noble endeavor. Whatever else *Rayuela* may have done, it certainly made the Latin American literary world aware of new possibilities. A good example of the kind of book Latin America was prepared for by *Rayuela* is Cabrera Infante's *Tres tristes tigres.* This is in no way a suggestion that Cabrera Infante is a follower or imitator of Cortázar. Far from it. And yet, when we realize that *Tres tristes tigres* is an assemblage, a kind of verbal scrapbook, then we must inevitably recall Cortázar's art of assemblage in *Rayuela.*

*Rayuela* must also be remembered whenever language, narrative structure, or the depiction of the artist within the work of art are discussed. *Rayuela* is a point of crystallization for so many subjects that one is tempted to set it at the head of a movement. This of course would be a falsification. Authors like Machado de Assis, Bioy Casares, Roberto Arlt, Juan Carlos Onetti, and Felisberto Hernandez, dead, forgotten or simply ignored for one reason or another, all did what Cortázar did. His importance lies in having done it all at the moment when he was able to make a huge impression on a new generation of readers and writers. Drawing lines between the writers of different generations is not difficult, especially in Latin America where two genres, satire and to a lesser extent romance have held such sway. That is, since most writers are working within the confines of a single genre, the essential traits of that genre soon begin to be common currency. What *Rayuela* is, then, is not so much an innovation as a gathering place in which an entire catalog of innovations is put on display.

### Jaime Alazraki (essay date 1978)

SOURCE: "Introduction: Toward the Last Square of the Hopscotch," in *The Final Island: The Fiction of Julio Cortázar,* edited by Jaime Alazraki and Ivar Ivask, University of Oklahoma Press, 1978, pp. 3-18.

[*Born in Argentina, Alazraki is an American educator and critic who has written extensively on Latin-American literature. In the following excerpt, he discusses philosophical themes raised in* Hopscotch *and compares the novel to Cortázar's short story* "The Pursuer."]

Cortázar's fictional world, . . . rather than an acceptance, represents a challenge to culture, a challenge, as he puts it, to "thirty centuries of Judeo-Christian dialectics," to "the Greek criterion of truth and error," to the homo sapiens, to logic and the law of sufficient reason and, in general, to what he calls "the Great Habit." If Borges's fantasies are oblique allusions to the situation of man in a world he

can never fully fathom, to an order he has created as a substitute labyrinth to the one created by a divine mind, Cortázar's stories strive to transcend the schemes and constructs of culture and seek precisely to touch that order Borges finds too abstruse and complex to be understood by man. The first stumbling block Cortázar encounters in this quest is language itself: "I've always found it absurd," he says [in Luis Harss and Barbara Dohmann's *Into the Main stream,* 1967], "to talk about transforming man if man doesn't simultaneously, or previously, transform his instrument of knowledge. How to transform oneself if one continues to use the same language Plato used?" He found a first answer in surrealism. As early as 1949 he defined surrealism as "the greatest undertaking of contemporary man as an anticipation and attempt toward an integrated humanism." Cortázar saw in surrealism not a mere literary technique or a simple esthetic stand, but a world view or, as he said in the same article [**"Irracionalismo y eficacia,"** *Realidad* (September-December 1949)], "not a school or an ism but a Weltanschauung." When surrealism settled for less than "an integrated humanism," Cortázar confronted some of its inconsistencies through the pages of *Hopscotch.* One of its characters, Étienne, says in chapter 99:

> The surrealists thought that true language and true reality were censored and relegated by the rationalist and bourgeois structure of the Western world. They were right, as any poet knows, but that was just a moment in the complicated peeling of the banana. Result, more than one of them ate it with the skin still on. The surrealists hung from words instead of brutally disengaging themselves from them, as Morelli would like to do from the word itself. Fanatics of the *verbum* in a pure state, frantic wizards, they accepted anything as long as it didn't seem excessively grammatical. They didn't suspect enough that the creation of a whole language, even though it might end up betraying its sense, irrefutably shows human structure, whether that of a Chinese or a redskin. Language means residence in reality, living in a reality. Even if it's true that the language we use betrays us . . . , wanting to free it from its taboos isn't enough. We have to relive it, not reanimate it.

The second obstacle Cortázar stumbles upon in this search for authenticity is the use of our normative categories of thought and knowledge, our rational tools for apprehending reality. He believes in a kind of marvelous reality (here again the affinity with surrealism is obvious). "Marvelous," he explains, "in the sense that our daily reality masks *a second reality* which is neither mysterious nor theological, but profoundly human. Yet, due to a long series of mistakes, it has remained concealed under a reality prefabricated by many centuries of culture, a culture in which there are great achievements but also profound aberrations, profound distortions."

Among those distorted notions which obstruct man's access to a more genuine world, Cortázar points a finger to our perception of death and to two of the most established concepts in the Western grasp of reality—time and space.

> The notions of time and space, as they were con-

ceived by the Greeks and after them by the whole of the West, are flatly rejected by Vedanta. In a sense, man made a mistake when he invented time. That's why it would actually be enough for us to renounce mortality, to take a jump out of time, on a level other than that of daily life, of course. I'm thinking of the phenomenon of death, which for Western thought has been a great scandal, as Kierkegaard and Unamuno realized so well; a phenomenon that is not in the least scandalous in the East where it is regarded not as an end but as a metamorphosis. [Harss]

As much as Cortázar sees the East as an alternative to this preoccupation with time and space, he also realizes that it cannot be an answer for Western man, who is the product of a different tradition, a tradition one cannot simply undo or replace. If there is an answer to the questions of time and space, it lies in a relentless confrontation with them in a manner similar to the struggle Unamuno memorably represented in the fight between Jacob and the Angel. "*Rayuela* [*Hopscotch*] like so much of my work," Cortázar says, "suffers from hyperintellectuality. But, I'm not willing or able to renounce that intellectuality, insofar as I can breathe life into it, make it pulse in every thought and word" [Harss]. . . .

Cortázar likes to think that with his novels, and more specifically with the long story **"The Pursuer,"** he begins to unloose the stylistic perfection with which his stories are knitted. He also believes that with this change he moves to a new stage in his development as a writer.

> When I wrote **"The Pursuer,"** I had reached a point where I felt I had to deal with something that was a lot closer to me. I wasn't sure of myself any more in that story. I took up an existential problem, a human problem which was later amplified in *The Winners,* and above all in *Hopscotch.* Fantasy for its own sake had stopped interesting me. By then I was fully aware of the dangerous perfection of the storyteller who reaches a certain level of achievement and stays on that same level forever, without moving on. I was a bit sick and tired of seeing how well my stories turned out. In **"The Pursuer"** I wanted to stop inventing and stand on my own ground, to look at myself a bit. And looking at myself meant looking at my neighbor, at man. I hadn't looked too closely at people until I wrote **"The Pursuer."** [Harss]

But, of course, the new linguistic mood he finds in this long story, and later in his subsequent novels, is not the deterioration of his previous style but a new form of expression which tackles more effectively the nature of his new concerns. Cortázar defines those new concerns as "existential and metaphysical" as opposed to his esthetic pursuits in the short story.

The truth is, though, as Cortázar well knows, that his short stories and his novels are motivated by a common search, by a quest for authenticity which is of one piece in both genres. Otherwise, how does one understand his own definition of *Hopscotch* [in *La vuelta al día en ochenta mundos*] as "the philosophy of my stories, as an examination of what determined, throughout many years, their substance or thrust"? *Hopscotch* articulates the same questions around which the stories are built; but if the novel is a reflection, an effort to brood upon those questions, the stories are narrative translations of those same questions. *Hopscotch* traces the mandala through which the characters of the stories are constantly journeying. Those characters do not speculate or intellectualize; they simply deliver themselves to the passions and games sweeping their lives, moved and battered by forces they don't understand. *Hopscotch* seeks to understand those forces, and as such it represents the intellectual bow from which the stories were shot. The proof that this is indeed the case lies in the fact that some of the central inquiries found in *Hopscotch* were already outlined in the early essays and reviews Cortázar wrote before and during his writing of the short stories. His tales were fantastic responses to those problems and questions which occupied his mind at the time and which eventually found a masterful formulation in *Hopscotch.* It goes without saying that *Hopscotch*'s hyperintellectual ponderings alone do not explain the stories; Cortázar combined his intellectual spurs with his own passions and phobias, and the latter are as enigmatic to him as to the reader.

If Horacio Oliveira seeks through the pages of *Hopscotch* a second reality which has been covered by habit and culture in our present version of reality, and Johnny Carter in **"The Pursuer"** perceives through intuition and artistic imagination dimensions of reality which have been buried by conceptualization, the characters of the stories also find their ultimate realization on a fantastic plane that is the reverse of that stiff reality to which habit and culture have condemned them. In **"Lejana,"** for instance, one of Cortázar's earliest short stories, the protagonist searches for a bridge at whose center she hopes to find that part of her self rejected and suffocated by family, friends and environment. She does find it, as a beggar waiting on a Budapest bridge, a beggar in whom she recognizes her true self, a sort of double whose reality bursts from her imagination, like a fantastic event, onto a historical plane. Similarly, the protagonist of **"The Pursuer,"** a jazzman modeled after saxophonist Charlie Parker, searches for "a reality that escapes every day" and that sometimes presents itself as "holes": "In the door," he explains, "in the bed: holes. In the hand, in the newspaper, in time, in the air: everything full of holes, everything spongy, like a colander straining itself. . . ." Those holes, invisible or covered for others, are for Johnny the residence of "something else," of a second reality whose door Johnny senses and seeks to open: "It's impossible there's nothing else, it can't be we're that close to it, that much on the other side of the door . . . Bruno, all my life in my music I looked for that door to open finally. Nothing, a crack. . . ." What is behind that door is a world that Johnny sees only on one occasion, through his music, but whose substance one glimpses throughout the narrative. A good example is the biography of Johnny written by Bruno: very well informed, very complete, very successful, but with one omission—the biographee. Or as Johnny puts it, "It's very good your book. . . . You're much better informed than I am, but it seems to me like something's missing. . . . Don't get upset, Bruno, it's not important that you forgot to put all that in. But Bruno, . . . what you forgot to put in is me."

Cortázar has acknowledged that Johnny Carter is a first draft of Horacio Oliveira, a precursor in that search which takes the protagonist of *Hopscotch* into a revision of the very foundations of Western culture—its writers and artists, its music and language, its philosophy and ethics, its religion and science—a task Oliveira undertakes together with his friends of the Serpent Club with the casualness and poignancy that makes fiction more credible and convincing than pure intellection. [In his *The Undiscovered Self,* 1957] Jung has said of Freud that "he has given expression to the fact that Western man is in danger of losing his shadow altogether, of identifying himself with his fictive personality and of identifying the world with the abstract picture painted by scientific rationalism." This is also Oliveira's concern; but to show that man has become "the slave of his own fiction, and that a purely conceptual world progressively replaces reality," as Jung has said of the products of man's conscious activity, Cortázar proceeds to disassemble that fictitious apparatus manufactured by culture to show that it has become a substitute of reality, a mask that must be removed if man is to regain touch with the real world and with himself. In this sense, *Hopscotch* is a devastating criticism of rationalism:

> . . . this technological reality that men of science and the readers of *France-Soir* accept today, this world of cortisone, gamma rays, and the elution of plutonium, has as little to do with reality as the world of the *Roman de la Rose* . . . Man, after having expected everything from intelligence and the spirit, feels that he's been betrayed, is vaguely aware that his weapons have been turned against him, that culture, *civiltá,* have misled him into this blind alley where scientific barbarism is nothing but a very understandable reaction.

As in **"The Pursuer,"** in *Hopscotch* reality lies also somewhere behind: "Behind all that (it's always behind, convince yourself that this is the key idea of modern thought) Paradise, the other world, trampled innocence which weeping darkly seeks the land of Hurqalyœa." How does one get there? How does one reach that center, the "kibbutz of desire" which Oliveira seeks? In his short stories the road is a fantastic event; the conflict between a hollow reality and one which, like an epiphany, reveals to the characters a time outside time and a space that transcends geometric space, resolves itself in metaphors that by defying physical laws appear as fantastic occurrences. In **"The Pursuer"** Johnny Carter peeps through those "holes" of a second reality via his jazz music; the artistic phenomenon becomes what it has always been—"a bridge toward true reality," in Nietzsche's dictum—but now Johnny transports his visions to the trivial act of riding a subway and indicts the fallacy inherent in our concepts of time and space. In *Hopscotch* our logical order of reason and science is described as totally absurd: "Reason is only good to mummify reality in moments of calm or analyze its future storms, never to resolve a crisis of the moment. . . . And these crises that most people think of as terrible, as absurd, I personally think they serve to show us the real absurdity, the absurdity of an ordered and calm world."

Oliveira muses on this absurd world when he concludes that "only by living absurdly is it possible to break out of this infinite absurdity." *Hopscotch* offers an answer different from the one found in the short stories and even in **"The Pursuer,"** where Johnny, as much as he lives a life which in Bruno's eyes can only be described as "absurd," engages in a life style of a musical genius who indulges in his allotted share of "absurdity"; it is music which in the end provides for Johnny a bridge to those "holes." The characters of *Hopscotch,* on the other hand, are unprofessional, simple, though extremely well-read and informed people who, as much as they live a bohemian life, share the pettiness and trivia of plain people.

Thus the solution *Hopscotch* presents to Cortázar's basic quest for authenticity is a kind of existential absurdity, a solution that also had a very strong appeal to surrealists since Mallarmé's *Igitur*: "Igitur is a person 'who feels in himself, thanks to the absurd, the existence of the Absolute.' After him the Surrealists will enlarge and maintain the domain of the absolute through this very same type of cult of the absurd which will tend to become the basis of artistic creation and a means of liberating art from the finite or natural aspects of things and beings." [Anna Balakian, *Surrealism: The Road to the Absolute,* 1959]. It is in this context that some of the most momentous chapters of *Hopscotch* should be read: the concert by Berthe Trépat, the death of Rocamadour, the encounter with the *clocharde,* the episodes of the board, the circus and the mental clinic. These seemingly preposterous situations impress us as absurd because they run against the grain of our accepted order, which for Oliveira has become absurdity at its best. For him, reason contains a sophism as huge as the world it has created, and logic leads to a gargantuan and catastrophic nowhere. To pull out from this dead end, Oliveira embarks on feats and situations which, though they offer him on one hand a route to further exploration of that dead end, act on the other hand as a modified virus of the same disease which hopefully will immunize him. And although *Hopscotch* presents no answers, no prescriptions for guaranteed salvation, it offers a possibility of reconciliation. Toward the end of his absurd odyssey Horacio meditates on the significance of his friend Traveler's last efforts to lend him a helping hand. Horacio seems to have reached the last square of his hopscotch:

> After what Traveler had just done, everything had something like a marvelous feeling of conciliation and that senseless but vivid and present harmony could not be violated, could no longer be falsified, basically Traveler was what he might well have been with a little less cursed imagination, he was the man of the territory, the incurable mistake of the species gone astray, but how much beauty in the mistake and in the five thousand years of false and precarious territory, how much beauty in those eyes that had filled with tears and in that voice that had advised him: "Throw the bolt, I don't trust them," how much love in that arm that held the waist of a woman. "Probably," Oliveira thought while he answered the friendly gestures of Dr. Ovejero and Ferraguto, . . . "the only possible way to escape from that territory is to plunge into it over one's head."

**Julio Ortega**    (essay date Fall 1983)

SOURCE: "Morelli on the Threshold," in *Poetics of Change: The New Spanish-American Narrative,* translated by Galen D. Greaser, University of Texas Press, 1984, pp. 54-9.

[*In the following essay, which was first published in the Fall 1983 issue of* The Review of Contemporary Fiction, *Ortega discusses the novel's paradoxical form and the significance of Cortázar's "mythical author" Morelli.*]

*Hopscotch* is many books in one, and one of these many books concerns Morelli, the author, or better still, the persona whose questioning of literature is also the convocation of another literature that implies this novel itself, along with its critical foundation and poetic open-endedness.

In "chapter" 22, Horacio Oliveira witnesses an accident in which a man is struck by a car on a Paris street. This man, who Horacio and Étienne visit in the hospital, turns out to be Morelli, a writer who the speakers of *Hopscotch* have read at length and who, as the central image of a marginal literature, rejects through the demands of his reformulating work the established literary currents. The speculation of the speakers of this novel, their need of a new formal system for a more radical poetic option, is generated in this questioning. [In an endnote, Ortega states: "Chapter 99 of *Hopscotch,* in which the characters discuss Morelli's ideas and projects after reading the Morelliana in chapter 112, is the key to understanding the importance of this author in the speculative debate lived by the novel's speakers. Cortázar's ideas, potentiated in a paradigm of his own radicalism in Morelli, are discussed by his own characters, which implies that they have read or are reading the novel itself as the author writes it. In this game of mirages and redoublings the novel *comments* on itself."]

Morelli's activity redoubles the formulation of the novel itself. In it, this apocryphal author lives the richness of a convergence of transgressions. The characters read his notes, they read the same novel that writes him, and thus witness the nucleus of a critical operation whose sign is the possibility of another novel, of another reader.

Several authors, several personae, Morelli is first of all the kind of writer one would like to glimpse on the threshold of his workshop. This nostalgic movement, which comes to us from the biography of the literary renewal that developed in the 1920s, is linked to another movement; Morelli is also the tacit writer who acts behind every major work, presupposing the fervor and abyss of a language of which we see the final product, rather than the vertiginous origin.

Through Morelli this origin is established in *Hopscotch* in its dazzling plurality, showing itself in the excess of its critical drama, implying the energy of its broad formal modification. But Morelli is even more. He is the mythical author, or the author as myth, of a literature that at times is able to reveal, in the self-referencing of its questioning, its ludic and critical reason, its interrogating fiction. [In an endnote, Ortega adds: "A new exchange in this hall of mirrors emerges from the possibility that Morelli himself may be the 'author' of *Hopscotch,* its metaphor. Morelli

is writing a novel and when Oliveira and Etienne visit him in the hospital he asks them to take back to his apartment a quinternion ('number 52 and put it in its place between 51 and 53,') which we immediately suspect involves *Hopscotch* in a self-reference. Morelli indicates also that the character he is interested in is the reader. And, in fact, the characters are readers of his work. A paradigm of the change itself that Cortázar is setting in motion, both authors coincide in a direct reference to *Hopscotch,* to attempt the novel as a subtraction, which is what the numbers at the end of each chapter indicate."]

It is not mere coincidence that the center of change in *Hopscotch,* the possibility of a verbal liberation that occupies and foretells itself—a center around which, in fact, our own literature has revolved, revealing to us its diverse matter in the testing of its transgressions—is the space that provokes Morelli. Provoked by this space of change, Morelli's game and drama, in other words, the formal discontinuity and the critical response, develop in turn the debate of the poetics of a novel that reconstructs itself starting from its negation as a novel.

Pierre Menard, the infinite author of the *Quixote,* might have been the paradigm of a literature that, with Borges and his poetics of "extenuation," we know reiterates itself in an *ars combinatoria* that makes us parties to the fiction of his myth. One generation later Morelli is perhaps another paradigm, because with Cortázar we have gained a literature that reconstructs itself and is liberated in the other figure it initiates, in the changed reader. [In an endnote, Ortega states: "*Menard/Morelli.* 'Pierre Menard, Author of the Quixote,' implies that literature has already been written, that the great authors already exist, and that the only thing which remains is to gloss these books and thus be those authors. This is a central idea in Borges; the themes are repeated, it is unnecessary to forge new metaphors. Morelli, on the other hand, wants to destroy literature and reinvent the use of the word, to rescue the mediating and analogical power of language and to modify not an abstract man, but a concrete reader. Morelli is marked by the modern critical foundation (Baudelaire, Mallarmé), but also by the great period of the crisis of naturalism (surrealism, Joyce, Pound) and lives the beginning of a literary reformulation, the utopia of a primordial language able to identify the certainty and celebration in poetry. But to systematize his creed would be to lose sight of its center, the speculation about change, revolving in search of a new language."]

A mythical author, or, the myth of the author, Morelli is thus a blank space, the generating center of the other novel that lives behind this one—because in writing *Hopscotch* Cortázar not only acted critically, in the vortex of his disruption, questioning the naturalistic tradition of his genre, but also questioned his own departure, his own tradition of change, establishing at the center of this redoubling of his writing the subtracted or despoiled space that Morelli and the Morellianas deduce. We could say that Cortázar attempts to establish the blank space of Mallarmé within the antirationalistic and nondualistic exploration of surrealism, but this formula might be incomplete, because, by being a generator of analogies, Morelli's blank space acts in the face of the profuse reality of the contemporary culture and situation, attempting a broad series of negations in its need to reevaluate the norms in a world that devalues all norms. Consequently, Morelli redirects those "forces . . . that advance in quest of their rights to the city" and also suggests the "punishment for having remembered the kingdom." A convergence of poetry and criticism, his sign is mediation.

Metaphorically, the speakers in **Hopscotch** also read in Morelli their own author, in the sense that Cortázar invents in Morelli the literature that invents him. This metaphorical level is not accidental. Whereas the three stages of dialectic thought imply a rationalistic and successive scheme, the three levels of "metaphoric thought" postulate a poetical and instantaneous conversion. Analogical language, which Borges attributed in "The Aleph" to mystics, pertains in fact to formal structures; the instant that coalesces the three sides of the "metaphor" or the various levels of the "figure" is no longer successive but simultaneous. The three "sides" of **Hopscotch,** which is a metaphor, are thus only one, which is why this reading by "leaps," like the game of hopscotch, renders better the multiplicity of that coalesced instant. The keenness of a speculative energy functions as the other side of the same imaginary form. As it shapes itself, the novel not only creates its critical dimension but also prolongs the communication of a poetic knowledge that can no longer be reduced to finalist categories or even to enlightening postulates, as some of the critics have wanted to believe. This poetic knowledge again legitimizes the notion of a reality whose center has been promised to us. Not by chance, the purpose of Morelli is to name once again, to recognize "the name of the day." This is the paradisiacal yearning of the novel: the search for the "Adamic language," for a language revealing the world and stating us, recovering in its genuine speech a common destiny. [In an endnote, Ortega adds: " '*Metaphoric thought.*' I am referring, obviously, to the classic scheme of the metaphor—two terms that provoke a third term—and not to the phrase called 'metaphoric,' which is a more or less fortunate comparison from which Cortázar wants to eliminate the inevitable link *as,* a link that in Lezama Lima, however, sets in motion the delta of complementary phrases which soon free themselves from their grammatical generator and become autonomous. On 'the demon of analogy,' see Cortázar's essay **'Para una poética'** (*La Torre,* no. 7 [Puerto Rico, July-September 1954]), which indicates some of the author's possible sources on this subject, especially the anthropological studies by Lévy-Brühl. See also the remarkable essay by Octavio Paz, 'La nueva analogía' (*Los signos en rotación* [Madrid: Alianza Editorial, 1971]); along with the fundamental essays by José Lezama Lima in *Introducción a los vasos órficos* (Barcelona: Barral Editores, 1970)."]

The speakers seek in Morelli, as they do in Zen, this central speaker, but Morelli in turn writes "as if he himself, in a desperate and moving attempt, had pictured the teacher who was to enlighten him." **Hopscotch** imagines itself in the novel written by Morelli; the readers reconstruct themselves in the options of **Hopscotch.** Mediation—the initiations of the despoilment—sets in motion

that search for an axial need, which literature reconvokes here starting from the *roman comique,* from the agony of questioning and the morals of nonconformity, from a defectiveness measured by reference to a surmised fulfillment.

In the initiation of the hopscotch, in this game of stages devised to conjugate in a single liberating movement the "earth" and "heaven" of an inherited code that must be changed, in this ironic and obsessive game, the novel jumps through Morelli's square—or Morelli's square infers the possibility of destroying the rules in order to rewrite them. The importance of the novel in Morelli, of the Morelli space in **Hopscotch,** is the seditious task of modifying through the new game of forms the density of a culture—the contemporary dark forest—that deceives through its partial solutions, and of taking the step that follows the restraint of the "blank page" and the lack of restraint of the *vases communicants.*

Among the many books contained in **Hopscotch,** the Morellianas are, then, the reading of one of them, the access toward its center, although clearly their reverberations can only be followed in the edifice itself of the novel.

The notion of change generated by **Hopscotch** begins with a poetic diction, which is resolved in an open prosody, and exchanges the traditional canons of "composition" for the aleatory possibility of "figures" in an analogical system. In the transformations of this system, which seek to modify the "purpose" itself of the genre, Morelli's book undoubtedly has a convocating role, not only because it links us to a debate that transcends the situation of our literature, but also because it commits our reading of the literary "prospects," establishing in that verbal profusion the standard of a radicalized demand with which we have won the right to a new freedom in the circulation of reading.

This Morellian reading thus proceeds from **Hopscotch** and returns to it. It is a spectrum of that novel, one of the several possibilities of choosing pages, convergencies, or places presented by every text that interacts with the center of a change. This also proves the plurality of a work whose reading, at the beginning of our creative maturity, prior to Lezama Lima's *Paradiso* and shortly after the Borgian library, begins another cycle of transformations in our literature. The other texts with a bearing on Cortázar's poetic narrative, **La vuelta al día en ochenta mundos** [**Around the Day in Eighty Worlds**] and **Ultimo round,** comment, I believe, on this modification starting from Cortázar's workshop, another spectrum of Morelli's workshop. Their tone is different, but their intent is similar; they refer other phases of critique (the questioning response) and of a celebration (the play of meaning) and their convergence in fervor and irony.

**Hopscotch** does not seek its center in a new "literary theory" but in a poetics of exclusions and integrations fulfilled in the possible entity of a language and an inquiry that alter the notion of what stands for real. This action—and the word *action* is reiterated for a reason—begins as a displacement, because this poetics (critique and the open desire for a revealing language) makes our absences clearer by communicating them with the irruption of a full presence. This demand enables us, at the same time, to see Cortázar in the light of the interrelationships he nurtures and liberates.

On the other hand, the text **"Algunos aspectos del cuento,"** a memorable talk given by Cortázar in Havana, helps us recover the tacit level found throughout these pages: that a literature of change establishes its own tradition, and that this movement begins with an acute consciousness of formal freedom, starting from which a short story or a novel first gain their specificity. It is after this fulfillment that Morelli speaks, on the threshold of another.

## Scott Simpkins   (essay date 1990)

SOURCE: " 'The Infinite Game': Cortázar's *Hopscotch,*" in *The Journal of the Midwest Modern Language Association,* Vol. 23, No. 1, Spring, 1990, pp. 61-74.

[*In the following essay, Simpkins discusses reader participation and authorial control in* Hopscotch.]

Every text can be played according to the reader's desires, but Julio Cortázar's **Hopscotch** specifically invites reader participation in its production. Intensely preoccupied with the reader's role in the text's creation, Cortázar offers an alternative plan, a "Table of Instructions," at the onset of the novel to encourage the development of multiple interpretations—the "many books" he ostensibly hopes the reader will find. The reader is urged to either follow the book as it is laid out, or to pursue the "second" book, the one suggested by Cortázar's alternative chapter arrangement. While readers can choose to deal with the novel in other ways as well, their inclusion in the assembly of the novel undeniably reveals a gaming instinct, an attempt to engage them in textual play which takes full advantage of "misreadings" usually discouraged by authors. Moreover, comments on the aesthetics of the multiple found in **Hopscotch** itself—especially those by an author named Morelli who argues for the reader's participation as the author's "accomplice"—reinforce this sentiment.

The reader is essential for such gaming and **Hopscotch** is an especially good example of textual play as it so clearly illustrates the concepts of "writerly" [see Roland Barthes, *S/Z: An Essay,* 1974] or "open" [see Umberto Eco, *The Role of the Reader,* 1984] texts in which the reader, in effect, is acknowledged as the text's final author. Yet, while seeming to encourage us to read the novel in more than one way (through his "Table of Instructions"), Cortázar actually attempts to guide the reader's "writing" of his text, perhaps inadvertently drawing our attention to his uneasiness with this appropriation of his role as textual director.

Cortázar even provides critical terms for the issue of reader participation in the novel. His differentiation between the "female-reader" and the "male-reader," for instance, serves as a useful beginning for such discussion despite the unfortunate sexist designations of his terms. [In an endnote, Simpkins notes that in an interview with Evelyn Picon Garfield, Cortázar remarked that "I ask pardon of the women of the world for the fact that I used such a 'machista' expression so typical of Latin American

underdevelopment . . . I did it innocently and I have no excuse. But when I began to hear the opinions of my friends, women readers who heartily insulted me, I realized that I had done something foolish. I should have put 'passive reader' and not 'female reader' because there's no reason for believing that females are continually passive. They are in certain circumstances and are not in others, the same as males."]

The female-reader desires an already finished text that requires no participation in its production. This reader, in effect, acquiesces when confronted with the task of reading, desiring instead the convenient commodity of a completed text. There is no gaming for this reader; indeed, the author has won even before the game begins.

But the male-reader faces the text head on, eager for an energetic encounter whose outcome is by no means forgone in the author's favor. In fact, authors can never win this game against male-readers; they are given only one move—the "initial" text—while the male-readers have a limitless number of moves to play what one of Cortázar's characters, in a slightly different context, refers to as "the infinite game."

Certainly, authors can employ strategies that attempt to wrest this control from the male-readers, but the success of such ploys is never more than illusory because these readers always have the final word, so to speak. Accordingly, notes to the reader, prefaces, introductions, a "Table of Instructions" in Cortázar's case—all attempts to control the male-reader's power, fail inevitably in the same manner that the initial control of the reader—the "main" text—fails. For the author remains perpetually unable to exert any final, authoritative power. That power rests in the hands of the male-reader.

And that is where the real game begins.

Faced with this dilemma, and undeniably placed on the losing side, authors such as Cortázar offer new projects for possibly gaining a stronger position in this field. A conscious gaming of the text, a plan to guide the male-reader's activities, offers a potential solution in this vein. Consider Cortázar's "Table of Instructions," a veritable key to such a plan. As part of a "cooperative game theory" based on the "formation of coalitions," to borrow Herbert De Ley's terms [in "The Name of the Game," *Substance* 55 (1988)], the Table is designed to initiate the play of the novel with a step toward balancing the impact of both the author's and the reader's moves.

In the authorial voice, with all the attendant reverberations of power, he begins by constructing a facade of textual possession. "In its own way, this book consists of many books," he writes, "but two books above all." Note that Cortázar initiates the persona of literary novelty here, positing a type of text which invites play rather than shunning the reader's ruinous (mis)interpretations. Unlike other books, he says, this one tries to be more than one—as though any other outcome were possible. Cortázar endeavors to make the inherent seem as though it were an elected choice. Because male-readers wreak havoc with texts, why not project a stance which appears to construct and invite this event? This is a crafty move by Cortázar.

Without it, the text (which can never be entirely "his" text anyway) would be vulnerable to innumerable misreadings that would dilute the authorial presence, a form of possession that is always at stake during such undertakings. But with the gesture of the "Table of Instructions," Cortázar guides the male-reader's free generation of the text. Or, rather, he creates the illusion of being able to do so, since it is a naive act of faith to believe that the author can wield any calculable influence on readers once the text is in their hands. This illusion, however, is a shrewd "strategy," in A. J. Greimas's use of the concepts as "a competence in interpreting the opponent's performance so that the subject may relate the acts and intentions of his adversary and assume a global representation of his knowledge, will, and power to act" ["About Games," *Substance* 25 (1979)]. In this regard, Cortázar is creating a ploy to dupe the reader into believing that the two together will create *their* novel, not *the author's novel.*

> Strategy is also competence at manipulation. Programs constructed by the subject are not all destined to lead straight to the goal. They often consist in "making believe" that one desires a certain objective and in making the opponent act accordingly. The opponent is then forced to act within and to the benefit of his enemy's more general program. [A] game of chess then becomes only a pretext. It forms the referential level on which there develops a cognitive activity of the second degree: a game of cunning and deceit.

Therefore, as Greimas concludes, "The efficacy of the player's programming depends, in final analysis, as much on the manipulations of his opponent's knowledge as on the actual moves which he constructs."

Cortázar continues his directive ploy by decreeing that "The first" of the books "can be read in a normal fashion," and "The second should be read by beginning with Chapter 73 and then following the sequence indicated at the end of each chapter." Not willing to abandon the reader in the event of "confusion or forgetfulness," he provides a list of chapter numbers outlining the second arrangement and points out that "Each chapter has its number at the top of every right-hand page to facilitate the search." Under the guise of encouraging a free reading of the text, he clearly tries to program the multiple readings, effectively maintaining a semblance of control over the male-reader's practice. If he is gaming, he certainly is stacking the deck in his favor.

Yet, can it be that Cortázar is playing a different kind of game with the reader here? Considering what his characters say in the novel, it appears that this is exactly what is happening. From the first page to the last (if these terms still apply in this case), he promotes a literary enterprise that runs counter to the reader manipulation that most authors can only hope for.

Evidently the reader is the sole agent for authors who want to make the most of a bad situation, namely, the myriad problems that accompany inherently polysemous texts. By shifting the arena of textual generation to include the reader as part of the authorial entity, Cortázar tries to turn this no-win situation into an acceptable equilibrium of a "saddle point." Obviously, the best example of this is Morelli's comments on the "reader-accomplice," even though similar statements appear earlier in the novel (earlier, that is, depending upon the order in which the reader deals with the text). In chapter 9, Oliveira praises Paul Klee for being "modest" about artistic possession of his paintings "since he asks for the cooperation of the viewer and is not sufficient unto himself." Once more, however, the reference to autotelic (or authortelic) texts offers the possibility that this situation can exist, in the same way that the "Table of Instructions" implies that the author can viably instruct the reader.

At the close of the shorter version of *Hopscotch,* Oliveira builds a web of string and thread in a room because it "made him happy," he says, and

> nothing seemed more instructive to him than to construct for example a huge transparent dodecahedron, the work of many hours and much complication, [and] to bring a match close to it later on and watch how a little nothing of a flame would come and while Gekrepten wr-ung-her-hands and said that it was a shame to burn something so pretty.

He found it "difficult to explain to her that the more fragile and perishable the structure, the greater the freedom to make and unmake it. . . . He liked everything he made as full of free space as possible, the air able to enter and leave, especially leave; things like that occurred to him with books, women, obligations. . . ."

Ostensibly, Oliveira offers a paradigm for approaching *Hopscotch* with this observation, noting the pleasure that accompanies intentional outside influences on the text. This becomes more apparent when the comments by Morelli among the "Expendable Chapters" are taken into account. [In an endnote, Simpkins adds that in *The Novels of Julio Cortázar,* 1980, Steven Boldly "notes that Oliveira's 'strings, the same that he uses in his mobiles, are an image of the open logic of the novel, of the mysterious relations between disparate objects and people.' "]

In chapter 62, the narrator notes that "At one time Morelli had been planning a book that never got beyond a few scattered notes" and offers an overview, apparently by Morelli, on this book which would be like

> "a billiard game that certain individuals play or are played at, a drama with no Oedipuses, no Rastignacs, no Phaedras, an *impersonal drama* to the extent that the consciences and the passions of the characters cannot be seen as having been compromised except a posteriori. As if the subliminal levels were those that wind and unravel the ball of yarn which is the group that has been compromised in the play. . . . as if certain individuals had cut into the deep chemistry of others without having meant to and vice versa, so that the most curious and interesting chain reactions, fissions, and transmutations would result."

This would yield a novel in which " 'standard behavior (including the most unusual, its deluxe category) would be inexplicable by means of current instrumental psychology'." " 'Everything would be a kind of disquiet,' " he concludes, " 'a continuous uprooting, a territory where psychological causality would yield disconcertedly. . . .' " Morelli's comments on this antiliterature aesthetic prompt much of the discussion about the reader's participation in the final construction of this type of novel. Moreover, this attitude is also expressed by characters who discuss Morelli's viewpoints. " 'What good is a writer if he can't destroy literature?,' " Oliveira says. " 'And us, we don't want to be female-readers, what good are we if we don't help as much as we can in that destruction?' "

In a statement on the *roman comique,* Morelli argues that " 'the usual novel misses its mark because it limits the reader to its own ambit; the better defined it is, the better the novelist is thought to be.' " He contrasts this with " 'a text that would not clutch the reader but which would oblige him to become an accomplice as it whispers to him underneath the conventional exposition other more esoteric directions.' " It is at this point that Cortázar's directions at the beginning of *Hopscotch* assume a new significance. They are, it now seems clear, such whispers, esoteric directions for constrained—but not constraining—productions by the male-reader. Morelli continues: his novel would contain " 'Demotic writing for the female-reader (who otherwise will not get beyond the first few pages, rudely lost and scandalized, cursing at what he paid for the book), with a vague reverse side of hieratic writing.' " This confirms Cortázar's surreptitious plan to maintain a position of advantage over the reader in this textual game in which the text is " 'out of line, untied, incongruous, minutely antinovelistic (although not antinovelish)'." He attempts to wrest control from the reader under a guise which promotes exactly the opposite activity.

Accordingly, even though novels such as *Hopscotch* are usually viewed as exemplary open works designed to engage the reader in the endless play of signification, in this case it appears that Cortázar is merely erecting a facade, a textual ploy utilized to lull the reader into a false sense of equal participation. If readers traditionally read a text any way they want to, Cortázar has beat them at their own game by making them produce the text the way *he* wants them to even though they remain unaware of this. He implies, for instance, that Morelli's novel would challenge the Western premises of reader subservience. In contrast to the romantic or classic novel, Morelli proposes to elevate the reader as an " 'accomplice,' " " 'a traveling companion' " so that " 'the reader would be able to become a co-participant and cosufferer of the experience through which the novelist is passing *at the same moment and in the same form*'." In this situation, the reader will be provided with

> "something like a facade, with doors and windows behind which there operates a mystery which the reader-accomplice will have to look for (therefore the complicity) and perhaps will not find (therefore the cosuffering). What the author of this novel might have succeeded in for himself, will be repeated (becoming gigantic, perhaps, and that would be marvelous) in the reader-accomplice. As for the female-reader, he will remain with the facade and we already know that there are very pretty ones among them. . . ."

It seems that Morelli—and apparently by extension, Cortázar—favors active readers because they can boost the signifying potential of a text by contributing forceful reconstructions to it. The author's influence upon the reader is a substantial portion of this activity, too, as the text serves to bridge thought between them. Morelli observes that " 'the true character and the only one that interests me is the reader, to the degree in which something of what I write ought to contribute to his mutation, displacement, alienation, transportation'." This is the stance Morelli offers—" 'to break the reader's mental habits,' " as one character describes it.

Regardless of the way *Hopscotch* is read, it is obvious that Morelli's game is essentially Cortázar's game, despite the distinct shortcoming that such a stance presupposes. When Morelli is instructing Oliveira on collating the notes for Morelli's novel before depositing it at his publishers, for instance. Oliveira is reluctant to undertake the task. " 'What if we should make a mistake . . . and get things all mixed up,' " he asks Morelli. " 'Who cares,' " Morelli replies. " 'You can read my book any way you want to'." Clearly this is one of those " 'winks at the reader' " that Morelli says are essential for good storytelling. And, even more clearly, we see Cortázar engaging in those same kinds of winks.

Yet the motivation for this seemingly good-natured abdication of authorial power needs to be more closely examined. Cortázar's extensive protests regarding his lack of desire for controlling the reader assume a suspicious hollowness after awhile, perhaps betraying his actual desire to remain the "leader" in the game of *Hopscotch.* [In an endnote, Simpkins adds: "I am using the term 'leader' in Martin Capell's sense as a designated captain for the overall game. However, Capell comments that 'Group formation is ordinarily characterized by a leader to whom more or less power over the members is given; in return, he is bound to treat them all with impartial or equal care.' Obviously, this is not the case with Cortázar's manipulation of the reader in *Hopscotch.*" See Martin Capell's "Games and the Mastery of Helplessness" in *Motivations in Play, Games and Sports,* edited by Ralph Slovenko and James Knight, 1967.] The text, in this sense, initiates an agon between the readers and Cortázar (through his characters and directions) while simultaneously serving as a site for disavowing this same activity. In other words, by pretending to waive his control over the reader, Cortázar tries to deceive the reader into following his guidance to the text. Thus, if the reader is an accomplice with the author (to incorporate Cortázar's term), the author nonetheless remains the leader of the group. "Accomplice," therefore, suggests the connotation of "accessory" rather than a participant of status equal to (or greater than) the author. In effect, those who adhere to Cortázar's purported plan of open interpretation are actually involved in a game of follow the leader. And Cortázar cannot conceal, despite his numerous efforts to do just that, who that leader is. For he is practicing the same form of reader guidance that essentially all authors practice: the attempt to establish a heavily orchestrated linkage between the author and the reader via the text.

Many readers apparently fail to recognize Cortázar's maneuver here, which attests to its success. Luis Harss and Barbara Dohmann, for instance, remark [in their *Into the Mainstream: Conversations with Latin-American Writers,* 1967] that "There is something healthy, in a communal art, about the novel that establishes its own premises." "Like the French anti-novelists," James Irby remarks [in "Cortázar's *Hopscotch* and Other Games," *Novel: A Forum on Fiction* 1, No. 1 (1967)], "Cortázar wants to involve his readers creatively in [the combination and rearrangement of its parts] so as to renew fiction as an instrument of perception." Some readers even accept his machinations as a necessary condition. While acknowledging that Cortázar creates an "overt, challenging and even cruel relationship to his reader," Sara Castro-Klarén argues [in "Ontological Fabulation: Toward Cortázar's Theory of Literature," in *The Final Island: The Fiction of Julio Cortázar,* edited by Jaime Alazraki and Ivar Ivask, 1978] that he is attempting to force his readers to contend with the recognition that our "being is inescapably invention." After providing a list of the game elements in the novel, Saúl Yurkievich asserts [in "*Eros ludens:* Games, Love and Humor in *Hopscotch*" in *The Final Island*] that "all are effects of . . . the playful attitude of the author, who wants to overwhelm his reader so that the latter undertakes *Hopscotch* playfully, so that he *reproduces* it by playing" (emphasis added). The healthiness, the discovery of self-identity, the "reproduction" of the author's imaginative construct—all of these elements point to an underlying game of manipulation which, through Cortázar's facade of equanimity, has gone largely unnoticed.

The portrayal of maladroit readers in the novel further reinforces Cortázar's uneasiness as he endeavours to coerce the reader into playing his game. [In an endnote, Simpkins adds: "Although this would obviously have no affect upon an ignorant reader, Cortázar remarked during an interview that in *his* reading of the novel, Oliveira does not commit suicide. (The issue is left undecided at the end.) . . . Cortázar explicitly portrays the reader who disagrees with the author's interpretation as someone to be pitied, perhaps implicitly revealing the desire for authorial control discussed in this essay."] After finishing this novel, nobody wants to be a female-reader, and once again this is a crucial point of Cortázar's plan. Cortázar is operating very much like Wordsworth who, in his Preface to *Lyrical Ballads,* claims that he is urging his readers to approach the poems on their own terms while he surreptitiously presents his own guide to the appropriate reading of them.

In an intriguing essay on chapter 34 of *Hopscotch* ["*Rayuela,* Chapter 34: A Structural Reading," *Hispanófila* 52 (September 1974)] J. S. Bernstein notes that the substance of its interlinear arrangement is essentially that of a reader commenting rather derisively upon an author's text (in this case, a section from Galdos's novel, *Lo prohibido*).

> It is a commentary . . . which, by denigrating its Galdosian source, calls the reader's attention conspicuously to itself. The commentary is hos-

tile and the interlineated text hardly reverential at all. Only to the extent that Cortázar chose Galdos, and not some other writer, can we say that he pays homage. But it is a homage paid to a sacrificial victim, a homage which exalts the victim only in order to heighten the majesty of the act of slaying him.

It seems unlikely that Cortázar would introduce this portrayal of an inconsiderate reader without some purpose in mind. Considering his valorization (through his characters and his Table) of the aggressive reader, it may seem at first that he is demonstrating the liveliness with which a reader may approach the text. Yet, the inherent viciousness, combined with the evidence of anxiety regarding the author's lack of reader control, suggest that Cortázar may well be attempting to illustrate the danger of taking this active form of reading too far. Those who fail to show reverent consideration for the author's project (i.e., the finished text) are viewed as cruel parasites who mangle the text and drain off its vital fluids, casting aside its desiccated husk once the gorging is over.

It is this sense that role of the "Table of Instructions," as a heuristic for reading the overall text, becomes evident. In game theory terms, it functions as a "bargaining" device for Cortázar, a "negotiation" which mediates between reader-response anarchy and the dictatorial author (not Cortázar!) who desires ultimate control over the final production of the text. The "pay-offs" for a game of this nature would result from a correlation between the relatively flexible guidance provided by Cortázar and an empathetic construction of the text by the reader. [In an endnote, Simpkins notes: "These game theory terms are taken from L. C. Thomas, *Games, Theory and Applications,* 1984."] To further employ gaming nomenclature, the Table serves as a type of "preplay jockeying" which gains its strength from the "power of disclosing one's strategy" [R. Duncan Luce and Howard Raiffa, *Games and Decisions: Introduction and Critical Survey,* 1957].

But if the reader wants to engage *Hopscotch* at a high level of gaming, this Table has to be approached warily because it is possible that Cortázar is, in reality, providing a false disclosure with this directive, thereby attempting to mislead the reader who then plays into his hands unwittingly. It serves as a move by Cortázar which assumes the equivalence of placing a chess opponent in "check." If the reader acquiesces—even aggressively, then this move becomes "checkmate" and Cortázar wins. ("Aggressive acquiescence" describes reading the novel actively, yet according to Cortázar's rules.) If, however, the reader can deliver a counter-move to the move of the Table, then play continues. With such a move, the infinite, or non-zero-sum, component of the game is activated.

In fact, Cortázar has engendered this situation himself simply by promoting the myth that authors can effect significant control over their readers—even if this control is the type of passive (in)direction offered in the Table. As Alfred MacAdam notes [in *Modern Latin American Narratives: The Dreams of Reason,* 1977], regardless of the directions for decoding the text, the reader still makes the final decision. Once the author has assembled the "materials" of the novel, "They are now in the hands of the reader, whose reading will connect the pieces." Of course, it is this connection of the chapters—in whatever manner the reader chooses—that removes the possession of the text from the author and places it firmly in the grasp of the reader. "Cortázar seems to have overlooked this aspect of reading in his desire to work some sort of disordering magic on the reader's sensibility," MacAdam contends. "He forgets that interpretation is a weapon which turns the text against its creator."

> the work, once in the world, acquires characteristics unimagined by the creator. It may horrify or delight him, but it *will no longer be his property.* What Cortázar wishes, therefore, is not something an artifact can give: he wants to change his reader, but he uses a tool that the reader will twist into something different. Whatever changes occur in the reader as he reads will be modified when the work is re-constructed in memory. There it will be organized and transformed, turned into an image of the reader's, not the artist's, mind. (emphasis added)

Although MacAdam fails to discuss the significance of the various reading strategies that can be applied to *Hopscotch,* he clearly identifies the powerlessness that authors both anguish over and somehow find delightful. In effect, Cortázar's stress on the benefits of the reader's version of the novel draws attention away from the negative side of this situation. This is one of his most cunning moves because, by not mentioning the anguish which attends a feeling of helplessness, he diverts the reader's focus instead onto the author's purported generosity (his encouragement of the reader's individual approach to the work). Since he has no real impact on the ways that readers interpret his novel, his gesture becomes transparent if viewed in this manner. To engage a metaphor from Martin Capell, Cortázar is playing a game in which mastery of helplessness is at stake. By successfully overriding the reader's usual misreadings of his text, he is able to remain in charge of the process of interpretation to the extent that the novel does, in fact, become *his* novel. Again, this intention betrays the inherent falsity of a stance offered under the guise of encouraging free readings of a work.

Cortázar attempts to remain in charge of the play of *Hopscotch* through the edict of the Table. To discourage the reader from settling for the shorter version, he leads us to conclude that the longer, interspersed version is the only entire one (even though chapter 55 is omitted from it). As a challenge to the reader's ego, moreover, he implies that only lazy, unimaginative readers will take the short route. (This is reinforced in the novel by the denigration of female-readers who would be satisfied with such a decision.) When Cortázar labels the extra chapters as "expendable," he ironizes this situation by indicating that for the female-reader, these chapters will indeed be of no use; but, for the aggressive, nonconformist reader, they will be crucial for a full production of the novel.

Yet some readers resist playing an assertive game with the novel, opting instead for the game established according to Cortázar's dictates (what Evelyn Picon Garfield calls [in *Julio Cortázar,* 1975] "the rules of the game that *is* the novel" [emphasis added]). [In *Julio Cortázar,* 1976] Rob-

ert Brody protests, for instance, the "disappointing element" of encouraging the activity of the male-reader, finding it a dereliction of responsibility by Cortázar. Brody, however, does not consider the participatory aspect of the accomplice's role in this contention, for the cooperation by the reader is actually a form of "passive mastery" by Cortázar in which the individual reader is subsumed into a larger body of readers, with the author controlling the game. "Invention or fabulation should not be equated with the unbridled or forgetful babbling of free association," Castro-Klarén contends. "Invention . . . is not a simple capricious denial of the known and a displacement toward any new image whatsoever, because as it moves from the form to the 'anti-form' or to the unknown, it is *critically thoughtful* of the form it parallels and transforms" (emphasis added). "If it is accepted," Yurkievich asserts, "the game acquires a positive character, instigating a code whose violation can entail unforeseeable damage." Steven Boldy remarks similarly that the novel

> is not a totally open, aleatory novel, nor, as many detractors and enthusers agree, is everything left to the reader. . . . The reader is drawn into bewildered but deep and critical commitment to his reading and involvement in the novel, by sometimes unconventional, but often conventional means, by the "aesthetic ruses" . . . , the misuse of which is decried by Morelli. [In an endnote, Simpkins states: "That Boldy uses a comment by Morelli to support his contention demonstrates the success of Cortázar's game plan. By creating characters who promote a playing of novels consonant with his apparent intentions, Cortázar uses these characters as members of his own team which then overwhelms the individual reader who is faced with more than one opponent. This is hardly 'fair play.' "]

And Bruce Morrissette concludes [in "Games and Game Structures in Robbe-Grillet," *Yale French Studies* 41 (1968)] that it is the influence of the " 'metaphysical' aspect of general game structure" which "protects the work from falling into the gratuity of a neo-Kantian 'free play of the faculties' conception of fictional art which might, if pushed to the limit, *reduce the creative process* to a kind of esthetic billiard game or acrobatic display" (emphasis added). All of these readers, however, resist the vast potential offered by textual direction beyond the author's control, relying instead upon the intervention of the author to tell them how to read. By accepting the author's dictum they have given up on the game of the text, engaging in a form of slavish subservience which leads to little more than sterile conformity.

This politeness or adherence to an author's project is by no means a full-fledged engagement of gaming. To play by Cortázar's rules is to play Cortázar's game—clearly not a game in which the players are equals. This sentiment is often supported by the notion of "fair play" (even though Cortázar himself fails to grant the reader this consideration, if the coercive elements of the Table are taken into account). Greimas observes that

> A game appears both as a system of constraints, reducible to rules, and as an exercise in freedom,

a distraction. Our first impression is that this freedom is limited to the single act of entering the game. At that point the constraining rules are voluntarily accepted. One is free to enter, but not to exit. The player can neither quit the game—he would be a coward—nor cease to obey the rules—he would be a cheater. The code of fair play is in its way as rigorous as the code of honor.

In fact, Cortázar has expressed dismay with those who do not play his game in exactly this manner. In an interview he noted: "In recent years, . . . reading the studies [on my works] has ended up by depressing me, since, in the last analysis, they establish the total negation of the author's invention and freedom" [Lucille Kerr, "Interview / Julio Cortázar," *Diacritics* (Winter 1974)]. Accordingly, the player who cooperates with Cortázar in his game of control is essentially handing him a trophy: his own novel (or rather, the ownership of the novel). This is an emblem of victory in gaming, one which denies the possibility of the reader's chance to snatch the trophy away from the author. As Greimas notes, "Victory is complete only if it is acknowledged by the opponent. In a game, it is not just a question of conquering [*vaincre*] but of convincing [*convaincre*], of obliging the opponent to share one's triumph."

How, then, is the reader to beat Cortázar at his own game? One of the most effective ways would seem to be to circumvent his directions in the Table and assemble the novel in a manner which leads to the most satisfying play of the text. This may involve deleting some chapters, for example, or arranging them in an order not readily apparent from an initial reading of it. J. S. Bernstein notes that, in a classroom reading situation, some students fail to initially decode the logic of the interlinear lines of chapter 34 and simply read the chapter in the usual progressive fashion. Even though this would appear to be a chaotic and useless undertaking, it can produce some surprisingly pleasant results for those students who read it "incorrectly" in this manner:

> they will encounter a text which seems totally obscure, except for some few phrases . . . which will appear as small breaks in the otherwise completely cloudy atmosphere of the chapter. They will be brought up sharply, both in surprise at finding some phrases which make coherent sense, and out of relief from the tedium of reading seven straight pages uncomprehendingly.

Another approach Bernstein discusses is reading the novel straight through from chapter 1 to 155. Without saying why, Bernstein feels "confident" that this form of the novel is "the one read by the majority of readers, particularly by those who believe that the intelligent reading of a novel demands the reading of every page of every chapter of the novel." One obvious explanation of this approach to the novel is that it is the conventional method of reading books in our culture, and many readers will inevitably resist playing a game of hopscotch with the book which involves jumping back and forth from one part to another. Cortázar's instructions explicitly discourage the 1-155 method, but readers who want to outwit the author could take this path as a means for securing victory

through the possession of their own "trophy." [In an endnote, Simpkins states: "In a revealing footnote, Brody points out that Cortázar reinforced the directions for the two-option reading in the Table after the first Spanish edition appeared by adding a sentence to subsequent editions.

> In the first edition we read, 'A su manera este libro es muchos libros, pero sobre todo es dos libros' ['In its way this book is many books, but above all it is two books']. . . . In the second and subsequent editions, one observes the additional: 'El lector queda invitado *a elegir* una de las dos posibilidades siguientes' ['The reader is invited to *choose* one of the two following possibilities'].

Clearly Cortázar tried to further restrict—and thereby manipulate—the production of his novel through this note on the reader's choices. However, Brody argues that this second sentence was introduced to assure readers that the plan announced in the Table was not 'a mere guise to fool the reader into reading Chapters 1-56 for a second time.' He concludes that 'By adding the new sentence, Cortázar implies that no such trick was intended, and that he was sincere in suggesting two books or two different ways of reading his book.'

Gregory Rabassa, who translated *Hopscotch,* noted that this new sentence does not appear in the English translation (which he based on the first Spanish edition) because Cortázar

> evidently didn't see fit to add what he had already added to the next Spanish edition. Therefore I am not sure what his purpose in putting in the specific instruction might have been, perhaps he meant to dumb it down to reach more readers. I do know that he was quite taken aback when he was scolded by an American reviewer . . . for making a reader go through the book twice. Julio said something to the effect that he would never ask anyone to read a book twice, much less this one. Like Borges, Julio liked to play games both with and on his readers, and it is difficult to tell what he is up to all the time (Letter to author, 21 September 1988)."]

Scrambling the arrangement of the novel would also yield an invigorating result. "Once all the fragments are known, they can and should be reviewed in any variety of combinations, revealing in a more and more organic way their implicit network of parallelisms, echoes, contrasts," James Irby observes. "In the realm of 'pure coordinates' there are no piecemeal progressions." This variation leads to the most rigorous manifestation of the "infinite game" Cortázar offers. Even though it may not (or even may) be the game he had in mind, it certainly engages in the type of play which the novel so clearly encourages. This play would generate endless chains of readings, with each gathering reverberations from all of the previous readings, thereby resulting in a lush web of interpretations far beyond the limited, superficial reading enforced by a designated plan of arranged chapters.

Perhaps the strongest evidence that suggests Cortázar himself hoped for a response of this nature can be found by turning once more to the "Table of Instructions." For there, at the end of his alternative chapter arrangement list, is a hyphen, implying that the reader's options are now open. At this point, the reader who is eager for a lively round of the "infinite game" can find authorial approval (if such reinforcement is needed). "Infinite players use the rules to regulate the way they will take the boundaries or limits being forced against their play into the game itself," James Carse asserts, [in *Finite and Infinite Games: A Vision of Life as Play and Possibility,* 1986], adding that "The rules are changed when the players of an infinite game agree that the play is imperiled by a finite outcome—that is, by the victory of some players and the defeat of others." [In an endnote, Simpkins adds: "Carse observes, in a statement which sums up Cortázar's strategy perfectly, that 'Infinite players do not *oppose* the actions of others, but *initiate* actions of their own in such a way that others will respond by initiating *their* own.' Moreover, the endless circularity of the final three chapters given in the list (-131-58-131-) further suggests that Cortázar is trying to prod readers to produce their own version of the novel beyond those he has suggested. A reader would not have to read these chapters over and over again for long without sensing that Cortázar is prompting a break away from his directions."] This is certainly true of *Hopscotch,* since Cortázar's directions in the Table are subverted by that final open hyphen, as if to imply that these are the rules—which, as we all know, are made to be broken.

---

**I don't believe I've ever written anything intellectual. Some works lean in that direction; for example, *Rayuela* emerges from a concrete fact and the characters begin to talk, so they launch into theories. Well, you and I can also theorize now if we like. But it's always on a secondary level. I wasn't born for theorizing.**

**—*Julio Cortázar, in an interview with Evelyn Picon Garfield in* The Review of Contemporary Fiction, *Fall, 1983.***

---

## Lucille Kerr    (essay date 1992)

SOURCE: "In the Name of the Author: Reading Around Julio Cortázar's *Rayuela,*" in *Reclaiming the Author: Figures and Fictions from Spanish America,* Duke University Press, 1992, pp. 26-45.

[*In the following excerpt, Kerr explores the problem of authorship in* Hopscotch, *focusing on the relationship between Cortázar and the fictional author Morelli.*]

By virtue of the dramatic and apparently revolutionary turn it gives to Spanish American fiction, Julio Cortázar's *Rayuela* [*Hopscotch*] (1963) represents a critical moment in the development of contemporary Spanish American literature. Though one might now question whether this text is in fact as subversive as it seemed to earlier readers,

it would be difficult to dispute *Rayuela*'s place within the modern Spanish American canon, or to challenge Cortázar status within Spanish American literary culture. I have chosen to begin with this title precisely because in *Rayuela*—a text noted for its radical questioning of some traditional notions about writing and reading narrative fiction—the author stands out as a concept to which Cortázar has paid considerable attention. The attention paid to that concept, and to different figures of the author, also appears to inform some of the unsettling directions taken by the novel as a whole.

The figure of the author appears to be a figure against which *Rayuela* launches a deadly attack. At the same time, however, there is a vigorous defense mounted by various figures of the author in and around this novel. Rather than disappearing or dying altogether, the author remains in sight as a problematical figure one may be led to read now one way, now another. As one rereads *Rayuela,* then, one finds significant evidence of how contemporary Spanish American fiction begins to pose questions about the figure of the author and about the attribution of authorship. But one also finds evidence of how Cortázar's apparent ruminations about the author's authority leads as much to the affirmation as to the denegation of authorial privilege and position.

What I propose to do is read Cortázar's novel through the inter-relation of authorial figures within it, and also through a sequence of interconnected and competing names (from outside as well as from within that text), which my reading will both construct and follow around it. *Rayuela* not only contains within its own pages but also draws into its orbit the names of familiar and foreign figures whose activity and identity inevitably return attention to the question of the author. In reading both the text to which the author's name is originally attached and others to which that name may be either overtly or obliquely connected, I also want to suggest how our own readings, as well as the texts upon which we focus, might address questions about the concept of the author. My reading of *Rayuela* may also appear to propose a program for reading "the author." . . . At the same time, however, it may also be that this reading of—and around—Cortázar's text merely performs the kind of reading that this complex concept and its competing figures requires, and which the readings of other texts pursue as well. Such a reading would anticipate, while also repeating, the meandering trajectory of the figures of the author to which *Rayuela* and, . . . other Spanish American narratives draw attention.

Given *Rayuela*'s seminal position within the modern Spanish American canon, and also its initial position in this study, it seems somehow appropriate to begin to talk about this text by looking at one of its first (and famous) pages, where the question of the author begins to be raised by Cortázar. As we remember, in *Rayuela*'s famous "tablero de dirección" ["table of instructions"], the reader is told that Cortázar's novel is really two books ("A su manera este libro es muchos, pero sobre todo es dos libros" ["In its own way this book is many books, but above all it is two books"]; translation mine). The first of these books comprises the initial 56 of its 155 chapters (the other 99 are to be regarded as "prescindibles" ["expendable"]); the chapters of this book are to be read in the order in which they appear. The second book, on the other hand, is composed of all but one of the text's printed chapters and is to be read according to the numerical scheme provided on this page of instructions. (This scheme is what likens the second book or reading—perhaps even all of *Rayuela*—to the titular game of hopscotch; to read the novel according to that model would, in a sense, be to read it "à la rayuela.")

The now famous directive of the "tablero" not only defines the novel's possible modes of organization. It also identifies the reader as a "guest-author" who has the option to choose how the book will be read, how *Rayuela* will come into existence. (In some of the subsequent Sudamericana imprints of the original 1963 edition, moreover, that invitation was made explicit: "El lector queda invitado *a elegir* una de las dos posibilidades siguientes" ["The reader is invited to *choose* one of the following possibilities"; translation mine].) The reading "à la rayuela" is proposed as a reading chosen, and thus authored, by the reader, whose primary role and privileged position are emphasized not only by this instructional preface but also by the literary theory explicitly proposed within *Rayuela's* pages. That theory, moreover, is presented as originating in a figure named "Morelli," a character-author whose poetics of the novel has generally been read as faithfully representing Cortázar's own position. The tablero has usually been seen as the text through which the author-figure surrenders his place of preeminence in, as well as his authority over, the book that is read. It would appear that such a place and such authority are transferred directly to the reader through this opening text. The reader is virtually invited to choose the text he or she wishes to read, by eliminating or retaining the "expendable" chapters.

According to the tablero, then, the text read by *Rayuela's* reader is a text over which the authorial subject figured by the introductory text (the figure that originally appears to be responsible for the novel) has no authority. However, this transfer of authority, one discovers, is quite problematical. Indeed, in the gesture by which an authorial figure seems to surrender his rights to the authorship of such a complex and self-conscious text as *Rayuela,* one can also read an affirmation of authorial privilege and position that is well suited for the novel in which it appears.

Given the tablero's position of anteriority and its instructional aims, it would appear as a text authored by a writer whose name is, or should be, Cortázar. This is the name of the empirical author whose virtual signature appears upon it. It is the name that identifies the author presumed to have written and signed the text and, as its original author and owner, to have staked a claim to it. The tablero's instructions, however, would seem to confound the author's place, if not the rights attached to his name, as it appears to open a path to the figure of another author.

The gesture by which the tablero's author-figure resituates the site of composition from one "side" of the text to the other (that is, from the place of the author to that of the novel's potential reader) is also a gesture that reasserts an original right of authorship. For it also asserts that the one who assigns that right to the reader authorizes himself (or is authorized by the place of authority he occupies) to make such an assignment, to propose how the novel might be read. Moreover, the freedom offered the reader-figure is the freedom to choose not among an unlimited number of texts (or readings) but between "two books" defined beforehand here in the tablero.

The choice put into operation will thus be a choice predefined and controlled—that is, already authored—by the figure who simultaneously proposes and implicitly proclaims his abdication of authority, his loss of control, over the novel. However, we recall that the table is a table (that is, a "board") of instructions, and that certain conditions would seem to obtain in a situation in which instructions are to be given. Obviously, one who gives instructions would appear to be situated in a position from which instructions or directions can in fact be given. Such a position may be a position that certifies prior mastery and, therefore, acknowledges the knowledge and privilege assumed to be held by the subject so situated in that position. But the position may itself also confer upon its occupant another (and perhaps new) kind of authority, an authority assumed not prior to but simultaneous with the positioning of that subject.

In the tablero the authorial figure would seem both to surrender and to confer upon himself the authority (that is, the authorial function) that is apparently ceded to the reader. Thus the author-as-teacher/instructor affirms his own identity as author/master through a directive (the virtually pronounced invitation) that would put in the place of textual authority a figure (that is, the reader) who, nonetheless, still requires some kind of instruction. The reader may well be proposed as *Rayuela's* virtual author. However, the conferral of such an identity (and, moreover, the right to such a title or role) is postulated, it must be remembered, by a figure whose own authoritative image is reinscribed within the text at precisely the moment when his authorial position appears to be surrendered.

The instruction table proposes, then, a theory of reading that is at the same time a theory of authorship. But such authorship is of a precarious sort, since the freedom granted the reader is a dubious freedom: the powers surrendered by the author, it seems, are the very powers that he also retains and keeps from his reader. Moreover, the place of the reader-as-author is explicitly legitimized by the figure whose apparent anteriority, and thus authority, would situate the reader as a belated author. That reader-author's late arrival places him in a somewhat equivocal position: he who comes after the text (in a position posterior to authorial activity) is authorized to move to a place somewhere ahead of it—to a position of anteriority from which one might author, as it were, *Rayuela's* reading.

One sees then that the reader, posited as a free agent, is the guest of a host whose apparent invitation sets up not so much a transfer of privilege and power as a dialectic of authority and authorship through which the authorial subject posited by the tablero assumes a somewhat deceptive position. One can, of course, read this relation between authorial and readerly figures as a partnership—a theoretical partnership that could be read as both foreshadowing and reiterating similar proposals from within and beyond Spanish American borders. That is, here in **Rayuela** of 1963 the proposal of this problematical relation between those figures precedes—anticipating in a decidedly critical fashion—modern critical theory's more recent notions about the figures of the reader and the author. (In some sense, one could argue that Cortázar's text, like a good many by Borges before him, is yet another of the precursors of, among others, the Barthes and Foucault essays discussed in chapter one. Borges is, of course, the Spanish American author to whom both European and North American critics and writers have often found it instructive to turn their gaze for considering these sorts of critical notions.)

This partnership prefigures (and, for some readers, might appear to put into practice) the theories of reading and authorship set forth in **Rayuela's** own pages. Oddly, this partnership, which both affirms and disavows the notion of a singular and original author, is proposed by still another (and apparently secondary) authorial figure. This figure, who is encountered only fleetingly and, yet, everywhere in the novel, is the character-author named Morelli. It is he who proposes within its body a set of literary theories often identified with the practice of Cortázar's novel. But his is also a problematical role, which is likewise prefigured here in **Rayuela's** tablero.

Though the name "Morelli" designates a fictional entity in the novel, his presence is established not by anything he says or does within its narrative chapters, but by what he has supposedly written and what gets repeated and discussed by some of **Rayuela's** own characters. Readers familiar with Cortázar's novel will recall how its narrative structure and story situate Morelli in both marginal and central positions. As we remember, **Rayuela** is composed of three sections. Chapters 1-36, headed by the phrase "Del lado de allá" ["From the Other Side"], and chapters 37-56, headed by "Del lado de acá" ["From This Side"], comprise what has generally been called its narrative, which is set in Paris and Buenos Aires of the 1950s. The oscillating narration in first and third person gives an account of the metaphysical and erotic "searches" undertaken or lived by Horacio Oliveira, the protagonist, first in Paris ("Del lado de allá") and then in Buenos Aires ("Del lado de acá"). Chapters 57-155, headed by the phrase "De otros lados" ["From Other Sides" (translation mine)], beneath which one finds the significant (though also problematically parenthesized) disclaimer "Capítulos prescindibles" ["Expendable Chapters"], contain a heterogeneous group of texts. Some of them relate episodes in the story of Oliveira, some present Morelli's literary thoughts and theories, and others appear as fragments extracted from the writings of other authors and incorporated into Morelli's notebooks (and Cortázar's novel). [In an endnote, Kerr states: "Among the other authors whose names appear to identify texts apparently cited, if not appropriated, by Morelli (and/or Cortázar) are: Claude Lévi-Strauss (chapter 59), Meister Eckhardt (chapter 70), José Lezama Lima (chapter 81), [Hugo von] Hofmannsthal (chapter 102), Anaïs Nin (chapter 110), Clarence

Darrow (chapter 117), Malcolm Lowry (chapter 118), [Lawrence] Ferlinghetti (chapter 121), [Antonin] Artaud (chapter 128), Georges Bataille (chapter 136), [Witold] Gombrowicz (chapter 145), and Octavio Paz (chapter 149)."]

Morelli is an author whose works have been read, revered, and recovered by Oliveira and his bohemian Parisian circle of friends. His name circulates within the text mainly as a sign of authorship. It virtually becomes a place where authorial activity is figured and through which the identity of the author may appear to be revealed, especially when this author is materialized as a personal figure in the story. But the mention of the name Morelli also places within the text a figure whose identity that name would suspend as much as solidify. In fact, Morelli materializes only briefly as a fictional character. Initially he is merely "un viejo" ["an old man"] injured in an accident witnessed by Oliveira (chapter 22); later he is identified as the person-author named Morelli, whom Oliveira and his friend Etienne go to visit in the hospital after his accident (chapter 154). [In an endnote, Kerr adds: "The naming of the chapters according to their assigned numbers in the text is deceptive, of course, since the reading sequence supplied by the table of instructions resituates, as it renumbers, them according to its own numerical and narrative scheme. Thus, chapter 154 is the thirty-first chapter after chapter 22, which is the forty-fourth chapter in the reading 'à la rayuela', or, viewed another way, chapter 22 is really chapter 44 and chapter 154 is really chapter 75."] There, the coincidence of identities (that of the initially unidentified "viejo" and that of the living author formerly figured only through the writings that bear his name) is revealed simultaneously to the characters and the readers of **Rayuela.**

This discovery gives an illusory fullness to an authorial figure whose presence is otherwise signaled not so much through the materialization of a personal character within the fiction as through the figuration of a writing subject constituted through a collection of texts that are read in the novel. We remember that Morelli's literary theories are not set forth as a textually unified or integrated body of principles, through which an illusion of authorial unity and presence might be created. They are instead dispersed throughout the novel's "expendable" chapters, and therefore interspersed within part of its narrative. (In a reading "à la rayuela" the chapters containing Morelli's literary theories are grouped with the chapters relating the Parisian narrative. Other of Morelli's heterogeneous notes and textual clippings are intercalated throughout the entire narrative from their "exterior" site in "De otros lados.")

The scattered notes figure Morelli as a fragmented, if not altogether absent, author-theorist—as an author who has no single or stable place within the text. The presentation of the "viejo" under the name Morelli restores the image of the whole author, while producing a figure whose days appear to be numbered. Indeed, one might argue that the introduction of Morelli into the narrative as a character-person at the very moment when, it is suggested, he appears to be about to die, can be read as an appropriate, even though anticipatory, figuration of the "death of an author." (After leaving the hospital, Etienne says to Oliveira: "En el fondo es un encuentro póstumo, días más o menos" ["When you come right down to it, it was a posthumous meeting, a question of days"].) [In an endnote, Kerr explains: "If one were to read the novel's chapters in chronological order, [Morelli's] death would appear to be imminent only in its final pages, since the text ends with chapter 155. However, if one were to read them 'à la rayuela,' this fatal scene would appear in the middle of the narrative as well as in the middle of the text as a whole. For, once Oliveira arrives in Buenos Aires, the 'capítulos prescindibles' interspersed with chapters 37-56 no longer advance directly Morelli's literary theories."] The absence already marked by the texts and theories he has supposedly composed, and which have been scattered throughout the novel (by another and apparently more primary author), are potentially literalized by a text that in so many other ways (as the tablero recalls) works to keep the figure of the author alive.

Indeed, Morelli the character-author, along with Morelli the name, seems to turn one's gaze to the scene of its imminent death and to expose both the appearance and disappearance of the name Cortázar. This last name is of course the name of the empirical author who has suggested the fictional character's impending death. It is also the name given to the textualized figure who survives the fiction of that fabricated author's demise. Morelli—whose role has been read as that of the literary "master absent from Hispanic culture in general" and here invented by Cortázar as a "mythical 'good-father' author" [Alfred J. Mac Adam, *Modern Latin American Narratives,* 1977], or as that of the "apocryphal author" or "tacit writer who works behind every major work" [Julio Ortega, "Morelli on the Threshold," in *The Review of Contemporary Fiction* (Fall 1983)], or as a "producto de las citas" ["product of citation"] and a "lugar de cruce de citas" ["point of citational crossings"]—is brought to life, while also being readied for death, at the hands of the figure whose role as author, or father-figure, derives some of its authority from the demise of another figure (that is, Morelli) who may otherwise appear to usurp the author's place. The name of the one (Morelli) thus competes with the name of the other (Cortázar) for the place of authorial privilege in this text. The name of the one or the other becomes a place of competition between different figures of the author.

Yet the figure who is left to die is revived as a textual authority, within the other fictional characters' reading and discussion of his texts as well as through the mere mention of his name. For instance, in a well-known key chapter (chapter 99), Oliveira and his Parisian group engage in a detailed discussion of Morelli's theories, which they have read, it seems, from the very same texts presented to the readers of *Rayuela.* This discussion—which brings Morelli back to textual life perhaps more than his appearance as a "person" in the hospital—takes place in Morelli's apartment, to which Morelli himself has given them the key (chapter 154). There, in the home of this author who has been ejected from his own place by an accident authored by another, they find his notebooks—original texts from which, presumably, Morelli's contributions to Cortázar's novel have been made.

Morelli's place is filled with his readers' rephrasings of his ideas about literature and language. His writings, at once originals and copies and collected in notebooks he himself has supposedly composed, are thus not only fragmented and scattered in the "Capítulos prescindibles" and throughout the reading "à la rayuela." They are also mediated by a group of readers who, in their discussions, would revise as well as review the author's theories. These texts belong to an author whose expendable work, placed as Morelli's materials and the characters' key discussion of his theories are in *Rayuela*'s margins (that is, in its "capítulos prescindibles"), is, of course, essential for what appears to be Cortázar's revolutionary literary project. Thus the discovery of the old man's name is the recovery of the name of an original, but also unconventional, author whose position in *Rayuela* is at best equivocal.

Morelli's name is both at the center and on the edges of things in the novel. His name appears to mark the place of an original author but also to identify the work of an author whose writing repeats, and is thus contingent upon, the work of others. In that he would figure the activity of his own literary father (Cortázar), whose attempt to propose a new beginning for the work of modern writers is materialized by the author named Morelli, Morelli (as both name and fictional entity) figures the critical nature of *Rayuela*'s confounding authorial practice and theory. [In an endnote, Kerr states: "Mac Adam reads this as Cortázar's attempt to invent not only a magisterial figure absent from the Latin American tradition, but also a conventional or 'traditional' model against which he—or his own text—could react and in relation to which he (or Morelli) could propose 'innovative' and 'transgressive' literary ideas. That the master to whom Cortázar alludes through the figure of Morelli may well be, or is in fact, Macedonio Fernández (1874-1952), whose *Museo de la novela de la eterna* (posthumous publication 1967) could be identified as the model for or fulfillment of *Rayuela*'s proposals, is suggested by . . ." numerous critics.]

Morelli is the author-reader and master-father invented by Cortázar, who is himself identifiable in such terms. That is, the name Cortázar would seem to designate a figure who is at once a belated reader of Morelli's work (as well as the work of other authors, who are also read by this fictional author) and a writer who makes that work appear to precede his own. The name of the one appears as both prior and posterior to that of the other; the name of the one is both subordinated to and supported by the name of the other. The author's place would seem to accommodate the figure of the one or the other author.

*Rayuela* has frequently been read as presenting Cortázar's own theories about language and literature in general and the novel in particular. In such readings, the name Morelli would appear to cover the name Cortázar, the name of the biographical author whose ghostly presence in the figure of the textualized author is also called forth by that name (that is, "Cortázar"). However, the name Morelli can also be read as revealing, rather than concealing, the name of the other author. As noted above, it has been suggested that *Rayuela* may well be the novel on which Morelli himself is working within the fiction and in which he tries to work out, if not put into practice successfully, the literary theories proposed in its pages.

However, if one identifies Morelli as the "source" of *Rayuela* itself (that is, as the source of both its fictional narrative and its literary theories), one posits for him a position literally equal, if not also superior, to that of Cortázar. The position held by the author (that is, both the biographical figure and the textualized subject), who is referred to through the name Cortázar, then becomes a crowded place indeed—a place in which the name Morelli is superimposed on (while supplementing and replacing) that of both the empirical author and the authorial subject figured by *Rayuela.* The name Morelli is positioned in something of a metaphorical relation to the name Cortázar, which all but jumps out from behind the transparency of Morelli's figure. (Moreover, if one accepts Cortázar's own identification of this figure as a double for the novel's protagonist, Oliveira, whom some have read as the novel's first-person narrator-author and who would thereby serve as but another cover for Cortázar, such and identification would further destabilize the frame of authorship, and the apparent singularity of any authorial name or place, in this text.) Each of these names remains identical to itself, but also becomes identified with the name of the other.

That the name Morelli is bound to the name Cortázar and that a good many readers have found it virtually impossible to talk about *Rayuela* without connecting the two is not surprising. Some of these connections go so far as to join—sometimes graphically—the two. When these names are written together to form the name of another author (that is, "Cortázar-Morelli" or "Morelli-Cortázar"), the doubled or divided name reveals what the name of one—if not both—of these figures already displays. When the names Cortázar and Morelli are bound together, two significantly specular figures emerge in the place of a single author. (Indeed, if one were to read the hyphen between the two names quite literally, respecting its etymological, original meaning as a sign written below two consecutive letters to indicate that they belong to the same word, the two names would have to be read as one.)

In this reunion of original authors, however, each also becomes the offspring of the other, each appears as a figure of anteriority and belatedness with respect to the other. Moreover, the figure of the two composite authors (or the composite figure of a single author) is irreducible to either of its proper names—though one of them, one might argue, is supposed to refer to a primary author who begets or creates the novel. Though, theoretically at least, Morelli may be seen to have a certain priority, from a perspective outside the text, his name bears no more than the appearance of a term that designates a character or copy. Yet it is precisely through such a secondary figure that the activity of the original author—and perhaps the problem of authorship itself—becomes inscribed with such vigor in *Rayuela.*

How, then, is one to read, or read through, the name of one or the other author? The name of the one not only leads to the name of the other; each seems ready to reveal and to hide the names of a variety of other authors. Indeed, the question of reading the author's name is ren-

dered all the more significant here because, within the text of the novel, Morelli's name is a name that also marks the place where the work of other authors may be read. The "morelliana" (that is, the materials from Morelli's notebooks, presented throughout the expendable chapters), as we recall, incorporate fragments of writing attached to and signed with the names of other authors. "Morelli" virtually hides those other names, while also becoming identified as but the name of the reader of those other authors, whose writings become identified with, even absorbed into, the figures of the author in *Rayuela.*

"Morelli" seems to fix in place (that is, within the text of *Rayuela*) the name of the author. But it also opens a space for the circulation of such a name and the figures (or names) of the author that seem to compete around it. The meaning of such a name would thus seem to arise from its relation to other such names and to the name Cortázar. However, one might argue that to get at the meaning of Morelli one ought to return to Cortázar, perhaps so as to consider other figures from which his own appearance or identity might seem to be derived or upon which he may have aimed to model his character.

Though one discovers that the name Morelli appears to have been chosen by Cortázar without any explicitly formulated authorial design, as one tries to situate and read its significance this name comes to resonate between one text, one author, and another. [In an endnote, Kerr adds: "This character-author is referred to only with a surname in *Rayuela.* He has no given name either in the novel or in Cortázar's notes. Moreover, in Cortázar and Barrenechea, *Cuaderno de bitácora de 'Rayuela',* one finds no authorial comments about the name itself nor any indication of what its original significance might have been. Thus, besides considering whether 'Morelli' may be but a cover for 'Macedonio,' one might also speculate about Morelli's onomastic antecedents (if not fictional models or thematic sources) in texts by other Argentine masters whose work Cortázar knew well, or in their sources—in Borges's Morell ('El espantoso redentor Lazarus Morell,' '*Historia universal de la infamia* ['The Dread Redeemer Lazarus Morell,' *A Universal History of Infamy*] [1935]), or Bioy Casares's Morel (*La invencion de Morel* [*The Invention of Morel*] [1940]), or Wells's Dr. Moreau (*The Island of Dr. Moreau* [1896], on which Bioy Casares is presumed to have drawn for his novel). One may also wonder whether Cortázar, who translated all of Poe's prose works (*Obras en prosa de Edgar Allan Poe* [1956]), may have somehow derived the name from the American author's 'Morella' (1834-35), which, aptly enough, can be read as a fable about the propriety of the proper name."] Indeed, one of the possible choices of nominal precursors through which to read Cortázar's Morelli leads to a name that refigures and repeats itself, as it moves to other texts and authors, without abandoning Cortázar or *Rayuela.* Moreover, the name Morelli within one or another context finally suggests that the name of one author may necessarily lead to the name of another. The author's proper name, perhaps even an authorial signature, seems always ready to embody—while also being unable to contain completely—both a critique and a consolidation of authorial originality and authority.

As we wander a bit with the name Morelli, hopscotching, as it were, to other names and signatures potentially hidden under as well as uncovered by it, we come across another problematical figure of the author—in fact, another figure named Morelli. Interestingly enough, it could appear that Cortázar's Morelli is prefigured by this other namesake who has become identified with the problem of authorship, and in whose name one might again raise the question of the author. The other Morelli to whom I refer is, of course, Giovanni Morelli (1816-91), the art historian known as the father of modern connoisseurship and the originator of the "Morelli-method," once considered a revolutionary theory of artistic attribution. Put forth in the late nineteenth century, Morelli's theory presented a theory for establishing the authorship of the work of art; it proposed a method for distinguishing an original painting from its copies. Purported to be a scientific method of attribution, Morelli's method provided a potentially authoritative return to the figure of the artistic author.

Essentially, Morelli proposed that the artist's identity (and thus, also, the work's authenticity—its status as an original) could be determined by examining the secondary or little noticed, and thus seemingly insignificant, details in a particular painting (for example, fingernails, hands, or ear lobes), instead of by reading its general patterns or overall design. The proper application of the method would lead to the restoration of the original artist's name in the case of incorrect attribution, and to the certification of a signature's authenticity in the case of unverified authorship. Morelli's theory was, in a way, a theory of signatures, of how artists sign their works through seemingly insignificant details. Such details, he proposed, are the sites through which a painting's true origins (that is, the singular identity of the original artist) are revealed. For it is there, in the "insignificant detail" (which, of course, is elevated to a position of the greatest significance by Morelli's method), that the artist virtually gives himself away.

This theory was not only a theory of what constitutes evidence of originality and authenticity—that is, a theory of authorship. It was also a theory of reading—a theory of how to read such evidence, how to read through the work to its singular, original author. But the author of this theory of artistic authorship was also a figure who played with the authorship of his own theory. Indeed, he would appear to have defied his readers to read the name of the author (that is, his own name) correctly. For Morelli originally attempted to obscure the origins of his theory by concealing his name beneath an alias, a false signature which, nonetheless, also gave away its author's identity. When he first published this work as a German translation of "original" Russian writings (1870s-1880s), he used the name Ivan Lermolieff, which is, if one reads it correctly, a partial anagram of Giovanni Morelli. (Moreover, the name of the "translator" of Lermolieff's writing is Johannes Schwarze—another alias of Morelli, who was fluent in German. This name, as one might expect, is but another play on "Morelli": "Giovanni," "Johannes," "John"; "Morelli"/moro, "Schwarze," "Black".)

Morelli's name, as well as his identity as an author, is thus both veiled and revealed by a succession of signatures that reinscribe, while also appearing to erase, evidence of original authorial activity. Morelli's "translated" work is an original designed to pass itself off as an authentic copy. This copy is a counterfeit whose originality is retroactively authenticated through the revelation of its author's name, which remains attached to, if not also completely obscured by, the name of another. Morelli signs his own name by signing or using the names of others, other names ("Lermolieff," "Schwarze") that both cover and copy his own. In the case of the name Morelli, then, the author of a theory that proposed a method for uncovering the name, the identity, of the original artist signs his work with a name that both displaces and consolidates the place of its own author and origins.

One can read Morelli's name as situated within complex relations of affiliation not only with the other names he would author as substitutes for his own, but also with those of established figures in art history. The Morelli-method, it is said, was proposed (like any new theory or method, perhaps) as an unconventional, revolutionary turn against the conventional theory and practice of his own discipline. Moreover, it appears that Morelli was not unconcerned with the issue of priority or originality within the discipline of art history. It has been suggested that he was so concerned to establish his own originality and authority that he failed to attribute to one or more of his colleagues their rightful authorship of parts of his own "original" theory.

Morelli's theory of artistic authorship was a theory that established his own place as the father, or author, of a new critical practice. It thus challenged the authority of the traditional figures whose places of paternal privilege he usurped, but from which he himself could also be displaced later. Within the history of art history, then, the name Morelli, the name of the father of connoisseurship, has become the name of an equivocal figure of authority. The figure of Morelli thus attaches itself to the images of many other authors, and the name Morelli continues to raise a variety of questions about the attribution of authorship.

Indeed, in Morelli's name one can read not just the literally affiliated figures of his namesake (or vice versa). Morelli also figures as the virtual father of another self-consciously affiliated author whose name as the "father of psychoanalysis" has clearly eclipsed the importance of that of the art historian. I refer, of course, to Freud, who, it turns out, in his well-known reading of Michelangelo's Moses ("The Moses of Michelangelo"), cites directly the name Morelli and the method of attribution from which Morelli's fame was derived. There, Freud draws attention not only to the similarity between Morelli's "method of inquiry" and the "technique of psychoanalysis." He also remarks upon the pseudonymous nature of Morelli's "original" signature and his own pleasure at learning of the Italian master's "concealed" but true identity.

Indeed, in his rereading of Michelangelo's Moses, Freud appears not only to draw openly on Morelli's method; he seems to copy surreptitiously the method for producing his signature as well. First, Freud's method for discerning how the Moses figure's pose should be read rests upon a reading of the insignificant details or clues to its composition. Freud's reading of those details leads back to the scene and psychological state immediately preceding the moment inscribed in the statue's pose to expose Michelangelo's supposedly intended original design. The homologous relation between the "insignificant detail" and an artistic origin (that is, either authorial identity or artistic psychology) in the methods of connoisseurship and psychoanalysis bring the figures of Morelli and Freud into virtual contact with one another. (This contact, as suggested below, may have proved characteristically problematical for the latter).

Given the methodological similarities of the Morelli and Freud methods for reading artistic works, as well as Freud's acknowledgment of Morelli's prior influence, one might be tempted to call this method the Morelli-Freud, or the Freud-Morelli, method. From this perspective, the identification of the method with only the one or the other author (or perhaps even with the two of them as a composite author) might seem an inaccurate attribution of authorship or authority. (In fact, a very suggestive reading of Morelli, Freud, and Sherlock Holmes has juxtaposed their methods as evidence not of singular originality but, rather, of a shared epistemology—as evidence of the emergence of an epistemological paradigm [that of the "conjectural method"] at the end of the nineteenth century.)

The intimate connection between Morelli's and Freud's methods, it has been conjectured, may also explain the homologous relation of their (real or virtual) signatures. For, when originally published in *Imago* in 1914, Freud's essay on Michelangelo appeared as an anonymous—an unsigned—article. Speculation about Freud's desire for anonymity assumes, as one might expect, problems with the idea of authorial filiation. It has been speculated that his pose of anonymity may have merely been imitative of Morelli's "taste for concealed authorship"; or it may have been a filial gesture of "unconscious rivalry with Morelli"; or it could be read as Freud's way of dismantling a "theological conception of art" through which one presumes that the discovery of the author's (that is, the father's) name constitutes accurate, and thus appropriate, access to the identity and meaning of the artistic work.

The explanation of this maneuver itself remains, of course, in the realm of conjecture, along with the answer to a question such as "who is the original or real author?" What one reads in this circulation of authorial names and signatures, as well as from the models of authorship those signatures and names (or their authors and referents) propose, are the alternately revealing and obfuscating effects that the appearance (or disappearance) of the name of the author may have. The name of the author—an apparently significant detail—also becomes a place of insignificance. But it is an insignificance that is nonetheless likely to be invested with a great deal of meaning. Indeed, the name becomes a place where significance and insignificance both meet and compete. In naming the author, as we are aware by now, one is likely to mean a number of things at once.

For example, we are yet pushed to ask, as we return again to *Rayuela,* what did Cortázar mean by the name Morelli? Is Cortázar's Morelli meant to figure the Morelli from art history, or does it refer perhaps to an author or character we have not yet considered (for example, most obviously, Borges's Morell, or Bioy Casares's Morel, or Wells's Moreau, or Poe's Morella, or, more obliquely, Macedonio Fernández; see notes 13, 19)? And, if it is meant to figure the art historian, for example, what, for Cortázar, would have been significant about such a figure? What would its meaning have been for him?

If one aims to discover the significance of this name, one takes up the text's (or the name's) invitation to read the name as meaningful rather than as arbitrary. One discovers that the name opens up a determined field of meanings but that the space of that field and its parameters are, as has been seen here, rather wide. The author's name seems to efface itself behind the names of its substitutes (that is, Morelli and his namesakes), but also seems to keep coming back from around or behind those other names. One discovers that the significance of this name would lie as much in its apparent arbitrariness as in its possible determined meanings. If, on the other hand, one does not presume that the name Morelli has some particular (and perhaps original) significance—that is, if one views the name or the figure of Morelli as insignificant, the name Cortázar becomes a convenient but confounding nominal cover. The name of the author would thus signify an author distanced from original or final meaning. It would appear to figure an author of unfixed significance.

What is significant is that either reading allows one to move from "Cortázar" to "Morelli" (and even to "Freud" and others), and back again, as one attempts to read *Rayuela,* or the names it proposes, properly. The move between the names Morelli and Cortázar appears to be an unavoidable move; each name provokes a shift to the other. The shift from one way of reading their names to another, and therefore from one theory of authorship or reading to another, is critical in reading *Rayuela.* Indeed, reading (or, rather, rereading) *Rayuela* seems to mean precisely that—reading between competing models of reading the figure of the author.

If this reading suggests that Cortázar is, in some way, not the (only) name of the author of *Rayuela,* it is because the author's name may well become a sign of instability, a sign of secondariness and subordination as well as of originality and authority. Such a sense of things would of course run counter to traditional notions about what the name of the author signifies and where it ought to lead in reading literary texts. Moreover, as one reads further around *Rayuela,* the author's name retains its position of instability while also recovering considerable authority. Such a problematical position, which emerges initially from within *Rayuela,* is, interestingly enough, underscored as well by another text that may seem to establish definitively *Rayuela's* authoritative and stable authorial beginnings. I refer to the 1983 *Cuaderno de bitácora de "Rayuela,"* published under the names of both Cortázar and Ana María Barrenechea, one of the author's best-known readers.

The logbook, which contains the author's original plans for his novel, purports to reauthor, in a way, the reading of *Rayuela,* the process of whose authorship by Cortázar the logbook would finally appear to reveal. But, appropriately enough, the juxtaposition of the names Cortázar and Barrenechea situates the two as complementary, if not also competing, author-figures. These figures meet and compete not only on the text's cover and title page, where they are explicitly united, but also throughout the book's pages, where they are implicitly joined in both Barrenechea's introductory study and Cortázar's personal notes. The name of the one may be read as vying with the name of the other for the primary position of authority in the *Cuaderno,* and by extension, perhaps, around *Rayuela.*

Published by Sudamericana exactly twenty years after *Rayuela,* the *Cuaderno de bitácora de "Rayuela"* is a heterogeneous text. [In an endnote, Kerr explains: "The *Cuaderno's* text comprises a reproduction of Cortázar's handwritten and variegated notes, whose originals were personally entrusted to Barrenechea by him and whose copies form the body of the logbook itself. It also contains a set of additional 'pre-textos' ['pre-texts'], which include the novel's originary episode called **'La araña' ['The Spider']** (this episode was elided by the author from the original novel but later published separately in *Revista iberoamericana* [1973]) and other typed manuscript materials and handwritten notes. The materials authored by Cortázar are appended to the original logbook pages, along with a lengthy 'Estudio preliminar' ['Preliminary Study'] composed by Barrenechea. Though the volume's contents would attest to its essentially heterogeneous nature, one reviewer sees the *Cuaderno* as a 'book of criticism' published by Barrenechea. I see the matter of authorial and generic identity as somewhat more problematical."] It combines the variegated writings of both Cortázar and Barrenechea. In introducing Cortázar's notebook pages, Barrenechea also introduces the problem of textual priority and authority, as she reviews, first, the tenets of genetic criticism she seeks to follow and, second, the relationship between Cortázar's notebook and his novel ("Estudio preliminar"). Within that preliminary essay, Barrenechea's introduction of Cortázar's original notebook pages takes a secondary position to the discussion of genetic criticism. This discussion legitimizes in general terms the attention given to "pre-textos" ["pre-texts"] such as Cortázar's logbook; it authorizes, in particular, her undertaking in the publication of the *Cuaderno* and her reading of its originary texts.

Barrenechea's presentation of the logbook grants a place of central importance to Cortázar's preliminary notes and aims to counter other readings that would subordinate the author's original ideas to the text that comes after them. Barrenechea confers upon the logbook an independent status and authority by which its comments are virtually elevated to a status equal to that of the novel that would otherwise supersede them. In the face of the authoritative, completed text that succeeds the originary notes, the "pre-textos" are restored by Barrenechea to their former position of authority. As set up by Barrenechea, the relation between the author's notes and the completed text both undermines and underwrites the privileged status of the one with respect to the other.

Barrenechea's reading of *Rayuela* through the logbook is presented as a rereading of the novel through the notes that reveal both the author's original dialogue with his fictional work and the process of writing and reading through which it was composed. Following Cortázar, Barrenechea proposes to read *Rayuela* as a dialogue between text and pre-texts. Through the reading now authorized by the logbook and the textual organization it allows Barrenechea to author, this dialogue also upends the apparently primary or secondary status of the one set of texts in relation to the other. Moreover, the configuration of the various pre-texts and her discussion of the relationships among them raise related questions of textual priority and privilege. They are questions that Barrenechea's reading seeks to address and that Cortázar, before her, considered. [In an endnote, Kerr states: "The organization of [*Cuaderno de bitácora de 'Rayuela'*] places Barrenechea's own text before that of Cortázar. Her 'Estudio preliminar,' which presents both a preliminary reading of Cortázar's logbook in virtual dialogue with *Rayuela* and a theoretical introduction to her own reading and his logbook texts, comes ahead of the notes first authored by Cortázar. Barrenechea's writing becomes its own 'pre-texto' for the 'pre-textos' that have occasioned her preliminary study, along with the publication of the logbook itself. At the other end, the *Cuaderno* closes with what Barrenechea calls 'otros pre-textos' ['other pre-texts'], the last of which is the originary episode or chapter of *Rayuela* ('La araña'), which is recuperated and once again revealed by Barrenechea, in the fashion of Cortázar, who preceded her. (. . . Cortázar first revealed and simultaneously restored this chapter some ten years after the novel's original publication.) She situates it (appropriately enough, one might argue) at the very end of the 1983 text. Indeed, that the text ends with 'pre-texts' that are themselves finally punctuated by an originary chapter is quite fitting for a volume dealing with *Rayuela,* to whose disruptive textual order its title openly alludes."]

The origins of this book are to be found, it seems, in the writing of not one but (at least) two figures, whose names and work have been tied together for many years. Barrenechea, entrusted with the logbook of which she is made proprietor by its original author and owner, assumes theoretical, as well as editorial, responsibility for Cortázar's writings. The work of one figure becomes the support for the writing of another; the writing of the one becomes the pretext for the work of the other. Each is proprietor of the text to which his or her name is attached. Yet each name, bound to the name of the other, puts into question individual rights of ownership and authority. Such are the relationships that have been made problematical by these authors individually in other texts and, here, together in the *Cuaderno.*

Barrenechea's name has long been connected to that of Cortázar (her readings of *Rayuela* are seminal; she is regarded as one of Cortázar's most important readers). Here in the logbook that connection is literalized in an overt fashion. As noted above, the logbook was published under the virtual signatures of both Cortázar and Barrenechea, under the auspices of the author and one of his most accomplished readers. Barrenechea appears all at once as a reader who edits, a copier who compiles, and a commentator who authors the text of another author.

The responsibilities attached to the different roles assumed by Barrenechea (the roles of a modern *scriptor, editor, compilator,* and *commentator*) combine within the performance of a single figure. They consolidate her authority and situate her as a competitor of Cortázar, the original author, even though she seems to be a secondary figure. Indeed, under the guise of a copier-compiler-commentator-editor, Barrenechea assumes a central, authoritative role in the *Cuaderno.* As she reads she also rewrites and organizes, much like the author she takes as her critical object. As she restores Cortázar's notes, and thus his retroactively recognized original activity, to a privileged position for the reading of *Rayuela,* her own activity seems to become more, rather than less, like that of an author—perhaps like that of a modern *auctor.*

In fact, Barrenechea's name appears on the text as the signature of Cortázar's coauthor, rather than as the signature of an editor or compiler of Cortázar's texts. Her name is virtually signed with the name Cortázar and appears in the place reserved for the name of the primary, and original, author. In the *Cuaderno de bitácora de "Rayuela"* the name of the author thus appears as a doubled or divided name, one that shifts the responsibility of authorship from one to another of the figures to which it would refer. The juxtaposition of names puts the work of the two authors on an apparently equal footing while also seeming to allow for the priority of one (Cortázar) over the other (Barrenechea). The author named by this text, it is tempting to suggest, is a composite figure, a figure designed by the texts of one and another author: Cortázar-Barrenechea or Barrenechea-Cortázar. [In an endnote, Kerr adds: "However, that the name Cortázar has greater value because of its presumed priority may well be declared, as convention would have it, by the book's title (the logbook named there is of course the text originally composed and owned by Cortázar) and the ordering of names on its title page. But within the text edited and authored by Barrenechea, this order and privilege are also reversed: Barrenechea's texts occupy approximately the first and Cortázar's the second half of its pages; and the index, which separates the names of the authors by placing each one over the list of texts attributed to him or her, literally exposes the division of authorship by textually distancing each name from the other."]

These names, and the figures they conjure up, are in one sense clearly distinguishable. The name of the author and the name of the critic refer to distinct subjects and discursive situations, and to different moments of signature. But in the publication of the *Cuaderno* and the reading produced by Barrenechea, who moves back and forth among Cortázar's texts as well as between her own comments and his writing, these names also come to identify the writing of the one with that of the other. Barrenechea, a formidable critic and trusted friend of the empirical author, inscribes her own critical presence within the texts of Cortázar. His writing is not only reshaped by her readings but also reorganized by her editing. The relation between their names suggests the uncertain state of authorship throughout the *Cuaderno de bitácora de "Rayuela."* As in the novel whose origins the *Cuaderno* purports to establish authoritatively and whose authorship it would doubly certify, the name of the author can be read here as a destabilizing sign rather than as an absolute marker of authorial singularity, priority, or originality.

In rereading *Rayuela* through the *Cuaderno* then, one may place the author's name in a position that would allow for the attribution of the text's ownership either to its original author or to one of its readers. (The latter move is, as we recall, apparently proposed by the tablero.) However, the idea of unequivocal authority over or ownership of the text is also precisely what the activities of Cortázar's renowned critical reader attenuate. The author's name, which here shifts between naming the authorial subject at the moment of writing and identifying the texts to which that name has become attached and through which its meaning is partially established, is reauthored as well as reread by Barrenechea.

That Cortázar is a name of distinction his writing and Barrenechea's readings would confirm; that this name is the name of the author of *Rayuela* the text's authorial signature would underscore. But, that this name is the single name that authorizes *Rayuela* or one's reading of it, or that this name is the only name that creates a place for the author, is open to question. Indeed, our wandering to the figure of Barrenechea, whose name circulates with that of Cortázar around the text of *Rayuela* would situate the name of the author in an unstable position. And the leap to the name Morelli (and from "Morelli" to "Freud," and back again to "Cortázar") would position the author's name so that it would be as ready to defend its authoritative place as to surrender that place to the authority of another author.

Such wanderings and leaps seem to mobilize each name, each place, of the author. Yet, this mobilization of the authorial proper name, and consequently the destabilization of the place given to the author, also reinvest such a name and such a place with considerable authority. The chain of names that leads away from Cortázar, and for which *Rayuela* unwittingly opens the way, also returns the author's name to a place of privilege. The shift from one name to the other may well intensify rather than attenuate the authority of such a name. The sharing of names of the author confers upon each of the author's figures a status that in one sense or another is both authoritative and authorial. As one reads, or reads around, *Rayuela,* then, the figure of the author seems to reclaim (if not retain) its own privilege under the names of a number of authors.

When one reads this text as originating with the writing of an authorial subject named Cortázar, or considers its connections to the work of a fictional author-figure named Morelli or his possible namesakes, or reads it as tied to the activities of a critic named Barrenechea, one is led around *Rayuela* and the questions it raises about the author's identity and activity. Such questions concern the meaning of the author's name or the nature of authorial rights and responsibilities, how authorial figures become endowed with authority, or how texts come to be read as authoritative, and so on. These are questions familiar and foreign to both modern criticism and to Spanish American fiction, where they continue to be debated rather than settled.

# FURTHER READING

## Bibliography

Francescato, Martha Paley. "Bibliography of Works by and about Julio Cortázar." In *The Final Island: The Fiction of Julio Cortázar,* edited by Jaime Alazraki and Ivar Ivask, pp. 171-99. Norman: University of Oklahoma Press, 1978.

Chronological listing of works by and about Cortázar.

## Criticism

Amaral, José Vázquez. "Julio Cortázar's *Hopscotch* and Argentinian Spiritual Alienation." In *The Contemporary Latin American Narrative,* pp. 157-65. New York: Las Americas Publishing Co., 1970.

Compares *Hopscotch* to James Joyce's *Ulysses* and argues that themes of failure and national tragedy are at the heart of Cortázar's novel.

Boldy, Steven. "*Rayuela.*" In *The Novels of Julio Cortázar,* pp. 30-96. Cambridge, England: Cambridge University Press, 1980.

Analyzes the major themes in *Hopscotch.* Boldy considers the significance of Paris and Buenos Aires, addresses the doppelganger theme, explores relationships between key characters, and considers the novel's ambiguous ending.

Brotherston, Gordon. "Intellectual Geography: Julio Cortázar." In *The Emergence of the Latin American Novel,* pp. 81-97. Cambridge, England: Cambridge University Press, 1977.

Focuses his discussion on the character Oliveira and the theme of identity in *Hopscotch.* Brotherston claims that "*Hopscotch* eclipses all Cortázar had written before it; . . . [and] stands as a point of reference for what has come afterwards."

Garfield, Evelyn Picon. "*Rayuela (Hopscotch).*" In *Julio Cortázar,* pp. 90-115. New York: Frederick Ungar Publishing Co., 1975.

Thematic and stylistic overview of *Hopscotch.*

Safir, Margery A. "An Erotics of Liberation: Notes on Transgressive Behavior in *Hopscotch* and *Libro de Manuel.*" In *The Final Island: The Fiction of Julio Cortázar,* edited by Jaime Alazraki and Ivar Ivask, pp. 84-96. Norman: University of Oklahoma Press, 1978.

Considers the theme of redemption through erotic transgression in *Hopscotch,* focusing on Oliveira's sexual encounter with Emmanuèle in Chapter 36.

Yurkievich, Saúl. "Eros ludens: Games, Love and Humor in *Hopscotch.*" In *The Final Island: The Fiction of Julio Cortázar,* edited by Jaime Alazraki and Ivar Ivask, pp. 97-108. Norman: University of Oklahoma Press, 1978.

Argues that themes of play, love, and humor in *Hopscotch* are liberating elements that counter the constraints of Western civilization.

Zamora, Lois Parkinson. "Art and Revolution in the Fiction of Julio Cortázar." In *Writing the Apocalypse: Historical Vision in Contemporary U.S. and Latin American Fiction,* pp. 76-96.

Comments briefly on *Hopscotch,* arguing that the novel is Cortázar's attempt to transcend the "boundaries of narrative genres and conventions."

## Interviews

Weiss, Jason. "The Art of Fiction LXXXIII: Julio Cortázar." *The Paris Review* 26, No. 93 (Fall 1984): 173-91.

Comments on the writing of *Hopscotch.*

Wolfowicz, Eugenia. "Julio Cortázar: A Conversation." *Antaeus* 60 (Spring 1988): 243-51.

Remarks briefly on the autobiographical elements of *Hopscotch.*

---

Additional coverage of Cortázar's life and career is contained in the following sources published by Gale Research: *Contemporary Authors,* Vols. 21-24 (rev. ed.); *Contemporary Authors New Revision Series,* Vols. 12, 32; *Contemporary Literary Criticism,* Vols. 2, 3, 5, 10, 13, 15, 33, 34; *Dictionary of Literary Biography,* Vol. 113; *DISCovering Authors Modules; Hispanic Literature Criticism,* Vol. 1; *Hispanic Writers; Major 20th-Century Writers;* and *Short Story Criticism,* Vol. 7.

# James Gould Cozzens

## 1903-1978

American novelist and short story writer.

The following entry presents an overview of Cozzens's career. For further information on his life and works, see *CLC*, Volumes 1, 4, and 11.

## INTRODUCTION

Cozzens is best known for insightful tales about the more or less privileged lives led by White Anglo-Saxon Protestant American professional men. Philosophical in approach, Cozzens's novels utilize little action but explore a wide range of ideas, including love, duty, and the law. Cozzens eschewed the modernist literary trends of his time, deliberately employing unfamiliar, archaic words, traditional literary structures, and moralistic Puritan themes; these choices caused many critics to regard his work as old-fashioned.

### Biographical Information

Cozzens was born in Chicago, Illinois, and grew up on Staten Island, New York. His father was a businessman whose ancestors include the Civil War-era governor of Rhode Island. His mother's family consisted of aristocratic Connecticut royalists who moved to Nova Scotia during the American revolt. Raised in an upper-class environment, Cozzens was educated at the Kent Academy Episcopal prep school and at Harvard University, which he left after his Sophomore year and the successful publication of his first novel *Confusion* (1924). While living in Canada he completed the historical romance, *Michael Scarlett* (1925), then taught school in Cuba and tutored in Europe. Following his marriage to Sylvia Bernice Baumgarten, he and his wife settled in Lambertville, New Jersey, where he wrote the remainder of his books and short stories. Although Cozzens initially received favorable critical acclaim for his writings and the Pulitzer prize for *Guard of Honor* in 1948, the literary community and reading public largely neglected his works.

### Major Works

Cozzens's novels—such as *Men and Brethren* (1936), *The Just and the Unjust* (1942), *Guard of Honor* (1948), and *By Love Possessed* (1957)—explore the moral conduct and self-disciplined lives of professional people, and span no more than a few days. Cozzens's central characters are almost always respected professionals, such as Dr. George Bull in *The Last Adam* (1933); Ernest Cudlipp, the Episcopal priest in *Men and Brethren*; Major General Beal, the commanding officer of a Florida military base in *Guard of Honor*; Abner Coates, the assistant district attorney in *The Just and the Unjust*; and Arthur Winner, the town lawyer in *By Love Possessed*. Typical of Cozzens's style is the

philosophical analysis of his protagonist's motivations. For example, the complexities of love and the tragedy of despair are explored in *Confusion,* in which Cerise D'Atree falls in love with Blair Broughton who dies in a car crash. That a doctor's medical responsibilities will ultimately guide his thoughts and actions is pivotal to the plot of *The Last Adam,* in which Dr. Bull works to curb a typhoid epidemic. In *By Love Possessed* Cozzens returns to the themes of love, passion, and reason in a story that follows a lawyer as he prepares to defend a young man falsely accused of rape. The story also explores the attorney's struggle with personal relationships and love. Law and its limitations, on the other hand, are the focus of *The Just and the Unjust,* in which the ideals of democratic justice are manipulated by the personal and social concerns of the people involved in a murder trial. In *Guard of Honor* duty and integrity are the principle elements examined in a story about a Major General who achieves an overseas command with the help of his friends and his unswerving dedication to the military.

### Critical Reception

Most critics readily acknowledge Cozzens's structural

clarity, facility with language, and his ability to create well-defined plots and characters. They also note the thoroughness of his research on such subjects as the law for *The Just and the Unjust* and Elizabethan history for *Michael Scarlett*. Some, however, fault his writing style as old-fashioned and aloof, citing, for example, his traditional approach to narrative, at times pompous vocabulary, conservative ideology, and a focus on wealthy professionals that appears elitist. Furthermore, a few commentators characterize his works as too philosophical and self-indulgent in their presentation of themes, suggesting that Cozzens's characters exist primarily to express his own views. Some also identify anti-semitic and racially biased themes in such works as *By Love Possessed*. Still, Cozzens's works continue to provoke admiration and controversy among critics.

## PRINCIPAL WORKS

*Confusion*  (novel)  1924
*Michael Scarlett: A History*  (novel)  1925
*Cock Pit*  (novel)  1928
*The Son of Perdition*  (novel)  1929
*S. S. San Pedro*  (novel)  1931
*The Last Adam*  (novel)  1933
*Castaway*  (novel)  1934
*Men and Brethren*  (novel)  1936
*Ask Me Tomorrow*  (novel)  1940
*The Just and the Unjust*  (novel)  1942
*Guard of Honor*  (novel)  1948
*By Love Possessed*  (novel)  1957
*Children and Others*  (short stories)  1964
*Morning Noon and Night*  (novel)  1968
*A Flower in Her Hair*  (novel)  1974
*A Rope for Dr. Webster*  (novel)  1976
*\*Just Representations: A James Gould Cozzens Reader*  (fiction and nonfiction)  1978
*†Selected Notebooks: 1960-1967*  (memoirs)  1984

*This work contains the novel *Ask Me Tomorrow*, excerpts from six other novels, short stories, essays, letters, reviews, and critical essays on Cozzens's work.

†This work was edited by Matthew J. Bruccoli.

## CRITICISM

### George J. Becker  (review date June 1949)

SOURCE: "Men at War," in *Commentary*, Vol. 7, No. 6, June, 1949, pp. 608-09.

[*Becker is an educator and author whose books include* Paris and the Arts, 1851-1896 *(1971) and* Master European Realists of the Nineteenth Century *(1982). In the following review of* Guard of Honor, *he contends that while*

*the military detail is authentic, the plot is weak and lacks objectivity and balance in its view of military life.*]

The slice of life or the cross-section has been used by novelists to give a balanced and objective view of a world too often subject to distortion because of faulty vision or special pleading. James Gould Cozzens, in his Pulitzer Prize novel, [**Guard of Honor**], uses the technique with skill and urbanity. Yet his very success brings the value of the device into question.

For millions of us, civilian as well as military combatants, the most abiding memory of the late war is of the gigantic and often apparently chaotic organizations of which we were a part. As sprawling army bases and posts rose in brick and concrete almost overnight, teapot tempests and departmental intrigues and jealousies loomed larger on the immediate horizon than the landing on Okinawa or the crossing of the Rhine. Conduct of the war, like that of any enterprise, depended on the nature and interplay of personalities. A fumbler in uniform was a fumbler still, raised even to a higher power.

What Mr. Cozzens gives us is the shock and pleasure of recognition. A score or more of representative people at a great army air base at Ocanara, Florida, live through forty-eight hours and 631 pages of a purely local crisis. For a time it is in question whether Major General Beal, commander of the base, will display the powers of judgment and stability to enable him in an administrative position to continue the rapid rise he has made as a "flying general." If it is less by intelligence than by his ability to inspire the intelligent devotion of others that he does come through, still there is the comforting assurance that the war is in good hands and men of good will do prosper.

It is both idle and ungrateful to ask that an author have written another novel than he did. Yet the careful lack of focus, the persistent effort to avoid an issue, the deliberate reaching out to obvious and trivial episodes in the lives of the characters, becomes here a fundamental flaw, negating the very literary skill that is everywhere apparent. This group of human beings is intrinsically no more interesting than any other similarly complex group, nor is the Ocanara air base shown to be any different in its essentials from a department store, or a labor union, or a metropolitan hospital, to choose at random from popular subjects of the cross-section technique. Indeed, except for the possible novelty of the military scene, there is nothing new here. On the evidence submitted by Mr. Cozzens, there is no reason to think that the war behind the lines is especially interesting or worth writing about.

Actually he starts a number of hares in the form of serious themes, any one of which would have provided an adequate focus for his book. In Benny Carricker and in General Beal, for example, we have tantalizing glimpses of the new man who has added the air to his dimensions. Benny, though not fully drawn, is convincing in his insouciant insubordination and pungent speech. Beal taking to the air while others resolve his problems for him is also memorable. He raises also the question of what kind of leadership a war demands, but though we are told at the end that Beal's qualities are more indispensable than those of Jo-Jo

Nichols, the Jove-like Deputy Chief of Air Staff, we never get at his essence.

The crisis in Cozzens' book deals with Jim Crowism at the base and in the community at large. Several characters exist only to exacerbate the tension by trying to see that justice is done. A nice sense of irony is displayed in some of the central scenes. But then, as personal crises are resolved, the social problem recedes, and it becomes clear that it is only a piquant element, not the real focus of Cozzens' concern.

Thus there is both too much and too little. There is a wealth of authentic detail, but the whole is a blur, a huge Delacroix canvas that becomes a little tiresome, no matter how engaging the parts. In short, the cross-section seems played out in serious writing except as an elementary device for readers who cannot keep their eyes on a complex object. What is needed is a more intensive application of the qualities of objectivity and balanced selection to a smaller segment of experience. Where an author has found value and meaning he should make it possible for the reader to disengage them. And where they do not exist, that itself is a meaning which needs to be brought into focus.

## Martin Price   (review date Autumn 1957)

SOURCE: "In the Fielding Country: Some Recent Fiction," in *Yale Review,* Vol. XLVII, No. 7, Autumn, 1957, pp. 143-56.

[*Price is an educator and author whose books include* The Restoration and the Eighteenth Century *(1973) and* Forms of Life: Character and Moral Imagination in the Novel *(1983). In the excerpt below, he praises* By Love Possessed *for its literary complexity and thorough presentation of the law, but faults the novel for its "tidy" picture of life and the insufficient development of the main character.*]

In its length, in its mannerisms, in its carefully "researched" presentation of a small town law firm, [*By Love Possessed*] bespeaks a long stretch of hard work. Its love of the machinery of the law or the Church recalls the work of Sinclair Lewis. And such speeches as Julius Penrose's sound like those Lewis was reported to deliver at bars while he was in the process of composing them. But Mr. Cozzens, unlike Lewis, retreats from comedy; in fact, the possibility of a comic view hangs like a threat over his hero, Arthur Winner. Mr. Cozzens allows himself a degree of contrivance in plot, particularly in his compressed time scheme (all takes place within forty-nine hours), and in the symbol of the clock with which the book opens and closes. But the contrivance is never allowed to register the novelist's detachment nor his control of his material. We are kept unremittingly within the point of view of Winner; we are expected to think with him even when the plot hints more than he sees. So that the book has a kind of drag in its point of view: neither the nimbleness nor the depth of Winner's awareness is sufficient to hold us, yet we have no novelist's presence to supply this deficiency, as Henry Fielding's does Tom Jones's. It is, perhaps, foolish to complain that Mr. Cozzens did not write a comic novel; yet his theme and situation all but command this.

> *By Love Possessed* binds together the powers of love and of time, of the mutable and uncontrollable, as against the rational and unchanging.
>
> —*Martin Price*

The clock which strikes three one afternoon and four two days later is one of the pieces collected by Arthur Winner's father, one of the adornments of the life of a skeptical Man of Reason. It shows a shepherd spying upon a nymph; surmounting them is an archer Cupid, and the motto reads "Omnia vincit amor." The book binds together the powers of love and of time, of the mutable and uncontrollable, as against the rational and unchanging. And all of the characters are revealed as actors in the comedy (one cannot resist the term) of mutability: the spectrum of love ranges from the savage coupling of an adulterous couple on a bare mattress in an empty room to the professed love of God. At every point it is love which undermines the stable edifices, the tenets of the law, the structure of personal loyalties, the gracious decorum of a good life. In the course of almost six hundred pages Mr. Cozzens builds a town, its leading citizens, their retainers and clients, their wives and children, their clubs and houses. When the callow brother of his secretary is charged with rape, Winner encounters the void of senselessness that haunts him through the novel. His interview with Ralph, performed with pained professional competence, shows Winner in beautiful control, able to penetrate evasions and delusions, confident of reaching truth, however saddening. The scene, in its solemn precision of anatomical detail, verges on *tour de force,* but it has considerable power; and it is to be set beside its counterpart later in the novel where Winner encounters the evangelical Mrs. Pratt with much less assurance. Except for these scenes, the book can hardly be said to have much dramatic force. The characters tend to talk interminably, as eager to reveal themselves in their fullness as the dead whom Dante questions. The speech is often authentic (although Mr. Cozzens is something of a ventriloquist) and it serves the valuable end of giving depth to the town and its society, and through them, to the central themes of the book. But, since Mr. Cozzens' gift is so little dramatic or pictorial, the book remains an endless translation of event into concept, of experience into meditation. And the thought is neither fresh nor rigorous enough to keep the book alive. One would cheerfully surrender all the Faulknerian parentheses Mr. Cozzens affects for the verve of Shavian debate; for this is primarily a novel of ideas, where images tend to become illustrations and characters consort like premises in a syllogism. The problem of time and change, for example, is developed through the Revere family, all descendants from an original Negro servant, with a line of succession to authority and a firmly preserved standard of diligence and skill. Or again through the antiquarian interests of Judge Lowe and others, the preservation of old houses and old names, the planting and cultivation of a pattern of dignity and order. Against these are set the changes of social status, the Revere boy who is no longer to be a servant, the Irish Catholic politician who may become a judge, the gardens that have gone back to wildness. All of this might have made for a rich and subtle pattern if only the statues could dance; at best they have amplifiers hidden within them and seem to speak, occasionally to orate.

There are troubling questions left by the book. Winner's last hour is largely given to noble platitude ("victory is in making do with uncertainties, in supporting mysteries"). The stable world has been inspected and exposed, but never quite assessed. Is it a world well lost, a world to be defended, or simply a world that can't work? Does Winner come to some expansive wisdom or to a drier practicality? Are the attitudes of the Winners and the Tuttles modified, transformed, simply displaced? There is neither the purgation of laughter nor the force of renewed life. For a novel which is pretentiously inlaid with countless allusions, which invokes such names as Pascal and Spinoza, which has tried for great internal complexity and intimations of universal truths, the hero's insight is late in coming and is hardly sufficient. One wishes that Mr. Cozzens had been able to impart more of the generous untidiness of life to his book or to impose more of the economy and wit of comic form. More or less art might have made the ambition less obvious and the work more impressive.

## Benjamin De Mott (essay date Winter 1957)

SOURCE: "Cozzens and Others," in *The Hudson Review,* Vol. 10, No. 4, Winter, 1957, pp. 620-26.

[*De Mott is an educator and novelist whose books include* The Body's Cage *(1959) and* A Married Man *(1968). In the excerpt, below, he faults Cozzens's novels for their overemphasis on professionalism and duty, their conventional plots, and a disregard for character development.*]

. . . Cozzens is capable on occasion of making his reader feel perceptive, aware of the difference between fantasy and fact and interested in their relationships, experienced enough to know that there is not so much elegance and order in life that anyone will be harmed by another glance at either, nor so little drabness and chaos as to permit the easy adoption of what is called A Balanced View. One knows quite well (despite the gassy paeans of the first reviews) that [*By Love Possessed*] is no masterpiece—Cozzens is not a major writer, however considerable he looks when compared with the common herd. He excites the senses with no new way of seeing and speaking, discovers no lost continents; both his range of feeling and his power of reflection are limited; as an observer and as a dramatist he is, as a rule, only deft. Moreover, though we learn from him something important about ourselves, we learn it not from a single book—not even from *By Love Possessed*—but rather from the shape of the career that this book has brought to a momentary climax. But to repeat, he can almost always be read without a suspension of common intelligence, and to say this is to say a good deal.

If the sense in which the new book gives point to Cozzens's career is to be specified, some sort of account—it can only

be brief—will have to be provided of the earlier novels. Probably the central observation to be made about these books (I exclude the juvenilia of course) is that all were marked by concern with professional competence in the workaday world. (*Ask Me Tomorrow* might be an exception, but for reasons that cannot be gone into here, I do not think it is.) Hemingway's professional knew bulls or fish, guns or wines—having taught himself; Cozzens's professional knew torts or bacteria, Latin syntax or the Gospel According to St. Matthew—having been to graduate school. On occasion Cozzens ventured outside the office: he was on the sea in *S. S. San Pedro* (1931) and in the air in *Guard of Honor* (1948). But neither of these regions was created as the habitation of romance or of heroism: the ship, like the law library, was to be taken as an instance of the always precarious triumph of a disciplined order of operations over the usually unmanageable chaos of nature. Watching his senior officers direct a freight loading, the Spanish first quartermaster of the *San Pedro* was moved to reflect on the degree to which the sight was all expressible as *tela*—a word of wide enough meaning to include not only the "Spanish sense of tone, texture, woven firmness," but also "the untranslatable value of a plan," and "that beautiful gift of the white man, the disciplined cooperation, speed, precision of people quick and certain about their duties." The abstraction thus defined was, for this officer, "the last perfect pleasure," and over the years Cozzens's responsiveness to it never lacked for critical notice.

> Cozzens is not a major writer, however considerable he looks when compared with the common herd. He excites the senses with no new way of seeing and speaking, discovers no lost continents; both his range of feeling and his power of reflection are limited; as an observer and as a dramatist he is, as a rule, only deft.
>
> —*Benjamin De Mott*

What this responsiveness signified, though, was difficult to say; while it was shared by many writers, old and new, it was shared with differences. Usually when the novel imparted information about trades—whether the pickpocket's or the stonemason's or the hackwriter's—it did so with a pretense of disinterest; Cozzens's fiction dropped the pretense. The author of *The Just and the Unjust* hardly bothered to disguise the truth that he cared more about the workings of the law than about the fate of the priggish Abner Coates and his girl; in book after book he interrupted his often quite conventional story with accounts of the innards of high callings and low—details of medicine, of church government, military organization, even of building construction—and always the preference was for the operation rather than for the operator. One tended to think of the accounts of technical proficiency as part of the writer's effort to contend against the modern consciousness that the triumphs of the organizing mind—or of Civilization—were unworthy of serious respect. But to accept this as their rationale required one to discount the fact that Cozzens's attitudes toward the particular modes of civilization he described were something less than positive.

Something far less, as it appeared on close inspection. Cozzens never dealt with the best artificers or with the best artifice—always with a bumbling lawyer who graduated at the bottom of his class, with a tumbledown eighteenth century mansion rather than with one that had been well preserved. Equally important, his novels all possessed the same ironic, somehow self-lacerating narrative design. The quartermaster of the *San Pedro* who gazed admiringly at his seniors did not know that his Captain was dying, that on this trip the ship would be mismanaged, that a debacle would result. In *The Last Adam* the well-equipped physician had a ten percent bile solution ready in the lab to do a blood culture, yet failed to recognize *bacillus typhosus;* men died as a consequence. The efficiency of the man of God in *Men and Brethren* cost him his health; he would step aside for a poorer administrator. The dull attorneys of *The Just and the Unjust* had a clear case and argued it doggedly, respecting the relevant points of law—but the case was lost. It seemed, in short, that Cozzens always had less than the full courage of his affections; wary of being caught out too baldly in the posture of a partisan of Order and Civilization, he everywhere indulged in self-protective irony which, though it hedged his bets, also obscured his meaning.

The irony is still present in *By Love Possessed,* and the narrative pattern is the pattern as before. The standards of a profession (finally of far more than a profession) are again set up for us to admire as a systematic ordering of experience; and again our discovery is that this system cannot hold anything fast, is, like any discipline, incommensurate to the roiling common chance of life. But this book advances beyond its own ironies. In its pages Cozzens gives as much to order, to style, to artifice, to made systems, made forms, as one suspects he has always, furtively, wanted to give. The first sentences of the book give us a key to the writer's new disposition of mind:

> Love conquers all—*omnia vincit amor,* said the gold scroll in a curve beneath the dial of the old French gilt clock. To the dial's right, a nymph, her head on her arm, drowsed, largely undraped, at the mouth of a gold grotto where perhaps she lived. To the dial's left, a youth, by his crook and the pair of lambs with him, a shepherd, had taken cover. Parting fronds of gold vegetation, he peeped at the sleeping beauty. On top of the dial, and all unnoticed by the youth, a smiling cupid perched, bow bent, about to loose an arrow at the peeper's heart. While Arthur Winner viewed with faint familiar amusement this romantic grouping, so graceful and so absurd, the clock struck three.

Had Cozzens ever written so before? On occasion (gold has been a favorite word of his from the beginning), but whatever the occasion one could be certain that a descent into flaccidity or looseness ("He was driving his new red

convertible, a flashy job") would come quickly. From the note struck here, though, there is not much lapsing. And the firmness of the writing is only an outward sign of the more general elevation of his matter, and intensification of his commitment, that Cozzens achieves throughout the book. This is not, to take a trivial example, the first clock in a Cozzens novel: there was a timepiece on the *San Pedro* whose "magnificence testified to the rightness of the world;" the D. A. in *The Just and the Unjust,* at a moment when his case was going well, relaxed to remark about an old clock he bought at auction: "I like clocks. If I had some money, I'd collect them." And whatever else we know about clocks, we know that they are an obvious enough symbol of the orderly structuring of experience. But the symbol is treated far more positively, and reverberates rather more interestingly, in Arthur Winner's ironic rumination than before. This clock is neither mere vulgarity nor mere mechanism, it suggests where its rules do not apply, and is, in addition, valuable, precise, the best in its kind.

In the latter respect it is like all the appurtenances of order in the book. Houses and public buildings are stately and solid—appreciated at one level for triple courses of brick and double cross-braced joists, at another for excellence of design. Where in earlier novels Cozzens was steadfastly unimpressed, sometimes even embarrassed, by the Chippendale pieces, the buildings of the Federal style, or the sayings of the Greeks that surprisingly turned up on his page, here he is always appreciative of the well made thing. He quite unashamedly lets us know of his approval of Shakespeare and of carillons, of winged gates with urn-tipped finials, sycamore drives, wild gardens of columbine and fringed gentians, music boxes of burled walnut, and the like. And his men of order are significantly improved by their association with these admirable contrivances. The lawyers and judges are no second raters, the hero has a strong sense of the fragility of the order his outer life represents but he is nevertheless a person distinguished in intelligence and feeling, a fair match for any shyster down from the city.

As already indicated, the sense of the fragility of order is the correct sense for this hero to have. Arthur Winner's aged partner turns out an embezzler, his own effort to isolate and control an outbreak of meaningless sensuality in lives that impinge on his own wholly fails. But the failure matters less than does the writer's accomplishment in working up, with an accumulating density of detail, a situation in which it is possible for the reader not only to perceive but to care about the difference between order and its opposite. In the earlier books senselessness—seen variously here as the murder trial of a farmer's idiot daughter, the life of a grimly respectable boarding house, the mean encounter of a pimply adolescent with a roadhouse slut in the back seat of a car—rarely seemed more drab than that which contended against it. (The difference between the criminals of *The Just and the Unjust* and their accusers was unimpressive, though the writer had no Dostoevskian moral to make.) What else could one expect when institutions and orders were studied at a level at which they were not seen to their own best advantage, where clumsiness only coped with clumsiness? To dramatize the distinction he cared about, Cozzens had, as it were, to forget his inhibitions, and that is what he has done in this new book. In at least one brilliant scene—a moment of well-executed legal interrogation—he has shown his reader that professional competence, whatever its ultimate failings, can locate the difference between itself and the world, can probe the rotten body of life and return with a truth.

How important is it that we know of this possibility? Well, the knowledge might check our paralysis of mind a little—that claim could be made for it. Ironists all, we surely intend to go on scorning our professional, order-making selves, mocking their claims of victory on this or that trivial field of battle; but it does us no harm to hear that in spite of ourselves we do recover certain truths as we labor, that at the worst we do return from professional frays undeceived. It may not even harm us to think for a spell that our best selves are our professional selves, cold as the thought is to contemplation. The point, I submit, is that this *is* a thought, at least when felt as fully as Cozzens makes it felt in the best moment in his book; that its force is negative does not invalidate it as criticism of representative contemporary character.

Approaching the moment of evaluation we think of course of a hundred reservations. As the size of Cozzens's audience would attest, there is more than a little lubriciousness in the recounting of the triumphs of the disorderly flesh. *L'esprit est toujours la dupe coeur*—well and good—400,000 copies. Also: to set up his distinctions as clearly as he has done, Cozzens has been forced into a kind of humorless social fantasy; the level of life he creates, extending out beyond isolated drives into a village, a club, a courthouse, is in 1957 a pure invention. Worse yet, the change in Cozzens's conception of his social world may owe as much to the reemergence between 1940 and the present of a vulgar plenty, as to any fundamental redefinition of his concerns on the part of the novelist. And finally one has to admit that, if *By Love Possessed* is an elegant, close-textured piece of writing throughout, it is also overlong and underdramatized. But judiciousness is, after all, a niggling virtue. The book deserves praise as a local success at the difficult task of elevating contemporary experience to the point at which it becomes interesting; it stands as a rare opportunity—rarer by far than even the most omni- of omnibus reviews can indicate—for the reader to lift himself briefly out of the sloughs of self-contempt into which the next new American novel he confronts will undoubtedly be determined to plunge him.

**Richard G. Stern**   (review date Winter 1958)

SOURCE: "A Perverse Fiction," in *The Kenyon Review,* Vol. XX, No. 1, Winter, 1958, pp. 140-44.

[*Stern is an educator, critic, novelist, and short story writer whose books include* Golk *(1960) and* Collected Stories *(1988). In the following unfavorable review of* By Love Possessed, *Stern faults the novel's structure, literary style, and character development.*]

The form of James Cozzens' latest novel is that of *The Ambassadors:* the book is organized around a central consciousness, an intelligent, middle-aged man who partici-

pates more or less directly in actions the evaluation of which leads to revaluation of his own experience and principles. A fine pattern for a novel, and one which Cozzens has successfully followed—though not so strictly—in *Men and Brethren* (1936), *Ask Me Tomorrow* (1940), and *The Just and the Unjust* (1942). Unfortunately, the structural principle of *By Love Possessed* is seriously flawed, and its materials are shoddy. The central intelligence, Arthur Winner Jr., the well-to-do lawyer who appraised the events and characters of the Delaware Valley town, Brocton, is sniped at throughout the book, but so inconsistently and arbitrarily that the values which are to be reappraised at the end have never been given a sensible presentation.

> Arthur Winner Junior—confusion in the moonlight; dismay among the roses! —was obliged to conceal as well as he could a crisis about which his single shamed consolation was that Hope [his first wife], anything but knowing, would never know what happened.

The interpolated mockery is so isolated in context that it seems as much mistaken intrusion as genuine qualifier. The real qualifying is done by the opposition of the two final clauses, and these, in all their contrived complexity, are the thoughts of Winner himself. Such thoughts seem to constitute what makes for right reason in this novel because nothing better is ever supplied.

Except at the very end. There, Winner's law partner, Julius Penrose, displaces him as the central intelligence, sits him down and teaches him what life is really about, what the true significance of the discoveries he has been making is, and what he should do about them. The structure of the book topples. As Winner staggers home through the streets of "Brocton, my Brocton!" the bitter sophistication ringing in his ears, the reader too is staggering in the realization that he has been led astray, and for over five hundred pages. The analyses of the events and characters Winner has supplied are all suspect. The effect of this conclusion may be gauged if we venture to substitute a similar *deus ex machina* for Maria Gostrey during the last scene of *The Ambassador.* Thus: Strether enters, full of the slowly-accumulated wisdom whose acquisition the book has charted, opens his mouth to speak, is sat down by the god and told, "Strether, dear boy, you have been beautifully, sublimely wrong from first to last. Let me sketch in the fine view for you." Such an ending reduces Winner's education to the level of a sweepstakes' winning, a sudden triumph which blots out the past. The Jamesian structure has been used—I think consciously—as a trick, a pointless trick, the result of which is a deformity of the sort that the author of the treatise On the Sublime says is due to "a single cause, that pursuit of novelty in the expression of ideas which may be regarded as the fashionable craze of the day."

Works of art frequently survive even serious structural flaws. *By Love Possessed* would not survive even if its overall make-up were as perfect as that of its model. And this is surprising, for Cozzens here attempts what he has done with great success ever since the two Cuban novels which he excludes from his canon, the panoramic presentation. Nearly a quarter of a century ago, in *The Last*

*Adam,* Cozzens had learned how to exhibit a town's crisis through a number of individual ones. Meanwhile, he had made a far more complex presentation in *Guard of Honor* (1948): there, two leading story lines, that of Ross and Beal, and that of Hicks, cut a swathe through a large number of individual careers and a number of important general crises in a manner reminiscent of Tolstoi. Although the burden of coincidence was a bit heavy, the total effect was one of spareness, the brilliant administration of a complex action. The panorama was incidental to the action, not close to its heart as is the case in *By Love Possessed,* where the urge to exhibit the scene seems to be nearly as strong as the urge to exhibit Winner's appraisal of it. Consequently, the expository devices are embarrassingly awkward and obtrusive; the list Winner's mother makes out at the beginning of the book which includes the names of many of the characters as in a *dramatis personae,* and which is gone over in detail by Winner; the frequent flashbacks which spring up at the sight of a plaque or a character and often go on for pages irrelevant to an action but not to sheer panorama, or to a Sherwood Anderson-like desire to write up the careers of all the characters as if this were what the novel were about. The clumsiness extends to the use of information one character gives another who must certainly have known it already: so Winner's second wife informs him that she used to run a girl's camp. (He has known her all her life and been married to her for some years. And there is no point in his not having known this fact. In novels, a wife, or husband, exists in no small part as a repository of all but the "to-be-treated" parts of the partner's past.) The story lines of this novel are largely replaced by the panoramic fill-in, elaborate detail, and by that most notorious feature of pretentious fictions, talk.

Cozzens has always had an eye peeled for the philosophic wiseacre, and he has usually been careful to separate his own reflective heroes from their burlesque counterparts by having the former denounce or make fun of the latter. So Ellery ridicules McKellar in *Ask Me Tomorrow,* Coates turns on Harry Wurts in *The Just and the Unjust,* and even Colonel Ross remembers Judge Schlicter's lapses into "discourse—no homelier word described it." Now, however, although the burlesque counterpart is present in the Roman Catholic proselytizer, Mrs. Pratt—"Ecstatic, she twittered: yes-yes; and mountains prepared themselves to be moved"—, her style is almost indistinguishable from that of Winner, Penrose, or the author himself. This book is swollen with tortuous lucubrations on every topic under the sun, honesty, tolerance, legality, sentimentality, old age, rationalism, and what have you. Almost everyone talks and talks and talks, in that style which will be memorable in the American novel as the most disserviceable, most inexcusably perverse of any but that of *A Fable.* Inversions—"With calm entire"; court-Latin syntax,

> Pushing hard, he managed to push it to play. A jar of cogs, forced, creaking and dubious, together, sounded;

Wardour Street diction—"the heart relucted"; cultural displays—

> "the small dome—like the side porches, innocent of utility; like the columns' capitals, a pure

aspiring to the solemn and to the noble, to putative glories of Greece, to supposed grandeurs of Rome";

tenth-rate philosophizing—

> The nature of the intimation could be seen—a query directed at human struggle and human failure, and at the kinds of victory attainable in life. Might all of them be forms of defeat: givings-up; compromises; assents to the second-best; abandonments of hope in the face of the ascertained fact that what was to be, was to be? . . .

and digested portions of selected texts—

> The heavy story needs no going over. To the height of this great argument, to justify to men these ways of nature, no tongue or pen ever successfully asserted anything—that was impossible.

This ambitious style, aiming perhaps at that of late James, succeeds in stifling what little life the book contains. No book could survive it.

All the critics of *By Love Possessed* whom I have read—Gill in *The New Yorker,* Cowley in the *N.Y. Times Book Review,* Ellmann in *The Reporter* and *The Chicago Sun-Times,* the anonymous *Time* reviewer—follow the blurb in pointing to a novelistic structure based on the theme of love. The novel is said to be a display of the varieties of love, the love which possesses and so perverts the proper functioning of human beings who become sentimentalists in the form of either fools or knaves. A word had best be said about such an organization. Thematic structures are of great importance in the 20th Century novel. (They were discussed briefly in the Spring, 1956, issue of *Western Review* as a way of contrasting the picaresque of Mann with that of Defoe.) A novel organized as variations on a theme runs into the peril of uncontrolled exhibitionism; it needs the support of another narrative method, either picaresque (as in *Felix Krull*), the memoir (Proust, *Dr. Faustus*), or the parodic epic (*Ulysses*). If the formal implications of the secondary technique are observed, then the thematic material can be distinguished as the crucial, underlying form. When the secondary convention is not observed, then the narrative collapses, and the thematic material looks like notes for a novel. A theme can be found to cover almost any disorganized book, but then it will be seen as the artificial, imposed form Proust talked about in *La Prisonnière.* (This was discussed in the Summer, 1956, issue of the *Kenyon Review.*) This, it seems to me, is the case of *By Love Possessed.* The novel stands at best as an immense prologue to a novel: all the vital relationships will appear in that alteration of the old relationships which Winner's discoveries entail. If the novel had begun shortly after the discoveries, gone back for the essential past, and then come up to deal with the difficult consequences, one could suppose an exciting novel as the result. Not, of course, the one here written.

A bad book, a labored book, and—God knows why—a popular book. For years Cozzens has been writing fine novels. He has won prizes, a Scribner contest in 1931, the Pulitzer Prize in 1948, been praised by influential critics

(De Voto, Fadiman), and had the Book of the Month Club's support four times, yet till now, his books have not sold well, and he has been almost entirely ignored by serious critics. One hopes that this most ornery of his books will not deflect serious readers from the fine ones, particularly from *Men and Brethren, Ask Me Tomorrow,* and *Guard of Honor.* It almost looks as if such fictional perversity as *By Love Possessed* exhibits was nurtured in that isolation which lack of serious criticism inflicts on serious writers.

## Frederick Bracher   (essay date 1959)

SOURCE: "Style and Structure," in *The Novels of James Gould Cozzens,* Harcourt, 1959, pp. 49-76.

*[In the following excerpt, Bracher explores Cozzens's use of description, alliteration, poetry quotes, and characters.]*

Until 1957, reviewers and the few critics who wrote of him at all were almost unanimous in praise of the lucid precision of Cozzens' style, and Bernard De Voto after the publication of *Guard of Honor* concluded that the author's reputation would rest largely on his technical achievements as a writer. This prediction seemed reasonably safe until the appearance of *By Love Possessed,* in which the occasional idiosyncrasies of Cozzens' basically classical style were at times exaggerated into the convolutions of the baroque, if not the eccentricities of the rococo. Malcolm Cowley, in a discerning review of the novel [in *The New York Times Book Review,* 25 August 1957], took gentle note of the change: "His style used to be as clear as a mountain brook; now it has become a little weed-grown and murky, like the brook when it wanders through a meadow."

Other critics were more harsh. Deploring "prose of an artificiality and complexity that approaches the impenetrable—indeed often achieves it," Dwight Macdonald [in *Commentary,* January, 1958] quoted excerpts to illustrate a whole gallery of supposed faults. The device is not very impressive to a reader who knows how easily stylistic effects can be distorted when sentences are removed from the field of force generated by their context; and Macdonald's bald lists of examples are certainly unfair. In an attempt to discredit Cozzens without damaging other writers notable for their complex meanderings, he adds,

> James's involutions are (a) necessary to precisely discriminate his meaning; (b) solid parts of the architecture of the sentence; and (c) controlled by a fine ear for euphony. Faulkner does meander, but there is emotional force, descriptive richness behind his wanderings. . . . Their style is complex because they are saying something complicated. . . .

Confronted with such arbitrary condemnation one can only try to make some further distinctions, not so much in the expectation of making converts among those who find Cozzens' latest style antipathetic as with the hope that his style may be seen for what it is, whether anyone likes it or not. The following is the kind of sentence hostile critics like to pin up on the wall as a horrible example:

> Here was Elmer Abbott, an Orcutt, a well-off man (with all that meant in the way of perfect freedom to quit himself like a man) so tame, so pridelessly relieved at the withdrawal of a false charge, at the permission to continue his namby-pamby round, keep his piffling post, his unpaid job's clung-to prerogative of inflicting on a captive audience his mediocre music, that he cried! [*By Love Possessed*]

This is knotty and mannered, and the alliteration is perhaps excessive. But in context this summarizing sentence is a deliberately rhetorical conclusion to a long passage (six pages) of meditation by Arthur Winner on Elmer Abbott's past. In the passage, Cozzens makes fully articulate the flashes of remembrance or intuition that occur in the mind of a principal character during the course of action or talk. The device is used constantly throughout the novels (it is especially effective in the brilliant scene with Mrs. Pratt in the garden); and if it is unrealistic in the strict sense that thought so fully explicated would take up much more time than a momentary pause in a conversation, the device is obviously intended to be taken with that willing suspension of disbelief which any convention, on the stage or in a novel, requires. Moreover, such meditative interpolations do not lack psychological realism. Cozzens is only articulating in precise detail a pattern of thought which perceptive minds might hit upon in flashes of intuition. The convention that readers are asked to accept is no more than the exposition of the full, coherent content of such intuitions. If the passages are neither euphonious nor simple, it is because they clearly were not meant to be; they are intended to arrest and challenge. In its context the sentence about Elmer Abbott is appropriate and functional in providing a deliberately rhetorical conclusion to the long interpolated meditation.

It should also be noted that the baroque style of *By Love Possessed* is neither completely representative nor entirely new. The eccentricities are exaggerated, to be sure, but they are exaggerations of tendencies already present, though kept under stricter control, in Cozzens' earlier novels. So far as sentence structure is concerned, Cozzens has two characteristic traits: a fondness for elaborate subordination which results in nests of parenthetical comments within subordinate elements, and a habit of appositival coordination in which one expression (noun, verb, modifier) is followed by others that explain and bear the same grammatical construction as the first. These traits, infrequent in dialogue, are common in meditative or descriptive passages.

> Though the waking mind clutched at its relief of recognizing the dream as such—not really real, not really happening, not really requiring such an anguished effort to grasp and to explain—the dreaming mind with desperate hypnagogic attachment would not let go, leave off. A running engine of phantasmogenesis, powerfully engaged again, pressed him to dream on; and, little as life, Dunky (could that man be still alive?) angrily, excitedly, confronted him. [*By Love Possessed*]

The two devices just illustrated are common as early as *Men and Brethren* (1936).

The words returned, of themselves, with unforced deliberation, over and over. Soon he was aware, without the distraction or the interruption of taking an interest in it, of the automatically increasing depth of his breathing, the modulation of his heart beat. Set, by the familiar practice of his will, on the deceptive threshold over which some people stepped to a supposed spiritual apprehension—where the senses, starved of nervous energy, were narcotized, kept no more check on actuality; where reason, deprived of ideas to work with abdicated, impotent; where Grace might very well appear, as Calvin supposed, irresistible—Ernest released himself.

Compare a typical passage from Faulkner which uses the same devices, especially the piling up of appositival absolute constructions.

> In the surrey with his cousin and Major de Spain and General Compson he saw the wilderness through a slow drizzle of November rain just above the ice point as it seemed to him later he always saw it or at least always remembered it— the tall and endless wall of dense November woods under the dissolving afternoon and the year's death, sombre, impenetrable (he could not even discern yet how, at what point they could possibly hope to enter it even though he knew that Sam Fathers was waiting there with the wagon), the surrey moving through the skeleton stalks of cotton and corn in the last of open country, the last trace of man's puny gnawing at the immemorial flank, until, dwarfed by that perspective into an almost ridiculous diminishment, the surrey itself seemed to have ceased to move (this too to be completed later, years later, after he had grown to a man and had seen the sea) as a solitary small boat hangs in lonely immobility, merely tossing up and down, in the infinite waste of the ocean while the water and then the apparently impenetrable land which it nears without appreciable progress, swings, slowly and opens the widening inlet which is the anchorage. [William Faulkner, *Go Down Moses,* 1942]

Cozzens' style is perspicuous, even when twisted and baroque, in the sense that its ornate complications serve to qualify, sharpen, and enrich an approximately specific meaning already established by the basic structure. In Faulkner the interminable increment of absolute phrases is cumulative: the meaning is not defined by an articulated structure but emerges as a kind of essence of the tangle of sentence elements, heaped up like branches on a bonfire—a glow that appears now and then dimly through the smoke and occasionally bursts free in bright flame. Though Cozzens' later style is, in rare instances, smokily obscured, it characteristically gives off a steady, dry light.

This is to say that Cozzens' style, although sensitive and ornate, is not poetic. The surface is dense and in the later novels often forbidding, but it is clear in the sense that the poetry of Pope is clear—the meaning not always easy to grasp on a first reading, but fully articulated and expressed if a reader makes the effort required by the compression and complication of the structure. The prose of Faulkner,

on the contrary, even when the structure is relatively simple, is suggestive rather than explicit; and it is ambiguous in the sense that, like poetry, it sometimes manages to express what cannot really be said. The one Cozzens novel that might be called poetic—both in its primary use of image and symbol and in the feeling it gives of being autogenetic, of having been discovered as an organic whole by the writer instead of being deliberately constructed—is *Castaway.* But even here the writing is sharp and precise. Cozzens seems to know, and to be able to say, exactly what he wants to express; as to ornament he would probably agree with Aristotle that "the perfection of style is to be clear without being mean." It is true that Cozzens' later style makes heavy demands on the reader, but it richly rewards those who still cultivate the art of full reading.

In addition to being complex and ornate in its structure, Cozzens' style is "literary" in the sense that the reflective and descriptive passages use a good many uncommon words, similar to the inkhorn terms of Elizabethan writers, and a wealth of half-quotations and allusions. Again, it is ridiculously easy to make fun of this vocabulary by compiling lists of outlandish terms from Cozzens' novels. Out of context they give a false impression of their frequency of appearance and a smack of the pedantic Latinism of Dr. Johnson's *Dictionary.* Actually, since such words are not common in the dialogue that makes up a large part of the novels, their frequency can easily be, and has been, exaggerated. They do not occur on every page but tend to cluster in occasional set pieces of rhetorical fireworks. While some of them—*anfractuosities, furibund,* or *successive*—make no obvious addition to the meaning, many of them (including most of those listed by Dwight Macdonald) make the precise discriminations appropriate to the literate sensibilities of the characters through whom comment on the action is made. Colonel Ross, who constantly quotes Milton and Pope, may be allowed an occasional word like *chicanery, senescence,* or *irruptive,* especially when, as in the last example, the word is so effectively used: "that horrid irruptive roar" of airplanes passing close overhead.

Apart from their preciseness of connotation, Cozzens seems often to use exotic words out of an almost Elizabethan exuberance, a simple delight in rich materials. Reminded of the phrase "an old style Princeton Seminary supralapsarian," Ernest Cudlipp interjects "What a marvelous word, by the way!" and rolls on his tongue its opposite, "infralapsarian," which he equates with "a dreary Arminianism, a mess of Methodist pottage." The orotund terms and the veiled allusion, are sharpened by contrast with the Anglo-Saxon earthiness of "Calvin would spit on them!" The rhetorical effect—colloquialism pointing up rhetorical opulence, and vice versa—is a marked characteristic of Cozzens' style, and it can be extraordinarily effective in puncturing a balloon, as in the following passage describing the Catholic Church's facility in dealing with the weakness of the flesh:

> But among the forewarned, forearmed faithful, such escapes were no occasion for panic, nor even for agitation. The strays were the devil's— bad; they worked evil; they spread confusion among pious or sacred thoughts and intentions;

but what would you? Evil's energies must flag, too; and when they flagged, means to recapture and recommit the unclean spirits had been appointed. Grace, failing to confine, still enabled contrition; mercy saved the contrite—just keep your shirt on! Meanwhile, nature must take nature's course. [*By Love Possessed*]

Similarly the studied, self-mocking, defensive artificiality of Julius Penrose's speech achieves an additional incongruity when used to describe some bald fact and gives a mild relish of irony to the style. Cozzens writes for an audience literate enough to enjoy deliberate virtuosity and able to look at the literary equivalent of late Victorian gingerbread architecture, not with Puritan outrage, but with amusement and affection.

These devices—the ornate complexity of sentence structure, the use of literary words, the excess of alliteration—give to parts of Cozzens' later novels their stylistic effect of slightly old-fashioned magniloquence. Cozzens is said to admire Macaulay, and he justifies his own style, by implication at least, when Arthur Winner contemplates the florid Victorian inscription in the lobby of the Union League Club:

> That epigraph embodied a seriousness of purpose still respectable. Were people really the better for not talking like that any more? Was there any actual advantage of honesty when high-sounding terms went out? Had facts of life as life is lived been given any more practical recognition? [*By Love Possessed*]

The bare, plain style recommended by Bishop Sprat for use by the Royal Society in the late seventeenth century is not the only possible style, and those who insist on its use in the novel seem to fall into the Puritan fallacy of assuming that all ornament is bad. Even at its most rhetorical, Cozzens' style in *By Love Possessed* is rich, sonorous, and masculine. The sentences are architectural in their feeling for rich materials and their concern for an explicitness of structure which baroque embellishment may cover but does not conceal. If the decoration is occasionally so literary as to approach the grotesque, at least it is determinate and perspicuous, sharp in the sunlight with no blurred, fuzzy edges. Its rhetorical opulence is a pleasant surprise in a day when the concept of unembellished functionalism has been so widely and unconsciously accepted that Renaissance splendor (as revealed, say, in a film like *The Titan*) comes as a shock to the average American.

Cozzens' magniloquence is not motivated by the pious reverence of the antiquarian; he uses Victorian mannerisms with a full, ironic awareness of their incongruity in an age which, as Julius Penrose notes, is cheap and maudlin. The ironically artificial speech of some of the characters provides them with a kind of defense against falsity, against too open a revelation of deep feeling. Lieutenant Amanda Turck's "wry phrasing" and intricately formed sentences [in *Guard of Honor*]—"I will stop drinking your valuable whisky, clean up these things, and with heartfelt thanks for your kindness and your cash outlay, make myself, as we said when I was young, scarce"—are not in the normal spoken style of even educated Americans. They are, as Nathaniel Hicks recognizes, defensive; and he is

touched by "this controlled and composed, yet ceaseless struggle . . . against that obsessive self-consciousness." He remembers her "in the terrible heat of yesterday's high afternoon pronouncing a little stiltedly: 'The Lybian air adust—' it was defensive, he could see now. It intended the irony, for what that was worth, both ways. Though she reeked, she thought, of sweat, she quoted Milton; and though she quoted Milton, she reeked, she thought, of sweat." Her wry raillery is "aimed at herself; her defense against everything."

The affected speech of Julius Penrose [in *By Love Possessed*]—"the finished phrases, in their level precision almost rehearsed-sounding, the familiar deliberately mincing tones that mocked themselves with their own affectation"—is likewise a defense against hurts to one's vanity. Though not in the ordinary sense realistic, they are realistically appropriate to the hypersensitivity of a proud, crippled man. Julius' habit of speech, ironic at his own expense, serves to hold strangers at arm's length while partially sharing, with old friends, "the privacy, or even secrecy, which alone, at some points, dignifies a man."

Cozzens' own sensibility may well be similar to that of Julius Penrose or Amanda Turck. In a letter written in 1955 he admits that the account of the young writer in *Ask Me Tomorrow* is to some extent autobiographical; and the theme of the novel is pride. Francis Ellery, over-sensitive and proud, interposes a series of masks between himself and the world, and Cozzens' use of a central consciousness in the later novels serves as a similar protective device. The point of view shifts in the early novels, but after 1933 it is only in *Castaway* that the author consistently speaks out in his own person. The entire action of *Men and Brethren* is seen through the sensibility of the Reverend Ernest Cudlipp; Abner Coates is unvaryingly the central consciousness of *The Just and the Unjust;* the melodramatic events of *By Love Possessed* are given us only as seen through the normally dispassionate eyes of Arthur Winner. In *Guard of Honor* a few incidents—General Beal on the target range, Sergeant Pellerino at the Knock and Wait Club, the WAC officers at breakfast—are narrated directly, but most of the action of the book is seen through the eyes of the youthful Nathaniel Hicks or the aging Colonel Ross. The device enables Cozzens not only to develop the theme of Hicks' moral education, but to attribute to the colonel a ripened wisdom which a sensitive author might hesitate to offer in his own right.

Another device that serves to establish an exact degree of separation between the author and his characters is the use of full names to designate the principal characters in *By Love Possessed.* A good many readers, including the parodists, have noted, sometimes with annoyance, the frequent repetition of the full name "Arthur Winner." The device may sound mannered, but it serves to establish the slightly formal tone that Cozzens seems to intend. Outside the Society of Friends no one in real life calls another person by his full name; normal idiom would require "Arthur," or "Art," or "Mr. Winner," depending on the degree of intimacy. These names are all used by characters in the novel, but none is really appropriate for the author's use. Garret Hughes, Julius Penrose, Noah Tuttle, and

Helen Detweiler are dramatis personae, not personal friends, and in **By Love Possessed** (as in **Guard of Honor,** where military titles are used) the slightly formal note struck by the repetition of the full names helps to detach the characters from the author and to stress the fact that, like actors in a play, their opinions are not necessarily those of their creator.

Cozzens' particular temperament may also be indicated in the frequency with which certain words are used. "Compunction" occurs over and over again throughout the novels, and its connotation—a faint suggestion of arrogance and guilt mingled with pity or sympathy—seems to define the author's contradictory combination of habitual feelings: protectively detached, oversensitive almost to the point of being finicky, yet worried and involved. The impression is reinforced, especially in **Ask Me Tomorrow,** by an excessive use of other words suggesting a kind of partial disengagement, or shrinking involvement: *mortifying, harassed, crest-fallen; qualms, chagrin, wounded feelings; quailed, shrank, recoiled.* Like his sentence structure, Cozzens' diction reflects his basically Pyrrhonistic temperament, his apoetic intelligence, and his troubled aloofness.

The intricately qualified observations and judgments of the Cozzens heroes are matched by the complexity and magniloquence of the style in which they think and speak, and a very conspicuous trait of this style is its frequent incorporation of quotations, half-quotations, and allusions. It is probably true, as suggested in **Ask Me Tomorrow,** that Cozzens no longer finds satisfaction in writing poetry, but the quotations indicate that he still finds poetry rewarding to read. The English poets of every age since the Renaissance are represented, and references to Shakespeare and the Bible are particularly frequent. Sometimes the quotations are unmistakably indicated by italics or quotation marks, as when Arthur Winner quotes from one of Hotspur's speeches or Julius Penrose recites a stanza from *In Memoriam.* More frequently they are worked unobtrusively into the structure of Cozzens' own sentences. On two of the pages describing the death of Warren Winner there are unacknowledged fragments of *Julius Caesar,* Keats, and Tennyson. An account of the orgies at the Osborne farm, known to the natives as Alcoholic Hill, concludes: "At any rate, the revels, silly or scandalous, now were ended." Mrs. Pratt makes a "fresh deviation into sense"; Arthur Winner thinks of the dimming "image of his late-espoused saint." The appropriateness of such fragments varies. Lieutenant Winner and Tennyson's eagle have obviously a good deal in common, and other fragments are more or less ironic. But some of the allusions are so recondite as to be easily missed by the average reader, who could hardly be expected to think of Sir Christopher Wren when Arthur Winner speaks of his father's monument. Many quotations have no apparent function beyond embellishment. Presumably they just occurred to Cozzens, as fragments from "Abide with Me," echoing the hymn tune played on the carillon, occur to Arthur Winner while he contemplates Colonel Minton's ruin.

The constant casual use of quotations in the novels has something of the effect of a genre of poetry popular in the eighteenth century—the "imitation." Like Pope's imitations of Horace, Dr. Johnson's "London" is neither a translation nor a new poem. The trick of writing an Imitation was to follow the content and plan of the original poem but to supply new, contemporary names and events and if possible to demonstrate a contemporary relevance in the thought of the "Ancients." The relevance might be ironic, as when Pope directed his Imitation of the first epistle of the second book of Horace not to that famous patron of poetry, the emperor Augustus Caesar, but to George II of England, notorious for his philistine scorn of literature and the arts. The effectiveness of a successful Imitation consisted partly in its demonstration of the idea, popular among neoclassic writers, that human nature did not change, that what oft was said could still be relevantly expressed. Partly, too, an Imitation was effective because it flattered the reader. Written for a small group of educated gentlemen, who could be counted on to be conversant with the Latin classics, an Imitation afforded the pleasure of a familiar Latin phrase turned to a new use. Whether the use was exactly apposite was not crucial; the pleasure of recognition was considerable, and it was increased by a flattering sense of belonging to a small, exclusive, superior group. The reader of Cozzens is likewise complimented by an implied offer of admission to the circle of educated professional people in whose mouths and minds the quotations appear.

Similar in use and effect to the quotations in the text are the epigraphs to the novels or to parts of novels. Some are ironic—for example, the text that introduces **The Just and the Unjust:** "Certainty is the Mother of Repose; therefore the Law aims at Certainty." Some are structural in the sense that they announce a theme. The quotation from Acts 2:37, "Men and brethren, what shall we do?" relates the title of the book to the central question answered in the novel. The epigraph to **Castaway** directs the reader to the parallel with *Robinson Crusoe;* the quotation from *Troilus and Cressida* at the beginning of **Ask Me Tomorrow** introduces the theme of frustrated youthful pride. But frequently the epigraphs have no clear, unmistakable relevance. Their significance must be seen, if at all, by peripheral vision, out of the corner of the eye rather than by direct examination. Ariel's speech to the earthbound Caliban beginning "I and my fellows/Are ministers of fate" and stressing his invulnerability to earthly weapons may strike the strictly logical mind as a baffling epigraph for **Guard of Honor.** But it has a kind of glancing relevance in its stress on the intractability of those inexorable forces which, despite our wishes and best efforts, determine a considerable part of what happens to us.

Similarly, the epigraph to **By Love Possessed** may have an indirect significance in addition to its explicit stress on the passage of time. It is taken from a speech by the weak and unhappy King Henry VI, who in the midst of battle wishes that he were a simple swain tracing the uneventful hours of a life that will in due time "bring white hairs unto a quiet grave"; instead of a king who, despite his rich surroundings, is waited on by "care, mistrust, and treason." Arthur Winner, too, had hoped for an ordered, blameless life but is forced to endure an increasingly heavy burden of dangerous responsibility. The epigraphs to the three main subdivisions of the novel are all stage directions, the first two only indirectly relevant. "Drums afar off" probably refers to *Coriolanus*, where the drums are a call to battle. "A noise of hunters heard" is from *The Tempest* and seems to be related to the metaphorical sounds—"Were they of hunting, of pursuers?" —which Arthur Winner takes as premonitory intimations of disaster. Both have a faintly ominous note and thus lead up appropriately to the short, climactic section headed "Within the tent of Brutus."

The parallel between the last section of *By Love Possessed* and Shakespeare's *Julius Caesar* is too striking to be missed, yet not easily generalized or defined. Helen Detweiler, like Portia too easily despairing, "fell distract,/And, her attendants absent, swallow'd fire." Julius Penrose, who like Cassius "smiles in such a sort/As if he mocked himself," gives Arthur (Brutus) wine to restore his spirits. Brutus, "arm'd so strong in honesty," accuses Cassius of condoning bribery.

> Shall we now
> Contaminate our fingers with base bribes,
> And sell the mighty space of our large honours
> For so much trash as may be graspéd thus?

Cassius' justification of himself is essentially Julius Penrose's insistence that in view of the factual situation principle must sometimes be shelved. Finally, paralleling Cassius' statement that "a friend should bear his friend's infirmities," Julius indicates that he knows, and is able to accept, still loving, the weakness that had led Arthur Winner into adultery with Marjorie Penrose. Those readers who, like most of Cozzens' generation, have studied *Julius Caesar* in school will find a reading of the last section of *By Love Possessed* enriched by half-recognized echoes from Shakespeare's play; just as the scene with Mrs. Pratt in the garden produces a faint resonance—inexplicable on logical grounds since the details are changed with the casual inconsistency of a dream—set up by parallels with Milton's account of the fall of man.

If Cozzens' style, with its usual lucid precision, its occasional deliberate flights of rhetoric, and its fondness for quoting from the "Ancients," might be described as classical, the same term could be used for another characteristic of his novels: a tight structure, based on the classical unities. The typical Cozzens novel is primarily dramatic; its purpose is the immediate presentation of significant character in action; and an important part of the action is what the characters think. In resolving the dilemma of what Joseph Warren Beach [in *The Twentieth Century Novel*, 1932] calls "subjective drama in the novel"—if it is to be drama, it must be presented rather than recounted or explained; if it is subjective, it must be told about since it cannot be presented through overt action—Cozzens follows the practice of Henry James. The description of internal, psychological experience is given as it occurs in the consciousness of characters in the novel, rather than by the author in his own person. In *Ask Me Tomorrow* Cozzens deliberately eliminated first-person observations from his original manuscript and lets his main character think about and comment on what happens. It is not necessary for him to "go behind" the consciousness of his characters, since those whose points of view he uses are apt to be, like Colonel Ross or Arthur Winner, almost preternatural in the sharpness of their perceptions, the breadth and depth of their understanding, and the articulate clarity of their thought and speech.

Cozzens does not trace the slow development of character molded by environment and experience over a long period of years. Instead, he confronts us at once with fully formed characters involved in some complication of critical action. The time covered by the novel is characteristically brief—several weeks in *The Last Adam* (the time required for the spread and crisis of a typhoid epidemic); three days in *The Just and the Unjust;* two days in *S.S. San Pedro, Guard of Honor,* and *By Love Possessed;* a day and a night in *Men and Brethren.* (*Ask Me Tomorrow* is an exception, both in the looseness of its structure and in the length of time covered.) Into these short periods Cozzens crowds relatively large casts of characters, a variety of crucial incidents, expository flashbacks sufficient to identify and explain both the persons and their actions, and a good deal of comment and speculation.

To present coherently and perspicuously this packed complexity of diverse material is a difficult technical problem even in a short novel like *Men and Brethren*. For the longer novels—*Guard of Honor* or *By Love Possessed*—the problem is fairly staggering. The author's awareness of the difficulty is made clear in a letter to his English publisher:

> What I wanted to write about here [*Guard of Honor*], the essence of the thing to be said, the point of it all, what I felt to be the important meaning of this particular human experience, was its immensity and its immense complexity. . . . I could see I faced a tough technical problem. I wanted to show . . . the peculiar effects of the inter-action of innumerable individuals functioning in ways at once determined by and determining the functioning of innumerable others—all in the common and in every case nearly helpless involvement in what had ceased to be just an "organization" . . . and become if not an organism with life and purposes of its own, at least an entity, like a crowd. . . . I would just have to write off as readers everyone who could not or would not meet heavy demands on his attention and intelligence, the imagination to grasp a large pattern and the wit to see the relation which I could not stop to spell out between this & that.

The first step in dealing with such a mass of material is a thorough job of organization, and this requires an intellectual effort which many novelists seem unwilling to make. Captain Hicks, in civilian life editor of a popular magazine, comments irritably, in a tone that suggests Cozzens is expressing his own feeling, on the irresponsibility of some modern writers of serious fiction. "One of you prose artists can screw up a simple, factual story until hell won't have it. You never know anything about organization of the material, and most of you won't learn; you think you know it all" [*Guard of Honor*].

In another connection Hicks speaks of the "austere beauty of order," and the phrase is an apt description of the effect of the Cozzens novels. Order is produced by "the important arts of selection and elimination" and a careful organization of the remaining details. The novels are as scrupulously organized as they are fully researched and documented, but despite the complicated ordering of events and the heavy load of accurate, detailed information carried, they never seem schematized or mechanical. Even so unsympathetic a critic as Irving Howe [in *The New Republic,* 20 January 1958] admits Cozzens' success in creating "the illusion of verisimilitude." The structure of the novels, though tight, appears organic.

***Guard of Honor*** is perhaps the best work to illustrate the point, since it incorporates an especially wide variety of material and the plan is simple enough to permit the bare bones of structure to be easily discerned. The novel opens with a superb account of an army airplane flying back in the late afternoon to Ocanara Air Base in Florida. The military personnel aboard are disposed in a stylized order based on rank. At the controls is General Beal, the commanding officer of AFORAD. Next to him, necessarily but significantly out of rank order, is his copilot, Lieutenant Colonel Carricker. At the foremost of the three navigators' desks is Colonel Ross, the Air Inspector. The other two desks are occupied by Captain Hicks and Lieutenant Amanda Turck, WAC. Behind them, on the pull-down seat by the door, is Sergeant Pellerino, the general's crew chief; and in the tail of the airplane, perched on the seat of a chemical toilet, is T/5 Mortimer McIntyre, Junior, a Negro from the Base Services Unit.

The arrangement reflects the chain of command, which in the Army determines the possession and flow of power, a main theme of the novel. The personnel aboard are key figures in the tense, two-day drama about to be enacted, and they represent the various lines of action that are brought to a practical, if not indubitably moral, solution by Saturday night. General Beal is the dramatic center of the network of events to come; his freezing on the controls when a collision seems imminent typifies the temporary loss of command around which so much later action centers. Carricker, the hot pilot, precipitates by his anarchic defiance of proper military procedure the racial conflict which is another main thread of action. Colonel Ross, the imperturbable man of responsibility, shows even in this introductory scene the qualities of rational, controlled efficiency which make him, in Mark Schorer's words [in *New York Herald Tribune Book Review,* 10 October 1948], the "thematic center" of the novel: he is the man who takes over and straightens out the messes produced by the impulsive or emotional behavior of others. Captain Hicks and Lieutenant Amanda Turck are the fated but as yet barely acquainted lovers; and the flight into Ocanara, with Hicks a hapless passenger, parallels his flight out of Ocanara at the end of the book, morally shaken and confused by the disruptive events of the past two days. Sergeant Pellerino represents the group of essential career technicians who really keep the air base operative and whose disciplined competence and assurance are contrasted with the bewilderment of the reserve officers, forced to fit themselves somehow into the immense, ordered confusion of the wartime Air Force. T/5 McIntyre, almost AWOL through ignorance and negligence, has gained the grudging assistance of Captain Hicks in getting back to the base,

and his place in the airplane suggests the racial injustice with which much of the subsequent action is concerned.

The flight to Ocanara serves as a kind of overture, sounding all the principal themes to be developed later in the novel. It begins as a routine operation, and in the early hours of the flight Cozzens sketches in, by means of very skillful flashbacks, the immediate background and present situation of each character. General Beal is being watched by the Air Force high command, who hope to give him, if he measures up to his present responsibilities, a major role in the later stages of the war. The account of Carricker's earlier heroism in combat reveals, along with the fact of his skill and physical courage, signs of his lawless, destructive individualism. The frustrating efforts of Judge Ross to get an assignment in the early days of the war, Captain Hicks' daily round of futile hack work, Amanda Turck's gallant efforts to overcome an ingrained maladjustment to life, all are interpolated into the account of the flight.

Thirty minutes from Ocanara, the persistent head-winds turn into a storm, and as the General attempts a landing in a thunder shower he narrowly misses a B-26 that slides into the runway ahead of him bearing one crew of the Negro medium bomb group who are to be tested and trained at AFORAD. The jolting disorder of the landing, with Lieutenant Turck sick and Sergeant Pellerino cut and bruised on the floor of the airplane, anticipates the only other violence directly presented in the book: the injury and drowning of the paratroopers at the review in honor of General Beal's forty-first birthday—the day on which he recovers the authority of command and qualifies as a full adult. Just as the flight to Ocanara serves as an overture to the grand opera that follows, so the whole novel serves as a kind of overture to the impending Götterdämmerung of the final assault on Japan. The first section ends with a superb curtain scene: in the glare of lightning flashes the whole party, from general to T/5, run just ahead of the thunder-shower for the Operations Building, Colonel Ross (the Prospero of this tempest) pausing characteristically to shepherd the new arrivals to shelter.

The multifarious activities of the Air Base—from high policy discussions among the generals to the routine problems of the WAC detachment and the Negro service units—are presented in a series of close-up shots, all organized around a carefully marked time scheme. The novel is divided into three main parts, entitled *Thursday, Friday,* and *Saturday.* Each of these parts is subdivided into numbered sections which cover shorter periods of time, usually about an hour. These sections often consist of several scenes in different places, the camera eye moving from one area of the base to another.

Section VII of *Saturday* covers the period just before lunch. The scene is the Base Hospital, and it involves Captain Hicks, Colonel Ross, General Nichols, Lieutenant Stanley Willis (the battered Negro pilot), and his father. That they are all present at the same time is due to a complex of earlier, apparently unrelated—but, as it turns out, providential—incidents. Section VIII includes a number of scenes, and all occur during and just after lunch. The first is at the Chechoter target range, where General Beal relieves his feelings by blasting targets with his 50-caliber machine guns and, as it turns out, solves his personal problems in his own unorthodox way. The second scene shows Sergeant Pellerino and the other master sergeants enjoying an after-lunch game of dominoes at the Knock and Wait Club. In the third scene Colonel and Mrs. Ross, discussing the Negro problem during a belated lunch at home, are interrupted by Mrs. Beal, who has tried to drown her worry about the general by drinking most of a bottle of Scotch and has come to the Rosses' house, drunk and sick.

Though they seem on the surface made up of random incidents, Sections VII and VIII are actually the turning point of the novel since they embody solutions to the two chief problems confronting General Beal. Both have been introduced in the *Thursday* overture. The first is the social and military problem of racial antagonism, which has become acute when Carricker smashes the nose of Lieutenant Willis, the Negro pilot of the errant B-26. The problem has been latent for some time: Army regulations permit no discrimination on account of race, but the Air Base is located in central Florida. In an attempt at compromise the local military authorities have established separate Officers Clubs, but the punching of the Negro pilot, magnified by rumor, leads the other Negro officers to organize a demonstration. They force their way into the main Officers Club and are arrested; the news leaks out to the papers, and General Beal gets a direct order from Washington: straighten out this mess without apparently backing down, without antagonizing the Negroes, and without obviously violating Army regulations against segregation.

The second major problem is personal and psychological. General Beal, accustomed to an active life as commander of fighter pilots, whom he likes and understands, has been going to pieces under the unfamiliar strain of sedentary, large-scale administrative command. He becomes acutely aware of his loss of assurance and authority when he freezes on the controls Thursday night and almost wrecks the plane. His abdication of authority is confirmed by his flighty behavior on Friday, and his lowest point comes on Saturday morning at the Base Hospital, where his arrogant demand for a sedative conflicts with the professional ethics of a disgruntled young doctor in uniform. One of Colonel Ross's many jobs is to keep the visiting general, who represents the Chief of Air Staff, from knowing that Beal has lost his grip.

Section VII shows Colonel Ross, by a masterly exploitation of accident and coincidence, settling, at least temporarily, the Negro problem. The father of the injured Negro pilot is flattered into accepting an artfully slanted but accurate version of the affair: Stanley Willis was not "beaten up"; he merely got into a squabble—"it had to do with flying"—with "another officer," and got punched in the nose. At the same time a reward is tacitly offered. If Stanley shows the ability to command (*i.e.,* if he is able to calm down the rebellious members of the Negro experimental bomb group), he will be made its commanding officer. After Colonel Ross has read the citation, General Nichols presents Lieutenant Willis with the Distinguished Flying Cross—which, like the Negro father, has providentially

arrived from Washington; and it is soon reported that Lieutenant Willis, having made a speech to the rebels, "does not think they will do it again."

General Beal's personal problem is solved over the target range, though the details are not reported until later. In a fantastic game of "chicken" played with fighter planes high in the air, he makes Carricker flinch.

> "Benny's had it close before; but I bet he never had it closer. . . . I moved in on him a little; and he hauled off fast, yelling: 'Stay away, damn it, keep away!'"

Having demonstrated, on Carricker's own primitive terms, that he is still as good a man as Benny, General Beal is restored; and he returns with vigor and assurance to the responsibilities that Colonel Ross has been bearing for him in the interim. The final episode—the accidental drowning of the paratroopers—serves to demonstrate, to the satisfaction of even the "hatchet man" from Washington, General Beal's complete recovery. In a burst of self-assurance, he contradicts his infallible, indispensable mentor, the Air Inspector.

> "This way isn't going to work," Colonel Ross said. "But you're the general."

> "You're damn right I am," General Beal said. "They have to prove to me they can't do it, not just say so."

At the very end of the novel, General Beal puts General Jo-Jo Nichols and by implication Colonel Ross in their proper places.

> He put his hand suddenly on Colonel Ross's shoulder. "Even Jo-Jo knows they could do without him before they could do without me. . . . Jo-Jo can talk to Mr. Churchill; but the war, that's for us. Without me—without us, he wouldn't have a whole hell of a lot to talk about, would he?"

Colonel Ross, "feeling the thin strong fingers, nervous but steadily controlled, pressing the cloth of his shirt," recognizes the gesture—the kindly hand of youth humoring yet firmly directing an aging subordinate. He accepts his position in the spirit of the lines from *Samson Agonistes* which have been running through his mind on the reviewing stand: with new acquist of true experience from this great event, and calm of mind, all passion spent. The final sentences of the book, while they imply another beginning in the interminable cycles of the war, round off this ordered cycle of minor tempest by introducing a different scale of proportion.

> The position lights of the northbound plane could still be made out by their steady movement if you knew where to look. The sound of engines faded on the higher air, merging peacefully in silence. Now in the calm night and the vast sky, the lights lost themselves, no more than stars among the innumerable stars.

*The Times Literary Supplement* (review date 6 May 1965)

SOURCE: "The Artless and the Arch," in *The Times Literary Supplement,* No. 3297, May 6, 1965, p. 356.

[*In the following review of* Children and Others, *the critic lauds Cozzens's ability to present the complexities of growing up.*]

[On] the evidence provided by the seventeen [stories] in *Children and Others,* Mr. Cozzens is probably at his happiest when working on a large canvas. "Eyes to See," the last story in the collection, is much the longest—more of a novella, really than a short story—and much the best. A fifteen-year-old boy is called home from school by his mother's sudden death, and, as the families gather for the funeral, Mr. Cozzens sets out for us most subtly young Maitland's growing awareness of all the complexities, cross-currents, and latent violence of adulthood. Childhood and adolescence are a recurring theme in many of the pieces, and all are beautifully shaped and full of meat. Two quite different ones are about war. In "Men Running" young Holcombe, a volunteer in the American Civil War, is suddenly faced with harsh and heavy responsibilities. Mr. Cozzens skilfully re-creates the authentic nightmare quality of war—that feeling of stepping on to a stage in order to take part in a play that has never been rehearsed.

**John Brooks**   (review date 25 August 1968)

SOURCE: "The I in Henry Dodd Worthington," in *The New York Times Book Review,* August 25, 1968, pp. 3, 33.

[*Brooks was an American critic, novelist and journalist. In the following review of* Morning Noon and Night, *he examines the novel's structure, Puritan themes, eccentric prose style, and plot.*]

In 1957, when James Gould Cozzens' *By Love Possessed* finally appeared, nine years after his last previous novel, *Guard of Honor,* it was instantly pronounced a masterwork by critical and popular acclaim and, an almost incredibly short time thereafter, it was dismissed (by what eventually came to be at least general critical assent) as a fake masterwork. On rereading, it seems to be neither, but rather a sound, skillful and entertaining portrayal of a part of American life marred, as Mr. Cozzens' earlier work had seldom been, by pretensions to both a style and a significance that were simply beyond its natural scope. One way and another, the book became a great *cause célèbre:* The reactions to it became, in themselves, a parable of the literary life, a write-it-your-self novel, obscuring the merits—obscuring the very being—of the novel that had actually been written.

Now, after a lapse this time of 11 years (broken by publication of *Children and Others,* a short-story collection), Mr. Cozzens has at last let a new novel go out of his workshop, and obviously he and it are very much on the spot. Has he bowed to the critics of *By Love Possessed* by returning to the simpler style and more manageable subject matter of his earlier novels? Or defied them by pressing the eccentric innovations of that book still further? Well, he has

done both, and neither—he has ignored the critics. Whatever else one may say for or against *Morning Noon and Night,* it makes clear beyond cavil its author's austere, magisterial, almost relentless disregard for literary fashion.

*Morning Noon and Night* sets out to be a searching study of the Puritan heart and mind (as *The Just and the Unjust* was of the American law, for example, and *Guard of Honor* of the American military). No character more than remotely mentioned in it is of other than Puritan ancestry. The world it describes is as parochially Eastern Anglo-Saxon Protestant as, say, that of Saul Bellow's *Herzog* is North American Jewish. Its hero and narrator is Henry Dodd Worthington, a successful management consultant in his sixties and beginning to feel his mortality intensely; its content is his memoirs.

Henry's background is classically genteel: father a Chaucer specialist at and finally president of a small, respectable Eastern college; grandfathers likewise professors; parents (like those of so many such people) distantly related to each other. His life story is unsurprising: placid campus boyhood; good prep school; sexual initiation at a genteel beach resort with a married neighbor lady of his parents' generation; Harvard; an abortive attempt to become a writer; marriage to the daughter of a high-church Episcopal clergyman; a few years' fling at a raffish job (maliciously arranged for him by a stern uncle) as a bill collector; the formation of the firm that is to bring him success; high-level, noncombatant military service in World War II; divorce; remarriage to a lifelong acquaintance who has been for some years his secretary.

At the time of his writing, his only daughter is bitterly facing her third divorce. His first wife, also embittered, is dying. His second wife is dead by what seems to have been suicide. He has come to realize that his relationship with his late beloved business partner was based in part on a cynical deception he had been guilty of as a schoolboy. Now, very much alone, he is asking himself, "What is this life? Who am I? What is this 'I' in me?"

A banal life, then; there is less story here than in any other Cozzens novel except *Castaway,* the other sport among the author's works. Surely this is intentional. Where Mr. Cozzens wants the highlight to fall is on Henry Worthington's style and ideas, the essence of his inherited Puritanism. His manner of telling his story is free-associational (and sometimes plain haphazard) rather than chronological or logically consecutive.

There is no attempt at suspense, the narration consisting of ruminations interrupted, not very frequently, by "stage plays of memory" in which the only action and dialogue occur. The first stage play (hardly one of memory) gives warning of what is to come. It is a description in elementary-science-textbook terms (sperm, Fallopian tubes, gametes, zygote), of the mating of his parents at which he was conceived. Here, as elsewhere, a tendency to laughably clinical exactitude and factual detail on the subject of sex seems to mask, or deny, embarrassment.

> **Always he inclines to sentence inversion, the passive voice, the ablative absolute, the long-obsolete usage, and other devices that create an effect, not so much of "old-fashioned grandiloquence" as of archness and pomposity.**
>
> —*John Brooks*

Henry's prose style is eccentric in the extreme. In the "stage plays," he inclines to nervous shiftings between the present and past tenses, and between the first and third persons. Where he uses the third person, he himself when younger often becomes "our Hank" or "our excited boy," as in the conventional fiction of a century ago. Always he inclines to sentence inversion, the passive voice, the ablative absolute, the long-obsolete usage, and other devices that create an effect, not so much of "old-fashioned grandiloquence" (a key phrase from *By Love Possessed*), as of archness and pomposity. Sometimes he writes purest old-fashioned Time-style: "In April died the old Secretary of Navy, and raised to his place was the Under Secretary."

And his ruminations? Henry (or "our Hank") thinks of them as "sagacity," partly in irony and partly not, but to the reader they come out as highly uneven in wisdom content. To the "Who am I?" query he replies, with resolute contempt for psychological self-analysis—perhaps inherited from a grandfather who was a renowned anti-Freudian—"Don't ask me." Here is a sampling of his apothegms:

"Legend's very nature must make for the struck pose, the formal stance, the act put on."

"Never the great and powerful, but only those of little or no real power will hurt for hurting's sake."

"The very fact that a man is a man and by that fact controlled (*homo est!*) is going to make him, reluct though he may, find—if not think, then feel—many very human things alien to him."

"Ingestion of beverage alcohol, not or not often to real excess, yet steady and systematic, has penalties."

Why does Henry talk, or write, that way? In part, it would seem, simply because he is something of a windbag when it comes to discussing himself. At times, the reader suspects that he has failed at human relationships not because of the excessive success-drive, the inherited streak of deviousness, and the sexual inhibition that he states or hints are the reasons, but because he has bored everybody close to him to distraction. But certainly he is not all windbag, as his huge professional success in management consulting (an occupation that is described, in the Cozzens tradition, with scrupulous fidelity) attests. There is a solid core of good sense, hard-earned skill, and natural perception in Henry. Perhaps his circumlocutory banalities are the outcome of an attitude toward the world more defensive than he cares to admit, and this is essentially a book about chronic embarrassment.

Since it certainly does not seem to have been so intended, and since it fails to deeply engage the reader's mind or heart as such, *Morning Noon and Night* has to be accounted a failure. Marquand's George Apley is pretty much of a bore (and so, for that matter, is Herzog) but the novels in which they appear succeed because of the authors' controlled mixture of irony and detached affection toward their heroes. Mr. Cozzens' attitude toward Worthington, as seen through Worthington's attitude toward himself, wavers uncertainly between irony and identification.

Because, along the way, Worthington expresses many ideas that the author himself has expressed in the past—a conservative outlook on human affairs in general, frank distrust of intellectual liberals, disdain for writers' conferences—and because of the tone of the whole book, one finds more than a hint here of a personal testament. Indeed, the reader wonders whether he is meant to discern the author's voice—the voice of one of the master craftsmen in American fiction in our time—behind Henry Worthington's valedictory, delivered after a last "stage play" in which Henry, as a boy, on a trip abroad with his parents, wanders out among classical ruins at sunset, knowing that in a few moments he will be ordered to bed, and thinks about the endings of things: "Good night, any surviving dear old Carian guests. Good night, ladies. Good night, all."

This reader, who has had so much pleasure in so many Cozzens novels and looks forward to more, certainly hopes not.

### John Updike   (review date 2 November 1968)

SOURCE: "Indifference," in *Picked-Up Pieces,* Alfred A. Knopf, 1976, pp. 416-22.

[*Updike is a prolific, Pulitzer Prize-winning American novelist, critic, short story writer, essayist, poet, and dramatist. In the review below, originally published November 2, 1968, in* The New Yorker, *he faults* Morning Noon and Night *for its stuffy, tedious, pessimistic, and pedantic style.*]

Beginning, forty years ago, with a style of sober purity, James Gould Cozzens has purposefully evolved a prose unique in its mannered ugliness, a monstrous mix of Sir Thomas Browne, legalese, and Best-Remembered Quotations. The opening chapter of his new novel, *Morning Noon and Night,* cloudy as a polluted pond, swarms with verbal organisms of his strange engendering. As Cozzensologists before me have discovered, there is no substitute for the tabulated list. We have the Unresisted Cliché:

> Here are clouds of witnesses, faces and forms in serried ranks . . .
>
> I don't intend here any telling in mournful numbers.
>
> Simply, the wood is not to be seen for the trees.

The Lame Echo:

To be sure, in this distraction of the mind, as through a glass darkly . . .

You have not world enough and time. . . .

I feel it leaves man as much as before the glory, jest, and riddle of the world.

The False Precision, the Legal "Or":

> . . . to inform yourself of any peculiarities or limitations of his that could have affected his observation or could now be coloring his report.

> . . . what they seem in our work or practice. I am not suggesting that I feel we are or ever could be ethically obligated. . . .

> . . . by elements of lust whether loving or unloving, a catalog longer or shorter of women . . .

The Vapid Expansion:

> What used to be, not just well enough, but often very good indeed, must be left religiously alone.

The Inversion Frightful, Capped by Cute Periphrasis:

> In eating employed now are partial dental prosthetic devices.

> Be that how it may, Nancy, as friends call her, will not refuse the rites mysterious of connubial love.

The Gratuitous Scientism:

> Penetrated, the microscopic cell is fertilized (in accepted language of the process, two gametes fuse to form a zygote).

The Infatuated Sonority:

> His course of ripe and ripe is running, and the rot and rot won't fail to follow. . . .

> Multitudinous as these remembered works of Nature may be, more multitudinous still, and by far, must be remembered works of man.

What Cozzens has set himself to achieve, and has, as he might say, so regrettably succeeded in achieving, is the literary equivalent for or capture of the all too veritably human quality of *stuffiness*. In tone and tedium, **Morning Noon and Night** is a four-hundred-page-long after-dinner speech.

The speaker is Henry Dodd Worthington; the dinner has been his life. Born at the turn of the century as the son of a small-college English professor, the narrator of this novel, after an acceptable education at an unnamed prep school and Harvard, and after shrugging off both teaching and writing as possible careers, drifted into employment with a Boston collection agency, and from this indifferent beginning rose to found Henry Worthington Associates, a management-consultant firm of prestige so immense that both he and the reader find it implausible. He has been twice married: his first wife, Judith, cuckolded and divorced him; his second, Charlotte, committed suicide. Violence, indeed, has made rather free with his relatives; his parents were asphyxiated in a hotel fire, and his two grandchildren were killed in the crash of a plane. Henry

(or "our Hank," as he jocosely calls himself) is of genteel Protestant background, an indirect descendant of President Franklin Pierce; during the Second World War he served as an Air Forces major, mostly in the Pentagon; his present preoccupations are the unhappiness of his daughter Elaine, now on her third divorce, and the composition of this memoir. The events of his life are not related consecutively but emerge as his memory rambles over the past; he ruminates at length upon such diverse matters as his grandfather's feud with the early Freudians, the tricks of management consultation, the technique of running an antiques shop, the sinking of the *Titanic,* the vagaries of chance, the nature of the Puritan heritage, the ups and downs and ins and outs of sexual "appetency," and (an unexpected obsession) the shabbiness of the literary world. Many of these essays, once the muddled sonority of the style is tuned out, possess interest, even a certain surly brilliance, but as a life the book lacks what it must have—life.

Elaine is the only character other than the narrator allowed to have any kind of a say; the novel's keystone scene is an interview between the distressed daughter and the stiff but sorry father, held in the courtyard of H.W. Associates' posh new suburban plant. But when, after seventy solid pages of authorial discourse, quotation marks appear amid the print and Elaine breaks into speech, she talks just like a little Henry, or (since without a doubt our Hank is pretty much our Jim) a little Cozzens. Listen to her:

> "So when Wilfred deflowered me I was pretty much, as the books say, unawakened."

> "You know; lovely Sue makes like softly panting while the geranium tree is planting. And doesn't that show what's up for grabs here is love forever true, and oughtn't he to latch onto it?"

> "You bet! Moving finger writes. Correct. And all my tears, or such as I've let drip, don't wash out a word."

Embarrassed, apparently, by her own wealth of literary tags, she admonishes her father, "Don't forget the expensive liberal-arts education you bought me. When it pays to, I can sound tolerably literate." But it doesn't pay; their conversation is lumpy with false wit and stilted slang and brittle with a supervisory knowingness—not a dramatization of her plight but an awkward exposition of it. So it is with the entire book. Henry's marriage to Judith, by all indications the deepest relationship of his life, is represented by some mocking paragraphs on newlywed lust, a potentially poignant but skimped account of their courtship, an unskimped theory as to how her father's anti-sexual High Anglicanism drove her decades later to promiscuity, a few cursory references to their divorce, a full exposition of Henry's financial advice to the antiques business she sets up in, and a glancing admission that now she is dying. She hardly speaks a sentence; for her one moment onstage, she is seen through her daughter's eyes distantly on a beach, coupling with a lover. Charlotte, the second wife, appears in Henry's account as a suicide note, as a glimpse of her in the shower (heavily misted by panting references to David and Bathsheba), and as an equable compliment to her secretarial ability. All the characters—wives, friends, business associates, service colleagues—are immersed, mute and all but immobile, in the tyrannous flow of Henry Worthington's disquisitional lava.

Now, to what extent does the author stand apart from his persona, as, say, John Marquand does from George Apley? How much of Henry's stuffiness is intentional caricature? Is his sluggish eclipse of the life he has lived a novelistic defect or an ironical comment? Mockery there is in abundance: Henry mocks his youthful ardor, his elderly dignity, his riskless wartime career, the little shams and maneuvers of his trade. His memory seeks out low moments: "mean actions of mine; uglinesses of greed or lust; shameful exhibitions of ignorance; deserved humiliations; mortifying follies and defeats." And the epigraph from Shakespeare's Sonnet 94, describing those who, "moving others, are themselves as stone," suggests that a self-portrait of a type of man and an implicit judgment were intended. But Marquand, even in his later novels, maintained an outsider's perspective on his Brahmins, whereas Worthington's voice and Cozzens' are indistinguishable, and the opinions of author and character merge in a ponderous, pessimistic morass of self-distrust and weary puzzlement.

Having troubled to invent a business profession for his alter ego, and having supplied a convincing amount of data and theory, Cozzens compulsively reverts throughout his narrative to the problems of the literary practitioner, to attacks upon "half-writer pretenders" and "liberal intellectuals." He includes a coy reference to the minor American writer Frederick Cozzens. He gives Henry, the supposed author of a million memos and directives, his own preposterously pedantic style, including the obligatory exotic words—*inappetency, erethism, furibund, condign, innominate, muliebrity, deontology.* Frequently heard is the rumble of hobby-horses being ridden by that ultra-conservative Cozzens displayed years ago in *Time*—a kind of male Ayn Rand who in this book must dote upon a fictional bank's status "in the best financial circles" as being "better regarded than the latter-day not always prudent House of Morgan," who speaks of Roosevelt's "near-senile megalomania" and the Kremlin's "dupes" and "expert perfidies and duplicities," and who seems pleasurably smitten by the speculation that a typhoon would have wiped out our scheduled invasion of the Japanese home islands had not the war been ended by the atomic bombs, which in passing are viewed as the "means to right a ceaselessly growing imbalance in Nature, to solve quickly and easily theretofore insoluble problems of excess population."

Not that political conservatives should be barred from the halls of fiction; rather, they should be better represented there, to relieve the present rather shrill unanimity on the left. Nor is author/alter-ego closeness an intrinsic handicap; *Herzog,* for example, is an excellent novel. Its superiority to *Morning Noon and Night* lies not only in Bellow's far livelier gift for conjuring up personalities but in his, and Herzog's, belief that a better world somewhere exists, that improvement can be sought and choices can be made. The illusion of free will, illusion or not, is necessary to a novel; excitement and import derive from the reality of human decision. As Henry Dodd Worthington describes himself, he has been always a product, a zygote formed by two fused gametes, in the grip, successively and simultaneously, of biology, heredity, social usage, sexual impulse, chance, and inertia. The turning points of his life—his marriage to Judith, his entry into the world of business, his enlistment in the Army Air Forces, his divorce and remarriage—are all seen as uncaused drift, "little governed by logic or demonstrable cause and effect." Herzog, at the end, can stop writing letters and set the table for a tryst, whereas Henry can only conclude that he knows nothing, that his life has been a "wandering directionless," a game of "blindman's buff—now sightlessly bumping into things, now surprised by sportive unreturnable blows." His memories—in the book's last, best flight, of imagery—are seen as ruined fragments and, far off, "a dozen or more aqueduct arches, commencing suddenly, suddenly ending, coming now from nowhere, now going nowhere." There is "thin final sunlight," and then "the child must soon be taken away to bed." A child is someone who lacks responsibility and power of choice; Henry Dodd Worthington, adviser to big business, labels himself as one. This vision of helpless, pointless process is at the heart of the novel's profound inaction, of its analyzed but unrealized events, and even of its reactionary style, seeping backward to include all those tired mottoes and phrases and clichés as if wryly to admit that nothing new can be said. Resigned pessimism is a defensible philosophy, and may be the natural end of American enterprise, but it makes for very dull fiction.

---

**What Cozzens has set himself to achieve, and has so regrettably succeeded in achieving, is the literary equivalent of the all too human quality of *stuffiness.* In tone and tedium, *Morning Noon and Night* is a four-hundred-page-long after-dinner speech.**

**—*John Updike***

---

Piqued by this book's curious badness, I turned to Cozzens' first full-length novel, ***The Last Adam.*** Though a trifle slick, with its climactic town meeting and its magnificent starring role for an aging screen idol (it *was* made into a movie, *Dr. Bull,* starring Will Rogers), it holds up well; the evocation of the Connecticut town of New Winton, the tight knit of weather and geography and people into a plot, the particularity and immediacy of every scene all show a mastery remarkable in a man of thirty. Cozzens then had more grasp of ordinary, middling America—or at least more willingness to transmute his grasp into art—than Hemingway and Fitzgerald ever showed. The hero of the novel, Dr. Bull, is sixty-seven, just about Henry Worthington's age, and he remembers the sentence from the Psalmist with which Henry begins his memoir: "I have been young and now am old." And cosmic nullity is present in both books: "Left to herself [a telephone operator in *The Last Adam*], and to what she could see of the universe, real and ideal were lost together in an indifference so colossal, so utterly indifferent, that there was no defining it." This colossal indifference, this abyss beneath society and conventional success, has always been with Cozzens, but as a threat, as a defining darkness, not as an all-swallowing enemy. From *The Last Adam* to *Morning Noon and Night,* the broad social scene of New Winton, primarily Protestant, has dwindled to one member of the Puritan aristocracy; class consciousness has narrowed to class loyalty. Cozzens has become like a Yale undergraduate in the earlier book: "He knew by now that he and his more intimate friends were right; or, at any rate, he could easily see that people who differed conspicuously in dress or behavior, in ideals or attitudes, were, as far as his college was concerned, wrong. His gray eyes considered all those in error with a level, complete indifference." Arthur Winner, of *By Love Possessed,* gave those not of his sort short shrift. Henry Worthington doesn't see them at all, they are squeezed into the remotest margins of his memoir, and there is nowhere to stand to see *him,* to judge him. Only the bitter vacuity of his conclusions betrays the possibility that somewhere along the way he went wrong.

### The Times Literary Supplement (review date 30 January 1969)

SOURCE: "Ponderosity," in *The Times Literary Supplement,* No. 3492, January 30, 1969, p. 116.

[*In the following negative review of* Morning Noon and Night, *the critic contends that Cozzens's attempt to expose "the reality beneath pretension" is undermined by a ponderous prose style.*]

The narrator of Mr. Cozzens's new novel [*Morning Noon and Night*] is Henry (Hank) Dodd Worthington, the sexagenarian founder and head of H.W. Associates, a firm of industrial management consultants preeminent in that field. The novel is presented in the form of a meditation on his life, or lives, and those of his ancestors, an inquiry that may be meaningful to others in so far as it is also an inquiry into the meaning of life at different ages and on different stages. H.W., the public figure, is as highly regarded as he is successful. But Hank has done many shameful things, the ill consequences of which he has avoided only by good luck; and the good management, in which his company specializes, is only the exercise of common sense in those chosen conditions where common sense gives an answer.

I remember a line of Montaigne's: *Amusing notion; many things I would not want to tell anyone, I tell the public.* I see what he means. Droll indeed the reflection that informing against yourself to one person is often imprudent, but not informing against yourself to the whole world. There you can count on a strange but true safety in numbers.

This reflection may be true of Montaigne or Mr. Cozzens or any other writer. But it is not true of Henry Worthington, whose confessions made to the whole world would do even more damage to the business reputation of himself and H.W. Associates than a private avowal; and well would he know it, if he had half the shrewdness he professes.

This basic flaw in the presentation of the novel is not concealed by the style which the author has given H.W. The descendant of a long line of professors and a broken line of writers. H.W., having taken his A.M. in English literature, has played with, but rejected, the ideas of teaching and writing. After starting in the "amusing" business of collecting debts in Boston, he has with the aid of inherited money and acquired school and college friends built up his consultancy business first in that city, then in the ultra-modernity of Madison Avenue, and finally in the Georgian replica of good taste outside New York City, having had a safe and successful war in the Air Force. He is very much a man of his times, not the phoney red who got worked up about Sacco and Vanzetti, the evils of the Depression and the threat of fascism, but the percipient man who broke only with the old establishment to establish himself with the new.

The way he expresses himself is a rococo version of the way in which Mr. Cozzens expressed himself in *By Love Possessed.* The rhythms are similar but exaggerated. Mr. Cozzens's literary hesitation becomes a stammer. Where one word will do justly, Mr. Cozzens uses a dozen and Henry Worthington a score.

> Normal aging's occasional distresses of sudden visceral ill ease, desultory muscle twinge, and hard-to-diagnose ache of bone and stiffening of joint visit me. Old skin, now too slowly renewed, suffers routine itches and allergy rashes. The breath of the image shortens, and, because it now sweats so easily, drafts need to be guarded against. Long ago glasses began to be required for reading. In eating employed now the partial dental prosthetic devices. Heating may soon have to be aided electrically. Yes many and sharp, if not yet very sharp, those numerous ills (the old mind is nervous and worrisome) inwoven with our frame.

His sentiments are often crudities condited in the recondite.

> . . . inappetency may well decide that a one only right name for the malodorous grapple, the damp assault on the subventral slit, the seesaw pump of in-and-out, the breakoff, spent and soiled, must be not *loving,* but, blunt and unvarnished *screwing.*

Mr. Cozzens is a deliberate writer, whose ponderosity is contrived to his own satisfaction. If the reader can take a short story cut so elaborately long, there is much in *Morning Noon and Night* which is shrewd or wise. The point of view, presented as H.W.'s (but the author's own?), has the merit of singularity; a complex attitude, apparently exposing the reality beneath pretension while really erecting an entirely different pretentiousness over the exposure.

## James A. Epperson (review date 8 December 1978)

SOURCE: "Eclipse," in *National Review,* Vol. XXX, December 8, 1978, pp. 1552-54.

[*In the following review of* Just Representations, *Epperson examines Cozzens's career, his fall from critical esteem, and argues that his work has significant literary merit.*]

Only twenty years ago, any list of our top-ranking novelists would surely have included the name of James Gould Cozzens. His short stories and novels had won prizes and critical attention. Six of his books had been selected by the Book-of-the-Month Club. *By Love Possessed* (1957) received all the acclaim a writer could hope for: commercial success as a best-seller, condensation in the *Reader's Digest,* a cover story in *Time,* $250,000 for the movie rights, and, in 1960, the prestigious Howells Medal for fiction, awarded every five years by the American Academy of Arts and Letters. One respected critic went so far as to suggest Cozzens as a nominee for the Nobel Prize. And such a suggestion seemed, at the time, perfectly apt. Cozzens had written a number of distinguished novels fully in the tradition of Hawthorne, Edith Wharton, and Henry James. One of them, *Guard of Honor* (1948), a fine novel by any standard and in any time, received the Pulitzer Prize and was called "the best American novel of World War II."

Such honors and distinction, one thought in 1957, would assure Cozzens of an enduring literary reputation. Yet now who reads his novels? Who not yet in middle age has even heard his name? He is certainly not read in college courses devoted to modern American fiction, where one naturally finds such contemporaries of Cozzens as Hemingway, Fitzgerald, and Faulkner—but also Jack Kerouac, Kurt Vonnegut, and William Burroughs, writers of little or no reputation in the late Fifties.

After about 1960, while other and perhaps less significant novelists rose to popularity, Cozzens virtually disappeared from our collective literary consciousness. His last book, *Morning, Noon, and Night,* received scattered and generally hostile notices when it was published in 1968, a bad year for books as for many other manifestations of American culture.

Perhaps now that the turmoil of the Sixties is fading, Cozzens' work may emerge from the curious limbo to which it has been assigned. The volume under review [*Just Representations: A James Gould Cozzens Reader*] is an attempt to help it do just that, to provide an introductory and comprehensive review of Cozzens' fiction in an omnibus that includes one complete novel (*Ask Me Tomorrow*), generous and relatively self-contained excerpts from six of his major books, and some stories, essays, letters, and reviews. Sandwiched between these chunks of Cozzens are appreciative essays by distinguished critics and men of letters. Professor Matthew J. Bruccoli, who edited the volume, has also contributed a perceptive biographical essay. In addition to the reprinted pieces by Jerome Weidman and Brendan Gill, there are four critical essays by academic writers, all of whom write appreciatively of Cozzens' art; in particular, Noel Perrin, Frederick Bracher,

and Richard Ludwig offer analytical commentary in support of their enthusiasm.

All the critics included in this volume are puzzled and rather aggressive about what they rightly see as the unjustified, almost conspiratorial, neglect of Cozzens by the critical establishment—that is by the majority of academic and "New York" literary critics. Explaining this neglect and overcoming it is largely the task of these critics and is, one assumes, the purpose of the anthology itself.

Several reasons are given for the sudden eclipse of Cozzens' once brilliant reputation, none of which seems convincing. Some point to Cozzens' obdurate refusal to grant interviews, to appear on talk shows, to become a celebrity. Such reticence, however, has not injured the esteem granted to Thomas Pynchon or (still) to J. D. Salinger, both of whom remain firmly and obsessively private. Others argue that Cozzens' style is too cerebral, too allusive, too controlled. Yet no one would deny cerebration, allusive reference, learning, or architectonic control in the writers named above, not to mention Mailer, Nabokov, Joyce Carol Oates, Bellow, John Hawkes, or Donald Barthelme—all writers whose works are regularly explicated in university lecture halls. The causes for this neglect of Cozzens must be found elsewhere, in the mysterious turns of literary fashion, and in the tremendous cultural upheavals of the last two decades, which fractured and then fragmented our literary ideologies.

We find a clue to these changes in the year 1957, the year of Cozzens' most successful novel, *By Love Possessed*—and also the year in which Norman Mailer turned in a new and astonishingly fruitful direction with the publication of his essay "The White Negro." At the same time, Kerouac published *On the Road,* a book that was to have an immense influence on the thoughts and deeds and writings popular in the Sixties. Both of these authors consciously rejected the novelistic *form* that they and Cozzens had inherited from a long American tradition, a form that Cozzens sharpened and refined in over three decades as a writer. His novels attempted to be "just representations" of men and manners in the twentieth century, judicious, realistic, objective, and accurate imitations of tone and detail. In contrast, the novel of the Sixties and Seventies was to be fact-and-fiction, *reportage,* polemics, or propaganda; it was to be autobiographical, plotless, solipsistic, or narrowly topical, and to range from the impressionistic to the surrealistic and absurd. Cozzens rigorously rejected these fashionable positions.

In addition, our most recent novels have played on (and perhaps played out) themes of anxiety, despair, violence, moral and spiritual relativism, and the blind aggressions of military, sexual, or social conflict. Cozzens' novels do not ignore these themes; to do so would have indicated a willful disregard of the stresses of our century. Nor does reconcile the problems these themes raise with sentimental or contrived solutions. Cozzens can be as bleak as Pynchon, as realistic as Mailer, and as ironically searching as Bellow.

Where Cozzens parts company with his contemporaries is in his ideological stoicism, his refusal to yield to despair or trendy nihilism, his steady belief that intelligence can impose form on experience, that excellence is necessary and possible, and that the abiding virtues in what we now pejoratively call the Puritan Ethic are indeed virtues. In other words, his novels celebrate and define the limits of honor, faith, education, hard work, dignity, loyalty, restraint, and the responsibility incumbent on those who possess (accidentally perhaps) social rank and material wealth.

---

**Cozzens' novels celebrate and define the limits of honor, faith, education, hard work, dignity, loyalty, restraint, and the responsibility incumbent on those who possess (accidentally perhaps) social rank and material wealth.**

*—James A. Epperson*

---

Cozzens, then, pursued subjects that might well be called old-fashioned and conservative—or, put another way, subjects that are worth conserving. His preoccupations naturally affected the way he wrote and the world he wrote about. He was a traditionalist who subordinated his ego, intelligence, and considerable skill to the demands of narrative and character. Honoring hard work, he worked hard and long at his craft, with a faith and diligence we cannot help but admire. His subjects came from that segment of American society, the privileged and educated elite, of which he unapologetically felt himself a part. (His essays on the Kent School and Harvard place him squarely and cheerfully among the Eastern gentry.)

His best books are about that class of Americans, professional people, doctors, lawyers, merchants, chiefs, going about their responsible and complicated lives with a sense of duty and compassion, sure of their abstract convictions but uncertain—as we all are—when the abstract collides with the concrete instance. It is this collision and the resulting incongruity that form the central interest of Cozzens' best novels. Lawyers discover that legalistic concepts of justice are inapplicable to matters of the human heart. Doctors, clergymen, and generals learn that the honorable and necessary principles of their professions, principles that have shaped their thoughts and actions, are inadequate to explain or control the complexities of experience. Despite these inadequacies, these limits (and Cozzens is a writer who explores our limitations), Cozzens' heroes retain their virtue and dignity even as they are disillusioned by experience. Perhaps this hard, classically stoic, even illiberal recognition of our limitations and helplessness accounts for Cozzens' unpopularity with the literary-critical establishment.

Or it may be, as Bruccoli argues, that Cozzens is in disfavor because he writes about those who are generally regarded as successful—the educated, intelligent, socially prominent, well-to-do. The liberal cliche, of course, has it

(to quote Bruccoli) that "success is a sign of corruption. . . . Cozzens alarms proponents of the higher failure." There may be truth in this comment. Only one other author of stature, Louis Auchincloss, has written with intelligence and knowledge of the nation's managerial and professional classes, a segment of our society by no means inconsequential or uncharacteristic. Yet Auchincloss, like Cozzens, gets short critical shrift in the pages of the literary quarterlies.

It is too soon to predict the reemergence of Cozzens as a major figure of American fiction. He died on August 9, ten days before his 75th birthday, the date on which this anthology was released. Like a character from one of his own novels, he must surely have been aware of the irony of this book's genesis and appearance, a project conceived and executed by academics who hoped to rescue him from oblivion. Personal oblivion came to him before he could know of the success or failure of this belated rescue operation. One likes to think that he did not much care, that a lifetime devoted to the writing of books in the best way he knew how was satisfaction enough. Whatever the case, his books will last because they are true, faithful, and intelligent. Those who know his novels will honor his memory. For those who have not yet read Cozzens' work, the omnibus serves as a fine introduction.

### Robert Scholes   (essay date 1979)

SOURCE: "Moral Realism: The Development of an Attitude," in *James Gould Cozzens: New Acquist of True Experience,* edited by Matthew J. Bruccoli, Southern Illinois University Press, 1979, pp. 44-62.

[*Scholes is an educator and author of several books on literature, including* Elements of Fiction *(1968) and* Textual Power: Literary Theory and the Teaching of English *(1985). In the following essay, he discusses the evolution of Cozzens's literary style and his rejection of romanticism in favor of moral realism.*]

The following quotations may be read as a dialogue. The first speaker is a young man in a novel of 1929. The second is an old man in a novel of 1942.

> That was what you did. You died. You did not know what it was about. You never had time to learn. They threw you in and told you the rules and the first time they caught you off base they killed you. Or they killed you gratuitously like Aymo. Or gave you the syphilis like Rinaldi. But they killed you in the end. You could count on that. Stay around and they would kill you.

> Don't be cynical. . . . A cynic is just a man who found out when he was about ten that there wasn't any Santa Claus, and he's still upset. Yet, there'll be more war; and soon, I don't doubt. There always has been. There'll be deaths and disappointments and failures. When they come, you meet them. Nobody promises you a good time or an easy time. I don't know who it was who said when we think of the past we regret and when we think of the future we fear. And with reason. But no bets are off. There is the

present to think of, and as long as you live there always will be.

The young man who spoke first was Frederic Henry in Ernest Hemingway's *A Farewell to Arms;* the old man who answered was Judge Coates in James Gould Cozzens's *The Just and the Unjust.* I do not wish to suggest that Cozzens in this passage is consciously and specifically attempting to rebut Hemingway. Rather, my intention in juxtaposing the two is to locate the unknown by its relation to the known—to make Cozzens's view of life clear by its polar opposition to the more familiar vision of the cosmos characteristic of Hemingway.

His view of life is certainly the right place to begin a consideration of James Gould Cozzens as a writer of fiction. This is true for a number of reasons. First, he is much more than most American writers of his generation a novelist of ideas. Second, and possibly because of the first reason, his technical development as a literary artist has been intimately connected with the development of his thought. This is not to say that he uses fiction (like George Orwell, for example) as a vehicle for polemical thought, but that a particular and very carefully worked-out attitude toward life operates in his fiction to determine the essentials of plot, character, and setting.

The speech of old Judge Coates from the end of *The Just and the Unjust* is characteristic enough to stand as a fair statement of the attitude toward life that dominates Cozzens's later and best fiction. But it is only characteristic. It is not an ultimate formulation, a solution to the problems of living. It represents a significant phase in his thinking, which is associated with much of his best work, but it represents a phase only—not the whole process of thought. The process is the important thing—the continuing development that began with his earliest fiction and is still in progress.

The early novels are *Confusion* (1924), *Michael Scarlett* (1925), *Cock Pit* (1928), and *The Son of Perdition* (1929). Cozzens was an undergraduate at Harvard when his first book was published—an event he has since regretted;

> It made me, in my own eyes, a real figure in literature, at once; an author of far too much promise to waste time any longer at schoolboy work. So I quit school and got at my career, started right in at what I thought was the top. In that way every natural fault was solidified, and it is taking all my effort now, in my mid-thirties, to wipe out those faults, to really learn to write. [Cozzens in an interview with Robert Van Gelder, "James Gould Cozzens at Work," *New York Times Book Review,* 23 June 1940]

This separation of the first four novels from the later works is not entirely a device of criticism on my part. Indeed, they were first dissociated by their author, who has failed to mention any of them in the lists of "Other Books by James Gould Cozzens" that appear opposite the title pages of his later works. That his repudiation of his earliest works is a result of their technical shortcomings can certainly be inferred from his statement just quoted, but there is yet another reason why at that time he found these early novels "much too painful to talk about."

> When I was that age I admired a friend of mine who got drunk at 9 o'clock in the morning. That is too early in life to begin to think of yourself as a writer. Because you are very young when you think a fellow who comes to your rooms early in the morning, already drunk, and is heaving bottles against near-by walls at noon, is entirely admirable. ["James Gould Cozzens at Work"]

The reasons for the repudiation of these first four novels were more than technical. In fact, the implication seems to be that it is the greenness of judgment rather than the technical faults which makes those first books "much too painful to talk about."

*Confusion* is a novel about a girl who develops a sensibility too exquisite to allow her to function in a world that has too little to offer her. In the matter of theme the book bears a close resemblance to a work published in the following year: *The Great Gatsby* by F. Scott Fitzgerald. Gatsby is described as having "something gorgeous about him, some heightened sensitivity to the promises of life, as if he were related to one of those intricate machines that register earthquakes ten thousand miles away." Cerise D'Atrée, the heroine of *Confusion,* has something of this same "heightened sensitivity to the promises of life." The descendant of an ancient French family, Cerise is given the best education the resources of her family and the intelligence of her two godfathers can provide. As she grows up, these two well-meaning gentlemen become aware that something has gone wrong. The more sensitive of the two, Tischoifsky, expresses it in this way:

> We gave her the past in full measure, we laid a foundation of exquisite sensibility and appreciation. It was to have been her most ready servant. It has turned on her and she is going to be its slave. You can see it. She has a remarkable instinctive taste in things. She has a youthful capacity for idealization, of course. Ordinarily the realization of life as it is—to use that for lack of a better phrase—would fall on semi-developed taste and immature appreciation. Both those safeguards we have obliterated in Cerise, we have put years and constant effort into obliterating. Now you see Cerise stripped of all protection except the unreliable slowness of experience to divulge the full force of disappointment. [*Confusion*]

Later the disenchanted bride, Jacqueline Atkinson, directly tells Cerise essentially the same thing about herself: " . . . I'd hate to see it happen to you. And you're one of the ones it would happen to. You're looking for more in life than there is. . . ." The death of Cerise in an automobile accident is meant, I am sure, to emphasize the world's inability to fulfill her, as well as to bring the story to a conclusion.

Fitzgerald and Cozzens in these two books both seem to feel that there is something wrong with a world that can not present such people as Gatsby and Cerise with "something commensurate to their capacity for wonder." The difference between the two novels—aside from any question of superiority of technique—is that *The Great Gatsby* is ripe Fitzgerald, while *Confusion* is very green Cozzens.

This motif of a sensitive young person destroyed by an indifferently cruel world is repeated in Cozzens's second book, *Michael Scarlett.* This is a historical novel, set in Elizabethan England, in which such characters as Nashe, Marlowe, Donne, Shakespeare, Southampton, and Essex figure prominently. But for all its period setting, the main outline of the story is very like that of Cerise D'Atrée. Michael Scarlett is "an exquisite youth" raised by a guardian, educated but sheltered—just as Cerise was. He comes as a young man into a Cambridge and a London alive with faction and is soon unwittingly embroiled. Shakespeare and Southampton speak of him:

> "I would have thought," commented Mr. Shakespere, "that my lord Essex, Mr. Marlowe, and Mr. Nashe between them dominated him wholly; they call, and he comes. A strange melancholy of indecision hath smitten you young people, Harry. Him chiefest of all."
>
> "I had not meant to hint I liked him less," answered Southampton quickly, "but that I pitied him more. It was an evil thing he ever came to London. See how an unplanned, undesired chain of event hath placed him in the saddle where he sits neither safe nor happy. Essex was fitted to taste in his championing of the high party. Essex requires aid at a duel (by irony, on Michael's behalf). Michael, with nice swordsmanship, saves the day and Devereux's life; yet so greviously hurting Captain Blunt that he transfers the popular leadership of his party from Essex to himself, which he neither wanted nor needed, and having, can neither manage nor hold. He doth not understand the issue, he cares little for the outcome. Those that do care, borrow his name to forward their own ends. Being confused and not comprehending, he hath submitted thus far." [*Michael Scarlett*]

Michael's death results from a senseless fight in which he attempts to enable Nashe, wanted for an accidental killing, to escape capture. Nashe refuses to flee, but fights by Michael's side until wounded.

In the last chapter of *Confusion,* "White Roses," the dying Cerise had gazed from her bed at a vase full of roses and mused that it was "strange that a rose which would presently die should be so beautiful." A rose figures in the closing pages of *Michael Scarlett,* too. Michael, bleeding to death in the snow, asks a mad prostitute to deliver to Southampton a memento he has carried in his shirt. He dies as she removes the object and inspects it.

> "How, a rose?" she murmured, "i' faith, a pretty wooden rose, yet much decayed and dry."
>
> She tossed it up and down as a child tosses a toy.
>
> "Poor rose, sweet rose," she sang, "yet thou'rt very dead."
>
> She looked at it for a space.
>
> "Prithee burn, rose," she said.
>
> It fell into the fire and was lost.

In each novel the roses, living or dead, seem to represent (clumsily, perhaps) the young person whose life and death has been the matter of the story. The suggestion that life is a sad affair because beautiful roses and exquisite young people must die in its confusion can only be described as sentimental. It is undoubtedly this sentimentalism, strikingly evident in the early novels, that makes their author so reluctant to discuss them.

It seems for a time in the third novel, *Cock Pit* (1928), that the familiar pattern of the first two is to be repeated. The story is set in Cuba against the prominent background of the sugar industry. The principal focus is on the daughter of an engineer at one of the mills.

Ruth Micks is not an "exquisite youth" as Cerise D'Atrée and Michael Scarlett were, but she is superior to and in conflict with her environment. The discerning bank manager, Mr. Britton, observes and judges her:

> He took a swallow of wine. Romanticists! His own practical mind made allowances for it as one would make allowances for the difficulties of a cripple.
>
> That cool and calculating efficiency of thought and judgment which made him one of the bank's most trusted managers appraised . . . them all. . . . He had nothing but admiration for Ruth, unlikely to criticize an intelligence which he felt to be understandable, like his own. Across it ran the softer stuff, the gentler, yes, stupider, sentiments of Mary and Maurice. Ruth went through them like steel through wax.
>
> No; he held that. Not steel. You missed Ruth altogether if you could see only that clean cutting power. That was superficial, a clear head working easily among muddled ones. His own clear head could recognize that with admiration, but there was something deeper, he knew, for he felt, totally unsentimental, an attachment for Ruth, a sense of understanding her, of seeing what none of these people saw, not even her father. His mind with a clearing flash, like the dropping of the jumbled pieces of a kaleidoscope into perfect pattern, held it there.
>
> By God, he thought, not surprised, for he had known it all along, he supposed; what a rotten shame! *Not even her father. . . .*
>
> An unutterable and very simple sadness came over him. It turned from Ruth, for that was the end he saw, not temporary, but a final frustration. [*Cock Pit*]

There is a hint in Britton's meditation, which occurs midway through the novel, that Ruth's story is to end in frustration as Michael's and Cerise's had, but it remains only a hint, ultimately belied by the plot. At the close of the story Ruth is a successful heroine, having conquered by her cleverness and courage the ruthless sugar baron, Don Miguel Bautizo. Don Miguel is not only defeated, he is made to like it, demonstrating that under his ruthless exterior beats the heart of a gallant gentleman.

The musings of Britton serve to illustrate a conflict that will prove most important for an understanding of Cozzens's novels. His opening condemnation of "romanticists" sounds a theme that recurs with increasing emphasis in Cozzens's work. The qualities Britton marks in those "romanticists" are "stupider sentiments" and "muddled" heads, which are opposed to the "understandable" intelligences and "clear" heads of Ruth and himself. Since it is Ruth's clear head that prevails in the novel, we may assume that the author shares to some extent in Britton's condemnation of romanticists. Yet the state of affairs pictured at the end of the story is clearly the result of a sentimental or romantic way of looking at life. To believe that a young woman may triumph over the armed rapaciousness of a large and powerful industry is surely the result of a sentimental conception of reality; and to believe that the unprincipled head of such an enterprise, a man who once quashed the report of a United States Senate Committee, is likely to turn out to be a cavalier old gentleman is even more romantic.

In this way a novel has been produced that specifically attacks muddled thinking and sentiment under the name of "romanticism" but which can be shown to be vulnerable to the same charges in regard to its plot and at least one of its characterizations. This then is the sort of book a young man who thinks that "a fellow who comes to your rooms early in the morning, already drunk, . . . is entirely admirable," might be expected to write. And this is the sort of book that a middle-aged man, who no longer finds such antics entirely admirable, might be expected to find it "painful" to have written.

Still the struggle between sense and sensibility was clearly joined in this novel, and, if the victory of sense was marred because it was achieved in a sentimental manner, there were to be other struggles. In the works of the eight years following the publication of **Cock Pit** in 1928, this conflict was renewed again and again. The vague antiromantic notions that began to take shape in **Cock Pit** were gradually formulated into a complete and consistent doctrine, most explicitly expounded in **Men and Brethren** (1936); and, finally, this doctrine has been qualified and enriched in the later works.

**The Son of Perdition** (1929), like **Cock Pit,** is a product of Cozzens's year in Cuba, but despite the similarity in setting, it is a very different book from its predecessor. It represents a considerable advance in technique: an attempt, perhaps not quite successful, to do more than was done in the early novels. And we can observe in it an important shift in thematic emphasis.

Cozzens's first three novels dealt with the efforts of young people to adjust to their environments. The exquisite youths, Cerise and Michael, perished without succeeding. The clear-headed Ruth triumphed, but in a sentimental way. The central conflict in **The Son of Perdition** occurs within a mature man. Joel Stellow is the Administrator General of the United Sugar Company, a post that gives him a truly despotic power. The company has its own railroads, its own banks, its own armed guards, even its own villages. Stellow chooses to exercise his power benevolently—insofar as this is compatible with the best interests of the United Sugar Company. And herein lies the central conflict of the novel.

The particular crisis that exposes this conflict is brought about by the arrival in Stellow's little kingdom of a dissolute American, Oliver Findley. Wherever Findley is, there is trouble. In part this is caused by his personal characteristics. He is a liar, a thief, and a drunkard; and these facets of his character cause their share of difficulties. But beyond this, there is something about him that seems to act as a catalyst, bringing into violent action the potential danger or evil latent in any given situation. He strolls into a sugar mill; a man is crushed in the machinery. He asks a bartender to drink with him; the man's boss enters and fires the bartender for drinking on duty. He seduces a Cuban girl; a whole complex of terrible intrafamily emotions, hitherto balanced against one another, are unbalanced, resulting in a murder. From the most serious to the almost trivial, trouble follows in the wake of Oliver Findley. He is thought to be the Devil by Pepe Rijo, the simple mayor of the United Sugar village of Dosfuegos. His relation to Stellow is adumbrated by the book's epigraph:

> —those that thou gavest me I have kept, and none of them is lost, but the son of perdition.
> —*St. John* 17:12.

Findley, of course, is the son of perdition; Stellow the man who tries to keep "those that thou gavest me."

When Findley turns up at a United mill, General Administrator Stellow tries to find a use for him. A ticket to Habana and fifty dollars are to be his reward for a little chore. Leaving Stellow's office, Findley appraises the great man:

> He wasn't sure, as he went out, that he understood Mr. Stellow—the man, that was, apart from the Administrator, the individual in contradistinction to the United Sugar Company. It was probably a shift from one to the other; from the Company, which asked what could be done with a liar and a thief, to the individual who tried to find a use in the face of that absolute nothing. A curious unemotional sympathy which would wish, for reasons too hard to guess, to give a human being a break where it was possible without hampering the Company. He wondered, struck by the thought, if Mr. Stellow, after these many years, had reached a point where he needed to believe that a human being could hamper the Company. [**The Son of Perdition**]

Stellow soon finds that Oliver Findley is not a man who can be given "a break." The son of perdition is caught stealing the same day. The Administrator, feeling that Habana is not far enough, decides to ship his guest to Bordeaux:

> "I don't believe you'll ever get back to Cuba again," he said. "That's all I care about, Findley. Wherever you go there'll be trouble, and it's not going to be here. It's too late to make you over, Findley."
>
> A change close to expression had moved Mr. Stellow's face; nothing direct, like pity or indignation. Only a trace of a sag, a contraction of the gray eyes. . . . Oliver Findley stood dumbly in the shadows, even his own relief lost in this final astonishment.
>
> For the first time he saw Mr. Stellow as a person. He saw him in the ultimate, incredible obvious-

ness of a human being apart from his position, divested of the small excrescences of habit and particular personality. Mr. Stellow was old, simply, and tired; as all men must be sooner or later. In the Administrator's last words had been also his own epitaph, and all his life, all that the eye had seen and the brain considered, could serve him no better than to make him understand it. [*The Son of Perdition*]

Findley is shipped off to Dosfuegos for further shipment to France. In the short space of time before he boards the ship he is the cause of an incident that affects Stellow not merely in his capacity as Administrator, but personally.

One of Joel Stellow's few friends, perhaps his only one, has been Vidal Monaga. Monaga is a fisherman, but because of his monumental family pride he is able to meet the Administrator as an equal. Findley casually seduces Nida Monaga, the daughter of Vidal. Nida's brother Osmundo suspects this seduction, and in his attack on Findley reveals to his father that his own relations with his sister are not purely brotherly. The old man, out of pride in his name, murders his son. He is imprisoned by the major of the village until Stellow can get there. On arrival the Administrator asks him to explain why he did it. Vidal explains that recent events have shown him that his son, now a grown man, did not know what it was to be a Monaga; and "Being sure of this, I saw that he would be better dead." Stellow, whose power is unlimited, has a report of accidental death prepared by his doctor. This effort to save his old friend from trial is frustrated by the man's pride in himself. Their conversation is overheard by Findley:

> "You are released from the Alcalde's order of arrest," said Mr. Stellow. "The matter is officially closed."
>
> It had never, reflected Oliver Findley, been open. Never in Mr. Stellow's mind, could it have been possible to allow the mechanical processes to grind up the simple stone of this old man. It went farther than that, no doubt. The wordless bond silently and invisibly held them too close. Such destruction would break down something of Mr. Stellow. Some saving faith.
>
> Oliver Findley thought of it, seeing clearly now, moved more than he would have thought possible. He saw too, the transparent farce of it. Mr. Stellow setting up himself against himself. Driving the mills and railroads on one hand, covering the face of the machines with the fiction of this necessary illusion on the other, sustaining futilely the legend of man and his dignity and freedom, long after the last remnants were dust under the revolving wheels. . . .
>
> In the electric lighted room Vidal Monaga said, "No señor. . . . That I could not do. . . . It is not much to be a Monaga to any one but me, señor. But I will be turned over to the authorities, please. . . . Because of justice. . . ."
>
> Finally Mr. Stellow answered: "As you wish." [*The Son of Perdition*]

To Findley, Monaga's refusal to avoid justice represents a victory for man over the machine: "the machine's inhu-

man beauty, the reason and might of the machine, confounded so inevitably by the rooted folly, the poor stubborn pride of man."

One of the major faults of the book lies in the difficulties presented by having as its central intelligence a character so depraved as Oliver Findley. How much weight can we put on such a summing up of action as that quoted above? To attribute to such a dissolute wretch the clear insight needed to judge others is an error on the part of the author, equivalent to attributing a gentlemanly soul to a rapacious sugar baron. To rely on such a character to sum up, in the closing lines of a book, the action just culminated, is a technical error stemming from the sentimental error.

Another difficulty in the novel lies in its somewhat disordered complexity. There are numerous minor actions and characters, most of which seem to belong to the plot rather than the theme, and which tend to blur the theme, making the need for clarification of it especially vital. That we are forced to rely on Findley for such clarification thus assumes even greater importance than it might in a better-ordered novel.

The significance of **The Son of Perdition** in the development of Cozzens's ethical attitude is that it represents a progress from the preoccupation with the problems of youth toward the less purely self-centered problems of mature individuals. The struggle within Stellow, between his duty to the company and his care for humanity—though sketched rather than developed in this novel—is a struggle that is more central in life than are the youthful flutterings of the early novels. But the book fails—aside from the technical difficulties—to give a moral order to the struggle presented. Other than a vague preference for people over machines, there seems to be present no unifying moral attitude. Is the triumph of humanity over the machine, acclaimed by Findley, punishment for Joel Stellow or vindication of him? Is Stellow's phrase of acquiescence to Monaga's desire—"As you wish"—the speech of a man who sees a higher truth than his own, or that of a man who has lost "some saving faith?"

This fuzziness of theme persists in the work of Cozzens for some years. His next works attempt by various devices to get around the problem of ethical attitude rather than to solve the problem by taking a stand. This is particularly noticeable in the two short novels, *S.S. San Pedro* (1931) and *Castaway* (1934).

It is probably best to consider these two short works together even though the full-length novel, **The Last Adam** (1933), was published before **Castaway**. These two novellas are experiments that have not been repeated, though they exhibit excellently some abilities and characteristics of their author. **The Last Adam,** however, is in the main stream of his development, where it appears as a marked advance over **The Son of Perdition** in the direction of the major novels.

**S.S. San Pedro** was first published as a prize-winning story in *Scribner's Magazine* in August of 1930. It is a fictionalized reconstruction of the actual events in the sinking of the S.S. *Vestris* in November 1928. The real disaster captured the journalistic imagination in its day because of some mysterious circumstances connected with the sinking. The ship left Hoboken bound for Brazil. She ran into heavy seas almost immediately, took on a list, and struggled ahead with cargo shifting and water entering the ship, probably through the submerged coal ports. The circumstance that disturbed the public so greatly was that the ship apparently had been in this state for a day and a night without sending out an SOS. A theory advanced was that the captain "seems to have been more afraid of salvage than he was of death" ["The Master of the *Vestris*," *Nation* 127, 28 November 1928]. The ship sank with considerable loss of life. Cozzens, working from the "transcript of the hearing before the U.S. Commissioner in New York" [Cozzens in a letter to Scholes, 14 March 1956] set about reconstructing one way in which such a disaster might occur. The events are seen through the eyes of the second officer, Anthony Bradell, and the Brazilian first quartermaster, Miro. The officer and the man, each extremely capable at his job, are unable to prevent the disaster. They can do nothing to avoid the ultimate, because of the structure of command, which requires action to be initiated at the top. Captain Clendening is overcome by a strange lethargy that renders him incapable of the necessary action. That this may happen is foreshadowed early in the book by the captain's doctor, who takes Bradell aside before going ashore and warns him about the captain's health:

> "The captain," he said very low to Anthony, "is an old man, Mr. Bradell."
>
> "What did you say, sir?" asked Anthony, taken aback.
>
> "People grow old, Mr. Bradell. They break down, they wear out." [*S. S. San Pedro*]

Dr. Percival, who gives Bradell this warning, has a face like a death's head:

> Doctor Percival's tight face was fleshless and almost gray. His lips sank in, rounded over his teeth. They were lips so scanty that you could see the line of the teeth meeting. His eyes, red-rimmed, lay limp in their sockets, appearing to have no color at all. Doctor Percival's intense pale gaze came out of holes covered with soft, semitransparent lenses. His head, one observed, jolted, was utterly hairless, and a pale-reddish star, a mark like a healed wound, lay across the crown. Every modulation of bone showed through a sere leaf of old skin. [*San Pedro*]

It is this face that Bradell sees at his side as he lies injured at the feet of Miro while the ship is about to founder. The story is told in a dispassionate "documentary" style, combining graphic observation of the physical details of the ship with the rather labored symbolism of the death-doctor. We are given an excruciatingly careful description of a foreordained event; thus no moral issues are raised. By choosing to depict the captain as the victim of forces beyond any man's control, Cozzens avoids the moral questions that might be raised had he made the problem the obvious one of the captain's weighing salvage costs against the possibility of weathering the storm. The whole of the action is carefully removed from the moral world of ethical choices.

*Castaway* is a story in many ways different from all of Cozzens's work, but bearing a closer resemblance to *S.S. San Pedro* than to any of his other books. It is the story of Mr. Lecky, cast away, not on a desert island but in a deserted department store. The epigraph is from *Robinson Crusoe:*

> . . . how infinitely good that Providence is, which has provided in its government of mankind such narrow bounds to his sight and knowledge of things; and though he walks in the midst of so many thousand dangers, the sight of which if discovered to him, would distract his mind and sink his spirits, he is kept serene and calm by having the events of things hid from his eyes. . . .

This epigraph is—like others of Cozzens's—an ironic one. It is precisely Lecky's fear of unseen dangers that destroys any possibility of his leading a peaceful existence in the great store. He is certain that there is someone else in the building: "the idiot" as Lecky calls him. Armed with a shotgun from the sporting goods department and a knife from kitchenware, he hunts the idiot down and kills him brutally. Then he discovers whom he has killed.

> Crouching as he turned up the fearful face, he bent his own face toward it, saw it again. His hand on the head, studying the uninjured side, Mr. Lecky beheld its familiar strangeness—not like a stranger's face, and yet it was no friend's face, nor the face of anyone he had ever met.
>
> What this could mean held him, bent closer, questioning in the gloom; and suddenly his hand let go . . . for Mr. Lecky knew why he had never seen a man with this face. He knew who had been pursued and cruelly killed, who was now dead and would never climb more stairs. He knew why Mr. Lecky could never have for his own the stock of this great store. [*Castaway*]

Presumably he has killed himself. One critic assures us that this is an allegory that "translates readily into half-a-dozen frames of reference (centering around a ritual of rebirth)" [Stanley Edgar Hyman, "James Gould Cozzens and the Art of the Possible," *New Mexico Quarterly Review* 19, Winter, 1949]. If one can believe that Lecky is a "God-Figure," and the idiot a "Devil-Figure" in a "dubious battle long ago joined," then perhaps their struggle has some large moral applications, but I find this conclusion as doubtful as the premises, which are very dubious indeed.

The descriptions of the store are as meticulous as those of the ship in *S.S. San Pedro,* and the inevitable action proceeds to its conclusion under the same uncommitted camera-eye. But this refusal on the part of the author to commit himself to a moral position could not be maintained in all his works. For, as Henry James said of Dickens, "a novelist very soon has need of a little philosophy. . . . When he comes to tell the story of a passion . . . he becomes a moralist as well as an artist. He must know *man* as well as *men*, and to know man is to be a philosopher"

[Henry James, "The Limitations of Dickens," *Views and Reviews,* 1908].

Cozzens's philosophy, which seemed rather fuzzy in **The Son of Perdition** (1929), was to appear in unmistakable clarity in **Men and Brethren** (1936). In an effort to isolate some of the elements that compose that clarified attitude, I will consider some of the short stories published between 1930 and 1938.

These twenty-one stories tend to divide into three groups. The largest group, comprising almost half of the stories, is composed of potboilers. The second group all deal with the same subject, a boys' preparatory school. The third group includes stories interesting primarily for the light they throw on themes treated at greater length in the novels. The groups can not be dealt with chronologically, for each of them covers nearly the entire span over which Cozzens wrote short stories. There is little that can be said about the potboilers, except to note that they get increasingly slick from first to last; but the prep school stories are significant in that they deal with young people in a way quite different from the treatment of exquisite youths in the early novels. The school in the stories, Durham, is unquestionably modeled on the Kent School in Connecticut at which Cozzens prepared for Harvard. It is relevant to note at this time that Cozzens's first published work appeared in the pages of the *Atlantic Monthly* while he was in the fourth form at Kent.

The occasion of this event was an article by Edward Parmalee in the January 1920 issue of the *Atlantic Monthly* that expressed disapproval of the boarding-school system, making the charge that rigid discipline stifled any impulses the boys might have to learn self-government, and asking the question, "would not better results be obtained by a less autocratic and a more democratic system of government?"

Young Cozzens's reply, entitled **"A Democratic School,"** made the point that institutions such as Parmalee was calling for did, indeed, exist and were successful. The prefect system, under which discipline was administered by three members of the sixth form appointed by the headmaster, and two members each from the fifth and fourth forms, elected by their peers, was a truly democratic system, he maintained, and added, "Perhaps it doesn't sound practicable, but then, it works." Note the emphasis on the practical and the present: "I will. . . offer the solution—not the visionary solution, but the solution that, in one school at least, works to-day." The young man who wrote the article on **"A Democratic School"** in 1920 seems in certain ways closer to the older man who wrote the Durham stories and the later novels than to the author of **Confusion,** which appeared only four years after the magazine article.

There are five Durham stories, the earliest appearing in 1930, the last in 1938. The only character who appears in more than one is the headmaster, Dr. Holt. The headmaster is an eminently practical man who understands equally well rebellious young people and demanding parents. The student and the school, as the individual and society in microcosm, provide a type of conflict that stimulates Cozzens to an extremely revealing series of comments on rebellious idealists in general.

**"Some Day You'll Be Sorry"** (*Saturday Evening Post,* 21 June 1930) is about a boy who nurtures a grudge against the headmaster. The boy's rebellion is based in part on some rather stimulating reading: "Smith III, as the saying goes, had read a book. It was Paine's *Age of Reason.*" The following observation on Smith by Cozzens is interesting for the generalization it leads to: "Smith III's intelligence was much too acute to waste its strength in a permanent and ridiculous war with his environment. Real rebels are rarely anything but second rate outside their rebellion; the drain of time and temper is ruinous to any other accomplishment."

**"Some Day You'll Be Sorry"** is an especially interesting story because of its autobiographical overtones. As Frederick Bracher pointed out some years ago, youth versus age is a major theme in Cozzens's work. Now as bits of biographical information begin to become accessible, it is apparent that one of the favorite pastimes of the elder Cozzens has been chastising the recollected figure of his youth.

> When, early in his fourth-form year, Smith III took occasion to inform the headmaster that he no longer believed in God, Doctor Holt sighed. Smith III's point had been that he did not see how he could honorably go to chapel when he considered the practice a superstitious farce. It is usual to hear most about the other side of these things—Shelley, at Oxford, is almost unbearably familiar—so it is worth a moment to consider Doctor Holt's position, confronted by a supercilious and impudent youth who appeared to get the only exercise he took from making trouble; who was very justly suspected of smoking without permission; whose marks were bad, and whose comments on life, society and the school were fitted nicely to the puerile sensation they made.

Smith III seems almost certainly to represent the way in which his own youth appeared to the very clear gaze of the maturing James Gould Cozzens in 1930.

A rather more mature rebel is presented in **"Guns of the Enemy"** (*Saturday Evening Post,* 1 Nov. 1930). This is a very fine story in which World War I descends on Durham in the form of a French officer. The ensuing conflict—among the agitated students, a young pacifist instructor, and Dr. Holt who sees the war as a monster that will destroy the youth to whom he is devoting his life—is endowed with a significance somewhat larger than that of a minor uprising in a small boy's school. "War was already enhanced by a noble solemnity and an emotional importance. Our attitude was, in fact, exactly that of America; with the special local result that when we took things hard, less than usual was said about it. When little is said, much must be taken for granted. As you know, what people took for granted was that we were fighting for humanity and could no longer allow the Germans to infest the earth." Dr. Holt does not share this attitude. He clearly sees the war as a horror, but he "had the courage—and courage it is if you value your reputation as a thoughtful man—to state: 'Our country, right or wrong.' Most people mistake the statement for jingoism, but it can be—and in Doctor Holt's case it was—the hard, honorable answer to an intolerable question." The man whose attitude disrupts the school is the young teacher, Mr. Van Artevelde. His pacifist leanings provoke a senseless physical assault from a student, whom Dr. Holt is then forced to expel. The school is threatened by a mass resignation in protest against the expulsion, but Dr. Holt, by main force of personality and skill in handling his boys, prevents this. Van Artevelde

> was, naturally, a socialist of some sort. In those years directly before the war, almost everyone who had the happiness to be young, intelligent and carefully educated was a socialist. This was in part simple intellectual snobbery, and the first cold wind from the world as it was blew it away, but Van was also an idealist, as well as being stubborn. To men of his temper, socialism's pathetic impracticality is not its worst argument; just as the principal charm of pacifism may be its dangerous unpopularity.

Durham figures only in the background for **"Total Stranger"** (*Saturday Evening Post,* 15 February 1936), another fine story, which won the O. Henry Prize. A boy is being driven back to school by his father, who is the object of a grumpy, misunderstanding rebellion on the part of the son. The father "could see no sense in breaking the simple, necessary rules of any organized society; and wasting time was worse than wrong, it was mad and dissolute. Time lost, he very well knew, can never be recovered."

The boy feels this way: "In my position, I supposed that he would always do his lessons, never break any rules, and probably end up a prefect, with his rowing colors and a football letter—in fact, with everything that I would like, if only the first steps toward them did not seem so dull and difficult. Since they did, I was confirmed in my impression that it was impossible to please him. Since it was impossible, I had long been resolved not to care whether I pleased him or not. Practice had made not caring fairly easy." On the trip an incident occurs that makes the son realize that his father was young once—is a human being. He begins to see that his father's is not an impossible goal reached by a perfect human being: "Unfortunately, I never did do much better at school. But that year and the years following, I would occasionally try to, for I thought it would please my father."

The last Durham story, **"Son and Heir,"** (*Saturday Evening Post,* 2 April 1938), is about another rebellious boy. This boy, an excellent hockey player, is embarrassed by his father's desire to push him. He tries to take out his resentment against his father and the school (the father is Durham '09) by disgracing Durham in a hockey game—not by playing badly, but by acting in an unsportsmanlike manner. Dr. Holt, in a locker room chat, helps him to grow up a little. The author comments: "Having no intent or volition of its own, he might guess that the world—surely it is the sum of a young man's possible education—would pay out to him, not with malice and not with pity, the things that were his."

The view of life implicit and explicit in these stories is con-

sistent throughout. It is the classic conservative view. The father who "could see no sense in breaking the simple necessary rules of any organized society" is pictured as a good man and a not unreasonable one. Dr. Holt, whose principal occupation in the stories is the conservative one of trying to hold together his little world in the face of disruptive influences, is presented sympathetically. The rebels are given short shrift. The name that persistently comes to mind as one reads these stories is Edmund Burke. The positive side: the organic conception of society; and the negative side: the fierce distrust and suspicion of rebels in general are both present. The particular hostility to the influence of Thomas Paine is characteristic of both Burke and Cozzens. Thus a reference to Paine in Cozzens's 1940 interview should not come as a surprise to us.

> This Summer I intend to spend many pleasant mornings hanging around court rooms because I plan to write a novel about a lawyer. "The Summer Soldier" probably will be the title. When Paine used that phrase he disdained the people who could be so described, he was calling on the men of his generation to forget their own concerns and fight for the ideal of the Revolution, to lose themselves in an ideal. He had no use for the militiamen who were willing to fight when they could afford the time, but wanted to spend most of the year raising crops, attending to business, taking care of their families.
>
> But as I see it there is a lot to be said for these Summer soldiers. The idealist, the intellectuals, haven't done any too well by the world. [Van Gelder, "James Gould Cozzens at Work"]

The attitude so clearly present in the short stories as early as 1930 is reaffirmed in this interview of 1940, and has remained an important factor in all Cozzens's later novels. The ethical attitude developed from the vague sentimentality of his earliest works through the various negations of what he calls "romanticism," "sentimentalism," and "idealism" to a firm position Cozzens calls simply "realism," and to which I have added the qualifying adjective, *moral,* to prevent any confusion of this ethical attitude with the literary or esthetic doctrine of realism. It was the development of this ethical attitude that enabled James Gould Cozzens to produce the works we now recognize as major.

## Colin S. Cass   (essay date Fall 1981)

SOURCE: "Cozzens's Debt to Thomas Dekker in *Ask Me Tomorrow,*" in *Markham Review,* Vol. 11, Fall, 1981, pp. 11-16.

*[In the essay below, Cass compares the characters and themes of Cozzens's* Ask Me Tomorrow *with Thomas Dekker's play,* The Pleasant Comedie of Old Fortunatus *(1599), contending that the play provided the basis for Cozzens's story.]*

When James Gould Cozzens finished his ninth novel, he wanted to call it "Young Fortunatus," but Alfred Harcourt dissuaded him "on the reasonable grounds that since he had never [sic] heard of *Old Fortunatus* most other readers wouldn't have, and might wonder, irked, what the hell I meant. The book didn't sell at all so it could have made no difference and I wish now I had used it." [Cozzens in a letter to James B. Merriwether, 27 March 1962]. The first edition was published in 1940 as *Ask Me Tomorrow.* Later it was republished in the Uniform Edition as *Ask Me Tomorrow or The Pleasant Comedy of Young Fortunatus.* During Cozzens's lifetime it received very little attention, a fact that evidently disappointed him. A year before his death he wrote to me and spoke as if he regarded it as his most underrated book:

> That promised account of the Spring Quarter course was wonderfully amusing (hell of a word; so I see sufferings of others as funny, huh?). Also it makes me wonder if for your projected purpose Ask Me Tomorrow (Uniform Edition text) might not be worth your looking at. Though not lacking 'literary milage' [sic] demands, it's fairly short, a virtue cardinal enough to excuse, perhaps, absence of Relevance ('Modren'), King Cong, sharks & (old aaf term) Nooky. Or do I really mean it happens to be the one book of mine that, finished, left me fairly content—no doubt because, not having tried to do too much, I wasn't forced to see chagrinned how short I came of all I aimed at to start. However: does anybody know a writer not dumb about his own work, so you judge. [Cozzens in a letter to Colin S. Cass, 15 July 1977]

The book now has a new opportunity to find an appreciative audience; it has been included in *Just Representations: A James Gould Cozzens Reader.* Reexamination should begin with the rejected title, which survived as a subtitle and has never been explained. Cozzens wanted to name his novel after the play by Thomas Dekker called *The Pleasant Comedie of Old Fortunatus,* and it's time we understood why.

Since students of Cozzens are apparently unfamiliar with *Old Fortunatus,* a synopsis may be helpful. The play concerns an unsuccessful old Cypriot named Fortunatus who, lost in a forest, meets the goddess Fortune. Calling him Fortune's minion, she offers him wisdom, strength, health, beauty, long life, or riches. When he prefers riches, she decries his foolish refusal of wisdom. Nevertheless, she bestows a purse that will be inexhaustible while Fortunatus and his two sons live. As Fortune leaves, she says contemptuously, "now goe dwell with cares and quickly die" (I.i.), but Fortunatus thinks, "If I die to morrow, ile be merrie to day . . ." (I.i.). So he returns, provides lavishly for his sons, Ampedo and Andelocia, and sets out to travel. Visiting Babylon, Fortunatus steals a hat that lets the wearer go instantly wherever he wants. Meanwhile, Andelocia squanders money and pious Ampedo spends none. Their father returns with the hat, but during a prideful speech he is interrupted by Fortune, who has reappeared to say that Fortunatus is "no sonne of *Fortune,* but her slaue" (II.ii.), whose fate is "to die when th'art most fortunate" (II.ii). Too late he regrets that he chose riches, but the goddess refuses to give his sons wisdom instead, and Andelocia gladly takes the purse as soon as Fortunatus dies.

The next scene is King Athelstane's court in England,

where suitors woo the king's daughter, Agripyne. Andelocia arrives with the same intention. His wealth attracts great interest, but it also provokes royal resentments and intrigues. Athelstane's daughter, wheedling Andelocia's secret, lulls him to sleep and steals his purse, as he learns when Shaddow, his servant, needing money, wakes him up. After the discovery Shaddow still needs to know, "Shal I buy these spices to day or to morrow?"

> To morrow? I, to morrow thou shalt buy them,
> To morrow tell the Princesse I wil loue her,
> To morrow tell the king, ile banquet him,
> To morrow, *Shaddow,* will I giue thee glad,
> To morrow pride goes bare and lust acold.
> To morrow will the rich man feede the poore,
> And vice to morrow vertue will adore.
> To morrow beggers shall be crowned kings,
> This No-time, morrowes-time, no sweetnes sings:
> I pray thee hence: beare that to *Agripyne* (III.i.).

Andelocia skulks back to Cyprus, steals his brother's wishing hat, and revisits England disguised as a jewel merchant. Seizing Agripyne, he abducts both princess and purse to a wilderness, where Vertue and Vice have earlier been seen planting trees. While Andelocia climbs in the tree of Vice, Agripyne escapes. Getting down, Andelocia also finds he has sprouted horns. He sleeps. The deities return, Fortune to prolong his life, Vice to scoff, Vertue to accept his repentance, remove his horns, and teach him to recover his purse and hat.

Agripyne, safe in England, has just been promised to the Prince of Cyprus when Andelocia and Shaddow enter disguised as Irish costermongers. They peddle apples of Vice to Agripyne and two courtiers, Montrosse and Longauille. When next seen, these three have horns, and Cyprus moans, "To morrow should haue beene our marriage morne, / But now my bride is shame, thy bridegrome scorne" (V.i.). Newly disguised as a French physician, Andelocia cures Montrosse and Longauille. He abducts Agripyne a second time, but having recovered his purse and hat, he releases her and cures her horn, then returns the hat to his brother. But Longauille and Montrosse are eager for revenge. Capturing the brothers, they shackle them both in stocks, where Ampedo dies of misery. Before the courtiers strangle Andelocia, he, like Old Fortunatus, regrets that he loved riches above wisdom and that he forgot his vows to Vertue. He dies. Athelstane arrives, Fortune and Vice appearing simultaneously. Vice overrules Athelstane's harsh sentence upon the murderers. Fortune rebukes Athelstane, but then gives him the purse with the admonition, "*England* shall ne're be poore, if *England* striue, / Rather by vertue, then by wealth to thriue" (V.ii.). At last enters Vertue, now resplendent, and asserts her dominance over Fortune and Vice. For proof, she enjoins, " . . . Looke but on *Fortunatus* and his sonnes: / Of all the welth those gallants did possesse, / . . . / Their glorye's faded and their golden pride" (V. ii.).

Dekker himself is indebted for this tale to still earlier sources, though the exact line of transmission has been debated. Henslowe's diary records the "First Part of Old Fortunatus" as performed in 1596 [see Mary Leland Hunt, *Thomas Dekker: A Study,* 1911]. We do not know whether Dekker wrote it, nor whether there was a second part; in November, 1599, however, Dekker was paid for "the hole history of Fortunatus," which he then immediately revised for court performance, 27 December 1599, as "A commedie called Old Fortunatus in his newe lyuerie" [see Fredson Bowers' "Introduction" to *The Dramatic Works of Thomas Dekker,* 1970]. These English dramatic renditions derive in turn from one or more of the editions of the German *Volksbuch,* the earliest having been published at Augsburg in 1509. But even they are not the true origin of the Fortunatus story, which "is an aggregate of very heterogeneous elements. . . . Scarcely any class of mediaeval fiction has failed to contribute to the medley . . ." [Charles H. Herford, *Studies in the Literary Relations of England and Germany in the Sixteenth Century,* 1886].

For the present purpose we need go no further than Dekker. Cozzens's titles, "Ask Me Tomorrow" and "The Pleasant Comedy of Young Fortunatus," place Dekker's influence beyond dispute, and nothing suggests that Cozzens was familiar with the *Volksbuch.* The nature of Dekker's influence, however, is less obvious. Juxtaposition of novel and play shows that Cozzens agrees with his source in some ways, yet values it especially for the contrasts it brings to mind and the corrections it invites.

Since Dekker divides his attention about equally between two protagonists, Fortunatus and Andelocia, with Ampedo an important secondary character, one might ask, to whom is Francis Ellery, the protagonist of **Ask Me Tomorrow,** being compared if he's called Young Fortunatus? The answer is, there is no exact parallel between Francis and any one character in the play. Fortunatus seems an obvious choice, but he is old. (He is younger in the first ten chapters of the *Volksbuch,* but there is no important correspondence between events there and in **Ask Me Tomorrow.**) True, his sons are young enough to be comparable with Francis, who is twenty-three. Moreover, Andelocia has the long speech about tomorrows and is engrossed in a love quest, as Francis is too, but as Fortunatus is not. As for Ampedo, he resembles Francis in other ways, being habitually censorious, unpleasant, and falsely virtuous. But neither brother is ever called "Young Fortunatus."

Not precisely analogous to any one character, Francis can be usefully compared to all three. Dekker's intentions are chiefly moral, and although Cozzens does not press his own conclusions, the playwright's topics also interest the novelist. Dekker, however, distributes his reflections among three characters. This creates disunity, for in Act II he dispenses with one protagonist and begins over with another. It also causes redundancy, Andelocia's story being substantially the same as his father's with the addition of the courtship. Had Andelocia been the character originally favored by Fortune, then sent to Babylon for the hat before going to England, the Fortunatus subplot could have been eliminated entirely, though popular familiarity with the folk tale probably militated against such a revision. In any case, Cozzens, whose books are tightly constructed, consolidates in one character what Dekker and his predecessors dispersed among three.

About pride, for example, Dekker makes the same conventional observations in both subplots. Before Fortune lifts him up, Fortunatus is "sorrowes heire, and eldest sonne to shame" (I.i.). But since "Riches make all men prowde" (II.Prol.), the old man's fate is interpreted in terms of pride: "Thy Sunne like glorie hath aduanc'd her selfe / Into the top of prides Meridian, / And downe amaine it comes" (II.ii.). His dying words are, "behold in me / The rotten strength of proud mortalitie" (II.ii.). Much the same is shown of Andelocia. King Athelstane resolves that "His pride weele somewhat tame . . ." (III.i.). Shaddow observes "what a horne plague followes couetousnesse and pride" (V.ii.). The murderers say the brothers' "pride should cost their liues" (V.ii.). And Fortune, explaining their demise, tells us "their ryots made them poore, / And set these markes of miserable death, / On all their pride . . ." (V.ii.). Plainly, Dekker means to say something about pride, yet the theme is grafted onto the action rather than evolving from it: "Since even in his maturest work Dekker showed little skill in structure, it is not surprising to find that 'Old Fortunatus' sins more than ordinarily; a part of the confusion no doubt arose from the successive recastings that the play suffered, especially the introduction of Vice and Virtue with their befogging relations to Fortune, and perhaps the relegation of Andelocia's serious wrong-doings to the chorus, for there is nothing in the action that deserves the punishment of death" [Mary Leland Hunt, *Thomas Dekker: A Study,* 1911].

Cozzens examines pride in Francis Ellery, who begins like Fortunatus as "sorrowes heire, and eldest sonne to shame." We meet Francis saying good-bye to his mother, who has nothing but sorrows to bequeath. On the contrary, to support her he must stoop to tutoring. But the novel diverges sharply here from its model. The story of Fortunatus doesn't really develop until the goddess makes him rich. But Cozzens studies pride in a character who never escapes the poverty he starts with. A realistic modern novel cannot be compared too closely, of course, to an allegorical Elizabethan play, yet this departure is instructive. The action is naturally more plausible than in the play, since Cozzens dispenses with the *deus ex machina*—goddesses with their magical purses, hats, apples, and the rest. He also substitutes Francis for the highly unrepresentative Cypriots. Not a hero, a villain, nor a minion of Fortune, Francis Ellery, wishing for a fortune he never gets, is one of us.

In him, pride is genuinely interesting to contemplate, since it is so persistent, troublesome, and familiar, yet so insecurely founded. Not the Cardinal Sin of the homilist, Ellery's pride is the unpleasant habit of the everyday egotist. He finds that "The virtue of the vice of pride was the impossibility of self-pity; and Francis's mind . . . to please him was obliged to show him always fortunate. . . ." Yet he chafes against "This damned business of being poor!," knowing that money always makes "its customary prompt appearance as the thing that mattered. . . . " *Old Fortunatus* suffers, especially for modern readers, because we sympathize too readily with the proud. When Fortunatus, accepting his good fortune, resolves that "If I die to morrow, ile be merrie to day," or when he provides handsomely for his hungry sons, or when he cheats the sultan who was hoping to cheat him, our condemnations are likely to be half-hearted. Cozzens mostly shares Dekker's disapproval of pride, yet in ***Ask Me Tomorrow*** pride is convincingly contemptible, as when Francis "was ashamed to think that far from admiring as he should the patience she [his mother] must show . . . , he detested her patience as a humiliation in itself, a wound to pride reaching through her to him." Recognizing a subject still worth reflecting upon, Cozzens disembalms it, considers it in believable characters, and offers some ironic observations about it.

One such observation is embodied in the epigraph from *Troilus and Cressida:*

> *Ajax,* Why should a man be proud? How doth pride grow? I know not what pride is.
>
> *Agamemnon,* Your mind is the clearer, Ajax, and your virtues the fairer. . . .

This epigraph is intelligible only in its Shakespearean context. Agamemnon, Ulysses, and Nestor are shrewdly flattering Ajax, the vain, doltish bruiser whom they mean to use against Hector while Achilles keeps to his tent:

> AJAX: Is he [Achilles] so much? Do you not think he thinks himself a better man than I am?
>
> AGAMEMNON: No question.
>
> AJAX: Will you subscribe his thought, and say he is?
>
> AGAMEMNON: No, noble Ajax; you are as strong, as valiant, as wise, no less noble, much more gentle, and altogether more tractable.
>
> AJAX: Why should a man be proud? How doth pride grow? I know not what it is.
>
> AGAMEMNON: Your mind is the clearer, Ajax, and your virtues the fairer. He that is proud eats up himself. . . .
>
> AJAX: I do hate a proud man, as I hate the engendering of toads.
>
> NESTOR: [aside] Yet he loves himself. Is't not strange? [William Shakespeare, *Troilus and Cressida,* II.iii.]

By itself, Cozzens's epigraph seems to deny that Ajax is proud, and we might expect that Ellery, lacking the fortune that makes Fortunatus proud, should likewise be without pride. Reconsidered in context, however, Ajax is evidently as proud as Achilles, yet too foolish to realize it. Similarly, pride is Ellery's most persistent motive, no matter how unwarranted it might seem. Ajax's fatuity is exploited by others, moreover, who recognize pride as his secret weakness and turn it to their own advantage. Quite the same can be said of Ellery, who requires some managing, but who is no match for Mrs. Cunningham. The novel closes as the waiter proclaims, *"Madame est servie!,"* thereby reminding us that despite his proud reluctance to do so, Ellery keeps serving her, much as Ajax serves Agamemnon.

*Old Fortunatus* is also about riches, though Dekker's thoughts are difficult to untangle. He probably intends conventional deprecations of worldly wealth, as when Fortune tells the old man, "Farewel, vaine couetous foole,

thou wilt repent, / That for the loue of drosse thou hast despised / Wisedomes diuine embrace . . . ." But Fortunatus and Andelocia are guilty of various offenses: covetousness at first, then foolish preference for riches over wisdom, then pride over their wealth, and still later, abuse of the gift of riches. Stirred together this way, the Cypriots' misdeeds make muddy moralizing, particularly when Ampedo is punished for the opposite crime of despising his wealth, and when Athelstane is finally rewarded despite a greed which far exceeds that of the Cypriots.

In ***Ask Me Tomorrow*** Cozzens divides the complex question of riches. Like Dekker, he dislikes covetousness. Just as Ellery is proud without Fortunatus's fortune, so he is covetous without getting what he covets. In the first scene, Fortunatus says, ". . . I am very poore and verie patient, Patience is a vertue: would I were not vertuous, thats to say, not poore, but full of vice, (thats to say, ful of chinckes)" (I.i.). It is a poor man's idle wish, and Fortune's timely gift keeps it from seeming any worse. In the novel's first chapter, Ellery has a similar speech: " 'God!' said Francis, 'I wish I had a hundred thousand dollars'." Besides recalling Fortunatus's wish, this passage echoes Cozzens's earlier remark about Italian adventurers (the passage occurs on p. 4 of the first edition, in the two-page prologue that Cozzens deleted from the Uniform Edition): ". . . Italian officers came in (perhaps with the wistful idea that they were going to meet and then easily marry a girl with a hundred thousand dollars) and sat and husbanded their drinks." Francis, who will not be handed any magical purse, may resent the imputation, but he exactly resembles these Italian adventurers. In this regard he is a realist's correction of Andelocia—not a suitor looking unsuccessfully for a bride to share his boundless fortune, but a penniless opportunist hunting a bride willing to share *her* fortune. Because he arrives empty-handed and plays on Lorna Higham's affection, Francis makes covetousness look more reprehensible than it seems in the Cypriots. He knows that "Authors were two for a nickel . . ." and that "two could and would live at least as cheaply and meanly as one." When proposing that Lorna nevertheless elope with him, he confesses—as if candor will change it—that "Of course I am trying to take advantage of you. Of course it isn't prudent, and so you are afraid." The prudent view is probably Gwen's:

> Gwen kept her eye on the main point. As well as a girl who had a right to something called romance . . . , Lorna was a valuable investment. . . . the finished product of invested money, . . . of invested time, . . . to fit her with special skills and accomplishments to keep house and raise children, not any old way, but in the style to which the sort of man she was meant to meet and marry would be accustomed. This fortunate man had conditions to fulfill; and one of them . . . was to lay on the line the cash to take up this investment. Then it would be time enough for him and Lorna to begin worrying about whether it was the nightingale and not the lark.

Seen this way ("The thought was sobering, one of those thoughts he tried to put aside. . . .") Ellery's proposal means that with Lorna he would either live "as cheaply and meanly as one," or accept financial rescue from the family whose prize investment he had coveted and stolen. Thus Cozzens, in a more believable tale than Dekker's, also renders covetousness more convincingly distasteful.

Dekker's Cypriots also prefer riches over wisdom—quite a different matter from coveting the wealth of others. Fortunatus explains his preference:

> Therefore dread sacred Empresse make me rich,
> My choice is store of gold; the rich are wise.
> He that vpon his backe rich garments weares,
> Is wise, though on his head grow *Midas* eares.
> Gold is the strength, the sinnewes of the world,
> The Health, the soule, the beautie most diuine,
> A maske of Gold hides all deformities;
> Gold is heauens phisicke, lifes restoratiue,
> Oh therefore make me rich . . . (I.i.).

Since Fortune tells him he'll be sorry, and the events prove her right, Dekker presumably agrees with her and means the old man's speech as a sample of folly.

But about the desirability of wealth Cozzens disagrees with Dekker, finding that Fortunatus's words are truer than Dekker knows. Wealth is examined most fully in the Cunninghams. Thanks to her late husband, Mrs. Cunningham needs no magic hat or bottomless purse, as her family's travels reveal. For Francis, indeed, *she* is his hat and purse. Such wealth ruins Fortunatus, but Mrs. Cunningham is another matter. Marrying her, Mr. Cunningham "considered himself the luckiest man in the world—without, Francis guessed, finding subsequently that he was very much in the wrong, either." Now a widow with two children, she is "as much a credit to her children as they were to her." There is even some conscious deification in the metaphors about her, as if to strengthen her resemblance to Dekker's goddesses, not his sinners: "Though personally she moved without a trace of ostentation, Walter, Francis, and Maggie, making in effect a train or suite, turned her entrance . . . into something of an event." Compare the stage direction in *Old Fortunatus*: "*Enter* Vertue, *crownd: Nymphes and Kings attending on her* . . ." (V. ii. 260). And again, "there was a bustle of people coming and going—proof enough that Mrs. Cunningham had arrived . . . Thousands at her bidding speed, Francis thought in the dazed levity of uncollected wits, and post o'er land and ocean without rest—." Francis's irony keeps this from being fulsome, but the allusion is to Milton's Sonnet XIX, where thousands at God's bidding speed.

Of course, Fortunatus goes too far in lauding riches. He says, "A maske of Gold hides all deformities" (I.i. 291), but all Mrs. Cunningham's money cannot mask her son's lameness. *Ask Me Tomorrow* is to some extent autobiographical, Cozzens having ". . . spent some months tutoring a nice kid who suffered from infantile paralysis while I also tried to act the published author. . . ." But even if the "nice kid" is the model for Walter Cunningham, Cozzens could not miss the coincidence that Dekker repeatedly mentions "deformity" in *Old Fortunatus*. There, physical deformity always implies depravity, as in the horns that sprout on characters given to Vice: "my body hornes must beare, / Because my soule deformitie

doth weare" (IV.i.). Walter, on the contrary, is one of literature's most delightful children, his deformity only heightening the comeliness of his character: "Walter's patience in his affliction, good temper, and politeness cost him, being expressions of a disposition, no special effort, and so perhaps deserved no special credit from the moral standpoint; but they were none the less ornaments to character." In fact, although Francis Ellery is "good-looking," spiritual deformities are more readily seen in him: "As for his character, he had what might as well be called a marked taste for wine and women, he was self-seeking and self-centered. . . ."

Fortunatus overestimates wealth again when he calls it "heauens phisicke, lifes restoratiue," as Cozzens concedes when Walter nearly dies of asthma.

> Preposterously, . . . there was notwithstanding no law, human or divine, against Walter, in an hour or less, being dead. . . . For years Walter's mother, and Maggie, and innumerable doctors had watched over him. . . . But, of course, it all could, maybe it all always did, go for nothing. . . .

Certainly, as Dekker says, gold will be no help against death. Yet the example of the Cunninghams suggests that wealth is far more compatible with a pleasing and virtuous life than Dekker allows.

For Dekker the choice is between riches and wisdom. But Cozzens observes that a Mrs. Cunningham can be both rich and wise, and that a Francis Ellery can be both poor and foolish. Cozzens even predicts some correspondence between wealth and wisdom, for "People who are poor, while they may be estimable and virtuous, confess in the fact of poverty an incapacity for mastering their environment. . . ." Fortunatus, categorically affirming that "the rich are wise," goes beyond Cozzens, yet rich Mrs. Cunningham never wears Midas ears, and poor Ellery does: "Given his choice, he would perhaps have preferred Mrs. Cunningham to mistake him for a sinister and dangerous schemer, weaving, resourceful and unprincipled, his subtle web; and that was good for a laugh, because she never could have made that mistake. There was only one fool there, and Francis was it." Ironies abound. Francis the tutor surely represents wisdom sooner than riches. But then he resents his job, and no riches are offered to him, though he covets them. Thus, there is no virtue in his lack of wealth. And although Mrs. Cunningham praises his learning, she is far wiser than he, and he is often downright foolish. Young Fortunatus thus lacks riches and wisdom as surely as Mrs. Cunningham has them.

It is not necessary to enumerate every correspondence between novel and play, but this study should not disregard the title Cozzens settled on: *Ask Me Tomorrow.* The exact phrase does not appear in *Old Fortunatus,* yet tomorrows are discussed at length, always to the same purpose: that a man like Fortunatus or Andelocia, who indulges in pleasant vices today, will regret them tomorrow. Just ask him.

Dekker calls his play *The Pleasant Comedie of Old Fortunatus,* yet it is pleasant and comical only in the technical sense of ending in a triumph for Vertue and a celebration of sorts. But the unhappy consequences of the characters' choices are unmistakable. All three characters are severely judged, their faults explicitly cause their grief, and all three die. In short, Dekker shows with melodramatic thoroughness that they reap what they sow. Whether people really do reap what they sow always interests Cozzens. Francis, worried because he is receiving no mail from Lorna, wonders whether his effort to seduce Faith Robertson is the reason:

> What about that detestable misbehavior of his in Milan? Rationally or irrationally, the inexpungeable suspicion of the anxious heart is that the gods may be just; that you reap what you sow; that the nature of things operates by an awful law, a sort of *lex talionis,* which, whether you revere or deride any given moral code, will take an eye for an eye and a tooth for a tooth, and complaining will not help you.

The allusion is to *Galatians* 6:7—"Be not deceived; God is not mocked: for whatsoever a man soweth, that shall he also reap"—and Cozzens returns to the other half of it when Francis recalls that in school his grades "had been *Ellery, 50,* or *45,* often enough (*Be not deceived, God is not mocked*—at least, not every time). . . ."

The possibility of such patterns is also mentioned in another connection: "as one thing follows another in life, patterns, often repeated, are formed. . . . Francis stood apprehensive, . . . wondering if . . . the pattern of a joke everybody knows might not be emerging. It begins with a man wishing; and then the man gets his wish and then (you could die laughing) he wishes he hadn't got it." This recalls Old Fortunatus, who wishes for gold, gets it, and then is sorry. But in exploiting such patterns, Cozzens avoids the simplistic thinking that mars Dekker's play. Francis gets no mail because he's been writing to the wrong address, not because he's reaping what he sowed. As for whether he will regret having gotten his wish to be in Cap d'Ail, the immediate answer is no. In other words, Cozzens lets it remain possible that the gloomy notion of a *lex talionis* "was most effective when half felt. . . . Put in words it sank to more or less imposing rodomontade." The beauty of Cozzens's plot, however, is that it is open-ended where Dekker's is too snugly closed. Having introduced the idea of reaping and sowing, Cozzens gives most attention to what Francis sows. And we see just enough reaping to realize that *Lex talionis,* though not an invariable law and sometimes accepting an eye for a tooth, is nevertheless more than rodomontade.

About this you need only ask Francis tomorrow, for his misdeeds are constantly catching up to him. For example, he decides to drink too much in Milan:

> "I'll have some brandy."

> He sat silent and defiant while the waiter was out.

> Tomorrow morning, when this triumph over the plaints of his better judgment would sicken him with exasperation, was somehow receding. Tonight, though diminishing hour by hour, magi-

cally expanded. . . . Tomorrow, on the other side of it, could take care of itself.

Tomorrow comes early, for nausea soon forces his undignified retreat, and weeks later the memory of this night still causes him fresh worry and disgust. The pattern repeats itself many times as Francis succumbs to temptations, only to regret them later. This behavior betrays a persistent childishness—ever interesting to Cozzens—in Francis and many adults. Francis knows that as a schoolboy what he needed "was a damned good licking, and never mind who was proud of what."

> But of course that was now, when a few long-ago beatings would seem well exchanged for . . . habits of discipline and application. . . . Offered the choice ten years ago he doubted if he would have . . . cared to insure the future at the immediate expense of his backside.

Yet as the Milan episode shows, he continues to let tomorrow take care of itself, and it continues to disoblige him.

From Francis's viewpoint the novel ends like a more pleasant comedy for Young Fortunatus than for Old. Though still without the girl or the fortune, Francis has scraped through two predicaments. Walter has survived the asthmatic attack that occurred partly because of Francis's dereliction, and ironically, Francis is even being mistaken for "the hero of the occasion." Thus, he has not lost his job. And he is leaving Cap d'Ail before Faith Robertson arrives, so Lorna still doesn't know about Milan.

A peculiarity, however, is that the title line is not spoken by Francis, but by Lorna. This does not mean that it is inapplicable to him. Francis, like Fortunatus and Andelocia, will see his good fortune differently in time, even though on the last page he is still saying of himself, "How fortunate! How fortunate he always was!" In addition, by giving the title line to Lorna, Cozzens recalls the other half of Dekker's thought—not only that the apparently fortunate man will judge his case differently tomorrow, but that it will also be judged by others. Lorna refuses to elope at once. But as to whether she'll marry him at all, she says, "It's rather a rotten trick, and I know it; but this has been a hell of a day. I can't think. I just don't know. Ask me tomorrow—I mean, if you still want to." What Lorna would respond tomorrow cannot positively be known, since Faith Robertson probably wouldn't "say anything about my making a pass at her." Nevertheless, we do know that Francis's pride will not let him ask the question tomorrow, since the idea of seeing Faith again is awkward. "In fact, I can't do it. Not with Lorna around." So the result is the same as if Lorna, knowing all, were to make some final denunciation. The open-ended plot, however, dispensing with such climactic confrontations, represents an obvious gain for realism.

There is a comparable gain in the treatment of Mrs. Cunningham. She, at the end, plays Vertue's part, but Cozzens adroitly conveys her judgment of Young Fortunatus without a hyperdramatic scene and without spoiling the irony that Francis continues serving her. Mrs. Cunningham has begun to judge Francis earlier, when after many provocations she has felt she must criticize his "whole attitude," thus joining his many other judges: "Through the years, how many people had found themselves . . . less and less pleased with Francis, and so, sooner or later, had felt . . . that they must speak to him about his whole attitude!" The first time, Mrs. Cunningham relents, thinking she must have misjudged him. She does for him what Fortune does for Fortunatus (II.Prol.) and what Vertue does for Andelocia (IV.i.)—gives him a second chance he really has not merited.

Predictably, her second judgment, like Vertue's, will be less lenient. Tomorrow or another day she will disapprove of Francis just as Lorna will, and then Francis, reaping what he has sown, will not seem so fortunate. Very tidily, in fact, Lorna's and Mrs. Cunningham's views of Francis converge two pages from the end as he imagines explaining his plight to Mrs. Cunningham:

> ". . . I happened to try to seduce a girl I didn't like very much at Milan. I was feeling depressed, and we'd had a couple of drinks, and she was there, and you know how it is—" A painful nervous laughter shook him. ". . . somehow I find the idea of seeing her again a little awkward. In fact, I can't do it. Not with Lorna around. What would you do, if you were I?"
>
> What, indeed? What advice from Mrs. Cunningham to the lovelorn? You could not easily imagine telling Mrs. Cunningham such a story; but you could imagine easily enough what she, what any woman, would say to the problem presented: *It serves you right!* My advice is; it serves you right.

## Irving Malin    (essay date Winter 1981)

SOURCE: "The Education of Francis Ellery," in *John O'Hara Journal,* Vol. 4, No. 2, Winter, 1981, pp. 32-8.

[*Malin is an educator and critic whose books include* William Faulkner: An Interpretation *(1957) and* Isaac Bashevis Singer *(1972). In the following essay, he examines the character development of Francis Ellery in* Ask Me Tomorrow.]

In *Just Representations,* a James Gould Cozzens reader, edited by Matthew J. Bruccoli, there is only one novel reprinted. This novel is *Ask Me Tomorrow,* first published in 1940. Bruccoli notes in his introduction that the novel is "uncharacteristically personal, drawing on Cozzens's experiences as a tutor in Europe." The brief description reverberates with meanings. In 1940 Cozzens was thirty-seven; he was able to be ironic toward his young hero, to have a "double view" of him.

My reading of the novel is not the usual kind for a Cozzens novel; it is intended to provoke criticism from professional Cozzens critics; they will probably see it as a perverse, overly symbolic explication which "deconstructs" the text. I believe that there are various ways of reading *Ask Me Tomorrow;* the fact that Cozzens himself made a few changes for Bruccoli's edition suggests that the author himself meant to offer variant readings, textual *transformations.*

I am not claiming great artistic value for *Ask Me Tomor-* *row.* It is not a mature work; it is not Cozzens's best novel. But it is a key one because it hints at the various themes the author developed in his later work.

The essay is brief. It suggests that Cozzens (consciously or unconsciously) used a kind of symbolic "shorthand." Surely all writing is "driven," "obsessive"—I am not bothered by Cozzens as "conservative," "moralist." The essay stresses the education of the hero, but it also underlines—in an oddly tentative manner—that "obsession" and "conservatism" are at war; their battle is, indeed, the vital struggle of Ellery's education.

The first edition of *Ask Me Tomorrow* begins with a lengthy description. We are told that "even at its occasional best, Florence is a forlorn city. It is not sad in any beautiful, comfortable way. It is really sad. It depresses you." This description is deceptive—we feel that the viewer of the scene is putting himself into it; he is the city. Although at this point we do not know the hero—or his special problems and longings—we notice that "depression" dominates his vision. And when we read about the "famous, decrepit churches; the heavy, meanly-placed palaces . . . ," we are strengthened in our belief. The entire description is perhaps, an accurate, "objective" one of Florence, but it also serves *symbolic purposes*—it compels us to read through the "externals" as it were, and to look closely at such words as "melancholy," "ruins," "no better rate." I suggest that the "lines" blur in the first paragraph; Cozzens wants us to observe the shifting perspectives not only of "Giotto's tower" but of the "newly arrived tourist"— the hero of this wise, brilliantly constructed novel.

Francis Ellery is fascinated by artistic patterns. He tends to observe things, people, designs in an unclear manner (unlike his mature creator). When we first meet him, he is sitting in his sick mother's hotel room in Florence. He is uncomfortable. His first words (after he looks at his watch) are: "I'd better keep moving." Francis is never easy-going; he wants to "keep moving" because he can be happy only when he does not *commit himself to anyone*— except himself. But he is an "artful dodger"—he tries as best as he can to hide his irritations, anxieties, and compulsions—and he is a charming young man who can easily blind others. The conversation is ambiguous; Francis and his mother hint at subjects, feelings, roles. We do not completely understand why he can't say warm words. Is he afraid of showing his feelings? Or is he a cold creator?

The scene, like the preceding description of Florence, is disturbing but artistically appropriate. The entire novel will deal with "incorrect" visions of the world; the gap between words and feelings and experiences; the intermixture of motives. It is, if you will, a mystery.

After Francis leaves his mother—he remembers that she "had probably been watching him from the window upstairs for him to wave"—he boards a "made-up" train. He is characteristically moving erratically, burdened by his suitcases, deadlines, inner turmoil. He finally discovers himself in the train compartment with Faith Robertson.

Francis is a "ladies man"—or so he thinks—and he treats women of his own age as convenient or dull prey. He jokes at their expense; he looks down at them. Thus when he speaks to Faith he acts a role he has written; he is not natural. It is ironic, of course, that he is quickly discovered by Faith. She says bluntly, "Why can't you be natural?" She continues: "Why do you bother to try to cut a figure?"

Francis is a writer. He is, however, so preoccupied with his roles as artist and lover and son that he cannot be "natural." He cannot do his tasks. He resorts to silly, immature ornamentation; he plays frivolous games. If it weren't for the fact that he understands, if only vaguely, his limitations, he would be merely a despicable clown. But Francis knows that he is self-destructive (even as he loves his games). He shifts ground—we remember his desire to keep "moving" and to make people and cities "move"— and he becomes depressed. He is a creature of lows and highs. Thus he broods about tomorrow: he "would just go on top to the end of his days never knowing where money for his next extravagance was coming from; yet never, probably, being quite destitute enough to have to give up thinking of extravagances." His "private chagrins" trouble and master him.

Francis, however, does not have the courage to move beyond brooding—to take serious action; he simply settles for literary or sexual allusions. (The novel is filled with such allusions. Cozzens counterpoints his hero's condition with others). And when he can't drown his sorrows, he rages against the world. He sits across from Faith; he sees a "disagreeable vision of Miss Robertson, in a state of beefy nature, grimly advancing her art on a bed with some Wop whose amorous taste was catholic enough to include anything he could get . . ." We should consider carefully such visions; Cozzens compels us to see through his hero by using ironic perspectives. Francis hates "beefy nature" because it offends his own unfulfilled aesthetic longings, but he continually dwells upon it. He, indeed, loves and hates all nature; he finds fault with it because it is *always outside*. It is ironic that he views Faith as "grimly advancing her art." He cannot *advance* his novelistic intentions; he muses about possibilities and future times to escape from present tedium. Why does Francis hate "wops"? Is it because Europeans in general are sure of themselves, their real worth? We are not told by Cozzens, but we are left with the unmistakable impression that he refuses to hold all the opinions of his hero. There is a double view here—and throughout the novel—which demonstrates Francis's severe disabilities.

Francis suggests to Faith—an interesting name in context—that they go to bed. Let tonight count; don't care about tomorrow—his words are hard-boiled. At the same time he thinks of Elizabethan love poetry. "The sweetest story ever told" is studded (and studied) with confusing motives. Francis is in love with his seduction, not Faith, and again he learns that his heroine—a character he creates—refuses his advances. Thus as the first chapter ends, he searches for "some concluding phrase" to control the now shaky situation. He can merely shrug and blurt out "good night."

When we begin to read the second chapter, we are put deliberately on edge. We meet Walter Cunningham, a student of Francis, who says: "I didn't get it all." He is physically crippled; he is mentally slow. There is an ironic parallel here. Although Francis plays with Latin lessons, demonstrating correct syntax, to the adolescent Walter, he recognizes dimly that he and the boy are in the same boat. The realization cannot last because it is painful and accurate. But even Walter "fools" him by knowing what *accipere* means and perhaps, in an expanded way, knowing that life is a series of accidents—of polio, of asthmatic suffocation, of grim misadventure.

Walter's mother is, of course, more knowledgeable, mature, and worldly. She apparently understands her son's and Francis's fears and limitations. Her words are full of meaningful(?) mystery. They threaten the young writer who cannot *place* her. Maggie, Walter's maid, is also disturbing. Francis goes everywhere with the Cunninghams and Maggie, but he remains "at home"; he is closed in by his dream-states: "Francis's mind took himself desconsolately away, wishing not for any single thing, but for vague new states of things which would comfort and relieve him according to his necessities!"

Cozzens introduces the skiing lessons. Francis teaches Walter how to manipulate his injured legs on snow. So much is made of these lessons—along with the Latin syntax—that we are tempted to view them as more than a plot-factor. They function symbolically. Does *Francis* want to "catch hold?" Can *he* move in a straight line?

Francis is in love with Lorna, a girl who inspires letters. He tells himself that he will convince her of his deep needs—again he acts an ill-conceived role. He is so self-centered that his letters to her—like his words to Walter or Mrs. Cunningham or even "beefy" Faith—are vain mirrors. He wants to be Donne or Spenser; he hopes to equal their roles as lovers and artists.

But Francis cannot even later bury Mrs. Cunningham's dog, Rose. He outrages the hotel management; he cannot control the situation. The juxtaposition of love letters and dog burial—he is inadequate in both cases—is admirably comic. Cozzens deflates "romance," showing us that Mrs. Cunningham's love for Rose is ironically warmer than Francis's cliché adorations of distant Lorna.

As Francis and the Cunninghams move to a ski resort, they shift perspectives. The natural scene is again used symbolically. Francis, for example, believes that the new hotel at Grindewald is a gloomy, empty place (like his depressive feelings), but he is surprised by quick changes in daylight. We are told that "those expanses of glass that served last night to let in the dark and to show the blind whirl of snow, let in now a blaze of sunlight." The shifting perspectives suggest that he is mistaken; things are a "blind whirl" while he does not have a *sure* picture of motives. It is little wonder that Francis is in acute "confused discomfort."

His discomfort increases when Miss Poulter, an employee at the hotel, tries to lure him to bed. (This is another example of Cozzens's use of parallels: she pursues him as he pursued Faith and pursues Lorna. Perhaps the parallel is meant to show the tables turned or, to use a more appropriate metaphor, the story rewritten.) Francis is lost in a novel he hasn't written; he is a constantly passive object.

His turmoil continues when Cozzens increases the tempo of events and characters. I do not mean to suggest that the pace—or the style—is manic. It is always "controlled," understated slow—and the fact that it is makes Francis's condition even more interesting.

Perhaps more intense than his fascination with Lorna, who seems, at least to us, a rather slight person, is his devotion to work. Francis sits in solitary confinement, trying to organize his thoughts and words—indeed, his life—and he "becomes" one fictional character after another: "To write, Francis had first to become this person; not as an act of deceit, but like a monologuist clapping on a cocked hat or turning up a collar to suggest an appearance that helped the part." The words, "monologuist" and "appearance," although not underlined, suggest his predicament. And, of course, when he cannot even put the right words on paper—or say the right ones to "real" people—he leans again on the external world—on what Cozzens calls "clumps of trees" or "patches of vegetation."

Francis tries to get closer to Lorna. He hints to Mrs. Cunningham that a change of scene would be beneficial. He exercises his will. The point is, however, that although he moves towards the impossible goal—is it Lorna? is it control over patterns? —he recognizes that "one thing follows another in life." Patterns are "formed" without his choice—occasionally they are appropriate for his ends; often they are not. In a convincing short passage Cozzens (through Francis) notes the comedy: "It begins with a man wishing; and then the man gets his wish; and then (you could die laughing) he wishes he hadn't got it."

The passage should be noted as an introduction to Francis's later thoughts about divine patterns. He remembers his Christian school days (as a youth), and he tells himself that he had been marked for life. Of course his religious views were not "fitting" then—or now! —because they suggest that he has, in the long run, little control over Lorna or himself. He is another character—not only in Mrs. Cunningham's "fiction" but in the Divine Plan. He believes in his immaturity that he is "helpless," especially when it comes to love: "Men who could not stop their longing did crazy things."

The closer Francis gets to Lorna, the "crazier" he becomes. There are several parties. At one he meets some friends of hers; these people are madly in love. Kirkland, the handsome Californian, and his married mistress, Mrs. Hartpence, seem out of control—even to him. But the ironies abound. When Francis borrows the car belonging to Mrs. Hartpence, he finds that it has a flat tire. There are several pages devoted to the confusion and non-movement. Cozzens again takes an ordinary incident and dwells upon its symbolic significance. When we remember Francis's almost-frantic movements and see his current "stasis," we feel that there is little hope for correct, thoughtful movement. I do not want to view Cozzens as a *symbolist*—he is not Poe! —but I believe that he sees symbols as a kind of attack. Perhaps Cozzens implies that Francis is immature because *he* confuses the symbol and what it stands for. Lorna is not accepted for what she *is;* Walter is manipulated—almost every person Francis en-counters he views as a symbol, not as a living, thinking individual.

Francis continues to daydream: "He could go back to Florence, and there were reasons why he ought to. He could really work on his book, get it done—maybe in a couple of months." His realistic vision is echoed in Cozzens's ironic view of his hero—and he concludes that Florence is a "hell-hole."

But his realism is not severe enough. I think that Mrs. Cunningham's lengthy comments to him at this point, after all his blunders, are dramatically appropriate. She is a "judge"—he thinks of her remarks as "indictments"—and her punishment, if you will, is handed down from above. She sees through his games with Lorna, Walter, herself, but even she is "seduced"—for her own ends? —by his charm.

Francis keeps his job. He is lucky (although he sees it only in terms of financial reward and convenience.) It enables him to stay away from his artistic endeavors. Cozzens, on the other hand, knows that Francis must *work* in order to gain self-control and knowledge.

Perhaps the most powerful passages in the novel occur now. Walter begins to have an asthmatic attack after a skiing expedition. (We have expected this attack because of Cozzens's careful plotting.) The boy becomes frightened; his fear infects Francis because it reinforces his deep sense of uselessness and uncontrollable designs. We can say the two are "brothers." There is great irony. Walter, recognizing his own plight, also senses his tutor's disturbance, and begins to assert his "mastery" of the world (while he almost dies).

Cozzens plays with the shadowy effects of the snow. He, in fact, uses the word "shadow" a few times. And the physical shadows serve as an effective reflection of the nature of Walter and Francis at this point: "The pale shifting shadow of the flag lifted and fell away . . ." The intermixture of motives, roles and designs is surely emphasized.

The closeness of Walter's death serves to underline Francis's rebirth as a mature, responsible man. Without thinking of his self-centered roles, fictions, games, he faces 'genuine,' hard facts of life. Francis may run back and forth, trying to save Walter, but his frantic behavior shows that he *cares* about him.

Although Francis dislikes the "European" ways of the physician who finally administers the life-saving injection, he has to admit the man's discipline, technique, and dedication—qualities he has lacked throughout the novel. "He thought of the doctor, whose manner with Walter, whose sympathy and intelligence, had been so different from what Francis wildly expected . . ." He goes on: "Recoiling in disgust from human beings, you had to recoil in another disgust, from your own recoiling . . ." This is not to imply that Francis is completely *saved*. (Who is?) He has, after all, merely begun to "grow up" and achieve wisdom. I find it interesting that he learns from a "spiritual father," the physician, and that this character is the first completely responsible male in the novel. Again, I do not want to offer a psychological reading; but I believe that

Cozzens, admiring the experience of, say, Mrs. Cunningham, nevertheless affirms that Francis must move beyond the "mother" (his own, Mrs. Cunningham) and learn from the men who control society. There is, of course, a sexist slant here—society is viewed as run by *dedicated men*—but we should not dislike Francis or the novel for this reason.

Francis puts off for tomorrow—at Lorna's request—his declarations of love. He is secure enough now to accept all accidents, unfulfilled designs of life. He finds wisdom—or at least some kind of commitment—by surrendering falseness of purpose, role-playing, melodramatic art. He becomes a realist; he is aware that his previous experiments were a kind of sham.

Francis's education is far from over—we remember that he is still a young man—but, like many of Cozzens's later, more mature heroes, he recognizes the need for straight thinking, clear vision, ironic perspective. We begin at the end of the novel to admire his own beginnings.

## Terry Teachout   (review date 28 February 1986)

SOURCE: A review of *Selected Notebooks: 1960-1967,* in *National Review,* Vol. XXXVIII, February 28, 1986, pp. 60-1.

[*Teachout is an American musician, editor, and essayist, whose books include* Beyond the Boom: New Voices on American Life, Politics, and Culture *(1990) and* Under Midwestern Eyes: Memories of a Lapsed Missourian *(1991). In the review below, he favorably assesses* Notebooks *as a valuable introduction to Cozzens's reflections on literature.*]

Matthew Bruccoli's 1983 biography *James Gould Cozzens: A Life Apart* contained a lengthy appendix of excerpts from a set of notebooks Cozzens began keeping three years after the publication of *By Love Possessed.* These blunt and unguarded journal entries revealed the real Cozzens—stoic, sardonic, full of unfashionable social and literary prejudices—with exceptional vividness, and it isn't surprising that Bruccoli received numerous requests to edit a more extensive selection from Cozzens's notebooks for publication. *Selected Notebooks: 1960-1967,* a hundred-page volume containing "most of the entries dealing with the practice of literature," is the result; anyone at all interested in the life and work of this country's most underrated novelist will find it endlessly intriguing. No great surprises, though; after all, it isn't very hard to deduce the Cozzens view of literature, modern and otherwise, from the deeply conservative philosophy that informs his fiction. (Well, there's one surprise, anyway: Cozzens admired Mary McCarthy.) Still, it's a pleasure to hear the acid voice of Julius Penrose—for that is what we hear throughout this slender volume—railing splendidly against Joyce, Proust, & Mann, Inc., advancing the lost critical cause of Somerset Maugham, and skewering distinguished contemporaries like Faulkner and Hemingway with an acuteness made possible by a mature, confident dogmatism. There is no index, an oversight hardly expected from an editor who is normally so omnicompetent as Mr. Bruccoli; one would also like to see at least a few of those unpublished entries "in which Cozzens commented on the news or quarreled with religious activities." But very fine all the same.

## Richard A. Posner   (essay date 1988)

SOURCE: "The Reflection of Law in Literature: 'Legal' Novels by Cozzens, Twain, and Camus," in *Law and Literature: A Misunderstood Relation,* Harvard University Press, 1988, pp. 79-88.

[*Posner is a lawyer and author of several books, including* The Economics of Justice *(1981) and* The Problems of Jurisprudence *(1990). In the following excerpt, he contends that* The Just and the Unjust *is not about the law, rather it is a story about the rite-of-passage of a young man.*]

. . . I begin in low key with a work that after more than forty years seems on its way to being recognized as a minor classic—James Gould Cozzens's novel *The Just and the Unjust,* a work so pervasively and accurately "about" law that one might think the author an experienced lawyer (he had no legal training). Yet this is an illusion; the book is not about law in any interesting sense.

The setting is a small town in an unimportant rural county, circa 1940. The ostensible subject is a murder trial that begins at the start of the novel and concludes at the end. The protagonist is the county's assistant district attorney, Abner Coates—young, able, but rather priggish—who tries the case for the prosecution along with the district attorney. The D.A. is in charge but Coates takes an active role, making the opening statement to the jury and examining several important witnesses. The trial reveals that the defendants—repulsive hoods named Howell and Basso—had, along with a third man, Bailey, kidnapped a drug dealer named Zollicoffer. After the ransom was paid, Bailey decided it would be unsafe to return Zollicoffer alive. On the way to the spot where the kidnappers were to drop Zollicoffer off, Bailey shot him, and Howell and Basso helped Bailey weight Zollicoffer down with leg irons and dump him into a river. Bailey later died fleeing the police. Although Howell and Basso do not deny having taken an active part in the kidnapping, it never becomes clear whether they authorized, knew about in advance, or participated in the murder. As Coates, the D.A., and the judge all emphasize to the jury in urging a verdict of first-degree murder (which would mean the electric chair), the defendants' lack of participation in the actual murder affects their guilt not a whit. Provided they participated in the kidnapping, as unquestionably they did, they are guilty of first-degree murder because Zollicoffer was killed in the course of a felony in which they participated. However, to the disgust of Coates, the D.A., and the judge (who dresses down the jury afterward), the jury convicts Howell and Basso only of second-degree murder. The author leads us to understand, through one of the wise old codgers who people the novel, that the jury has exercised its prerogative of nullifying a law that it considers unjust—the felony-murder rule, a legal fiction that punishes a felon who is not a murderer as if he were one.

While the trial is wending its way to its surprising conclusion—for the reader is given no clue that the jury might fail to convict the defendants of first-degree murder—Coates is both getting engaged to be married and agreeing to run for D.A. (the incumbent is leaving for another job). It is understood that Coates cannot lose the election; he is a Republican, and Republicans always win in this county. But to agree to run he must overcome his aversion to the local Republican boss, who Coates fears will interfere in the D.A.'s office, though in fact the boss is pretty straight. The suspense in the novel is focused not on the trial, which seems a foregone conclusion but is not, but on whether Coates will overcome what are plainly priggish scruples to marrying his utterly charming childhood sweetheart and accepting the tremendous career opportunity opened up by the D.A.'s impending departure.

From this brief summary it should be plain that *The Just and the Unjust* is not really about trial strategy, the legal profession, the felony-murder rule, or the power of juries to acquit lawlessly, and thus that critics miss the point when they accuse Cozzens of "belligerent legalistic conservatism" [John P. McWilliams, Jr., "Innocent Crime or Criminal Innocence: The Trial in American Fiction," in Carl S. Smith, John P. McWilliams, Jr., and Max Bloomfield, *Law and American Literature: A Collection of Essays,* 1983]. This is a rite of passage novel, a *Bildungsroman.* The hero is a prissy kid at the beginning and a man at the end, having assumed family responsibilities and learned the difference between pure forms (of law, of career advancement) and sordid realities (law may diverge from the lay sense of justice, politics influences promotions), as well as the need to compromise, to moderate demands, to scale down ideals, to trim absolutes, to empathize—with the Republican boss, and above all with his sweetheart, to whose feelings Coates is remarkably insensitive at the beginning of the novel. The work has none of the resonance of *Hamlet* or the *Iliad* but is recognizably part of the same broad category of works, in which youthful idealism becomes tempered with realism through a series of crises.

That the law is rather a detail in all this, as revenge is rather a detail (though an essential one) in the other works, can be made clearer by a comparison with another and finer Cozzens novel, *Guard of Honor,* perhaps the best American novel about World War II. Set in Florida, it recounts a brief period in the administration of an air base by a young major general. He is champing at the bit to be sent overseas to do more fighting (he had held a major command in the North African campaign). But we soon understand that his command of the base, which involves dealing with domestic crises that have no martial dimension (race relations, a training accident), is an important preparation for the major combat command that he is slated to assume next—and that, with nice irony, is the command of fighter cover for the invasion of Japan, which of course never took place. Again it is a rite of passage novel, with the professional setting, in this case military, again incidental. The hero, at first insufficiently worldly-wise to handle senior administrative responsibilities, like Coates matures in the course of the novel by meeting the challenges of everyday life.

If either novel were about the *professional* challenges of its protagonists—if either one showed lawyers correcting their legal errors or generals correcting their military errors—they would not have much appeal, even to members of these professions. A novelist with neither legal nor military training is unlikely to have significant insights to impart at the level of actual practice, though [there are] some exceptions to this rule. . . .

---

# FURTHER READING

## Bibliography

Bruccoli, Matthew J. *James Gould Cozzens: A Descriptive Bibliography.* Pittsburgh: University of Pittsburgh Press, 1981, 193 p.

    Extensive bibliography of Cozzens's writings, including related literary criticism, reviews, and biographical books and pamphlets about the author.

## Biography

Broccoli, Matthew J. *James Gould Cozzens: A Life Apart.* New York: Harcourt, 1983, 343 p.

    Examines Cozzens's life and works.

## Criticism

Chamberlain, John. "Writer of Character." *New York Times Book Review* (August 8, 1978): 10-11.

    Review of *Just Representations: A James Gould Cozzens Reader* focusing on the main themes of Cozzens's work.

Garrett, George P. "Whatever Wishful Thinking May Wish: The Example of James Gould Cozzens." In *The Sorrows of Fat City,* pp. 83-90. Columbia: University of South Carolina Press, 1978.

    Favorably comments on Cozzens novels, the characters in his works, and the personal aspects of his life that have affected his writings and his relationship with the reading public.

Hicks, Granville. *James Gould Cozzens.* Minneapolis: University of Minnesota, 1966, 47 p.

    Examination of several of Cozzens's earlier works, up to and including *Children and Others* (1964).

Lewis, R. W. "The Conflicts of Reality: Cozzens' *The Last Adam.*" In *Seven Contemporary Authors: Essays on Cozzens, Miller, West, Golding, Heller, Albee, and Powers,* edited by Thomas B. Whitbread, pp. 1-22. Austin: University of Texas Press, 1968.

    Identifies *The Last Adam* as a "pattern novel" and discusses its various strengths and weaknesses.

"The Hermit of Lambertville." *Time* LXX, No. 10 (2 September 1957): 72-4, 76-7.

    Overview of Cozzens's life and career.

Additional coverage of Cozzens's life and career is contained in the following sources published by Gale Research: *Concise Dictionary of American Literary Biography, 1941-1968; Contemporary Authors,* Vols. 9-12R, 81-84 (obituary); *Contemporary Authors New Revision Series,* Vol. 19; *Contemporary Literary Criticism,* Vols. 1, 4, 11; *Dictionary of Literary Biography,* Vol. 9; *Dictionary of Literary Biography Documentary Series,* Vol. 2; *Dictionary of Literary Biography Yearbook, 1984*; and *Major 20th-Century Writers.*

# Tomson Highway

## 1951-

Canadian dramatist.

The following entry provides an overview of Highway's career through 1994.

## INTRODUCTION

One of Canada's most highly regarded dramatists, Highway is primarily known for his award-winning plays *The Rez Sisters* (1986) and *Dry Lips Oughta Move to Kapuskasing* (1989). In these works Highway uses Native humor, language, and mythology to address the effects of European colonization on Native North American cultures, the realities of reservation life, and contemporary Native issues. Commenting on the numerous influences evident in Highway's work, Denis W. Johnston has stated: "Highway is perhaps the first Canadian member of the international tradition of accomplished writers who work in their second language. Among playwrights, this tradition included Samuel Beckett in French and Tom Stoppard in English. Like them, Highway delights in linguistic estrangements and paradoxes. Furthermore, the fact that Highway's first language is Cree contributes to his unusual dramatic style."

### Biographical Information

Born in northwest Manitoba, Canada, Highway spoke only Cree until age six when he began attending a Roman Catholic boarding school. He stayed there until age fifteen, returning to his family for only two months each year. A musical prodigy in high school, Highway studied music in Canada and England and later obtained degrees in English and music from the University of Western Ontario. After spending several years working for various Native support organizations and with Canadian writer James Reaney, Highway stated that he "started writing plays, where I put together my knowledge of Indian reality in [Canada] with classical structure, artistic language. It amounted to applying sonata form to the spiritual and mental situation of a drunk." Highway was also the artistic director of Native Earth Performing Arts, Inc., Toronto's only professional Native theater company, until 1992.

### Major Works

*The Rez Sisters* and *Dry Lips*, the first two works of a proposed cycle of seven plays, are set on the fictional Wasaychigan Hill Indian Reserve on Manitoulin Island, Canada. *The Rez Sisters* involves seven women, who plan to go to the world's largest bingo game in Toronto, and a male Nanabush—the Ojibway name for "The Trickster"—a Native mythological being who can assume various guises and who is a central figure in Cree culture. While the women experience many difficulties, Highway emphasizes

the importance of creativity and humor in their lives. He has stated: "I'm sure some people went to *Rez* expecting crying and moaning and plenty of misery, reflecting everything they've heard about or witnessed on reserves. They must have been surprised. All that humour and love and optimism, plus the positive values taught by Indian mythology." *Dry Lips* revolves around a female Nanabush and seven men (who are mentioned but do not appear in *The Rez Sisters*). Considered less optimistic than *The Rez Sisters*, this work addresses such issues as alcoholism, rape, violence, and misogyny. Johnston has observed that "we find in *Dry Lips* a litany of disturbing and violent events, set within a thin frame of hopefulness."

### Critical Reception

Critical reaction to Highway's works has been generally positive. Both *The Rez Sisters* and *Dry Lips* have won numerous prizes, including the prestigious Dora Mavor Moore award, and Highway has been called, by Johnston, "the most important new Canadian playwright to emerge in the latter half of the 1980s." Although sometimes considered stronger in characterization and humor than in plot, *The Rez Sisters* and *Dry Lips* have been acclaimed as revealing portrayals of reservation life and as insightful examinations of the cultural, religious, environmental, and societal issues confronting Natives in a contemporary, urban-oriented world. Critics note, however, that the spiritual insights and ultimately hopeful messages revealed in these works have universal implications. Highway himself has stated: "Native culture is beautiful, Native language is beautiful, Native mythology is beautiful and powerful, [and these] are very relevant, increasingly so, as time goes on. At a time in our history, as a community of human beings, when the world is about to get quite literally destroyed, and all life forms have a very good chance of being completely obliterated—at a crucial time like this, Native people have a major statement to make about the kind of profound change that has to come about in order for the disaster to be averted."

# PRINCIPAL WORKS

*The Rez Sisters*   (drama)   1986
*Aria*   (monologues)   1987
*Dry Lips Oughta Move to Kapuskasing*   (drama)   1989
*The Sage, the Dancer, and the Fool* [with Rene Highway and Bill Merasty]   (drama)   1989

# CRITICISM

## Ray Conlogue   (essay date 21 November 1987)

SOURCE: "Mixing Spirits, Bingo and Genius," in *The Globe and Mail,* Toronto, November 21, 1987, p. C5.

[*In the following excerpt, Conlogue discusses* The Rez Sisters *within the context of Highway's life and culture.*]

Tomson Highway has long black hair, worn straight and loose. There is no mistaking that he is a native person—he will even call himself an Indian, but the word is tongue-in-cheek nowadays—and his commitment to his heritage is profound. That much he has shown in a play called *The Rez Sisters,* which came out of nowhere last year to win the Dora award for best play.

*The Rez Sisters* is being remounted by Toronto's Factory Theatre. That's why, this particular afternoon, Highway is found sitting at the piano in the Factory Theatre's green room, basking in late autumn sunshine. He may have just happened to be there, but the image has the composed quality of an artist mindful of such things. In either case, it is dramatic: a black glossy piano and a black glossy mane of hair.

Highway embodies the customary contradictions of living in two worlds at once, native and white, but he embodies them with special intensity because, simply put, he is outrageously talented. He grew up speaking Cree, not learning English until his teens—but he speaks it now with a fluid and untrammelled eloquence. And although as a child on a Manitoba reserve, he witnessed privation and brutality of every kind, he exudes a startling serenity.

"Indisputably bad things happened to my people," he says. "But it's water under the bridge. Now we have to deal with it, cure it."

Highway, who is 28 years old, is deeply attached to the spirituality of his people. Their religion was badly battered by the traders and missionaries and battered worse by the move off the reserves to the white cities. But it survives nonetheless, and it underlies *The Rez Sisters*.

The play is set on Manitoulin Island in Georgian Bay, which is a long way from Highway's home on a reserve in northern Manitoba. But it is a place he knows well; he moved there to start a theatre company after graduating from Western University.

One of the things that struck him, after having lived some years in the big white cities, was the way people in isolated communities give a mythical quality to their own lives. "Even in a few years, certain people's adventures become legends. Near where I lived on Manitoulin, there had been a lady who played bingo with such ferocity that she became the queen of bingo. She's dead now, but her spirit still hovers over the bingo hall." He smiles. He is not sanctimonious about these things. "It's a neat way of making your life more fun than it might have been."

Out of such stories, and the sense of fun underlying native culture—an idea he returns to frequently—Highway began to fashion the story of seven women on this reserve. The story focuses on a huge bingo game they have heard of, which is going to take place in Toronto. They set off on an epic journey to the Big City, which none of them has seen before. On their journey they are accompanied by a seagull, played by an actor; the bird embodies Nanabush, the trickster spirit at the core of native religion.

As the play develops, the story pushes out in several directions. Only two of the women can actually see the magical bird, one of them being a retarded girl who has suffered terrible abuse in her life.

"This trickster is so central to our system of spiritual belief," says Highway. "It's a connection to this great energy, or God, which most people perceive only in moments of extreme crisis. Or when they are close to death, and can see into the spirit world."

In the case of the retarded young woman, he was thinking of a true story of a girl from his home reserve who was raped by several white men on a backwoods road. She was retarded, but, to make doubly sure of not being identified, they beat her and gouged out her eyes. They needn't have troubled—she froze to death before she was found.

In recounting this story, Highway's customary serenity and composure cracks somewhat. There is a terrible anger as he states quietly that the white men, who were known, have never to this day been prosecuted. "The racism is real. And the sexism. Men are here"—he gestures—"and women are here, and Indian women are here." His hand hovers near the floor.

Then he leaps imaginatively back into the world of the play, of the thoughts that this terrible story inspired. "I began to imagine that when the girl is lying there in the snow, the seagull comes to her. In my version, in the play, she doesn't die. The bird says, 'Not yet.'"

And that is the young woman, gifted with second sight, who accompanies the group to Toronto.

People who have seen the play are struck by Highway's extraordinary empathy with women.

"I am sensitive to women because of the matrilineal principle in our culture, which has gone on for thousands of years. Women have such an ability to express themselves emotionally. Men are all clogged up. And as a writer, you want to express emotion."

As a writer, especially in the theatre, you also want to work in a tradition. Highway's knowledge of theatre comes from his studies at Western University, where he met and was deeply influenced by James Reaney. "Seeing the Donnelly Trilogy was one of the great moments for me. With those characters, the mother and father of the Donnelly clan, James Reaney is putting down roots. They become characters that remind me of Mother Earth and Father Sky in our stories."

The Donnellys were real people, but folklore gave them a great dimension, which Reaney incorporated into his play. "I love folklore," says Highway. "How stories go from mouth to mouth and the figures become huge and heroic."

At university, he also familiarized himself with Western theatre, and the influences are interesting to notice. In *The Rez Sisters,* one of the women continually repeats that she "wants to go to Toronto." Is there Chekhov in this?

Highway laughs. "Oh sure, there is *The Three Sisters* in there, and a little bit of Michel Tremblay's *Les Belles Soeurs.*"

He is open to such influences, but they never dominate in his play. "People often tell me when they see the play, even if it is in English, that these are not French women or English women, but Indian women who are speaking."

One very good reason for that is that Highway writes his plays in Cree before he writes them in English. "It's hard for native writers to write in a language that isn't theirs. I wasn't fluent in English till my late teens. So my dream life is in Cree. And so are my first drafts."

Highway is fond of the explosive nicknames that exist in his culture, which often become permanent names. "Names like Shot on Both Sides, or One Foot in Hell. Or Highway.

"I'm a full-blooded Cree. Nobody knows where my name comes from. It may be an Irish name, borrowed from an early trader."

This also accounts for the names of the characters in the play—such as Emily Dictionary. "My home reserve is half Cree and half Chipewyan. There was a Chipewyan family with a name we couldn't pronounce, so we changed it to the nearest thing: Dictionary."

The eternal play on words and ideas is part of what makes Cree "such a funny language. You laugh all the time when you speak it. In spite of the violence on the reserve, the rhythm of the language is funny. It must have something to do with the Trickster being at the centre of it."

It is difficult for whites to understand how a deity called the Trickster could be central to any culture—one of the perennial problems between natives and whites. Highway tries to clarify it by comparing the Trickster to Christ. "He occupies a central role for us, just as Christ does for you. But there are three important differences. Trickster has a sense of humor. He was never crucified. And he is neither male nor female."

By the absurd construction of having to say that he is neither male nor female, Highway underlines the inadequacy of the English language to describe reality as seen by a native.

But at the same time, the otherness of the native view of the world has survived immersion in white culture. "The missionaries think that they killed off the Trickster," says Highway, "but we don't think so. To my mind, the Trickster has been passed under the table for 200 years. Those guys in Hastings Street (Vancouver's skid row) who have been drunk for 25 years—you see the Trickster in them, clawing to come back to life."

In the face of so much human destruction and tragedy, it is tempting to see something Pollyanna-ish in Highway's optimism. But it is not like that to him. He is well aware of the destruction—"the Indian you meet is a drunk, and the reserves are full of inner-directed rage and violence"— but he does not see why this should lead the observer to lose sight of the other side of native reality.

"Our mythology is strong. Our dream world is filled with the most extraordinary creatures. Freud and Jung would have had a holiday travelling in Manitoba. And these dreams are relevant to the way this country breathes."

> I am sensitive to women because of the matrilineal principle in [the Cree] culture, which has gone on for thousands of years. Women have such an ability to express themselves emotionally. And as a writer, you want to express emotion.
>
> —*Tomson Highway*

Highway's personal salvation comes largely from his father. "My dad has a unique charismatic personality. Just by his example, we wanted to do well by him. So we took what he taught us tacitly: that you take the most positive aspect of your culture and do what you can with it. So my brother is a dancer and I am a writer."

When *The Rez Sisters* opened last year in Toronto, it was overlooked by most of the media. It was presented in the

Native Canadian Centre, which nobody had been to before, and it ran very briefly on slim funding.

But the few people who saw it were passionately committed to the show. They threw all their votes into it for the Chalmers Award last year and helped it to win the Dora for best new play.

For Tomson Highway, this was a vindication of his own talent, and of the people who inspired and performed the play. "It was a thrill to be nominated for a Dora beside people like Margaret Hollingsworth, whose writing had electrified my imagination."

So the Rez Sisters made it to Toronto after all, and won the biggest bingo game of all.

---

**Daniel David Moses, Delaware poet and playwright, on *The Rez Sisters* :**

The majority of Native people, forced to inhabit ignored, economically disadvantaged areas called reserves, are not encouraged to regard their own lives as important. The accomplishment of *The Rez Sisters* is that it focuses on a variety of such undervalued lives and brings them up to size. The passion that drives the characters is suddenly easy to recognize and the theatrical daring that invites the audience members to play a game of Bingo along with the play's characters is both a pleasure and a measure of the playwright's wisdom. We literally play along, experiencing for ourselves the Rez Sisters' passion.

*Daniel David Moses, in* Canadian Fiction *Magazine,*
*1987.*

---

**William Peel   (review date Winter 1990)**

SOURCE: A review of *The Rez Sisters,* in *Canadian Theatre Review,* No. 65, Winter, 1990, pp. 62-4.

[*In the following excerpt, Peel discusses the characters and narrative structure of* The Rez Sisters.]

Tomson Highway succeeds in creating a striking cast of characters who reveal both blemishes and beauty, and possess, on the whole, great human dignity. His ***The Rez Sisters*** tells the tale of seven Indian women living on a reserve in northern Ontario who one day decide to travel to Toronto to attend "the Biggest Bingo in the World." The women are sisters, half-sisters, and sisters-in-law, and their ages range from the 20s to the 50s. The polarities and contradictions of their characters reflect the polarities and contradictions of the world in which they live: poverty-stricken, crude and cruel, and at the same time rich in beauty, vitality, and tenderness.

Highway has carved out a number of memorable portraits. Among these are Pelagia Patchnose who hammers shingles onto the roof of her house, when she'd much rather use her bingo-won hammer to knock some sense into the band chief and get the reserve's roads paved; Philomena

Moosetail whose aspirations to gentility are directed into an unrelenting pursuit of "bathroom beautiful"; Emily Dictionary, a former battered wife and motorcycle gang member, who keeps the name of her abusive ex-husband, "the man who made me learn to fight back"; and Marie-Adele Starblanket who at 39 has had 14 children (each one designated by a board in her 14-post white picket fence) and who now battles cancer.

Highway's achievement lies not only in the characters he has created, but in his masterful orchestration of the action through which these characters are revealed. Before becoming a playwright, Highway trained as a classical musician, and he brings a truly musical sense of composition to the structuring of his work. One scene in particular, a fight at the reserve's general store/post office involving all seven women, is a masterpiece in terms of rhythmic development and the interweaving of a variety of voices. Another, the women's manic fund-raising campaign for their trip to Toronto, is superbly theatrical in its mimed, ever-accelerating action. In fact, from the opening moments to the end of the play, Highway's compositional control and acute sense of dynamic rhythm never fail to impress.

As a playwright Highway openly acknowledges his debt to James Reaney and Michel Tremblay, and the inspiration of the latter is particularly evident in ***The Rez Sisters***. Obviously Highway had Tremblay's *Les Belles Soeurs*—

---

**Highway on Native mythology:**

We have a mythology that is thousands and thousands of years old, which was almost destroyed, or some of it obliterated, by the onslaught of missionaries and affected by Christian religion.

But, I suppose, when you do that to something, inevitably, the spirit of it survives even more strongly, and the mythologies too. It's coming back, it's still very much alive. It just went underground.

It's still very much alive in our spirits, although it's not an intellectual thing necessarily. But the spirit is still infused with it—our people. And the vitality, and the relevancy of it, and the immediacy of it are very much with us. Whereas we have people—and the way our writing is coming on proves it—that you know there is this connection with God. There is a spirituality that still is so powerful and beautiful and passionate! Whereas, in the case of mainstream culture here on this continent, both American and Canadian, we find that the mythology that they came over with is—their relationship to that mythology is really an academic relationship. It's not a living thing any more. So it was lost along the way.

*Tomson Highway, in an interview with Hartmut Lutz,*
*in* Contemporary Challenges: Conversations with
Canadian Native Authors, *Fifth House Publishers,*
*1991.*

complete with its "Ode to Bingo"—very much in mind as he wrote. Yet Highway's voice is distinctively his own. The depth of his characterizations and the original flair of his compositional ability cannot be denied.

**Robert Cushman**   (review date 15 April 1991)

SOURCE: A review of *Dry Lips Oughta Move to Kapuskasing,* in *The Globe and Mail,* Toronto, April 15, 1991, p. C3.

[*In the following excerpt, Cushman asserts that* Dry Lips Oughta Move to Kapuskasing *is a powerful play about misogyny.*]

***Dry Lips Oughta Move to Kapuskasing,*** which opened Saturday at the Royal Alexandra Theatre in Toronto, begins with magic. At the side of a great, bare, tilted platform, white with a black surround, stands a figure, recognizably and traditionally Indian. The figure gestures, and snow falls.

After this descent another, more prosaic. A sofa is lowered from the flies. Visible upon it is a naked male body. A female in black underpants detaches herself from it, and begins to dress. Actually she dons, slowly, a monstrous pair of false breasts. Music sounds: *The Stripper,* played plaintively and incongruously on a mouth organ. Not a word spoken and already we have been moved—beautifully, comically and with enormous theatricality—from the ideal to the painfully real and on again to the satirical-grotesque. . . .

Playwright Tomson Highway's characters live, for the most part, like poor whites; they have adopted rock-bottom American values. This is not a play about racial prejudice; it couldn't be since there are no non-Indian characters. It is about what people do to themselves under pressure, though the pressures may be externally imposed. Especially it is about what men do to women.

This is the most powerful play I have seen about misogyny, and it is fitting that it should be the work of a man. The cast contains one woman, in a multiple role, but eight men; for the most part, their view of women is accurately summed up in the opening dumbshow. The extreme case is Big Joey (Ben Cardinal), whose wife is the one with the falsies; he is virtually prostituting her as part of a blackmail scam. His ambitions to run a radio station conflict with those of his pudgy victim Zachary (Gary Farmer) to get money to open a bakery. Big Joey cannot stand the sight of female blood, and his phobia led to culpable negligence at the birth of his son (in a barroom, by the light of a juke box). Seventeen years on, he watches while the boy commits an especially brutal rape.

The scene in which Joey explains himself is one of the play's weakest, matched by one in which the baker takes on the Christian God, defying Him to justify the misery in which the community is living. These both sound like the playwright being painfully explicit. He also spreads himself so that his play, though actually tightly plotted, seems to sprawl. But the weaknesses are those of talent and ambition. At times he writes with horrific power; more often he deploys a barbed, juicy laughter that ex-

ploits and explodes masculine obsession and masculine bluster. Sometimes he suggests a grown-up Sean O'Casey. Urban-sharp this Highway may be, but he belongs in the line of ethnic comedy that periodically rejuvenates the Anglo-American theatre. When this line breaks through, as Indian writing now has, it does us a double service; it introduces us to new scenes and puts us in touch with old ones. At moments we seem to be reaching back to the roots of the theatre.

A crisis finds Pierre St. Pierre (Graham Greene, at the furthest remove from his wisdom-incarnate role in *Dances With Wolves*) posed at a window, pulling a nightcap on and off as he wrestles between the demands of sleep and conscience. The sequence is prolonged past the limits of farce, and becomes agonizingly tense. We desperately want him to do the right thing, and know how easily we ourselves would do the wrong one.

Greene also has a protracted clowning triumph as a hockey referee, slithering around on invisible ice, in abject fear of the game and the unseen players. These players are the women on the reserve and it is these sporting ambitions that put the fear of whatever it is into most of the males. The men literally fall backward with astonishment when they first hear about it. But they recover.

The women in the play, even more than the men, have a rich variety of names and labels: from Gazelle Nataways to "that awful dictionary woman" to the eponymous Dry Lips. The men end up hooting the dismissive title line, Big Joey once more in the lead.

Cardinal's Joey, balefully unrelenting, makes a strong negative pole in a group otherwise composed of weaklings, misfits and the odd doomed idealist. They have all—Tom Jackson, Gary Farmer, Billy Merasty, Dwayne Manitowabi, Kennetch Charlette, Doris Linklater—appeared in the play before, at Theatre Passe Muraille in Toronto or in Manitoba, and they are an ensemble.

The arrival of this show at the Royal Alex is an event. One hopes that a general audience, subscribers or otherwise, will fill a large theatre for a major new play. This is a matter of economics, but also of morale and of ultimate value. If the Canadian theatre is to mean anything, it cannot skulk forever in holes and corners.

**John Bemrose**   (review date 29 April 1991)

SOURCE: "Native Grace: An Indian Reserve Struggles for Salvation," in *Maclean's Magazine,* Vol. 104, No. 17, April 29, 1991, pp. 60-1.

[*In the following review, Bemrose praises the humor and moral of* Dry Lips Oughta Move to Kapuskasing.]

Last summer, as armed Mohawks stood guard at their barricades in Oka, Que., a new image of Canada's native people forced itself on the national consciousness. But such defiance is only one aspect of the current Indian struggle for greater self-determination. Early this month at Toronto's Royal Alexandra Theatre, native people staged a different kind of event—the production of Tomson Highway's award-winning play, ***Dry Lips Oughta***

*Move to Kapuskasing.* The bitter tragicomedy first appeared at the city's Theatre Passe Muraille two years ago. But its remounting at the plush Royal Alex—where it is the first Canadian play in eight years—marks a special triumph for an Indian cultural community determined to raise the profile of its concerns and its achievements.

Pride in those achievements was in evidence at the theatre earlier this month as native people in formal evening attire mingled under the television lights with the well-to-do opening-night crowd. In part, the celebrity atmosphere was a carryover from last month's Academy Awards show when one of the stars of *Dry Lips,* Toronto actor Graham Greene, was an Oscar nominee for his role in Kevin Costner's *Dances With Wolves.* The glitter contrasted starkly with the events portrayed onstage. For all its broad humor, Highway's vision of life on Wasaychigan Hill, a fictional Manitoulin Island reserve, is as bleak as the morning after a week-long binge. Like so many native communities, Wasaychigan Hill is destroying itself in a black orgy of substance abuse and violence. Only its frayed links to traditional values and a kind of gamy courage hold it back from complete disintegration.

Highway's earlier hit play, *The Rez Sisters,* focused on Wasaychigan Hill's women, who made an epic comedy of their journey to a big-city bingo game. In *Dry Lips,* Highway turns his attention to the men. They are a pathetic if oddly endearing lot. Of the seven native males in the play, five are drunks, fools or both. The remaining two, Dickie Bird Halked (Kennetch Charlette) and Simon Starblanket (Dwayne Manitowabi), are youths struggling to escape the community's collective nightmare. But Simon is killed in a pointless accident, while Dickie Bird's inner demons—he has been left speechless by a mysterious childhood trauma—drive him to commit a brutal rape.

All the men of Wasaychigan Hill are caught in a vortex of angry passivity. Even the authority figure, Big Joey (Ben Cardinal), is a bully obsessed with past memories. By contrast, the women of the reserve—who appear mostly through the eyes of the men—positively brim with creativity and initiative. That has helped inspire a deep strain of misogyny. When Big Joey is pressed to explain why he stands by passively during Dickie Bird's attack on Simon Starblanket's fiancée, Patsy Pegahmagahbow (Doris Linklater), he blurts out that he hates all women for taking power away from the men.

Fortunately, Highway, a Cree born 39 years ago in Brochet, Man., leavens Wasaychigan's anguish with humor of a very high order. The chief vehicle of the play's comedy is a loquacious bootlegger named Pierre St. Pierre, played by Greene. The gap-toothed, jut-jawed drunk is the utter antithesis of dignity: he shamelessly cadges beer and chugalugs it a bottle at a time. Greene is simply brilliant in the role. When he appears as the referee for an all-women's hockey game, his physical comedy has the stumbling insouciance of Buster Keaton. St. Pierre is also, in his way, the poet of the reserve, as he sums up with wonderful exaggeration and malapropisms the exploits of the women hockey players. His repeated recitation of their outlandish names, including Big Bummed Pegahmagah-

bow and Dry Lips Manatawagan, grows more deliciously funny every time.

While all the comic sections of the production have an engaging buoyancy, a certain heaviness creeps in elsewhere. Much of the play concerns Dickie Bird's search to discover his true father and understand the causes of his dumbness. It is a tedious quest, unable to bear the dramatic importance that Highway places on it. Part of the problem is Charlette's too-frenetic performance. Even more critically, Highway has not found a language adequate to his characters' rage and pain. That makes the climactic rape scene—which involves the brutal use of a crucifix—a bloody but emotionally unaffecting affair.

---

**Dry Lips Oughta Move to Kapuskasing is more than a play about conditions on Canada's Indian reserves. It is a reminder that when the cultural underpinnings of a society crumble, chaos is not far behind.**

**—John Bemrose**

---

The result of those failures is that *Dry Lips* breaks in half between beguiling comedy and less effective tragedy. Still, much of the production soars above that split, including Carlos del Junco's haunting accompaniment on the blues harp. Also successful is the use of the Ojibwa trickster figure, Nanabush (Linklater), who hovers like Puck in the background, an invisible influence on the characters. In one scene, she waggles an enormous pair of false buttocks and causes the reserve's baker, Zachary (Gary Farmer), to break into a chorus—he has no idea why—of *Hot Cross Buns.*

The drama's earthiness and gallows humor are important gifts from native people to a society that has all too often lost sight of such qualities. *Dry Lips* is also a warning. Wasaychigan Hill's predicament can be seen as being symbolic of the larger society that surrounds it—a society that may itself be bent on self-destruction in more subtle or socially acceptable ways. In that sense, *Dry Lips Oughta Move to Kapuskasing* is more than just a play about conditions on Canada's Indian reserves. It is a reminder that when the cultural underpinnings of a society crumble, chaos is not far behind.

**Gitta Honegger   (review date Winter 1992)**

SOURCE: "Native Playwright: Tomson Highway," in *Theater,* Vol. XXIII, No. 1, Winter, 1992, pp. 88-92.

*[In the following laudatory review of* Dry Lips Oughta Move to Kapuskasing, *Honegger discusses the play's plot, character, and main themes.]*

A non-Native theatergoer sees a play written by a Native playwright. It is one of the most exciting plays she has seen in a long time. The all-Native ensemble has developed a uniquely cohesive acting style, rarely seen on our stages. The work is a brilliant combination of Western and Native performance traditions. The observer, a theater professional herself, with extensive training in Western theater has no problem ranking the work (very highly) within the canon of Western drama. She is much more limited in her resources to define adequately, let alone do full justice to that "other", "Native" dimension, that enriches and transcends the European conventions. Already the quotation marks reveal the perspective of the speaker which necessitates a special care in the use of language, and specifically, of misleading generalizations such as "Native Drama" or "Native Theater." The playwright, Tomson Highway, is Cree, one of the "First Nations" in Canada, which is the preferred term there. Accordingly, the sensibility that informs his play is Cree.

Although I have for some years now involved myself in the histories of some of the Native peoples, their different performance traditions, and the present situation, particularly of American Indians, I am in no position to adequately illuminate the intricate texture of the play within the rich and diversified heritage of Native traditions. My emotional response, overwhelming as it was, comes from my own cultural and personal experiences. The play generously led me into its world, its tragic dimensions as well as its wonderful comedic spirit. This world as I perceive it, in all its contemporary vitality, takes on its full life and meaning only within the ancient circle of myths which hold the origin and still safeguard the continuity of its people. I consider myself an invited, privileged guest at the periphery of that circle. I cannot speak from within it. I feel that at this point in our shared history on this continent it is important to establish one's perspective and acknowledge one's limitations.

Although a great critical success in Canada, no major American publication has reported about the recent production of Tomson Highway's *Dry Lips Oughta Move to Kapuskasing*. Somewhat unexpectedly, this tough, unsentimental yet deeply compassionate play with its feisty humor and unrelenting tragic drive became a triumphant, sold out hit at the Royal Alexandra, Toronto's historic landmark of Continental, West End and Yankee showbiz glamour. It marks the first major commercial breakthrough of a Native writer. The playwright, a long time favorite of reservation and urban theater audiences across Canada, is virtually unknown in the United States. He should be introduced here as a powerful voice in the theater with important stories to tell. He might inspire our Native writers to share their stories on the stage. Perhaps even more importantly, the success of this play should inspire our Artistic Directors and producers to turn their attention to Native writers.

In a time when American theaters have become programmatically committed to the challenge of reflecting an ethnically diversified society on stage, it is still surprising how little attention has been paid to the development and presentation of plays by and with Native American artists. It is all the more surprising since Native American poets and novelists have made extraordinary, internationally acclaimed contributions to contemporary literature. This is

not to say that Native American playwrights don't exist. To name just a few: Hanay Geiogamah comes to mind immediately. As a playwright, director, teacher and producer he has made crucial contributions toward the development of a Native American Theater; Bruce King, a powerful, tough writer of the Vietnam generation, generated some interest a while ago. More recently, William Yellowrobe, Jr. is a name, practically the only name, that comes up regularly in conversations about Native American drama. But no Native American playwright has achieved the recognition of a Scott Momaday, Leslie Silko, James Welch, Linda Hogan, not to speak of the most recent mega-stars of the contemporary literary scene, husband and wife-team Louise Erdrich and Michael Dorris.

By contrast, in Canada, 39 year old Tomson Highway has first gained national attention with *The Rez Sisters*. Its sequel, *Dry Lips Oughta Move to Kapuskasing* should firmly establish him as one of the leading voices in the English speaking theater. As all of his plays, (as well as many other Native playwrights' works), it was first developed by Native Earth Productions, Toronto's only and arguably, North America's foremost professional Native theater company, of which he is also Artistic Director.

While *Rez Sisters* follows the journey of seven women to the world's largest Bingo game, *Dry Lips* concentrates on seven men from the same reservation. In both plays, the rich heritage of the northern Woodland nations intersects with the legacy of colonialization in a contemporary Native world, presented as the fictitious Wasaychigan reserve on Manitoulin Island.

In Larry Lewis's fluid production of *Dry Lips* the set pieces are flown in from above. Before the play begins, and when not in use, the shabby furniture pieces are visibly suspended in the fly space, with a hockey game in process on the old black and white television set. What may at first seem a convenient way of changing the scenery also conveys the essential tension of the play: the handed down clutter of the dominant culture looms over a bare stage, soon to cut into the expansive, mythic space of the ancient woodland, with its present inhabitants suspended between tribal dreams and colonized nightmares.

The play's central dreamer is Zachary Jeremiah Keechigeesik, 41 years old, an average kind of guy with a pregnant wife and basic American dreams of sex and a little status and money. He wants to have his own bakery on the reservation. We first get to know his (sizable) ass, framed in a spotlight, as he lies sleeping on his friend's shabby sofa, with a life size Marilyn Monroe poster in the back. A voluptuous leg drapes itself around his bottom, followed by the regally voluminous body of a Native woman. She puts on black stockings, paper-maché tits and ass and a hockey sweater. It is Gazelle Nataways, the reservation's femme fatale and captain of the newly formed women's hockey team, the Wasy Wailerettes. The kiss she plants on Jeremiah's ass leaves a red pair of lips on his buttocks. It will soon become the stuff for blackmail by her present boyfriend, Big Joey, tough guy of the Rez and his devoted admirer, Creature Nataways who happens to also be her husband. Eventually the comedy will evolve from a puck that gets lost in a heated hockey match, with Jeremiah's wife and Gazelle getting into an impassioned fight over territorial claims on Zachary. The puck will be found stuck in Gazelle's ample bosom just in time to have the Wasy Wailerettes advance from a local team of reservation rebel women to the Ontario to the National and finally the Aboriginal Women's World Hockey League. Somewhere during the performance, the ass we saw at the beginning suddenly connects via its synonym to another dreaming stage character, who turned into an ass with the help of a woodland trickster whose name happens to be synonymous with the embattled object of the hockey match. And sure enough, at the feet of Marilyn/Titania, this big Native bottom is transported into a Midwinter Night's Dream by another woodland trickster of Chippewa origin: Nanabush, mythic survivor, transformer, clown and healer with great spiritual power, histrionic talent and indestructible humor.

Language further confounds the situation. As Highway explains in a program note, in contrast to European languages there is no gender differentiation in Cree and Chippewa, the first languages of the characters in his play. This means that in theory the trickster as the central hero figure in Native mythologies doesn't have to be exclusively male or female. In **Rez Sisters,** Nanabush was a man, a beautiful dancer who transformed into mythic birds of life and death. Now Nanabush is a woman.

It is Nanabush who activates the dreams and plays all the female characters. They are Native women in the grotesquely exaggerated guises of femininity shaped by the cliches of the dominant culture. On the surface, this Nanabush appears as an oddly assimilated aboriginal *Lulu,* the comic subversion of her colonized men's sexual fantasies who ends up as the tragically brutalized victim of alcoholism and the delusions of an imposed religion. But this is also Nanabush, the shaman, who is taking all seven men into a dream world, knowing that "before the healing can take place, the poison must be exposed. . . ." Highway prefaces the play's published version with this quote by Lyle Longclaws.

Doris Linklater, of considerable size and magnificent in her power, moves through the transformations of sexual stereotypes with such commanding dignity that the portrayals of these women never seem exploitative. There is a special concentration to her performance, an integrity of knowledge, compassion and intent which she shares with the dancers of sacred Native ceremonies. It seems to come from an uncompromising, uncompromised commitment to the responsibility involved in the (sacred) task of enactment. It informs every transformation, whether she does a hilarious deadpan strip, twirling the tassels on her nipples with deadly arrogance, or tiptoes in as Patsy, the shy young woman in love with the young dreamer, Simon Starblanket; whether she dances with the magnificent feather bustles, or does an impersonation of the old Catechist God sitting on a potty in white wig and beard and black lace stockings.

Zachary's dream intersects with the dreams of his buddies, Big Joey, ruthless, merciless and macho, Creature Nataways, hopelessly in love with him, and Spooky Lacroix, a born again Christian. All are 39 years old, and together they had participated in the famous siege at Wounded Knee in 1973. The shared memory of their youth, with its legacy of violence and abandoned dreams haunts them to account for their own lives and their effect on the next generation.

At the depth of the tribal nightmare is a rape performed with a crucifix by the 17 year old victim of Fetal Alcohol Syndrome, on a young woman who is the only person still connected to the old native traditions. At the height of the four buddies' comic nightmare is a hockey match that involves their wives who have organized the team to reaffirm their power. A team member's fateful slip on the ice elicits the emotional exclamation which gives the play its cryptic title. The match is refereed by Pierre St. Pierre, an old toothless bootlegger, played by Graham Greene in a dazzling virtuoso clown act which is all the more astonishing after his composed performance of Kicking Bird, the charmingly worldly Lakota holy man in *Dances With Wolves.* He is all alone there on the ice, on skates, surrounded by phantom women. His body language and facial expressions visualize in hilarious details the women's frenzied encounter while trying to keep his balance. His consummate performance is further proof of the extraordinary range of this actor and confirms what those of us who had seem him on stage in New York knew all along: at 38, he is one of the most powerful actors around. Neighboring Stratford should remember this Toronto based actor when they are casting a Falstaff or Macbeth, to name just the most obvious possibilities. He can play anything.

Between the crucifix and the lost puck, Highway takes us on a rollercoaster dream ride that drives towards the confrontation with the reckless circumstances of the disturbed boy's birth in a speakeasy, next to a jukebox, with Gazelle Nataways stripping on top of it, just as his mother is about to pass out in a drunken stupor. The events are locked deep inside the mute boy's head as unspeakable mysteries. The only key handed to him by his born again uncle Spooky Lacroix is the cross. Everyone had a part in that hellish night. Everyone had avoided facing up to the truth of their own irresponsibility, their dependence on the self-perpetuating cycle of the dominant culture's destructive forces. As the drama erupts in all its phantasmagoric horror through everyone's alcohol drenched unconscious, the child reenacts the classic tragedy at the threshold of Western consciousness: He penetrates his mother, in the figure of Nanabush who is also enacting the young woman. Through these transformations, he is also violating Nanabush, the spiritual center of his culture, and he does it with the ultimate symbol of Western civilization. In the production, the traumatized boy repeatedly stabs the cross into the earth. The young woman stands in front of the jukebox which has transformed into a bizarre altar. She slowly lifts her skirt to reveal her blood soaked panties while blood is dripping from the cross in the boy's hand. With the cross symbolizing the rape of the earth that sustains his culture, his desperate act is also an act of tragic self-immolation. It is an eerie reminder of both Oedipus blinding himself and of Jocasta's suicide. The rape becomes the ritual enactment of gender separation, first introduced through language and enforced through violence.

Nothing is just what it seems. Resonances of Western drama and Native customs mirror each other and refract the collisions and convergences of influences in contemporary Native cultures. Indian names that refer to certain characteristics or incidences in a person's life echo the descriptive names in classic comedy. Underlaying the street/*rez* smart lingo is the poetry of idioms that have traversed layers of linguistic residues, Native and European. There is a special music to the soft pitch and gently punched rhythm of the characters' Cree tinted English, which is counterpointed by passages in Cree and Chippewa. Behind every surface emblem there is a dream image that contains the past, both ancient and immediate, tribal and personal. The speak-easy's flashing lights which encircle the stripper, give way to the calm glow of a full moon that frames the young woman who teaches her lover to dance the old way. Behind the kitschy life-size madonna statues in Spooky's house lurks the desperate face of his pregnant sister, with a huge bloated belly, a big rosary around her neck and beer bottle in her hand. The nightmare contains the healing process: The comedic imagination, ancient gift of the trickster, outsmarts the terror: Storytelling as performance in process is a triumphant proof of continuity: a culture creates itself anew through each act of telling, of performing.

Motifs of birth are woven throughout: Only pregnant women or women with many children qualify for the hockey team. Spooky's and Zachary's wives are pregnant, so is Patsy, fiancee of Simon Starblanket who dreams of going to Rosebud to dance with the Sioux and ends up accidentally killing himself, as he pursues Dickie Bird with a loaded gun. Early in the play he shared his haunting vision of an Indian baby waiting to be born:

> . . . I have my arms around this rock, this large black rock sticking out of the ground, right here on this spot. And then I hear this baby crying, from inside this rock. The baby is crying out my name. As if I am somehow responsible for it being caught inside that rock. I can't move. My arms, my whole body, stuck to this rock. Then this . . . eagle . . . lands beside me, right over there. But this bird has three faces, three women. And the eagle says to me: "the baby is crying, my grand-child is crying to hear the drum again."

As he is telling the story to Zachary who is thinking about his bakery and the equipment he needs, Nanabush as Patsy, enveloped in shimmering circles of feathers appears like a mysterious, wailing bird. Simon continues:

> There's this noise all around us, as if rocks are hitting the sides of houses-echoing and echoing like in a vast empty room—and women are wailing. The whole world is filled with this noise.

Simon, too begins to wail, then he continues:

> Then the eagle is gone and the rock cracks and this mass of flesh, covered with veins and blood, comes oozing out and a woman's voice somewhere is singing something about angels and god and angels and god. . . .

Zachary replies with his dream which is considerably sim-

pler and with more predictable, comically solvable consequences: He tells Simon that he dreamt waking up at Gazelle Nataway's place with no shorts on and his pants ripped in the middle.

In the end, Zachary wakes up in his own house with his own wife, played by Nanabush, entering with their baby. It is a real baby, a beautiful, naked, Indian baby girl which she hands to the naked Indian man on the sofa. The final tableau is fully earned in the context of the play. It is filled with strength and free of sentimentality. Nanabush's healing gift to her people becomes Highway's generous gesture to the audience who at this point has also been cleansed to accept the gift of continuity in the right spirit.

What is perhaps most impressive and enviable from the point of view of a visitor from the U.S. is the depth of the company, which makes for the remarkable consistency of their performance style. It is a dazzling combination of Vaudevillian humor, the tough critical edge of a Brechtian approach to characterization and, at the core of it all, the transformational skills of the tricksters, the clowns, the story tellers and dancers of ancient Native origins. What is also quite astonishing is the actors' versatility. Gary Farmer, remembered from the film *Powwow Highway* for his whimsically challenging portrayal of Philbert, the young Indian reclaiming his native spiritual powers in junk littered ancestral landscapes, plays Jeremiah with just the right mixture of an all too human foolishness and a touching, albeit endangered humanity. Tom Jackson is a popular singer-songwriter with matinee idol charisma. He turns Spooky Lacroix into a spindly bigot with pot belly and thinning hair. Every one of the actors gives a performance that is testimony to an impressive Native talent pool which should also serve as a model and a challenge to U.S. theaters.

**Tomson Highway with Robert Enright  (interview date December 1992)**

SOURCE: "Let Us Now Combine Mythologies: The Theatrical Art of Tomson Highway," in *Border Crossings,* Vol. 1, No. 4, December, 1992, pp. 22-7.

[*In the interview below, Highway discusses his upbringing, Native literature, mythology, and the structure of his plays.*]

[*Enright*]: *You were born on a trap line 176 miles north of Lynn Lake in the upper reaches of Manitoba. What was that experience like?*

[Highway]: Back in the early '50s it was very basic. There were 12 in my family and most of us were born in tents and we lived in tents almost year 'round. In the summer time we travelled by canoe and in the winter time we travelled by dog sled. We lived a very nomadic life; my father trapped in the winter and fished in the summer and hunted in between. It was an exquisite lifestyle.

*A dozen children! Your family was almost its own tribe.*

Yes. It was beautiful. I mean, we weren't in a state of constant ecstasy but we certainly weren't unhappy, either, even though it was very harsh in the winter. It's always been easy for me to go back to those days in my mind.

*Doesn't Philomenia say in* **Rez Sisters** *that the place gets in your blood, you can't get rid of it and it can't get rid of you? Is that a reference to the way you feel about the North as well?*

Yeah. I go back as often as I can, twice a year on average, once in the winter and once in the summer. I believe that a sense of place applies to everybody. Where you come from, where your roots are—all that is extremely strong. I don't think anybody really is able to get rid of it.

*So even when you're not in the North, when you're working in Toronto, or attending a play in Edinburgh or Paris, there's a way in which it will constantly come back and renew you?*

Yeah. I come back because of that and certainly having family up there makes it even more necessary to return. But I've frequently thought about going to live in Europe again. We live in the age of FAX machines and telephones, so you really can live anywhere on the face of the earth and still do what you do, or at least do what I do, and I have this fantasy of living in Paris.

*Why would that be your fantasy?*

For a number of reasons. I've been there many, many times over the years and I love the city, the language and the sense of anonymity the culture provides. I wouldn't go and live there forever, but a two- or three-year stretch would be nice. But I'd have to come back; I mean, I love this country too much. Part of the reason I'd want to live in a situation like that is to avoid the pressures. You do get a tremendous number of requests to speak here, to do this interview there, do this charity, do that benefit, sit on this committee or that board. After a while it gets to be too much. The demand on your time is extreme and privacy becomes a rare commodity.

*Has that become a problem for you?*

To a certain extent. I certainly do seem to get a lot of demands on my time. I haven't had a new play produced in four years because I just haven't had any time to write. The other reason I'd like to live in Paris comes out of my personal life. I'm proud of the fact that I'm considered to be among a group of artists whose statements are unequivocally direct and honest. But it's also earned me a certain degree of notoriety, not to mention a certain number of enemies, and after a few vicious attacks on your own person you can be hurt. I just don't have time to deal with that kind of hatred. So there's a certain part of me that wants to hide away.

*Have the attacks come about because of the frankness with which you've presented aboriginal culture?*

Well, it goes beyond aboriginal culture. The material I write is layered and certainly a very obvious layer is the aboriginal component. But I think I've studied enough Western and other art to have achieved a level of sophistication where I write beyond the specifics of my aboriginal background and get to the universal human condition. At this point in my career I'm really heavily into the whole gender issue, the male/female dichotomy, the sexual hierarchy, which is an area that knows no racial boundaries.

Partly because these things are layered constructions, they can be very easily misunderstood and a lot of people do misunderstand them. I've been called everything from a racist to a sexist and I've been accused of purposely promoting racism and sexism. It reached the point where I've been called the living reincarnation of Satan. I've come across situations where people I used to know will refuse to talk to me on the street. I've even had people who are very Christian, and supposedly very kind and loving, turn and walk away from me.

*But surely you're not surprised? After all, you were raised in residential schools where the discrepancy between the practice and the preaching of Christianity must have been fairly apparent.*

In a perverse sort of way I'm almost thrilled by the occurrences, because they represent tangible proof that the theory and the practice are two entirely different animals. Which is an opinion I've always held.

*I want to pick up this notion of your sophistication coming out of the study of Western culture. The plays are highly canny in a theatrical way. I mean Pierre St. Pierre is a kind of Mr. Malaprop; he tells a character "not to contribute your elders," for "contradict." He plays with language and makes bizarre, unconscious mistakes. Now, you must be aware that there are characters going back to Shakespeare and the Restoration who abuse language in just that way. When you conceive of a play and its characters, do you deliberately build in a literary tradition which doesn't necessarily have anything to do with the aboriginal culture you're writing about?*

It's not a deliberate choice. But there's two or three answers to that question. In order of importance, the first answer is that I find the whole process of writing to be so difficult, so painful, so humiliating and so humbling that I'm grateful for anything that works. The actual act of writing is an act of desperation at the best of times. So the first answer is that ultimately those characters and situations came out because I really didn't have a choice. There's a point where they start running on their own and they pull you. Secondly, those kind of characters are universal—they're story-telling conventions that exist in every culture. The concept of the hero is a universal and so is the heroic myth. And the comic or clown character. I also have a strong musical background and I believe that the process of writing plays is very much a musical act. Ultimately, you seduce an audience, you lull it into a kind of hypnotic state. To me the human mechanism responds naturally and subliminally to the concept of rhythm, the origins of which lie with the basic beat of the human heart.

*Is that one of the ways you structure your plays, as if they were musical arrangements?*

Yes, and that's the way it works psychologically on the human brain and on human emotions. You can subdivide that whole note, which is the beat of the human heart, into quarter notes, eighth notes, sixteenth notes, thirty-second notes, and complex configurations thereof, including variations and combinations of pitch, meaning, counterpart, harmony and so forth. What I'm saying is that I transfer all that knowledge into the construction of a line.

> The material I write is layered and certainly an obvious layer is the aboriginal component. But I think I've studied enough Western and other art to have achieved a level of sophistication where I write beyond the specifics of my aboriginal background and get to the universal human condition.
>
> —*Tomson Highway*

*You score your language and the rhythm of the play that closely?*

It's not a conscious process but ultimately that's what it boils down to. I'll give you a very blatant example. I find it comes naturally to create one character as a legato and contrast him with a staccato, so that in **Dry Lips Oughta Move to Kapuskasing,** there are the two guys who enter the play at the very top, one of whom, Creature Nataways, is a staccato character, and then the character with him is Big Joey, who talks in monosyllables. Then there are lyrical characters like Simon Starblanket who's full of dream visions and lilting, vaulting passages. And there are other variations, not all of which I can explain. Ultimately, for me writing a play is very much like writing a symphony.

*You also use music more directly. The wail of the harmonica is used throughout* **Dry Lips,** *as is Kitty Wells. Are these part of the symphonic play you're making, as well? How do these songs and instruments interact with your musical characters?*

During the initial productions of a new play, I'm usually very much a part of the rehearsal process. I usually end up playing the role of musical director, being very precise about choosing the music and choosing the rhythms of the music. If I want a drum to go boom boom I say so and if I want to change that drum to go digga dum, then I say that and we put it in. For instance, in **Dry Lips** the first musical sound you hear, other than the human voice, is the harmonica. In **Rez Sisters** it's the drum. Those are choices I made. And at the opening there's an upward climbing glissando, sort of like the opening of Gershwin's "Rhapsody in Blue." That was a very deliberate choice. I said to the harmonica player, "I would like you to start out with a trill on the low A flat, A flat combined with B flat, and then I would like you to do this glissando climbing all the way up to the high B flat above the high C." That's the way I talk in the rehearsal process.

*I thought you'd given music up after you stopped playing classical piano, but you haven't given it up at all. You've just found a different way for it to operate in your art.*

Absolutely.

*You said earlier that there's always a hero. One of the things your plays seem to do is to create a mythology of the com-*

*mon folk. You have a female bingo player who's a legend for playing 27 cards simultaneously; another of your characters actually drinks a Kitty Wells record, presumably out of affection. These are stories that are part of a common mythology; if we were living in Greece, one assumes they would be our Olympians. Are you conscious of creating a substitute mythology?*

Yes. One of my most passionate pursuits when I was at university was the study of mythology. Mostly European—specifically classical Christian, Celtic and Teutonic mythology—and its application in literature by the artists of those respective cultures. The first example that surfaces in my mind is William Butler Yeats. In Teutonic mythology, the most obvious example is Richard Wagner. And then, of course, there's Cree mythology. And making a comparative study of all those traditions of story-telling.

*Was this a systematic study?*

Very much so. I did go out and very specifically apply myself to the study of these mythologies. At some point I found out the process of myth-making is the same in every culture and it comes from a very basic human impulse—the need to communicate. To make people laugh, to make people enjoy and celebrate life. Let's say there was a party in a hotel room and the party got raided. The actual party was on the second floor. People are getting arrested but this one guy, who is the pusher, jumps out the window. It's only the second floor, so he takes off, unharmed and unheroic. But by the time the incident has gone from story-teller "A" to story-teller "X" a whole year has passed. By now the guy jumped out of the 15th floor of the hotel and hung on by his fingernails the entire time the police were investigating the party participants. He becomes a character of heroic proportions.

*Robert Graves has done an exemplary job with the Greek myths in showing their actual historical and social beginnings. What intrigues me about your process is you also inherit a culture that already exists, the culture of the trickster Nanabush. The mythology is complete and intact. So how do you remake that mythology and continue to make it live? Can you pick it up and transform it, mix it with other stories without any worry?*

I think with communication technology as highly developed as it is now it's pretty well impossible for a person to limit himself to his own specific mythology. Even though I come from northern Manitoba and from a Cree background, I've become very much a part of mythologies worldwide. I don't resist the impulse to create the characters that I do. And I don't resist the impulse to combine mythologies because ultimately I believe they are universal and that their archetypes are all the same. I was really surprised at the response to **Dry Lips** because I didn't realize that non-Native people were so ignorant of their own mythology. Putting it in the bluntest way possible, I was shocked to discover main-stream audiences knew more about the size of Elizabeth Taylor's breasts, Michael Jackson's most recent nose job and Madonna's most recent fuck than they did about their own systems of gods and goddesses. So that a Cree Indian from caribou country ended up knowing more about Hera and Zeus, about

Apollo and Dionysius, about Mars and Mercury and about the roles they played within that society, than the people the stories belonged to.

*So I assume as a result they didn't understand the importance of the central characters in your plays, either?*

That's right. **Dry Lips** is the story of Hera and Zeus. Zeus was forever philandering because the Greeks were very much into the celebration of the sensual, visceral self. It's the same with Cree mythology.

*This is the Zeus who had the imagination and the capability to turn up on earth in any number of guises—a swan or a bull.*

Or a calf and so forth. He would come down and make love to mortal girls and then he'd go back up and Hera, the Queen of the Sky, would find out about it and shake the universe. Thunderbolts would fly and earthquakes would happen—that's the way the Greeks explained these natural disasters. So if you dig through all the layering in **Dry Lips** what happens at the simplest level is that Hera Keechigeesik—which in Cree means "Hera of the great sky"—finds her husband Zachary Jeremiah—I couldn't name him Zeus but I got close enough—in bed with another woman. Hera characteristically flies into a jealous rage and beats the living daylights out of the other woman, knocks a puck out of her bosom and only when that puck is released, after the whole world has been turned upside down, do things come back to normal. And it's Hera who is like a puppet mistress who manipulates her husband's dream world. Ultimately she puts back into his hands the reincarnation of herself and so you get the return of the goddess. A lot of people didn't understand that. All they saw was a woman being treated brutally.

*That's a convincing explanation. Because you could be accused of being sentimental at the end of* **Dry Lips**, *in the way that you create the perfect aboriginal family in a kind of flawless, harmonic world. Coming out of the horror of the bar room scene and of the crucifix rape, the ending seems positively saccharine.*

I put it in the dream context for a number of reasons. Number one, I wanted to make a distinction between so-called aboriginal societies and so-called industrialized societies, whether we're talking about the Indians of North America or the aboriginals of Australia. Putting it very simplistically, the collective intellect of industrialized society has been developed to such a high degree at the expense of its spiritual centre. Whereas, with aboriginal cultures it's the reverse. We're not a highly intellectualized or highly technologized society but we haven't sacrificed our spiritual centre. And extending that idea one step further, our spiritual centre is very much expressed in the way our dream world operates. Our dream visions affect our day-to-day lives and, certainly for North American Indian culture, our dream life is every bit as important as our physical, conscious life.

*The cynical response to that would be that aboriginal people are probably a hell of a lot better off in their dream life than in their real life. In lots of cases that seems to me to be a kind of cop-out.*

That's part of it. I don't know if cop-out's the word for it. I think that's being judgmental.

*And equally cynical?*

Yeah. I'm not passing judgement on these notions. At least, I don't wish to. We place such a tremendous amount of importance on the way our dream world works that I never thought that it could be considered a cop-out. Let's put it less pessimistically and call it a release. But I think that regardless of how you wish to judge the respective societies, it is beyond argument that these two comparative states exist.

*Do you want the plays to be free of judgement?*

I don't think so. I think that ultimately if they were not judged, if they were not criticized, if they did not generate emotional and other responses, then I wouldn't be doing my job.

*Let me ask about judgement in another way. In* Dry Lips *there are two characters: Spooky Lacroix, a ridiculous, babbling Christian, and then there's Simon Starblanket, who wants the return of the drum, of the dance and of Nanabush. He wants to make the spiritual life powerful again. My sense is that as a playwright you have more sympathy with Starblanket than you do with Spooky.*

I think it's inevitable that your writing will be coloured by your own point of view, by your own attitude towards the world and everything within it. Certainly coloured with your own experience. I've had a very specific type of experience with Roman Catholicism and so the play—and Spooky Lacroix—are coloured by that. It's unfortunate that my experience with Roman Catholicism has been what it is. Spooky Lacroix's opening speech, which is something about the end of the world being at hand, is taken almost verbatim from the mouth of a Jehovah's Witness.

*Christianity isn't a neutral mythology for you though, is it? It can't be for someone who has been damaged by that mythology. Dickie Bird has such a rage in him that it leads him over the edge. I don't sense that you view Christianity as just being another neutral mythology that you can take this from and that from to layer your play so that it becomes more resonant and more dense.*

I have every reason to fight when I think what Christianity has done to me personally, never mind what it has done to my race. It's been an act of monumental dishonesty, monumental two-facedness. To have it hammered into your head by so-called figures of authority (the priests and nuns and teachers) that sex and the human sex organs were disgusting and dirty instruments of the devil—at a time when your own sexuality is at such a delicate place of development—was deeply confusing. But then to turn that around and have ten-year-olds victimized by a priest who goes around diddling little boys. What I'm angry at is those priests who said one thing and then when the lights went out, they did the complete opposite. It's like a game. They're like that woman at the hotel this morning. The victim doesn't end up being the loser; it's the aggressor who debases himself and debases life. I think that truth should be told.

*Were you sexually abused yourself?*

Absolutely. Everybody was.

*Do you mean at the Guy Hill Residential School in The Pas?*

Yeah. It's been off the record so far, but I'll tell you what happened. There was this Brother—and he wasn't the only one—who was our supervisor. We were 30 beds of ten- to 12-year-old boys in the Intermediate Boys Dormitory. We were far away from home and our parents had no input whatsoever into our education. And they had no control over our teachers. There was no such thing as a PTA, for instance. Anyway, this Brother would put us to bed at 8:30 and we'd all be kneeling at our beds in our pajamas and he'd take us through the rosary. Then he'd turn the lights off and we'd all start falling asleep. About half an hour later he'd come through the dormitory in the dark and go from bed to bed and wank off little boys. He was a French guy with a very thick accent and I'll always remember that as he'd do this he'd go, "It's big, eh, it's big." The Hail Marys from the rosary were still ringing through your head. Through the course of the six years that this guy was at Guy Hill he must have gone through 300 boys, all of whom are now between the ages of 35 and 45, and many of whom are now lawyers and businessmen. Sooner or later that kind of activity is going to come up.

*Is this Brother still alive?*

He was quite old back then, so he's probably dead. But that's just one story. There are so many others. So to this day my experience is coloured with that singular act of dishonesty. I mean they lied to us.

*You haven't yet written about that experience, of the massive hypocrisy involved.*

Not yet.

*I gather that prior to your encounter in the residential school system, you hadn't had much sexual experience?*

No. It happened when I was ten. It's a very vulnerable time, just when you're entering puberty.

*You have been accused by some feminists and by some aboriginal women of being sexist because of what happens to women in your plays.*

I think I could boil it down to two or three women out of a raft of thousands, most of whom are totally in support of and who understand the material. Just because a few women misunderstand, misinterpret the material is no reason to condemn all of them as being unintelligent, for instance.

*Do you have a personal sense of taboo within your own tradition and culture?*

No, I don't think one should be frightened of violating one's culture. I think that the role of any artist in society is to criticize that society, to force that society to look at its own imperfections. In a sense the role of the artist is the role of the shaman in traditional, pre-Christian Indian society. Shamans were the visionaries who led that society

into the future, who outlined the path that society was to take.

*And outlining that path can be cruel and can expose raw nerves?*

Well, I think that if society makes certain mistakes, then it's the role of the artist/visionary to tell society that it's made a mistake here, correct it, and then we'll move on. In the particular instance we've been talking about, the Roman Catholic church has made a tremendous error. And it should correct it and then either move on or die.

*I once interviewed a Native jazz drummer who was scrupulous about not using sacred rhythms in his music. He felt a sense of taboo, even in the free-wheeling world of improvisational jazz. I was struck by his adherence to this self-imposed limitation and I'm wondering if there's anything about the world you live in that you would feel discomfort in exposing to a mainstream audience. Maybe even because you don't want to be critical at this point in the history of aboriginal culture.*

I don't know. I often stand alone in these situations, which is why I've got myself into trouble in the past. I don't necessarily subscribe to that opinion. I don't think any religion or any society should be so holy as to be untouchable. I don't think that any icon should be put on a pedestal because once you put it on a pedestal it's too easy to tear down.

*So is Nanabush—a figure who operates on both sides of the gender and sexual spectrum—susceptible to attack? He's a mischievous figure, a trickster, he's always getting into trouble and is in some senses dangerous. Or am I going too far?*

No, I think he should be dangerous, I think he should push people right to the edge. I think—when he needs to be—he should be absolutely horrifying.

*Does he ever get diabolical?*

I think Nanabush is perfectly capable of it. I think he's capable of anything that the human heart is capable of, that God is capable of. I think God is ultimately Nanabush and by extension what he/she represents. God, the Great Spirit, whatever you wish to call this being. I think that God is every bit as capable of diabolical cruelty and evil as are human beings. He embodies beauty and incredible love and ecstasy and all these things. I also think that God is every bit as capable of being as enormous an asshole as that blonde was this morning. She's not the only one. They're an archetype and they're everywhere. Men treat women like that. And women have been angry about it for many generations, and are now doing something about it. But to go back to your question, no, nothing is too sacred to attack.

*You use humour in a liberating kind of way. Is that tendency something that comes naturally out of your life and culture, or is it a strategy for taking some of the pressure off events in the plays that may get pretty hard to take?*

Both. My favourite activity is to laugh. And the Cree culture is hilarious, the language is hilarious. When you speak Cree you laugh constantly. But the other side of it is that to make a statement that is brutally honest, you have to count upon incredible hilarity and incredible ridiculousness. And so the plays are structured in such a way that you do have to laugh at what seem to be the most inappropriate moments. But it works. It happened in *Dry Lips* time and time again. There's a scene where Zachary Jeremiah basically tells God to fuck himself. And people were crying. But then all of a sudden God is sitting up there on a toilet. You know, in drag as a woman with boobs hanging out and everything. And then people started to laugh. So there they were, laughing and crying at the same time.

*Speaking about mixed emotions, because of your experience in The Pas, did you use the Helen Betty Osborne incident in the crucifixion rape scene?*

I think the more specific application of the figure of Helen Betty Osborne comes in *Dry Lips*. I think the act that was committed up in The Pas back in 1971 has a complex metaphorical resonance. Because of society's response to the crime, she might as well have been raped with a crucifix. Did the church stand up for that girl, did the city council, the town council of The Pas? As they went to church every Sunday and prayed to their god, did they come back after church to stand up for that girl? Did the white women in that community stand up for another woman? No. I think those kinds of acts and those kinds of mistakes should be trumpeted.

*You often describe one play as the flip side of the other. When you initially conceived of* **Rez Sisters,** *did you know immediately that there was another play you would do very quickly and that it would be a mirror image?*

No.

*So* **Dry Lips** *came out of* **Rez Sisters** *after you realized what you could do with it?*

I don't know that it was that easy. Ultimately it was so difficult to do that I was just grateful that it came out the way it did. I mean, a lot of it is a happy accident. I'm just very fortunate. I'm so desperate at certain points that I'll write anything.

*But after you had done* **Rez Sisters,** *you did sit yourself down and say, Okay, now I want to do a play about seven men where hockey is the governing metaphor rather than seven women obsessed with bingo?*

Yeah, I think that was a rational choice.

*Am I right in thinking that 'beauty' means usefulness in Cree and Ojibway? It's an interesting way of looking at art, isn't it, that it has a social message as well as an aesthetic one?*

That's right, it is an interesting way of looking at things.

**David Richards**   (review date 5 January 1994)

SOURCE: "Bingo as the Way of Escape, at Dismal Odds," in *The New York Times,* January 5, 1994, pp. C15, C21.

[*In the following review of the New York production of* The Rez Sisters, *Richards criticizes the play for its poorly plotted scenes and adolescent humor.*]

It's Toronto or bust for the seven impoverished Indians whom the Canadian playwright Tomson Highway calls **The Rez Sisters.**

That's where "the biggest bingo in the world" is about to be held. As the raucous women envision it with mounting excitement and a feverish gleam in their dark eyes, hitting the $1 million jackpot is how they'll change their hardscrabble existence on the Wasaychigan Hill Indian Reserve in Ontario. "When I win" is how they begin their wishful sentences. No one says, "If I win."

You don't need a crystal ball to predict the outcome of Mr. Highway's 1986 play, which opened last night at the New York Theater Workshop. For all their gumption, his characters are up against hopeless odds, in society as well as the bingo hall. Still, the drama, which has won awards in Canada, has to be more surprising than this ramshackle staging would suggest.

Mr. Highway, a Cree, may be writing about a mythical community, but **The Rez Sisters** ("Rez" is short for reserve) is rooted in harsh realities. Joblessness, prejudice and alcoholism are endemic. The old sustaining Indian rituals have died, replaced by the platitudes of consumerism and country-western music. While his women don't lack for get-up-and-go, they really have no place to go to. Surely, this is material for some pungent conflicts.

Unfortunately, all of the playwright's shortcomings, and none of his assets, are readily apparent in the production that the New York Theater Workshop has put together in collaboration with the American Indian Community House. He plots scenes clumsily and states points baldly. When the dialogue is meant to be ribald, it rarely rises above the level of adolescent bathroom humor. And if you want to know what it all adds up to, well, grizzled Pelajia Patchnose (stone-faced Gloria Miguel) is more than happy to tell you.

"Kinda silly, isn't it, this business of living." she mutters, after the flashing bingo lights have been extinguished and she and her sisters are settling back into the dreariness of their welfare lives. "But what choice do we have? . . . I figure 'we gotta make the most of it while we're here.'"

Mr. Highway's strongest gift, an ability to capture flamboyant personalities with their defenses down, remains largely unexploited. All the actresses belong to various tribes and several are sisters in real life, so their credentials would appear to be in order. Few of them, however, show signs of theatrical sophistication. Raw gusto, more than anything else, distinguishes their collective endeavors. (There are also two men on the fringes of the story. One beats a large drum and chants accompaniment. The other portrays the star-spangled bingo master, a defecating sea gull and the ominous nighthawk, a harbinger of death.)

The principal acting area is marked off by a semicircle of birch trees, and seven brightly painted chairs, grouped in clusters, serve as the van that takes the women on their long drive to Toronto. But if the two directors. Linda S. Chapman and Muriel Miguel, have chosen to approach the play nonrealistically, their imagination seems to have dried up immediately afterward. All through **The Rez Sisters** you find yourself thinking that it needn't be this dull.

After all, one of Mr. Highway's characters, Marie-Adele Starblanket (Shella Tousey) has 14 children and is dying of cancer. Emily Dictionary (Murielle Borst), a barely reformed hellion with a tattoo on her shoulder, lost the love of her life, a woman, in a motorcycle accident. That indefatigable busybody Veronique St. Pierre (Lisa Mayo) has two equal sources of distress: a mentally deficient adopted daughter (Hortensia Colorado) and an erratic stove.

The garish Annie Cook (Elvira Colorado) sees herself as a country-rock star, a proposition that might be easier to accept if Ms. Colorado carried a tune better. As for loquacious Philomena Moosetail (Muriel Miguel again), her dyed and painted head is bursting with gossip and visions of the new toilet she'll purchase with her lucre from the bingo tables.

They may not be delicate souls, but they should be more affecting than they're allowed to be here. Ms. Tousey, who projects wan, unwavering strength beautifully, is pretty much alone in demonstrating that she knows how to navigate a stage. And the nighthawk makes short work of her.

Before the Rez sisters spread out their bingo cards and go for the big pot, the audience is invited to participate in a warm-up game. The cash prize, paid on the spot to the winner, is $20. The sum is not princely, granted. But this way, at least, it cannot be said, that everybody leaves the New York Theater Workshop empty-handed.

### Roberta Imboden   (essay date Spring 1995)

SOURCE: "On the Road with Tomson Highway's Blues Harmonica in *Dry Lips Oughta Move to Kapuskasing*," in *Canadian Literature,* No. 144, Spring, 1995, pp. 113-24.

[*In the following essay, Imboden discusses the role of the blues harmonica player in* Dry Lips Oughta Move to Kapuskasing *stating that while the player does not participate in the drama as a character, "the musician's absence-presence is crucial for the full development of the play's potentiality."*]

Tomson Highway observes in the Production Notes that precede his play **Dry Lips Oughta Move to Kapuskasing**:

> The 'sound-scape' of **Dry Lips Oughta Move to Kapuskasing** was mostly provided for by a musician playing, live, on harmonica, off to the side. The 'dream-scape' of the play is laced all the way through with Zachary Jeremiah Keechigeesik's 'idealized' form of harmonica playing, with a definite "blues" flavor.

The harmonica player invites the reader/audience to enter the dream, but the link between the play and the Blues warrants a preliminary explanation.

The blues is the music that arose from the recently freed slaves of the United States at the end of the 19th century. The Hayes Compromise of 1877 ended the hopes of Afro-Americans for authentic political participation in American life. This law caused the withdrawal of federal troops from the South, troops who were perceived as a buffer against white southern prejudice. By 1896 the Civil Rights Act of 1875 was declared unconstitutional and a situation of apartheid existed, for the doctrine of "separate but equal" was the law. The blues emerged out of this socio-political setting.

The spirituals, which came directly out of the slavery experience, at once resemble and differ from the blues in that both forms of music emerge from the suffering of slavery and move toward transcendence, but the transcendence of the spirituals involves life after death, whereas that of the blues involves only that of historical reality on earth. The blues, although sometimes referred to as "secular spirituals," are totally secular. "The blues are about black life and the sheer earth and gut capacity to survive in an extreme situation of oppression." Not surprisingly, the blues have strongly sexual overtones since on this earth the only possession the Afro-American had was the body, the body that must be celebrated.

The blues music emerges from the horror of the failed reconstruction of the South, but its power lies in the affirmation of the Afro-American self as it transforms itself through song. Thus, the structure of the blues moves from the tragedy of a lost dream, lost in the tragedy of the Post-Civil War South, toward a transcendence of this agony within the visceral affirmation of the Afro-American self.

The role of the Blues harmonica is one that parallels that of the Blues itself. Known as "the French harp," this instrument is well suited to the songs of a people hungering for a freedom that they have, yet do not have. Since the mark of the slave had been the absolute curtailment of all movement, trains and buses are important images in the Blues. Because the harmonica player could easily mimic trains, the sound of locomotives, the symbol of movement, of freedom, the harmonica was the ideal Blues instrument. Furthermore, the harmonica is seen by Blues experts as having a considerable expressive range, more volume, more versatility than the other instruments that were used by the Blues musicians. The harmonica, more easily than other instruments, can mimic the human voice.

Although Tomson Highway's characters have a very different history from that of the Afro-Americans in the South after the Civil War, the Blues harmonica suits well the situation of the Native People who are also struggling with a freedom that they have and do not have, toward some form of transcendence, some affirmation of the self. Thus, the Blues harmonica is an excellent medium of exodus for Highway's characters on the road toward meaningful liberation. This harmonica is the music the leads the characters from the poisons, sufferings, of their present state, on a journey that takes them toward a new world.

The Blues harmonica player does not participate in the play as one of its characters. Nevertheless, the musician's absence-presence is crucial for the full development of the play's potentiality. The placing of the musician on the side is symbolic of the assertion of a dynamic intertextuality by forces outside the text upon the actual play itself. Outside forces are always potentially disruptive, but in this case, this outside historical force, the suffering of the Afro-Americans of the Post-Civil War South, is interwoven into the play in such a way as to add a powerful, supportive new dimension. The eruption of an outside into the work has tremendous transformative potential for two different reasons. (1) The sound of the Blues harmonica sings of free movement and the possibility of transcendence. (2) The concept of performance, as personified in the semi-invisible musician, also carries within its process the transformation of the text. In the new idea of performance, the work that is being performed is opened up to the forces outside it. "[P]erformance can be defined as an activity which generates transformations, as the reintegration of art with what is 'outside' it, an 'opening up' of the 'field.'" Since, in a sense, the musician is performing Highway's play, the musician takes the characters on a journey that will allow them to move outside the confines of their narrow, sordid existence, toward the transformation of their lives.

The tools of Northrop Frye and Jacques Derrida will be helpful to the reader/audience who must accompany the characters on this journey. Although these critics are so obviously dissimilar, analyzing the play from these two different perspectives will add two different, but meaningful, dimensions to the deciphering process. The use of Frye will reveal an exodus that moves from the bondage of misery to freedom, whereas the use of Derrida will lead the characters, as well as reader/audience, on a journey from the present moment of this misery back, back in time, beyond time, toward the origins that allow such an exodus to take place.

Deep within the rhythm of the Blues harmonica lies a hidden impetus that finds the characters within the world of tragedy, not that of an apartheid American South, but that of a Native People's reservation that bears all the marks of an apartheid North. But this Blues harmonica, with its images of movement, of trains toward true freedom, will direct the characters from the present world of tragedy to the road of satire. On this road the characters will be given the weapons of liberation; they will see clearly all that is wrong with their society. A powerful light will shine upon them and they will understand their reality. They will see in the lucid light all vices, depravities, cruelties, all the demonic forces that have imprisoned them in a labyrinth of darkness, of violence. Highway will expose for them the torture and crucifixion of their women, the destruction of the vulnerable foetal brain of their children through foetal alcohol syndrome and the premature, senseless, violent death of their young men. But the Blues harmonica will give hope, will give the characters the gut capacity to survive, will tell the people on this reservation that the road from Corinth to Thebes is not caught within the strange circular path of the moebius strip.

Now, a brief look at what this circular path is, this structure of classical tragedy, is necessary. If one uses Sophocles' *Oedipus Rex* as an example, the structure becomes clear. Points A and B on the opposite sides of the circle are Corinth and Thebes. No way out of this enclosed circle is possible except through ostracism, exile, death. At first, on the road from Corinth to Thebes, while one watches

Oedipus fleeing his fate of parricide and incest, as predicted by the Delphic Oracle, the reader/audience thinks that true escape is possible. But as the play progresses, every step that every character in the play takes on the road to Thebes from Corinth is really a step on the road to Corinth from Thebes. Corinth represents the irreparable fate of the past. Thebes seemingly represents the freedom to create one's own destiny of the future. But Oedipus, in fleeing his past, his fate, is actually moving toward it of his own free will. Similarly, Big Joey, in attempting to flee the fate of misery on the reservation, goes to Wounded Knee in 1973. But instead of finding liberation from his fate, he finds murder and assassination. When he returns to the reservation, he brings with him the hatred and violence of the South Dakota site. Seething in hatred and despair, he becomes responsible for the three strikingly tragic events of the play: the damaged birth of his son, Dickie Bird, whom he refuses to recognize, the brutal crucifix rape of Patsy by Dickie Bird, and the subsequent accidental, suicidal death of her lover, Simon. His hatred has both caused and allowed Black Lady Halked to drink constantly for the three weeks preceding Dickie Bird's birth. This same hatred allows him to watch silently as Patsy is raped. Every one of these events can be seen as one of the steps that binds Big Joey and his people more securely than ever in their agonizing fate of impoverishment.

This tragic structure is one of narrowing inevitability in which all the characters move closer and closer to hell. The plagues of Sophocles' Thebes, which threaten to kill all life, would have killed all life here as well, but the achingly beautiful strains of the Blues harmonica are heard. Somewhere within their feverish brains, the characters, through the Blues, become aware of an opening in the tragic circle. Somewhere, on this earth, within history, some form of transcendence of this agony is possible. The Blues song purges anguish, horror, just as did the ancient plays of the Greek tragedians. The harmonica, with all its range and versatility, tells them that this narrow hell is not all that exists. The Blues harmonica places them on the road toward satire which will give them the code that leads them out of the Corinthian-Theban impasse. As Frye reminds us, this world of satire is often a wasteland, a desert, but, in this case, because the Blues harmonica continues to play, the desert is not that of the wilderness and death of the ancient Greek exiles. Rather, it will be the desert of Moses and his followers going to the Promised Land.

The weapons of satire that break the structure of the tragic circle are: militant irony, burlesque, caricature, wild, obscene humour, the hallmarks of satire. The militant irony contains a sharp-edged attack against all that the characters see. The militant aspect contains the passion and the irony contains the intellectual ability to invert reality so that contradictions are unearthed, so that the present reality is juxtaposed with an ideal of Wounded Knee that has been absolutely defiled. Instead of being a source of transcendence, Wounded Knee casts a long shadow of devastating drunkenness, brutal rape, razor-edged misogyny and accidental death over the reservation.

The burlesque, wild, obscene humour that works with this

militant irony on the wasteland road of satire, allows the characters, and ourselves, the reader/audience, to have the courage to face the horrors with a bravery that otherwise would not have been possible. A drunken nine months pregnant Black Lady Halked, looking very much like the Virgin Mary, suddenly appears in the bright spotlight in mid-air, trying very hard to become more inebriated than she already is. A few scenes later the reader/audience realizes that the mid air is held up by a jukebox. This same drunken Virgin, in the Dickie Bird Bar, giving birth astride this jukebox to a brain-damaged child, is the epitome of this type of humor. So too are all the appearances of Nanabush as she, in true Rabelaisian manner, romps through the play wearing either false, gigantic rubberized breasts, belly or bum. This burlesque humor allows the characters and the reader/audience to see the demonic, chaotic labyrinth in which the characters live in such a caricatured manner that a liberating process begins. The gross exaggeration is so close to the truth that a shock occurs. What appears as wild exaggeration on the printed page or on the stage is a faithful representation of the tragedy of reservation life. But the burlesque humour creates a distancing effect allowing the recognition that what is portrayed is so absurd that surely it is not normal and natural; it is not given. Surely another way must be better. The grotesque humour creates a sense of utter chaos, but, ironically, this realization of chaos means that a certain kind of freedom exists, the freedom that comes from not having to destroy the rigid structures of society, for in this play there is no society. Hope lies in the realization that such unbounded freedom is the stuff with which to build a new world. The zeitgeist of the Postmodern world suggests that it is only upon ruins that creativity takes place. The world of satire is a world of ruins, of pure anarchy. Within the Frye perspective, the world of comedy, which succeeds that of satire, rises from the chaos of anarchy toward the creation of a new society. The most paradigmatic example of this new society is the wedding banquets that end so many comedies, banquets to which the entire human community is invited.

The musical strains of the Blues harmonica fit beautifully into this bawdy world, for "the most expressive and dominant theme in blues is sex." Here Nanabush can bump and grind and strip and kiss men's bums to her heart's content. Here the harmonica can sing the agony and praises of the only possession that these characters have: their bodies.

Then, faithful to those who have been on the road of bawdy, Bakhtinian carnivalesque satire, Highway moves the play in the last scene, from the desert wasteland of satire to the Promised Land of comedy. Suddenly the dreamscape of the Rabelaisian world disappears as Zachary awakens from the dream that has been the play, and all the elements of the comic world are neatly in place, including the happy ending.

Through the comic classical twist in the plot that is clearly manipulated by the intelligence of the author, the play moves from the world of satire where chaos reigns to a new order that is that of a new society. Here we see Zachary united with his wife Hera and their infant daughter. The reader/audience realizes that the mayhem of the pre-

vious scenes, the riotous drunkenness that leads to brain damage, rape, and suicide was Zachary's nightmare. Now the scene is one of peace and love. Even the less harmful, but, nevertheless, disruptive actions of the earlier scenes were all a play within the sleeping brain of Zachary. In the opening scene of his play dream, he awakens naked on the couch of Gazelle Nataways. Panic ensues when he realizes the situation. What will Hera say? To make matters worse, he cannot find his shorts and he discovers the marks of a woman's lips in lipstick on his bum. Throughout the dream play, his male friends, who have found his shorts, threaten to send them to Hera. The threatening complications that could perhaps destroy Zachary's relationship with his wife are suddenly removed by the manipulated twist of Zachary's awakening. Zachary had indeed fallen asleep naked on a couch, but it was a couch in his own house. His shorts are missing, but Hera discovers them beneath the couch. The lipstick mark is indeed on his bum, but the conveyor of the kiss is Hera. Thus, in a sense, from the point of view of the reader/audience, a reconciliation has occurred. The furious Hera of Zachary's dream is serenely happy with the now happy, rather than harassed, Zachary. Furthermore, the reader/audience recognizes that Hera, Zachary and their infant daughter are the proper and desirable society that all have desired. The proper act of communion occurs with the reader/audience who feels that "this should be".

The new society that Highway depicts is an interesting one. Hera and Zachary's name's are rooted in Western culture. Hera was the wife of Zeus and Zachary was the Hebrew Testament prophet. But Hera speaks Cree to Zachary, and a powwow bustle hangs over the poster of Marilyn Monroe on the wall. It would appear that the ingredients of the new society are composed of the richest roots of Western and of Native society. The bustle hanging over the photograph appears to imply that the richest roots of Native society can become more powerful than some of the more superficial, glossy Hollywood aspects of Western society.

Frye says that the new society of comedy is pragmatically free, free from the old obsessions that haunt tragedy and satire. Oedipus's obsession with parricide and incest, Antigone's obsession with the burial of her brother, and Big Joey's obsession with the massacre at Wounded Knee have vanished, along with the classical comic blocking character, Big Joey, himself, a constant source of hatred and violence. This pragmatic freedom exercises itself visibly as Zachary lifts his infant daughter high into the air in an act of exaltation, of celebration. She is the future and, freed of ancient poisoning obsessions, she will be able to create her own new world. The shape of that world is not defined, as it never is in comedy.

But that world will be founded upon reality, rather than upon illusion. Big Joey and Simon had lived with the illusion that traveling to Wounded Knee would free them from the grinding poverty and misery of the reservation. The Marilyn Monroe poster, with no powwow bustle draped over it at the beginning of the play, can be interpreted as a symbol of illusion. Norma Jean, the original name of Marilyn Monroe, was a signifier of the real, but the face of the woman named Marilyn on the poster is an image of illusion that led to drug abuse and suicide. Now, at the end of the play, this illusion is exorcised.

In true Frye fashion, one of the great myths of the Judaeo-Christian culture has been accomplished. An exodus has occurred. To the strains of the Blues harmonica, the characters have boarded the train and traveled the road from the fallen world of tragedy to the new world of comedy through the chaos of satire. The Blues harmonica, through the structure of its music, through its singing the human heart out of its anguish toward transcendence and exodus, has enabled the characters to accept and to use the weapons of satire so that they could tread the difficult road toward comedy, the land of milk and honey. Moses is the invisible musician of the harmonica. True to scriptural tradition, once the characters have arrived in the new world that has been promised, the music of the Blues harmonica ceases. Moses never reaches Israel. Only his people do. Our harmonica player has expired in the desert. Once the world of freedom has been created, the Blues Harmonica, the instrument of liberation, has fulfilled its purpose, is no longer needed.

In Derrida's poetic piece *Cinders,* whose 1991 publication by the University of Nebraska has an excellent introduction by Ned Lukacher, the concept of "cinders" becomes the primary tool through which to understand what Derrida means by the non-presence within language. Derrida's theory concerning language, the written language, in particular, states that in order to read language properly, the reader must pay attention to the site within language, within the word, which is haunted by a lack, a kind of absence. This absence is "irreducible to either presence or absence," On the one hand, non-presence threatens all meaning, but on the other, it presents a promise that calls one to undertake a journey that can never be fully accomplished toward the origins of language, of the universe itself. Lukacher makes clear that it is Derrida's concept of "cinders" that inaugurates the journey toward the reading of the absence/presence. Cinders precede words; they are the "clinging to language of something beyond language," "the quarks of language." The call, the clinging of something entirely other, is that of the "You," the Other, the Nameless One that can never be named. The reader must, in reading the word, listen to the "inaudible song, prayer," this quark of language, and in so doing, take a journey to the "there" where the cinder is, "on the far side of Dasein, just on the edge of its Being-in-the-world." It is here, "there," on the border between speech and the silence of that which lies beyond the universe of language that the cinder lies. It is there, where it beckons to an unreachable site "that is not to be conceived or experienced spatially," where "the voice of the Other burns in the silence," at the site of the first all-burning, the original holocaust that marked the big bang, the all-incineration that brought being, the universe, into existence. Derrida's methodology thus takes the reader to the Alpha moment of time.

The undertaking of the Derridean journey toward that Alpha moment will reveal that we need not mourn the death of the Blues harmonica player. We must find her/him again by making a reverse journey through the play. Toward the end Highway states that Zachary "sleep-walks through the whole lower level of the set, almost as though he were retracing his steps back through the whole play. Slowly, he takes off his clothes item by item, until, by the end, he is back lying naked on the couch where he began the play . . . ." Let us now walk backward with him.

In the final scene, two very important things occur in relation to this backward journey. Hera speaks Cree, and in her laugh one hears the laugh of Nanabush which, because it is wordless, carries one toward the silent ringing that lies beyond language. As the androgynous trickster of Native religion who is the mediator between ourselves and the Great Spirit, Nanabush is the perfect guide toward the big bang of the all-burning, the originary moment of creation. One also hears the silent ringing in the inaudible song of the Cree words, the song that is promised in the cinders that cling to language. The combination of the spoken Cree and the laugh of Nanabush will take the characters and the reader/audience on the road, back through the world of satire, through the world of tragedy. But the world beyond tragedy takes on the characteristics of a Derridean, rather than of a Frygian space. This world is one of shimmerings, of flickering fires, of space beyond language, rather than the green new world of Frye's romance. Frye's world of romance is the world at the time of its birth and infancy. Derrida's shimmering world is the space beyond the origin of our world, the space that moves one toward that moment of the all-burning, that moment of the birth of the cosmos. The laugh of Nanabush, the laugh beyond language, will guide us back to this world where all things are possible, the world before poison is poured into the ear of the king and into the minds of the Highway characters in the fallen world of the tragic circle.

In the land of satire, the Blues harmonica player will join us on the road so that we can more easily follow the laugh of the trickster. The musician will readily follow her. In the Production Notes Highway states that "the sound of this harmonica . . . under-line[s] and highlight[s] the many magical appearances of Nanabush in her various guises." We need the structure, the rhythm, the cathartic sorrow and hidden promise of the Blues to prevent us from going astray.

Perhaps more than anything else, the language of Cree(as well as Ojibway), that Hera speaks and that many of the characters speak throughout the play, makes possible Zachary's retracing sleep-walk journey. Hera's words of Cree enable the reader/audience, the characters, to set out on the journey of sensing the non-presence in her words that leads us to the cinder that clings, that calls us through its inaudible song. For a non-Native reader/audience, the hearing of the Cree language is a defamiliarizing experience that causes an awareness, in an acute manner, of the absence that clings to the words, to the silence that haunts them. Re-immersion in the play through Zachary's walk backward takes the reader/audience once again to the dramatic hockey game of the women and the wild narration of that game in Cree. Such an extended defamiliarizing experience can then apply to the words of English that inform most of the play.

The final words of the fatally wounded young Simon allow us to follow the cinders of words on the journey toward the hockey game, with its barrage of Cree words. Simon, who has dreamed of restoring Native spirituality to his people, utters these words: "Kammoowanow . . . apple . . . pie . . . patima . . . neetha . . . igwo Patsy . . . n'gapeetootanan . . . patima . . . apple . . . pie . . . neee." The cinder that clings to every English word is accentuated by the juxtaposition with the Cree words. "Apple" and "pie," the most familiar and everyday of words, appear to develop an unrecognizability, an inaudibility that makes them strangely alien, as if the meaning that they usually convey is absent. A mysterious code is presented to us, a code that is augmented by the pauses that the dying Simon places between his words. This sense of the absent meaning of the code calls the audience toward something, towards the laugh of Nanabush. The call toward this journey is facilitated by the Blues harmonica, an audible song, whose sound, with its familiarity, urges us onward. Since the harmonica, a great simulator of the human voice, is without words, this instrument is a perfect vehicle for calling the characters beyond the world of language toward the silent ringing.

The stage directions say, "From the darkness of the theatre emerges the magical flickering of a luminescent pow-wow dancing bustle." The two bustles "play" with each other, looking like two giant fire-flies. Another stage direction says, "The shimmering movements of the bustle balloon out into these magical, dance-like arches." The luminescent shimmerings are the cinders of the fires of the original all-burning toward which all language takes us. The presence of Nanabush is strongly associated with shimmering fire.

But one must recognize also in the shimmering fire the semi-invisible figure of the Blues harmonica player who has now become silent. This player was the initial absence/presence that called the characters toward the original all-burning. By means of an audible song, the Blues harmonica called everyone toward the inaudible song which the strains of the music always promised. The Blues harmonica is now part of that inaudible song.

We, the reader/audience and the characters, cannot reach that unreachable Other who is the origin of this wondrous activity, but the words of the languages lead us toward the Other. This is the journey that Zachary takes as he sleep-walks backward through the play. This journey is toward the "place for giving, rendering, celebrating, loving," for it is the site of the promise of the giving of the original, all-burning moment of creation, the promise of the name of the Nameless Other beyond Being that holds everything in being. A nice comic twist occurs within the last scene when Zachary, who has just awakened from his walk toward the origins of time, to a fresh world that still shimmers with the fires of creation, holds aloft in a triumphant gesture, his infant daughter, who, as yet, is a nameless one.

Thus, a strange dialectical movement pervades the play: one is the exodus of those fleeing bondage, and one is the free falling through time of those seeking the origin of the giving which created the universe. Perhaps the cinders of the dying words of Simon, the one who most passionately wanted to journey toward the shimmering fire of Nanabush, are one of the most important guides on that free falling journey. Both movements involve journeying on a road that is perilous, but one must remember that the greatest facilitator on that road is the Blues harmonica. Perhaps on a journey toward his own roots, songs of free West Africans, the harmonica player sings the audible song that makes the journey possible. The harmonica expresses the sorrow and, in the luminescent shimmerings of Nanabush with which it is so closely joined, promises the joy of liberation that permeates the lives of those who are "en marche," those who are on the road.

---

# FURTHER READING

## Criticism

Grant, Agnes. "Canadian Native Literature: The Drama of George Ryga and Tomson Highway." *Australian-Canadian Studies* 10, No. 2 (1992): 37-56.
> Compares Highway's *The Rez Sisters* to George Ryga's *The Ecstasy of Rita Joe*.

Kirchhoff, H. J. "International Authors Festival." *The Toronto Globe and Mail* (23 October 1989): D7.
> Discusses the awarding of the 1989 Wang Festival Prize to Tomson Highway.

Loucks, Bryan. "Another Glimpse: Excerpts from a Conversation with Tomson Highway." *Canadian Theatre Review*, No. 68 (Fall 1991): 9-11.
> Interview in which Highway discusses his work and his role as a voice for Native culture.

Nunn, Robert. "Marginality and English-Canadian Theatre." *Theatre Research International* 17, No. 3 (Autumn 1992): 217-25.
> Examines the themes in *Dry Lips Oughta Move to Kapuskasing*, asserting that Highway presents three responses to white hegemony.

Petrone, Penny. "1980-1989." In her *Native Literature in Canada: From the Oral Tradition to the Present*, pp. 138-81. Toronto: Oxford University Press, 1990.
> Discusses Highway's major works along with those of other Native Canadian writers.

Preston, Jennifer. "Weesageechak Begins to Dance: Native Earth Performing Arts Inc." *The Drama Review* 36, No. 1 (Spring 1992): 35-59.
> Traces the development of Native Earth Performing Arts Inc., a Native theater company in Toronto, and their productions, including several of Highway's plays.

Rainwater, Catherine. "Community of Dreamers." *Canadian Literature* 15, No. 130 (Autumn 1991): 169-70.
> Asserts that Highway emphasizes spiritual rather than biological bonds between humans in his *The Rez Sisters*.

Townsend, Martin. "A Very Limited Edition . . . a Word-struck Wordsmith . . . Out of Afghanistan: New Drama Books Set the Canadian Stage." *Quill and Quire* 55, No. 3 (March 1989): 76-7.
> Provides a favorable review of Highway's *The Rez Sis-*

*ters.* Townsend praises "Highway's good sense of comic rhythm and the novelty of the play's setting."

Usmiani, Renate. "The Bingocentric Worlds of Michel Tremblay and Tomson Highway: *Les Belles-souers* vs. *The Rez Sisters.*" *Canadian Literature,* No. 144 (Spring 1995): 126-40.

    Comparative reading of the two plays.

Wigston, Nancy. "Nanabush in the City." *Books in Canada* 18, No. 2 (March 1989): 7-9.

    Presents an overview of Highway's life and work.

---

**Additional coverage of Highway's life and career is contained in the following source published by Gale Research:** *Native North American Literature.*

---

# Leonid Leonov

## 1899-1994

(Full name Leonid Maximovich Leonov) Russian novelist, dramatist, short story writer, and essayist.

The following entry presents an overview of Leonov's career.

## INTRODUCTION

A major figure in Soviet literature, Leonov is known for works in which he explored political and social issues in post-revolution Soviet society. Known for their psychological and philosophical complexity, Leonov's works address such themes as the conflict between the individual and society, the moral dilemmas associated with revolutionary upheaval, and the antagonism between urban and rural cultures. Although Leonov supported the 1917 Bolshevik Revolution and was committed to Communism throughout his life, he nonetheless openly explored the realities and hardships associated with radical social change. Employing complex symbolism, extensive figurative language, and stream-of-consciousness narrative techniques, Leonov was once described by noted Russian author Maxim Gorky as "a master of his craft" who "deftly [chose] from the inexhaustible riches of our language precisely those words of which the illustrative and musical magic is most convincing, excluding from among them every superfluous element." Leonov's works are acknowledged for their insightful depiction of the Russian character, and for this reason they have been compared to those of Russian masters Fedor Dostoevsky, Nikolai Gogol, Leo Tolstoy, and Ivan Turgenev.

### Biographical Information

Leonov was born in Moscow. His father was a poet and journalist who was arrested for anti-Tsarist activities and later exiled to Archangel, where he published a newspaper. Educated in Moscow, Leonov later worked for his father's newspaper as a theater critic and proofreader. During the Russian Civil War—which lasted from the mid-1910s into the early 1920s and involved "Red" Soviet forces, who gained decisive power in the October 1917 Revolution, fighting off "White" Russian anti-Communist insurgents—Leonov served in the Red Army, primarily as a war correspondent. He edited the newspaper of the Fifteenth Inzenskaia Division in 1920 and worked for the newspaper of the Moscow Military District from 1921 to 1922. After his demobilization, he published a short story collection, *Dereviannaia koroleva* (1923), but his first real success came in 1924 with the publication of his novel *Barsuki* (*The Badgers*). The subsequent success of *Vor* (1927; *The Thief*) brought him a measure of political as well as artistic success. "He had arrived," as R. D. B. Thomson has observed, and was soon elected to the governing board of the Union of Soviet Writers. Prior to the 1930s, writers

in the Soviet Union were not heavily restricted, but with the emergence of socialist realism, a Marxist aesthetic theory calling for the didactic use of literature, art, and music to develop social consciousness in the evolving socialist state, and the beginning of the Stalinist purges, Soviet writers suffered more intense scrutiny. These developments had dramatic implications for Leonov's career. Leonov's fifth novel, *Doroga na okean* (1935; *Road to the Ocean*), was almost immediately suppressed and from the mid-1930s through the 1940s his works came under official attack. No new editions of his novels were issued until 1947, and his play *Metel* (1939; *The Snowstorm*) was suppressed in 1940 during rehearsals for its Moscow premiere. Except for the novella *Vziatie Velikoshumska* (1944; *The Taking of Velikoshumsk*), Leonov did not publish any new extended prose works until 1953—the year of Stalin's death—when he published *Russkii les* (*The Russian Forest*). He instead devoted his efforts during this period to dramas. From 1946 to 1970, Leonov served as a Deputy to the Supreme Soviet of the U.S.S.R. A substantially revised version of *The Thief* was issued in 1959, and in 1963 he published *Evgenia Ivanovna*, a novel which he had begun in the mid-1930s. Leonov also wrote criticism and essays and published two fragments of an untitled novel-in-progress during the 1970s and 1980s. He died in Moscow in 1994.

## Major Works

The central theme in Leonov's works is the conflict between the demands of society and the needs of the individual. In his writings about the revolution, he often focused on marginalized participants who did not fully understand what was occurring. *The Badgers,* for instance, set in the early 1920s, centers on a group of peasants in the remote Russian countryside who reject the Soviet government and engage in guerilla warfare against Soviet officials and the Red Army. Leonov used this story to address the conflict between the urban proletariat and the peasantry. The major figures in the novel are brothers: Semyon, who returns to the countryside after a brief stay in Moscow and becomes the leader of the partisans, and Pavel, who remains in Moscow after leaving his home in the village and becomes the commander of a Red Army unit. Pavel is able to explain the complexities of the revolution to his brother and finds a peaceful solution to the conflict. In the words of Valentin Kovalyov, "Pavel distils the features of the hero of the time, a revolutionary, a man of great inner strength and strongly-held convictions." *The Thief*, a psychological novel set in 1920s Moscow, centers on Vekshin, a Bolshevik and veteran of the Civil War who, confused by the New Economic Policy, decides that his wartime efforts were in vain and becomes a thief in order to subvert what he sees as an economy based on private property and dominated by "enemies of the revolution." Vekshin longs for moral certainty even as he commits immoral acts and eventually realizes the fallacy in his behavior. Much of the story is narrated by Firsov, a participant in the story as well as a writer who is writing a book about the characters in the novel; the story unfolds on two planes—the "real" events and Firsov's literary version. In 1959 Leonov published a revised version of the novel. One of the major differences is Leonov's depiction of Vekshin. In the first version, he elicited Firsov's sympathy, but in the second the protagonist has been stripped of his favorable qualities and, as quoted by Vera Alexandrova from the revised version, "we graphically see the futility of Firsov's attempts . . . to save the image of Vekshin, which until recently still held his sympathy—even if somewhat shaken—but which is now almost hateful to him." Leonov's next major work was *Sot'* (1929; *Soviet River*), an epic, socio-political novel set in a remote northern province where a factory is being built. Concerned with the industrialization of the countryside, the story dramatizes the conflict between the forces of Russia's future, symbolized by the Soviet leaders who are organizing the factory's construction, and those of Russia's antiquity, symbolized by the hermit monks who for centuries have lived in the forest and perpetuated old customs and beliefs. Ultimately, the factory builders succeed in overcoming both the ignorance of the people and the obstacles of nature. Marc Slonim has observed that for Leonov, *Soviet River* depicts "the blind irrational forces man must control within and outside himself." The action in *Road to the Ocean* centers on a conspiracy against the government and spans two years, 1933 and 1934. It's multi-leveled plot is interrupted by numerous predictions for the future and flashbacks that range from the Civil War to the 19th century. The novel is also distinguished by the stream-of-consciousness technique Leonov used to describe the characters and by its numerous philosophical debates. The focus of *Road to the Ocean,* according to R. D. B. Thomson, is the "new 'positive hero' of socialist realism." The principal character is Kurilov—a party official and a man of great moral authority who had fought with the Bolsheviks in the Red Army; approaching death, he reflects on his career and the future and history of the Soviet state. The novel is also notable for its villain, a former White officer named Gleb Protoklitov, who tries desperately to conceal his past. Similar in scope to *Road to the Ocean, The Russian Forest* focuses on the struggle between two scientists over the best methods of forest management. The hero Vikhrov is honest, patriotic, and views the forest as a source of life, while the villain Gratsiansky embodies deception and death. Commenting on the characters, Slonim has observed that Leonov's in-depth exploration of Gratsiansky "is accompanied by the confrontation of past and present in the light of Russia's historical heritage, by the opposition of the rational and the elemental, of self-centered egotism and creative collectivism—in short by all Leonov's favorite themes." The struggle between the two men is an allegorical one, representing their differences over what they feel would be the best government for Russia. Valentin Kovalyov has observed that the "image of the mighty forest occupying vast spaces of the great country is a symbol of the people, and its inexhaustible strength and vitality."

## Critical Reception

Leonov was dedicated to the social and political causes of Communism, which, according to Slonim, "Leonov interpreted . . . idealistically, not in terms of a doctrine derived from Marx and Lenin but as one of the variations of radical humanism." Kovalyov described Leonov as a man of "passionate civic commitment," and Leonov himself once told Alexander Lysov that he "plants a tree for the sake of future generations with no hope of seeing it bear fruit." Critical discussion of Leonov's works often centers on themes of individual morality, happiness, and purity, and the relation of the individual to society. Commentators have noted that Leonov's villains are often more interesting than his heroes and that his works are sometimes overwritten. One of the most divisive questions among Leonov's critics has been his relationship to Dostoevsky. Many commentators have noted extensive similarities between the works of the two novelists; however, while some scholars have argued that Leonov was deeply concerned with moral, philosophical, and psychological problems, others have insisted that he was not at all motivated by the intense concern with ethics, morality, and religion that characterized Dostoevsky's writings. Alexandrova, for instance, has questioned "the view of some Russian critics abroad that, were Leonov free in his creative work, he would have become a 'Soviet Dostoyevsky.'" Critics have also questioned whether Leonov was simply a dogmatist or a truly subversive writer who managed to escape severe repression. Remarking on the "seeming conventionality" of Leonov's career, Thomson has argued that "of all the Soviet writers, Leonid Leonov is the most individual. His elaborate style, his highly personal thought and imagery, his characteristic range of heroes, and above all the acute conflicts on which his works are built . . . distinguish his books from those of his compatriots and contemporaries."

# PRINCIPAL WORKS

*Dereviannaia koroleva* (short stories) 1923
*Barsuki* [*The Badgers*] (novel) 1924
*Rasskazy* (short stories) 1926
*Gibel' Egorushki* (short stories and novellas) 1927
*Vor* [*The Thief*] (novel) 1927; revised edition, 1959
*Provintsialnaya istoriya* [*A Provincial Story*] (drama) 1928
*Untilovsk* (drama) 1928
*Sot'* [*Soviet River*] (novel) 1929
*Sarancha* [*The Locusts*] (novella) 1930; published in journal *Turkmenovedenie;* also published in journal *Krasnaya Nov'* as *Saranchuki,* 1930
*Usmirenie Badadoshkina* [*The Taming of Badadoshkin*] (drama) 1930
*Skutarevski* [*Skutarevsky*] (novel) 1931
*Doroga na okean* [*Road to the Ocean*] (novel) 1935
*Polovchanskie sady* [*The Orchards of Polovchansk*] (drama) 1938
*Metel* [*The Snowstorm*] (drama) 1939
*\*Volk* [*The Wolf*] (drama) 1939
*Obyknovenny chelovek* [*An Ordinary Man*] (drama) 1941
*Nashestvie* [*The Invasion*] (drama) 1942
*Lyonushka* (drama) 1943
†*Vziatie Velikoshumska* [*The Taking of Velikoshumsk*] (novella) 1944; published in journal *Novy Mir*
*Zolotaya kareta* [*The Golden Coach*] [first publication] (drama) 1946; revised edition, 1956; revised edition [first publication], 1964
*Russkii les* [*The Russian Forest*] (novel) 1953
*Sobranie sochinenii.* 6 vols. (novels, novellas, dramas, short stories) 1953-55
*Begstvo mistera Mak-Kinli* [*The Flight of Mr. MacKinley*] (screenplay) 1961; published in journal *Pravda*
*Evgenia Ivanovna* (novel) 1963
*Literatura i vremia* [*Literature and the Times*] (criticism and essays) 1964; enlarged edition, 1976
‡"Dymkov's View of the Universe" (novel fragment) 1974; published in journal *Nauka i zhizn;* revised edition, 1984; published in journal *Novy Mir*
‡"The Last Outing" (novel fragment) 1979; published in journal *Moskva*

*This play is also known as *Begstvo Sandukova* (*The Flight of Sandukov*).

†This novella is also translated as *Chariot of Wrath.*

‡These are excerpts from an unpublished and untitled novel-in-progress.

# CRITICISM

## Maxim Gorky (essay date 1932)

SOURCE: A foreword to *Soviet River,* translated by Ivor Montagu and Sergei Nolbandov, 1932. Reprint by Hyperion Press, 1973, pp. v-vi.

[*One of the former Soviet Union's most popular authors, Gorky is considered one of the framers and foremost exponents of Socialist Realism. In the following essay, which was originally published in 1932, Gorky remarks on Leonov's artistic development.*]

I am not a critic and I do not feel inclined to 'explain' an artist; I well remember that when critics undertook to 'explain' me, they attributed to me intentions of which I was innocent and deeds I had never done. All that is said below is just a note by an old writer on his young comrade-in-arms—though of another generation. It is neither censure, nor is it praise, it is merely an attempt to tell how I see Leonid Leonov.

He is one of the most prominent of the group of modern Soviet authors who are continuing the task of Russian classical literature—the task of Pushkin, Griboyedov, Gogol, Turgenev, Dostoyevsky and Leo Tolstoy. It is early yet to speak of the power of his talent—that power, like every other, develops through exercise. Nobody could have foreseen that Dostoyevsky, the author of a weak and even pitiful story *Poor People,* would ever become capable of writing the caustic *Notes from the Underworld,* or of creating *The Brothers Karamazov.* Leo Tolstoy's *Childhood* did not make it possible to foretell that one day he would create *War and Peace.*

None the less, it seems to me already that Leonov's powers are increasing with remarkable rapidity, and that, from **The Badgers** to **The Thief** and from **The Thief** to **Soviet River,** the distance he has covered is so great that I, for my part, know no instance of such rapid and indisputable growth in our old Russian literature. This growth is indicated by the complexity of the subjects he now handles with bold assurance, as well as by the increasing euphony of his language, the individuality of his style. He is particularly successful in his development of stylistic technique, and every new story, every new book he writes, strikes a more and more convincing note. While **The Thief** sometimes gives us the impression of being over-burdened with words—**Soviet River** is written in a language of symbolic harmony.

The word, clothing of truth and falsehood, characterises a man just as does the deed—and Leonov endows each of his heroes with a strongly-emphasized, individual manner of speech. Not every gifted author succeeds in this. Leonov deftly chooses from the inexhaustible riches of our language precisely those words of which the illustrative and musical magic is most convincing, excluding from among them every superfluous element. Master of his art, he hardly ever describes, he always draws pictures, using words as a painter his paints. His style lacks the hysterical hastiness of Dostoyevsky, so popular with many, a hastiness which often makes the dialogues of his heroes seem to their reader like an incessant clamour of the afflicted. More and more frequently in Leonov's pattern do we encounter the powerful strokes of Leo Tolstoy, strokes by means of which Tolstoy achieved, with such great pains, such magnificent plasticity of illustration. If we may say of Tolstoy that he 'forged his books out of iron'—and of Turgenev that he cast his out of copper and silver—then Leonov must be regarded as operating with a very complex alloy of metals. In his descriptions of landscape often echoes Tyuchev's 'nature-lyricism,' while in the delineation of his figures we can perceive the sharp, acute precision of Lermontov's prose. In a word—Leonov is a bee who gathers his honey from all the flowers that abound in it.

Quite consciously do I measure Leonov by so high a standard, quite consciously place him in one rank with the greatest figures of our old literature—Leonid Leonov himself forces one to approach him thus with the highest claims.

## Helen Muchnic (essay date 1961)

SOURCE: "Leonid Leonov," in *From Gorky to Pasternak: Six Writers in Soviet Russia,* 1961. Reprint by Vintage Books, 1966, pp. 276-303.

[*A Russian-born American educator and critic, Muchnic has written extensively on Russian literature. In the following excerpt originally published in 1961, she remarks on Leonov's influences and his artistic development.*]

In 1932 an article on Leonov in the Soviet Encyclopedia spoke disparagingly of his early work as having been "abstract" in the manner of the Symbolists and influenced by Dostoevsky, and congratulated him on having "surmounted" Dostoevsky. Leonov, then thirty-three years old, had been publishing for about ten years. He had begun with short stories; had written a play, *Untilovsk,* and four novels, *The Badgers, The Thief, Sot'* (translated as *Soviet River*), and *Skutarevsky,* which had brought him to the attention of the public and elicited the praise of Gorky, who declared that the writing of this very gifted young man would one day merit "serious study," if he abandoned his "aestheticism" and turned his vigorous prose to good account.

Leonov's earliest work was not social-minded. His stories were stylistic experiments, inspired by a purely literary interest. Some were fairy tales, **"Buriga," "The Wooden Queen," "The Jack of Diamonds," "Valya's Doll,"** in which woodland sprites or playthings figured as main characters; others were essays in various forms: in the uncanny and the grotesquely humorous, **"Egorushka's Destruction"** and **"An Incident with Jacob Pichunk"**; in the Biblical parable and the Oriental prose poem, **"Ham's Departure," "Khalil," "Tuatamur"**; in pathos, **"The End of an Insignificant Man," "Petushikhin Notch"**; in satire, **"A Record of Certain Episodes Made in the Town of Gogulev by Andrew Petrovich Kovyakin."** All were derivative; manifestly Leonov was "playing the sedulous ape," copying E. T. A. Hoffmann, Remizov, Blok, Leskov,

Gogol, Dostoevsky, Gorky. Endowed with an unusually acquisitive ear, he enjoyed making the most of his verbal facility, mastering dialects—including Tartar for the sake of **"Tuatamur"**—steeping himself in all manner of rhythmic prose; interested, in short, in making himself a writer. He gives the impression of one for whom the activity—one is tempted to say the game—of writing was, initially, more important than any theme, much less any "message." No personal experience, no belief compelled him. He tried out subjects and styles, was dexterous in playing with artistic effects; but since he was a man of neither passion nor conviction, his work, unlike Blok's, Mayakovsky's, Pasternak's, even Gorky's and Sholokhov's, was the work of a follower, not a leader.

The stories with which he began were semiserious, gently tender, romantically pathetic. And there was implicit in them a teasing, insoluble comparison between the artificial and the real, between the game and actual being, between toys or fairy-tale creatures and real men and women. When the black chessboard queen becomes a woman with whom a chess player falls in love and then turns out to be the bride of his best friend, "Even in chess," he remarks, "as I have long since felt, the kind of situation must exist in which a woman is unfaithful only for the sake of unfaithfulness, a situation in which there is mystery and all kinds of magic." A fancy such as this, on the borderline between the dream and actuality, is the kind that Blok and the Symbolists were using to express their most intimately evanescent, their most complicated experiences. In Leonov's hands it turns to sentimentality and triteness; and the manner in which a potentially original and personal theme is here made platitudinous is indicative of a characteristic duality of Leonov's mind: fascination with excursions into unknown realms on the one hand, and desire for comfort on the other. Leonov was affected by the atmosphere of experimentation which prevailed when he started to write, just as later he was to fall in with another dominant tendency. But his experiments were differently motivated from those of the introspective Symbolists, or of such speculative novelists as Pilnyak and Olësha, or even of such limelight seekers as Mayakovsky. There was less boldness in him, a kind of cautious effacement of personality, an unwillingness to cultivate whatever capacity for individual experience he might have had. From the first, he seems eager to use his unquestionable cleverness not to impose himself but to get a hearing, and without being natively devoid of distinctiveness and intensity, chooses to suppress the one and to dilute the other.

He was published in experimental journals—*Shipovnik, Literaturnaya Misl', Krug, Russkiy Sovremennik;* in a literary quarrel with Vakhtangov, he defended what was later scornfully referred to as "personal psychologism"; and when in 1927 he was asked by an interviewer: "Whose method, among classical writers, do you consider most appropriate for depicting our contemporary world?" he answered, "F. M. Dostoevsky's, given sufficient strength and understanding." Three years later, however, on a similar occasion, he replied that although he himself had learned most from Dostoevsky, "by the irony of fate" he had "flunked" because of him. Dostoevsky's psychological analysis was "static," he had decided, not suitable for describing the contemporary world, and his style was "long drawn out, verbose." Between these two opinions had come friendship with and encouragement from Gorky, and the publication of the Dostoevskian novel which had "flunked" him, *The Thief.* Now his consciousness became a battleground on which Dostoevsky and Gorky fought for his allegiance. Gorky scored an easy victory. For despite his earlier enthusiasm, Dostoevsky had never been firmly entrenched in his mind. It had been Dostoevsky's trappings and gestures that had impressed Leonov, not his essence; and just as from Leskov he had borrowed the form of the *skaz* (i.e., of the extended anecdote, comically related in semiliterate speech) but not that starkness of tragedy which makes Leskov's work powerful, and from Gogol the element of grotesque humor but not his sense of terror, so he had caught Dostoevsky's fascination with complex and abnormal states of mind but nothing of his philosophic depth or psychological imaginativeness.

And yet, however naïve his use of Dostoevsky, he was apparently more deeply stirred by him than by the other writers whom he imitated, for in the works that lean most heavily on Dostoevsky, there is a subjective strain, a touch of intimacy, which has always been rare with Leonov, and which was completely "surmounted," it would seem, under the influence of Gorky and other Soviet commentators. Strongly Dostoevskian was the short story of 1922, **"The End of an Insignificant Man."** It had to do with a geologist, Likharëv, who, caught in the hard days that followed the Revolution, obliged to endure cold, hunger, illness, and intellectual isolation, becomes involved with a set of "arty" characters, whose pretentious arguments are a cover for mental chaos and the absence of moral principles, and who finds it all but impossible to continue his writing; but having returned to it, Likharëv is persuaded by a demonic hallucination, a "Fop" who visits him during his heart attacks, that his work is of no importance, while the paper it is written on might serve a useful purpose in warming his room. Although the "Fop" is an obvious replica of Ivan Karamazov's bourgeois devil, though he talks and looks and acts like him, and has the same function of belittling a thinker's efforts and forcing him to doubt himself, the scene in which Likharëv burns his manuscript is genuinely moving. So also is another Dostoevskian episode, his sister's death. This occurs at the moment when, at long last, Likharëv has found it possible to resume his work. He is so engrossed in it that when his sick sister calls to him, he selfishly refuses to be interrupted; and she, realizing the situation, stifles her cries of pain and, to spare him the death agony, sends him out on a fictitious errand. He goes, aware of the ruse, but, too cowardly and selfish not to take advantage of it, wanders about the streets until he knows she must have died. Passages such as this indicate that Leonov had a feeling for the intricacies and ironies of Dostoevsky's moral situations, the poignant tragedy of his pathetically isolated men, but more for the Dostoevsky of *Poor Folk* than of the major novels.

In **"The End of an Insignificant Man,"** just as in *Poor Folk,* society forms the background for the pitiful individual. But in **The Badgers,** his first novel, which followed immediately upon this story, Leonov reversed the design and made a social theme its center. He dealt here with one aspect of the establishment of Soviet power, the struggle between city and country, which he represented in the fortunes of two brothers, Simon and Paul Rakleev, who, taken as children from their native village to Moscow, part company there and meet again only at the end of the story. Paul, rebelling against maltreatment at the hands of his employer, runs away to become a factory worker and a Communist; Simon, after a period in the army, returns to the village, ends up as leader of a guerilla band that defies the Bolsheviks, and is in the outcome confronted by his brother, who, transformed into Comrade Anton, has arrived as commander of a punitive expedition. After a hazardous and daring struggle, Simon submits to the new power: the forward-looking Communist city has overcome the backward, recalcitrant country. . . .

After **The Badgers** came **The Thief.** Its central figure, the passionate Mitka Vekshin, is modeled on Dmitry Karamazov and is, like Raskolnikov, an honest criminal who is ultimately regenerated; the woman he loves, Man'ka Dolomonova, nicknamed Viuga (i.e., blizzard), reminds one of both Grushenka and Nastasya Fillipovna (as well as of the enchantress who inspired Blok's *Snow Mask* and *Faïna*). Manyukin is another Marmeladov, and there are several more minor personages in the tradition of Dostoevsky's insulted and injured. It was noted by Gorky that in this novel one had, as with Dostoevsky, "the elemental riot of instinct," and by others that the idea of the contradictions between the individual and society was basic in the book; that its leading characters were "individualists" and "sufferers" whose suffering "purified" their souls; that all of them were more or less unbalanced and full of reflectiveness, doubt, and inward struggle; and that structurally its main figures, like Dostoevsky's, served as "crooked mirrors" in which the others were reflected, so that they came to play an almost symbolic role, Manyukin standing for the "disintegration of personality," Ageyka for the "descent of the individual to crime," Pchkov for rejection of the world, etc. Today Leonov is spoken of as having been influenced by the "psychologism" of the twenties, and **The Thief** does not appear in the six-volume edition of his collected works. But although **The Thief** is so obviously Dostoevskian that it often reads like a pastiche, Leonov's differences from Dostoevsky are more striking than the similarities. He writes for a different reason; his interests, themes, emphases are all different. The intricate plot of this novel, more intricate than that of **The Badgers,** and more justifiably so, is closer to André Gide's structures than to Dostoevsky's; and its basic theme, which, elaborating the speculations of his early stories, is a musing on how art is related to life, is also Gide's kind of theme, not Dostoevsky's. Like that of *The Counterfeiters* it is developed on two levels: there is the story itself of Mitka Vekshin, the thief, and the story that the writer Firsov writes about him, the "real" events and their literary version proceeding along parallel lines. The characters themselves want to be written about; they take the writer into their confidence and comment on his work both while it is in process and afterwards, while Firsov is more than an observer: he takes part in the action, even, to a degree, manipulates events, and his book about Mitka comes out before Mitka's story is finished. All this creates an atmosphere of mystification, in which a drama of guilt and passion is acted out. The implication is that however close to life the writer may think himself to be, however much involved he may be in it, life itself escapes him. For his involvement is never complete; and with all the influence he may exercise, he is primarily an observer and commentator, not an actor.

But another kind of artist is introduced in this novel, one whose art is not of the intellect but of skill and daring. And so often does Leonov subsequently return to the experience represented by this type of artist that, as one soon realizes, it must be fraught with symbolic import for him, must stand in his mind for some cherished ideal, perhaps the one most intimately cherished of all. Like that moment in Thomas Hardy's *Under the Greenwood Tree,* when the plaintive cry of "the small bird being killed by an owl" pierces the stillness and passes "into the silence without mingling with it," so in **The Thief** there is an incident which, though it has no vital bearing on the plot, remains most memorable and most poignant. This is an episode which concerns Mitka's sister Tanya, who, having been lost for many years, is finally rediscovered as the famous Guella Vel'ton, a daring performer on the trapeze, the chief attraction of a traveling circus. Her act is called *shtrabat* and we are told that

> it was considered old-fashioned, but Vel'ton had complicated it with hazardous details, and her unaffected grace welded the whole of it into the complete triumph of a youthful, skillful body. . . . Her agility rose to deadly daring that gave *shtrabat* a cruel and terrible beauty.

She had been trained in this work by a pathetic, lonely old clown, part of whose story is given as follows:

> At the height of his career he earned his bread with his "little ones." In circus language this is called "strap-turning the mill." Head down, his feet grasping the trapeze, he held the strap in his teeth and slowly unwound his children who hung on it. A rapid drum roll, as at executions, accompanied the fateful moments. In the buzzing shaft of the spotlight the children fluttered about, over the sand, the pitiable tinsel of their wings glistening: butterflies! . . . The calamity was trite, as if invented by a bad author. When the mill was unwound, the piece of strap which is clenched in the teeth, and which had rotted, tore apart, and the butterflies fluttered to the sand. An agitated, uniformed attendant was already running toward them, but the father hung with the bit of strap in his teeth, afraid to understand its sudden lightness.

Tanya also dies in the performance of her act. Before stepping into the arena for what is to be the last time, she says to the old clown—she who is now famous, who is "that night the center of attention, precisely she herself and not the mysterious name of her performance":

> "You know, I still haven't got used to the idea that I am a regular circus performer. My whole life seems an attempt to do what is impossible for man to do. I love my work, Pugel, because I know how much labor I put into it when I first

> started. How I cried when I couldn't do it! . . . Do you remember? . . . Work, when you love it, is jolly; then even failures are jolly."

There follows a description of Tanya beneath the enormous dome, gracefully poised on the trapeze, fastening herself to it in the midst of thunderous applause, her body "yearning to fly."

> With quickened consciousness Tanya measured the distance to that point in the air beyond which the noose would not permit her to go. A colossal recklessness took possession of the artist as she glanced at the rows, where like a mountain of vegetables, human faces lay close together; a terrible fear floated up from them. The moment split into a thousand particles and they crumbled into other moments, imperceptible to the mind. Tanya darted down, and it was as if time had stopped. Then, everyone saw the light blue, longish body hanging like a faded flower; but this in no way entered their consciousness. Tanya hung there; dead, she seemed to be looking at the dead light of the lampion; the noose had lifted her chin.

This episode appears to be unintentionally symbolic, not of Leonov's themes but of himself, the only instance in all his productions when unconscious experience has been permitted to take conscious, artistic form. Just as the pitiful cry of the unseen bird expressed all Hardy's bitterness at the tragedy of innocent and helpless creatures and was the most intense note in his book, although its suggestion of fatal cruelty was not borne out in the story, so Tanya's death, in my opinion, strikes the central, deepest note of Leonov's work, and is emotionally, if not structurally, the climax of **The Thief.** In somewhat the same way as the poor, anonymous small bird sums up the core of Hardy's tragic tales, the irrational and irremediable suffering of inoffensive creatures, and as the leap from a high tower, the sudden fall, and the moment of vision or dazzling illumination stand in Dostoevsky's work for passion or a supreme act of will, so the perilous circus stunt seems to express Leonov—the daring exploit that requires skill and training as well as courage, an artistic defiance of death, in which a human being attempts to do what is superhuman before a frightened and fascinated audience. Presently, as the sound of Dostoevsky's voice recedes to be replaced by Gorky's, this symbol is metamorphosed into a useful and rational form, suitable for conveying the message of Socialist Realism. . . .

---

**Although *The Thief* is so obviously Dostoevskian that it often reads like a pastiche, Leonov's differences from Dostoevsky are more striking than the similarities. He writes for a different reason; his interests, themes, emphases are all different.**

**—*Helen Muchnic***

---

Among Soviet authors, Leonov stands out for what Gorky called his "strong, clear, juicy" prose, and for his genuine feeling for elemental forces. His writing throbs with the excited sense of the chaotic and destructive violence of nature which stimulates man to incredible exertion. He needs enthusiasm to write, and it is adventure, danger, the utmost straining of nerve and muscle that rouse him to enthusiasm. But he cannot let nature stand alone. Like the medieval theologians for whom gross earth had meaning only as an allegory of the divine—the shining sun signified Jesus Christ, the unplowed field the unregenerate mind of man, and the frisking lambs in spring the happily converted heathen—so Leonov sees swarming locusts as "the enemy," floods and fires as unbridled passion, and the forest as the greatness of Russia's land and people. Nature rages in his novels only that man may subdue it; the Russian man, that is, the good citizen of the U.S.S.R., who conquers it in time of peace as he conquers enemy nations in time of war. Clearly enough, Leonov's predilections jibe with the official demands of the state, and it is unlikely that he has needed to change himself to become accepted; he has simply utilized a native admiration for strenuously won success to both political and literary advantage. Early in his career, his docile, acquisitive mind had welcomed a publicly authorized theory and method; it gave him opportunity to indulge his thirst for knowledge, his verbal facility, and a genially unreflective optimism. Gorky's formula had proffered, in effect, the means of letting the mind rest, while giving it the illusion of discovery. Once the subject was supplied, the method indicated, the feeling ordained—once, in short, Leonov had adopted Socialist Realism—it became his duty to do what he most liked to do: extol great enterprise and the valor of his countrymen, assimilate their modes of speech, and acquire information about their processes of labor. His duties and tastes so happily coinciding, he followed his inclinations and filled his works with narratives of success, portraits of victorious men, and borrowed erudition: disquisitions on lumbering and forestry, on power plants and railroads, with settings and dialects that ranged over the length and breadth of Russia, and a whole gallery of scientists with their stores of specialized knowledge of engineering, surgery, mathematics, theoretical physics—not to mention more recondite fields, such as the history of chronometry. Thus for an understanding of power transmission one might read *Skutarevsky,* for railroad engineering *Road to the Ocean,* for the theory of conservation and the practice of forestry *The Russian Forest,* and any novel or play for a lesson in elevated patriotism.

On this basis, Leonov has accomplished now and then something like *tours de force,* as when in *The Taking of Velikoshumsk,* he succeeds in endowing an armored tank with personality and in making it convincingly the hero of a decisive battle; or as when in *The Russian Forest,* a long, uninterrupted university lecture becomes the eloquent kernel of an epic tale of war and reconstruction. The latter instance is structurally reminiscent of Dostoevsky. Does not "The Legend of the Grand Inquisitor" stand in the same relation to *The Brothers Karamazov* as Vikhrov's lecture does to *The Russian Forest*? But here, as always with Leonov, the literary echo is purely stylistic. In substance and feeling, nothing could be further from Dos-

toevsky, or for that matter from any other important Russian writer of the past, since the one element that most inspired Russian literature in its great period was precisely that to which Socialist Realism gives least encouragement and for which no doctrine can make provision: an interest in human beings in themselves, not only as exemplars of a prescribed morality, mere ciphers in an ideological ledger, as Leonov's people always are, even at their most complex—like those three elder brothers conceived in the womb of Socialist Realism, Skutarevsky, Kurilov, Vikhrov, with their marked family resemblance to one another and to their Marxist progenitors Lenin and Gorky. If it be objected that all fictional heroes represent ethical ideals, that Pierre Bezukhov and Andrey Bolkonsky, Prince Myshkin and Ivan Karamazov might also be entered in an account book of virtues and vices, the answer is that these men were not created for purposes of illustration and that the difference in artistic method between them and Leonov's creations is like the difference in logic between induction and deduction. Nowhere in Leonov's novels will one find any revealing comment on the human situation, any subtlety, novelty, or convincing portraiture. His characters are contrived images of human beings. At first, wanderers in search of something they can prize, victims of accident, fate, or circumstance, dissatisfied or miserable rather than unhappy, uncommitted and uninvolved, engaged in play, fantasy, invention, they entertain, pretend, and cheat; their personalities and opinions clash, but they are incapable of passionate debate, and life flows on somewhere beyond and beside them; then, having been made masters of events, "engineers of human souls," they still remain incomplete, peripheral beings of whom life demands a part of themselves only, making use of their specialties, not of their whole selves. There is not one among them whose action involves the entire man. They are cleverly constructed plaster models of civic virtue, presented not in sympathetic understanding, but through a haze of sentimental kindliness toward suffering, which casts a rosy glow on the horizon. This rosy glow is obligatory; it brightens the foreground, shows life *sub specie utopiae,* makes tragedy impossible.

And yet, through the stereotypes of theme and manner a more personal pattern emerges, the pattern of a romantic admiration for what is individually heroic. The acrobat's fatal act, of course, cannot be meaningful to one who rejects the whole concept of tragedy and does not believe in chance or fate, for whom man himself is fate, tragedy only a sentimental term for weakness, and life is interesting, important, and "true" only when humanity, through supreme ingenuity and effort, wins against tremendous odds. Tanya's leap into the void beneath the dome of a circus tent becomes the aviator's flight into enemy-infested skies or into interstellar space; or it is transformed into the bold experiments of the far-seeing scientist, or the endurance and intrepidity of men and women on perilous missions in wartime. What is man to Leonov? More and more what society wants, or judges him to be, and less and less what he is to himself—a development which is indicative of Leonov's own process of increasing conformity to public demand.

If, however, Leonov is praised in the Soviet Union for his

"correctness," is hailed as the "patriot-author," and is held up as an example of one who has been able to overcome the initial error of his views, it must be admitted, in all fairness, that his eminence has been come by honestly. For however strong his love of popularity, he cannot be called a time server. His is apparently the more complicated case of a man who, in need of ready-made dogma, develops, through ambition coupled with the honest weakness of self-distrust, a moral sense so resilient and an intelligence so flexible that the one can adopt astonishing reversals of belief and the other provide ready justifications for them. There is even something like logic in his development, a kind of organic progression from a degree of independence to complete submission. When the critics of his early work, and Gorky most of all, pointed out the "right," indeed the only acceptable, direction to him, he followed it eagerly, since he wanted to be told where to go. His is not, therefore, the story of coercion but of persuasion, operating on a gifted, acquisitive, adaptable being, as curious about ideas as any literary mind of Soviet Russia, the quickest to grasp the ins and outs of scientific enterprises, to catch the forms and intonations of dialects, and to appreciate all processes of reason—all, that is, except that of independent thought, of which he has never been capable. At no time was Leonov's thinking vigorous and original, nor his disposition rebellious. The inquiring attitude and the preoccupation with philosophic questions, exhibited in his early stories, were soon abandoned in favor of accumulating facts; the possibility of rigorous thinking was relinquished for the easier process of gathering information; and an inclination to irony, pathos, and tragedy was replaced by a simple-minded acceptance of men's feelings and a formula for judging human events. By no means merely facile, but intelligent and gifted, Leonov is a very interesting example of talent that lacks independence and needs to lean on well-formulated, officially accepted articles of faith. Nor is it so paradoxical as on the surface it might seem to be, that the best established of Soviet "realists" is, at bottom, an aesthete attracted to schemes of writing rather than to the substance of art.

The truth of the matter seems to be that Leonov is interested in neither people nor ideas, that his major concerns are and always have been dogmatic to a degree, that this was true even in his early work when he experimented with forms of narrative in the manner of his favorite authors, and that this has remained true when experiments in propaganda have succeeded experiments in style. In both stages he has been concerned with effectiveness, not with the matter but the manner of discourse. Intellectual and moral questions were early solved for him; he asked, and the answers were given. There had been a brief moment when restless outlawry, perilous amusements, and uncontrollable passion had seemed enchanting to him. But this was soon made purposeful, and a serious social aim reduced artistic intention to frivolity. For seriousness in "realistic" works is impossible when, as in fairy tales, everything must end happily, whatever outcome may be demanded by the logic of characters and events. At the beginning Leonov had been inspired by that which for the artist is the most serious of all frivolities, the essential, gratuitous delight in invention and expressiveness, although in his case the very nature of delight had been dictated by

the favored literary mood at the time of his debut. Then, still moved by the desire to be in favor, and under the influence of an aestheticism which confuses art and propaganda and recognizes no other legitimate motive than the will to "serve" the nation by elucidating and inculcating official dogma, he transformed entertainment to usefulness, drowned his art in mistaken patriotism, and diluted his affection for hard-won achievement and his love of exciting adventure to an insipid, childlike optimism.

But if one sees in his work a progressive relinquishment of fantasy, of the personal vision, of independent speculation, if one sees him as having been persuaded by the enticements of a popular philosophy to reverse his views and interests, one is also bound to recognize that what he gave up never constituted that imperative necessity which rules genuine artists. One cannot see him as another Mayakovsky who "stepped on the throat of his own song." Mayakovsky, having had much to lose, was inspired by his very martyrdom to creative vigor. Exalting at the top of his voice the agony of his self-willed repression, he made himself a tragic hero and endowed literature with the eloquent utterance of his pain and his will. But Leonov has had only a desire to sing, no song to step on, nor much more than his playfulness to sacrifice. If his reversal has reduced a genuine, if timid, gift to commonplace, he has been either unaware of the loss or has thought himself well compensated by the rewards of comfort. At any rate, he seems to have accepted his descent to public favor without qualm or protest. Of the true state of mind of one who has written so little about himself, it is, naturally, impossible to tell. And it may be that the progressive loss of gaiety and humor in Leonov's work, its increasingly ponderous discursiveness, are signs of some unhappiness. But this is pure conjecture. Outwardly there is nothing to indicate dissatisfaction. His themes are the "right" themes, and they are dealt with in the "right" way.

**Vera Alexandrova    (essay date 1963)**

SOURCE: "Leonid Leonov (1899-)," in *A History of Soviet Literature: 1917-1964, From Gorky to Solzhenitsyn,* translated by Mirra Ginsburg, 1963. Reprint by Anchor Books, 1964, pp. 203-21.

[*A Russian-born critic, Alexandrova originally published the book from which the following excerpt is taken in 1963. Below, she provides an overview of Leonov's career, focusing on his novels.*]

Many young writers begin their literary careers with a work they call a novel. On closer acquaintance it quickly becomes obvious that their book can scarcely be called a novel by the standards normally set for this literary form. "In order to construct a novel," said Chekhov, "it is necessary to have a good knowledge of the law of symmetry and the balance of masses. A novel is an entire palace, and the reader should feel free in it, neither astonished nor bored as in a museum. Sometimes he must be given a rest both from the hero and the author. This can be accomplished with a landscape, or something amusing, or a new twist in the plot, new characters. . . ." [Quoted by A. Serebrov in *Chekhov in the Recollections of Contemporaries,* Moscow: State Publishing House for Fine Literature, 1952.]

Leonid Leonov is one of the relatively small company of genuine novelists who know "the law of symmetry and the balance of masses."

Leonov was born in 1899 in Moscow, the son of a self-educated peasant poet who was at one time the chairman of the Surikov Literary and Musical Circle (the poet Surikov was also of peasant origin). Later, Leonov's father joined the literary group which called itself "Sreda" (Wednesday) and which attracted at the turn of the century many young men who subsequently became famous writers, including Bunin, Leonid Andreyev, and others. Leonov's grandfather owned a grocery store in Zaryadye, the market district in the old section of Moscow. A stern manner and great kindness were the most striking characteristics of this unusually colorful man, whom Leonov later used as the model for Bykhalov in his novel *The Badgers.*

Leonov's earliest memories were of 1905, when the terrorist Kalyaev assassinated the Grand Duke Sergey Alexandrovich. During the same year the future writer's father was arrested for publishing two pamphlets. The boy was twice taken by his grandmother to visit his father in prison. After twenty months in prison his father was released, but was exiled soon afterward to Arkhangelsk, where he remained even after the expiration of his term of exile. Leonov visited his father in Arkhangelsk several times, and the north made a great impression upon him, later reflected in a number of his works (particularly *Sot*).

Leonov received his elementary education at the city school in Moscow. His favorite teacher was Mitrofan Platonovich Kulkov. In 1925, when the young writer's works were first translated into German, he wanted to present a copy of the German edition to his old teacher, but the old man was no longer alive: both he and his wife (also a teacher) had died in the early part of the Civil War. Leonov later gave the name of Kulkov to the teacher of General Litovchenko, one of the characters in the novel *The Taking of Velikoshumsk* (1944).

During the Civil War, Leonov joined the Red Army as a volunteer, but was freed in 1921 in order to continue his education. At that time Leonov planned to study painting. When he returned to Moscow, he found none of his relatives or acquaintances there, except his mother's cousin, the locksmith Vasiliev, who readily accepted the young man into his home. But Leonov insisted on repaying his uncle's hospitality by helping in his locksmith's shop. For a long time afterward, he "toiled over the smoky forge." Later, the famous Russian graphic artist Falileyev took an interest in the young writer, and it was while living in his studio that Leonov wrote *The Petushikhino Breakthrough* and *The End of a Little Man.* Falileyev introduced Leonov to some well-known artists and literary figures of the mid-1920s. These included two publishers—Koppelman (of the Shipovnik Publishing House) and Sabashnikov. On hearing several of the young writer's stories, both of them offered to publish a volume of the pieces.

This initiated a new phase in Leonov's life—the beginning of professional literary activity.

Leonov's first stories—**"Buryga," "The Wooden Queen,"** and the longer tale *The Petushikhino Breakthrough*—were merely gropings for a theme, merely attempts to relieve the pressure of ideas and images that filled his mind. **"Buryga"** is an imp who, after a complicated series of adventures, finds himself far from his native woods, in distant Spain, with the cook of a "Spanish count," and his only friend, an old dog. **"The Wooden Queen"** is a little poem in prose, inspired by a long December evening and the flute song of a blizzard. The most interesting of these first "trials of the pen" is *The Petushikhino Breakthrough.* It is a tale of village life on the eve and in the early days of the revolution. Amid a tangle of human destinies the writer singles out the warm image of the quiet boy Alyosha, filled with a tender love of the world, living like a fragile azure flower somewhere at the edge of a forest.

In this tale we find Leonov's first use of lyrical digression, reflecting on the meaning of the large events of the time. These digressions were later to be given a firm place in Leonov's works. In this story Leonov devotes his lyrical digression to the distant future: "The troubled days will pass, we shall put on velvet trousers, sit down around electric samovars, and recall, and recall the dance of frantic rainless winds . . . when our guiltless Mitkas, Nikitkas, and Vasyatkas went without shrouds or coffins to public, crossless graveyards. . . . We shall recall how we fought for our right to be Red. . . ."

Fame came to Leonov early, with *Kovyakin's Journal.* This *Journal* is kept in the name of an old resident of Gogulev, a decaying hamlet forgotten by the powers that be. There is a humbled quality in Kovyakin, reminiscent of Gogol's Akaky Akakievich, but in contrast to Akaky, Kovyakin is a man well pleased with himself.

But neither *Kovyakin's Journal* nor *The End of a Little Man* marked Leonov's emergence as a major literary figure. This was accomplished by his first novel, *The Badgers* (1925), reflecting the early years of the revolution, which "reshuffled the cards" in such a way that the "game" proceeded according to new, unheard-of rules, under which "non-trump yokels beat true-born kings."

The novel is built on two planes: the village and the city. The poor peasant Savelin sends his two sons, Pavel and Semyon, to the city to learn new ways of earning a livelihood. They go to live with a former neighbor who had moved to Moscow and now owns a stall in the Zaryadye district, where the wretchedly poor village has long been disposing of its human "surpluses." The enterprising ones among these "surpluses" survive the harsh ordeal and "make their way in the world." Others, the seekers after "justice," remain at the bottom.

Leonov knew Zaryadye very well from frequent childhood visits to his grandfather. It was like a second home to him, and his novel captures the very air of the bustling market district in pre-revolutionary days. We see Zaryadye both on "a crisp December morning," and on a quiet evening in April, filled with the festive ringing of Lenten church-bells, its odors floating steadily along—"solid and slow, like a procession of well-fed Zaryadye tomcats."

Fate early separates the Savelin brothers. The elder, Pavel, lame, unlucky, and disgruntled, goes to work in a factory. Semyon, thoughtful and more even-tempered, adjusts himself to Zaryadye. Here he falls in love with a merchant's daughter, Nastya, but the merchant refuses the poor suitor, and Semyon harbors a deep grievance against him for this refusal.

With the outbreak of the revolution the brothers' paths diverge still further. Semyon is drawn back home. Their village, called Vory ("Thieves"), has long been engaged in litigation with a neighboring village, Gusaki ("Ganders"), over Zinkin meadow. The revolutionary government resolves this old dispute in favor of Gusaki. Its decision gives a new turn to the ancient quarrel: the Vory peasants, who feel wronged by the new authorities, become enemies of the Soviets, secretly hoping that "all this smashing business may make the city crumble into dust."

The pretext for an open rising against the new government is provided by the searches and requisitioning of grain. Semyon becomes the leader of the rebellious villagers. The peasants leave the village, intending to withdraw into the woods. A procession of carts loaded with the wretched peasant belongings heads for the forest, but on the way one of the ringleaders breaks down and exclaims: "Brothers, peasants . . . there's really no place for us to go!" And this cry from the depth of his heart serves as a signal for retreat. Most of the peasants turn back. But Semyon, with a group of other intransigents, becomes a partisan. They make their headquarters in the woods, living in dugouts like badgers (hence the title of the novel). They are joined by Nastya, Semyon's old love. She puts on trousers, and lives and fights together with the partisans.

Supported by the local peasantry, the partisans make flying raids against the representatives of the government, terrorizing them. The center sends army units to fight the rebels. With them comes Semyon's brother, Pavel, who became a Communist in the early days of the revolution. When he learns that Semyon leads the "badgers," Pavel arranges a meeting with him, at which, without revealing his present mission, he tries to convince his brother that, "historically," the village must follow the "Soviets," and that "there is no future for it without the Communists." But even without this naïve propaganda, the "badgers" are shaken with the coming of spring: their longing for the land becomes too strong.

Leonov was one of the first writers to depict the "Green" village—the village which rebelled against the Reds, but did not accept the Whites. He also sought to show the socio-political development of the peasant masses, awakened by the revolution.

The reader will encounter many of the characters of *The Badgers* in the writer's later works. The quiet, inwardly illuminated hatmaker Katushin will reappear in *The Thief* as the master mechanic Pchkhov. In the same novel Manka Vyuga (also Masha Dolomanova) is reminiscent of Nastya, of *The Badgers.* But there is one quality in *The Badgers* which makes it difficult for the reader to become

involved in the novel's narrative flow: the writer does not seem to be genuinely interested in the destinies of his heroes. Leonov attempted to overcome this flaw in *The Thief* (1927).

In this novel, against the broad background of the outskirts of Moscow during the NEP period—a period of officially acknowledged retrenchment from revolutionary policies in the face of the country's backward economy— Leonov gives us the first picture of the socio-political conflict which has arisen within the revolution. The hero of the novel is Mitka Vekshin, the son of a railroad watchman at a small, out-of-the-way siding. Impulsive, impressionable, and restless, he plunges wholeheartedly into the revolution from its very start; he fights with reckless courage in the ranks of the Red Army at the front, wins a decoration, and soon becomes a commissar.

After the end of the Civil War, Mitka goes to Moscow. The demobilized soldiers look askance at the growing profusion of goods in the store windows which only yesterday were nothing but shattered glass. In the beginning Mitka is not disturbed by these changes. "With mocking attention, he looked at all of this as the work of his own hands, flattering himself with the secret thought: 'I wanted it, and it appeared; I will not want it and it will go.' " But one day, as he stands by a store window, lightheaded with hunger, looking at the tempting display of tasty delicacies, a woman approaches the store. She is obviously the wife of a NEP man, "elegant and splendid like an Arabian morning." "With simple courtesy," Mitka stretches his hand to open the door for her. But she takes his gesture amiss and strikes his hand. That evening Mitka gets drunk and from then on rapidly begins to roll downhill.

Sinking to "the lower depths," Mitka becomes something of a celebrity and virtually the leader of a gang of thieves. Here, too, as at the front, his candid and impulsive character wins him many friends. He is joined by his old chum of Red Army days, Sanka Babkin. But Mitka himself is not impressed with his new career as a safecracker. To him, theft is not a profession, but a "persuasion," (as banditry is to Nomakh, the hero of Yesenin's unfinished play). He steals out of protest, but he does not feel that he has broken with his past. "I belong, I'm one of them," he says with feeling to Manka Vyuga (Masha Dolomanova), his childhood friend whom he meets again "at the depths," where she has become "gang queen." "I can still die if necessary," he continues. "But I am not a man to peep through keyholes. Didn't I fight? No, no! Allow a hero not to boast of his heroism."

The allusion to "keyholes" refers simultaneously to two characters in the novel: the chairman of the house committee, Chikilev, a little Soviet pettifogger, about whom "even the pencil feels too disgusted to write," and Mitka's former fellow soldier Atashez, who now occupies an important post in the economic apparatus. Atashez tries to explain to Mitka that the NEP does not mean the end of the revolution, but merely its adoption of "new forms." With his whole direct and impressionable nature Mitka is repelled by these explanations. And the entire background of the novel—the crowded and squalid life in the little apartment in the Blagusha district, with its kindly but scatterbrained café singer Zinka; the Bundyukovs, who love their quiet so much that they prefer to remain childless; the former landowner Manyukin, who earns a livelihood as an entertainer in the Blagusha all-night taverns—all this background merely brings into sharper relief the moving restlessness of the novel's only sincere and honest character—the thief Mitka Vekshin.

But Mitka is not the only hero of the novel. He has an interesting rival in the person of Nikolay Zavarikhin, a young fellow who comes to Moscow from the village in the hope of striking it rich (his trunk is stolen by Manka Vyuga at the station). "Everything was remarkable about him: his great height, as of a man who drew himself up to deliver a blow, the banked fire of his hard, pale-blue eyes, the leather trimming of his fancy felt boots . . . and his gay mittens, so brightly decorated, you'd think their maker was singing a song as he worked, and tracing out its wonderful refrains in color" (these gay and vivid colors mark the verbal mastery of Leonov himself). Nikolka hates the city and yet is drawn to it. He despises the city folk for their easy work and agile hands, but he knows that only the city can give him an opportunity to utilize his extraordinary acquisitive talents. He challengingly presents himself as a "bourgeois," adding: "But now there will be a new breed of bourgeois—without bellies. There won't be anything to stick a knife into." Nikolka's sullen, close-mouthed peasant strength is best expressed in his remark denying the assertion that strong men never cry: "That's rot! A strong man cries when he has nothing to put his strength to."

The writer Firsov, in whose name the narrative is often told, and who represents Leonov himself, remarks that "Mitka and Zavarikhin were spawned in the same hour by the earth, indifferent in her creative rage. The first goes down, the second up. When their paths cross, there are catastrophes, revulsion, and hatred. The first will die a death cruel and splendid; the second will make a three-time fool of death. Both are right: the first, in his honesty and will; the second, in his strength. And both are harbingers of the awakened millions."

Official criticism did not wait for the appearance of the last chapters of the novel (it ran serially for several months in the magazine *Krasnaya Nov*); it descended upon Leonov for exaggerating "the mud-faced danger" supposedly emerging from the NEP-time village. Obligingly, Leonov altered his original intention in mid-course: Mitka does not die, but leaves Moscow for the remote provinces where he becomes a lumberjack, thus breaking his ties with the criminal underworld. Zavarikhin's subsequent fate is indicated in passing in the early pages of the novel: by his large-scale trading in hemp, Nikolka will ultimately win glory for his peasant name not only at home, but also abroad. But we are told about this outside the framework of the story itself; at the end of the novel Zavarikhin is still a small-time owner of a stall in a dark corner of the market place.

The changes made by Leonov in the course of writing the novel as a result of critical attacks are obvious even to the naked eye. However, the reasons for his sense of failure with this work are much more complex, and expressions of dissatisfaction crop up in many places in the novel. What is the source of Leonov's feeling that the novel, on which he has "expended almost all of himself," is in some sense a failure? Some clues to this may be found in his comments on his alter ego, the writer Firsov: "Not loving the things he had to write about in those years, Firsov was afraid of touching Mitka, who appeared to him as a dark, subterranean force, a flame which, once it has broken through, subsides and flares again, momentarily changing form and color. . . . Firsov did not love Mitka enough to tell the truth about him, about the reasons why, in the end, he dropped out of the life he had won by dint of so much suffering and effort."

These lines help us to understand Leonov's sense of creative failure in connection with *The Thief.* Leonov the artist was unquestionably aware of the moods of disappointment with the results of the revolution which existed in Soviet society. During the years when he was writing the novel, disillusionment with the NEP caused many suicides among the young men who had fought in the Civil War and had been fired with the ideas of Wartime Communism. These suicides included the gifted trade-union leader Yury Lutovinov, the proletarian poets Kuznetsov and Khvastunov, and the brilliant peasant poet Sergey Yesenin.

Another conflict emerged and became widespread in the village: awakened by the revolution, the peasant youth was longing to spread its wings, but it felt hamstrung by the duality of the government's policy. Leonov himself was more in sympathy with Mitka than with Zavarikhin; but—like his alter ego Firsov—he *did not love him enough* to tell the whole truth and defend him from the attacks of his critics.

Among the failures of *The Thief* one must include the image of Mitka's youthful love, Masha Dolomanova, who later, through her husband, the thief Aggey, became the "gang queen," Manka Vyuga. In some of her traits she is kin to Dostoyevsky's Grushenka in *The Brothers Karamazov.* Dostoyevsky's influence may be traced in many pages of *The Thief,* particularly in the portrait of the former landowner Manyukin, who, from the writer's many oblique hints, appears to be Mitka's real father. It is felt also in the picture of Mitka's loyal friend Sanka Babkin, and especially of the latter's wife, Xenia.

Despite its flaws, however, *The Thief* is a novel of great scope, with a well-developed plot. Among the writer's most successful moment there is the meeting between Mitka and his sister Tanya, who left the parental roof before him and joined a circus where, thanks to the devotion of Pugel, her instructor, she became a celebrity as an aerialist. Her love affair with Nikolka Zavarikhin and her early death during a circus performance are particularly poignant.

*The Thief* had a most extraordinary history. At the end of 1959 the novel, which had not been reprinted since the middle of the 1930s, was issued in a new edition. From the preface to this edition the reader learns that *The Thief* has undergone a radical revision, which took Leonov two years to accomplish. In a brief note to the new edition, Leonov says the following:

> The author has reread the book written more than thirty years ago, with pen in hand. To intervene in a work of such long standing is as difficult as stepping for a second time into the same creek. But it is always possible to follow the dried-up bed, listening to the crunching of the pebbles underfoot and looking without fear into the hollows that are no longer filled with water.

In this brief preface every word is a riddle. Why was it necessary to "intervene" in a work written more than thirty years ago? The very comparison of the novel to a "creek" is unconvincing (*The Thief* was not a creek, but a wide river). And how did the water vanish from this "creek"?

A comparison of the two versions reveals that, in revising the novel, the author sought to strip both leading characters of all the traits which had elicited the reader's sympathy—sometimes against the author's will. Leonov achieved this by whittling down the importance and attractiveness of the images of Mitka and Zavarikhin. The digression in which Leonov indirectly admits his failure "to love Mitka enough" is also deleted. In its place we find the harsh and disapproving lines: "Approximately by the middle of the book, we graphically see the futility of Firsov's attempts . . . to save the image of Vekshin, which until recently still held his sympathy—even if somewhat shaken—but which is now *almost hateful to him*" (italics mine—V.A.).

The devaluation of Zavarikhin is still more drastic. He is depicted as a coarse and cynical man, ready to trample down the lives of even those who are near to him for the sake of his interests, as he has done with his fiancée, Tanya Vekshina. The new edition has also been purged of the intimation that Zavarikhin would win renown both at home and abroad through successful trade: he now ends in a concentration camp. In the earlier version Zavarikhin fell in love at first sight with Manka Vyuga, who stole his trunk at the station when he first arrived in Moscow, but he never saw her again, and never looked for her. In the new version he sometimes thinks of her after "a grueling day in the camp." And he never learns that Manka Vyuga also "suffered, revenged herself, and fell, again and again, until at last she came to rot away her days quite near" the place of his own exile.

The *Literary Gazette* (February 7, 1960) published some interesting comment on the new version of *The Thief:*

> Once upon a time, the twenty-three-year-old Leonov, back from the southern front in the Civil War, was struck by the contrasts of NEP-time Moscow. He thought about many problems that seemed insoluble to him at the time— problems connected with the future of his generation, with the search for a place in life. . . .

But the present version of the novel, according to the *Literary Gazette,* "is a condensation of certain thoughts which have stirred Leonov over three decades; it is a debate of the firmly convinced and experienced writer with his own younger and wavering self."

To the present-day Leonov, the entire 1927 version is a gross political error, and he spares neither effort nor his heroes in order to "correct" his novel. And so, the large river of his earlier narrative has, in fact, dwindled in the later edition to a "dried-up creek."

Having failed, in the latter 1920s, to create a "hero of the epoch" in the images of Mitka Vekshin and Nikolka Zavarikhin, Leonov did not abandon hope that he would still succeed in finding him. He shifted his attention to another milieu, whose active elements devoted themselves to work in the first Five-Year Plan for the industrialization of the country.

*Sot* (1929) was the first major literary dealing with the industrialization theme. The idea of building a cellulose-paper combine in the North originates with the chairman of the Province Executive Committee, Potyomkin, who spent his youth, until his army days, as a lumber floater, and who was later a worker in a paper-manufacturing plant. The abundance of forests and available men, and the paper shortage in the country lead Potyomkin to the idea of building a paper factory. As he dreams of it, he becomes more and more enthusiastic and, together with some "knowledgeable people" in the region, he develops a plan for a mighty combine. In his mind's eye Potyomkin already sees an island of industry in the midst of a vast peasant ocean. Thanks to his persistence, Potyomkin succeeds in obtaining approval for his project from the center.

Of course, the novel's interest does not lie in the history of this construction project, but in the men depicted in it. For the first time, the reader of the late 1920s was offered a work reflecting, not the lives and feelings of individuals, but the epoch in the totality of its components. The center of the narrative is held by Uvadyev, one of the leaders of the project and an ex-foreman of a paper factory. After the end of the Civil War his life was spent in responsible but uninteresting work. Uvadyev's credo is simple and direct: "In our age it is necessary to think big: in terms of dozens of factories, thousands of hectares, millions of people. . . ." The workers on the new project, "Sot-Stroy," to which Uvadyev is now assigned, dislike their new chief. One of them says to him: "You have no understanding of a workingman, you are a hard master!"

The young engineer Favorov is closest to Uvadyev in his outlook. He sees the current period as a parallel to the days of Peter the Great, who also used "the whip, and drove in endless piles to drain the wide expanses of the Russian swamp." In brief, the novel presents a generation of men who are "economic workers, co-operators, men of the American type." At the other pole, rarely looked at, are the workers and peasants and, even further, the monks who are living out their days in the woods.

There is little communication among most of Leonov's characters in *Sot.* Uvadyev finds it difficult to speak a common language even with his own mother. A worker's widow and a worker herself, Varvara Uvadyeva sharply criticizes the way of life enjoyed by her son and the other "commissars." Accustomed to poverty, she is angered "at even the slightest evidence of comfortable living." She leaves her son, goes to live somewhere in a cellar, and finds a job as a switch operator on a streetcar line. "I refuse to be a flunkey. I may be a fool, but I'll be my own fool!" To escape loneliness, Varvara marries an elderly man who earns his livelihood by selling portraits of "the leaders" in the market place.

In *Sot,* as in *The Thief,* Leonov paints a graphic picture of the life and moods of the Moscow back streets, where Varvara goes to live with her husband. The motley population of the district consists of workers, erstwhile ladies who are now selling sweets in the market, and petty "NEP-men." All these people are united in their hatred of the powers that be.

Leonov does not succeed in presenting Uvadyev as the "hero of the epoch." Against his wish, the artist in him shows his central character as a stony hulk in whose vicinity no living thing can grow: his wife Natalya leaves him; his affair with a young girl, the daughter of an engineer employed on the project, ends in failure. Uvadyev escapes from his personal disasters into work, leaving Moscow for the construction site.

The novel also offers a striking picture of life in the remote northern province and the small town of Makarikha, around which the new construction is developed. The reader is astonished by the persistence of the old social forms. A locomobile sent from the center makes its appearance in the town square. A group of peasants examines the machine with curiosity, and a conversation ensues which is reminiscent of the opening pages of Gogol's *Dead Souls.* " 'Look at all those tubes!' one of the peasants exclaimed, yawning solely from excess of feeling. The peasant eye was teased and tempted by the lubricating tubes which fairly seemed to beg for transfer to the home-brew apparatus. 'Come a second revolution, and we'll have to take it all apart again; you can get ruptured on the job!' added another, not without enthusiasm."

Leonov does not minimize the antagonism between the government and the working people. Once, when a dam bursts on the project and the workers toil on its repair without sparing themselves, Uvadyev wants to praise one of them, who plunged into the work with particular disregard of himself. He says to the worker: "But you are really one of ours!" In reply he hears the sullen and intractable: "I'm nobody's, I am my own. You think you rule me? You like the voiceless ones; they lick your boots, but keep a rope for you in a dark corner."

Acute need fills the peasants' hearts with bitterness. Observing the endless cases of iron and nails arriving at the construction site, a peasant says to his fellow villagers: "They'll build for you! I carted cases from the station the other day. . . . Iron and iron, pure-blooded iron, peasants! And we must plead like beggars for a nail or a horseshoe." Suffering from shortages of the barest essentials, the peasants do not conceal their disapproval of the "squandering waste" attending the construction project.

For all his loyalty to the regime, Leonov did not want to conceal that, under the conditions which developed by the late 1920s, "socialist construction" did not further the consolidation of the country, but, on the contrary, hastened the process of class differentiation in the new society.

In his tireless search for a dynamic and positive hero epitomizing the period of construction, Leonov stumbled upon a large theme which for many years became his central preoccupation. It was the theme of *fathers and sons.* Though not, of course, new in Russian literature, the theme was highly interesting in its new interpretation: for the first time in Russian literature, the writer—himself a young man at the time—gave his sympathy, not to youth, but to the "old men." This was particularly apparent in the novel *Skutarevsky* (1932) and in *The Road to the Ocean* (1935).

Along with novels and shorter works Leonov has written a number of plays: *The Orchards of Polovchansk* (1936-38), *The Wolf* (1938), *An Ordinary Man* (1940-43), and others. I shall forego analysis of these plays, since Leonov is at his weakest as a dramatist. His plays remind one of icebergs, nine-tenths of which are submerged under water. Many of the decisive events in the lives of most of the characters seem to have taken place before the opening of the play and quite outside its framework. The only exception is *The Invasion,* written in 1942.

Hitler's attack on the Soviet Union in June of 1941 and the defeats sustained by the Red Army for almost two years were a great shock to Russia, and most of all to the upper strata of Soviet society; the latter turned out to be the least prepared for these defeats. A detailed characterization of these moods will be found in Chapter 16, devoted to literary developments during and after the Second World War. No writer in the Soviet Union failed to reflect this bitter period in his work. Like others, Leonov was deeply shaken, and responded with his play *The Invasion.*

The action of the play unfolds in a small provincial town on the eve of its surrender to the Germans. The center of action is the family of Doctor Talanov. The old doctor has decided not to leave his native town, feeling that its people will have even more need of his help during the occupation than in peacetime. Just before the arrival of the Germans, the doctor's errant son, Fyodor, returns home after imprisonment. Fyodor has had a stormy youth: he killed the woman he loved, was sent to prison, then to a concentration camp. Since he has never written them from the camp, the doctor and the rest of the family fear Fyodor. During his years in the concentration camp he may have grown hardhearted. He might even go over to the Germans.

While the doctor is talking with his son, the chairman of the Executive Committee, Andrey Kolesnikov (the fiancé of Talanov's daughter Olga), calls on him and tries to convince him to evacuate. As Andrey enters, Fyodor manages to slip behind a screen. Kolesnikov confides to the doctor that he will also remain in the city for underground work. Fyodor inadvertently turns over a chair and comes out of his hiding place. He offers to help Kolesnikov, but the latter refuses, distrusting him. There is an exchange of caustic words. Kolesnikov gives the impression of a man who has lost his bearings. After he leaves, Fyodor says to his father: "I am not an artilleryman, Father, but *this gun isn't working any more*" (italics mine—V.A.).

On the day when the Germans arrive, Fyodor disappears, intensifying still further the apprehensions of his family. In the occupied city the Germans live as if they were sitting atop a volcano: every day some German soldiers and officers are killed. The assassinations are attributed to Andrey Kolesnikov, but the Germans fail to capture him. All the greater is the astonishment of the Talanov family when the mysterious partisan, captured by the Germans and brought to their home, turns out to be Fyodor and not Kolesnikov. Afterward Fyodor is taken to the prison cellar, where he meets other Soviet partisans. Threatened with death before a firing squad, he is asked by the other prisoners why he posed as Kolesnikov and showed such heroism. Sullen and sparing of words, he replies: "I prolonged your lives . . . and I ask for no receipt." Fyodor is shot, and several hours later the city is retaken by Soviet troops.

For a full appreciation of Leonov's play, we must return to Mitka Vekshin, whom Leonov did not "love enough" to tell the whole truth about him. The emotions which Leonov experienced during the bitter war years helped him, more than fifteen years later, to give just due to Mitka and the other young people who had been critical of the Soviet regime, and whose true worth Leonov had failed to see.

The boldness and unexpectedness of Leonov's reorientation is brought into sharp relief by the fact that Soviet critics and the theater directors who produced the play refused for a long time to reconcile themselves to the idea that the hero of the play was not the Communist Andrey, but an erstwhile concentration-camp prisoner.

The short novel *The Taking of Velikoshumsk* is so fragmented that it can scarcely be called a novel. This is somewhat—but not altogether—camouflaged by the fact that three of its protagonists bear the same name, Litovchenko: the tank-corps general who arrives to inspect the front; the young driver of the famous "203" tank, who plays an important role in the story; and the elderly peasant woman into whose house the general comes to warm himself.

The background of the story is formed by the roads of the Soviet advance, described with remarkable vividness. Like "splinters in the river of war," the returning people and cattle flowed along these roads: "lean cows with sorrowful Biblical eyes pulled ramshackle carts, and old men walked alongside, helping the beasts to reach home. Small flocks of peasant children, often four of them under a single piece of sacking, looked with uncomplaining smiles at their mothers who trudged along with tightly drawn lips, with nothing to rely on in the world except their own hands, now hanging limply down their sides. . . ." And all around the caravans returning to their own ruins lapped "the bitter sea of peasant trouble."

The rather weakly delineated plot of the novel is balanced by the history of the famed "203" tank, whose crew is proud of its military biography. This crew consists of the tank commander Sobolkov, whose wife and children are left behind in distant Altay, and who has won the respect

and love of his men by his comradely warmth and courage; the tank's gunner, the merry, hard-drinking Obryadin, about whom the radioman Dybok says: "You're a friend to the whole honest world, Obryadin, but you'd be a king among loafers!" The tank driver, after the death of his predecessor, is the young Vasya Litovchenko. All of them are linked by the bonds of love for one another and for their tank. After the last and most violent encounter with the enemy, only Vasya and Dybok remain alive, and Dybok swears eternal devotion to his friend.

The underlying meanings of the conversation between General Litovchenko and his old schoolteacher Mitrofan Platonovich Kulkov are highly significant. Like Leonov, Litovchenko did not find his teacher among the living, but saw him in a dream. The teacher and the general sat silently in this dream, and "there was a profound question in the old man's silence: how will history repay for the irredeemable human suffering caused by the war?"

Litovchenko is deeply stirred by Kulkov's question. He feels as if he were "at a lesson, thirty years ago." And he begins to tell the old man about the coming material blessings to be brought by the still incompletely realized program, and about the "sage from Gori" (i.e., Stalin). But the humanist teacher, unreceptive to high-flown rhetoric, is not to be placated by future perspectives. To all of Litovchenko's arguments about a shining future, Kulkov replies: "To seek friends in the future is the fate of loneliness."

The Soviet general's dispute with his own conscience ends as abruptly as it began, but it throws a new light on the question that arises in the minds of Soviet people along the roads of the advance: what "price" will the Soviet government set on the country's unprecedented feats of self-sacrifice, how will it reward the people of our time, dressed "in the tattered army coats of death"?

After the publication of *The Taking of Velikoshumsk*, Leonov was silent for almost ten years. It was not until the end of 1953 that he came forward with a new novel, *The Russian Forest*, and, a year later, with the play *Golden Carriage*. These works (especially the play) contribute little that is new to the writer's extensive literary "economy," and the new novel is artistically weaker than many of Leonov's previous works.

The literary portrait of Leonov cannot be completed without at least a passing glance at the question of Dostoyevsky's influence upon his work. This influence was mentioned in the discussion of *The Thief*. It is especially evident in Leonov's treatment of his heroines, including Nastya (*The Badgers*), Masha Dolomanova, and Xenia, Sanka's wife (*The Thief*), Liza Pokhvistneva (*The Road to the Ocean*), and others. It may be felt, further, in Leonov's language, although his style is richer and more vivid. Like Dostoyevsky, Leonov makes wide use of the wealth of suffixes and prefixes in the Russian language to lend the desired shading to what, for one reason or another, he does not want to say directly and openly.

Nevertheless, I would question the view of some Russian critics abroad that, were Leonov free in his creative work, he would have become a "Soviet Dostoyevsky." Dostoyevsky's central concern was with ethical and religious problems, which determined the entire character of his work. Leonov is alien to moral, religious, and philosophical preoccupations. He is an accomplished artist, who perceives the world through images. But his spiritual and emotional world is devoid of that intensity with which Dostoyevsky's works were so profoundly charged.

---

**Ernest J. Simmons on Dostoyevsky and Leonov:**

Dostoyévsky's influence . . . is much . . . pronounced in the art of Leoníd Leónov (1899-), one of the most distinguished Soviet novelists. His early tale, "The End of an Insignificant Person" (1924), is a striking pastiche of Dostoyévsky. The story is built around a savant who starves to death during the famine period, and the question is raised whether the positive gains of a revolution justify the terrible wastage of human life and culture. In Leónov's first full-length novel, *The Badgers* (1925), a typical Dostoyévskian psychological approach is employed in the development of characters cast against a background of revolution. The theme is the fierce antagonism between town and village represented in two brothers, one a city-bred communist, the other a village *kulak*.

*Ernest J. Simmons, in his* An Outline of Modern Russian Literature (1880-1940), *Cornell University Press, 1943.*

---

## R. D. B. Thomson (essay date April 1966)

SOURCE: "Leonid Leonov," in *Forum for Modern Language Studies,* Vol. II, No. 2, April, 1966, pp. 264-73.

[*In the essay below, Thomson examines themes of flight, genius, and morality in Leonov's works.*]

Leonid Leonov (born 1899), novelist and playwright, might seem to be the most conventional of Soviet writers. He has written a novel about the Civil War (*The Badgers,* 1924) and another (*The Thief,* 1925-7) about the NEP period; in the thirties he produced a novel (*The River Sot',* 1930) about industrialisation, and devoted another (*The Road to the Ocean,* 1933-5) to the new "positive hero" of socialist realism. The Second World War drew three more works from him, and the death of Stalin was followed by the last of his novels to date, (*The Russian Forest,* 1950-3) often regarded as the first swallow of the "thaw". His work might almost serve as a miniature history of Soviet literature.

This seeming conventionality disappears on closer acquaintance. Of all Soviet writers Leonid Leonov is the most individual. His elaborate style, his highly personal thought and imagery, his characteristic range of heroes, and above all the acute conflicts on which his works are built; all these features distinguish his books from those of his compatriots and contemporaries.

Leonov has drawn his material principally from the clash of human individuality and personal morality, and throughout his life he has attempted to find some equation relating them. Over the years, however, the balance of these two themes in his work has shifted gradually but conclusively, to such an extent that his works of the last decade effectively reverse the values affirmed in his early work.

For Leonov, human individuality is synonymous with creativity—and the basic conflict of his works sets the tragic but creative hero against the sterile and envious villain. This theme is not new in Russian literature; it goes back to Pushkin's "little tragedy", *Mozart and Salieri,* a work, incidentally, to which Leonov frequently makes explicit reference in his own novels and plays. In Pushkin's dramatic poem the genius and the craftsman are confronted with one another. No one can appreciate the genius Mozart better than the honest craftsman Salieri: "You are a god, Mozart, and you don't realise it"; but at the same time Salieri revolts against a system of values which can allow the irresponsibility of a genius to outshine the painstaking industry of the craftsman: "There is no justice on earth, but there is none above either". In a vain attempt to redress this injustice, Salieri poisons Mozart. In terms of earthly justice, Salieri certainly has a better claim to inspiration—but it is still Mozart who remains the genius. Morality is no guarantee of creativity.

Dmitry Vekshin, the hero of Leonov's first important novel, *The Thief,* had been one of the most brilliant commissars in the Red Army during the Civil War; but his mercurial temperament had led him into a grave breach of discipline—he murdered a prisoner—and he has been expelled from the Party. At the end of the War he is faced not only by the traditional difficulties of the demobilized service-man, but also by the stigma of expulsion from the Party. He is further demoralized by the introduction of the New Economic Policy, a temporary relaxation of the controls on private enterprise; Vekshin regards this as a betrayal of the Communist ideals for which he had fought in the Civil War, and he becomes a thief, devoting his ingenuity and courage to undermining a society which he now repudiates. His protest, however, is made in the name of the Revolution, and however low he sinks he remains loyal to this goal. Accordingly Vekshin is not regarded as a traitor; and Leonov plays down the criminal and anti-social aspects of his activities. It is rather Communism that is on trial, and its ability to harness and make creative use of Vekshin's boundless energies. It is this dilemma which lies at the heart of the novel; it also dominates the course of Leonov's later development.

Leonov's admiration for his hero runs very deep. Vekshin is [Leonov stated in *Vor* (1928)] "the best that mankind can produce", and he is associated with an image that is to colour Leonov's work for many years, the image of "flying". The word carries many overtones; there is the idea of being raised above the rest of humanity, of being conspicuous, of being superior; then again there is the idea of danger and therefore heroism; finally there is the suggestion of aspiration, the inability to be satisfied with what has been achieved. All these ideas are present in the comment that Vekshin is a "planet that has broken out of its orbit", and its associated images.

Vekshin's career is paralleled in the figure of his sister, Tanya, the trapeze artist. Her star turn, the *shtrabat,* a dangerous leap across the circus, with no safety-net below her, provides another version of his "flight", or challenge to the accepted conventions of humanity. Like her brother, she takes a pride in constantly inventing new difficulties and overcoming them. She too can never rest on her laurels. But for Tanya the end is tragedy; she misses her footing and falls to her death.

Vekshin himself is driven by the same urge to self-destruction. His motto is "upwards and onwards"; he refuses to be satisfied, even when his immediate goal has been achieved. Above all, he rejects happiness, for that implies a final achievement, or at least a coming-to-terms, and consequently an abrogation of man's duty to aspire "upwards and onwards", "Happiness is always bourgeois: happiness is when there's no further to go, when everything has been achieved". On the other hand, his antithesis, the loathsome bureaucrat Chikilev dreams of the day when men will be happy to order. And even the Communists in the book regard happiness in terms of social and physiological organization: "You'll be able to manufacture it like goloshes or light-bulbs". But the world is not to be judged by the logic of an earth-bound Salieri. Creativity and tragedy are not to be measured in terms of morality and happiness.

In Leonov's scheme of values suffering and tragedy are inseparable from "flight". They provide the only evidence of spiritual vitality, evidence that has to be constantly reasserted by new exploits. Indeed, a tragic outcome is the only really consistent end for Vekshin himself. Leonov, however, holds out a tentative prospect of regeneration for his hero: "How Mitya fell among lumberjacks, how he was beaten at first, and then welcomed . . . how he regained the name that he had lost: all this lies outside the scope of the present narrative". This ending hardly provides a satisfactory solution to Vekshin's restless aspirations, but oddly, this idea of salvation through communal labour contains a prophecy of Leonov's own later development.

Leonov's need for an optimistic end to Vekshin's career comes from his belief that the same qualities are inherent in the Bolshevik Revolution. Vekshin cries: "The Revolution is first and foremost a flight, upwards and onwards, upwards and onwards". On the other hand the doubters see the Revolution in terms of a brave but pedestrian slog. The déclassé aristocrat Manyukin writes: "Perhaps you'll tell me that the train is still deep in the tunnel, hasn't yet burst out into the blue glimmer at the far end? But hasn't the tunnel gone on rather long? What if there's no way out of it?" The whole idea of flying is an assertion of the creative leap, the stroke of genius, the very negation of the patient but earth-bound industry of Salieri. Not surprisingly, however, Leonov baulked at associating the tragic overtones of this image with the Revolution. On the other hand the "tunnel" raises the question: if the Revolution is no more than that, is it worth anything at all?

With the publication of **The Thief** Leonov won instant recognition as one of the most important Soviet Writers. Gorky marked him out for special attention and his works began to be translated in the West. By 1929 he had been elected first chairman of the new Party-controlled Union of Soviet Writers. He had arrived. One could guess at this change in Leonov's status from the works alone. His heroes are now no longer underdogs and rebels, but men at the top of the tree, prominent commissars and world famous scientists. The concern with creativity and tragedy, morality and happiness, however, still remains the dominant motif in the work of Leonov's second period (1929-1936), though these values are now subtly redistributed.

---

**Leonov has drawn his material principally from the clash of human individuality and personal morality, and throughout his life he has attempted to find some equation relating them.**

**—R. D. B. Thomson**

---

With the intensification of the drive towards industrialization and collectivization in 1928, the cult of individualism, so characteristic of Soviet literature during the earlier twenties, began to be officially discouraged in favour of the new ideal of collectivism. This convention, too, is reflected in Leonov's novels of the period. Thus the individualist scientist Skutarevsky (in the novel of the same name) is finally reconciled with the party and the rest of his people in the closing pages. On a deeper level the commissar Kurilov, in **The Road to Ocean,** debarred from Party activity by a fatal illness, is amazed to discover that Communism has richly equipped him for human relationships. He makes new friendships and finds himself actually capable of love.

Yet these men are recognizably Leonov heroes. Professor Skutarevsky is working on the wireless transmission of electricity, a new variant of the leap of creative energy, depicted in **The Thief.** He actually drives his car like an aeroplane, commenting: "Flight—that's man's natural state: everything else is just a blasphemous lowering of the norm". Kurilov indulges in flights of imagination, dreaming of his Utopia Ocean, "the capital of men who fly naturally and effortlessly". So it is not surprising that Leonov still speaks in the same terms of the Revolution. "You're a pedant: you're afraid of risks: but the Bolsheviks too took a risk in 1917".

On the other hand "flight" still retains its tragic associations for Leonov. The cosmonauts, envisaged by Kurilov, return from their first space-flight, dead or blinded by their experiences. "We learnt that in Ocean too there were tragedies, but ones more worthy of man's lofty estate". For Skutarevsky: "Flight—that's the only way for a man to die". Accordingly Skutarevsky recognizes the ominous signs of a heart-attack just at his moment of triumph; and

Kurilov collapses just when love seems to have humanized him finally.

For all this, however, the tragic images of Skutarevsky and Kurilov are somewhat muted. They are sick men, middle-aged, and, ironically, they are even more isolated and conscious of their isolation than Vekshin had been. They are both aware that the best of life is behind them, that they will not live to see the glorious future for which they have worked. Their devotion to the cause has left them with no personal interests or private life. This gives them a pathetic, almost sacrificial, air which overshadows their more obviously heroic qualities. Skutarevsky joins the Party only after a series of shattering blows in his private life and his work. But there is no real tragedy here: the safety-net of Party-membership is waiting for him. As for Kurilov, the act of flying has been suspended and made static: "he was like a bridge and people passed over him into the future".

These new heroes are loyal, respectable Soviet citizens. They find fulfilment, not in flying in the face of society, but in identifying themselves with it. Individualist though they are, they achieve their happiness only when they have finally shed their individuality. In *The Thief,* the idea of flight had been a condition of life, an expression of the need to intensify experience by danger and courage, and as such it contained for Leonov and his heroes a sort of happiness, even though this sometimes involved the rejection of happiness in its more conventional forms. But now happiness has become a different sort of right, one that can, and indeed must, be earned: "All work entitles a man to bread, but only creativity entitles him to happiness; and tomorrow all work will be creative". Chikilev, with his desire to make people happy to order, would have welcomed the suggestion.

The word "creativity" too has changed its meaning; it is no longer opposed to patient industry, but has become a consequence of it. Kurilov's service to the Party has been loyal and persevering, but no more than that; his life is an example, not a challenge. Creativity now is simply a reward for services rendered. It is no longer an aesthetic concept, but an ethical one. Undeniably, Salieri deserves to be a better composer than Mozart. Does this necessarily make him so?

Somewhat apart from these heroes stands the ex-White officer Gleb Protoklitov, the villain of *The Road to Ocean.* Because of the need to conceal his past with the Whites, his life since the Civil War has been a succession of falsehoods, fake biographies and desperate bluffs. Yet in this deeply compromised character, and his hopeless situation (for Gleb's ultimate ruin is never in doubt), Leonov discovers unsuspected riches. At times the figure of Gleb dominates the entire work.

Leonov tries in vain to alienate the reader from his villain—notably in the horrific scene where Gleb attempts to murder one of his old comrades, now blackmailing him—but Gleb obstinately retains the reader's sympathy. The men who hunt and betray him are infinitely more repulsive than Gleb himself. Admittedly, he speaks of Kurilov as enviously as Salieri of Mozart: "He is like a great planet, and I his insignificant satellite", but he too shares in this image of flight. Kurilov even observes that Gleb "would make a good airman". This is not just a coincidence. Gleb Protoklitov really does recall the Vekshins. His life represents a new variation on theirs. Faced with the prospect of annihilation he refuses to come to terms. He exists in defiance of the law and even of his creator, Leonov. Inevitably, the flying image covers him too. Mozart has been poisoned, but his music is still better than Salieri's.

*The Road to Ocean* is Leonov's most ambitious novel, in its formal experimentation and the importance of the issues it raises. However, after initial approval, it ran into savage criticism, and within a year of its first appearance it had been virtually suppressed. Leonov must have felt this painfully, for after producing five novels in the twelve years 1924-1935, his next appeared only in 1953. In the meantime, he turned to the stage.

The years following *The Road to Ocean* were the years of the great purges, and the change in Leonov's fortunes was undoubtedly caused, at least in part, by a spiteful personal campaign, which can be traced back as far as November, 1933. This campaign took various forms: attacks on Leonov's personal vanity, distortions of the content and meaning of his works, and, more insidiously, suppression of all his pre-1936 works. Altogether some forty editions of his novels had appeared up to 1936; none was to be issued again until 1947, one of them (*Skutarevsky*), only after Stalin's death, while another (*The Thief*) has never been re-published in its original form. This campaign continued with a series of vicious attacks on Leonov's plays of 1937-40, culminating in violent denunciations of *The Snow Storm,* then (November 1940) undergoing rehearsals at the Maly theatre. The play, which had been performed successfully in the provinces, was immediately suppressed and Leonov himself disgraced. It seems likely that only the war saved him from annihilation.

Leonov's fall was almost as meteoric as his rise. In 1929 he seemed to be standing at the top of the tree. A personal friend of Gorky, Chairman of the Union of Soviet Writers, and with an international reputation as a novelist, he seemed unchallengeably secure. Yet within seven years he had lost the friendship of Gorky, his books had been virtually suppressed, and after Gorky's death he does not seem to have been considered even as a candidate for a post in the Union.

These changes are inevitably reflected in his works. His new heroes are no longer men with important positions at the hub of affairs, but provincial figures, in agriculture, industry or local administration. They lack the individuality of Leonov's earlier heroes; the stress is on modesty, efficiency, unobtrusiveness; one of these plays is actually called *An Ordinary Man,* and the characters in it drink a toast to "heroic ordinariness". Many of these men are engaged in "creative" work, but they are no longer associated with images of flight. Like Kurilov, they are at best "bridges". Professor Skutarevsky had driven his car as if it was an aeroplane; Professor Vikhrov, the hero of *The Russian Forest,* prefers to go on foot.

Leonov's heroes are almost always older than their creator. None of them has found personal happiness; each of them is sadly aware that he will not live to see the entry into the Promised Land, whose prospect has dominated and given meaning to his life. Inevitably it seems to the older figures that their successors will enjoy the triumph too easily, without having shared in the efforts or sacrifices that had made it possible; they look for some evidence that their children appreciate their work and are worthy of inheriting it. Leonov himself perhaps shared the feelings of his ageing heroes, for from 1936 onwards he begins to depict the younger generation.

It is here that the image of flying re-appears. The younger heroes—or more often heroines—are associated with gliding or parachute-jumping; sometimes, by extension, they serve in tanks or submarines. These militaristic images reflect, of course, the years in which the plays were written; but these displays of courage and heroism, while seeming to echo the Vekshins' self-destructive challenge to the void beneath, are no longer sought for their own sake, but serve as demonstrations that these boys and girls are "entitled to happiness". Where the Vekshins had been testing their potentialities to their furthest limits, these new heroes are simply undergoing initiation, or rather confirmation, ceremonies, which they invariably complete successfully.

In the better works of this period, the younger heroes and heroines prove their mettle by moral, as much as physical courage. Both aspects can be seen in *The Russian Forest,* where the heroine, Polya Vikhrova, is parachuted behind the German lines in the Second World War, and falls into Nazi hands. As she prepares for interrogation, "she realized that she was nearing the critical, decisive moment, for which the whole of her previous life had been only a preparatory run-up—and then a selfless, headlong flight, whose height and duration determine a man's true value". This image might seem to recall the Vekshins, but there are important differences. For the Vekshins flying had been a continual challenge; for Polya it is a performance once and for all. The Vekshins prove nothing beyond their own vitality; once Polya's "true value" has been determined, the main business of her life has been settled.

This leads to a re-appraisal of the whole ideal of flying. Leonov now concentrates less on the creative leap involved, and more on the training and preparation of his parachutists and gliders. This in turn produces a new image, the mountains, "the eternal heights of human happiness" in *An Ordinary Man,* "glaciered heights" in *The Russian Forest,* the Pamir mountains in *The Golden Coach,* and the patient endeavour involved in climbing them. To the Salieris of the world all flight is an affront.

But what is the point of this flight-cum-mountaineering symbol? For now even its "title to happiness" is questioned. Polya says: "What do people aspire to? Some people say—to happiness; but that's not right in my opinion. You should aspire to purity. Happiness is just the chief reward, a sort of makeweight to purity". Sometimes happiness is actually suspect; in *The Golden Coach* Marka, having got her mother's permission to marry the man she loves, feels "ashamed of her happiness . . . as if she had committed the gravest crime of her life". In the same play a whole family is disparaged with the words: "They have

everything you could ask for, everything—except hardship and happiness". Leonov now rejects conventional happiness as contemptuously as he had done in *The Thief*: "Happiness is always bourgeois", but his standpoint has completely changed. He does so no longer in the name of human aspiration, but of moral purity.

These developments are only logical extensions of the tendencies revealed in *The Road to Ocean.* In the case of the "villains" the progression is equally clear. But, where Protoklitov had been merely doomed, the later villains are described as "corpses", "ghosts", or "returned from the dead", until in *The Golden Coach* the cast-list is headed by the name of Shchelkanov, who is characterized simply by a yawning blank, since no actor is required to play the part. Although Shchelkanov is heard knocking on the door, scurrying up and down the passages outside, he never actually materializes on stage. He is the logical culmination of Leonov's villains: his very existence is, as it were, questioned, while at the same time his character is brilliantly delineated. Yet, in another sense, Shchelkanov is also the final statement of that will to self-destruction that drives so many of Leonov's characters to their doom.

The villain of *The Russian Forest* is a similar type. Gratsiansky had been trapped into working as an informer for the Tsarist secret police; but instead of emigrating after the Revolution, he had elected, like Protoklitov, to stay in the Soviet Union. This only increases his difficulties—he is subjected to various pressures from anti-Soviet agents abroad, and finally, during the Second World War, blackmailed into spying for the Nazis.

Like Shchelkanov, Gratsiansky's life too is a void. His much-vaunted work in the archives proves to be the destruction of all record of his past before it can fall into the hands of the Soviet Secret Police. Even what there is of his life has to be annihilated. He has contributed nothing to the science of forestry except malicious attacks on the hero Vikhrov's life and work. Finally, when these attacks seem to have been crowned with success, and Vikhrov's disgrace is imminent, Gratsiansky intervenes on his behalf: "The destruction of his opponent would have involved annihilation for him too". Vikhrov's life allows Gratsiansky a vicarious existence and provides him with an identity; without it he would be revealed as nothing.

Is Gratsiansky then just another envious Salieri? The Tsarist chief of police foretells his later fate thus: "As you decline, so your blood will turn sour with unfruitfulness and envy of your neighbour, his health, his talents, his digestion, and even the torments of his spirit. . . . No doubt, in failing to make yourself a Prometheus, you will contrive to turn yourself into a vulture feeding on one; with the years, you will come to love this intense, almost creative delight in devouring his liver, drowning his voice, blackening his character, in the hope of resembling him at least in the colour of your face". Fated to survive for another thirty years after these words, Gratsiansky, even though no Prometheus, yet creates such an illusion of independent life that, as prophesied, it is "almost creative".

So Leonov's treatment of the subject of Mozart and Salieri comes full circle. Professor Vikhrov is [according to

Leonov, as quoted in F. Vlasov, *Poeziya zhizni* (1961)] "good, wise, industrious, well-educated, talented, but no more than that": it is Vikhrov who is the Salieri. For Shchelkanov and Gratsiansky, as once for the Vekshins and Gleb Protoklitov, merely to continue to be constitutes a fantastic challenge to non-existence: it is a trapeze-act that cannot but end in disaster. Even though he is only half-alive, perhaps even because of it, Gratsiansky's existence is nearer to a creation out of nothing ("almost creative") than Vikhrov's patient industry.

It is hardly possible to envisage any further development of the types of Vikhrov, Gratsiansky and Shchelkanov. They are all in their different ways final statements, and indeed in the twelve years since **The Russian Forest** Leonov has produced only one new work, the unworthy and unrepresentative **Mr. McKinley Runs Away.** Instead, he has devoted his energies to revising his most controversial works, notably **The Thief, The Snowstorm** and **The Golden Coach.**

Here too Leonov might seem to be conforming to one of the "traditions" of Soviet literature; but unlike other Soviet revisions, Leonov's are dictated less by political or ideological considerations than by the logic of the author's own development. In fact he began to produce these revisions at just the time when other Soviet classics were being re-issued in something like their original form.

The most extensive of these revisions is **The Thief,** of which the last third has been almost completely recomposed. But there is no need to read even that far to see that Leonov has now reversed his earlier verdict on Dmitry Vekshin. In 1927 Leonov had been at pains to justify his thief to the Communists; in the new version he shows that people guilty of this sort of antisocial behaviour are not welcome in Communist or any society. The image of Vekshin's "flight" has accordingly been replaced by that of his "fall". His once noble aspirations are now parodied and Leonov's own earlier enthusiasms unmercifully mocked. Veksin was once "a planet that had broken out of orbit"; that image has been replaced in the later version by the words: "a fragment of human spray, torn from the flame-wrapped crucible of humanity", a phrase equally suggestive of alienation, but now presenting a picture of blind senselessness, rather than of superhuman aspirations.

It is notable too that Leonov now devotes less attention to the brilliance of Tanya's *shtrabat* than to her training, "the mechanics of this unusually impressive turn"; it is now not the challenge to the void beneath, but "simply the number of difficulties overcome that created the value of her show". The idea of flight is finally compromised when the shallow young suitor in the new version of **The Golden Coach** talks of taking Marka to the Pamir mountains by aeroplane.

Moreover, by reducing the complexities of human creativity to "morality", and finally "purity", Leonov has killed the idea of tragedy too. Tragedy arises from the incompatibility of conflicting ideals; when there is only one criterion of conduct, then the tension arising from the clash of different systems of value disappears.

The drastic solution of judging all human conduct by the yardstick of "purity" might at least resolve the contradictions in Leonov's attitude to the Revolution. In his early work he had associated it with his tragic imagery: "The Revolution is first and foremost a flight", even though he had shirked the tragic consequences of the image in both **The Thief** and **The Road to Ocean.** Now, in **The Russian Forest,** the Revolution is defined as "not just a struggle for a fairer distribution of the good things of life, but, first and foremost, for human purity."

The contradiction may have been resolved superficially, but Leonov's work still aches with a sense of disenchantment. In the first version of **The Golden Coach,** Leonov had returned to the doubts expressed in **The Thief,** and answered them triumphantly: "We have passed the darkest tunnel now—only the last defile remains. Look, you can see the sea and the shore." In the revised version, however, this remark has been omitted. On the other hand, Maria Sergeyevna in the same play, realizing that her life has been ruined by her failure to marry the man she loved, and that it is too late now to repair the error, cries: "Then at least let our children, at least our children! . . .". But the unfinished sentence carries no assurance that the next generation will be any more fortunate or successful. Indeed, when, in the latest (1964) edition, the children do repair this error, they prove, ironically, only to have perpetuated it.

Leonov has made several attempts to suppress his fascination with the theme of flight; sometimes it was harnessed to the needs of society, as in Kurilov and Vikhrov; sometimes it was sublimated into acts of heroism or self-denial, as in the young heroines of the third period; sometimes, as in Protoklitov and Gratsiansky, it went underground; it seemed indestructible. Now, at last, in the revised versions of his profoundest works Leonov has finally settled his account with creativity. There is no tragedy now. Happiness, in whatever guise, seems further off than ever. Nothing remains but morality.

And Leonov himself? He is always ready to discuss the second version of **The Thief,** and is fond of recalling, in this connection, a conversation with his former friend and teacher, Maksim Gorky. The older man had raised the idea of an author actually meeting one of his own fictional heroes in real life: "Suppose he saw that he had overrated him and, out of sheer disillusionment, killed him." "Something like this", says Leonov, "happened to me. In this new version I kill Vekshin dead."

Salieri has killed Mozart again.

### Leonid Leonov with Roland Opitz   (interview date 1972)

SOURCE: An interview, translated by David Marks, in *Soviet Literature,* No. 10, 1975, pp. 174-82.

[*The following interview was conducted in East Germany in 1972 and later published in* Sinn und Form *and* Literaturnaya Rossia. *Below, Leonov discusses his writing process and the themes that interest him.*]

[*Opitz*]: *Leonid Maximovich, we should like to talk to you about your writing. First of all, may we ask you about the way your novels are conceived. What inspires you to write: experiences or images, ideas or observations?*

[Leonov]: I must say that I do not think in political or philosophical categories. I lived in the times I described, I saw a lot including those people who were to fall victim to the crucible of change, who could not withstand its searing heat.

This is probably how all creation is conceived, not only in the case of writers. With Copernicus and Galileo, was it a formula, or was it not rather a kind of premonition which told them that something was not quite clear? It was this intuition which led them on. The intellect can only attain what the soul already knows. With me it always begins with a painful, insuperable obsession. I am haunted by some images or by some combination of words, and I have a vague feeling that here is where I must search. It can be a snatch of a phrase overheard in a conversation, or a feeling of some threat, defencelessness or incredible sorrow, which like a fan sucks in everything which makes up the writer's life. One evening my wife shook me by the shoulder and shouted: "You've got a daughter, you know! Can't you at least look at her!" It seemed to me that this was happening far away on another planet. You must sacrifice everything: the love for your daughter, your last twenty kopecks, a good salary—everything!

*Did all of your novels have beginnings like these?*

Yes. Talking of **The Badgers,** it was prompted by an exclamation. Pantelei Chmelev, one of the main characters in the novel, when he first saw the moon through a telescope, cried: "I'm looking at the moon, and it's all pitted!" All his life he had thought that the surface of the moon was smooth. Maybe something does exist, something else, unseen, hidden from our eyes? The surface may be smooth, but maybe something is hidden behind it, so we must continue searching. I began my search, and the result was a novel. **Road to the Ocean** began with the song: "Travel to the ocean, you're fifty years old, soon it will be too late". It goes on: "You're sixty years old. . . ." This theme worked its way deep into my soul. Ocean is a fairy-tale whose secret we cannot penetrate, and at the same time it is the road to eternity.

*Is not* **Skutarevsky** *written under the influence of those times, the trials of counterrevolutionaries, the members of "Industrial Party", and so on?*

I was not very interested in trials, but I was interested in people and personalities. Take Petrygin, for instance, and also the invincible tenacity of man in flight. The theme of Arseni interested me less than might have seemed, though it does interest me still, and the Arseni theme appears again in my new novel.

*You once wrote that the idea of the novel was born under the impression of Brueghel's picture* The Hunters in the Snow . . .

Not all of **Skutarevsky** was conceived under the impression of the picture, but only the opening melody, the barely perceptible snatches of a melody, some quiet sounds.

*In any case the great artist of the era of the first victorious bourgeois revolution gave a creative impulse to the writer of the era of the first victorious proletarian revolution?*

I like Brueghel for the multi-plane quality of his paintings. A writer is not only judged on his material or on his plot, for any theme can be embodied in various ways. The milieu is also important. I can close a book and continue to wander through the places where the action unfolds, and you can do the same with Brueghel. I learnt much from him, including composition in two or three planes. Milieu is bound up not only with the theme and the plot, but also with colour. A page of a book should be seen not only as a text, but as a ladder which helps one to break into the writer's inner world. You can also wander through Brueghel's paintings, and as far as you go, even to the very horizon, you will meet interesting people. The pictures beckon you into the distance, and what immediately meets the eye is not the only interesting thing. I love Brueghel's paintings for their "literary" quality; you can read them like stories. I love Brueghel for the human smile you see in his pictures, for their mysterious aura. This is also why I like Hieronymus Bosch. In Brueghel's work algebra is subjected to harmony, just as in Dürer's. I like his Flandria, with its blend of the concrete and the apocalyptic. I like the musicality of *The Hunters in the Snow,* where the birds are as "organic" as a musical note. If you take away the birds you will ruin the whole picture. I find that I can "get inside" his picture and identify myself with one of the hunters: I feel close to these people. I do not like all of Brueghel's pictures: I like *The Tower of Babel* much less, but I very much like *The Carrying of the Cross,* and I am enraptured by the charming humour of *Children's Games* and the kind peasant hands in his other paintings. Brueghel's *The Parable of the Blind* figures in my short novel **Evgenia Ivanovna.** I did see a scene like that in real life, and I was greatly moved. For Brueghel it is very important how he embodies any idea he may have.

*Tell me about the process of creation in your own case.*

That is an old question. In the 20s on Gorky's initiative a special section was established in one of our magazines, devoted to world classic writers under the heading, "How They Worked". Today too young writers would find this interesting. A French critic once wrote of Flaubert that he would even get up at night in order to correct some inappropriate adjective. But another, more accurate adjective would give another characteristic to the hero, and so he had to change all the actions and all the behaviour of that person. That in turn affected the description of the milieu, the room and even the weather. There is nothing accidental in a work of art and there can be nothing superfluous. Flaubert would make more and more crossings-out until he had completely defaced the painstakingly-written text! And all because of one adjective! The writer's gift is a joy and a curse. After a long and intense search he may at last find the right detail, or draw the line which connects all twenty-five coordinates, but still he must cross everything out, change everything once more. It is simply hard labour.

I have never derived pleasure from my work. I have always wanted to get a book over with quickly, to get rid of it! If the author lets his characters out of his sight for even a single day they will devour him and everything around. They become ghosts which will torment their creator until he drives them into the book, from which they cannot escape. You might, for instance, write a five-word rejoinder, which for some reason you need to extend by two words. This extends the bounds of the narrative incredibly, and creates new possibilities. What does your character do at home, when no one can see him? What does he dream about in his sleep? What could he not confess, even to himself? Sometimes all this is not important for the novel itself, but just in case, for achieving an absolutely accurate diagnosis of the character. A hero, once created, is hard to deal with. He becomes an independent personality. He is unwilling to submit to my wishes, and puts up a stubborn fight. I might demand something of him, and though I know what he is thinking about, he will not say a word. You fight him like a real person. You live among images. In *The Thief* it is said that the whole world speaks only in the seven languages of the characters. Things can go to extremes. You remember Kurilov from *The Road to the Ocean*, the man who could quite easily have worked in the Politbureau? He was suffering from a very serious and extremely agonising illness: hypernephroma, a malignant tumour of the kidneys. You cannot imagine anything more painful than that pain. Recall Firsov, and what he said about the "naked man" and his hidden "sacred pimple". I undressed Kurilov, took everything from him, layer by layer, to see what sort of person he was, and he lives on without diminishing in stature.

Recently I suffered a kidney complaint and while I was in hospital I studied Kurilov's illness through and through. I sympathised so much that one day, as I was going upstairs, I had a real attack. The pain was unbearable and I could not move a muscle. Following long and fruitless investigations, the doctor asked me to show him exactly where the pain was. I showed him and he exclaimed: "My dear fellow, the kidneys are two fingers lower than that."

I had studied the illness thoroughly, and I felt it deeply, but its anatomical aspect quite escaped my attention.

*Does this merging with your characters go parallel with your work on composing a piece?*

Composition often presents many difficulties. After all, we live in very difficult times. There is so much information that we are overwhelmed. You have to be brief. It is sometimes difficult for me to read Walter Scott now. . . . It is as though you were slogging to America in a horse-drawn carriage, when you could get there and back twelve times in the same time. That is why sketches are vital to composition. For instance, *Russian Forest* has two lines: the Polya line from 1941 to 1942, and the Vikhrov line from 1886 to 1942. In order to describe these characters you could write as much as you like about each of them. Could Polya have gone to the Bolshoi Theatre, when she moved to Moscow? Of course she could: she had come from the country, thirsting for knowledge, and she had heard much about Moscow. But this would only be a dot, a cross along her line, while Vikhrov remains on the sidelines. On the other hand, could Vikhrov go grouse-shooting? That of course would be completely in keeping with his character,

but it would do nothing to develop Polya's image. The essence of the novel is Vikhrov's relationship with his daughter, and so I found points which bring the two into contact. Where do the twenty-five roubles come from? A suspicion grows in Polya's mind: maybe he really is a bad man? Then other elements are brought into the narrative: Knyshev, Gratsiansky and finally the whole of Russia.

This is where you need a sketch to see how to distribute your material. I distribute the material for a new book among "various tiers" of my mind, though at this stage I still do not know what is superfluous and should be discarded. Before you write something you should take a bird's eye view at the material, look at the theme as a whole.

*What sort of conditions do you write in?*

I prefer to work in the mornings, usually till three or half-past three. I am over seventy, and people of that age tire more quickly. I used to work evenings as well, as many as eleven hours a day. But subconsciously the work goes on the rest of the day and night as well. You always work in two or three shifts. The melting process must not be interrupted. Vital corrections come in one's sleep, like the rat-tat-tat of a submachine-gun. This night-work reminds one of the experiment they used to do in physics lessons at school: particles of some substance are sprinkled onto a plate, and a violin bow is drawn along its edge. The vibrations make the particles form up in a certain order, and lines appear.

It is necessary to revise and re-write. Formerly I was not so thorough about this, and I underestimated certain possibilities of the word, but now I have become capricious and demanding. Re-writing melts down the raw material, and only when you are utterly in control of the material can you obtain a product of high quality. A good poem is not written at one go, and the poet takes at least three days moulding it and remoulding it in his mind before it pours out onto the paper.

Most of all I love working to quiet music which forms a kind of sound screen. My table must be tidy, there must be no distractions. Chekhov and Dostoevsky wrote with their desks pushed to the wall. The fewer things in the room the better. Creation is emanation, self-irradiation. If one's study is cluttered, there is no room for irradiation.

I am afraid of my working-table, and this fear has always been with me. Every finished page is a spoiled page for it could have served to create a great work. After a time there is so much finished paper that moving house or going on holiday becomes a complicated problem: I can never find anything, and the thing I need is not in its usual place, and this makes work difficult. But if the article has been cast, and if it gives the inimitable ring you longed to hear, then you feel that you have created something, have achieved something, and that is your reward. When I finish a novel I am overcome by a feeling of terrible fatigue. I am utterly exhausted, devastated.

*Where do you find rest?*

In the garden. It allows me to switch off entirely. If I had not become a writer I would probably have become a gardener. I love my good, mute friends. You must look after them well, though, for they are silent when they are not happy. Three times a day I go up to every plant to see how it is growing. The cacti are especially interesting, entirely wrapped up in themselves, growing in the desert, they give off no moisture and they need nothing from their environment: they have their own world. I have been growing orchids and many other interesting plants for many years. Do you know why it is good to spend time with flower-growers? You go up to a complete stranger, two or three Latin names pass between you, and it is immediately clear who the man is. I constantly used to give my cacti to botanical gardens, to the Academy of Sciences and Moscow University. Remember how in **The Road to the Ocean** Protoklitov gives his collection of clocks away? He sat the precedent and I simply followed his example. In the same way Firsov acquired a checked overcoat in **The Thief,** and I bought one myself much later.

---

**I am carried away by powerful passions, by situations when the passions reach their fieriest heat, their culmination, and everything else ceases to have any meaning. This is what one should write about, and it is what I have always tried to write about.**

**—Leonid Leonov**

---

*What is particularly important for you when writing?*

Do you remember the story of the Eastern tsaritsa whose husband told her after a feast that she had been drinking from the gilded skull of her own father? This woman thought up her revenge. She changed beds with her servant girl, and when the girl's lover came in the night, the tsaritsa welcomed him with caresses. Later she turned on the light, and the man grew afraid, for the price of loving the tsaritsa was death. She, however, persuaded him to save his life by killing the tsar.

I am carried away by powerful passions, by situations when the passions reach their fieriest heat, their culmination, and everything else ceases to have any meaning. Then the gnashing of teeth can be heard, and an incredible tension arises in relations between people. This is what one should write about, and it is what I have always tried to write about. A book like that will never leave a reader indifferent.

I do not like when everything is too direct, though. The actor Yershov was guilty of this sin in the Art Theatre's production of my play **Untilovsk** in 1928. Buslov's rebellion, expressed in his monologue, constitutes the very core of the play but still it should not be shouted. The actor should first speak very loudly, and then he should make an abrupt shift to a different tone where he speaks quietly. That has a much stronger effect. Untilovsk (a name composed of the English "until", the Russian word "*util*",

which means "garbage", and which should remind one of "reptiles") is a mire which can suck a man down. It is something like the shelf by a Russian stove, warm and cosy. Then there is the winsome Vaska, and Buslov has forgotten the lessons he should be giving, and the Komsomol choir. This is the situation he must get out of.

After the war we wanted to create a new theatre, a theatre in which the inner world of the hero would find a very accurate reflection. The actor must convey every psychological nuance very correctly. Unfortunately one of the main participants in this theatre died. He was the actor and director Mikhoels. He was a good actor and would have risen to this task. He should have played Rakhuma in **The Golden Carriage,** a part that needs to be played subtly and tactfully to make a stronger impact. It would be absolutely wrong to cast a jolly fat man for Rakhuma, for he is living in the hard postwar years, and things are going badly for him.

*In your opinion, can literary studies help to reveal the intrinsic qualities of your work?*

I always feel a bit uncomfortable with people who spend whole months and even years studying my books. Of course this work can be very meaningful if it does not become mere re-telling, but sooner or later the reader would understand the sense of the book without its help. Literary scholars would do better to write about the main themes in my books. Take **"Buryga,"** one of my first short stories. In that story you can really find everything that moves me, everything that I only developed later: the forest, the circus, love of one's country, burning sadness, and the legend-like and mysterious powers of the forest. The poet is infected by his main theme and thereafter constantly returns to it.

*Does that apply to the novel you are now working on?*

It will contain many things. I do not like talking about unfinished work. You arouse curiosity, and it can turn out that you disappoint expectations. A writer should not tease his public, rather he should sit at his desk and work to produce a good book for them. But still, I will say that I have really been writing this book all my life. My first thoughts on it went into the weak, utterly bad story which I wrote in 1922. That story was not published, and I will never publish it. Going further back, I wrote a poem when I was seventeen, in which the autumnal tune rings out. It is saturated with the mood of homelessness and the motif of compassion. My first poems were generally bad, but I want to say in immodest justification that big trees bear fruit late. This motif appeared in various forms again and again, blended with quite different melodies, and rings out here and there in my books. I began intensive work on the new book in 1948 and 1949, and after writing **Russian Forest** and revising **The Thief,** I came back to these themes again and again, but I had to break off work for reasons of a personal nature. I came back to this book for the fourth time, and now I am working on it with utmost concentration and determination. If a theme can grip a person to such an extent, then there must be something real behind it. But the book will not be finished in the near future.

*What is the theme of the book?*

I am interested in the limits of the human mind's potential. I do not miss one article on astrophysics. We probably still have not true ideas of the laws of nature. Sometimes I feel that nature is like the Buddhist lama who gazes at people with indifference. Even when a beautiful girl walks along he just looks past her and preserves his imperturbability. Kurilov understood much as he was dying. Once I was visited by a student who wanted to write on the theme of death in Leonov. Well, of course, that is nonsense and stupidity, but I am concerned as to whether much is not revealed to a man at the moment of his death. I would like to create my own model of the world, but I do not know if I will be successful. My new book will also feature Katya, the little girl of whom Uvadyev, a character of my novel *The Sot,* dreams. Over the years Katya has grown up and has come to understand many things. When you picture for yourself the world of tomorrow you must first of all think of human personality. You must look forward and try and solve some of our problems, as if from the future. I am interested in democracy. It only makes sense if you awaken initiative in many people, and this is the basic problem of democracy. As the world already has three and a half thousand million people, and this number is growing fast, not every person can develop his abilities as he would like to. Everybody needs a minimum of well-being, and if someone wants his personality to blossom further: well, take a piece of paper, sit down and develop, express yourself, and then we will read what you have written.

We live in a critical period of history. The fate of the whole world depends upon decisions which people will make in the coming years, and that is why the writer's word is acquiring more weight. I have always striven to participate in unfolding the future for the whole of mankind, or, to put it more simply, I see myself as an interpreter standing between life and the reader. I take hold of phenomena which are taking place daily before the reader's eyes, but which he cannot always realise or assimilate, and I deduce a formula which I offer for him to work on.

## Marc Slonim   (essay date 1977)

SOURCE: "Leonid Leonov: The Psychological Novelist," in *Soviet Russian Literature: Writers and Problems 1917-1977,* second revised edition, Oxford University Press, 1977, pp. 198-212.

[*A Russian-born American critic and educator, Slonim wrote extensively on Russian literature. In the following excerpt, he provides an overview of Leonov's works, focusing on psychological themes, and argues that Leonov placated official Soviet tastes to the detriment of his talents.*]

In introducing Leonov to the Soviet readers of the 'twenties Gorky called him a disciple of Dostoevsky. What made him say this was not any similarity of ideas— Leonov did not share the political and religious opinions of the master—but a similarity of approach to character and to plot structure. Like Dostoevsky, the young Soviet writer possessed an almost morbid curiosity about the complexities of mind and flesh, a bent for exploration of the unconscious, and an unfailing interest in hidden moti-vation and subterranean drives. When critics blamed Leonov for not showing his heroes at work, he answered that he preferred to take them out of their daily environment and to leave them alone, facing their own thoughts and conscience. "It is difficult to remain in solitude and have oneself as the interlocutor, in such a situation we discover what a man is worth." If Leonov were left alone, in creative solitude, he would have undoubtedly followed the "Dostoevskian" line. Yet this genuine and natural psychological bent was curbed and at times distorted by external pressure. Too often he was compelled to yield to the social demands of his times, and many of his artistic failures or lengthy periods of silence were due to his incapacity to solve a conflict within himself or to rise above historical contingencies. Whenever he dealt with tragic characters in crisis, describing twisted minds and depraved passions in a highly romantic, ornamental, and symbolic prose, he attained literary fulfillment; but as soon as he attempted to pursue the weary road of didactic realism and to produce stereotyped happy endings and socially useful "new heroes," he became redundant and unconvincing. This rift undermined his work and prevented him from realizing fully the possibilities of his unusual literary talent. In fact, he remains, even with all his defects, one of the most original Soviet writers. Fortunately, the Moscow critics do not try to pretend that he is a true socialist realist: his work is outside the official literary encampment.

Leonid Leonov, born in Moscow in 1899, the son of a journalist who was of peasant stock, graduated from a *gymnasium,* and then served in the Red Army. In 1922 he settled in the capital and published his first tales: **"The Wooden Queen,"** obviously suggested by the Serapion Brethren with whom Leonov had a great deal in common; **"Tuatamur,"** written in a rhythmic poetic prose, the story of a Tartar khan who suffers from unrequited love for the beautiful Ytmar; and **Kovyakin's Diary,** the description of a sleepy provincial town, where the Revolution has degenerated into a caricature of itself because it has to deal with "smug citizens" and "dead souls." The striking stylistic qualities of these tales attracted general attention. They certainly indicated that their young author owed a great deal to Leskov, Remizov, Bely, and Zamyatin, but they showed too, that he had his own approach to literary material. The opulence of his language, which was studded with flowery epithets and involved metaphors, was matched by the emotional complexity of his chief characters.

An opponent of naturalism and of the novels of manners or environment, Leonov was mainly interested in man's doubts and sufferings. He was attracted by problems which he regarded as the natural outgrowth of the individual's intricate relationship with the universe and society. In *The End of the Little Man* (1925), Leonov's first important short novel, he raised the same problem that Zamyatin had dealt with in "The Cave." His scholarly hero, Likharev, who is about to complete a study on Mesozoic fossils, is so disturbed by the bloodshed and horrors of the revolutionary upheaval that life loses all its meaning for him. A catastrophe has smashed his old world to smithereens and nobody needs books or scientific research any longer: all that people actually care for is food and fuel.

A morsel of bread and a stick of wood are of far greater importance than culture; a holocaust leaves little room for illusions. People of Likharev's own class are no better than the "new barbarians," and all this had become clear "from that very day when the steel wing of a tremendous earthquake had swept over Russia, and somebody armed with a whip had hustled her out of darkness into a new, flame-breathing space where hundreds of thunderous tubas were bellowing like steers—whereupon the earth had begun to spin around the sun twelve times faster than before." Likharev knows that "the soul is frozen just like the water in the pipes," there is no salvation for a little man, crushed by the Revolution, and he burns his manuscript. This short novel belongs to a whole series of stories devoted to the collapse of the old intelligentsia and its culture.

The cruelty and insensibility of peasants who beat a horse thief to death is the theme of another, earlier work by Leonov, *The Breakthrough of Petushikhino* (1923), written in a lyrical mood; here, however, the grim picture of evil in man is counterbalanced by the image of Alyosha, a sickly lad who feels the spell of spring as a revelation of God and who longs for justice and kindliness.

From this preparatory stage in his career, Leonov turned to what was his true literary vocation—long, epic-like narratives built on several levels and including various social strata. Gorky believed that Leonov proceeded "by jumps" and that he leaped from the tale to the novel, but such a statement seems very debatable: Leonov's development as a writer was organic, and from the beginning he was much more of a novelist than a short-story-teller.

Leonov's *The Badgers* (1925) was as typical of the revival of the traditional novel form as Fedin's *Cities and Years* which came just before it. In this lengthy book Leonov deals with two Russias: the pre-revolutionary Russia of bearded Moscow merchants who rule with an iron hand over their families and employees, and the new Russia of young rebels growing up unsuspected in the merchants' very homes and warehouses. The beautiful and willful Nastya is in revolt against her rich family, and the brothers Senya and Pasha, two peasant lads painfully making their living in Nastya's father's firm are ready to blow up the entire old order. Pasha joins the revolutionaries, and Senya, desperately in love with the unattainable Nastya, goes through many adventures during the war and the Revolution before winning her. Deeply rooted in his rural background, he finally becomes the leader of rebellious peasants who refuse to yield to Communist rule. They hide in the forests like badgers, and it is Pasha who commands the troops sent by Lenin's government to quell the uprising. The village represents the anarchical, instinctual element, and is contrasted with the city, which is hated by the peasants and is symbolized by the Communist Party. "We are millions," says Senya, "we give bread and blood and strength . . . we are the soil, and we are going to destroy the city." Thus the conflict of the two Russias shown in the first part of the novel acquires an entirely different meaning in the second part in which the peasants are shown as enemies of urban and rational Communism. Although Leonov's interpretation of the Revolution seems close to that of Pilnyak, it is offered more as a hypothesis than as an affirmation, and the author of *The Badgers* apparently wonders about the philosophical implications of the issue he has raised.

**"Legend of Kalafaat,"** a story-within-a-story in *The Badgers,* caused a good deal of distress to Soviet censors and was eliminated from further editions of the novel. In it Leonov describes a Tsar of peasant folklore who wants to have all the stars filed away, to issue passports to all the beasts of the forest, and to register every herb. When he finally carries out his project, "everything became sad. The groves turned silent, clearings became overgrown with underbrush . . . All nature was completely messed up. Even the bear became sickly: what with the passport and all, he did not know any more whether he was a beast or a man." Next Kalafaat decides to build a tower as high as the skies, and it takes him twenty years to do it: "twenty years to him, twenty centuries to us." When the tower is completed Kalafaat begins climbing to its top. He climbs for five years, but when he finally reaches the flat roof and looks around him, he lets out a howl worse than any beast's. While he has been ascending the inner stairs, the tower, under his enormous weight, has been gradually sinking into the ground: for every step he has been taking upward, the tower has been sinking the same distance underground; despite all his trouble he has not gotten an inch above the earth's level. Moreover, during his futile ascent nature has done away with all his seals and passports—and the birds and beasts are enjoying themselves again in the free forests and blooming fields.

The **"Legend of Kalafaat"** has often been cited as a symbolic interpretation of the peasant's attitude toward the building of Communism. It has, however, a wider significance: Kalafaat personifies the principle of blind bureaucracy, of a mechanical order that challenges nature and kills life and joy. Like Leo Tolstoy, the author of *The Badgers* hailed simplicity, naturalness, and conformity to organic laws as the highest moral virtues—without, however, sharing either Tolstoy's religious beliefs or his moral dogmatism. In any case, *The Badgers* did not try to formulate a message and its value, which is unquestionable despite its shaky structure and the strange coincidences in the plot development, lay in the author's gift for presenting in an impressive, dynamic, and yet poetic manner the conflict of generations, classes, mentalities, and temperaments. The psychological characterization of its heroes lacked, perhaps, the depth we will find in Leonov's later novels, but he did succeed in populating his vast narrative with many different kinds of human beings and in giving a broad picture of Russia and its basic problems.

Leonov's next and perhaps his best novel, *The Thief* (1927), was a great step forward from *The Badgers.* It deals with modern Moscow and with a very special section of life there, and its tone and structure are obviously inspired by Dostoevsky. Here the characters and events are depicted under a double aspect: through the author's exposition and through the eyes of Firsov, a writer, whose diary carries notes for a novel about the same characters and the same environment. This device of a "mirror gallery" (which André Gide used so successfully in *The Counterfeiters*) makes the structure of *The Thief* somewhat sophisticated. No less intricate is its plot, which unfolds a startling panorama of the Moscow underworld under the NEP. [In a footnote, Slonim adds: "The theme of the criminal underworld appears very seldom in Soviet literature; between 1930 and 1955 it was banned from fiction, and the reader of Soviet novels had the impression that crooks, thieves, and murderers simply did not exist in Soviet society."] Mitya Vekshin, the central figure of the novel, a former commissar in the Red Army and a Party member, is a kind of Soviet Raskolnikov. A romantic rebel, disappointed with the "retreat" of the NEP, he becomes a thief and the leader of a gang of criminals. He challenges law and society but is tormented by remorse and persecuted by the furies: once he had killed in cold blood a captive White officer, and a sense of guilt gnaws him still. The "anti-heroic" NEP adds to his anxiety and feeling of frustration. Temperamentally he is an individualist, politically an idealist disgusted with surrounding reality. His pals are the grim, taciturn bandit Ageika, haunted by his own isolation; Manyukhin, a former landowner who earns his living by telling off-color stories in dives and taverns and behaves like Marmeladov, his literary predecessor; and the heartless Chikilyov, a cynical nihilist who distrusts and loathes his fellow men, striking the pose of the Dostoevsky's "Notes from the Underground." Chikilyov says that "thought is the source of suffering, and whoever will destroy it will be eternally honored by mankind." Mitya is also surrounded by "infernal" women, such as the proud Masha Dolomanova, whose love is a torture and a delight, and by prostitutes and gangsters. They all move in a feverish twilight of danger and passion; they spend hours in morbid introspection while drinking in clandestine night clubs; they humiliate, hurt, and offend one another. Masha, who both adores and fights Mitya, makes him alternatively miserable and ecstatic, without ever arriving at the fulfillment of her love. "The best fictions of old mankind are God and Love," says Leonov, and all his protagonists search for truth and warmth as a possible escape from their impasse. They are all plagued by pain, anguish, and struggle, and they know that such is their human lot. The Communist Matvey tells his sister Zina, who is also in love with Mitya, that some day man will know and measure everything, and that great happiness will result from such rational awareness. But the voluptuous Zina laughs at him: "Happiness without torment? Made on an assembly line? Impossible!" The writer Firsov does not wish to depict socially useful types and exclaims: "But what if I am interested in the hidden roots of man? . . . There is no other task as poignant as to scrutinize man face to face."

The pathologically warped characters and the dramatic plot of **The Thief,** which depends on murder, suicidal drives, and the clash of passions, remind us quite obviously of Dostoevsky. The moral denouement of the novel is, however, not a religious one. Mitya is purged by suffering, "the fire of his soul burns him clean," but his recovery and his awakening to new life are due to social causes: the rebel promises to become a citizen and accepts the pattern of the Soviet community. The Communist critics felt that this ending was not strong enough, and that the individualist Mitya had not passed through an "ideological conversion." They also reproached Leonov for the morbid atmosphere of his novel and the "decadent psychological introspection." They missed the fact that **The Thief,** despite all its melodramatic devices, has a variety of excellently drawn characters, and is striking in its use of different levels of the Russian language, including the slang and vernacular of various social groups. [In a footnote, Slonim adds: "Leonov, unfortunately, took these criticisms quite seriously, and began to rewrite **The Thief.** He published in 1959 a new, expurgated version of the novel in which the pernicious effects of individualism are clearly condemned."]

It was obvious from whatever Leonov wrote in the 'twenties that his fiction was rooted in moral and psychological problems, and in the late 'twenties, when the first Five-Year Plan demanded new sacrifices, he began wondering whether the requirements of the collective state could be reconciled with the aspirations of the individual. In his remarkable **Stories About Unusual Muzhiks** (1930) the basic conflict is impressively illustrated. Ivan, a deaf-mute carpenter who has never known success or love, attends a village meeting that is to decide the fate of a blacksmith, who has been caught stealing horses. There is but one blacksmith in the village, whereas there are several carpenters. The peasants stare at Ivan: everybody knows that he is innocent. Yet crime calls for punishment—the equilibrium between the law and transgression must be restored, and someone has to pay. Ivan is chosen as an expiatory victim, and the villagers embrace him and promise him a good burial as he is led off to his death. The community has demanded and obtained human blood to furnish a deterrent and to maintain justice.

The same contradiction between the blind rules of society and the personal life of an individual is brought out in other works by Leonov, but he gradually began to accept Communism as the supreme judge and settler of such conflicts. Like many fellow-travelers of the period he suppressed his own doubts and hesitations. The industrialization of the country supplied him with a new argument in favor of the rulers who, regardless of the cost in lives and energy, were accomplishing an historic mission in a backward nation. It was not the social command but a sincere feeling for the revolutionary transformation of the country and his desire "to bring literature closer to life" that determined the subject matter of Leonov's next novel.

**Sot'** or **Soviet River** (1930), published with a foreword by Gorky that placed Leonov very high among contemporary writers and declared that his words "shine," was inspired by the Five-Year Plan. The action takes place in millennial forests, in forlorn hamlets, in the chapels of the Old Believers (Schismatics), in medieval monasteries, and on the shores of rivers in a remote Northern province. Ignorant *muzhiks* and superstitious monks still talk of the advent of the Antichrist and listen to seventeenth-century chants, but new men and machines invade the peace of this wilderness. Moscow needs cellulose and paper; the plan calls for an erection of paper mills on the banks of Sot'. Thousands of workmen and technicians shatter the stillness of the forests; a dam is built to harness the turbulent waters of the river. A deadly struggle ensues between the pioneers led by the chief engineer, the Communist

Uvadiev, and the monks and peasants, stirred up by Vissarion, a former Imperial army officer. Like Senya of ***The Badgers,*** Vissarion hates the city. Man has no need of this crazy realm of machines, huge towns, and artificiality, he declares. Only people who are living in the simplicity of a communion with nature are obeying the Divine Law. To save mankind from the iron age of impiety, corruption, and technology, a new invasion of barbarians is needed: Vissarion has fantastic dreams of Mongolian hordes that will sweep over Europe and Russia in a purifying torrent of blood and fire; Communism will perish along with the old and false civilization, and luxuriant crops of grain will grow freely upon its ruins. But Vissarion's phantasmagoria amounts to no more than impotent raving, and he dies an ignominious death.

The anti-Soviet conspiracy proves less dangerous than the enmity of the elements. Symbolically, they both stem from the same source—from the blind irrational forces man must control within and outside himself. The builders have to conquer land and river inch by inch, and only through perseverance do they finally overcome the fury of the river and the insidiousness of the people's ignorance and reaction. The theme of the "conquest of nature" is parallel to that of the conquest of man; and the opposition of the past to the present takes more dramatic form than the same confrontation in ***The Badgers.*** It is curious that in all these conflicts the writer seems ambivalent: he is nostalgic toward the past and has a great love of nature; his sympathy, however, goes finally to the rational man who imposes his will over storms and floods and destructive passions. In ***The Thief*** the elemental rages throughout the novel. In ***Soviet River*** it explodes but is curbed, despite almost insuperable difficulties. Uvadiev, the leader of the workmen, the puritanical, almost inhuman hero, becomes an abstract symbol: if Leonov wanted to embody the ideal Communist in this "iron-like" character, he most certainly created a misfit.

---

**Leonov interpreted Communism idealistically, not in terms of a doctrine derived from Marx and Lenin but as one of the variations of radical humanism.**

—*Marc Slonim*

---

Stylistically, ***Soviet River*** is an accomplishment: the combination of archaisms, of regional idiom, of neologisms originated under the Soviets, and literary stylization forms an attractively bright verbal pattern. Some secondary characters, such as the engineer Burago, an intellectual planner, or Renne, Suzanna's old-fashioned father, or Uvadiev's powerful mother, who is reminiscent of Gorky's creations, are extremely vivid and aesthetically successful. ***Soviet River,*** one of the best books about the Five-Year Plan, fortunately lacked the blaring rhetoric which spoiled most of the works devoted to the same subject in the 'thirties; it represented, however, Leonov's official salute to

Communism. Like most of the intellectuals of the same decade, he interpreted Communism idealistically, not in terms of a doctrine derived from Marx and Lenin but as one of the variations of radical humanism. He also insisted that the chief motivation of the intellectuals who were giving their support to the regime was their desire to "serve the people," that dream of the Populists, which has always been one of the most powerful determinants in the development of the Russian intelligentsia.

Leonov's effort to make a complete adjustment to the new order is clearest in ***Skutarevsky*** (1932), a novel about an old scientist whose cautious, almost hostile, attitude toward the Communists gradually changes into a friendly acceptance of their aims and methods. His son Arseny, however, calls the Five-Year Plan "enthusiastic hysterics," gets involved in a counter-revolutionary conspiracy, and kills himself. The clash between father and son symbolizes, in an inverted fashion, the opposition of two eras and two mentalities. Their strange relationship, Skutarevsky's domestic complications, his love for a young girl whose embrace he refuses, leaving her to a younger rival, and the suggestions of sabotage and imperialistic intrigue make the plot involved and fairly melodramatic, as is often the case with Leonov. It is obvious that the campaign against non-Party technicians and the trials of 1930-31 were to a certain extent reflected in the novel, but Leonov came to the defense of the intelligentsia and affirmed its loyalty; he could not, however, refrain from depicting imaginary or real conspiracies, and accepting the sensational revelations of enemy activities which, according to the claims of the Security Police, were taking place all over the country. But the character of Skutarevsky and the painful process which led him to a political conversion were treated with intelligence and subtlety. As for the new Communist man (this time called Cherimov), Leonov again failed to make him come alive.

More complex but less convincing is ***Way to the Ocean*** (1935), a novel with excellent passages that fails to become an artistic whole. It was certainly Leonov's most ambitious attempt to create a truly Communist work, but he succeeded only in the parts devoted to the pre-revolutionary past and in the portrayals of negative characters; the sketches of virtuous heroes and the panorama of beautiful times to come seem strained and pompous. The composition of ***Way to the Ocean*** is very intricate: it is built on several levels, with the chronological sequence of the narrative being constantly interrupted by flashbacks or predictions of the future. It is quite possible that Leonov, conscious of the prominent place occupied by the problem of time in modern European literature (especially in works by Proust, Joyce, Mann, Virginia Woolf, Faulkner, and others) wished to introduce it into Soviet literature. Unfortunately, he lacked a firm point of view, and his treatment of time often becomes obscure and blurred.

The plot of the novel centers around Kurilov, an old Communist and director of a local Siberian railroad, who is very ill; the approach of death makes him think of the years gone by and of the people he has known—of Liza, whom he loves and who torments and illuminates his last days; of her husband, the surgeon Ilya Protoklitov, whose father, a Tsarist official, had sentenced Kurilov to prison and exile; of Ilya's brother Gleb, a former White officer who had wormed his way into the Party. The unmasking of Gleb and of a conspiracy against the regime and the intricate relationships of Kurilov, Liza, and the surgeon form the core of the story and are described in the present tense. The reminiscences of all the protagonists make up the second level of narrative, and the third level gives a vision of the future (in three separate chapters) along with predictions of war (apparently with Japan), of a revolution in China, of new formidable weapons of destruction, of a Communist army led by a Negro commander. There is a description of Ocean, the world capital somewhere near Shanghai, and a resplendent picture of Communism, toward which all the hopes and achievements of mankind will converge, even as all the streams and rivers find their way into the mighty ocean. Above all individual destinies will shine the bright star of collective action and "service for the people."

Despite all his utopian excursions into the future, which merge with Kurilov's dreams, Leonov failed to make Kurilov a new hero: he portrayed him as a nice ordinary fellow, a romantic, who looked no different than other, non-Communist personages. The grandiloquence of style and the overdramatization of plot added to the heaviness of this artificial work. Critics, writers, and readers received it without enthusiasm, and this lack of success affected Leonov so deeply that he decided to stop writing novels and, in fact, his next one did not appear until eighteen years later, in 1953. Between 1936 and 1946 he turned to the stage and wrote twelve plays. Eleven of them were produced by leading Moscow theaters but the twelfth, *The Blizzard,* was killed by the censors and not released for publication until 1963.

Leonov's ideological and psychological complexity made his plays stand out among Soviet productions, but he often was too eager to fulfill the political requirements of his times. His best play was *Untilovsk,* an exposé of provincial evil and boredom, staged in 1928 by the Moscow Art Theater; one of its main characters Chervakov, reminiscent of Chikilyov of *The Thief,* is a cynical philosopher who laughs at idealists and liberals, and who maintains that "everything on earth has the hole in which it is destined to disappear, just as man is gulped up by his grave." Critics reproached Leonov for having made Chervakov more interesting than his life-affirming opponents.

A characteristic dramatic work of Leonov is *The Orchards of Polovchansk* (1936). In its first version the playwright opposed Makkaveyev, head of a large family, the creator of gardens, and a man of purposeful and fruitful life, with Pylyayev, a superfluous man. With its lyrical and symbolic scenes, the drama had a consistency of mood and tone. But after the purges and trials Leonov wrote a second version in which he made Pylyayev a secret foreign agent, and the whole play became a melodrama centered around the discovery of subversion. *The Wolf* (1938) was simply a potboiler about saboteurs, cunning villains, and noble police investigators. *An Ordinary Fellow* (1940), a comedy, is slightly better and does not show that eagerness to please the masters of the day which Leonov had

displayed in other dramatic works. During the war he overcame his political servility in two outstanding plays, *Invasion* (1942) and *Lyonushka* (1943). The first is a study of an embittered character who changes under the pressure of circumstances; Fyodor Talanov had attempted to kill his wife and was sentenced to hard labor. He is released and returns home just when the Germans overrun his native town. The disappointed and lonely outcast, an enemy of the Soviet regime, emerges reluctantly from his shell and avoids contact with other people. Their sufferings, however, lead him finally to forget his own troubles; he helps the victims of the Nazis and becomes active in the underground resistance. When caught he pretends to be Kolesnikov, the leader of Red guerrillas whom the Germans are vainly trying to arrest. In order to protect Kolesnikov and his men, Talanov is ready to die. His mother understands what he is attempting to do and identifies him as Kolesnikov, thus accepting and blessing his sacrifice. He is hanged by the invaders, and dies at peace with his conscience. This is his redemption: the "lonely wolf," as he called himself, has given his life for the people to whom he belongs, for the country he cannot help loving. The gradual "conversion" of Talanov and the dramatic incidents of *Invasion* make it one of the most breathtaking of war plays. Some theaters, however, tried to "correct" Leonov and gave undue prominence to Kolesnikov, in order to stress the role of the Party in the ultimate victory over the Germans.

In *Invasion* the hero's parents, the kind and rather Chekhovian doctor Talanov and his forthright wife Ann, are presented as "average Russians." The interest in national traits is even more distinct in *Lyonushka,* a symbolic drama, "a popular tragedy," as the author calls it. Lyonushka, a peasant girl, is in love with a badly burnt flier whom the guerrillas are hiding in their forest camp. Lyonushka wants to bring hope and joy to the dying man, and stages songs and dances for him. The strange scenes of Russian revelry serve as a symbolic background to the flier's agony. The play has an intricate psychological design and a remarkable merging of tragic elements, folklore motifs, patriotic emotions, and allegorical allusions. Theatrical directors were afraid of it: it was obviously not a realistic drama, and it contained dangerous formalistic devices and ideological deviations. From the literary standpoint it is a very interesting work even though it can be accused of rhetoric and intellectualism. Less intellectual, but also intricate and definitely symbolic is Leonov's short war novel, *The Taking of Velikoshumsk* (1944), in which the themes of war and defense of the motherland are treated in elaborate prose. It tells the story of an old battered tank and its crew, whose members, despite individual differences, represent the basic unity of Russia. Realistic details of combat mingle with the image of the tank as a living person; characterizations of generals and soldiers are as valid psychologically as they are symbolically, and the whole plot, although perfectly believable in terms of military operations, has a hidden philosophical meaning—again dealing with the essence and fate of Russia, its traditions and its aspirations. The extent to which this problem preoccupied Leonov is shown by *The Russian Forest,* a huge novel published in 1953. Here again Leonov resorts to multi-level composition. The story deals with the deforestation of Russia and the struggle between Vikhrov, an honest and patriotic scientist for whom the forest is the source of life, and his enemy and rival, Gratsiansky, an embodiment of deception and the death instinct. The exploration in depth of this villain is accompanied by the confrontation of past and present in the light of Russia's historical heritage, by the opposition of the rational and the elemental, of self-centered egotism and creative collectivism—in short by all Leonov's favorite themes. The treatment of time is much more skilled than it was in the **Way to the Ocean** and Leonov deals now only with the past and the present, making but vague hints about the future.

The beginning of the novel is perhaps its best part: it depicts the arrival in Moscow of Polya, Vikhrov's daughter, her wanderings through the streets, and her youthful intoxication with whatever she sees. She is so thrilled and elated that she sends a telegram of welcome to herself. The charm and freshness of Polya and her wondrous impressions are rendered with a poetic sweep reminiscent of early Leonov. It is not, however, completely devoid of the author's customary ambivalence. Polya makes a pledge to Lenin in the Mausoleum to be a good girl and a good Communist; the scene resembles the taking of a religious vow by a novice in front of the holy relics of a Christian saint. Later Polya is swept into the whirlwind of war and behaves like a heroine when imprisoned by the Germans behind their lines. But neither the description of war nor the treatise on forest preservation, including a thirty-two-page lecture by Vikhrov on the subject, hold the attention of the reader. Dramatic episodes from Gratsiansky's shady past or from Vikhrov's virtuous youth hardly relieve the monotony of an overwritten work in which villains are more interesting than the characters in whom the author wishes to incarnate the high qualities of the new Communist man. Here again, Leonov, eager to march in step with the "army of Communism," tries to be what he is not. It does not suit him to make sermons and glorify dogmas. This is confirmed again by his short novel **Evgenya Ivanovna** (1965), a moralizing and pseudo-patriotic tale about the fate of a Russian *émigré* woman.

Leonov's work is long-winded and heavy; verbal twists, bizarre metaphors, poetic embellishments render his style baroque, at times obscure and often artificial. There is an overabundance in his multi-level compositions. His novels resemble old mansions with dark passages, recesses, winding staircases, corridors, wings, and annexes. What saves these voluminous productions from being overwhelmed by their own weight is Leonov's dramatic sense and his psychological insight. He develops his themes like musical motifs, and he is deeply interested in moral and philosophical problems. Above everything else, he is attracted by man's complexity, which is paralleled in his work by linguistic complexity. He likes a rich, inflated, rhetorical, literary idiom just as he likes to portray human beings with emotional deviations, ranging from fads to neuroses and psychoses. Leonov is preoccupied with the ambivalence of human nature, by the drawing power of evil and the need for supreme justice, by our desire for sublimation and the urge for self-abasement. His work is perhaps the only significant counterpart in Soviet literature to the Western

psychological fiction of the 1930's. The question remains, however, whether Leonov did use his talent to full capacity; it is probable that his deliberate endeavors to conform limited his freedom of self-expression and curbed his natural development.

## George Harjan    (essay date 1979)

SOURCE: "Leonov's Early Prose" and "Re-evaluation of Values: Second Version of *The Thief* and *Evgenia Ivanovna*," in *Leonid Leonov: A Critical Study,* Arowhena Publishing Co., 1979, pp. 11-25, 181-90.

[*An educator, novelist, and critic, Harjan has written extensively on Russian literature. In the following excerpt, he surveys Leonov's early stories, discusses differences between the first and second versions of* The Thief, *and remarks on* Evgenia Ivanovna.]

Leonov stated that his entrance into literature began with a story called **"Buryga"** ("Buryga"); most editions of his collected works open with this short story. A great deal of effort has been spent in interpreting this fairytale-like miniature. Many scholars speaking about Leonov's early works pointed to his dependence on E. T. A. Hoffmann (1776-1822) and Hans Christian Andersen (1805-1875), but few were specific about **"Buryga."** True, Buryga faintly resembles Hoffmann's "Klein Zaches, genannt Zinnober," but it is not the borrowing of the plot, the literary dependence on the celebrated German romanticist that matters here. **"Buryga"** is a typical Russian story with a Russian setting and, most important, with rich, colorful, racy Russian language. And yet, the writer almost grotesquely begins his story in a manner of the Russian fairytale but places it, curiously enough, in Spain. "There lived in Spain a Spanish count and he had two sons: Rudolf and Vania [diminutive of Ivan]."

This Spanish count has nothing in common with Spain and we think that Leonov parodies some early Russian romantic stories. Buryga is a small, imp-like forest dweller, who blends well with his Russian environment, with various traditional fairytale-like forest ambiences. The narrative is kept in a *skaz* manner and the writer shows considerable knowledge of Russian folklore. Future translators will encounter a difficult task because of the fecundity of Leonov's Russian.

Buryga lives happily in the forest, he is at home with the plants, with the mushrooms, with the animals and with the sky as well as with the gremlins, the ghosts and the various spirits of his green habitat. All goes well until progress marches on and the entire forest is cut down. Already in **"Buryga"** Leonov shows a predilection for rendering the material animistic: "One morning the axes began to sing loudly, gaily they crackled with the bluish hands and began to promenade and kiss around; where they kiss there is death." Buryga runs away and when he encounters human beings, begins his new adventure. Men are stupid, heartless, greedy and cruel. A miracle happens; Buryga becomes a "man" and lands in a circus. One day he is thrown up to the trapeze by the circus torturer who, being drunk, does not throw him high enough; like a muffin Buryga falls down onto the sand. Osip Ivanovich, the clown, takes him backstage while the public gaily laughs. "When the clown was carrying him, Buryga ached all over his body and they looked into each others eyes. In the bright light thousands of eyes were watching them and no one noticed anything; thousands of long ears listened to them and they did not hear a word what these two *skomorokhs* [old Russian term for an entertainer, a clown] said to each other. And here is what they said: 'I love you very much Buryga'. . . . 'I love you too, Osip Ivanovich . . . very much! Because . . . you are very much like one of us, forest people.' "

After many adventures, Buryga, half-frozen, finally is picked up by the count's maid (that's when the story begins) and settles down in the count's household, but he fares no better there and does not last very long. He is expelled from the house and is taken in by Sharik, the watchdog (unlike humans, he had a compassionate heart). After awhile Buryga, longing for his forest, decides to go to his home country and leaves on foot.

We have dwelt so long on this short story because it is typical of early Leonov; it shows his bold experimentation with the language and his considerable knowledge of it. In this charming story we also have the juxtaposition, which will be of paramount importance for the writer's later work, of so-called civilization and simple, naive Russian village life. Buryga is endowed with the characteristics of a simple, long-suffering Russian peasant, deeply rooted in his native soil.

Another short story, **"Valina Kukla" ("Valya's Doll")** 1923, also betrays the traits of a fairytale. The doll, to Valya's great chagrin, runs away with the tin soldier to America, to the state of Orinoko. *Ex abrupto* the narrative changes from the dream world of a child into mean reality: the happy couple quarrels. The handsome tin hussar does not cope with American reality, he becomes a plumber and the perfidious doll runs away to Van'ka Vstan'ka—a sort of Russian humpty dumpty who is by far more adaptable to the American Dream. Being a doll with a weight attached to its base so that it will always recover its standing position, he opens up a tavern, becomes rich. The tin soldier dies of grief.

The end, which faintly reminds us of Chekhov's nostalgic mood, is fitting; it brings us to the third reality: Valya grows up and forgets about her toys and dolls.

Very interesting and cleverly constructed is the **"Dereviannaia Koroleva" ("The Wooden Queen")** 1923, published together with **"Valya's Doll"** and **"Bubnovy Valet" ("The Knave of Diamonds")**. It is a story of a lonely man, Izvekov, who plays chess by himself, dreaming up the most impossible combinations. The reader feels that the main character goes mad, he falls in love with the wooden queen, goes down onto the chess board, saves the queen and feels voluptuously happy and frightfully small and insignificant at the same time. The magic spell is broken; it was all a daydream which is interrupted by the arrival of his friend who wants to play chess with him.

**"The Knave of Diamonds"** is a similar story except that this time it is the knave of diamonds, a playing card, who falls in love with Helen, a girl of fourteen, and is crushed when she becomes engaged and marries a real man, not a knave from a deck of old, soiled cards. The end again is characteristic. Reality is sad; when Helen becomes forty she comes back to her dream and sheds bitter tears, kissing her knave of diamonds.

The similarity of Leonov's early stories to Andersen's fairytales has been often pointed out. A certain influence is undoubtedly discernable in the writer's creativity, but how important is it? Russian folklore abounded in fairytales, and since this genre was popular in Russia, the reader, or for that matter the listener, avidly absorbed the foreign material in this form. This tradition dates back many centuries when the first "magic stories" were recorded in ancient Russian literature. Even the hagiographic, patristic literature contained the lure, the wonder of distant and marvelous countries. Leonov was steeped in the tradition of Russian fairytale (how many countries in Western Europe could boast such wealth of this folkloristic genre?) and utilized it, giving it a contemporary setting. But even that is not important; what is so significant is the way he dealt with his material. The early Leonov is a highly *original* writer and his highest achievement lies in that magnificent perspicuity and imaginativeness of the Russian language.

Soviet scholars, with the exception of V. Kovalev and A. M. Startseva, treat Leonov's early prose sparingly; it is strange that they ignore one Russian writer, who in our view, had considerable influence on his early writing. When we think of **"The Wooden Queen"** as a melange of Romantic and Realistic elements, we are struck by the fact that N. V. Gogol (1809-1852), who definitely deserves our closest scrutiny in reference to Leonov's early output, is hardly mentioned. Most likely, this omission stems from a certain shyness on the part of modern scholars to place Gogol within the confines of Romanticism; they would prefer to see the great writer a Realist. There is no doubt, however, that such stories as **"The Wooden Queen"** or **"The Knave of Diamonds"** have definitely certain affinities with the latter's "Nevsky Prospect," not in the language, not in the structure of the stories but in the amazing blending of dream and reality, this intentional and painful depiction of human cognizance. Leonov always claimed Dostoevsky to be his master and teacher, but Dostoevsky was indebted to Gogol among other writers.

Very interesting, if not curious, are the responses of various present day scholars to Leonov's early prose. Z. Boguslavskaya, in [*Leonid Leonov*, 1960], claims that the writer was lost in the turmoil of NEP (New Economic Policy), hence his "strange" prose of that period. V. A. Kovalev, one of the most knowledgeable scholars, claims in his study [*Romany Leonida Leonova*, 1954] that: "The dependence on decadent works is particularly evident in **'The Wooden Queen'**: everything is stylized, the language which lacked concrete expressiveness, the image of a dream . . . and the queen who comes to life with her eyes of a snowstorm and Blok's notion of the snowstorm raging outside. Such storms were far from demands of the contemporary events and were unacceptable." As a comment on this puerile outburst, we remind the reader that as late as the 1950s another Soviet writer, Boris Pasternak, utilized just that motif in *Doctor Zhivago* and did it success-fully.

A more sober and sensitive appraisal of Leonov's early prose is given by A. M. Startseva [in *Tvorchestvo Leonida Leonova,* 1969]. One could not agree more with her penetrating analysis of **"The Wooden Queen."** According to her:

> it seems that the writer, with complete self-assurance imitates the style of the symbolist poets. . . . But the meaningful infantility of the symbolist style is contained in the genre pictures of a short story. And that created an unexpected alloy which makes **"The Wooden Queen"** not only a polemical work, but a parody as well. A reality of the two unkempt bachelors with their soup of yesterday, their fat female cook [Natasha the witch], their unpleasant habitat, enters the Romantic imagination, the tale of 'life of beyond' the 'marvelous day'. . . . In **"The Wooden Queen"** we witness Leonov's artistry create a buffeted multi-plane imagery interwoven with the development of the plot. In this respect, this seemingly light short story is a perfectly constructed work of art.

One could also add that coupled with the perfect, mathematical construction of the story (after all, it is supposedly an imaginary chess game) is the rhythm of this dream-like tale. It reaches its crescendo when the man gets on to the chess board to defend the queen, and when the author describes with magnificent insight and amazing tactility the finely chiselled and polished hand of the object of his adoration. But then it is not surprising, for Leonov was interested in sculpture and devoted much of his time to wood carving.

This would conclude the first phase of our discussion of Leonov's early prose, but it is imperative to mention one more story, which is closely linked to his ethnographical aspirations. In 1924, in the almanac *Krug* (*The Circle*) No. 3, appeared another story which shows the writer's interest in folklore and experimentation with the local Archangel Saga and its linguistic peculiarities. **"Ghibel' Egorushki"** (**"Egorushka's Undoing"**), was written in March of 1922.

It is a strange story, deeply rooted in Russian folklore; its vocabulary definitely attests to that. Just to mention a few examples, Leonov freely uses words which would be incomprehensible to the inhabitant of Central Russia; *vzvoden'* (the tidal wave), *malica* (a male upper garment), *oshkuy* (the white bear), *ostroga* (harpoon) and many others. It is strange that many Soviet specialists in North America failed to realize that the various Siberian dialects, as well as the dialects of Arctic Russia, are very different from the language of Central and Southern Russia.

**"Egorushka's Undoing"** has definite and close affinity to Russian folklore, to the speech of the inhabitants of Arctic Russia and, more interesting, to Gogol's "Terrible Vengeance." One could also add, but few readers would realize, that it also has close ties with works by the almost forgotten Russian-Ukrainian writer Orest Somov (1793-1833), particularly with his "Evil Eye." We have no way

of knowing whether Leonov ever heard of Somov, but we do know that such luminaries as Pushkin and Gogol were indebted to him, if not for brilliance of style, then for certain highly original ideas. It is also plausible that the description of Egorushka's plight, with the stern Arctic weather, the loneliness of the fisherman and the hunter, and the intrusion by the monk Agapy who has all the qualities of an evil genius, have close relationship to the usual amplitude of West-European and Russian Romanticism. Compare, for example, the story with Pushkin's "Hussar," Gogol's "The Terrible Vengeance," or Somov's "Evil Eye" and "The Kievan Witches," or for that matter, although Leonov always denied any connection, with M. Bulgakov's (1891-1940) *Master and Margarita.* Leonov could not have read Bulgakov's novel, which was published posthumously in the 1960's, but he most certainly has been acquainted with Goethe's *Faust,* which has all the inventory of the Romantic set up. At any rate Egorushka's riding into the imaginary land on some imaginary horses shaped like strange birds, and his tragic undoing, bears close resemblance to Gogol's irrevocable and tragic motives, Bulgakov's satirical escapades—the flight of Margarita and her maid, as well as the exit of Woland and his entourage (in *Master and Margarita*)—and we might add D. Merezhkovsky's (1865-1941) Kassandra, as well as Bryusov's Renata in the *Fiery Angel,* with her extraterrestrial trips.

With all this interdependence of ideas, we could claim that the most important element in Leonov's story is the true Russian folklore, the life of the simple Russian hunter and an amazing poetical sustenance of a budding great Russian writer. Here we move to another no less striking aspect of Leonov's prose: his so-called ornamental style. He was not the only one to have written in this manner but he might have been the best.

It is interesting that the second phase of Leonov's creativity (this, of course, is an arbitrary subdivision for our scrutiny) departs from the original Russian source and moves to a more exotic territory. One should, however, not be unduly surprised at the novelty of the writer's subject matter; after all Russian history was closely linked with the history of the Near East (Caucasus), the Arabic and Turkic invasion of Central Asia, the greatness of Samarkand and the splendor of Khoresm, and, the forgotten vitality of Khersones and various Greek colonies in the Crimea and the Ancient Southern Rus'. The most lasting and obviously terrifyingly painful memories which made their imprint on Russian minds were the Tartar invasions and the subsequent subjugation, which became known as the Tartar Yoke.

Amazing was this locust-like movement of the people. Merciless and senseless were the slaughter and exploitation of the various Russian principalities and in the states in Asia, Eastern Europe, as well as in China. The Arabic invasion brought culture to the primitive, often semi-barbaric peoples in Western Europe; the Tartars, on the other hand, brought nothing but grief and suffering.

In some of Leonov's early poetry some traces of Blok's defiance, the challenge to Western Europe are discernable. In **"Khalil"** and **"Tuatamur"** he explores a universal, an all-human trait in dealing with the conquerors; in this respect his short stories are tightly linked to the tradition of Arabic and biblical heritage. **"Khalil"** was written in September of 1922. It is a story of two lovers: Khalil' and Bayalun' who consummate their earthly love but turn away from each other because both are striving for the unattainable, divine volatile love, in this case the moon, which is a common motif in the Arabic and Persian literature. The story is highly stylized and encrusted with the voluptuous ornamental design. Written in the form of fourteen *kasydas* (songs), it reminds the reader of songs of Scheherazade, the miniatures of *One Thousand and One Nights,* of the intricate tales of Apuleius of his *Golden Ass* or of the later Latin Golden short stories. Compare for example the usual beginning of the Latin Golden stories: "Drop me a coin and I will tell you a golden story" (golden at that time meant popular; hence *The Golden Ass,* and "The Golden Prose" of Pyphaforas) with Leonov's beginning of **"Khalil"**: "Give me a pipe and coffee or drop me a small silver coin onto the rug or tell me quietly 'Saliam' (Peace) . . . and I will reward you with fourteen *kasydas* about Khalil', the memory of whom did not remain in the hearts of people, because he did not remain in the hearts of people, because he did not spill anybody's blood, did not crush anybody's hearts by vain reveries, and, did not build useless cities."

**"Khalil"** however is more than a poetical exercise in prose, it also marks a certain departure—one could almost say—it hints at the break with Romanticism. Therefore the ending of this charming story: "May the Prophet protect you from Khalil's fate."

**"Tuatamur"** (written in May, 1922, published by M. and S. Sabashnikov in 1924) deals with the life of an aging Tartar warrior, who apparently participated in the battle of Kalka (1223) when the Tartars decisively defeated the Russian forces, which were weakened by internal strife and internecine wars. All his life the warrior of Genghis Khan was destructive—he fought bravely, conquered many distant lands and burnt down many towns and villages—but in the process he lost his own soul, he was no man anymore. Strangely enough, the plot of this story is woven around love of Ytmar', a magnificent warrior-like girl, the daughter of Genghis, for a vanquished hero. Tuatamur, who loves the girl, is incapable of any positive action; fearless in battle, he is impotent confronted with this tragic event. Ytmar' commits suicide.

As Friedrich Scholz so incisively pointed out in his introduction to *Leonov, L. M.: Rannie Rasskazy,* the young writer showed an astounding linguistic ability to deal with certain ethnographical illusions. His use of Turkish words and idioms introduced in such a way, that even though a Russian does not understand them, their placement in a texture, the loom of the story, makes them comprehensible to the reader.

In **"Ukhod Khama"** (**"Ham's Departure"**) Leonov deals with a biblical theme of Noah's flight with his family. It is a sheer phantasy, and the writer manipulates several events in the *Bible*: The flood, the building of the ark, the curse and the blessings over his children (Genesis 6:9). Leonov also adds the story of Jacob and his father's bless-

ing as to the firstborn child (Genesis 27). Ham's undoing has a new twist; he is wronged by his brothers and his father (who lies with Ham's wife). Distrustful of God he embarks upon a voluntary exile.

After the stylized legends of **"Khalil"** and **"Tuatamur"** with their solemn euphony, and linguistic decorativeness skillfully interwoven with the *skaz* manner, in keeping with the Tartar inscriptions left over to us from the times of the reign of the Golden Horde (the Tartar state on Volga River), Leonov moves back to a Russian setting. [*Petushikhinsky prolom* (*Petushikha's Breakthrough*)] is a curious tale and introduces Leonov's musings about Russia, Revolution and its effect on Petushikha—a small Russian village. Some Soviet scholars claimed that there is duality in Leonov's tale. The writer set out to describe the primitiveness, the cruel life of Russian peasants yet he failed to show the real "breakthrough" of Petushikha; the ossifying element is too strong in the story, nothing can break the old tradition, the vulgarity and the animalistic basis of its existence. And all this in spite of the fact that the village undergoes a certain transformation; the peasants hear that the tzar is no longer there and the country is ruled by "deputies" who later are swept away by the "bolshaks" (Bolsheviks).

Some critics also claimed that *Petushikha's Breakthrough* is a poorly constructed tale; it has no central idea and is nothing but a series of short miniatures loosely connected. But such was not the purpose of the tale. The seemingly disjointed plot of the story only underlines the chaotic conditions, the breaking up of the old life. The style of the story, which some critics called a "poem," is pure rhythmical prose. In this Leonov does not really depart from his ornamental "oriental" tales in spite of the fact that the action takes place in a Russian village. A number of situations in the story will recur in the writer's later works, but his main preoccupation here is the reflection on the Russian Revolution, the metamorphosis of the horse thief Talagan into a political activist. (Compare some of the characters in Pasternak's *Doctor Zhivago*). When everybody is dressed decently, when Utopia reigns supreme, when all remember the famine and forever forget it, Russia's future and the painful cogitation over the country's fate are embodied in Petushikha with the writer's doleful exclamation in Chapter Sixteen:

> Oh sheaf of wheat, hearken to muzhik's voice,
> give him a kernel the size of a log;

the famine takes its toll and the peasants begin to eat clay.

Stylistically this rhythmical prose has almost biblical connotations; hence the beginning of some of the chapters: (And the One and Only spake) "People call it famine but we call it death, those mortal years of Resurrection. Indeed, really our road to Heaven is marked by dead bodies."

Linked with these almost mystical-religious connotations of the above mentioned passages are further bold experimentation in style and bold linguistic performance of a virtuoso; this tale marks the beginning of Leonov's preoccupation with—and deep concern about—the fate of the

Russian village before and after the Revolution and the subsequent NEP period.

Leonov's next tale, [*Konets melkogo cheloveka*] *The End of a Petty Man,* also deals with the post-Revolutionary times "when all over Russia resounded steel wings of unthinkable upheavals." Likharev, the main character in this tale, is a world famous paleontologist. He is cast overboard by the events which are incomprehensible to him. Leonov makes it clear that the eminent professor is and always has been a hermetic personality, not to say a selfish man. His vision always was directed to the past, and for all his study of life, was unable to recreate it. Now he is reduced to an animal-like existence, to the struggle for survival. Later the writer will contrast, as it were, "the petty man" to Professor Pickering in *Evgenia Ivanovna.*

Leonov was not unique in treatment of the plot of this psychological tale. Many other Soviet writers, particularly B. Pilniak (pseudonym of B. A. Vogau, 1894-1941) and E. I. Zamiatin (1884-1937) were also preoccupied with the theme of Revolution versus individual. Without drawing an unfair and invidious comparison one could claim that this tradition dates back to A. S. Pushkin's "The Bronze Horseman." In Leonov's tale we clearly discern his dependence on Dostoevsky's style and experience.

Much was written about Dostoevsky's influence upon Leonov's early prose but in *The End of a Petty Man* it is particularly manifest. Like Dostoevsky, the writer utilizes the Petrograd motif (though at the time of Dostoevsky it was majestic but cold St. Petersburg); there are some other similarities: Likharev is out of touch with reality, in his agony he is confronted by *fert* (named Titus in the original version), the distant relative of Ivan Karamazov's devil. The imagery and certain situations of *The Double* are also compelling. Equally true are the philosophical discourses by *fert* who urges the professor to burn his manuscript—his life-long work.

In our opinion, Leonov uses all of Dostoevsky's literary components in this tale (as well as those of Gogol), but falls short of—perhaps luckily—emulating the great Russian writer. And all this in spite of the religio-philosophical and moral undertones of Likharev's and *fert*'s quest for modern Utopia. In this story Leonov continues in the path of Dostoevsky a precursor of modern social and psychological science-fiction.

In one of the conversations, *fert* mockingly describes the future of mankind: "The sky will be paved with concrete, streetcars will furrow the clouds. Bread will be made of air . . . people will wear velvet trousers." Likharev flings himself at his tormentor, he suddenly realizes that the sister who lived and took care of him is dead, that he is starved and decrepit and that he is dying of hunger and a weakened heart.

Here Leonov arrives at an objective reality; in Likharev's last moments of consciousness before his death, he walks outside his apartment and, burning with curiosity, greedily looks through the window at the dead body of the petty man.

In [*Zapisi nekotorykh epizodov, sdelannye v gorode*

*Goguleve Andreem Petrovichem Koviakinym*] *Koviakin's Notes,* Leonov continues to probe the changes which took place in a provincial town after the Revolution. *The Notes* are a curious blend of *Petushikha's Breakthrough* and *The End of a Petty Man.* The story, or series of episodes, is narrated by Koviakin himself whose habit it was to write down everything that happened during certain "solemn and festive" occasions. The construction of the *Notes* is oddly close to Pushkin's *Tales of Belkin;* the traces of Dostoevsky and particularly those of Gogol are discernible in it. Koviakin's letter which follows the Preface to *Koviakin's Notes* is kept within "style absurd." Many scholars have also found in *Koviakin's Notes* a similarity with Pushkin's *The History of the Village of Goriukhino,* and certain echoes of *Manners of Rasteriaeva Street* by Gleb Uspensky (1843-1902) and of *Little Town of Okurov* by M. Gorky (pseudonym of A. M. Peshkov, 1868-1936). But Leonov is still an original writer: he intentionally draws certain parallels to situations in the works of the above mentioned writers and at times parodies them.

In the first part of *The Notes* the writer proves to be an able satirist, with the propensity for *genre grotesque,* capable of creating petty comical personages. The vulgar (*poshly*) poetry of Mr. Koviakin enhances and unfolds the petty person and his stagnant and vulgar environment. The town of Gogulev is a swamp, a pond in bloom, and self-satisfied little fish Koviakin feels comfortable in it. In this story Leonov once again shows a great linguistic adroitness and culture; some of the comical situations and personages remind us of M. Zoshchenko's (1895-1958) characters.

In the second part of *Koviakin's Notes* the mood of the story changes; it becomes its own philosophical pendant. Koviakin worries about the fate of his town and that of Russia. He is a pacifist who notes that the war brought grief to the town but no changes, except that the coffin maker has now branched out in his business: he makes and sells wooden legs as well. Koviakin screems against the war; he is against the spilling of blood:

> "Young people should not be killed." "Why don't the people settle down and work in peace"? "States are also unnecessary, the more states there are, the more blood is spilled."

The most persistent question with which Koviakin was preoccupied was the collision of man and society; for Leonov too it was a very painful question. Koviakin muses over the origin of man: "Man came from the ape, and the ape came from a wolf, and the wolf came from a flea and the flea came from moisture, and the moisture from boredom."

Koviakin runs to the priest who calms him by stating that it was the Almighty who created man. A friend, however, taunts him again: "The priest lied to you to have power over you. That's how its going to be nowadays, the one who lies best will have the power. There is no Almighty, He also originated from boredom."

*Koviakin's Notes* are not only a caricature-like description of the provincial life, but also a serious reflection over the fate of man, not only confronted by the Revolution but his role in this world in general. We don't know what subsequently happened to Koviakin's further musings; he departs from Gogulev. Leonov will try to solve this Dostoevskian problem in his later works.

By the middle of the Twenties, Leonov was a recognized and promising writer. His reputation and creative activity at the same time were hotly debated. His political attitudes in literature were disputed; he was dubbed a "fellow traveller." . . . In the Soviet Union today he is an accepted and recognized talented writer. The passions of yesteryear have died down, but until recently his early prose was largely neglected or interpreted as that of imitative character. Everything is falling into place, however, and in spite of divergence of opinions of various Soviet critics Leonov's early output is regarded, with all its shortcomings, as an interesting and original creativity. Much emphasis is placed now on his engagement in the Revolutionary and Civil War activity; the interpretation of Leonov's early works acquires the tendentious hue so prevalent in the works of the nineteenth century Russian writings. In Western Europe and in North America he begins to occupy a venerable if controversial position. But even now his critics do not speak with an unequivocal voice. . . . Christoph Brümmer insists in his dissertation that Leonov's early prose was purely apolitical but another, Friedrich Scholz in his short but interesting introduction to *Leonid Leonov: Rannie Rasskazy* (Wilhelm Fink Verlag, Munich, 1972) takes issues with Brümmer's thesis.

We can only agree with Scholz who states so succinctly in his introduction that Leonov's early works were not of an imitative character. The writer found himself. He grew up in the great tradition of Russian literature which he furthered. His diversity was astounding: peasant stories with the worry about the future of Russia, combining his highly original language based on folklore, his excellent knowledge of Russian and Russian Patristic literature, his whimsical literary fantasy **"Buryga"** (with its question of progress and subsequent immigration; compare *The Flight of Bulgakov*) and the highly stylized "oriental" stories. Leonov would next embark on longer works, and as early as the fall of 1923 he begins to work on the first novel *Barsuki* (*The Badgers*). We will encounter many stylistic and ideological situations and elements of his early prose in this short but interesting novel.

. . . . .

Leonov, like most prominent Soviet writers, does not limit himself to literary creativity alone. He publishes a number of political articles, and some touch upon everyday current problems. He is consistently elected to membership in the Supreme Council of the USSR. He is active in the administrative work of various Russian literary publications; notably *Oktiabr'* (member of the editorial board 1958-61), *Literatura i Zhizn'* (1954-57) and *Teatral'naia Zhizn'* (since 1958). As a member of the government and of various cultural and literary organizations, he travels a great deal: to Britain, Bulgaria, Yugoslavia, Italy, France, Czechoslovakia, India and other countries.

In 1959 he was once again awarded the Order of Lenin. In spite of his many activities he did not idle in his creative

writing. . . . [Never] satisfied, or simply changing his mood, he edited and re-edited his play *The Golden Coach;* he became a member of the Council of the Ministry of Cinematography; in 1953 he began to publish his collected works in five volumes (actually, with the addition of *The Russian Forest* it became six) and in 1960 started to publish his works again—thoroughly rechecked and augmented, in an edition of nine volumes; this is the best collection to date.

All of this is overshadowed by the rewriting of one of his first novels, *The Thief.*

The second version provoked a great deal of controversy both in Russia and abroad. Perhaps we can dismiss some Western critics as "shoddy craftsmen" who did not bother to read the novel thoroughly. But certainly there were both objective and subjective reasons for the controversy. The objective reasons are as follows: after 1950 many Soviet writers, no doubt under pressure, began to rewrite their earlier works to fit the "dictates of the times" (official Soviet critical euphemism). We shall cite only a few well-known writers. Yuri Libedinsky (1898-1959) changed his novel *The Commissars* in 1953 and restored the original version in 1956. The novel was eventually changed again by an editorial board in 1965. In 1945 Fadeev published his now famous *The Young Guard* which dealt with the Soviet underground activities in Krasnodon against the German invaders. It was based on factual material; all of the young partisans perished. The novel was enthusiastically greeted in Russia, but after 1947 it was persistently pointed out to the writer that he had not sufficiently stressed the role of the older members of the Communist Party. Fadeev sincerely believed he had erred and, accordingly, he added a number of "outstanding" personages in his novel. The innovations of the years from 1953 to 1956 were crucial in Soviet letters. Disillusioned by changes he could not adapt to, Fadeev committed suicide.

The most glaring example of the forcible and voluntary rewriting of a work is that of *Quiet Don* by Mikhail Sholokhov. A well-known American scholar of Soviet literature, in an interesting article, points to a number of factual, episodical and textual changes undertaken by Sholokhov. The most telling changes of political hue were carried out in 1953, and all these were ruthlessly thrown out by the author in 1956.

The subjective reason for confusion in interpreting Leonov's new version of **The Thief** might have been a somewhat misleading statement of the writer himself in his short Foreword (*Ot avtora*) to it. In fairly free translation it reads:

> The author, with a pen in his hand, reread the book written more than thirty years ago. It is difficult to interfere with such a work, just as it would be difficult to enter for the second time an old stream of long ago. Nevertheless it is possible to walk in the shallow waters listening to the crunching of the pebbles, safely looking into the places at former whirlpools which are now bereft of water.

This sounded like recanting to many Western readers. It also confused some of the Soviet critics. V. A. Kovalev, in his excellent chapter "The second birth of the novel *The Thief*," begins by stating that the writer has matured. Leonov may have omitted something the first time, and did not see certain imperfections which he corrected in the second version.

"These are actually two different novels. The first one will have an historical interest for the reader, the second will have a longer life ahead of it" [V. A. Kovalev]. He then proceeds with a sensible and sensitive analysis of the novel. E. Starikova in her notes to the novel in the third volume of the nine-volume edition seems to have found reasons to disagree. Still, she says that "although it retains the original plot, composition and the factual basis, the novel is a different work in its ideological and stylistic contents."

It is useless to discuss why Leonov did write a new version and whether he had the right to do so; the writer seems to be pleased to be coming back to his works. We can only try to see *how* he did it and what changes were brought about in his second version. One thing is certain—Leonov did not do it under any political pressure. On the contrary, at times, he seems to use his revisions as a way of "settling the score" with either himself or the critics who had viciously attacked him at times in the past, and there are many "private evocations" in the novel which cannot be discussed here. We should bear in mind that the novel was rewritten between 1956 and 1959—the most liberal time in Soviet literature of the postwar period.

The plot and the subject matter of the novel's second version differ very little from the original. Externally there are some changes but these are insignificant. The original novel consisted of a prologue (not identified as such) and four parts. The second version consists of a formal Prologue, Parts I to III, then the Epilogue. Both novels are approximately the same length. The only change in the plot is the ending. Mit'ka is not saved; the author does not preclude such a possibility but he places the responsibility for his rescue on Firsov, who might have contrived such a possibility in the novel.

Most of the characters are retained in the second version: Mit'ka, Don'ka, Zina Balueva, Maniukin, Chikiliov and others. While the action is the same, the novel is still different from the first version. What are the changes? First of all, the style and linguistic composition are different. All the luxuriant superfluity in Leonov's language is cut out. The narrative is taut and less extravagant than in the original novel. We must admit, however, that we miss certain original statements which were enlivening but whose removal made the narrative more precise. Some minor episodic changes were introduced. All in all we feel that the writer has matured considerably—his hand is surer and readers can sense Leonov's many years of writing experience. But even that is not the most important change in the book.

As in the first version, Mit'ka is the central character but how different he is now. In the first version the thief had an aura of romanticism, almost that of martyrdom. But he went wrong, he did not take account of what was happening around him. He was strong and there was always hope for his salvation. In the second version he appears like Lermontov's demon after his second fall. He is a cruel, even petty, self-centered thief. Even during the Civil War he commits a gratuitous crime by senselessly killing a White Guard officer. Mit'ka is at a dead end. He has satiated all his desires, but his most heinous crime is his total indifference to the people around him. He sinks so low that he lives off Zina's money without ever asking where it comes from. And yet he shudders at the thought of becoming like Agei, a hysterical murderer, who also began as a thief claiming that he was rectifying social injustices. Mit'ka is a defeated man and his erstwhile friend Artashez (Atashez in the first version) understands this. That is why Leonov cut out some lengthy conversations between the two friends.

If Mit'ka undergoes such a change, the other characters must change also. Most of Mit'ka's companions do not treat him with the great respect he received in the first version. True, he still has his faithful friend San'ka ("the bicycle") but even he rebels after Mit'ka tries to break his friend's relationship with his wife. In the end Mit'ka prevails, and drags San'ka back to the world of crime. For this his friend fires at him twice but misses.

Very different is the personality of Masha Dolomanova ("the blizzard"). In spite of certain "infernal" qualities she had in the first version, she was "beautiful, mysterious, blizzard-like, a lady beautiful of Aleksandr Blok" [V. A. Kovalev]. In the second version she is cynical, warped, with a psychotic personality, clever enough to destroy and torture people. She feels Mit'ka has wronged her and wants to avenge herself. She could have eliminated him long ago as cruelly as she had done Agei (whom she betrayed to the criminal investigation department), but she wants to torture her former lover. And Mit'ka, in his egocentricity, is blind to the fact that she no longer loves him. Man'ka, a movie actress, now uses her beauty to entice and destroy. She even plays a lethal cat-and-mouse game with Firsov. At the very end of the novel he realizes that it was she who provoked Agei's demise and also dropped into Don'ka's suitcase a piece of evidence, proof of the latter's collaboration with the police. Firsov, for the first time, sees Man'ka the way she is: "Suddenly, something secret, disgusting, blotched, something that Firsov so passionately longed to forget, became more and more evident in that woman. These signs probably were the traces of Agei's embraces."

There are other characters who undergo a change in the second version of the novel. Chikiliov becomes a fuller, more developed, and therefore more disgusting character. Maniukin ends up without resurrection (although there are some short notes in Firsov's book which mention such a possibility) and in this he gains as a personage; he becomes a sad rather than a pitiful character.

Zavarikhin, like Mit'ka, is changed radically. He no longer has the redeeming qualities he had in the first version. Consequently he himself divides people into consumers and those to be consumed. Accordingly his relationship with Tanya is changed. He is the taker. The only reason he wants to marry her is to improve his financial situation.

He takes her but the wedding is postponed, and she dies before it happens.

Tanya is still very attractive to readers, but now "real" and earthy, she loses the inexplicable charm she had in the first version. The critic Kovalev declines to discuss it, but one has a feeling he wished she had not been changed. In fact, he claims that Tanya as a character is outside of the realm of the milieu of the novel. In a way, the highly romanticized heroine becomes somewhat pitiful, although the fear of death she has acquired (and which proves in the end her undoing) explains her desire to marry Zavarikhin. The catastrophe of *shtrabat,* her daring act, is the only way for her. She would surely have perished anyway.

A very important change takes place in Firsov's position in the novel. Leonov has a critical attitude towards his ubiquitous protagonist. His role in the novel is so complex that the reader at times has difficulty in comprehending who is speaking and passing the judgement, Leonov or Firsov. To make it all the more complex, Leonov's Firsov lives his "independent" life and in turn creates a reflection of himself. It is difficult at this point to assess fully Firsov's role in the novel. Suffice it to say that the writer uses him often to express his own ideas on the creative processes, the role of the writer in society, on literature in general and Soviet literary criticism in the past. At times it looks as if Leonov was settling the score with some of his former denigrators; the novel is full of allusions, insinuations and hints which still might be investigated fully.

Reading the second version of the novel, one has a distinct feeling that Leonov has matured, and that he is not afraid to fall into the "whirlpools of yesteryear." But we discern a certain fatigue and bitterness on his part. His wit is mordant, his invectives are sarcastic. The criminal world is not romanticized, it becomes vulgar. A good case in point is the description of one of the last *shalmans.* Everything in that den is permeated with the smell and the signs of decay: the dirty walls, the ruffled-up palm tree, "the five tired men playing their mandolins, making indecent, ugly gestures with their right hands."

Pchkhov is still Mit'ka's conscience. He is stricter, not as vociferous as in the first version, but occasionally almost sententious. He passes the judgement on Mit'ka the thief. "Thief" in the second version acquires a general symbolic meaning. Almost everybody in the novel is a thief, including Firsov who finally admits it, saying that he rummages through people's lives. In his final conversation with Mit'ka, Pchkhov advises: "To begin with you should go to communion." And when Mit'ka haughtily asks how he proposes to save him, Pchkhov replies: "Like He used to do." This is a curious turn of events. As we know, the word God is spelled with a small letter in the Soviet Union. The evocation of Jesus Christ pardoning the penitent thief is telling, not withstanding the fact that the continuation of the passage indicates Mit'ka's realization that personal salvation lies within himself. There is a ray of hope, if not for Mit'ka, at least for Firsov. Having escaped Masha Dolomanova's clutches, Firsov turns and goes away abruptly. It is a beautiful early spring day and the last word Leonov uses in his novel is *the thaw.* The second

version is an interesting literary document which most probably will provoke some heated discussion for a long time to come. We must agree with those critics who claim that though similar in content, both novels differ in their ideological and social make-up. They will continue to exist as two interesting but separate entities.

We shall now turn to another work which, although far removed from *The Thief* could provide us with answers to some nagging questions.

[*Evgenia Ivanovna*], considered by most critics the most perfect of Leonov's works, was published in 1963. It was marked 1938-63, but, as was proven beyond a doubt, was conceived at some time in the period from 1924 to 1934, in October of which year, Leonov participated in the festivities of the Valley of Alazan in Soviet Georgia.

It would be interesting to follow Leonov's creative process; twenty-five years is a considerable length of time for any writer, and in it one matures and is enriched by further life experiences. The world itself shows appreciable change in the cognizance of the readers. Leonov stated: "I made one copy of *Evgenia Ivanovna* but returned to it every three years, thus instead of one, I collected 5 or 6 copies—versions. And each one served as a certain whetstone for trying the sharpness of will and pen." V. A. Kovalev had the good fortune to look at various copies, written from 1926 to 1943; in each of these, the character who would become Mr. Pickering was still called Mr. Harkraider. He concluded that the real date of composition should be 1938, for at that time the writer began to muse about the fate of post-Revolutionary Russia. In this respect, as one critic remarks, *Evgenia Ivanovna* is linked to such plays as *The Snowstorm, The Wolf* and *The Orchards of Polovchansk.*

Readers both in Russia and abroad met the tale enthusiastically. But most of them—and that included many critics—saw in it supreme mastery of language and style, and Leonov's usual wit and simple and somewhat naive plot. Stripped of any deeper meaning, the plot is indeed simple. Zhenia, a young girl in love, follows a White officer, Stratonov, into exile without realizing what the Civil War is all about. After half a year in Constantinople, Stratonov leaves her penniless. With great difficulty she reaches Paris where life is no less hard for her, and is just about to embark upon a life of a prostitute, when by luck she meets Mr. Pickering, a world-renowned English archeologist who offers her a position as his secretary. Both travel a great deal, and Zhenia (Jenny) once again entrusts her fate to a man who marries her. Here the writer could have concluded his tale with the Cinderella-like ending but he continues. Mr. Pickering, the husband, notices that his wife is homesick and offers her a trip to Russia. Evgenia Ivanovna's happiness is clouded by guilt feelings towards Stratonov. She hears that he was killed while serving in the Foreign Legion.

The couple goes to the Soviet Union, and, to Zhenia's surprise, the guide turns out to be Stratonov himself. A lively argument ensues between the former lovers. Evgenia Ivanovna has the upper hand, her husband, has to watch passively the outcome of this mental struggle (he does not know anything but senses that his happiness is in jeopardy). Stratonov, utilizing the festive mood of wine-pressing time in Alazan, tries desperately to remind Zhenia of their former love, but in vain. Evgenia Ivanovna at this moment notices the first symptoms of pregnancy—she is bearing an English child—and the couple leaves the Caucasus to go "home." That is to Evgenia Ivanovna, a mysterious and distant country.

Leonov could have ended his tale here. Evgenia Ivanovna is no longer a Russian (even her name is spelled with Latin letters), but he continues the story to say that a year later Evgenia Ivanovna dies as a result of postnatal complications. The writer who so lavishly describes the Caucasus ends his tale almost cursorily. Leonov abruptly terminates the narrative with the almost parenthetical remark that the English never part with their country, having that magic ability to take it with them wherever they go. But as for the Russians, ". . . as in the past: attempts of our exiles to take with them a handful of severe Russian snow to the countries of more temperate climate ended in failure—it invariably melted." A true Russian could not be deracinated, that would mean for the emigrant certain spiritual death.

*Evgenia Ivanovna* is sheer poetry. The tale has often been linked to the Russian classical tradition of Pushkin and Lermontov. But Leonov considered it a psychological work. We add that it is a social, and philosophical work as well. The writer touches upon many problems: the fate of humanity, the futility of any upheaval or revolution. Most important, it investigates the fate of the Russian people and the returning emigrants. Stratonov is a mechanically correct Soviet citizen (here we have a variation on the theme of *The Snowstorm*), but he does not even care about the Russian people. Both Pickerings understand this, particularly when he wants to prove how barbaric Soviet people are by showing them the defiled bower in which the Russian writer Griboedov, once upon a time, proposed to Nina Chavchavadze, his wife-to-be. He wants to cover up his wicked deed (the desertion that caused Zhenia's grief) with declamatory statements that he returned to Russia to help to build up the country. The spineless members of intelligentsia who frothed at the mouth (but only a little) were equally guilty in the ensuing chaos, as were members of that noxious segment of the pernicious population of the old Russian Empire, who strove to create a social experiment in the country. Neither understood nor loved Russia.

In this lyrical tale, Evgenia Ivanovna is a tragic figure. Having left her country almost involuntarily, she subsequently loses her identity, rather like George Bernard Shaw's Eliza Doolittle. And her kind husband Pickering (for these are *Pygmalion* names, Pickering and Higgins) is incapable of saving her. A leaf torn from its stalk withers and dies. There is nothing more tragic than to be uprooted, no matter how severe one's homeland can be, and nothing more ignominious than deportation from one's own country. In light of the events of recent years, one can see how right and how prophetic Leonov was.

## Harold B. Segel   (essay date 1979)

SOURCE: "The Gathering Clouds: On the Eve of War" and "The War Years," in *Twentieth-Century Russian Drama: From Gorky to the Present,* Columbia University Press, 1979, pp. 295-304, 305-17.

[*An American educator and critic, Segel has written extensively on Russian literature. In the following excerpt, he discusses* The Orchards of Polovchansk *and* The Invasion, *two of Leonov's plays.*]

International events in the 1930s were followed with intense interest in the Soviet Union. The triumph of fascism in Italy and Germany and the Japanese invasion of China were viewed as ominous developments of profound potential danger to the Soviet state. The defeat of the Loyalist cause in Spain and the gradual clarification of German and Japanese political goals in Eastern Europe and Asia, respectively, made the threat of war no longer merely a possibility but a virtual certainty. The necessary preparations began to be undertaken in the late 'thirties; this meant above all the raising of the military to a level of preparedness but also the psychological conditioning of the people to the hardships and sacrifices that lay ahead.

This preparedness for war became the focus of much literature of the period. Of the plays devoted to the subject, only a few succeeded in rising above the level of outright propaganda. The best of these were: *Polovchanskie sady (The Orchards of Polovchansk,* 1938), by the major Soviet novelist Leonid Leonov (1899-); *Feldmarshal Kutuzov (Field Marshal Kutuzov,* 1939), by Vladimir Solovyov (1907- ), one of the more able writers of historical drama in the USSR; and Aleksandr Afinogenov's *Nakanune (On the Eve,* 1941).

Apart from dramatizations of his novels *Barsuki* (*The Badgers,* 1927) and *Skutarevsky* (1934), Leonov has a number of original plays to his credit: *Untilovsk* (1928), about life in an out-of-the-way community in Siberia; *Provintsialnaya istoriya* (*A Provincial Story,* 1928), a somber picture of rural life; *Usmirenie Badadoshkina* (*The Taming of Badadoshkin,* 1930), about a NEP profiteer; *The Orchards of Polovchansk* (1938); *Volk* (*The Wolf,* 1939), also about preparedness for war and the efforts to quash enemies within the Soviet state; *Metel* (*The Snowstorm,* 1939, 1962), the (better) original version of which develops a novel contrast between two brothers, a corrupt Soviet official and a sympathetically conceived émigré, and was suppressed during rehearsals at the Maly Theater; *Obyknovenny chelovek* (*An Ordinary Person,* 1940-41), Leonov's only designated "comedy," about false values in life represented by the ultimately unsuccessful materialistic ambitions of a mother for her daughter; *Nashestvie* (*Invasion,* 1942) and *Lyonushka* (1943), both about Russian heroism during the war; and *Zolotaya kareta* (*The Golden Coach,* 1946-55), the original version of which was another casualty of Party suppression, dealing with the psychological and emotional complexities of readjustment to peace among the residents of a devastated provincial town immediately after the war.

*The Orchards of Polovchansk* is Leonov's best-known and, at the same time, most problematic play. It can also serve as something of a paradigm of the acrobatics—and compromises—of revision in which Leonov has had to engage, especially in the 1930s and '40s, in order to overcome objections that his stylistic individualism and psychological complexity obscure ideological purpose.

Reminded of Chekhov by the summertime country setting, the orchard motif, the family milieu, and the play's largely static quality, critics have long imputed a Chekhovian character to *The Orchards of Polovchansk.* At some level, Chekhov clearly figured in the conception of the work, but in its conceptualization aspects of Chekhovian dramatic technique barely extend beyond the external. *The Orchards of Polovchansk* dramatizes the intrusion of hostile, alien elements into a tranquil and happy family atmosphere. The family is that of the Makkaveevs, headed by the family patriarch, the earthy, life-loving, and hardy Adrian Makkaveev, a character more familiar to readers of Gorky than of Chekhov. Makkaveev's accomplishments are a testament to his productive capacity. On the former estate of a nobleman he has cultivated a magnificent fruit orchard in which he can justifiably take pride. This is the most obvious Chekhovian element in the play. Makkaveev's orchard is meant to recall that of *The Cherry Orchard* and his successful working of the land is intended as an example of what could be accomplished in Soviet times. The orchard that symbolizes a way of life coming to an end in Chekhov's play now becomes a symbol of a reborn Russia. Because of his rough-hewn and dynamic character the temptation also exists to view Makkaveev as an extension of Chekhov's Lopakhin. There are similarities, certainly, but Makkaveev's gilt-edged revolutionary background (he underwent campaigns of the Civil War) and immense love for the land set him far apart from Lopakhin. Given his origins, his shrewd business sense, and

his drive, Lopakhin could more easily have become a NEP speculator than a Makkaveev.

Makkaveev's productive capacity is emphasized by the family situation as well: seven children by two wives (the second much younger than himself), six of them boys. With the exception of his youngest son, a cripple, the men of the family are all successful in their careers, all patriotic and heroic—true sons of their father. The exception of the youngest son is explained by a moral code of Russian drama . . . , namely that the offspring of an illicit union is stigmatized by some physical defect. With Makkaveev's youngest son the suspicion is firmly implanted that his birth resulted from a wartime affair between Makkaveev's second wife, Aleksandra, and a shadowy character named Pylyaev.

The surprise reappearance of Pylyaev after an absence of eighteen years offsets the mood of joyful family reunion occasioned by the return home for a brief stay of Makkaveev's oldest sons and his daughter, Masha, and injects into the play its major element of intrigue.

The return of Makkaveev's children sets the stage for a Chekhovian drama of family relationships explored against the background of a provincial estate in summer. But the anticipation of the Chekhovian mood is unfulfilled. The arrival of the children is unobtrusive and undramatic, and the children themselves are paragons of virtue in their respective ways. Hence, the placid family setting remains essentially unchanged in dramatic terms. There is a great deal of the usual sort of family small talk and the incidents that go together to make up a family reunion, but none of the subtle character interaction of a Chekhovian drama materializes.

Leonov attempts to create interest by injecting a note of suspense regarding the delay of one son, Vasili, who is in the navy and has been away on a secret and dangerous submarine assignment, presumably in the Baltic. Late in the play, the Makkaveevs learn that Vasili was killed in an accident while on the assignment, but since he is then invested with the aura of a national hero no scene or scenes of visible remorse occur and the suspense evoked by the anticipation over his arrival and failure to appear really leads nowhere. To compensate, as it were, for the loss of Vasili, Leonov introduces the character of a young officer (Otshelnikov) who was a friend of Vasili, who is the bearer of the sad tidings of his death and with whom Makkaveev's daughter will become romantically linked.

Whatever dramatic interest *The Orchards of Polovchansk* generates stems from the play's negative forces—Pylyaev and the gathering clouds of war. Neither of these, to be sure, has anything to do with Chekhovian drama. Pylyaev emerges instead out of the ample Soviet tradition of the "wrecker," who filled the Soviet stage to overflow in the paranoid 1930s. In an earlier version of the play, Leonov's conception of the character was considerably different. Related more to the common figure of the unassimilable malcontent of Soviet literature of the '30s, Pylyaev (named Usov in the earlier version) was originally an unsuccessful, bitterly frustrated, Salieri-like man envious of his friend Makkaveev's accomplishments and determined to ruin his domestic happiness. Bowing to criticism principally from theatrical administrative quarters that the play lacked political content, Leonov reworked Usov into the sinister anti-Soviet schemer Pylyaev, thereby transforming the drama itself from a psychological study of Ibsenian resonance into a sociopolitical play in which themes of patriotism, heroism, obscure political intrigue, and impending conflict contend awkwardly for balance with ingredients of Chekhovian style. The problems raised by the transformation of the character of Usov-Pylyaev eluded a satisfactory solution; once the integrity of the original conception was compromised, neither the dramatic characterization nor the play itself fully recovered. The Moscow Art Theater rehearsed the play for fifteen months before its première in 1939, delayed largely by the difficulties the actor N. N. Sosnin experienced in trying to infuse life into the role of Pylyaev. After nearly three years work on the play, and the exceptionally long rehearsal period, **The Orchards of Polovchansk** had a run of just thirty-six performances and to generally poor reviews.

Playing on ironic contrast, Leonov times the reappearance of Pylyaev to coincide with the scheduled arrival of Makkaveev's children. Although he is very sparing of details concerning the reasons behind Pylyaev's return visit after so long an absence, he leaves little doubt: a) that Makkaveev's youngest son is really the illegitimate offspring of Pylyaev and Aleksandra and that Pylyaev wants to see him again; and b) that Pylyaev who, it is established, has spent time in prison, has been up to further wrongdoing and is a fugitive from the law. From the instant he appears Pylyaev is wholly unappealing: insinuating, presumptuous, conniving. But at the same time he is presented as so shadowy, that the characterization never truly coheres. The result is that the Pylyaev-Aleksandra-Makkaveev relationship arouses some interest but not enough to sustain the play as a whole. At the end of the work, moved no doubt by what he considered a sense of dramatic symmetry, Leonov has Pylyaev arrested by the same Otshelnikov who brings the news of Vasili's death and with whom Masha falls in love.

More convincing an aspect of **The Orchards of Polovchansk** is the ominous aura of imminent war. Significantly, Makkaveev's oldest sons are in the armed forces: Vasili, who was killed, and another son on military maneuvers in the very vicinity of Polovchansk. The sounds of tanks, artillery, and rockets reverberate throughout the play underscoring in a sense the fragility of the calm reigning at Polovchansk. It is also made clear against whom the military precautions are being taken. The Germans and Japanese are mentioned directly on a few occasions and as if to emphasize the point Makkaveev frequently recalls his fighting against the Germans (possibly in World War I and certainly in the "intervention" during the Civil War).

Leonov's efforts to re-create the atmosphere of Chekhovian drama and to enrich the intrigue of his play by introducing an evil and mysterious figure such as Pylyaev fail. But where **The Orchards of Polovchansk** does succeed is in capturing the sense of evil encroaching on a calm, orderly way of life. The sounds of war games are distant at first, but they continue to draw nearer with a portentous

insistence. In trying to strengthen the underlying meaning of his play it is possible that Leonov was operating symbolically both with the death of Vasili and the ironically juxtaposed arrival of Pylyaev. If Vasili's untimely death foreshadows the death of many heroic young men in the war to come, then Pylyaev's reappearance seems to suggest the impossibility of ever fully eradicating evil from life. . . .

The years 1941 to 1945 produced, expectedly, a rich harvest of plays about the war. Most were schematic exercises in the propaganda of heroism and nationalism. There were a few, however, that stood above the ordinary, such as *Dym otechestva* (*Smoke of the Fatherland*, 1942), a joint effort by the Brothers Tur (the collective pseudonym of Leonid Tubelsky, 1905-61, and Pyotr Ryzhey, 1908- ) and Lev Sheynin (1905- ); *Russkie lyudi* (*The Russian People*, 1942), by the best-known Russian writer of the war period, Konstantin Simonov (1915- ); **Nashestvie** (**Invasion,** 1942), by Leonid Leonov; and *Front* (1942), by the popular Ukrainian playwright Aleksandr Korneychuk (1905-72). . . .

A familiar setting (a small Russian town in the initial period of the war), familiar characters (an anti-Red former Russian émigré, Mosalsky; a heroic Communist, Kolesnikov; compromising Russians anxious to preserve their skins at any cost, Fayunin and Kokoryshkin; "good" Russians, Dr. Talanov and his family; hard-as-rock Germans, Wiebel, Spurre, and Kuntz), and a familiar "happy ending" (the final-curtain liberation of the occupied town by Soviet parachutists) reappear in Leonov's best-known and most frequently performed war play, **Invasion.** But as the world of the drama is entered, the terrain seems distinctly less recognizable than a first glance indicates. If partisan resistance and heroics dominate the action of such plays as *Smoke of the Fatherland* and *The Russian People*, the thrust of **Invasion** moves in a very different direction. War is the inescapable fact of Leonov's play; it is the background against which everything in the drama has to be viewed and against which everything, indeed, has to be measured. Yet within this context the dramatist's concern shifts from the epic to the lyric, from the drama of the group to the drama of the individual. This shift enabled Leonov to write a play which has flaws (the *deus ex machina* triumphant ending is trite and weak) but which deserves to be considered one of the most interesting of the war period and one reflecting a sincere effort on the part of the dramatist to work the familiar stuff of war into an intellectually and psychologically more provocative experience than the rousing patriotism of most of his contemporaries' plays.

Psychology is the key word here, the indisputable focus of **Invasion.** At the core of the drama is an inquiry into the psychologically transformative power of war's suffering, a power sufficient to metamorphose an arrogant, self-centered, young ne'er-do-well into a man possessing the spiritual courage to sacrifice himself so that a better man (in a civic sense) might live. The subject of this metamorphosis is the erring son, Fyodor, of the town doctor, Talanov. In the first draft of the play the cause of Fyodor's rupture with his family is his (innocent) involvement in a political crime. In the final version, it is because of a sordid love affair about which, perhaps wisely—from a dramatic point of view—Leonov is very sparing of details. Apparently incapable of killing himself (rather than the woman he is involved with), Fyodor breaks with her— temporarily—and returns to his father's home after an absence of three years. Shortly thereafter, the town is occupied by the invading Germans. The residents begin to adjust to the drastically changed pattern of their lives and it is the process of adjustment that Leonov chooses to dramatize rather than the more conventional heroics of resistance. The restlessness and recalcitrance of Fyodor seem impervious to change, however, until the pivotal episode of the play occurs: the brutal assault by Germans on the teen-age Aniska, the granddaughter of the Talanovs' servant, Demidevna. Typical of Leonov's low-keyed approach throughout the play, the assault on Aniska (like all other brutalities in *Invasion*) is relegated to an offstage action, only the effects of which are shown onstage. Aniska's assault becomes the turning point in Fyodor's life. The horrible violation of innocence succeeds in cracking the wall of arrogance and self-interest narcissistically nurtured over several years. An inner compulsion to atone, to reestablish contact with the collective is born and requires only the proper catalyst to realize itself. This comes when a local Communist official, Kolesnikov, now presumably a partisan fighter (again, this is implied by Leonov but not spelled out in the dramatic action) is given shelter in the Talanov home after he is brought there, wounded, by Fyodor's sister, Olga, a schoolteacher. Fyodor's earlier relationship with Kolesnikov (in Act I) was marked by a kind of resentful acrimoniousness. But now the wounded (and hunted—there is a price on his head) Kolesnikov crystallizes as the instrument of Fyodor's self-transformation and regeneration.

When it becomes apparent that the Germans have traced Kolesnikov to Dr. Talanov's house and will arrest him the moment he leaves it, Fyodor takes Kolesnikov's place. Since neither Fyodor nor Kolesnikov are familiar faces to the Germans, the ruse goes undetected. The possibility of revelation arises in the third act of the play during the interrogation of Fyodor at which his own parents are present. But at the crucial moment, when they perceive what is happening, the Talanovs resist the naturally human impulse to divulge their son's true identity and thus save his life, aware perhaps intuitively of Fyodor's spiritual need. The final act of Fyodor's personal drama, when his self-fulfillment at last is attained, comes in the fourth and last act. In a prison cell awaiting execution Fyodor is not at once automatically accepted by his fellow Russians as Kolesnikov's surrogate, worthy of being executed *as* Kolesnikov. The inmates debate the matter and finally accept Fyodor in recognition of his undeniable heroism. He and two other prisoners die before the others are rescued in a daring surprise raid by Soviet parachutists.

The ending, and the few genuflective references to Stalin's military leadership preceding it, produce the only really discordant notes in an otherwise subdued psychological drama almost wholly devoid of heroics, strident patriotism, and overt political propaganda. The subdued quality of *Invasion,* which sets it apart from most Russian plays

about the war, is carefully developed from the beginning of the action with the lack of hysteria among the townspeople in the face of the German occupation to the very moment when Fyodor quietly confronts his death. As I pointed out earlier, virtually all brutalities and heroics are kept offstage and introduced only in so far as they have any bearing on the activities and relationships of characters onstage. The actual occupation of the town by the Germans is not dramatized as the focus shifts entirely to the process of adjustment by the townspeople and their efforts to preserve a semblance of a normal routine of life within the framework of occupation. Aniska's brutalization occurs offstage and produces no emotional excesses onstage. The murder of German occupation officers by Kolesnikov and his guerrillas is never seen by the audience. The seizure of Fyodor is also kept offstage as well as his death and the appearance at play's end of the parachutists who appear out of nowhere in the sky.

If there is less overt action in a physical sense in Leonov's play than in other Russian war dramas, it is also true that significant character interrelations and transformations proceed from action rather than from words or from the confrontation of opposing personalities. Leonov's technique in this respect is nowhere better observed than in Fyodor's metamorphosis and the emotion-charged (if emotion-less) interrogation scene in Act IV where his parents are faced with the agonizing decision whether or not to reveal to the German authorities that their son is not Kolesnikov. In the first instance, the virtual absence of any "soul-searching" on Fyodor's part articulated in the form of a soliloquy or in dialogue with other characters may create the impression that his metamorphosis is inadequately or improperly motivated. But this is not the case. The transformation is not arrived at suddenly; it is not overt or theatricalized. It springs from the circumstances of Fyodor's private life and his psychological state at the moment he beholds the battered body of Aniska before him. In keeping with the low-keyed mood of the entire play the transformation of Fyodor is not, therefore, thrust suddenly upon the audience but disclosed piecemeal, unobtrusively, and only through action.

On the formal level one further aspect of *Invasion* invites comment—Leonov's extensive use throughout the play of long, detailed stage directions. These not only fulfill the primary function of providing precise information on attire, gesture, and props but at times are so literary and narrative as to seem aimed principally at a reader. Certainly, to the director and actors their imagery, humor, and irony are of no particular value. Reflected here is not just a concern for the manner in which the dramatist wishes his work brought to the stage, but the dissatisfaction with the limitations of the dramatic form on the part of a writer ultimately more at ease with the expansiveness of the novel. Some of the best examples of such stage directions occur in the dramatically effective third act in which Fyodor, impersonating Kolesnikov, is interrogated in the presence of his parents, and at the very beginning of Act IV. Looking more closely at the directions especially in Act III, one has the distinct impression, moreover, that Leonov was striving for something even beyond narration. The room in which the interrogations are conducted is filled with a variety of characters, Russian and German alike. When the Germans are first introduced into the scene, the stage direction calls for their moving in a rigid, wooden manner reminiscent of pasteboard figures or puppets: "Now guests of a secondary significance are visible. They are pasteboard, with the restricted movements of mannequins. At the non-Russian speech of the new arrivals, Kokoryshkin peeped out and then seemed even to shrink in size."

In the light of other directions in the same act it is apparent that Leonov sought not only to convey the impression of something non-human about the Germans through their physical movements, but also to introduce an element of the grotesque into the scene. Consider, for example, the directions governing the movements of the German officer Spurre and the Russian flunkey Kokoryshkin. Spurre has just come into the room and Kokoryshkin begins to greet him. But before he finishes Spurre obviously mistakes him for the prisoner Kolesnikov. Kokoryshkin barely perceives what is happening when the German grabs him by the collar and rushes him out of the room. The first part of the stage direction reads as follows: "Like a little feather he turns Kokoryshkin around with his back to the door and leads him with his extended arm. They exit rhythmically, as though dancing, leg to leg and face to face. Kokoryshkin offers no resistance and is just very afraid of stepping on Spurre's toes. . . ." For stage directions such as these employed, above all, to reinforce through physical movement and gesture language the already grotesque character of the entire act one has to go back to the comic art of a Gogol or Sukhovo-Kobylin whose inspiration at least for the act should not be discounted.

## Leonid Leonov with Alexander Lysov (interview date 26 April 1983 and 20 June 1987)

SOURCE: An interview in *Soviet Literature,* translated by Evgeni Filippov, No. 5, 1989, pp. 161-65.

[*In the following interview, which is based on talks between Leonov and Lysov that took place on April 26, 1983, and June 20, 1987, Leonov remarks on the difficulty of writing and the place of art in the twentieth century.*]

Everyone entering Leonov's house leaves the world's mundanities and vanities on the doorstep. The personality of the owner, the feeling of concern he exudes, the time that seems to flow at a different pace in his study lined with books—ancient tomes, "books constantly in use" with worn gilded bindings, and the latest publications and periodicals—everything creates a "philosophical atmosphere", makes you aware of "the age-old concerns of the world waiting to be resolved" without, however, inducing a sense of guilt if you failed to address yourself to the task. Conversations with Leonid Leonov are always unique and unpredictable. Scattered over time, separated by the boundaries of understatement and questions that remained unasked, they complement one another, echo one another leaving an impression that the conversation has never stopped. There are so many questions I would like to have asked that I sometimes feel as if I were standing

at the door of Leonov's flat, a nervous chill running down my spine.

The moral focus of Leonov's quests is "the large, genuine humanity", "all together", "united, perhaps, still only in its noble aspirations, but already standing on the threshold of unity." This noble, throbbing ideal informs everything Leonov says, whether he is talking about "the wisdom of ancient writers", tragic distortions in the course of science, nature or human history, the ethical consequences of the religious crisis, spiritual improvement or contemporary epistemological aspects of morality. The same high values are used as a yardstick of the "crevasses" which were formed in the 20th century as a result of the "volcanic displacement of concepts, forces and values", and which have "cut across continents, families and human hearts."

According to Leonov, a true artist "does not portray himself", "does not preach on his own behalf," "as a person inhabiting his time," he is committed to outlining the "thinkable ideal", strives to attain a new level of moral oneness with the great whole of the human race, and he rejects everything that is extraneous, "inessential", "not prompted by concern about tomorrow" and consequently distorting the natural "order of things."

. . . . .

[Leonov]: The search in art is always the search for truth and universal harmony; it is a tireless quest of justice, of the challenges and goals of civilisation, a keen awareness of its tragic course. . . . The most powerful ideas, themes and aspects of themes are those the author holds nearest as a person. The underlying law is the same as the law which governs energy transfer without conductors: in order to reach the receiver, the energy charge should be great, and greater, the larger the distance to be covered. Such a high level of maturity of ideas can be observed in our major authors who have set a standard of excellence. The main thing by which you can judge an author is what guided him, what events of his life could have prompted this or that plot, how are his ideas rooted in his times, what did the artist find interesting and how he reacted? In my own case, there are some pointers in the legend about the "furious Calaphat" or say, Pchkhov's narrative about the escape of Adam and Eve who cry on the edge of the Garden of Eden while the Antipode invites them to go *further* and take a roundabout path. I have in one way or another experienced and thought about all this, but in my novels it does not spring from me, in this sense, my novels are not autobiographical.

[Lysov]: *In your tribute to Tolstoy, speaking about an artist of the future (it might as well be the end of the century) you name among the many missions of the artist the task of recording "how our difficult era fits into the mainstream of humanity". Today, it is one of the main questions in our literature. Can I address this question to you paraphrasing it as follows, what is the distinguishing feature of continuity processes in the 20th century, and the complexity of continuity in art?*

Great epoch like ours have strong winds blowing which turn the main ideas of mankind *en face* and "in profile". In order to arrive at the true substance and direction of these ideas, it is necessary to go to the root of things and find one's own place accordingly. Above all, one must adhere to the basic principles of humanity, the classical notions of Justice, Goodness and Beauty. These are the pillars of every world view, given the modifications brought by the specific nature of the times. You will remember my character Firsov who reflects about the "seven ideas" clad in historical garb. Morality understood in this way is the theatre of action for the whole history. I have a good deal to say about it in **The Thief,** in the discussions between Vikhrov and Seryozha in **Russian Forest,** in **Skutarevsky:** think about the conversation between two brothers. In the body of human values, only an indifferent person cannot locate his place: in order to be oneself, and find one's place in time, one must love, believe, have pity and compassion. To me, these concepts are much broader than passing fads or trends—they are not about "personal" loyalty to, say, Comrade Kalinin or Voroshilov. It is a different kind of loyalty. Without this higher sense of involvement neither human civilisation, nor the existence of the human race are possible . . . With prophetic insight into many features of the future, Dostoevsky dreaded most the upheavals and changes the future would inevitably bring to human morality. Dostoevsky's perception of the world took shape at a time when literature drew on solid, time-tested material, strong and reliable like old wood from which wonderful violins could be made. At that time there was no ambiguity about the notions of "eternity", "God", "motherland", "the people", "man in general". The Revolution did not merely change the former climate, but displaced and bared many concepts, they became contradictory. Writing today is a tricky business. The material is raw, you plane a board, and suddenly it twists. But tomorrow, this too may be obsolete.

It is an important, unwieldy epoch we are living in, I don't think an artist has ever been confronted with such difficulties . . . How to convey the cruel experience of the 20th century? In these conditions of polarised concepts and aberration of ideas, how does one determine the true value of things and pick one's bearings in depicting the world split asunder? Many meanings have been shifted, but the words have remained the same: I still have to call a desert a "desert", ecstasy "ecstasy" and people "people". So, I for one, cannot vouchsafe that I have managed to express the genuine content of my times.

*Your* **Spiral,** *if I understand it correctly, opens with a diagnosis of the distortion of human ideas in the 20th century: "Sometimes dictionaries gave such widely diverging definitions of the same words, denoting everyday, and not only philosophical objects, as if the very chemistry of life was different on the opposite sides of the cleavage." Can this moral crisis lead to a global tragedy?*

Yes, **Spiral** is short on optimism in the accepted sense. But optimism can be derived from tragic knowledge as well. One must look with unblinkered and honest eyes at the future and the tragic events that it may hold in store for us as a consequence of the many mistakes we make ourselves, but also of various survivals of our civilisation which are hard to get rid of.

*But there must be a realistic way towards "reinstating" humanitarian values.*

The ethical and the spatial worlds intersect in an invisible point to form a crucifix—a genuine human personality can only be formed if one passes through this crucifix. Nothing is dearer than the individual. Mikhail Gorbachev has expressed the idea that the interests of humanity are above the interests of class. This is a very important statement. Culture is what welds the human race into a single organism. Man, humanity . . . There are no other values, and many, if not all of them, were discovered in the past. It is through commitment to what is human that much of what has been lost can be retrieved. This is necessary in order to "be", and not just to "be seem to be", not to eke out a bleak existence in "the dark desert of the world". It is the catechism for daily life and for the processes going on deep under the surface. Everything proclaimed today coincides remarkably with the ideas preached by Pushkin's *Prophet.* Even if "the sinful tongue" has not yet been torn out of our heads, there is a pressing need for new departures, for the truth, something through which the whole mankind must pass. In our country, the quest for truth must redress many mistakes made either due to haste or to ignorance. We have left cruel and harsh times behind us: we were ploughing through uncharted deserts, without making detours—and the results were bound to affect our morality . . . The terrain of history is always rugged: there are mountains and valleys, ravines and precipices. I see contradictions coming to a head, and I pray to God that they should be resolved peacefully. Today, we see only the early signs of change: perestroika was preceded by a prolonged and grim period when terrible blunders and incredible overloads were explained away by promises of a bright future (which includes the present). As a result, we have run up a huge debt to our posterity.

To sum up, if one looks at all these processes, the complexity of the 20th century lies in the fact that the destinies of humankind have focussed in it. The October Revolution, in resolving many world problems, triggered a series of great historic events, both in the short and especially in the longer term. We passed through several historical stages and cleared many hurdles within several years. The problems being tackled in this century determine the road of the world for the future. Everything that happens to us, any choice we make is important not only for us, but for our descendants. We would do well to recall the work of the forester, not only as a profession, but as a moral symbol: one plants a tree for the sake of the future generations with no hope of seeing it bear fruit.

. . . . .

The hand can barely commit to paper the fast-changing dimensions: the infinitely small particle "flying in lepton" with the speed of light, the Demiurge playing with a Leviathan in-between "acts of creation", the swirling primary substance, the ringing "waterfall" of history. I am in a hurry to learn something more about what seems most important, ever hoping to discover the magic "sesame". In the midst of these travails, I hear the muted voice of Leonid Leonov, thoughtful, groping for the right word: "I always stand before a mysterious curtain as it were. Behind it are strange, wonderful lives, and I am anxious to look at them. I feel like a child waiting to go to the circus—a treat and a mystery."

**Valentin Kovalyov   (essay date November 1986)**

SOURCE: "Leonid Leonov's Path," in *Soviet Literature,* No. 484, November, 1986, pp. 143-49.

[*In the essay below, Kovalyov provides a brief overview of Leonov's career and remarks on the themes of his major novels.*]

Leonid Leonov is a remarkable writer, a craftsman who has left an important mark in the history of Soviet literature.

The characters he has created (Skutarevsky, Kurilov, Vikhrov, Fyodor Talanov, Vekshin, Evgenia Ivanovna, Gratsiansky, Chikelev) are comparable in stature to the major characters in Russian and world classical literature. They give an idea of this nation and its complex internal development.

Leonid Leonov was born on May 31, 1899. He matured socially in the early years of the revolution when he worked as a war correspondent.

After being demobbed from the Red Army in 1922 Leonov took up writing. He wrote stories and novellas such as *Buryga, The End of a Little Man, Kovyakin's Notes,* etc. From the beginning he was interested in moral and philosophical questions and invested his plots with drama and psychological insight. He revealed a penchant for complex composition and a rare gift of verbal portrayal. Critics noted the influence of the Russian realists—Gogol, Dostoevsky, Tolstoy, Saltykov-Shchedrin and Maxim Gorky on his writing.

Leonov's manner was extremely original: he depicted the revolution as perceived by those who stood on the sidelines of the main events and did not have a good grasp of what was happening (peasants in a remote forest village; conservatively minded metropolitan intelligentsia; a salesman in a provincial town). This oblique reflection of the time, so the writer felt, gave him a better insight into the destinies and experiences of "the little man" in the stormy years of revolutionary upheaval and into the contradictory phenomena of the post-revolutionary years.

His first novel, *The Badgers,* published in 1924, looked at the dramatic social cleavages in the Russian countryside after the revolution, the tragic delusions and waverings amongst some of the peasantry. The "badgers" are the peasants in a remote hamlet in the Russian hinterland who have lost their sense of direction in the face of the turbulent change that swept away age-old traditions; rejecting Soviet power, they took to the woods in order to "weather the storm". The "badgers" are led by Semyon Rakhleyev. A man of peasant stock, he had spent some time in Moscow trying, without success, to better himself socially (it was his ambition to become a merchant).

Semyon is opposed by his brother, Pavel. Like Semyon he has moved to the town in search of a livelihood. But his life takes a different turn. He gets a job in a factory where he learns of the proletarian struggle through personal experience. He becomes a commander of a Red Army unit and it is in this capacity that he encounters his brother. Pavel, who was himself a peasant not so long ago, quickly sizes up the complex situation and finds a peaceful solution to the conflict. To him, the "badgers" are not the enemies of the revolution but bewildered people who have temporarily lost their way. The image of Pavel distils the features of the hero of the time, a revolutionary, a man of great inner strength and strongly-held convictions.

The writer draws affectionate portraits of peasants, admiring their common sense, native intelligence and sharp tongues. But he does not idealise them, and he is aware of how much still needs to be done to usher the peasants into the modern age.

*The Badgers* brought Leonov fame in the Soviet Union and abroad (the novel was translated into German and Spanish as early as 1926).

In 1927 he published his second novel, ***The Thief.*** Like *The Badgers* it looks at the recent past—the first half of the 1920s. The novel is set in a Moscow suburb. Its characters include a ruined landowner, a cabaret singer, a cinema actress, a wealthy peasant (*kulak*), and other human flotsam of the ancient régime, as well as the underworld.

The author describes his novel as psychological. *The Thief* comes to grips with important social problems, such as the individual and revolution, the position of man in the complex contemporary world, contours of an emerging new morality, and so on. Maxim Gorky's influence is discernible in the author's keen interest in the human psyche, the mentality of people who have dropped out of the mainstream of life, and the broadly humanist perspective. At the same time Leonov borrowed something of the manner and artistry of Dostoevsky, and this shows in his meticulous psychological analyses. There are also echoes of some of the characters and plot motifs of his great predecessor. The novel's hero, Dmitri Vekshin, an ex-Red Armyman who used to take part in daring cavalry charges, does not understand the rationale of the New Economic Policy (NEP) launched by the Soviet government. Feeling that this would bring back all the Philistines and all the "have beens", he becomes a thief. He justifies his fall by saying that in this way he is fighting against the enemies of the revolution, the new speculators, profiteers and Philistines. Gradually and painfully, he realises the fallacy of his antisocial behaviour.

Thirty years later the author, dissatisfied with the first edition of *The Thief* undertook a thorough revision of the novel. He changed the overall conception and the main characters, as well as the language and style.

He takes a new look at Dmitri Vekshin. His involvement on the side of the revolution had not turned the working-class lad into a truly new person. There was a discrepancy between the humane cause for which he was fighting and his cold and arrogant attitude to people. Vekshin is a type of person who takes part in the revolution spontaneously, pursuing only personal aims and unable to grasp the great social significance and humanism of the revolution.

In the second edition greater prominence is given to the narrator, Firsov. He is an intelligent and observant person who tends to take a somewhat biassed view of things, and often interprets facts in a "literary" way. In giving us a detailed description of Firsov's approach to writing, Leonov airs some of his own views on the artistic process and formulates his principles of the philosophical-psychological novel.

The novel is full of reflections on the complex inner world of the contemporary man, the difficulties of overcoming mutual misunderstanding, alienation, fear of life, and the danger of spiritual emptiness. Leonov's vision embraces the whole predicament of man in its contemporary meaning.

It is interesting to note that when *The Thief* was reissued in the United States in 1968 it was the first edition that was chosen. "People there believe that writers here work on the government's orders," says Leonov. "In Berkeley a lady came up to me and exclaimed theatrically: 'Why, why did you have to alter *The Thief*?' She had not read the second edition, but she glibly assumed that I had changed the novel on somebody's orders."

After *The Badgers* and *The Thief* critics were inclined to regard Leonov as an artist who had found his theme. Before long, however, they had to eat their words. Leonov wrote his novel, *The River Sot* (1929), and the novella, *Locusts* (1930).

*The River Sot* is a socio-political novel devoted, in Leonov's words, "to the history of the clash between aggressive novelty and Russian antiquity, the history of the first encounter between the machine and the ignorant grassroots." Sot is the name of a river flowing through the boundless northern forests. The pristine silence is invaded by the noise of human voices, axes, and the roar of machines. A major factory is being built. The backward country is being industrialised, rural life is changing, and these changes undermine the influence of the local hermit monks, the custodians of old ideology and customs. The 20th century comes into conflict with the 16th. The new wins in travail and difficult struggle.

---

**Leonov's vision embraces the whole predicament of man in its contemporary meaning.**

*—Valentin Kovalyov*

---

Dramatic changes in the economy were accompanied by changes in people's minds. The author showed the new world and the new man. The main character of *The River Sot* is the Bolshevik Uvadiev, chief of the construction project. Behind a forbidding facade, he hides tenderness and idealism: "Somewhere yonder, on a glittering horizon beneath the rainbows of the future, this crude solider saw a little girl. She was no more than ten and her name was

Katya. It was for her sake that he was going into battle and facing hardship." The happiness of future generations is gained in hard day-to-day battles and work, the writer seems to say.

Gorky described the novel as a vivid example of how genuine literature had become involved with the new socialist reality and he praised Leonov's skill in composition and style: *The River Sot* is written with "symphonic clarity." And in 1931 Gorky gave this assessment of Leonov's skill: "From the inexhaustible wealth of our language Leonov skilfully selects the vivid and sonorous words whose magic is particularly convincing. There is hardly a superfluous word in his books. A master of his craft, he never narrates but always portrays using words as an artist uses paint."

*The River Sot* is a major work of socialist realism, and it begins the cycle of Leonov's novels in the thirties about the drive to build socialism and the emergence of a new mentality (*Skutarevsky, The Road to the Ocean*). *Skutarevsky* (1933) is about scientists, the Soviet intelligentsia. The central figure is Sergei Skutarevsky, a major Russian physical scientist who openly took the side of the people in the October Revolution. The novel describes Soviet scientists of the older and younger generation (Cherimov). In drawing the character of Fyodor Skutarevsky, the hero's artist brother, Leonov makes us aware of the difficult decision that faced an artist who was at first suspicious of the October Revolution. The author ridicules decadent trends in art and poetry in the 1920s. The novel offers an impressive panorama of the hectic creative atmosphere of the First Five-Year Plan, the historical optimism of the Soviet people and their confidence in the triumph of socialism.

As in his earlier works, Leonov probes into the spiritual world of his contemporaries, their mode of thinking, and their views. The reader is not told about the practical activities of the characters alone. He is given insight into their souls and their philosophy of life.

*The Road to the Ocean* (1935) plunges into the thick of contemporary life. The action spans two years—1933-1934. But the plot is not confined to these time limits. There are flashbacks into the past, both the recent past (the Civil War) and the more remote past (the 19th century) in search of the roots of contemporary phenomena. He traces the origins of social types and accompanies the characters in the novel in their imaginary "travels beyond the horizon" into the distant future.

The principal character, Kurilov, a member of the "Old Bolshevik Guard", is presented as the "focal character" of his time; he has tremendous moral authority over people; he is a generous, expansive man who makes easy contact with other people.

The novel has many strands. Several inherently interconnected plots develop simultaneously. There are flashbacks, the characters are described through a "stream of consciousness" technique, there are frequent rambling philosophical debates and psychological disputes. From time to time the epic narrative is broken by lyrical and topical digressions.

In the 1930s Leonov made a number of aesthetic statements. The most comprehensive of these was his speech at the First Congress of Soviet Writers in 1934. He said: "We live in an atmosphere ionised by the progressive ideas of the age. Our country today is a giant laboratory where new morality, new ethics and new socialist humanity are being forged." Leonov pointed out that art "is becoming a major instrument in the moulding of the new man". The thematic range of literature has changed in socialist society. Literature has ceased to be "a mirror of the domestic life of the individual. Today all personal concerns emerge from the privacy of the room into workshops, clubs, laboratories and into the streets." The mind of the contemporary man, stressed Leonov, can only be fully revealed by portraying him in his professional milieu, because profession is "the social drivebelt" linking the individual with his times.

*The Road to the Ocean* was the last novel Leonov wrote in the twenties and the thirties. The decade that followed was devoted to drama.

He wrote his first stage adaptations of his work (*The Badgers, Skutarevsky*) back in the 1920s and early 1930s. In the 1920s Leonov wrote the plays *Untilovsk* and *The Taming of Badadoshkin.* These were followed by *Polovchansk Gardens* (1937), *The Wolf* (1938), *The Snowstorm* (1940), *An Ordinary Man* (1941), *The Invasion* (1942), *Lyonushka* (1943), and *The Golden Coach* (1946).

The plays of the 1930s and 1940s reflected the atmosphere of the gathering storm in the pre-war years, and the nation's battle against fascism. Among the more popular plays were *The Invasion* (about the Soviet people's struggle against German occupiers in a Russian town) and *The Golden Coach* (about the life of a Soviet town after fascist invaders were driven out). These were much produced by theatres in the Soviet Union, as well as in France, Britain, Czechoslovakia, Yugoslavia, Poland, Hungary, and other countries.

During and after the Second World War, Leonov was active as a journalist and literary critic. His letters **"To an Unknown American Friend"** (1942-1943) evoked a wide response abroad. They are a reminder to people everywhere of their responsibility for the destinies of civilisation, a call for joint action on the part of all nations against fascism and Hitler's aggression. His articles celebrating the Great Victory were long remembered by readers.

In 1944 *Pravda* published his story **The Storming of Velikoshumsk** about Soviet military operations in the victorious closing stage of the war. The story gives close-up portraits of Soviet soldiers, officers and commanders.

In the post-war decades Leonov returned to prose-writing. The 1950s saw the publication of a sweeping epic and philosophical novel *The Russian Forest* (1953) and the second edition of *The Thief* (1959). He continues to write non-fiction (*In Defence of a Friend* is a piece about nature conservation. *Talent and Work* is about the writer's craft: *A Wreath to Gorky, A Word About Tolstoy,* etc. deal with the classical heritage.) In his numerous interviews published in Czechoslovakia, Yugoslavia, the GDR, Bulgaria, the USA, and other countries, Leonov expresses his view of the mission of art in the present era and speaks about his plans.

*The Russian Forest* won the Lenin Prize. In terms of structure it is similar to *The Road to the Ocean,* bringing together the story of the present (the first year of the Great Patriotic War) and lengthy digressions into the past; as a result, the reader gets an idea of a whole era in the history of the nation ending with the war years.

The focal conflict in the novel is between scientists who espouse different scientific ideas. One of them (Vikhrov) is concerned with nature conservation and favours a progressive scientific method of forest utilization; the other (Gratsiansky) rejects that principle and demagogically claims that it restricts the use of timber resources in the economy. The argument over a purely economic problems is just the tip of the iceberg. Behind it lies genuine concern for the nation's future in one case, and indifference to the country's destiny and the interests of the people, in the other. Locked in battle were humanism and selfish individualism; the creative spirit on the one hand and malice, envy and spiritual impotence on the other; historical optimism, strength of spirit and a decadent philosophy and the petty mentality of a loner and an outcast.

Vikhrov is a man of great ideas dedicated to the noble goal of protecting nature and increasing his country's wealth. Thinking about his mission and about the new socialist era Vikhrov wrestles with the problem, "what should be his role in it?" Having found a solution, he follows his chosen path unswervingly.

The image of the mighty forest occupying vast spaces of his great country is a symbol of the people, and its inexhaustible strength and vitality. The author makes the theme of the forest a vehicle for his ecological ideas and his philosophy of nature.

The novel treats of many other themes and problems, such as the heroism of the Soviet people in the Great Patriotic War; the hideous essence of fascism; the complicated moral dilemmas of the time; the spiritual maturing of youth (in the character of Polya Vikhrova).

*The Russian Forest* reveals Leonov's skill both as novelist and dramatist. It is not fortuitous that the novel has inspired several stage versions. It is interesting to note that the problems of the forest are considered with such scientific competence (in the fields of forestry, botany and biology) that specialists have borrowed Leonov's arguments to justify their ideas about forestry. This novel tells us more about the author's personality than any other. It reveals his vast erudition in diverse areas of modern life and history, his passionate civic commitment, his broad horizons, his ability to put the concrete problems of the Soviet Union in the context of the aspirations of the whole of mankind.

To Leonov's heart are close and dear the words of Mikhail Gorbachev spoken in his statement over Soviet television about the decision of the Government of the Soviet Union to extend the unilateral moratorium on nuclear tests till January 1, 1987 based on socialism's adherence, as a social system, to the cause of peace and its profound realisation of its responsibility for the fate of civilization.

The 1960s saw the publication of two new works by Leonov: a screenplay *Mr MacKinley's Flight* (1960) and a novella *Evgenia Ivanovna* (1963). The former is an impassioned, almost political plea for peace, the latter—begun before the war and completed in the 1960s—tells the tragic story of a young Russian woman who emigrated during the Civil War.

For a long time Leonov has been working on a major new novel. Two extracts from it, *Dymkov's View of the Universe* and *The Last Outing* (in which the author offers his models of the Universe, and shows pictures of the devastation of the earth in a hypothetical atomic war) were published in 1974 and 1979. The first of these fragments was published in a new edition in 1984. These are philosophical and futurological novellas within the novel.

Like any major artist, Leonov expresses the national traits of his people. His originality is felt in his gravitating to the realism of Gogol, Dostoevsky, Tolstoy, Chekhov, Alexander Ostrovsky and Maxim Gorky. He has the awareness of the spirit of the people and the civic commitment that have always been a hallmark of Russian classical literature. He is in love with Russia and has profound insight into the Russian national character.

Leonov's books are a wonderful wellspring of knowledge of the Russian people in the modern epoch, their heroic deeds, their love of their country, and deep feeling of internationalism. Gorky said of the young Leonov that "he has the makings of a major Russian writer, very major." We can now fully appreciate how prophetic and profoundly justified these words were.

### *The Times,* London    (obituary date 11 August 1994)

SOURCE: An obituary in *The Times,* London, August 11, 1994, p. 17.

[*In the obituary below, the critic provides an overview of Leonov's career.*]

Leonid Leonov, one of the major literary figures of Soviet Russia, received two Stalin Prizes, and was a senior member of the Praesidium of the Union of Soviet Writers. In the 1930s he was a fiction editor of the leading journal *Novy Mir.* Maxim Gorki spoke of his "strong, clear, juicy prose", and Edmund Wilson wrote that he was possessed of "a literary sophistication very rare in Soviet literature".

But, while widely accepted in the Soviet Union (his books have been published there in editions amounting to more than three million copies), he was a controversial writer in the West. Some have taken him to have been a Marxist dogmatist from the start; others, more perceptive, claimed to see in him the most subversive Soviet writer to have escaped serious persecution. He was seldom called a time-server.

Leonid Maksimovich Leonov was the son of an "obscure journalist" (as he called him) and village poet who was exiled to the north of Russia from 1905 to 1910 for anti-Tsarist activity. Leonid was educated at Moscow Third Gymnasium, became a reporter on the Red Army newspaper, and fought for the Red Army in the Civil War.

He began writing in 1922 under the aegis of the Serapion Brothers, a literary group of "fellow travellers", of which Zamyatin, author of the famous dystopia *We,* was the leading theorist. Until about 1928 Russians were more or less free to write as they liked but by 1932, with the promulgation of "socialist realism", they were shackled, as they were to remain until recently.

Leonov's first stories were not at all social in intent nor was he initially much interested in politics; rather, he was influenced by Balzac, the story-teller, and Dostoevsky. In *Konets melkogo cheloveka* (1924), *End of a Trivial Man,* he experimented with *skaz* (the Russian style, started by Leskov, in which a colloquial and idiosyncratic first-person narrator tells the story): it is about a scientist who is led by his double—a transparently Dostoevskian device—to destroy the results of his work. Some have seen in it a creative writer's prophetic despair at things to come, a kind of bitter announcement of literary suicide.

In the same year Leonov published a novel, *Barsuki*—translated into English as *The Badgers* (1947)—which moved towards a more conventional realism. But *Vor* (1927), translated as *The Thief* (1931), is by common consent his best novel: an ex-commissar with blood on his hands becomes the leader of a gang of criminals, but undergoes a Dostoevskian reformation. Into this book Leonov introduced himself as a novelist who is writing a novel, but about other characters than in this novel.

There is no telling in what direction Leonov might have gone had he chosen to leave Russia. But he remained—and, under later severe criticism from the regime, rewrote and quite ruined this, his best work, in a conformist version published as late as 1959. It is therefore proper to read it in its original version.

But although he stayed, Leonov—who never denounced other writers as his near contemporaries Sholokov and Fadeyev notoriously did—produced the most ambiguous and enigmatic novels of any writer who appeared to toe the official line.

In each of them there is some element that could be taken as critical of the regime, though Leonov always arranged matters so that he could not be seriously criticised. Both *Sot* (1930), translated as *Soviet River* in 1931, and *Skutarevsky* (1932), translated under the same title (a name) in 1936, are ostensibly patriotic "Five Year Plan" novels, and the "good Communists" come out on top. But each deals zestfully with sabotage, describing anti-Communists with Dostoevskian depth and some evident relish. Moreover, the latter novel is openly experimental (it has three story-lines, as well as a novelist as a character) in a manner not supposed by "socialist realists" to be wholesome.

Nor could Leonov shake off the then supposedly bad influence of Dostoevsky. His last novel of substance was *Russkiy les* (1953), translated in 1966 as *The Russian Forest,* an allegorical attack—well before the so-called Thaw of 1956—on Stalin's purges and labour camps, with a powerful thread of ecological feeling for Russia's natural resources.

His plays are skilful suspense dramas which had much success on the stage. The filmscript **Begstvo mistera Mak-Kinli** (1961), **Mr McKinley's Flight,** was a tedious satire on Western politicians, and could have been written especially to please the Soviet censors. Earlier, just after the war, two plays by him had been suppressed.

In 1942 Leonov gave as his recreations "gardening, rearing cactuses, and motoring". In that year he lost an eye while fighting the Germans outside Leningrad. He married the daughter of the publisher N. V. Sabashnikov in 1923.

He is likely to be remembered as the author of **The Thief** (original version)—and as a writer who just might have gone on to greatness had he been allowed freedom to write as he wished. His friend Boris Pilnyak, a more original novelist, tried desperately to please the authorities, but was wholly unable to do so—and perished as a result of the purges. Leonov, in one sense more sophisticated, seems to have been able to control his own impulses more efficiently; but it is impossible to decide how ironic he intended to be.

He will always be of interest to the student of Soviet literature, though it is doubtful if the issue of the extent of the sincerity of his commitment to socialist realism, and to Marxist-Leninism itself, will ever be resolved. Do his better novels represent a struggle within himself, or are they deliberately ironic? This is the question critics ask, and will continue to ask. He remains a paradigmatic example of a writer whose genius was eventually crippled by his obligation to an ideology.

---

# FURTHER READING

### Criticism

Gibian, George. "Versions of a Soviet Inferno." In *Interval of Freedom: Soviet Literature During the Thaw, 1954-1957,* pp. 106-44. Minneapolis: University of Minnesota Press, 1960.
   Discusses Alexander Gratsiansky, the principal antagonist of *The Russian Forest,* as an example of the negative Soviet character type "closest to the old-fashioned Stalinist villains."

Klimenko, Michael. Review of *Literatura i vrem'ja,* by Leonid Leonov. *Books Abroad* 39, No. 3 (Summer 1965): 360-61.
   Remarks favorably on Leonov's collection of essays dealing with literary criticism, politics, and travel.

Plank, D. L. "Unconscious Motifs in Leonid Leonov's *The Badgers.*" *Slavic and East European Journal* 16, No. 1 (Spring 1972): 19-35.
   Analyzes a minor incident from *The Badgers,* Sergej Polovinkin's seduction of Anna Brykin, focusing on unconscious motifs and anonymity.

Simmons, Ernest J. "Leonid Leonov." In *Russian Fiction and Soviet Ideology: Introduction to Fedin, Leonov, and Sholokhov,* pp. 89-61. New York: Columbia University Press, 1958.
   Surveys Leonov's literary career, focusing on his novels.

Sosa, Michael. Review of *The River,* by Leonid Leonov. *World Literature Today* 50, No. 3 (Summer 1985): 451.
   Remarks on the protagonist of *Soviet River* and faults the translation as "woefully inadequate."

Starikova, Ekaterina. *Leonid Leonov.* Translated by Joy Jennings. Moscow: Raduga Publishers, 1986, 219 p.
   Surveys Leonov's career. In this edition, Starikova's monograph is bound with Leonov's *On Craftsmanship,* a collection of five essays including "A Word on Tolstoy" and "Dostoyevsky and Tolstoy."

Struve, Gleb. "Leonov." In *Russian Literature under Lenin and Stalin: 1917-1953,* pp. 98-105. Norman: University of Oklahoma Press, 1971.
   Focuses on *The Badgers* and *The Thief.* Struve notes Leonov's use of stories within his novels, particularly "The Tale of the Furious Kalafat" in *The Badgers,* and Leonov's debt to Dostoevsky.

Thomson, R. D. B. "Leonov's Play *Zolotaja kareta.*" *Slavic and East European Journal* 16, No. 4 (Winter 1972): 438-48.
   Discusses the themes of *The Golden Coach,* the changes Leonov made in the play's different versions, and its place in Leonov's artistic development.

"Robbing the Thief." *Times Literary Supplement,* No. 3386 (19 January 1967): 54.
   Reviews *The Thief* and *The Russian Forest.* The critic laments Leonov's revisions of the earlier novel and states that the latter novel "compares unfavorably" with Leonov's early works.

Additional coverage of Leonov's life and career is contained in the following sources published by Gale Research: *Contemporary Authors,* Vol. 129; *DISCovering Authors Modules;* and *Major 20th-Century Writers.*

# Mark Leyner

## 1956-

American short story writer and novelist.

The following entry provides an overview of Leyner's career through 1995.

## INTRODUCTION

Best known for comedic and satirical fiction often characterized as chaotic and irreverent, Leyner is a prominent contemporary writer who blends literary experimentation with elements of contemporary American life and popular culture, including scientific advancement, mass marketing, and the electronic media. Leyner has stated: "I feel linked to artists who launched their careers reading billboards aloud in the back seats on family trips, who spent their formative Saturday mornings cemented to their television screens with crazy glue, who grew up fascinated by the rhetoric of pentecostal preachers, dictators, game show hosts, and other assorted demagogues. . . . I said in an article once that we need a kind of writing that the brain can dance to. Well, that's the kind of writing I'm trying to write—thrashing the smoky air of the cerebral ballroom with a very American ball-point baton."

### Biographical Information

Born in Jersey City, New Jersey, Leyner is the son of a well-known lawyer. Fascinated with politics and current events at an early age, he avidly tracked the news both in print and on television. He also developed an interest in literature and read such diverse authors as Percy Bysshe Shelley, Joseph Conrad, William S. Burroughs, and Jack Kerouac. Leyner first took up serious writing while in high school, where he wrote a column for the school newspaper. After spending nearly a year in Europe and Israel, Leyner attended Brandeis University as a student of creative writing and literature. In 1977 he graduated and entered a graduate writing workshop at the University of Colorado at Boulder. There, Leyner's writing attracted the attention of a group of experimental writers called the Fiction Collective, who published his first book, *I Smell Esther Williams* (1983). Leyner earned his graduate degree from the University of Colorado in 1979 and returned to New Jersey. He worked at a number of teaching and copywriting jobs before the publication of *My Cousin, My Gastroenterologist* in 1989, which allowed him the opportunity to devote his time exclusively to writing.

### Major Works

In an interview with John and Carl Bellante, Leyner stated that he finds *I Smell Esther Williams* to be "pretentious," "juvenile," and "very derivative of the New York school of poetry." In addition to twenty-six short stories, the book includes a play, a dialogue, and a number of col-

lages composed of random narrative sketches. Leyner's next work, *My Cousin, My Gastroenterologist,* is similarly a composite of prose fragments, described by one reviewer as "a kind of postmodern *Arabian Nights*." Incorporating a variety of popular culture images and symbols, the collection highlights Leyner's focus on the mass media. The protagonist of the novel *Et Tu, Babe* (1992) is a popular young author named Mark Leyner around whom all life on earth revolves. Seen by many as a critique of America's celebrity-oriented culture, *Et Tu, Babe* explores the limits of individual stardom and importance. In *Tooth Imprints on a Corn Dog* Leyner continues to address and satirize the vagaries and idiosyncrasies of popular culture and contemporary society, including technological innovation, commercialism, and celebrity.

### Critical Response

Although many critics applaud Leyner's satire and parody, some have raised concerns over the anecdotal nature of his prose, the flippancy of his style, and an apparent tendency toward megalomania. Michiko Kakutani has stated in a review of *Et Tu, Babe* that a reader "begins this demented book amused and entertained and finishes it reeling from anecdote overload." In discussing *Tooth Imprints on a Corn Dog*, she has further noted that Leyner's prose pieces "are clever and amusing and willfully superficial." Rick Marin considers Leyner's fiction to be "likably self-absorbed," with the author, as evinced in *Et Tu, Babe*, writing "about what he knows and loves best—himself." However, Leyner's focus on the excesses of contemporary American society has routinely earned critical praise. Commenting on *My Cousin, My Gastroenterologist*, William Severini Kowinski has asserted: "At last readable literature has been made from the peculiar material of contemporary life, the stuff other fiction leaves out."

---

# PRINCIPAL WORKS

*I Smell Esther Williams, and Other Stories* (short stories)　1983
*American Made: New Fiction from the Fiction Collective* [editor, with Curtis White and Thomas Glynn] (short stories)　1986
*My Cousin, My Gastroenterologist* (short stories)　1990
*Et Tu, Babe* (novel)　1992
*Tooth Imprints on a Corn Dog* (short stories)　1995

---

# CRITICISM

**Charlotte M. Meyer**　(review date March-April 1984)

SOURCE: A review of *I Smell Esther Williams*, in *American Book Review*, Vol. 6, No. 3, March-April, 1984, p. 15.

[*Meyer is an American educator. In the review below, she lauds Leyner's collection of short stories* I Smell Esther Williams, *finding the prose to be "chaotic and exhilarating."*]

[*I Smell Esther Williams,* a] collection of twenty six short fictions, reads as if Leyner went to sleep or put himself into a trance to write them; they have the same exhilarating mixture of chaos and suggestiveness as sleep-talking. The title is absurdly evocative, a rich joke, but it is only one little monkey in an enormous, crowded barrelful. This has got to be among the funniest, most innovative fiction around. Here is a good sample, the opening to one of my favorites, **"A Bedtime Story for My Wife"**:

> The clock on the Hudson City Savings Bank billboard says 6:30, indicating nothing but the hands' exhaustion—it was so thrilling five minutes ago & now that seems like another life, when all the cars accelerated down Newark Avenue like they'd lost their brakes and some of the passengers, some of the women, craned their necks in the wind and their religious medals pulled against their necks and were held rigid in the draft of the wind and the dashboard saints bared their teeth to this speed and the sky went vermillion and then purple and then deep blue

and then black like four blinks of the eye and the clock's hands just fell limp . . .

Almost all of the stories are insanely disjointed on the surface, on the level of logic, but at second glance each is clustered like the petals of some exotic asymmetrical bloom. The internal consistency of the stories originates more out of tone and mood than content. None of them is plotted in any conventional way, yet each is based on a sequence of association that has all the inevitability of a traditional story.

The twenty six of them are constructed in a variety of formats. **"Octogenarians Die In Crash"** is a play in five scenes. **"Blue Dodge"** is all in dialogue. **"I Smell Esther Williams,"** the longest, is a collage of random bits and pieces—narratives, sketches, musical notation, movie scripts, and dialogues, such as this one, given here in its entirety, called

### TEENAGE CHRIST KILLERS

Mother: Where were you?

Moshe: Out.

Chaim:

Mother: Where!?

Moshe: Just out.

Chaim:

Besides variety in format, there is a "veritable cornucopia" of moods: stories of satire, of sad love, of frustration, of pure joy. The stories are highly topical and outrageously exploit the delicious comedy in the banal reference: Slurpies, mood rings, Maalox, Otis elevators, patio pools. (Yes, it's Donald Barthelme's "dreck" again but without the coyness that sometimes overtakes his writing.) There are innumerable cameo references to the rich and the famous as well. Watch for Ted Kennedy, Johnny Mathis, Carlo Ponti, Brooke Shield's mother and many, many more.

Leyner jimmies open ideas and attitudes that once seemed safely established and sealed in language. There is an endless array of parodies of writing styles—but he has shaken them loose from the burden of content and the presuppositions of values these earlier styles carry.

> Susan and Jill were so excited! They'd primped for weeks and the day had finally come! Is there anything more beautiful than a pair of girls consumed by romance! Jill stood in front of the mirror! Her underpants were a "yellow-pages" print! "Howard will flip!" Susan assured Jill!

The stories are finally *about* language: they are full of unheard-of associations, mixed metaphors by the cascading streamful, fantastic transmogrifications of the familiar into the strange, lists of disparate items held together in newly-invented categories, distortions in space and time (compressions, extensions, negations, telescopings, magnifications, and other perceptual alterations). The book is very rich.

But hasn't it all been "done before," as certain more traditional critics allege when they attempt to discredit this kind of writing (a strange condemnation, isn't it, to come from those who uphold literary tradition)? The answer is yes, of course, and so has the criticism of this kind of writing been "done before." Recall the famous condemnation of John Donne's poetry by Samuel Johnson. "The most heterogeneous ideas are yoked by violence together," he complained (as he probably does right now, wherever he is, about Leyner). Here was T.S. Eliot's classy reply two centuries later: "But a degree of heterogeneity of material compelled into unity by the operation of the poet's mind is omnipresent in poetry." And against the charge that Donne's poetry is "artificial," Eliot answered, "The effect, at its best, is far less artificial than that of an ode by Gray" (or, in Leyner's case, than a short story by Hawthorne). When Eliot rebuts Johnson's charge that Donne's style was too complex, he answers for Leyner as well: "It is to be observed that the language of Donne is as a rule simple and pure. . . . The *structure* of the sentences, on the other hand, is sometimes far from simple, but that is not a vice; it is a fidelity to thought and feeling." And finally here is Eliot's exhortation—which Leyner has already heeded—about the need to bind experience and language:

> Our civilization comprehends great variety and complexity, and this variety and complexity, playing upon a refined sensibility, must produce various and complex results. The poet must become more and more comprehensive, more allusive, more indirect, in order to force, to dislocate, if necessary, language into his meaning.

But it is only an academic exercise to connect Leyner to his predecessors. It is much more interesting in his case to look ahead than behind because his work points so confidently toward the future of fiction.

### Welch D. Everman (review date November-December 1990)

SOURCE: "The Same Pink as Pepto-Bismol," in *American Book Review,* Vol. 12, No. 5, November-December, 1990, pp. 16, 21.

[*Everman is an American writer and educator. In the following review of* My Cousin, My Gastroenterologist, *he cites numerous references to popular culture in Leyner's fiction, theorizing on the relationship between the act of writing and contemporary electronic mass media.*]

Reading the pieces in Mark Leyner's *My Cousin, My Gastroenterologist* is like sitting in front of an ultrahightech video monitor and flipping back and forth through the channels, from this to that to this and back to that again. It's all here and all perfectly familiar—the quiz shows, the kiddie shows, the late movies, the news broadcasts, the talk shows, MTV, and of course the commercials. The monitor flickers like a strobe light, and it's up to the viewer to put the bits and pieces together, to make a program of what he sees and hears.

There are stories here—the story of kids' show host Big Squirrel who is also a ninja assassin, the story of a graduate of the Wilford Military Academy of Beauty who is sentenced to die in a custom-built Mies van der Rohe electric chair for allegedly attempting to crash a commercial jetliner into the Queen Elizabeth II—but the stories are twisted, broken, interrupted again and again by other stories and stories-within-stories, stories that appear and disappear with the flick of a remote control. *My Cousin, My Gastroenterologist* is a kind of postmodern *Arabian Nights,* and its vocabulary is the "violent vocabulary of the u. s. a.," the vocabulary of the electronic media.

> "what color is your mozzarella? i asked the waitress it's pink—it's the same color as the top of a mennen lady speed stick antiperspirant dispenser, y'know that color? no, ma'am, i said it's the same pink they use for the gillette daisy disposable razors for women . . . y'know that color? nope y'know the pink they use on the wrappers for carefree panty shields? nuh-uh well, it's the same pink as pepto-bismol, y'know that color? oh yeah, i said"

Leyner is a realist, and his reality is the reality of the electronic media, the new hyperreality, more real than your hand in front of your face. For better or worse, this is our reality, too. We know what we know—the color of mozzarella, the most up-to-date treatment for kidney stones, what Elvis was really like—because we've seen it all on TV.

Back in the thirties, Walter Benjamin suggested that the camera was replacing the human eye as the arbiter of the real. In the 1990s, nothing is real until it is seen through the camera. Is it raining outside? I turn on the weather channel. How do I feel about being a homosexual carpenter in the wilds of Montana? I find out by watching other gay Montana-based carpenters on *Oprah.* I can turn on the local news to see what I've been up to today.

Leyner's reality is the one we all share, and in his writing he can assume that we know all about hockey ("tonight at madison square garden the new york rangers disemboweled the boston bruins' goalie, brought a hibachi onto the ice, roasted his intestines and served them on toast points to the howling hometown fans"), cellulite exercises ("we're doing the nine or ten beautifully firming things you can do for your derriere"), wild life ("the hippopotamus feeds on soft vegetation"), and soft drinks ("I think Tab tastes like raw sewage"), just as Homer could assume that his listeners knew of Odysseus, Achilles, and the stories of Olympus.

> "This [football] play is shown over and over and over and over and over and over again, in slow motion, fast motion, isolated camera, pixilated camera, thermographic camera, and finally X-ray vision which shows leaping skeletons in a bluish void surrounded by 75,000 roaring skulls."

The camera offers us what the human eye could never see on its own, the really real, and it can repeat that reality again and again. Electronic media are simply better than the eye, and better than memory. Their possibilities are infinite.

The other day, my two-year-old son and I were watching a videotape of *Bambi.* When Bambi's mother was shot by hunters, Charlie became upset, grabbed the remote control, and rewound the tape until Bambi's mom reappeared. He had discovered the real possibility of immortality.

> "Huck is heavily into a Bertolt Brecht/Barbra Streisand thing. Later we go to the Thalia and sit through a double feature of *Mother Courage* and *Yentl*. During the climactic scene in *Yentl* where Barbra Streisand eats 300 salted herrings to prove to the other rabbinical students that she is macho, Huck weeps uncontrollably and vomits."

Leyner understands how the media work to flatten and homogenize culture. All celebrities, real or fictitious, are equal—Barbra Streisand, Bertolt Brecht, Huck Finn, Walid Jumblatt, President Bush, the 50-foot woman, Michael Jackson, Bruce Lee—as all events, real or fictitious, are equal, because they all appear in the same space, on the same screen. In the same way, Leyner's writing brings together seemingly disparate elements, not in a kind of Surrealist juxtaposition but in a leveling process that makes no distinction between, say, Big Bird and Charles Manson, who might very well find themselves seated side by side on the Carson show or on *Hollywood Squares*.

> "i had 225 mortal illnesses my doctor painted a grim picture of each disease he did my leukemia in acrylic on canvas"

In a reality in which all things are the same, in which all differences are leveled, there is no difference between metaphor and the literal. To paint a grim picture is to paint a grim picture. There is no need for interpretation here. There is no meaning beneath the surface of the words, because the words are only surface.

Like the discourse of the electronic media, Leyner's discourse reads itself.

> "If you want to be successful in life, he said, everything you do must be an act of patricide. . . . Even when shaving—each whisker you shave off is your father's head. And if you're using a twin blade—the first blade cuts off the father's head and as the father's neck snaps back it's cleanly lopped off by the second blade."

Leyner suggests that everything and anything we say or do is informed by "the violent vocabulary of the u. s. a.," that the media speak through us even in those moments when we speak the most revolutionary thought, the killing of the father who is the source of the Law.

> "wasn't it mallarme who said, 'when a superhuman being shampoos its hair, it thinks of death?'"

Probably not, but here it is not the accuracy of the quotation that is important but the act of quoting in itself. To quote is always to quote out of context, or rather it is to decontextualize, then recontextualize what is being placed within the quotation marks.

But in the new media reality, who quotes and who is quoted? Are the media only saying what we say, or have we learned to say only what the media say?

---

> **Leyner's stories are full of unacknowledged quotations that most readers will recognize immediately. His sources are mass culture—TV shows, advertising, popular songs—and Leyner repeats once again those phrases and brand names we have heard so often that they seem natural, right.**
>
> **—*Welch D. Everman***

---

Leyner's stories are full of unacknowledged quotations that most readers will recognize immediately ("In high school, I loved to rock 'n' roll, a hot dog made me lose control"). His sources are mass culture—TV shows, advertising, popular songs—and Leyner repeats once again those phrases and brand names we have heard so often that they seem natural, right. These are the familiar phrases that seem to say what we want to say. They express our thoughts. They make thinking and speaking easier, because they supply us with thoughts and the words to speak them. And why not? It's a complicated world, and we deserve a break today.

And yet, like everything else in Leyner's writing, these quotations, while recognizable, are misquoted, somehow off-center, disrupted from within themselves, as when the Queen of England says to one of Leyner's narrators: "Y'all come back and visit Buckingham Palace real soon, y'hear."

The words are familiar, but they no longer say what we want them to say.

> "Well, to make a long story short. . . ."

What is Leyner up to here? Are these stories with titles like **"Colonoscope Nite"** and **"The Suggestiveness of One Stray Hair in an Otherwise Perfect Coiffure"** supposed to be funny? Yes, of course, and they are. So is Leyner poking fun at the electronic media, critiquing them by using and exposing the techniques and the language of the media themselves? Are these works parodies?

The parody critiques by using the techniques and the form of what it parodies, but it does so in a way that exaggerates, exposes, and lays bare those techniques and that form. The parody is a parasite that lives off the host form, that indeed could not come into being and survive without the prior existence of its host.

Leyner's writing is parodic/parasitic in this way, but there is something more going on here. The parody is a negative critique, a making-fun-of. Like a parasite, it seems to aim at the destruction of the host form, which means, in turn, the destruction of parody as well, for the parody is an instance of the form it parodies. The work of the parody, once begun, is irreversible.

Leyner's project, however, is negative and positive—negative insofar as it is parody but positive insofar as there seems to be a genuine affection here for what is being critiqued. Is it possible that Mark Leyner loves *The Patty Duke Shows, The Beverly Hillbillies,* and professional wrestling, in the same way as, say, Andy Warhol loved Campbell's soup cans and Marilyn Monroe?

It's possible.

Because it is irreversible, the parody is relatively easy to write and to read. Leyner's writings, on the other hand, are not, because they move in two directions at once. He criticizes and makes fun of our American mass culture, and yet only one steeped in that culture could write what he writes, just as only the reader who is steeped in that culture could read those writings. As in the works of Andy Warhol, the photographs of Cindy Sherman, or the songs of Laurie Anderson, there are no simple resolutions in Leyner's writings, only questions with no apparent answers.

Like: Was Ronald Reagan the president of the United States, or was he an actor who played the part of the president on TV?

As Leyner's wildly funny and profoundly serious pieces make clear, there is no reality beyond the reality of the mass media, no point of reference beyond the slogans and the catch-phrases by which one might decide what is real and what is not. But is this bad news or good news?

Or is it just news?

> "who are the new intellectuals who are the new aesthetes now that the old new intellectuals and the old new aesthetes have been decimated by the self-decimating ramifications of their old new ideas?"

Good question. Perhaps the new intellectuals and the new aesthetes are not intellectuals or aesthetes at all but players in an infinite game without resolution, without closure, without winners or losers. Perhaps they are the ones who are not afraid to make fun of/have fun with reality, no matter what its form might be. If this is Mark Leyner's game, he is a hell of a player.

## William Severini Kowinski    (review date January-February 1991)

SOURCE: "Welcome to the '90s," in *The Bloomsbury Review,* Vol. 11, No. 1, January-February, 1991, p. 20.

[*Kowinski is an American book reviewer. In the following review of* My Cousin, My Gastroenterologist, *Kowinski praises Leyner's prose style and hails the author as "a voice to watch in the nineties."*]

Fiction readers as well as writers watch for what that smarmy public relations type in "A Hard Day's Night" called "an early clue to the new direction." In these particularly perilous times, we're on the lookout for new styles and substances that can help us sort out where we've been and where we're going, as a society and as individuals. Besides which, the novel form requires a certain amount of novelty to keep going and continue growing.

Mark Leyner has been touted as the largest antidote to American minimalism—or as some would describe it, the

Wimp Lit—that's dominated the literary field of dreams and launched a thousand gleaming paperback originals. There's no doubt that Leyner is different. In [the pages of *My Cousin, My Gastroenterologist*], worlds and words collide, and deep soul searches are likely to be interrupted by a commercial for hemorrhoid cream; in other words, the surrealism of real life today.

It's not that Leyner's prose is unprecedented—in fact, it's his mixtures that are original. He's a hybrid of William Burroughs and Dave Barry, Henry Miller gene-spliced to Woody Allen. This is the fiction of colliding sound bites, of a dream life spent zapping through a reality totally composed of cable TV channels, genre paperbacks, *National Geographic,* pornography, and medical instrument catalogs.

Aside from the specific content of Leyner's wildness—and you can quote from any page at random:

> An enormous Caucasian fat man in plaid Bermuda shorts spraying Windex on the front windshield of a Datsun 280-Z with a Playboy rabbit dangling from the rearview mirror gets a cramp and calls out, Grandma! Grandma!

What's great about this prose is that it works for readers. After promising starts in the sixties—Bob Dylan, Ronald Sukenick—there's been an imaginative slumber in advancing this kind of high-stepping, hijinking, very American surrealism. Everybody thought this should work: a constant assault of images simultaneously mundane and mind-boggling, grafted onto mutated pop fiction and media forms. It seldom has, but now Leyner pulls it off. There's enough punch and surprise in the prose for the moment-to-moment success that nontraditional narrative needs to hold us, even long enough to sense the poetic structures of these individual pieces. At last readable literature has been made from the peculiar material of contemporary life, the stuff other fiction leaves out.

With this book, Leyner becomes a voice to watch in the nineties. He may even be a new type of writer.

## Lewis Burke Frumkes    (review date 27 September 1992)

SOURCE: "Who's the Cutest One of All?," in *The New York Times Book Review,* September 27, 1992, p. 14.

[*In the following review of* Et Tu, Babe, *Frumkes discusses what he considers instances of "unrelenting megalomania, narcissism and disjointed narrative flow" in Leyner's novel.*]

Just as *Finnegans Wake* is one long swim that begins (*in medias res*), "riverrun, past Eve and Adam's, from swerve of shore to bend of bay," and ends 628 pages later, "A way a lone a last a loved a long the," suggesting the cyclical nature of life and death, *Et Tu, Babe* is one long paean to its author, Mark Leyner, a self-promotional concert that begins, "Dear Peter Guzzardi [his editor], As you know, I am not your average author," and ends 169 pages later with "Call 1-800-T-LEYNER today for an exhortatory message from Mark Leyner to his fans recorded in the heroic hours before his disappearance! Stay on the line to record your personal words of support for the man whom food-and-lifestyle authority Martha Stewart has described as having 'the face of an angel and the glands of a god!' . . . Help disseminate the incendiary words of this visionary warrior by ordering additional copies of Mark Leyner's majestic masterworks for your family, friends and co-workers," suggesting that Mr. Leyner . . . how shall I say it? . . . has probably already made some preliminary advances toward self-reflections in a pool.

Nevertheless, Mr. Leyner, whose previous books are *I Smell Esther Williams* and *My Cousin, My Gastroenterologist,* is not without talent or undroll in his contemporary Joycean, Hunter Thompson-on-who-knows-what, stream-of-consciousness sort of way. If you are prepared to put up with the unrelenting megalomania, narcissism and disjointed narrative flow in this novelistic pastiche of pop-cultural images, sci-medical terminology and cosmo-scatologica, you will be treated to some genuinely creative and amusing writing, as when Mr. Leyner satirizes the biotech craze: "Phallotropin—if I'm not mistaken—is a patented form of synthetic penile growth hormone (PGH). The drug was originally developed as an otological drop to facilitate ear wax removal. Then, a number of men who inadvertently ingested the solution orally began to notice significant penile growth. . . . I also know that the writer Mark Leyner has supposedly signed a multimillion-dollar contract to be the spokesperson for Phallotropin."

Mr. Leyner can be perverse without being pornographic, erotic in an almost surreal way: "Then one of them—I think it was Felice—puts my face into her freshly shaven armpit, which smells slightly but deliciously of teenybopper b. o. and she says 'count backwards from 100' and the next thing I remember is waking up and it's Rosh Hashanah, U.S.A., in the 1990's."

He can also be delightfully inventive: "Later on in the afternoon, we took a couple of bottles of scotch up to the rooftop patio and we played this drinking game that Mark invented. You listen to one of those talk-radio stations and every time you hear the word 'the' or 'and' you have to take a drink." And by the book's end he even has Katarina Witt (c'mon, Mark, not Katarina too), the beautiful Olympic skater, fantasizing about him after his purported disappearance: "I recently competed in the World Figure Skating Championships in Stuttgart. It was the climax of my program, I was doing a triple Salchow and, right in the middle, in midair, I just left my body and there I was with Mark again—this was during the most important international competition of the year! Well, it turns out that, in my disembodied state, I didn't do a triple Salchow, I did a septuagesimal Salchow—that's 70 rotations in the air!"

The truth is, Mark Leyner, despite all the ego, displays not just one *jeu d'esprit* in *Et Tu, Babe,* he displays 70. I'm not surprised that several members of the press, according to the jacket copy, have dubbed him "the cult author of the 1990's." Mr. Leyner is a very funny man who has written a very twisted book.

## Michiko Kakutani    (review date 13 October 1992)

SOURCE: "Who Is Mark Leyner? A Legend in His Own Mind," in *The New York Times,* October 13, 1992, p. C17.

[*Kakutani is a regular reviewer for* New York Times. *In the following mixed review of* Et Tu, Babe, *she praises its inventiveness and irreverence but faults the book's satirical density or "anecdote overload."*]

Who is Mark Leyner? According to the fictional testimonies offered in his cheerfully warped new novel, he is "the most intense, and in a certain sense, the most significant young prose writer in America." Stephen Hawking supposedly didn't publish *A Brief History of Time* until Leyner had "reviewed the book's fundamental theorem" and given his approval. Martha Stewart supposedly hailed him as "the writer who single-handedly brought a generation of young people flocking back to the bookstores after they had purportedly abandoned literature for good." And Harold Pinter supposedly called Leyner's play *Varicose Moon* "achingly beautiful": "I think it will be unnecessary for playwrights to write any new plays for some time now: *Varicose Moon* should suffice. In fact, I think it would be vulgar for playwrights to burden the public with their offerings given the creation of this coruscating masterwork." The fictional Leyner says of himself:

> I'm only 36 years old; I've achieved international notoriety as a best-selling author, body builder, martial artist; I make more in a year from product endorsements than most people make in a lifetime; I've got a multi-million-dollar headquarters with a guard tower, gatehouses, patrol dogs, armed sentries, a vast warren of underground tunnels; I've got a gorgeous wife and an entourage of gofers and sycophants.

This description, of course, is both a sendup of America's celebrity-obsessed culture and a fantasy self-portrait of the real-life Mark Leyner, a 36-year-old writer who achieved college cult fame with his last novel, *My Cousin, My Gastroenterologist* (1990). The fictional Leyner depicted in the pages of *Et Tu, Babe* is a monster of egotism, a show biz-literary tycoon of formidable wealth, a Rabelaisian consumer of drugs, women and bizarre experiences, a paranoid and possibly dangerous eccentric pursued by the Federal Bureau of Investigation.

Beautiful women—including Sonia Braga, Elle Macpherson, Claudia Schiffer and Katerina Witt—sing the praises of his remarkably muscled body, while less famous fans line up to buy coffee-table books featuring photos of him in the nude. There are Leyner dolls in the toy stores, and Leyner cartoons on TV. The television show "The American Sportsman" asks Leyner—as well as Ken Follett and Whitley Strieber—to go to Australia to hunt bandicoots with aboriginal boomerangs, and Bergdorf's charges $3,500 for a hand-carved Baccarat crystal bottle of Team Leyner perfume.

Who is this fictional Mark Leyner? Picture Arnold Schwarzenegger, Michael Jackson, Keith Moon, Donald Trump and Howard Hughes all rolled into one. Picture Citizen Kane, the Terminator and the character played by

Mick Jagger in "Performance" merged into a single person.

And what of the narrative style used by Mr. Leyner to depict his fictional alter ego? It, too, is a crazy hybrid: William S. Burroughs crossed with Michael O'Donoghue, Jack Kerouac crossed with Sam Kinison. Told in short, discontinuous takes, the story of the fictional Mark Leyner is a long shaggy-dog tale, packed with scatological digressions, ribald fantasies, Dali-esque dream sequences, and weird bits of manically distorted information.

The reader learns of such bizarre phenomena as weight-loss camps for terrorists; penile-growth hormones; medical cheese sculptures (sculptures of human organs, made of mozzarella and havarti), interactive computerized laser-video players that insert Mr. Schwarzenegger as the actor in any movie ("*The Diary of Anne Frank* with Arnold Schwarzenegger as Anne Frank, *West Side Story* with Arnold Schwarzenegger as Tony, *It's a Wonderful Life* with Arnold Schwarzenegger instead of Jimmy Stewart") and "visceral tattoos," that is, tattoos inscribed on people's internal organs with radioactive isotopes.

In the course of *Et Tu, Babe,* the fictional Leyner begins to run amok. He starts kidnapping his promising writing students, to insure that they won't one day become a threat to him, and he steals a vial of Abraham Lincoln's breath from the National Museum of Health and Medicine. The F.B.I. starts moving in on him, and his paranoia turns to justified fear.

For the reader, his adventures make for a dizzying read, by turns funny, outrageous and sophomorically twisted. But while *Et Tu, Babe* attests to Mr. Leyner's vitality as a writer—his inventiveness, irreverence and shrewd ability to satirize the wretched excesses of a society obsessed with fame—a little bit goes a very long way. Because the narrative is so crammed with anecdotes, jokes and grotesqueries, the effect is similar to sitting on a Disneyland ride several times. Or spending several hours with a garrulous and narcissistic dinner guest who's cranked up on Benzedrine and high on his own ego. One begins this demented book amused and entertained and finishes it reeling from anecdote overload and more than a little sick of the author's willful hipness.

### Mark Leyner with John Bellante and Carl Bellante (interview date July-August 1993)

SOURCE: "A Leaner and Meaner Mark Leyner," in *The Bloomsbury Review,* Vol. 13, No. 4, July-August, 1993, pp. 5-7.

[*In the interview below, Leyner discusses his literary influences and preferences, his research sources, and his thoughts on the writing process.*]

So daunting is the mythic image author Mark Leyner—rhymes with complainer—paints of himself in his latest literary exploit, *Et Tu, Babe,* that the prospect of encountering him might have sent shivers through lesser mortals. Instead, the diminutive, albeit muscular, fellow who greeted us at the door of his temporary lodgings on the edge of the University of Colorado campus turned out to be one

regular guy—within carefully controlled limits. The blue jeans, Oakland Athletics T-shirt, and ostentatious cowboy boots he sported had a premeditatedly unpremeditated quality, the hallmark of his ever-slippery literary libertarianism.

Notably absent were any remnants of Team Leyner, that fictious squad of devoted underlings dedicated to making their boss the most conspicuous name in contemporary cultural chronicles. In their wake was his wife, Arleen, whom he depicts at the conclusion of *Et Tu, Babe* as putting him through an especially messy divorce. We remarked, somewhat naively, how nice that the two of them were still together, despite their novelistic aftermath, only to learn later, much to our mutual consternation, that Mark and Arleen are indeed separated and entangled in new relationships. Too reticent to confess, or the never-ending process of re-inventing oneself? Leyner never lets on, one way or the other.

Ex-Mrs. Leyner in the course of our discourse resembled the dormouse during Alice's Mad Tea Party: awakening fitfully from bouts of slumber to mutter semi-intelligible rumblings—like worrying whether our tape recorder had clicked off.

As for the scenario in progress, it approximated a contemporary *Alice in Wonderland:* two erstwhile journalists situated at the foot of his royal bed while the hookah-less caterpillar strove vaingloriously to impart wisdom. (Leyner was continually in the process of lighting a cigarette, but never managed, due to the intensity of our discussion. Or so one, or both, would like to believe.)

Leyner's insights about the grueling art of promoting a book were also unexpectedly human: exhaustion from the three to four hours of sleep per night he averaged; an avowed aversion to all airplanes and airports he attended; and not least, the dizzying mixture of excitement, hilarity, and confusion he harbors about becoming America's latest inflatable cult figure.

In keeping with that last perception, Leyner apologized for the cramped accommodations gamely endured for the length of our talk. He made assurances that when next our paths crossed, the atmosphere would reflect his deservedly megalomaniacal reputation—an assertion, it should be noted, as worthy of a grain of salt as any other he made that day. But therein lies the fun of mixing it up with Mark Leyner: separating fact from fabrication, showman from charlatan. If he so chooses not to recognize the disparity, who can blame the rest of us for enjoying the joyride?

On the afternoon we met, Leyner was in an outspoken frame of mind, although it did take a few minutes to break through his perfectly sensible schizophrenia regarding the press—whether to court or condemn.

[*The Bloomsbury Review*]: *Your prose has been compared to such surrealistic stand-up comedians as Steven Wright. Do you worry more about how your writing reads aloud, or how it appears on the page?*

[Leyner]: Doing readings has made me pay a lot more attention to how a passage sounds. But when I'm writing, I'm more attuned to how it reads on the page. It's a very pragmatic question, because if you happen to be doing a number of readings while you're also in the course of writing a book, then you'll be very aware of how the new one's going to sound. And that will affect the writing. On the whole *Et Tu, Babe,* reads very well out loud. That's because, as you get more notoriety as a writer, you're asked to read more. It's a very practical kind of influence. And I'm not averse to allowing that motivation to shape my work.

I really love readings. I've made a conscious effort to be a good performer. Some people don't, but it's something you have to think about, an entirely different discipline. You can't just get up and read as you would to yourself when writing. It's a transforming experience when you're performing. It took me a couple of years to understand the difference, but I'm pretty good at it now. When I'm really on, I'd compare what I do to stand-up comedy. Some critic in Los Angeles described me as the first stand-up fiction writer, or some such phrase. I don't mind that description, I feel very much like that when I'm performing. You get your timing down. You know how long to wait so you don't step on laughter. They're all Borscht Belt tricks in a way, but that's what you have to do. In all honesty, I'm influenced by stand-up comedy in a formal way, but I don't know Steven Wright's work all that well. Usually, I'm not that familiar with the writers people say I'm influenced by. It's always interesting for me to see.

*Another possible influence, in terms of your jagged and unruly narrative style, must be the* Monty Python *television series.*

Sure. But let's say I never made a point of sitting down every week to watch it. Of course, readers believe that, because some similarities undoubtedly exist. It's just that people are so positive certain writers served as antecedents or progenitors for my work. William Burroughs, for example, comes up a lot in reviews and articles about me. In reality, I've only read bits and pieces of *Naked Lunch* and nothing else. I have great respect for him, but that's not the same as trying to emulate his writing.

*Then you don't even think his impact is subconscious.*

I know it's not. I know why I do what I do. It's not mysterious.

*Would you say you're more influenced by pop culture than by contemporary literature?*

I'm not interested in contemporary literature at all, because I don't read it. There are two main currents that have conflated to form my style. One is a pretty rigorous education in literature. Those are the authors I still read.

*Laurence Sterne's literary oddity,* Tristram Shandy, *comes to mind. You both share a cavalier attitude towards accepted methods of storytelling.*

Yes, I know that novel. But my influences are really much more traditional than that. Like *The Iliad* and *The Odyssey.* John Keats' *Odes.* Shelley. The *Essays* of Charles Lamb I love very much. And Baudelaire, Rimbaud, Mallarmé. ["Nothing is to me more distasteful than that entire complacency and satisfaction which beam in the counte-

nances of a new-married couple." Charles Lamb (1775-1834) "There are in every man, at every hour, two simultaneous postulations—one towards God, the other towards Satan." Charles Baudelaire (1821-1867) "The poet makes himself a seer by an immense, long, deliberate derangement of all the senses." Arthur Rimbaud (1854-1891) "The flesh is sad, alas, and I have read all the books." Stephane Mallarmé (1842-1898)]

*Does that mean you read the last three in the original French?*

I can read them in the original French when there's a facing page with English. [Laughter.] I try to go back and forth. I do like to learn how the poem reads in French, because that's how it was meant to work, obviously. But what kills me is that people expect my major influences to be authors whose styles are similar to mine. And I tend not to like those writers for some reason.

*Kurt Vonnegut, for instance.*

Another writer whose work I can honestly say I've never read. I have very antique tastes in poetry, fiction, and drama. When it comes to nonfiction, my reading is very contemporary. I'm much more omnivorous, as far as that goes.

*Biographies?*

Yes, biographies. Books about the Philadelphia Mafia. This species of mammals I'm interested in—naked molerats—I just got a book about. I've got this wonderful *Taste of Paradise* by Wolfgang Schifflebusch, a cultural anthropological study of chocolate, tobacco, alcohol, and spices. It's fabulous. So my interests in nonfiction are eclectic, to say the least.

*That's quite apparent in your writing.*

Not to mention lists of magazines. *Scientific American. Science News. Sassy.* Boxing magazines. *People.*

*Do you ever pick up supermarket tabloids as a source of information?*

No. The stories are too close to the fiction I eventually come up with. There's no need for me to read supermarket tabloids because somehow I end up creating tabloids of my own. So they're of no interest to me.

*We recently interviewed Tama Janowitz who said she actually invented plot twists [in* The Male Cross-Dresser Support Group *(1993)], which turned out to be true, that later appeared in newspaper headlines. Does that phenomenon ever occur with you?*

I hate when that happens.

*Can you remember any particular examples?*

That's a risk you take when you deal with anything topical, or when you incorporate celebrities into your work. Because the currency of that celebrity is volatile. I use Paula Abdul somewhere in the book, very fleetingly. Still, you don't know, by the time the novel comes out, what will have happened to Paula Abdul? The half-life of these people amounts to nothing. Also, something could happen to her; she could lose her legs, but it's too late, the book is out. Or she fades away into nothingness, that could happen in the course of a year or two. There's a part in **Et Tu, Babe** where a daughter is talking to her mother, and she's saying, "Mom, I don't understand Mia Farrow. How could one woman love sensitive artists like Woody Allen, Andre Previn, and then be married to someone like *Frank Sinatra*? Who calls women cunts and broads." And they have this discussion. Then this whole controversy occurs with Woody Allen, which was very disturbing to me. As the author of this book, I didn't quite know how that was going to change the texture or fabric of that bit I did. It didn't completely subvert it, but it came close. That's the sort of risk you take.

*Have you seen Woody's latest,* Husbands and Wives?

No.

*It's really eerie how so many of the events depicted were probably going on at the time the film was being shot. The movie appears to have amounted to a self-fulfilling prophecy.*

Strangely enough, **Et Tu, Babe** turned into a self-fulfilling prophecy itself. It's a book about the apparatus of celebrity-making, which I am now a part of in a very real way. It's what takes me all over the country.

But to return from a number of different tangents, the way pop culture has affected me more than any other influence is in a formal manner. The formality of television, for instance. Not the content of it at all. But its formal grammar, its kineticism, its ability to juxtapose thousands of images against each other in 30-second and 60-second ads.

*Which raises another issue:* **Et Tu, Babe** *does reflect a short attention span typical of the American public. To say nothing of the entire notion of sound bites.*

I'm certainly aware that there's a fortuitous match between my work at the moment and the sensibility of people who also have grown up on television. But my decisions to write the way I do had more to do with starting out writing poetry, and then seeing if I could make a kind of prose that was as dense with event, surprise, humor, and lyricism. Which had no dead spots. I think I really started coming up with these ideas when I was a sophomore or junior in college. When you'd read a long book like George Eliot's *Middlemarch,* for example, where if you're in a rush you can skip entire sections. If somebody visits a country home, there will be 25 pages describing the front lawn that the reader has to cross to get to the front door. If there's a test the next day, by all means get to the door. You don't need to read all that. Now, of course, being an older and more serious reader, I wouldn't skip that passage. There's probably wonderful stuff in there, details that turn out to be important, some psychological tapestry that's been painted by this description. I thought at that time, though, I didn't want to write books that include transitional passages which merely serve to move characters from room to room. Or which explain how a person is related to someone else. I want every sentence to be unskippable, very intense and charged. That's how I started developing my style. I didn't say to myself I wanted to come up with something which approximates the jagged feeling of a day of television. Although they *are* very similar.

*In a sense you're redefining the whole concept of what a novel is, or what a novel is capable of doing. Including the way you use yourself as a comic presence. Can you define how you differ from, and conversely resemble, the protagonist of* **Et Tu, Babe**?

I exaggerate certain characteristics. It's an extreme hyperbolic version of myself. But if you scale it back, turn down the volume, look carefully at all the details, it's very much me. Many of the details of the book are true.

*Ever had any complaints from people whose life stories you incorporate into your work?*

Not this book so much. After all, my dog can't complain. Martha Stewart, whom I also mention, likes it. Actually, we got to be friends through that, which is part of that weird life/art relationship we were discussing before. The Mark Leyner in the novel and the *real* Mark Leyner have been forged into this indistinguishable lump by the media and my own ambitious machinations. It's hard to tell what the interior, or exterior, of either of us is. But the book itself is the first novel made up entirely of jacket copy. On the outside and the inside. Even the photo of the author and the blurbs. Most people think I've made up all the blurbs on the book. Which I didn't, because I do all those things in the book. So it's funny; I've encouraged some sort of Chicken Little syndrome, where no one believes anything I say anymore. There are some people to whom I could say anything and they'd believe me. I'll admit, a lot of extraordinary things have happened in my life.

*So, one of your points is that fact and fiction, in your experience at least, are inextricably linked.*

I've always been fascinated by that issue—the way the creation of public figures has hybridized fact and fiction. Or the way we promote idealized images of ourselves to acquaintances in our intimate life. The whole business of fact and fiction is never as clear as people make it. It's quite fuzzy.

*Another way of looking at it is that "fact" per se only happens in the present, the "now." Once it becomes part of the past, or a person's recollection, it becomes fiction.*

Fictionalization starts the instant a phenomenon is perceived by an observer. A fictionalizing component occurs in the very sensory perception of an event. What we're seeing, hearing, touching, smelling is not the entirety of the event, it's some version which we've been biologically evolved to have. From the very beginning of an experience, it's not fact or fiction, but simply how we tend to look at it. This false opposition between the two is just rampant throughout our lives. When I got the idea to do **Et Tu, Babe,** that angle was what I most enjoyed. I've always had this interest in using real people, though I'm certainly not the first writer to do it. For instance, the poet Frank O'Hara used real people throughout his poetry.

*Even people he didn't know?*

No, not to the extent I do. His focus was more on people he knew, about having lunch with so-and-so. But I never felt any need to restrict myself to people I really knew. My latest book is the story of someone who flips himself into the television, so that he can hang around with these famous celebrities. That's what I've tried to do.

*Did a Hollywood producer really use the phrase, "Et tu, babe" ad infinitum when talking with you?*

No, but I did meet a producer who used the expression "babe" as a coda to every sentence, the first person in my life who'd ever *done* this. To have a person actually speak like that made a big impression on me.

*And he managed to speak that way without any sense of self-consciousness.*

None. In fact, I was in Las Vegas once, and I tried to say "babe" one day to lots of people. The response I got was nothing. No one thinks you're being funny, it's a real dialect out there. But that producer inspired my artistic decision somehow.

---

**I want every sentence to be unskippable, very intense and charged. That's how I started developing my style. I didn't say to myself I wanted to come up with something which approximates the jagged feeling of a day of television. Although they *are* very similar.**

**—Mark Leyner**

---

*Could that mean you've aspirations to dabble in the movie business?*

I'm about to have some heavy meetings in L.A. I was in Los Angeles last week for preliminary discussions. Then I'll be back with Fox and various other studios about some television/movie ideas. Some of them mine, others other people's. It hasn't always been an ambition of mine, but now I'd like to give it a try, sure. To be moved out to Los Angeles for some months and write a few episodes for some series. That would be fun.

*Would such projects reflect your personal style of surrealism, or would they be more what viewers expect to see on your average TV program?*

You know, someone once told me—I think it was Jay McInerney [*Bright Lights, Big City* (1984)]—that the best thing that could happen is to get paid a ton of money to work on a project, and it's never made. So you never have to be embarrassed by it. That's a writer's dream of the L.A. experience. Don't misunderstand me. I think there are some good things on TV. My viewing tends to be along the periphery. Mostly pure television like CNN and ESPN, the weather, and home shopping networks. Infomercials I enjoy watching. The actual network shows, I don't even know what they are. I never watch them. I prefer events. Any big news event I love to see how it's being covered. The Gulf War had me glued to the set, or

the Olympics. I watch a lot of sports on television; I'm a big sports fan. *The Simpsons* is a wonderful show. If I could do something that was good, and if it could really have a bit of flavor of what my work is like, that would be great. We'll see what happens.

*How seriously can readers take the scientific information that pops up in your books? For example, that thousands of people in American compulsively pull their hair out.*

Trichotillomania. Yeah, that's real. But these numbers tend to be inflated by support groups for the disease. Somewhat. Still, it's hard to imagine 30 million people compulsively pulling their hair out. Because I think we'd see the hair around somewhere.

*Seriously, though, we've never met anyone guilty of that habit. Not that it isn't a hilarious image.*

I've met people who play with their hair, but don't actually pull it out in great gobs, or handfuls. Nevertheless, in **Et Tu, Babe,** just about all the medical stuff is real and appropriate. Not just some name I found and stuck in.

*There is a definite science-fiction undercurrent in your work, however.*

Again, I've immunized myself against certain questions and accusations by not ever reading these kinds of things. The only science-fiction book I've ever read is *Neuromancer* [1984] by William Gibson. And that was only after people had accused my work of being cyber-punk: "You better see what you're being compared to." I got this question asked a lot, because there is science in my fiction. But, obviously, that doesn't make me science fiction. There are also references to pop culture, books, and so on.

I try to include what I see and hear and know as much as possible. So, of course, science is going to be there. Pop culture is the same way—these are the disenfranchised areas of our society, traditionally, in terms of literature. Only recently has science fiction been taken seriously at all. The inclusion of pop culture in books is still considered unusually suspect.

*Literary slumming.*

Yes, it's still an issue. That seems ridiculous to me. Unfortunately, the scientific references are the most salient point to a lot of readers.

*Oddly enough, this subject brings us back to your habit of glossing over descriptive passages in novels. Does it bother you that Americans, with their aversion for technical details, might be reluctant to humor your scientific esoterica?*

Yeah, I guess people probably skip that sometimes. Usually, my object is not to make the books difficult, not to confuse people. I want what I'm doing to be accessible so that readers can enjoy it the way I intended. I'll explain what I mean. I don't say there are 20 to 30 million people who suffer from trichotillomania, then expect you to look it up, come back, and laugh. I'm not trying to lord over the reader because I have some amateur knowledge of matters scientific.

*Do these little tangents require much research? Or are they simply tasty tidbits you've accumulated mentally over the years?*

I get this digest every week—*Science News*—which I read carefully. And I always read the science section of *The New York Times* every Tuesday. I buy *Scientific American* or *Discovery* every now and then. I'm just interested. I keep my eyes open, it could be in *Newsweek* or *Time*. I jot facts down. I don't find I have to go out and make a special effort of fishing out this information.

*By recreating your own persona, you seem to be fooling around with the whole area of authorial voice. To an extent you're practically suggesting, "It doesn't matter who I am. Just enjoy my writing and shut up." Much as Vladimir Nabokov might have done.*

[Laughter.] Satirizing authorial voice is not a concern of mine at all. I've tried to develop a style that maximizes my freedom as a writer. Doing it as I've done gives me the most latitude—with myself as narrator, and being able to wander back and forth between actual autobiography and complete fantasy. I'm constantly after a structure which unleashes my imagination. My methods have nothing to do with satirizing authorial voice: That's much too academic for the way I think. I'm very practical as a writer. Very much a writer and not an academic when I look at these problems, and the way I enjoy solving them. My approach is much more nuts-and-bolts. Much more about the process of being a writer. One can talk about matters like this, and it's valid. Because I've done this, it does raise some interesting questions about the whole notion of authorial voice.

*Do you plan in terms of a large arc as far as the plotline is concerned?*

Depends on the book. **My Cousin, My Gastroenterologist** no. That book was intended to be read like you'd enjoy one of those candy samplers. Pick and choose, put it away, come back, pick and choose. **Et Tu, Babe** is best appreciated from beginning to end. I had a very simple notion of how it should work, which is illustrated by the bedspread I'm sitting on, remarkably enough. [The bedspread is a series of oval patterns.] See, we've all been brought to this room for a reason. [Laughter.] This is the exact shape I had for the book, and how it was going to work. I had no idea how I was going to do it, but I figured Team Leyner would reach some kind of apogee in the middle of the book, when it would be most powerful. The Leyner character would be at his most megalomaniacal. His delusions of grandeur would be full-blown. Then gradually, the Team Leyner minions, personnel, and staff would start deserting him. Until, at the end, there's no one. My dog, Carmella, even deserts me. I was telling someone recently *Et Tu, Babe,* as compared to my other books, reminds me of Jane Austen. It's so tightly plotted. Of course, this is very relative—people who don't know my work read *Et Tu, Babe* and say, "This is so wild, this novel. It goes everywhere." But to me it's the most novelistic of anything I've done.

*Was the way in which the novel begins to fall apart towards the end meant to reflect the hero's literal and figurative decline as well?*

Yeah, but again, I was feeling constricted by the book itself. At the beginning of the chapter you refer to, I say something about being depressed by the eccentricity of the narrative. Also, at the time I was writing that part, all kinds of things were going on in my life. My ability to pay attention to a long chapter wasn't there. I realized in order to do it, I had to work in miniature and make it more interesting for *me*. I just wanted to explode the book a bit at that point. [Gesturing once again at the oval patterns on his bedspread.] But I didn't want to destroy the curved skeleton of the book I'd made. So I had to keep sneaking in little bits and pieces of information that were significant in terms of the narrative. My favorite method, as far as that goes, is the game show written in the form of a play. Because at that point, I had a sense of what the length of the book should be. [169 pages of compact prose, to be precise.] It was getting to be time to get rid of a lot of the characters so that the Leyner character could be alone at the end and we could have the whole section with everybody claiming to have been with me in those final hours and whatnot. But I didn't want to go through the tedious process of narrating how people were getting sick of me and leaving. Especially at this point where I was very impatient with that subject. So I came up with this game show idea—I don't know how exactly—and within the game show context the contestant picks Team Leyner as a category. Through that, I managed to get rid of four or five characters and explain why they left, and work in comic material that was lots of fun for me and the reader. Also, it's a pretty fucking interesting narrative device.

*As a character you grow further and further removed from the story itself, until you're simply somebody other characters refer to.*

Yes, because I wanted to disappear from the book. In the last chapter I don't exist at all. I don't even exist as a narrator anymore, because I've gone and disappeared. But the great trick of *Et Tu, Babe* is the last part of the book, which is oral history. The last person to talk is Jessica Hahn, describing how they confiscated my laptop, then her testimony about this ends abruptly. She says, "He was in mid-sentence when they wrested away his final remaining possession—yes, his laptop! —and he di—." Of course, that means I've been making up everybody's oral history. Because my character is relentless in his exploitation of other people to aggrandize himself. Otherwise there's no reason why, just because they take away my laptop, Jessica Hahn's statement about it should end in mid-sentence. I consider it an interesting little knot at the end.

*Do you specifically attempt to write books on the shortish side, so that every detail is reduced to its barest essential?*

Some of these considerations are very practical. You live on your advance for a while, but you can't take forever writing a book unless you're not depending on that income. These are funny things most people don't realize. You need to finish, and hand the book in so you can get the rest of your advance. But I don't really think that was the real reason for *Et Tu, Babe*'s length. In general I want to write books that are about 200 pages or so. Not much more, not much less. I just have a notion that's a nice length. I'd like people to be able to read my books in a couple of sittings. Because I think the experience of reading my books in a short period of time makes the density of pleasure that I'm after even more powerful, more concentrated as opposed to reading over a longer period of time. A book should be good enough to take in one quick dose.

*Have you reached the stage where you can basically survive on the money you make writing?*

Oh, yeah. For the past two, two and a half years. This is all I do now, which sometimes strikes me as *so* remarkable. No matter what else happens to me—say, I even get a television show or do movies, win the Nobel Prize—that will stand as the most profound thing that's happened to me in my life.

*Funny. Virtually every author we've talked to says more or less the same. They feel almost guilt-stricken they're actually making a living doing what they love.*

You just never think you're going to be able to do that. You know, I came out of the writing program at the University of Colorado, and the myth you're fed to live by is that you'll go teach, write books not many people are going to read, and that's your life. But I never wanted that. For a while I was ready not to regard myself as a writer anymore. Right before *My Cousin, My Gastroenterologist* was published, I said to myself, "Okay, this is enough. I can keep writing and enjoying it, as I would, say, in playing tennis or chess. I'm not going to think of myself as a writer anymore because I don't want to become a fiction collector, or just a small press writer who has to become an academic." There's nothing wrong with that, but I simply wanted to do something else. Because I'm very ambitious. This is a long way of saying that my schooling never prepared me for what the life of a writer is. It's interesting for me to hear other writers feel the way I do. I've never discussed it with anyone. But I can't imagine a more earth-shattering change in my life ever again.

*A few final questions. How did you end up settling in Hoboken?*

I'm from around there originally. From Jersey City, which is nearby. After graduate school I moved to Washington, D.C., to be with a girlfriend. Then I moved back to Jersey because my father had an interest in a restaurant in Jersey City, and I helped him for a while. Hoboken was the place to move to at that time. A cheap alternative to living in Manhattan. It's right across the river.

*Finally, did you honestly go to a motel to teach your dog how not to sit, as the* Times *article states?*

[Laughter.] No. That was sort of cheating on William Grimes. I had that idea a couple of days before the interview. This dog of mine is intractably disobedient. She really doesn't *know* how to do anything. We're together all day all the time, so there's no need for her to know. We're very much in synch—she senses when to leave me alone to write. She also understands to give me about eight hours before she can start bugging me. About five or six o'clock she just comes over and says, "That's enough. We need to go out and play." I've been lazy about training her. Actually, lazy is an understatement. So I knew she'd jump all over Grimes when he came to my place. And I was in

the shower and thought, "Here's a funny idea." This is how to handle the media, though. You always like to have a few good lines beforehand. And it's always wonderful to see it work. You plant these ideas. Like the headline of the whole piece—"America's Best Built Comic Novelist"—I had a feeling they would use that when I told Grimes, in an offhanded manner, "You know even more than being known as the best comic novelist, I'd like to be known as the best built comic novelist." I didn't expect the cover with the headline, but it's always nice to see your sinister plots take wing.

*Therefore, even when you're being interviewed, you're inventing a persona.*

Certainly for that one. Because it was such a big deal. I was dealing with something that was potentially life-changing. What's happened to me since *Et Tu, Babe* is another whole stage. As far as this interview with you guys, no. [Indicating his less than grand motel room.] It's hard to create a persona for yourself in this environment. [Laughter.]

*Tell us about your work habits. For instance, the hours you keep, what you prefer to write on.*

I've gotten used to computers whenever I can compose on them. I used to write in longhand, and then transfer. But now I don't need that extra step. I love this new Mac Classic I just bought. It feels like it's part of you after a while. But don't get me wrong. I'm interested in calligraphy, Japanese and Chinese characters. So there's still something I love about seeing words on a white page. I'll do that too, sometimes at night in bed. I value that process.

*That you work on a computer isn't terribly surprising, considering your prose has the shape of being refined, re-refined, and then refined again. While some of your sentences can be quite long, there's usually not a superfluous word in them.*

My stuff is very, very worked-out. I spend a lot of time on sentences. I can spend a whole day getting a couple right. I recently wrote an essay about Keith Richards for *Spin Magazine*. They had me go spend some time with him one afternoon. It was great.

*Is he a hero of yours?*

Twenty years ago he was, and I still admire him. That's what the essay came to be about—what it's like to meet someone you idolized long ago. Internally, there seemed to be two trajectories at this meeting. I'm very aware of myself now gaining a certain kind of notoriety for my work. So I feel like there's an internal direction to my life. Meeting him was the inverse of that. I was thrown back chronologically, psychologically to a time when I was an anonymous person, obeisant to this idol of mine. To have both happen at the same time sort of made me ill. I was rather nauseous after meeting him. Later I realized it was because we'd both smoked about 800 cigarettes. I was probably just suffering from nicotine poisoning. [Laughter.] I enjoy the first theory much more.

But getting back to my original point, I wrote that piece and the people at *Spin* were great about it, although it had to be cut somewhat. Nevertheless, in the most well-meaning way, every time they tried to edit my writing in the most essayistic parts, they just ruined it. Not that their changes were stupid, but I am careful. You can't just chop my stuff up. Now I'm going to have to rewrite the parts they rewrote to repair them. They're very nice people, but I'm absolutely meticulous about how the language works. You can't mess around with it.

---

**I've always been fascinated by the way the creation of public figures has hybridized fact and fiction. Or the way we promote idealized images of ourselves to acquaintances in our intimate life. The whole business of fact and fiction is never as clear as people make it.**

**—*Mark Leyner***

---

*Apparently, one of your first editors complained about your punctuation, or lack of it.*

I mean, it's amazing they published that book *My Cousin, My Gastroenterologist*.

It's completely unpunctuated, completely disconnected. *Et Tu, Babe* is a very different story. You can see why it would be published at this time, do well, and get lots of attention. But that other book! It certainly gives one faith there are good editors in mainstream publishing.

*You appear to be a bit reticent about discussing your first book* I Smell Esther Williams. *Explain what there is about it you don't like.*

A lot of it is very pretentious. It seems rather juvenile to me. First of all, much of it is very derivative of the New York school of poetry. Writers like Frank O'Hara and John Ashberry. Some of it tries to show off how erudite I am, what a wonderful vocabulary I have. These flaws are forgivable, but I don't have to like the damn book anymore. If people ask what should I read of yours, I'll answer *My Cousin, My Gastroenterologist* and *Et Tu, Babe*. I don't imagine I'll ever think ill of those books. But *I Smell Esther Williams* was written in Colorado when I was a graduate student. I was only 22.

*Describe your feelings about returning to your alma mater since achieving success.*

It always gives me a "Hail the Conquering Hero" kind of buzz. I wish the person in graduate school could have seen the article written about me in *The New York Times Magazine* and thought, "God, isn't it great that could happen to someone!" Going through the process now is wonderful and very fulfilling, but you're so involved, and it's hard work. If you want to keep up that media attention, you work at it. These tours are pretty grueling. So you never get a chance to sit back and feel "Ah, am I famous! This is great!" Sometimes you have little glimmers, but I'd like

to have some science-fiction trick where I could pull in the younger me and let him share this experience. Many of those feelings come back when I'm in Colorado. I have to admit it's nice to lord over some of these people and show off what a big shot I am. "I don't have to teach!" [Laughter.]

### Michiko Kakutani (review date 7 March 1995)

SOURCE: "From a Cool Dude in a Hip, Literary Mood," in *The New York Times,* March 7, 1995, p. C18.

[*In the review below, Kakutani finds the short stories included in Leyner's collection* Tooth Imprints on a Corn Dog *to be "clever and amusing and willfully superficial."*]

Reading Mark Leyner's new collection of short pieces [*Tooth Imprints on a Corn Dog*] isn't like reading a book exactly. It's more like spending several hours with the Comedy Channel on cable television, or a long evening with a couple of teen-agers on acid. Imagine Beavis and Butt-head morphed with William S. Burroughs or Michael O'Donoghue crossed with Eugène Ionesco; then picture the twisted products of their imaginations projected on one of those big-screen television sets, with the volume turned all the way up. The results are intermittently hilarious, but also silly and highly sophomoric.

Essentially a collection of pieces Mr. Leyner wrote for assorted publications (including *The New Yorker* and *The New Republic*), *Tooth Imprints on a Corn Dog* ostensibly addresses a variety of subjects like fatherhood, the Miss America pageant, muscleman culture, sperm banks and the Menendez brothers' trial, but each piece is really just an excuse for Mr. Leyner to joke around and free-associate about his favorite preoccupations: namely, arcane skin diseases, bizarre technological innovations and the consequences of contemporary celebrity.

As in his last book, *Et Tu, Babe*, Mr. Leyner purveys an image of himself as a willfully hip, ardently narcissistic dude with a cheerfully warped sense of humor. As he writes in the introduction, "I'm just the cream-soda-swilling, crotch-scratching, irascible, coughing-up-indigestible-bits-of-grizzle-from-some-meat-on-a-stick, surly, greasy overalls-over-candy-colored-latex-mini-kimono (my work uniform when I'm in the throes of a novel or a play), don't-bother-me-till-halftime kind of guy that society has made me."

In another piece, he writes: "Each morning and before I leave for any social function, I gargle with Johnny Walker Black. I think that women like that tinge of hard liquor on a man's breath in the middle of the day; it contributes to that aura of insouciant menace that the 90's woman finds so alluring and so refreshing after a decade of male angst."

Mr. Leyner's fictional alter ego and the other characters who appear in these pieces tend to speak the same idiosyncratic lingo of non sequiturs and hyperbole, trading wisecracks and oddball observations with self-conscious panache.

In **"Young Bergdorf Goodman Brown"**—a playlet that's

supposed to be a takeoff on Hawthorne's tale "Young Goodman Brown"—a rabbi speaks of meeting extraterrestrials in a sub-basement of Bergdorf Goodman, while Mr. Leyner's own fictional persona seriously contemplates paying $3,450 for a miniature Giorgio Armani backpack for his daughter's Barbie. In **"The (Illustrated) Body Politic,"** senators cover themselves with arcane tattoos attesting to their power and connections. And in **"Oh, Brother,"** a high-powered lawyer argues that twin brothers have murdered their sweet, nurturing parents because they had become convinced—through hours of television watching—that such pleasant parental behavior was highly abnormal.

The satiric impulse behind such stories, of course, involves simple exaggeration of an already bizarre reality, and a similar technique informs Mr. Leyner's manic depictions of a futuristic world filled with peculiar new services and products: miniaturized Barbie dolls that can clean out clogged-up arteries and perform other surgical procedures; post-cold-war clothes manufactured by defense-industry giants ("a single-breasted, three-button, linen-and-viscose-glen-plaid suit from McDonnell Douglas"; a "heather-gray cotton V-neck cardigan from Raytheon"); on-line posters whose "image changes according to which celebrity is most popular for your child's particular demographic niche," and self-service, drive-through liposuction clinics.

Highly attuned to the effluvia of contemporary pop culture, Mr. Leyner deliberately focuses on the glossy surface of life. Indeed, many of these pieces take as their theme America's obsession with image: **"Hulk Couture"** is a tongue-in-cheek ode to bodybuilders and their bulked-up physiques; **"Immoral Allure"** suggests that crime may not pay, but that it may lend its practitioners a glamorous beauty and allure, and **"Dangerous Dads"** gives new fathers tips on how to maintain a macho image.

But while some of these pieces are laugh-out-loud funny, they tend to have the emotional afterlife of a mayfly. In fact, in sending up our appearance-mad society. Mr. Leyner has consciously or unconsciously created pieces that echo the very culture he intends to spoof: pieces that are clever and amusing and willfully superficial.

### Rick Marin   (review date 27 March 1995)

SOURCE: "Buffing Up Is Hard to Do," in *Newsweek*, Vol. CXXV, No. 13, March 27, 1995, p. 68.

[*In the following review, Marin favorably assesses Leyner's collection of short stories,* Tooth Imprints on a Corn Dog, *praising its comical and satiric elements.*]

Mark Leyner isn't the best-selling writer in America, but he may be the buffest. With just 135 pounds on his 5-foot-7 frame, the author of *My Cousin, My Gastroenterologist* and *Et Tu, Babe* can bench-press 220 without breaking a sweat. He's a little guy who goes to the gym to get huge,

even though fiction is where Leyner does all his heaviest lifting.

His new book, *Tooth Imprints on a Corn Dog* is a willfully random collection of magazine humor pieces, lunatic ravings and one-liners composed "while listening to Mahler in the afternoon." In a brief three-pager called **"The (Illustrated) Body Politic,"** Leyner conducts a mock-investigative report on tattoos worn by U.S. senators: "A DNA double helix attached to a ball and chain means: 'My sibling is a convicted felon'." Elsewhere, his febrile mind dreams up new fragrances ("Bastard," made from the pineal glands of death-row inmates) and transposes Nathaniel Hawthorne's "Young Goodman Brown" to a ludicrously extravagant New York department store in a playlet dubbed **"Young Bergdorf Goodman Brown."** Leyner, 39, is a hyperbolist, a wild exaggerator of his own world and the one around him. With his pumped-up prose and steroidal satire, it's easy to see why he's become the new Hunter S. Thompson to the online generation. He's a hero in cyberspace, if not in the literary establishment. You could call him the Quentin Tarantino of cult fiction: they both have an obsession with pop ephemera and a wickedly violent sense of humor. And although *Tooth Imprints* is Leyner's most accessible opus to date, it is emphatically not for everyone. Then again, what good book is?

"I really don't like there to be a line in my book that isn't in neon," Leyner says. Sitting in the orderly basement office of his modest house in Hoboken, N.J., he rails good-naturedly against "depressing books about people in trailers" getting more literary respect than comic novels, which he complains have become a "disreputable" genre. An award winner for his college fiction at Brandeis, Leyner toiled in obscurity for years, writing fiction for little quarterlies and ad copy for medical journals like Urology Today. Then *The Mississippi Review* ran one of his short stories in an all-cyberpunk issue, Harper's reprinted it and suddenly he had a big agent and a big contract for his 1992 novel *Et Tu, Babe*—a brilliant riff on celebrity culture starring a famous musclebound writer named Mark Leyner who surrounds himself with a corporate entourage ("Team Leyner") of bodyguards and minions.

Likably self-absorbed, Leyner writes about what he knows and loves best: himself. His rambling semiautobiographical style is his strength and weakness. He's so nonlinear that you can pick his books up and put them down on just about any page—which is why he's giving his next novel a beginning, middle and end. "Jerry Lewis's remake of Marcel Proust's *Remembrance of Things Past*" is how he describes the new work-in-progress. Facing down 40 must be maturing him. Paternity is a running theme in *Tooth Imprints*. Leyner's 21-month-old daughter, Gaby, inspired **"Dangerous Dads,"** an essay instructing aging gonzo dudes how to reconcile "history's honorifics of virility—'brigand,' 'defiler,' 'conquistador,' 'warlord' "—with being a sensi-guy father. Even buff bad boys have to grow up sometime.

**M. G. Lord**  **(review date 23 April 1995)**

SOURCE: "Part Poetry, Part Jai Alai," in *The New York Times Book Review,* April 23, 1995, p. 12.

[*In the following review of* Tooth Imprints on a Corn Dog, *Lord criticizes Leyner's tendency to write self-referential and self-promotional fiction.*]

I first encountered Mark Leyner's name in the Mystery Quote contest on Echo, a computer bulletin board. In the competition players guess the author of unidentified texts, and wrongly attributed to Mr. Leyner were some wildly dissimilar bits of prose: excerpts from Gore Vidal's spoof of Christianity, *Live From Golgotha;* the film maker Derek Jarman's thoughts on Caravaggio; and a hard-boiled detective story from Bill Pronzini's collection *Son of Gun in Cheek* in which a woman is killed by having the air sucked from her lungs with a vacuum cleaner.

Even more startling is how plausible these guesses were. Mr. Leyner's first three books—*I Smell Esther Williams, My Cousin, My Gastroenterologist* and *Et Tu, Babe*—are not conventional narratives. Often scatological, rarely predictable, they most closely resemble the long, loopy yet occasionally brilliant monologues of the psychiatric patient Sylvia Frumkin, which Susan Sheehan first recorded 12 years ago in "Is There No Place on Earth for Me?" and reprised in the recent anniversary issue of *The New Yorker.*

Perhaps because they were originally published in various magazines, many of the pieces in Mr. Leyner's latest book, *Tooth Imprints on a Corn Dog,* are more accessible. Many also seem to have been written according to this formula: To achieve humor, insert outrageous nouns into a traditional story.

The recipe produces sentences such as this: "Several friends and I hiked to the old hydroelectric plant on the outskirts of town; we cut our fingers and pledged never to use any word associated with French deconstructionism, including 'liminal,' 'endo-colonization' and 'simulacrum.' " And this: "When I'm not crisscrossing the globe, honing my connoisseurship of the physical arts—an avocation that has taken me from the fighting-cockroach parlors of Rangoon and wet T-shirt contests at Khmer Rouge ruby mines to the self-service drive-through liposuction emporia of Boca Raton and Easter brunch with a self-mortification cult in Montclair, New Jersey—I body-build."

Readers may immediately recognize Mr. Leyner's literary precedent—the formula used in Mad Libs, a party game popular with generations of junior high school students.

When Mr. Leyner's satire works, it works well. He is brilliant at inventing facetious products to make a political point. Commenting on the sad shape of the post-cold-war defense industry, he concocts a "Swords Into Plowshares" clothing line that features boxer shorts made by Martin Marietta. And he exposes the sleaziness of classroom advertising by removing its subtlety—inserting actual brand names into passages from Shakespeare's *Antony and Cleopatra.*

Mr. Leyner's mature comedy, however, is often upstaged by his not-so-mature fixation on potty jokes. I also wish he would write more about the world and less about himself. His self-mockery looks troublingly like self-promotion, especially when—for the third or fourth time—he mentions his well-known agent.

To a degree, Mr. Leyner's songs of himself are tongue-in-cheek. He flirts with being a poseur: "I'll play the elegant, mordantly witty belletrist whose writing combines the delicacy and voluptuousness of poetry with the rigor of science and the vivacity of jai alai." Yet even he seems to know that there is such a thing as too much self-indulgence. How else to explain this insight in his essay on a sperm bank? "As a writer," Mr. Leyner observes, "the notion of being paid to masturbate does not seem odd to me in the least."

---

## FURTHER READING

### Criticism

Gehr, Richard. Review of *My Cousin, My Gastroenterologist,* by Mark Leyner. *VLS,* No. 85 (May 1990): 7.
> Positive review of *My Cousin, My Gastroenterologist* in which Gehr notes that the book "radiates experimentalism."

Grimes, William. "The Ridiculous Vision of Mark Leyner." *The New York Times Magazine* (13 September 1992): 34-5, 51, 64, 66.
> Feature on Leyner's life and works.

Harris, Michael. Review of *Et Tu, Babe,* by Mark Leyner. *The Los Angeles Times Book Review* (11 October 1992): 6.
> Negative review in which Harris states that Leyner "[jams] together pop genres and spoofs of genres, weird science, police reports and references to classic literature into a glop of information overload."

Krist, Gary. Review of *Et Tu, Babe,* by Mark Leyner. *The Hudson Review* XLVI, No. 1 (Spring 1993): 239-46.
> Negative assessment of *Et Tu, Babe* in which Krist states "ultimately [I] found the book tiresome."

O'Hara, J. D. "They Have the Words, Sometimes the Tune." *The New York Times Book Review* (21 September 1986): 46.
> Negative assessment of *American Made,* asserting that the volume contains "those commonplaces, from paranoia and irrelevance to bad grammar and circular reasoning, that have given such collections a bad name."

Review of *American Made,* edited by Mark Leyner. *Publishers Weekly* 229, No. 26 (27 June 1986): 82.
> Notes that the stories that compose this anthology are "marked by a feeling of despair and pointlessness."

Sales, Nancy Jo. Review of *Tooth Imprints on a Corn Dog,* by Mark Leyner. *People Weekly* 43, No. 16 (24 April 95) 27-8.
> Discusses parody and satire in *Tooth Imprints on a Corn Dog.*

Skow, John. "You'll Flip." *Time* 140, No. 15 (12 October 1992): 90.
> Argues that the irreverence and disjointedness of *Et Tu, Babe* reflects the short attention spans of contemporary American youth.

Yardley, Jonathan. "Stand-Up Comic Novelist." *Book World—The Washington Post* (4 October 1992): 3.

> Favorable review of *Et Tu, Babe,* discussing the cultural references employed in Leyner's fiction.

**Interview**

Phillips, W. Glasgow. "Last Bite." *The San Francisco Review of Books* 20, No. 2 (May-June 1995): 14-15.

> Interview in which Leyner discusses works-in-progress.

---

**Additional coverage of Leyner's life and career is contained in the following sources published by Gale Research:** *Contemporary Authors,* **Vol. 110; and** *Contemporary Authors New Revision Series,* **Vol. 28.**

---

# Hugh MacLennan

## 1907-1990

(Full name John Hugh MacLennan) Canadian novelist and essayist.

The following entry presents an overview of MacLennan's career, focusing on his novels. For further information on his life and works, see *CLC,* Volumes 2 and 14.

## INTRODUCTION

A distinguished figure in modern Canadian literature, MacLennan is known for his vivid portrayal of the Canadian character and experience. Although his novels usually address regional concerns, critics have observed that his skillful craftsmanship and sensitive exploration of such broad themes as father-son relationships, various manifestations of the abuse of power, and the social and moral disintegration of the twentieth century, have made his works accessible to readers around the world. As J. E. Morpurgo has stated: "Among Canadian novelists Hugh MacLennan was the most consistent in his ability to create an essentially Canadian mythology without abdicating the novelist's responsibility to be at once idiosyncratic and universally comprehensible."

### Biographical Information

A fourth-generation Nova Scotian of Highland Scots heritage, MacLennan was born in Glace Bay on Cape Breton Island, a coal-mining town in Nova Scotia, where his father ran a medical practice. When MacLennan was eight the family moved to Halifax, which served as a naval base during World War I, and his father joined the Canadian army. In December 1917 a munitions ship collided with a relief ship in the Halifax harbor, causing an explosion which destroyed a large portion of the town and killed almost 2,000 people. MacLennan witnessed the devastation caused by this accident and later used the event as the focal point of his first published novel, *Barometer Rising* (1941). MacLennan's father constantly encouraged him to excel in both athletic and scholastic endeavors, particularly tennis and classical Greek and Latin studies. From 1924 to 1928 MacLennan studied at Dalhousie University in Halifax, graduating with a Governor General's medal for classical studies and a Rhodes scholarship. During the next four years MacLennan continued his studies in classics at Oxford University in England. Upon graduation, he applied for a position in the classics department at Dalhousie, but, after being turned down in favor of an Englishman, began his doctoral studies at Princeton University in 1932. While at Princeton, MacLennan began writing fiction; his first published work, however, was his doctoral dissertation *Oxyrhynchus* (1935), which examined the social and economic causes of the decline of an early Roman colony in Egypt. In 1935 MacLennan began teaching history and classics at a pri-

vate boys' school in Montreal. Following the popular and critical success of his first two novels, *Barometer Rising* and *Two Solitudes* (1945), MacLennan resigned his teaching position in 1945 to devote himself to his literary career. Although he received numerous awards and honors during the following years, his subsequent works were generally less successful financially, and in 1951 he returned to teaching part-time at McGill University, where he remained until his retirement in 1979.

### Major Works

Set during World War I, *Barometer Rising* focuses on Neil Macrae, a disgraced young military officer who returns to Halifax in 1917 to wreak vengeance upon Colonel Wain, the officer who falsely blamed him for a bungled mission, and to resume his romantic relationship with Penny, the colonel's daughter. Before Macrae can carry out his plan for revenge, two ships collide in the harbor causing an explosion which kills many of the town's residents, including Colonel Wain. Neil demonstrates his heroism during the cleanup effort following the explosion and subsequent blizzard; he is reunited with Penny at the novel's end. *Barometer Rising* is considered an important expression of the increased spirit of nationalism and independence that arose in Canada during the early part of the twentieth century. On the twenty-fifth anniversary of the novel's publication, William H. New commented on the allegorical nature of the novel, observing that "the two generations into which the central characters divide . . . represent the young Canada and the controlling Great Britain; the explosion which figures as a prominent event in the story represents both the First World War and the political severance between Canada and Britain, which historically accompanied it. The novel is also a work that can be read with interest outside Canada, for the conflict that it depicts is ultimately not limited by national boundaries." Focusing primarily on the period between the world wars, MacLennan's *Two Solitudes* examines the conflict between Canada's Catholic, French-speaking heritage and its Protestant, English-speaking one. Through an assorted cast of characters—including a wealthy Quebec landowner, a writer, and an English-Canadian industrialist—the novel explores the social and political conflicts between English and French Canadians, suggesting that the two cultures should resolve their differences. Set partly in a fictive Ontario town and partly in New York and Princeton, *The Precipice* (1948) delineates a romance between a Canadian woman and an American engineer while simultaneously comparing and contrasting American and Canadian views on material success, technology, and religion, particularly the guilt-complex as derived from Canadian Puritanism. Noted for its authentic local color and dialogue, *Each Man's Son* (1951) centers on Dr. Daniel Ainslie, a physician in a small Canadian mining town on Cape Breton Island who is troubled by insecurity about his religious faith, his relationship with his father, and his wife's inability to bear children. Desiring a child to restore meaning to his life, Ainslie adopts a boy named Alan, the orphaned son of a local boxer. *Return of the Sphinx* (1967), the sequel to *Each Man's Son,* centers on Alan Ainslie's troubled relationships with his children during the social and political turmoil in Quebec during the 1960s. One of MacLennan's most successful novels, *The Watch That Ends the Night* (1959) explores the insecurities of Canadians who grew up between the world wars by relating the impact of international events on the narrator, his wife, and her former husband. Widely translated, this novel is noted for its psychological insight, characterization, and humor. MacLennan's last novel, *Voices in Time* (1980), is similarly concerned with international events. Set in the year 2039 after a nuclear holocaust has destroyed most of civilization, *Voices in Time* relates the efforts of an elderly man to make sense of the letters, diaries, and videotapes left to him by two of his relatives, a German historian who participated in Nazi atrocities and a radical Canadian television personality who provoked social disturbances during the 1960s. *Voices in Time* garnered praise for its sophisticated exploration of humanity's abuse of power.

**Critical Reception**

Critical reaction to MacLennan's work has been mixed. Although he received three Governor General's awards for fiction—for *Two Solitudes, The Precipice,* and *The Watch That Ends the Night*—and two for nonfiction—for *Cross-Country* (1949) and *Thirty and Three* (1955)—some critics have faulted his methods as outdated and have lamented what they consider his tendency toward didacticism. Many scholars have, however, praised his concern with the human condition, his exploration of the Canadian character and the tensions in Canadian society, his efforts to combine realism and symbolism, and his interest in the theme of power. Remarking on *Voices in Time,* which many critics regard as MacLennan's most accomplished work, Elspeth Cameron has stated that MacLennan's "enduring central theme has been the choice facing all men: whether power is to be used for constructive or destructive ends, a theme he has treated with increasing complexity and impact." Commenting on MacLennan's literary career, Canadian novelist Robertson Davies has observed that "Hugh MacLennan has not written nice books, but the best books of which he was capable, and they have not always been easy or friendly reading. Always there has been that exploration of his very own Canadian consciousness, which has thrown up boulders of philosophical disquisition on what might have been the smooth lawns of his story-telling. He has refused to bury the rocks and roll the lawns, and has taken the consequences of his decision." While MacLennan's works have not been greeted with universal acclaim, his gift for eliciting understanding and appreciation of Canada and its people have established him as an important and influential figure in Canadian literature.

---

## PRINCIPAL WORKS

*Oxyrhynchus: An Economic and Social Study* (nonfiction)  1935
*Barometer Rising* (novel)  1941
*Two Solitudes* (novel)  1945
*The Precipice* (novel)  1948
*Cross-Country* (essays)  1949
*Each Man's Son* (novel)  1951
*Thirty and Three* (essays)  1955
*The Watch That Ends the Night* (novel)  1959
*Scotchman's Return, and Other Essays* (essays)  1960; also published as *Scotman's Return, and Other Essays,* 1960
*Seven Rivers of Canada* (essays)  1961; also published as *Rivers of Canada* [revised edition], 1962
*Return of the Sphinx* (novel)  1967
*The Other Side of Hugh MacLennan: Selected Essays Old and New* (essays)  1978
*Voices in Time* (novel)  1980
*On Being a Maritime Writer* (nonfiction)  1984

---

## CRITICISM

### Robert H. Cockburn   (essay date 1969)

SOURCE: *"Two Solitudes,"* in *The Novels of Hugh MacLennan*, Harvest House Ltd., 1969, pp. 47-69.

[*In the following excerpt, Cockburn provides an in-depth analysis of character, theme, and setting in* Two Solitudes. *Overall, he finds the first half of the novel aesthetically and intellectually superior to the second.*]

The title of MacLennan's second novel has long since passed into the language as a common descriptive phrase of Canadians; and *Two Solitudes* is probably still the best-known of his books. MacLennan wrote it, one feels certain, because of the importance of the theme; here was a chance to examine the major rift in Canadian life; here, concomitantly, was the chance for MacLennan to establish himself solidly in the role of sociological historian, of spokesman, as it were, for Canada. Edmund Wilson has written that

> Mr. MacLennan seems to aim . . . to qualify, like Balzac, as the "secretary of society," and one feels that in his earnest and ambitious attempt he sometimes embarks upon themes which he believes to be socially important but which do not really much excite his imagination. An example of this, it seems to me, is . . . *Two Solitudes.* [*O Canada* (1965)]

On the contrary, one feels that MacLennan's imagination was excited by the theme—the first part of the book surely proves this—but that he fails to find enthusiastic critical approval rather because he refused to make a conscientious effort at sustained artistry. There is a suggestion to support this idea in an essay of the author's [in *Scotchman's Return*]:

> . . . I published at the height of the King era a book called *Two Solitudes* which sold more copies in Canada than any Canadian novel since *Maria Chapdelaine*. Literary merit had no connection with this sale; the book merely happened to put into words what hundreds of thousands of Canadians felt and knew.

MacLennan seems almost to be daring us to attach too much importance to "literary merit"—instead, we are meant to applaud because he got his message over, loud and clear. But, after all, since MacLennan has chosen to deliver his nationalistic campaign through the medium of fiction, he has to be judged as a craftsman. While the overall impression left by *Two Solitudes* is perhaps more disappointing than that imparted by *Barometer Rising,* MacLennan has, to a great extent, improved his technique. And there is no denying that this novel said, in 1945, a number of things which the average Canadian reader was himself too inarticulate to express; in its day, *Two Solitudes* came as both a revelation and a confirmation of a situation—the French-English problem—that was, and still is, significantly and importantly Canadian. The title is drawn from Rainer Maria Rilke:

> Love consists in this,

> that two solitudes protect,
> and touch, and greet each other.

The story begins in 1917 in the riverside parish of Saint-Marc, Quebec. Almost immediately the plot takes shape; it develops through personal conflicts among major characters, conflicts which mirror the French- vs English-Canadian predicament.

Athanase Tallard is the protagonist of the first half of the novel. He comes of a long line of anti-clerical seigneurs, is better educated and far wealthier than anyone else in the parish, and is the local M.P. Despite his disenchantment with the power wielded by his church, he is proud of his heritage and of his own people; he has been frustrated by his failure to help them move ahead, before it is too late, into a new, steadily progressing world. The conscription crisis is raging, and Tallard is in favour of full mobilization.

Vehemently opposing him is Father Beaubien, the parish priest. He is proud of having, through his own efforts, built the largest church for forty miles around: "It was larger even than the largest Protestant church in Montreal where millionaires were among the parishioners. And Saint-Marc numbered less than a hundred and thirty families." Beaubien is sincere, but a simple man and in many ways a narrow-minded one: "Quite literally he believed that God held him accountable for every soul in the place." He epitomises both the weakness and the strength of the Roman Catholic clergy in Quebec; it is through men such as himself that the Church controls the population—yet he stands for a more traditional, and probably happier, way of life than that which is encroaching from the outside. Saint-Marc is cut off from the main current of world and national affairs, and the priest wants things to remain that way: "Let the rest of the world murder itself through the war, cheat itself in business, destroy its peace with new inventions and the frantic American rush after money. Quebec remembered God and her own soul, and these were all she needed." Beaubien is against the war and defies conscription. So there is, first of all, a conflict between these two men; Tallard aligns himself with the wider world of national responsibility while Beaubien stands for narrow provincialism.

Tallard brings two English Canadians to the village. John Yardley is a retired Nova Scotian sea-captain and a Protestant. Huntly McQueen, shrewd and calculating, is "rapidly becoming one of the richest men in Canada," and represents, in the novel, the Scots-Canadian businessmen who control Quebec Province from Montreal: "Being an Ontario Presbyterian, he had been reared with the notion that French Canadians were an inferior people, first because they were Roman Catholics, second because they were French." Yardley decides to buy a farm and stay on, and McQueen broaches the idea of building a power dam on a local river—it would bring in a factory, which in turn would produce revenue for the debt-ridden parish. Beaubien opposes both moves: he regards factory towns as beds of sin and intends to keep his people on the land, and he has no use for "English" men: "No English Canadian had ever owned land in this parish." Tallard, who has heretofore only seen the proposed location of the dam as a scenic spot, and who distrusts businessmen of McQueen's stripe, is nevertheless attracted to the proposition because it promises a chance for his people to develop their own resources. Also, however, he spots a personal opportunity. The site is on his property and, feeling his career in parliament to be a failure, he sees a chance to make a name, money, and a new position for himself.

In less than twenty pages MacLennan has established the thematic framework of his novel by showing the numerous antagonisms inherent in such a situation: French against English; Catholic against Protestant; Quebec against Montreal; old against new. Tallard, his priest, and McQueen are caught up in a maelstrom of differences and Yardley will be trapped in the middle.

Tallard has two sons, Marius, by his first wife, and Paul, by his second wife, Kathleen. Paul, in the first half of the novel, is just a boy; largely ignored by his father, he is comforted by, and becomes a close friend of, Yardley. In the full course of the book, however, he and his brother come to enact on a different level the same conflict that besets their father and priest.

Marius is a university student and a Quebec nationalist. Like Father Beaubien, he loathes the British and is an unswerving Catholic. Rifling his father's desk, he comes across some writing criticising the Church. He regards this as heretical and considers his father not only a traitor to his race for his stand on conscription, but now a traitor to his religion as well. Jansenism, puritanical Catholicism, is the trouble with Marius; his nature is secretive, and he feels himself to be an outcast within his own family. Kathleen, who is not much older than himself, he both resents for superseding his own mother, a nun-like woman, and desires for her beauty. But Tallard, whose time has largely been given to politics, must share the blame for Marius' attitude; he has not been a companion to his sons and is, for all his logic and intelligence, a distant, rather cold man. This lack of parental consideration has spurred Marius' alienation.

We see Marius at a political rally in Montreal, howling against conscription, his ego inflated by applause. Accused by an English soldier of being a "yellow son of a bitch," Marius smashes him to the ground and goes into hiding "to keep out of the army in order to defy the English and assert his rights as a French Canadian. And he would be doing even more than that. He was saving himself for his career, a career that he knew now would be a crusade." Thus, depth is added to the already internecine atmosphere of the plot.

Tallard's wife, Kathleen, provides yet another conflict within the story. She hates Saint-Marc. Of Irish descent, she comes from Montreal and her main desire is to live there again. Saint-Marc regards her as a foreigner and condemns her "for not having a child a year." The marriage of Tallard and Kathleen is a very weak link in the plot. She comes of a working-class background, has had no education to speak of, and has held jobs as a salesgirl and a hat-check girl "in one of the fashionable hotels." Sex was her favourite extracurricular activity and Tallard met her in bed, and "to her surprise" asked her to marry him

when his first wife died. This strikes one as being extremely improbable when the contrasting social backgrounds of the two are taken into consideration. MacLennan never satisfactorily explains Tallard's infatuation; it is suggested that Kathleen's "lush body" is the only reason.

Kathleen's apparent purpose in the novel is to make Paul half- "English." She is successful there. Also, she adds another dimension to Tallard's dilemma. Kathleen figures in the weakest episode of the first part of the book, a love-making scene with a returned army major. One sees here how easily MacLennan falls, when discussing sex, into the romantic clichés of the women's magazines:

> "You're miraculous! Are you always like that?"
> "Are you?"
> "No."
> "I'm not either."
> etc.

Such clumsy writing makes a sham of MacLennan's pretensions to realism and, of course, forms a hollow spot in what is, for the most part, an interesting and convincing story.

Father Beaubien learns of Tallard's "heretical" writing from Marius, and eventually takes him to task on this score and also for his "failure" in having only two children. In one of the best scenes in the book, Tallard is confronted by the priest in his library. The latter's narrowness is painful to read about: prints of Voltaire and Rousseau he mistakes for family portraits, and he distrusts the many English books on the shelves. But this ignorance is countered by his insight into Tallard's character. They discuss Marius and Beaubien asks, "Have you ever shown a father's natural feeling toward him? Have you ever really gone out of your way to help him?" Tallard has decided to send Paul to an English school so that he'll learn to mix naturally with English boys and so he can get a scientific education. Beaubien insists upon a French, Catholic school and flays Tallard for backing "materialism" and war.

Shortly afterwards, Marius, bitterly cynical and on the run, returns and goes into hiding. In the ensuing confrontation the fanatical priest threatens Tallard, who has refused to back down on the factory scheme, with a disclosure that shocks and weakens the older man: Marius has known, and this we now see to be the underlying cause of his rebellion, that on the night of his mother's death his father slept with Kathleen in a hospital room near that containing the body.

Marius is captured and taken off to the army. An informer, Janet Methuen, gave him away; she is Lardley's daughter, and turns informer because her husband has died fighting in France. Also, and more importantly, she is an agent, and a victim, of her social background; having married into the English "aristocracy" of Montreal, she has been trained to despise the French. Yardley remonstrates with her and she replies: "It makes me furious, all this pampering of them. It's time they were brought to heel." Beaubien taunts Tallard with what has happened and with having let Paul, who has been their companion on their vacations, associate with Janet's young daughters. He demands that Tallard, once and for all, dismiss the plan for the factory—if he refuses, his name will be read out in church; every voter in his constituency will know that he is condemned.

The outcome is tragic and manifold: the Tallard family is ostracised in Saint-Marc, and Kathleen turns upon her husband, accusing him of being an old fool. He and Paul join the Presbyterian Church in Montreal, and the family moves to the city. As Part One (1917-1918) of the novel ends, Tallard is hanging on to his final shred of hope—that the factory will be built and that the money from it will vindicate him, in his own eyes and Kathleen's.

With Part Two (1919-1921) the first half of the novel finishes in a satisfactorily inevitable fashion. The last meeting between Tallard and McQueen is convincingly portrayed. They were to have been partners in the factory scheme but now McQueen has backed out—he refuses to go ahead with plans in conjunction with a man toward whom Saint-Marc is antagonistic. In reply to Tallard's furious protests that this will mean his ruination, McQueen answers: "Come, Tallard, be reasonable. You French-Canadians make too much trouble for yourselves—far too much." Tallard is broken, bewildered, and embittered:

> He remembered a sentence of McQueen's and gave it a different twist: "The tragedy of French-Canada is that you can't make up your minds whether you want to be freethinking individuals or French-Canadians choosing only what you think your entire race will approve . . ." Like all you English, free with advice! But do they ever help a man? Do they ever stretch out a hand? Do they ever really want us to have a chance?

Three years pass, and Tallard dies. On his deathbed he calls for a priest and returns to his Church. Marius, a law-student now, is jubilant. His young brother is confused, and as Athanase breathes his last, Marius and Kathleen fight for possession of Paul. Kathleen wins, and the first half of *Two Solitudes* closes with her and her son in a cramped Montreal apartment. Tallard has died bankrupt.

The plot of the first half of *Two Solitudes* is, despite a few flaws, extremely convincing and satisfactory. This is because the plot and its characters contain the theme within themselves. It is through the actions and personalities of the characters that the theme becomes clear; and the plot develops logically out of these actions and the natures which incite them.

Tallard, we realise, is a man caught between two views of life, each of which is pulling him in a different direction. He scorns his Church, yet he returns to it in the end; he is repelled by McQueen, but he can't help envying the wealth and progress for which the man stands; he loves Saint-Marc and its old ways, yet he is certain that it is his duty to radically alter the tempo and flavour of the parish. MacLennan handles internal revelation far more competently in this novel than he did in *Barometer Rising.* Thematic ideas are contained principally in dialogue, rather than in contemplation, and thus become far more credible

and vital. Tallard's debates and conversations with Beaubien, McQueen, and Yardley are heavily weighted on the thematic side, but, when one takes into account the circumstances of the plot, this is not objectionable. Here, for example, is Tallard speaking to Yardley:

> "The trouble with this whole country is that it's divided up into little puddles with big fish in each one of them. I tell you something. Ten years ago I went across the whole of Canada. I saw a lot of things. This country is so new that when you see it for the first time, all of it, and particularly the west, you feel like Columbus and you say to yourself, 'My God, is all this ours!' Then you make the trip back. You come across Ontario and you encounter the mind of the maiden aunt. You see Methodists in Toronto and the Presbyterians in the best streets of Montreal and the Catholics all over Quebec, and nobody understands one damn thing except that he's better than everyone else. The French are Frencher than France and the English are more British than England ever dared to be. And then you go to Ottawa and you see the Prime Minister with his ear on the ground and his backside hoisted in the air. And Captain Yardley, you say God damn it!"

MacLennan has said [in *Scotchman's Return*] that this is "a passage which dozens of strangers mentioned when they wrote to me about the book." Obviously, MacLennan was able to put into words what a great many Canadians felt but were unable to define; and, generally speaking, such material is fitted—as here—effectively into the pattern of the first half of the novel.

Tallard is by no means simply a vehicle for the theme. One sees him to be driven by his own nature, by his sense of family pride and his disillusionment in not having lived up to his own expectations. He has lost his first wife, whom he loved deeply but whose aversion to sex he deplored, and finds himself, when we come to the novel, too old and staid to satisfy Kathleen. Politically, he has never attained high rank, and his career—as well as his second wife—has alienated him from his sons. He is hurt by the parish's rejection of him, however his growing bitterness is not directed only against them but against himself as well. He stands to make a fortune by the factory, and thus his scorn for both his priest and his business partner is mixed with guilt. Because we understand Tallard's temperament we believe in these divisive conflicts.

He is a man beset by many dilemmas, all of which combine to crush him in the end. Like Hamlet he is indecisive; like Lear he wrecks his own family life and the order of his "state"—for McQueen goes on to build the factory alone, and Saint-Marc is transformed; like Michael Henchard he is a victim of his own environment; there is something of Prospero about him, too: through the life he plans for Paul—partially, one must remember, out of selfish motives stemming from divided loyalties—he hopes that, one day, there will be reconciliation and new hope. Clearly, Tallard is a tragic figure; flawed by pride, a vacillating sort of stubbornness, and ambitious but well-meaning gullibility, he falls from fortune to misery and is wiped out. Certainly his misfortune is more than he deserves, and we are moved to pity. Do we, however, consider him a tragic *hero*? How much "greatness" is there in Tallard? and how much "goodness?" Unfortunately, there is little, if any, of either. He is the outstanding figure in *Two Solitudes,* and is very real—but, like most of MacLennan's heroes, he is too much given to self-pity and to an almost painfully sincere sense of purpose. Where one looks for stoic humour or strength there is only bitterness, irresolution, and weakness. One sympathises with Tallard, one understands him and hopes for him—but one neither likes nor admires him.

The sympathy that is generated for him derives from the actions not so much of himself as of others; one is reacting against McQueen, Beaubien, Marius and Kathleen instead of for Tallard. From a technical standpoint he unifies the first half of the book. It is because of the relationships that others have with him that the plot develops, and with it the theme. Each of the other major characters gains importance and holds our interest mainly because of his involvement with Tallard.

This is true of Huntly McQueen. His relationship with Tallard resembles, in several ways, Donald Farfrae's association with Henchard. In each case a cold, practical businessman is brought into a backwater; his up-to-date, progressive ideas shatter the old order, and the main representative of that order gets caught up in a predicament of his own making, cannot cope, and eventually is driven, broken and penniless, to his death.

The minute McQueen saw the falls of Saint-Marc he thought of power and profit; Tallard had seen them all his life and only thought them beautiful. McQueen respects Tallard's authority, but sums him up as being "probably a poor businessman." To Athanase, McQueen belongs to that class in Montreal on whom dollars grow "like barnacles; and their instinct for money was a trait no French-Canadian seemed able to acquire."

MacLennan's explanation of his background contributes greatly to our belief in McQueen's character. The fat son of poor Presbyterians, he came up the hard way—on the Bible and on beatings at his school. His intelligence carried him through university, after which he inherited a dying business and made it flourish. Discovering that he had this flair, he devoted his life to business. Aside from being a trustee in the Presbyterian Church he has virtually no outside activities; money is an end in itself, an end justified by his nightly prayers for his dead, strict mother; he is unmarried and "no woman with a bosom could be quite a lady in his eyes." Tough and unscrupulous, he is so dedicated to his way of life that he believes himself to be a fair and honest man. His moral values and his business "ethics" are practically one and the same thing.

McQueen has, because of his wealth and financial acumen, been accepted almost as an equal by Montreal's social elite; he moves among his fellow barons of St. James Street comfortably and is taken into the confidence of leading Westmount families. It is when one sees McQueen in his own particular environment that he becomes especially life-like. In *Barometer Rising* one couldn't take Geoffrey Wain seriously because he was too "flat" a character—one never sufficiently understood why he acted as he did nor

what he was really like. McQueen is, in a sense, a rounded, believable Wain; the reader knows his early background and his present one, is a party to his thoughts, and sees his special brand of reasoning develop and take form in action. MacLennan forces us not only to detest McQueen, but also to give him our grudging respect.

One may not respect Marius, but, again, one finds him a thoroughly convincing figure. His fanaticism is a logical development of his dedication to his saintly mother; of the "traumatic shock" he suffered that night in the hospital; of his father's unintentional rejection of him; and of the disturbing, sensual presence of Kathleen. The end result of these factors is Marius' alliance with Beaubien and the subsequent action. Marius is not a simple, flaming separatist, but a young man reacting in a realistic manner to psychological and environmental influences. His cynical disillusionment, hypocrisy, and misguided sincerity and dedication all help to make him a solid, living presence.

MacLennan deals briefly with Beaubien's early life—enough so that we find his beliefs and actions a natural element of the context. His simple, one-sided personality would not hold up were it not for the fact that one is always aware of his power; he shows himself a good judge of human nature, speaks with vitality, and his presence is constantly reflected, even when he is not on the scene, in the conversations and contemplations of other characters, minor and major—notably Tallard.

Janet Methuen is just as real in her way as Beaubien is in his. She is neurotic, misguided, and singularly unpleasant. Once more, this can be explained by her background. Having married into Town of Mount Royal society from more humble origins, she has been twisted by her desire to live up to unfamiliar but socially desirable standards. Early on, her nature was being moulded into a sort of conformity that MacLennan detests: "Her voice was a clipped imitation of the British. The Englishwomen who had run the finishing school to which her mother had sent her had done all they could to prevent her from talking or thinking like a Canadian." Barely thirty, she is lean and severely English in dress and appearance. She rations herself on food, is willing to go hungry "to make herself feel worthy of the British." In the first half of the novel Janet serves a triple purpose: her young daughters meet Paul at Saint-Marc; she betrays Marius, thus giving impetus to Tallard's ouster from the parish; and she, along with McQueen, enables MacLennan to deal in considerable depth with a branch of society that is just as distinctively Canadian as the parish on the Saint Lawrence.

The above characters are successful; one believes in them, finds their actions and beliefs the logical result of their environments and natures. There are, however, two characters who are not fully believable and who do not fit comfortably into the first-half context—Kathleen and Yardley.

Kathleen, we have already noted, is a bizarre choice for Tallard to have made. This awkwardness might have been partially overcome had MacLennan invested her with some sort of distinction, or at least force. But she is a phantomfigure and never comes alive. About all one knows about her is that she is too young for Tallard, out of place in his home, and self-centred and aloof in her relationships with other human beings, including her son.

Nor can one reconcile oneself completely to Yardley's presence in the novel. Taking into account his nautical life, MacLennan has endowed him with an artificial leg and a flow of witticisms uttered in the Maritime vernacular. It is hard to believe that such a man would choose Saint-Marc as his home; but he wants to be near his daughter, and an old ship-mate of his hailed from the parish—this we are meant to take as sufficient justification for his removal to a hot-bed of French-Canadian Catholicism.

Nonetheless, his role is clear. He is, because of his down-East background, able to view the Quebec situation with detachment; he is the chorus of the tragedy. As such, his comments are usually valid and helpful in illuminating the theme. Where the trouble comes in is in his personality. Despite his salty and often ungrammatical dialect he is given to reading Shakespeare and to playing chess; he is kindly, benevolent, and always has the right answer, is the second of a line of "sages" in MacLennan's novels. Besides acting as the chorus, he becomes a second father to Paul and moulds him, as best he can, to his own far-seeing, non-fanatical attitude. When the novel moves into its second half, Yardley, having left Saint-Marc, seems much more acceptable; but stumping his hearty way about the parish he strikes a jarring note.

If Yardley represents the homespun Maritimer, Major Dennis Morey, the man who sleeps with Kathleen, is the Spirit of the West. He praises Winnipeg to the skies, and one suspects that he was included as a "filler" to build up the over-all image of Canada for the reader. Also, he may have had a few talks with Neil MacRae in France:

> ". . . Canada isn't England, and too many Canadians try to pretend it is, generally they're the rich ones, and they pay the money and make the choices. Does our Western prairie look like anything in England, for God's sake? Then why try to cover it with English architecture?" He shrugged his shoulders. "After a while they'll get another idea. They'll pretend we're exactly the same as the States. And they'll start to imitate ideas from down there. But is there anything in the States like the Saint Lawrence Valley? For that matter, is there anything in the States like us—the collective us?"

This has the familiar ring of the MacLennan lecture, but it is rendered credible by being expounded in the course of conversation.

It can be seen, then, that the majority of the leading characters unify and illuminate, through their personalities, and actions, the plot and the theme. The awkward, unsure treatment of theme so noticeable in *Barometer Rising,* has, except for a few minor recurrences, disappeared in the first half of *Two Solitudes.* While the characters do, of course, symbolise divisive elements in the Canadian population, they are by no means simply vehicles for MacLennan's opinions. We can see, as we read, why there is distrust on one side and condescension on the other, why the problem is so intricate and explosive. But at the same time we have an affinity with the actors and are caught up in the tragic course of their lives.

Another major strength, and one tightly interwoven with the single unity of characterisation, plot, and theme, is the setting. We move, for the most part, between Saint-Marc and Montreal. The leisurely, time-honoured pace of life in the parish is memorably portrayed: Polycarpe Drouin's general store with its jumble of merchandise and perpetual checker games; Tallard's house, "built by the first member of the family who came to Canada in 1672;" the local customs and the local characters—all make a lasting impression on the reader. MacLennan draws these scenes with affectionate honesty. He also captures the spirit of Montreal, and there are fine general descriptions of that city. But, because he is dealing with Montrealers such as Mc-Queen and Janet, these pictures of a locale and its special life are often satire:

> It was a huge stone house on the southern slope of Mount Royal. Harvey Methuen's family was decidedly rich, the money coming from government bonds and stocks in breweries, distilleries, lumber, mines, factories and God knew how big a block of Canadian Pacific. It was a large family and every branch of it lived in stone houses with dark rooms hung with wine-red draperies, and they all had great dark paintings on their walls framed in gilded plaster.

Here is a snapshot of Paul's school in the city:

> . . . the school bowed heads for a short prayer and then stood at attention and sang *God Save the King,* looking up to the picture of King George, draped with the Union Jack, their eyes lighting at the same time on the large group-photograph that also hung behind the platform, containing the picture of . . . the men who formed the guiding committee of the board of governors.
>
> . . . . .
>
> The boys never worried themselves about national problems of any sort; indeed, they did not know they existed. Their home was the English section of Montreal; as a result of what everyone told them, their country was not Canada but the British Empire.

Sociological information, one sees, is effectively conveyed through such descriptions. MacLennan's sympathies, it is plain, do not lie with England. One wonders, however, whether such criticism of Canada in 1917-1921 is helpful or even meaningful. She was a young country, and it was only natural, given her history, that she should identify with Great Britain—it is only very recently that Canada has come to grips with the problem of self-knowledge. On the other hand, one cannot deny that MacLennan is right to emphasise the harmful effects of what he, one suspects, would call secondhand tradition. It nourished, in the upper levels of English-speaking society, the attitude which was partially responsible for Janet Methuen's betrayal of Marius—an inhuman action—and, generally speaking, a patronising discrimination toward French Canadians by the denizens of Westmount and the Town of Mount Royal.

If one were to choose a typical landscape description of MacLennan's, the following would be as good as any:

> That afternoon it blew cold from the northeast, the wind built itself up, towards evening the air was flecked with a scud of white specks, and then the full weight of the snow began to drive. It whipped the land, greyed it, then turned it white and continued to come down hissing invisibly after dark all night long until mid-morning of the next day. For a few days after that the river was like black ink pouring between the flat whiteness of the plains on either side. Then the frost cracked down harder, the river stilled and froze. Another blizzard came and covered the ice, and then the whole world was so white you could hardly look at it with the naked eye against the glittering sun in the morning. The farmhouses seemed marooned. . . .

MacLennan is not fond of figurative language—metaphors and similes are few and far between in his writing. The strength of this spare prose lies in its clarity; ordinary language is used to convey the sense of something seen and remembered. To the reader such pictures are real; if he is familiar with Montreal or the Saint Lawrence Valley, say, the impact is immediate, and he is liable to give the author more credit than he deserves, artistically speaking. Familiarity negates, to some extent, the lack of an original or really exciting prose style, but certainly straight-forward visual, often sensuous, description serves its purpose admirably.

One outstanding fault in the novel is a deliberate tilting of the story towards an American audience. "Since the confederation of the provinces into the Dominion of Canada just after the American Civil War, a Tallard had always sat in parliament in Ottawa." This is far too explicit, and is a blatant concession to the American reader. If Americans don't know the date of Confederation or the location of Canada's parliament, let them look up the details elsewhere. A more flagrant and annoying instance reads: "A year ago Drouin had introduced another decoration for the store-front, a small bracket over the door holding three faded flags. One was the Red Ensign of the British Mercantile Marine with a Canadian crest in the corner." A Canadian reader was bound to be indignant at the assumption that he did not know what his own flag looked like. It is as if an American writer were to describe his flag not as "the stars and stripes," but rather as "a design originated by Betsy Ross, who lived in Philadelphia. . . ." MacLennan's audience is, after all, predominantly Canadian—and most Canadians, one imagines, particularly if they are as concerned about nationalism as MacLennan is, will resent this clumsy bowing and scraping toward the south.

Except for this flaw, the banal bedroom scene, and the disturbing presence of Kathleen and Yardley, the first half of *Two Solitudes* is skilfully and convincingly written. One sees in microcosm, and begins to comprehend, a major problem that besets this country. More important, one arrives at this understanding through being involved in the tragic predicament of living characters. Here, in the first two hundred and twenty-five pages of *Two Solitudes,*

MacLennan comes very close indeed to creating a "whole which is harmonious."

Nothing like as much can be said for the second half of the book. George Woodcock has written that

> If *Two Solitudes* had ended with Tallard's death, it would have been a moving and cohesive book. But up to this point it merely presents the problem of racial relations; it does not have the logical completeness of presenting a solution, and this MacLennan seeks, at the expense of his novel, in its later chapters. ["A Nation's Odyssey: The Novels of Hugh MacLennan," in *Masks of Fiction,* edited by A. J. M. Smith, 1961]

—and he is right, as is Desmond Pacey, who [in his *Creative Writing in Canada,* 1961] calls the second half "much inferior." In this part of the book, structure, plot, characterisation, theme, and style all collapse, and one finds it hard to understand how a man who had been writing at the top of his form up to now could be responsible for this turgid shambles.

We leap a gap of thirteen years, from Tallard's death to 1934. Heather, Janet's younger daughter, breaks away from the cloying restrictions of the elite society in which she has been brought up and falls in love with Paul. The two of them meet at Yardley's Montreal apartment—he has left Saint-Marc, which by now has long been a factory town. Paul has, since his father's death, travelled across Canada on various jobs and has played professional hockey to put himself through college; he has taken a degree and, with Kathleen remarried, is entirely on his own. He has intentions of becoming a novelist, and he and Heather are together for only a short time, for he wants "to see the world" and Part Three of the novel, 1934, ends with him outward bound from Halifax Harbour.

Five years flash by and we find ourselves in 1939, the final quarter of the book. Paul has, in the interim, not only been a seaman; he has sold short stories to American magazines and, on the strength of his Canadian degree, has gone to Oxford. (His college, like MacLennan's, was Oriel.) There he began work on a novel and he has come to Greece to finish it. Unable to, however, and homesick, he has planned his return to Canada.

Back home, Yardley has returned to Nova Scotia. He lives in a lodging house in Halifax where Janet and Heather have been visiting him. Janet is worried about Heather's having discarded her proper social circle (She has been studying art in New York.) and also about her lasting infatuation for Paul. Yardley, having rebuked his daughter for her attitude, dies. The scene dealing with his death is easily the best in the second half of the book. Paul has come back, and he and Heather are secretly married in Halifax. Three unmemorable chapters are given to their honeymoon trip to Montreal via the Gaspé. In Montreal, Paul refuses to concede to Janet's wishes for him, and gets down to work on a novel. He visits Marius, who lives with his wife and a slew of children in a grubby working-class neighbourhood; the older brother is an impoverished lawyer, and his bitter nationalistic idealism has become almost his sole purpose of existence.

As the novel moves to its close, Heather and her mother—who does not know of the marriage—are vacationing in Maine. McQueen, who has remained Janet's intimate advisor, is encouraged by her to persuade Heather to break with Paul. This forces Heather's hand, and her mother, when she learns the truth, feigns a serious attack. As this is going on, the war begins, and Paul, who is to enlist the following day, arrives to join his wife. Heather has at last made a clean break with her mother and all that she stands for; but reconciliation on Janet's part is implied at the end.

The plot of the novel finishes there. But then comes an incredibly poor, if brief, concluding chapter. We are given a quick cross-country tour of Canada, we read of its preparations for war, and, finally, we are subjected to this fuzzy piece of pontifical philosophising:

> Then, even as the two race-legends woke again remembering ancient enmities, there woke with them also the felt knowledge that together they had fought and survived one great war they had never made and that now they had entered another; that for nearly a hundred years the nation had been spread out on the top half of the continent over the powerhouse of the United States and still was there; that even if the legends were like oil and alcohol in the same bottle, the bottle had not been broken yet. And almost grudgingly, out of the instinct to what was necessary, the country took the first irrevocable steps toward becoming herself, knowing against her will that she was not unique but like all the others, alone with history, with science, with the future.

This paragraph is, regrettably, an almost inevitable conclusion; for MacLennan, in the second half of *Two Solitudes,* is primarily interested in proselytizing. The plot and the characters are subjected to the theme, and as a result the theme degenerates into a tiresome lecture.

A plot is sustained by the actions of its characters, actions which must, in a realistic novel, develop from convincing emotions and beliefs, which in their turn must stem from believable, living, personalities. The two protagonists here, Paul and Heather, are, artistically speaking, failures. Paul is meant to symbolise, through his union with Heather, the desired harmony of French- with English-speaking Canada. But he is just as unreal as his mother. One never really learns why he has developed into the person he is—only that he had a tough time in the depression, that he went to sea and to Oxford, etc. Rather than take the time to illuminate Paul's character in Part Three, MacLennan hurriedly jumps to Part Four, anxious, seemingly, to deliver his message. Our discomfort with Paul is generated in large part by this emptiness of understanding. He steps into the second half of the book a ready-made hero. He does too many things which, taken together, have a "romantic" aura about them: labourer to hockey-star to sailor to Oxford man to novelist. Indeed, by the time he gets to Greece—just twenty-nine—his hair is, in the best women's-magazine tradition, "foxed with grey."

It is apparent that Paul is mainly a projection of the author himself—not entirely an autobiographical figure, but certainly one whose activities bear a striking resemblance to MacLennan's. This is borne out not only by Paul's time

at Oriel and in Greece, but, more obviously, through his ideas on the novel. There is no good reason for his being a novelist, and one can only suppose that this was done so as to give the author a chance to air, and defend, his own views on writing about Canada. One sees that Paul's developing attitude is the same as was MacLennan's:

> In every city the same masses swarmed. Could any man write a novel about masses? The young man of 1933, together with all the individuals Paul had tried to create, grew pallid and unreal in his imagination beside the sense of the swarming masses heard three stories below in the shuffling feet of the crowd. For long minutes he stood at the window. To make a novel out of this? How could he? How could anyone? A novel should concern people, not ideas, and yet people had become trivial.

This refers to that novel MacLennan tried to write before the war—the one with "an international setting." By the time Paul goes on his honeymoon, his artistic philosophy is carried to the conclusion that, as we have seen earlier, MacLennan himself reached. Heather (Dorothy Duncan?) has read Paul's now-finished book. Her criticism leads him to exclaim,

> "Maybe I shouldn't have chosen a European scene. Of course, Europe is the focus . . ." He jumped up and began walking back and forth. "My God!" he shouted, "I've been a fool! A year's work! Heather—I've wasted a year's work!"
>
> She looked at him in excitement. Her thoughts were on the same track as his own. "Paul, why didn't you set the scene in Canada?"

Paul follows this up with the following argument:

> Must he write out of his own background, even if that background were Canada? Canada was imitative in everything. Yes, but perhaps only on the surface. What about underneath? No one had dug underneath so far, that was the trouble. . . . Canada was a country no one knew. . . . There was the question of background. As Paul considered the matter, he realised that his readers' ignorance of the essential Canadian clashes and values presented him with a unique problem. The background would have to be created from scratch if his story was to become intelligible. He could afford to take nothing for granted. He would have to build the stage and props for his play, and then write the play itself.

*Two Solitudes* preceded MacLennan's first volume of essays, *Cross Country,* the contents of which were all written after the novel was published. So this passage is his first declaration in print of what he has set out to do, and why he is following the pattern that he does; in that respect it is both interesting and informative. But, seen in its entirety, this passage does not read much like a thought process and, unfortunately, could be taken as a justification, or defence, of the methods employed in writing *Barometer Rising* (a belated reply to critics?) or *Two Solitudes.* "A novel should concern people, not ideas, and yet people had become trivial." thought Paul. Here we see ideas taking over, and Paul's own reality is diminished.

MacLennan tends to fall back on a style which wrecked *Barometer Rising,* but which had all but disappeared in the first half of *Two Solitudes.* Stilted philosophising takes the place of internal revelation. Here is Paul as he works on his new novel:

> Out of the society which had produced and frustrated him, which in his own way he had learned to accept, he knew that he was at last beating out a harmony. . . . In all his life, he had never seen an English-Canadian and a French-Canadian hostile to each other face to face. When they disliked, they disliked entirely in the group. And the result of these two group-legends was a Canada oddly naive, so far without any real villains, without overt cruelty or criminal memories, a country strangely innocent in its groping individual common sense, intent on doing the right thing in the way some children are, tongue-tied because it felt others would not be interested in what it had to say; loyal, skilled and proud, race-memories lonely in great spaces.

If one assigns these ideas to MacLennan as well—and one must—there is a discrepancy, petty though it may seem; in this novel we have seen English- and French-Canadians "hostile to each other face to face;" McQueen and Tallard, Marius and the soldier who accosted him, and, shortly now, Janet and Paul. Paul, then, is emasculated by the author's style; he is like Neil MacRae—a humourless hollow man, and too obviously an unreal symbolic figure for us to identify with him.

Heather has no real impact. She acts as a foil for Paul's usually turgid polemics and is in all respects an extremely commonplace heroine; like Penelope Wain, she is mature, intelligent, attractive, and strong-willed but loyal to Paul. She is used mainly as a commentator on the faults of Montreal high society, and is a representative of new tolerance and harmony between the English and French. Also, she is employed—as was Penny—as a weapon against Canadian restrictions on women who desire a career of their own.

As protagonists, both Paul and Heather fail because they never capture our imagination or admiration. The ideas they extol are interesting enough, but, as in *Barometer Rising,* these ideas lose their attraction because one is always conscious that one is reading a work of fiction—the frequent interruptions while dreary characters deliver lectures diminish our interest; MacLennan, as a craftsman, never makes up his mind whether to fish (write fiction) or cut bait (write non-fiction), and this indecisiveness is all too apparent to the reader.

The other four major characters are more successful. McQueen retains his pompous stupidity and Janet her neurotic unpleasantness. The two of them, along with Daphne, Heather's older sister, enable MacLennan to continue in this half of the book his sarcastic satire of their background. These three, and other peripheral figures, live in the pages because they speak far more than they think, and MacLennan's handling of dialogue—he has a good ear for regional accents and idiom—is crisply competent.

Yardley sagaciously admonishes us and the characters until he dies, but he is more believable now that he is out of Saint-Marc. His reminiscences of his years at sea as he lies dying appeal to our emotions and imagination more than anything else in this half of the novel; these memories are vivid and have a sensory quality that typifies MacLennan's writing at its best. And then, this:

> It was strange how a man's life passed like a ship through different kinds of weather. . . . Wonder in childhood; in the twenties physical violence and pride in muscles; in the thirties ambition; in the forties caution, and maybe a lot of dirty work; and then, if you were lucky, perhaps you could grow mellow. It seemed to Yardley that with the talent and the courage there was no limit to what a man could obtain out of life if he merely accepted what lay all around him. But knowledge was necessary; otherwise beauty was wasted. Beauty had come to him late in life, but now he couldn't have enough of it. It was something a man had to understand. Pictures and colours, for instance, and fine glass.

This thematic undertone which we first noticed in *Barometer Rising* with Angus Murray—of thankfulness for the wonder of life—we will next see, in greatly expanded form, in *The Watch That Ends the Night.*

These characters, however, do not play a large enough part to rescue the second-half plot from the protagonists. Other debilitating factors—closely related, as we have seen, to the failure of Paul and Heather—are the crippling structure, the dead weight of thematic context, and an almost incomprehensible falling-off of technique. The structure is arranged, first of all so as to bring a mature Paul and Heather together, and secondly to bring them to the brink of the Hitler War, which, it is suggested in that disastrous concluding chapter, will forge a new national unity. The theme controls the structure and the characters, both of which aspects wreck the plot.

The first half of *Two Solitudes* is one of MacLennan's most disciplined and coherent efforts at craftsmanship. Clearly, however, he was artistically negligent in the second half of the book. Once one moves from 1921 to 1934 one finds oneself in a new story. The connexion between the halves is tenuous at best. The characters do, of course, provide a link, but one is concerned mainly with Paul's theorising and his affair with Heather. One misses the fiery Marius and Tallard's sad battle against overwhelming odds. Not only is unity of time and action lost, but also the unity of place, the intricate and meaningful contrast between Saint-Marc and Montreal. From a tightly knit, intelligently written, and believable tragedy we move into what is supposed to be a confident reconciliation—only to find it a boring, fragmentary denouement. With the death of Tallard, MacLennan's imagination failed him; falling back on his own experience and private philosophy he tried to keep the theme going; it did, but the novel stopped dead. Giving every credit to the first half of the book, one must in the last analysis condemn the author for starting a job and failing to finish it. The last one hundred and forty-one pages are a flimsy excuse for fiction; the halves of the novel are themselves solitudes.

**Alec Lucas    (essay date 1970)**

SOURCE: "Constructing a Canada," in *Hugh MacLennan,* McClelland and Stewart Limited, 1970, pp. 10-17.

[*In the following excerpt, Lucas remarks on the main themes of MacLennan's fiction.*]

MacLennan served a long apprenticeship to his trade. He never woke to find himself famous. His was a long, slow climb beset by graduate studies, newspaper work, and the chalk-and-blackboard-chore of teaching at Lower Canada College (1935-1945)—as well as by his failure to publish his first three works of fiction: an international novel, *So All Their Praises,* completed at Princeton (1933), *Man Should Rejoice* (1937), another international novel, and *Augustus* (1939), a radio play. The tale of these works is a sad one, and the compounding of the inherent difficulties and loneliness of writing with such want of success must have almost crushed MacLennan's resolve. A publisher had taken the first book, but the poor man's almost immediate insolvency gave his young author little chance to savour the wine of good fortune. The second novel fared worse. It never found a publisher, but was read widely (in a limited way), no fewer than twenty-one editors having seen the manuscript before it reached the end of its dispiriting tour of the publishing houses. As for the radio play, it now rests with the other unpublished works in McGill's MacLennaniana. Yet these manuscripts, for all their want of success, do commemorate their author's struggle to master his craft and do point the way he would take in his later books. They centre on his favourite topics—the past (as comment on the present), political issues (not, however, Canadian, but American and European), and lonely young intellectuals searching for a place in the sun.

Like all ill winds these misadventures as a writer gained MacLennan something. They removed all dangers of premature recognition, certainly, and put him to school to a crotchety master, experience, from whom he learned methods of composition and structure and a lasting lesson when, one day in May, 1939, he received a long letter about *Man Should Rejoice.* As an unintentionally ironic comment on the title, the letter began with greetings but continued dishearteningly through a catalogue of reservations until it reached its final "deep regrets." After this missive, MacLennan gave up his attempts to write an international novel and set to work at once on *Barometer Rising,* recognizing for the first time the "inadequacy of large non-Canadian themes" for his fiction. Like Paul Tallard, he discovered that his early work "was wrong," because he had disregarded "his own native background." MacLennan had also listened attentively to his wife, herself an author of merit (Dorothy Duncan, undoubtedly the prototype in general of Paul's wife, Heather, and of Catherine Martell) who advised him "to see Canada as it was and to write of it as [he] saw it" ["**On Discovering Who We Are,**" in *Cross Country*]. For MacLennan this became a dictum. In all the years ahead he remained a loyal adherent to what he called "serious social fiction," long after the defection of many who had once marched under its banner. As late as 1966, he contended as confidently as he had a quarter-century before "that a literature can have no blood and earth in it unless it has deep roots in the au-

thor's own society" ["**An English-Speaking Quebecker Looks at Quebec,**" speech given in Vancouver, February 9, 1966].

MacLennan, again like Paul Tallard, saw the novel as a social force, and became a realist as much by circumstance as by choice. If he wanted to write about Canada convincingly, he had, he insisted, to reconstruct the background and set his own stage. The "general run of Canadian fiction" until then formed, as he evaluated it, "a handicap, repeating itself with reverberations of ancient traditions" and taking the Canadian scene for granted without ever defining "its essence." He had the task of "creating a perspective" for Canadian fiction that would include and explain the nature of the regional for Canadians and present the general scene for the international public so as to reveal how the processes shaping the destiny of Canada gave the country meaning in the world at large. MacLennan's is not a flags-and-bunting Canadianism, but simply a faith that internationalism for Canadians does not necessitate their going beyond their national boundaries. He thought it possible to concentrate on the country without denying it an international setting, so long as the Canadian "experience" selected should "reach out into the world." Writing in English, MacLennan had, willy-nilly, the language to do the stretching, and he was equally certain the nation was rich with experiences.

Despite these aims MacLennan is neither journalist, nor historian, nor sociologist *manqué* writing fiction. If he felt obliged to analyze Canada's political and cultural heritage, he did not think the novel a fictionalized documentary like Dos Passos's *U.S.A.* For him it remained a story presenting a true-to-life social situation as a focal point for the study of vital and interesting human beings. It should also contain a "mystery," not as a literary "jigsaw puzzle" or as a "private language" as in much modern fiction, but as a vision uniting facts in an organic whole like Tolstoy's *War and Peace,* "the greatest novel ever written" ["**The Future of the Novel as an Art Form,**" in *Scotchman's Return, and Other Essays*].

MacLennan's sights are high here, but the aim discloses how far his model for "historical" fiction differs from the traditional form in Canadian literature. "Designing and equipping the stage" where the nation could watch itself acting out its own destiny was not merely a matter of reconstructing this stage, but of integrating it with the drama. He was not essentially interested in the romance of Canadian history. This had no bearing on his novels, except peripherally as in *The Precipice,* when Lucy, in a reverie, contemplates the "trail of the voyageurs" as she gazes out over Lake Ontario. It was only later, in his book of essays, *Seven Rivers of Canada* (1961), that he made a large place for it, but as a fictional mode he has always thought it unsuited to the country. Sir Walter Scott, for his historical romances, could draw on centuries of tradition in a nation whose "essence" had long been defined. For Canadian authors there was no such indigenous tradition and no such "essence." The historical romance was a transplant that falsified our history. For all that books of the kind may have some relevant sense of time and even more of place, they pertained only superficially to the society in which they were set. They assumed what MacLennan, in keeping with his theory of the novel, felt obliged to detail and assess. Consequently, in his fiction, place is both background and foreground, and time, both individual and historical.

These characteristics dominate his first novel [*Barometer Rising*]. Halifax, a microcosm of Canadian society in the First World War, assumes the role of a major character, setting the standards of the behaviour of the people, and motivating them and presiding over their lives like a rich and whimsical aunt among poor relatives. In Halifax MacLennan was on familiar ground, but his success in describing it derives especially from his re-creation of the scenes of the munitions explosion (December 5, 1917) and of the following blizzard with such effect that they have much of the immediacy of the actual events.

MacLennan's later work reveals the same stress on geography and history. Saint-Marc-des-Erables, Grenville, Broughton, with their loves, hopes, honesty, courage, humour, gossip, scandals, bickering, bigotry, and loneliness, are not the idyllic towns of romance, nor are they gritty Peyton Places—MacLennan's belief in the essential dignity of man precluded such a presentation. They are simply little places that he tries to read in their own terms: Saint-Marc, a French-Canadian village struggling to maintain its old ways against the threat of English-Canadian and modern suburban society; Grenville, a southern Ontario town stuffy with a century of puritanism; Broughton, a coal-blackened mining centre, grim with Scottish Calvinism and generations of back-breaking labour.

A member of the so-called school of urban realists, MacLennan has made Montreal his special preserve. On one hand, he seems to find it attractive as a romantic world—not as a big, bad place where poor Nelly goes astray—but one beckoning young men to try their fortunes where the stakes are high. "Love her," he observes; "and she will give you her heart, though not her purse" [*The Watch that Ends the Night*]. Moreover, since he was a small-town boy, cities, as "My Author Husband" suggests, do perhaps have a meaning for him that those who have known nothing else can only guess. On the other hand, their skyscrapers, out-topping the spires of the churches, and their suburban sprawl of houses, caught in a net of TV antennae, are for him symbols of the modern world's new faith and new culture. This was one of his reasons for choosing Montreal in his effort to ascertain the essence of the country. Equally important was the fact that there the two cultures most deeply involved in making its history and in forming its character come face to face.

Montreal is the setting of three MacLennan novels—*Two Solitudes, The Watch that Ends the Night,* and (with a bow to Ottawa) *Return of the Sphinx.* Perhaps several Montreals would be more accurate, since the city of the thirties and the city today are hardly similar. Nor to Paul Tallard was it quite the same as to George Stewart or to Alan Ainslie. When, in *The Precipice,* MacLennan leaves Montreal for New York, he loses the touch that enabled him to catch the very set and manner of the Canadian me-

tropolis, "l'immuable entité qui donne à notre ville son âme," as critic Naim Kattan expresses it.

---

> **Although MacLennan writes city novels, they occasionally and significantly centre on the agrarian myth, a belief that man for his betterment can and should ally himself with nature *vis-à-vis* society.**
>
> **—Alec Lucas**

---

Only in the first sections of *Two Solitudes* (aside from Martell's boyhood interlude in a New Brunswick lumber camp) does MacLennan select a rural setting for his fiction, and this early work, though no country romance, is certainly no novel of the soil. Yet his books are frequently fresh and bright with appreciations of the beauty of nature and with scenes that evoke some awareness of the spread and mettle of the land as the characters take their parts on an almost continental stage: an old French Canadian, Athanase, returning home in the Laurentian evening, when it is "sunset in Ontario, late afternoon in the Rockies, mid-afternoon in British Columbia," or an English-Canadian urbanite, George Stewart, caught at this moment on a winter night:

> All the way down the frozen St. Lawrence the moon gleamed on the steeples of the parishes, it threw the shadows of horses pulling farmers' sleighs home from bingo parties in the church basements, it brought down into the valleys the huge shadows of hills.

Such passages are relatively few, however, and, moreover, while they do imply space, they never quite give the novels a quality of spaciousness. Sometimes, too, the attempts to place the narrative in a national setting become obtrusive, as in the account of Athanase's death. While the broken man breathes his last, the novel offers the information that "the red-haired Presbyterian nurse from Prince Edward Island" was surprised to see the dying man's wife at prayer.

Although MacLennan writes city novels, they occasionally (and significantly) centre on the agrarian myth, a belief (and for years a staple of Canadian fiction) that man for his betterment can and should ally himself with nature *vis-à-vis* society. In his first (unpublished) novel, Nova Scotia took on an Eden-like role, and there are hints in the rest of his work that nature can become a haven of security notwithstanding Angus Murray's aggrieved comment that "It was too easy to be sentimental and tell one's self that the pioneers were superior." Memories of a summer garden permeate the harsh present of Neil Macrae's life; Lucy's door-yard flower beds signify a world of beauty and vitality impinging on her puritan asceticism; dreams of fishing at the old farm haunt the unhappy Dr. Ainslie; and Alan Ainslie's summer cottage becomes his only asylum in defeat. Although these are isolated illustrations of

Arcadianism, MacLennan does supply evidence that it had an almost religious hold on him. "It is no accident," his essay **"Help Thou Mine Unbelief"** reads, "that farmers, close to the mysteries of germination, growth and death in the plant and animal world, are as a group more religious today than industrial workers." And it is no accident, surely, that at the conclusion of *The Watch that Ends the Night,* George Stewart finds consolation "in the cathedral hush of a Quebec Indian summer," or that the even more distraught Alan Ainslie takes centre stage in this tableau:

> The vast land. Too vast even for fools to ruin it all. . . . [and] looking over the lake he at last accepted that he had merely happened into all this . . . . loveliness that nobody could understand or possess, and that some tried to control or destroy just because they were unable to possess or understand it. . . . He thanked God he had been of it, was of it.

For all this, the dominant nature in MacLennan's novels is of another kind—dark mines and shark-infested seas. MacLennan escapes the depressing naturalism and the tedious domestic realism of the novels of the twenties and thirties; his material posed similar problems. Since, however, he chose to handle historical facts and large social and political issues, he was perhaps even more challenged to retain an imaginative approach to his subject, because in by-passing the demesne of romance he ran the risk of wandering off into a wasteland of didacticism. In order to balance the big impersonal theses he wished to develop, he was forced to introduce many details to humanize and lend authenticity to the lives and the world he described. At times the practice produces such a red herring as concludes this vignette: Bruce "looked up from the right front wheel and smiled at her. He was wearing a tweed jacket over gray flannel trousers"; or the kind of staginess and irrelevancy (though it might perhaps pass for local colour) in which a French-Canadian seigneur stuffs his pipe, not with tobacco, but with "Hudson's Bay," and an habitant "shoots a stream of tobacco juice from the corner of his mouth [hitting] a stone with a loud smack." This technique irritates even more when the irrelevancies are inaccurate—when *Chloë* turns up as an old-fashioned waltz (perhaps intended, as an ironical aside on Lassiter's dancing or his inability to recognize a fox trot), or when white-throated sparrows sing in August deep in southern Ontario.

These are only motes in a beam of realism that does create an illusion of reality. But one hardly harsh enough, it would seem to the modern reader, to raise an eyebrow, let alone loud voices of protest. Yet Penny's child, born out of wedlock, was sufficient to bar the doors of many schools to *Barometer Rising,* and MacLennan's love scenes, which may now appear sentimental or sometimes gauche, were such that one critic of *Two Solitudes* advocated the author's giving notice in future when similar sinful situations were pending. The reader at least might then preserve the sanctity of the heroine's bedroom if neither she nor the novelist was willing to preserve her virtue. No such simple warning as "Sexual Interlude" could save MacLennan from another critic who, like a fiery St.

George rushing into battle in the *Presbyterian Recorder,* strove to slay this literary dragon, this defector from Calvinism and decency, whose works were destroying the morality of a nation. MacLennan stood his ground and, threatening a lawsuit, drove his adversary to seek refuge in a polished, though tepid, retraction.

### David Arnason    (essay date Fall 1972)

SOURCE: "Canadian Nationalism in Search of a Form: Hugh MacLennan's *Barometer Rising,*" in *Journal of Canadian Fiction,* Vol. 1, No. 4, Fall, 1972, pp. 68-71.

[*In the essay below, Arnason discusses MacLennan's formulation of a Canadian consciousness in* Barometer Rising *and* Two Solitudes.]

Hugh MacLennan published his first novel, **Barometer Rising,** in 1941. Since that time, he has become the "grand old man" of Canadian novelists, an assessment that has little to do with his age or the quality of his achievement, but is rather an acknowledgement that the development of a Canadian consciousness is paralleled in the development of his work.

Success did not come easily or quickly to MacLennan. He wrote two novels, **So All Their Praises** (1933) and **Man Should Rejoice** (1937) which were never published. Both were concerned with broad international issues. It was only when MacLennan narrowed his scope and turned to a Canadian subject that he did succeed. That success was marked by the Publication in 1941 of **Barometer Rising,** the first novel written in Canada, by a Canadian, in which a peculiarly Canadian consciousness manifests itself.

Since that time, MacLennan has continued to expand his vision of Canada and Canadian consciousness. At the same time, his importance has been recognized, and a growing body of critical study of his work is available. Unfortunately, certain critical clichés have prevented a balanced assessment. The first of these is that MacLennan has, in some incomprehensible way, suffered "a failure of imagination", and the second is that he is a sociologist in disguise. Neither of these views will stand close scrutiny.

A reassessment of **Barometer Rising** must begin with MacLennan's second novel, **Two Solitudes.** In it, he has created his vision of the artist as a young man, in the person of Paul Tallard. Though Paul Tallard comes from a very different background from Hugh MacLennan, he is the young artist who discovers the difficulty of dealing with broad world themes, and turns back to his Canadian roots. The insights, values and ideas that Paul gains in **Two Solitudes** mirror MacLennan's aesthetic and ethical views.

For instance, in **Two Solitudes,** Paul gains an insight into the problem of writing a Canadian novel:

> he realized that his reader's ignorance of the essential Canadian clashes and values presented him with a unique problem. The background would have to be created from scratch if his story was to become intelligible. He could afford to take nothing for granted. He would have to

build the stage and props for his play, and then write the play itself.

It is an insight which MacLennan himself shares with his character, and it accounts, in part, for some of the successes and some of the failures of MacLennan's work.

The basis of Paul's insight is an assumption that the reader will be ignorant of things Canadian. Who, then, is this hypothetical reader? Obviously, he is not a thinking modern Canadian, or else he should know something of the "essential Canadian clashes and values" and the kind of stage-business that Paul envisions would be superfluous. Is he then some outsider, some American or English, or non-Canadian-Canadian literary creature to whom the author offers his work with built in apologies? This appears to be the case and many of the excesses in MacLennan's work spring from an assessment of his audience that is parallel to the assessment that Paul makes. Why else would a man suffering from shell-shock, obsessed by thoughts of revenge and desperately hungry for love be permitted by his artistic creator to think: "The Citadel itself flew the Union Jack in all weathers and was rightly considered a symbol and bastion of the British empire" [*Barometer Rising*].

Why else would a wounded alcoholic doctor, seconds before he is to deliver a proposal of marriage be permitted to pause and contemplate irrelevantly that

> " . . . Halifax, more than most towns, seemed governed by a fate she neither made nor understood, for it was her birthright to serve the English in time of war and to sleep neglected when there was peace. It was a bondage Halifax had no thought of escaping because it was the only life she had ever known; but to Murray this seemed a pity, for the town figured more largely in the calamities of the British Empire than in its prosperities, never seemed able to become truly North American".

These examples are typical, and they are by no means isolated instances. Throughout both *Barometer Rising* and *Two Solitudes* action is continually interrupted by contemplations about Canadian society, Canada's place in the world and the forces that operate in Canada's Usually, these thoughts do not arise as any consequence of the action and seem to exist purely as apologia to the un-Canadian reader. Sometimes they seem to be meretricious interpolations on the part of the author, a difficulty in form that arises from MacLennan's inability to handle his narrative with skill.

In part, though, MacLennan's insight is a valid one. At the time of his writing *Barometer Rising,* there were not many people in Canada who thought of themselves as essentially Canadian, and so some of the stage business is not so superfluous as it might first appear. Now, thirty years later, when people can refer to themselves as Canadians without feeling that there is something embarassing or pretentious about the use of the word, MacLennan's self-consciousness seems particularly clumsy. In retrospect, any battle that has been won seems disproportionate to its causes. Today, we wonder whether Canada, as a nation,

can survive. Thirty years ago the problem was not whether Canada survived, but whether it existed at all.

Since MacLennan is very much concerned with ideas, it is necessary to examine some of the ideas that he considers important. That is to say, since MacLennan is building "the stage and the props for his play" it might be worthwhile to examine them before we look at the play itself.

First, MacLennan's conception of Canada's possibilities seems to be based on an idea of corporate spiritual energy invested in the state. The wars in *Barometer Rising* and *Two Solitudes* are testimony to the expended energy of the Europeans. The first world war, MacLennan feels, will leave only madness, contempt, despair and an "intolerable burden of guilt" in Europe, because the war is the "logical result" of the Europeans "living out the sociological results of their own lives". Canada's role in the future will be to "pull Britain clear of decay and give her a new birth" [*Barometer Rising*]. MacLennan is a bit less overtly didactic and somewhat more dramatically convincing in his treatment of European decadence in *Two Solitudes.* First, the reader is given a picture of a cultured, wealthy, Parisian woman, the carefully wrought product of an European civilization caught, fascinated, waiting for a brutal German to debase her sexually. It soon becomes apparent, as MacLennan moves toward the lecturers tone in which he is most comfortable that she is an analogue for one part of Europe and the brutal porcine German is an analogue for the other. As Paul retraces in his mind the progress of his novel *Young Man of 1933,* we find that an effete, wasted civilization that has abandoned itself to machines and cities and has forsaken God is powerless to resist the resurgence of totemism, magic and brutal atavism, in fact, the whole *danse macabre* that "had burst out of the unconscious" and found its focus in Hitler.

Speaking for MacLennan, Paul says "the same brand of patriotism is never likely to exist all over Canada. Each race so violently disapproves of the tribal gods of the other I can't see how any single Canadian politician can ever imitate Hitler—at least, not over the whole country." MacLennan clearly feels that the future is Canada's. In *Barometer Rising* he confidently and optimistically foresaw Canada as "the central arch which united the new order." A trifle more subdued in *Two Solitudes,* he sees Canada acting "out of the instinct to do what was necessary" taking the first steps to self-knowledge, aware that she is "not unique but like all the others, alone with history, with science, with the future." This view of Canada is not, however, as chastened as it may first appear. The war is leading the rest of the world to self-destruction while it leads Canada to self-knowledge.

Against this backdrop of historical inevitability, MacLennan sets his props: his own ideas and attitudes, and his impressions of what are typically Canadian ideas and attitudes. MacLennan clearly distrusts certain aspects of progress. In *Barometer Rising* his characters deplore the mass production of ships, and regret deeply the passing of honest craftsmanship. In *Two Solitudes* Paul sees the machine behind Hitler, "the voice of God the Father no longer audible through the stroke of the connecting rod." Angus Murray in *Barometer Rising* has a theory that

" . . . this war is the product of the cities." Paul Tallard in *Two Solitudes* sees "the new city-hatred (contempt for all things but cleverness)" as the foundation for anti-semitism, class warfare and economic jealousy. The conscienceless American engineer of *Barometer Rising* is the typical product of the city.

On the other hand, MacLennan clearly feels a deep emotional attachment to certain aspects of the old order. The simple, God-fearing farmer-fisherman of Cape Breton epitomize for him the enduring values. Tied both to the sea and the land, governed by the natural rhythms of the earth, they are honest and noble. Alec McKenzie of *Barometer Rising* and Captain John Yardley of *Two Solitudes* function as archetypal figures, symbols of human potentiality against whom the other characters may be measured.

This is not to say that MacLennan is opposed to change. Indeed, there are many things about the old order that he resents—the desperate and cold materialism of men like McQueen, the aristocratic conventions of people like Col. Wain and The Methuens which lead them to debase the country in which they live and which gives them their living, and the narrow religious bigotry of Alfred Wain and Father Beaubien. Change offers not only the hatred of the cities and the brutality of the machine, but also the possibility for growth and renewal, for the fulfilling of destiny and the achievement of self-knowledge. The drastic and accelerated change occasioned by the war are the flames from which Canada will arise, Phoenix-like, to take its rightful place in the world.

Canada, as MacLennan sees it, and presumably as Canadians themselves think of it, is the product of two cultures. On the one hand, it is tied to England and "a world without England would be intolerable" [*Barometer Rising*]. On the other hand it is tied to the United States by "a frontier that was more a link than a division." Uniquely, it partakes of the two cultures. MacLennan clearly sees a dialectic at work, and Neil McRae expresses it: " . . . if there were enough Canadians like himself, half-American and half-English, then the day was inevitable when the halves would join and his country would become the central arch which united the new order." The same kind of dialectic functions in *Two Solitudes* in which Paul Tallard becomes the synthesis of the French-Canadian and English-Canadian cultures. Here, though, the symbolic form of the dialectic functions against MacLennan's thesis that the cultures are in fact solitudes and must co-exist rather than merge. The title of the novel is from a poem by Rilke, and is part of a definition of love, another example of MacLennan's incurable optimism.

There is one more significant idea that must be mentioned, and that is the sense of geography that MacLennan feels is part of the Canadian vision and which becomes, in his novels, an important device. In *Two Solitudes,* Heather paints a picture and asks Paul to comment on it. When he sees it, he (or else the author—there is some confusion) notices " . . . she had missed the vastness of such a scene, the sense of the cold wind stretching so many hundreds of miles to the north of it, through ice and tundra and desolation." It is an error that MacLennan has no intention

of making. The sun that sets on Halifax makes long shadows in Montreal, glints on the prairies and beams down from high noon on Vancouver. MacLennan seems determined to create a vision of Canada as at least a geographical reality if not a social one, and he loses no opportunity to tie a description of a particular place into a vision of the whole continent.

A set of ideas provides the stage and the props for MacLennan's play: the background is the historically inevitable achievement of destiny and self-knowledge by a young and vigorous country pulled from the outside by two cultures and from the inside by two cultures, caught between the old and the new. The props are certain attitudes and representative characters. Against this is to be set a play which will be an artistic whole, and which will utilize this stage and these properties. Obviously enough, since a nation is a composite of its individuals, the play will concern itself with the achievement of individual destiny and self-knowledge.

It is fashionable to claim that the failures in MacLennan's novels are the result of a failure of imagination. This is not an adequate assessment. The failures that occur are usually the result of a failure to handle with skill the technical form of the novel and sometimes the result of the misapplication of an unbalanced talent.

First, every novel must have a voice, a presumed narrator who tells the story. In the case of *Barometer Rising* the voice is that of an omniscient author who sees everything, who can move about at will and permit the reader to share the thoughts, feelings, and vision of various characters. At times he exists independently of any character and observes and comments for himself. Like the characters themselves, he is limited to a present and retrospective vision, and none of the unfortunate dramatic ironies of the "dear and gentle reader" school of omniscient author intrude themselves. When the voice speaks for itself, and when it operates at some distance from the characters, it is observant, acute, and incisive. When it moves closer, though, it runs into problems. Too often we begin with the description of a character's thoughts, and find that the anonymous voice has taken matters out of their hands and is commenting itself. For example, [in] *Barometer Rising* we discover Wain contemplating Alec MacKenzie. "Wain puffed a lungful of smoke against the windowpane", at this point the anonymous voice is watching from outside. "MacKenzie was the only man in the world capable of upsetting his apple cart, of cancelling out all the patient work he had done in Halifax since his return from France"—now we have moved into Wain's mind and are observing his thought. "But the big man had no notion of this"—so far, so good. "When he had accepted the job and brought his wife and family to Halifax he had never guessed that it had been Wain's motive to make him a dependent". By this point there is some considerable doubt as to whether Wain is thinking or the narrator has taken over.

The result of this unsureness in the handling of point-of-view is that the characters are blurred. At times the thoughts of the characters are authentic and individual; at other times they are not. Penny, for instance, is distinctly feminine much of the time, but when she contemplates the Nova Scotian scene, and the anonymous voice intrudes, she could be Neil, Murry or anybody else:

> Her eye wandered back to the freighter sliding upstream a commonplace ship, certainly foreign and probably of the Mediterranean origin, manned by heaven knew what conglomeration of Levantines, with maybe a Scotsman in the engine room and a renegade Nova Scotian somewhere in the forecastle. The war had brought so many of these mongrel vessels to Halifax, they had become a part of the landscape.

Besides blurring the identity of the characters, the authorial voice also blurs the action and interferes with the dramatic power of the narrative. MacLennan's chief skill lies in his ability to write sustained passages of descriptive narrative. This is obvious in his powerful description of the events leading to the explosion and the chaotic action thereafter. He chooses to dissipate this power by his refusal, in the first half of the book, to sustain his focus on any action. As the action approaches a climax, the focus shifts and the dramatic tension created is lost. To be sure, this shifting focus is obviously intentional. The unfulfilled nature of the characters calls for unfulfilled action, and provides a striking contrast to the sharp decisive nature of the action in the latter part of the book, as the cathartic effect of the explosion impels the characters to self knowledge and the fulfillment of their destinies. In theory, it is a fine idea, and as an outline for a novel it has a compelling symmetry. Unfortunately, in practice it is unsatisfying, and even more unfortunately MacLennan is incapable of supplying any richness of imagery and metaphor to make up the deficiency.

It is frequently pointed out that the explosion in ***Barometer Rising*** operates as a kind of *deus ex machina* which dispenses an arbitrary, though poetic justice. It interferes with the action, and prevents the confrontations that the early development of the book would seem to demand. For instance, Neil does not encounter Geoffrey Wain until he is safely dead, and the triangular relationship between Neil, Penny, and Angus creates none of the difficulties inherent in the situation. This is quite simply explicable, though, in terms of MacLennan's aesthetics. Just as Canada itself must work out its destiny in terms of individual self knowledge, so must each of the characters in the novel. Confrontation leads to victory or defeat, but not to the kind of self knowledge that MacLennan wants to delineate. The explosion prevents Neil from confronting Colonel Wain and Angus from confronting Neil. Instead, it makes each confront himself and learn to understand himself. At the end of the novel each of the characters is oddly isolated and self contained. There has been no development of relationships; but then, that is not what the novel is about. Though Penny and Neil are reunited physically as they ride together on the train, each is completely separate and distinct; that is to say, no communication goes on between them. Neil does not even know that he is a father when the novel ends.

This argument does not absolve the novel of weakness in its close. The process of self-discovery is not particularly convincing, and MacLennan's refusal to permit relationships to grow and change limits the novel and is frustrating to the reader. The argument does absolve MacLennan of much of the charge that his imagination is limited. He does not fail to develop interpersonal relationships because he cannot envision them, but because he chooses to concentrate on the individual's relationship with himself.

Another defect in the novel occurs as a result of MacLennan's use of characters in his novel both as props in his stage setting and participants in the action. The characters are too obviously symbolic. Col. Wain and Alec MacKenzie represent two facets of the old order, Angus Murray represents the transition and Neil and Penny represent the new order. MacLennan makes the mistake of overestimating the obtuseness of his readers, and to make sure that nobody has missed the point allows Angus Murray to sum up the symbolic action in a neat little precis:

> There was Geoffrey Wain, the decadent of military colonists who had remained essentially a colonist himself, never really believing that anything above the second rate could exist in Canada, a man who had thought it necessary to lick the boots of the English but had merely taken it for granted that they mattered and Canadians didn't. There was Alec MacKenzie, the primitive man who had lived just long enough to bridge the gap out of the pioneering era and save his children from becoming anachronisms. There were Penny and Neil MacRae, two people who could seem at home almost anywhere, who had inherited as a matter of course and in their own country the urbane and technical heritage of both Europe and eastern United States. And there was himself, caught somewhere between the two extremes, intellectually gripped by the new and emotionally held by the old, too restless to remain at peace on the land and too contemptuous of bourgeois values to feel at ease in any city.
>
> We're the ones who make Canada what she is today, Murray thought, neither one thing nor the other, neither a colony nor an independent nation, neither English nor American. And yet, clearly, the future is obvious, for England and America can't continue to live without each other much longer. Canada must therefore remain as she is, noncommittal, until the day she becomes the keystone to hold the world together.

All in all though, struggling under the symbolic load they must carry and with their thoughts continually being wrenched away from them by the author, the characters do remarkably well for themselves. Angus Murray is not a very convincing alcoholic, and is perhaps a bit too clear sighted, but he does seem motivated by genuine concerns, and his responses are convincing. Penny Wain does not convince us of her brilliance, but does convince us of her femininity. Colonel Wain, though a megalomaniac is not much more a parody than many real-life colonels. Alec MacKenzie, though a bit too good to be true, is acceptable. The Neil of the first part of the novel and the Neil of the second part are each in his own way convincing. Neil number one is indecisive and paranoid, and his actions confirm this. Neil number two is smugly selfish and competent, as is shown by his handling of things after the explosion. The difficulty is that it takes an unusually powerful ability to suspend disbelief to be convinced that the two are one, and that is a chief flaw in the book. We have seen no flashes of the old Neil or the Neil to come in the shuffling character of the first part of the book, and so we are not convinced at his change. The peripheral characters—Aunt Maria, Roddy and the rest who have escaped the symbolic load and who don't do much thinking are all quite delightful.

Style is as much an aspect of form as it is of thought and it is in respect of style that the novel has its chief virtues and its chief faults. MacLennan's greatest strength is in pure narrative description. His point by point description of the Halifax explosion is as good as anything of its kind in Canadian literature, or any other literature, for that matter. His description of the details of the landscape are deft and sure and he can characterize people with swift, sure and precise detail. Where he is weakest is in his handling of metaphor, and his novel loses strength from his inability to make vivid and animate comparisons. His ear for dialogue is not particularly good. The speech of his characters is a bit bookish at best, and collapses at moments of deep emotional stress, as may be seen by the stilted conversation between Neil and Penny at their first confrontation. John Yardley's accent in **Two Solitudes** is chiefly the result of his inability to pronounce the "a" in "that", though he can pronounce the same sound well enough in other words. Finally, a tendency to prefer latinate forms, possibly as a result of his training in the classics, leads MacLennan at times to such infelicities of expression as "she welcomed the lassitude as an anodyne to thought" [**Barometer Rising**].

In the end, a novel is not judged by weighing of its good points and weaknesses and the drawing up of a balance sheet. It must stand on its own, apart from the author's intent and its significance as a philosophic document. On these terms, **Barometer Rising** is a limited success. MacLennan has taken the subject of national consciousness in Canada and given it a form that is convincing. Unfortunately, the novel is weighed down by a lot of stage business that reduces its immediacy and vitality. The clutter is in part a weakness in MacLennan's writing, but another part of it is sheer historical necessity. An evolving Canadian consciousness found its first firm voice in MacLennan, and if that voice is a bit self-conscious, surely that is understandable.

In a conversation between Margaret Laurence and Robert Kroetsch in a book called *Creation,* an interesting passage occurs:

> L: You know, I read Kipling, and what the hell did Kipling have to do with where I was living? And that isn't to say that we shouldn't read widely, but it is a good thing to be able to read, as a child, something that belongs to you, belongs to your people. And you and I might have sort of subconsciously had a compulsion to set down our own background.
>
> K: I've suspected that often. We want to hear our story.

Laurence and Kroetsch speak of "our people" and "our story", and unselfconsciously regard themselves as Canadians. I don't think it is too much of an overstatement to say that their easy acceptance of the Canadian fact owes something to the ground broken by Hugh MacLennan.

**Patricia A. Morley    (essay date 1972)**

SOURCE: "MacLennan's Early Novels: Life Against Death," in *The Immoral Moralists: Hugh MacLennan and Leonard Cohen,* Clarke, Irwin & Company, 1972, pp. 37-52.

[*In the following excerpt, Morley discusses MacLennan's treatment of puritanism and sexuality in* Barometer Rising, Two Solitudes, *and* The Precipice.]

In his study of the psychoanalytical meaning of history [*Life Against Death,* 1970], Norman O. Brown describes Freud's theory of the dualism which underlies human conflicts, a dualism which Freud sees in terms of two basic instincts driving men towards life or death. This dualism is grounded in the very nature of life. Freud describes the instincts in terms of a "pleasure principle" and a "reality principle." The latter is the cause of repression, the pillar on which Freud's theory of psychoanalysis rests. Brown finds the source of Freud's pessimism in this hypothesis of an irreconcilable conflict between human instincts: between Eros or sexual love, seeking to preserve and enrich life, and the death instinct, seeking to return life to the peace of death. Brown is attempting to account for the forward movement in Freud's thought, since many of Freud's later ideas are not in agreement with his earlier ones, and go beyond Freud to an optimistic theory of human life and history. Brown posits a primal unity, differentiation through antagonism, and final harmony or "redemption" in the reunification of the instinctual opposites. He argues that death, properly understood, is not the enemy of life.

In seeing these instincts as a dialectical unity rather than an antagonistic dualism, Brown's thesis is similar to the metaphysic which underlies the fiction of D.H. Lawrence. Lawrence's essay, "The Crown" (1915), uses an imaginative rather than a didactic technique to show the dynamic interrelationship of these opposites as necessary to one another. "The Lion and the Unicorn are fighting for the Crown." The two fight everlastingly, in a "divine discontent," for the Crown of Life: "And there is no rest, no cessation of the conflict. For we are two opposites which exist by virtue of our inter-opposition." And what does Lawrence intend by his two mythical beasts from the old nursery rhyme? Darkness and light, flesh and spirit, power and love, activity and passivity—as in the yin and yang of Taoist thought, the list is endless.

I suggest that Lawrence's attitude is very close to Brown's, where-as MacLennan's is similar to Freud's as here defined by Brown: namely, it posits a duality to be fought out rather than a dialectic between two very different but equally necessary forces. MacLennan, like Lawrence, is a moralist. Both men regard the body and sex, given certain conditions, as *good.* But MacLennan's metaphysic differs from that of Lawrence and Brown with regard to the desirability of the instincts which are not loving and peaceful, or life-seeking, in MacLennan's terms. His Puritan heritage would incline him to see the forces of life and death as forces for good and evil, irreconcilable opposites. MacLennan has interpreted his Calvinist heritage as basically life-denying, since in his experience the conviction of sin was necessarily accompanied by fear and guilt. Thus it became, for MacLennan, a death force. The patterns of imagery in his fiction and the alignment of his characters (as sympathetic and admirable, or the opposite) all centre in this contrast of life and death. And puritanism, as MacLennan defines it, is placed on the side of death.

MacLennan's early novels, *Barometer Rising, Two Solitudes* and *The Precipice,* will appear at first sight to constitute a consistent attack upon puritanism. In *Barometer Rising,* these attacks are casual rather than thematic. The consistency here is in MacLennan's underlying attitude, not in the frequency of his attacks. The social environment which forms the background for the major portions of these novels—the city of Halifax, the Protestant community of Montreal, the Roman Catholic parish of Saint-Marc-des-Érables, and the Ontario town of Grenville—is depicted in each case as uncompromisingly puritan. Various anecdotes and references widen the picture to include all of Canada and much of the United States. "God help us," exclaims Dennis Morey in *Two Solitudes,* "why do people hate beauty in this country the way they do?" He claims that puritan attitudes have ruined the city of Winnipeg. Similarly, Bruce Fraser says in *The Precipice* that until the Grenvilles of Canada are "debunked" from top to bottom, there will be no fun and no future for anyone in Canada.

Halifax provides the setting for *Barometer Rising,* and for one chapter in *The Precipice,* where the city is described as being dominated by Calvinists who think it more moral for a man to buy a bottle of whisky and drink it in secret in the park than to drink it comfortably in public. In *Barometer Rising,* the puritan environment of Halifax has necessitated Penny's three years of "secrecy and abnegation," years of bitterness during which she has been unable to enjoy beauty.

The Protestant community of Montreal is represented by the Methuen family and by a group of Presbyterian businessmen, especially Huntly McQueen and Sir Rupert Irons. . . . Our present concern is his [McQueen's] attitude towards women, and towards pleasure in general. Although he admires Janet Methuen (the exact opposite of the sensuous Kathleen), he considers the prospect of marriage "embarrassing." The Methuen family distrusts physical beauty in women, who are "expected to be irreproachable wives and solid mothers of future Methuens, not females who might stimulate those pleasures the men of the family believed had caused the ruination of the Babylonians, Greeks, Romans, French . . . and various other minor races of the world." Dennis Morey, the officer who meets Kathleen Tallard in a Montreal hotel, describes his wife in terms similar to that of the Methuen ideal: irreproachable as a wife and mother, undeniably good, but totally lacking in imagination and humour.

One might suspect at this juncture that MacLennan does not admire goodness, but this soon proves to be an error. The Methuens admire art, but only when both art and artist are socially acceptable. Janet suspects the soldiers whom she serves in a war canteen of being immoral merely because of their rough language, and she and her Methuen in-laws appear to be totally incapable of appreciating the simple goodness of a man like Captain Yardley, her father, or the fine qualities of a young man like Paul Tallard. Both Paul and Heather, in their twenties, run away from Montreal to escape the strait-jacket of their background.

In the parish of Saint-Marc, the atmosphere is almost as puritan as it is in Grenville. Father Beaubien is described as having an eye for the length of the girls' dresses, and as seeing the devil every time a boy puts his arm around a girl when the moon is full. Father Beaubien maintains an atmosphere in the parish which Kathleen, Tallard's Irish wife, finds repressive. Preparing for dinner in Montreal with Dennis Morey, she dresses and makes up her face as she has not dared to do in Saint-Marc.

Marius Tallard, Athanase's son, both fears and despises sex. He is fascinated by the pictures of nude women in his father's art books: "They signified only the female being he did not know, the being which was beautiful and dangerous and at the core of sin." The sensual beauty which Kathleen embodies both repels and attracts him. He feels that she has made the atmosphere of the house "mysteriously evil, warm with sin." It is not just her beauty but its sensual quality which Marius fears. His puritan attitude has been inherited from his mother, whose memory he worships. Marie-Adèle, Athanase's first wife, had estranged herself from Athanase soon after their marriage and had sought to make a devotional piety her whole life. After her death, Athanase thinks that his first wife never lived for life, "but in order to die, in order to enter the Kingdom of Heaven."

In *The Precipice,* the town of Grenville makes itself felt as a personal character. Although there are five parts in the novel, the first, dealing with Grenville, occupies one half of the whole. It concentrates on the town's puritan attitudes, for the problems of the chief characters can only be understood against this background. Matt McCunn describes puritan towns such as Grenville as prematurely old: old, "like respectable women" before they ever start living. Lucy Cameron's Uncle Matt is a non-puritan individualist, of whom the townsfolk strongly disapprove. Talking with Matt in the Grenville drugstore, Lucy encounters Ike Blackman, the town's most disreputable character. Using Ike, Matt and the Greek waitress, MacLennan humorously sketches the town's disapproval of drink, sex and Ike's avoidance of "honest work." MacLennan depicts puritanism as working through social approval or disapproval to limit and restrict freedom. Lucy realizes that, in a town like Grenville, personal freedom will necessarily be accompanied by a bad reputation.

The negative and repressive influence of puritanism is represented in Part One by deathly images of blankness and freezing, of walls and rigid molds. Lucy feels the town to be closing in around her, "freezing her into the mold of a perpetual childhood." She feels that if she remains there, it will be like facing a blank wall for the rest of her life, or like passing thousands of days and nights with nothing to show for them "but the slow stain of unused time." She is sure that the influence of puritanism had acted to contain her father's violent energy, and she imagines the violence of the family sunk like stones beneath the surface of a pond, rigid (corpse-like) beneath a glaze of respectability.

As Lucy wrestles with the problem of whether or not to marry Stephen Lassiter, a violent storm rages outside. Lucy and Jane sit inside with the shutters firmly closed. Jane feels safe and secure, but the storm suggests the life which Jane is attempting to shut out. Before the end of Part One, Lucy has decided to leave Grenville and marry Stephen. She has chosen to live fully and to deny her puritan background which forbids divorce. In New York, alone with Stephen, she remembers a sleigh ride in her childhood when her ears had been badly frozen. She pictures her sheltered life as a child wrapped up against the winter: "Now her whole soul seemed to be unfreezing." Puritanism had originally attempted to shield people from evil, as a child must be protected from the cold. In our own century, MacLennan feels, it has succeeded only in blighting or killing what it had attempted to preserve.

Each of MacLennan's early novels uses houses to symbolize puritan and non-puritan characteristics in their owners. The Wain family house in *Barometer Rising,* described as being typical of the history and character of the town, is forbidding, rather than gracious or beautiful. The shutters have been placed on the inside where they can be useful. Inside, the mood is the same. The furnishings reflect a sombre dignity, not beauty or joy. As an adult, Penny loves only the garden and thinks of the rest of the house as an "incubus." This word, and similar suggestions of a deadening burden or oppressive nightmare, are frequently used by MacLennan in connection with puritanism. The Wain house represents the puritan suspicion of beauty. It is also identified with the stifling, restricting influence which MacLennan associates with puritanism, and suggests by images of blankness and freezing in *The Precipice.* In *Barometer Rising* the heavy oak front door of the Wain mansion, weighted with a brass knocker, is seen by Penny as a symbol: "Her family had shut her in from the world when she was young; it had shut her out from itself when she had ceased being a child." After the death of her father in the explosion, Penny says she can never live in the house again. As she goes with Neil to find Jean, she realizes with a sense of shock that she has left home for the last time. There is a suggestion here of the rebirth-through-death pattern which runs through all MacLennan's novels.

The Cameron house in Grenville has passed through two stages. Under Lucy's father there had been neither gardens nor colour, only blistered tan paint and unsoftened lines. Since it is exactly the kind of house that old John Knox Cameron would choose to live in, its harshness is identified with his character. An earlier Scot had added the brown paint and the harshness. MacLennan describes the Scotch and Scotch-Irish as roughening everything they touched: "It would be another hundred years before any part of English-speaking Canada could hope to be rid

of what they had done to it." (Little did MacLennan suspect, in 1948, what Canada would be like a mere twenty years.)

Under Lucy's care, the imposed ugliness has been stripped off, and the house transformed. Now beautiful and gracious, it is described as being the outward expression of her personality. MacLennan thus uses the house to show both the puritan character of old John Knox and the non-puritan character of Lucy, and to suggest that we must consciously struggle to cleanse ourselves of the puritan aversion to beauty and joy. In *Two Solitudes,* Yardley's farm in the parish of Saint-Marc is a symbol of non-puritan joyous acceptance of life. Yardley is both proud and pleased to see his first crops growing and his animals thriving. The Methuen and McQueen mansions on the Montreal mountain are status symbols of their owners' concern with financial and social success. These houses seem to entomb their occupants and cut them off from life, like the Wain front door.

We have seen how MacLennan emphasizes, in his first three novels, that the Canadian social environment is strongly puritan. His characters are also presented largely in terms of this concept, which is an obsessive concern in MacLennan's first four novels. Each novel has a contrasting set of characters, puritan and non-puritan by his definition, who are for or against life. The plot structures in *Two Solitudes* and *The Precipice* depend upon a clash of values between these opposing groups. In *Barometer Rising,* puritanism is less important to the structure, which is tightly built around the historic explosion of 1917 in Halifax harbour. Puritan characters have a relatively minor part here, as compared to their major role in the next three novels. Penny's relations, Uncle Alfred and Aunt Maria, are lightly and humorously sketched. They are shown as narrow-minded and self-righteous. Just enough details are given to explain why it is that Penny cannot bear to be alone with them when she is feeling depressed. Alfred's chief interest is the Presbyterian church in which he is an elder, and his chief talent, the ability to estimate the collection value of any congregation to within a half-dollar. MacLennan gives us a more modern version of a puritan in Geoffrey Wain. Wain is a materialist who despises his nephew Neil for his lack of interest in money, and a hypocrite who pays lip service to one sexual code while practising another. Wain's contempt for his mistress Evelyn is really based upon a contempt for sex. These life-denying puritan characters are set in opposition to the hero and heroine of *Barometer Rising,* who affirm life in a spirit of generosity and optimism.

In *Two Solitudes* the puritan values of Janet Methuen, of the Methuen "tribe" in general, and of the Calvinist businessmen such as McQueen and Irons, are opposed to those of the non-puritan characters such as Kathleen Tallard, Captain Yardley, Heather Methuen and Paul Tallard. Athanase Tallard, a character in conflict, has both puritan and non-puritan characteristics.

The prevailing attitudes of the puritan town of Grenville, represented primarily by Jane Cameron, her father old John Knox Cameron, and his aunts, are contrasted with the non-puritan behaviour of Lucy Cameron and her uncle, Matt McCunn. Lucy's family background is given in some detail. Her father had been brought up by two maiden aunts who had made his life a "Calvinistic horror," forbidding him toys as a child and making him afraid of his sex when he grew older. The efforts of these two Scots had apparently been only too successful, for as an adult "John Knox had been hard even for an Ontario small town to take, where the Scotch-Irish are chocolate-brown with Calvinism."

---

**MacLennan emphasizes, in his first three novels, that the Canadian social environment is strongly puritan. His characters are also presented largely in terms of this concept, which is an obsessive concern in MacLennan's first four novels. Each novel has a contrasting set of characters, puritan and non-puritan by his definition, who are for or against life.**

**—*Patricia A. Morley***

---

Stephen Lassiter, like Athanase Tallard, is ambivalent. At first sight he appears to be free of puritan inhibitions, and he regards the Grenville attitudes towards drink and sex with amused condescension. It later appears to Lucy that Stephen, even when drunk and in bed with another woman, is more of a puritan than she herself has ever been. Stephen, like her sister Jane, cannot accept weakness in himself. Both are terrified of appearing to be weak or in error; both refuse to accept the Christian promise of forgiveness of sin; both are shown as being obsessed with guilt. Even when they no longer believe in God, as Marcia points out, the old guilt-habit stays. MacLennan has described his intention in **The Precipice** as an attempt to find "a common denominator between U.S. and Canadian tradition which I believe exists in the Puritan background of both countries" [quoted in Hugo McPherson, "The Novels of Hugh MacLennan," *Queen's Quarterly* (1953-54)]. The prefatory note in this novel refers to the journey "which the puritans began more than three hundred years ago when they lost hope in themselves and decided to bet their lives on the things they could do rather than the men they were." This restless, discontented urge to accomplish ever greater feats is seen by MacLennan as a drive towards nothingness—hence the title image.

Jane is described as being Grenville's collective conscience. Most of the town's inhabitants make sensible compromises with their puritan code; Jane does not:

> She was the only one of them who followed, in thought and life, all the principles of the religion and morality which the entire Protestant part of the country professed to honor. The great crimes had no reality for her whatever. She had never in her life seen an act of deliberate wickedness. It was quite natural for her to believe that sex

was the dirtiest thing in the world, and near to the root of all evil.

Jane loves music and plays well herself. Lucy marvels that anyone could enjoy music as Jane obviously does and yet still consider it unimportant. Jane's attitude reflects the puritan suspicion of beauty and the puritan emphasis on utility. As Lucy listens to Jane's playing she becomes aware of a deep and repressed passion of which Jane herself is unaware. Jane's unconscious sexual frustration is revealed in her playing of the Beethoven "Appassionata": "One would expect her to be at her best in a Bach fugue, but it was only in these slow movements of Beethoven, where religion mingled with a deeply sublimated sexuality, that Jane really found herself in music."

The hypocrisy of the contemporary puritan attitude towards sex is revealed in the talk between Jane and Lucy after they have learned from a neighbour that Stephen is already married. Jane is concerned with keeping up the appearance of respectability, rather than with truth. Lucy insists that she has done nothing of which she should be ashamed, but Jane paints such a vivid picture of whispering gossipmongers that Lucy is reduced to shame. Lucy is represented in Part One as being slightly puritanical, in MacLennan's sense, in so far as she has not been able to completely purge herself of the fear of sex implanted in her in childhood. She is pictured as making a determined effort to use her mind to free herself from this fear, "fear of nothing but what people like Father put into our minds when we were helpless children." [In an endnote, Morley adds: "In a letter to John Gray, 1951, MacLennan wrote: 'My mortal quarrel with Calvinism was not that it denied realities but that it inculcated into children the idea that God was each man's personal enemy and that a man committed a sin merely by existing.' MacLennan Papers, quoted in Alec Lucas, *Hugh MacLennan*, 1970."] Despite her efforts to overcome her puritanism, Lucy is shocked to discover that Stephen is married and that his attitude towards divorce is extremely casual. Her whole background denies the possibility of her marriage to such a man, and she struggles to discard "the superstitious sense of taboo under which she had been reared." Matt McCunn, her uncle, encourages her to marry Stephen. Like Captain Yardley in **Two Solitudes,** Matt is a vigorous, tolerant and happy man who accepts life. Lucy remembers that in her childhood her whole world had seemed larger whenever Matt had come to their house.

Janet Methuen, in **Two Solitudes,** is very similar to Jane Cameron. Janet and Jane represent the puritan attitudes which MacLennan sees in Canada, "a land still so near the frontier that in most of it everything was black or white, uncomplicated, where wickedness was barely intelligible unless it were sexual." When Janet receives word of the death of her husband overseas, her puritan belief that emotions must be restrained and hidden makes her struggle to face the villagers as if nothing had happened. She returns to Yardley's farmhouse and retires to her bedroom. Unfortunately for Janet, the walls are thin and she can overhear the story which her father is telling the Tallards. Yardley's humorous anecdote of the horses and their two "hard-shell" Baptist owners, and Janet's neurotic hysterical reaction to this anecdote, set the puritan and nonpuritan attitudes in stark relief. Yardley relates that Calvin Slipp, owner of the stallion "Okay," had "hated Luther's guts" ever since Luther, owner of the mare, had beaten him to the position of church deacon. Under cover of the noise of a Baptist prayer meeting, the two horses are brought together. Janet has been listening upstairs with mounting feelings of horror and embarrassment, and she finally climaxes Yardley's story with hysterical screams.

Yardley, whom Paul later describes as "just a natural man," accepts the idea of sex as normal and natural for both people and animals. Janet does not. When he suggests to her that she should remarry, she calls his suggestion horrible, and considers his idea that "people are not so different even from animals" to be so peculiar as to verge on insanity. When her father is near death, Janet sits by his side from a sense of duty, afraid to show her feelings, for fear of seeming sentimental. Yardley thinks, sadly, that she has been worried about something ever since he could remember, and he is afraid that it is partly his fault. Perhaps if he had had a better education, she would have respected him more, and he would have been able to teach her to find enjoyment in life. "But her mother had made the child ashamed of him, and then her own conscience had made her ashamed of being ashamed, and after that there was no end to the impasse between them."

In opposition to the puritan attitudes represented most strikingly by Janet Methuen and Jane Cameron, MacLennan affirms the value of beauty and pleasure. But let no one think that his aversion to puritanism has turned him into an advocate of free love. In no other connection does MacLennan's serious moral attitude towards life show more clearly than in his idea of mature sexual love. In *The Precipice,* he defines mature love as being "a matter of endurance, a matter of wisdom and care." From his novels it is clear that he believes sexual relations should involve the whole person and should entail permanent ties and responsibility. MacLennan's first three novels suggest that feminine beauty reflects moral character, that beauty and goodness are intimately connected in a woman. His heroines (Penny Wain, Heather Methuen, Lucy Cameron) are all women whose beauty of character has had a transforming effect upon their external appearance. Similarly, in each of these novels MacLennan shows women whose beauty is simply physical. The surface beauty of these women—Wain's mistress Evelyn, Daphne Methuen, Nina Cameron, Stephen's first wife Joyce, and his mistress Gail Beaumont—does not reflect any corresponding beauty of spirit. MacLennan believes that beauty without goodness is unsatisfying.

Penny Wain, who fancies herself to be plain, is described as being transformed by contact with another person: "In conversation her face opened and disclosed a sympathetic and comprehensive mind." The heroine of *Two Solitudes* discovers her own beauty in Paul Tallard's eyes after they have fallen in love. Earlier, Paul has reacted with scornful amusement to Heather's admiring description of her honey-blond sister Daphne: "It must be a full-time job, being Daffy." Daphne has been shown to resemble her mother Janet, being cold, hard and priggish, even as a child. After Daphne's marriage to the titled Englishman,

Noel Fletcher, Heather realizes that she has been foolish to admire and envy Daphne for her beauty. She now sees her sister's beauty as a weapon, a destiny, her only wealth. Suddenly, Heather feels freed from her lifelong dependence upon her sister. She judges Noel and Daphne, and condemns their whole attitude towards life: "They had nothing whatever she wanted, for all they possessed was a cold surface beauty and his ability, motivated by a mechanical sensuality, to counterfeit the fire she knew was still alive in the world, somewhere, if she could find it."

The love which Heather and Paul have for one another embodies MacLennan's idea of mature love, where sex is part, but only part, of a total relationship. Paul and Heather have no sooner met, as adults, and fallen in love, than MacLennan separates them physically for five years. During this separation their mental and spiritual intimacy continues to grow. She is not afraid to open to him in letters, so that he feels towards the end of this period that he knows her better than when he left Canada. Just before his return, an incident in Athens reveals MacLennan's moral attitude towards sex. A German strength-through-joy ship is in port. Paul watches a German Nazi with an attractive French woman at a nearby café table. Paul despises the German for his crudity and considers casual sexual relationships only another form of loneliness. After Paul and Heather are married, he tells her that his love is "for always."

In *The Precipice,* Stephen tells Lucy she is "simple and decent and lovely." He finds her to be beautiful in a way that few women are any more, and he contrasts her beauty with the soulless sophisticated beauty of his first wife. He asks Lucy if she thinks, seeing Joyce's picture, that she could be generous or warm. Lucy's sister Nina is depicted, like Joyce, as vain and self-seeking. Lucy fears that Nina will only make Bruce more restless, instead of helping him. Stephen tells Lucy that Nina will never get what she wants because she will never give enough, and that "Nina is the last girl, as a type, that a wise man would choose to go to bed with." After the war we see Stephen's prophecy coming true. Nina's dissatisfaction and unhappiness are caused by her selfishness, which is actually spoiling her physical beauty.

There are five main scenes in *Barometer Rising* which are concerned with sexual relationships. In some of these the lovers have MacLennan's approval, while in others they do not. His underlying attitude as to the proper and improper use of sex is shown indirectly but clearly. In the first such scene, on Sunday evening in the Wain house, Angus Murray and Penny Wain are somewhat inhibited, and MacLennan might be accused of puritanism under his own definition. Penny, although twenty-nine and a mother, is shy, "daintily awkward" as a young colt. The inhibitions of this scene reflect the author's moral attitude. He cannot approve of sexual relations between these two, for Penny is to be reunited with Neil. (Yet in the Canadian social climate of the forties, the sheer fact that Penny has had a child out of wedlock is sufficient to make MacLennan very much the *immoral* moralist. Alec Lucas notes that Penny's child was responsible for keeping *Barometer Rising* out of many a school, and that the love scenes in

*Two Solitudes,* conservative as they now appear, were so daring at the time as to give rise to the request that the author give the reader notice in future when similar sinful situations were pending, so that they might be skipped over.)

In the second scene, Mamie, the madam of a brothel, has the author's approval because she represents *agape* or unselfish concern for the welfare of others. As she tries to help Murray out of his depressed mood, her face is kindly. She criticizes her girls for not caring, and she uses her earnings to support her children in the countryside. MacLennan uses Murray's drunkenness as a technical device for introducing prophecy: " 'Though I speak with the tongues of men and of angels and have not charity'—his voice broke—'Mamie, you're a good girl. . . . You just want us all to be one big happy family.' "

The next two love scenes consist of two pairs of incidents set in a curious counterpoint. The married love of Jim and Mary Fraser, who genuinely and deeply care for one another, is set against the relationship of Geoffrey Wain and his mistress Evelyn, who despise each other. Wain considers Evelyn his social inferior, and despises her vulgarity. Evelyn hates Wain and uses sex as a weapon for material advancement. MacLennan emphasizes their mutual scorn and disdain. The scene in Evelyn's apartment is followed immediately by a short scene in Prince's Lodge, where Jim and Mary Fraser have a teasing but loving conversation before their "rendezvous in bed."

Shortly after, MacLennan shows both couples on the following morning. In one short paragraph describing Wain waking in Evelyn's bed, MacLennan preaches a sermon on the undesirability of sex divorced from love:

> To Geoffrey Wain, the sunlight coming in through Evelyn's faded lace curtains . . . was vaguely insulting. . . . Evelyn had fallen asleep naked, too lazy to put on the nightgown she had discarded over the side of the bed. . . . The deadness of expression caused by sleep robbed her of all attractiveness. Her slightness . . . now seemed a defect . . . her breath had an odour of acetone which displeased him too, although it never occurred to him that in this respect he was the greater offender.

Why should the sunlight be insulting? Why should Evelyn be condemned as "lazy"? MacLennan's moral disapproval colours every line of this paragraph. He shows that nothing is really attractive or pleasurable, and that there is neither beauty nor joy in such a relationship. The view of untidy backyards and garbage which Wain sees out the window is identified with the affair. By contrast, the sunlight which the Frasers enjoy with their breakfast is not insulting, but dazzling, brilliant. They are happy as they eat breakfast together and argue good-naturedly on their way to the train. The parallel structure serves as an indirect comment on the use and abuse of sex.

Finally, there is the love which Penny Wain and Neil MacRae have for one another. This love has been consummated before Neil went overseas. Both Penny and Neil relive it in memory. For Penny, the experience had a quality almost sacramental: "into thy hands I commend my spir-

it." Neil remembers the peonies by their bed, full-blown and fragrant, a symbol of consummated love. There is no inhibition in MacLennan's handling of this love scene. The description is both passionate and delicate. The lovers, although unmarried at the time, seem to be permanently committed to one another by their act. As Penny and Neil go together to find Jean at Prince's Lodge in the last chapter, Penny feels that she is tied to Neil, "a prisoner of his maleness because once she had wanted him and he had refused to forget it." Their difficult progress through the dark night becomes for Penny a symbol of the inevitability of the permanence of their relationship. Why inevitable? There is no apparent necessity in the events themselves, although Jean's foster parents have been conveniently disposed of. The inevitability follows from MacLennan's ethic, that sexual relations should mean permanent and total involvement of the whole person.

Compare this with Lucy Cameron's relations with Steve Lassiter. Their wedding night is distanced by placing it in Lucy's memory, as with the Montreal love scene in *Barometer Rising.* In *The Precipice,* as in the earlier novel, there is a sense of reverence towards the experience, a sense of wonder and joy. Even after several years of marriage, Lucy maintains her feeling of wonder and gratitude for her position as Stephen's wife, and for his physical candour which has effaced the last traces of puritan shame she has brought with her into marriage. Against the puritan attitude of condemnation MacLennan affirms, like D.H. Lawrence, that sex is good and is to be enjoyed with reverence and thankfulness.

But only under certain conditions. When Lucy thinks of Stephen and Gail together, the violence of her imagination makes her actually shake. She imagines scenes, "natural as health were she a part of them, obscene and terrible and unjust when they were of Stephen and Gail." Sexual relations, then, are to be considered natural as health, or obscene and terrible and unjust, depending on the context. On the next page, Marcia relates an anecdote about multiple marriages and the resulting confusion for the children of such marriages. Lucy recoils in horror. Her children must never be subject to this. Whereas earlier she had spoken broadly and tolerantly of forgiving adultery, even of expecting it in a man such as Stephen, she now realizes that she cannot live long in a state of suspense and dishonesty. Although these remarks belong to dramatic fictional situations, the entire context convinces the reader that Lucy's opinions are also MacLennan's. Marital fidelity is depicted as being necessary for psychological health.

*Two Solitudes* reveals the same underlying attitude towards sex as the earlier novels. Kathleen has spent the night with Athanase Tallard at the time of his first wife's death. He is convinced that she is thereby responsible for his renewed will to live. And he knows that he will always be grateful to her for this. They are married, but later cease to interest one another, since the marriage has been based more on sexual attraction than on their whole personalities. Earlier, when Athanase had been rejected physically by his first wife, he had found that he could be neither "a celibate nor a cynical boulevardier." Athanase is seeking the permanent and complete union which

MacLennan holds up as the ideal. It is part of Athanase's tragedy that he fails to find happiness in marriage, as he fails to find it in other areas of his life.

There are two exceptions in the early novels to MacLennan's general attitude towards sex as involving a permanent commitment. In *Two Solitudes,* there is the encounter in a Montreal hotel between Kathleen and the strange officer Dennis Morey. Secondly, there is an incident in *The Precipice* where Nina refuses to spend the night with a young airman in Halifax. MacLennan indicates that she should have done so. Nina is condemned for failing to meet a human need, the boy's excessive fear and loneliness. These episodes are not in MacLennan's general pattern. Both might be described as versions of the New Morality, where each individual situation must be judged uniquely by love's concern for another's need. Kathleen tells herself that her encounter with Morey has happened in accordance with some deep necessity, "that even though for others it might be a sin, for her at this particular time it had been good." MacLennan made Morey his mouthpiece for a violent attack on Canadian puritanism, and perhaps felt compelled to let the situation arrive at its logical conclusion. In the next chapter, Kathleen remembers her husband and son, and wonders if her act has harmed them. It is probable that her doubts here echo MacLennan's own uneasiness with the situation.

The incident may also have a bearing upon MacLennan's rejection of Kathleen in the later parts of the novel. In Part One, Kathleen is presented as amoral rather than immoral; her movements are sexually provocative, but are also "of an earthy gentleness, almost of a strangely individual innocence." She is described as being easy-going and accepting. By working as a hat-check girl in a hotel, she is fulfilling herself, using her one talent which is to be herself. Both her son Paul and her husband Athanase depend heavily upon her. When she has been absent in Montreal, Paul feels her return makes the world once again gay and full of wonder. Athanase has credited her with renewing his will to live on the night his first wife died.

In contrast to this earlier treatment, MacLennan's later treatment of Kathleen is strangely scornful and condescending. After Athanase's death she seems no longer admirable. Her fragrance, warmth and softness, once so wonderful to Paul, are now unable to relieve his loneliness. Kathleen leaves the dishes unwashed and the beds unmade while she seeks enjoyment outside the apartment; and Paul, left to find his own amusement, does these jobs for her. Paul feels that she is "still herself yet somehow much less than she had been before." Her smile, although sincere, is "still somehow automatic." Why is MacLennan, a most careful writer with regard to style, reduced to using the word "somehow" twice in consecutive sentences? I suggest that it is the author's moral bias, suppressed earlier, now rising to reject Kathleen. Thirteen years later, at her second marriage, Paul finds the ceremony shocking: "The food being blessed was stale; indeed it had already been eaten." Kathleen and her new husband, Henry Clayton, have already lived together for some time, and MacLennan's condemnation of this is symbolized by the ugliness of the physical conditions of their marriage:

the background traffic noise, the excessive heat and humidity, the ink-blotted register. Paul tells himself that his attitude is senseless, but he cannot change it, and Kathleen's parting words are a request for her son's forgiveness. MacLennan's rejection of Kathleen, in the second and third parts of *Two Solitudes,* is one of the most striking examples of the ambivalence which results from his refusal to see any connection between the puritanism which he is attacking and his own moral values.

With the single two exceptions discussed above, MacLennan's early novels condemn casual sexual relations. The behaviour of a man like Noel Fletcher, which might appear as unpuritanical and thereby liable to MacLennan's approval, is condemned as "mechanical sensuality." The relations of Gail Beaumont and Stephen Lassiter are "obscene and terrible and unjust." In MacLennan's serious and moral definition, the right use of sex is part of a total and permanent relationship. Only within this context is sex natural as health. With MacLennan, as with the historic Puritans, morality is the first concern.

### Hugh MacLennan with Ronald Sutherland    (interview date Spring-Summer 1976)

SOURCE: An interview in *Canadian Literature,* Nos. 68-69, Spring-Summer, 1976, pp. 40-8.

*[In the following interview, MacLennan discusses various influences on his writing.]*

*[Sutherland]: How long have you been here in Quebec, Hugh?*

[MacLennan]: I came to Quebec the fall of 1935 to teach for Lower Canada College and live in at $25.00 a week. I came late in the term, because they simply had to get somebody else, I suppose. And I've been permanently based in Montreal ever since then.

*Did you come directly from the Maritimes?*

Directly from Halifax. I did not have a job. I got my Doctor's degree at Princeton during the depths of the depression, and it was difficult to get any kind of job at that time. I was in Roman History and a Rhodes Scholar. Terry McDermott, who ended up as Ambassador and Commissioner at various places, was the secretary of the committee that gave me a Rhodes' Scholarship, because I was defeated in Nova Scotia. But there was a special one loose at the time, and I was actually a Rhodes Scholar for Canada at large.

*Where were you going to university? Dalhousie?*

I went to Dalhousie. I did Honours Classics there.

*When did you leave Dalhousie?*

I graduated in 1928 and went to Oxford the next fall, then Princeton. I would sooner have gotten a job then, but there just weren't any jobs in 1932. Only about five per cent of Rhodes Scholars got any jobs at all.

*Did you want to go back to the Maritimes, or did the economic conditions force you to leave?*

I very much wanted to go back, but I couldn't get a job there, and that was the thing, I think, which was very damaging in the Maritimes then. Less so now. The casualties in the first world war had been abnormally heavy, and once the war was over there was a depression all over the Maritimes. They never had a 1920's boom down there. The old establishment didn't particularly encourage people who really weren't members of it to remain, but at any rate I couldn't get a job. Indeed, a post was vacant in my field at Dalhousie, and the chairman was a Yale man. A very small department, of course—they all were then. He simply told me that an Englishman was applying, and that was it, although he didn't like the English. The same thing happened with a vacancy in Saskatchewan. The Chairman called me and said, "I am afraid you haven't got a chance because an Englishman is applying." The Englishman hadn't any higher qualifications than I had and was only coming here in order to get into the States, which was where he eventually went.

*Do you still consider yourself a Maritimer?*

I never did. I'm a Nova Scotian.

*A Nova Scotian?*

Anybody who says he comes from the Maritimes, ninety-nine times out of a hundred he is from New Brunswick. They never call themselves New Brunswickans. Perhaps they don't like the word. Otherwise, you are a Nova Scotian, or from the Island, or Newfoundlander, or from the Atlantic Provinces, in my case Cape Breton.

*Do you think there is a particular mystique shared by people from Nova Scotia or any part of the Maritimes?*

I do. I think it's because there is a sense of community. It's very beautiful country where people know each other. I'm not saying that in the old colonial days of Newfoundland the government was honest, because it wasn't, but I would say the governments in the Island, Nova Scotia and New Brunswick, have been universally pretty honest for the reason that politicians know they couldn't get away with anything else. People know too much about each other down there. They are democratic countries. Montreal, the rest of Canada, Toronto—they aren't democratic, they're simply controlled by corporations.

*Are the Maritimes still democratic?*

They're democratic in the sense that they do manage a good many of their local affairs. For example, the developers began to do damage in Halifax, but they've been, to some extent, stopped. An attempt was made to develop Point Pleasant Park. They got nowhere. No, the people down there are much more straightforward and outspoken than they are here.

*Can you see your upbringing in the Maritimes having an influence on your writing? You've not written a great deal about the Maritimes comparatively speaking.*

I was influenced by Nova Scotia, and also by the kind of education I had. Years ago I came to the conclusion that urban-dwellers—people like Norman Mailer, Mordecai Richler or John Dos Passos, who grew up in cities—don't see details. But they have a wonderful sense of surge of movement. Now when Hemingway was growing up he spent a great deal of time in the country, and Hemingway will describe a situation or landscape by the minutest intuitive selection of detail, and he will use the *mot juste* again and again and again. That's why he is such a vivid kind of writer. City living is having its effect on me. My next book will be in a far more surging kind of prose than I have ever written before—there's a slight element of this in some of the writing in certain sections of ***Rivers of Canada.*** The kind of writing or style that I used before is more reflective than what I feel now, living in Montreal.

*Are you saying that the Maritimes have an essentially rural effect?*

Don't forget the sea. Five thousand miles of coastline in Nova Scotia. When I was reading Homer as a kid, particularly *The Odyssey,* he was describing what I had all around me. Many of the poems in the Greek Anthology could have been written of Nova Scotia, and when I went to Greece the first time and again even more the second time, because the second time I was able to get out to sea a bit, it was very like the coast of Nova Scotia. If you stand out on Cape Sounian, remove the Temple of Neptune, and look inland, it's just like looking in beyond Peggy's Cove up St. Margaret's Bay. The ground cover is slightly different, but the same granite outcropping, the same formations. Now my neighbour, Tasso Sikiris, who is a Greek, went down with his wife to Nova Scotia last year, just about this time in September—they went around the Cabot Trail in Cape Breton, went through the valley and around the North Shore. Tasso called me up and said, "My God, you're absolutely right!" Once I saw a picture that my old friend, Ewing Irwin, had in his house here in North Hatley, and I said, "Ewing, that's somewhere up in Cape Breton isn't it?" "God, no," he replied, "That's Delphi."

*So there's no accident about the affinity you've had with Greek legend?*

No, not at all.

*Do you think that growing up in Nova Scotia has influenced the themes of your books?*

Actually, classical education, particularly Roman History, is the most perfect preparation for living today, especially the later Roman Empire in the period of disintegration. I wasn't studying that at Halifax, I was reading the elementary basic classics of the Golden Ages, but my research at Princeton involved that period. Boiled down in the long run, it was the decline and fall of the Roman Empire through the wrong end of the telescope. The Roman tax system was about the same as ours, and therefore doomed. The bureaucracy was doomed. We're going much faster than they were. We're much more efficient at ruining ourselves, but ultimately money, you see, became worthless. It took a long time, but once it passed a certain point—we're just on the verge of passing it now—it just went off to practically nothing—which meant agrarian feudalism. In our age it would mean, of course, some sort of urban feudalism, which would be far more explosive.

*Far more explosive?*

Oh, yes, it will probably destroy us.

*Feudalism in what way?*

Well, I mean, the working man today may be making a lot of money, but the government's taking half of it. There's no government, just bureaucracy. It doesn't seem to me to matter who's Prime Minister any more.

*And this you regard as a new kind of feudalism? Man becomes a serf again?*

He's becoming just that. He always tended to be. But a dictatorship of the Proletariat means a dictatorship of the leaders of the Proletariat. They drive around in Cadillacs and everything else, with hoods to keep the boys in order.

*Of course, some of the labour leaders have a tendency to disappear these days, like James Hoffa.*

That happens. It all reminds me of the Roman barrack room Emperors, the gangster Emperors. If you ever go to Florence, don't miss looking through the Portrait Gallery of the Roman Emperors. It tells you more than you get in books.

*Let me ask you another question. You are considered one of the foremost interpreters of Quebec and the solitudes of Quebec. Do you think that your Maritime background has had some influence or has helped you to interpret Quebec?*

I think so because I had absolutely no trouble at all, not even being able to speak French at the time and knowing very few French Canadians, interpreting how French Canadians felt. They regard everybody who is non-French as *Anglais*. But, of course, that's not so. The Scotch, as you know, had in many ways a worse history than the French Canadians ever had. The chiefs sold them and transported them some way or other with them as soldiers for the English and so forth. Leo Rowse, the great historian of All Souls, was a Cornishman. He read one of my essays in **Scotchman's Return** and said only a Celt could have written it. He was saying that a Celt has a dog-whistle sound that an Anglo-Saxon simply doesn't get and which an Anglo-Saxon finds very irritating. Of course, the Anglo-Saxons on the whole are much abler administrators and much more reliable people. At any rate, I knew what it was like to be in a minority, because the Celts were.

*How were they in a minority in Cape Breton?*

They were a minority in Nova Scotia, and while they were proud people and never felt a sense of inferiority, there was something underneath. The Annapolis Valley was pro-Loyalist Yankee. A lot of them came from Massachusetts. The Loyalists, of course, were not the way the Americans said—all coming from the upper classes. If you look at the shipping lists of boats that went into Saint John, you will find that every trade right down to tinkers, all classes of people were there. Some of them were upper class. For instance, the Bishop of New York, the Anglican Bishop became the Archbishop of Nova Scotia as a Loyalist. Many of them came from West Chester County, some from Connecticut and some of them even came from North Carolina. As Loyalists they were more British than the King in some ways, as they tended to be in Ontario. But there was another thing about Nova Scotia in the 19th

century. It was a tremendous sea power—the little town of Yarmouth with a population of about six thousand people built, sailed and manned one sixty-fourth of the entire shipping of the world from about 1850 to the end of the century. In sailing ships of wood, which they built themselves, Nova Scotian or Maritime ships—mostly Nova Scotian but there were some from New Brunswick—were about the fourth largest fleet in the world. The British were first, I suppose the Americans might have been second, who was third I don't know, but they were fourth. Anyway, fourth or fifth. The Cunard Line was founded in Halifax and the White Star Line was founded in St. John. Those provinces in the 19th century were not provincial. Quebec and Ontario were much more provincial. A man who became the Admiral of the Fleet, Provost Wallace, was born and went to school in Halifax county.

*You think then, that the fact that the people of Scottish descent were a minority in Nova Scotia has given you a lever to interpret Quebec?*

I think it probably has, although I never thought of it at the time. Yes, I think it probably did, because I always felt in a minority. My family left Cape Breton when I was seven, coming to Halifax. I thought Haligonians were different people. I liked them very much. I loved Halifax, but people had names like Smith and Brown and Robinson and so forth. Halifax seemed to me a terribly exciting place. It still does.

*Have you found any other sort of spiritual affinity with Quebec that helped you to develop your novels and your writing about Quebec?*

Well, I think it's true that the Scotch and the French people have had an intuitive understanding of each other. God knows where the Highlanders would have been if their Chiefs hadn't made an alliance with France. I spent a winter in Grenoble about ten years ago. I remember I was very amused by this old retired French colonel who said to me, *"Monsieur, est-il possible de visiter l'Ecosse sans visiter l'Angleterre?"* I found out that he hated the English, but being *Ecossais* made a difference, being *Ecossais* and *un écrivain*. Everybody knows that the French seldom invite foreigners into their homes, but somehow or other people began inviting us out and we were in about fourteen different homes in Grenoble, which is very unusual.

*Of course, in Quebec there are a lot of Scotch.*

I'll bet that one third of them have Scottish blood. The Fraser Highlanders were disbanded here. If Rocket Richard doesn't have Highland blood in him, I'd be very surprised.

*It would be interesting to find out. But when you came up to Montreal, did you like the place?*

Immediately. I loved it. I don't like it now. It was the finest city in America seven years ago. Look at it now. It's a concrete jungle.

*In your writing have you never had the desire to write more about the Maritimes? How do you pick your themes?*

They pick me. The first book I wrote was unsuccessful. It was mixed up with Nova Scotia. I had some bootleggers in it, and it was set more or less in the States—people, the sea and so forth. The next one I tried to set in Europe with some Americans in it, but I wasn't close enough to it. Then *Barometer Rising* occured to me. I have to write about what I absolutely know, and I had almost to make a map to write about Canada then. I had to because early perceptions are the things that count, and this all came about when my second novel had been reviewed by the twenty-first New York publisher, and the agent had simply put my name on it and sent it in. The review said, "We don't know who your writer is. He doesn't write like an American and he doesn't write like an Englishman. Who is he? There's something missing." So, I thought O.K., I can't get away from it. Then I thought of Aristotle's idea of recognitions—nobody could recognise within a social novel where the conflict would lie if they didn't know anything about the country. Even Canadians knew nothing about the country. So I made the city the hero of *Barometer Rising* and thought it might last for nine months, and I'm amazed that it's still published.

---

*Two Solitudes* **came out of a dream in which I saw some tall blond man, a total stranger, and a short stocky dark man shouting at each other at the tops of their voices, both of them quite likeable people who just simply couldn't understand each other at all, and some boy said, "Don't you see they're both deaf."**

**—Hugh MacLennan**

---

*Have you consciously tried to map the country in that way?*

It's hard to say that specifically. After *Barometer Rising* came out, an old friend of mine, an Englishman, was killed in an accident in the war. He had been in the publishing business, had been with Constable in New York, but he had lost his job in the depression as did everybody else. When he read *Barometer* he sent me a letter saying, "This is not Canadian literature, it's Nova Scotian." He asked me why I didn't consider setting a novel in Quebec. It's the centre of Canada, if anything is. Well, I'd already started it, because *Two Solitudes* came out of a dream in which I saw some tall blond man, a total stranger, and a short stocky dark man shouting at each other at the tops of their voices, both of them quite likeable people who just simply couldn't understand each other at all, and some boy said, "Don't you see they're both deaf." How the book was structured as it was, don't ask me. I have no idea how it formed itself. I felt the material was so rich I could have gone on forever.

*Where did you get the material? How did you find out about the attitudes?*

I got absorbed in them, and in Quebec. I should say this because it's very definitely true, and I want to acknowledge it though I didn't realize it at the time. I had a

French-Canadian colleague who was a Protestant, Monsieur Peron, a man of enormous integrity and intelligence, a delightful personality and tough as all hell. The French-Canadian Protestants were sort of an underground in those days. He could call an election within a decimal point. He was very strong as a French Canadian. He disliked the Catholic Church intensely, blamed it for practically everything that was wrong here. When I finally finished *Two Solitudes,* I still had the job at Lower Canada. Mr. Peron was a very tough critic of things, and the highest praise that book ever got was when I gave him a copy on a Friday afternoon and he read it over the weekend. He came back and said there was nothing the matter with it.

*Did you use him as a model for Tallard?*

Absolutely. But unconsciously. Monsieur Peron was a very poor man. He had two sons and a daughter. How in the name of God he educated the whole lot of them, I do not know. He never got more than $2,400 a year, and he had his own house, at least part of it, and he rented the other part of it. Both of his sons have succeeded tremendously. Fernand, the younger son, is now Professor of, I think Bio-Chemistry, down in M.I.T., and René, the elder, has been very successful in business.

*You mentioned before that* **Barometer Rising** *was a Nova Scotian novel and not a Canadian novel. Is it possible for this contradiction to exist? Can you see any pan-Canadian attitudes or are the writers here strictly regional and must they be regional?*

Well, I think that in so far as the novel has got to have a physical basis, all novels are regional in some way. *War and Peace* isn't, because it's the whole world. *Two Solitudes* isn't truly regional. *The Watch That Ends The Night* isn't regional. The reception *Barometer* got in Canada was so remarkable that it must have stirred up echoes from one end of the country to the other. I got letters from all over the place. It seemed to echo so many of our attitudes. It was a book with something of a contrived plot, though the plot turned out to be almost dead accurate as I found out later. But I didn't know that when I wrote it.

*In what way?*

Larry MacKenzie, who had been overseas with the 85th Nova Scotians, asked me if I got into any trouble about the book. I said no. A lot of people in Halifax said it was obscene and that sort of thing. Actually there was a case, and strangely enough I knew the people involved or at least some of them, of a man from an old Halifax family who had been with the 25th Regiment, which was decimated on, I think, the 19th of July, 1916, in the Somme battles. The colonel was a very ruthless man who was actually an Englishman, a ranker, who accused one of the soldiers of cowardice. The man might possibly have been shot, I don't know.

*You didn't know this story before?*

I didn't know it then, but how can I be sure? You get things through the pores.

*Do you find then that it's quite possible to be completely re-*

gional and at the same time to embrace a kind of pan-Canadian attitude?

I think so. I have always seen Canada as a part of the history of the world and there has never been any universal literature that started on a local basis, except maybe the Greek, and even it probably didn't. But that was the original Western civilization. The Romans had to learn from Greek models, how to adapt them to Latin, and in the final Ode of the third book of Horace—I have built a monument more enduring than bronze and higher than the royal seat of the Pyramids and so on—he ends up by saying, I was the first man to tune the Roman lyre to Grecian measures. Take the Renaissance. It was first of all Italian. Just think back to the time that Queen Elizabeth came to the throne. The only thing scholars could read really was Latin. Then Greek was coming in. They were learning some Greek, because Erasmus had come there to teach Greek. What was there of the European? Rabelais, Montaigne had just published around 1580. There was Chaucer and Malory and that was about it, before the great flowering came.

*Are you saying there's no question of isolation of a culture?*

Yes. It just means tuning the lyre to Grecian measures you may say, but I have no use for regionalism in itself although some of it can be charming. I always used to be irritated at being called a Canadian writer—I was a writer who was a Canadian.

*Let me ask you another thing, what do you consider to be the major influence on your writing career?*

This may sound stuffy, but in a practical way one sentence of Aristotle that the drama depends on the ability of an audience to recognize what the drama is about. I had to build a stage for the earlier books. Nearly all the academics at the time were criticizing me for doing this. Back in the 1950's, people who later became violent literary nationalists—who shall now be nameless—were bawling me out for not joining the English angry young men and so forth. I'd been to Cambridge for a year. That, and I suppose living in North Hatley, made an enormous difference to my understanding of how people live. I knew practically everybody in this village and I used to work in the garden with some French Canadians. I recall the lovely story of what would happen if the Germans won the war. My French-Canadian friend said that he would still be on one end of the saw, but the man of the other end would be an Englishman.

*All of these influences together then have resulted in your writing the way you do?*

I suppose so, but truly it's not profitable for a writer to analyse how he does things while he's still working, except in a technical way. The thing that must have had an enormous influence on how I looked at things was that I was something of an athlete when I was young, and I would sooner have been a Wimbledon champion than to be well known as a writer. When I was in my early twenties, I'd never thought of being a novelist; it just happened.

*You say that when you wrote* **Barometer Rising** *you had to*

consciously set the stage for your writing. Has that stage now been set, do you think?

It's been set. By the time I finished **The Precipice** I decided that I didn't have to do that any more. With **Each Man's Son,** when I sent it to Boston, I just opened right up, didn't tell them anything about the situation. And I was told that I would have to write some kind of a preface, because nobody in America, not even in Boston, could believe in a kind of Calvinism as rigid as I had described. But I don't think such prefaces are necessary any longer.

*Young writers today no longer have the same task. Good.*

I think it might be relevant to say too that Gabrielle Roy had to do the same thing. Her book came out, *Bonheur d'occasion,* six weeks after **Two Solitudes** did. Neither of us knew of each other's existence. Roger Lemelin had to do it to some extent too. But Lemelin's work was of much more popular nature. *La Famille Plouffe* practically put the rural, small-town film business out of commission, because that long series of "La Famille Plouffe" not only trained a lot of French-Canadian actors and showed how to move people around the stage in television, but it brought up all manner of contemporary problems in French-Canadian life. Its influence was prodigious.

*Do you often go back to The Maritimes?*

I do like to get back to The Maritimes, to Nova Scotia, any part of it, but especially Cape Breton.

### Warren Stevenson   (essay date Winter 1977)

SOURCE: "A Neglected Theme in *Two Solitudes,*" in *Canadian Literature,* No. 75, Winter, 1977, pp. 53-60.

[*In the essay below, Stevenson argues that the idea of "individual self-awareness" is an important though neglected secondary theme that adds to the unity of* Two Solitudes.]

It has become almost a commonplace of criticism of Hugh MacLennan's **Two Solitudes** to say that the novel succeeds brilliantly up to the end of the twenty-ninth chapter, portraying the death of Athanase Tallard, but is less convincing in the last twenty-three chapters portraying the symbolic resolution of the theme in the education and maturation of the members of the second generation, Paul Tallard and Heather Methuen, and their eventual marriage. The following quotation from critic George Woodcock is in this respect typical: "If **Two Solitudes** had ended with Tallard's death, it would have been a moving and cohesive book. But up to this point it merely presents the problem of racial relations; it does not have the logical completeness of presenting a solution, and this MacLennan seeks, at the expense of his novel, in its later chapters" ["A Nation's Odyssey: The Novels of Hugh MacLennan," *Odysseus Ever Returning,* 1970]. I think the time has come for a reassessment of this position. To my knowledge, the only critic who has dissented from the majority view of the concluding chapters of **Two Solitudes** is Robert D. Chambers, who observes [in "The Novels of Hugh MacLennan," in *Hugh MacLennan,* edited by Paul Goetsch, 1973]:

The second half of *Two Solitudes* has been criticized as over-written and unconvincing, and it is interesting to note that MacLennan has allowed some pruning for the paperback and school editions. Nevertheless, the latter parts of the novel carry through his vigorous assault on the pillars of Canadian respectability, and his closing picture of intelligent Canadian youth facing with tolerance and humanity the problems of their generation seems made of stuff that will adhere.

It has also become a commonplace of criticism of *Two Solitudes* that [as George Woodcock states in "Hugh MacLennan," in *Hugh MacLennan*] "the idea of Canadian unity becomes the main symbolic theme," which MacLennan attempts to embody in the lives of his characters. Without pretending to deny the primacy of the theme of Canadian self-awareness and unity, I would like to suggest that the novel contains an important subsidiary theme which most critics have overlooked and which helps to unify the novel. I refer to the theme of individual self-awareness, worked out in terms of a contrast between two types of persons, those who learn to come to terms with what MacLennan calls "the ultimate solitude" and those who don't. The title thus has another dimension than the French-English dichotomy to which it is usually applied. The quotation from Rilke which constitutes the novel's epigraph is an important clue to its meaning: "Love consists in this, that two solitudes protect, and touch, and greet each other." Rilke was almost certainly referring to individuals, not societies, though it would be pedantry to attempt to limit the range of applicability of the quotation; and the novel's dedication which precedes the epigraph, "To Dorothy Duncan with admiration and love," suggests that MacLennan was also thinking of individuals and their personal relationships.

To anticipate my argument briefly: those characters in the novel who learn to come to terms with "the ultimate solitude" are most notably Captain Yardley, Paul Tallard, and Heather Methuen, who becomes Paul's wife. The characters who most dramatically fail to come to terms with the ultimate solitude are Athanase Tallard, his second wife Kathleen, his son by his first marriage Marius, such satiric figures as Huntly McQueen, General Methuen, et al, and Janet Methuen. Of Captain Yardley MacLennan writes:

> Though Yardley had never had an academic education, he had slowly learned how to read books and how to think. As a sailor, and then as a ship's master, he had known solitude in strange places. He was persuaded that all knowledge is like a painted curtain hung across the door of the mind to conceal from it a mystery so darkly suggestive that no one can face it alone for long. Of ultimate solitude he had no fear, for he never let himself think about it. But he knew that if he once started, fear would be there.

With its overtones of T. S. Eliot's concept that most people cannot bear very much reality, this passage may seem to contradict rather than confirm my argument. But clearly, Yardley has learned how to handle solitude and the fear which lurks within the recesses of the human mind surrounding the "mystery."

The passage I have quoted is followed by a longer one in which Yardley reminisces about an experience in the tropics, when he spent an afternoon leaning over the taffrail and watching sharks and barracuda "gliding through ten fathoms of sunlit water below. . . . Self-centred, beautiful, dangerous and aimless: that was how they had been, and he could never forget it." In this symbolically important passage, the sharks and barracuda represent the undirected passions. One is reminded of the beautiful, dangerous (for Athanase), and fundamentally self-centred and aimless Kathleen, gliding about the Tallard seignory house. Like Athanase, she is basically lacking in self-knowledge. One is also reminded of Marius Tallard, who is described as follows addressing an anti-conscription meeting:

> Marius Tallard was drunk with a new knowledge of himself. He stood in the big hall before the meeting with his feet apart, swaying from the hips, his arms folded across his chest. Now and then his right arm shot out and the long fingers of his hand wove gestures in the air. His white teeth flashed rare and bitter smiles in his white face. His black hair was loose on his long, narrow skull. He pulled emotion out of the crowd and threw it back at them.

Marius' white teeth and "long, narrow skull" remind one of the sharks and barracuda. His "new knowledge of himself" is spurious, a dangerous and deceptive substitute for the true self-knowledge of a Captain Yardley. Like the *anglais* capitalist Huntly McQueen, Marius remains fixated on the memory of his dead mother. His Oedipus complex leads him into conflict with his father and the social authority his father represents.

Marius' opposite number is of course his half brother Paul, who in the latter part of the novel reaches a truer understanding of himself as a result of his travels and writing. Yardley's words to Paul on the occasion of his father's death pick up the theme of solitude and the failure of Athanase to come to terms with it: "I tell you how it is, Paul. You father being a Catholic again—if that's what it means, the candles and the things by the bed—well it means he got lonely and wanted to be what he'd been all his life, I guess. Or maybe it means something else so big I can't understand it." The only hint of self-knowledge on the part of Athanase is the extent to which he seems to have consciously brought Paul up as a synthesis of the two cultures.

Following the death of his father, Paul makes a symbolic ascent of Mount Royal which represents by anticipation his quest for true knowledge, including self-knowledge. The attainment of vision (in the deepest sense of the term) is portrayed symbolically in the panoramic view of Montreal which greets Paul from the summit, in the paragraph beginning: "He was breathless from his climb, but now he was on top of the mountain and could see the whole city spread out beneath him." This passage anticipates Paul's attainment of a comprehensive overview of Canadian society as it is to be expressed in his as-yet-unwritten second novel. At the end of the chapter in which this passage occurs, MacLennan indicates that an important ingredient in Paul's continuing maturation is the "loneliness" which "struck right through him." In this respect he is contrasted to his mother: "And he knew now that although her smile was as sincere as possible, it was still somehow automatic, a gesture as natural and unconscious as the sway of her hips when she walked, and that behind it her mind was a stranger."

Parallel to Paul's development is that of Heather, who impulsively leaves Huntly McQueen's pretentious dinner party and the company of the predatory Fletchers (cf. the sharks and barracuda) to make her own ascent of Mount Royal, which is contrasted to Paul's climb by being made in an automobile at night and taking her to a lower eminence of the mountain. The beneficent effects of solitude are again suggested: "It was wonderful to be alone." At twenty-three Heather feels she has reached a crisis in her life. So far she has followed the Methuen pattern, attending school in Lausanne for two years and studying French as a social accomplishment rather than as a help to her in the province of Quebec. She has also had her debut and picked up a college degree. Unlike her sister Daphne, she has not rushed into a prestigious marriage, and her mother is beginning to consider her a social liability. Her painting, paralleling Paul's interest in writing, is her only asset other than the Methuen money, which she has not helped to earn. Unwilling to become a St. James Street wife, she finds that Canadian discrimination against women stands in the way of any career she might choose for herself except the most conventional. Her vision from the Westmount summit of the mountain, from which "only a portion of the city could be seen," parallels Paul's more comprehensive vision in its symbolic connotations and is really different rather than inferior to his, as her exclamation "Oh, lovely!" and the delicate description of the moon-coloured scene suggest.

When Kathleen marries the American Henry Clayton, thus merging her identity in the American melting pot, Paul experiences the most intense loneliness of his life thus far: "If loneliness is a man's inability to share his feelings with another, Paul had never been as lonely in his life as he was now. The whole ceremony seemed shocking to him." As for Kathleen, whose possession represents "the only real purpose Henry Clayton had ever known," her fading physical charms are portrayed as a surrogate, a sweet substitute for a sense of inner purpose which Clayton lacks and Paul is in the process of acquiring. As MacLennan remarked earlier apropos of Athanase: "Incredible, that for most of a lifetime a man could imagine that beauty was enough, or that women could satisfy the ultimate solitude."

In contrast to Athanase, to whom women were "necessary," Paul undergoes a lengthy period of relative sexual abstinence during his European venture. Heather similarly sees through the "cold surface beauty" and "mechanical sensuality" of Daphne and Noel Fletcher. The intellectual pursuits of Paul and Heather (she is reading the post-war novelists as well as painting; he wants to be a writer) are paralleled by those of their spiritual mentor, Captain

Yardley, who is interested in astronomy and, with Paul's help, begins studying Greek at seventy-six. MacLennan suggests that both Yardley and Paul are learning to come to terms with the ultimate solitude, and that for Paul the process involves physical as well as mental effort (he is a graduate of the University of Montreal and has had a brief career as a hockey player):

> For a long time now it had been growing, all through his teens, and getting steadily tighter. It woke him nearly every morning, except when he was physically exhausted after a hard game. It was more than a physical state of nerves; it was a quality of mind, breeding a kind of solitude of its own.

This may be compared with a passage earlier in the novel in which MacLennan remarks of the Canadian soldiers returning home from the First World War: "Some had learned peace through an ultimate knowledge of themselves."

The loneliness within Paul the acceptance of which leads to self-knowledge finds its objective correlative in the sense of desolation in the northern forests as he recalls a trip to Lake Superior on a lake boat:

> A sunset burned through Fort William and Port Arthur and hurled gigantic shadows of the grain elevators forward on to the trembling waters of Thunder Bay. . . . As night closed over the ship the colour had died, and nothing was left but the sounds of millions of shallow waves turning over in the darkness, an astringent wind keening blindly out of the empty forest to the north, the quick spatterings of lifeless fresh water whipped by the wind over the waist of the ship and wetting the deck. It was only a few days later, away from this sense of desolation in the heart of a continent, that they were passing so close to shore in eastern Ontario he could look into the windows of houses when the lights were on after dark. He had seen men reading in arm chairs and children going to bed, and once a naked woman thoughtfully combed her hair before a window, her lips open as though she were singing to herself. The ship had passed and left her there, strangely transfigured.

Here the description of the landscape reminds one of certain Group of Seven paintings, such as J. E. H. MacDonald's "The Lonely North," and the naked woman combing her hair before the window and singing like a mermaid or a wood-nymph symbolizes the spirit of the land. The result is what Robertson Davies has somewhere called a kind of northern mysticism In coming to terms with the inner loneliness, Paul is also coming to terms with the outer loneliness, and the growth of MacLennan's protagonist towards self-knowledge parallels a similar development in the young nation.

In *The Watch That Ends The Night* George Stewart makes a canoe trip to Lake Superior and likewise confronts the spirit of the lonely land, which MacLennan explicitly compares to Group of Seven paintings. This spirit finds its individual parallel in that of Catherine, who was "strangely solitary in her core," and in that of Jerome

Martell, who as a boy confronted the loneliness of the New Brunswick forests. The repetition of the quotation from Rilke in the later novel, and George Stewart's statement that "She [Catherine] and I had protected and touched and greeted each other reasonably well in the past nine years, but Jerome was a part of her core," show that each of the three protagonists is invested with a measure of the solitude that characterizes the theme of the earlier novel. And when Jerome tells George that Catherine "must be enabled to live her own death" and makes it possible for George "to live her death with her," the concept of losing one's life in order to gain it is given a radically Christian emphasis which contrasts with the more existential treatment of the theme in *Two Solitudes.*

When Paul ships out of Halifax harbour aboard a merchantman, he seems to be trying to emulate Captain Yardley, his spiritual father. But Paul's travels are also a kind of preparation for his vocation as a writer, a self-chosen period of solitude. They are also a way of testing his love for Heather. In a hotel bar in Athens Paul witnesses a scene involving a German seducing a French woman which seems symbolic of the changing face of European society, and may be contrasted to the nude Canadian woman singing to herself. Following this scene, MacLennan describes Paul's recurring feeling of loneliness: "the city surrounded him like a giant presence of loneliness. It was no new feeling; most of his life he had known it, and now it was recurring again like a periodic disease. . . . He wondered if Heather had ever felt as he did now. Two solitudes in the infinite waste of loneliness under the sun." This is the only occurrence in the novel other than the title and the epigraph of the phrase "two solitudes"; and it is significant that, in its context, it refers not primarily to the fact that Paul is of French and Heather of English extraction, but to the existential and individual aloneness which both characters are learning independently to face as part of maturation. The passage from which I have just quoted ends with Paul rejecting the opportunity to have a casual affair with a woman sitting at a nearby table, and the statement: "He wasn't equal to that kind of loneliness today." Again, there is the solitude of those who learn to come to terms with their existential loneliness, and the solitude of those who don't. MacLennan suggests that the latter kind of solitude is potentially dangerous, causing wars and other social upheavals:

> Athens could be London, Rome, New York, Paris, Berlin or any other great city. This was where it had started. In the city. Any city. . . . the new city-hatred (contempt for all things but cleverness) of the slum man for the Jew, the owner for the worker, the worker for his fear of himself, the bourgeois for his own thoughts in the dark, the hatred of them all for the old men washing their hands.

These thoughts are directly related to the novel Paul is trying to write, "Young man of 1933." The chapter ends with the theme of solitude taking on overtones portentous of the coming catastrophe:

> Below in the Hodos Stadiou isolated figures still prowled with the furtive urgency of single men alone in a city after dark. In the far distance,

somewhere in the streets beyond the Place de la Constitution, the horn of a taxi with a short circuit in its ignition system howled like a wolf in the darkness.

When Paul returns to Canada and marries Heather, MacLennan emphasizes the solitude of the lovers in a way that reminds one of a line from Kahlil Gibran: "Let there be spaces between your togetherness." A good example of this is when Paul spends an hour talking with some French-Canadian fishermen, and Heather feels temporarily bereft. The description of the gulls and gannets at Percé Rock parallels that of the sharks and barracuda earlier:

> The gulls must be diving like mad down the line of the cliffs. She remembered them as she had seen them yesterday wheeling out over the water about the rock; beautiful, aloof, cruelly competent, and farther out were the gannets with wingspread wider than a swan's and rusty eyes. When the gannets dipped their wings they plunged to the water like bombs.

Again there is a symbolic suggestion of the destructive course of the undirected passions and a hint of the impending war.

Brooding about his book "Young man of 1933" and the as-yet-unrealized subject of his next novel—the changing shape of Canadian society—Paul contrasts the state of affairs in Canada with that in Europe: " 'The same brand of patriotism is never likely to exist all over Canada. Each race so violently disapproves of the tribal gods of the other. I can't see how any single Canadian politician can ever imitate Hitler—at least, not over the whole country.' " Rabid nationalism of the Hitleresque variety finds its Canadian counterpart in Paul's half brother Marius, who claims he is not a fascist, but is obsessed by thoughts of "a pure race, a pure language," and seems to Paul to be binding himself in a strait-jacket.

Opposed to the failure of self-knowledge leading to disaster is the sense of wonder and ability to grow which Captain Yardley retains until his death—an event which leaves his daughter Janet "prostrate with grief, not knowing that grief is always for the self." Now Janet feels things falling away from her, "leaving her solitary in the way of life to which she had bound herself." Hers is the loneliness of those who have not learned to come to terms with their solitude. This failure of self-knowledge manifests itself objectively in her opposition to the love of Paul and Heather. The same is true of Janet's sole remaining prop, Huntly McQueen, who attempts to separate Paul from Heather by shunting him off to an obscure teaching job in British Columbia.

The conflict between the older and younger generations is integrated with the wider theme by the suggestion that the generation of Janet Methuen and Huntly McQueen and Sir Rupert Irons is responsible for permitting the rise of Hitler, and hence for the coming war. "Had there ever been a time in human history like the present, when the older generation was blind to nearly every vital issue for which their children were prepared to fight and die?" Another anticipation of *The Watch That Ends The Night.* When Janet fakes a heart-attack upon learning that

Heather is married to Paul, the old bridge-playing doctor who attends her and gives equivocal answers to Heather's questions also seems to represent the older generation and its failures. When Paul confronts the doctor, demanding the truth about Janet's health, it is as though the younger generation is confronting the older generation with its mistakes which have led up to Munich. And when Paul confronts Janet with the news that he is going to enlist, it's as though he is emphasizing the need for the generations to stand together in this time of crisis: " 'I don't want to do it. Everything that's in me cries out against the waste of the only talent I've ever had. But I've got to go. And when I'm gone, I'd like to know that you and Heather are together.' " The impending war emits sparks which are jumping the gap between the two different kinds of solitude. But Paul's kind of solitude is also protecting and touching and greeting Janet's.

The concluding chapter departs from the private lives of the novel's human characters to emphasize the coming together of the nation's energies to meet the wartime crisis. The portrayal of the autumnal face of the Canadian landscape reminds us that the country both human and natural is the real hero of this novel. The theme of solitude—what MacLennan previously described as "race memories lonely in great spaces"—is also evident, along with its counterpart, the theme of self-awareness:

> Then, even as the two race-legends woke again remembering ancient enmities, there woke within them also the felt knowledge that together they had fought and survived one great war they had never made and that now they had entered another . . . And almost grudgingly, out of the instinct to do what was necessary, the country took the first irrevocable steps towards becoming herself, knowing against her will that she was not unique but like all the others, alone with history, with science, with the future.

Canada in relation to the European countries is like Paul and Heather in relation to the older generation: neither has made this war, but both recognize the importance of seeing it through. And like Paul and Heather, Canada is approaching self-knowledge and the self-sufficiency that comes from an acceptance of the ultimate solitude.

### Robert D. Chambers    (essay date Winter 1979-80)

SOURCE: "Hugh MacLennan and Religion: *The Precipice* Revisited," in *Journal of Canadian Studies/Revue d'études canadiennes,* Vol. 14, No. 4, Winter, 1979-80, pp. 46-53.

[*In the essay below, Chambers discusses* The Precipice *as an examination of "developments in modern North American consciousness."*]

A few years ago, in the course of a review [in *University of Toronto Quarterly* (Summer 1971)] of critical opinion about Hugh MacLennan's novels, I summarized—perhaps cavalierly—the general response to *The Precipice* (1948): "a disaster on every count." That judgment was directed at the novel's techniques, particularly MacLennan's tendency to deploy character and incident in such a didactic way as to undermine the book's fictional impact. In that respect, I do not recant: *The Precipice* has flaws of procedure which appeared in MacLennan's fiction as early as *Barometer Rising* (1941) but which retreated somewhat in its magnificent successor, *Two Solitudes* (1945). In reacting negatively to the fictional techniques of *The Precipice,* many critics—including myself—have tended to overlook the book's intellectual value, allowing impatience with its contrived characters and situations to distract from its ambitious and, I now think, significant theme. Hence this belated revisit.

It can be argued that MacLennan's novels are primarily linked by the theme of opposition between historical forces which untidily, though dynamically, overlap in modern Canadian society. That theme has interesting variations: embryonic Canadianism versus an outdated colonialism (*Barometer Rising*); the French-English conflict in Quebec (*Two Solitudes*), revisited by MacLennan himself two decades later (*Return of the Sphinx*); the residual nightmare of Calvinism imposing itself upon a fresh dawn of Humanism (*Each Man's Son*); the tensions created in human relationships by a dramatic juxtaposition of the 1930s and the 1950s (*The Watch That Ends The Night*). It would not be difficult to fit *The Precipice* into this way of seeing MacLennan's novels: it, too, deals with opposition, between Canadian values and American goals, here symbolically joined in the marriage of Lucy Cameron and Stephen Lassiter. The success of that marriage remains a possibility on the last page, even in the final words, of the novel. *The Precipice* is thus a book which develops essentially through a slow process of revelation. In effect, MacLennan looks at the traditional—and stereotyped—differences between Canada and the United States, and then looks beyond them towards a perceived similarity arising from their shared experience of religion. That complex, and clearly ambitious, theme serves to set *The Precipice* slightly apart from his other novels; it takes us, moreover, to the heart of MacLennan's intellectual—indeed human—concerns.

The intellectual background to *The Precipice* is established in an introductory prose passage to the novel:

> Gaze up at the Empire State and R. C. A. Building, watch the Skymaster circle into LaGuardia with its bellyful of executives, see the shop girls staring at rubies and pearls reposing like a mogul's concubines in the window of Van Cleef and Arpels, the roar of the fight crowd in the Garden, look at the festoons of toilet paper descending upon the hero who makes his Roman progress up the avenue, see the greatest flash of them all shoot through cloud-rings into the stratosphere.

The nature of MacLennan's imagery here is important: we are meant to think of New York City as the focus of all life; the airplanes bringing back the executives from the farthest reaches of capitalist enterprise; the goal of wealth caught in the image of the poor shop girls cut off by windows (which give visual access but also physically restrain) from jewels of inestimable value; the roar of the boxing crowd at the Garden, together with the popular hero seen as "Roman" conqueror—indications of secular violence and the glory of sheer power; finally, the "greatest flash of them all," the A-bomb drop on Hiroshima which, to thoughtful people, confirmed the appalling posibility of a scientific daemon dethroning the traditional God of compassion and love. Greed, sex, and violence are here raised to the nth degree and combined into a kind of horrified vision of a world without any redeeming impulse (confirmed in this parade of epithets: "Empire," "Skymaster," "bellyful," "mogul's concubines," "Roman progress" and so on). With this backdrop of images, MacLennan gives us the vital link with the past:

> How near are you then to the end of the journey which the puritans began more than three hundred years ago when they lost hope in themselves and decided to bet their lives on the things they could do rather than on the men they were?

Here is the import of MacLennan's historiographical view: between the 1640s, when the Puritans fled religious persecution to that New World designed in their imaginations for free men's wordship, and the 1940s, when modern North Americans have abandoned the God of their fathers and erected instead the same false idols which finally brought down the Roman Empire—MacLennan sees a basic transfer from divine to secular, from inner values to outward things, from a reverence and awe at the mystery of life to an acquiescent worldliness in part fostered by science's stunning domination of nature.

MacLennan's approach, suffice it to say, is hardly novel: the process of rendering unto Caesar has bothered philosophers and prophets for a very long time. What is important is his choice to apply this perception to the whole of North American experience, seeing that stretch of history (despite regional and national differences) as unified by a single factor—the inevitable having to, and yet not knowing how to, cope with the legacy from its puritan past. Although MacLennan applies this notion to the history of North America during the past three hundred years, it also has a direct and personal relevance. At least two of his most interesting characters—Daniel Ainslie in ***Each Man's Son*** (probably based on MacLennan's father) and George Stewart in ***The Watch That Ends The Night*** (a partial portrait of MacLennan himself)—need to come to terms with a background in which puritan values of a negative and inhibiting kind have been at work.

In ***Each Man's Son,*** MacLennan refers to this problem as "an ancient curse" and repeats the phrase at several later points in the novel. It is a theme which causes MacLennan some difficulty, since the dramatization of something so abstract as a "curse" must of necessity remain nebulous, as in this conversation between Daniel Ainslie and Dougald MacKenzie:

> " . . . There's something cold about those New England Loyalists. Something—I don't know myself what it is."
>
> "I do, Dan." MacKenzie smiled. "They don't see ghosts. And after all, can you name any type in history more ridiculous than a Scotch Presbyterian? If you can't laugh at him, you'll be tempted to murder him."

Ainslie bridled. "What do you call yourself?"

> "A Scotch Presbyterian." MacKenzie was still laughing, but he checked himself. "Our people were poets once, before the damned Lowlanders got to us with their religion. The old Celts knew as well as Christ did that only the sinner can become the saint because only the sinner can understand the need and the allness of love. Then the Lowlanders with their Calvinism made us ashamed of living. The way it's made you ashamed."

Here, the reader is asked to accept some kind of direct relationship between the historical spread of Calvinism in Scotland and the mental anguish of a modern-day medical doctor in Cape Breton. MacLennan strives to establish each of his characters by reference to that background. It becomes, for Daniel Ainslie, the central fact in his process of understanding himself:

> A shaking rage began to mount within him. There is no God, he kept repeating to himself. God is nothing but an invention of mad theologians who have told generations of men that He is the all-seeing Ancient of Days who at the same time damns men and loves them. The theologians, not Jesus, have tried to convince us that God, out of His infinite loving-kindness and tender mercy, out of His all-wise justice, has decided that nearly all human beings are worthless and must be scourged in the hope that a few of them, through a lifetime of punishment, might become worth saving.

Notice that MacLennan describes persuasively the theological perversion of the Christian word into a dogma which promotes a sense of human worthlessness. As a piece of writing, the passage ironically reveals the twisted logic of the Doctrine of the Elect; it does not, however, convince us that it is happening as a particular mental rhythm in the consciousness of Daniel Ainslie. MacLennan's tendency is to let the theme overwhelm the character who is supposed to be experiencing it:

> Now he had something specific to be angry about, and Ainslie let his rage build upon itself. Underneath all his troubles, he told himself, lay this ancient curse. He thought desperately of Margaret and desperately of himself, and he knew that it was his fear of the curse which had hobbled his spirit. The fear of the curse had led directly to a fear of love itself. They were criminals, the men who had invented the curse and inflicted it upon him, but they were all dead. There was no one to strike down in payment for generations of cramped and ruined lives. The criminals slept well, and their names were sanctified.

It is surely significant that this passage drifts away from Ainslie towards an historical perspective on the devastating impact of Calvinism.

MacLennan took a long stride towards solving this technical problem with the decision to write ***The Watch That Ends The Night*** as a first-person narrative. The creation of George Stewart, and the ability to fuse his voice with the kinds of intellectual concepts which MacLennan wished to dramatize, led to passages such as the following:

The terror is simply this. God, whom we have been taught to regard as a loving Father, appears indifferent. God, whom we have been taught to regard as all-just, is manifestly unconcerned with justice as men understand the meaning of that word. Why should Catherine have to suffer like this? Why should a scoundrel have health and she none?

You may think I make too much of this. I don't think I do, because these considerations lie very deep in all of us, even in atheists.

All of us are children at heart. What gives the child the desire to grow and acquit himself well is his hope of winning his parents' love. Without this hope, why struggle? Why care?

But the child becomes middle-aged, and who then can fulfill the father's role? Reason can't do it for long. Ability and success are makeshifts. A man may install his wife or children in the role of his god, as the sanction for his existence and his reason for being. A woman, more naturally integrated into the scheme of nature than modern man seems to be, may find no difficulty at all. But a man, apparently, needs a god. So in the Thirties we tried to make gods out of political systems, and worship and serve them.

But the trouble is that none of these substitutes abides. The time comes when the wife dies, and then what is there? The time comes when children go away. The time comes when the state is seen for what it is—an organization of jobholders.

Then, though we may deny it, comes the Great Fear. For if a man cannot believe that he serves more than himself, if he cannot believe there is meaning in the human struggle, what are his chances of emotional survival? We may assert that as flies to wanton boys, so are we to the gods who kill us for their sport. But we can't live long believing this.

Human dignity forbids it.

Here, the articulation of basic human needs, and the relationship of those needs to the long traditions of religion and theology, are filtered with impressive success through the individual psychology of George Stewart. And this technical feat accounts for the impressive and mature impact of *The Watch That Ends The Night.* But it is in the earlier book, *The Precipice,* despite its technical flaws, that MacLennan worked out most fully his approach to religion.

Seek first the father. This is MacLennan's replacement, given the findings of modern psychology, of the older formula—"Seek first the Father." Part I of *The Precipice* is a particularly interesting set of variations on this theme, which is related to three characters with quite diverse backgrounds.

Lucy Cameron is the middle daughter of a rigid Calvinist father—John Knox Cameron—whose obsession with outward respectability has stifled his human impulses. Brought up by two aunts, both Biblical literalists, John

**In *The Precipice,* MacLennan looks at the traditional—and stereotyped—differences between Canada and the United States, and then looks beyond them towards a perceived similarity arising from their shared experience of religion.**

**—*Robert D. Chambers***

Knox Cameron had early learned to trade off genuine friendship for cold respect, and had so successfully instilled that twisted sense of values into his domestic life that his three daughters had grown up desperately sheltered in the backwater of Grenville (a small Ontario town fictionally located in the Trenton-Belleville area). MacLennan catches the essence of Cameron domesticity in small, but memorable, moments: Lucy's wanting so much to please her father, because he had arranged a winter sleigh-ride, that she allows her ears to freeze rather than spoil his "happiness." The eldest sister, Jane Cameron, has become a sad carbon copy of her father; Lucy, by way of contrast, is given the possibility of growth through MacLennan's subtle handling of flower images. From the book's outset, Lucy is constantly associated with her flower garden, always with interesting symbolical touches:

> "If you wanted to grow a new flower [she says to her neighbour Bruce Fraser] or a new vegetable—I mean something entirely different, a mutation—where would you choose to live?"

> "I don't know! Does it make any difference?"

> "It makes quite a lot. Burbank went to California. I don't think I ever realized what a hard country this is until I seriously tried to grow flowers in it."

Later, when Lucy has made an emotional commitment to Stephen Lassiter—an act of identification which deeply violates her family tradition of emotional suppression—MacLennan appropriately places her in her "ruined" autumn garden, thus symbolically showing her in transition from adolescent to mature love.

If John Knox Cameron fits into the tradition of emotional denial often associated with the negative side of Calvinism, the father of Stephen Lassiter relates to its "positive" side—a tremendous release of energy into the world of affairs. It is, in fact, a concept which gives the novel its name, as Lucy Cameron's unfrocked uncle, Matt McCunn, explains:

> "You know what I told Lassiter? I told him that when New York burns, efficiency will be the cause of it. He didn't get the point so I tried again. I asked him if he believed in progress, so of course he said he did. So I told him the most progressive animals the world had ever seen had been the Gaderene swine. That didn't do any good, either. He'd never heard of the Gaderene swine."

This image of a blind and unheeding force, being swept towards its destruction because it is possessed of an evil which it has no power to resist, is MacLennan's notion of the residual effect of Calvinist theology on the consciousness of modern Americans, one which he returns to powerfully at the novel's close:

> "The other night after we heard about the atomic bomb I began to think of the Americans the way you do—like a great mass of people and not as individuals. I saw them moving in a vast swarm over a plain. They had gone faster and farther than any people had ever gone before. Each day for years they had measured out the distance they'd advanced. They were trained to believe there was nothing any of them had to do but keep on traveling in the same way. And then suddenly they were brought up short at the edge of a precipice which hadn't been marked on the map. There they were with all their vehicles and equipment, jostling and piling up on the front rank. For of course the ones behind didn't know the precipice was there and couldn't understand why the ones in front had stopped advancing. The pressure from behind kept increasing on the front ranks and they were all shouting at each other so loudly nobody could hear anything."

MacLennan carefully establishes Stephen Lassiter's background in relation to this pattern of images: Stephen is one who doesn't know that the precipice is there. His early experience, rather like Lucy's, had its sheltered component—a dimension of genteel life arising from his mother's "old New England stock." But we know, of course, to seek first the father, who, in Stephen's case, came of hardworking and grimly-religious folk in rural Missouri. Stephen thus grew up feeling "a little guilty because his boyhood had not been hard enough," and was thus early imbued with a need to equal his father's toughness. (Much is made, in the early chapters of the book, of Stephen's delight to dominate on the tennis courts; it is what his father would have described as giving a man an "edge.") Unlike Lucy, whose basic fear was that she might give way to her emotions, Stephen fears that he will never become as hard and ruthless as his father. And so Stephen, largely unaware of this basic driving force, rushes along the road of success towards the precipice.

In utter contrast is the case of Carl Bratian, a name which—depending on how one pronounces it—may suggest a kind of aggressiveness linked in MacLennan's mind with the stereotype of the "brash" American. Carl Bratian's father was a saint, a kindly and innocent immigrant who, measured by the terms of American success, amounted to nothing. Carl was not to emulate that pattern, but rather to inch his way from the slums to the very peak of achievement in the get-rich-quick world of advertising: "He was living in an age of anxiety, but the anxiety did not touch him." Bratian's ride to the top has become possible through imagination, hard work, and cynicism, but especially by putting himself—so unlike his father—absolutely first.

I like to think of Part I of *The Precipice*—in which MacLennan intertwines the lives of Lucy, Stephen, and Carl—as a fictional study of the earliest phase of religious experience. A personality is shaped, a process is begun—but the consciousness of these things remains hidden: there is as yet no intellectual awareness of *why* one has become *what* one has become. Lucy's need of new life (she is a lovely bud that urges to blossom), Stephen's youthful masculine assertiveness (it is, after all, his decisiveness which initially attracts Lucy to him), Carl's instinctive sense that the top can be reached—all these MacLennan cleverly roots in their respective pasts. It may be that they also come trailing clouds of glory from their Heavenly Father, but MacLennan's eye is on the worldly fathers who have placed an imprint on them that they are both too young to understand and too helpless to resist.

In Part II of *The Precipice,* MacLennan uses Bruce Fraser as a vehicle for exploring the next important stage of religious experience—sexuality.

The narrative background of Part II is intriguing. Bruce Fraser (also from Lucy's home town of Grenville) plunges into the heady atmosphere of New York City, which MacLennan has already established in utterly materialistic terms:

> . . . for even God seemed irrelevant in this region of random lights encased in thousands of cells of invisible ferroconcrete between the earth and the sky.

Bruce is on a brief wartime leave, and MacLennan imaginatively responds to the opportunity of placing a quiet and inexperienced Ontario lad against the glaring lights of the great metropolis. What will be played out is Bruce's first act of sexual consummation, an experience which leads to some real ambivalence on Bruce's part:

> Less than half an hour later, watched in the dim light by still another of Marcia's New England ancestors, Bruce Fraser came to the end of a trail he had been following since adolescence; and in the conflicting tensions of the moment he was not sure whether he had crossed the frontier of a deeper mystery or merely entered the first of a long series of empty rooms.

These "conflicting tensions," symbolically representing the angelic sublimation and earthbound animality of women, are dramatized respectively in the persons of Lucy Cameron Lassiter and Marcia Stapleton (Stephen Lassiter's twice-divorced sister). MacLennan thus has Bruce Fraser act out an age-old mythical pattern, for he at once satisfies with Marcia his carnal yearning (despite Marcia's puritan ancestor looking down upon him from a gilt picture frame) but also remains spiritually in love with Lucy, who throughout this sequence is beautifully etherealized despite her roles as wife and mother:

> Among all the individual girls to be seen in the crowds of New York, a stranger passing Lucy on Fifth Avenue would hardly notice her at all. Yet the question as to whether she was beautiful or not made no difference today whatever. For him she had a quality far greater than any objective beauty of figure or features. She had the power of making him think of beautiful things, of lifting his imagination.

MacLennan is thus complicating his notion of religion by

adding the dichotomous element of sexuality—"a deeper mystery" or "a long series of empty rooms"? In this process, Marcia Stapleton is associated with the bright hard surface of modern life while Lucy emerges as "from an earlier segment of time," a clear indication that a purer sense of religious impulse lingers on, almost unnoticed, in the modern Babylon.

In Part III of *The Precipice,* MacLennan continues this developing drama of religious experience with a further stage—death. Here, appropriately, we are given a World War II background, with a series of short transitional sections which MacLennan handles with great skill. Bruce Fraser comes to contemplate the fact of human mortality when he is shot down over German territory. He escapes, but injuries push him to the sidelines of the war, and from that detached perspective he develops the habit of reflecting on his own experience:

> Battles of all kinds are a colossal sensuality. You can't think, except to do your job almost mechanically, but the moment the height of the danger passes you feel with an incredible intensity. That's when you discover your buried self. You get so close to the buried *you*—that part of us that the mind of Ontario tries to censor out of existence—that sometimes you become afraid of yourself. [In an endnote, Chambers adds: "In an article entitled **'Help Thou Mine Unbelief,'** collected in *Cross-Country,* MacLennan indicates that the source of Bruce Fraser's wartime reflections was his own conversation with a young airman during the war."]

Back home in Grenville, Jane Cameron has turned Lucy's flower garden into a "victory" vegetable garden, thus satisfying her urge for useful things by destroying beautiful things. To the south of the 49th parallel, Marcia Stapleton—now a nurse—has also encountered her buried self, this time in the form of the helpless and hopeless war victims who pass through her hands on their way to death. But the shock of that experience brings also a form of recognition: " 'Sometimes people have to find themselves in hell before they can see there's a way out of it'." And there is a sense of death, too, in the marriage of Lucy and Stephen. They move from New York City back to Princeton, where Stephen went to university, but his inability to go back home again, his foolish desire to recapture his youth, suggest a potential dilemma in both his career and his marriage.

In *Religion and the Rise of Capitalism,* R.H. Tawney conveys the immense tension of puritanism by comparing the puritan mentality to a coiled spring—it must either explode outward and scatter destruction in its wake, or rebound intensely inward upon itself, and so destroy itself. MacLennan strives, in Parts IV and V of *The Precipice,* to apply this image to the characters of his novel. In Part IV, the shadow of the Faust legend hovers about the narrative: Lucy, conscious that Stephen has fallen into the Mephistophelian grip of Carl Bratian, struggles to break through to the core of his problem. His symptoms are clear enough to her—an unhappiness so intense that even his taking of a young mistress cannot sufficiently explain his lonely and puzzled middle-age existence. In a series of

memorable passages, including a particularly interesting sequence in which Marcia Stapleton moves beyond psychoanalysis to conversion within the Roman Catholic faith, MacLennan ties Stephen firmly to the puritan tradition:

> . . . the long line of lean men threading west out of New England, no poetry in them, no music, but the necessity of believing that westward things were better, over every mountain a valley richer than the last, carrying wherever they went the qualities that made them unlike any other people who had ever lived, the great refusal to be satisfied, to rest and sit down, the unwillingness to be content which was as hard as a rock in the soul. First the Lord had hounded them, and when the Lord grew remote, they had hounded themselves.

The tension mounts for Lucy and Stephen (there is a fine sequence in which MacLennan associates Stephen with the loneliness of all-night bars and jazz joints in New York City). The breaking point comes when Lucy, conscious that Stephen is all but lost to her, uses the pretext of war's ending to return to Canada with her two children.

Part V of *The Precipice*—the final section of the book—covers the archetypal ground of spiritual regeneration. Here, MacLennan completes the pattern developed in the earlier parts of the novel by concentrating within Stephen Lassiter's character the dilemma posed by the puritan tradition: at what point does North American immersion in the material world threaten the onset of spiritual death? At what point does one perceive the existence of the precipice?

This dilemma is imaginatively heightened by an interesting pattern of images. In Part V, MacLennan frequently places his characters—especially Bruce, Lucy, and Stephen—as watchful and brooding insomniacs, symbolically caught between the darkness and the light. The image is also worked into the fabric of the conflict between what MacLennan calls "the materialistic fallacy" and the awareness of "the buried self ":

> At one time during the war Myron Harper had worked for three weeks without once leaving the wing of the plant where his office was. He had worked in a room without windows, air conditioned, with indirect lighting and sound-proofed walls. Suppose the electricity had failed and the clocks had stopped and he had emerged from that office at a certain moment of dawn or sunset—could he have known whether it was going to be night or day?

Appropriately, it is the horror of Hiroshima—that "greatest flash of them all"—which leads to the novel's final resolution. Looked at in one way, Hiroshima was the fateful indication that modern technology had carried modern man over the precipice: thus Lucy's decision to seek out Stephen again and offer her love as he wrestles with the daemon of modern puritanism. With her help, Stephen is finally able to cope with—

> . . . . the voice which for more than a century had been driving the bold and generous ones out

of a thousand Grenvilles all over North America, driving them away to cities which had lost all touch with the towns, driving some into a transplanted Asiatic luxury they could never understand, launching others into a rootless technology in which they could never do enough to appease the unknown monster on the other side of the door, leaving them unforgiven and longing helplessly for the purity and safety of a childhood to which none of them could ever return.

It has not, I think, been generally noticed by students of MacLennan's work how closely the themes of *The Precipice* anticipate those of *The Watch That Ends The Night*. The triangular relationship of Lucy, Stephen, and Bruce—the redeeming love of a wife for her spiritually lost husband, the withdrawal of a rival love so that the wife and husband may find each other again—clearly foreshadows the roles of Catherine, George, and Jerome in the later novel. In *The Precipice,* MacLennan traces the developments in modern North American consciousness (both Canadian and American) as it meets the challenges of the "fallen" world—notably the need to cope with sexuality and human death and, above all, the relentless assault of the puritan tradition. As such, MacLennan's treatment of the external world—the "rootless technology" that threatens to obliterate the deeper need for spiritual wholeness—is an early fictional expression of values that were to emerge more forcefully in Canadian writing, especially in the books of George Grant.

*The Precipice* thus poses some fundamental questions about the quality of modern life in North America. As I have indicated earlier, MacLennan's handling of these themes is hampered on the technical side by a mode of presentation which had not as yet found a way, without self-conscious didacticism, to dramatize ideas that he felt deeply about. The technical gift which finally solved that problem was George Stewart [in *The Watch That Ends The Night*]:

> The clouds crossed the sky, country rains washed the gardens, moons shone on the lake and the hillsides, cicadas sang in the August grass, boys and girls fell in love. In the early October of that year, in the cathedral hush of a Quebec Indian summer with the lake drawing into its mirror the fire of the maples, it came to me that to be able to love the mystery surrounding us is the final and only sanction of human existence. What else is left but that, in the end? All our lives we had wanted to belong to something larger than ourselves. We belonged consciously to nothing now except to the pattern of our lives and fates. To God, possibly. I am chary of using that muchmisused word, but I say honestly that at least I was conscious of His power. Whatever the spirit might be I did not know, but I knew it was there. Life was a gift; I knew that now. And so, much more consciously, did she.

We can only speculate how much George Stewart owes intellectually to those earlier night watchers of *The Precipice.*

**Stephen Bonnycastle**   (essay date Winter 1979-80)

SOURCE: "The Power of *The Watch that Ends the Night,*" in *Journal of Canadian Studies/Revue d'études canadiennes,* Vol. 14, No. 4, Winter, 1979-80, pp. 76-89.

[*In the following essay, Bonnycastle provides a structural analysis of MacLennan's novel, focusing on the protagonist's consciousness and MacLennan's recurring passages of lyrical description.*]

*The Watch that Ends the Night* has had a notable success in Canada and abroad. There seems to be agreement that it is MacLennan's best novel, and a fairly general consensus that it is one of the most important novels in the body of Canadian literature. Many critics have written about it, either in short reviews published soon after the novel appeared in 1959, or in longer articles which have often formed parts of books on MacLennan. The topics most often discussed are the nature and credibility of the three major characters, and the quality of the ending, which is reflective and didactic. What has not been explained satisfactorily is the enormous power which this novel has had for many readers. Many people have an affection and a reverence for *The Watch that Ends the Night* which gives it, for them at least, a unique status in Canadian literature. After referring to some of the existing literature on the novel, I would like to suggest why this is so. Among professional readers—critics and professors—the novel has fared much worse. There are interesting reasons for this, as well.

Jerome Martell, orphan, soldier, doctor, socialist, refugee from Auschwitz, and finally spiritual healer, has attracted a variety of comment. Almost everyone finds his escape down the river in the wilds of New Brunswick a wonderful, compelling piece of writing; but several commentators do not find him a satisfactory character. F.W. Watt says [in "Letters in Canada, 1959—Fiction," *University of Toronto Quarterly* (1960)] that Martell's saintliness turns to smugness at the end of the novel, and Robert Cockburn says [in *The Novels of Hugh MacLennan,* 1969] that he becomes a "soulful superman," and that it is impossible to believe in him. Many people have remarked on the resemblance between Martell's life and that of Norman Bethune. [In "Jerome Martell and Norman Bethune," in *Hugh MacLennan,* edited by Paul Goetsch, 1973] Keiichi Hirano, a Japanese critic, is morally outraged that MacLennan should have started with a fascinating and admirable prototype, and watered him down into a conventional hero of sentimental romance. He maintains that having Martell return to Canada as a religious visionary (rather than stay in China as a committed communist) is a cheap way of making him an easily assimilable hero, who will not shock or disappoint narrow-minded Canadian readers. There is no hard evidence that MacLennan used Bethune as the basis for Martell, but the argument is interesting nevertheless. If Martell is a vulgar cliché, then the novel is seriously flawed.

Catherine, the wife of Martell and then of George Stewart, has received bad press on the whole. Watt says that she is complacent, rather than strong and mature; Cockburn says that she is merely a torchbearer for Stewart's philosophy, and that she never comes alive as a character in her own right. Robertson Davies reports [in "MacLennan's Rising Sun," in *Hugh MacLennan*] that she seems to him a "spiritual vampire, living on the vital force of others," although he acknowledges that she may seem a legitimate heroine to some readers.

George Stewart, the narrator of the book, arouses the most interesting variety of opinions. Cockburn says that it is impossible to identify with Stewart, and so the novel loses a great deal of interest. Woodcock maintains [in his *Hugh MacLennan*, 1969] that although Stewart is the most authentic of the three main characters, he is not entirely convincing, because he embodies a lot of material taken from MacLennan's own life. Watt says that Stewart is mawkish and genteel, and Warren Tallman says [in "An After-Glance at MacLennan," *Canadian Literature* (Summer 1959)] that he is boring and garrulous, and implies that he is an utter failure as a character. Robertson Davies, however, likes Stewart, and feels that he has intelligence, insight, worth, and strength, even though he appears weak.

Since the conclusion of *The Watch that Ends the Night* consists largely of Stewart's reflections on, and responses to, the forces of life and death around him, critics who dislike the character find the ending intolerable. Tallman says that Stewart is remarkable for "handing out crashing complacencies on almost every imaginable major consideration in life," and Lucas [in his *Hugh MacLennan*, 1970], Woodcock, and Buitenhuis [in his *Hugh MacLennan*, 1969] agree that the ending is too like a sermon to be acceptable in a novel. Cockburn says that Catherine's illness inspires mere orotundity on George's part, and Edmund Wilson feels [in his *O Canada*, 1965] that the novel ends in a "spasm of revelation that will leave you disappointed because unconvinced." On the other hand, Walter O'Hearn [in "A Sense of Wonder Preserved and Shared," in *Hugh MacLennan*, edited by Goetsch] finds MacLennan's sense of wonder, and his ability to share it, inspiring; and Davies says that *The Watch that Ends the Night* is "plainly the work of a man of extensive and subtle intellect." [In an endnote, Bonnycastle states: "My general feeling about *The Watch that Ends the Night* is similar to Walter O'Hearn's, and in some ways this essay is an expansion of his remarks on the novel."]

I have assembled this selection from the published opinion about *The Watch that Ends the Night* to show to what extent the criticism of novels consists of direct value-judgments passed on individual characters. This is natural, and it has its parallel in the teaching of literature. It is a common pedagogic method to ask a group of students what they think of Hamlet as a person, as though he were someone they had just met. Most people can respond to this kind of question more easily than to questions about literary structures and techniques. Gossip about characters can be as interesting as gossip about mutual acquaintances.

What is dissatisfying about value-judgments is their extreme relativity. When Cockburn says that none of the main characters in the novel is believable, this may indicate more about the critic than the novel. It may be that he finds few characters in literature believable, and that he would say the same thing about the Jesus of the Gospels, or about Macbeth. Value-judgments are useful to start debate, but if you do not move beyond them the conversation is usually unprofitable. Similarly, when Warren Tallman says that he does not like Stewart's ruminations, it is helpful to learn later in the review that he is unsympathetic to reflective literature in general. "Surely MacLennan," he says, "must be aware that what the artist has to tell us is likely to be valuable by virtue of his capacity to represent experience rather than by virtue of any parallel capacity to comment upon it." But *how likely* is it that Tallman's generalization is true? Proust, Pasternak, and Thomas Mann are all exceptions to it. MacLennan would presumably be glad to find himself in this company. Once again, the value judgment, and the accompanying theory, show the limitations of the critical approach, and they contribute little to our understanding of the novel.

In the face of this problem, what approach can we adopt? I would like to suggest two ways in which one might hope to avoid the relativity of value-judgments. The first is to recognize that people read in different ways; because of differences in their backgrounds, their assumptions about life, and their experience of literature, the processes which occur when different people read vary enormously. Any particular reading of a novel is the result of the interaction between a way of reading (or strategy of interpretation) and the text to which it is applied. If the ways of reading can be classified, then it should be possible to predict what will happen when a particular strategy of interpretation encounters a particular text. The body of criticism related to *The Watch that Ends the Night* is instructive, because three main strategies have been employed on it.

The first way of reading is also the most common, and in some ways it is the most exciting. It is usually practised unconsciously, and people who read this way sometimes assume that it is the only 'natural' way to read. In this process, the reader pretends that what is recounted in the book is something which is actually happening, before his very eyes. This kind of reading is like hallucinating, and the hallucination which the reader forms must be credible—that is, it must agree with what the particular reader has come to accept as credible. The most involving adolescent reading is often done this way; you actually think that Cyrano or Hamlet or Jane Eyre is a person who is living through the experiences which those books describe. You may or may not identify with that person, but you take him or her as real. This way of reading leads to disappointment verging on outrage when a character does something improbable, because that breaks the illusion and shatters the hallucination. There have been innumerable readers of *The Watch that Ends the Night* who have found Jerome inspiring, Catherine a woman to love, and George Stewart a trustworthy friend, reflective and wise. The bitterest critics can be those who hope for this kind of experience, and then are disappointed; once the hallucination is shattered, there seems to be nothing left which is worth having. You need to shift to a different strategy of interpretation to be interested in the novel after it has lost its power as realism.

A second strategy of interpretation which has been applied to *The Watch that Ends the Night* is to treat it as an allegory for the development of Canada or the Canadian consciousness. Alec Lucas, for instance, wonders if Catherine is an allegorical figure representing Canada; she is courageous in becoming mature, although she has physical problems stemming from her childhood, and she is inclined to withdraw from the public. George Stewart, on the other hand, is Canadian liberalism; he reaffirms his faith in Canada after his trip to Russia. In a similar vein, Dorothy Farmiloe says [in "Hugh MacLennan and the Canadian Myth," in *Hugh MacLennan,* edited by Goetsch] that in the account of Martell escaping down the river in his canoe, "Hugh MacLennan is giving us his version not only of the Canadian character, but of the Canadian myth." "When Jerome accepts urban living—in his case, Montreal—and final involvement on the world front, his destiny and Canada's have moved into the present." This strategy of interpretation is more complex than the first, because to employ it the reader must have two stories in his mind, the one he is reading, and another, more fundamental story, which is reflected in the novel and which constitutes its most powerful meaning. If you are looking for the parallels as you read, you will be less sensitive to credibility in the novel, not simply because you are not taking it as reality, but also because for you the real story is the hidden one which you are decoding from the novel. This method of reading has an ancient and venerable basis in the interpretation of the Bible. The parable of the Good Samaritan was interpreted by the Fathers of the Church as follows:

> The fate of the traveler represents the fall of the human race into the hands of demons; he is Adam, who has left Jerusalem, the heavenly city, for Jericho, the world. The Samaritan is Christ, the inn is the Church, the promise to return is the Second Coming. [Frank Kermode, *The Genesis of Secrecy,* 1979]

Here the paradigm story is that of the eschatological fate of man; because that story had such tremendous importance, it seemed proper to project it into the seemingly simple account of one man helping another. To a Canadian critic, the development of Canada could have a similar paradigmatic significance.

A third strategy for interpreting *The Watch that Ends the Night* is to search it for archetypal patterns. George Woodcock, for instance, sees Martell as an embodiment of the heroic wanderer, Catherine as the *princesse lointaine* of mediaeval romance, and Stewart as "the dolorous knight, full of chivalrous notions which seem out of place except in the romances." The method here is for the critic to propose a typology of characters which he has assembled from somewhere else, and then project it onto the characters in the story. When it is well done, this method is very stimulating; it suggests new relationships between the characters, and it highlights aspects of the story which before were shadowy. This is the kind of criticism expertly practised by Northrop Frye and by some psychoanalytic critics. It is similar to the second strategy, in that it sees the story to be interpreted as a reflection of something more fundamental; only instead of this being a second narrative, which develops in time, it is a cast of characters of

a relatively fixed nature. Searching for a cast which will be universally valid, and would cast light on the fundamental structures of narrative, is a subject of some current, and highly interesting, research.

These three ways of reading novels (as reality, as allegories of another story, or as embodiments of a typology of characters) produce different experiences in the people who employ them, and critics often want to demonstrate that their way of reading is the correct one, sometimes by saying that the author clearly intended his novel to be read in a particular way. It is possible, for instance, to show that Hugh MacLennan has been interested in the development of Canada, from which one might deduce that *The Watch that Ends the Night* should be read as an account of that development. Or one might show that certain archetypal patterns which appear in the novel also appear in the rest of his fiction, which might lead one to believe that the novel should be read in this way. The urge to police the reading of the novel, and impose a single interpretation, is perfectly understandable, especially in professional teachers, who are asked to perform a large number of policeman-like activities, such as correcting spelling, setting deadlines, and marking exams. Also, when you discover a new and interesting approach to a novel, it is easy to believe that it must be the only right way of dealing with it. But there is no need for uniformity in readings; the only acceptable rule for a community discussing the novel is that a reading must 'cover' as much of the novel as possible—that it not clash with or leave out major elements in the novel. So there will be some readings which are inadequate, because they do not cover the story; but there may be many which are acceptable and illuminating.

The first way I have proposed for avoiding a welter of value-judgments is to distinguish between different strategies of interpretation, and to find the correlation between each strategy and the reading which it produces. But if we end up with a welter of readings, what progress has been made? The progress is, in fact, quite satisfying: now there is something to discuss, and a way of discussing it. Instead of assertion and counterassertion about the merit of *The Watch that Ends the Night,* or about the credibility of its leading characters, it is possible to describe methods of reading and predict the results. And instead of presenting value-judgments as though they were facts, this analysis shows how the evaluation of one text can vary enormously, depending on the use to which it is put. This realization can have a powerful liberating effect, and improve dialogue enormously.

The second way of going beyond assertion and value-judgment is in some ways more ambitious, because it aims to describe the book *before* the various strategies of interpretation go to work on it. The method is to search for structures within the text which *any* interpretation will have to take account of—elements or patterns which are so important that they must be reflected in any reading which is to be considered acceptable. [In *Critique et vérité,* 1966] Roland Barthes speaks of this as working out the "empty" structure of the text, which will be relatively free of ideology, and can serve as the basis for discussion. When the basic structure of the work is established, then the various kinds of interpreters can go to work on it: Christian critics can breathe Christian interpretations into it, Marxists can make it a Marxist allegory, archetypal critics can map the empty structure onto their categories, and those searching for the Canadian identity can adapt the patterns to their purposes.

A number of critics have made perceptive comments about the basic structures in *The Watch That Ends the Night,* and most of these have to do with the relations between the main characters. Paul Goetsch points out [in "Too Long to the Courtly Muses," *Canadian Literature* (August 1961)] that Catherine, Martell, and Stewart all come to possess the same wisdom about life, and that George's early life is remarkably similar, in terms of spiritual insecurity, to those hours when Jerome is drifting down the river in his little canoe. Both Goetsch and Lucas have remarked on the opposition between Martell and Stewart: Stewart is secular and controlled, while Martell is wilder, more irrational, and more religious in nature. Goetsch proposes the interesting comparison between this pair of characters and the two main characters in Thomas Mann's *Dr. Faustus*: Serenus Zeitblom, the rational and civilized narrator, and Adrian Leverkühn, the demonic composer. Warren Tallman points out that Martell's experiences are subordinated to the narration of George Stewart. [In "The Relation of Structure to Theme in *The Watch that Ends the Night*," in *Hugh MacLennan,* edited by Goetsch] Barry Thorne remarks on the similarities of the two rebellions of Catherine and Stewart, and says that Martell acts as a scapegoat for Stewart. An interesting characteristic of critics who discuss structural properties of novels is that they seem less inclined to make direct value-judgments about the novel or its characters. They seem more concerned with understanding the novel than with evaluating it, although the quality of their attention to it suggests what value they place upon it.

My aim in this essay is to describe two structural features of *The Watch that Ends the Night,* and to establish their significance. Their existence is perfectly clear, and you do not need any sophisticated critical technique to see them; but they have been given little attention in the critical literature on the novel, and they allow us to account for the power of the novel in a new and satisfying way. The first feature of the novel is that it is essentially about the consciousness of George Stewart and the progress he makes in coming to terms with the world. [In an endnote, Bonnycastle adds: "That George Stewart's consciousness is the centre of the novel has been pointed out by Peter Buitenhuis in his book on MacLennan. But he praises the novel, as does George Woodcock, for a number of small achievements—good renderings of Canadian scenes, for instance—as though the novel were a series of *tableaux*. My argument is that the real quality of the novel lies not in its diversity, but in its unity, in what Stewart comes to realize in his consciousness."] The second feature is the recurrence throughout the book of passages of lyrical beauty describing either natural scenes or urban landscapes. These passages have a mystical quality, and they strongly suggest a pantheist view of the world—that is, that the world, and man within it, are essentially unified, at harmony and at peace. When Stewart fully realizes the signifi-

cance of these passages, the novel is at an end; and the ending is satisfying because it ties together these two fundamental structures in the book. Furthermore, these two features of the book seem to be part of its 'empty' structure: any reading of the novel has to take account of them, and many existing readings are inadequate because they do not. Finally, these features of the book suggest comparisons between it and other works of literature which are generally considered to be among the finest works by western authors (I am thinking of Wordsworth, Proust, and Spinoza), so my structural analysis of the novel leads to an implied evaluation of it which is much higher—indeed, of an entirely different order—than that which has generally been accorded it.

George Stewart is the narrator of *The Watch that Ends the Night.* We see events through his eyes, and we see what he can see and what he can know about. We have direct access to his mind much of the time. In contrast we never have a direct view of Martell or of Catherine, except when Stewart reports things which they have said. So it is natural that both these characters, who have enormous influence on Stewart, appear not as realistic, down-to-earth characters, but rather as larger-than-life, mythic figures, who are in some ways sketchily presented. These characters *are* larger than life to Stewart, and that is the way he presents them. The same phenomenon occurs in *Hamlet.* The hero gives the audience a lot of information about his father, who appears to have been an ideal king. But this is an image which *Hamlet* is creating in his own mind, and we do not need to take it as the truth. Like the ghost of *Hamlet's* father, Martell and Catherine may, to some readers, be compelling characters; but to criticize the novel because they are not convincing *in themselves* misses the mark. They need to be convincing to Stewart, and play a legitimate role in his development. [In an endnote, Bonnycastle adds: "George Woodcock judges the novel to be MacLennan's 'most brilliant failure in the proper function of a novelist, which is to present human relationships that in their own terms are convincing.' "]

Stewart has been criticized as a boring, dull man, and in one case this evaluation is accompanied by high praise for the incident in which Martell, as a child, escapes from the lumber camp in his canoe. The excellence of MacLennan's portrayal of this incident obscures, I feel, the real merit of *The Watch that Ends the Night.* Martell is a driven man, a man of action, relatively impervious to the world around him. Stewart is a reflective man, who is slow to act, because he takes things into his mind, thinks about them, and is affected by them. Some readers would prefer to read about Martell, others about Stewart; the contrast between the two is stark. Consider the nature of the episode on the river. Everyone in it is driven by necessity. Jerome's mother is driven by her sexual hunger to take to her bed a man for whom she has no feeling. That man is driven by her withering scorn to murder her. Jerome is driven by fear for his life to escape from the man. His canoe is swept down the river by the current. The exhilaration and the exhaustion produced by this kind of violent narrative is exciting, but it is a minor element in *The Watch that Ends the Night,* and not its central concern.

The central concern of the book is George Stewart's progress from spiritual infancy and dependence to maturity and a full relation to the world. This progress occurs partly because Stewart makes an effort to understand what is going on around him. One critic feels that this subject involves too much reflection for it to be the focus of a successful novel, but of course some of the most admired works in literature have this kind of development as their main theme. They show how a character can achieve a stable relationship with the world around him; on this basis he is able to take meaningful action and engage in reliable commitments. *Hamlet, Great Expectations, Middlemarch, A la recherche du temps perdu, The Magic Mountain,* and *Zen and the Art of Motorcycle Maintenance* all share this theme. Like **The Watch that Ends the Night,** they contain episodes of violence, and characters who are driven by forces which they do not understand and are powerless to resist. But their main concern lies elsewhere.

---

**The central concern of *The Watch that Ends the Night* is George Stewart's progress from spiritual infancy and dependence to maturity and a full relation to the world.**

**—Stephen Bonnycastle**

---

What progress does Stewart make in his psychological life? Following his childhood and the brief period when he discovers his love for Catherine, there seem to be five stages in his development. (i) While he is putting himself through university, and teaching in the boarding school, he has no confidence that he can do anything which is really productive. He is not in control of his life, he does not like what he is doing, and he thinks of himself as a parasite. (ii) He feels ignorant of the world until he makes his trip to Russia; he then realizes that he is not more ignorant than many people who have been confidently theorizing about communism. He returns to Canada determined to find out something about his own country, and he is less at the mercy of his inferiority complex. (iii) When he achieves a reputation in broadcasting, largely because he has been able to predict the events leading to the war, he begins to feel that he may have some economic security in the world. This reduces the crippling anxiety from which he has suffered. (iv) When he marries Catherine he establishes a home and feels a rewarding love both for his wife and her child; he has wanted this for a long time. (v) In the final section of the book Stewart learns how to live with the knowledge that his wife will die soon; he not only accepts this, but he achieves, with her, a tranquillity and a joy in life in spite of her fate.

What is the nature of the wisdom which George Stewart acquires in the course of the novel, and tries to pass on to the reader? This is a difficult question, and it is in some ways presumptuous to condense an answer from the novel, which is itself economically written; but for the purposes of my argument a summary will be useful. Stewart's wisdom is the result of his search for security in the world. He needs more than economic or emotional security, although they too are necessary. He is searching for an absolute security, which nothing can call into question. This is related to the second structural feature of the novel which I mentioned earlier, the recurrence throughout the novel of passages in which, for a moment or an hour, Stewart contemplates nature in a vision of tranquillity. Here are two examples:

> The November silence was so profound that the crack of a breaking stick carried a mile. . . . The lake itself was shallow as most Laurentian lakes are with the spruce coming down to the water and parts of the shoreline were cemeteries of gray stumps bleached smooth and eroded to fantastic shapes and the water was the colour of amber. Strangest of all was the effect of the sun that afternoon; less than a month from the winter solstice, the sun was so low that its light streamed almost parallel between the sky and the earth.

> April had turned into May and the world was bright and clear: cool air and warm sun, a powder of buds on the hardwoods, fields skunk-cabbage green against the heavy viridian of spruce and fir, the muscles and bones of the land visible as an athlete's under the light dust of its first verdure. . . . When I got out of the car there was a sough in the firs and I wished I had been here at dawn when the birds sang. Little waves danced on the lake, ferns had sprung in fiddleheads, trilliums were white stars under the trees and the daffodils Catherine had planted five years ago swayed in the breeze like golden dancers.

This kind of vision can also occur in the city:

> It was exciting on the campus with the sound of creaking feet as the students hurried past clamping their ears; there was the recurrent excitement an extremely cold night gives you even in Canada. The evening star was yellow in a tiny green corona caught in a net of bare branches over the little observatory and behind us, high over the university and the hospitals that hug the city's crest, the hospitals I had come to know so well, Mount Royal slumped like a stationary whale in an arctic sea, the huge lighted cross in its brow blazing eastward toward the Catholic end of the city.

It is extremely difficult to give the proper kind of attention to passages such as these when they appear in the midst of criticism instead of where they belong in the novel. One is not prepared for them, and the eye slides over them too easily. What they have in common is acute perception of the natural world (similar to that in Coleridge's best poetry) which produces a sense of underlying beauty so strong that it takes away any fear or insecurity which the individual might have. The beauty does not resolve Stewart's nagging doubts and anxieties, but for the moment it makes him forget them.

The recurrence of passages like these forms an important

feature of the novel because they induce a state of mind which is very similar to that which Martell creates in Stewart at the end of the novel. After his experiences in concentration camps, and in the east, Martell has acquired a preternatural stillness, an inner calm, which is imperturbable; Stewart calls it "an absolute serenity, a total sureness." Unlike Stewart, Martell is not dependent on nature for this—on an accidental flash of brilliant beauty; he can develop it in himself, and cause it to flow from himself to others. This ability gives him an otherness, almost as though he were a piece of inanimate nature. He tells Stewart:

> Think of your life as lived. Think of yourself as annihilated. Then death won't matter. Then fear will go away because there will be nothing left to fear. I learned that in Auschwitz from a Jewish rabbi who also knew some medicine. I learned how to do it, too.

This is said just after Catherine's operation, when Stewart is in a state of exhaustion and despair. His loathing of her helpless suffering, which amounts to a disgust at life itself, is transformed in his newly awakened spirit:

> Something new and strange had begun to happen to me. Light seemed to be shining inside of me when I stepped outside and walked down the driveway toward the city. The weather had turned still warmer, and on the precipices of the mountain tiny rivulets of icy water were making musical sounds. . . . The chaos which had been dark within me for days had disappeared and my soul was like a landscape with water when the fog goes and the moon comes out and all the promontories are clear and still.

This is another of the moments of heightened consciousness which Stewart has experienced at intervals throughout the novel. But in the face of his wife's illness and impending death, he uses what Martell has told him to answer questions which have been preoccupying him since the beginning of the novel—what is the purpose of life, and what is the larger entity to which one can submit one's life, and be enlarged? When he was a child, God served this purpose; then during the depression he turned to social action and the possibilities of communism, until he became disillusioned with that. Following his marriage to Catherine, she seems to have become his reason for existence, and now that he must face her death and the possibility of life without her, he moves beyond his reliance on her.

The final stage in Stewart's progress, which is evoked in the epilogue to the novel, is like a return to the first stage, because much of what he says is couched in religious language. These four pages seem to me the finest in the novel, because MacLennan reaches a solution to the problem, and a conclusion to his narrative, with a tenderness, a delicacy, and an honesty of which the finest writer would be proud. Through Catherine's joy in the passing days of her remaining life, Stewart sees that existence is worth the pain which it involves, and there is a joy in what he says which we associate with all that is best in the religious vision of life. But his assertions are much more guarded than is common in religious discourse, and they are the more exhilarating for that:

> In the early October of that year, in the cathedral hush of a Quebec Indian summer with the lake drawing into its mirror the fire of the maples, it came to me that to be able to love the mystery surrounding us is the final and only sanction of human existence.

In this conclusion MacLennan achieves a gentle and timeless pantheism, a vision of the earth and all that it contains, in which the members of a living community praise their common life.

My principal argument is that MacLennan's rendering of this vision is by far the most exciting thing, intellectual or emotional, about *The Watch that Ends the Night,* and that in itself this is an outstanding achievement. To place it in an appropriate context, I would like to compare it with the achievement of three other authors. (I am not suggesting that there is direct influence at work between any of these authors; there may be, but this is not relevant to what I would like to establish.) What Wordsworth, Proust, Spinoza, and MacLennan have in common is (i) a pantheist vision of the world, in which each individual can attain a harmony with his surroundings, and in which evil is ultimately impotent; (ii) each author is concerned with how an individual can achieve a new beginning in his life, which will allow an inner calm to take charge over, and put into perspective, the mass of petty, silly, or annoying elements of life; and (iii) each author has had this effect on countless readers, who respond with gratitude and admiration. These similarities raise the question, does Hugh MacLennan deserve a place in our intellectual economy—in the order of Canadian literature—comparable to that occupied by Wordsworth in English literature, Proust in French literature, or (the greatest claim of all) that of Spinoza in the history of philosophy? This question demands much more thorough and expert investigation than I am capable of giving it here, but pointing out some of the striking parallels between these four authors will indicate some of the areas which such an investigation might cover.

William Wordsworth's enormous reputation and influence, both now and in his own time, have been due to his ability to define a new relationship between man and nature, one opposed to the city-centred high culture of the 18th century and its aristocratic foundation. Like George Stewart, Wordsworth was deeply involved in the outstanding ideological conflict of his generation, the French Revolution; and just as Stewart was disappointed by the failure of the Russian Revolution to improve life in Soviet Russia, so Wordsworth was dismayed to watch the infant French republic degenerate during the Reign of Terror and finally become an oppressive empire under Napoleon. Wordsworth abjured politics entirely; he was thrust into a deep depression; he was plagued by doubts about his own worth and about his role in society. He was rescued from this unhappy state, almost literally, by nature: he returned to his native Lake District, and he found in its rugged grandeur an image of perfection which was capable of raising his spirit to exaltation. Wordsworth's finest work, *The Prelude,* is about this twenty-year process of growth, crisis, and recovery. At the end of the poem he casts himself in the role of a teacher, passing on his vision to others:

> Prophets of Nature, we to them will
>     speak
> A lasting inspiration, sanctified
> By reason, blest by faith: what we have
>     loved,
> Others will love, and we will teach them
>     how. . . .

His success in this role is the foundation of his greatness.

Wordsworth's pantheism is clearly and beautifully expressed in one of his shorter poems, the "Lines composed a few miles above Tintern Abbey." He returns to the Wye Valley near the Welsh border, and he is suddenly struck by the effect which the *memory* of this place has had on him during the previous five years: it has given him hours of peace in the midst of noisy cities; it has given him an inner calm which has made him more considerate to others; and finally, it has provided him with moments of vision which have settled his doubts about himself and the world:

>                               I have felt
> A presence that disturbs me with the joy
> Of elevated thoughts; a sense sublime
> Of something far more deeply interfused,
> Whose dwelling is the light of setting
>     suns,
> And the round ocean and the living air,
> And the blue sky, and in the mind of
>     man:
> A motion and a spirit, that impels
> All thinking things, all objects of all
>     thought,
> And rolls through all things.

This is his classic statement of pantheism. The experience produces in him

>                     that blessed mood,
> In which the burthen of the mystery,
> In which the heavy and the weary weight
> Of all this unintelligible world,
> Is lightened. . . .

The burden "of all this unintelligible world" is precisely what George Stewart feels at several points in the course of *The Watch that Ends the Night,* and, like Wordsworth, he is rescued from it by rediscovering his harmony with the natural world. The vision of that harmony is the main thing which both Wordsworth and MacLennan pass on to their readers.

Marcel Proust's great novel, *A la recherche du temps perdu,* is similar to Wordsworth's *Prelude* in many ways. Both works are autobiographical; both authors experience a vision at the end of the story which gives them the impetus to sit down and dedicate themselves to writing the work; and both authors are rescued by their vision from despondency and an aimless life. Both authors are deeply concerned with memory, and it could be plausibly argued that each provides the most compelling account of the functioning of memory in his own language. Both are acute observers of human psychology. Wordsworth is impressed with how "the mind of man" works in a marriage with nature; Proust is concerned with how the imagination takes an experience, like a seed, and develops a vast structure in the memory from the tiny germ. Even a name, such as that of a noble family or of a city, can provide an image which is then invested with love and connected to a host of ramifications, so that when you actually meet the individual, or visit the city, you are acutely disappointed because the reality does not correspond with what you had imagined.

The melancholy produced by this experience, repeated over and over again, provides the background against which Marcel's visions occur. They are rare (perhaps half a dozen in the three thousand pages of the novel), and they are extremely compelling. The first occurs when Marcel, as an adult, tastes a piece of cake dunked in tea. This recalls, completely and passionately and involuntarily, his childhood days when his aunt used to give him *Petites Madeleines* saturated with tea. The final vision occurs when several experiences similar to this one occur in rapid succession, transporting him integrally into his past, and he recovers a part of his childhood which he thought he had lost for ever. Marcel had concluded that the universal rule of life is that the passing of time reduces our experiences and disappoints our expectations; but these moments of involuntary memory, by eliminating time, give him access to eternity. As a result, they are similar to Wordsworth's moments of vision, and to George Stewart's flashes of tranquillity and acceptance in *The Watch that Ends the Night.* Here is Marcel's response to his first experience of the vision:

> No sooner had the warm liquid, and the crumbs with it, touched my palate than a shudder ran through my whole body, and I stopped, intent upon the extraordinary changes that were taking place. An exquisite pleasure had invaded my senses, but individual, detached, with no suggestion of its origin. And at once the vicissitudes of life had become indifferent to me, its disasters innocuous, its brevity illusory. . . . I had ceased now to feel mediocre, accidental, mortal.

The repeated qualities of these experiences are that they provide enough joy to make death seem unimportant; they supply him with the only true pleasure, "fécond et véritable"; they give him access to his true self; and they show him what art ideally should be—the reproduction in a book or a painting of what you hear, listening in silence to an inner reality.

Proust differs from Wordsworth and MacLennan in locating his vision within himself; the visions of Wordsworth and MacLennan involve nature more directly. The essential similarity is that for all three there are moments of consciousness which provide the anchor for the rest of life, and which you try to hang on to, but which seem inevitably transient; all three progress because they develop a way of grasping these moments and drawing on their power. Wordsworth and Proust achieve this by creating works of art; for MacLennan it is achieved in the final pages of his novel, through reflection on experience. Proust says, in a passage to which all three authors would subscribe:

> The greatness of true art . . . is to discover, to repossess, and to make known the reality which we put far away from our daily lives, and which recedes in the distance as our conventional knowledge of the world becomes denser and more impermeable. We substitute conventional knowledge for this reality, and we are in grave danger of dying without having known it—this reality which is in fact our [true] life.

For all three authors, it is possible for a man to live his whole life and fail to realize what is most valuable in it. The calling of these authors is to awaken readers from such a slumber. It is easy to understand why there is a religious feeling in the works of all three.

The acknowledged greatness of Proust's novel, or of Wordsworth's poetry, does not prove the greatness of *The Watch that Ends the Night,* although these works provide relevant standards of comparison. MacLennan is seeking to embody a vision as fundamental, as difficult, and (I think) as compelling as that of Proust or Wordsworth; it demands the same dedication, the same sincerity, the same struggle with language, and the same tenacious contemplation of fundamental values. Those critics who think of MacLennan as the author of a sentimental romance have missed the central element of *The Watch that Ends the Night.*

It is unusual to compare a novelist to a philosopher, but Spinoza is a useful figure to bring into this argument, because he is the pantheist philosopher *par excellence,* and he illustrates what Wordsworth, Proust, and MacLennan have in common. I am not concerned with the deductive method which Spinoza uses, or with the absolute rightness of his position, although these are of great interest, and not just to professional philosophers. I am concerned with his fundamental aim, with the magnitude of his achievement, and with the profound respect and admiration which he has inspired.

Spinoza's most direct statement of his purpose as a philosopher occurs at the beginning of the fragment entitled 'On the Improvement of the Understanding':

> After experience had taught me that all the usual surroundings of social life are vain and futile; seeing that none of the objects of my fears contained in themselves anything either good or bad, except in so far as the mind is affected by them, I finally resolved to inquire whether there might be some real good having the power to communicate itself, which would affect the mind singly, to the exclusion of all else; *whether, in fact, there might be anything of which the attainment would enable me to enjoy continuous, supreme, and unending happiness.* [my italics]

Wordsworth and Proust would have agreed that the rewards of ordinary life seem small in comparison with the "continuous, supreme, and unending happiness" to which they have found access. [In his *Spinoza,* 1962] Stuart Hampshire has said of Spinoza that "no other modern philosopher of equal stature has made such exalted claims for philosophy, or had such a clear vision of the scope and range of philosophical thinking. He conceived it to be the function of the philosopher to render the universe as a whole intelligible, and to explain man's purpose within the universe." This is the ethical purpose of Wordsworth, Proust, and MacLennan, as well.

Spinoza held that the universe is unitary—that all the manifestations of nature are part of one immense unity. (He was a pantheist because he maintained that this totality of the universe is equivalent to God, and therefore God has no existence outside the universe, but instead exists throughout the universe.) Since the universe operates in a rational manner, it is possible for man to understand it; and because man is part of the universe, it is possible for man to understand himself. Most men, most of the time, are compelled to act by forces which they do not understand, as is George Stewart when he reaches the depths of despair during Catherine's operation at the end of the book. It is possible, however, to rise above destructive feelings and enter into the harmony of the universe. This is the encompassing happiness which Spinoza thought could be achieved by right thinking. The mystical fervour which this happiness inspires is similar to the feeling evoked at the end of *The Watch that Ends the Night.*

Many of the major romantic writers in Germany, France, and England found Spinoza's philosophy, and his attitude of mind, extremely attractive. They shared his belief in a universe at harmony with itself, and they agreed with him that the mind can apprehend that harmony. After a century of being reviled as an atheist, Spinoza was adopted as a model by some of the most eminent authors of the romantic period. Goethe, for instance, reported, "I am reading with Frau von Stein the *Ethic* of Spinoza. I feel myself very close to him, although his spirit is much deeper and purer than my own." [In an endote, Bonnycastle notes: "All these admiring reactions to Spinoza are taken from Thomas McFarland's outstanding book, *Coleridge and the Pantheist Tradition,* 1969."] Coleridge, describing his own intellectual progress, said, "Strong feeling and an active intellect conjoined, lead almost necessarily, in the first stage of philosophising, to Spinosism." Matthew Arnold, describing the unusually broad appeal of Spinoza to non-philosophers, wrote:

> A philosopher's real power over mankind resides not in his metaphysical formulas, but in the spirit and tendencies which have led him to adopt these formulas. . . . Propositions about substance pass by mankind at large like the idle wind . . . [but] Spinoza . . . has inspired in many powerful minds an interest and an admiration such as no other philosopher has inspired since Plato.

In 1877 Ernest Renan, author of the celebrated *Vie de Jésus,* said that all enlightened people realized that the man who had the strongest sense of the divine in the 17th century was Baruch Spinoza. The atheist had been canonized.

I have dwelt on the response to Spinoza because the response of many readers to MacLennan is similar, and the reasons for it are probably the same. In Spinoza we find a man who avoided publicity and recognition, who had none of the advantages of wealth or position, and who lived as an outsider after being rejected by the Jewish community in his native Holland. In spite of this he achieved, by his own efforts, by the discipline of his life, a transcendent peace and happiness which seemed to raise him above the smaller concerns of ordinary life. He might have claimed that his tranquility came to him because he was unusual in some way. He might have claimed that he had been favoured by God. But his whole philosophy says the opposite, because according to it no one has special status in the world. His happiness came through identifying with the whole world, through raising his vision above short-term goals. It was therefore available not just to himself, or to a small group of initiates, but to everyone. Near the end of *The Watch that Ends the Night,* George Stewart sees "an old Jewish man, poorly dressed but serene, staring up at the clouds sailing over the mountain." His serenity is like that of Spinoza. The rabbi in Auschwitz, who teaches Jerome that ultimately there is nothing to fear in life, is communicating Spinoza's strength of mind. Similarly, the wisdom which this book offers has all the attraction which Spinoza exerted on the 19th century. People love it for the same reasons.

If in *The Watch that Ends the Night* MacLennan succeeded in embodying a vision which bears comparison with those of Wordsworth, Proust, and Spinoza, it is worth noting that in one respect his vision is even more encompassing than theirs. Those of Wordsworth, Proust, and Spinoza entail a sacrifice which is generally agreed to be enormous. That sacrifice takes the form of a withdrawal from the world, an almost hermitlike retreat from the centers of power and activity, accompanied in each case by some scorn of the normal pleasures and activities of man. Spinoza begins his famous declaration which I quoted earlier by saying that "all the usual surroundings of social life are vain and futile"; Wordsworth speaks of "all the dreary intercourse/Of daily life"; and for Proust, real happiness cannot be found in either friendship or love. These attitudes are accompanied by physical withdrawal: Spinoza to his solitude in the Hague, Wordsworth to his small circle of friends in the north of England, and Proust to his cork-lined study in Paris. It is accurate to say that, in each of these cases, the affirmation of their vision depends on their rejection of normal human life; this gives the vision much of its intensity, and, to some extent, its poignancy.

In contrast to these authors, MacLennan's vision is self-sustaining, and it does not depend on shutting out a large segment of the world. Its thrust is in the opposite direction, towards including and affirming the value of the world. At the beginning of the novel, during the depression of the thirties, George Stewart is driven to hatred of his parents, of society, of himself, and he denies the existence of God. As the novel progresses, all of these positions are reversed, until at the end he realizes that even a life threatened with imminent death can be filled with joy. This is one way in which the novel affirms the value of life. A second way is through the deep sympathy which MacLennan seems to feel for all his characters. Even minor characters, such as the headmaster of the school where Stewart taught, are redeemed and presented positively, rather than ridiculed and excluded from the novel's range of sympathy. *The Watch that Ends the Night* conveys an almost Shakespearean love of the world, because

all the minor characters are treated in this way. Finally, MacLennan repeats several times in the book that 'millions of people' are aware of what the novel is expressing at its most intense moments. This is said of the emptiness of life during the depression, of Jerome's excruciating experience in the concentration camp, of the despair of Stewart when Catherine is near death, and of his joy at achieving a momentary understanding of the universe. So MacLennan is not acting as a prophet, dispensing a new vision of the world and man's place in it to a group of initiates; he is attempting something more difficult—to articulate and make available a common wisdom which we all possess, hidden though it may be.

I am suggesting, then, that *The Watch that Ends the Night* possesses a visionary power similar to that of Wordsworth, Proust, and Spinoza, and that its vision does not depend, as do theirs, on rejecting a large part of the world. Such an achievement should have been universally acclaimed, and yet the novel has been criticised much more than it has been praised in print. I would like to conclude by offering an explanation for this apparent injustice.

I think it is difficult for critics to respond appropriately to a novel with the visionary intensity of *The Watch that Ends the Night.* Literary critics are usually widely read, and normally they have already established a deep affection for, and a profound relation to, a number of books. These attachments help to create the critic's own vision of life, and a new novel which tries to alter that vision is not likely to succeed—unless the critic has already been influenced by a similar writer, such as Wordsworth or Proust, in this case. So a didactic novel, unless it makes a conquest of an experienced reader, is likely to be rejected. In reviewing the novel, such a reader will examine both the style and the content looking for reasons why he was not moved, and (as with Wordsworth and Proust) several may be found. But this reader will be unable to account for the effect the novel has had on others who, for one reason or another, are more open to it.

The second reason that *The Watch that Ends the Night* has been less than well received is that it is very short in relation to the vision it presents. A long and sometimes difficult novel like that of Proust, or like *Dr. Faustus* by Thomas Mann, makes such demands on the reader (both in concentration and in time) that by the end he is more likely to be won over to its philosophy than he is by a short novel. This is a matter of the psychology of reading, and there is an analogy in human relations. A person whom you meet casually may not make you want to engage in a long-term friendship; but if you are forced to spend several weeks with that person, often you find that you become deeply attached to him, that he enriches your life, and that he changes your outlook in ways which you would never have predicted. I think a similar process can occur when certain novels, conceived on a large scale, are read. A short novel which is easy to read, like *The Watch that Ends the Night,* cannot gain its adherents in this way. It seems inappropriate to criticize a novel because it provides such a vision in a concentrated form, but this may help to explain why its real merit has not been widely recognized. I realize that readers who do not respond to *The*

*Watch that Ends the Night* are not likely to become more receptive by listening to arguments about it. Time, and the reading public, will establish the place of the novel. What I hope to have offered is a valid explanation why many people feel an intense, and unusually personal, gratitude toward Hugh MacLennan. It is due to his power to enlarge the lives of his readers, in ways which are almost beyond comprehension. Beginning to understand how this takes place can only make the acquisition more profound, and the debt more lasting.

### Elspeth Cameron   (essay date Autumn 1981)

SOURCE: "Not With a Whimper: Hugh MacLennan's *Voices in Time,*" in *World Literature Written in English,* Vol. 20, No. 2, Autumn, 1981, pp. 279-92.

[*In the following excerpt, Cameron examines MacLennan's thematic treatment of technology and power.*]

"If I have been prophetic in my earlier novels, it would not be pleasant if I were prophetic in this one," Hugh MacLennan commented [to Burt Heward in "Masterful Novel Protests Humanity's Ignorance," *Citizen Ottawa,* (27 September 1980)] of his latest novel, *Voices in Time.* Certainly if a mighty nuclear blast such as the one he describes taking place near the end of this century were indeed to shake the world down to a few hundred inhabitants, it would be horrendous. This explosion in *Voices in Time* is MacLennan's concept of what could conceivably be mankind's darkest hour.

Although he boldly sets his events in the years after this holocaust, his intention had nothing to do with futuristic science fiction: "I tried to avoid any semblance of science fiction," he wrote [in a letter to Cameron dated May 29, 1980]. "Critics will call the book 'Orwellian,' but I don't think it owes anything to Orwell, who died before the H-bomb" [letter from MacLennan to Cameron dated March 1, 1980]. If his interest did not lie in playing the clever game of imagining details of life in the aftermath, what is the point of this novel's setting?

MacLennan has been fascinated with explosions since December 1916. That month, his father was invalided home from service as a doctor in Shorncliff Hospital, a Canadian medical unit near Dover, to the great relief of his wife, his daughter, and his nine-year-old son. Less than an hour after the small family walked into the house MacLennan's mother had rented for the occasion, it blew up. MacLennan's father, thinking he smelled gas, had gone down into the basement to investigate—with a lighted match. Although no one was seriously injured in the explosion that resulted, the house was for some months uninhabitable. This event was nothing short of traumatic for the young MacLennan, who would later retell it in his first short story, **"An Orange From Portugal."** To him, it had meant that the coherent world of his childhood, about which he had already become anxious during his father's year overseas, was shattered. The family Christmas he had hoped to spend in their new house became instead a makeshift affair in a Halifax hotel.

This dramatic homecoming prepared the way for the ef-

fect of the famous Halifax explosion, which took place almost exactly one year later on 6 December 1917. Whatever general sense of a stable universe the boy had managed to reassemble during the year was annihilated in the largest man-made explosion before the atom bomb. MacLennan's own painstaking description of this event, first in an essay called, significantly, **"Concussion,"** and then in his first published novel, **Barometer Rising** (1941), testifies to the major impact it had on him. But only partly. For the ten-year-old boy who wandered the streets of Halifax saw more than he ever recorded later of the bloody anguish of the explosion's victims. Earlier enthralled by the glamour of war heroics, he was then sickened. It was not difficult to guess at his state of mind two months later, one bitter February day in 1918, when sleighs hastily carried him off with his classmates to crouch behind the sheltering hills of the local golf course in anticipation of yet another explosion (which never actually occurred) while an ammunition ship lay ablaze in the Halifax New Ocean Terminal. In none of these three instances—his father's catastrophe in 1916, the Halifax blast of 1917, or the threatened explosion of 1918—was destruction planned. Human carelessness and irresponsibility had been the catalyst each time.

To a greater or lesser degree, MacLennan's personal struggle to understand the causes and consequences of these fearsome situations lies behind much of his fiction and a good number of his essays as well. Why, he has always wondered, has man been driven to invent and improve on things that explode and destroy? And, once man has invented the means to bigger and better blasts, why has he treated them with such carelessness and irresponsibility? Beyond that, what conceivable relationship could such "creations" bear to other creations such as works of art or, more generally, the very genesis of the known world itself?

In **Barometer Rising** MacLennan explored the implications of the Halifax explosion in human terms. Indeed, the explosion itself lies at the novel's heart, forming the pivot on which the plot line turns. He wrote the novel backwards, deciding first on the resolution that would follow his "catastrophe" (which he thought of in both senses—colloquially as trauma, and technically as the Greek term for the high point of his drama) and then working towards the story that would feed into it. The result, he was and still is convinced, was too superficial. Although from a technical standpoint the limitations of this method of writing forcefully shaped his material, he always felt that somehow the novel did not reflect the complexities of life. From a philosophical viewpoint, its conclusion seemed lightweight: "Probably what bothered me about the novel was the unavoidable necessity of making the explosion a *deus ex machina.* Also, the deliberate limitations I imposed on myself for the sake of the market" [MacLennan to George Barrett, October 20, 1941]. To use the Halifax explosion as a *deus ex machina* was simply too convenient. Although it effectively blasts the new world free of the old, it too neatly resolves the affairs of his characters: the villain, Colonel Wain, exposed in vice and destroyed; the child, Jean, left free of her adopted parents so that her real parents, recently reunited, might now claim her. This resolution was too deterministic—it suggested a purposeful

God somewhere who had an interest in human life. It did not demonstrate to MacLennan's satisfaction that human choice might play a significant role in human events.

In *Two Solitudes* (1945), MacLennan continued his examination of this theme in a quite different way. Although he did not centre on any one explosion as he had in *Barometer Rising,* he thought of the collective explosions that constituted war as a major issue. His main concern at the time was Canada, but he consciously attempted to find in his specifically Canadian situation an analogy to international events. He struck that analogy in what he called Canada's "state of becoming." He had observed that in Canada, loyalty to the region or group frequently impeded the development of an allegiance to the nation as a whole. Optimistically, he thought that a true pan-Canadianism was about to emerge, and he considered that this trend away from petty allegiances to a wider loyalty had potential as a useful example of behaviour to war-torn Europe. "I see Canada as a bridge," he wrote to a friend as he was about to begin *Two Solitudes,* "a bridge with the ends unjoined. I don't believe there can be a synthesis until the ends are joined. I am trying to go ahead on the assumption that the failure of our people even to understand the necessity of joining the ends of the bridge is responsible not only for our own national schizophrenia [the French-English split], but breakdown as well. In that state of 'becoming' I seem to detect the possibility of a universality for a writer who attempts to write out of the Canadian scene" [MacLennan to Barrett, October 20, 1941]. If Canadians could overcome their group loyalties to "protect and touch, and greet each other," in the words of his epigraph from Rilke, if the two solitudes could manage love, then perhaps the various nationalisms in Europe that had led to war could be transposed into peaceful co-existence. In *Two Solitudes,* by contrasting Huntly McQueen, another power-hungry character like Colonel Wain, who is appropriately fascinated with technological and industrial "progress," with the creative writer Paul Tallard, whose very life represents the mutation of English and French divisiveness into a purposeful unity, MacLennan examined how destructive and constructive tendencies in human life related to each other in a moral framework.

That entire concept can be illustrated in one compact and striking image in the novel. Captain Yardley recalls being deep in contemplation while stranded in the tropics. Over the side of the drifting ship he sees

> the fish gliding through ten fathoms of sunlit water below. Sharks and barracuda moved in their three-dimensional element, self-centred, beautiful, dangerous and completely aimless, coming out from a water-filled cavern hidden beneath the promontory and slipping under the ship's keel, fanning themselves for seconds under the rudder, then circling back into the cavern again . . . The memory of that hour had never left him. Self-centred, beautiful, dangerous and aimless: that was how they had been, and he could never forget it.

The moral implication of the juxtaposition of the predatory sharks and barracuda with the ship's keel and rudder is profound. Man as individual or as nation has the choice:

he can act selfishly, randomly destroying whatever gets in his way, or he can purposefully steer his life on a productive course.

In his third novel, *The Precipice* (1948), MacLennan's approach to the problem lay in two new directions: first, in a comparison of Canada to the United States; second, in the application of Freudian psychology to the issue. Probably drawing on J.B. Brebner's astute observation of the cultural lag between Canada and the United States in *The North American Triangle,* MacLennan speculated, "I think that Canada has been, is, and may be in the future, more fortunate than the United States . . . For it seems that nothing but catastrophe can check the furious progress of Americans into a still more bleak and dangerous desert of technology than they have reached now. The very vastness of the apparatus their genius has created stands over them now like a strange and terrible master. Every man, as Sophocles said years ago, loves what he has made himself. Canadians have as yet fallen in love with no such Frankenstein. And, as a result of this, our future is more clearly in our own hands" ["**On Discovering Who We Are,**" in *Cross Country*]. In his title, *The Precipice,* drawn from the biblical parable of the Gaderene swine who mindlessly rushed in droves over a precipice to their deaths, MacLennan located the external result of the dark side of human ingenuity in the technological "advances" made in America and in the parasitical field of advertising designed to manipulate the public to accept technology's goals as their own. There is a lesson in that tragic nation of sharks and barracuda, he demonstrates. His indictment of the America lifestyle emerges in a brief image, reminiscent of Yardley's speculations in *Two Solitudes,* in which he compares New York to "a giant aquarium teeming with ancient and invisible life: raw, terrible, humorous, brave and infinitely various." Canadians, by virtue of the time lag of forty or fifty years, have the opportunity to take the lesson to heart and direct their nation's fate more purposefully. And from a Freudian point of view, the male need to devise weapons that kill and destroy on a grander and grander scale is a displacement of the sexual drive. As Bruce Fraser confesses about his war experience, "Battles of all kinds are a colossal sensuality . . . the moment the height of the danger passes you feel with an incredible intensity."

Appropriately, the novel ends with the world-rending explosions of Hiroshima and Nagasaki—testaments to fine technological "progress" but also, ironically, to the incredible moral "retardation" of the United States. Facing his nation's irrational drive to destruction forces the novel's protagonist, Stephen Lassiter, to face the same impulses in himself. Pulling back just in time at the edge of the precipice, he can make a new start.

In his next novel, *Each Man's Son* (1951), MacLennan turned the kaleidoscope of his enduring interest in man's pursuit of power to reveal a new emphasis. He picked up the doctor character from *Barometer Rising* and placed him centre stage; he drew back from a consideration of American technology and advertising to look instead at raw physical power in the form of a prizefighter, Archie MacNeil.

As was made amply clear not only in his novel but also in a couple of essays he wrote shortly after he finished *Each Man's Son*—"Power and Love" and "A Layman Looks at Medical Men"—doctors had become symbolic to him in a highly idiosyncratic way. Just as Angus Murray in *Barometer Rising* stands for the healers in war and is sharply opposed to the megalomaniac Colonel Wain, who revels in the power to destroy, Dr. Ainslie represents MacLennan's idea of the highest human example of power used purposefully with love. Whereas Dr. Murray is a minor character, a somewhat ineffectual, rootless man slipping into alcoholism, Dr. Ainslie is presented as a powerful and stable character, central to his community, with wide visions of a further stage to his career which will enlist his talents even more effectively for the benefit of mankind. His conflicts are not those of Dr. Murray, whose debates with Colonel Wain seem to need a resolution from outside himself in the form of the Halifax explosion. Ainslie's conflicts are imagined as internal: he undergoes a crisis of conscience and guilt that his powers have not always been tempered with sufficient love. The resolution of that conflict in Ainslie was seminal in MacLennan's developing analysis of the problems he addressed. Ainslie cannot reason his way to a solution; he feels or intuits it. His resurgence of faith is also linked to the natural world:

> A world without purpose, without meaning, without intelligence; dependent upon nothing, out of nothing, within nothing; moving into an eternity which itself was nothing. With a slow movement, as if coming out of a deep sleep, Ainslie sat up and looked at the sky. With longing for continuance brimming in his blood, he had looked ahead on his days and seen total emptiness. He had reached his core. And there he had stopped. He got to his feet and looked down at the brook. In that moment he made the discovery that he was ready to go on with life.

MacLennan thus demonstrated the importance of the lessons of organic growth and continuity lying all around us in nature. Ainslie's vocation is felt through contact with nature in an experience that might be called "mystic."

In contrast to Dr. Ainslie, the boxer Archie MacNeil applies his powers destructively. Where Ainslie heals, MacNeil pounds and pummels his way to the top and, in turn, is pounded and pummelled into a declining phase of his career. He is punished for his marked neglect of his wife and son by losing them: his wife through his own final explosion of physical violence; his son, with great moral significance, to none other than Dr. Ainslie, who will adopt him.

In *The Watch That Ends the Night,* MacLennan moved his examination of the use and misuse of power onto a much more sophisticated plane. In his earlier fiction he had located the constructive and destructive tendencies in separate characters: the former he portrayed as heroes, the latter as villains. Now he saw that both impulses exist in each individual, and he set about presenting characters who demonstrated this fact.

This dramatic insight was probably the result of his deep consideration of the whole question in an essay entitled "Joseph Haydn and Captain Bligh" that he wrote in 1953 during the early stages of his novel. In this essay, he attempted to resolve the apparent paradox that the same society could spawn both these men: "As Haydn represents the spiritual grandeur of the eighteenth-century imagination, Bligh represents its irresponsibility." In his essay, MacLennan turns from Haydn to consider more recent "geniuses." For a time, he speculates, scientists like Einstein have been the "creative men" of the modern world—until Hiroshima, that is. Seeing the consequences of their inventions, their genius became "beclouded," just as Haydn's might have been had he concerned himself with the dark underside of his own culture. Just as he had done in his essays "Power and Love" and "A Layman Looks at Medical Men," MacLennan turned to medicine as the most recent field of "genius." Not surprisingly, Dr. Albert Schweitzer, who denied his own not inconsiderable talent for music to give his healing services to thousands, stands as an example of "the highest aspirations of our social conscience." Because of this gradual incorporation of social conscience into the lives of all citizens, MacLennan concluded "the twentieth century is better than the eighteenth." And he looked forward to an even better future: "after this age of transition, the shadow of Captain Bligh [will have] been removed from the whole world."

This essay, with its theory of an evolutionary development away from a society split between destroyers like Captain Bligh and creators like Haydn, towards one in which responsibility for the evil in the world is accepted by all men, marks a crucial stage in MacLennan's treatment of power and reflected accurately the means by which he would demonstrate it in his next novel. In *The Watch That Ends the Night,* the central character, George Stewart, is flanked by a man and a woman each of whom possesses to a dramatic degree both creative and destructive powers. Jerome Martell, whose surname means "hammer," is as aggressive and powerful as Archie MacNeil the boxer. He is a warrior whose natural element is the battlefield of the Spanish civil war. Yet, like Dr. Ainslie, he is also capable of tremendous healing powers as a doctor—powers, in fact, that go beyond simple medical skills. Catherine, almost conversely, has undeniable creative strength, not only in her obvious talents as an artist, but also in her fierce love of life itself and the positive energy she draws on to stay alive despite her fatal illness. But in Catherine, too, is the power to destroy, to hold men dependent on her so that she can sap their strength; she is partly the "spiritual vampire," as Robertson Davies once observed [in "MacLennan's Rising Sun," *Saturday Night* (28 March 1959)]. It is the recognition of this duality in the two people most important to him that helps to trigger George's profound and final insight: in him, too, and in Everyman the same forces are at war. As he comments: "There it was, the ancient marriage of good and evil, the goodness of this day and the compulsive evil people must see and know, but the sky dominated in the end. Pale and shining, it told me that our sins can be forgiven."

In an image reminiscent both of Captain Yardley's speculations about the sharks and the ship's rudder in *Two Solitudes,* and of Dr. Ainslie's descent to the "total emptiness" at his "core," George describes his own encounter with the destructive impulses deep inside himself and the inner urge for order and purpose that counters it. When the strain of Catherine's illness is finally too much for him to bear, he thinks, "Could I . . . believe that this struggle had any value in itself?"

> At first I couldn't . . . My subconscious rose . . . the greedy, lustful, infantile subconscious, indiscriminate and uncritical discoverer of truths, half-truths and chimeras which are obscene fusions of foetal truths, this source of hate, love, murder and salvation, of poetry and destruction, the Everything in Everyman, how quickly, if it sways him, can it obliterate the character a man has spent a lifetime creating! Then a man discovers in dismay that what he believed to be his identity is no more than a tiny canoe at the mercy of an ocean. Shark-filled, plankton-filled, refractor of light, terrible and mysterious . . .
>
> . . . And the earth was without form, and void; and darkness was on the face of the deep.
>
> . . . And the spirit of God moved upon the face of the waters. And God said: *let there be light:* and there was light.

Christian ethics had always hovered close to MacLennan's treatment of this theme: now they were explicit. In a letter [dated March 21, 1959] to his friend and editor at Macmillan's, John Gray, he described the experience of writing the novel, which he at first titled "Requiem," as a "revelation." "In absolute humility I felt that the Lord touched me at the end of this novel and I was only thankful I didn't quite break under the final strain," he confessed.

For a man who had come to believe that the great war was within, that to control the destructive impulses and channel energy into creative or at least purposeful outlets was the challenge facing Everyman, the era of the sixties appeared to be an unaccountable moral lapse of civilization. The student revolution, the sexual revolution, the musical revolution—all seemed like the most primitive self-seeking and destructive behaviour. MacLennan soon termed it a "psychic crisis" and set about understanding it as best he could for purposes of his next novel. That novel he would name *Return of the Sphinx,* for it seemed to him that the old Oedipus legend applied to what he saw. Relying heavily on a book called *Sex in History* by G. Rattray Taylor, he considered the psychic crisis to be evidence of a "matrist" era arising in reaction to the "patrist" phase that had culminated in two world wars. As Taylor defined it, a matrist era displayed open rebellion against authority in any form, sought personal comfort and decadence and eschewed discipline in any form. To MacLennan, this seemed to go far in explaining what otherwise must have seemed inexplicable to one who in **"Joseph Haydn and Captain Bligh"** had outlined the steady moral progress of the Western world. Now he seized on Taylor's theory that such progress was cyclic, not linear. Such theories melded well with his own. To tame the primitive drive to violence, man needed self-discipline; he must sacrifice personal gratification for the sake of others. If the whole era were

undergoing an undisciplined phase, explosions and destructive violence were predictable.

MacLennan's depiction of the explosive violence in Quebec appeared to anticipate the October 1970 FLQ crisis, although *Return of the Sphinx* was really based on the political rhetoric and sporadic bombing incidents that had marked the sixties. The October Crisis, however, shocked and frightened MacLennan and provoked him to continue to probe the causes of human destruction. In an article in November commissioned by the Toronto *Telegram,* he reviewed his two "Quebec" novels—*Two Solitudes* and *Return of the Sphinx*—in an attempt to understand the political crisis that had just occurred. With what by now was an ingrained reaction to disruptive violence, he described recent events in Quebec as but one surface manifestation of what he termed "the mid-20th century volcano" ["Quebec Crisis Bares the Agony of Youth," *Telegram* (21 November 1970)]. The notion of a powerful potential explosion lying underneath apparent events just waiting to be triggered would eventually find its way into his next novel.

*Voices in Time,* which was not to appear for another eleven years, was to be his most penetrating analysis of the theme that had intrigued him from his youth. To understand more fully the answers to those enduring questions about the use and abuse of power, he turned to the theories of the New Biologists who at that time were applying evolutionary data to a study of modern man's behaviour.

Reading Robert Ardrey's books *African Genesis* and *The Territorial Imperative* evoked a passionate response from MacLennan. "When Keats first looked into Homer," he wrote off to Ardrey, "he could not possibly have felt more like Cortes than I do after looking into you. Everything has conspired to make the reading of your work the most exciting reading I ever did in my whole life" [MacLennan to Robert Ardrey, May 4, 1969]. Ardrey had theorized that man's nature was dual: as he put it, *"The command to love is as deeply buried in our nature as the command to hate."* Basing this theory on the emergence in prehistory of *australopithicus africanus,* a flesh-eating ape that used the antelope bone to kill its prey, but was also capable of self-sacrifice in the interests of survival of the species, Ardrey had postulated that the genes of modern man reflected this same double impulse. The urge to kill (and to create the weapons to do so) and an altruistic impulse both were man's genetic inheritance.

Everything had conspired to make MacLennan receptive to this theory. He had already depicted this double impulse in the three main characters of *The Watch That Ends the Night;* he had used psychological theory as a base on which to construct *Return of the Sphinx* in order to show how a whole era can fall prey to the destructive urges in man and ignore complementary altruistic action. Beyond that, he had been working on his nonfiction study *Rivers of Canada* for republication, and his imagination had been gripped by the notion of vast eons of geological time which the history of Canada's rivers suggested.

> ***Voices in Time** concentrates on a full and complex dramatization of how and why an explosion that almost wipes out all species, including mankind, could occur and offers MacLennan's deepest probing of man's nature yet.*
>
> *—Elspeth Cameron*

All these influences converged to deepen the religious faith he had experienced has he completed ***The Watch That Ends the Night.*** Now, specifically, his idea of "God" was intimately linked with evolution: "The God I believe in," he told members of the Canadian Club in Vancouver in May 1968, " . . . is the God who manifests Himself in evolution, in all living creatures." God, in other words, was revealed in that impulse to self-sacrifice that characterized the species. As he wrote in his *Telegram* article, underneath all known events were "causes so mysterious that I am convinced they are lodged in the evolutionary process itself. What some New Biologists have called 'the Keeper of the Kinds' permits no species to threaten the survival of all species, including itself."

To set his story ***Voices in Time*** in a future setting was neither unprecedented nor surprising for MacLennan. In a pair of short experimental pieces in the fifties, he had already used a futuristic milieu to make satirical comments on the cold war. And both settings hinged on an explosion—the blowing up of the moon as a "necessary" episode in the space race between Russia and the West. But, as MacLennan once commented of Field Marshall Haig's behaviour in World War I: "it seems to me far more important to discover how such a man could act like that than to orbit a hunk of metal around the sun" [MacLennan to Gray, January 4, 1959]. In both essays, [**"The Finding of the Way"** and **"Remembrance Day: 2010"**], his criticism of man's ingenious technology is scathing. His futuristic setting in ***Voices in Time*** was also in keeping with his recently heightened awareness of prehistory in the New Biology and in his own revisions of ***Rivers of Canada.*** This awareness gave him a sense of perspective that he wanted to reflect in his novel, a feeling that, as he put it, "Time to me now is like an expanding universe." As he himself concluded, this was a perspective gained by virtue of his age: to see time this way, he commented [in *Conversations with Canadian Novelists,* 1973], "is something . . . one perhaps has to be older to do."

***Voices in Time*** concentrates on a full and complex dramatization of how and why an explosion that almost wipes out all species, including mankind, could occur. This novel offers MacLennan's deepest probing of man's nature yet. In it he attempts to answer the questions he had posed from the start—questions which always centred on explosions.

Certainly the most explosive character in the novel is Timothy Wellfleet. A carryover from the characters in ***Return***

*of the Sphinx,* Timothy is a creature of the sixties, caught in a matrist era and loving every minute. Timothy is a man who lives for the present, in the present, without thought for others or for the consequences of his actions. Through him, MacLennan attacks the media in the same way that he had attacked advertising in ***The Precipice.*** To MacLennan, the methods of modern media provided a perfect example of the misuse of power: "For nearly a decade," he had remarked in his *Telegram* article, "TV screens have been inviting the most inflammatory irresponsibles to sound off and for entertainment purposes have given full exposure to anyone who wants to shock or propagandize . . . However, the murder of truth, as always, leads to the murder of people." Timothy, whose TV news program is called "This is Now"—a phrase gleaned from something a woman had said to him during orgasm—is one of those "inflammatory irresponsibles" whose deliberate distortion of truth through sophisticated media techniques leads to the murder of a man who (unknown to him) is his stepfather, Conrad Dehmel.

Dehmel, a German survivor of a concentration camp, is the victim of a whole era in which the destructive impulses of men have been elicited and organized by Hitler. Hanna Erlich, Dehmel's Jewish girlfriend, observes once, "Hitler talks directly to the volcano underneath the rules." Dehmel has already had ample opportunity to observe such behaviour in his own father—another megalomaniac colonel like Wain, a "boy-man" who has "played" as a naval officer in World War I. Like MacLennan, Dehmel's idealization of things military has been reversed into horror. Dehmel, then, is a more complex character than Timothy, in that he has actually felt and acted upon both impulses. His initial attraction to war enables him later to pose as a Gestapo officer so that he can help Hanna and her father escape from Germany; but his essentially purposeful mission is trapped in "the collapsing vaults of history."

Taken together, Dehmel's experience of two world wars and Timothy's of the "psychic crisis" of the sixties represent the decline and fall of the Western world as it moves towards its own destruction. The genetic impulse to destroy (and to create the weapons to do so) culminates in the Destructions in which a "computer balls-up" triggers a nuclear explosion that almost destroys the world. Almost. MacLennan dramatizes the "keeper of the kinds" in operation: "Something profound and mysterious, something blessed and almighty in the genes of humanity, has created a taboo against these [nuclear] bombs . . . They invented what were called 'clean bombs,' which had a destructive power less than that of the nuclears but nevertheless tremendous." Dehmel comments on one occasion, "the creative energy of the universe will . . . interfere with human ingenuity."

The novel's central character, however, is neither Timothy nor Dehmel, but Timothy's older cousin, John Wellfleet. He has survived the Destructions and, somewhat like MacLennan himself, looks back over that "expanding universe" of time, to make sense of the voices from the past. A young man called André Gervais, born after the great nuclear blast, has come to the old man with a couple of metal boxes which have been uprooted from the wreckage.

In these boxes marked "Wellfleet" are shards of his family history that his mother has saved—letters, tapes, diaries, even a videotape of Timothy's October 1970 television show. These are the "voices in time" which John Wellfleet must arrange into an intelligible chronicle. His purpose in doing so is to provide young André Gervais and his friends with a demonstration of the danger man poses to himself as these young people set about constructing a new society. His methods of doing so are those of the artist himself, which is to say, they are creative.

By interweaving the separate stories that arise from the materials in the boxes, old John Wellfleet gains profound insight into mankind and achieves a perspective on life which enables him to see the broad patterns in human behaviour. Formerly caught in an egocentric consideration of the troubles he himself has known, he can ultimately see that Dehmel has suffered more than he himself ever has, he can understand and even forgive Timothy's loathesome, irresponsible behaviour. Even the Destructions, he comes to appreciate, were "so impersonal that there was no more malice in them than in a combined earthquake and volcanic explosion on a global scale."

MacLennan's novel is a profound paradigm of the human condition. Man's creative abilities are juxtaposed with the ingenuity that seems, at first glance, to be the same thing. They could not, MacLennan demonstrates, be more different. The purposeful drive represented by André Gervais to build a new civilization and by John Wellfleet, whose jagged and powerful tale will stand as a moral guide to such builders, is at the opposite extreme from the aimless ingenuity of the "boy-men" who play at war, the technological experts who build and misuse mass media equipment, or the inventors of computers and nuclear bombs. This is the way the world ends, MacLennan asserts in a parody of the one major twentieth-century poet with whom he consistently disagreed, not with a whimper but with a bloody, great bang. In an image that reverberates from his previous work, and now drew force from the New Biology, those bent on destruction in October 1970, a mere prelude to the Destructions themselves, move in for the kill like sharks and barracuda: "Unseen and with precision—my God, and with such beautiful haughtiness—they had moved out of the Great Barrier Reef of unidentified humanity to plant the bomb, to seize the hostages, then had faded back unseen into the Barrier Reef from which they were hurling their ultimatums like conquerers."

The sense of "mysterious" and "unseen" forces behind human action in **Voices in Time** bears testimony both to that "God of evolution" MacLennan had come to believe in and to the strangely hypnotic compulsion to turn God-given gifts to destructive purposes which is the deeply rooted heart of darkness in Everyman.

### Barbara Pell    (essay date Spring 1991)

SOURCE: "Faith and Fiction: Hugh MacLennan's *The Watch That Ends the Night*," in *Canadian Literature*, No. 128, Spring, 1991, pp. 39-50.

[*In the following essay, Pell examines religious and spiritu- al themes in* The Watch That Ends the Night, *arguing that the novel's primary subject is a "search for religious peace—a truce between man's spirit and his fate."*]

There is an inherent tension, even conflict, between faith and fiction. The modern realistic novel has a professed mimetic relationship to the post-Christian era we live in that is artistically inimical to acts of grace and expressions of faith. This conflict is somewhat analogous to the crisis in modern theology which has attempted to respond to people's spiritual need in an age bereft of God. Neo-orthodox and liberal theologians have struggled, from opposite directions, to provide a "theology of mediation" between the religious tradition and the modern mind. Neo-orthodoxy, led by Karl Barth, has emphasized revelation and the Word of God as the timeless and timely answer to man's quest, while liberal theologians, such as Paul Tillich, repudiate past dogma and redefine God in terms of man's "existential experience."

Similarly, modern religious writers who find their vision and vocation no longer coincide with the spirit of the age are, like modern theologians, attempting to communicate a vision of God to a godless world. And, like the theologians', the novelists' dilemma resolves itself into two possibilities: do they offer a dogmatic, theological answer imposed from outside onto their characters' struggles, or can they realize a spiritual solution arising out of the existential experience of their characters?

Paradoxically, this godless age could be extremely propitious for religious fiction. In this century, society has been stripped of religious complacency and materialistic security; many people are asking the basic questions of existence for which Christians have always claimed to have The Answer. But dramatizing a religious vision within the creative logic of realistic fiction can cause almost insurmountable tensions and problems for the artist. And communicating this vision to a sceptical world requires infinite talent and tact.

Religious novelists therefore, *as novelists,* must have as strong a commitment to their *art* as to their faith. Traditionally, the novel has been seen as a reflector of reality. Therefore writers of realistic fiction, though their convictions of a Higher Reality will influence their themes and form, cannot falsify life. They must admit evil, suffering, disbelief and temptation—in other words "sin"—into their world along with righteousness and belief. They must honestly portray the agonies of doubt along with the fervour of faith. Above all, they cannot impose an ultimate solution on the existential struggles of the characters *deus ex machina,* nor miraculously transpose their finite quests into an infinite realm. These artistic problems must be worked out with great care within the novel itself. The struggle for religious meaning against doubt and sin cannot be expounded as abstract dogma. It must be integrated into the fabric of the plot, presented as dramatic conflict arising out of the convictions of the characters, and resolved with fidelity to the artistic logic of the fiction and the finite complexities of life.

In other words, Christian novelists who wish to communicate their religious vision through realistic fiction to a post-Christian society must portray realistically and dramatically the action of God's grace in fallen nature. And all serious religious novelists have found a tremendous struggle between the demands of their art and their faith, their fidelity to fallen nature and their commitment to divine grace. As François Mauriac asked: "How can I reconcile so distorted a view of the human animal with the faith I claim to have in his vocation to sanctity?" [quoted in Philip Stratford's *Faith and Fiction: Creative Process in Greene and Mauriac,* 1964.] And in the end he could not, and he ceased to write novels.

Let me explain how one of the founding fathers of modern Canadian fiction, and the self-appointed spokesman for Canada in the twentieth century, attempted to resolve this artistic tension in his works, and more particularly in his finest novel. In four books of essays and seven novels, Hugh MacLennan chronicled the historical maturation of Canada from colonialism to atomic *angst* and paralleled it with his own personal spiritual journey from Calvinism to Christian Existentialism. In a sociological oversimplification, he generalized his personal experience of the joyless and inhibiting Cape Breton Calvinism into a national identity crisis, and his own religious quest for a theology for the modern age, "a new vision of God," into the spiritual pilgrimage of the twentieth century.

In two of his essays [from ***Cross-Country***], **"Help Thou Mine Unbelief"** and **"A Second Look,"** MacLennan warns: "History reveals clearly that no civilization has long survived after that civilization has lost its religion." But, if "the state of mind resulting from our loss of the sense of God's nearness constitutes the greatest crisis of our time," this loss of faith is due to the dominance of science and rationalism in our society. And the *apparent* incompatibility of science and religion within the modern mind he ascribes to the evils of a "puritan education" that exchanges mysticism for materialism:

> So the end-product of puritanism has been enthroned, science unreconciled with religion, and by what seem to be logical steps we have been led into the solitude of a purposeless universe. This is what I believe to be the essence of the spiritual crisis we face. We are alone and we are purposeless.

However, MacLennan feels that now "with the churches all but empty shells, the hunger for a believable religion may well be stronger than at any time in world history since the reign of Caracalla." And he does not believe that traditional Christian doctrine contains "a countervailing idea great enough and sustaining enough to save society from totalitarianism and our own souls from the materialistic desert in which they now wander." He calls for a "reconstruction of Christian theology" to forge "new symbols" for a "new vision of God." Scientists must develop "a genuine synthesis of knowledge" and from it formulate new "concepts of God" compatible with "modern scientific discoveries" and intelligible to a scientific, industrial society. It is, perhaps, the refusal of science to undertake this commission that led MacLennan to search for a theology of mediation, a redefinition of God for modern man, in the world of his fiction.

MacLennan's greatest assets as a novelist, most critics agree, are the traditional virtues of interesting plots, narrative action pieces, well-realized characters, and vivid settings that were his professed aim in order to "entertain" his readers. Unfortunately his greatest defect, and this also often over-rides his virtues, is that MacLennan was first and foremost an essayist. The conflict between his desire to instruct—and we have seen that this most often had a religious motivation—and his responsibilities as a novelist to "entertain" is constantly felt in his works. Although this dual commitment results in technical weaknesses, it also gives his books the universal layers of meaning that "if they do not make them great, at least make them much more than ordinary romantic-idealist novels intended for well-meaning members of the Book-of-the-Month Club" [George Woodcock, *Hugh MacLennan,* 1969]. But the tension between faith and fiction may account for the fact that MacLennan's novel writing grew increasingly slower and more difficult over the years.

The essential pattern that emerges from MacLennan's fiction is remarkably similar to that which Gordon Roper describes as characteristic of those "spiritual biographies" written in Canada between 1880 and 1920:

> The novel traces his [the central character's] doubts, loss of faith, and his search for a new religious position, unorthodox and undogmatic, or for some substitute "religion." The chief problems are the inspiration of the Bible, the presence of pain and evil in the universe, and the divinity of Christ; solutions are found in Pantheism, universalism, and a belief in "Brotherhood," "true Christianity," the "living Jesus of the Gospels." [Carl F. Klinck, editor, *Literary History of Canada: Canadian Literature in English,* 1965]

For in many ways MacLennan's very traditional novels are fighting the theological battles of the nineteenth century. His heroes repudiate the doctrines of Calvinism but cannot free themselves from its psychological legacy of guilt; they deny the reality of God in the world and then desperately search for alternative "religions" to console their emptiness and anxiety. But all humanist solutions—social, political, materialistic, even personal relationships—ultimately fail them, and they must eventually find a spiritual Absolute to give their lives meaning and purpose.

This general pattern is developed in progressive stages, and with growing disillusionment, through MacLennan's novels. In ***Barometer Rising*** (1941) Neil Macrae and Penny Wain triumph over the repressive forces of Calvinism and colonialism to enter an optimistic future. While there is still confidence that politically Canada can forge a "new order" that will unite the old and new worlds, the lovers can find personal salvation in integrity, self-knowledge and human love. The idea that individual lives might be part of "a pattern possessing a wider meaning" is only a peripheral theme. In ***Two Solitudes*** (1945), although the struggle for Canadian unity is dramatized in all its tragic, and religious, complexity in the first part, MacLennan imposes a symbolic solution on the second half. Paul Tallard and Heather Methuen in their marriage represent an end to the puritan tyranny of the past (both Catholic and Protestant) and to racial enmity. Their "personal religion" is founded on self-knowledge and love and humanistic optimism, but again there is a wise old man in the background hinting at a larger "pattern" which sanctifies the whole of life.

*The Precipice* (1948) is an overly-schematized analysis of the legacies of puritanism without God in Canada and the United States. Having escaped the sexual hypocrisy of Calvinist Canada, Lucy Cameron finds that the American inheritance is compulsive materialism. MacLennan, however, never clearly defines either the problem ("the precipice") or the solution. This is a transitional novel. Since humanist, political answers are now seen to have failed MacLennan's "well-meaning generation," he turns to the personal, religious vision which has only been hinted at in the previous novels, expressing it in didactic rhetoric. Marcia converts to Roman Catholicism, and Lucy becomes the personification of "grace" in her acceptance and forgiveness of her husband's sins, but neither answer is a convincing outcome of the plot. *Each Man's Son* (1951) recapitulates most of MacLennan's previous religious themes. Daniel Ainslie, too, suffering "the ancient curse" of Calvin, attempts to justify himself through hard work and to achieve immortality through a son. Repudiating God, he faces existential meaninglessness. But in a melodramatic and moving conclusion he comes to see that only selfless love can conquer sin and guilt. The dramatization of human conflict, doubt, despair and love in this novel gives it a vitality that overcomes the occasional thematic rhetoric.

MacLennan embodies the whole pattern of this spiritual pilgrimage in his finest novel, *The Watch That Ends the Night* (1959), and finally arrives at his twentieth century "shrine": a radical redefinition of God to answer the existential dilemma of modern man, a redefinition with suggestive affinities to the liberal Protestant theology of Paul Tillich. An analysis of this novel reveals MacLennan's theology for a post-Christian culture, and his solution for the modern Christian novelist's problem of writing a religious novel for a secular society. However, while *The Watch That Ends the Night* is autobiographically sincere and didactically powerful, its theological thesis ultimately compromises its fictional form and undermines its narrative resolution.

MacLennan said that during the writing of *The Watch That Ends the Night* he shed "the intellectual skin" that his generation had worn:

> So long as I wore it myself, my novels had been essentially optimistic. I had believed the barometer was really rising; I had believed . . . that the two solitudes were bound to come together in Canada. But my last two novels [*The Watch That Ends the Night* and *Return of The Sphinx*] have been tragic. My original title for *The Watch* was a dead give-away; it was *Requiem*. Requiem for one I had loved who had died, but also for more: requiem for the idealists of the Thirties who had meant so well, tried so hard and gone so wrong. Requiem also for their courage and a lament for their failure on a world-wide scale. . . . What *The Watch* was trying to say in the atmosphere of its story was that the decade of the 1950's was the visible proof of my generation's moral and intellectual bankruptcy. [**"Reflections on Two Decades,"** *Canadian Literature* (Summer 1969)]

Since the "basic human conflict" is spiritual, MacLennan decided to "write a book which would not depend on character-in-action but on spirit-in-action. The conflict here, the essential one, was between the human spirit of Everyman and Everyman's human condition" [**"The Story of a Novel,"** *Canadian Literature* (Winter 1960)]. Although the theme is the spiritual dilemma of the modern world, and the setting spans the century and the globe in its allusions, this novel is focused on the personal religious quest of Hugh MacLennan in the character of George Stewart.

The narrator, George Stewart, has many obvious similarities to MacLennan: he is a writer and university professor, living in Montreal with his wife, who is dying of a rheumatic heart condition. But George is also the Everyman of his generation, "a generation which yearned to belong, so unsuccessfully, to something larger than themselves." This articulation of the religious theme of the book recalls William James' definition of "religious experience" [in his *The Varieties of Religious Experience,* 1902]: "that we can experience union with *something* larger than ourselves and in that union find our greatest peace." The search for religious peace—a truce between man's spirit and his fate—is the premise and substance of *The Watch That Ends the Night* as we can see in a theological exegesis of the novel.

Beginning in Montreal in February 1951, George leads the reader gently into a series of flashbacks which span four decades before returning to the present. And, in a pattern repeated throughout the novel, he prepares us theologically for the events he then dramatizes. He tells us that as a boy he had been religious and believed in a personal, living God. Unlike MacLennan's other heroes, George did not suffer the repressions of a strict Calvinist upbringing. Nevertheless, in the disillusionments of the Thirties, like millions of others, he lost his faith in religion, in himself, and in the integrity of human society. And the manifest injustices of the world, symbolized for him in his wife's illness, have increased his rejection of any divine Power. So, in the hubristic, self-centred Fifties he finds his religion, his "rock" and his "salvation" in the palpably moral life and love of Catherine. As Goetsch has pointed out [in "Too Long to the Courtly Muses: Hugh MacLennan as a Contemporary Writer," *Canadian Literature* (Autumn 1961)], "George belongs to the stock type of naive narrator," and MacLennan is deftly preparing us to see his rash confidence (covering a basically insecure nature) corrected by the passage of time and new religious insights.

Catherine Carey-Martell-Stewart represents a quasi-divine "spiritual force" in George's life. She is primarily characterized by the "spirit" or "Life-Force" which has developed in her in response to her life-long struggle against her "fate"—her rheumatic heart. Therefore, in words which MacLennan later borrowed for **"The Story of a Novel,"** George says that this spirit has become for him "the ultimate reality": "I think of this story not as one conditioned by character, as the dramatists understand it, but by the spirit and the human condition." And this spirit is the "sole force which equals the merciless fate which binds a human being to his mortality." It is her strength and her knowledge that "all loving is a living of life in the midst of death" that George leans on for years until he is forced to develop his own spiritual resources.

---

**Although the theme is the spiritual dilemma of the modern world, and the setting spans the century and the globe in its allusions, *The Watch That Ends the Night* is focused on the personal religious quest of Hugh MacLennan in the character of George Stewart.**

**—Barbara Pell**

---

Among George's generation, in which "so many of the successful ones, after trying desperately to hitch their wagons to some great belief, ended up believing in nothing but their own cleverness," towers the mythological figure of Jerome Martell, Catherine's first husband and George's spiritual father. He too is larger than life, "more like a force of nature than a man," and for the narrator he epitomizes the anguished decade of the Thirties. In Part v of the novel MacLennan recreates Jerome's heroic story. An illegitimate orphan who escapes from his mother's murderer in a New Brunswick logging camp, he is finally adopted by a devoutly religious clergyman and his wife in Halifax. His life has the symbolic dimension of a modern *Pilgrim's Progress;* we are told that during his youth "he had really thought of himself as a soldier of God. He believed the Gospels literally, and they meant far more to him than they could mean to most people, because he had such a desperate need to belong." But the horror and guilt of World War I had destroyed his religion, forcing him to seek absolution in medicine and politics for the senseless killing.

Of the mid-thirties, George says:

> This was a time in which you were always meeting people who caught politics just as a person catches religion. It was probably the last time in this century when politics in our country will be evangelical, and if a man was once intensely religious, he was bound to be wide open to a mood like that of the Thirties.

Jerome is one of many who divert the passions that no longer serve a traditional God into this neo-religious faith. Having failed to fill "the vacuum left by his lost religion" with Catherine's human love, he seeks salvation through humanistic works:

> I used to dream of a city on top of a hill—Athens perhaps. It was a great privilege to enter it. I used to dream that if I worked hard all my life, and tried hard all my life, maybe some day I'd

be allowed within its gates. And now I see the fascists besieging that city. . . .

Confronted by the spectre of Original Sin in capitalist exploitation and fascist evil, Jerome embarks on a crusade to save mankind in the Spanish Civil War. But he is all too aware that his City of Civilization is a substitute for Bunyan's Celestial City, the City of God, as he articulates half of the theme of this novel:

> A man must belong to something larger than himself. He must surrender to it. God was so convenient for that purpose when people could believe in Him. He was so safe and so remote. . . . Now there is nothing but people. . . . The only immortality is mankind.

When the political gods of the Thirties are discredited, however, George and his generation sell out their ideals in exchange for personal peace and affluence:

> In the Thirties all of us who were young had been united by anger and the obviousness of our plight; in the war we had been united by fear and the obviousness of the danger. But now, prosperous under the bomb, we all seemed to have become atomized. . . . The gods, false or true, had vanished. The bell which only a few years ago had tolled for us all, now tolled for each family in its prosperous solitude.

It is at this point that Jerome Martell returns from the dead, in the manner of Christ, to witness to the second half of the theme: what every man "requires to know and feel if he is to live with a sense of how utterly tremendous is the mystery our ancestors confidently called 'God.' " He has had an unorthodox and existentialist vision of Jesus in his prison cell: "He wasn't the Jesus of the churches. He wasn't the Jesus who died for our sins. He was simply a man who had died and risen again. Who had died outwardly as I had died inwardly." It is this vision that has given him the courage to affirm the value of life in the face of death.

Part VII, the end of the novel, illustrates most clearly the difficulty of expressing and dramatizing a religious vision within the dynamics of a realistic narrative. Faced with his wife's imminent death, George reacts as Everyman, subconsciously revolting against the emptiness of existence: "For to be equal to fate is to be equal to the knowledge that everything we have done, achieved, endured and been proud and ashamed of is nothing." MacLennan resorts to a theological interlude in Chapter iv, in which George explains man's need for a god and the insufficiency of all the various substitutes: reason, success, wife and family, political systems and the state. When they fail, he is prey to the "Great Fear," the existential anxiety that God is indifferent and life is meaningless; this *angst* threatens to obliterate his identity. Then, using analogies of music—the melodies of Bach and Beethoven—he attempts to describe the spiritual experience that finally resolves "the final human struggle" between the "light and dark within the soul" into an ultimate harmony (paraphrasing 1 Corinthians 13:7):

> . . . which is a will to live, love, grow and be grateful, the determination to endure all things,

suffer all things, hope all things, believe all things necessary for what our ancestors called the glory of God.

This union of the spirit of Everyman with the "Unknowable which at that instant makes available His power, and for that instant existing, becomes known" is, in theological terms, mysticism. It is this "mystical approach to a vision of God" which MacLennan has invoked in his essays [in **Cross-Country**] as a new theology of mediation for the twentieth century. This vision defeats the modern death wish, vindicates God to scientific man, justifies the human plight and celebrates life: "it is of no importance that God appears indifferent to justice as men understand it. He gave life. He gave it. Life for a year, a month, a day or an hour is still a gift."

In the final chapters of the novel, MacLennan attempts to dramatize this theology in his fiction. But the mystical encounter of the anguished George with the revenant Jerome, who teaches him to confront death by dying to self, is neither dramatically compelling nor realistically convincing. The characters have become puppets "wired for sound" by the didactic commentator offstage. And in the Epilogue, the world of the realistic novel has been completely transposed into a metaphysical abstraction:

> All our lives we had wanted to belong to something larger than ourselves. We belonged consciously to nothing now except to the pattern of our lives and fates. To God, possibly. I am chary of using that much-misused word, but I say honestly that at least I was conscious of His power. Whatever the spirit might be I did not know, but I know it was there.

As I suggested in my introduction, MacLennan's analysis of the modern spiritual dilemma and his "theology of mediation" have suggestive similarities (though no documented debt) to Paul Tillich's doctrine of "the courage to be." According to Tillich [in *The Courage to Be*, 1952] (and MacLennan dramatizes this failure in the experiences of Jerome Martell and George Stewart), as popular faiths for the twentieth century, "the courage to be as a part" and "the courage to be as oneself" are ultimately disappointing: "the former, if carried through radically, leads to the loss of the self in collectivism and the latter to the loss of the world in Existentialism."

However, Tillich offers an alternative. This is the "courage to be" which "is the courage to accept oneself as accepted in spite of being unacceptable," and which also takes into itself death and meaninglessness. The source of this courage is "absolute faith . . . which has been deprived by doubt of any concrete content." But this act of the courage to be is a manifestation of "the ground of being" which is God, and "the content of absolute faith is the God above God." This new vision of God transcends the old doctrines of theism: God as a vague symbol, God as a Person in divine-human encounter, and "the God Nietzsche said had to be killed because nobody can tolerate being made a mere object of absolute control"—MacLennan's Calvinist God. Rather, "the courage to be is rooted in the God who appears when God has disappeared in the anxiety of doubt."

In **The Watch That Ends the Night,** George Stewart's religious quest may be illuminated by reference to Tillich's ideas. The inner harmony and death to self which George finally arrives at is an experience of "mysticism," defined by Tillich as "the striving for union with ultimate reality, and the corresponding courage to take the non-being which is implied in finitude upon oneself." And George's final affirmation of life is what Tillich calls "the self-affirmation of being-itself":

> There are no valid arguments for the "existence" of God, but there are acts of courage in which we affirm the power of being. . . . Courage has revealing power, the courage to be is the key to being-itself.

In this novel MacLennan has attempted to translate this existential theology into dramatic action. Most critics agree on the importance and clarity of the theme of this novel, and on the sincerity and intensity of feeling which give it persuasive power. However, the problem for MacLennan, as for all modern religious novelists, is to dramatize his faith in terms of realistic fiction. And the critics have also noted that this, his best novel, nevertheless suffers from a non-dramatic ending, a transposition of character conflict from physical reality into metaphysical abstraction.

The parallels which I have noted with liberal Protestant theology may help to explain some of the problems which critics have had with the ending of **The Watch That Ends the Night** and also with MacLennan's later novels. MacLennan's solution to the problem of writing a religious novel in a godless society, as I have suggested, is a redefinition of God to answer the modern questions about meaning and purpose within the existential situations of his characters. His emphasis is on natural and liberal theology, as opposed to revealed and neo-orthodox theology. As a result, MacLennan's view of God, like that of most liberal theologians, is philosophical, hypothetical, and subjective. Tillich, for example, has repudiated "those elements in the Jewish-Christian tradition which emphasize the person-to-person relationship with God": the personalistic image of God, the personal nature of human faith and divine forgiveness, the idea of divine purpose, and the person-to-person character of prayer and practical devotion. These qualities, traditionally portrayed by religious writers to dramatize God's interaction with this world (for example, in the works of Graham Greene), seem also to be absent from MacLennan's concept of God. His "new vision of God" is that synthesis of science and mysticism which modern man can accept, but God is no longer a Person with an objective reality independent of man's perception of Him. A relationship with this transcendent, impersonal Deity is difficult to portray dramatically. This is one of the reasons why, when MacLennan does portray the existential questions with great realism and complexity and conviction, his theological answer often seems arbitrary and artificial. As a result, George Stewart's ultimate encounter with the divine is distinguished by didactic sincerity and rhetorical intensity—but metaphysical unreality.

Furthermore, MacLennan has been unable to sustain this optimistic "new vision of God" in his later novels. **Return** *of The Sphinx* (1967) replays the conflict between the races and the generations of *Two Solitudes,* but because this novel is MacLennan's elegy for lost idealism, there is no attempt at an optimistic fictional resolution. The lesson here is that every generation must repeat the universal religious quest—from the death of God, through false ideologies, to spiritual grace—but now in a world of moral, spiritual and humanistic disintegration. In the Epilogue, therefore, MacLennan is forced to offer his larger vision of the grace operating in nature that he has not honestly been able to dramatize in his plot. Alan Ainslie's vague, pantheistic optimism lacks even the theological content of the resolution of *The Watch That Ends the Night.* And, more seriously, it is in rhetorical opposition to the atmosphere and implications of the entire novel. Finally, in the ambitious scope of *Voices in Time* (1981) MacLennan portrays a civilization destroyed by man's ignorance and evil, offering only a feeble spiritual hope in the mysterious "God of evolution." The religious pilgrimage of the twentieth century seems to have ended, for MacLennan, back in the wilderness of man's self-destruction.

MacLennan was a didactic writer, and his religious perspective was a dominant part of that larger world view of history and sociology—particularly regarding the development of the Canadian identity—that determined all of his novels. He often repeated the D. H. Lawrence dictum: "the novel 'treats the point where the soul meets history' " and he admired the evangelical fervor of writers who have "made the novel a mighty instrument for human understanding" [quoted from *The Other Side of Hugh MacLennan,* edited by Elspeth Cameron, 1978], feeling that he too must offer his solutions to the spiritual dilemmas of our world. Since he believed that "in any novel, content should be more essential than form" [Donald Cameron, "Hugh MacLennan: The Tennis Racket Is an Antelope Bone," in *Conversations with Canadian Novelists,* 1973], there is always the danger in MacLennan's art that his faith will distort his fiction. Since his religious concerns predisposed him toward thesis novels, his greatest weakness was the tendency to manipulate plot and character development toward a theological solution. Therefore, his structures often appear schematically contrived; the endings do not grow naturally out of character or action but are conceived thematically and invoked externally. His major characters are inevitably vehicles for his ideas and spokespeople for his rhetorical interludes, which are not well assimilated into either plot or characterization.

If MacLennan is obviously more of an essayist than a stylist in his novels, this, too, is partly a result of his faith. For he scorned the modern technical experimenters who, he feels, all seem to denigrate life: the famous contemporary writers of America and Europe who have devoted "their immense technical abilities to the dissection of cowards, drunkards, weaklings, criminals, psychotics, imbeciles, deviates, and people whose sole common denominator seems to be a hatred of life and a terror of living" [*The Other Side of Hugh MacLennan*]. This was not MacLennan's vision. In an era of spiritual disintegration his artistic vocation was not so much to seek "to forge the uncreated conscience of his race as to reforge a conscience that

has been fragmented" [*The Other Side of Hugh MacLennan*].

This is an admirable, if unfashionable, theological enterprise. But can it be realized within the artistic form of the realistic novel, a form which is equally unfashionable in the context of postmodernism? While affirming that "there are no religious novels *per se,*" Charles Glicksberg [in *Modern Literature and the Death of God,* 1966] nevertheless acknowledges the accomplishments of religious novelists such as Mauriac and Greene in whose words "religion is presented as experience, as spiritual conflict, as vision and aspiration, struggle and search and suffering, not as codified theology." In the tradition of the great religious novelists, Hugh MacLennan also dramatically portrayed the spiritual conflicts of modern man and, particularly in *The Watch That Ends the Night,* attempted to narrate a spiritual resolution which arises out of existential experience. That his fictional narrative tends to become "codified theology" in the conclusion is, I believe, partly a result of his didactic, thesis-centred style and partly a product of the abstract liberal theological model which he invokes as his solution, but which could not sustain his fiction.

---

# FURTHER READING

## Bibliography

Cameron, Elspeth. "Hugh MacLennan: An Annotated Bibliography." In *The Annotated Bibliography of Canada's Major Authors,* edited by Robert Lecker and Jack David, pp. 103-53. Downsview, Ontario: ECW Press, 1979.
    Lists books, essays, and reviews by MacLennan as well as citations and annotations for criticism on his works.

## Biography

Cameron, Elspeth. *Hugh MacLennan: A Writer's Life.* Toronto: University of Toronto Press, 1981, 426 p.
    Traces MacLennan's life and artistic development, with a chapter devoted to each novel.

## Criticism

Bartlett, Donald R. "MacLennan and Yeats." *Canadian Literature,* No. 89 (Summer 1981): 74-84.
    Remarks on the "Yeatsian overtones" in *Return of the Sphinx.*

Cameron, Elspeth. "MacLennan's *Sphinx:* Critical Reception & Oedipal Origins." *Journal of Canadian Fiction* 30 (1980): 141-59.
    Discusses the critical reception of *Return of the Sphinx* and the books that influenced the novel's conception.

Daniells, Roy. "Literature: Poetry and the Novel." In *The Culture of Contemporary Canada,* edited by Julian Park, pp. 1-80. Ithaca, N.Y.: Cornell University Press, 1957.
    Overview of Canadian literature in which Daniells comments on *The Precipice* and praises MacLennan for identifying "religion and not the class struggle as our chief problem and the true enigma of our society."

Davis, Marilyn J. "Fathers and Sons." *Canadian Literature,* No. 58 (Autumn 1973): 39-50.

Focuses on the theme of Calvinist guilt in MacLennan's *Each Man's Son.*

Goetsch, Paul. "Too Long to the Courtly Muses: Hugh MacLennan as a Contemporary Writer." *Canadian Literature,* No. 10 (Autumn 1961): 19-31.

Examines MacLennan's early novels, focusing on his treatment of nationalism, history, and motive.

Hyman, Roger. "Too Many Voices, Too Many Times: Hugh MacLennan's Unfulfilled Ambitions." *Queen's Quarterly* 89, No. 2 (Summer 1982): 313-24.

Discusses the critical reception of *Voices in Time* and states that the futurist structure of the novel "is the ideal form for the worst of MacLennan's didactic excesses."

Hyman, Roger Leslie. "Hugh MacLennan: His Art, His Society and His Critics." *Queen's Quarterly* 82, No. 4 (Winter 1975): 515-72.

Thematic analysis of MacLennan's novels, focusing on his depiction of Canadian character and identity.

Jones, D. G. *Butterfly on Rock: A Study of Themes and Images in Canadian Literature.* Toronto: University of Toronto Press, 1970, 197 p.

Comments on *Each Man's Son, The Return of the Sphinx,* and *The Watch That Ends the Night* in the context of Canadian literature.

*Journal of Canadian Studies* 14, No. 4 (Winter 1979-80): 3-121.

Special issue devoted to MacLennan.

MacDonald, Larry. "Psychologism and the Philosophy of Progress: The Recent Fiction of MacLennan, Davies and Atwood." *Studies in Canadian Literature* 9, No. 2 (1984): 121-43.

Examines the theme of political and social unrest in works by Robertson Davies, Margaret Atwood, and in MacLennan's *Return of the Sphinx* and *Voices in Time.*

MacLulich, T. D. *Hugh MacLennan.* Boston: Twayne Publishers, 1983, 142 p.

Biographical and critical survey.

Magee, William H. "Trends in the Recent English-Canadian Novel." *Culture* X (1949): 29-42.

Remarks briefly on the distinctly Canadian themes in *Barometer Rising* and *Two Solitudes.*

Tallman, Warren. "Wolf in the Snow, Part One: Four Windows on to Landscapes." *Canadian Literature,* No. 5 (Summer 1960): 7-20.

Comments on the depiction of Canadian life in *Each Man's Son* and four other novels by different authors.

Woodcock, George. *Hugh MacLennan.* Toronto: Copp Clark Publishing Company, 1969, 121 p.

Examines MacLennan's essays and novels, arguing that the nonfiction works are "statements on life" and that the fictional writings are openly didactic.

————. "A Nation's Odyssey: The Novels of Hugh MacLennan." In *Odysseus Ever Returning,* pp. 12-23. Toronto: McClelland and Stewart, 1970.

Remarks on the nationalist themes of MacLennan's novels.

————. *Introducing Hugh MacLennan's "Barometer Rising."* Toronto: ECW Press, 1989, 75 p.

Detailed analysis of *Barometer Rising,* covering the novel's critical reception, themes, and structure.

Zezulka, Joseph. "MacLennan's Defeated Pilgrim: A Perspective on *Return of the Sphinx.*" *Journal of Canadian Fiction* IV, No. 1 (1975): 121-31.

Discusses the human dilemma and crisis in Western history depicted in *Return of the Sphinx* and *The Watch That Ends the Night.*

**Interviews**

Cameron, Donald. "Hugh MacLennan: The Tennis Racket Is an Antelope Bone." In *Conversations with Canadian Novelists,* pp. 130-48. Toronto: Macmillan of Canada, 1973.

Discussion of MacLennan's novels, focusing on theme.

Twigg, Alan. "Hugh MacLennan: Patricius." In *For Openers: Conversations with 24 Canadian Writers,* pp. 83-96. Madiera Park, British Columbia: Harbour Publishing, 1981.

Discusses MacLennan's career, influences, and the inspiration for several of his works.

Additional coverage of MacLennan's life and career is contained in the following sources published by Gale Research: *Contemporary Authors,* Vols. 5-8 (rev. ed.), 142; *Contemporary Authors New Revision Series,* Vol. 33; *Contemporary Literary Criticism,* Vols. 2, 14; *Dictionary of Literary Biography,* Vol. 68; *DISCovering Authors Modules;* and *Major 20th-Century Writers.*

# Mountain Wolf Woman

## 1884-1960

(Also known as Little Fifth Daughter, Xehaciwinga, and Haksigaxunuminka) American autobiographer.

The following entry presents an overview of Mountain Wolf Woman's life and career.

## INTRODUCTION

A member of the Winnebago tribe, Mountain Wolf Woman is the author of the critically acclaimed *Mountain Wolf Woman, Sister of Crashing Thunder* (1961). An evocative recounting of the author's life, the autobiography is highly regarded as an authoritative document of Winnebago history and customs. Written in collaboration with a white author, the book, with its copious notes and fidelity to Mountain Wolf Woman's voice, is also lauded for successfully avoiding the loss of tribal identity often arising from Native-White literary collaborations.

### Biographical Information

Born in East Fork River, Wisconsin, Mountain Wolf Woman was a member of the Thunder Clan of the Winnebago tribe. Initially raised in Black River Falls, Wisconsin, she frequently moved with her family in accordance with hunting and growing cycles. She did, however, receive two years of formal education while living in Tomah, Wisconsin. At a later date, she resumed her studies; these, however, were again interrupted when her older brother forced her into an arranged marriage. She eventually divorced her first husband and remarried Bad Soldier, also a member of the Winnebago tribe; between her two marriages, she had eleven children and several grandchildren. Mountain Wolf Woman first met her adopted niece, anthropologist Nancy Oestreich Lurie, in 1945, and she was eventually asked by Lurie to record her life story. She traveled to Ann Arbor, Michigan, in 1958 and stayed with Lurie while they worked on the book. Mountain Wolf Woman died of complications from pneumonia and pleurisy at her home in Black River Falls in late 1960, never seeing her autobiography published.

### Major Works

Mountain Wolf Woman and Lurie began to seriously work on what would become *Mountain Wolf Woman, Sister of Crashing Thunder* in the late 1950s. Unsatisfied with the initial results, which resulted in a few pages of text, Lurie asked Mountain Wolf Woman to elaborate and expand on her memories. Using a tape recorder, Mountain Wolf Woman dictated her story in Winnebago and then in English. The tapes were later replayed to Mountain Wolf Woman, at which time a list of additional topics upon which Mountain Wolf Woman wanted to ruminate was compiled. After additional tapes were made, Lurie

began translating the tales into conventional English; to accomplish this, Lurie worked with Frances Thundercloud Wentz, a grandniece to Mountain Wolf Woman, who compared the English and Winnebago versions. The result yielded *Mountain Wolf Woman, Sister of Crashing Thunder*. The book relates Mountain Wolf Woman's girlhood, education, and marriages; her contributions to her family; and her role in Winnebago society as a daughter, wife, and mother. *Mountain Wolf Woman, Sister of Crashing Thunder* is further recognized as an evocative and insightful account of Winnebago history and culture, relating the Winnebagos' numerous relocations, tribal customs and rituals, and views on gender.

### Critical Reception

Scholars assert that *Mountain Wolf Woman, Sister of Crashing Thunder* is exceptional in terms of its focus on Winnebago life, the events surrounding its composition, and its intended audience. Because Lurie kept such detailed accounts of her attempts to render Mountain Wolf Woman's tale into "good English" and reprinted them in appendices, critics note that the subject's voice is not lost and that the problems normally precipitated by Native-

White collaboration are not an issue. They additionally note that since the work was originally told in Mountain Wolf Woman's native tongue and to a family member, her intended audience was—first and foremost—other Native Americans.

---

# PRINCIPAL WORKS

*Mountain Wolf Woman, Sister of Crashing Thunder: The Autobiography of a Winnebago Indian*   (autobiography)   1961

*This work was edited by Nancy Oestreich Lurie, translated by Frances Thundercloud Wentz, and contains a foreword by Ruth Underhill.

---

# CRITICISM

## Nancy Oestreich Lurie   (essay date 1961)

SOURCE: A preface and appendix to *Mountain Wolf Woman, Sister of Crashing Thunder: The Autobiography of a Winnebago Indian,* edited by Nancy Oestreich Lurie, The University of Michigan Press, 1961, pp. xi-xx, 92-108.

[*An American educator, editor, and critic, Lurie was adopted into the Winnebago tribe as an adult and was considered a niece of Mountain Wolf Woman. At Lurie's urging, Mountain Wolf Woman began the process of telling her life story. In the first part of the following excerpt, taken from the preface to* Mountain Wolf Woman, *Lurie discusses the composition of the autobiography, her relationship with and impressions of Mountain Wolf Woman, and Mountain Wolf Woman's adherence to Winnebago customs. In the second part of the excerpt, which is taken from one of Lurie's appendices to the book, she relates the events surrounding Mountain Wolf Woman's death.*]

Autobiographies are published for a variety of reasons. Authors often disclaim any personal importance but justify making their memoirs public because of close association with the great people and stirring events of their time. Individuals whose roles are of obvious historical significance frequently explain that a sense of social responsibility requires that they make known the underlying influences and motivations of their actions. Mountain Wolf Woman has told her story for a reason that is at once simpler and more complex than those usually adduced. Her niece asked for the story. Among the Winnebago Indians, a strong sense of obligation to relatives prevails, as well as the reciprocal sense of right to call upon them as the need or desire for favors may arise. The fact that the kinship in this case is one of adoption and not of blood makes it no less binding from a Winnebago point of view.

Our relationship stems from my adoption by Mountain Wolf Woman's parallel cousin, Mitchell Redcloud, Sr.

According to Winnebago reckoning, they are classified as brother and sister because their fathers were brothers. Thus, Mountain Wolf Woman is my aunt. I had met Redcloud during the summer of 1944 in the course of my first field work among the Winnebago. When I began my senior year at the University of Wisconsin the following fall, I learned that Redcloud was a cancer patient at the Wisconsin General Hospital on the university campus. I visited him frequently and my questions about Winnebago culture helped relieve the tedium of existence in a hospital ward. In time he came to believe that our association had been preordained. Despite frequent and intense periods of pain, Redcloud forced himself to instruct me as fully as possible about his people, even writing long accounts of Winnebago customs to present to me when I appeared during hospital visiting hours. He was eventually scheduled for surgery, and fearing that he might not survive the operation, presented me with a cherished and valuable legacy—adoption as his daughter. I thus acquired a Winnebago name, a clan affiliation, and a host of relatives upon whom I could rely in continuing the task Redcloud and I had begun. Redcloud's condition precluded the traditional announcement of such an adoption at a public feast, but he did write of it to Mountain Wolf Woman and evidently told other Winnebago during the year he lived following the operation.

Thus, when I met Mountain Wolf Woman in the summer of 1945 while working at the Winnebago community of Black River Falls, Wisconsin, she greeted me as her niece. My aunt soon proved to be not only a valuable informant, but a good friend as well. Her personality and her own experiences as an individual became as interesting to me as the ethnographic data about the Winnebago which she could provide. I felt that her autobiography would be of great interest both as a literary document and as a source of insights for anthropological purposes. I was inspired, naturally, by the fact that the first full-length autobiography of an American Indian edited and published by an anthropologist, Paul Radin, had been that of a Winnebago, Crashing Thunder. The example set by Radin in 1920 has been followed by the publication of a number of autobiographies of American Indians and other native peoples. However, few such life histories have been collected from women. Therefore, Mountain Wolf Woman's story takes on particular significance in scholarly terms, since it is the account of a woman from the same tribe as Crashing Thunder. However, I knew Mountain Wolf Woman almost a year before I learned that she is the sister of Crashing Thunder. Thus, a unique opportunity was presented to obtain an autobiography which would be valuable not only for its own sake but also for its comparative importance in regard to Radin's work.

Mountain Wolf Woman readily agreed to my request for her story, but a great deal of time elapsed before we could actually begin work on the project. In the first place, I realized that a request of such magnitude would require a commensurate gift as a matter of reciprocal kin obligations. I was obliged for many years to use any field funds I received for more general research on the Winnebago. Then there were technical problems. Mountain Wolf Woman's household was crowded with small grandchildren she was rearing and she did not have the leisure or quiet to write her story in the Winnebago syllabary script, let alone in English which she would find even more difficult. Furthermore, I was fully occupied for several years with teaching and other research.

It was not until 1957 that I could begin to give serious thought to the long-delayed work with Mountain Wolf Woman. By that time she was able to put her household in the temporary charge of an adult granddaughter in order to stay with me. Thanks to the Rackham Fund for Faculty Research of The University of Michigan and to the Bollingen Foundation, grants-in-aid were provided to finance the project.

I notified Mountain Wolf Woman that work could begin and she traveled from her home at Black River Falls to Milwaukee where I met her and accompanied her on the rest of her journey to Ann Arbor, Michigan. This incident is duly noted in her autobiography as it was her first airplane flight. We worked together at my home for almost five weeks during January and February of 1958.

We began our task by discussing the best manner of procedure. She soon became accustomed to using a tape recorder and decided she preferred it to writing her story in the Winnebago syllabary script that her brother had employed. She also chose to speak Winnebago rather than English as it allowed for easier recall and discussion of events. However, to aid me in the task of translation, she repeated the entire story on tape in English using the Winnebago recordings as a guide. Since the account was told directly to me, it was natural for Mountain Wolf Woman to gloss over details of Winnebago culture and history. I have therefore made notes for each chapter providing more extensive data on matters which may be of further interest to the reader. The first day's work proved highly disconcerting to me. Mountain Wolf Woman told her entire story on less than half a reel of tape. Although I endeavored to hide my feelings, my disappointment must have been evident since she observed that the story could be made much longer on the basis of the many notes I had made in conversations with her during earlier periods of field work. I said that I would really like to hear all the stories again to be sure that I had understood them correctly. A knowing smile crossed her face and she said, "This is just a start to show where we will go, like beginning of a book."

She began her story again, eliminating what she recognized as meaningless details, expanding and adding events more pertinent to her own experiences. She recounted episodes already familiar to me and many new ones.

The completed autobiography thus consists of the second or long account of Mountain Wolf Woman's life, supplemented where necessary from the shorter account or from other data such as the English version of the narrative or comments made in the course of our work but not transcribed on the tapes. . . .

The transcription of Mountain Wolf Woman's story was doubtless one of the most pleasant ways imaginable of doing "field work." Mountain Wolf Woman is a delightful companion, witty, empathic, intelligent and forthright.

During the course of our work she thought of herself as a visiting relative. When my teaching schedule interrupted our work, she found ways to occupy her time, and even between daily recording sessions she was never idle. Indeed, she is incapable of idleness and equates personal contentment with useful activity. She sewed clothing for herself, and even split wood for the fireplace when she felt in need of exercise. Because my birthday occurred during the course of her visit she decided to make me a gift in the form of elaborate floral beading of the buckskin dress I wear for lectures of a popular nature, explaining, "The girls wearing fancier dresses to powwows nowdays."

She looked upon our main task as fun rather than work, although she expressed surprise that "just talking" could be so physically tiring, and confided that she never appreciated that I must really work quite hard as a teacher. However, beds had to be made, dishes washed, and the house put in order each morning before I dared suggest we sit down beside the tape recorder.

Mountain Wolf Woman was pleased to have my study as a room all to herself where she slept and could retire to read, sew or write letters to her children. She also appreciated the fact that our house has running water, but most of our electrical appliances struck her as more trouble than they are worth. She particularly distrusted the electric stove, since she is accustomed to cooking at a wood-burning range or over an open fire out-of-doors. Thus, on days when both my husband and I were away teaching, she chose to prepare her meals at the living room fireplace, even baking bread in the embers as a surprise for us when we returned in the late afternoon. In fact, Mountain Wolf Woman gradually transformed our home into a Winnebago household with activity centered about the fireplace in the living room. The recording equipment was shortly moved from the acoustical isolation of my study to the living room. Consequently, the tapes contain peripheral sounds of doorbell, telephone, cat meows, and my husband's footfalls. However, the greater ease Mountain Wolf Woman felt in working amidst the bustle of daily living more than compensated for these technical imperfections in the recordings.

When telling her story, Mountain Wolf Woman would settle herself comfortably in a large chair, fold her hands in her lap, close her eyes and begin to relive events as she recalled them. Sad incidents often caused tears to well up, and funny stories evoked chuckles.

Mountain Wolf Woman likes to refer to herself as an "old Winnebago lady." This is an accurate self-assessment because among the Winnebago age carries connotations of wisdom and dignity. It also carries the privilege of speaking frankly on the basis of knowledge and understanding derived from observing the world for a long time.

Considered very pretty in her youth, Mountain Wolf Woman's face still reflects this basic beauty and the deeper beauty of serene old age. Her dark, expressive face is attractively contrasted with her perfectly white hair, which is always combed straight back into a neat bun. Although she often dresses "like a white lady," she usually wears a style of clothing typical of Winnebago women of her age.

This consists of a full cotton skirt topped by a loose, collarless blouse reaching just to the waist. She likes to wear large fringed shawls for special occasions but considers coats and sweaters far more practical for working out-of-doors. Her short stature and style of dress suggest a stolid obesity, but this effect is dispelled by the quick grace of her movements.

Like many Winnebago women, she never wears a hat, but binds a silk kerchief tightly about her hair, bringing the ends together in a neat knot above her forehead. Her ears are pierced and though she now wears earrings only in the lobes, the helices of her ears show small punctate marks. Traditionally, Winnebago women wore five or six pairs of long earrings dependent from the edges of their ears.

Throughout Mountain Wolf Woman's stay I regretted that it was not possible to have a microphone constantly recording her conversation. Our mealtimes and periods of domestic activity were enlivened by her spontaneous observations and comments. Frequent good-natured teasing increased the effect of living in a Winnebago household. Aunts stand in a joking relationship to their nieces' husbands and I had warned my husband that our guest might tease him. She did, accusing him of laziness in providing for her wants in the way of food and firewood. She had never met my husband before her visit to our home and in a moment of serious conversation with me she expressed her approval of him in traditional Winnebago terms, "Kind, a good worker, and not jealous-hearted." However, in talking to him she frequently engaged in the outrageous coquetry appropriate to their relationship. The English term "Honey," as a form of affectionate address amuses Mountain Wolf Woman and so she usually called my husband, "My Honey, Add." One night as we watched a television commercial concerning a preparation for coloring hair, she turned seriously toward my husband and mimicking the simpering voice of the young woman on the screen, she asked, "Honey, what color would you like me to dye my hair?"

Television is still a rather novel experience for Mountain Wolf Woman, but she had purchased a set for her own home shortly before coming to visit us. She reasoned shrewdly that since she would not be home to supervise her young granddaughters, the television set would be an inducement for them to stay home at night. An interesting result of television viewing at Ann Arbor was revealed in a letter from Mountain Wolf Woman upon her return to Black River Falls.

She evidently recalled a program in which small scale models were used to illustrate how the Russians might land an unmanned rocket on the moon. By remote control the rocket disgorged a jeep-like vehicle which rolled about taking pictures and transmitting them back to earth. The presentation was designed to be frightening and I had been properly disturbed by the impersonal awesomeness of such technological speculations. However, Mountain Wolf Woman has lived far longer than I have and has seen the transition from horse to airplane without feeling a sense of threat to her individuality. Her letter, while indicative of her brief schooling, illustrates her remarkable abil-

> **Mountain Wolf Woman likes to refer to herself as an "old Winnebago lady." This is an accurate self-assessment because among the Winnebago age carries connotations of wisdom and dignity. It also carries the privilege of speaking frankly on the basis of knowledge and understanding derived from observing the world for a long time.**
>
> **—*Nancy Oestreich Lurie***

ity to organize new information into meaningful patterns, reducing the extraordinary to comprehensible and even comfortingly amusing terms.

> My dear neice.
>
> I'm writing to thank you that money you sent me [payment for moccasins and other items I had ordered]. and I'm going to tell you a story. You alway like old story. about the moon. long time ago when the world new old time of different tribe were against each other. that time [a Winnebago] went away from his people when he came back to his home war came and kill whole town and this man he trace them he follow them to and he got to where they come from. he there toward morning. that time indian chief alway live right in middle of the town. he new [knew] where the chief son and his wife. so the peoples were slept real deep. he went in cut chief son head of [off] and his wife too. and he took both heads and went up to the moon. when the moon full moon you could see him he's carry two human head in his hand. his name is Sheiganikah he is at right in moon. true American indian already he is there yet.
>
> I heard russia want it to get their befor us. when I was their [there, at Ann Arbor] once I was start telling you about this and we start talking about something else so I didn't finish it. When I was young my good old dad and my uncle use to tell story in the evening. we all love listening story that the time my dad told this story about the brave man and the moon.
>
> Mr. Sheiganikah
> it mean some kind of bird
>
> I hope you like the story. hope to hear from again. from your Aunt . . . tell my honey Add Hi.

Aside from the fascinating implications of her story for the Department of State, the letter tells a great deal about Mountain Wolf Woman. She had set no price on the materials I had ordered and considered my payment more than she would have asked as a fair price. Thus, the story is offered to even the balance, a state of affairs the Winnebago like to maintain. She is also conscious of the importance I place on sources of information and the meaning of words. Her sense of orderliness is shown in her choice of a story to send me. It ties up a loose end of conversation begun during her visit. Finally, instead of merely signing the letter as my aunt, she stresses the relationship to both my husband and me in her final statement.

To Mountain Wolf Woman, aunt, friend and informant, I extend my heartfelt thanks for allowing her autobiography to be published both for its own personal appeal and for the insights it may offer scholarly investigators. . . .

. . . . .

And now the story is truly ended. Mountain Wolf Woman died quietly in her sleep the morning of November 9, 1960, the very day that I also received notification that the galleys of her narrative were ready for me to proofread. Thus, it is possible to add this final commentary while my descriptive notes concerning Mountain Wolf Woman remain in the present tense.

Mountain Wolf Woman had returned to her home at Black River Falls after a visit at the home of one of her children. She apparently caught cold in the course of sealing windows and otherwise preparing her house for the winter. At her request, neighbors drove her to the clinic at Black River Falls where her condition was diagnosed as pleurisy and pneumonia. After a week's stay at the clinic she appeared to be recovering and told visitors that she intended to go home on November 9. However, when I went to Black River Falls for the funeral, I learned that she had told one close relative that she did not want to worry her children, but that she really meant she was going to her spiritual home. Whether or not this is apocryphal is unimportant; it is in keeping with Winnebago expectation that people who are good and wise and old are privileged to foretell their own deaths. After all, Mountain Wolf Woman reported just such a prophecy from her own husband.

The funeral arrangements reflected the varying religious affiliations among the Winnebago. Conservative relatives and friends held a brief version of the traditional Winnebago wake at a community some distance from Black River Falls; her own peyote beliefs were represented in a well-attended peyote meeting held at her home the night before her burial; and on Saturday, November 12, 1960, she was laid to rest at the mission cemetery at Black River Falls after Christian services at the mission church.

Many Winnebago are understandably distressed by the apparent evidence of religious confusion in the holding of two or more different kinds of rituals when a Winnebago dies. Nevertheless, when I saw the several hundred people gathered from near and far to pay their last respects, my own feeling was that the three rituals were somehow fitting and proper. Mountain Wolf Woman's own life had included participation in all three religions and while she considered herself a peyotist, she retained virtues of generosity and obligation to kindred of her traditionally Winnebago childhood. She accepted Christianity in her baptism and confirmation at a mission boarding school. Finally, she found in the peyote religion a deep sense of spiritual understanding and experience. Her many friends and relatives in these different religious groups all desired most

earnestly to express their grief in their loss and their respect for her memory in the way each found most meaningful.

### Gretchen M. Bataille and Kathleen Mullen Sands (essay date 1984)

SOURCE: "Culture Change and Continuity: A Winnebago Life," in their *American Indian Women: Telling Their Lives,* University of Nebraska Press, 1984, pp. 69-82.

[*Bataille and Sands are both American critics, educators, and editors who specialize in Native studies. In the following excerpt, they survey Mountain Wolf Woman's life, work, and heritage.*]

The purpose for the writing of *Mountain Wolf Woman* is different from almost all other ethnographic autobiographies. Where other recorder-editors often recorded women's stories as an incidental part of fieldwork, Nancy Lurie specifically requested the story and did so as an adopted niece of Mountain Wolf Woman [whom she knew as "Aunt Stella"]. With Mountain Wolf Woman in the position of aunt, and with the power of age and wisdom such a position connotes, it was both appropriate and necessary that she instruct her niece in the ways of the tribe. The association was one of long duration, for Nancy Lurie and Mountain Wolf Woman had met in 1945 in Black River Falls, Wisconsin. It was not until 1958 that recording actually began, allowing thirteen years of friendship and kinship to have developed.

Unlike the field methods used earlier, Lurie used a tape recorder and made a record of the life story both in Winnebago and in English. This, of course, allowed Mountain Wolf Woman to do some degree of immediate editing as she translated her own material. Lurie also notes that passages were omitted from the final manuscript at the request of the narrator. "She told me a number of things that happened, particularly when she went to get her grandchildren in the state of Washington, that she didn't want in the book. I respected her wishes. They were interesting but not all that vital to the completeness of her story" [personal correspondence, Nancy Oestreich Lurie, 30 July 1980].

Obviously the element of selection was still in operation, but the decision here had been given to the informant and was not assumed by the recorder. Lurie describes the story as being "told *to,* not *through,*" her. Of the recording sessions, Lurie comments:

> My Winnebago isn't all that good, so often I wasn't sure of what she was saying until we replayed [the tapes] and she told her story in English, and then I went over the Winnebago tapes with a highly competent bilingual woman, Frances Thundercloud Wentz. . . .

Of the final published autobiography, Lurie says, "It was her story as she wanted to tell it. I had some reservations about her comments about the traditional religion, but she did not, so they stayed in as she told them. She got to hear herself exactly as she told her story on tape before it was committed to paper or published."

Ruth Underhill, in the foreword to the narrative of Mountain Wolf Woman, makes comparisons with Paul Radin's autobiography of Mountain Wolf Woman's brother, Crashing Thunder, describing Radin's book as more dramatic, more artistic; in short, she sees it as more "literary." Comparing herself with Radin, Lurie noted that she was not collecting data in the field; Mountain Wolf Woman stayed at her home. She asked few questions during the narration, checking with Frances Wentz about translation details later, after Wentz had worked through the Winnebago tapes. . . . Of Radin's work she wrote:

> Sam's story, *Crashing Thunder,* was written in the Winnebago syllabary by Sam himself for Radin. In the D. Appleton Century version Radin added other data he had collected from Sam and his brother Jasper to fill out the story. . . . I don't know if Sam was aware of the additional material before the book came out. But, unlike [other subjects of white-Native collaborations], Sam and Stella could review what they said, and had the opportunity to edit before publication if they wished.

Lurie sees the two Winnebago autobiographies as reflecting fundamental differences between males and females. She writes, "Mountain Wolf Woman's autobiography is a predictable reflection of the greater self-confidence enjoyed by women in comparison to men in a culture undergoing rapid and destructive changes" [**Mountain Wolf Woman**]. Women's tasks of caring for children and family did not change despite acculturation. Reflecting her own self-confidence, Mountain Wolf Woman does not tell a story of self-aggrandizement. Although she is aware of her strengths, she sees herself more as a transmitter of culture, one who is a link between the historical life of her people and the future generations. Indeed, it is her female roles of mother, wife, grandmother, and provider that concern her most.

---

**The complete narrative of *Mountain Wolf Woman* is a chronological and factual account of its narrator's life. There are dramatic moments, but these events are handled so matter-of-factly by Mountain Wolf Woman that the reader doesn't always appreciate the anxiety which must surely have accompanied the moments.**

**—*Gretchen M. Bataille and Kathleen Mullen Sands***

---

Lurie describes Mountain Wolf Woman as "witty, empathic, intelligent, and forthright," and it is this personality that comes through in the narrative. Lurie's comments in the preface are instrumental in preparing the reader to like the narrator before reading the autobiography. It is clear that the relationship that had been established between Lurie and her narrator provided the best possible means of recording a life story with an editor. Lurie is careful to point out her methodology and to indicate where she has supplemented the narrative with her own materials.

Mountain Wolf Woman provides only superficial information on Winnebago history, information that is supplemented by Lurie in the notes. The Winnebagos were subject to many removals, causing one writer to refer to them as the "Wandering Winnebago" [Ed Shannon, "The Wandering Winnebago," *Frontier Times,* August-September, 1971]. Although contemporary American Indians reject the labels "nomadic," "transient," and "roaming" to describe travel to follow game or to find new and better locations to live, the term "wandering" perhaps aptly describes the aimless movements to which the Winnebagos were subject at the whim of the United States government.

Before 1864 the Winnebagos had been forced to move several times over a thirty-two-year period. From the Green Bay area, the Winnebagos had settled in southern Wisconsin by 1832, but after the Black Hawk War, the Winnebagos were resettled by the government in northeastern Iowa near the present city of Decorah. By 1848 there was an increasing number of white settlers in Iowa, and the Winnebagos were once again moved, this time to Todd County in north-central Minnesota. By 1855 the tribe had negotiated a move to southern Minnesota to avoid having to move west of the Missouri River; but in 1863 the Winnebagos were loaded on boats and sent down the Minnesota River to their next home, Crow Creek, in the Dakota Territory. This proved to be a disastrous move and, reacting to the desperate starvation conditions of Crow Creek, Winnebago leaders led the people to Nebraska to seek help from the Omaha Indians. Finally, after years of moving and being moved, the Winnebagos were settled in Thurston County, Nebraska. This final move was the only one initiated by the Indians themselves rather than the government. Although attention has usually focused on those Winnebagos who were moving, one group remained in Wisconsin, near Black River Falls, the entire time. Today the Winnebago tribe remains divided: one group lives on a reservation in Nebraska and the other group lives as nonreservation Indians in Wisconsin.

This history of movement and forced migration is part of Mountain Wolf Woman's tribal history. The influence of this past on her life is clear; she found moving around not a chore, or a burden, but an accepted element of her life. In her life story, Mountain Wolf Woman recalls the many journeys she made—journeys to find work, to be with her husband, or to care for children or grandchildren.

Mountain Wolf Woman begins her narrative by relating the events before her birth, referring particularly to the history of Winnebago removals. From the beginning it appears that Mountain Wolf Woman was aware of the way the Winnebagos had been treated, and she wished to place herself within this context of tribal history.

Born in 1884 in East Fork River, Wisconsin, Mountain Wolf Woman soon moved to Black River Falls. As a child she attended school for two years in Tomah, Wisconsin, but when her family moved to Wittenberg she had to change schools, remaining there only a short time before she married. Her first marriage, arranged by her brother, ended, and she remained in Black River Falls until her marriage to Bad Soldier. Her itinerary after that marriage included moves from Hatfield, Wisconsin, to Wakefield, Nebraska, on to South Dakota, back to Nebraska, and finally a return to Black River Falls. During this time there were shorter trips to trap muskrats, to dig yellow water-lily roots, to hunt deer, or to pick cranberries. She once journeyed as far as the Northwest because of her concern about her grandchildren. This acceptance of family responsibility is not surprising, for, as Winnebago educator Woesha Cloud North writes of the Winnebagos, "It is a practice . . . for a grandmother to take on the responsibility of her children's children where there is no longer parental supervision or because of death or other reasons" [*Informal Education in Winnebago Tribal Society with Implications for Formal Education,* 1978]. Clearly Mountain Wolf Woman viewed this as a normal responsibility. In all of her moves Mountain Wolf Woman seemed keenly aware of the necessity of the travel and moved with ease. She was not tied down to a specific geographical location; even near the end of her life she moved her house itself from one location to another. The experiencing of many locales is an outward manifestation of the explorative nature of the narrator, a nature that prompted her to try peyote as well as to participate in traditional Winnebago ceremonies, to believe in a Christian god in the heavens with the same faith that allowed her to believe the Winnebago story of Sheiganikah living on the moon. That she went to live with an anthropology professor and her husband and became a part of the routine of yet a different environment further attests to Mountain Wolf Woman's adaptability.

Adaptability to cultural change as well as geographical change is suggested in other ways. Throughout the narrative Mountain Wolf Woman refers to changes she has observed during her lifetime. The relative ease with which she discusses or sometimes casually mentions certain events or different ways of doing things belies the profound transformations in Winnebago culture during Mountain Wolf Woman's lifetime. Cloud North summarizes some of the effects of these changes, particularly on the Nebraska Winnebagos, but also on the Wisconsin group:

> Traditional informal education or cultural transmission was to assist the boy or girl to grow as a responsible person and social being into adulthood of the Winnebago society. The conquest of the Winnebago people, their forced removals, and later a reservation existence in which their lives were taken over by the paternalistic system of the Bureau of American Indian Affairs and other outside influences, both moral and religious, made serious inroads on these educational practices.

There were changes in the material culture, changes symbolized by "metal teaspoons for clam shells to scrape the corn off the cobs." Long ago the metal teaspoons of the Europeans had been substituted for the sharpened clam shells that had traditionally been used to prepare corn, but

the use of clam shells had persisted as well. Mountain Wolf Woman appears comfortable with both the old and the new. She values the continuities in the culture, but readily adapts to necessary changes. She realizes that long ago her father did not need a license to hunt deer, but that adherence to a different legal system had become necessary. After recounting the entire fasting ritual of her brother Hagaga, Mountain Wolf Woman says, "Today they do not do that any more."

Mountain Wolf Woman writes openly about her first menstrual period, recreating for the reader the fears she had as she fled into the woods alone. The tradition of isolation, common in many tribes, was also one which would ultimately be dropped. Irma Bizzett, a Winnebago woman and now a student at Iowa State University, said her mother told her she had been put in an isolation lodge during her first period and after giving birth to her first three children, but by the time Irma was born in 1949, this custom was no longer practiced.

In the shorter version of her life story that is published as an appendix to the longer autobiography, Mountain Wolf Woman is philosophical about the past and all of the changes that she has observed, changes that are made manifest through the relationships within the tribe:

> In the beginning people loved each other. They even would all live in one house, never disagreeing. We too used to live this way. . . . We were never at odds with one another, nor quarrelling nor scolding one another. Mother and father never scolded any of us; however, we were probably well behaved. They never used to scold me. Now children are not like that. They are even against their own parents. . . . That is how it is today.

The complete narrative of **Mountain Wolf Woman** is a chronological and factual account of its narrator's life. There are dramatic moments—her unwanted first marriage and the journey to Washington to retrieve her grandchildren, for example—but these events are handled so matter-of-factly by Mountain Wolf Woman that the reader doesn't always appreciate the anxiety which must surely have accompanied the moments. Literary conventions are not ignored, however. Lurie admits to making some changes in tenses, clarifying idiomatic expressions, and inserting words necessary for clarification. But the wording and tone of the original Winnebago is retained, rendering the text closer to Winnebago expression than conventional English, but making it no less literary.

Because Mountain Wolf Woman's life spanned much of the twentieth century, one can note her changing attitudes toward the institutions around her. In particular, she had experience with formal education, the organized church, and the United States and local governments. Unlike Helen Sekaquaptewa or Anna Shaw, Mountain Wolf Woman did not attend school for very long or in a consistent fashion. But she did attend school, first at Tomah and later at Wittenberg, leaving to get married. She realizes that a casual attitude toward school education no longer prevails, however, noting that the Indians of the past would not have stayed home just so the children could attend school. She recognizes that "they can no longer act in this way." She herself was disappointed at having to leave school, but she accepted the necessity of marriage according to tribal custom. She adhered to tradition, but she was grateful that her mother offered her an acceptable way out by telling her that when she was older she could do as she wished.

Traditional Winnebago education included naming ceremonies to teach a child to recognize clan and family relationships, story telling, fasting and vision quests for boys, fasting associated with menstruation for girls, curing and healing, and preparations for a vocation within the tribal structure. Mountain Wolf Woman had received this education, and, although she was an eager learner when she was in school, she was pleased that she had not missed out on traditional Winnebago tutoring. For a time, when Winnebago families stayed close together, such informal education could continue alongside public education. Irma Bizzett recalls being given a name by her grandfather (during a story-telling session) when she was a child. Her daughter, fourteen years old in 1981, also received a name from her grandfather as they sat around on a Sunday afternoon telling traditional stories after returning from Christian church services. Geographical distance from family and tribe, however, makes weekly story-telling sessions and ceremonies less likely to be experienced by children. But the Winnebagos, like other tribes, have learned to adapt to change.

Mountain Wolf Woman's funeral epitomized her allegiance to three religions, an amalgamation which she apparently did not find difficult to handle. Raised as a traditional Winnebago, Mountain Wolf Woman participated faithfully in Winnebago ceremonies, including the scalp dance and the medicine dance. She was also a practicing Christian, but the religion that made her faith whole was the Native American Church and her participation in peyote meetings: "I joined the medicine lodge. I was once a Christian. Then, when we went to Nebraska I ate peyote which is even a Christian way. Three things I did. But peyote alone is the best."

Minnie Littlebear was born in 1898 and lives in Nebraska. When she was interviewed by Woesha Cloud North and asked if a Christian prayer is said at the Naming Ceremony, she answered, "It's all the same to the Winnebago. It's all the same god, Ma-una." Paul Radin has pointed out [in *Primitive Religion: Its Nature and Origin,* 1937] similarities to Christianity in traditional Winnebago religion, and his description of the Medicine Dance—"the whole ceremony is the reiteration of one basic theme, the proper method of passing through life in order to be reborn again"—suggests why Mountain Wolf Woman and other Winnebagos may so readily have incorporated both religions into their belief system.

Mountain Wolf Woman relates two important visions: one that occurred as a result of two nights of traditional dancing; and the other a vision of Jesus she had after participating in a peyote ceremony. She attributes both visions to her faithfulness to the necessary rituals of the ceremonies. Her account of these visions further suggests that she believes it is possible, perhaps even desirable, to participate

fully in more than one religion. This may have been a way of answering those critics within the tribe who condemned the peyote eaters. In fact, one of the most negative responses from the Winnebago community was that the book and, by extension Lurie and Mountain Wolf Woman, were seen as promoting the Native American Church. The traditional Winnebagos resented Mountain Wolf Woman's comments on the Medicine Lodge. Asked about negative reactions, Lurie wrote, "YOU BET! It has only been since my return for extended work the last three summers that I've overcome the image as a promoter of the Native American Church." Such factionalism is not unusual, however, and clearly demonstrates that the narrative is the life of one Winnebago woman and cannot be seen as necessarily representative of all Winnebagos.

The narrator was aware of the Winnebago removals and the allocation of parcels of land that had occurred before her birth. She learned to skillfully manipulate government agencies to obtain necessary help: first, for some of the old people; secondly, in arranging to get her grandchildren back to Wisconsin; and, finally, in getting her own house moved when it became necessary. The government intruded upon the lives of the Winnebagos during World War II. The narrator's most intimate comments reflect her emotions at the time her son was wounded; that event produced her strongest outpouring of grief:

> It was early in the morning when they brought the telegram. I was the first one to go to the berry place. I thought to myself, I will go before the white people arrive. I went to where they had finished picking and when I got there I wept. I prayed to God and I cried as hard as I could cry. I was crying quite a distance from the other people. I cried as loud as I could and cried as much as I wanted to. That is the way I cried. Then when I got enough crying, I stopped crying. When I stopped crying my anxiety seemed to be relieved. Then, after I cried it out, this pain in my heart, I felt better.

The repetition of the words *cry, cried,* and *crying* emphasizes her grief, and through repetition in the narrative itself, she purges herself of tears.

---

**Mountain Wolf Woman serves as a model of an autobiography that combines an individual narrative told by the subject with ethnographic detail supplied by a recorder-editor.**

**—Gretchen M. Bataille and Kathleen Mullen Sands**

---

Mountain Wolf Woman describes her emotions at other times—her reluctance to marry, the pain of leaving her daughter in Washington, and her sorrow at her husband's death—but most of her feelings are discussed with the resigned acceptance of one who has experienced much of life's sorrows and joys and has learned to accept both as a part of the natural order of things. She sees herself as separate from white people and accepts the Winnebago position in relation to the rest of society in the same un-emotional and flat manner: "I do not know why, but whatever the white people say, that is the way it has to be. I guess it must be that way."

Although Mountain Wolf Woman became experienced with the institutions of white society, she held tenaciously to the traditions of her people. Religion was just one aspect of her adherence to traditional ways; she also expected proper behavior at the dances, she recognized the value of old age, and she perpetuated the oral tradition in her own way. Speaking of old age, she said, "The old people were supposed to be respected. 'Respect those old people,' mother and father used to say to us. That is what we used to do. We respected the old people, but today they do not respect the old people."

Fred Rice, a Winnebago from Nebraska, expresses similar dismay: "Nowadays the kids laugh at the old people when they speak Winnebago." Later in the book, Mountain Wolf Woman explains the power of age: "If you give food to an old person and he really likes it, that is very good. The thinking powers of old people are strong and if one of them thinks good things for you, whatever he wishes for you, you will obtain that good fortune."

She participates in the transmission of tales early in the narrative when she tells the story about stealing beans from mice; but she admits the difficulty of remembering the oral stories, recalling the story-telling sessions with her father:

> Then father used to say, "All right, prepare your bedding and go to bed and I will tell you some stories." I really enjoyed listening to my father tell stories. Everybody, the entire household, was very quiet and in this atmosphere my father used to tell stories. He used to tell myths, the sacred stories, and that is why I also know some myths. I do not know all of them anymore, I just remember parts of stories.

Her greatest tribute to the oral tradition is the narrative of her own life. Her autobiography is a collection of stories that are linked by the journeys and adventures of the central character, Mountain Wolf Woman. She describes herself as a trickster of myth, remembering events before her birth, later "always the one who is spoiling things," the one who sees visions, and who has bridged the gap between myth and reality, having now ridden through the sky, albeit in an airplane, to bring her life story together with the life of Nancy Lurie. The final tale ties the narrative together, gives it purpose, and provides a conclusion that is appropriately literary:

> Once when I came back from Nebraska one of my relatives had died. His name was Fish Back. Mitchell Redcloud, Sr. He had three sons. One time he had told me a young white girl was going to come to Black River Falls and that she was his daughter. He even gave her a Winnebago name. Therefore, she was my niece. All of our relatives liked her very much. That is how it was.

She thought a lot of us too and she liked Indians. She was an only child. When the Indians talked about their affairs, whatever they knew she knew more. She helped the Indians. She wanted me to do her a favor. "Auntie," she said, "if you come and visit me we will write down Indian stories

---

**An excerpt from *Mountain Wolf Woman, Sister of Crashing Thunder***

When they finished the medicine dance somebody said, "About this time they usually peel and dry slippery elm." They used to tie it in a bundle and white people bought it. They paid a good price for slippery elm. "All right," father said, "we can do that. We are a big family and thus we will be able to eat." That is what they did. Mother and her young ones put up a tent next to my grandfather's home and we lived there. Those who were strong went away some place with a wagon and some household goods. Where the trees were very dense they stopped and they asked for the slippery elm from the white people who owned the woods. They called it slippery elm; it is something like the elm tree. They asked, "Could you not give that kind to us so that we can make something to sell?" The white people said, "Help yourself, do whatever it is that you are talking about."

Then they walked about and looked at the trees and wherever they saw a slippery elm they skinned it. They cut the bark from the base of the tree and pulled it loose up to the very top of the tree. Then they slashed it off and it fell down like folding cloth. The trees were easily peeled. Even one tree produced a lot of bark. They measured the bark with their arms and cut it to that length. They made piles big enough for a person to carry on his back and when they had a load for everyone they started back to wherever they were camping. The women peeled off the outer bark with jackknives. They made drying racks and hung up all the bark. They dried a lot of bark and tied it in bundles. In a short time they made many bundles. Only the drying took a long time. They took the bundles to some town where the white people bought slippery elm. They used to come and visit those of us who were living at home and bring us food. Then they went away again to the big forest where they travelled about gathering slippery elm. Today they no longer do that. Today the white people who have timber land keep it for themselves. Years ago it was not that way and the white people used to say, "Help yourself, do whatever it is that you are talking about." They looked for slippery elm and they prepared it to sell. Whatever the situation they always found something to do and were able to obtain food for themselves by such methods. Whatever the circumstances, the Indian is always doing something useful.

*Mountain Wolf Woman, in her* **Mountain Wolf Woman, Sister of Crashing Thunder: The Autobiography of a Winnebago Indian,** *edited by Nancy Oestreich Lurie, The University of Michigan Press, 1961.*

in a book." That is why I am here, saying this at her home. I even rode in an airplane, and I came here. And here I am, telling in Winnebago how I lived my life. This I have written.

The autobiography of Mountain Wolf Woman, ethnographic to be sure, much more closely approaches literature than do most of the life stories collected by anthropologists. When Paul Radin first published *The Autobiography of a Winnebago Indian* in 1920, he was pessimistic about the abilities of outside investigators to get much accurate information about a culture. He wrote that it was only "on rare occasions" that they were successful. The autobiography of Mountain Wolf Woman presents one such "rare occasion," for, by letting Mountain Wolf Woman tell her own story, Lurie was able to publish a life narrative with very little editing. The bonus is that Lurie, as an anthropologist, was able to anticipate what might be confusing to readers and add that information in the notes and appendices. *Mountain Wolf Woman* serves as a model of an autobiography that combines an individual narrative told by the subject with ethnographic detail supplied by a recorder-editor.

## Melissa Hearn (essay date Fall 1992)

SOURCE: "Iterative Score from a Singulative Motif: Mountain Wolf Woman's Song of Herself," in *A/B: Autobiography Studies,* Fall, 1992, pp. 254-72.

[*In the essay below, Hearn discusses the existence of rhetorical devices, particularly the use of an iterative narrative style, in* Mountain Wolf Woman, *which she describes as "a series of teaching stories" about Winnebago history, customs, and beliefs.*]

Scholars have concluded that anthropologists often have imposed their Euro-centric biases on Native American life stories and that educated Native people have often followed certain European narrative forms. However, anthropologist Nancy Lurie, who recorded and annotated *Mountain Wolf Woman, Sister of Crashing Thunder: The Autobiography of a Winnebago Indian,* belongs to a group of post-World War II anthropologists who [according to Hertha D. Wong in her 1992 *Sending My Heart Back Across the Years*] "are acutely self-conscious about the personal and cultural assumptions they bring to their examination of other cultures." Mountain Wolf Woman's autobiography, therefore, is a valuable document for studying and understanding Winnebago culture.

In order to produce a bicultural autobiography which is to be regarded as authentic, proposes Arnold Krupat [in his 1985 *For Those Who Come After: A Study of Native American Autobiography*], one must work from a primary source, such as a tape recording, and one must scrupulously translate the concepts from the original language. According to Krupat's criteria, Lurie's method is a model of responsible editing and translating. Lurie's attention to language and her respect for Mountain Wolf Woman's own translation and interpretation of her story allow Mountain Wolf Woman to continue "the oral tradition in her own way" [Gretchen Bataille and Kathleen Mullen Sands, *American Indian Women: Telling Their Lives*]. Lurie's attention to details of verb tense and Mountain

Wolf Woman's involvement in the translating and editing process further enhance the text as a document for narrative analysis.

Mountain Wolf Woman offers her story upon request as a gift to Lurie, whom she regards as a kinswoman, while she visits in the professor's home. Lurie informs the reader that the recording sessions were held regularly in her living room by the fireplace in which Mountain Wolf Woman often cooked meals for Lurie's family. Therefore, under Mountain Wolf Woman's guidance, the setting complements the custom of instructive storytelling, and her life story is transformed into a vehicle for Lurie's education. In this way Mountain Wolf Woman avoids the tribal taboo of bragging, while she carefully avoids relating, for the most part, incidents which would be embarrassing to others. [In a footnote, Hearn adds: "The veiled identity of her brothers, for instance (Paul Radin's Crashing Thunder uses his brother's name as an alias), may allow Mountain Wolf Woman to tell stories about them."]

Although less is known about women and their life narratives, scholars agree that "women were considered upholders of tradition" [Hertha D. Wong, "Preliterate Native American Autobiography: Forms of Personal Narrative," *MELUS* 14, No. 1 (1987)]. Accordingly, Mountain Wolf Woman's narratives in her autobiography, *Mountain Wolf Woman, Sister of Crashing Thunder,* might be regarded not as traditional teaching stories, but as teachings of tradition. According to Gretchen Bataille and Kathleen Sands, rather than making herself into a heroine, Mountain Wolf Woman "sees herself more as a transmitter of culture, one who is a link between the historical life of her people and the future generations."

Since much of a Native woman's life was often spent in the company of children and other women, women's teachings were quite likely shared in life stories with children and younger adults, allowing both audiences to draw their own conclusions about such issues as proper behavior. Accordingly, it seems reasonable to place Mountain Wolf Woman's stories, as told to Nancy Lurie, in the context of autobiographical "forms that were shaped by the cultural patterns of the tribe but were modified according to the needs of a new audience, purpose, and setting" [Wong].

Mountain Wolf Woman's narratives comprise a series of teaching stories, varied in tonal quality by Mountain Wolf Woman's wit and humor, as well as more serious modes of discourse. The translations of the stories themselves are deceptively unadorned, and for the uninitiated, they are inseparable from Lurie's extensive notes on Winnebago culture. In this manner, Lurie allows [according to Bataille in her "Transformation of Tradition: Autobiographical Indian Women," in Paula Gunn Allen's 1983 *Studies in American Indian Literature: Critical Essays and Course Designs*] "Mountain Wolf Woman to tell her own story as free from intrusion as possible." The combination of Lurie's explanations and Mountain Wolf Woman's teachings provides an exceedingly dense and multilayered text, sustained by the richness of Mountain Wolf Woman's iterative narrative style.

In *Narrative Discourse,* Gérard Genette defines the singulative as the narration of "what happened once." In contrast, he defines the iterative as "narrating one time what happened *n* [any number of] times." Analyzing the structural forms in Marcel Proust's *Remembrance of Things Past,* he concludes that the iterative is communicated in French through the imperfect tense, "what used to happen" and by the implied synthesis of a singulative scene into a paradigm, which stands for a classification of events. What Genette discovers in Proust is that the iterative takes over the narrative, rather than merely serving to summarize the singulative as it does in classical European narration.

Such forms of modernism or anti-romanticism in Proust's work are amazingly similar to the iterative techniques of Winnebago storytelling when translated into English verb tenses by Mountain Wolf Woman and Frances Thundercloud Wentz, a bilingual Winnebago speaker and Mountain Wolf Woman's grandniece. In *Mountain Wolf Woman* we find frequent use of the imperfect, words and phrases such as "always" or "one time," and summary statements, such as "It was very pleasant to live in a rush wigwam." According to Nancy Lurie's personal correspondence with Arnold Krupat, the phrase Paul Radin translates from Winnebago as "I have been told" is more accurately translated, "It is said." Lurie's awareness of the more faithful translation implies an understanding of iterative practice in the original language. Mountain Wolf Woman's iterative rhetorical devices convert an overwhelming number of the singulative stories into paradigms.

In fact, because of Proust's extensive use of the iterative, Genette connects *Remembrance of Things Past* with the autobiographical mode in his response to critics, *Narrative Discourse Revisited.* However, even though there are structural correspondences in the two narrations, Proust's chronicle of a decadent culture in no way shares the purpose of Mountain Wolf Woman's narrative. Nonetheless, narrative discourse theory serves to illuminate aspects of Mountain Wolf Woman's teachings, just as many personal narratives by Native people reveal a body of practical, shared wisdom.

Although Mountain Wolf Woman is telling her life story in the expanded narratives, she repeatedly reverts to the iterative mode. The events thus become part of a teaching story, adapted for the present time and audience, which instructs on different levels. According to Bataille, Native autobiographies of Mountain Wolf Woman's period—the 1930s through the 1950s—reveal that:

> Despite their fears of losing the old ways, the women survived and continued to provide direction for the people. . . . The old ways are not forgotten, but they are seen as unworkable in a new social order.

Therefore, the stories uncover a wealth of Winnebago heritage, in spite of Mountain Wolf Woman's assimilation. Her narratives record the stories of the way historical events are placed in Winnebago life, the meaning of an inherited sense of place, the details of Native healing practices, the importance of visions, spiritual rites and experiences, Winnebago protocol, and tribal traditions. Since the reason for telling her stories is in the nature of tradition and social protocol and since much of this knowledge can be taught without speaking of that which is sacred, most of her teachings focus on these realms. For the purposes of this study, these categories are artificially separated, whereas in the narrative they are inseparable parts of a body of teachings.

The focus on tradition and social protocol is further emphasized by the structure of the narrative which follows a seasonal pattern, as do the customs and lives of the people. The narrative design also follows a circular pattern, ending with the beginning, as Mountain Wolf Woman's relates her reason for telling the stories:

> She [Nancy Lurie] helped the Indians. . . . She wanted me to do her a favor. "Auntie," she said, "if you come and visit me, we will write down Indian stories in a book." That is why I am here, saying this in her home . . . telling in Winnebago how I lived my life.

Although the narratives are not arranged exactly as Mountain Wolf Woman told them, she helped with the organization of the narratives, rearranging certain stories to fit appropriately into the structural pattern. This favor to Lurie, a kinswoman, who with her research had helped the Winnebago with their lawsuits and who had offered Mountain Wolf Woman the gift of an airplane trip and a visit in her home, is part of tradition and protocol. Nancy Lurie's gifts are being returned because she performed a kind act, she respected Winnebago language and culture, and she asked for a favor in the right way.

The stories and their teachings reveal Mountain Wolf Woman's respect for her niece. They are not traditional tribal narratives of trickster or culture heroes and therefore do not dwell on the origin of tribal custom and beliefs, but they are identified by Mountain Wolf Woman as stories, and they are told in the iterative manner of teaching stories. Bataille and Sands assert, "With Mountain Wolf Woman in the position of aunt, and with the power of age and wisdom such a position connotes, it was both appropriate and necessary that she instruct her niece in the ways of the tribe." Mountain Wolf Woman's words, "telling in Winnebago how I lived my life," proclaim the paradigm for this classification of story telling and situate the narrative within a tradition and its protocol. The fact that Lurie felt compelled to illuminate the narrative with her knowledge of Winnebago culture in her extensive notes also emphasizes Lurie's sense of the iterative nature of the utterances over the singulative.

Although Mountain Wolf Woman points to her adaptation to several aspects of the dominant culture, adaptation and independence are part of the present, iterative mode of Winnebago teachings. Certainly her experience does not represent all Winnebago practice. Her life may have departed from certain old ways, yet she presents the Winnebago world view as a vital part of her life. According to Bataille and Sands: "She values the continuities in the culture, but readily adapts to the necessary changes."

Her story does not reveal any self-indulgent aspects of

American romantic individualism. Yet individual freedom, balanced with regard for communal acceptance, is integrated into a value system in which exceptions to the rules are allowed under certain appropriate circumstances. Therefore, Mountain Wolf Woman's narrative, even at its most singulative, or individualistic, is still representative of the iterative, tribal narrative of experience and teachings.

In Mountain Wolf Woman's autobiography, outside events or historical circumstances are secondary to familial and tribal happenings which take place in reaction to these events. Hertha Wong contends that "Family relations in general serve as the central organizing device of her self-narration." Moving to Nebraska as part of the government removal plans, attending boarding school, and having her son return from World War II are important to her story of family and traditions. However, the events are treated as catalysts for attending to kinship, tribal, and communal duties. Significant political occasions or government policies are mentioned because of the way they affect the family, not because the narrator places herself within a linear, historical progression of events.

Furthermore, Wong suggests:

> Perhaps Mountain Wolf Woman's apparent lack of chronological structure is a more accurate reflection of the pattern of her life, which focused on the smaller fluctuations of daily life and family, rather than on the grander shifts of philosophical awakenings.

For example, in connection with having to leave school to follow her family during seasonal hunting trips, Mountain Wolf Woman mentions casually, without condemnation, that she has forgotten many parts of her father's stories. Thus her education through the Winnebago methods and her education through the white methods interrupted each other, but "that is the way with Indians," she concludes. This final iterative comment on these events indicates that without question family traditions (seasonal hunting trips) take precedence over personal interests (Mountain Wolf Woman's enjoyment of school).

In an amusing anecdote, related by Nancy Lurie in the preface, Mountain Wolf Woman writes a letter to Lurie in which she recounts a traditional story about the figures one can see on the moon. Mountain Wolf Woman tells Lurie not to worry about the Russians getting to the moon first since the American Indian is already there. The story is a gift in return for Lurie's cash payment for Mountain Wolf Woman's handwork. It reveals Mountain Wolf Woman's emphasis on a relationship with the cosmos, in contrast to Lurie's focus on the significance of political events.

---

**Mountain Wolf Woman's narratives record the stories of the way historical events are placed in Winnebago life, the meaning of an inherited sense of place, the details of Native healing practices, the importance of visions, spiritual rites and experiences, Winnebago protocol, and tribal traditions.**

*—Melissa Hearn*

---

In addition to Mountain Wolf Woman's feeling of connection to the sky, she reveals the essence of her inherited sense of earthly place through her iterative narration. After she returns with her second husband to live at Black River Falls, part of their ancestral territory, the land they built their house on is sold out from under them. They had intended to buy the land; moreover, they felt they had a right to it since they had erected a house there. Her anger in the story is directed toward the white buyer: "You have lived here a long time. Whatever land you were going to buy, it would seem that you would have bought it long ago." Although she understands the historical relationships with whites and land sales in the area, she regards the greed of the white man as unconscionable and his encroachment as a violation of her sense of inherited place and her right to the land on which they had settled. This confrontation is singulative, but it provides a paradigm for her connection to Black River Falls and her tribal story about sense of place.

An earlier story of her father imparts his sense of inheritance which again is more cosmic and tribal than legal. Lurie notes that after the United States government gave up trying to force the Winnebago out of the Black River Falls area, they offered the tribal members forty-acre homesteads. Since her father was Thunder clan, he felt that he had no business deciding on land matters, which were the province of the Bear clan. Her mother, however, took a homestead, sensing that this was necessary in order to secure an authorized piece of land for the future. Mountain Wolf Woman's iterative comment precedes the relation of this incident and explains her parents' misunderstanding of the dominant culture's perception of land as property, rather than part of an inherited place of shared abundance and livelihood:

> [M]y parents did not realize what they were doing . . . Indians did not look ahead to affairs of this sort. They never looked to the future. They only looked to the present insofar as they had enough to sustain themselves. This is the way Indians used to live . . . "I do not belong to the Earth," he [her father] said.

To belong to the earth in this sense means having one's personal freedom and sense of tribal tradition invaded and becoming trapped by the economics of farming. This concept becomes even clearer when Bad Soldier, her husband, sells their farm in Nebraska so that they can return to live closer to their relatives in Black River Falls. "Well," he said, "we are our own masters. Who is boss over us?"

In notes six and nine to Chapter Five, Lurie humbly explains her own cultural barriers to interpreting Mountain Wolf Woman's stories about land. The principle barrier consists of the concept that being a landholder does not confer status in Winnebago terms as much as being one's own master. However, this does not interfere with the Winnebago feeling for tribal inheritance of place and family, which keeps Mountain Wolf Woman and many others from staying on the Nebraska reservation lands. Implicit in Mountain Wolf Woman's iterative statements is a perception of communal place that is fluid, depending on the seasons and the customs for survival, yet located in a homeland. For instance, she tells about moving to trap muskrats or to gather food: "Eventually it was time to pick blueberries and we moved away to pick blueberries."

Her sense of inherited place is connected with the spiritual communion of family as well as with the land itself. Although she accepts the displacement of her children as they grow up and leave home, she often feels uncomfortable in her realization that they are far away from kin and have no traditional relationships to rely on. To secure her own sense of place while she is travelling, she remarks in English in a dining car full of soldiers that because her son is a soldier, all soldiers are her sons. She is rewarded by the respect of the soldiers and by having one address her as mother. As Wong asserts, "Within her Winnebago sense of relatedness, Mountain Wolf Woman's notion of family extends beyond biological connections." This singulative incident further illustrates an iterative teaching about the ability to call on kinship relationships to create an awareness of place and belonging that goes beyond physical space.

Although Mountain Wolf Woman discloses that she is knowledgeable about Native medicines, she devotes little actual storytelling to healing, other than to declare its power and to communicate the protocol for passing on such knowledge. For example, when her sister first shares peyote with her, we learn more about teaching procedure than healing procedure through her iterative mode. Before Mountain Wolf Woman's child is born, her sister tells her, "When people are in that condition [labor], they use peyote. They have children without much suffering." The incident is singulative, but the quotation is iterative. Her sister shares the healing knowledge that she has learned in Nebraska and offers Mountain Wolf Woman the option to use it by expressing herself in the historical present. Mountain Wolf Woman's conclusion is iterative, although it is in past tense: "My sister did that for me," implying her approval for her sister's teaching and kindness.

When Mountain Wolf Woman receives the teachings of an elder healer, her grandfather [interpreted by Lurie as "first Cousins twice removed"], she gives more attention to the protocol on how one asks for this information and to the explanation of the spiritual dimension of the medicine than to the teachings themselves. Note seven for Chapter Seven reveals Lurie's scientific bias, describing the "magical features" in the use of native medicines. Since Lurie has not asked for the favor of medicine teach-

ing, since she apparently would not accept the spiritual aspects of such teaching, and since she was writing the book to be published for the general public, Mountain Wolf Woman has enough reasons for this singulative silence in the text. This rationale may explain her reluctance to elaborate on certain information even though she allows the old healer to speak for himself on these matters.

As Mountain Wolf Woman briefly quotes the healer's teachings, we recognize the iterative phrasing implicit in her reproduction of his use of the future tense:

> You will prescribe Indian medicines. . . . The power will all be yours. You are not yet holy, but these medicines are holy . . . these medicines are going to talk to you . . . If you put your mind to it intensely, that is where you will have your power.

Mountain Wolf Woman interrupts the quotation, saying that, at the time, she did not understand all of this. Nevertheless, her story reveals the way the spiritual power works for a healer through the medicine. Also omitted is any explanation about whether or not she did come to an understanding of this power. However, her healing practices such as midwifery and her taking responsibility for getting people to hospitals, acceptable customs to Lurie and her non-Native audience, are mentioned.

---

**In Mountain Wolf Woman's autobiography, outside events or historical circumstances are secondary to familial and tribal happenings which take place in reaction to these events.**

**—Melissa Hearn**

---

Mountain Wolf Woman describes several visions with prophetic interpretations. These are the distinct visions of individuals, told in the singulative, but the iterative comments provide a paradigm for the prophetic importance of vision. During the third night of her fast, which she undergoes at the onset of her menses, she dreams of horses. In the conclusion of this narrative, she supplies the iterative tags "always" and "used to" to proclaim its consequences and to verify the traditional qualities of the singulative event: "I must have been one who dreamed about horses. I believe that is why they always used to give me horses." This is also the time of great power for women as givers of life, so fasting would be expected to bring powerful visions for women. Later in the narrative, Mountain Wolf Woman mentions a gift of horses from her adoptive Sioux family to show the high regard in which she was held by them, but it also verifies her prophecy and the importance of the dream vision.

On other occasions, she gains a singulative vision in the iterative framework of prescriptive forms for observing ritual. She begins the story of her peyote vision, "I was sitting with bowed head. We were all sitting with bowed heads. We were supposed to ponder." In her dream there is a storm, and the people have nowhere to turn, except to Jesus. She thanks the god who gave her life and feels "a sensation of great joyousness." The closing of the vision narrative concerns the holiness of the peyote way in general:

> But if someone sees something holy at a peyote meeting, that is really true. They are able to understand things concerning God. I understood that this religion is holy. It is directed toward God.

Rhetorically she casts the meaning of her particular visions as a part of the iterative practices of the peyote cult as a whole. Other references to peyote visions affirm its reliable truths and iterative practice.

Similarly, Mountain Wolf Woman's rendering of her singulative vision of the German soldier is a cautionary tale about the proper observance of ritual. Even though Mountain Wolf Woman is a Christian and a peyotist, she is critical of the "conservative" or traditional people who do not observe the forms of the scalp dance. After some participants go back to their cars and tents to sleep, Mountain Wolf Woman and a few others keep dancing. At this point in her narrative, she warns against holding a ceremony "without feeling any reverence for it." However, inherent in these warnings is the iterative characterization of the ways that ceremonies have always been and should continue to be. Her reward for proper observance is a vision of the dead soldier to whom she speaks. Her nephew responds to her story of the vision so as to confirm the ritual prophecy of the vision in its iterative sense—this is the way it would always be and so it continues:

> "Well, Aunt," he said, "you respected that scalp dance from the beginning. You were taking part when it ended . . . You spent the time properly. That is what you did. You spoke the truth when you said that we beat them . . . Whatever good luck was to have befallen him we won for ourselves."

In this instance, her singulative vision requires an iterative response because its meaning is more communal than personal.

The special powers of the elderly to communicate with the spirit world and their visionary powers are also a component of the iterative message in the singulative stories. Of the grandfather from whom she obtains the knowledge of medicines, she observes:

> The thinking powers of old people are strong and if one of them thinks good things for you, whatever he wishes for you, you will obtain that good fortune. That is what they always said.

One of Mountain Wolf Woman's earliest memories is of an elderly man returning an earthly favor with a spiritual gift. Her mother asks her sons to fulfill the man's dying wish, which is to be carried outside. To repay them, he prophesies that whenever the boys eat skunk meat, his favorite food, if they offer tobacco and think of him, they will have their wish granted. Mountain Wolf Woman uses these stories and the iterative mode to illustrate the respect that should be shown to old people and to emphasize their spiritual importance: "That is what we used to do. We respected old people, but today they do not respect old people."

Although social protocol is not completely separate from the spiritual aims of an individual in the Winnebago culture, such connections in Mountain Wolf Woman's narrative are often taken for granted when codes of behavior are emphasized. The reasons for doing and saying the right things, such as showing respect for elders, may be intrinsically linked to regard for spiritual concerns, but codes for social behavior related through iterative rhetorical devices comprise one of the strongest features of her teachings. Again this may be due to her perceived audience, Nancy Lurie and the uninitiated non-Native reader. In the education of children, codes of behavior and introduction to traditions would come before an understanding of the deeper spiritual meanings attained through fasting and vision. Thus her audience would stand in an analogous relation to children, who would learn the ways of the culture and their deepening significance as they grew up.

One of the teachings of Winnebago protocol is that some customs are not revealed. In describing her initiation into the medicine society, for example, Mountain Wolf Woman reports that "they did all the things they still do when they have a medicine dance. They even 'shot me.'" However, the death and rebirth ritual is not delineated or explained. In a singulative incident, she tells of one woman, who was heavy, and could not fall properly when she was shot, no matter how they tried to teach her. How one was to fall or how one was initiated is thus not depicted, but the protocol, a proper way of doing it is stressed without describing the details.

Even though Mountain Wolf Woman turns away from some of the ways of the medicine lodge when she becomes a Christian and a peyotist, she reveals that she has retained respect for the traditional ways. Her story of the scalp dance ceremony shows that she preserved her reverence for ceremonies by what she tells us and what she does not. In a particular case, Nancy Lurie translates "old religious ways" from ". . . when they spoke about *that*" (emphasis added) for the elucidation of the audience. However, it may be a significant breach of protocol, illustrated by Mountain Wolf Woman's use of the iterative mode, to speak of or name sacred rites.

On the other hand, Mountain Wolf Woman's narrative is full of detailed description of daily activity. Accordingly, instructions on how to perform activities in the right manner are expressed in the iterative. In the chapter entitled "Livelihood," summer berry picking illustrates the industry of the Winnebago. According to Mountain Wolf Woman's pronouncement, "Thus the Indian came through history." Lurie interprets this "curious phrase" to mean that "the Winnebago are always adaptable and self-sufficient, not that they traditionally sold blueberries to whites." Mountain Wolf Woman's iterative remark, typical of her concluding utterances throughout the narration, portrays not only the enterprising activities of the Winnebago, but the communal and cooperative dimension of such harvests.

The polite way to treat relatives and in-laws also comes through the iterative mode of Mountain Wolf Woman's narrative. The gentle teasing used to balance favor toward children and to promote modesty is disclosed through the comments on her own birth: "I was the last child—'Poor quality' they used to say of that one." When Mountain Wolf Woman arrives at her first mother-in-law's house, she brings gifts for the female relatives and receives gifts in return. Although her major point in the conclusion concerns the arranged marriage, which turned out to be an unhappy one, protocol is also noted in her observation, "That is the way they used to do." She also goes against her own better judgment when she is initiated into the medicine lodge by her mother-in-law because "She asked me very nicely . . . I will do graciously what she asks me to do, but after that I will do what I want to do." Proper protocol, noted by a concluding paradigm, in this case, asking in the proper way, commands at least temporary compliance.

On the other hand, the way her oldest brother advises Mountain Wolf Woman on her second marriage requires her to take his suggestion seriously, but not necessarily to comply with it. He points out that Bad Soldier "knows how to take care of himself. If you make a home someplace, then I will have someplace to go to visit." According to the explanatory notes, Mountain Wolf Woman later clarified for Lurie in English the meaning of her commitment. Mountain Wolf Woman's older brother's wanting to visit her and his wise appraisal of her future husband held considerable weight with her in making her own decision to marry. This was more significant to her than her younger brother's promise that she was required to fulfill with her first marriage. Her older brother's utterance, translated in the future tense but indicative of the future perfect "I would have," signifies his desire to see his sister and for her to be happy. Her explanation, supplied by the editor, suggests that her consideration of Bad Soldier is based on the way serious suggestions should be made among siblings.

Protocol is a major consideration in making requests as well as complying with kinship obligations. In asking for the knowledge of Indian medicines, Mountain Wolf Woman is careful to ask in the right way, which includes appropriate gifts, concern for the welfare of her grandfather, and the appropriate feeling of respect, demonstrated by her words, "Indian medicines help people." She records his reply, revealing his approval of her following protocol: "You said something worthwhile. You have asked for a very good thing. You said a good thing. You are going to have something valuable." The pattern of this particular story and conversation is more iterative and ritualistic than singulative. The iterative instruction is apparent in her reward. Although the exact words must come from each individual when making a request, the attitude of proper respect must be implicit in those words. However, improper demonstrations of respect are not rewarded. For instance, the neighbors who bring the grandfather food, but who are "always talking about it" are not honoring the man, but are looking for approval from others. Mountain Wolf Woman uses the iterative "always" in this instance to illuminate the boundaries of protocol.

Other negative examples, which flag improper behavior, are drawn from Mountain Wolf Woman's first marriage. When her mother-in-law initiates her into the lodge, Mountain Wolf Woman explains, "She did not give me that big otterskin bag they wanted to give me. She was selfish." Even her own husband disapproves of his mother's breaking her promise to give Mountain Wolf Woman the bag. Selfishness is clearly a transgression that the mother-in-law deserves to be shamed for committing. Protocol in this story has less to do with the tradition of the lodge than the way one treats others—the condemnation of selfishness indicates that this story illustrates a paradigmatic experience and is, therefore, iterative.

In contrast, Mountain Wolf Woman's second husband bought new dishes for her with money left to him by his mother. He tells her, "If my mother were living, she would not begrudge you anything she had." The conditional tense in Mountain Wolf Woman's quotation of his statement expresses the iterative mode, highlighting the code for generous behavior that a proper mother-in-law would show a good daughter-in-law. Thus his statement is a compliment to both his wife and his mother from him and from Mountain Wolf Woman in her retelling the story.

As a foil, Mountain Wolf Woman tells the story of how she rejects her first husband because he is jealous. She uses the iterative to describe his continued violation of what should be their mutual trust in each other:

> He used to accuse me of being with other men. That made me angry. I hated him. He used to watch me too. So, I said to him one time, "No matter how closely you watch me, if I am going to leave you, I am going to leave you!" . . . That is what I did to him.

His unsuitable actions and attitude toward her seriously violate marital protocol and are clearly not to be tolerated. His story is a prototype of bad faith. Her family gladly accepts her back, generously offering her a harness and buggy hitch to help her move. Her family's response illustrates the familial and social code of generosity and the trusting relationship between relatives, differentiating her own relatives from her first husband and in-laws. [In a footnote, Hearn writes: "Mountain Wolf Woman's stories also illustrate the polite way to treat distant relatives and friends."]

Mountain Wolf Woman's affirmation of the importance of gift-giving and ways of spiritual validity contrast with that of her brother, Crashing Thunder. His story is structured around giving up the old ways. She confesses, "At one time I thought it [traditional religious practice] was just empty talk." However, proper observances of etiquette require her participation in the dance, which leads to vision and her validation of Winnebago tradition. Even this significant spiritual revelation is supported by the iterative context of protocol. Similarly, numerous other stories signifying proper behavior, though having less serious consequences or rewards, are important enough to enter the narrative with iterative commentary.

> **Mountain Wolf Woman's stories are not traditional, tribal stories, but they are stories of tradition.**
>
> —*Melissa Hearn*

Equal in emphasis to protocol, or the forms for showing proper respect for one individual to another, are Mountain Wolf Woman's teachings on tradition or the oral practice of handing down culture. Certain practices, exemplified in the stories, signify cultural values, which may include forms of protocol, but which are often more inclusive. In addition, Mountain Wolf Woman's narrative communicates the peyote tradition, which was passed on to the Winnebago. Although Mountain Wolf Woman, like many informants who gave their stories to anthropologists, adapted to the changes in Winnebago life and adopted other traditions, she did not completely desert her original culture. Her iterative voice in the narrative is associated with the great respect she still has for traditions, which she does not find to be mutually exclusive with her conversion to the peyote way and its inclusion of Christianity. Her respect for a variety of traditions is acknowledged by her funeral services. Nancy Lurie records that:

> Conservative relatives and friends held a brief version of the traditional Winnebago wake . . . ; her own peyote beliefs were represented in a well-attended peyote meeting . . . ; and . . . she was laid to rest at the mission cemetery at Black River Falls after Christian services at the mission church.

In fact, respect for the beliefs of others is itself a tradition of the nonproselytizing religions of Native peoples.

Although most of the spiritual traditions are covered [elsewhere in this article], spiritual tradition as the center of life also is reflected in traditional social behavior associated with the peyote religion. As Mountain Wolf Woman explains, "Whenever there were peyote people they all came forth. . . . Every Saturday night we had a meeting." The hostility of the conservative people towards the peyotists is characterized by their desire to break up the social/spiritual unit. They threatened to "scatter us," explains Mountain Wolf Woman. "They watched us with harmful intent." The importance of the tradition of communal life is expressed through Mountain Wolf Woman's story of how a group might be punished. Thus noncommunal living can be a direct threat to survival. Although Native religions were not missionary in character or principle, apparently the introduction of the pan-Indian/Christian practice of the peyote band was threatening to Winnebago tradition. Perhaps their reaction was based on the many disastrous effects of Christian missions on Native peoples.

Mountain Wolf Woman's concern about her daughter's move to Oregon also reflects the strength of the tradition of communal living and family obligations. Without relatives around to care for her daughter's family in times of trouble, Mountain Wolf Woman feared for them, especially because of her son-in-law's "craving for liquor." She advises him, "Do not do there as you behave here. It is very far, that Oregon, I am not always going to know what you are doing." This last negative phrase implies that "always knowing" and being there to help out are the cultural norms.

When Mountain Wolf Woman herself lived away from her family, she preferred to live near other Native people, such as the Sioux. Her connection to the Sioux community is revealed by her adoption. Other Native families joined her and her husband after they went to South Dakota, and they all trapped and worked together. Mountain Wolf Woman reinforces the communal tradition by commenting on the group's trapping success, which contrasts with her preceding story of the single-family farm in Nebraska with all its debts.

The tradition of family responsibility is told through the story of her return to Oregon to take her daughter's children home with her when the daughter's husband leaves and she is unable to care for the children. Mountain Wolf Woman reports, "The little children lived at my house. They went to school and they stayed there with me and they grew big." Her emphasis in this story is on the iterative parable concerning the importance of the education and health of the children and their eventual reunion with their mother. Mountain Wolf Woman also raises another grandchild after her son and his wife are separated. When she receives word from a distant relative that the mother is not caring properly for the child, Mountain Wolf Woman takes appropriate action. The story of the Uncle's words enforce the tradition: "I thought that if you had your own grandchild you would take good care of it." Mountain Wolf Woman concludes with the iterative statement, "That is what he said." Such a statement verifies the significance and the appropriateness of her relative's information and delicate reminder to her of her duty. Family responsibility is thereby corroborated by the message and its medium.

Various other family traditions which involve taking care of relatives are related through the rhetorical devices of the narrator. When an old man interrupts the peyote ceremony with insults to Squeaking Wing, the speaker, the younger man claims kinship in order to disperse the insult and show respect to the drunk: "That is my uncle who is speaking. What he is saying does not matter. He is just petting me." Nancy Lurie explains the reticence of Squeaking Wing to criticize the old man as an illustration of "Christian forbearance", however, the claim of family ties and the teasing kinship tradition are paradigmatic circumstances under which such forbearance is granted without the speaker's losing face.

The tradition of family connection and helpfulness is illustrated throughout the narrative. Such traditions as teaching through gentle ridicule, illustrated in the humorous story of the waterlily root, and joking relationships with in-laws, represented in the story of Mountain Wolf Woman's brother-in-law, Red Horn, are lively illustrations. The concluding sentences to these stories are iterative statements reaffirming the importance of traditions.

Honors, on the other hand, do not come merely through the kinship traditions. They must be earned, usually through following tradition. Since Mountain Wolf Woman avoids bragging about herself, her singulative deeds are often implied through iterative narration. When Mountain Wolf Woman is asked to become a member of the medicine lodge, for example, she explains that this is because of the respect the lodge members had for her mother-in-law. However, her own mother says about Mountain Wolf Woman, "They are saying something good. . . . She is going to earn something for herself." Such an honor would, of course, be worthwhile, and Mountain Wolf Woman's initiation would confirm her "right to be a lodge member." The honor earned is the right to participate in the traditional rites. Also earned by singulative deeds, which are silent in the text, is the respect of her Sioux adoptive parents. The adoption itself is an honor and the gift of four horses signifies their respect. Mountain Wolf Woman comments, "They thought a lot of me, those Sioux brothers, sisters and uncles." In her stories, then, tradition and family relations are cultural paradigms and signs of virtue.

Winnebago traditions (and the kinship obligations associated with them), however, are not always easy for Mountain Wolf Woman to comply with, especially in the case of her first marriage. She reflects on her experience in the iterative mode, "That is how they used to arrange things for young women in the past. They made the girls marry into what ever family they decided upon." The marriage is part of a kinship obligation to her brother, and her mother explains that her brother will be embarrassed if she does not comply. However, her mother also confides to the unhappy bride that "When you are older and know better, you can marry whomever you yourself think that you want to marry." Mountain Wolf Woman states, "I did not forget it!" Therefore, built into the tradition of arranged marriages and respect for the honor of one's brothers is some flexibility. Once compliance with the tradition has taken place, the individual can assert her right to happiness.

Another cultural tradition Mountain Wolf Woman implies through the iterative repetition in her teaching stories is independence. When she takes care of the elderly, she honors traditional Winnebago protocol, but she also provides as much independence as possible for them. She offers gifts and brings food for her grandfather, but she also buys him a small stove so that he can fix his own food. She reports his reply, "Now I will be able to cook for myself," and concludes with an iterative remark, "and that is what he did." The sense of cultural approval of the tradition of self-sufficiency is also repeated in another story in which Mountain Wolf Woman helps an elderly, neglected woman to help herself.

Similarly, Mountain Wolf Woman insists on her own independence. When she goes to Oregon to see her daughter, she takes a job that her son-in-law finds for her. Nancy Lurie assures us in a note that "this was intended and understood as thoughtful concern for her welfare. It enabled her to earn money and not be dependent on her daughter." Mountain Wolf Woman also refuses her grandchildren's offers to live with them, saying: "Not until I am much older. When I am so old that I cannot care for myself, then you can take care of me." These words are introduced by the iterative tag, "I always say," implying the importance of the tradition of independence. She is particularly angry that her house at Black River Falls is regarded as the same as those who had houses built for them, because she provided material and bought the fixtures. The white agent's lack of acknowledgment of her independence receives her scornful reproach.

Mountain Wolf Woman's stories are not traditional, tribal stories, but they are stories of tradition. The iterative voice proclaims and communicates her Winnebago heritage to her non-Native audience. This is not an autobiography that has taken on the European forms of the confessional or the success story as some early Native American autobiographical narratives have been described. In addition, although the narration of her life story exists primarily because of the desire of an anthropologist, this anthropologist is also a younger relative who deserves to be taught. As Paula Gunn Allen points out about the continuance of traditional teachings:

> As teacher, the woman is the link between one generation and the next; thus, if she fails to teach her children, she has failed herself and her tribe. Women represent continuity and completeness. If women fail to pass on their contributions, they cause the circle to be broken, the sacred tree to die.

Through its iterative rhetorical forms, Mountain Wolf Woman's narrative reveals a tradition of responsible teaching passed down from one generation of women to the next.

### Susan Gardner (essay date October 1992 & February 1993)

SOURCE: " 'And Here I Am, Telling in Winnebago How I Lived My Life': Teaching Mountain Wolf Woman," in *College Literature,* Vol. 19, No. 3 & Vol. 20, No. 1, October, 1992 & February, 1993, pp. 233-36.

[*In the excerpt below, Gardner discusses the literary aspects of* Mountain Wolf Woman.]

[*Mountain Wolf Woman, Sister of Crashing Thunder*] enjoys an unusual popularity for academic texts; it has been continuously in print for 31 years. Reasons for its enduring reputation include the upsurge of interest in American Indian literature and women's studies. Originally its editor, anthropologist Nancy Lurie, thought that an autobiography by her adoptive aunt Stella would be interesting in itself and, as the subtitle indicates, as a gender-specific comparison with the autobiography of Mountain Wolf Woman's brother Crashing Thunder produced by Paul Radin. But neither of these is an autobiography in such conventional Western senses as "confessional in form, exploring the inner labyrinth of the psyche, recording the emotional vibrations of the writer as well as the cultural milieu, documenting historic events and the autobiographer's relationships with members of society, encompassing both the inner and public lives of the subject over a lengthy period of time" [Gretchen M. Bataille and Kathleen Mullen Sands, *American Indian Women: Telling Their Lives,* 1984]. David Brumble does in fact claim that Sam Blowsnake ("Crashing Thunder") was making a shift in American Indian autobiographies parallel to the conversion narrative of St. Augustine. It most certainly is an account of salvation; but with Radin's heavy editorial control, the "autobiography" is difficult to evaluate. Radin described it as a "rake's progress" and compared Blowsnake to Candide. Such an imposition of Western categories on a non-Western text is understandable, but also misleading. Thanks to Arnold Krupat's detailed study of American Indian autobiographies as "original, bicultural composite composition" in *For Those Who Come After,* the complexities of rendering an "authentic" Indian voice (when no traditional Indian would even have thought of "producing"—I use the word advisedly, for most "autobiographies" were dictated through interpreters—an autobiography) can be understood as a process whereby Western culture appropriates "the other" in its own terms. . . .

Bataille and Sands, in *American Indian Women: Telling Their Lives,* do accept Mountain Wolf Woman's narrative as "literary," by which they mean techniques usually associated with literature: "dialogue, expression of inner emotions and responses to events, a first-person omniscient viewpoint, latitude in handling time and sequence of events, and an awareness of audience." But such techniques are not limited to self-consciously literary artifacts, and Mountain Wolf Woman's is not such an artifact. When Mountain Wolf Woman narrated in Winnebago what she thought was her complete story, which Lurie then asked a grandniece of Mountain Wolf Woman's to translate into English, Lurie was very disappointed. Mountain Wolf Woman used no more than a half reel of tape, and this version is included as Appendix A. . . . Lurie transformed her aunt's seemingly random and schematic recollections (which to Mountain Wolf Woman, of course, were not) into a form familiar to Western readers. Unlike many previous bicultural composers, Lurie makes no claims of having had no influence on her narratee's story; she meticulously outlines every step (and also resorts to extensive notes to add information for us that Mountain Wolf Woman assumed, correctly, any Winnebago relative—such as her niece—would understand). The narrator's intended audience, then, is Winnebago, not us. In a sense, we eavesdrop on a private conversation. Unlike Radin, who borrowed from previous narratives by Crashing Thunder, including some which may not even be by Crashing Thunder but reflect Radin's understanding of Winnebago (male) culture over many years, Lurie scrupulously set out her own methodology and motivation. Also, Crashing Thunder's text (one of them, at least) was *written* in a Winnebago syllabary by Crashing Thunder, whereas Mountain Wolf Woman *told* her story as a favor to her niece. This composition process can illuminate . . . culturally differing notions of self, role, and society, and lead them to question what "literature" in a Western sense has conventionally meant.

> **Mountain Wolf Woman's intended audience is Winnebago. In a sense, we eavesdrop on a private conversation.**
>
> **—*Susan Gardner***

One result of Lurie's and Mountain Wolf Woman's collaboration is, as David Murray has commented [in *Forked Tongues: Speech, Writing and Representation in North American Indian Texts,* 1991]:

> [a] typical multi-layered sandwich, where we are given a foreword, a preface, the text with extensive footnotes, then the first brief version of her life given by Mountain Wolf Woman, which she extended when she saw Lurie's disappointment—indicating the role of white expectations in the creation of such texts. . . . At several points Lurie refers to "literary" and "scholarly" criteria which decided the style of the English version. Unfortunately [and rather like Bataille and Sands] she never develops what she means by these terms, and when we look at all of the layers of the "sandwich," questions of authenticity [and, I would amplify, "authorship"] become even more confusing. What role . . . does a letter from Mountain Wolf Woman, written in non-standard English . . .ü play in the combination of voices? . . . We are offered either her poor written English—which leaves us at a distance from her "real" voice, though it is her own actual product—or a translation of her speaking Winnebago which uses all the (white) literary and scholarly resources available to recreate a sense of her real presence and speech.

However, rather than a static sandwich (in which Mountain Wolf Woman's contribution in English would represent a dab of mustard), what we have is a plurivocal, indeed intervocal text that does not pretend to answer, only to raise, issues of cultural translation. This is hardly a feature of American Indian texts alone, but exploring Krupat's principle of original, bicultural composition encourages students to ponder Western notions of "authorship"/ownership and textual authority.

Comparing Mountain Wolf Woman's two narratives reveals at least three constant themes in her life (and other Winnebagoes'): frequent travel to visit a wide network of kin separated by various Federal policies, and in search of work and a syncretically satisfying spirituality in a time of drastic change. . . . Both start with "Mother" (not with "I") and both show her own satisfaction as mother, wife, and provider. She is no proto-feminist, and women's studies courses will properly teach her narrative as an illustration of non-Western gender arrangements. The original narrative, moreover, suggests that she did not "love" her second husband, marrying, as she did the first time, due to the patriarchal constraints imposed upon her by her brothers, not her father. The expanded narrative contains moving descriptions of her grief when her second husband dies, as well as when her son is reported wounded in World War II. The extended introspection, which Bataille and Sands regard as "literary," is to my mind a Western convention satisfying our notions of individual subjectivity. Mountain Wolf Woman's own sense of self is more action-oriented: "This is what I do. That is the way I am."

---

**David Murray on the authenticity of *Mountain Wolf Woman*:**

[One] feature of . . . anthropological autobiographies is the stress in prefaces and introductions on the personal bonds of friendship between editor and subject. Nancy Lurie, following in [Paul] Radin's footsteps, elicited the life story of Mountain Wolf Woman, who was, in fact, Crashing Thunder's sister, and her introduction gives a warm and intimate picture of the old lady and her stay in Lurie's household. Lurie's text is a typical multi-layered sandwich, where we are given a foreword, a preface, the text with extensive footnotes, then the first brief version of her life given by Mountain Wolf Woman, which she extended when she saw Lurie's disappointment—indicating the role of white expectations in the creation of such texts. After all this, there is commentary on both texts by Lurie. At several points Lurie refers to 'literary' and 'scholarly' criteria which decided the style of the English version. Unfortunately she never develops what she means by these terms, and when we look at all the layers of the 'sandwich', questions of authenticity become even more confusing. What role, for instance, does a letter from Mountain Wolf Woman, written in non-standard English, and reprinted in Lurie's introduction, play in the combination of voices? It has a very different sort of claim to authenticity from that of the rest of the text, which was spoken in Winnebago but is given to us in an English which is not like that of the letter. We are offered either her poor written English—which leaves us at a distance from her 'real' voice, though it is her own actual product—or a translation of her speaking Winnebago which uses all the (white) literary and scholarly resources available to recreate a sense of her real presence and speech, in all its resonances.

*David Murray, in his* Forked Tongues: Speech, Writing and Representation in North American Indian Texts, *Pinter Publishers, 1991.*

---

## Hertha Dawn Wong   (essay date 1992)

SOURCE: "Literary Boundary Cultures: The Life Histories of Plenty-Coups, Pretty-Shield, Sam Blowsnake, and Mountain Wolf Woman," in *Sending My Heart Back across the Years: Tradition and Innovation in Native American Autobiography,* Oxford University Press, 1992, pp. 88-116.

[*In the excerpt below, Wong discusses the creation of Mountain Wolf Woman's autobiography and the volume's focus on family, education, and marriage.*]

In 1958, thirty-eight years after Sam Blowsnake wrote his autobiography [*Crashing Thunder*] in the Winnebago syllabary, his sister Mountain Wolf Woman narrated her life story to her friend, adopted niece, and amanuensis, Nancy O. Lurie. Traveling from Black River Falls, Wisconsin, to Ann Arbor, Michigan, Mountain Wolf Woman stayed with the Luries for five weeks as a visiting relative. During that time, Mountain Wolf Woman spoke her life story in Winnebago into a tape recorder; then [according to Lurie] she "repeated the entire story on tape in English using the Winnebago recordings as a guide." With the assistance of Mountain Wolf Woman's grandniece, Frances Thundercloud Wentz, Lurie translated the Winnebago into "literary English." According to anthropologist Lurie, Mountain Wolf Woman did not have the intense problems adjusting to reservation life that plagued her brother. Like him, she had a traditional Winnebago upbringing, and like him, she converted to the peyote religion. Unlike her brother, however, she made the transformation from the old ways to the new ways with apparent ease. According to [Lurie's preface], "Mountain Wolf Woman's autobiography is a predictable reflection of the greater self-confidence enjoyed by women in comparison to men in a culture undergoing rapid and destructive changes." Mountain Wolf Woman's "greater self-confidence" has to do with "the greater continuity and stability of female roles," as well as her older age at the time of relating her autobiography (she told her story at the age of seventy-four, while her brother wrote his before the age of forty-five), not to mention her favored status as the baby of the family.

Lurie provides a candid and detailed explanation of when, why, and how she collected Mountain Wolf Woman's life history. In Appendix B [of *Mountain Wolf Woman, Sister of Crashing Thunder*], she acknowledges the "element of coercion" involved in the fact that she "manipulated the kinship structure for [her] own purposes," asking her aunt for a favor that could not, because of the Winnebago sense of familial obligation, be denied her. She also describes her relationship with Mountain Wolf Woman, the interview setting (Lurie's home), her own editorial principles, Mountain Wolf Woman's character, Winnebago character in general, traditional Winnebago male and female roles, dominant themes, and Mountain Wolf Woman's storytelling skills. Throughout the autobiographical account, she adds footnotes to clarify meaning, tone, or performance. Mountain Wolf Woman, like Plenty-Coups and Pretty-Shield, was a gifted storyteller and "an accomplished mimic," often taking on the voices of various speakers. Besides mimicking, she would often "relive events as she recalled them," crying or chuckling whenever she felt moved to do so. Lurie, however, makes no attempt to incorporate performance cues into Mountain Wolf Woman's translated narrative. Instead, she limits her commentary to footnotes, a preface, and an appendix. The familiar pattern of framing the life history of the speaker between the authenticating and expository sections of the editor continues. In Appendix A, Lurie includes Mountain Wolf Woman's first attempt at telling her life story—a very brief account that disappointed Lurie so evidently that Mountain Wolf Woman retold each story in fuller form.

Mountain Wolf Woman's oral autobiography, tape-recorded by Lurie in 1958, relates her experiences of traveling, growing up, marrying, being initiated into the medicine lodge, converting to peyote, joining a Christian church, learning Winnebago medicines from her grandfather, and caring for her family. As Mountain Wolf Woman, whose name was given to her by an elderly woman from the Wolf clan, discusses the domestic details of food collection and preparation and family relations, she intersperses humorous anecdotes and old stories. Mountain Wolf Woman narrates a humorous personal story about how as a little girl gathering yellow waterlily roots with her mother and sisters, she imitated her older sister. Observing her sister tie a waterlily root in her belt (to ward off anything bad that might affect her pregnancy), the little girl did the same—much to the amusement of those gathered. Gretchen Bataille and Kathleen Sands point out [in their *American Indian Women* (1984)] that rather than "cast themselves in heroic molds," female Indian autobiographers tend "to concentrate on everyday events and activities and family crisis events." In general, this seems true of Mountain Wolf Woman's narrative.

---

**Family relations in general serve as the central organizing device of Mountain Wolf Woman's self-narration. Grandparents, parents, siblings, husbands, children, and grandchildren provide the context for her life.**

**—*Hertha Dawn Wong***

---

In contrast to her brother's dramatic cultural and religious conflicts, which shape his autobiography, Mountain Wolf Woman's rather placid autobiographical account is anecdotal. According to Ruth Underhill [in her foreword to ***Mountain Wolf Woman***], "No particular pattern appears other than the slow change from the life of an illiterate Indian food gatherer to that of a responsible church member who lives in a modern house, travels in Pullman trains, and believes in the Christian heaven." Underhill's comments reveal her cultural bias, which assumes an evolution from "illiterate Indian food gatherer" to "responsible church member," as though living in the "modern" world necessarily erases one's Indian identity. Perhaps Mountain Wolf Woman's apparent lack of chronological structure is a more accurate reflection of the pattern of her life, which focused on the smaller fluctuations of daily life and family, rather than on the grander shifts of philosophical awakenings. Theorists of autobiography note a similar associational structure (rather than a linear narrative with identifiable beginnings, middles, and ends) and a similar emphasis on the minutiae of domestic detail (rather than on worldly actions) in the writings of many Euro-American women as well. Rather than assume "no particular pattern" other than the obvious pre-contact/post-contact experience, it is more appropriate to reconsider

notions of what constitutes a "pattern." Focusing on the daily fluctuations of family relationships is suitable for a woman who had eleven children, thirty-eight grandchildren, and nine great-grandchildren, especially since she raised many of them herself.

Even though Mountain Wolf Woman focuses on family and communal activities and the domestic rhythms of her life, there are two dramatic personal incidents that she spends more than the usual time narrating. The events are related to each other and, not surprisingly, linked to family. Her education and her first marriage were personal crises for Mountain Wolf Woman. She criticizes her family for disrupting her education and for forcing her to marry an unworthy man. Mountain Wolf Woman explains that at age nine she attended school for two years in Tomah, Wisconsin. Although she enjoyed being there, her parents took her out of school to travel with the family as they followed the harvesting and hunting cycles. Years later, as a teenager, she returned to school. There she met Nancy Smith, an Oneida and "the girl's matron." Together they cruised around on their bicycles, rode horses, participated in Indian dances, and enjoyed themselves. When her family suddenly removed her from school again, she had no idea why. "Alas, I was enjoying school so much," says Mountain Wolf Woman, "and they made me stop." She did not discover until she returned home that she was going to be married. Her mother explained: "It is your brother's doing. You must do whatever your brother says." Because she could not embarrass her brother or violate the taboo that might end in suffering for him, Mountain Wolf Woman had to submit to his wishes and to this marriage. She found out from her mother how this came about. It seems her "older brother had been drinking and was asleep." When Sam Blowsnake awoke, he found a man fanning mosquitoes from his face. To dispense a debt of gratitude for this kindness, her older brother promised his sister to the solicitous man.

Mountain Wolf Woman conveyed her anger and resentment even as she fulfilled her familial duties. As Mountain Wolf Woman's mother combed her weeping daughter's hair in preparation for her soon-to-be married status, she said: "Daughter, I prize you very much, but this matter cannot be helped. When you are older and know better, you can marry whomever you yourself think that you want to marry." The dutiful daughter never forgot her mother's words. Throughout her description of the marriage arrangement (an economic exchange), the trials of the marriage, and the divorce, Mountain Wolf Woman refers to her first husband as "that man," refusing even to name him. After two children and several unhappy years with "that man," Mountain Wolf Woman left him. Shortly thereafter, once again with the intervention of a brother (this time her eldest brother, the true Crashing Thunder), and with her consent and approval, Mountain Wolf Woman married Bad Soldier, with whom she lived happily until his death in 1936.

Just as Pretty-Shield's narrative is punctuated by interruptions from grandchildren, an intrusion of contemporary Indian life on the stories of the past, family, particularly grandchildren, permeates Mountain Wolf Woman's story.

Family relations in general serve as the central organizing device of her self-narration. Grandparents, parents, siblings, husbands, children, and grandchildren provide the context for Mountain Wolf Woman's life. She ends her narrative with accounts of corresponding with her children now "scattered over great distances," raising her grandchildren, and narrating her life story to her "niece." Family relations, then, determine the scope and nature of her life and even its narration. With her Winnebago sense of relatedness, Mountain Wolf Woman's notion of family extends beyond biological connections. One brief anecdote illustrates this. On a trip to Oregon to visit one of her daughters, she learned that a son of hers had been wounded in Germany. On her train trip back to Wisconsin, she and her granddaughter sat at a table in the dining car with two young men "wearing khaki uniforms." "I am going to eat with my sons," she said to them. " 'Whenever I see somebody wearing khaki, I always think that might be my son.' The boy across from me got up," she continues. " 'My mother died when I was born. I never had a mother. Now I have a mother,' he said. Then he shook my hand." The worried mother, far from her Wisconsin home and her wounded son, mothered those who were near.

Mountain Wolf Woman shares certain themes with Plenty-Coups, Pretty-Shield, and Sam Blowsnake. Like them, she discusses her participation in dances and ceremonies. Also, she continues to highlight the differences between the old days and the present. Even though she has adjusted to the new ways and does not seem embittered about such enforced change, she recalls that in the old days, "[w]e respected the old people, but today they do not respect the old people." Since she is now one of "the old people," this change has deep meaning for her personally. Likewise, she speaks wistfully of the days when "Indians were real Indians."

---

**Additional coverage of Mountain Wolf Woman's life and career is contained in the following sources published by Gale Research:** *Contemporary Authors,* **Vol. 144 and** *Native North American Literature.*

# Abraham Polonsky

## 1910-

(Full name Abraham Lincoln Polonsky; also wrote under the joint pseudonym Emmett Hogarth with Mitchell A. Wilson) American filmmaker, screenwriter, and novelist.

The following entry provides an overview of Polonsky's career through 1988.

## INTRODUCTION

Polonsky is best known for three films: *Body and Soul* (1947), *Force of Evil* (1949), and *Tell Them Willie Boy Is Here* (1969). These works, like his novels and other screen- and teleplays, concern individuals who, though they are embroiled in social and political corruption, struggle, ultimately, against their circumstances for a measure of redemption. A former member of the American Communist Party and a lifelong socialist, Polonsky was "blacklisted," not allowed to work, in Hollywood for twenty years after he refused to cooperate with Joseph McCarthy's House Un-American Activities Committee. Many critics, citing the thematic and aesthetic richness of Polonsky's first major works in film, count the two decades in which he was prevented from developing his craft among the most unfortunate effects of McCarthyism.

### Biographical Information

Polonsky was born in New York City to Russian-Jewish immigrant parents. He studied literature and philosophy at the City College of New York, receiving his B.A. in 1932. He then attended Columbia Law School, from which he received his LL.B. in 1935, and soon began working for a law firm in New York. It was also during this time that Polonsky's social and political ideals led him to join the American Communist Party. Pursuing his interest in writing, Polonsky worked briefly on the radio series *The Goldbergs.* Soon after, he gave up practicing law and devoted his energies to teaching at City College and writing for radio shows, including Orson Welles's *Mercury Theater of the Air.* After publishing his first major novel, *The Enemy Sea,* in 1943, Polonsky was offered a job at Paramount Pictures as a screenwriter. Before accepting the offer, however, Polonsky volunteered to serve in World War II. After returning from Europe in 1945, he worked for Paramount on a number of screenplays. He eventually became disenchanted with the frivolous nature of the work, however, and left to work at Enterprise Productions, an independent film company started by his friend, actor John Garfield. Hired initially to "tweak" a few scenes in a problematic screenplay about a boxer, Polonsky rewrote the entire film, which was released in 1947 as *Body and Soul.* Following the great success of this film, he was hired by Garfield and producer Bob Roberts to write and direct a second film for Garfield. Having learned the rudiments of directing by watching and con-

sulting with Robert Rossen during the filming of *Body and Soul,* Polonsky began his new project with a spirit of experimentation. The resulting film, *Force of Evil,* was well received critically, particularly in Great Britain, but failed to attract large audiences. Having never hidden his political affiliations, Polonsky was called before the House Un-American Activities Committee in April 1951. After invoking the Fifth Amendment and refusing to cooperate with the committee's demand that he divulge the names of other communists, Polonsky was banned from working in Hollywood for seventeen years. During this time, however, he wrote fiction and criticism, and worked on various screen- and teleplays under assumed names. In deference to those who lent their names and to passively promote the half-truth that many of the most successful movies of the era were actually written by blacklisted writers—a cynical joke of the blacklistees—Polonsky has never revealed the extent of his work during this time. The blacklisting effectively ended in 1968 when he received co-screenwriting credit for *Madigan,* and Polonsky soon returned to directing. After the commercial failures *Tell Them Willie Boy Is Here* and *Romance of a Horse Thief* (1971), Polonsky returned to fiction. Although he has written several screenplays since then, he has not directed another film.

## Major Works

The proposition that capitalism necessarily entails greed and corruption informs all of Polonsky's work. His first original screenplay, *Body and Soul,* presents the story of Charlie Davis (played by Garfield), a poor, young boxer who gets mixed up with corrupt fight promoters. Polonsky's script uses the boxing world to illustrate the nonstop drive for profit in contemporary, capitalist society. A study of capitalism as the mirror image of the criminal underworld, *Force of Evil* is the story of two brothers: Joe Morse, a lawyer who works for the Mob; and Leo, who runs a small-time, illegal lottery operation. Leo is killed after refusing to work for the syndicate Joe represents; in the end Joe comes to accept the fact that he played a part in Leo's death and that within a corrupt system, everyone is corrupt to some degree. *Force of Evil* is particularly noted for its lyrical dialogue, which many critics describe as blank verse. *Tell Them Willie Boy Is Here* centers on a chase: when a Paiute American Indian, Willie Boy (played by Robert Blake), accidentally kills his girlfriend's father, he and the woman (played by Katherine Ross) are pursued by the local sheriff, a sympathetic character (played by Robert Redford) whose understanding of the situation makes him ambivalent about carrying out his official duty. The film ends with a climactic confrontation between Willie Boy, the sheriff, and an angry mob bent on revenge. *Tell Them Willie Boy Is Here* is noted for its sensitive depiction of Native Americans and their treatment by the United States government, its cinematography, and Polonsky's direction of the actors, notable especially in Redford's performance as what many critics consider the film's main character.

## Critical Reception

Polonsky's films have garnered predominantly favorable critical responses. *Body and Soul* was one of the most popular films of 1947 and earned both Polonsky and Garfield Academy Award nominations. *Force of Evil* is widely regarded as one of the best films of the immediate postwar period, gaining in popularity over time, despite being seen by some as too demanding for mass audiences. His films are known for thematic complexity, focusing on the ramifications of capitalist politics. Polonsky is praised for the technical skill of his filmmaking and his accomplished dialogue. William Pechter argues that *Force of Evil* deserves to be included "in any mention of the handful of most remarkable directorial debuts in American movies."

---

# *PRINCIPAL WORKS

*The Goose Is Cooked*  [with Mitchell A. Wilson, under joint pseudonym Emmett Hogarth] (novel) 1940
*The Enemy Sea*  (novel) 1943
*Body and Soul*  (screenplay) 1947
*Golden Earrings*  [with Frank Butler and Helen Deutsch; based on the novel by Yolanda Foldes] (screenplay) 1947
†*Force of Evil*  [with Ira Wolfert; based on Wolfert's novel *Tucker's People*] (film) 1949
*I Can Get It for You Wholesale*  (screenplay) 1951
*The World Above*  (novel) 1951
*A Season of Fear*  (novel) 1956
*Madigan*  [with Howard Rodman and Harry Kleiner; based on the novel *The Commissioner* by Robert Dougherty] (screenplay) 1968
†*Tell Them Willie Boy Is Here*  (film) 1969
†*Romance of a Horse Thief*  [with David Opatoshu and Joseph Opatoshu] (film) 1971
*Avalanche Express*  (screenplay) 1979
*Zenia's Way*  (novel) 1980
*Monsignor*  [with Wendell Mayes] (screenplay) 1982

*In addition to the works listed here, Polonsky wrote numerous screen- and teleplays under the names of other authors while he was blacklisted. Neither Polonsky nor the authors who lent their names have disclosed the titles of these works. Note that in this list bracketed information next to film titles refers to screenwriting credit only.

†These films were directed by Polonsky.

---

# CRITICISM

### Evelyn Sager   (review date 13 June 1943)

SOURCE: "Aboard an Oil Tanker," in *The New York Times Book Review,* June 13, 1943, pp. 12, 14.

[*In the following mixed review, Sager praises Polonsky's vivid descriptions and dramatic sensibilities, but finds* The Enemy Sea *anticlimactic at key moments.*]

The merchant seaman has been rescued from his role of obscurity within the past year by several first-hand reports of terror, endurance and courage at sea. The stark facts of the hunt—the submarine stalking the slow, lumbering merchant fleet—need none of the artistry of fiction to supply color and climax.

Fiction, on the other hand, can deal with these same grim facts—as Abraham Polonsky does in **The Enemy Sea**—and out of the facts draw a pattern of purpose and hope. **The Enemy Sea** is facile melodrama; the story of a fated oil tanker, and the entangled lives of several of those on board. A bald telling of the tale would make a superb movie scenario; all the sure-fire ingredients are there—action, brawls, intrigue and suspense. But there is a third-dimensional quality to **The Enemy Sea**. The author is telling more than an adventure story. To him, the struggle aboard the tanker *Aruba* is comparable to the bigger struggle now going on—the easy-living man of the democracies pitted against the ruthless workings of a fascist organization.

Aboard the *Aruba,* on what is to prove her last voyage, are two passengers on a special assignment; Danny McCloud, a reporter, and Carrie Tennant, an ace photographer, are covering the trip on a tanker as a joint stunt for a popular magazine. Soon after leaving the harbor of Galveston, several strange incidents cause Danny to suspect that this is no ordinary tanker. Before he can fit his clues and suspicions into a tidy solution, the ship is taken over by a Nazi submarine with the help of several fascist officers serving in key positions on the tanker. According to the Nazi plan, the oil carried by the betrayed tanker is to be used to refuel a group of German submarines operating in that area; when the oil has been transferred, the *Aruba* and her crew are to be torpedoed. Only the traitors are to survive, to repeat the pattern of destruction with another tanker and her crew.

Summoning resources of ingenuity and strength that he did not know he possessed, Danny attempts to defeat the Nazi plan, by escape, by trickery and by cajolery. He fails each time. The superior physical force and disciplined organization of the Nazis seem too powerful to be overcome by a small, unarmed group. Danny, Carrie and the majority of the crew are saved not by their own efforts, but by a weak link in the seemingly infallible Nazi system.

Despite the author's outstanding gift for sketching a vivid, dramatic scene, his narrative is strained and often anticlimactic. Through Danny, we are constantly groping for the meaning behind each episode, probing the nature of the other characters and analyzing his own reaction to brute force. This adds considerable depth to the novel, but impedes the action.

The author himself, we are told, has served in the merchant service. He writes of the men with deep sympathy and admiration; one of the finest bits in the book is his portrait of the big, impassive Negro steward. Polonsky writes sensitively, too, of the spirit and moods of the sea—particularly of the enemy sea where death is a daily caller.

## Bosley Crowther  (review date 27 December 1948)

SOURCE: "At Loew's State," in *The New York Times,* December 27, 1948, p. 16.

[*Crowther was an American film critic and journalist long associated with the* New York Times. *In the following positive review, he argues that* Force of Evil *reveals Polonsky as a director of "imagination and unquestioned craftsmanship."*]

It may be that **Force of Evil,** which opened . . . on Christmas Day, is not the sort of picture that one would choose for Yuletide cheer. It's a cold, hard, relentless dissection of a bitter, aggressive young man who lets himself get in too deep as the lawyer for a "policy racket" gang. And as such it is full of vicious people with whom the principal boy associates, it reeks of greed and corruption and it ends in death and despair.

But for all its unpleasant nature, it must be said that this film is a dynamic crime-and-punishment drama, brilliantly and broadly realized. Out of material and ideas that have been worked over time after time, so that they've long since become stale and hackneyed, it gathers suspense and dread, a genuine feeling of the bleakness of crime and a terrible sense of doom. And it catches in eloquent tatters of on-the-wing dialogue moving intimations of the pathos of hopeful lives gone wrong.

Written by Abraham Polonsky and Ira Wolfert from the latter's acid book, *Tucker's People,* about the "numbers racket," and directed by Mr. Polonsky, too, it gets right at the matter of petty gambling from the bottom to the top. It gives a fair understanding of the vast and monstrous scale on which the "numbers" business is established. And it hints obliquely at political hook-ins.

But this isn't the main thing about it. Racketeers are still racketeers and the operation of "numbers" is special but not unique. The main thing about this picture is that it shows, in plausible terms, the disintegration of a character under the too-heavy pressure of his sense of wrong.

In their up-from-nothing lawyer who gets himself in too deep on the moral excuse that he is doing it for his brother, a middle-aged man, Mr. Polonsky and Mr. Wolfert have some real things to show about the practical operation of the psychology of crime. And in the frenzied romance of this tough lawyer with a decent but daring little girl, they say something rather disturbing about lust for the dangerous and unknown.

They do it in startling situations and in graphic dialogue, in shattering cinematic glimpses and in great, dramatic sweeps of New York background. New to the business of directing, Mr. Polonsky here establishes himself as a man of imagination and unquestioned craftsmanship.

True, he was very fortunate in having John Garfield play the young lawyer in the story, for Mr. Garfield is his tough guy to the life. Sentient underneath a steel shell, taut, articulate—he is all good men gone wrong. And a new little actress named Beatrice Pearson is something of a lucky feature, too. With her innocent, worldly demeanor, her shyness yet forwardness, too, and a voice that would melt a pawnbroker, she points up the pathos in the tale.

But Mr. Polonsky's direction of Thomas Gomez, who does a fine, tense job as the small-time brother of the tough guy; of Roy Roberts, who plays Tucker, the big boss, and of half a dozen others shows that he has the stuff. In this particular picture, produced by Bob Roberts for Enterprise, we have a real new talent in the medium, as well as a sizzling piece of work.

## Frederic Morton  (review date 3 June 1951)

SOURCE: "Modern Mind," in *New York Herald Tribune Book Review,* June 3, 1951, p. 11.

[*Morton is an Austrian-born American novelist, historian, biographer, critic, and educator. In the following mixed review, he finds that while* The World Above *is rich in evocative details and acute observations, Polonsky's characters become conduits for a dogmatic political philosophy that he feels overshadows the literary merits of the novel.*]

[**The World Above**] is a huge, restless book attempting to give scope to the spiritual bafflement which has overtaken Western civilization today. Mr. Polonsky has charged—and partially smothered—his second novel with much of the modern mind's burden.

The central figure is a young psychiatrist named Carl

Myers. From the very outset we find him in an intensely up-to-date dilemma: brilliant but impoverished, he strives for the objectivity and humanitarianism of science in a ferociously competitive climate. The story of his double-edged fight—for worldly recognition and against the means by which he must seek it—is essentially the story of this book.

*The World Above* follows Carl's career through many places. We watch him struggle out of the tenements of New York's East Side; we see him waiting and busboying his way through Hopkins and Harvard, studying at Vienna, participating in the second world war. His soul, however, remains a battleground between ambition and principle. It is only as the chief of a large hospital that, in a convulsion of courage, he sees himself becoming a true physician, however fumbling, to all humanity. At last he also finds personal fulfillment in the woman he loves.

Carl, however, is exceptionally strong. He alone, among the main characters of the book, can prevail against the abrasive challenges of our culture. His friend, David, a latent homosexual, cracks under the desperate endeavor not to be himself. Sandy, Carl's quick, sensitive mistress, grows blunted after her first contact with wealth. His brother, Bill, becomes an anonymous casualty of the big war. And Curtin, Carl's jovially dynamic colleague, sells himself in the end to expediency.

Mr. Polonsky relates the lives of these in rich detail. Being a perceptive observer, he has much to say. And he says it well. I will not soon forget his ability to render the texture and immediacy of mental states or to reproduce the cunning of paranoia.

But this book is never as good as it should be. The people in *The World Above* behave spontaneously only in intervals. They have a habit of falling into the same uniform eloquence that reduces them after a while to becoming mere channels for a near-Communist philosophy; a philosophy born of a narrow intellectual bitterness which sees only the conditions that caused it, not the full consequences that would attend its success. The imposition of so inelastic and twisted a viewpoint also flattens the figure of Carl, though the phases of his development are individually well depicted, they do not coalesce into a satisfying portrait.

It is unfortunate that a book of considerable literary virtues should have such drawbacks. Mr. Polonsky's remarkable verbal power never forsakes him. Too often, however, his poetry is stymied by his dogma.

### John Envers   (review date August 1951)

SOURCE: A review of *The World Above,* in *The Canadian Forum,* Vol. XXXI, No. 367, August, 1951, pp. 115-16.

[*In the following mixed review of* The World Above, *Envers lauds Polonsky's descriptive capabilities but finds the novel stylistically inconsistent.*]

If Mr. Polonsky has not written a best seller this time, it can hardly be ascribed to want of talent but rather to lack of economy and care. *The World Above* struck this re-

viewer like a badly edited manuscript, not quite ready for typesetting. The book has divergencies of style ("he didn't" and "he did not," both within the short space of a few lines; the exclamation "Agh!", so frequent during early passages, later turns into a humble "Ah!"); an occasional spelling error; faults in minor detail, which might easily irritate a reader acquainted with particular circumstances (an Englishwoman would never refer to an officer in the British Women's Force as "The Lieutenant"). On the other hand, there are memorable moments that surely rank with the very best descriptions in contemporary anthologies. These are, alas, generally followed by long and labored paragraphs, unfamiliar words limping behind each other. This novel has, indeed, all that is required to make it attractive to the public: war, violence, sexual inversion, the occasional profanity; it shows Freudian psychologists at work and play; it arranges for wives to jump into bed with men not their husbands; it usefully comments on our time and sometimes manages to instruct; finally, it is long and offers no conclusion or solution to the problems under discussion. In spite of this, [this critic] fully admits having enjoyed *The World Above*—not for what it attempts to be, but for what it is. With the mentioned provisos, the various emotional and actual adventures of Dr. Carl Myers make for good, usually absorbing entertainment. It is, however, suggested that the author re-issue this work after some conscientious checking and much cutting.

### Abraham Polonsky with William Pechter   (interview date Spring 1962)

SOURCE: "Abraham Polonsky and *Force of Evil,*" in *Film Quarterly,* Vol. XV, No. 3, Spring, 1962, pp. 47-54.

[*In the following interview, which was conducted entirely through correspondence, Polonsky discusses the filming of* Body and Soul, *his adaptation and direction of* Force of Evil, *and his thoughts on the Blacklist and Hollywood's fear of Communists in the 1950s. In the essay that frames the interview, Pechter discusses Polonsky's career, focusing on* Body and Soul *and* Force of Evil.]

In 1949, a writer, whose experience, with the exception of two previous screenplays and two unmemorable novels, had been primarily in radio, made an adaptation of an unsuccessful, journalistic novel to the screen, and directed a film of it. The event would not seem to be a particularly auspicious one nor much of a novelty for Hollywood, where every other day finds one hack adapting the work of another hack. Nor would it have been much more promising to know that the film made use of several elements that were sufficiently familiar—the bad-good guy involved in the rackets who finally goes straight, the ingenue who tries to reform him, etc. Yet, apparently, to have known all this was not to know enough. How else to account for the fact that out of it all was created an original, moving, and even beautiful work, whose only tangency with clichés was at the point at which it transformed and transcended them? I think it is accounted for by that phenomenon which never ceases to be somehow both inexplicable and unpredictable: the presence of an artist.

But the event was, perhaps, not quite so unpredictable as I may, somewhat Hollywoodishly, have made it sound. The artist's name was Abraham Polonsky, and his film was *Force of Evil;* previously, he had written the original scenario for the film *Body and Soul. Body and Soul* did not lack acclaim; although independently produced, it won an Academy Award, and was financially successful. *Force of Evil* was without acclaim or appreciation; noticed only by the British film periodicals, it was allowed to die its quiet death, a gangster film with only muted violence, a love story without romantic apotheosis, a Hollywood film without the Happy Ending. Both *Sight and Sound* and *Sequence* had cited it as among the most original films of its year, and it still occasionally crops up in catalogues of neglected works. Lindsay Anderson, in his close analysis of the last sequence of *On the Waterfront* which appeared in *Sight and Sound* several years ago, invoked *Force of Evil* as foil to that film's operatic dishonesty. The habitual British reader may have caught the aptness of the comparison; for the American one, it must have been merely a little baffling.

In theme and meaning, *Body and Soul* and *Force of Evil* form an extraordinary unity. In each, the hero, played in both cases with a combination of tough cynicism and urban dreaminess by the late John Garfield at his most characteristic, allows himself to become involved with certain forces of corruption, only, finally, to revolt against them, and attempt to wrench himself free. In both films, the hero is not moved to this final breach without first having caused some irrevocable violence to those most close to him, and both films end not with some cheap and easy redemption, but deep in *Angst* and ambiguity. "What can you do? Kill me? Everybody dies," are the final words of *Body and Soul,* as the fighter says them to the gambler whose fight he has refused to throw. The effect is not entirely pessimistic; there is a certain heroic implication in the fighter's assertion of his moral triumph, inalterable even in death; still, the fact remains that a life is not this casually disposed of, and the audience demands some compensation for the lack of final Uplift. This it got, in *Body and Soul,* in the physical excitement of the prizefight scenes, photographed so dynamically by James Wong Howe on (!) roller skates, and in the reliable familiarity of the fundamental story line: ambitious slum boy battles way up to success. It is the kind of story that allows the audience the illicit thrill of a vicarious participation in the somewhat unscrupulous rise of the hero without the guilt that belongs properly to him. So, despite the frequently rich and even lyrical language of the film, its often striking images of city life, and the sense of flexible and sensitive human relationships which managed to cluster about the success story's rigid central structure, despite, that is to say, the presence of artistry, it was officially recognized by the Academy of Motion Picture Arts and Sciences as a work of art.

*Force of Evil* is not so immediately likeable a film; it is without such direct compensations for its underlying sadness. Unlike the fighter of *Body and Soul,* Joe Morse, the hero of *Force of Evil,* is not so simply and understandably the product of social determinations. We first see him as a successful lawyer; he is not fighting to escape poverty,

but to annex greater wealth. Nor is he unaware of the nature of his involvement, or without moral understanding. One is never certain that the fighter of *Body and Soul* is wholly aware of his moral predicament; but Joe Morse acknowledges full responsibility, without even pleading the excuse of weakness. By his own admission, he is "strong enough to get a part of the corruption, but not strong enough to resist it." But this is not so much weakness as a perversion of strength, a defect not in quantity but in kind. The progress of *Force of Evil* is that of the painfully gradual burgeoning of a moral imagination—if you prefer, a conscience. It is not miraculously achieved by romantic love, but only attained after the death of Joe's older brother, whom he had tried both to advance and protect within the racket in which they become involved. It is the relationship of the two brothers which is the central love story of the film—the Freudian "family romance"—a love thwarted mutually by guilt, and ending in anguish. In terms of plot, the film ends utterly without stereotypic satisfactions: the older brother is killed; Joe is about to confess to the police, and inevitably to be punished; there is no final, solipsistic kiss. "I decided to help," are Joe's last words as the film concludes, after he has found his dead brother's battered body. It is a moment entirely free from the pieties which customarily attend such a regeneration, nor has it any of that sense of straining to engage some good, gray abstraction like "Society," which hangs so heavily over the last sequence of *On the Waterfront. Force of Evil* ends in moral awakening, but it reaches out not so much toward society as toward community, even communion; a sense of the oneness of human involvement without any diminution of that involvement's ineluctable guilt.

Were this all, one might have simply a film of the tenderness, sensitivity, and, I believe, somewhat vitiating softness of, say, *They Live By Night.* Even *Sight and Sound* tended to relegate *Force of Evil* to the status of a sympathetic but "minor" film; I think this is other than the case. The film was said to be overly literary, and there is no doubt that it is a work which relies heavily on its language; perhaps, we are still not entirely free of the tyrannical dogma that language is not properly an element of film. To observe that the language of *Force of Evil* is beautiful in itself may not be quite to the point. The impression of that language is of for the first time really hearing, on the screen, the sound of city speech, with its special repetitions and elisions, cadence and inflection, inarticulateness and crypto-poetry; much as Odets had brought it to the stage. As in Odets, the effect is naturalistic, and, as in Odets, it is achieved by an extreme degree of mannerism, artifice, and stylization. But the astonishing thing about *Force of Evil,* more obvious now, perhaps, in the light of such more overtly experimental works as *Hiroshima, Mon Amour,* is the way in which the image works with the word. Nothing is duplicated, or supererogatory. Even in so simple an instance as that of the heroine's face in close-up, as the first person narrative runs "Doris wanted me to make love to her," is the relationship of word to image complementary rather than redundant. The soundtrack is the image slantwise; refracted through an individual consciousness; and, to that extent, interpreted. Throughout the film, Joe is constantly commenting upon the action, telling us not only what he and the others think, but even describing his own, overt actions as we see him engaging in them. It is this kind of awareness and volition which is alien to the conventional melodramatic hero; and it is interesting to note that it is a departure from the novel which is related in flatly omniscient third person. The effect of all this off-repetition, with its language overlapping image and language overlapping language is finally quite different from that of the very similar devices of *Hiroshima, Mon Amour.* In that film, the final effect is merely rhetorical and consciously Artistic; in *Force of Evil,* the language takes on the quality of incantation, and imparts an almost choric resonance to the Cain and Abel myth which lies at the film's center.

The more one sees *Force of Evil,* the closer one gets to the film's center, the more one becomes aware of that central myth, and the formal means by which it is exposed. The language becomes a kind of insistent music, and the images move congruently with an extraordinary purity freedom. A brief conversation is composed from a remote angle above a gracefully, curving stairway; the moment exists both in and independent of the plot; and, independently, it is startlingly beautiful. Such imagery proliferates throughout the film, from the simplest of conversational exchanges to the complexly moving vision of Joe running senselessly down a deserted Wall Street at night, knowing that never again will he be able to return to his "fine office up in the clouds." *Force of Evil* is, actually, a very impure film; it *is* literary and dramatic, but only insofar as the film *is* a literary and dramatic medium, and no further. Beneath and beyond that, there is the autonomous beauty of poetic diction; the aesthetic paradox that what is harrowing in life may be that and be also beautiful in art. And the final passage of the film, in which, in the pervasive grayness of the early morning, Joe discovers his brother's body at the base of an arching bridge, from the desolate rocks upon which it has been discarded, "like an old rag," is both immensely harrowing and starkly beautiful. It is a descent to "the bottom of the world," to a kind of hell; the symbolic death that must be suffered before regeneration. "Because, if a man can live so long, and have his whole life come out like rubbish, then something was horribly wrong . . . and I decided to help."

[The "interview" with Abraham Polonsky related below was conducted entirely through correspondence. I have taken the liberty of some slight rearrangement so that there might be a clear relation of answer to question, but the words remain unchanged. Therefore, while the exchanges may occasionally approximate the give and take of conversation they may be accepted as having the value of written reflection, such as that may be.]

.  .  .  .  .

[Pechter]: *Would you begin by giving me some idea of your background before you began working in films? Somewhere I picked up the information that you originally wrote for radio, and, if my memory doesn't play tricks, I recall reading a radio script of yours in the old* Quarterly of Film, Radio, and Television. *I also seem to remember hearing that you taught for awhile at the University of Southern California and even the City College of New York, although I am not sure of the chronology (i.e., before or after film-*

*making), and virtually certain that I must have dreamed the latter. Would you also refer to your published fiction and film criticism?*

[Polonsky]: I led the usual restless street life: gang (East Side); schoolboy (P.S. 32, 57, De Witt Clinton); teacher (CCNY, A.B.); Law (Columbia); volunteer in politics (Democrat, Anarchist, Radical, Confused). I taught at City College from 1932 to the war; never taught at the University of Southern California. I am familiar with the learned professions (teaching and law), the vagrant ones (sea, farm, factory), and the eternal ones (marriage, fatherhood, art, science). The most extraordinary shock in my life was not the war which I survived, but the films which I did not. I always wrote, produced little motion in life and never stopped talking.

My first novel (*The Discoverers*) was accepted, announced, advertised by Modern Age Books and then withdrawn as unreadable. I retired to silence in art, action in politics, and gibberish in radio (Columbia Workshop, Orson Welles, Goldbergs, and I forget). Two potboilers (Simon and Schuster, Little, Brown). The war (O.S.S.). My blueberry pie was Paramount.

Excluding the movies for the moment, I managed a semi-serious return to the novel with *The World Above,* and, after being blacklisted, *The Season of Fear.* These attempts were laced with some short stories, criticism, and genteel scholarly editing (*Hollywood Quarterly, Contemporary Reader*).

The guerrilla life I pretended to practise in the war I played with some amusement and frequent disgust in the jungle of TV as a blacklisted writer. Likewise in films. Those minor victories and major defeats admit no obituaries at the moment.

*How did you begin your work in films?*

By accident. I signed with Paramount before going overseas. However appalled as I was by the industry and its product, the medium overwhelmed me with a language I had been trying to speak all my life.

*Since I am under the impression that it is not extensive, would you mention all of your screen credits, official and unofficial, if the latter case is such?*

Credits. *Golden Earrings:* direction, Mitchel Leisen. Assigned to an incredible romantic melodramatic stew, I painstakingly studied gypsy life under the Nazis (they were incinerated) and very cleverly worked the whole thing around to something else. The film, starring Marlene Dietrich, appeared as an incredible romantic melodramatic stew. I never could sit through it. I know there isn't a single word or scene of mine in it, but I was instructed to rejoice in the credit which I shared with two old hands, Helen Deutsch and Frank Butler.

*Body and Soul:* original screenplay; direction, Robert Rossen.

*Force of Evil:* screenplay with Ira Wolfert from his novel, *Tucker's People;* my direction.

*I Can Get It For You Wholesale:* screenplay based on

Weidman's own treatment which simply kept the title of the novel. A comedy of sorts, directed by Mike Gordon with Dan Dailey, Susan Hayward. It was a stopgap for me to return to Europe to write another book and set up *Mario and the Magician*. Before I left, Thomas Mann told me he felt his exile was beginning all over again since fascism was inevitable in America. The novel I completed years later. No one wanted to finance the film.

I returned to Hollywood and made a deal with Sol Siegel at Twentieth to write and direct a picture, but the blacklist intervened.

*Was your scenario for* **Body and Soul** *a wholly original work, or was it derived from some other source?*

It's an original screenplay. A folk tale from the Empire City.

*Was Rossen to direct the movie from the time of the script's inception, or did he only come to do it through the contingencies of film production?*

Rossen was hired after the script was done.

*Did your work on* **Body and Soul** *end with the scenario?*

No.

*Were you present on the set during shooting?*

Continuously.

*Of course, it is easy to look knowing in retrospect, but to judge from Rossen's other work,* **Body and Soul** *would seem to have closer affinities with* **Force of Evil** *than with the other films of his, even in the elusive matter of visual style. Or am I just second guessing?*

There was a struggle during the shooting to prevent Rossen from rewriting the script and changing the ending. In fact he shot an alternate finish in which the fighter is killed and ends up with his head in a garbage can. I think a comparison of *Body and Soul* with *The Hustler* might indicate not only the uses Rossen made of the former but where his temperament and style inevitably lead him.

---

**We had that big Hollywood machine which the success of *Body and Soul* had delivered into our hands and we didn't mind seeing what we could do with all that horsepower. But the blacklist took the machine away from us.**

**—Abraham Polonsky**

---

*Are you satisfied with the realization of* **Body and Soul** *as a film?*

I liked **Body and Soul.** It was a surprise to see something I had written become film. I have an animal faith that survives moral weakness and defeat. To urge this against Rossen's metaphysical identity with everyday cynicism

and the journalism of sense and sex indicated the realities of film making. Our resources on the set were immense: Garfield, James Wong Howe, Robert Aldrich, Lyons and Parrish, Don Weiss, Pevney. A slew of directors emerged from the film. Rossen's talent is force applied everywhere without let-up. My only concern was to save it from parody, except where deliberately I had kidded *Golden Boy* and that dear old violin. However, I'm not so sure any more that the obvious isn't one of the strengths of film language. If so it violates a bias of my nature.

*What attracted you about* Tucker's People *as an original source?*

Experiment. Garfield and Roberts suggested that I direct. I had already been brooding over this notion. Being a novice didn't prevent me from sharing all the illusions and frustrations of more seasoned writers. I was under fire long before I knew I had volunteered.

I knew *Tucker's People*. It had an allegory, true then and even more bitterly apt today; a milieu and characters familiar as my own habits; a hint of the language of the unconscious I could use as dialogue. In realization, necessities of the medium evaporated the allegory leaving great uncharted reefs of symbolism to wreck the audience; the people emerged except where I agreed to wrong casting; and the language almost obeyed my intention to play an equal role with the actor and visual image and not run along as illustration, information, and mere verbal gesture (wisecracks, conventional middle class slang, elevated notions drawn from the armory of Longfellow and Hemingway).

*In the course of adaptation, you altered the novel rather radically, excising some characters and events, combining and condensing others. What particular problems did you feel were fundamental to your decisions in making the adaptation? I don't mean so much with regard to* Tucker's People *in particular as with the question of adapting to the screen in general.*

I no longer remember anything except the days Wolfert and I spent endlessly talking along the beaches. Under the windy sun we didn't reason so much as proclaim discoveries. In effect, we eliminated the discursive power of the book and substituted for it so to speak centers of suggestion. We reimagined the novel as if it were an aborigine again. Then it became obvious that some characters would play larger roles and others disappear. Adapting a book to film is fundamentally a moral crisis. Assuming the intention is serious, the book is not chosen to be translated for non-readers but because still embedded in the conception is a whole unrealized life whose language is a motion of images. Where a book is unfulfilled a frightful problem arises. The film, if successful, is a critique of the author's failures. I am a coward here and prefer my own stories.

*Do you have any particular conception of the nature of the medium? One of the original reviewers of* **Force and Evil** *(Robert Hatch in* The Nation, *as I recall) suspected the presence of blank verse, and was duly horrified; but even admirers of the film have characterized it as "literary." Does this have any meaning to you? Do you have any ideas* *about the relation of word to image in the film; yours, and, perhaps, the film in general?*

I've heard them talk in talking pictures. Might talkies be like the opera? The main thing is the music but O the joy when the singers act and the songs are poetry. Let's pretend, I assumed for *Tucker's People* (**Force of Evil**) that the three elements, visual image, actor, word, are equals. (After all, the human personality is the medium of total human expressiveness. After all, language has been a medium for an art or two.) I didn't project anything important, just an experiment in which each of my resource was freed of the dominance of the other two. I was too inexperienced to invent novel visual images or evoke great performances. And certainly there was nothing in my literary record to suggest a New Voice. All I tried to do was use the succession of visual images, the appearances of human personality in the actors, and the rhythm of words in unison or counterpoint. I varied the speed, intensity, congruence and conflict for design, emotion and goal, sometimes separating the three elements, sometimes using two or three together. As for the language, I merely freed it of the burden of literary psychology and the role of crutch to the visual image. Blank verse? No. But the babble of the unconscious, yes, as much as I could, granted the premise that I was committed to a representational film. It was a method I would have tried again and again until solved. After all, we had that big Hollywood machine which the success of **Body and Soul** had delivered into our hands and we didn't mind seeing what we could do with all that horsepower. But the blacklist took the machine away from us. While we had possession, like those bicycle fanatics at Kitty Hawk, we couldn't wait to waken in the morning, knowing that each day would surprise us. We had the right feelings. Only our plane never flew.

*Would you say you have been influenced by any other filmmakers?*

Vigo.

*Mention has been made in a way I think might be valid of Odets as a literary influence. What is your opinion of this?*

We both derive from Jewish jokes and street quarrels. I live dangled between the formal and argot without solution. I've tried to avoid American Standard Movie dialogue which is a genuine Hollywood convention. But I can write it and have for a living.

*What film-makers do you particularly admire?*

I like going to the movies.

*What Hollywood films have you thought commendable since the late 'forties?*

I seem to remember liking some but I can't remember which.

*Is there an identity of theme and meaning between* **Body and Soul** *and* **Force of Evil***?*

Yes, but in **Force of Evil** every character and situation is compromised by reality while **Body and Soul** is a folk tale.

*Eric Bentley has made the point that in both Elia Kazan's* On the Waterfront *and Arthur Miller's* A View from the Bridge *there is, scarcely beneath the surface, an apologetics for each of their respective positions on political informing, a certain acting out of private crises; informing being the crucial act in both works, good in the former and evil in the latter.* **Force of Evil** *ends with the hero about to confess to the police, and "help" them. I do not mean to suggest that the final act is ever simply this, but do you feel that there is any political parable underlying the conclusion to your film?*

Not a parable, a fact. The hero is about to confess to the police because that was the way we could get a seal. There was an allegory underlying the film. It got lost somewhere and had nothing to do with confession or avoidance. Bentley is certainly right in his estimate of those works although the distinction between good informing and bad escapes me. One informs not only to escape punishment and regain acceptance but to share once again in the authority of the state. It is a hard life outside the pale.

*Do you believe or know that you were blacklisted?*

I know it and I believe it.

*How did you discover this?*

I was told by the studio, my agent, the newspapers, Congress, and my landlord.

*How is one blacklisted; I mean, what is the typical nature of the process?*

One is named in a hearing by an informer, or one is summoned to the hearing in person. The consequences are the same.

*Do you know of particular individuals who were behind the blacklist, or was its authority always kept anonymous?*

The cold war was behind the blacklist and everyone participated from those on the political right through those who had no politics. It was like collaboration under the Nazis. And it was like the resistance. The spectrum took in everything human including the inhuman.

*Did you ever appear before the House Un-American Activities Committee?*

Yes.

*Was there any opportunity for compromise in order to "clear" yourself?*

Then and now and frequently in between.

*John Cogley, in his* Report on Blacklisting, *observes that there was virtually no political content in the films of the blacklisted, and when it did exist it was usually in the form of so generalized a commitment to democratic ideals and justifiable revolution as could be subscribed to by any member of the audience but the most avid Hitlerite. Do you agree? Would you ascribe this to lack of intent, or lack of accomplishment? Or lack of talent?*

Hollywood radicals were mainly moral humanists and their films when they reflected anything at all showed a concern for the suppressed elements in human life. Political programming of any sort, left, middle, right, couldn't ever appear because producers wanted to make money.

When political programming did appear as in the so called anti-communist pictures they were made in deference to the climate and not from the usual expectation of profits. Cogley's argument that blacklisting radicals is silly because they're too stupid or talentless to use the film for direct Marxist propaganda is jejune. He is talking about journalism, not story telling.

*Do you have any thoughts on the career of Edward Dmytryk, who went from the Hollywood Ten to "exoneration," and eventually was to film such a tribute to conformity as* The Caine Mutiny?

He probably thought it was capitalist realism.

*It has been suggested that John Garfield's political difficulties and debarment from Hollywood work was a considerable influence in accelerating his early death. Do you have any opinion on this?*

Yes. He defended his streetboy's honor and they killed him for it.

*In the publisher's blurb for* **The Season of Fear,** *it was implied that you left film-making voluntarily in order "to go abroad and devote [yourself] to serious fiction." Aside from the thinly veiled, characteristic cultural snobbery, is there any truth in this?*

No.

*Inasmuch as you have any such self-image, do you regard yourself primarily as a novelist or film-maker? Or both?*

Neither. If I were younger you might say I had promise.

*Were you aware of the sympathetic reception accorded* **Force of Evil** *in* Sight and Sound *and* Sequence?

Yes.

*Was their appreciation of any personal importance to you?*

Pure oxygen.

*Was* **Body and Soul** *a financial success?*

Very much so.

*Was* **Force of Evil** *commercially successful?*

No.

*Do you have any criticisms of the latter film's distribution?*

It got lost in the general dissolution of Enterprise studios. Had we stayed in business we could have rescued it and made some money.

*How did you come to use Beatrice Pearson [who plays the romantic lead opposite John Garfield in* **Force of Evil**]?

She was brought to my attention by Martin Jurow, now a considerable producer himself. He worked for our company at that time.

*Where had you seen her previously?*

Nowhere.

*What became of her?*

She was in a few films and disappeared. They didn't know how to use her.

*In what work are you engaged at present?*

Grub Street.

*Have you had any opportunity to make films since* **Force of Evil?**

No.

*Have you imagined any new subjects you would have particularly liked to work into a film?*

Indeed I have.

*Do you see any possibility for your prospective return to work in the film?*

No.

*What are your plans for the future?*

None.

. . . . .

The interviewing of an artist is chancy; the pitfalls are familiar. On one hand, there is that kind of gulling Lindsay Anderson suffered at the hands of John Ford in his well-known *Sequence* interview; on the other, those dreary chronologies of how The Studio mutilated this film, and how They butchered that. Both alternatives may be valuable in their way (and the Anderson piece, I believe, does reveal, even inadvertently, a good deal of Ford's nature as an artist), but I was interested in achieving neither. Existing somewhere in that uncharted area between the put-on and the death toll, I tend immodestly to think that my "encounter" with Abraham Polonsky was something of a success. In anticipating critical intelligence of the artist, one proceeds at one's own risk. In Polonsky, I found this sort of intelligence, and the ability to articulate it.

Not all of the questions were answered as thoroughly as they might have been, but I conceived my role not as inquisitor; I was not out to "get all the facts"; rather, to open up certain areas for discussion, to that extent which Polonsky was interested in going into them. Politically, for example, it may be observed that, although the specters of the blacklist and the House Un-American Activities Committee are pointedly raised, no question is put as to Polonsky's actual political affiliations. I don't think of this as an evasion. My own attitude toward the pursuit of this line of questioning (from an anti-Communist position, it may not be irrelevant to add) is simply: So what? The fact remains that Abraham Polonsky, having earned the right to work in Hollywood on the terms which Hollywood unfailingly understands, those of having proven the ability to show a profit, was denied the exercise of that less-than-glorious right. The fact is that, since 1949 a filmmaker whom I regard as one of the richest talents to have appeared in Hollywood in the past fifteen years (and, I believe, the richest literary talent to have appeared in the American film) has not been able to work in films. One need not respond emotionally to that fact. One need not respond emotionally to any fact.

**Lindsay Anderson on *Force of Evil*:**

Only five years ago Abraham Polonsky, a writer, directed his first film in Hollywood—*Force of Evil,* the story of two brothers, one sharp, one stupid, caught in a situation of civic and political corruption. [Unlike the fates of the brothers in *On the Waterfront,* played by Marlon Brando and Rod Steiger, in this film] the outcome was reversed: the dumb brother is killed, the shyster is brought by tragedy and by love (the girl in this case no shy wallflower, thank heavens, but a proud and morally pugnacious innocent) to a sense of shame, and an acknowledgement of moral responsibility. A film without tricks, but highly individual in writing and direction; with enough genuine human feeling in it to allow for a sense of humour; finely acted, with a most sensitive study by John Garfield of the central character; a last sequence which enclosed and expressed the essential significance of the fable in a series of stern, forlorn, authentically poetic images. A film which attracted little attention, and less favour.

And where is the director of *Force of Evil* today? It remains his only film. He has been banished from Hollywood for his political sympathies. Abraham Polonsky is not working in the American cinema just now.

> *Lindsay Anderson, in his "The Last Sequence of* On the Waterfront," *in* Sight and Sound, *January-March, 1955.*

**Abraham Polonsky with Eric Sherman and Martin Rubin   (interview date November 1968)**

SOURCE: An interview in *The Director's Event: Interviews with Five American Film-Makers,* Atheneum, 1970, pp. 3-37.

[*Sherman is an American educator and screenwriter. In the following interview, conducted in November 1968, Polonsky discusses* Force of Evil *and* Tell Them Willie Boy Is Here *and reflects on being blacklisted by producers in Hollywood. In the introduction to the interview, Rubin compares the main themes and techniques of the two films.*]

In 1948, a 39-year-old screenwriter and novelist named Abraham Polonsky directed his first film, *Force of Evil.* Soon after, he was called to testify before the House Un-American Activities Committee and was blacklisted by the movie industry. He disappeared completely from the world of over-the-counter motion picture production. The film he left behind him, although quickly forgotten by amnesiac American critics, indicated the loss of one of the most talented post-Wellesian film-makers.

After twenty years of writing left-wing novels, sub-rosa screenplays, and articles for obscure journals, Polonsky has returned to directing with *Tell Them Willie Boy Is Here,* a major production for Universal Studios. *Willie Boy* confirms that Polonsky's talents have not only remained intact after the bizarre turns of his career, but have matured astonishingly during his enforced inactivity.

The plots of his two films are rigorously simple. In *Force of Evil,* two brothers, played by John Garfield and Thomas Gomez, see themselves on opposite sides of their corrupt milieu. Garfield, young, ambitious, is the Organization's sweet-talking lawyer who pressures representatives of a virtually non-existent law force on the one hand, and manipulates and consolidates all the cosmopolitan vices for his boss, Tucker, on the other. Gomez, older, haggard, runs a small-change numbers bank for the simple, honest folk. Garfield tries to force Gomez into the syndicate. Gomez resists in order to maintain his "honor." Abetted by a rivalry over Beatrice Pearson, who is as yet uncorrupted, their mutual destruction becomes inevitable.

*Willie Boy* is based on a historical incident which occurred in 1909. Willie (Robert Blake), a strong-willed Indian, is intent on removing Lola (Katherine Ross) from the sterile and dehumanizing Indian reservation. Coop (Robert Redford), a self-confident sheriff, tries to pacify government agent Elizabeth Arnold (Susan Clark), with whom he is engaged in a love-hate affair, and other white reservation landlords. Willie Boy is forced to kill Lola's father, and, although it is not considered bad for one Indian to kill another, it provides a good excuse to eliminate the troublesome Willie from the otherwise docile reservation tribes. Coop and a large posse track down Willie and Lola for the remainder of the film. As in *Force of Evil,* the outcome is inevitable.

Within these deceptively simple plot frameworks, Polonsky concentrates on developing a complex series of parallel relationships. These parallels do not really clarify or even contrast one another; they instead create ambiguous and shifting frames of reference. Every aspect of a Polonsky film has a parallel aspect which acts upon the other to create a distorted echo, much like the "murmurs from history" the director refers to in the interview.

In *Force of Evil,* Garfield's major corruption is set alongside Gomez's minor corruption; Beatrice Pearson's suppressed impurity is set alongside Marie Windsor's open amorality; the vagueness of the criminal Tucker is set alongside the invisibility of Hall, the crusading Special Prosecutor. These relationships induce us to draw parallels which only confuse the issues—we begin to wonder if Gomez's corruption is so minor, if Pearson is as pure as her exterior (*i.e.* the taxicab scene), and whether the force of evil in the film emanates from law or crime. Rather than producing black-and-white contrasts, these parallels tend to merge nihilistically into a mixed ambiguity. The gray dawn of the descent into hell at the end of *Force of Evil* brings us to the point where all imagined values are annihilated, and, like Garfield, we have no other choice but to start over again.

In *Willie Boy,* the development is similar but more extreme. Willie and Lola, the hunted lovers, are paralleled by Coop and Elizabeth, the hunters. In an extraordinary chase which constitutes the major segment of the film, no one really chases anyone. By the first night of the indeterminately long manhunt, Willie and his pursuers are within a few feet of each other. The terms "hunter" and "hunted" become relative. We sense that Willie is passively chasing his destiny, while Coop is actively escaping his.

As in *Force of Evil,* a tension between past and present overlays the more personal frames of reference. In *Force of Evil,* this conflict is almost surreal: the classical decor of the interiors, the references to July 4 and 1776, and the obvious overtones of Cain and Abel clash insanely with a story of gangsterism, the numbers racket, Wall Street, and wire-tapping.

*Willie Boy* begins where *Force of Evil* ends. Rather than a surreal opposition of concrete symbols of past and present, *Willie Boy*'s vision of history is stark and barren; only the murmurs are left. The past is realized in the filtered remnants of a dead, mythic Old West: Barry Sullivan's stories of the good old scalphunting days, Willie's relics from his Indian heritage—his ghost shirt and his pagan burial. The present is characterized by several dozen small American flags and a huge, carefully measured chair which await President Taft's arrival; as Polonsky says, "It's so specific that suddenly it's irrelevant." The future is remote; at one point, Willie questions the existence of eternity. When Lola says, "They'll chase you forever," Willie replies, "How long is that?"

The blankness of the historical frameworks surrounding the characters, particularly Willie, makes the generalized wish for annihilation more compelling. The merely symbolic death in *Force of Evil,* when Garfield goes "down, down, down . . . to the bottom of the world," is no longer sufficient. Annihilation must be total. Accordingly, Willie (in a sense) and Lola commit suicide, and Willie's body is burned. In each case, the results are positive: Lola's suicide prolongs Willie's life; Willie's death renders absurd the last great posse, the final enactment of the charade of the Old West; the burning of Willie's body awakens a dormant sense of identity in his fellow Indians. In *Willie Boy,* Polonsky's view of history becomes bleak, apocalyptic— to resolve the ambiguous and immobilizing conflicts between past and present, the past, with all its remnants and relics, must be willfully destroyed. The last line of the film is, "Tell 'em we're all out of souvenirs."

Polonsky's visual style reflects this division of frames of reference. He uses very little middle ground between long-shot and close-up. The long-shots, which presuppose an outer framework (in this sense, they are the more "historical" shots), are rarely shown from the character's eye-level. One recalls the opening overhead shot of *Force of Evil,* which shows people scurrying like ants in the streets of New York, and the low-angle shots of the Indian reservation in *Willie Boy,* in which the government agent's house seems about to topple over while a huge mountain looms behind it. Appropriately, the characters appear most futile in the long-shots: in *Force of Evil,* Garfield running senselessly down an empty city street, Beatrice Pearson perched awkwardly on a mantle where Garfield has left her stranded; in *Willie Boy,* the high-shots of the posse wandering around, the sense of absurd pantomime in the long-shot of Coop shooting Willie, the final shot of the posse members dancing grotesquely around Willie's funeral pyre. The characters achieve their greatest emotional reality and integrity in close-up—when an outer framework is omitted. The apotheosis of this is the "Garden of Eden" love scene between Willie and Lola, in which the background and foreground are almost totally blacked out—by telephoto lens, darkness, and close-up—until Polonsky cuts to a terrifying long-shot of Lola's family closing in on the lovers.

Polonsky's characters are caught between frames of reference which complicate values to the point of producing moral inaction. But when their confusing alternatives are eventually removed, they inevitably slip into the path of a predetermined impulse to destroy the outer frameworks (whether historical, political, or social) which simultaneously create and splinter identities in a modern world. Then, as Polonsky says of Garfield's moral awakening at the end of *Force of Evil,* "There's no problem of identity when you have no identity left at all. In your very next step, you must become something."

The following interview was conducted at Mr. Polonsky's office in Universal Studios, California, in November 1968.

. . . . .

[Polonsky]: The trouble with interviews is that everything sounds so damned intended and pompous. It's like someone writing a review of his film after he's made it. A great deal of just plain *living* goes into making a film—that's the pleasure of it—and the interviews never reflect that. They reflect Seriousness and Significance and all that. That's like saying a love affair is all about the time you had these kids. But that's not what it's about, is it? Those are just some of the things that happened. And these interviews always sound like that to me. So, I forgive you, if you forgive me!

I came to make *Force of Evil* because Bob Roberts [the producer] and John Garfield asked me to direct a film. At that time I hadn't the slightest notion that it was possible for me to direct. I'd only written two films: one at Paramount called *Golden Earrings,* which was completely rewritten by Frank Butler, and *Body and Soul,* which was a success of sorts. I had been on the set all the way through *Body and Soul,* and Roberts and Garfield thought it would be an interesting idea if I directed. It was a time of interesting ideas, just after World War II, with plenty of trouble beginning in the United States in political matters. We were all more or less involved with certain radical attitudes and a great sense of loss—who had really won that war?

I knew the novel *Tucker's People* by Ira Wolfert and was fascinated by it. The book had a clear parallel to Fascism. I mean, that's an ordinary metaphor you find in all economic writing and in the poetry of left-wing journalism: gangsterism is like capitalism, or the other way round. I don't know if that's true, but anyhow it's a metaphor when you're desperate.

The great thing about success in Hollywood is that everything you say is considered potentially profitable. So, even though this was a particularly arty subject—arty for a studio film—I proposed it and they accepted it.

I arranged for Ira Wolfert to write the first draft of the screenplay. What he wrote was good, but it was clearly Ira Wolfert writing a screenplay from *his* novel. It's very difficult for a novelist to escape his work, and that would go for me, too, I think, if I were to adapt any of my own novels. Eventually I wrote the screenplay, based on his treatment, the book and our conversations. People who read the screenplay were a little upset by it at first—the language put them off. I know how to write in my own way, but not necessarily in the convention of energetic moving picture dialogue. *Force of Evil* wasn't anything like that and it was a little upsetting to them. But, as I told you, success carries you past all such habitual hesitations. So we made it.

[*Sherman and Rubin*]: *Why did you use classical décor in the film, particularly in Tucker's house and in Garfield's office?*

Why not? The audience immediately accommodates to that as being recognizable, significant, weighty—suggesting power and authority. Therefore, when you come to portray this story, which is actually a destructive analysis of the system, the decor gives you the tension that's necessary to disrupt the given situation.

*Were you attempting an even broader contrast between the decor and what was going on inside of it?*

That was the technique of the whole film: unfinished polar relationships. I used the rhythmic line of the dialogue sometimes with the images, and sometimes against the images. In that Tucker scene when they are walking down the stairway, the voices are right on mike but the people are a mile away. I did that all the time. It was the style of the film.

*Another example might be the café scene with Gomez and the Bauer character [Tucker's bookkeeper]. When Gomez is kidnapped, it's very different from the usual gangster violence. The dramatic and visual tone of the scene was quite muted, and the music was like a religious dirge. In other words, there was a very noticeable air of detachment, of alienation from the images.*

You said it! [Laughs.]

*Could you go more specifically into why you were trying for this note of disruption?*

To create a sense of general anxiety. When you do a thing like that, what you do is utilize the *familiar* as a way of calling attention to the fact that it's not so familiar after all.

*Why did you give so much emphasis to that first shot of Garfield and Tucker going down the stairs? In other words, why did you use a long take?*

They're on their way to hell, you see. But in the beginning, it looks like they're coming down a grand staircase. It's only later that you find out where they're really going.

*So, you intended a definite parallel between that and the final scenes?*

"Down, down, down." Right. Also, there's a knocking on the door downstairs, as in *Macbeth,* isn't there? Death is coming! [Knocks twice on desk.]

*Another way in which* **Force of Evil** *differs from the average gangster film is that you never show the Law Crusade.*

*We never see the law enforcement people, particularly that Special Prosecutor, Hall, who is always talked about.*

I originally had a scene with the Law, but I eliminated it. After all, who cares about *them?* I mean, with all their talk about law and order, they're not really saying anything. I'm for law enforcement—but not against *me.*

*This made the Law much more ambiguous. By making it so remote, you seem to tie it up with the remote fate that these people are dealing with.*

The Law is just another representative of the general evil in which we all exist. I mean, it's nice that someone comes and helps you when you're being robbed or beaten up. I like that. But that's not a metaphysical argument. I'd rather have it that *you* helped *me* and didn't have a badge. You just helped me because you saw me suffering, not because you were the Law.

*Why did you attach so much importance to telephones throughout the whole film?*

Well, first of all, they're useful . . . but they're more than useful. The telephone is a dangerous object. It represents dangerous kinds of things. I don't like instant communication. I like it to take a long time before I understand you and you understand me. In the film, it forms the structure of the characters' relationships. Everybody is tied up with this phone. Garfield makes his call to order the raid, right? And he makes this call a number of times in the film. It's his way of communicating with one world and receiving messages from another. I had a big telephone made so that it would loom very large in the foreground of those close-ups. I guess the telephone was any easy symbol for the connections between all the different worlds in the film. These worlds communicate with each other through telephones instead of feelings. We're getting our messages in *signals,* not *feelings.* Sometimes these messages are correct, and sometimes, even when you hear them, they're incorrect. And to have your telephone tapped, we know now, is the way we communicate with our government and law enforcement agencies. It's our last means of direct representation except for an occasional riot.

*In the novel, much more time is given to the character of Tucker. Why is he a shadowy figure in the film?*

It was necessary for what I was trying to do. The more shadowy Tucker is, the more omnipresent the feeling of what he represents.

*There seemed to be a direct parallel between Tucker and the Law on the other end of the telephone.*

Exactly. You see, the people live in a lane, and on both sides of this lane are vast, empty places. On one side, it says LAW, and on the other, it says CRIME. But, in fact, you can't tell one from the other. Except for the messages you get on this phone, it's hard to know. All I can tell is what happens in this lane, and the rest are murmurs from space outside. It's just history talking to us—murmurs from history.

*How much freedom of choice is there in this lane?*

Any *single* person can stop anytime, I feel. I don't know

if a *thousand* can, but I know any single one can. I believe that. Sometimes, if you stop, you make all the others stop. If you stop believing *that,* you've become the establishment, the organization, the syndicate.

*Can this one person ever stop outside of corruption?*

Why not? I don't think the nature of life is to be corrupt. Nor do I think the nature of life is to be good. I mean, the nature of man is to *be there,* as any other animal is there. That's why we invent our moralities. That's the way we handle the world. The fundamental relationship between people is *moral.* That's our social invention—in place of instinct.

*I wasn't too clear about the man that Bauer meets in front of the bus with a password. Was he a gangster or a lawman?*

I don't remember. In the film, I have two kinds of people around: cops and gangsters. I don't remember which side this particular person was on, because I made that up as I went along. It wouldn't matter to me whether he was one or the other. I can't remember now what I had in mind with that character. I'd have to see the film again, which I refuse to do because I can only see how bad it is. That film, you know, is fundamentally a failure.

*The end of the film, where Garfield "returns to society" saying, "I decided to help," is again different from the ending of a normal gangster film. But it also seemed different from the way the story was leading. Do you think this was some real kind of rebirth, or was it the logical development of his character throughout the film?*

It was a mixture of cop-out . . . and significance. It was a gangster film, and in those days, censorship was much stronger. So, in a way, his last sentence had to say, "I'm going to see that something is done to get rid of all this corruption." People say that to themselves all the time, and I wouldn't consider that, as you must know, a significant remark then or now. That's not the way things happen. How much history do we have to have happen to know that?

So, it was partly a cop-out. It was saying to the censor, "Look. It's O.K. Don't worry about it. He had a change of heart." But that was *completely* on the surface. I didn't mean it at all. What I really meant were all those words at the end and all those images: "Down, down, down."

At the end of the picture, in Garfield's case, it's like being left back in school. I remember in Thomas Mann's *The Magic Mountain,* when he talks about Hans Castorp's youth. Hans is in school, and he gets left back—and what a *relief* it was to get left back! Because *then* you don't have to get ahead anymore. A kind of liberation and freedom comes from failure. What I tried to do there was to get the feeling that, having reached the absolute moral bottom of commitment, there's nothing left to do but commit yourself. There's no longer a problem of identity when you have no identity left at all. So, in your very next step, you must become something.

In general, that's what the ending was: vague. But then changes in personality are always vague. You only know long afterwards whether they had any significance.

*It seemed to me that you framed the cycle of Garfield's corruption. In other words, at the end of the film, a light is flashing outside the exit of the nightclub when he leaves, and near the beginning of the film, a lot of emphasis is given to the light flashing outside the window of Tucker's office. I interpreted that one as sort of an entrance light, as the other was an exit light. Does Garfield's corruption start right there, which I don't think is true, or, does anything start when he's in Tucker's office at that time?*

What happens in Tucker's office is not the beginning of his corruption, but that it is called to Garfield's attention. That's the thing. I don't think you begin to get corrupted at any particular moment. You're *already* corrupted when you first begin to notice it.

Life's a kind of corruption, as you live it. Life's a kind of dying, as you live it. You receive messages, as from these telephones, or you receive messages from other people, and slowly you're aware that you're immersed in something. But you don't believe it, because you think you can handle it. And *true* corruption starts at that moment. Because if you realized that you *couldn't* handle it, your corruption would begin to be over. It would be on its way out, wouldn't it? It's that sense of power or control over yourself, that you don't really have, which leads to your tragedy.

*Thomas Gomez, who played Garfield's brother, felt that he maintained some kind of integrity because he was only involved in small-time corruption, nickel and dime gambling. But Garfield points out to him, truthfully, that they are in some way equal.*

Sure. Gomez was even worse: he felt he had an ethical basis. It's even true in American society today. Small businessmen feel ethically superior to trusts, and our laws reflect it. The base of the bourgeois ethic by which we all live in our society is the small businessman. He sits in his shop; he's honest; he deals well; everybody takes advantage of him—and out of him come all the disasters. That's why Tommy Gomez feels he's an honest man; he reflects the whole society.

*What about Bauer, the bookkeeper who informs the police? The film gives particular emphasis to his doom. For example, when the numbers bank is raided, there's a shot of him on the floor which is the exact same shot used when he's killed in the restaurant. Why should we feel that Bauer's more doomed than the other characters, particularly Thomas Gomez?*

Gomez thinks he's in charge of his life. Bauer knows he's not. Then, Bauer is an accountant. He has the account books of our society. They balance out, don't they? In the end, one side is equal to the other. God knows what happens in between—which is all this terrible life people lead.

Bauer is the accountant of the whole picture. Therefore, he feels, "I'm only keeping the books! I'm doing something perfectly proper and reasonable. I do nothing but add numbers. What am I guilty of?" And all the while he feels terrible because he knows he's involved in the whole thing.

A man who feels he's doing something reasonable and

who's suddenly caught short is the *perfect* betrayer. You know, if you don't have very strong moral principles, it's hard for you to betray other people. You really have to be committed to do that. That's Bauer.

*How does he differ from Thomas Gomez, who also feels that he's not responsible?*

Well, Thomas Gomez is in a way like Bauer. But Gomez is the employer. He's carved out this little niche which is fundamentally illegal. And he runs this operation as if it were a human society. He takes care of Doris [Beatrice Pearson]. He takes care of his people. He doesn't want them to get into big trouble. He doesn't want his brother to bring him into the big syndicate and involve him in the *big* corruptions of society. He has this little island of human loyalty, human relations, and benevolence, and that's the way he justifies what he does. It makes him feel like a man, and they want to take away his manhood by making him part of the machine.

So he's different from Bauer, because he's in control. Bauer knows he's in control of nothing, and therefore he never fights. How can he fight? He runs like a rat. That's what he is: a rat, keeping the books.

*What is Garfield trying to get out of Gomez?*

He wants his brother to be his brother—and to forgive everything.

*Then why does he victimize him?*

Because he's trying to *save* him. If he just let Gomez go down, Gomez would have no problem. But he's his brother, so he's going to save him—and he kills him. Gomez keeps saying, "Stop trying to save me! You'll kill me! Because you're no good!" This is the classical mythological relationship between these kinds of brothers—all brothers.

*But does Garfield ever try to destroy Gomez, rather than save him?*

They're both trying to destroy each other. The older brother, Gomez, had to live a bad life and a hard life, and he says to Garfield, "I made all these sacrifices for *you*. *You* are the favored one, and *you* have the blessing there." It turns out that this blessing is a disaster. The younger brother finds out that you can't do anything with this blessing in the world, except turn it into power. If you turn it into power, you turn it into corruption.

In that sense, you can interpret everything that one person does for another as a way of destroying him. Everything is double-edged in our relations. The way all stories take on their dynamism is that everything has its double nature. You do a thing for this side, and it's the other side that becomes apparent. As you shift from one side to another, one becomes more dominant over the other. Love becomes death and hate—all love, depending on how you make your choices.

In the end, Gomez is doing everything in his power to make sure that his brother destroys him, because *then* his brother is guilty. Garfield says it all the time, doesn't he? "Why are you trying to do this to me? I'm trying to save you! Do you want to make me feel guilty?" And Gomez says, "You *are* guilty!"

*Even with the classical décor the visual tone of the film seemed stark, almost barren.*

The cameraman was George Barnes, who, as you know, was probably one of the best cameramen we ever had in this town. He had deep-focus long before other people used it, before Welles and Toland hit it. Now, for years Barnes had been photographing mostly older actresses, making them stay young and beautiful—you know how that's done.

We did a few days' testing and looked at the rushes, and they were beautiful and vague. That is to say, it was the standard romantic photography that he'd been doing, which was absolutely against everything I intended to do in this picture. Jimmy Howe, who photographed **Body and Soul,** doesn't shoot that way at all. He's very clear and precise and naturally anti-romantic. I was used to that, since I'd seen Howe every day on the set of **Body and Soul.**

I tried to tell George what I was looking for, but I couldn't quite describe that to a cameraman, because I didn't know what to say. I went out and got a book of reproductions of Hopper's paintings—Third Avenue, cafeterias, all that back-lighting, and those empty streets. Even when people are there, you don't see them; somehow the environments dominate the people. I went to Barnes and I said, "This is kind of what I want." "Oh, that!" He knew right away what "that" was, and we had it all the way through the film. He never varied from it once he knew the tone I wanted.

*The New York exteriors that you used in the film were strange. What were you trying to do with them?*

Just what you said. I was trying to make strange exteriors. Just as Tucker's apartment and the offices are full of the nature and power of our society, so are the exteriors full of their beauty and the symbols of their significance: the bank-fronts, the church, the Palisades, the great bridge. Of course, you die at the foot of the bridge, but that happens all the time—we fall off our monuments. We spend our lives falling off our monuments.

*The opening shot of the film shows a huge crowd. As the film progresses, it becomes less populated, and the final exteriors are deserted.*

Well, by the end, Garfield's flying. He's flying down his dreams or illusions or whatever you want to call them. He's flying to that bridge, and the world gets emptier and emptier. Finally, the only things that are left are his dead brother and this girl—and she's as much a victim as his brother.

One of the scenes that I particularly like takes place after Gomez's numbers bank is raided. Garfield's sitting outside the courtroom, and all these people come out. They have just been let out on bail; everything's arranged. And these people coming out are a freak show, a real one, except for this darling girl. I mean, these people are really beaten. Even if they had had all the success in the world, it's already been stolen from them.

I felt that that scene was shot just the way it should be: the texture of it, the look of it—it's so bedraggled and empty. And then, when Garfield meets the girl, I use a romantic image, through the translucent glass doors of the courthouse. Completely romantic—the complete opposite of the milieu. As if to say that you can still hold on to something beautiful and delicious despite everything. Of course you can! That's the cheat. Garfield still thinks so, because he's not finished yet, is he? Going down those steps. I kind of liked that scene. I thought it was successful.

*Why do you consider the film a failure?*

Well, it was my first film, and I think there's a difference between what I really intended to do and what came off. I didn't know *how*. And then, despite good reviews, it wasn't a successful picture at the box office. Of course it was a difficult picture, and, of course, it was experimental in a way, deliberately experimental. But, nevertheless, I thought that the general weight of it would be obvious, that people would feel it. But it wasn't felt except by very sophisticated audiences.

*Did you try to correct these "failures" in* **Willie Boy?**

**Willie Boy** is totally different. There's no relation between the two films, except as I'm related to both of them. The technique is different. Everything in the world of the film is charged with my meanings, everything is present, you see, so I know I don't have to work so hard to make them available. It'll happen anyway. So it's much simpler . . . *apparently* much simpler. If you wrote a sonata when you were twelve, and then you wrote one when you were fifty, they'd be different, wouldn't they?

*Could you tell us about your experience with the blacklist? What were you doing between* **Force of Evil** *and* **Willie Boy?**

After I finished **Force of Evil,** I went to Europe to write a novel. The blacklist, of course, had begun to operate by then, although it hadn't yet taken on that momentum and destructive energy in the industry. Blacklisting is part of the political behavior of all societies: you put your friends in and keep your enemies out. But it takes on its own momentum, too. It becomes a *thing* with its own life, which has nothing to do with its original intentions.

I'd written this novel, and then I came back here to work at Twentieth-Century Fox. I knew that it would have been safer to stay in Europe—but not really, because not everybody is suited for exile. I think you have to have a temperament for it. Also, the only kinds of exiles that I admire are those who are doing everything in their power to overthrow the government at home, so they can get *back*. Otherwise, you might as well emigrate and get it over with, finish it off and become another person—if they let you.

Now it wasn't that bad—yet. But it was happening. Instead of staying in Europe, I came back here. I was subpoenaed to appear before the committee. I appeared, and was blacklisted.

I made a living all those years mainly by writing for television under pseudonyms. I did a very good show, too,

called *You Are There.* At the height of the whole blacklist, a couple of other blacklisted writers and I were doing shows about free speech and personal liberty. You know: Galileo, Milton, Socrates, and so on. But we weren't doing it for that reason; we were just making a living.

Then, by and by, the Hollywood producers started appearing in cloaks and black hats, in obscure corners of remote cities—and giving us jobs fixing up scripts. Very shortly we were making just as much money, if not more, than before, but we were doing infinitely worse work. That was the way the blacklist period was.

I sometimes wonder why I didn't go right down and start working in the underground film movement which was in existence then. I don't know why. It never occurred to me at the time. One of the reasons was: I didn't want to do any pictures at all . . . I think.

So I turned myself into a writer, in a way. I'd only directed once, right? I didn't consider myself a director. I considered that I *had* directed. But I'd always been a writer of sorts. I became interested in some little, lefty, avant-garde magazine in New York, and I wrote articles for it. The blacklist world slowly ground to a halt with the McCarthy-Army hearings. It did not disappear after the defeat of McCarthy, but it no longer terrorized those people who gave employment. Now they appeared openly. In fact, some of them, like Otto Preminger, just ignored it. He hired Dalton Trumbo and paid no attention to it. Of course, it was soon discovered that if you paid no attention to it, nothing happened. And finally, some three or four years ago, that happened to me.

Frank Rosenberg, who is a producer at Universal, asked me to write a television pilot. Since I had plenty of money at that time, as a blacklisted writer, there was no particular reason for me to do a television show. I was making a good living fixing up rotten movies. So I said, "I'll do it if you put my name on it." In that way, I though I was getting rid of the possibility of ever having to do it. My name was submitted to whatever the network was. A generally discouraging kind of report came back, which in a sense said, "Get somebody else. Let's not start this up again." When that happened, Jennings Lang, one of the vice-presidents of Universal, called and told the network to go to hell. And they said, "O.K., we'll go to hell." So there I was, able to do that pilot under my own name.

Then Rosenberg prepared the film *Madigan.* The screenplay was being written by Howard Rodman. Rodman and Rosenberg, for their own reasons, didn't get on very well—this happens. So Rosenberg asked me to work on the screenplay. But this was under my own name, you see. After checking with Rodman to make sure that he wouldn't be working on it, I came out here and did some rewriting.

Soon after that, Jennings Lang proposed that I write and direct what we call a "one-twenty," which is a two-hour film for television. Before this, Philip Waxman, who was to be the producer of this television film, had come to me with a book called *Willie Boy.* I proposed that we make it into a "one-twenty." This is not a very good deal for a producer of a "one-twenty" since you get very little money compared with what you get for a feature film. But Lang—he was at the heart of the whole operation as you can see—thought that we could make a feature film out of it. Waxman took his chances. I wrote the script, and they liked it. And I cast it with their help, and they liked it. And I made it, and they liked it. That's the way it happened. Don't ask me if I like it!

*What was it about* Willie Boy *that particularly interested you?*

When I read the book originally, I didn't see anything interesting enough in it for me to make a film. I had no particular interest in the Old West or in the New West, or the Old East or the New East, or anything like that. Then, when I was writing *Madigan,* one day I suddenly saw the story, the Willie Boy incident, in a different way. It had nothing to do with the Old West or the New West. It had to do with most of the young people I knew today, living in a transitional period and being driven by circumstances and values they couldn't control. And at that point, I thought it would be an interesting story to do, because then I could play around with this romantic investment we have in the past, along with a lack of comprehension for the realities of the present, and show these two things pushing one way and another. When I saw that, I called up Waxman and said I'd do it.

This picture is intended for young people not yet committed to the disasters of history. If I had one specific intention in my mind, it was to tell my feelings about this to your generation. Not to mine. If mine doesn't know that, to hell with 'em. They should know it by now—and you should know it by now, too. I have a particular feeling about this general problem. Not just because they're Indians, but because this is a general human situation. It's fundamental to human history—this terrible thing that we do. Civilization is the process of despoiling, of *spoliation* of people, which in the past we considered a victory, but we now suspect is a moral defeat for all.

My feeling about this film, in making it, was to address it to your generation and say, "This is what I think about this. This is the way I feel about this. This is the way I see it. This is what this experience is—and you should know it."

By the way, how did you like Bobby Blake, who played Willie Boy? Did you accept him?

*Completely. I wasn't too sure if Katherine Ross fit into the part of Lola at the beginning, but I think she got better as she got a little more violent.*

That was the hardest thing in the film. You must accept Blake as an Indian in 1909. I think any first-rate actor can handle most roles, but to look like it, too, is the hardest thing to accomplish. And I think he made it; he actually seems to look like that person, and he certainly is that person as an actor. Toughest part in the picture.

Ross had the same problem. I mean, how does one become an Indian girl? I tried to overcome that difficulty by making her an Indian girl who wanted to be a white girl. So, wherever she's not really Indian, you say, "Well, that's because she's trying to make it with the whites." Then you finally accept her anomalous position, and she plays into the part. It works out kind of nicely, I think. Of course, you know, in history, no one knows who Lola is, as a person. She's a name from history, that's all.

*The grayness of the rocks in the film reminded me of brimstone.*

Great rocks, weren't they?

*I felt that the film was starting at the end of* **Force of Evil,** *going down, down, but going far beyond that.*

**Force of Evil** dealt more with what they used to call *angst.* This film ignores that. It starts long after we're used to *angst.* It's too serious to worry about generalized metaphysical anxiety. And that's what I meant when I said that I don't want to look at that other picture again. The point of view seems so limited to me.

*The chase was handled unusually. You seemed to eschew all melodramatic value—suspense, people catching up to other people, decreasing distance between the pursued and the pursuer, and so on.*

Well, I treated it as a formal structure. I took the whole chase and changed it from someone chasing someone to just a formal structure, like writing a fugue, see, so that you wouldn't get mixed up in the pursuit but pay attention to the meaning.

I had it written out originally as a real chase, with events and so on, which you do to make it interesting. Then it occurred to me, just before I started to shoot those scenes, that I didn't really care very much about that. What did that have to do with my story? With what I meant? What I did was reorganize all that into this formal structure. I treated the ambush in that way, too.

*I had no sense of time throughout the film. This seems unusual for a chase film, where time is usually so important. It was as if time stopped.*

Well, why do you think that happened?

*At one point Lola says, "They're white. They'll chase you forever." And Willie says, "How long is that?"*

". . . less than you think." It has no duration, has it? Which is why I finally formalized the chase, because if I had used that chase in a dramatic way, I would have brought chronological chase time in and destroyed the picture, I thought.

*When Willie leaves the Twenty-Nine Palms oasis, several locations are repeated. This gave a great sense of futility to the whole chase; it seemed as if he were retracing his steps. Was this intended?*

Well, everything is kind of intended. But sometimes intended things have magnificent results in a direction opposite to what you hope for. Then you're happy to see it and take advantage of it. [Laughs.] Hooray for accident! Father of us all!

*Outside of the four main characters—Blake, Ross, Robert Redford [the sheriff], and Susan Clark [the government agent on the reservation]—everybody else seemed almost irrelevant.*

Right. But of course everybody's characterized, you see. No one is just a neutral thing, or else the motion picture would be unseeable. But, at the same time, I want these other characters to be the environment just like the stones, the sky, the water, and everything else—with these four living creatures in it. When many persons are your environment, are within your life, the prime question is one of focus.

*One character who stood out among the posse was Calvert [Barry Sullivan].*

He wishes he could live a little again, because everything seems so boring now. Our main use of the Western, in our mythology of pleasure, is to deny its reality and substitute what we like to imagine our history was for what really happened. Everybody does that with history; it makes the present more tenable. So Barry Sullivan plays out this untenable mythological Western, you see. For example, he says to Redford, "Your father was lucky. He died when it was still good to live."

He also says, "I was telling them about the year your daddy and me followed a party of Comanche two hundred miles into Mexico. We brought back six scalps that time." And sitting around that fire with the posse are three Indians! Indian police, who are out chasing this other Indian. The posse members never pay any attention to whether these Indians react to this. All the conversation about Indians, even at the end, is done in the presence of Indians, who are not supposed to have any reality. They're not supposed to think like Indians—they just exist. And we do that all the time, of course, with people whom we think are inferior to ourselves.

But I put in a slow alteration in mood. These Indians finally start to identify with Willie, and then they start to get pretty hostile, and finally Redford says, "Bury him," and they burn him!

*The turning point seems to occur when Lola's body is brought up, and the other Indians say that they think she killed herself in order to save Willie, not that she was murdered by Willie. That seems to be where these Indians started to swing over.*

That's right. And that sort of thing actually happened in history. In real life, unlike in the movie, Willie had committed suicide early in the story. They had twelve posses out looking around for a man who no longer existed.

I used that general feeling of identification, developed between Willie and the other Indians, which arose from the fact that the posse couldn't capture him. Therefore, an Indian was making some kind of stand, in that sense, at a time when Indians made no stands at all. 1890, I think, was Wounded Knee, the last of the Indian massacres. About two hundred Indians, who were wearing those ghost shirts, were wiped out. The Sioux believed if they wore the ghost shirts, white bullets couldn't go through. When Willie runs at the end, you know he's not trying to escape, if you're really tuned in, because he's wearing a ghost shirt. He put his father's ghost shirt on.

Also, Lola killed herself because they would have surely caught Willie if she had stayed with him. Alone he had a chance. Well, instead of making a stand at Twenty-Nine Palms, he really *escaped*. They couldn't catch him; therefore, Lola hadn't died in vain. After that, he was ready to do what he wanted. In other words, she didn't kill herself for nothing: he did escape. But after that, he had no reason to be free anymore.

*The Susan Clark character, the woman agent on the reservation, was benevolent toward the Indians yet had very little real understanding of the situation.*

Yes, I think she did a marvelous job of creating the establishment—humanized, but at the same time, infinitely dangerous and infinitely involved. I wanted to show that, despite all of Clark's sympathies for the Indians and her desire to help them, her concern is only with sanitation, education, health. She doesn't have a spiritual concern. She's helping them, and Willie says, "Yeah, she's a helper!" What he means is, "Who wants that kind of help? We don't need any help. We just have to *be*. Our problem is to *become* someone." But Lola doesn't know that until the very end.

We don't really admit the Indians' existence, because their existence means that we don't really belong here. They have no being, except anthropologically.

*In this light, the only character who "becomes" is Willie Boy. He becomes through his death.*

That's right. This is a story of an anti-hero, to use popular phrases, who is Redford, and of a real hero, who is Willie. A real hero is someone who fulfills his destiny. And an anti-hero is one who struggles to find his identity in a destiny that he refuses to fulfill. What he's really fighting against is the power structure, the organization, the set-up. Willie is struggling with that, too, but he has a real destiny to fulfill. He's a hero. All he has to do is become himself, and he does. What else can a poor Indian do?

*In the filming of Willie, it doesn't look like he's making choices along the way. It looks like every step he takes is pre-destined. On the other hand, every step that Redford takes looks like he's making choices—the way he carries himself, rides his horse, follows Willie's trail. Willie has laid the trail; Willie is the one who had to step there.*

Exactly. And that's what's good about Redford's performance. That's why I called him Coop in the film: Gary Cooper, the great Western sheriff. And he plays this role with a great deal of uneasiness. I think he does it very well.

*When Willie and Lola were making love in the orchard, you cut to a long-shot of the people closing in on them. That was one of the darkest love scenes I'd ever seen.*

It's what happened in the Garden of Eden—after they ate of the tree. It's shot like a Garden of Eden scene. They're completely nude, and yet their nudity is irrelevant. They're not nude; they're in their skins. That's their costume for that scene.

*You inter-cut a lot between the two love affairs: Willie and Lola, and Coop and the Susan Clark character.*

I treat both love affairs as a single affair, being acted out by different people at different times. All during the story, that's what it is.

*The whole thing is who acts out what part. For example, there's an obvious sense of Willie and Lola consummating the affair for the other two people.*

That's right. That's where the significance comes in. That's the way I make the social significance work without having anything to do with it.

*All through the film, the town is awaiting a visit from President Taft. The local officials prepare for his arrival by constructing a chair large enough to hold him and by deploying an extravagant number of small American flags all over the place. Again, this seemed to do away with any surface political or social intonations to the story. You see all these flags, and that settles that!*

[Laughs.] That's it! You see these flags and this immense chair for Taft to fill, and what more can you ask of a President? It's so specific, that suddenly it's irrelevant.

*About the end, the burning of Willie's body. The posse comes for souvenirs . . .*

Something to show for all of it! They have to have something to show for all this work they've done—this chase, the money, all this nonsense they've invented.

*What does Susan Clark's inscrutable expression to Redford at the end mean?*

Well, ask yourself this question: What do you say to a man who finds himself a prisoner of a situation which he feels he must play out? He feels he must fulfill a role in this situation in order to become a man. And the moment he does so, he realizes that's precisely the one way he *can't.* In that last scene, he now knows this, and he's washing the blood off his hands. What do you say to him? Nothing. How do you look at him? What do you do? You stay away from him! What does she do? She stays away from him. And that's the end of the film, as far as she's concerned. By the way, while we were filming it, it was Redford who urged this approach.

*So this man thought he had a job to do, and he thought he would define himself by doing it . . .*

Not necessarily to *kill* Willie. Coop didn't go out to kill him, just to capture him. He was *prepared* to kill him. I suppose to be prepared is somehow already to have killed.

*But he did kill Willie, and in doing so he destroyed himself. But, by the nature of his self-definition, it had to be done. When we were discussing* **Force of Evil,** *I asked you how much freedom of choice these characters have. Did Coop have a choice* not *to commit this act?*

Well, he offered Willie and therefore himself the choice to go peacefully, but after Coop had killed him and discovered that Willie's rifle wasn't loaded he knew that there had been no choice after all.

And it's that irony, which is in all events, that defeats all the illusions we have about the choices that we make up for ourselves. *Long* before that event, we have committed ourselves to courses of action which are folly and disaster.

And all along the line, we invent choices which we think are real but are just cover-ups.

I think that's the nature of the fake morality that we live by. We invent right and wrong, so that we seem to be making very good choices all the time—and that's a trap! Long before that, we've committed the disaster. And all these choices that we seem to be making are not choices at all.

That's why, long after terrible historical events pass, people say, "But I didn't know!" "I didn't know what was going on in those camps." "I didn't know that was what the war meant." "I didn't know that he was going to die." "I didn't know she was going to be so unhappy." Those are the great *I-didn't-know's.* You've heard them all over. Popular fiction, whether in television, films, novels, or plays, is made of these false *I-didn't-know's.* That's what you call sentimental writing. That's the pornography of feeling. And that's the way we cop-out, to use a favorite phrase of your generation.

*At the end, these people who are breaking up the fire look extremely desperate and futile. They're not really breaking up anything.*

No, they're not. They've got nothing to bring back. These Indians burn Willie's body because you could burn the bodies of chiefs in those days. I originally had a line in the script about that, but I took it out—too noble. Now he's burned beyond salvage, and there's nothing to bring back except cinders. So the posse rides in and starts pulling the fire apart—a boot, a shoe, an ear, *anything* to bring back. And they're dancing around this fire, trying to find something. Then Sheriff Wilson goes up to Coop and says, "God damn it, Coop, what've we got to show for it? What will I tell 'em?" And Coop says, "Tell 'em we're all out of souvenirs."

And that's what I want to tell everybody. Never mind all those souvenirs that they keep pushing down on us, all the sacrifices *they* made in the past. I don't care about them. The past is not now. It's just a souvenir, and we shouldn't be bound by souvenirs. If we are, we're not going to live here long. Well, you know that. We're not living here long anyway. They've extended our life expectancy but decreased our chances of living long.

*Is there any affirmation in this dark ending?*

Well, we know *they're* in the dark; *we* don't have to be. Willie isn't in the dark. Coop isn't in the dark anymore either, is he?

*Although Coop may not be in the dark, will his next step be of his own choosing?*

Far from it. That's why there should be no movement between Redford and Susan Clark at the end that gives you any sense of warmth or affection. It would obscure the ending. It would make you feel, "Oh, well anyhow, Love goes on!" We didn't have anything like that. By then, she knows this man, doesn't she? She comes at Coop's moment of disillusionment, which is Willie's triumph, since he's become himself. And she doesn't do anything. She doesn't weep a single tear, she doesn't show any kindness toward Coop. She just passes him by.

You only kiss returning soldiers in real wars. In these kinds of wars, which, in a certain way, are much more important than real wars, you don't do that. There's no comfort and no company. You're alone, and you want to be alone, and Coop is alone at the end of the story. He walks away from history.

In effect, he says at the end, "It's no use explaining how all these things come about, because all you do is explain. The terrible thing is that they happen." Historical explanations and moral explanations, and explanations of tenderness and love, and *all* such explanations, are irrelevancies beside the fact, as you look at the fact. Now, you look at this fact and face it. I say that to you and anyone. Know this fact and face it.

### Abraham Polonsky with James D. Pasternak and F. William Howton   (interview date 1971)

SOURCE: An interview in *The Image Maker,* edited by Ron Henderson, John Knox Press, 1971, pp. 17-27.

[*Pasternak is an American film director, screenwriter, and educator. Howton is an American sociologist and film critic. In the following interview, Polonsky discusses the impetus for making* Tell Them Willie Boy Is Here *and describes his career as a filmmaker before and after the blacklist.*]

[*Pasternak and Howton*]: *Tell us about your new project.*

[Polonsky]: I have three. One of them is *Childhood's End* by Arthur Clarke, which Universal bought for my company to make into film. Another is an original screenplay by me called *Sweet Land,* which Universal bought for my company to do, and a third is one I haven't sold to anyone yet, *Mario the Magician* by Thomas Mann.

*You've been working on that property for quite a while now, haven't you?*

I got it from Thomas Mann in 1950. He was living, in those days, in California. I've known his daughter for a long time, and I'd already directed *Force of Evil.* I got in touch with him and we had a discussion about my notions of directing it, which wasn't to be exactly the way he wrote it. He gave me an option on it, and I went to Europe to try to set up the project, but was unable to raise any money for it. No one was really interested at that time.

*Why?*

In 1950 everybody thought fascism was old hat. I think that was the real reason for it. In any event, when I was blacklisted, I had to drop it. So, the first thing I did, when I got to direct **Willie Boy** and had the project set up at Universal, was to get in touch with Erica Mann, and I got it back. But, of course, in all these years my notion of how it is to be done changed. Fundamentally, it's the same discussion I had with Thomas Mann. It was at that time that Thomas Mann said to me that he thought fascism was coming to the United States and he advised me to leave the country. He said he was going to England, and did in fact go to Switzerland. He had just finished *Faustus.* I disagreed with him and didn't come.

*Is* Mario *your most immediate project?*

I think it is. My problem, of course, is to get it financed without telling them what I'm doing, which is very difficult to do.

*Isn't that easier to do, though, because you're dealing with a classic? It has a kind of built-in acceptance for the studio mentality?*

Well, our studios are not impressed by Thomas Mann.

*Yes, but it would make it easier for* you, *an impressive director, to bring in an impressive property. I'm trying to psych out the twisted psyche. . . .*

They don't have a twisted psyche! Their psyche is extremely clear. There's nothing twisted about studios: They know what business they're in. They don't *understand* what business they're in, but they know what it is. I mean, they don't know how to operate very well, because they have a tendency to make money in the way in which they are accustomed to making money, which is, to do again what has already been successful.

*You mean to make a film of the film that was a film originally?*

It's even worse than *that*! It's to be immediately up to date with what has already gone out of fashion. It's hard to escape that in the studios, because—to use your words—they're trying to psych out the market. And when the market has changed radically, as it has in the last five or six years, I would imagine for them (it has been changing over the years) they keep insisting that that market still exists out there, even when they say, "no, it doesn't really exist any more," we're going to adjust to it. So, now when they say they're going to do youth films, and in a sense are like the people in *Vogue* magazine who have a youth consultant, that's the youth market, this is what youth likes now, then they do youth films, whatever they think youth loves. "Youth" is, of course, a fiction—*their* youth, at least, is a fiction. Actually (they) would like to make pictures that appeal to the television market, that is to say, the widest possible market. They would like every film to appeal to every possible audience. And when they get something like that, they're very happy.

*I gather you don't endorse the thesis, which is fashionable, that the big studios' dominance of the industry is somewhat passé, that the success of comparatively low-budget films, medium-low budget films, has been so impressive that the studios are more and more inclined to simply lease out their facilities and not, in fact, the entrepreneurs themselves?*

Well, that's going on obviously with some of the studios, especially if they're in the stages of potential bankruptcy. But I would say that the new money coming in will ultimately go back into some sort of studio operation, especially if they want to stay in the television business, where you need a studio operation, since films for television and television series are made under studio control, unless you can't make them for the price.

*Isn't that how the property of* **Willie Boy** *was originally conceived by them, as a television film?*

That was a device. What actually happened was that Jennings Lang, a vice president at Universal, who was in charge of the whole television operation, said that if we brought *Willie Boy* in under television, then he, on his own, could OK going ahead with the project. He was *certain* that if I wrote the script they would turn it into a feature, and as a matter of fact they did at once—the minute I handed them the script.

*Mr. Polonsky, could you tell us how you changed your mind? I think you had an original impression of the* Willie Boy *book as being not especially interesting for a screenplay and a movie.*

There's no particular reason why I should write a western, or any other genre film, although I'm interested in genre films, but I didn't see how it was relevant to me. Not that you only do films that are relevant to yourself when you're trying to make your living as a writer in the film industry, although they do become so. I talked about it with others a little and I suddenly realized that the events in the story had taken the exact sequence of the western myth: the actual historical events had taken that sequence. That interested me.

*Which myth? The myth of the western American movie, or the western myth?*

Oh! The way I always put it is that the western genre film deals with the Western Myth, an illusion. I'd always enjoyed those films myself, as a young man. Now the illusion of the West as a kind of Paradise Lost—in which for a small period Americans lived in this strange and marvelous world, this frontier in which all kinds of heroic sentiments were generated, and in which an idea of what the American was was most clearly presented: the adventurer in search of the Good Life. But, of course, the Paradise Lost was genocide for the Indians, and, in fact, Ford in *Cheyenne Autumn* had that too in effect. But the very great western directors kind of know that, even as they're dealing with and eulogizing the myth in terms of its excessive nature.

*An exploitation of the myth?*

Of course. Suddenly, I saw that in fact this myth was still operating—as a notion of American life—and that it was possible to tell the story and set in motion a counter-myth to it. But I wanted the film to have the clarity of a myth and not be overly psychologized, because if you overly psychologize the relation between the characters you destroy the mythic quality in which the events determine what is really going to happen.

*Is that why the language is very spare, very lean?*

And the remarks are kind of gnomic, so to speak—little balls of words like stones and rocks that I dropped. There are only one or two scenes that are really dramatic scenes in a normal motion picture narrative sense. They just drop these words, and they're not very relevant as dialogue, even; in fact, the film could be silent, almost, and still work.

*Would you elaborate on the counter-myth theme?*

The counter-myth is genocide. Now, of course, some of the critics, even those who *loved* my picture, speak of the scene in the poolroom as representing my political opin-

ion, which is absurd, since it's kind of a take-off on a Mark Twain-*Huckleberry Finn* kind of scene in which some of the poolroom hustlers and river characters are making the usual remarks they make in a poolroom. They like to talk about democracy a lot and what he's really saying, of course, is very funny. When a character says, for example, "Let's hear a cheer for President Taft, but not to me. That's the inequality in the country . . . I pay my taxes," and so on—that's supposed to be a funny scene, and hardly represents any political opinions I might *possibly* hold! I included it really in a way to remind people of Mark Twain.

*And also, it's there to give a democratic idea when he speaks of what democracy can do for an Indian.*

That's right. And it's supposed to be amusing rather than pretentious and important. It's certainly not my idea of what democracy is, if I know what my idea of democracy is. I begin to doubt it occasionally. So, the counter-myth is the genocide theme.

Now, the film is embedded in the whole notion of racism, and it's not against it in any kind of way, as if that were the point of the film. It just takes that for granted. What I do is assume that the western myth is fundamentally racist, even though the question never comes up, but just the way the Indian appears in the mythology of American life: an invisible person. They're the original exiles in this country. And, of course, that third factor came into mind when I finally became interested in it because I've been a kind of invisible exile myself, in my own country, for twenty years.

*And you, like Willie Boy, refuse to be invisible.*

But I was luckier than he was, because I didn't believe in the Indian notion of the earlier days of not committing suicide, because if you committed suicide, you lost your relationship to whatever future there was after death. So what the Indians did was charge into the enemy and have the enemy kill them so that they died heroically in battle, which is exactly what Willie does on top of the mountain, because he could have killed the sheriff Coop, with any of those three shots which is demonstrated in the attack on the posse.

*You wanted to, it seems, say something from your generation's perspective to youth of today through this film that has some relationship to your being blacklisted for twenty years. You have also mentioned that you think of this film as a "free gift" of entertainment. How do you relate these two conceptions of* **Willie Boy**?

I think it's important to know that, to begin with, I didn't make this film for any market. I assumed in the very beginning, when it became possible to make this film, which was an accident and a miracle of a sort, to get the right to direct a film after twenty years and spend $2,300,000 of their money, it's impossible, and when the impossible occurs, it's like a miracle. So I made this film, with the notion in mind that it was probably unlikely that, first, I would ever finish it, because it's possible you might not finish it, and secondly, I probably wouldn't make another film again as a director, because it's very hard to be a director in Hollywood. The director is the most dangerous man in the business and usually he is circumscribed in various kinds of ways; the old producer-supervisor system was set up to control the director.

*You mean from the Thalberg days?*

Oh, yes, sure. The whole point about it was that the director was an employee, and not the maker of the film. The maker of the film was the producer. Now this has been changing, of course, in recent years, and never was really true; it was true financially, but never was true in the case of the really important directors, because they, in some way, were always making their films, using products, stories, handed to them of which they had very little choice. In a very significant way, they were actually making their films, and there now would be no film history or film classes if they *hadn't* been doing it. You would have had nothing but sociology as a way of studying film. This would have been a product made in those days; it would have had its audience; it was made for this kind of an audience; it was made like *The Saturday Evening Post* stories, or whatever stories were being made then, and when the time passes the product is gone, has been consumed, and can never be reconsumed, because it's so boring, dated, and gone.

Now what makes that not true is the fact that the directors really operated during this period and created the medium as you now know it. Walsh did it, Ford did it, von Stroheim did it, all the ordinary American directors in one form or another did it. In recent years it's been recognized that this is so and now that they begin to speak of film as an art form, why, of course everybody becomes very self-conscious about that, and begins to make films that reproduce the discoveries made in the other arts—to imitate them, so they feel it's more artistic that way—but fundamentally I would say that the contribution made by the older directors is even more significant in that sense, but they didn't think so. It's better to make movies than works of art.

*You said that you spent 20 years directing films in your mind. Surely you must have lived vicariously in the films of others. What filmmakers are you interested in?*

It's hard for me to remember the films of those 20 years—there are all the American films that were made and all the foreign films that were made. When I made that remark, it was made because I'd been challenged by a peculiar question. The question was in praise of me; it embarrassed me. It went something like this: "How come, after not directing a film for 20 years and having only made one before, this is such a good picture?" I don't know how to answer that question, so what I said was I've been directing films in my mind for 20 years and I've had a lot of experience.

Of course, it's based on another notion which I think I share with some people that being a director is something in your mind and not just a question of techniques. The techniques of directing a film are really trivial, I would say. The techniques are not trivial in the sense that the more experience you have the more valuable your resources are when you begin to approach a subject. That's

really true. But you elect yourself to be a director the way you elect yourself to be a writer, or elect yourself to be a revolutionary, or your elect yourself to be a prophet. There's no evidence except the conviction in your own mind and whatever sympathy you feel for works similar to what you have in mind. Having elected yourself, you try to get somebody to let you practice this new profession you've chosen for yourself. If it's a revolutionary, it's a revolution; if it's a director, it's a film; if it's a writer, it's a novel; if it's a painter, it's a picture. Now, there's quite a wasted election from that, naturally, but some are not wasted.

*Would you elaborate on what you mean when you say that the technique of directing a film is trivial?*

There's nothing trivial about the technique; what's trivial is your control over it. In the commercial picture the fundamental resource is the actor. There is enough resource in the studio, if your election is correct, that you are able to draw upon it very freely, and in terms of what your notion of your film is. In the elaboration of all the techniques into film, you are almost able to assume others' talents as your own. That demands a certain kind of temperament, a certain kind of intelligence, a certain talent.

The precondition of a certain kind of elaborate technical training, like the one that makes you a surgeon, is not the same thing that makes you a director. And somewhere along the line before you elect yourself director or get the job, you've done something in film. In my case, I had been a screenwriter. And being a screenwriter is in effect to do all the things you talk about by assuming that someone would show you how to do it if you had to do it. The screenplay is evidently a strategy for making a film.

*So on the basis of two films you've learned on the job and you're ready to make your first film?*

On the basis of my past I am willing to say that I am willing to re-elect myself on the next occasion. I don't know if this makes it clear, but I really think that you can watch a thousand films, if you're a writer, of course, or an editor and have worked on many films, but being a director is a unique kind of thing, like being a novelist or being a painter, and most of us share that unique ability in some sense, but not as much as others.

*You wrote* **Body and Soul** *before you directed* **Force of Evil?**

Right. ***Body and Soul*** was a situation where the writer turned out to have more influence with the producer and the studio than the director did, which is very bad for the director, Bob Rossen. But it didn't hurt Rossen because after he made that film, he became an important director.

*What were your impressions of Rossen? Did you ever agree on an interpretation?*

I never interfered, actually, on the interpretation of the movie. We discussed it all the time in the sense that I had opinion, that Rossen had opinions, or anyone else had opinions. That's not interference; it was a normal, healthy situation. The genuine interference that I posed had to do with the fact that Rossen was a writer, and his conceptions of what a scene should be began to alter as he directed the film. He would like to bring out elements that I suppressed, for example.

*Like what?*

Well, I think he is more sentimental than I am, in the main, and also his force comes from the application of a great deal of energy—unrelenting exercise of energy throughout the picture. He was in an unfortunate position because if I hadn't been there, he would have been able to rewrite scenes to make them happen that way. No one would have objected, but with me objecting, he wasn't able to do that.

*Isn't it rather atypical for the writer to have as much influence compared to the director as you described?*

Right. And it happened because of the personal relations that had been established so quickly between Garfield, who played the lead, myself, and Bob Roberts, the producer—between myself and Enterprise Studios which is the *very* reason that I was able to direct there. In other words, I think it was a question of personality, I suppose—I don't know what the words are for this—it was my relationship to the whole project that gave them the confidence that I could direct.

*Did Rossen have another ending he wanted to shoot?*

Yes. He suggested another ending to the story which was really carrying through my ending which was very ambiguous. Rossen said it should end as a real tragedy, and he wrote such an ending. And we decided to shoot them both because it was the end of the picture. In Rossen's ending Garfield gets shot and rolls through the ashcans, and they fall on top of him, and he's dead among the garbage of history. Then we shot my ending which was more ambiguous, in the sense that Garfield says that everybody dies, and he walks off. He may or may not die, but what's so unusual about that? Everybody may or may not die all the time.

So we screened both versions the next day and Rossen got up and said, "we'll use Polonsky's," and that was the end of it. He agreed. So I would say that in the main our relationship was good, although in memory Rossen probably resented it a lot. But people always resent you when they disagree with you, and they don't win. I suppose that's the normal kind of thing. Anyway, if you've been in politics a little bit, you take it for granted; after all, I'd been a teacher and I was quite used to it. And also, to having my way!

*Before we get to* **Force of Evil,** *tell us about the group of radical artists you formed while working in the industry during the 1940's.*

"Radical artists" is wrong, because that means their art was radical, and that's not true. They were a group of *social* radicals with a rather wide spectrum of opinion with the more traditional Communist Party attitudes as the center of it, in some kind of way, with all kinds of variations all around it: liberal Democrats, Socialists, and so on. That was the community and it was significantly involved in both state and city politics at the time, and I merely dropped into it like I was at home, since I'd been in it to begin with.

*Was there a hard-core conservative group of people?*

There always is. Because the studio represented the same spectrum of American life you found elsewhere. There were conservatives, liberals, radicals, and so on. But there were more radicals than usual in that particular small community, because of the people that had been drawn on for the motion picture industry out of New Deal times. In normal times, it wouldn't be that way, because I don't think that artists are politically more radical than other people in general. They sometimes think they are, but it very often turns out they're not.

I would say that artists—the writers of that time, *especially* the writers of that time—were more significantly *left en masse* in Hollywood than later, and even before. You must also remember that the writers had been the leaders in the struggle with the producers in unionization for the writer's union. They had been beaten several times, but finally they won and had a great deal of coherence among themselves. So they were important. In the community. Recently, when I was in France, everybody in Europe wanted to know if there was really a social film movement going on among certain writers and directors which was cut off by the McCarthy movement, and the answer is yes. But it wasn't an esthetic movement in the sense that social realism is an esthetic movement. It was a generalized political awareness existing in a number of people who were trying to make films that reflected this in one way or another when they had an opportunity to do so, but that opportunity in Hollywood is very limited.

Probably the most socially aware films are often made by what could be called conservative directors like Frank Capra, because what we consider socially aware is a sentimental attitude toward the goodness of man, and getting together and working things out right, and getting rid of injustice. That's a political attitude, of course, but it's generalized, like breathing, as opposed to not breathing. It could hardly be called a *definite* political attitude.

*You say this movement was cut off. What themes would this movement have brought to the screen if it had not been cut off?*

I don't know. It's impossible to predict because what cut off the movement was something that was happening elsewhere in the United States on an even larger scale. So that was cut off in the entire United States, which is what we mean by the McCarthy period. You must remember that the main political fight that took place in the United States about this time and toward the last years of the war, and right after it, was a struggle in the trade union movement, the CIO and the structure of the left-wing leadership. And that movement was an enormous movement in American life, and its consequences were fatal because that made it possible for McCarthy to operate against people who lost their allies, because the main allies in that movement, of course, were the organized trade unions, and what had happened during the building of the CIO and all the alliances around that among the bourgeoisie.

But really and truly, the triumph of McCarthyism was in effect the cutting-off of a generalized social movement which began before the war, and identified itself then with the objectives of the war. As the war changed, when it was over, and the battle was drawn between the two victors, that social movement came to an abrupt halt as United States policy changed, and the internal life of the country changed. So the witchhunt against the Hollywood people was, in a sense, a consequence of that generalized defeat, I would say, and it's gotten a lot of attention because everybody knew who these people were.

*Do you consider* **Force of Evil** *an expression of the fear of this movement?*

Not only that, but an expression of the conflict. Because *Force of Evil* was made during the main rush of that period. The Hollywood Ten had already been in trouble, and we were already conducting campaigns for them. This may be one of the reasons people still look at *Force of Evil* and find something in it, aside from whatever esthetic things they find interesting.

*Was the film specifically attacked?*

No, what they did was attack all the films written by these people regardless of content. They really picked on the ones made during the war period with lines such as "We can get on with the Russians, they're not so bad," like *Mission from Moscow*—a film written by a man who was not even a radical, Howard Koch. But he was blacklisted because of that.

---

> During the blacklist I wrote books, I wrote articles, I carried a picket sign against the Korean War, I continued to live. You see, a whole life went on at the same time in every sense of the word.
>
> —*Abraham Polonsky*

---

*Was there an anticipation of the McCarthy attack?*

Oh, yes. By the time the war was over, the Hollywood Writers' Mobilization had began to harden its attitudes, too. People who were in it began to drop out. They tried to make films about the returning veteran, his rights, etc. They tried to repeat again the objectives of World War II, the promise to humanity which had been in that, all the usual things, the political hangovers. And the attack had already started because it was going on in the unions. And then, as if to crystalize it in Hollywood, a strike, led by the Conference of Studio Unions, was called which was an attempt to shake off their leadership. That was a very devastating strike because it destroyed almost all the good unions in Hollywood like the story-editors unions. The screenwriters guild, in effect, sided somewhat with the Conference of Studio Unions and when that strike was lost, the leadership in the screenwriters union changed, too.

What I'm trying to say is that you're not dealing with an isolated event in American life, but merely the focus of such an event that happened in Hollywood. It merely reflected what was going on throughout the country.

Hollywood's first reaction to the blacklist, when they subpoenaed the nineteen (of whom the ten are part), was to react furiously against it. They formed the Committee for the First Amendment, which had almost every single writer, director, and actor in Hollywood on it. But by the time the first hearings were held in Washington—I think by the time that plane got back with them—the Committee for the First Amendment was in a state of absolute disillusion. I went to the various meetings of the Committee, of course, and no one was there at the second meeting. I remember Humphrey Bogart walking around the room saying to everybody: "You sold me out! I was in Washington, and you sold me out!" He said, "The hell with all of you. If you don't want to fight, I'll take care of myself!" And he stormed out of the room.

*People like John Howard Lawson were such obvious main targets that his jail sentence was inevitable. Could you have played ball and adapted, and compromised?*

Of course, that was offered to everybody, including John Howard Lawson. People who were more profoundly involved in radical politics than Lawson made the switch, and very often appeared before the committee as what they called "expert witnesses," and made a career of it.

*A career?*

A career of being expert witnesses. They functioned as the main advisors to those committees.

*What would you have been required to do and what difference would it have made in your development?*

They asked me if I would give the names of people I knew had been involved in certain radical activities, and if I would provide those names—they didn't want too many, just a few to establish the fact that I was cooperative—then I could just go on doing what I was doing.

*Then you would have continued to get directing offers?*

Of course, they guaranteed them.

*You might have made* **Funny Girl***?*

No, I might have made a whole series of Kazan pictures.

*There were others, like Rossen and Kazan, who talked. What were your decisions at the time? Did you talk them over with your wife?*

It never occurred to me as a possible action. I mean, I never thought of doing that. I knew it existed as a possibility because it had been offered to me, and I had seen it operate around me, but it never even occurred to me, the way it doesn't occur to me to hit you on the head and take your purse. Now, of course, you might say, "what would you do if you were hungry and starving?" Well, our attitude is that nobody should have been hungry and starving in that time because it wasn't that situation. I know from experience and from knowledge that lots of people were forced to talk about their friends when they were captured by the enemy in Germany, Italy, maybe even Russia, too. And did. Some did; some didn't. Just what the limits of resistance are in these cases is doubtful; we don't really know. We just know that some do and some don't. We know that some last longer, and some don't. I don't take any moral position on that because I think to do so is an ungenerous attitude toward the problems of living. Life can be extremely difficult and, at points, people survive under any circumstances they can. It may not be worth surviving, but that's a kind of *post facto* decision that people make, you know.

I don't believe that's a serious judgment to be made on people, when you know all the circumstances of it, even in the case of the people who talked before the Committee. My feeling toward them is that they did what I consider a bad thing. I'm sorry they did it, and I'm not interested in being their friends, or anything like that, but people do that in life. People live a long time, and act badly very often. But that should not upset your general attitude toward what should be done.

*How can it help then?*

No, what you do is do what should be done, according to how you conceive how things should be done, if that's the kind of thing that interests you. And when some fall off, they fall off, that's all. That's the way it happens. I mean, in the general biology of humanity it's a very common occurrence. Maybe that's the way evolution works, I don't know.

*You were natural and spontaneous; it wasn't a matter of ruminating?*

No, when you start to ruminate, you get into trouble. If you start to ruminate on the question of betrayal, you are in the process of betraying, very often. You don't necessarily have to do so, and may not, but then you have a lot of self-punishment and self-pity going on all the time. And that's the worst form of punishment the enemy can accomplish, I guess. To make you think, my God, how good things would have been, if I'd only cooperated! What a lifetime of punishment that must be.

*You mentioned the price paid by the people who cooperated; but didn't you pay a price, too? You referred on another occasion to working on "rotten pictures" for TV or for Hollywood. This must have been an unpleasant experience.*

You're assuming that we did nothing else. In any case, I wrote books, I wrote articles, I carried a picket sign against the Korean War, I continued to live in a more general way than just being a writer working in Hollywood, as I do now. So the life wasn't that narrow and sterile. You see, a whole life went on at the same time in every sense of the word. That's why you just don't make a film, you live it, too. You're making a film and all the while you're watching to see if it happens.

*Do you find it ironical that you went out of filmmaking, at least in the official sense, at the beginning of the McCarthy era, and now you're coming back with a big bang at the time we seem to be moving into a new period of repression?*

It doesn't strike me as ironical at all. It strikes me as significant. What I mean: I feel like a [judas goat].

*I'm not sure you want to comment on this, but at present the attacks on the mass media by Agnew, and the deliberate use of the mass media, especially television, by Nixon, suggests to many people that a new version of McCarthyism is building up which will take as its focus of interest the writers and artists and producers in the mass media. Do you see it that way?*

You must remember that Nixon was one of the main McCarthyites. It was Nixon who red-baited Helen Gahagan Douglas out of her job in Congress, and he made his career in Washington as such a person; now he's the President of the United States. He's just changed his advertising agency, that's all, not his opinions. I agree with the New Left: I think there's a wider blacklist now than there was then. While I was in Europe, I remember reading an editorial in the *New York Times* on the existence of a blacklist in the Department of Health, Education and Welfare. It's obviously true that if you are in the peace movement today, you get arrested, they take your picture; if you're a physicist or a scientist, you can't get a job in any place that has anything to do with government contracts. I think Agnew's attack is characteristic of such a period, and I think the fact that the networks are laying down in front of it is very recognizable to me.

*I find it interesting that both of your films, **Force of Evil** and **Willie Boy**, are derived from the two essentially American film genres.*

See, I think genres, like other social habits, speak for us in terms of summaries of the way we see life. We live out the genres as we live out the myths and rituals, because that's the way we systematize our relationship to society and our relationship to other people. I think anthropologically speaking it has very deep connections with the role of religion in life. I would assume that I am essentially a religious person of some sort, at least in the sense that I try to make things signify as if there were some ultimate significance all the time—the ultimate significance sometimes being something that's not so ultimate after all. That's a question of temperament, personality, belief, and so on. I like gravitation—it's the gravitation that operates when I select themes, characters, meanings, and stories. And I am going to assume without deciding on it, that that'll probably happen with everything I do one way or another.

I don't think that the development of genres in the art forms are accidents. I think they're fundamental to the way art operates on our life. I don't think I make works of art in any deliberate sense—like I'm going to make an artistic film. I don't think that way. But, for instance, if I were to make a film outside the commercial media, inexpensively, you know, about some little thing, intended for a different kind of audience, or a smaller audience, it would then adopt a genre of whatever art form appealed to a smaller audience.

So in the long run, they're inescapable. Now, always, of course, as art advances, what you do is destroy the genre in one form or another, and reconstruct it in some other form, ultimately. If we leave out faddism, since by nature I'm not attracted to fads, and reject them deliberately. But genre is not a fad.

**Force of Evil** *is essentially a study of polarities. You have an evil man who is a little man and you have an even more evil man who's a big man, and in between you have a fat, heart-aching slob, Leo. Did you mean Leo to be humanity, torn in between and unable to make a decision, helpless in the midst of all these forces at work?*

Well, I don't think he's a slob, because I don't think about humanity, of course. But I do think that most of us are able to work out a pattern of behavior in society in which we can accept a role we don't want to play in general for the benefits we get immediately by not recognizing what the implications are. So, Leo is able to say, "Gee, I just run a small business, I'm good to my help, it's not really a bad thing I'm doing, everybody depends on me, and now you want to get me involved with something big and terrible" because he doesn't realize that that relationship is inevitable. And his brother's superiority to him as a person or as an intellectual is that he knows that you can't be slightly pregnant with evil in this society, you're dealing with it all the time, it's part of your life, and it's manipulating you as you think you're manipulating it. So Joe, in effect says, "Let's manipulate it and let's beat it, and take the advantages," and his brother says, "You'll become an evil man. You'll be Cain. You'll be a murderer." And Joe says, "I'm not the murderer, the whole thing is the murderer and we don't have much choice anyhow, so let's beat it. We have to survive. Let's be on top instead of on the bottom, because on the bottom you're doing the same thing, except it's doing it more to you than you to it." This relativity in values, which to each of the people seems to be ultimate, are fundamentally not ultimates at all, and this relativity of values is coextensive with the entire morality of our society, I would say. And all societies, perhaps, I don't know, except the one we hope someday will come, which will not be like that.

*I find it interesting that the flaw in Joe's development as a fictional character is his desire to maintain the sense of family, to protect his brothers, and it brings his ultimate downfall. In* **Willie Boy** *you have a hero who refuses to participate in the family relationships of, let's say, a tribal society. And this also brings his downfall. What were you saying in 1948, about families?*

I've been trying to see some families in 1970. I'm looking very hard, but I can't see any. In the older Jewish environment, the family center was a source of strength, because it formed a cooperative effort in a hostile society. We were able to draw force from it, and allies. The tribal structure of the Indians is a disaster for them today. It's a disaster for the Africans, too, isn't it? Because in the context of modern technology, it has no strength to win. Willie is not a reservation Indian, he's not a white man either, although he's a partial success in the white world. He's a success in the white world by refusing to be white, and he's a success in the Indian world by refusing to be an Indian, and in that sense is able to exist as himself. But the moment the event starts, which he sets off, and he does an Indian thing, he runs off with the girl who's now his wife, now the old ritu-

als and habits of his particular inherited myth, which is disaster for the Indians, begin to operate. And the more he becomes an Indian, the more impossible it becomes for him to live. And when he's really and truly an Indian in the end, he's like all the Indians, he's dead.

*One final question: What advice would you give a young writer-director with ambitions to direct a feature?*

Don't go to Hollywood. I would give myself the same advice, too!

### Jack Shadoian   (essay date 1977)

SOURCE: "The Genre's 'Enlightenment', the Stress and Strain for Affirmation: *Force of Evil* (1948)," in *Dreams and Dead Ends: The American Gangster/Crime Film,* The MIT Press, 1977, pp. 134-48.

[*Shadoian is an American critic and educator who has written extensively on various aspects of the cinema. In the following excerpt, he analyzes* Force of Evil *as an example of the gangster film, arguing that the conventions of the genre provide an apt framework for the main thematic focus of Polonsky's work, namely a critique of capitalism.*]

After making this film [**Force of Evil**], his first, director Abraham Polonsky became a casualty of the blacklist, and he did not resume directing until 1969. The scarcity of his output and his sacrifice to the cause have combined to draw special attention to a small but ambitious film that, unusual though it may be, fits comfortably into the genre and works intelligently within its structure. I feel that the film picks up much power by bringing its concerns to the underworld for articulation. **Force of Evil** urges recognition of not only the utility but also the value of a film genre.

Polonsky's discussion of **Force of Evil** in two separate interviews indicates, should the film itself fail to, that he had a lot on his mind to crowd into a seventy-six-minute melodrama. The seriousness of his aim—an examination of the sick soul of modern man living within a capitalist system—is apparent. How successfully his themes are realized is debatable. Polonsky has gracefully admitted his failure:

> It was my first film, and I think there's a difference between what I really intended to do and what came off. I didn't know *how*. And then, despite good reviews, it wasn't a successful picture at the box-office. Of course it was a difficult picture, and, of course, it was experimental in a way, deliberately experimental. But, nevertheless, I thought that the general weight of it would be obvious, that people would feel it, but it wasn't felt except by very sophisticated audiences. [*The Director's Event: Interviews with Five American Film-makers,* edited by Eric Sherman and Martin Rubin, 1972]

I find this a curious response in several ways. First of all, I think he underrates the film, but the artist is often his most severe critic since he alone knows what was in him trying to get out and how far the results may have fallen short (the audience sees only the results). It is also gratifying (and unexpected) for the "experimental" filmmaker to suggest that it might have been his own inadequacies of execution and strategy, and not the audience's dimness, that were responsible for failure (it would have been easy, as is common, to excoriate mass taste). The big issue here is whether movies ought to be made in disregard of their audience. Polonsky implies that they ought not to be, that an awareness of the public is part of the filmmaker's discipline, and that one measure of a movie's quality is how widely and discernibly it communicates. Perhaps he is right. Movies are part of a *popular* culture; they are not a private art, like poetry, designed for the individual connoisseur. *Force of Evil,* with its thematic complexity and literate dialogue, miscalculates its level of intelligibility to a general audience (or did in its day, at any rate). The presence of John Garfield is its only surefire commercial asset, but he cannot dispel the privatistic nature of the "experiment." It is a distinctive film with a genuine personal stamp, but that is maybe one of the reasons for its understandable lack of commercial success.

Polonsky was shrewd enough, however, to adapt his thoughts to a solid genre. It may be that the genre hinders him somewhat, obscuring his critique and forcing his themes into an awkward obliquity. My own view is that the icons and conventions of the genre give what might have been maudlin a hard, steely edge. The genre's inherent viciousness prevents an imbalance toward a soggy humanism. The austere, sober mood plays off nicely against the typical kinetics of this kind of film, making Polonsky's points more, not less, noticeable.

The story is about a group of unhappy, guilty people involved, in one way or another, with the numbers racket. John Garfield plays Joe Morse, a lawyer gone crooked in the hope of a cool million. His older brother Leo (Thomas Gomez) runs a small numbers bank that goes broke because of Joe's high ambitions. Joe also causes, indirectly, Leo's death. Upon discovering Leo's dead body, Joe experiences a change of heart and, with the support of Doris Lowry (Beatrice Pearson), Leo's former secretary with whom he has fallen in love, decides to cooperate with the law.

Garfield was, at the time, at the tail end of his extraordinary popularity. He was the people's star. He had the true urban/ethnic vibes, a ghetto authenticity in manner and speech. He projected guilt better than anyone else on the screen, and nowhere so movingly as in *Force of Evil.* [In an endnote, Shadoian argues that it "is not too farfetched to suggest that it was Garfield's own guilt that was being conveyed in roles like this. Garfield retained his leftist ties and sympathies throughout his career. Being a leftist in theory and a wealthy film star must have been a hard line to walk. His old friends disowned him as a sellout, and he was too much of a maverick, an individualist, to survive in the movie industry. At last hounded and persecuted by HUAC, he died of a heart attack in 1952, at the age of thirty-nine. His lower-class, antiestablishment manner was something audiences were receptive to for well over a decade."] The character of Joe Morse betrays his kind; he feels superior to Leo and his scraggly band of employees. Yet he is a sensitive man, with a conscience. His cynicism

is a front. He is a man divided against himself who doesn't, deep down, believe in what he says, who is pained and hurt by what he is doing to others. His drive to succeed is based on a specious philosophy whose moral shabbiness he is at last made to confront. He knows he is not better than others (that his advantage is merely power), yet talks himself into thinking that he is. An unhappy man, his only moment of joy is at the end when, crushed by circumstances, he is released from his false self-conception.

What is unusual in Joe Morse's characterization is his self-awareness. He acknowledges his acquisition of power, his impulse of greed, with atypical (in a hero) candor. Introspection is anathema to most American films; characters normally do things without knowing why, or if they do, it is just implied. They don't stop to articulate or explain and slow the movie up. In *Force of Evil,* though, we become very interested in observing the rhetorical con job Joe Morse performs on himself and the modifications of it on the sensitive register of Garfield's face.

The central relationship is between Joe and Leo, a set of Cain-and-Abel variations smoothly joined to the superficial level of the action. After their mother's death, Leo has sacrificed himself to put Joe through college, and he resents Joe's success. The brothers are estranged, having not seen each other for years prior to their first meeting in the film. Joe is handsome, self-admiring, a smoothie. Leo is ugly, harried, and tyrannical. Both are corrupt, though Leo protests his morality, a morality the film progressively undermines. They love each other as brothers, and each insists that what he does or has done is for the other's welfare. They clash throughout, philosophically and emotionally. Joe tries to relieve his guilt by making his brother rich. Leo's intense refusals have a touch of perversity. He too is guilty, envious. Ultimately, he is blinder than Joe, and no more morally upright. After one confrontation, Joe tells Doris, "I pretended to make him [join Tucker] and he pretended to be forced," an insight Leo is incapable of. He continues to protest his "honesty," an old-world figure who cannot risk admitting to himself that his bitter, hardworking life has been in the service of corruption.

The nuances of their relationship revolve around the brother-versus-brother situation and its timeless, dramatic, biblical qualities. For all their superficial differences, Leo and Joe are the same: they are brothers. They cannot see that they do the same thing, are bound together by both love and corruption. And they cannot see because in following the ways of the world their natures, and their true knowledge of things, have been warped. Polonsky is getting at what living in the American economic system does to people, Leo and Joe and everyone else. Capitalism promotes greed and greed causes hatred, envy, guilt, and fear.

At the top of the moral muck heap created by the itch for money and success is Tucker, Joe's boss, a former gangster gone legit with Joe's lawyer know-how. (The first shot of Tucker is of his hand reaching out above his massive safe to take money from Joe.) He lives with his wife Edna in a cold and almost ludicrously ostentatious apartment filled with classical statuary. Tucker is all money; as a human being he is as unfeeling and meaningless as the decor surrounding him. He cannot, or does not, perform sexually. Edna, making a play for Joe, says her husband is like "a stone," reminding us of the statues. Edna herself is not more lifelike. Living with Tucker has made her remote to her own sexuality. She pursues Joe with a mechanical tenacity, playing seductress in a timbreless, soft monotone creepily lacking any inflection of true passion. Her conquest of Joe would mean a total enslavement; Tucker would own his soul and Edna his body. Joe reads her lust accurately as an exercise in power and refuses her advances, telling her that if she wants to break somebody to go break her husband. It is a sign of the hero's potential salvation.

Tucker and his wife are morally diseased; their cancer is incurable. The rest are involved in what seems to be a losing struggle with their moral natures. Polonsky shows us how people give up, get resigned, betray each other when they live in a society that says grab, succeed, and forces people into corruption to stay alive. Capitalism causes rifts in the human community. *Force of Evil* is a gangster/crime film with Wall Street as its locale. (The opening shot is an extreme high angle showing people scurrying like insects along and across city streets.) The force of evil is American business, symbolized by Wall Street. "Business" is the recurrent theme. Wally, Ficco's henchman, tells the informer Bauer that his outfit is in "business." (Later, Ficco has both Bauer and Leo killed.) Leo protests he runs an honest "business." Joe runs Tucker's "business" and talks to Bauer about loyalty to the firm. Even Hall, the prosecutor after Tucker, falls into the category. Joe says, "Hall's in business, and Tucker's his stock in trade." Business is the American way of life, and because it is ingrained, legal, and philosophically supportable, its destructiveness remains unnoticed until an analysis is made of it. *Force of Evil* is such an analysis.

Polonsky claims that the ending—Joe deciding to help Hall (a figure never seen)—was a concession to get a seal and that what he really wanted was for Joe to face his own defeat. That would have been victory enough; the character's decision to reform did not need to be stressed. It provides a false note of social reform, as though one man's evidence might cure an entire city of corruption. Polonsky wants to have Joe morally reborn, but inwardly. There is much in the film, besides, that implies the humane reconstruction of society would be a long and perhaps impossible task. Joe's farewell to his posh law office foresees a repetition of his own career; the office is waiting for a "smart young lawyer trying to get ahead in the world." Joe says to Doris, with unsentimental accuracy, "I didn't have enough strength to resist corruption, but I was strong enough to fight for a piece of it." But it is Leo who hits the nail on the head in the following conversation with his wife, who is arguing against his giving in to Joe:

> SYLVIA: You're a businessman.
>
> LEO: Yes, I've been a businessman all my life, and honest, I don't know what a business is.
>
> SYLVIA: Well, you had a garage, you had a real estate business.
>
> LEO: A lot you know. Real estate business. Liv-

ing from mortgage to mortgage, stealing credit like a thief. And the garage—that was a business. Three cents overcharge on every gallon of gas, two cents for the chauffeur and a penny for me. A penny for one thief, two cents for the other.

Business is all, and it is evil. Little guy or big guy, it makes no difference; the blight of profit is all-pervasive. Also, Joe's "I decided to help" is in a context of a brother dead, a love disrupted, and (presumably) an upcoming term in jail.

Edna tells Joe that he's "not strong or weak enough" a man to take her, and she is right. Joe's weakness, however, is his salvation; strength of the kind Edna demands would make him into an other Tucker. He's the man in the middle, torn by good and bad. Instead of receiving Edna, he seeks out Doris, as fascinated by her image of innocence as she is by his image of corruption, and it is her faith in him that allows for his turnaround. Another choice is made for him by Leo's death. Leo has a weak heart and he is old. He tries to back out of the business, but it is too late; years of toil and anguish have done him in. As long as Leo lives, he and Joe will be at each others throats, Leo bellyaching about Joe but really voicing his own frustration and Joe trying to clear his conscience by pushing Leo into an office on Wall Street, "up in the clouds." The battle between them would be prolonged forever, with no "discovery" possible. When Joe literally "sees" Leo's dead body, all that is finished. He has no excuse not to start afresh. He must stop thinking about his brother and attend to himself. Contemplating Leo's mangled corpse dumped on the rocks near the river under the bridge, he is released from his conflict and his former values. Leo's bodily annihilation liberates Joe by annihilating his morally gangrenous identity.

Doris is an important element in Joe's liberation. Indebted to Leo for giving her a job, she is prone to defend him against Joe, but Joe exerts a power over her—sexual, of course, but more than that. His confidence and success appeal to her shy, guarded temperament. Joe dallies with her, secure that his virility and charm will carry the day. But this seemingly frail girl is made of stronger stuff than he allowed for. Joe learns that Doris can't be treated as a toy, but it is partly her experience of him that strengthens her.

Joe is so impatient with her innocence that he tries his best to demean her, to make her low enough to satisfy the demands of his cynicism. What he thinks and says about her, though, is in part true (Doris accepts his roses *and* his hundred-dollar-a-week job). She does have the desires he says she does—human ones, corrupt ones—and he does her a service by bringing her out of her shell of propriety and sentimentality. She is forced by her love for him to face herself, the truth behind her angelic mask. She undergoes the painful process of understanding what she is, as opposed to what she tries to be. She grows up, transformed from a child ignorant of the ways of the world to a woman who can love strongly enough to sustain a man suffering acute agonies of conscience. Her high, soft voice, almost annoyingly well mannered at first, eventually carries some of the best, most sensible dialogue ever written for a movie actress. The film does not allow her to remain sheltered and innocent. She must assume responsibility for herself and others.

Why the script of *Force of Evil* remains unpublished when many lesser scripts are readily available in paperback is a mystery, since it is among the most beautiful of the American cinema. Polonsky departs from the tough, predictable, snappy idiom of the gangster/crime film. What he supplies, Andrew Sarris calls a "crypto-poetry" [see Sarris's *Interviews with Film Directors,* 1969]. Whatever it is, nothing quite like it has been heard on the screen in English since. The dialogue is full of verbal echoes; people speak a strange, incantatory language, with phrases repeated like musical notes. The wonder is that it works so well as dialogue—not as poeticized speech but as the poetry of speech. The performers have to be given much of the credit. Polonsky's dialogue is good, but it is above all splendidly *spoken,* with naturalness, spark, credibility, and beauty. Polonsky says he was trying for the "babble of the unconscious" [Sarris, *Interviews*]. The first-person narration has some of that quality, the images shown evoking ideas and emotions in the speaker that get uttered in a fluid, uncensored form. (Where Joe's narration is coming from we never learn, but in time, it must obviously be after the events described. Perhaps we can assume it is from prison or some milieu that enforces meditation and recollection.) Polonsky's achievement, though, is much greater than imitation stream of consciousness. Lines like Doris's "I don't wish to die of loving you," spoken from within a grimy telephone booth, fuse the sordid and the tragic, the prosaic and the poetic. The line evokes a classicism seasoned by centuries, a theatrical language naturalized and humanized into an ordinary eloquence.

Polonsky's script is a model of how literary values can be put to use in the film medium, how images and ideas can be synthesized, blended, and made to reinforce each other. Most "literate" film dialogue is a pompous embarrassment to actors who have unlimited freedom of movement through space and time. Polonsky prevents his talk from being stilted and artificial by conceiving his film world as something in between dream and reality. *Force of Evil* does not so much record or analyze as evoke. It contemplates humanity. It has little, basically, to do with the numbers racket. Its focus is on how people live, and have been forced to live, for centuries. American capitalism being merely the latest and most stifling form of human misery, separating man from his world and from his fellow humans. The film has a specific locale, but it is given to us in a hazy, surreal way. The characters speak a language appropriate to their milieu but seem as well to be abstracted from the particulars of that world, as though the drama they are enacting has occurred many times before throughout human history. *Force of Evil* has a timeless, frozen quality, antithetical to realism. History is evoked through analogy and allusion—July 4, 1776, the classical decor, the Cain and Abel myth, the church music playing softly, then more insistently over the scene of Bauer's death and Leo's capture, the poetic diction. What is happening to Joe and everyone else is the same old story; there is nothing new under the sun. Polonsky integrates it into

a modern setting and a gangster tale by counterpointing image, music, and dialogue and letting each add its separate dimension of meaning without breaking any of the requirements of a representational film. The genre itself provides a modest, unassuming but sturdy framework that prohibits deleterious lapses into pretension and ornateness.

The principle of repetition and contrast so apparent on the verbal level is also consciously employed in the visual scheme, but less obviously. One thinks immediately of the great Russian silent films, of montage as meaning, but Polonsky's method is more discreet, the exigencies of the commercial cinema necessitating a subtler approach to visual significance. The opening shot looks down from a great height upon Wall Street, and the theme of high and low, descent and ascent, is sustained to the very end. All the characters literally have their ups and downs, with Joe traversing the greatest distance. Joe's descent to Leo's body beneath the bridge is photographed and edited to make a climax of the motif. It takes him forever to get there. He works his way down in a lateral zigzag, moving up into and then across the frame. Time seems to stretch, and the symbolic overtones of dawn, rocks, river, and bridge supply a thematic gravity rarely attempted with such rhetorical abandon. Characters are linked by the motif. There is a startling dissolve from Bauer (the frightened accountant) being dragged down the stairs in a police raid to Joe going down a long flight of stairs to meet Tucker, who has symbolically pulled Joe down into the hell over which he presides. (An earlier scene has both men descending a long, curved staircase while hatching strategies about the upcoming fix on the number 776, "the old liberty number.") Ficco's thugs hoist Leo up the stairs of the restaurant in a grotesque but moving version of the calvary of Christ.

The telephone is also a recurring motif. We are not told it is significant, but so much that is important involves the telephone that it accumulates an inescapable weightiness. [In an endnote, Shadoian adds: "There is an article to be written on telephones in a genre that seems suspended between Vince Barnett's wanting to shoot one in *Scarface* [in 1931] and Lee Marvin finally doing it in *Point Blank* [in 1967]. The suggestion is not an idle one (compare the uses of the telephone in *Little Caesar, T-Men, The Public Enemy, Gun Crazy, The Big Heat, 99 River Street, Kiss Me Deadly, The Brothers Rico,* and countless other films.)"] Polonsky has this to say:

> The telephone is a dangerous object. It represents dangerous kinds of things. I don't like instant communication. I like it to take a long time before I understand you and you understand me. In the film it forms the structure of the characters' relationships. . . . I had a big telephone made so that it would loom very large in the foreground of those close-ups. I guess the telephone was an easy symbol for the connections between all the different worlds in the film. These worlds communicate with each other through telephones instead of feelings. [Sherman and Rubin, *The Director's Event*]

Polonsky also uses his characters as repetitive signs.

Leo—sweaty and turbulent; Doris—thin and shy; Joe—healthy and authoritative; Bauer—mousy and quaking; all are rigid enough in look and behavior for Polonsky to use them in the first half of the film as replicas from scene to scene. They appear and we think "that kind of woman, that kind of man" the way we might observe a style of furniture or a kind of plant. Not being strong enough to fight their condition, they take their place, in the beginning, among the other fixtures of their world. They seem mechanical and drugged, and oblivious of their condition. By a gradual process, Polonsky reveals them as individuals—hurt, in pain, and confused. Pressured by demanding events, they are unable to continue taking refuge in their roles. They come alive as people and modify their status as signs. Those whose moral nature has been crushed entirely and who have no capacity for change—Tucker, Edna, Wally, Ficco—remain serviceably stiff icons throughout.

The dark look of [*film*] *noir,* though not as intense as in *The Killers,* dominates. [*The Killers* (1946), which Shadoian discusses in an earlier chapter, was directed by Robert Siodmak; written by Anthony Veiller, who adapted the short story by Ernest Hemingway; and was photographed by Woody Bredell and David S. Horsely.] Interior decor is stark, arid, and grim. Shadows abound, and what light there is is usually harsh and uneven. Several scenes take place in near-total darkness. The shoot-out between Joe, Ficco, and Tucker has them all crawling around in the dark, hunting each other like animals. Framing is always careful, pointed. Long shots isolate people as either the clumsiest or most vulnerable points in the frame (Joe walking down a deserted Wall Street, Doris left sitting on top of a lobby mantelpiece, Bauer's nervous entry into an office suddenly full of outsiders), while close-ups are used not so much for intimacy but to convey terror and alarm (Joe's eyes peering over the transom of his office door, Bauer shot in the face). One interestingly framed shot is in the restaurant scene between Leo and Bauer. Leo has always been solicitous of Bauer, touching him, protecting him, leading him home. Now, though, they are separated by a table, indicating the gulf between the two caused by Bauer's decision to betray Leo. Polonsky frames so that Leo is at one side of the table and Bauer at the other—to the far left and the far right of the frame, respectively. Between them, directly in the middle at a background table is Wally, who has worked on Bauer to set Leo up. Prior to Leo's entrance, Polonsky also conducts a shadow game between Wally and Bauer. Wally has been, almost literally, Bauer's shadow. As they wait for Leo (Bauer in foreground, Wally in background), Bauer lifts his arm to drink and the shadow Wally makes on the wall raising *his* arm to drink is perfectly timed to Bauer's gesture. Bauer and Wally are joined against Leo.

The exteriors are something else. *Force of Evil* is one of the few gangster/crime films interested in the beauty of the city. Normally, the city is either "there," as in *Kiss of Death*—an authentic backdrop to what is going on with no particular attitude attached to it—or is seen negatively (*The Public Enemy, Angels with Dirty Faces,* a good percentage of gangster films). George Barnes gets marvelous shots of city streets and buildings that we sense are differ-

ent without knowing quite why, because we do not expect the city to be beautiful. But a feeling for the magnificence of the city is the only explanation for the unsettling effect of these shots. Cities, in and of themselves, are clearly not the cause of misery or crime. A deserted Wall Street at dawn seems as pure as any travelogue waterfall. The film's conclusion is the climax of its odd pictorial beauty, a series of breathtaking long shots of Joe completing his downward quest to be reborn. Here, at the city's edge, the dawn casts a splendor on everything. Joe begins his descent accompanied by a solo wind instrument moaning in high register. The river breeze blows foliage into motion while a string orchestra soars into melody. Joe strides by a lighthouse symbolic of his moral awakening and finally reaches Leo's broken body sprawled on the rocks. Even this image, however, is more awesome than horrible, conveying truth, not terror. Depending on one's taste, the effect of this finale is either bombastic or stirring. The voice-over narration is actually understated, but the music and visuals are rhetorically ponderous. Personally, I don't mind being clobbered by photography so imaginative and deeply felt. The chromatic climb of the music matched to Doris and Joe's resolute upward movement—the last shot—completes the attempt at sublimity. I think it works, if only because its scope and weight take us by surprise, and leave our senses stunned.

As in *Kiss of Death,* a Christian framework appears to be operating although exactly how is even less clear than in the former film. The upshot of all the betrayals—Bauer betrays Joe through Leo, Joe betrays Leo through Tucker—seems to be that Leo dies for everyone's sins. The biblical drift of Joe and Leo's relationship is confirmed when Leo specifically alludes to the Cain and Abel myth in his anger toward Bauer. At the point of his lowest emotional state, his life crumbling about him, Joe, sleepless, walks dazedly down Wall Street at dawn toward a huge, centrally framed church, his small figure overwhelmed by the surrounding architecture. (The shot is framed so that the church has special emphasis among the equally imposing high-rise office buildings. The point seems to be that it is there, in the midst of greed and evil, but ignored.) Joe appears to be progressing toward it—the shot is held so we may ponder its importance—but it is far away, and it becomes apparent that he has not chosen it as his destination (he has still greater woes to suffer). Bauer's betrayal of Leo is infused with the symbolic overtones of bread and water, and the peculiarity of it is most evident to a viewer. In taking Bauer home, Leo pulls up at a bakery for Bauer to buy some rolls. In the background of the shop is a church entrance. After buying the rolls, Bauer flees from Leo and runs toward the church with the rolls. When Leo follows, Bauer ducks into the alley adjoining the church, the place where he is to meet Wally and set up Leo's betrayal, and cringes. Leo, more concerned with Bauer than himself, flings the rolls away and yells at Bauer, "You want to live to eat these rolls, don't you?" Later, Bauer awaits Leo in the restaurant and specifically orders and drinks water. When Leo arrives, he is, as his dialogue suggests, ready to die, but he does not expect it will be through Bauer or under these circumstances. After Wally kills Bauer, his hired thugs carry Leo up the stairs to choral music, each arm propped, Leo's expression and agony reminiscent of Christ's. It is through Leo's death that Joe is redeemed.

One accepts Polonsky's vision of change because of the sadness that has preceded it; a more cynical man could not have brought it off. Polonsky gets an unusual depth of feeling from his performers, and the sorrow of life is made quite eloquent. *Force of Evil* does not speed, clatter, or contort as much as other films in the genre—it has very little "action"—but it broods and reflects insightfully. And it is not only symbolic and metaphoric. It condemns, rather boldly, the connections among politics, business, and crime, and its images of the gangland boss and the corrupt lawyer have perhaps a greater veracity than more melodramatized versions. Its view of crime as business equates the two. Tucker's organization is seen as a huge corporation taking over the independent businessman (not that Polonsky has anything favorable to say about free enterprise—Leo is no answer, he's part of the problem). Hall's wiretapping is as underhanded as Tucker's policies. The cops are terrible—brutal, unfeeling, paid off. And the people are infected by the disease. The cycle of corruption is complete. Crime is now organized and legitimate, creating jobs for large numbers of workers who are either oblivious to what they are involved in or prefer not to think twice about it. What most gangster/crime films skim over, or treat indirectly, *Force of Evil* bluntly acknowledges.

### Larry Ceplair (review date 14 June 1980)

SOURCE: "Creative Forgetting," in *The Nation,* New York, Vol. 230, No. 23, June 14, 1980, pp. 730-31.

[*In the following excerpt, which offers a mixed review of* Zenia's Way, *Ceplair argues that while the novel's narrator is intelligent and observant, the title character remains flat and one-dimensional.*]

In his fourth novel, *Zenia's Way* (his first in thirty years), Polonsky explores the effects on two people, Ram and Zenia, of participation in six decades of political history. He juxtaposes two political events widely separated in time and place—a Palmer raid episode in New York City and a Palestine Liberation Organization raid in Israel—as a means of viewing where he started and where he has arrived.

Polonsky has discovered, as a result of the many forms of political terror he has witnessed or been told about, that no matter how inhuman the raid appears, human connections grow between captors and captured. He also believes that the quality of the cause, not the form of the terror, determines the nature of the attachments formed. The P.L.O. raiders, more efficient and ruthless than the Palmer raid Feds, are portrayed much more sympathetically. The Palestinians represent a cause, the liberation of a people, while Stair, the Fed, represents a bureaucracy and follows orders he finds morally repugnant and illegal.

Another lesson that Polonsky learned much earlier and has repeatedly expressed in his best novels and screenplays (notably *Body and Soul, Force of Evil* and *Tell Them Willie Boy Is Here*), is that people can, within limits, control their destinies. Even though individuals are continually snared in the webs of other people's plans, they remain free to choose and to act. Polonsky's heroes, then, are the paradoxical—he would say dialectical—people: liberated captives.

The novel is strongest when the narrator's voice dominates. It is the voice of an intelligent, observant and wise man. Ram has seen and heard much, and still has maintained balance and perspective. Zenia, the character of the title, however, is a failed creation. She is portrayed as the center of young Ram's world, the model for his adult consciousness and the magnet electrifying his last days. Polonsky has intended her to be a vital, inspiring figure—she is neither. Her character and her words lie flat on the page, in the main because she is fully formed before the narrative begins. Polonsky, too, has suffered a lapse of memory: he has forgotten that he achieved his greatest art through characters who are involved in the process of becoming.

### Terry Curtis Fox (review date 8-14 October 1980)

SOURCE: "Faith on the Left," in *The Village Voice,* Vol. XXV, No. 41, October 8-14, 1980, p. 49.

[*Fox is an American playwright and screenwriter. In the following positive review of* Zenia's Way, *he describes the novel as "a true political tragedy."*]

Abraham Polonsky is one of the most curious and compelling figures in the history of American film, a man who refuses to fit into any simple, definable mold. When he was blacklisted in the '50s, he had directed only a single film (*Force of Evil*) and was credited with only three scripts (*Body and Soul* among them). Perhaps for this reason, Polonsky did not—like Joseph Losey or Jules Dassin—go to Europe to maintain his filmmaking career. Instead, he wrote (quite profitably) anonymous scripts, often about free speech for the likes of *You Are There,* and two novels—*The World Above,* which came out the day he appeared before HUAC, and *A Season of Fear,* about a writer who signs the loyalty oath. Polonsky never repented of his leftism as a "folly of youth"; indeed, both movies he directed after the blacklist was lifted are explicitly political: *Tell Them Willie Boy Is Here,* a western allegory about race war that finally established Polonsky's critical reputation as a director, and *Romance of a Horsethief* a Jewish comedy about revolution. Both films failed at the box office and Polonsky turned to work on a novel, *Zenia's Way.*

The book is unlike any screenwriter's novel ever written. Its structure—two interconnected stories about the same people, seen first when the protagonist, Ram, is a young boy and his Aunt Zenia a major formative influence, and later when Ram is 60 and Zenia 80—is decidedly anti-cinematic. It is explicitly concerned with the interconnection between American Judaism and the American left, and the continued importance of the Soviet Union to each.

The first half takes place just after the Russian Revolution and pivots on Zenia's decision to return to her birthplace; the second half is set in Israel, where Zenia has fled following Soviet anti-Semitism. It is purposely written in the archaic (but never awkward, and often beautiful) syntax of translated Yiddish, a language used here not as a crass joke but as a poetic dialect. And it is also pure Polonsky. The issues it describes are precisely those found in the writer's films, and its mixture of tempered pessimism and hard-edged optimism is precisely what has made his work so much more important than its quantity would indicate.

One might expect *Zenia's Way* to be a sentimental memoir of an aging leftist, but it is nothing of the sort. Polonsky uses the first half of the book to establish why Jews—strangers in all countries—would be moral leftists, allied with other immigrant cultures. Ram's first love is an Italian girl whose family contains gangsters and Communists, a mixture of the corrupt and the idealistic, central to Polonsky's vision. This is then employed to show Israel as a country that must exist *and* as a base to understand the Palestinians as holding the same historical place as Jews in Christian lands. *Zenia's Way* manages something few other works I know have even attempted: it upholds Israel without being Zionist, and credits the justness of the Palestinian cause without giving a bit of sympathy to terrorism.

Like *Willie Boy,* Polonsky's only non-Jewish work, *Zenia's Way* is a true political tragedy, a work about a moment when history destroys its participants. The Soviet Union is the hope and destroyer of Jews, Israel a necessity that invites catastrophic violence. By casting an unsentimental eye on the major contradictions of Jewish leftism, Polonsky has reconfirmed his faith. The man who told us that because "everybody dies," moral action is possible, has written a novel in which, because "everything mattered except all of it," hope is possible even when expectation is not.

### Christine Noll Brinckmann   (essay date 1981)

SOURCE: "The Politics of *Force of Evil:* An Analysis of Abraham Polonsky's Preblacklist Film," in *Prospects: The Annual of American Cultural Studies,* Vol. 6, 1981, pp. 357-86.

[*In the following excerpt, Brinckmann discusses the ways in which* Force of Evil *deviates from the traditional gangster film, manipulating the genre's conventions to emphasize its political theme, namely the critique of capitalist society. She argues that while the film balances politics with emotional and spiritual intensity, its thematic and formal complexity accounts for its lack of popularity with mass audiences. She also suggests that the film's most serious flaw is its inconsistent depiction of the law as the mirror image of the criminal underworld.*]

*Force of Evil* was the first film Abraham Polonsky directed, and it is not without structural flaws. It is, however, a rare work of art in that it is poetical, popular, and political at the same time. Unlike other political art in which the balance between message and aesthetic form is usually uneven and the difficulties the artist had in creating an imaginative framework around his or her statement can be felt throughout, *Force of Evil* shows no seams. Although revealing the corruption of the capitalist system, the information it gives cannot be subtracted from its fic-

tional, emotional impact, and although its effect on the viewer is agitational, there is no proposition for practical action.

The reasons for this unique blend are probably to be found in the fact that the filmmakers were less alienated from their work than other Hollywood artists. Instead of catering to other people—the producers, the masses, the critics—they made a film that first of all was to comply with their own tastes and political beliefs, even though it was subject to a number of practical and economic restrictions.

The mentality out of which *Force of Evil* evolved was that of creative intellectuals who had worked within the movie industry but whose independent spirit and leftist political awareness did not fit into the Hollywood system. [In an endnote, Brinckmann adds: "As Dorothy B. Jones's study on 'Communism and the Movies' has shown, it was practically impossible to smuggle Marxist ideas into movies produced by the big studios: 'The very nature of the filmmaking process which divides creative responsibility among a number of different people and which keeps ultimate control of content in the hands of top studio executives; the habitual caution of movie-makers with respect to film content; and the self-regulating practices of the motion picture industry as carried on by the Motion Picture Association, prevented such propaganda from reaching the screen in all but possibly rare instances.' 'Communism and the Movies: A Study of Film Content,' in John Cogley, *Report on Blacklisting I: The Movies* (Fund for the Republic, 1956). For Polonsky's views on the problematic, see especially his article in *Film Culture* 50-51 (Fall-Winter 1970)."] This is not to say that they looked down upon popular art—there was no elitist or puritanical distaste for the movies and no cynical contempt for mass audiences. On the other hand, there was no overall didactic impulse to enlighten the masses either. The filmmakers did not perceive themselves as missionaries of political ideas, and they knew they had to make money in order to survive. Even though the film is original and bold, it also employs popular movie patterns, and it contains nothing to offend the censors. And even though Polonsky was closely in touch with the political situation and knew that he might not get another chance at directing a film, the production of *Force of Evil* implied no acts of personal martyrdom; the time of the blacklist was close but had not yet begun. . . .

*Force of Evil* was an independent production, produced by the newly established Enterprise studios. Independent production companies, which had been a marginal phenomenon during the 1930s and 1940s, suddenly started to burgeon after World War II. In 1946, the economic prospects of the movie industry looked highly promising. Audience attendance had reached its peak. It was before television had made its significant impact and before the postwar baby boom began to keep young couples at home. The antitrust suit had not yet forced the studios to divest themselves of monopoly holdings and to break up their vertical integration with movie theaters. The British market was still intact. It was therefore little wonder that movies were considered a particularly safe investment and that it was comparatively easy to find the money necessary for a new film project.

Independent production companies could thus spring up and become an alternative to the Hollywood establishment. They were, however, mostly funded by the same type of investors and, therefore, basically controlled by the same free-enterprise ideology as the big studios. They also had to use the same channels of distribution and to show their films at the same theaters to audiences shaped by, and accustomed to, Hollywood. While it was thus rather unlikely that independent productions would differ drastically from the usual Hollywood fare, they did provide a slight opening for divergent, innovative talent. Things could be handled on a more personal basis and with less rigidity than in the big studios, and there was also some ambition to avoid stale patterns and be at least moderately experimental (and it made commercial sense, too).

Enterprise Productions went into business in 1946 and soon merged with Roberts Productions, an independent studio founded by the producer Bob Roberts and the actor John Garfield. One of Enterprise's first releases, and its most successful, was *Body and Soul* (1947), directed by Robert Rossen, written by Abraham Polonsky, photographed by James Wong Howe, and starring John Garfield and Lilli Palmer. Though not a particularly expensive production, its credits include a number of well-known names. Moreover, the film tapped a popular genre and made use of the narrative patterns and visual style of its day. *Body and Soul* is a prizefight picture, told in first-person flashbacks and set and photographed in the dark, expressionist-realist tones of film noir. It is the story of a ghetto hero who has made his way up only to realize that in boxing he has to face the same corrupt and corruptive forces he had set out to avoid. After sacrificing personal happiness and moral values for fame and material wealth, he finally acknowledges that he has sold himself and walks out on his oppressors.

The social criticism contained in this story is more detailed and consistent than in comparable films. Although it is never obtrusive enough to occupy center stage, the information conveyed about commercialism in prizefighting and the moral stance taken by the protagonist tend to affect us in more than a superficial way. Apart from its underlying message, *Body and Soul* is also memorable for employing a black actor in a fairly important character role. In other respects, however, the film is more or less conventional and not even altogether successfully so. Lilli Palmer's acting is wooden, the dialogues are sometimes stilted and sentimental, some of the scenes move clumsily, and the film seems too long.

*Body and Soul* immediately became a big hit, reaping substantial profits and winning an Academy Award. As the laws of the market demanded, Enterprise decided to repeat its success with another, relatively similar film. John Garfield, as one of the cofounders and investors of the production company, as well as one of its chief assets as an actor, planned to star in a comparable role. Again Abraham Polonsky wrote the script, but this time he was to direct the film as well. Because Polonsky had been on the set during the entire production of *Body and Soul,* work-

ing closely with the movie crew and especially with Garfield, assisting (and fruitfully contradicting) the director, he seemed well qualified for the job.

Abraham Polonsky was brought up in New York, in a socialist Jewish milieu. He attended City College in the 1930s—when it was a center of political and ideological controversy—joined a number of Marxist discussion groups, and taught classes in English literature. Later graduating from Columbia Law School and earning his living as a lawyer, he soon began to write fiction as well. He gave up law for radio writing in 1939, and at the same time became involved in union work for the Communist party. During the war, Polonsky joined the Office of Strategic Services and was sent to Europe. Before his departure, he had signed a contract with Paramount Studios to become a screenwriter. After moving to Hollywood, Polonsky worked on several scripts, none of which was filmed in the form in which it was written, became an editor of the critical journal *The Hollywood Quarterly,* and again took part in radical politics and union struggles. It was only after he had moved to Enterprise Productions that his career as a creative screen artist finally got under way, and it was only then that he could combine his political and artistic identities in his film work.

At Paramount, Polonsky's original talents and political energies had gone unnoticed. But within the small Enterprise group of dedicated movie workers with their dynamic esprit-de-corps, he suddenly came into his own. His friendship with John Garfield, another New York Jew who held similar, if intellectually less articulate, political beliefs, proved especially constructive, but Bob Roberts, the producer, also defended the project against the other, less enthusiastic financiers. Polonsky soon obtained almost total control over the production of *Force of Evil:* He rewrote the script (originally written by Ira Wolfert after his novel *Tucker's People*), selected the locations, influenced the camera style, lighting, and music score, and supervised the editing. *Force of Evil* is thus one of the few films of the 1940s that can rightfully be called the work of an auteur. As Polonsky's own comments on the film show, he considered and still considers it to be *his* film, a work of art that evolved out of a complex set of personal and political decisions.

When *Force of Evil* was released in December 1948, the fate of Enterprise Productions was already sealed. Consequently, the film did not receive proper publicity. It was distributed by MGM in an inexpensive, listless way and advertised as another gangster thriller. [In an endnote, Brinckmann adds: "Promotion materials (issued in 1949; filed at Lincoln Center Library) characterized *Force of Evil* with the following slogans: 'Sensational story of a numbers king whose number was up!' 'He wouldn't live within the law—or without love.' 'He challenged the underworld and busted the numbers game wide open.' 'He fought with the woman he loved and made love to the woman he hated.'

At the same time, the publicity experts advised exhibitors not to stress the controversial contents of the film:

> When you exploit *Force of Evil,* don't take a controversial attitude on the perils of local gam-

bling. Don't crusade for better local conditions or improvements, unless such a drive is already underway at the time of your play dates: then play safe and merely cash-in with picture tie-ins. Spearheading such a drive, or participating aggressively, might have unpleasant repercussions for your theater. You can, however, institute a campaign for city-wide endorsement of your engagement by enlisting the support of influential people.

The pressbook also suggests valuable promotion ideas:

> CRIME DOESN'T PAY. *Force of Evil* is a thriller-diller example of the fact that crime doesn't pay; so seize every opportunity to bring it to the attention of the public—at sports events, in bowling alleys and pool-rooms, recreation centers, with spot announcements at end of radio crime programs &c.

And:

> STOP THESE MEN! Prepare 40x60 lobby board containing tough-looking heads of John Garfield and other male members of the cast, under above headline and describe under each head the manner in which that person is a 'menace' to society. Finish up with picture billing and play date announcement. Strong stuff for patrons who like their pictures hard-boiled and exciting."]

Although a few critics mentioned it favorably, *Force of Evil* soon disappeared from the screen. It did not reach its audience until it was rediscovered by television in the 1950s, but it has remained a kind of intellectual cult movie ever since.

Abraham Polonsky wrote one more script, *I Can Get It for You Wholesale* (1951), before he was blacklisted. As an avowed Marxist, a member of the Communist party and one of the most active participants in Hollywood's radical efforts, he was named by several "friendly witnesses" and summoned before the House Un-American Activities Committee (HUAC). Realizing that he could no longer find work in the film industry, Polonsky moved back to New York. He started to write for television under a pseudonym and eventually also resumed his work as a screenwriter, using other writers' names as fronts (because neither Polonsky himself nor the writers concerned have disclosed which films he wrote, this part of his career remains to be discovered). [In an endnote, Brinckmann adds: "In *Film Culture,* Nos. 50-51 (Fall-Winter, 1970), Polonsky gives his reasons for not disclosing which films he wrote during the blacklist period:

> It might not be damaging today to name the films I worked on during this blacklist period, but I think it's up to the persons who lent their real names to this purpose to name the films, not me. I don't see why they should do so. There would probably not be any harm, except to them personally perhaps. I mean, it's a very difficult thing to be a writer who's writing, and occasionally someone else writes something but your name is on it. That's the greatest sacrifice you can demand of a friend. And to say later, 'I want to distinguish between this and that' seems to be

absurd, because I don't think there are any great major works of art now going under false pretenses.

> But perhaps as history the exact credits are important. If the situation were reversed, I don't know what I would do. I wouldn't do anything. I guess, unless I felt it was a bad thing that I was keeping something from someone, but that's because I'm an old Puritan. But in general I don't think the inaccuracies of these credits, due to the blacklisting, is a bad thing. I think it's better to let the past be the way it is. And instead let us writers make our usual claims that we wrote all the good pictures and everyone else wrote all the bad ones. In that way the guerrilla warfare continues."]

It was not until 1968 that Polonsky's name was allowed to appear on the screen again (in *Madigan,* directed by Don Siegel), and not until 1970 that he got another chance at directing a film (*Tell Them Willie Boy Is Here*).

Strangely enough, but in accordance with the usual practice of HUAC and the studios, Polonsky was not blacklisted on account of *Force of Evil.* Inconspicuous, commercially unsuccessful, and not to be categorized as pro-Russian, the film did not arouse the interest of the Committee. Stranger still, but probably because of its poor distribution, *Force of Evil* was not recognized as a radical film by scholars of the blacklisting period either. John Cogley mentions Abraham Polonsky only as the writer of *Body and Soul,* and Dorothy B. Jones, in her extensively researched content analysis of postwar films, "Communism and the Movies," does not mention him or *Force of Evil* at all. Obviously, the film had not begun to reach its audience by 1956.

It is difficult to convey an impression of *Force of Evil* by summarizing its plot, as so much depends on the way images and sound coexist, function on their own, or are dialectically set against each other.

One has to imagine sets and locations photographed in what Polonsky wanted to be the equivalent of Edward Hopper's style in painting: "Third Avenue, cafeterias, all that backlight, and those empty streets. Even when people are there, you don't see them, somehow the environments dominate the people" [see Eric Sherman and Martin Rubin, *The Director's Event: Interviews with Five American Film-makers,* 1970].

City architecture and the empty clarity of the 1940s interiors are depicted with a predominance of rectangular planes and a clear distribution of masses, resulting in a simple sense of perspective. Each scene has a precise iconic identity, rich in symbolic overtones. An overall gloomy, stark style rather than a glossy visual one imparts an atmosphere of anxiety, reinforced by the claustrophobic quality of some of the sets and a film noir taste for shadows, almost total darkness, and the nervous flicker of neon signs. This was not the usual style of the cinematographer, George Barnes, who was famous for the romantic glow of his pictures.

The clarity and poetical economy of the images are matched by the soundtrack, which, although highly complex, is equally lucid and expressive. It consists of three separate strands: the music score, the dialogue and noises connected with the action, and a voice-over narration, commenting on and sometimes poeticizing the scenes. Poetry is, however, not limited to the voice-over—it is as much a quality of the dialogue, in fact one of the most original and most beautiful features of the film. As Polonsky has said in an interview, "the language almost obeyed my intention to play an equal role with the actor and visual image and not run along as illustration, information, and mere verbal gesture" [see William Pechter, "Abraham Polonsky and *Force of Evil,*" *Film Quarterly,* Vol. XV, No. 3 (Spring 1962)]. And it is the poetry of the language as applied to the Wall Street locale or the sordid atmosphere of betting offices, courtrooms, taxicabs, and bars that gives the film its intensity.

*Force of Evil* tells the story of Joe Morse, a young lawyer who has made his way up from the Jewish ghetto to a Wall Street office. He is played by John Garfield and endowed with the inimitable Garfield personality—dynamically virile, persevering, hotheaded, tough, yet strangely sensitive. Joe Morse is a character destined to undergo radical changes. One is immediately made aware of this by the two functions he has in the film: as a fictional character, blindly and ruthlessly involved in the action, and as a voice, commenting on the action as if it had happened long ago and to a much younger, less mature person. But in spite of the spiritual distance, there is a strong rapport between the voice and the character on the screen, and the voice-over somehow manages to emphasize the emotional sensitivity of Garfield's face.

The opening scenes show Joe Morse on the eve of the Fourth of July, contriving a scheme to destroy all the betting offices or "banks" connected with the numbers racket. By manipulating the results at the racetrack, the number 776 will be made to come up, and all the bettors who have traditionally chosen this number will consequently win—enough to make the numbers banks go bankrupt and to give Joe Morse's boss, Tucker (Roy Roberts), full control over the racket.

During the planning and execution of this scheme, one sees Joe functioning as a shyster lawyer, energetically trying to come to grips with the intricacies of the racket, on the one hand, and the law, on the other. But whereas he is highly successful in pulling the necessary strings, he fails to save his brother, one of the "bankers" involved. Leo Morse (Thomas Gomez), a rigidly moral person, runs his numbers bank like a benign patriarch, suppressing the fact that the nature of his business connects him inescapably with illegality and crime. Consequently, he considers Joe's proposition morally contaminating and refuses to play the part that would save him. This is emotionally taxing for Joe, for Leo has sacrificed his own career in order to put him through law school.

In the course of the action, Joe has Leo's betting office raided by the police. This event thoroughly upsets Leo's patriarchal enclave—his young secretary, Doris (Beatrice Pearson), quits her job, and his bookkeeper (Howard Chamberlain) becomes an informer, both to the police and to Tucker's men. Aware of the pressures Leo's stance puts

on Joe and of the security risk involved, Tucker tries to double-cross Joe. He has his phone tapped by Hall, the special prosecutor and a mysterious figure looming in the wings of the plot. But Joe has been warned. He clears out his safe and deserts his law office, never to return. Tucker's response to this is the attempt to have Leo kidnapped, using the bookkeeper as a decoy. In an ill-fated assault, the bookkeeper gets shot and Leo, too sick to endure the shock, dies of heart failure. Dismayed by his brother's death, for which he holds himself responsible, Joe takes revenge on Tucker and Tucker's Mafia partner, Fico. In a dramatic shoot-out conducted in Tucker's office, he kills both men.

The scenes leading up to this final confrontation differ widely in tone. The encounters with Tucker's racket are crisp and fast, showing Joe in full control of the situation. The meetings of the two brothers are gloomy and slow, Leo Morse presenting himself as an insurmountable obstacle whose irrationality resists every argument. Emphasizing this difference, Tucker's environment looks pompously expensive, while Leo's office is depicted as a dark, narrow trap. Even Leo's physical appearance expresses his painful intractability—he is fat, unhealthy, elderly, and seedy. But most of all it is his traditionally Jewish rhetoric of futility, guilt, and victimization that characterizes the scenes between the brothers and makes it clear to us from the beginning that Joe will be unable to save Leo.

There is, however, a third kind of scene that is set in still another tone and reveals another aspect of Joe's character. During the first confrontation with Leo, Joe meets Doris, his brother's gentle, innocent secretary. It is through Doris, who is fascinated by him yet terrified at becoming contaminated, that Joe begins to see himself in a new light. Their encounters oscillate between romance and disillusionment, attraction and repulsion, hope and despair. And although their relationship is dissonant and dynamic in its own right, it serves as a mellow, almost peaceful counterpoint to the aggressiveness and speed of the main plot. Images of flowers, jewelry, softly swinging dresses and domestic paraphernalia characterize most of the scenes with Doris, and her pure, intensely serious voice, even when talking about Joe's world, seems to come from an entirely different place. But Doris is not a weak character, and her firmness runs parallel to Joe's energetic rashness and enforces the sense of determination the film conveys. It is thus significant for the final breakthrough (as well as romantically appropriate) that Doris follows Joe after the shoot-out to find his brother's body.

The shoot-out is the climax and ending of Joe's involvement with the numbers racket, but it is neither the climax of his emotional development nor the end of his ideological struggles. Although his belief in his career as Tucker's lawyer has been shaken, Joe's decision to disappear with the money is dictated by egotism and practical necessity rather than by moral disgust. And his final turning against Tucker is shown as the outcome of his grief rather than the result of a mature analysis of the situation. The film defers Joe's full change until the very last, separating it from the scenes of violent action by images of pure symbolic movement and lyric intensity. Joe is seen running down Wall Street, descending to the bank of the Hudson River at the first rays of dawn. It is now that the metaphors of ascent and descent, and of day and night, that have been recurring throughout the film acquire their full significance. Joe is forced to sink to depths deeper than the slum from which he came and to endure a night as dark as hell so that he may undergo a purification and attain a new, dynamically positive personality.

The final voice-over, spoken while Joe turns back from his brother's body and starts walking up again toward the city with Doris, expresses the flow of energy from grief to future action:

> I found my brother's body at the bottom there, like an old dirty rag nobody wants. He was dead and I felt that I had killed him. I turned back to give myself up to Hall. Because if a man's life can be lived so long and come out this way, like rubbish, it's something that is horrible and has to be ended one way or another. And I decided to help.

In his review of *Odd Man Out* (Carol Reed, 1947), Polonsky states that this film is

> . . . actually a stereotype of realism and the literary form of melodrama. Its content, as differentiated from its mechanical form, is essentially anti-realistic, a consideration of a metaphysical and not a social struggle. In treating social events it is necessary to know their precise historical conditions in order to evaluate the operation of moral choices. [*Hollywood Quarterly* 2 (July 1947)]

What Polonsky resents is that images with an intensely realistic impact are used to depict a story only vaguely rooted in reality. One does not know the "object of the terror, the suspense, the suffering, the meanness," as one gets no information about the organization for which the protagonist is fighting. For example: "We do not know in what sense it represents the population or some part of it. We do not know why the police must suppress it." For Polonsky, it is not sufficient to show that a fictional character is seriously engaged in a conflict of some sort. The audience has to be put into a position to judge whether this conflict is meaningful in its own right as well.

---

**It is typical of Polonsky's work to cut across the traditional distinctions between fiction and factual information, fantasy and politics, entertainment and serious art.**

**—*Christine Noll Brinckmann***

---

Applied to his own film, Polonsky's theory makes a lot of sense. The lives of Joe and Leo Morse and of Doris and other characters are explained in terms of socioeconomic struggles. Public and private affairs, the characters' business identities and their personal lives, merge into each other. All situations and relationships are permeated by the same central conflict: the question of whether it is possible to be financially successful without becoming corrupt. Essentially a moral issue, this question has as much bearing on personal decisions as it has on the evaluation of the structure of society.

Polonsky's strategy of combining the personal and political is especially evident in the scenes between Joe and Doris. Traditionally limited to the expression of personal feeling, love scenes in gangster movies usually function as moments of emotional relief. Without denying the romantic aspects of love, Polonsky breaks with this tradition by placing Doris within the arena of racket decisions and police raids. The conversations between Joe and Doris revolve around Joe's part in the numbers scheme, moving swiftly back and forth between love making and ideological conflict, until one becomes inseparably entwined with the other. Joe and Doris are alternately seen in business locales and romantic places, using offices and courtrooms for passionate conversations and the steps of Trinity Church or Doris's kitchen for discussion of corruption and contamination.

Sometimes the atmosphere of the setting is transformed by purely visual means, as in the scene at the courthouse, when the profiles of Joe and Doris appear as romantic silhouettes on the translucent panes of the door. Totally out of keeping with the bleak environment, this image is "the complete opposite of the milieu. As if to say that you can still hold on to something beautiful and delicious despite everything." As Polonsky further points out, the image expresses Joe's point of view: "Garfield still thinks so, because he is not finished yet" [Sherman and Rubin, *The Director's Event*]. While combining the worlds of sordid business and romantic love, the image also comments on the futility of fleeing from one into the other.

If one of the strategies of the film is to show how the protagonists are personally affected by the system, another one is to keep their antagonists as impersonal, unsympathetic, and static as possible. Tucker in particular, the boss of the racket, remains a cipher. Portrayed by Roy Roberts as more like a business executive than a gangster, he lacks the charisma that usually distinguishes the villain of a plot. As we learn nothing about his past and are never allowed to participate in his decisions, we never get inside the character. Consequently, Tucker comes to stand for the system that motivates him or, as Polonsky puts it, "the more shadowy Tucker is, the more omnipresent the feeling of what he represents" [*The Director's Event*].

One of the achievements of the film is to emphasize the fact that the real source of conflict transcends the characters—that the "force of evil" cannot be personalized in the usual, fictional way. The audience has to accept the socioeconomic system instead of the racketeer Tucker as the main antagonist of the plot. The spectator is thus asked to think about the part this system plays in his own life. But Polonsky's strategy could, of course, have the reverse effect as well: As an antagonistic force in a fictional plot, the system could be divested of its connection to the real and become part of the fiction. It could play the traditional role of fate, of evil in general, or stand for an overall sense of inevitability, uncontrollability, or obstruction. In each case the political impact of the film would be weakened.

One of the main devices used to prevent this effect is to set the film in authentic locations. Contrary to the prevailing Hollywood style, the exteriors of *Force of Evil* were shot in New York City. Wall Street, Trinity Church, the bank of the Hudson River, and other locales are allowed to play themselves, as it were, and give a documentary touch to the film. Their monumentality and symbolic connotations—as the site of the Stock Exchange and the leading banks of the Western world—already signify to the audience the spirit of free enterprise. Authenticity is thus "naturally" accompanied by symbolic significance, the symbols depicted being part of the audience's reality.

Another, related feature of the film is the numbers racket, a lottery that was, and to some degree still is, immensely popular with the lower classes. By using the numbers game as one of the pivotal points of the plot, Polonsky introduced a commonplace phenomenon with which everybody was familiar, although it did have an element of the illegal and mysterious. It was, therefore, possible to let the numbers banks play two simultaneous roles: as the natural place where the numbers business would be conducted and, metonymically, as representatives of the real banks, "establishments for the custody, loan, exchange, or issue of money" (*Webster's New Collegiate Dictionary*). The Wall Street environment, then, serves several purposes. While it sets the action in locations that are at the same time realistically authentic and authentically symbolic, it also enforces the duplicitous use of the word "bank." Again, fictional world and reality are fused in an intricate way.

It is typical of Polonsky's work to cut across the traditional distinctions between fiction and factual information, fantasy and politics, entertainment and serious art. Considered in this light, one of the most relevant features of *Force of Evil* is that it uses the framework of the gangster genre as a foil for its divergent content. It would not be correct, however, to maintain that Polonsky started out with a political message that he then tried to disguise as popular fiction. As the production history shows, his assignment was to create a popular movie (with progressive overtones), and the more radical content of the film only materialized as he went along. But even if the choice of a popular genre was a given, it did not run contrary to Polonsky's style and inclinations. His other scripts and films are characterized by the same strategy of employing fictional patterns in order to undercut their conventional structures, though *Force of Evil* remains the most explicit example. The documentary, or semidocumentary, is not a mode of expression Polonsky has attempted.

The gangster qualities of *Force of Evil* are prominent enough to have induced several film historians to classify it as a prime example of the genre. Jack Shadoian in his *Dreams and Dead Ends: The American Gangster/Crime Film* and Stanley J. Solomon in his *Beyond Formula: American Film Genres* have both used it to illustrate the development of the gangster film in the 1940s. But *Force of Evil* does not "fit comfortably into the genre," as Shadoian has it; nor does it portray evil as "one of the perva-

sive elements of modern life, its source seeming to lie *within* man," as Solomon claims. The way Polonsky makes us aware of the corrupting influence of the system rather than the corrupt nature of individual people already serves to contradict Solomon, and the way the personal and the political are combined in the main characters is another instance of deviating from the usual pattern. There is, however, further evidence on this point, which will also help to explain how Polonsky avoids the pitfall of fictionalizing the social forces he depicts.

In his seminal article "The Gangster as Tragic Hero" (written in 1948, the year *Force of Evil* was made), Robert Warshow traces several basic qualities of the American gangster film. One of them concerns the nature and filmic depiction of the gangster's criminal activity, which are reflected in its function for the audience:

> The gangster's activity is actually a form of rational enterprise, involving fairly definite goals and various techniques for achieving them. But this rationality is usually no more than a vague background: we know, perhaps, that the gangster sells liquor or that he operates a numbers racket; often we are not given even that much information. So his activity becomes a kind of pure criminality: he hurts people. Certainly our response to the gangster film is most consistently and most universally a response to sadism; we gain the double satisfaction of participating vicariously in the gangster's sadism and then seeing it turned against the gangster himself. [Robert Warshow, *The Immediate Experience*, 1972]

*Force of Evil* is, however, not at all vague about the particulars of the criminal setup. Much time is occupied with pointing out how the numbers banks work and how their bankruptcy is to be engineered. Although the film is not repetitious—it is in fact so terse that audiences are sometimes at a loss—many scenes or parts of scenes are dedicated to minor details: We are told about betting habits, about the way police detectives spy on numbers banks dressed up as bus supervisors, or how incriminating objects should be dropped before the police enter, as they cannot serve as evidence unless found in the defendant's hands. The audience is confronted with relentless explanations that often transcend the dramaturgical necessities of the plot.

*Force of Evil* deviates from the typical gangster picture also in that it does not supply sadism in the way Warshow describes it. Neither Joe Morse nor Tucker is presented as sadistically inclined, and the physical violence that does occur on the screen—the police raid of Leo's office, the kidnapping scene in which the bookkeeper is shot—has masochistic overtones rather than sadistic ones. In each case we see how a group of more or less anonymous men assault defenseless people; and in each case we sympathize with the assaulted, although we also feel that their pain and misery are to some degree self-inflicted or, in Leo's case, even sought. As for the final shoot-out in Tucker's office, which could have provided a scene of grim violence, its crucial moments take place in almost complete darkness. There is no way of knowing who fires at whom with what success and, consequently, no way of experiencing vicarious sadistic pleasure.

Apart from its avoidance of sadism, *Force of Evil* also refrains from presenting the typical, significant gangster career. As Warshow points out,

> . . . we are always conscious that the whole meaning of this career is a strive for success: the typical gangster film presents a steady upward progress followed by a very precipitate fall. Thus brutality itself becomes at once the means to success and the content of success—a success that is defined in its most general terms, not as accomplishment or specific gain, but simply as the unlimited possibility of aggression.

In *Force of Evil* the action begins at a point where the "steady upward progress" has already reached its climax. Thematically, the myth of the American dream is present throughout the entire film, but experientially it is almost absent. If Joe Morse is still seen as fighting against all odds, his fight no longer leads him upward. While he succeeds in engineering the numbers scheme, this success is accompanied by the failure to persuade and save his brother. And while he manages to kill his adversaries, he loses or gives up all he has achieved during his career as a gangster lawyer. The film is thus not a story of economic, material success, and it does not end with a "very precipitate fall."

One could, of course, argue that Warshow's categories do not fit every gangster film and, in fact, do not have to do so—that it is their very "archetypicality" that makes them an inappropriate tool for the analysis and classification of *individual* works. Further, Warshow only speaks about films in which the gangster is the hero, whereas the term "gangster film" includes all kinds of pictures in which gangsters appear. It is true that Joe Morse is not even presented as a genuine gangster—he is a gangster's lawyer—and that the real gangster of the story is the shadowy, marginal figure of Tucker. But the plot of the film is continuously, if dialectically, evocative of Warshow's gangster syndrome, as is the character of Joe Morse. The battle for material success and power is the model *against* which the film is set, as sadism is the attitude one expects but never sees. The typical career of the gangster hero, from the slums to the lonely summit of a powerful syndicate, is the career Joe renounces. [In an endnote, Brinckmann adds: "Other gangster films of the time also tend to move away from Warshow's pattern. But instead of evoking it as *Force of Evil* does, they drop it altogether in favor of a different type of story and a different hero personality. In pictures like *Kiss of Death* (Henry Hathaway, 1947), *They Live by Night* (Nicholas Ray, 1948), or *Side Street* (Anthony Mann, 1949), the protagonist is a simple, basically innocent young man who got involved in crime only because he was too weak to extricate himself from bad influences or to resist the temptation of the moment."]

In an interview with Pasternak and Howton, Polonsky commented on the significance of film genres and their transformation in art:

> . . . I think genres, like other social habits, speak for us in terms of summaries of the way we see life. We live out the myths and rituals, because that's the way we synthesize our relationship to society and our relationship to other people. I think anthropologically speaking it has very deep connections with the role of religion in life. I would assume that I am essentially a religious person of some sort, at least in the sense that I try to make things signify as if there were some ultimate significance all the time—the ultimate significance being something that's not so ultimate after all. . . . I don't think that the development of genres in the art forms are accidents. I think they're fundamental to the way art operates on our life. . . . So in the long run, they're inescapable. Now, always, of course, as art advances, what you do is destroy the genre in one form or another, and reconstruct it in some other form, ultimately. [*The Image Maker*, edited by Ron Henderson, 1971]

Apart from being a convenient vehicle for telling a story and attracting a mass audience, a film genre is, then, a way of structuring the world. And it supplies the artist with a presystematized framework that can be further paraphrased, transformed, or used as a foil for a dissident perception of reality. In *Force of Evil*, Polonsky has made use of the genre in all these ways, re-emphasizing some of the established gangster film statements about society, modifying others, and evoking a number of traditional patterns without fulfilling them, transferring the energies they carry to a different cause.

Highly aware of his own strategies, Polonsky has commented on several subtle ways in which he has transformed the genre. One of these involves the use of music. In the kidnapping scene, we hear a kind of religious dirge instead of the usual musical equivalent for violence and aggression, introducing a "note of disruption" that alienates us from the images as well as from our sense of expectation. Polonsky chose this way of presenting the scene in order to "create a sense of general anxiety. When you do a thing like that, what you do is utilize the *familiar* as a way of calling attention to the fact that it's not so familiar after all" [*The Director's Event*].

In the same interview Polonsky explains the significance of the telephone in *Force of Evil*. A mode of communication that figures large in most gangster films, the telephone usually emphasizes the technological ease with which the racket network functions, and expresses the isolation and refrainment from personal, emotional contact it involves. By using a specially made oversize telephone, which sits in the foreground of some images like an enormous black contraption, Polonsky at once acknowledges the symbolic convention and takes it to obtrusive extremes. At the same time, he exploits the (visual) anonymity and functional sameness of the people engaged in telephone conversations in order to indicate a sense of identity between them. When Joe Morse speaks first with his boss, then with the police, there seems to be a "direct parallel between Tucker and the Law on the other end of the telephone." Or, as Polonsky further elaborates, "The people live in a lane, and on both sides of this lane are vast, empty places. On one side, it says LAW, and on the other, it says CRIME. But, in fact, you can't tell one from the other."

Again, one of the traditional metaphorical devices of the gangster genre is used in a more salient, ideologically more pointed way. The equation of crime with business in general, of the criminal world with society, or of gangsterism with Americanism becomes the equation of crime with the established countermeasure directed against it, the law itself.

Whereas the gangster features of *Force of Evil* are evident in the factual setup of the plot, in most of the personnel involved, and in the iconography of many scenes, the dramatic core of the film goes back to a much older, almost timeless mythical source. It is the archetypal conflict between Cain and Abel, the story of how one brother turns against the other or, more generally, of how men are unable to understand and tolerate each other. Like the myth of Cain and Abel, the film revolves around egotism, distrust, and discordance, ending in the death of one of the brothers.

Cain and Abel are, however, one-dimensional characters who represent evil and good, respectively—the provocation inherent in Abel's priggish righteousness is not in the foreground of the biblical fable, and Cain has to bear the full punishment for the deed. Contrary to this, the film incriminates both brothers. Although Joe resembles Cain in that he is violent, selfish, and irreverent, and Leo resembles Abel in his gentleness and morality, Joe is also characterized as responsible, repentant, and able to reform, whereas Leo is rigid, irrational, and despairing and tries to put the blame on his brother. It is as much Leo's rigidity and eagerness to victimize himself as it is Joe's involvement in the racket that finally results in Leo's death. Moreover, Joe wishes to help his brother, and this desire increases until it becomes the primary motive of all his actions. That his reform comes too late to save his brother is a tragic coincidence. Joe's sense of guilt is, therefore, gratuitous to some degree, and it functions as a redeeming quality. Purified rather than contaminated, Joe is now able to dedicate himself to the fight against the forces that caused his own corruption and his brother's death.

The myth of Cain and Abel thus does not provide the skeleton of the plot, because the deviations from it are more significant than the similarities. Again, Polonsky has drawn from a well-known pattern without following its implications, and again the film profits from the strategy. For one thing, the familiarity with the myth sets up audience expectations. For another, it furnishes a moral framework within which the characters can be evaluated. Joe and Leo themselves often conjure up the specter of fratricide, adding emotional intensity to their discordance. But, most of all, the biblical connotations of the myth give an aura of seriousness, dignity, and weight to the film.

The deviation from the myth also serves to save *Force of Evil* from the danger of becoming "melodramatic" in Polonsky's sense of the word. For the Cain and Abel story could have provided the same kind of metaphysically oriented, eternally humanitarian, nonconcrete, nonrealistic thrust Polonsky criticized in his review of *Odd Man Out*. As it is, however, *Force of Evil* does not allow such an interpretation. Apart from its significantly different ending, which alone would make a metaphysical reading some-

what difficult, and apart from the way Joe and Leo Morse differ from Cain and Abel, the film also shows how the brothers have been shaped by their environment. Because the economic system rather than some innate moral deficiency has to be held responsible for their mistakes, *Force of Evil* is not about the evil eternally and inescapably present in the human race.

But the pattern of the two discordant brothers does have some allegorical overtones, and their being brothers is more than a neat coincidence of the plot. Not a very convincing pair of siblings, their family resemblance showing neither physically nor spiritually, Joe and Leo Morse represent two alternatives, two almost complementary ways of being. This is evident in their characters, as well as in their attitudes and their ability to adjust to the system.

Joe has decided to use his education and intelligence in order to make as much money as possible, no matter how immoral the means. "I had not enough strength to resist corruption, but I was strong enough to fight for a piece of it," he tells Doris. No longer able to see the difference between being a gangster's lawyer and doing a gangster's business, he is on the verge of becoming a gangster himself. Leo, on the other hand, has no education and is not as smart as his younger brother. He has tried very hard to earn his living honestly but has been forced by bitter circumstances to go into the numbers business. Looking back on his life, he too is no longer able to discriminate between legality and illegality:

> I've been a businessman all my life, and honest,
> I don't know what a business is. . . . Real estate
> business, living from mortgage to mortgage,
> stealing credit like a thief. And the garage, that
> was a business. Three cents overcharge on every
> gallon of gas—two cents for the chauffeur, and
> a penny for me. A penny for one thief, two cents
> for the other.

The brothers demonstrate that whatever you do, you get caught in the mesh of corruption. Dramatically opposed in all important respects, they represent a wide range of contamination, and their being brothers only adds to the sense of totality conveyed. The generality inherent in the motif of the two brothers has thus been employed to express a political statement.

The discussion so far has concentrated on Polonsky's attempts to render a critical analysis of the capitalist system. By focusing on concrete details, by introducing authentic materials, or by transforming the genre or myth employed, *Force of Evil* disrupts the fictional conventions and succeeds in drawing a detailed and manifold picture of the system. All these strategies appeal to, and depend on, the mental capacity of the audience to grasp the meaning of the deviations and understand their bearing on reality. But the film is not an essay on capitalism, and nothing would be achieved if the audience could not respond emotionally as well. In a work of fiction, the analytical insights have to be aligned with the emotional impact of the story—or the story will appear stale and ultimately unconvincing. Although stories have a strong tendency to absorb all kinds of material, they suffer easily from being didactically overloaded. It is, therefore, as necessary to keep the emotional experience of the audience intact as it is to protect the political message from being smothered in the magic of fiction.

Polonsky's strategy to achieve the right balance consists first of all in shifting the main emotional impact from the story to what could be called the "spiritual intensity" of the film—intensity of character, feeling, atmosphere, or poetical presentation in general. As has been indicated before, the plot itself does not fulfill the requirements of a gangster story (or of other genre fiction, for that matter): It does not portray the rise and fall of a criminal hero; it does not focus on personal violence; it refrains from melodrama; it shows little dramatic interaction between the protagonist and his antagonists; and the love story is neither supplementary nor pathos-ridden, nor does it furnish the pivotal point of the action. Although tightly knit and determining each scene logically, the plot of *Force of Evil* is also too restrained, too terse, too symbolical, and too open-ended to involve the audience emotionally. Instead of participating in the actual incidents of the story, one is induced to watch them from a detached point of view.

This detachment is, however, counterbalanced by the high emotional intensity that characterizes the film. For one thing, *Force of Evil* is permeated by an overall sense of anxiety present even in its most romantic scenes. Visually, this anxiety is expressed through the narrowness, darkness, and bleakness of most of the locales—much of the film takes place at night, in confined interior spaces or in Leo's office, to which daylight is not permitted. But claustrophobia is not only expressed through the images (as it is in many a film noir of the period). One of the characters actually suffers from it, and it can thus be vicariously experienced by the audience. When one of Leo's employees explains to the police how he was trapped in his car after it had been pushed off the road into the river, they insist nonetheless that he ride in the narrow back of the van. His reaction is extreme, providing the film with one of its most agonizing moments.

Other scenes also impart a sense of acute physical discomfort—for example, when the police burst the door of Leo's bank open, regardless of the group of people crowded behind it; or when the police injure the bookkeeper's ear, which he will cover with one hand for the rest of the film; or when Leo's heart condition manifests itself, so that his fatness and hysterical irritation are felt as a constant threat to his life; or when Joe gets so drunk at the nightclub that he is hardly able to speak. All these scenes have a harrowing, anxiety-raising quality, because one is forced to experience empathetically what it feels like to be physically hampered or disabled.

Another way in which the film raises anxiety is by repeatedly introducing situations of frustration and impotence. A frequent instance of this is provided by the telephone, through its threatening capacity to exert remote control over people and through its constant liability of being tapped. It is mostly the main character who experiences—and conveys—this anxiety, for his impatience and dynamic agility make him all the more prone to frustration. In spite of all his bustling activity and dreamlike presence of mind, Joe is not able to control what is going on. His ac-

tions are almost inevitably reactions, and he is always either just in time to forestall greater loss or already too late to prevent disaster. Consequently, the audience feels a growing sense of uneasiness and nervous urgency, and it is only at the end that one is able to breathe freely again.

Polonsky attributes this climate of anxiety to the prevailing political experience of the period in which the film was made. *Force of Evil* can be considered an expression of the fear that spread in the leftist movement as American policy changed in the postwar years, and of the traumatic insight that the movement was to be curbed and destroyed. But the anxiety in the film is not only a reflection of the historical situation. It also serves to emphasize the general sense of alienation and impotence inflicted by a dehumanized and corrupt economic system. Anxiety is thus part of the basis of the film and, therefore, a particularly appropriate sensation to be imparted to the audience in order to keep it in a state of emotional agitation.

Anxiety is, however, not the only intense emotion the film evokes. For one thing, *Force of Evil* is steeped in melancholy that is both painful and sweet. It is the feeling that accompanies the remembrance of things past, especially memories of one's youth, and it is created by the voice-over, on the one hand, and Joe Morse's youthful enthusiasm, on the other. As the voice-over is spoken from a vantage point above the film and sufficiently removed temporally to allow a contemplative stance, the scenes presented become less imminent and the situation appears no longer hopeless: If the main character has survived and matured into a personality capable of narrating his own story with feeling and insight into its general significance, we may be reassured that anxiety, frustration, and dismay can be overcome.

For another thing, the aesthetic structure of the film serves to suspend our anxiety. The poetry of the language, as well as the beautiful texture of the images, heightens the feeling of reassurance, while both add overtones of lyrical assonance and the excitement of intense compression and expressiveness. Through the mythical symmetry of the motif of the two brothers, the recurrent patterns of descent and ascent, and the metaphorical framework of day, night, and morning, the film conveys a sense of aesthetic control strong enough to counterbalance the experience of being at the mercy of a hostile, uncontrollable system. [In an endnote, Brinckmann adds: "Simon O. Lesser, in *Fiction and the Unconscious* (1957), holds that it is one of the major functions of form to relieve free-floating anxiety: 'The highest achievements of form, it may be conjectured, are due to the double requirement of having to subdue the quotient of anxiety which is always with us as well as the anxiety which may be aroused by the subject matter of a particular story.' Through our positive response to form, 'we are paying homage to the superego, not simply attempting to deceive or conciliate it, but asseverating our devotion and our unqualified acceptance of its demands.' "] In a way, the voice-over is a manifestation of this control, too. Free-floating, capable of entering the film at any given moment, divested of a visible source and omniscient in its understanding, the voice is as much that of the filmmaker as it is that of Joe Morse. A creative authority, it is able to conjure up forces and counterforces, to cope with dismay and passion, and to explain the significance of it all as far as it is explicable.

Apart from the highly charged atmosphere of *Force of Evil,* it is chiefly the spiritual energy of the protagonist that keeps the audience involved, and like the emotions of anxiety and reassurance it contributes to the effectiveness of the statement the film attempts. Joe Morse's personality comes across equally strongly in romantic scenes and in business encounters—even in brief moments of trivial occupation, like climbing stairs or opening a door. As portrayed by John Garfield, the character of Joe Morse is endowed with a depth and swiftness of feeling irresistibly attractive and with emotional and physical energies bound to make the audience identify with him. Polonsky was well aware of Garfield's powers: "Garfield was the darling of romantic rebels—beautiful, enthusiastic, rich with the know-how of street intelligence. He had passion and a lyrical sadness that was the essence of the role he created as it was created for him" [see Polonsky's introduction to *The Films of John Garfield,* by Howard Gelman, 1975].

Although empathetic identification with the main character (and a glamorous star at that) is a phenomenon usually connected with escapist Hollywood movies, it can be put to different uses as well. What Polonsky attempted to achieve through his star was different already in that it was to function in a differently structured film: As has been indicated before, the Garfield character serves as a center of emotional intensity in a rigorously condensed plot loaded with thought and information. But it also serves to give an emotionally and, to some degree, politically satisfactory ending to *Force of Evil.*

Again the device of the voice-over is responsible for the way in which the main character is experienced. Garfield's split identity, the fact that he exists in the present as well as the past, serves to disentangle him from the events on the screen. For the voice-over makes it quite clear that what we see is the past, which has to be lived through and overcome, and that the point we are to reach is a point at the end of the film, or even outside it. Although this does not drain Joe's screen activities of their dynamic quality, they seem to occur on a plane once removed from the central awareness of the film. Joe's energy is thus not completely integrated into, and at the disposal of, the plot. He has a kind of surplus power that, together with his invulnerability (also guaranteed by the voice-over) and his charisma, makes him a hero figure who can continue after the plot of the film has exhausted itself.

The ending of *Force of Evil* is bound to disappoint those who pay too much attention to the plot, ignoring its functional, almost allegorical character and not acknowledging the implications of the voice-over. David Talbot and Barbara Zheutlin give evidence of this fallacy in their comment on Joe Morse's descent to the bank of the river: "His descent is so long and steep, and the sight of his dead brother so terribly final that it is evident Morse will never fully regain his humanity—despite his declared intention of turning himself in to the district attorney" [*Creative Differences: Profiles of Hollywood Dissidents,* 1978].

But how can he "never fully regain his humanity" and at the same time be capable of telling his story the way he does? And isn't it precisely the steepness and length (and pace) of his descent that give him the energy to turn around and make a new beginning? There is, moreover, the metaphor of night and morning used again and again, visually as well as verbally, to characterize Joe's moral awakening. The finality of his brother's death cannot interfere with the tremendous energy he gains in the course of this experience, especially as it is the price he has to pay for his purification. It is, then, certainly a strategy of Polonsky's to invest Joe Morse with more spiritual intensity than the plot requires. Joe is set up as a contagious center of energy, a kind of energizing spirit of revolt who bursts the fetters of the system to prove that it is possible to live outside it. And his experience could not be conveyed effectively if the powers of the protagonist were limited to the self-contained fictionality of a story.

In his review of *The Best Years of Our Lives* (William Wyler, 1946) Polonsky finds fault with the ending of that progressive and in many respects exemplary film:

> Unfortunately, in the *Best Years,* as in most social-problem fiction, the artist falls into the trap of trying to find local solutions in existence for the social conflicts, instead of solving them in feeling. This is, of course, the industry's demand for happy endings. . . .
>
> Fascism is solved with a punch; a bad marriage by the easy disappearance of a wife; the profound emotional adjustment of a handless veteran by a fine girl; the itchy conscience of a banker by too many drinks. The future is not to be predicted out of such formulas. [*Hollywood Quarterly* 2 (1946-47)]

Polonsky objects to the way the picture first "exposes the fraud of America's promises to its soldiers" then finds cheap and—at best—individually convincing solutions for their problems. In his own film, Polonsky has avoided covering up insoluble problems with happy endings; in fact, he does not offer any solutions or practical suggestions at all. The shooting of the two racketeers will clearly not make a difference to the system; Leo's death is shown as inevitable, no matter what Joe might have done; and Leo's life proves that there was no way of escaping corruption. Reality is thus depicted as endlessly frustrating, but it is the explosive power of pent-up frustrations that may ultimately lead to relief. The only "solution" or positive experience *Force of Evil* offers is a "solution in feeling," that is, a solution that makes the audience aware of its own anger and the potential to break free and strive for change, in spite of the all but utopian chances to win. [In an endnote, Brinckmann continues: "Whether Polonsky's political strategies in *Force of Evil* can be considered to constitute a Marxist film aesthetics I do not know. It is a question raised in one way or another by most of his critics and interviewers. Polonsky himself has commented on what the attitude of the Hollywood left was in respect to a Marxist aesthetics:

> Their attitudes (about film) reflected—to a certain extent—what was going on in the Soviet Union, which had destroyed the dynamic aes-

thetic movement of its late 1920s. So they thought of aesthetics in terms of social content. To them, the social content of a film *was* its aesthetic. If the Party line of progressive social ideas or progressive subjects were treated in a film—*that* was communist aesthetics. [Talbot and Zheutlin, *Creative Difference*]

Polonsky clearly dissociates himself from this attitude, and justly so, as I hope to have demonstrated."]

If this interpretation sounds overenthusiastic, it is because the flaws of the film have not been discussed. *Force of Evil* is not all it could have been—wrong casting of some of the minor characters (especially Marie Windsor as Tucker's wife) and a few scenes that are too sparse or too sketchy to fulfill their aesthetic functions are shortcomings that could have been avoided. But they are probably due only to the small budget of the film, and they do not seriously detract from its merits. There are, however, a few points that concern the political effect of *Force of Evil,* and these have to be raised.

For one thing, *Force of Evil* has a pregnancy, an over-terseness that makes it difficult to grasp the film's full meaning at first viewing. In the light of its intended political impact, this could be detrimental, and one can argue that Polonsky sacrificed some of the agitational effect of his film in an effort to achieve aesthetic perfection. Instead of making music, words, and images work together, one repeating and elaborating on the message the others convey, he has made his film say different things on different levels simultaneously. Moreover, all of its scenes are short, and nothing is said twice—a policy of communication appropriate for poetry or philosophical discourse, perhaps, but not for a motion picture aimed at an audience accustomed to the redundancy of Hollywood movies and in the habit of seeing a film only once.

A related problem is Polonsky's strategy of using a popular fictional pattern as a vehicle for political content. As the box-office figures indicate, *Force of Evil* did, in fact, alienate its audience, and it is quite conceivable that its mixture of popular appeal and poetical sophistication is responsible for its failure. In the mood for escapist entertainment and expecting to see a gangster movie, the audience may have felt cheated, and many people may have been the less inclined to engage themselves in aesthetic subtleties and ideological analysis.

With a running time of only seventy-eight minutes, *Force of Evil* is also at the lower end of the usual scale. This is partly the result of a few substantial cuts Polonsky made in the course of shooting the film and partly aesthetically motivated. In a letter he wrote to me [dated March 7, 1979], Polonsky commented on his omissions from the original script and his reasons for making them. I shall quote from this letter extensively because it touches on a number of questions raised throughout this article, and also because it refers to a flaw in the film that I shall subsequently discuss.

> Originally, the screenplay began and ended with the court trial. After I shot the first half of the court scene which would then in narrative se-

quence lead to the present film, the original script returned to the court for the conclusion.

Naturally in shooting the courtroom scenes they were scheduled to be shot together. I did the first part of a good section of it as I recall and when I saw the rushes decided this would destroy the entire film so I just junked the whole concept.

My reasons for doing this were aesthetic and political. Aesthetically, it destroyed the continuing sense of the present which I wanted to be the feel of the film. The voice-over took the place of the original mechanical flashback technique and gave the sense of Morse meditating upon the nature of what he was living through, rather than supplying mere narrative elements in the story.

Politically, I didn't want Joe Morse to be co-operating with the police and the law in any way or to be seen doing so. What he was doing was co-operating with what was suppressed in his own nature and in the society in which he found himself. There is just enough dubious hinting for the censors to believe it might be the law of the land he was talking about, but for me, it was the law of history he meant. Naturally, I had no practical suggestions in the film for political organizations since even now as we search, we still don't find.

Of course the elimination of two courtroom scenes made the film shorter. But you must also remember that in those days, films that were an hour or more long were considered long enough and it's only now that the habit of making much longer films has become a feature of the feature film. A feature film, like a novel, should be long enough, but after that, it's either long enough or too long, and the question is aesthetic. I assume that your question means perhaps that you would feel more fulfilled if the film were longer.

I made two other cuts in it. One dealt with the bookkeeper's home life with his wife. I shot that but it seemed extraneous when I edited the film and I left it out. The second part I cut out was a very long scene between Doris and Joe which was a kind of monologue on his part filled with prophecy underlined with personal loneliness. I liked it well enough but in the three or four times I showed the film to audiences, they seemed to find this a place to be very restless. In the end I reduced it to a minimum so that it served merely a narrative function.

While these things shortened the film, I intended not too long a film in the beginning. It was basic to the style and verbal relation with the images. But I did not deliberately make it as short as it became, originally. That happened to it. But it seemed to be all that it had to be, so there I paused.

Two kinds of flaws have to be distinguished in *Force of Evil*: its inability to reach the masses, on the one hand, and its intrinsic shortcomings, on the other. Although not reaching the audience it was initially made for is a serious deficiency, it can be attributed to Polonsky's lack of experience with movie audiences outside New York and Los

Angeles or outside his own political environment. The film has meanwhile proved to have a strong appeal to more sophisticated audiences, and its terseness, experimental nature, and ideological commitment are precisely the qualities responsible for its success.

The film contains, however, one major inconsistency that is bound to weaken its political impact. It is the ambiguity or contradictoriness with which the law and Joe Morse's attitude toward it are treated. On the one hand, the film insinuates that the law is a kind of mirror image of the racket—as impersonal (using the telephone to assert itself), as threatening, and probably as corrupt. On the other, there is no unmistakable evidence of this. Hall, the special prosecutor, never appears on the screen in person, and we have no way of knowing what his real intentions are. It is, however, ideologically inconceivable not to consider the law as part of the "system": Either the law would appear to be so weak as not to deserve anybody's respect or the system would be a minor problem indeed. If Joe decides to cooperate with the law, his decision implies an acknowledgement of the system and, therefore, a denial of all for which his own purification and liberation stand.

Polonsky's statement that he had to compromise in order to pass the censors is an honest and acceptable explanation of this inconsistency. But his additional remark that what he actually meant was the "law of history" is, of course, irrelevant for the audience. Joe Morse's final words, in which he informs us that he "turned back to give myself up to Hall," are much too explicit to be taken metaphorically.

I shall conclude this article with a review that appeared in *Variety* after *Force of Evil* was released in 1948. It is an exemplary document in several respects. The mouthpiece of the movie industry, *Variety* puts its finger on the film's most salient deviations from the usual Hollywood fare, pointing them out as artistic shortcomings instead of political strategies. This may prove how seismographically the response of the audience could be predicted. But it also proves to what degree a critic faithful to the standards of the industry could renounce his or her perceptions, evaluating them contrary to the film's intentions as if the review had been written with tongue in cheek:

> *Force of Evil* fails to develop the excitement hinted at in the title. It's a missout for solid melodramatic entertainment, and will have to depend upon exceptionally strong exploitation and the value of the John Garfield name for box office. Makers apparently couldn't decide on the best way to present an expose of the numbers racket, winding up with neither fish nor fowl as far as hard-hitting racketeer meller is concerned. A poetic, almost allegorical interpretation keeps intruding on the tougher elements of the plot. This factor adds no distinction and only makes the going tougher. [*Variety* (24 December 1948)]

**Terence Butler   (essay date Autumn 1988)**

SOURCE: "Polonsky and Kazan: HUAC and the Violation of Personality," in *Sight and Sound,* Vol. 57, No. 4, Autumn, 1988, pp. 262-67.

[*In the following excerpt from an essay in which he compares the works of Polonsky and Elia Kazan—who cooperated with Joseph McCarthy's House Un-American Activities Committee (HUAC), though he shared many of Polonsky's political ideals—Butler examines the main themes of Polonsky's works, focusing on* Tell Them Willie Boy Is Here *and* Romance of a Horse Thief.]

Abraham Lincoln Polonsky was one of the many casualties of the House Un-American Activities Committee in Hollywood, Elia Kazan a self-justifying collaborator with the same committee; yet their roots in the Communism of the Depression ensure a strong, if contradictory, relationship between their films. Both are central to the political concerns of postwar American cinema. By their time the populism so dear to Frank Capra and John Ford (the little man assailing urban corruption; the independent-mindedness of the frontier) may have been to some degree still culturally pervasive; but such confidence in the power of the people and of the individual was rather misplaced in an America that had witnessed expansion in the big corporations and the spread of McCarthyism.

The work of Polonsky and Kazan is necessarily a search for, as much as an assertion of, value. Each film-maker was led back to an exploration of his—and America's—immigrant prehistory (Polish Jew in Polonsky's case, Greek in Kazan's), the dilemma of HUAC intersecting with that of American identity. For them America was tough, exploitative and—contrary to Horatio Alger myth—took a psychological toll even of those who survived the encounter with it. In such a context HUAC seems not so much an aberration of the American character, involving as it did in the requirement of naming names the setting of self-preservation above personal morality. As Lillian Hellman wrote in one of the less contested statements in her HUAC memoir *Scoundrel Time:* 'The children of timid immigrants are often remarkable people: energetic, intelligent, hardworking; and often they make it so good that they are determined to keep it at any cost.'

Of the two men, Kazan was the first to begin directing films. Yet it was not until after he had named names before HUAC that his work gained force and depth—partly out of his need to account for his changed political position. Kazan's early work is often rather impersonal, too readily revealing the shallow side to the liberalism of pre-HUAC Hollywood—as with *Gentleman's Agreement,* which sees anti-semitism as a matter of individual failing rather than as a social problem. This is not the case with Polonsky: *Body and Soul,* directed in 1947 by Robert Rossen from Polonsky's first solo screenplay, and *Force of Evil,* Polonsky's 1949 directorial debut, are disturbing *film noir* studies of a dangerously power-oriented pro-WASP America with little regard for those who have not made it to the top of the heap. In *Force of Evil*'s Bauer, the frightened Jewish small-time gaming accountant who informs to hoodlums and thuggish police alike, Polonsky diagnosed American society as conductive to the informer even as HUAC was barely under way.

Much of the Communist contribution to Hollywood, particularly that of a more direct kind, now seems sadly unprogressive—such as the wartime scripts of CP luminaries

John Howard Lawson for *Action in the North Atlantic* and Dalton Trumbo for *Tender Comrade,* CP sloganeering merely working to reinforce the simple-minded populism that all war governments like to promote. If a CP member, Polonsky was not largely out to toe any party line. His scripts are particularly striking in the complex way they examine how social roles influence individual motivation, an achievement arguably only matched among CP screenwriters by Richard Collins in his script for Don Siegel's *Riot in Cell Block 11.*

Indeed Freud seems to have influenced Polonsky as much as Marx; and like the also blacklisted liberal director Bernard Vorhaus (*So Young So Bad*), he sees as a major obligation of society the cultivation of an integrated personality in the individual. **Body and Soul** and **Force of Evil** were made under the auspices of John Garfield's short-lived Enterprise studios. Garfield had made his name in the 1930s acting in plays like Clifford Odets' *Golden Boy* at New York's radical and experimental Group Theatre (where Kazan also acted). That Odets was a major influence on Polonsky is acknowledged in the manner **Body and Soul** and **Force of Evil** contribute to the Garfield image, the 'poetic realism' of their dialogue and the former film taking its boxing milieu from *Golden Boy.* As with Odets, Polonsky's socialist commitment proceeds from a conviction of the need to overcome the powerfully divisive impact of the drive for material success on American society.

Before his untimely death at the height of the Hollywood witchhunts, Garfield had made his own the character of the *Golden Boy*-type young man tragically alienated from lower-class origins by the drive for success. Moving towards a desperate plea for social justice, **Force of Evil** is particularly memorable in its handling of the Garfield image. Unable through Jewish origins to attend the right college like his partner in law practice, Garfield's Joe Morse has nevertheless made himself rich working as a prominent hoodlum's lawyer. But Leo, Joe's elder brother, ekes out a living running a small illegal gaming concern that is in danger of being swallowed up by one or other of the large crime organisations; and when Leo dies from a heart attack on being abducted by thugs, Joe is moved to take a stand against the corruption around him.

Revenge sagas—typically involving a hero stung into action by the killing of a family member—proved popular fare for 50s America, perhaps because they provided a diversion from the treachery encouraged by HUAC (Kazan's *On the Waterfront,* Anthony Mann's *The Man from Laramie*); but if **Force of Evil** may have some resemblance to this cycle, it is finally set apart from it by avoidance of cathartic identification with a violent hero. The film's true climax is not Joe's showdown with hoodlums but his awakening to social responsibility at the discovery in the last sequence of his brother's corpse dumped in a grimy waterway. If censorship here necessitated Joe resolving to tell the police all he knows, this is not allowed to diminish the power of the film's close. Since Polonsky has shown the police as hardly capable of clemency, it would seem that Joe may be completely washed up by this action. Thus the film looks forward to the insistence on the broken man as hero of *The Big Knife,* Odets' anti-

Hollywood play of the following year, and to the reckless humanism of **A Season of Fear,** Polonsky's anti-McCarthyist novel ('We're getting so that nothing else counts except survival and I say to hell with survival').

The American CP could hardly be considered to constitute a totalitarian threat, as HUAC asserted: its failings (a reluctance to condemn Stalinism, the branding as heretics of those making alliances with liberals) met with criticism from party members like Polonsky and drove others to leave an already dwindling party. In some part HUAC seems to have been an attempt to bring into disrepute the New Deal of the 1930s—a time when America was sustained not so much by free enterprise as by reforming federal intervention. In any event, most of those blacklisted—whether CP members or otherwise—were no more than liberals and humanists in the New Deal mould. For all the trumpeting about freedom of the individual, the HUAC period was—as suggested by Fred Zinnemann's *High Noon* and Arthur Miller's play *The Crucible*—a time of isolated individuals striving to uphold their principles in the face of the mob.

Some of those of a left-wing background who became friendly witnesses even contributed to the anti-Communist paranoia by claiming that they were simply acting to oppose left-wing totalitarianism. Such a claim fails to stand up. Polonsky exposed its crucial flaw when he asked of Budd Schulberg, Kazan's scriptwriter on *On the Waterfront* and *A Face in the Crowd:* 'Why did he become an informer when they forced him to? Why didn't he become one before they forced him to?' (quoted in *Naming Names,* Victor Navasky). . . .

Blacklisting meant that Polonsky was only ever able to find sporadic creative independence in the American cinema. Even scripts for which he was able to take credit after the blacklist (**Madigan, Avalanche Express**) ended as crudely directed action thrillers, their moral complexity inadequately inflected. Yet, over twenty years after **Force of Evil,** Polonsky did manage to direct **Tell Them Willie Boy Is Here,** one of the best of the self-critical Westerns of the early 1970s; and soon afterwards came **Romance of a Horse Thief** which, like Kazan's *America, America,* has sadly only in France achieved reasonable distribution and found a discerning critical response. If slim, Polonsky's directorial output remains indispensable, particularly for the ease with which it skirts the kind of confusion of values that led Kazan to spiritual emptiness.

**Willie Boy** is about a Paiute Indian who becomes the quarry for a posse when he flees with his girlfriend after accidentally killing her possessive father. The film harks back to such memorable HUAC explorations of scapegoating as Nicholas Ray's *Johnny Guitar* and Alan Dwan's *Silver Lode,* as well as films such as Robert Aldrich's *Kiss Me Deadly* and Rossen's *They Came to Cordura* that—in contrast to much of Kazan's work—responded to HUAC by viewing America's avowals of individualism in terms of a shabby vanity. Polonsky had already dealt with the latter theme in his anti-HUAC novel **A Season of Fear,** an examination of the arrogant and complacent psychology of a government employee whose career advances due to the impact of the blacklist on his department; but *Willie Boy's* elaboration is particularly ambitious: while the majority of the posse's members clothe their actions in a heroic frontier romanticism, they are clearly especially galvanised by the need to put on a show during the visit West of President Taft.

Not only here does Polonsky reject the kind of idealisation of America's past Kazan expressed in his later work: the Paiutes are also incisively portrayed. In becoming a hero to his people, the fugitive Willie confirms them in their insularity and refusal to join the modern world. Polonsky is aware of the problems inherent in identification with a minority. Reacting against feeling an outsider for having worked among whites, Willie is increasingly absorbed by the fanatical, terrorist identification with his people that his predicament invites. Aptly the opposition in the movie's early scenes between Willie and John Vernon's poolhall thug and subsequent posse member echoes Robert Wise's *Odds Against Tomorrow*, which a blacklisted Polonsky clandestinely helped script, where Harry Belafonte's black power acolyte and Robert Ryan's down-at-heel racist work as mirror images of an essentially impotent social disaffection.

In his portrayal of Willie, Polonsky eschews the masochistic identification with the underdog so common in the cinema of Nicholas Ray; and *Willie Boy* also refuses to accord a direct moral authority to those in socially responsible jobs, contrasting with the majority of postwar liberal movies—notably early Kazan movies like *Gentleman's Agreement* and *Panic in the Streets* where society is protected by respectively a journalist and a health inspector. Elizabeth Bowman, the reservation worker, has become as embittered as Willie in her struggle to be an independent woman in what is unfairly a man's world; and prey to a scornful proto-feminism that seems more a reflection of her wealthy upbringing than a valid response to her situation, she instinctively resents Willie and tends to see him simply as a chauvinistic male who has abducted a girl. Such ambivalence towards men also propels Elizabeth to Robert Redford's Marshal Coop, a man of liberal persuasion, but for whom a relationship with her is made something of a test of his manhood by her displays of hostility to him.

If Polonsky may here be recalling a tendency among certain CP colleagues to lose sight of themselves in their political posturing, he does not see hypocrisies in the behaviour of those of a left/liberal persuasion as proof—like Kazan—of the impracticability of what they claim to stand for, or—like Rossen in *Lilith*—of a basic tragic fallibility to people; for him it is that people claiming any persuasion can be divided against themselves in a divided society. Polonsky has always tended to criticise society rather than the individual. This is why if in *Willie Boy* the relationship of Coop and Elizabeth evokes the wanderer-home antinomy familiar to the Western, Polonsky makes no claims about man-woman relationships being inherently antagonistic (as Kazan does in his novels) and portrays this particular relationship as, if not uncommon, capable of being changed.

For all his circumspection, Polonsky finally articulates in *Willie Boy* as strong a trust in the possibility of a straight-

forward humanity as in *Force of Evil*. The vehicle for this is Willie's friend, Lola. Education has given her independent-mindedness and an ability to assimilate into society on her own terms; and she goes with Willie of her own choice, not to conform to tribal dictates. It is thanks to her presence that Willie's violence is more threatened than real. We never know whether Lola dies from her own hand or from Willie's; but it seems that physically incapable of continuing the flight, she may have chosen death in an attempt to stem the anger and bitterness confirming Willie on his trajectory to terrorism. Like Stavros with Hohannes in [Kazan's] *America, America*, Willie could have accepted Lola's death as the price of his survival; but he disconsolately retraces the route they have travelled together, and when Coop kills him, he finds that Willie has faced him with no bullets in his gun. If tragic, Willie's death does provide a way for the humanity of Lola to permeate the relationship of Coop and Elizabeth. When Elizabeth witnesses a dejected Coop wiping Willie's blood from his hands, she seems at once to acknowledge a vulnerability to Coop and to appreciate the sad and lonely nature of Willie's dying.

The tone of *Romance of a Horse Thief* is more relaxed than in Polonsky's previous films. Central to the film is the mellowing of the relationship between the poor Jew Kradnik and the middle-class student revolutionary Naomi—initially, he in embittered isolation like previous Polonsky heroes, she priggish but confused rather like Elizabeth Bowman. Although the film is set in Russian-occupied Poland in the early part of the century, its world is a sunlit one shot through with the type of gentle nature imagery that has often underscored humanism in the American cinema, as in the famous close of Milestone's *All Quiet on the Western Front*—with the reaching out for a butterfly—or in pantheistic New Deal movies like *Our Daily Bread* and *Grapes of Wrath*.

Polonsky's aim is not so much nostalgia for past ideals as the idealisation of the world he portrays. His earlier films deal with the violation of personality, and in *Romance* he fashions a world where it is possible to live without hate, where people find self-respect through respecting one another. In neat antithesis to Kazan's trophy symbolism, Polonsky places a priority on the notion of gift, recalling the eponymous tokens of Mitchell Leisen's *Golden Earrings*—his first script credit—and the yellow scarf given to Lola by Willie which functions as a symbol of his continuing humanity: thus, given a horse by a countess for sexual pleasures, Kradnik does not keep it as a trophy but trades it to acquire a present for Naomi and a dowry for his sister.

Whereas Kazan portrays the family as all too susceptible to the competitive pressures of society, Polonsky is concerned here with reconciliation between generations—a theme evident even in the inception of the film, which was developed by David Opatoshu (who plays Kradnik's father) from short stories by his father. Unlike Kazan in *East of Eden*, *Splendor in the Grass* and *America, America*, Polonsky does not criticise his hero's father for failure to maintain an authority that would seem proper to his role: Kradnik comes to appreciate his father even as a man of compromise, the old man placing the protection of his family above the preservation of patriarchal self-esteem. Thus (unlike the typical Kazan hero) freed from exalted notions of male conduct, Kradnik is not too deeply emotionally scarred by being reduced through deprivation to live by stealing horses.

A contempt for Europe has at times been part of the propaganda of American identity. General Patton's famous speech to troops before the invasion of Sicily imputed a heroic legacy to his Italian and German American soldiers by comparing their European counterparts as the product of stock who failed to emigrate to apparent freedom; and the same equation is at least implicit in *America, America* in the contrast between self-help Stavros and his beaten-down father. In its recognition of the need to respect origins properly, Polonsky's work counters such sentiments. In *A Season of Fear,* Professor Strom, a refugee from Nazi Germany, places value on the notion of exile, having found immigration a depersonalising process and as such one that has left him vulnerable to the intimidation of HUAC. In *Romance* Kradnik is signally spared the compromise of Strom in what for Polonsky is a statement of the liberating potential of socialism.

Kradnik is without the illusions of Kazan's Stavros: initially heading for America to escape conscription in Russia's war with Japan, he lampoons the idea of a heroic destiny awaiting him in the American West. In any event, he returns to rescue Naomi from prison, outwitting Cossack troops with the help of—among others—his father. When Kradnik heads again for the border, it is with a varied crew of friends and relatives—Polonsky's way of saying that America should be for everybody. Their renewed sense of personal worth suggests that these refugees will be able to assimilate into American society on their own terms; unlike Kazan's Greek Americans, they should not need to display ethnicity as a means of hiding from both guilt about origins and a desperate need to be accepted.

Ultimately Kazan and Polonsky provide complementary outlooks of tragedy and potentiality. Of course Kazan may never really have been able to distance himself from his portrayal of heroic posturing and conformity to recognise in this the tragedy of how most people live their lives; yet, as a romantic masquerading as a pragmatist, he seems all the more relevant to the Reagan era, his work telling us much about the evasions of American culture. Although Polonsky would probably be sneered at by many

of today's Marxists with their ambitions to scientific rigour, there is value in his call to America to adopt a humanist rather than epic interpretation of its history. Suspicious of America's romanticisation of its frontier past, he sees a more vital past lying among the poor of Europe who must be accorded their own integrity in the flow of history for America to find genuine self-respect. HUAC may have scored its victories, but the spirit of John Garfield still waits to find peace.

---

## FURTHER READING

### Criticism

Canham, Kingsley. "Polonsky: Back Into the Light." *Film,* No. 58 (Spring 1970): 12-15.

> Overview of Polonsky's life and career, focusing on *Force of Evil* and *Tell Them Willie Boy Is Here.*

Cannon, Lee E. Review of *The World Above,* by Abraham Polonsky. *The Christian Century* 68 (2 May 1951): 561-62.

> Favorable discussion of *The World Above,* in which the critic finds the novel written with insight, emotion, and honesty.

Crowther, Bosley. Review of *Body and Soul,* by Abraham Polonsky. *The New York Times* (10 November 1947): 21.

> Favorably comments on Polonsky's screenwriting and Robert Rossen's direction of *Body and Soul.*

Pechter, William. "Parts of Some Time Spent with Abraham Polonsky." *Film Quarterly* XXI, No. 2 (Winter 1968-1969): 14-19.

> Recounts a day on the set of *Tell Them Willie Boy Is Here,* presenting Polonsky's comments on various performance and technical aspects of filmmaking.

Zheutlin, Barbara, and Talbot, David. "Abraham Polonsky." *Creative Differences: Profiles of Hollywood Dissidents.* Boston: South End Press, 1978, pp. 55-99.

> Overview of Polonsky's life and career, including discussion of his education, introduction to Hollywood, political and artistic development, and work during and after being blacklisted.

---

Additional coverage of Polonsky's life and career is contained in the following sources published by Gale Research: *Contemporary Authors,* Vol. 104; and *Dictionary of Literary Biography,* Vol. 26.

# ☐ Contemporary
Literary Criticism

## Indexes

Literary Criticism Series
Cumulative Author Index
Cumulative Topic Index
Cumulative Nationality Index
Title Index, Volume 92

# How to Use This Index

## The main references

### list all author entries in the following Gale Literary Criticism series:

*BLC* = *Black Literature Criticism*
*CLC* = *Contemporary Literary Criticism*
*CLR* = *Children's Literature Review*
*CMLC* = *Classical and Medieval Literature Criticism*
*DA* = *DISCovering Authors*
*DC* = *Drama Criticism*
*HLC* = *Hispanic Literature Criticism*
*LC* = *Literature Criticism from 1400 to 1800*
*NCLC* = *Nineteenth-Century Literature Criticism*
*PC* = *Poetry Criticism*
*SSC* = *Short Story Criticism*
*TCLC* = *Twentieth-Century Literary Criticism*
*WLC* = *World Literature Criticism, 1500 to the Present*

## The cross-references

### list all author entries in the following Gale biographical and literary sources:

*AAYA* = *Authors & Artists for Young Adults*
*AITN* = *Authors in the News*
*BEST* = *Bestsellers*
*BW* = *Black Writers*
*CA* = *Contemporary Authors*
*CAAS* = *Contemporary Authors Autobiography Series*
*CABS* = *Contemporary Authors Bibliographical Series*
*CANR* = *Contemporary Authors New Revision Series*
*CAP* = *Contemporary Authors Permanent Series*
*CDALB* = *Concise Dictionary of American Literary Biography*
*CDBLB* = *Concise Dictionary of British Literary Biography*
*DLB* = *Dictionary of Literary Biography*
*DLBD* = *Dictionary of Literary Biography Documentary Series*
*DLBY* = *Dictionary of Literary Biography Yearbook*
*HW* = *Hispanic Writers*
*JRDA* = *Junior DISCovering Authors*
*MAICYA* = *Major Authors and Illustrators for Children and Young Adults*
*MTCW* = *Major 20th-Century Writers*
*NNAL* = *Native North American Literature*
*SAAS* = *Something about the Author Autobiography Series*
*SATA* = *Something about the Author*
*YABC* = *Yesterday's Authors of Books for Children*

**A. E.** . . . . . . . . . . . . . . . . . . . . . . . . **TCLC 3, 10**
See also Russell, George William

**Abasiyanik, Sait Faik** 1906-1954
See Sait Faik
See also CA 123

**Abbey, Edward** 1927-1989 . . . . . . **CLC 36, 59**
See also CA 45-48; 128; CANR 2, 41

**Abbott, Lee K(ittredge)** 1947- . . . . . . **CLC 48**
See also CA 124; CANR 51; DLB 130

**Abe, Kobo** 1924-1993 . . . . . **CLC 8, 22, 53, 81**
See also CA 65-68; 140; CANR 24;
DAM NOV; MTCW

**Abelard, Peter** c. 1079-c. 1142 . . . **CMLC 11**
See also DLB 115

**Abell, Kjeld** 1901-1961 . . . . . . . . . . . **CLC 15**
See also CA 111

**Abish, Walter** 1931- . . . . . . . . . . . . . . **CLC 22**
See also CA 101; CANR 37; DLB 130

**Abrahams, Peter (Henry)** 1919- . . . . . **CLC 4**
See also BW 1; CA 57-60; CANR 26;
DLB 117; MTCW

**Abrams, M(eyer) H(oward)** 1912- . . . **CLC 24**
See also CA 57-60; CANR 13, 33; DLB 67

**Abse, Dannie** 1923- . . . . . . . . **CLC 7, 29; DAB**
See also CA 53-56; CAAS 1; CANR 4, 46;
DAM POET; DLB 27

**Achebe, (Albert) Chinua(lumogu)**
1930- . . . . . **CLC 1, 3, 5, 7, 11, 26, 51, 75;**
**BLC; DA; DAB; DAC; WLC**
See also AAYA 15; BW 2; CA 1-4R;
CANR 6, 26, 47; CLR 20; DAM MST,
MULT, NOV; DLB 117; MAICYA;
MTCW; SATA 40; SATA-Brief 38

**Acker, Kathy** 1948- . . . . . . . . . . . . . . **CLC 45**
See also CA 117; 122

**Ackroyd, Peter** 1949- . . . . . . . . . . **CLC 34, 52**
See also CA 123; 127; CANR 51; DLB 155;
INT 127

**Acorn, Milton** 1923- . . . . . . . . **CLC 15; DAC**
See also CA 103; DLB 53; INT 103

**Adamov, Arthur** 1908-1970 . . . . . **CLC 4, 25**
See also CA 17-18; 25-28R; CAP 2;
DAM DRAM; MTCW

**Adams, Alice (Boyd)** 1926- . . **CLC 6, 13, 46**
See also CA 81-84; CANR 26; DLBY 86;
INT CANR-26; MTCW

**Adams, Andy** 1859-1935 . . . . . . . . . **TCLC 56**
See also YABC 1

**Adams, Douglas (Noel)** 1952- . . . **CLC 27, 60**
See also AAYA 4; BEST 89:3; CA 106;
CANR 34; DAM POP; DLBY 83; JRDA

**Adams, Francis** 1862-1893 . . . . . . . **NCLC 33**

**Adams, Henry (Brooks)**
1838-1918 . . . . . . **TCLC 4, 52; DA; DAB;**
**DAC**
See also CA 104; 133; DAM MST; DLB 12,
47

**Adams, Richard (George)**
1920- . . . . . . . . . . . . . . . . . **CLC 4, 5, 18**
See also AAYA 16; AITN 1, 2; CA 49-52;
CANR 3, 35; CLR 20; DAM NOV;
JRDA; MAICYA; MTCW; SATA 7, 69

**Adamson, Joy(-Friederike Victoria)**
1910-1980 . . . . . . . . . . . . . . . . . . **CLC 17**
See also CA 69-72; 93-96; CANR 22;
MTCW; SATA 11; SATA-Obit 22

**Adcock, Fleur** 1934- . . . . . . . . . . . . . **CLC 41**
See also CA 25-28R; CAAS 23; CANR 11,
34; DLB 40

**Addams, Charles (Samuel)**
1912-1988 . . . . . . . . . . . . . . . . . . **CLC 30**
See also CA 61-64; 126; CANR 12

**Addison, Joseph** 1672-1719 . . . . . . . . . **LC 18**
See also CDBLB 1660-1789; DLB 101

**Adler, Alfred (F.)** 1870-1937 . . . . . **TCLC 61**
See also CA 119

**Adler, C(arole) S(chwerdtfeger)**
1932- . . . . . . . . . . . . . . . . . . . . . . **CLC 35**
See also AAYA 4; CA 89-92; CANR 19,
40; JRDA; MAICYA; SAAS 15;
SATA 26, 63

**Adler, Renata** 1938- . . . . . . . . . . . **CLC 8, 31**
See also CA 49-52; CANR 5, 22; MTCW

**Ady, Endre** 1877-1919 . . . . . . . . . . . **TCLC 11**
See also CA 107

**Aeschylus**
525B.C.-456B.C. . . . . . . . . **CMLC 11; DA;**
**DAB; DAC**
See also DAM DRAM, MST

**Afton, Effie**
See Harper, Frances Ellen Watkins

**Agapida, Fray Antonio**
See Irving, Washington

**Agee, James (Rufus)**
1909-1955 . . . . . . . . . . . . . . . **TCLC 1, 19**
See also AITN 1; CA 108; 148;
CDALB 1941-1968; DAM NOV; DLB 2,
26, 152

**Aghill, Gordon**
See Silverberg, Robert

**Agnon, S(hmuel) Y(osef Halevi)**
1888-1970 . . . . . . . . . . . . . . **CLC 4, 8, 14**
See also CA 17-18; 25-28R; CAP 2; MTCW

**Agrippa von Nettesheim, Henry Cornelius**
1486-1535 . . . . . . . . . . . . . . . . . . **LC 27**

**Aherne, Owen**
See Cassill, R(onald) V(erlin)

**Ai** 1947- . . . . . . . . . . . . . . . . . . **CLC 4, 14, 69**
See also CA 85-88; CAAS 13; DLB 120

**Aickman, Robert (Fordyce)**
1914-1981 . . . . . . . . . . . . . . . . . . **CLC 57**
See also CA 5-8R; CANR 3

**Aiken, Conrad (Potter)**
1889-1973 . . . **CLC 1, 3, 5, 10, 52; SSC 9**
See also CA 5-8R; 45-48; CANR 4;
CDALB 1929-1941; DAM NOV, POET;
DLB 9, 45, 102; MTCW; SATA 3, 30

**Aiken, Joan (Delano)** 1924- . . . . . . . **CLC 35**
See also AAYA 1; CA 9-12R; CANR 4, 23,
34; CLR 1, 19; DLB 161; JRDA;
MAICYA; MTCW; SAAS 1; SATA 2,
30, 73

**Ainsworth, William Harrison**
1805-1882 . . . . . . . . . . . . . . . . . **NCLC 13**
See also DLB 21; SATA 24

**Aitmatov, Chingiz (Torekulovich)**
1928- . . . . . . . . . . . . . . . . . . . . . . **CLC 71**
See also CA 103; CANR 38; MTCW;
SATA 56

**Akers, Floyd**
See Baum, L(yman) Frank

**Akhmadulina, Bella Akhatovna**
1937- . . . . . . . . . . . . . . . . . . . . . . **CLC 53**
See also CA 65-68; DAM POET

**Akhmatova, Anna**
1888-1966 . . . . . . . **CLC 11, 25, 64; PC 2**
See also CA 19-20; 25-28R; CANR 35;
CAP 1; DAM POET; MTCW

**Aksakov, Sergei Timofeyvich**
1791-1859 . . . . . . . . . . . . . . . . . **NCLC 2**

**Aksenov, Vassily**
See Aksyonov, Vassily (Pavlovich)

**Aksyonov, Vassily (Pavlovich)**
1932- . . . . . . . . . . . . . . . . . . . **CLC 22, 37**
See also CA 53-56; CANR 12, 48

**Akutagawa Ryunosuke**
1892-1927 . . . . . . . . . . . . . . . . . **TCLC 16**
See also CA 117

**Alain** 1868-1951 . . . . . . . . . . . . . . . **TCLC 41**

**Alain-Fournier** . . . . . . . . . . . . . . . . . . **TCLC 6**
See also Fournier, Henri Alban
See also DLB 65

**Alarcon, Pedro Antonio de**
1833-1891 . . . . . . . . . . . . . . . . . . **NCLC 1**

**Alas (y Urena), Leopoldo (Enrique Garcia)**
1852-1901 . . . . . . . . . . . . . . . . . **TCLC 29**
See also CA 113; 131; HW

**Albee, Edward (Franklin III)**
1928- . . . . . . **CLC 1, 2, 3, 5, 9, 11, 13, 25,**
**53, 86; DA; DAB; DAC; WLC**
See also AITN 1; CA 5-8R; CABS 3;
CANR 8; CDALB 1941-1968;
DAM DRAM, MST; DLB 7;
INT CANR-8; MTCW

**Alberti, Rafael** 1902- . . . . . . . . . . . . . **CLC 7**
See also CA 85-88; DLB 108

**Albert the Great** 1200(?)-1280 . . . . **CMLC 16**
See also DLB 115

**Alcala-Galiano, Juan Valera y**
See Valera y Alcala-Galiano, Juan

**Alcott, Amos Bronson** 1799-1888 . . **NCLC 1**
See also DLB 1

**Alcott, Louisa May**
1832-1888 . . . . . . . **NCLC 6; DA; DAB;**
**DAC; WLC**
See also CDALB 1865-1917; CLR 1, 38;
DAM MST, NOV; DLB 1, 42, 79; JRDA;
MAICYA; YABC 1

**Aldanov, M. A.**
See Aldanov, Mark (Alexandrovich)

**Aldanov, Mark (Alexandrovich)**
1886(?)-1957 . . . . . . . . . . . . . . . **TCLC 23**
See also CA 118

**Aldington, Richard** 1892-1962 . . . . . . **CLC 49**
See also CA 85-88; CANR 45; DLB 20, 36,
100, 149

**Aldiss, Brian W(ilson)**
1925- . . . . . . . . . . . . . . . . . **CLC 5, 14, 40**
See also CA 5-8R; CAAS 2; CANR 5, 28;
DAM NOV; DLB 14; MTCW; SATA 34

**Alegria, Claribel** 1924- . . . . . . . . . . . **CLC 75**
See also CA 131; CAAS 15; DAM MULT;
DLB 145; HW

**Alegria, Fernando** 1918- . . . . . . . . . . . **CLC 57**
See also CA 9-12R; CANR 5, 32; HW

**Aleichem, Sholom** . . . . . . . . . . . . . . **TCLC 1, 35**
See also Rabinovitch, Sholem

**Aleixandre, Vicente**
1898-1984 . . . . . . . . . **CLC 9, 36; PC 15**
See also CA 85-88; 114; CANR 26;
DAM POET; DLB 108; HW; MTCW

**Alepoudelis, Odysseus**
See Elytis, Odysseus

**Aleshkovsky, Joseph** 1929-
See Aleshkovsky, Yuz
See also CA 121; 128

**Aleshkovsky, Yuz** . . . . . . . . . . . . . . . **CLC 44**
See also Aleshkovsky, Joseph

**Alexander, Lloyd (Chudley)** 1924- . . **CLC 35**
See also AAYA 1; CA 1-4R; CANR 1, 24,
38; CLR 1, 5; DLB 52; JRDA; MAICYA;
MTCW; SAAS 19; SATA 3, 49, 81

**Alfau, Felipe** 1902- . . . . . . . . . . . . . . **CLC 66**
See also CA 137

**Alger, Horatio, Jr.** 1832-1899 . . . . . **NCLC 8**
See also DLB 42; SATA 16

**Algren, Nelson** 1909-1981 . . . . **CLC 4, 10, 33**
See also CA 13-16R; 103; CANR 20;
CDALB 1941-1968; DLB 9; DLBY 81,
82; MTCW

**Ali, Ahmed** 1910- . . . . . . . . . . . . . . . **CLC 69**
See also CA 25-28R; CANR 15, 34

**Alighieri, Dante** 1265-1321 . . . . . . . **CMLC 3**

**Allan, John B.**
See Westlake, Donald E(dwin)

**Allen, Edward** 1948- . . . . . . . . . . . . . **CLC 59**

**Allen, Paula Gunn** 1939- . . . . . . . . . . **CLC 84**
See also CA 112; 143; DAM MULT;
NNAL

**Allen, Roland**
See Ayckbourn, Alan

**Allen, Sarah A.**
See Hopkins, Pauline Elizabeth

**Allen, Woody** 1935- . . . . . . . . . . **CLC 16, 52**
See also AAYA 10; CA 33-36R; CANR 27,
38; DAM POP; DLB 44; MTCW

**Allende, Isabel** 1942- . . . . **CLC 39, 57; HLC**
See also CA 125; 130; CANR 51;
DAM MULT, NOV; DLB 145; HW;
INT 130; MTCW

**Alleyn, Ellen**
See Rossetti, Christina (Georgina)

**Allingham, Margery (Louise)**
1904-1966 . . . . . . . . . . . . . . . . . **CLC 19**
See also CA 5-8R; 25-28R; CANR 4;
DLB 77; MTCW

**Allingham, William** 1824-1889 . . . **NCLC 25**
See also DLB 35

**Allison, Dorothy E.** 1949- . . . . . . . . . **CLC 78**
See also CA 140

**Allston, Washington** 1779-1843 . . . . **NCLC 2**
See also DLB 1

**Almedingen, E. M.** . . . . . . . . . . . . . . . **CLC 12**
See also Almedingen, Martha Edith von
See also SATA 3

**Almedingen, Martha Edith von** 1898-1971
See Almedingen, E. M.
See also CA 1-4R; CANR 1

**Almqvist, Carl Jonas Love**
1793-1866 . . . . . . . . . . . . . . . . . **NCLC 42**

**Alonso, Damaso** 1898-1990 . . . . . . . . **CLC 14**
See also CA 110; 131; 130; DLB 108; HW

**Alov**
See Gogol, Nikolai (Vasilyevich)

**Alta** 1942- . . . . . . . . . . . . . . . . . . . . . **CLC 19**
See also CA 57-60

**Alter, Robert B(ernard)** 1935- . . . . . . **CLC 34**
See also CA 49-52; CANR 1, 47

**Alther, Lisa** 1944- . . . . . . . . . . . . . . **CLC 7, 41**
See also CA 65-68; CANR 12, 30, 51;
MTCW

**Altman, Robert** 1925- . . . . . . . . . . . . . **CLC 16**
See also CA 73-76; CANR 43

**Alvarez, A(lfred)** 1929- . . . . . . . . . . **CLC 5, 13**
See also CA 1-4R; CANR 3, 33; DLB 14,
40

**Alvarez, Alejandro Rodriguez** 1903-1965
See Casona, Alejandro
See also CA 131; 93-96; HW

**Alvaro, Corrado** 1896-1956 . . . . . . . **TCLC 60**

**Amado, Jorge** 1912- . . . . . . **CLC 13, 40; HLC**
See also CA 77-80; CANR 35;
DAM MULT, NOV; DLB 113; MTCW

**Ambler, Eric** 1909- . . . . . . . . . . . . **CLC 4, 6, 9**
See also CA 9-12R; CANR 7, 38; DLB 77;
MTCW

**Amichai, Yehuda** 1924- . . . . . . **CLC 9, 22, 57**
See also CA 85-88; CANR 46; MTCW

**Amiel, Henri Frederic** 1821-1881 . . **NCLC 4**

**Amis, Kingsley (William)**
1922-1995 . . . . . **CLC 1, 2, 3, 5, 8, 13, 40,**
**44; DA; DAB; DAC**
See also AITN 2; CA 9-12R; 150; CANR 8,
28; CDBLB 1945-1960; DAM MST,
NOV; DLB 15, 27, 100, 139;
INT CANR-8; MTCW

**Amis, Martin (Louis)**
1949- . . . . . . . . . . . . . . . **CLC 4, 9, 38, 62**
See also BEST 90:3; CA 65-68; CANR 8,
27; DLB 14; INT CANR-27

**Ammons, A(rchie) R(andolph)**
1926- . . . . . . . . . **CLC 2, 3, 5, 8, 9, 25, 57**
See also AITN 1; CA 9-12R; CANR 6, 36,
51; DAM POET; DLB 5; MTCW

**Amo, Tauraatua i**
See Adams, Henry (Brooks)

**Anand, Mulk Raj** 1905- . . . . . . . . . . . **CLC 23**
See also CA 65-68; CANR 32; DAM NOV;
MTCW

**Anatol**
See Schnitzler, Arthur

**Anaya, Rudolfo A(lfonso)**
1937- . . . . . . . . . . . . . . . . . **CLC 23; HLC**
See also CA 45-48; CAAS 4; CANR 1, 32,
51; DAM MULT, NOV; DLB 82; HW 1;
MTCW

**Andersen, Hans Christian**
1805-1875 . . . . . . . . **NCLC 7; DA; DAB;**
**DAC; SSC 6; WLC**
See also CLR 6; DAM MST, POP;
MAICYA; YABC 1

**Anderson, C. Farley**
See Mencken, H(enry) L(ouis); Nathan,
George Jean

**Anderson, Jessica (Margaret) Queale**
. . . . . . . . . . . . . . . . . . . . . . . . . . **CLC 37**
See also CA 9-12R; CANR 4

**Anderson, Jon (Victor)** 1940- . . . . . . . **CLC 9**
See also CA 25-28R; CANR 20;
DAM POET

**Anderson, Lindsay (Gordon)**
1923-1994 . . . . . . . . . . . . . . . . . **CLC 20**
See also CA 125; 128; 146

**Anderson, Maxwell** 1888-1959 . . . . . **TCLC 2**
See also CA 105; DAM DRAM; DLB 7

**Anderson, Poul (William)** 1926- . . . . **CLC 15**
See also AAYA 5; CA 1-4R; CAAS 2;
CANR 2, 15, 34; DLB 8; INT CANR-15;
MTCW; SATA-Brief 39

**Anderson, Robert (Woodruff)**
1917- . . . . . . . . . . . . . . . . . . . . . **CLC 23**
See also AITN 1; CA 21-24R; CANR 32;
DAM DRAM; DLB 7

**Anderson, Sherwood**
1876-1941 . . . . . . . . **TCLC 1, 10, 24; DA;**
**DAB; DAC; SSC 1; WLC**
See also CA 104; 121; CDALB 1917-1929;
DAM MST, NOV; DLB 4, 9, 86;
DLBD 1; MTCW

**Andouard**
See Giraudoux, (Hippolyte) Jean

**Andrade, Carlos Drummond de** . . . . . . **CLC 18**
See also Drummond de Andrade, Carlos

**Andrade, Mario de** 1893-1945 . . . . . **TCLC 43**

**Andreae, Johann V.** 1586-1654 . . . . . . **LC 32**

**Andreas-Salome, Lou** 1861-1937 . . . **TCLC 56**
See also DLB 66

**Andrewes, Lancelot** 1555-1626 . . . . . . . **LC 5**
See also DLB 151

**Andrews, Cicily Fairfield**
See West, Rebecca

**Andrews, Elton V.**
    See Pohl, Frederik

**Andreyev, Leonid (Nikolaevich)**
    1871-1919 ................... **TCLC 3**
    See also CA 104

**Andric, Ivo** 1892-1975 ............. **CLC 8**
    See also CA 81-84; 57-60; CANR 43;
    DLB 147; MTCW

**Angelique, Pierre**
    See Bataille, Georges

**Angell, Roger** 1920- ............. **CLC 26**
    See also CA 57-60; CANR 13, 44

**Angelou, Maya**
    1928- .... **CLC 12, 35, 64, 77; BLC; DA;**
                                      **DAB; DAC**
    See also AAYA 7; BW 2; CA 65-68;
    CANR 19, 42; DAM MST, MULT,
    POET, POP; DLB 38; MTCW; SATA 49

**Annensky, Innokenty Fyodorovich**
    1856-1909 ................. **TCLC 14**
    See also CA 110

**Anon, Charles Robert**
    See Pessoa, Fernando (Antonio Nogueira)

**Anouilh, Jean (Marie Lucien Pierre)**
    1910-1987 ...... **CLC 1, 3, 8, 13, 40, 50**
    See also CA 17-20R; 123; CANR 32;
    DAM DRAM; MTCW

**Anthony, Florence**
    See Ai

**Anthony, John**
    See Ciardi, John (Anthony)

**Anthony, Peter**
    See Shaffer, Anthony (Joshua); Shaffer,
    Peter (Levin)

**Anthony, Piers** 1934- ............. **CLC 35**
    See also AAYA 11; CA 21-24R; CANR 28;
    DAM POP; DLB 8; MTCW; SAAS 22;
    SATA 84

**Antoine, Marc**
    See Proust, (Valentin-Louis-George-Eugene-)
    Marcel

**Antoninus, Brother**
    See Everson, William (Oliver)

**Antonioni, Michelangelo** 1912- ..... **CLC 20**
    See also CA 73-76; CANR 45

**Antschel, Paul** 1920-1970
    See Celan, Paul
    See also CA 85-88; CANR 33; MTCW

**Anwar, Chairil** 1922-1949 ........ **TCLC 22**
    See also CA 121

**Apollinaire, Guillaume** .. **TCLC 3, 8, 51; PC 7**
    See also Kostrowitzki, Wilhelm Apollinaris
    de
    See also DAM POET

**Appelfeld, Aharon** 1932- ....... **CLC 23, 47**
    See also CA 112; 133

**Apple, Max (Isaac)** 1941-........ **CLC 9, 33**
    See also CA 81-84; CANR 19; DLB 130

**Appleman, Philip (Dean)** 1926- ..... **CLC 51**
    See also CA 13-16R; CAAS 18; CANR 6,
    29

**Appleton, Lawrence**
    See Lovecraft, H(oward) P(hillips)

**Apteryx**
    See Eliot, T(homas) S(tearns)

**Apuleius, (Lucius Madaurensis)**
    125(?)-175(?) ............... **CMLC 1**

**Aquin, Hubert** 1929-1977......... **CLC 15**
    See also CA 105; DLB 53

**Aragon, Louis** 1897-1982........ **CLC 3, 22**
    See also CA 69-72; 108; CANR 28;
    DAM NOV, POET; DLB 72; MTCW

**Arany, Janos** 1817-1882........ **NCLC 34**

**Arbuthnot, John** 1667-1735.......... **LC 1**
    See also DLB 101

**Archer, Herbert Winslow**
    See Mencken, H(enry) L(ouis)

**Archer, Jeffrey (Howard)** 1940- .... **CLC 28**
    See also AAYA 16; BEST 89:3; CA 77-80;
    CANR 22; DAM POP; INT CANR-22

**Archer, Jules** 1915- ............. **CLC 12**
    See also CA 9-12R; CANR 6; SAAS 5;
    SATA 4, 85

**Archer, Lee**
    See Ellison, Harlan (Jay)

**Arden, John** 1930- .......... **CLC 6, 13, 15**
    See also CA 13-16R; CAAS 4; CANR 31;
    DAM DRAM; DLB 13; MTCW

**Arenas, Reinaldo**
    1943-1990 ............. **CLC 41; HLC**
    See also CA 124; 128; 133; DAM MULT;
    DLB 145; HW

**Arendt, Hannah** 1906-1975 ........ **CLC 66**
    See also CA 17-20R; 61-64; CANR 26;
    MTCW

**Aretino, Pietro** 1492-1556 .......... **LC 12**

**Arghezi, Tudor**.................... **CLC 80**
    See also Theodorescu, Ion N.

**Arguedas, Jose Maria**
    1911-1969 ............... **CLC 10, 18**
    See also CA 89-92; DLB 113; HW

**Argueta, Manlio** 1936-............ **CLC 31**
    See also CA 131; DLB 145; HW

**Ariosto, Ludovico** 1474-1533........ **LC 6**

**Aristides**
    See Epstein, Joseph

**Aristophanes**
    450B.C.-385B.C......... **CMLC 4; DA;**
                                 **DAB; DAC; DC 2**
    See also DAM DRAM, MST

**Arlt, Roberto (Godofredo Christophersen)**
    1900-1942 ............ **TCLC 29; HLC**
    See also CA 123; 131; DAM MULT; HW

**Armah, Ayi Kwei** 1939-.... **CLC 5, 33; BLC**
    See also BW 1; CA 61-64; CANR 21;
    DAM MULT, POET; DLB 117; MTCW

**Armatrading, Joan** 1950-.......... **CLC 17**
    See also CA 114

**Arnette, Robert**
    See Silverberg, Robert

**Arnim, Achim von (Ludwig Joachim von**
    **Arnim)** 1781-1831 ......... **NCLC 5**
    See also DLB 90

**Arnim, Bettina von** 1785-1859.... **NCLC 38**
    See also DLB 90

**Arnold, Matthew**
    1822-1888 ..... **NCLC 6, 29; DA; DAB;**
                                 **DAC; PC 5; WLC**
    See also CDBLB 1832-1890; DAM MST,
    POET; DLB 32, 57

**Arnold, Thomas** 1795-1842 ...... **NCLC 18**
    See also DLB 55

**Arnow, Harriette (Louisa) Simpson**
    1908-1986 ............... **CLC 2, 7, 18**
    See also CA 9-12R; 118; CANR 14; DLB 6;
    MTCW; SATA 42; SATA-Obit 47

**Arp, Hans**
    See Arp, Jean

**Arp, Jean** 1887-1966................. **CLC 5**
    See also CA 81-84; 25-28R; CANR 42

**Arrabal**
    See Arrabal, Fernando

**Arrabal, Fernando** 1932- ... **CLC 2, 9, 18, 58**
    See also CA 9-12R; CANR 15

**Arrick, Fran**..................... **CLC 30**
    See also Gaberman, Judie Angell

**Artaud, Antonin (Marie Joseph)**
    1896-1948 ................ **TCLC 3, 36**
    See also CA 104; 149; DAM DRAM

**Arthur, Ruth M(abel)** 1905-1979.... **CLC 12**
    See also CA 9-12R; 85-88; CANR 4;
    SATA 7, 26

**Artsybashev, Mikhail (Petrovich)**
    1878-1927 ................. **TCLC 31**

**Arundel, Honor (Morfydd)**
    1919-1973 ................. **CLC 17**
    See also CA 21-22; 41-44R; CAP 2;
    CLR 35; SATA 4; SATA-Obit 24

**Asch, Sholem** 1880-1957 .......... **TCLC 3**
    See also CA 105

**Ash, Shalom**
    See Asch, Sholem

**Ashbery, John (Lawrence)**
    1927- ...... **CLC 2, 3, 4, 6, 9, 13, 15, 25,**
                                         **41, 77**
    See also CA 5-8R; CANR 9, 37;
    DAM POET; DLB 5; DLBY 81;
    INT CANR-9; MTCW

**Ashdown, Clifford**
    See Freeman, R(ichard) Austin

**Ashe, Gordon**
    See Creasey, John

**Ashton-Warner, Sylvia (Constance)**
    1908-1984 ................... **CLC 19**
    See also CA 69-72; 112; CANR 29; MTCW

**Asimov, Isaac**
    1920-1992 ... **CLC 1, 3, 9, 19, 26, 76, 92**
    See also AAYA 13; BEST 90:2; CA 1-4R;
    137; CANR 2, 19, 36; CLR 12;
    DAM POP; DLB 8; DLBY 92;
    INT CANR-19; JRDA; MAICYA;
    MTCW; SATA 1, 26, 74

**Astley, Thea (Beatrice May)**
    1925- ..................... **CLC 41**
    See also CA 65-68; CANR 11, 43

**Aston, James**
    See White, T(erence) H(anbury)

**Balzac, Honore de**
1799-1850 . . . . . . . **NCLC 5, 35, 53; DA; DAB; DAC; SSC 5; WLC**
See also DAM MST, NOV; DLB 119

**Bambara, Toni Cade**
1939-1995 . . . . . **CLC 19, 88; BLC; DA; DAC**
See also AAYA 5; BW 2; CA 29-32R; 150; CANR 24, 49; DAM MST, MULT; DLB 38; MTCW

**Bamdad, A.**
See Shamlu, Ahmad

**Banat, D. R.**
See Bradbury, Ray (Douglas)

**Bancroft, Laura**
See Baum, L(yman) Frank

**Banim, John** 1798-1842 . . . . . . . . NCLC 13
See also DLB 116, 158, 159

**Banim, Michael** 1796-1874 . . . . . . NCLC 13
See also DLB 158, 159

**Banks, Iain**
See Banks, Iain M(enzies)

**Banks, Iain M(enzies)** 1954- . . . . . . . CLC 34
See also CA 123; 128; INT 128

**Banks, Lynne Reid** . . . . . . . . . . . . . . . CLC 23
See also Reid Banks, Lynne
See also AAYA 6

**Banks, Russell** 1940- . . . . . . . . . CLC 37, 72
See also CA 65-68; CAAS 15; CANR 19; DLB 130

**Banville, John** 1945- . . . . . . . . . . . . . . CLC 46
See also CA 117; 128; DLB 14; INT 128

**Banville, Theodore (Faullain) de**
1832-1891 . . . . . . . . . . . . . . . . . . NCLC 9

**Baraka, Amiri**
1934- . . . . . . . . **CLC 1, 2, 3, 5, 10, 14, 33; BLC; DA; DAC; DC 6; PC 4**
See also Jones, LeRoi
See also BW 2; CA 21-24R; CABS 3; CANR 27, 38; CDALB 1941-1968; DAM MST, MULT, POET, POP; DLB 5, 7, 16, 38; DLBD 8; MTCW

**Barbauld, Anna Laetitia**
1743-1825 . . . . . . . . . . . . . . . . NCLC 50
See also DLB 107, 109, 142, 158

**Barbellion, W. N. P.** . . . . . . . . . . . . . . TCLC 24
See also Cummings, Bruce F(rederick)

**Barbera, Jack (Vincent)** 1945- . . . . . CLC 44
See also CA 110; CANR 45

**Barbey d'Aurevilly, Jules Amedee**
1808-1889 . . . . . . . . . . NCLC 1; SSC 17
See also DLB 119

**Barbusse, Henri** 1873-1935 . . . . . . . TCLC 5
See also CA 105; DLB 65

**Barclay, Bill**
See Moorcock, Michael (John)

**Barclay, William Ewert**
See Moorcock, Michael (John)

**Barea, Arturo** 1897-1957 . . . . . . . . TCLC 14
See also CA 111

**Barfoot, Joan** 1946- . . . . . . . . . . . . . CLC 18
See also CA 105

**Baring, Maurice** 1874-1945 . . . . . . . . TCLC 8
See also CA 105; DLB 34

**Barker, Clive** 1952- . . . . . . . . . . . . . CLC 52
See also AAYA 10; BEST 90:3; CA 121; 129; DAM POP; INT 129; MTCW

**Barker, George Granville**
1913-1991 . . . . . . . . . . . . . . . CLC 8, 48
See also CA 9-12R; 135; CANR 7, 38; DAM POET; DLB 20; MTCW

**Barker, Harley Granville**
See Granville-Barker, Harley
See also DLB 10

**Barker, Howard** 1946- . . . . . . . . . . . . CLC 37
See also CA 102; DLB 13

**Barker, Pat(ricia)** 1943- . . . . . . . CLC 32, 91
See also CA 117; 122; CANR 50; INT 122

**Barlow, Joel** 1754-1812 . . . . . . . . . NCLC 23
See also DLB 37

**Barnard, Mary (Ethel)** 1909- . . . . . . . CLC 48
See also CA 21-22; CAP 2

**Barnes, Djuna**
1892-1982 . . . **CLC 3, 4, 8, 11, 29; SSC 3**
See also CA 9-12R; 107; CANR 16; DLB 4, 9, 45; MTCW

**Barnes, Julian** 1946- . . . . . . . . . CLC 42; DAB
See also CA 102; CANR 19; DLBY 93

**Barnes, Peter** 1931- . . . . . . . . . . . . CLC 5, 56
See also CA 65-68; CAAS 12; CANR 33, 34; DLB 13; MTCW

**Baroja (y Nessi), Pio**
1872-1956 . . . . . . . . . . . . TCLC 8; HLC
See also CA 104

**Baron, David**
See Pinter, Harold

**Baron Corvo**
See Rolfe, Frederick (William Serafino Austin Lewis Mary)

**Barondess, Sue K(aufman)**
1926-1977 . . . . . . . . . . . . . . . . . . . CLC 8
See also Kaufman, Sue
See also CA 1-4R; 69-72; CANR 1

**Baron de Teive**
See Pessoa, Fernando (Antonio Nogueira)

**Barres, Maurice** 1862-1923 . . . . . . . TCLC 47
See also DLB 123

**Barreto, Afonso Henrique de Lima**
See Lima Barreto, Afonso Henrique de

**Barrett, (Roger) Syd** 1946- . . . . . . . . CLC 35

**Barrett, William (Christopher)**
1913-1992 . . . . . . . . . . . . . . . . . . CLC 27
See also CA 13-16R; 139; CANR 11; INT CANR-11

**Barrie, J(ames) M(atthew)**
1860-1937 . . . . . . . . . . . . . TCLC 2; DAB
See also CA 104; 136; CDBLB 1890-1914; CLR 16; DAM DRAM; DLB 10, 141, 156; MAICYA; YABC 1

**Barrington, Michael**
See Moorcock, Michael (John)

**Barrol, Grady**
See Bograd, Larry

**Barry, Mike**
See Malzberg, Barry N(athaniel)

**Barry, Philip** 1896-1949 . . . . . . . . . TCLC 11
See also CA 109; DLB 7

**Bart, Andre Schwarz**
See Schwarz-Bart, Andre

**Barth, John (Simmons)**
1930- . . . . . . **CLC 1, 2, 3, 5, 7, 9, 10, 14, 27, 51, 89; SSC 10**
See also AITN 1, 2; CA 1-4R; CABS 1; CANR 5, 23, 49; DAM NOV; DLB 2; MTCW

**Barthelme, Donald**
1931-1989 . . . . . . **CLC 1, 2, 3, 5, 6, 8, 13, 23, 46, 59; SSC 2**
See also CA 21-24R; 129; CANR 20; DAM NOV; DLB 2; DLBY 80, 89; MTCW; SATA 7; SATA-Obit 62

**Barthelme, Frederick** 1943- . . . . . . . . CLC 36
See also CA 114; 122; DLBY 85; INT 122

**Barthes, Roland (Gerard)**
1915-1980 . . . . . . . . . . . . . . CLC 24, 83
See also CA 130; 97-100; MTCW

**Barzun, Jacques (Martin)** 1907- . . . . CLC 51
See also CA 61-64; CANR 22

**Bashevis, Isaac**
See Singer, Isaac Bashevis

**Bashkirtseff, Marie** 1859-1884 . . . NCLC 27

**Basho**
See Matsuo Basho

**Bass, Kingsley B., Jr.**
See Bullins, Ed

**Bass, Rick** 1958- . . . . . . . . . . . . . . . . CLC 79
See also CA 126

**Bassani, Giorgio** 1916- . . . . . . . . . . . . CLC 9
See also CA 65-68; CANR 33; DLB 128; MTCW

**Bastos, Augusto (Antonio) Roa**
See Roa Bastos, Augusto (Antonio)

**Bataille, Georges** 1897-1962 . . . . . . . CLC 29
See also CA 101; 89-92

**Bates, H(erbert) E(rnest)**
1905-1974 . . . . . . **CLC 46; DAB; SSC 10**
See also CA 93-96; 45-48; CANR 34; DAM POP; DLB 162; MTCW

**Bauchart**
See Camus, Albert

**Baudelaire, Charles**
1821-1867 . . . . . **NCLC 6, 29; DA; DAB; DAC; PC 1; SSC 18; WLC**
See also DAM MST, POET

**Baudrillard, Jean** 1929- . . . . . . . . . . . CLC 60

**Baum, L(yman) Frank** 1856-1919 . . . TCLC 7
See also CA 108; 133; CLR 15; DLB 22; JRDA; MAICYA; MTCW; SATA 18

**Baum, Louis F.**
See Baum, L(yman) Frank

**Baumbach, Jonathan** 1933- . . . . . . CLC 6, 23
See also CA 13-16R; CAAS 5; CANR 12; DLBY 80; INT CANR-12; MTCW

**Bausch, Richard (Carl)** 1945- . . . . . . CLC 51
See also CA 101; CAAS 14; CANR 43; DLB 130

**Baxter, Charles** 1947- . . . . . . . . . . CLC 45, 78
See also CA 57-60; CANR 40; DAM POP; DLB 130

**Baxter, George Owen**
See Faust, Frederick (Schiller)

Baxter, James K(eir)  1926-1972 .... **CLC 14**
See also CA 77-80

Baxter, John
See Hunt, E(verette) Howard, (Jr.)

Bayer, Sylvia
See Glassco, John

Baynton, Barbara  1857-1929 ..... **TCLC 57**

Beagle, Peter S(oyer)  1939- ........ **CLC 7**
See also CA 9-12R; CANR 4, 51;
DLBY 80; INT CANR-4; SATA 60

Bean, Normal
See Burroughs, Edgar Rice

Beard, Charles A(ustin)
1874-1948 .................. **TCLC 15**
See also CA 115; DLB 17; SATA 18

Beardsley, Aubrey  1872-1898 ..... **NCLC 6**

Beattie, Ann
1947- .... **CLC 8, 13, 18, 40, 63; SSC 11**
See also BEST 90:2; CA 81-84; DAM NOV,
POP; DLBY 82; MTCW

Beattie, James  1735-1803 ....... **NCLC 25**
See also DLB 109

Beauchamp, Kathleen Mansfield  1888-1923
See Mansfield, Katherine
See also CA 104; 134; DA; DAC;
DAM MST

Beaumarchais, Pierre-Augustin Caron de
1732-1799 .................... **DC 4**
See also DAM DRAM

Beaumont, Francis  1584(?)-1616 ...... **DC 6**
See also CDBLB Before 1660; DLB 58, 121

Beauvoir, Simone (Lucie Ernestine Marie
Bertrand) de
1908-1986 .... **CLC 1, 2, 4, 8, 14, 31, 44,
50, 71; DA; DAB; DAC; WLC**
See also CA 9-12R; 118; CANR 28;
DAM MST, NOV; DLB 72; DLBY 86;
MTCW

Becker, Carl  1873-1945 ......... **TCLC 63**
See also DLB 17

Becker, Jurek  1937- ........... **CLC 7, 19**
See also CA 85-88; DLB 75

Becker, Walter  1950- ........... **CLC 26**

Beckett, Samuel (Barclay)
1906-1989 ...... **CLC 1, 2, 3, 4, 6, 9, 10,
11, 14, 18, 29, 57, 59, 83; DA; DAB;
DAC; SSC 16; WLC**
See also CA 5-8R; 130; CANR 33;
CDBLB 1945-1960; DAM DRAM, MST,
NOV; DLB 13, 15; DLBY 90; MTCW

Beckford, William  1760-1844 .... **NCLC 16**
See also DLB 39

Beckman, Gunnel  1910- .......... **CLC 26**
See also CA 33-36R; CANR 15; CLR 25;
MAICYA; SAAS 9; SATA 6

Becque, Henri  1837-1899 ........ **NCLC 3**

Beddoes, Thomas Lovell
1803-1849 ................. **NCLC 3**
See also DLB 96

Bedford, Donald F.
See Fearing, Kenneth (Flexner)

Beecher, Catharine Esther
1800-1878 ................. **NCLC 30**
See also DLB 1

Beecher, John  1904-1980 .......... **CLC 6**
See also AITN 1; CA 5-8R; 105; CANR 8

Beer, Johann  1655-1700 ............. **LC 5**

Beer, Patricia  1924- .............. **CLC 58**
See also CA 61-64; CANR 13, 46; DLB 40

Beerbohm, Henry Maximilian
1872-1956 ............... **TCLC 1, 24**
See also CA 104; DLB 34, 100

Beerbohm, Max
See Beerbohm, Henry Maximilian

Beer-Hofmann, Richard
1866-1945 ................ **TCLC 60**
See also DLB 81

Begiebing, Robert J(ohn)  1946- ..... **CLC 70**
See also CA 122; CANR 40

Behan, Brendan
1923-1964 ........ **CLC 1, 8, 11, 15, 79**
See also CA 73-76; CANR 33;
CDBLB 1945-1960; DAM DRAM;
DLB 13; MTCW

Behn, Aphra
1640(?)-1689 ...... **LC 1, 30; DA; DAB;
DAC; DC 4; PC 13; WLC**
See also DAM DRAM, MST, NOV, POET;
DLB 39, 80, 131

Behrman, S(amuel) N(athaniel)
1893-1973 ................... **CLC 40**
See also CA 13-16; 45-48; CAP 1; DLB 7,
44

Belasco, David  1853-1931 ......... **TCLC 3**
See also CA 104; DLB 7

Belcheva, Elisaveta  1893- ......... **CLC 10**
See also Bagryana, Elisaveta

Beldone, Phil "Cheech"
See Ellison, Harlan (Jay)

Beleno
See Azuela, Mariano

Belinski, Vissarion Grigoryevich
1811-1848 ................. **NCLC 5**

Belitt, Ben  1911- ................. **CLC 22**
See also CA 13-16R; CAAS 4; CANR 7;
DLB 5

Bell, James Madison
1826-1902 ............. **TCLC 43; BLC**
See also BW 1; CA 122; 124; DAM MULT;
DLB 50

Bell, Madison (Smartt)  1957- ...... **CLC 41**
See also CA 111; CANR 28

Bell, Marvin (Hartley)  1937- ..... **CLC 8, 31**
See also CA 21-24R; CAAS 14;
DAM POET; DLB 5; MTCW

Bell, W. L. D.
See Mencken, H(enry) L(ouis)

Bellamy, Atwood C.
See Mencken, H(enry) L(ouis)

Bellamy, Edward  1850-1898 ...... **NCLC 4**
See also DLB 12

Bellin, Edward J.
See Kuttner, Henry

Belloc, (Joseph) Hilaire (Pierre)
1870-1953 ............... **TCLC 7, 18**
See also CA 106; DAM POET; DLB 19,
100, 141; YABC 1

Belloc, Joseph Peter Rene Hilaire
See Belloc, (Joseph) Hilaire (Pierre)

Belloc, Joseph Pierre Hilaire
See Belloc, (Joseph) Hilaire (Pierre)

Belloc, M. A.
See Lowndes, Marie Adelaide (Belloc)

Bellow, Saul
1915- ...... **CLC 1, 2, 3, 6, 8, 10, 13, 15,
25, 33, 34, 63, 79; DA; DAB; DAC;
SSC 14; WLC**
See also AITN 2; BEST 89:3; CA 5-8R;
CABS 1; CANR 29; CDALB 1941-1968;
DAM MST, NOV, POP; DLB 2, 28;
DLBD 3; DLBY 82; MTCW

Belser, Reimond Karel Maria de
See Ruyslinck, Ward

Bely, Andrey .............. **TCLC 7; PC 11**
See also Bugayev, Boris Nikolayevich

Benary, Margot
See Benary-Isbert, Margot

Benary-Isbert, Margot  1889-1979 ... **CLC 12**
See also CA 5-8R; 89-92; CANR 4;
CLR 12; MAICYA; SATA 2;
SATA-Obit 21

Benavente (y Martinez), Jacinto
1866-1954 ................... **TCLC 3**
See also CA 106; 131; DAM DRAM,
MULT; HW; MTCW

Benchley, Peter (Bradford)
1940- ...................... **CLC 4, 8**
See also AAYA 14; AITN 2; CA 17-20R;
CANR 12, 35; DAM NOV, POP;
MTCW; SATA 3

Benchley, Robert (Charles)
1889-1945 ............... **TCLC 1, 55**
See also CA 105; DLB 11

Benda, Julien  1867-1956 ......... **TCLC 60**
See also CA 120

Benedict, Ruth  1887-1948 ........ **TCLC 60**

Benedikt, Michael  1935- ........ **CLC 4, 14**
See also CA 13-16R; CANR 7; DLB 5

Benet, Juan  1927- ................ **CLC 28**
See also CA 143

Benet, Stephen Vincent
1898-1943 ........... **TCLC 7; SSC 10**
See also CA 104; DAM POET; DLB 4, 48,
102; YABC 1

Benet, William Rose  1886-1950 ... **TCLC 28**
See also CA 118; DAM POET; DLB 45

Benford, Gregory (Albert)  1941- .... **CLC 52**
See also CA 69-72; CANR 12, 24, 49;
DLBY 82

Bengtsson, Frans (Gunnar)
1894-1954 .................. **TCLC 48**

Benjamin, David
See Slavitt, David R(ytman)

Benjamin, Lois
See Gould, Lois

Benjamin, Walter  1892-1940 ..... **TCLC 39**

Benn, Gottfried  1886-1956 ........ **TCLC 3**
See also CA 106; DLB 56

Bennett, Alan  1934- ..... **CLC 45, 77; DAB**
See also CA 103; CANR 35; DAM MST;
MTCW

**Bennett, (Enoch) Arnold**
1867-1931 . . . . . . . . . . . . . . . **TCLC 5, 20**
See also CA 106; CDBLB 1890-1914;
DLB 10, 34, 98, 135

**Bennett, Elizabeth**
See Mitchell, Margaret (Munnerlyn)

**Bennett, George Harold** 1930-
See Bennett, Hal
See also BW 1; CA 97-100

**Bennett, Hal** . . . . . . . . . . . . . . . . . . . . . **CLC 5**
See also Bennett, George Harold
See also DLB 33

**Bennett, Jay** 1912- . . . . . . . . . . . . . . **CLC 35**
See also AAYA 10; CA 69-72; CANR 11,
42; JRDA; SAAS 4; SATA 41;
SATA-Brief 27

**Bennett, Louise (Simone)**
1919- . . . . . . . . . . . . . . . . . **CLC 28; BLC**
See also BW 2; DAM MULT; DLB 117

**Benson, E(dward) F(rederic)**
1867-1940 . . . . . . . . . . . . . . . . . **TCLC 27**
See also CA 114; DLB 135, 153

**Benson, Jackson J.** 1930- . . . . . . . . . **CLC 34**
See also CA 25-28R; DLB 111

**Benson, Sally** 1900-1972 . . . . . . . . . . **CLC 17**
See also CA 19-20; 37-40R; CAP 1;
SATA 1, 35; SATA-Obit 27

**Benson, Stella** 1892-1933 . . . . . . . . **TCLC 17**
See also CA 117; DLB 36, 162

**Bentham, Jeremy** 1748-1832 . . . . . **NCLC 38**
See also DLB 107, 158

**Bentley, E(dmund) C(lerihew)**
1875-1956 . . . . . . . . . . . . . . . . . **TCLC 12**
See also CA 108; DLB 70

**Bentley, Eric (Russell)** 1916- . . . . . . . **CLC 24**
See also CA 5-8R; CANR 6; INT CANR-6

**Beranger, Pierre Jean de**
1780-1857 . . . . . . . . . . . . . . . . **NCLC 34**

**Berendt, John (Lawrence)** 1939- . . . . **CLC 86**
See also CA 146

**Berger, Colonel**
See Malraux, (Georges-)Andre

**Berger, John (Peter)** 1926- . . . . . . **CLC 2, 19**
See also CA 81-84; CANR 51; DLB 14

**Berger, Melvin H.** 1927- . . . . . . . . . . **CLC 12**
See also CA 5-8R; CANR 4; CLR 32;
SAAS 2; SATA 5

**Berger, Thomas (Louis)**
1924- . . . . . . . . . **CLC 3, 5, 8, 11, 18, 38**
See also CA 1-4R; CANR 5, 28, 51;
DAM NOV; DLB 2; DLBY 80;
INT CANR-28; MTCW

**Bergman, (Ernst) Ingmar**
1918- . . . . . . . . . . . . . . . . . . . **CLC 16, 72**
See also CA 81-84; CANR 33

**Bergson, Henri** 1859-1941 . . . . . . . **TCLC 32**

**Bergstein, Eleanor** 1938- . . . . . . . . . . **CLC 4**
See also CA 53-56; CANR 5

**Berkoff, Steven** 1937- . . . . . . . . . . . . **CLC 56**
See also CA 104

**Bermant, Chaim (Icyk)** 1929- . . . . . . **CLC 40**
See also CA 57-60; CANR 6, 31

**Bern, Victoria**
See Fisher, M(ary) F(rances) K(ennedy)

**Bernanos, (Paul Louis) Georges**
1888-1948 . . . . . . . . . . . . . . . . . . **TCLC 3**
See also CA 104; 130; DLB 72

**Bernard, April** 1956- . . . . . . . . . . . . . **CLC 59**
See also CA 131

**Berne, Victoria**
See Fisher, M(ary) F(rances) K(ennedy)

**Bernhard, Thomas**
1931-1989 . . . . . . . . . . . . . **CLC 3, 32, 61**
See also CA 85-88; 127; CANR 32;
DLB 85, 124; MTCW

**Berriault, Gina** 1926- . . . . . . . . . . . . **CLC 54**
See also CA 116; 129; DLB 130

**Berrigan, Daniel** 1921- . . . . . . . . . . . . **CLC 4**
See also CA 33-36R; CAAS 1; CANR 11,
43; DLB 5

**Berrigan, Edmund Joseph Michael, Jr.**
1934-1983
See Berrigan, Ted
See also CA 61-64; 110; CANR 14

**Berrigan, Ted** . . . . . . . . . . . . . . . . . . . **CLC 37**
See also Berrigan, Edmund Joseph Michael,
Jr.
See also DLB 5

**Berry, Charles Edward Anderson** 1931-
See Berry, Chuck
See also CA 115

**Berry, Chuck** . . . . . . . . . . . . . . . . . . . . **CLC 17**
See also Berry, Charles Edward Anderson

**Berry, Jonas**
See Ashbery, John (Lawrence)

**Berry, Wendell (Erdman)**
1934- . . . . . . . . . . . . **CLC 4, 6, 8, 27, 46**
See also AITN 1; CA 73-76; CANR 50;
DAM POET; DLB 5, 6

**Berryman, John**
1914-1972 . . . . . . **CLC 1, 2, 3, 4, 6, 8, 10,
13, 25, 62**
See also CA 13-16; 33-36R; CABS 2;
CANR 35; CAP 1; CDALB 1941-1968;
DAM POET; DLB 48; MTCW

**Bertolucci, Bernardo** 1940- . . . . . . . . **CLC 16**
See also CA 106

**Bertrand, Aloysius** 1807-1841 . . . . **NCLC 31**

**Bertran de Born** c. 1140-1215 . . . . . **CMLC 5**

**Besant, Annie (Wood)** 1847-1933 . . . **TCLC 9**
See also CA 105

**Bessie, Alvah** 1904-1985 . . . . . . . . . . **CLC 23**
See also CA 5-8R; 116; CANR 2; DLB 26

**Bethlen, T. D.**
See Silverberg, Robert

**Beti, Mongo** . . . . . . . . . . . . . . **CLC 27; BLC**
See also Biyidi, Alexandre
See also DAM MULT

**Betjeman, John**
1906-1984 . . . **CLC 2, 6, 10, 34, 43; DAB**
See also CA 9-12R; 112; CANR 33;
CDBLB 1945-1960; DAM MST, POET;
DLB 20; DLBY 84; MTCW

**Bettelheim, Bruno** 1903-1990 . . . . . . **CLC 79**
See also CA 81-84; 131; CANR 23; MTCW

**Betti, Ugo** 1892-1953 . . . . . . . . . . . . . **TCLC 5**
See also CA 104

**Betts, Doris (Waugh)** 1932- . . . . **CLC 3, 6, 28**
See also CA 13-16R; CANR 9; DLBY 82;
INT CANR-9

**Bevan, Alistair**
See Roberts, Keith (John Kingston)

**Bialik, Chaim Nachman**
1873-1934 . . . . . . . . . . . . . . . . . **TCLC 25**

**Bickerstaff, Isaac**
See Swift, Jonathan

**Bidart, Frank** 1939- . . . . . . . . . . . . . . **CLC 33**
See also CA 140

**Bienek, Horst** 1930- . . . . . . . . . . . . **CLC 7, 11**
See also CA 73-76; DLB 75

**Bierce, Ambrose (Gwinett)**
1842-1914(?) . . . . . . . **TCLC 1, 7, 44; DA;
DAC; SSC 9; WLC**
See also CA 104; 139; CDALB 1865-1917;
DAM MST; DLB 11, 12, 23, 71, 74

**Billings, Josh**
See Shaw, Henry Wheeler

**Billington, (Lady) Rachel (Mary)**
1942- . . . . . . . . . . . . . . . . . . . . . . **CLC 43**
See also AITN 2; CA 33-36R; CANR 44

**Binyon, T(imothy) J(ohn)** 1936- . . . . **CLC 34**
See also CA 111; CANR 28

**Bioy Casares, Adolfo**
1914- . . . **CLC 4, 8, 13, 88; HLC; SSC 17**
See also CA 29-32R; CANR 19, 43;
DAM MULT; DLB 113; HW; MTCW

**Bird, Cordwainer**
See Ellison, Harlan (Jay)

**Bird, Robert Montgomery**
1806-1854 . . . . . . . . . . . . . . . . . **NCLC 1**

**Birney, (Alfred) Earle**
1904- . . . . . . . . . . **CLC 1, 4, 6, 11; DAC**
See also CA 1-4R; CANR 5, 20;
DAM MST, POET; DLB 88; MTCW

**Bishop, Elizabeth**
1911-1979 . . . . . . **CLC 1, 4, 9, 13, 15, 32;
DA; DAC; PC 3**
See also CA 5-8R; 89-92; CABS 2;
CANR 26; CDALB 1968-1988;
DAM MST, POET; DLB 5; MTCW;
SATA-Obit 24

**Bishop, John** 1935- . . . . . . . . . . . . . . . **CLC 10**
See also CA 105

**Bissett, Bill** 1939- . . . . . . . . . . **CLC 18; PC 14**
See also CA 69-72; CAAS 19; CANR 15;
DLB 53; MTCW

**Bitov, Andrei (Georgievich)** 1937- . . . **CLC 57**
See also CA 142

**Biyidi, Alexandre** 1932-
See Beti, Mongo
See also BW 1; CA 114; 124; MTCW

**Bjarme, Brynjolf**
See Ibsen, Henrik (Johan)

**Bjornson, Bjornstjerne (Martinius)**
1832-1910 . . . . . . . . . . . . . . . **TCLC 7, 37**
See also CA 104

**Black, Robert**
See Holdstock, Robert P.

**Blackburn, Paul** 1926-1971 . . . . . . **CLC 9, 43**
See also CA 81-84; 33-36R; CANR 34;
DLB 16; DLBY 81

**Bottoms, David** 1949-............ **CLC 53**
See also CA 105; CANR 22; DLB 120;
DLBY 83

**Boucicault, Dion** 1820-1890...... **NCLC 41**

**Boucolon, Maryse** 1937-
See Conde, Maryse
See also CA 110; CANR 30

**Bourget, Paul (Charles Joseph)**
1852-1935 ................. **TCLC 12**
See also CA 107; DLB 123

**Bourjaily, Vance (Nye)** 1922- .... **CLC 8, 62**
See also CA 1-4R; CAAS 1; CANR 2;
DLB 2, 143

**Bourne, Randolph S(illiman)**
1886-1918 ................. **TCLC 16**
See also CA 117; DLB 63

**Bova, Ben(jamin William)** 1932-.... **CLC 45**
See also AAYA 16; CA 5-8R; CAAS 18;
CANR 11; CLR 3; DLBY 81;
INT CANR-11; MAICYA; MTCW;
SATA 6, 68

**Bowen, Elizabeth (Dorothea Cole)**
1899-1973 ...... **CLC 1, 3, 6, 11, 15, 22;
SSC 3**
See also CA 17-18; 41-44R; CANR 35;
CAP 2; CDBLB 1945-1960; DAM NOV;
DLB 15, 162; MTCW

**Bowering, George** 1935-........ **CLC 15, 47**
See also CA 21-24R; CAAS 16; CANR 10;
DLB 53

**Bowering, Marilyn R(uthe)** 1949-... **CLC 32**
See also CA 101; CANR 49

**Bowers, Edgar** 1924- .............. **CLC 9**
See also CA 5-8R; CANR 24; DLB 5

**Bowie, David** .................... **CLC 17**
See also Jones, David Robert

**Bowles, Jane (Sydney)**
1917-1973 ................. **CLC 3, 68**
See also CA 19-20; 41-44R; CAP 2

**Bowles, Paul (Frederick)**
1910- ........ **CLC 1, 2, 19, 53; SSC 3**
See also CA 1-4R; CAAS 1; CANR 1, 19,
50; DLB 5, 6; MTCW

**Box, Edgar**
See Vidal, Gore

**Boyd, Nancy**
See Millay, Edna St. Vincent

**Boyd, William** 1952-........ **CLC 28, 53, 70**
See also CA 114; 120; CANR 51

**Boyle, Kay**
1902-1992 ..... **CLC 1, 5, 19, 58; SSC 5**
See also CA 13-16R; 140; CAAS 1;
CANR 29; DLB 4, 9, 48, 86; DLBY 93;
MTCW

**Boyle, Mark**
See Kienzle, William X(avier)

**Boyle, Patrick** 1905-1982......... **CLC 19**
See also CA 127

**Boyle, T. C.** 1948-
See Boyle, T(homas) Coraghessan

**Boyle, T(homas) Coraghessan**
1948- ........ **CLC 36, 55, 90; SSC 16**
See also BEST 90:4; CA 120; CANR 44;
DAM POP; DLBY 86

**Boz**
See Dickens, Charles (John Huffam)

**Brackenridge, Hugh Henry**
1748-1816 ................. **NCLC 7**
See also DLB 11, 37

**Bradbury, Edward P.**
See Moorcock, Michael (John)

**Bradbury, Malcolm (Stanley)**
1932-.................... **CLC 32, 61**
See also CA 1-4R; CANR 1, 33;
DAM NOV; DLB 14; MTCW

**Bradbury, Ray (Douglas)**
1920- ........ **CLC 1, 3, 10, 15, 42; DA;
DAB; DAC; WLC**
See also AAYA 15; AITN 1, 2; CA 1-4R;
CANR 2, 30; CDALB 1968-1988;
DAM MST, NOV, POP; DLB 2, 8;
INT CANR-30; MTCW; SATA 11, 64

**Bradford, Gamaliel** 1863-1932..... **TCLC 36**
See also DLB 17

**Bradley, David (Henry, Jr.)**
1950- .................... **CLC 23; BLC**
See also BW 1; CA 104; CANR 26;
DAM MULT; DLB 33

**Bradley, John Ed(mund, Jr.)**
1958-.................... **CLC 55**
See also CA 139

**Bradley, Marion Zimmer** 1930-..... **CLC 30**
See also AAYA 9; CA 57-60; CAAS 10;
CANR 7, 31, 51; DAM POP; DLB 8;
MTCW

**Bradstreet, Anne**
1612(?)-1672 ...... **LC 4, 30; DA; DAC;
PC 10**
See also CDALB 1640-1865; DAM MST,
POET; DLB 24

**Brady, Joan** 1939- .............. **CLC 86**
See also CA 141

**Bragg, Melvyn** 1939- ............ **CLC 10**
See also BEST 89:3; CA 57-60; CANR 10,
48; DLB 14

**Braine, John (Gerard)**
1922-1986 .............. **CLC 1, 3, 41**
See also CA 1-4R; 120; CANR 1, 33;
CDBLB 1945-1960; DLB 15; DLBY 86;
MTCW

**Brammer, William** 1930(?)-1978 .... **CLC 31**
See also CA 77-80

**Brancati, Vitaliano** 1907-1954..... **TCLC 12**
See also CA 109

**Brancato, Robin F(idler)** 1936-..... **CLC 35**
See also AAYA 9; CA 69-72; CANR 11,
45; CLR 32; JRDA; SAAS 9; SATA 23

**Brand, Max**
See Faust, Frederick (Schiller)

**Brand, Millen** 1906-1980.......... **CLC 7**
See also CA 21-24R; 97-100

**Branden, Barbara** ................ **CLC 44**
See also CA 148

**Brandes, Georg (Morris Cohen)**
1842-1927 ................. **TCLC 10**
See also CA 105

**Brandys, Kazimierz** 1916- ........ **CLC 62**

**Branley, Franklyn M(ansfield)**
1915- ...................... **CLC 21**
See also CA 33-36R; CANR 14, 39;
CLR 13; MAICYA; SAAS 16; SATA 4,
68

**Brathwaite, Edward Kamau** 1930-... **CLC 11**
See also BW 2; CA 25-28R; CANR 11, 26,
47; DAM POET; DLB 125

**Brautigan, Richard (Gary)**
1935-1984 .... **CLC 1, 3, 5, 9, 12, 34, 42**
See also CA 53-56; 113; CANR 34;
DAM NOV; DLB 2, 5; DLBY 80, 84;
MTCW; SATA 56

**Braverman, Kate** 1950- ........... **CLC 67**
See also CA 89-92

**Brecht, Bertolt**
1898-1956 ...... **TCLC 1, 6, 13, 35; DA;
DAB; DAC; DC 3; WLC**
See also CA 104; 133; DAM DRAM, MST;
DLB 56, 124; MTCW

**Brecht, Eugen Berthold Friedrich**
See Brecht, Bertolt

**Bremer, Fredrika** 1801-1865 ..... **NCLC 11**

**Brennan, Christopher John**
1870-1932 ................. **TCLC 17**
See also CA 117

**Brennan, Maeve** 1917-............. **CLC 5**
See also CA 81-84

**Brentano, Clemens (Maria)**
1778-1842 ................. **NCLC 1**
See also DLB 90

**Brent of Bin Bin**
See Franklin, (Stella Maraia Sarah) Miles

**Brenton, Howard** 1942-........... **CLC 31**
See also CA 69-72; CANR 33; DLB 13;
MTCW

**Breslin, James** 1930-
See Breslin, Jimmy
See also CA 73-76; CANR 31; DAM NOV;
MTCW

**Breslin, Jimmy** ................. **CLC 4, 43**
See also Breslin, James
See also AITN 1

**Bresson, Robert** 1901-............ **CLC 16**
See also CA 110; CANR 49

**Breton, Andre**
1896-1966 ..... **CLC 2, 9, 15, 54; PC 15**
See also CA 19-20; 25-28R; CANR 40;
CAP 2; DLB 65; MTCW

**Breytenbach, Breyten** 1939(?)- .. **CLC 23, 37**
See also CA 113; 129; DAM POET

**Bridgers, Sue Ellen** 1942- ......... **CLC 26**
See also AAYA 8; CA 65-68; CANR 11,
36; CLR 18; DLB 52; JRDA; MAICYA;
SAAS 1; SATA 22

**Bridges, Robert (Seymour)**
1844-1930 ................. **TCLC 1**
See also CA 104; CDBLB 1890-1914;
DAM POET; DLB 19, 98

**Bridie, James** .................... **TCLC 3**
See also Mavor, Osborne Henry
See also DLB 10

**Brin, David** 1950-................ **CLC 34**
See also CA 102; CANR 24;
INT CANR-24; SATA 65

**Buchner, (Karl) Georg**
1813-1837 ................ **NCLC 26**

**Buchwald, Art(hur)** 1925- .......... **CLC 33**
See also AITN 1; CA 5-8R; CANR 21;
MTCW; SATA 10

**Buck, Pearl S(ydenstricker)**
1892-1973 .... **CLC 7, 11, 18; DA; DAB;
DAC**
See also AITN 1; CA 1-4R; 41-44R;
CANR 1, 34; DAM MST, NOV; DLB 9,
102; MTCW; SATA 1, 25

**Buckler, Ernest** 1908-1984 .... **CLC 13; DAC**
See also CA 11-12; 114; CAP 1;
DAM MST; DLB 68; SATA 47

**Buckley, Vincent (Thomas)**
1925-1988 ................... **CLC 57**
See also CA 101

**Buckley, William F(rank), Jr.**
1925- ................... **CLC 7, 18, 37**
See also AITN 1; CA 1-4R; CANR 1, 24;
DAM POP; DLB 137; DLBY 80;
INT CANR-24; MTCW

**Buechner, (Carl) Frederick**
1926- ................. **CLC 2, 4, 6, 9**
See also CA 13-16R; CANR 11, 39;
DAM NOV; DLBY 80; INT CANR-11;
MTCW

**Buell, John (Edward)** 1927- ........ **CLC 10**
See also CA 1-4R; DLB 53

**Buero Vallejo, Antonio** 1916- ... **CLC 15, 46**
See also CA 106; CANR 24, 49; HW;
MTCW

**Bufalino, Gesualdo** 1920(?)- ........ **CLC 74**

**Bugayev, Boris Nikolayevich** 1880-1934
See Bely, Andrey
See also CA 104

**Bukowski, Charles**
1920-1994 ........ **CLC 2, 5, 9, 41, 82**
See also CA 17-20R; 144; CANR 40;
DAM NOV, POET; DLB 5, 130; MTCW

**Bulgakov, Mikhail (Afanas'evich)**
1891-1940 ....... **TCLC 2, 16; SSC 18**
See also CA 105; DAM DRAM, NOV

**Bulgya, Alexander Alexandrovich**
1901-1956 ................... **TCLC 53**
See also Fadeyev, Alexander
See also CA 117

**Bullins, Ed** 1935- .. **CLC 1, 5, 7; BLC; DC 6**
See also BW 2; CA 49-52; CAAS 16;
CANR 24, 46; DAM DRAM, MULT;
DLB 7, 38; MTCW

**Bulwer-Lytton, Edward (George Earle Lytton)**
1803-1873 .............. **NCLC 1, 45**
See also DLB 21

**Bunin, Ivan Alexeyevich**
1870-1953 ........... **TCLC 6; SSC 5**
See also CA 104

**Bunting, Basil** 1900-1985 .... **CLC 10, 39, 47**
See also CA 53-56; 115; CANR 7;
DAM POET; DLB 20

**Bunuel, Luis** 1900-1983 .. **CLC 16, 80; HLC**
See also CA 101; 110; CANR 32;
DAM MULT; HW

**Bunyan, John**
1628-1688 ...... **LC 4; DA; DAB; DAC;
WLC**
See also CDBLB 1660-1789; DAM MST;
DLB 39

**Burckhardt, Jacob (Christoph)**
1818-1897 ................ **NCLC 49**

**Burford, Eleanor**
See Hibbert, Eleanor Alice Burford

**Burgess, Anthony**
**CLC 1, 2, 4, 5, 8, 10, 13, 15, 22, 40, 62,
81; DAB**
See also Wilson, John (Anthony) Burgess
See also AITN 1; CDBLB 1960 to Present;
DLB 14

**Burke, Edmund**
1729(?)-1797 .... **LC 7; DA; DAB; DAC;
WLC**
See also DAM MST; DLB 104

**Burke, Kenneth (Duva)**
1897-1993 ................ **CLC 2, 24**
See also CA 5-8R; 143; CANR 39; DLB 45,
63; MTCW

**Burke, Leda**
See Garnett, David

**Burke, Ralph**
See Silverberg, Robert

**Burke, Thomas** 1886-1945 ........ **TCLC 63**
See also CA 113

**Burney, Fanny** 1752-1840 .... **NCLC 12, 54**
See also DLB 39

**Burns, Robert** 1759-1796 ............ **PC 6**
See also CDBLB 1789-1832; DA; DAB;
DAC; DAM MST, POET; DLB 109;
WLC

**Burns, Tex**
See L'Amour, Louis (Dearborn)

**Burnshaw, Stanley** 1906- ..... **CLC 3, 13, 44**
See also CA 9-12R; DLB 48

**Burr, Anne** 1937- ................. **CLC 6**
See also CA 25-28R

**Burroughs, Edgar Rice**
1875-1950 ................ **TCLC 2, 32**
See also AAYA 11; CA 104; 132;
DAM NOV; DLB 8; MTCW; SATA 41

**Burroughs, William S(eward)**
1914- ....... **CLC 1, 2, 5, 15, 22, 42, 75;
DA; DAB; DAC; WLC**
See also AITN 2; CA 9-12R; CANR 20;
DAM MST, NOV, POP; DLB 2, 8, 16,
152; DLBY 81; MTCW

**Burton, Richard F.** 1821-1890 .... **NCLC 42**
See also DLB 55

**Busch, Frederick** 1941- ... **CLC 7, 10, 18, 47**
See also CA 33-36R; CAAS 1; CANR 45;
DLB 6

**Bush, Ronald** 1946- ............. **CLC 34**
See also CA 136

**Bustos, F(rancisco)**
See Borges, Jorge Luis

**Bustos Domecq, H(onorio)**
See Bioy Casares, Adolfo; Borges, Jorge
Luis

**Butler, Octavia E(stelle)** 1947- ..... **CLC 38**
See also BW 2; CA 73-76; CANR 12, 24,
38; DAM MULT, POP; DLB 33;
MTCW; SATA 84

**Butler, Robert Olen (Jr.)** 1945- ..... **CLC 81**
See also CA 112; DAM POP; INT 112

**Butler, Samuel** 1612-1680 .......... **LC 16**
See also DLB 101, 126

**Butler, Samuel**
1835-1902 ...... **TCLC 1, 33; DA; DAB;
DAC; WLC**
See also CA 143; CDBLB 1890-1914;
DAM MST, NOV; DLB 18, 57

**Butler, Walter C.**
See Faust, Frederick (Schiller)

**Butor, Michel (Marie Francois)**
1926- ............. **CLC 1, 3, 8, 11, 15**
See also CA 9-12R; CANR 33; DLB 83;
MTCW

**Buzo, Alexander (John)** 1944- ...... **CLC 61**
See also CA 97-100; CANR 17, 39

**Buzzati, Dino** 1906-1972 .......... **CLC 36**
See also CA 33-36R

**Byars, Betsy (Cromer)** 1928- ....... **CLC 35**
See also CA 33-36R; CANR 18, 36; CLR 1,
16; DLB 52; INT CANR-18; JRDA;
MAICYA; MTCW; SAAS 1; SATA 4,
46, 80

**Byatt, A(ntonia) S(usan Drabble)**
1936- ................... **CLC 19, 65**
See also CA 13-16R; CANR 13, 33, 50;
DAM NOV, POP; DLB 14; MTCW

**Byrne, David** 1952- ............... **CLC 26**
See also CA 127

**Byrne, John Keyes** 1926-
See Leonard, Hugh
See also CA 102; INT 102

**Byron, George Gordon (Noel)**
1788-1824 ..... **NCLC 2, 12; DA; DAB;
DAC; WLC**
See also CDBLB 1789-1832; DAM MST,
POET; DLB 96, 110

**C. 3. 3.**
See Wilde, Oscar (Fingal O'Flahertie Wills)

**Caballero, Fernan** 1796-1877 ..... **NCLC 10**

**Cabell, James Branch** 1879-1958 ... **TCLC 6**
See also CA 105; DLB 9, 78

**Cable, George Washington**
1844-1925 ............. **TCLC 4; SSC 4**
See also CA 104; DLB 12, 74; DLBD 13

**Cabral de Melo Neto, Joao** 1920- ... **CLC 76**
See also DAM MULT

**Cabrera Infante, G(uillermo)**
1929- ............ **CLC 5, 25, 45; HLC**
See also CA 85-88; CANR 29;
DAM MULT; DLB 113; HW; MTCW

**Cade, Toni**
See Bambara, Toni Cade

**Cadmus and Harmonia**
See Buchan, John

**Caedmon** fl. 658-680 ............. **CMLC 7**
See also DLB 146

**Caeiro, Alberto**
See Pessoa, Fernando (Antonio Nogueira)

Cage, John (Milton, Jr.) 1912- ..... CLC 41
See also CA 13-16R; CANR 9;
INT CANR-9

Cain, G.
See Cabrera Infante, G(uillermo)

Cain, Guillermo
See Cabrera Infante, G(uillermo)

Cain, James M(allahan)
1892-1977 .............. CLC 3, 11, 28
See also AITN 1; CA 17-20R; 73-76;
CANR 8, 34; MTCW

Caine, Mark
See Raphael, Frederic (Michael)

Calasso, Roberto 1941- ........... CLC 81
See also CA 143

Calderon de la Barca, Pedro
1600-1681 ............... LC 23; DC 3

Caldwell, Erskine (Preston)
1903-1987 ........ CLC 1, 8, 14, 50, 60;
SSC 19
See also AITN 1; CA 1-4R; 121; CAAS 1;
CANR 2, 33; DAM NOV; DLB 9, 86;
MTCW

Caldwell, (Janet Miriam) Taylor (Holland)
1900-1985 .............. CLC 2, 28, 39
See also CA 5-8R; 116; CANR 5;
DAM NOV, POP

Calhoun, John Caldwell
1782-1850 ................. NCLC 15
See also DLB 3

Calisher, Hortense
1911- ......... CLC 2, 4, 8, 38; SSC 15
See also CA 1-4R; CANR 1, 22;
DAM NOV; DLB 2; INT CANR-22;
MTCW

Callaghan, Morley Edward
1903-1990 ..... CLC 3, 14, 41, 65; DAC
See also CA 9-12R; 132; CANR 33;
DAM MST; DLB 68; MTCW

Calvino, Italo
1923-1985 ..... CLC 5, 8, 11, 22, 33, 39,
73; SSC 3
See also CA 85-88; 116; CANR 23;
DAM NOV; MTCW

Cameron, Carey 1952- ........... CLC 59
See also CA 135

Cameron, Peter 1959- ............ CLC 44
See also CA 125; CANR 50

Campana, Dino 1885-1932 ........ TCLC 20
See also CA 117; DLB 114

Campanella, Tommaso 1568-1639 .... LC 32

Campbell, John W(ood, Jr.)
1910-1971 ................... CLC 32
See also CA 21-22; 29-32R; CANR 34;
CAP 2; DLB 8; MTCW

Campbell, Joseph 1904-1987 ....... CLC 69
See also AAYA 3; BEST 89:2; CA 1-4R;
124; CANR 3, 28; MTCW

Campbell, Maria 1940- ....... CLC 85; DAC
See also CA 102; NNAL

Campbell, (John) Ramsey
1946- ............... CLC 42; SSC 19
See also CA 57-60; CANR 7; INT CANR-7

Campbell, (Ignatius) Roy (Dunnachie)
1901-1957 .................. TCLC 5
See also CA 104; DLB 20

Campbell, Thomas 1777-1844 .... NCLC 19
See also DLB 93; 144

Campbell, Wilfred ............... TCLC 9
See also Campbell, William

Campbell, William 1858(?)-1918
See Campbell, Wilfred
See also CA 106; DLB 92

Campos, Alvaro de
See Pessoa, Fernando (Antonio Nogueira)

Camus, Albert
1913-1960 .... CLC 1, 2, 4, 9, 11, 14, 32,
63, 69; DA; DAB; DAC; DC 2; SSC 9;
WLC
See also CA 89-92; DAM DRAM, MST,
NOV; DLB 72; MTCW

Canby, Vincent 1924- ............. CLC 13
See also CA 81-84

Cancale
See Desnos, Robert

Canetti, Elias
1905-1994 ....... CLC 3, 14, 25, 75, 86
See also CA 21-24R; 146; CANR 23;
DLB 85, 124; MTCW

Canin, Ethan 1960- ............... CLC 55
See also CA 131; 135

Cannon, Curt
See Hunter, Evan

Cape, Judith
See Page, P(atricia) K(athleen)

Capek, Karel
1890-1938 ...... TCLC 6, 37; DA; DAB;
DAC; DC 1; WLC
See also CA 104; 140; DAM DRAM, MST,
NOV

Capote, Truman
1924-1984 ...... CLC 1, 3, 8, 13, 19, 34,
38, 58; DA; DAB; DAC; SSC 2; WLC
See also CA 5-8R; 113; CANR 18;
CDALB 1941-1968; DAM MST, NOV,
POP; DLB 2; DLBY 80, 84; MTCW

Capra, Frank 1897-1991 .......... CLC 16
See also CA 61-64; 135

Caputo, Philip 1941- ............. CLC 32
See also CA 73-76; CANR 40

Card, Orson Scott 1951- .... CLC 44, 47, 50
See also AAYA 11; CA 102; CANR 27, 47;
DAM POP; INT CANR-27; MTCW;
SATA 83

Cardenal (Martinez), Ernesto
1925- ................. CLC 31; HLC
See also CA 49-52; CANR 2, 32;
DAM MULT, POET; HW; MTCW

Carducci, Giosue 1835-1907 ....... TCLC 32

Carew, Thomas 1595(?)-1640 ....... LC 13
See also DLB 126

Carey, Ernestine Gilbreth 1908- .... CLC 17
See also CA 5-8R; SATA 2

Carey, Peter 1943- ............ CLC 40, 55
See also CA 123; 127; INT 127; MTCW

Carleton, William 1794-1869 ...... NCLC 3
See also DLB 159

Carlisle, Henry (Coffin) 1926- ...... CLC 33
See also CA 13-16R; CANR 15

Carlsen, Chris
See Holdstock, Robert P.

Carlson, Ron(ald F.) 1947- ........ CLC 54
See also CA 105; CANR 27

Carlyle, Thomas
1795-1881 .. NCLC 22; DA; DAB; DAC
See also CDBLB 1789-1832; DAM MST;
DLB 55; 144

Carman, (William) Bliss
1861-1929 ............. TCLC 7; DAC
See also CA 104; DLB 92

Carnegie, Dale 1888-1955 ........ TCLC 53

Carossa, Hans 1878-1956 ......... TCLC 48
See also DLB 66

Carpenter, Don(ald Richard)
1931-1995 ................... CLC 41
See also CA 45-48; 149; CANR 1

Carpentier (y Valmont), Alejo
1904-1980 .......... CLC 8, 11, 38; HLC
See also CA 65-68; 97-100; CANR 11;
DAM MULT; DLB 113; HW

Carr, Caleb 1955(?)- .............. CLC 86
See also CA 147

Carr, Emily 1871-1945 ........... TCLC 32
See also DLB 68

Carr, John Dickson 1906-1977 ...... CLC 3
See also CA 49-52; 69-72; CANR 3, 33;
MTCW

Carr, Philippa
See Hibbert, Eleanor Alice Burford

Carr, Virginia Spencer 1929- ....... CLC 34
See also CA 61-64; DLB 111

Carrere, Emmanuel 1957- ......... CLC 89

Carrier, Roch 1937- ..... CLC 13, 78; DAC
See also CA 130; DAM MST; DLB 53

Carroll, James P. 1943(?)- ........ CLC 38
See also CA 81-84

Carroll, Jim 1951- ............... CLC 35
See also AAYA 17; CA 45-48; CANR 42

Carroll, Lewis ........... NCLC 2, 53; WLC
See also Dodgson, Charles Lutwidge
See also CDBLB 1832-1890; CLR 2, 18;
DLB 18, 163; JRDA

Carroll, Paul Vincent 1900-1968 .... CLC 10
See also CA 9-12R; 25-28R; DLB 10

Carruth, Hayden
1921- ...... CLC 4, 7, 10, 18, 84; PC 10
See also CA 9-12R; CANR 4, 38; DLB 5;
INT CANR-4; MTCW; SATA 47

Carson, Rachel Louise 1907-1964 ... CLC 71
See also CA 77-80; CANR 35; DAM POP;
MTCW; SATA 23

Carter, Angela (Olive)
1940-1992 ...... CLC 5, 41, 76; SSC 13
See also CA 53-56; 136; CANR 12, 36;
DLB 14; MTCW; SATA 66;
SATA-Obit 70

Carter, Nick
See Smith, Martin Cruz

**Carver, Raymond**
  1938-1988 ... **CLC 22, 36, 53, 55; SSC 8**
  See also CA 33-36R; 126; CANR 17, 34;
  DAM NOV; DLB 130; DLBY 84, 88;
  MTCW

**Cary, Elizabeth, Lady Falkland**
  1585-1639 ................... **LC 30**

**Cary, (Arthur) Joyce (Lunel)**
  1888-1957 ............... **TCLC 1, 29**
  See also CA 104; CDBLB 1914-1945;
  DLB 15, 100

**Casanova de Seingalt, Giovanni Jacopo**
  1725-1798 ................... **LC 13**

**Casares, Adolfo Bioy**
  See Bioy Casares, Adolfo

**Casely-Hayford, J(oseph) E(phraim)**
  1866-1930 ............. **TCLC 24; BLC**
  See also BW 2; CA 123; DAM MULT

**Casey, John (Dudley)** 1939-........ **CLC 59**
  See also BEST 90:2; CA 69-72; CANR 23

**Casey, Michael** 1947-............. **CLC 2**
  See also CA 65-68; DLB 5

**Casey, Patrick**
  See Thurman, Wallace (Henry)

**Casey, Warren (Peter)** 1935-1988... **CLC 12**
  See also CA 101; 127; INT 101

**Casona, Alejandro**................ **CLC 49**
  See also Alvarez, Alejandro Rodriguez

**Cassavetes, John** 1929-1989........ **CLC 20**
  See also CA 85-88; 127

**Cassill, R(onald) V(erlin)** 1919-... **CLC 4, 23**
  See also CA 9-12R; CAAS 1; CANR 7, 45;
  DLB 6

**Cassirer, Ernst** 1874-1945 ....... **TCLC 61**

**Cassity, (Allen) Turner** 1929- .... **CLC 6, 42**
  See also CA 17-20R; CAAS 8; CANR 11;
  DLB 105

**Castaneda, Carlos** 1931(?)-........ **CLC 12**
  See also CA 25-28R; CANR 32; HW;
  MTCW

**Castedo, Elena** 1937- ............ **CLC 65**
  See also CA 132

**Castedo-Ellerman, Elena**
  See Castedo, Elena

**Castellanos, Rosario**
  1925-1974 ............ **CLC 66; HLC**
  See also CA 131; 53-56; DAM MULT;
  DLB 113; HW

**Castelvetro, Lodovico** 1505-1571..... **LC 12**

**Castiglione, Baldassare** 1478-1529 ... **LC 12**

**Castle, Robert**
  See Hamilton, Edmond

**Castro, Guillen de** 1569-1631........ **LC 19**

**Castro, Rosalia de** 1837-1885 ..... **NCLC 3**
  See also DAM MULT

**Cather, Willa**
  See Cather, Willa Sibert

**Cather, Willa Sibert**
  1873-1947 ....... **TCLC 1, 11, 31; DA;
    DAB; DAC; SSC 2; WLC**
  See also CA 104; 128; CDALB 1865-1917;
  DAM MST, NOV; DLB 9, 54, 78;
  DLBD 1; MTCW; SATA 30

**Catton, (Charles) Bruce**
  1899-1978 ................... **CLC 35**
  See also AITN 1; CA 5-8R; 81-84;
  CANR 7; DLB 17; SATA 2;
  SATA-Obit 24

**Cauldwell, Frank**
  See King, Francis (Henry)

**Caunitz, William J.** 1933- ......... **CLC 34**
  See also BEST 89:3; CA 125; 130; INT 130

**Causley, Charles (Stanley)** 1917-..... **CLC 7**
  See also CA 9-12R; CANR 5, 35; CLR 30;
  DLB 27; MTCW; SATA 3, 66

**Caute, David** 1936-............... **CLC 29**
  See also CA 1-4R; CAAS 4; CANR 1, 33;
  DAM NOV; DLB 14

**Cavafy, C(onstantine) P(eter)**
  1863-1933 ................. **TCLC 2, 7**
  See also Kavafis, Konstantinos Petrou
  See also CA 148; DAM POET

**Cavallo, Evelyn**
  See Spark, Muriel (Sarah)

**Cavanna, Betty** ................... **CLC 12**
  See also Harrison, Elizabeth Cavanna
  See also JRDA; MAICYA; SAAS 4;
  SATA 1, 30

**Cavendish, Margaret Lucas**
  1623-1673 ................... **LC 30**
  See also DLB 131

**Caxton, William** 1421(?)-1491(?)..... **LC 17**

**Cayrol, Jean** 1911-............... **CLC 11**
  See also CA 89-92; DLB 83

**Cela, Camilo Jose**
  1916- ........... **CLC 4, 13, 59; HLC**
  See also BEST 90:2; CA 21-24R; CAAS 10;
  CANR 21, 32; DAM MULT; DLBY 89;
  HW; MTCW

**Celan, Paul** ...... **CLC 10, 19, 53, 82; PC 10**
  See also Antschel, Paul
  See also DLB 69

**Celine, Louis-Ferdinand**
  .............. **CLC 1, 3, 4, 7, 9, 15, 47**
  See also Destouches, Louis-Ferdinand
  See also DLB 72

**Cellini, Benvenuto** 1500-1571 ........ **LC 7**

**Cendrars, Blaise** ................. **CLC 18**
  See also Sauser-Hall, Frederic

**Cernuda (y Bidon), Luis**
  1902-1963 ................... **CLC 54**
  See also CA 131; 89-92; DAM POET;
  DLB 134; HW

**Cervantes (Saavedra), Miguel de**
  1547-1616 ........ **LC 6, 23; DA; DAB;
    DAC; SSC 12; WLC**
  See also DAM MST, NOV

**Cesaire, Aime (Fernand)**
  1913-.............. **CLC 19, 32; BLC**
  See also BW 2; CA 65-68; CANR 24, 43;
  DAM MULT, POET; MTCW

**Chabon, Michael** 1965(?)- ......... **CLC 55**
  See also CA 139

**Chabrol, Claude** 1930-............ **CLC 16**
  See also CA 110

**Challans, Mary** 1905-1983
  See Renault, Mary
  See also CA 81-84; 111; SATA 23;
  SATA-Obit 36

**Challis, George**
  See Faust, Frederick (Schiller)

**Chambers, Aidan** 1934- ........... **CLC 35**
  See also CA 25-28R; CANR 12, 31; JRDA;
  MAICYA; SAAS 12; SATA 1, 69

**Chambers, James** 1948-
  See Cliff, Jimmy
  See also CA 124

**Chambers, Jessie**
  See Lawrence, D(avid) H(erbert Richards)

**Chambers, Robert W.** 1865-1933... **TCLC 41**

**Chandler, Raymond (Thornton)**
  1888-1959 ................. **TCLC 1, 7**
  See also CA 104; 129; CDALB 1929-1941;
  DLBD 6; MTCW

**Chang, Jung** 1952- ............... **CLC 71**
  See also CA 142

**Channing, William Ellery**
  1780-1842 ............... **NCLC 17**
  See also DLB 1, 59

**Chaplin, Charles Spencer**
  1889-1977 ................... **CLC 16**
  See also Chaplin, Charlie
  See also CA 81-84; 73-76

**Chaplin, Charlie**
  See Chaplin, Charles Spencer
  See also DLB 44

**Chapman, George** 1559(?)-1634...... **LC 22**
  See also DAM DRAM; DLB 62, 121

**Chapman, Graham** 1941-1989 ...... **CLC 21**
  See also Monty Python
  See also CA 116; 129; CANR 35

**Chapman, John Jay** 1862-1933 ..... **TCLC 7**
  See also CA 104

**Chapman, Walker**
  See Silverberg, Robert

**Chappell, Fred (Davis)** 1936-.... **CLC 40, 78**
  See also CA 5-8R; CAAS 4; CANR 8, 33;
  DLB 6, 105

**Char, Rene(-Emile)**
  1907-1988 ........... **CLC 9, 11, 14, 55**
  See also CA 13-16R; 124; CANR 32;
  DAM POET; MTCW

**Charby, Jay**
  See Ellison, Harlan (Jay)

**Chardin, Pierre Teilhard de**
  See Teilhard de Chardin, (Marie Joseph)
  Pierre

**Charles I** 1600-1649 ............... **LC 13**

**Charyn, Jerome** 1937- ........ **CLC 5, 8, 18**
  See also CA 5-8R; CAAS 1; CANR 7;
  DLBY 83; MTCW

**Chase, Mary (Coyle)** 1907-1981 ...... **DC 1**
  See also CA 77-80; 105; SATA 17;
  SATA-Obit 29

**Chase, Mary Ellen** 1887-1973....... **CLC 2**
  See also CA 13-16; 41-44R; CAP 1;
  SATA 10

**Chase, Nicholas**
  See Hyde, Anthony

Chateaubriand, Francois Rene de
1768-1848 ................ NCLC 3
See also DLB 119

Chatterje, Sarat Chandra    1876-1936(?)
See Chatterji, Saratchandra
See also CA 109

Chatterji, Bankim Chandra
1838-1894 ................ NCLC 19

Chatterji, Saratchandra .......... TCLC 13
See also Chatterje, Sarat Chandra

Chatterton, Thomas   1752-1770 ....... LC 3
See also DAM POET; DLB 109

Chatwin, (Charles) Bruce
1940-1989 ............. CLC 28, 57, 59
See also AAYA 4; BEST 90:1; CA 85-88;
127; DAM POP

Chaucer, Daniel
See Ford, Ford Madox

Chaucer, Geoffrey
1340(?)-1400 ... LC 17; DA; DAB; DAC
See also CDBLB Before 1660; DAM MST,
POET; DLB 146

Chaviaras, Strates   1935-
See Haviaras, Stratis
See also CA 105

Chayefsky, Paddy ................. CLC 23
See also Chayefsky, Sidney
See also DLB 7, 44; DLBY 81

Chayefsky, Sidney   1923-1981
See Chayefsky, Paddy
See also CA 9-12R; 104; CANR 18;
DAM DRAM

Chedid, Andree   1920- ............. CLC 47
See also CA 145

Cheever, John
1912-1982 ...... CLC 3, 7, 8, 11, 15, 25,
64; DA; DAB; DAC; SSC 1; WLC
See also CA 5-8R; 106; CABS 1; CANR 5,
27; CDALB 1941-1968; DAM MST,
NOV, POP; DLB 2, 102; DLBY 80, 82;
INT CANR-5; MTCW

Cheever, Susan   1943- .......... CLC 18, 48
See also CA 103; CANR 27, 51; DLBY 82;
INT CANR-27

Chekhonte, Antosha
See Chekhov, Anton (Pavlovich)

Chekhov, Anton (Pavlovich)
1860-1904 ..... TCLC 3, 10, 31, 55; DA;
DAB; DAC; SSC 2; WLC
See also CA 104; 124; DAM DRAM, MST

Chernyshevsky, Nikolay Gavrilovich
1828-1889 ................ NCLC 1

Cherry, Carolyn Janice   1942-
See Cherryh, C. J.
See also CA 65-68; CANR 10

Cherryh, C. J. ................... CLC 35
See also Cherry, Carolyn Janice
See also DLBY 80

Chesnutt, Charles W(addell)
1858-1932 .... TCLC 5, 39; BLC; SSC 7
See also BW 1; CA 106; 125; DAM MULT;
DLB 12, 50, 78; MTCW

Chester, Alfred   1929(?)-1971 ....... CLC 49
See also CA 33-36R; DLB 130

Chesterton, G(ilbert) K(eith)
1874-1936 ......... TCLC 1, 6; SSC 1
See also CA 104; 132; CDBLB 1914-1945;
DAM NOV, POET; DLB 10, 19, 34, 70,
98, 149; MTCW; SATA 27

Chiang Pin-chin   1904-1986
See Ding Ling
See also CA 118

Ch'ien Chung-shu   1910- ........... CLC 22
See also CA 130; MTCW

Child, L. Maria
See Child, Lydia Maria

Child, Lydia Maria   1802-1880 .... NCLC 6
See also DLB 1, 74; SATA 67

Child, Mrs.
See Child, Lydia Maria

Child, Philip   1898-1978 ........ CLC 19, 68
See also CA 13-14; CAP 1; SATA 47

Childress, Alice
1920-1994 .. CLC 12, 15, 86; BLC; DC 4
See also AAYA 8; BW 2; CA 45-48; 146;
CANR 3, 27, 50; CLR 14; DAM DRAM,
MULT, NOV; DLB 7, 38; JRDA;
MAICYA; MTCW; SATA 7, 48, 81

Chislett, (Margaret) Anne   1943- .... CLC 34

Chitty, Thomas Willes   1926- ....... CLC 11
See also Hinde, Thomas
See also CA 5-8R

Chivers, Thomas Holley
1809-1858 ................ NCLC 49
See also DLB 3

Chomette, Rene Lucien   1898-1981
See Clair, Rene
See also CA 103

Chopin, Kate
........ TCLC 5, 14; DA; DAB; SSC 8
See also Chopin, Katherine
See also CDALB 1865-1917; DLB 12, 78

Chopin, Katherine   1851-1904
See Chopin, Kate
See also CA 104; 122; DAC; DAM MST,
NOV

Chretien de Troyes
c. 12th cent. - .............. CMLC 10

Christie
See Ichikawa, Kon

Christie, Agatha (Mary Clarissa)
1890-1976 ...... CLC 1, 6, 8, 12, 39, 48;
DAB; DAC
See also AAYA 9; AITN 1, 2; CA 17-20R;
61-64; CANR 10, 37; CDBLB 1914-1945;
DAM NOV; DLB 13, 77; MTCW;
SATA 36

Christie, (Ann) Philippa
See Pearce, Philippa
See also CA 5-8R; CANR 4

Christine de Pizan   1365(?)-1431(?) .... LC 9

Chubb, Elmer
See Masters, Edgar Lee

Chulkov, Mikhail Dmitrievich
1743-1792 ................... LC 2
See also DLB 150

Churchill, Caryl   1938- ... CLC 31, 55; DC 5
See also CA 102; CANR 22, 46; DLB 13;
MTCW

Churchill, Charles   1731-1764 ........ LC 3
See also DLB 109

Chute, Carolyn   1947- ............ CLC 39
See also CA 123

Ciardi, John (Anthony)
1916-1986 ............. CLC 10, 40, 44
See also CA 5-8R; 118; CAAS 2; CANR 5,
33; CLR 19; DAM POET; DLB 5;
DLBY 86; INT CANR-5; MAICYA;
MTCW; SATA 1, 65; SATA-Obit 46

Cicero, Marcus Tullius
106B.C.-43B.C. .............. CMLC 3

Cimino, Michael   1943- ............ CLC 16
See also CA 105

Cioran, E(mil) M.   1911-1995 ...... CLC 64
See also CA 25-28R; 149

Cisneros, Sandra   1954- ...... CLC 69; HLC
See also AAYA 9; CA 131; DAM MULT;
DLB 122, 152; HW

Cixous, Helene   1937- ............. CLC 92
See also CA 126; DLB 83; MTCW

Clair, Rene ..................... CLC 20
See also Chomette, Rene Lucien

Clampitt, Amy   1920-1994 ......... CLC 32
See also CA 110; 146; CANR 29; DLB 105

Clancy, Thomas L., Jr.   1947-
See Clancy, Tom
See also CA 125; 131; INT 131; MTCW

Clancy, Tom. .................... CLC 45
See also Clancy, Thomas L., Jr.
See also AAYA 9; BEST 89:1, 90:1;
DAM NOV, POP

Clare, John   1793-1864 ...... NCLC 9; DAB
See also DAM POET; DLB 55, 96

Clarin
See Alas (y Urena), Leopoldo (Enrique
Garcia)

Clark, Al C.
See Goines, Donald

Clark, (Robert) Brian   1932- ........ CLC 29
See also CA 41-44R

Clark, Curt
See Westlake, Donald E(dwin)

Clark, Eleanor   1913- ........... CLC 5, 19
See also CA 9-12R; CANR 41; DLB 6

Clark, J. P.
See Clark, John Pepper
See also DLB 117

Clark, John Pepper
1935- ............ CLC 38; BLC; DC 5
See also Clark, J. P.
See also BW 1; CA 65-68; CANR 16;
DAM DRAM, MULT

Clark, M. R.
See Clark, Mavis Thorpe

Clark, Mavis Thorpe   1909- ........ CLC 12
See also CA 57-60; CANR 8, 37; CLR 30;
MAICYA; SAAS 5; SATA 8, 74

Clark, Walter Van Tilburg
1909-1971 .................. CLC 28
See also CA 9-12R; 33-36R; DLB 9;
SATA 8

**Crane, Stephen (Townley)**
1871-1900 ...... **TCLC 11, 17, 32; DA;**
**DAB; DAC; SSC 7; WLC**
See also CA 109; 140; CDALB 1865-1917;
DAM MST, NOV, POET; DLB 12, 54,
78; YABC 2

**Crase, Douglas** 1944- ............. **CLC 58**
See also CA 106

**Crashaw, Richard** 1612(?)-1649 ...... **LC 24**
See also DLB 126

**Craven, Margaret**
1901-1980 ............. **CLC 17; DAC**
See also CA 103

**Crawford, F(rancis) Marion**
1854-1909 ................. **TCLC 10**
See also CA 107; DLB 71

**Crawford, Isabella Valancy**
1850-1887 ................. **NCLC 12**
See also DLB 92

**Crayon, Geoffrey**
See Irving, Washington

**Creasey, John** 1908-1973 .......... **CLC 11**
See also CA 5-8R; 41-44R; CANR 8;
DLB 77; MTCW

**Crebillon, Claude Prosper Jolyot de (fils)**
1707-1777 .................... **LC 28**

**Credo**
See Creasey, John

**Creeley, Robert (White)**
1926- ..... **CLC 1, 2, 4, 8, 11, 15, 36, 78**
See also CA 1-4R; CAAS 10; CANR 23, 43;
DAM POET; DLB 5, 16; MTCW

**Crews, Harry (Eugene)**
1935- ................. **CLC 6, 23, 49**
See also AITN 1; CA 25-28R; CANR 20;
DLB 6, 143; MTCW

**Crichton, (John) Michael**
1942- ................ **CLC 2, 6, 54, 90**
See also AAYA 10; AITN 2; CA 25-28R;
CANR 13, 40; DAM NOV, POP;
DLBY 81; INT CANR-13; JRDA;
MTCW; SATA 9

**Crispin, Edmund** ................. **CLC 22**
See also Montgomery, (Robert) Bruce
See also DLB 87

**Cristofer, Michael** 1945(?)- ........ **CLC 28**
See also CA 110; DAM DRAM; DLB 7

**Croce, Benedetto** 1866-1952 ...... **TCLC 37**
See also CA 120

**Crockett, David** 1786-1836 ....... **NCLC 8**
See also DLB 3, 11

**Crockett, Davy**
See Crockett, David

**Crofts, Freeman Wills**
1879-1957 ................. **TCLC 55**
See also CA 115; DLB 77

**Croker, John Wilson** 1780-1857 .. **NCLC 10**
See also DLB 110

**Crommelynck, Fernand** 1885-1970 .. **CLC 75**
See also CA 89-92

**Cronin, A(rchibald) J(oseph)**
1896-1981 ................. **CLC 32**
See also CA 1-4R; 102; CANR 5; SATA 47;
SATA-Obit 25

**Cross, Amanda**
See Heilbrun, Carolyn G(old)

**Crothers, Rachel** 1878(?)-1958 ..... **TCLC 19**
See also CA 113; DLB 7

**Croves, Hal**
See Traven, B.

**Crowfield, Christopher**
See Stowe, Harriet (Elizabeth) Beecher

**Crowley, Aleister** ................. **TCLC 7**
See also Crowley, Edward Alexander

**Crowley, Edward Alexander** 1875-1947
See Crowley, Aleister
See also CA 104

**Crowley, John** 1942- ............. **CLC 57**
See also CA 61-64; CANR 43; DLBY 82;
SATA 65

**Crud**
See Crumb, R(obert)

**Crumarums**
See Crumb, R(obert)

**Crumb, R(obert)** 1943- ........... **CLC 17**
See also CA 106

**Crumbum**
See Crumb, R(obert)

**Crumski**
See Crumb, R(obert)

**Crum the Bum**
See Crumb, R(obert)

**Crunk**
See Crumb, R(obert)

**Crustt**
See Crumb, R(obert)

**Cryer, Gretchen (Kiger)** 1935- ...... **CLC 21**
See also CA 114; 123

**Csath, Geza** 1887-1919 .......... **TCLC 13**
See also CA 111

**Cudlip, David** 1933- .............. **CLC 34**

**Cullen, Countee**
1903-1946 ...... **TCLC 4, 37; BLC; DA;**
**DAC**
See also BW 1; CA 108; 124;
CDALB 1917-1929; DAM MST, MULT,
POET; DLB 4, 48, 51; MTCW; SATA 18

**Cum, R.**
See Crumb, R(obert)

**Cummings, Bruce F(rederick)** 1889-1919
See Barbellion, W. N. P.
See also CA 123

**Cummings, E(dward) E(stlin)**
1894-1962 ...... **CLC 1, 3, 8, 12, 15, 68;**
**DA; DAB; DAC; PC 5; WLC 2**
See also CA 73-76; CANR 31;
CDALB 1929-1941; DAM MST, POET;
DLB 4, 48; MTCW

**Cunha, Euclides (Rodrigues Pimenta) da**
1866-1909 ................. **TCLC 24**
See also CA 123

**Cunningham, E. V.**
See Fast, Howard (Melvin)

**Cunningham, J(ames) V(incent)**
1911-1985 ................. **CLC 3, 31**
See also CA 1-4R; 115; CANR 1; DLB 5

**Cunningham, Julia (Woolfolk)**
1916- ..................... **CLC 12**
See also CA 9-12R; CANR 4, 19, 36;
JRDA; MAICYA; SAAS 2; SATA 1, 26

**Cunningham, Michael** 1952- ....... **CLC 34**
See also CA 136

**Cunninghame Graham, R(obert) B(ontine)**
1852-1936 ................. **TCLC 19**
See also Graham, R(obert) B(ontine)
Cunninghame
See also CA 119; DLB 98

**Currie, Ellen** 19(?)- ............... **CLC 44**

**Curtin, Philip**
See Lowndes, Marie Adelaide (Belloc)

**Curtis, Price**
See Ellison, Harlan (Jay)

**Cutrate, Joe**
See Spiegelman, Art

**Czaczkes, Shmuel Yosef**
See Agnon, S(hmuel) Y(osef Halevi)

**Dabrowska, Maria (Szumska)**
1889-1965 ................. **CLC 15**
See also CA 106

**Dabydeen, David** 1955- ........... **CLC 34**
See also BW 1; CA 125

**Dacey, Philip** 1939- .............. **CLC 51**
See also CA 37-40R; CAAS 17; CANR 14,
32; DLB 105

**Dagerman, Stig (Halvard)**
1923-1954 ................. **TCLC 17**
See also CA 117

**Dahl, Roald**
1916-1990 ...... **CLC 1, 6, 18, 79; DAB;**
**DAC**
See also AAYA 15; CA 1-4R; 133;
CANR 6, 32, 37; CLR 1, 7; DAM MST,
NOV, POP; DLB 139; JRDA; MAICYA;
MTCW; SATA 1, 26, 73; SATA-Obit 65

**Dahlberg, Edward** 1900-1977 ... **CLC 1, 7, 14**
See also CA 9-12R; 69-72; CANR 31;
DLB 48; MTCW

**Dale, Colin** ..................... **TCLC 18**
See also Lawrence, T(homas) E(dward)

**Dale, George E.**
See Asimov, Isaac

**Daly, Elizabeth** 1878-1967 ......... **CLC 52**
See also CA 23-24; 25-28R; CAP 2

**Daly, Maureen** 1921- ............. **CLC 17**
See also AAYA 5; CANR 37; JRDA;
MAICYA; SAAS 1; SATA 2

**Damas, Leon-Gontran** 1912-1978 ... **CLC 84**
See also BW 1; CA 125; 73-76

**Dana, Richard Henry Sr.**
1787-1879 ................. **NCLC 53**

**Daniel, Samuel** 1562(?)-1619 ........ **LC 24**
See also DLB 62

**Daniels, Brett**
See Adler, Renata

**Dannay, Frederic** 1905-1982 ....... **CLC 11**
See also Queen, Ellery
See also CA 1-4R; 107; CANR 1, 39;
DAM POP; DLB 137; MTCW

**D'Annunzio, Gabriele**
1863-1938 ................. **TCLC 6, 40**
See also CA 104

**Danois, N. le**
See Gourmont, Remy (-Marie-Charles) de

**d'Antibes, Germain**
See Simenon, Georges (Jacques Christian)

**Danticat, Edwidge** 1969- ......... **CLC 91**

**Danvers, Dennis** 1947- ........... **CLC 70**

**Danziger, Paula** 1944- ........... **CLC 21**
See also AAYA 4; CA 112; 115; CANR 37;
CLR 20; JRDA; MAICYA; SATA 36,
63; SATA-Brief 30

**Da Ponte, Lorenzo** 1749-1838.... **NCLC 50**

**Dario, Ruben**
1867-1916 ....... **TCLC 4; HLC; PC 15**
See also CA 131; DAM MULT; HW;
MTCW

**Darley, George** 1795-1846........ **NCLC 2**
See also DLB 96

**Daryush, Elizabeth** 1887-1977.... **CLC 6, 19**
See also CA 49-52; CANR 3; DLB 20

**Dashwood, Edmee Elizabeth Monica de la Pasture** 1890-1943
See Delafield, E. M.
See also CA 119

**Daudet, (Louis Marie) Alphonse**
1840-1897 .................. **NCLC 1**
See also DLB 123

**Daumal, Rene** 1908-1944........ **TCLC 14**
See also CA 114

**Davenport, Guy (Mattison, Jr.)**
1927- .......... **CLC 6, 14, 38; SSC 16**
See also CA 33-36R; CANR 23; DLB 130

**Davidson, Avram** 1923-
See Queen, Ellery
See also CA 101; CANR 26; DLB 8

**Davidson, Donald (Grady)**
1893-1968 .............. **CLC 2, 13, 19**
See also CA 5-8R; 25-28R; CANR 4;
DLB 45

**Davidson, Hugh**
See Hamilton, Edmond

**Davidson, John** 1857-1909....... **TCLC 24**
See also CA 118; DLB 19

**Davidson, Sara** 1943- ............. **CLC 9**
See also CA 81-84; CANR 44

**Davie, Donald (Alfred)**
1922-1995 ........... **CLC 5, 8, 10, 31**
See also CA 1-4R; 149; CAAS 3; CANR 1,
44; DLB 27; MTCW

**Davies, Ray(mond Douglas)** 1944- .. **CLC 21**
See also CA 116; 146

**Davies, Rhys** 1903-1978........... **CLC 23**
See also CA 9-12R; 81-84; CANR 4;
DLB 139

**Davies, (William) Robertson**
1913-1995 ..... **CLC 2, 7, 13, 25, 42, 75,**
**91; DA; DAB; DAC; WLC**
See also BEST 89:2; CA 33-36R; 150;
CANR 17, 42; DAM MST, NOV, POP;
DLB 68; INT CANR-17; MTCW

**Davies, W(illiam) H(enry)**
1871-1940 .................. **TCLC 5**
See also CA 104; DLB 19

**Davies, Walter C.**
See Kornbluth, C(yril) M.

**Davis, Angela (Yvonne)** 1944- ...... **CLC 77**
See also BW 2; CA 57-60; CANR 10;
DAM MULT

**Davis, B. Lynch**
See Bioy Casares, Adolfo; Borges, Jorge
Luis

**Davis, Gordon**
See Hunt, E(verette) Howard, (Jr.)

**Davis, Harold Lenoir** 1896-1960.... **CLC 49**
See also CA 89-92; DLB 9

**Davis, Rebecca (Blaine) Harding**
1831-1910 .................. **TCLC 6**
See also CA 104; DLB 74

**Davis, Richard Harding**
1864-1916 .................. **TCLC 24**
See also CA 114; DLB 12, 23, 78, 79;
DLBD 13

**Davison, Frank Dalby** 1893-1970 ... **CLC 15**
See also CA 116

**Davison, Lawrence H.**
See Lawrence, D(avid) H(erbert Richards)

**Davison, Peter (Hubert)** 1928- ..... **CLC 28**
See also CA 9-12R; CAAS 4; CANR 3, 43;
DLB 5

**Davys, Mary** 1674-1732............. **LC 1**
See also DLB 39

**Dawson, Fielding** 1930- ........... **CLC 6**
See also CA 85-88; DLB 130

**Dawson, Peter**
See Faust, Frederick (Schiller)

**Day, Clarence (Shepard, Jr.)**
1874-1935 .................. **TCLC 25**
See also CA 108; DLB 11

**Day, Thomas** 1748-1789............. **LC 1**
See also DLB 39; YABC 1

**Day Lewis, C(ecil)**
1904-1972 ........ **CLC 1, 6, 10; PC 11**
See also Blake, Nicholas
See also CA 13-16; 33-36R; CANR 34;
CAP 1; DAM POET; DLB 15, 20;
MTCW

**Dazai, Osamu** .................. **TCLC 11**
See also Tsushima, Shuji

**de Andrade, Carlos Drummond**
See Drummond de Andrade, Carlos

**Deane, Norman**
See Creasey, John

**de Beauvoir, Simone (Lucie Ernestine Marie Bertrand)**
See Beauvoir, Simone (Lucie Ernestine
Marie Bertrand) de

**de Brissac, Malcolm**
See Dickinson, Peter (Malcolm)

**de Chardin, Pierre Teilhard**
See Teilhard de Chardin, (Marie Joseph)
Pierre

**Dee, John** 1527-1608 ............. **LC 20**

**Deer, Sandra** 1940- ............... **CLC 45**

**De Ferrari, Gabriella** 1941- ........ **CLC 65**
See also CA 146

**Defoe, Daniel**
1660(?)-1731 .... **LC 1; DA; DAB; DAC;**
**WLC**
See also CDBLB 1660-1789; DAM MST,
NOV; DLB 39, 95, 101; JRDA;
MAICYA; SATA 22

**de Gourmont, Remy(-Marie-Charles)**
See Gourmont, Remy (-Marie-Charles) de

**de Hartog, Jan** 1914- ............. **CLC 19**
See also CA 1-4R; CANR 1

**de Hostos, E. M.**
See Hostos (y Bonilla), Eugenio Maria de

**de Hostos, Eugenio M.**
See Hostos (y Bonilla), Eugenio Maria de

**Deighton, Len** ............. **CLC 4, 7, 22, 46**
See also Deighton, Leonard Cyril
See also AAYA 6; BEST 89:2;
CDBLB 1960 to Present; DLB 87

**Deighton, Leonard Cyril** 1929-
See Deighton, Len
See also CA 9-12R; CANR 19, 33;
DAM NOV, POP; MTCW

**Dekker, Thomas** 1572(?)-1632....... **LC 22**
See also CDBLB Before 1660;
DAM DRAM; DLB 62

**Delafield, E. M.** 1890-1943 ....... **TCLC 61**
See also Dashwood, Edmee Elizabeth
Monica de la Pasture
See also DLB 34

**de la Mare, Walter (John)**
1873-1956 .... **TCLC 4, 53; DAB; DAC;**
**SSC 14; WLC**
See also CDBLB 1914-1945; CLR 23;
DAM MST, POET; DLB 162; SATA 16

**Delaney, Franey**
See O'Hara, John (Henry)

**Delaney, Shelagh** 1939- ........... **CLC 29**
See also CA 17-20R; CANR 30;
CDBLB 1960 to Present; DAM DRAM;
DLB 13; MTCW

**Delany, Mary (Granville Pendarves)**
1700-1788 .................. **LC 12**

**Delany, Samuel R(ay, Jr.)**
1942- ............. **CLC 8, 14, 38; BLC**
See also BW 2; CA 81-84; CANR 27, 43;
DAM MULT; DLB 8, 33; MTCW

**De La Ramee, (Marie) Louise** 1839-1908
See Ouida
See also SATA 20

**de la Roche, Mazo** 1879-1961 ...... **CLC 14**
See also CA 85-88; CANR 30; DLB 68;
SATA 64

**Delbanco, Nicholas (Franklin)**
1942- .................... **CLC 6, 13**
See also CA 17-20R; CAAS 2; CANR 29;
DLB 6

**del Castillo, Michel** 1933- ......... **CLC 38**
See also CA 109

**Deledda, Grazia (Cosima)**
1875(?)-1936 ............... **TCLC 23**
See also CA 123

**Delibes, Miguel** ................. **CLC 8, 18**
See also Delibes Setien, Miguel

**Delibes Setien, Miguel** 1920-
See Delibes, Miguel
See also CA 45-48; CANR 1, 32; HW;
MTCW

**DeLillo, Don**
1936- ..... **CLC 8, 10, 13, 27, 39, 54, 76**
See also BEST 89:1; CA 81-84; CANR 21;
DAM NOV, POP; DLB 6; MTCW

**de Lisser, H. G.**
See De Lisser, Herbert George
See also DLB 117

**De Lisser, Herbert George**
1878-1944 ................... **TCLC 12**
See also de Lisser, H. G.
See also BW 2; CA 109

**Deloria, Vine (Victor), Jr.** 1933-.... **CLC 21**
See also CA 53-56; CANR 5, 20, 48;
DAM MULT; MTCW; NNAL; SATA 21

**Del Vecchio, John M(ichael)**
1947- ....................... **CLC 29**
See also CA 110; DLBD 9

**de Man, Paul (Adolph Michel)**
1919-1983 ................... **CLC 55**
See also CA 128; 111; DLB 67; MTCW

**De Marinis, Rick** 1934-........... **CLC 54**
See also CA 57-60; CANR 9, 25, 50

**Demby, William** 1922-....... **CLC 53; BLC**
See also BW 1; CA 81-84; DAM MULT;
DLB 33

**Demijohn, Thom**
See Disch, Thomas M(ichael)

**de Montherlant, Henry (Milon)**
See Montherlant, Henry (Milon) de

**Demosthenes** 384B.C.-322B.C. ... **CMLC 13**

**de Natale, Francine**
See Malzberg, Barry N(athaniel)

**Denby, Edwin (Orr)** 1903-1983..... **CLC 48**
See also CA 138; 110

**Denis, Julio**
See Cortazar, Julio

**Denmark, Harrison**
See Zelazny, Roger (Joseph)

**Dennis, John** 1658-1734........... **LC 11**
See also DLB 101

**Dennis, Nigel (Forbes)** 1912-1989.... **CLC 8**
See also CA 25-28R; 129; DLB 13, 15;
MTCW

**De Palma, Brian (Russell)** 1940-.... **CLC 20**
See also CA 109

**De Quincey, Thomas** 1785-1859 ... **NCLC 4**
See also CDBLB 1789-1832; DLB 110; 144

**Deren, Eleanora** 1908(?)-1961
See Deren, Maya
See also CA 111

**Deren, Maya** .................... **CLC 16**
See also Deren, Eleanora

**Derleth, August (William)**
1909-1971 ................... **CLC 31**
See also CA 1-4R; 29-32R; CANR 4;
DLB 9; SATA 5

**Der Nister** 1884-1950........... **TCLC 56**

**de Routisie, Albert**
See Aragon, Louis

**Derrida, Jacques** 1930-........ **CLC 24, 87**
See also CA 124; 127

**Derry Down Derry**
See Lear, Edward

**Dersonnes, Jacques**
See Simenon, Georges (Jacques Christian)

**Desai, Anita** 1937- ...... **CLC 19, 37; DAB**
See also CA 81-84; CANR 33; DAM NOV;
MTCW; SATA 63

**de Saint-Luc, Jean**
See Glassco, John

**de Saint Roman, Arnaud**
See Aragon, Louis

**Descartes, Rene** 1596-1650 ......... **LC 20**

**De Sica, Vittorio** 1901(?)-1974 ..... **CLC 20**
See also CA 117

**Desnos, Robert** 1900-1945....... **TCLC 22**
See also CA 121

**Destouches, Louis-Ferdinand**
1894-1961 ................. **CLC 9, 15**
See also Celine, Louis-Ferdinand
See also CA 85-88; CANR 28; MTCW

**Deutsch, Babette** 1895-1982 ....... **CLC 18**
See also CA 1-4R; 108; CANR 4; DLB 45;
SATA 1; SATA-Obit 33

**Devenant, William** 1606-1649 ....... **LC 13**

**Devkota, Laxmiprasad**
1909-1959 ................. **TCLC 23**
See also CA 123

**De Voto, Bernard (Augustine)**
1897-1955 ................. **TCLC 29**
See also CA 113; DLB 9

**De Vries, Peter**
1910-1993 .... **CLC 1, 2, 3, 7, 10, 28, 46**
See also CA 17-20R; 142; CANR 41;
DAM NOV; DLB 6; DLBY 82; MTCW

**Dexter, Martin**
See Faust, Frederick (Schiller)

**Dexter, Pete** 1943-............ **CLC 34, 55**
See also BEST 89:2; CA 127; 131;
DAM POP; INT 131; MTCW

**Diamano, Silmang**
See Senghor, Leopold Sedar

**Diamond, Neil** 1941- ............. **CLC 30**
See also CA 108

**Diaz del Castillo, Bernal** 1496-1584.. **LC 31**

**di Bassetto, Corno**
See Shaw, George Bernard

**Dick, Philip K(indred)**
1928-1982 ............. **CLC 10, 30, 72**
See also CA 49-52; 106; CANR 2, 16;
DAM NOV, POP; DLB 8; MTCW

**Dickens, Charles (John Huffam)**
1812-1870 ...... **NCLC 3, 8, 18, 26, 37,
50; DA; DAB; DAC; SSC 17; WLC**
See also CDBLB 1832-1890; DAM MST,
NOV; DLB 21, 55, 70, 159; JRDA;
MAICYA; SATA 15

**Dickey, James (Lafayette)**
1923- ........ **CLC 1, 2, 4, 7, 10, 15, 47**
See also AITN 1, 2; CA 9-12R; CABS 2;
CANR 10, 48; CDALB 1968-1988;
DAM NOV, POET, POP; DLB 5;
DLBD 7; DLBY 82, 93; INT CANR-10;
MTCW

**Dickey, William** 1928-1994 ...... **CLC 3, 28**
See also CA 9-12R; 145; CANR 24; DLB 5

**Dickinson, Charles** 1951-......... **CLC 49**
See also CA 128

**Dickinson, Emily (Elizabeth)**
1830-1886 ....... **NCLC 21; DA; DAB;
DAC; PC 1; WLC**
See also CDALB 1865-1917; DAM MST,
POET; DLB 1; SATA 29

**Dickinson, Peter (Malcolm)**
1927- .................... **CLC 12, 35**
See also AAYA 9; CA 41-44R; CANR 31;
CLR 29; DLB 87, 161; JRDA; MAICYA;
SATA 5, 62

**Dickson, Carr**
See Carr, John Dickson

**Dickson, Carter**
See Carr, John Dickson

**Diderot, Denis** 1713-1784 .......... **LC 26**

**Didion, Joan** 1934-..... **CLC 1, 3, 8, 14, 32**
See also AITN 1; CA 5-8R; CANR 14;
CDALB 1968-1988; DAM NOV; DLB 2;
DLBY 81, 86; MTCW

**Dietrich, Robert**
See Hunt, E(verette) Howard, (Jr.)

**Dillard, Annie** 1945-............ **CLC 9, 60**
See also AAYA 6; CA 49-52; CANR 3, 43;
DAM NOV; DLBY 80; MTCW;
SATA 10

**Dillard, R(ichard) H(enry) W(ilde)**
1937- ....................... **CLC 5**
See also CA 21-24R; CAAS 7; CANR 10;
DLB 5

**Dillon, Eilis** 1920-1994........... **CLC 17**
See also CA 9-12R; 147; CAAS 3; CANR 4,
38; CLR 26; MAICYA; SATA 2, 74;
SATA-Obit 83

**Dimont, Penelope**
See Mortimer, Penelope (Ruth)

**Dinesen, Isak**.......... **CLC 10, 29; SSC 7**
See also Blixen, Karen (Christentze
Dinesen)

**Ding Ling**....................... **CLC 68**
See also Chiang Pin-chin

**Disch, Thomas M(ichael)** 1940-... **CLC 7, 36**
See also AAYA 17; CA 21-24R; CAAS 4;
CANR 17, 36; CLR 18; DLB 8;
MAICYA; MTCW; SAAS 15; SATA 54

**Disch, Tom**
See Disch, Thomas M(ichael)

**d'Isly, Georges**
See Simenon, Georges (Jacques Christian)

**Disraeli, Benjamin** 1804-1881 .. **NCLC 2, 39**
See also DLB 21, 55

**Ditcum, Steve**
See Crumb, R(obert)

**Dixon, Paige**
See Corcoran, Barbara

**Dixon, Stephen** 1936-..... **CLC 52; SSC 16**
See also CA 89-92; CANR 17, 40; DLB 130

**Dobell, Sydney Thompson**
1824-1874 ................ **NCLC 43**
See also DLB 32

**Doblin, Alfred** ................... **TCLC 13**
See also Doeblin, Alfred

Dobrolyubov, Nikolai Alexandrovich
    1836-1861 ................. NCLC 5

Dobyns, Stephen 1941-............ CLC 37
    See also CA 45-48; CANR 2, 18

Doctorow, E(dgar) L(aurence)
    1931- ..... CLC 6, 11, 15, 18, 37, 44, 65
    See also AITN 2; BEST 89:3; CA 45-48;
    CANR 2, 33, 51; CDALB 1968-1988;
    DAM NOV, POP; DLB 2, 28; DLBY 80;
    MTCW

Dodgson, Charles Lutwidge 1832-1898
    See Carroll, Lewis
    See also CLR 2; DA; DAB; DAC;
    DAM MST, NOV, POET; MAICYA;
    YABC 2

Dodson, Owen (Vincent)
    1914-1983 ............. CLC 79; BLC
    See also BW 1; CA 65-68; 110; CANR 24;
    DAM MULT; DLB 76

Doeblin, Alfred 1878-1957....... TCLC 13
    See also Doblin, Alfred
    See also CA 110; 141; DLB 66

Doerr, Harriet 1910- ............. CLC 34
    See also CA 117; 122; CANR 47; INT 122

Domecq, H(onorio) Bustos
    See Bioy Casares, Adolfo; Borges, Jorge
    Luis

Domini, Rey
    See Lorde, Audre (Geraldine)

Dominique
    See Proust, (Valentin-Louis-George-Eugene-)
    Marcel

Don, A
    See Stephen, Leslie

Donaldson, Stephen R. 1947-....... CLC 46
    See also CA 89-92; CANR 13; DAM POP;
    INT CANR-13

Donleavy, J(ames) P(atrick)
    1926- ............. CLC 1, 4, 6, 10, 45
    See also AITN 2; CA 9-12R; CANR 24, 49;
    DLB 6; INT CANR-24; MTCW

Donne, John
    1572-1631 ...... LC 10, 24; DA; DAB;
                              DAC; PC 1
    See also CDBLB Before 1660; DAM MST,
    POET; DLB 121, 151

Donnell, David 1939(?)-........... CLC 34

Donoghue, P. S.
    See Hunt, E(verette) Howard, (Jr.)

Donoso (Yanez), Jose
    1924- .......... CLC 4, 8, 11, 32; HLC
    See also CA 81-84; CANR 32;
    DAM MULT; DLB 113; HW; MTCW

Donovan, John 1928-1992 ........ CLC 35
    See also CA 97-100; 137; CLR 3;
    MAICYA; SATA 72; SATA-Brief 29

Don Roberto
    See Cunninghame Graham, R(obert)
    B(ontine)

Doolittle, Hilda
    1886-1961 ..... CLC 3, 8, 14, 31, 34, 73;
                              DA; DAC; PC 5; WLC
    See also H. D.
    See also CA 97-100; CANR 35; DAM MST,
    POET; DLB 4, 45; MTCW

Dorfman, Ariel 1942-.... CLC 48, 77; HLC
    See also CA 124; 130; DAM MULT; HW;
    INT 130

Dorn, Edward (Merton) 1929-... CLC 10, 18
    See also CA 93-96; CANR 42; DLB 5;
    INT 93-96

Dorsan, Luc
    See Simenon, Georges (Jacques Christian)

Dorsange, Jean
    See Simenon, Georges (Jacques Christian)

Dos Passos, John (Roderigo)
    1896-1970 ...... CLC 1, 4, 8, 11, 15, 25,
                        34, 82; DA; DAB; DAC; WLC
    See also CA 1-4R; 29-32R; CANR 3;
    CDALB 1929-1941; DAM MST, NOV;
    DLB 4, 9; DLBD 1; MTCW

Dossage, Jean
    See Simenon, Georges (Jacques Christian)

Dostoevsky, Fedor Mikhailovich
    1821-1881 ...... NCLC 2, 7, 21, 33, 43;
                        DA; DAB; DAC; SSC 2; WLC
    See also DAM MST, NOV

Doughty, Charles M(ontagu)
    1843-1926 ................. TCLC 27
    See also CA 115; DLB 19, 57

Douglas, Ellen.................... CLC 73
    See also Haxton, Josephine Ayres;
    Williamson, Ellen Douglas

Douglas, Gavin 1475(?)-1522........ LC 20

Douglas, Keith 1920-1944 ....... TCLC 40
    See also DLB 27

Douglas, Leonard
    See Bradbury, Ray (Douglas)

Douglas, Michael
    See Crichton, (John) Michael

Douglass, Frederick
    1817(?)-1895 ....... NCLC 7; BLC; DA;
                              DAC; WLC
    See also CDALB 1640-1865; DAM MST,
    MULT; DLB 1, 43, 50, 79; SATA 29

Dourado, (Waldomiro Freitas) Autran
    1926- .................... CLC 23, 60
    See also CA 25-28R; CANR 34

Dourado, Waldomiro Autran
    See Dourado, (Waldomiro Freitas) Autran

Dove, Rita (Frances)
    1952- ............. CLC 50, 81; PC 6
    See also BW 2; CA 109; CAAS 19;
    CANR 27, 42; DAM MULT, POET;
    DLB 120

Dowell, Coleman 1925-1985........ CLC 60
    See also CA 25-28R; 117; CANR 10;
    DLB 130

Dowson, Ernest (Christopher)
    1867-1900 ................... TCLC 4
    See also CA 105; 150; DLB 19, 135

Doyle, A. Conan
    See Doyle, Arthur Conan

Doyle, Arthur Conan
    1859-1930 ......... TCLC 7; DA; DAB;
                              DAC; SSC 12; WLC
    See also AAYA 14; CA 104; 122;
    CDBLB 1890-1914; DAM MST, NOV;
    DLB 18, 70, 156; MTCW; SATA 24

Doyle, Conan
    See Doyle, Arthur Conan

Doyle, John
    See Graves, Robert (von Ranke)

Doyle, Roddy 1958(?)-............ CLC 81
    See also AAYA 14; CA 143

Doyle, Sir A. Conan
    See Doyle, Arthur Conan

Doyle, Sir Arthur Conan
    See Doyle, Arthur Conan

Dr. A
    See Asimov, Isaac; Silverstein, Alvin

Drabble, Margaret
    1939- ........ CLC 2, 3, 5, 8, 10, 22, 53;
                              DAB; DAC
    See also CA 13-16R; CANR 18, 35;
    CDBLB 1960 to Present; DAM MST,
    NOV, POP; DLB 14, 155; MTCW;
    SATA 48

Drapier, M. B.
    See Swift, Jonathan

Drayham, James
    See Mencken, H(enry) L(ouis)

Drayton, Michael 1563-1631........ LC 8

Dreadstone, Carl
    See Campbell, (John) Ramsey

Dreiser, Theodore (Herman Albert)
    1871-1945 ....... TCLC 10, 18, 35; DA;
                              DAC; WLC
    See also CA 106; 132; CDALB 1865-1917;
    DAM MST, NOV; DLB 9, 12, 102, 137;
    DLBD 1; MTCW

Drexler, Rosalyn 1926- .......... CLC 2, 6
    See also CA 81-84

Dreyer, Carl Theodor 1889-1968.... CLC 16
    See also CA 116

Drieu la Rochelle, Pierre(-Eugene)
    1893-1945 ................. TCLC 21
    See also CA 117; DLB 72

Drinkwater, John 1882-1937...... TCLC 57
    See also CA 109; 149; DLB 10, 19, 149

Drop Shot
    See Cable, George Washington

Droste-Hulshoff, Annette Freiin von
    1797-1848 ................. NCLC 3
    See also DLB 133

Drummond, Walter
    See Silverberg, Robert

Drummond, William Henry
    1854-1907 ................. TCLC 25
    See also DLB 92

Drummond de Andrade, Carlos
    1902-1987 ................... CLC 18
    See also Andrade, Carlos Drummond de
    See also CA 132; 123

Drury, Allen (Stuart) 1918-........ CLC 37
    See also CA 57-60; CANR 18;
    INT CANR-18

Dryden, John
    1631-1700 ........ LC 3, 21; DA; DAB;
                              DAC; DC 3; WLC
    See also CDBLB 1660-1789; DAM DRAM,
    MST, POET; DLB 80, 101, 131

Duberman, Martin 1930-........... CLC 8
    See also CA 1-4R; CANR 2

Dubie, Norman (Evans) 1945-...... CLC 36
See also CA 69-72; CANR 12; DLB 120

Du Bois, W(illiam) E(dward) B(urghardt)
1868-1963 ...... CLC 1, 2, 13, 64; BLC;
DA; DAC; WLC
See also BW 1; CA 85-88; CANR 34;
CDALB 1865-1917; DAM MST, MULT,
NOV; DLB 47, 50, 91; MTCW; SATA 42

Dubus, Andre 1936-... CLC 13, 36; SSC 15
See also CA 21-24R; CANR 17; DLB 130;
INT CANR-17

Duca Minimo
See D'Annunzio, Gabriele

Ducharme, Rejean 1941-.......... CLC 74
See also DLB 60

Duclos, Charles Pinot 1704-1772 ..... LC 1

Dudek, Louis 1918-.......... CLC 11, 19
See also CA 45-48; CAAS 14; CANR 1;
DLB 88

Duerrenmatt, Friedrich
1921-1990 ...... CLC 1, 4, 8, 11, 15, 43
See also CA 17-20R; CANR 33;
DAM DRAM; DLB 69, 124; MTCW

Duffy, Bruce (?)-................. CLC 50

Duffy, Maureen 1933-............ CLC 37
See also CA 25-28R; CANR 33; DLB 14;
MTCW

Dugan, Alan 1923-.............. CLC 2, 6
See also CA 81-84; DLB 5

du Gard, Roger Martin
See Martin du Gard, Roger

Duhamel, Georges 1884-1966 ....... CLC 8
See also CA 81-84; 25-28R; CANR 35;
DLB 65; MTCW

Dujardin, Edouard (Emile Louis)
1861-1949 ................. TCLC 13
See also CA 109; DLB 123

Dumas, Alexandre (Davy de la Pailleterie)
1802-1870 ....... NCLC 11; DA; DAB;
DAC; WLC
See also DAM MST, NOV; DLB 119;
SATA 18

Dumas, Alexandre
1824-1895 ............. NCLC 9; DC 1

Dumas, Claudine
See Malzberg, Barry N(athaniel)

Dumas, Henry L. 1934-1968 ..... CLC 6, 62
See also BW 1; CA 85-88; DLB 41

du Maurier, Daphne
1907-1989 ........ CLC 6, 11, 59; DAB;
DAC; SSC 18
See also CA 5-8R; 128; CANR 6;
DAM MST, POP; MTCW; SATA 27;
SATA-Obit 60

Dunbar, Paul Laurence
1872-1906 ...... TCLC 2, 12; BLC; DA;
DAC; PC 5; SSC 8; WLC
See also BW 1; CA 104; 124;
CDALB 1865-1917; DAM MST, MULT,
POET; DLB 50, 54, 78; SATA 34

Dunbar, William 1460(?)-1530(?) .... LC 20
See also DLB 132, 146

Duncan, Lois 1934-.............. CLC 26
See also AAYA 4; CA 1-4R; CANR 2, 23,
36; CLR 29; JRDA; MAICYA; SAAS 2;
SATA 1, 36, 75

Duncan, Robert (Edward)
1919-1988 .... CLC 1, 2, 4, 7, 15, 41, 55;
PC 2
See also CA 9-12R; 124; CANR 28;
DAM POET; DLB 5, 16; MTCW

Duncan, Sara Jeannette
1861-1922 ................. TCLC 60
See also DLB 92

Dunlap, William 1766-1839....... NCLC 2
See also DLB 30, 37, 59

Dunn, Douglas (Eaglesham)
1942-..................... CLC 6, 40
See also CA 45-48; CANR 2, 33; DLB 40;
MTCW

Dunn, Katherine (Karen) 1945-..... CLC 71
See also CA 33-36R

Dunn, Stephen 1939-.............. CLC 36
See also CA 33-36R; CANR 12, 48;
DLB 105

Dunne, Finley Peter 1867-1936.... TCLC 28
See also CA 108; DLB 11, 23

Dunne, John Gregory 1932-........ CLC 28
See also CA 25-28R; CANR 14, 50;
DLBY 80

Dunsany, Edward John Moreton Drax
Plunkett 1878-1957
See Dunsany, Lord
See also CA 104; 148; DLB 10

Dunsany, Lord................. TCLC 2, 59
See also Dunsany, Edward John Moreton
Drax Plunkett
See also DLB 77, 153, 156

du Perry, Jean
See Simenon, Georges (Jacques Christian)

Durang, Christopher (Ferdinand)
1949-.................... CLC 27, 38
See also CA 105; CANR 50

Duras, Marguerite
1914-...... CLC 3, 6, 11, 20, 34, 40, 68
See also CA 25-28R; CANR 50; DLB 83;
MTCW

Durban, (Rosa) Pam 1947-........ CLC 39
See also CA 123

Durcan, Paul 1944-............ CLC 43, 70
See also CA 134; DAM POET

Durkheim, Emile 1858-1917 ..... TCLC 55

Durrell, Lawrence (George)
1912-1990 .... CLC 1, 4, 6, 8, 13, 27, 41
See also CA 9-12R; 132; CANR 40;
CDBLB 1945-1960; DAM NOV; DLB 15,
27; DLBY 90; MTCW

Durrenmatt, Friedrich
See Duerrenmatt, Friedrich

Dutt, Toru 1856-1877.......... NCLC 29

Dwight, Timothy 1752-1817...... NCLC 13
See also DLB 37

Dworkin, Andrea 1946-.......... CLC 43
See also CA 77-80; CAAS 21; CANR 16,
39; INT CANR-16; MTCW

Dwyer, Deanna
See Koontz, Dean R(ay)

Dwyer, K. R.
See Koontz, Dean R(ay)

Dylan, Bob 1941-...... CLC 3, 4, 6, 12, 77
See also CA 41-44R; DLB 16

Eagleton, Terence (Francis) 1943-
See Eagleton, Terry
See also CA 57-60; CANR 7, 23; MTCW

Eagleton, Terry ................... CLC 63
See also Eagleton, Terence (Francis)

Early, Jack
See Scoppettone, Sandra

East, Michael
See West, Morris L(anglo)

Eastaway, Edward
See Thomas, (Philip) Edward

Eastlake, William (Derry) 1917-..... CLC 8
See also CA 5-8R; CAAS 1; CANR 5;
DLB 6; INT CANR-5

Eastman, Charles A(lexander)
1858-1939 ................. TCLC 55
See also DAM MULT; NNAL; YABC 1

Eberhart, Richard (Ghormley)
1904-............... CLC 3, 11, 19, 56
See also CA 1-4R; CANR 2;
CDALB 1941-1968; DAM POET;
DLB 48; MTCW

Eberstadt, Fernanda 1960-........ CLC 39
See also CA 136

Echegaray (y Eizaguirre), Jose (Maria Waldo)
1832-1916 ................. TCLC 4
See also CA 104; CANR 32; HW; MTCW

Echeverria, (Jose) Esteban (Antonino)
1805-1851 ................. NCLC 18

Echo
See Proust, (Valentin-Louis-George-Eugene-)
Marcel

Eckert, Allan W. 1931-........... CLC 17
See also CA 13-16R; CANR 14, 45;
INT CANR-14; SAAS 21; SATA 29;
SATA-Brief 27

Eckhart, Meister 1260(?)-1328(?) .. CMLC 9
See also DLB 115

Eckmar, F. R.
See de Hartog, Jan

Eco, Umberto 1932-........... CLC 28, 60
See also BEST 90:1; CA 77-80; CANR 12,
33; DAM NOV, POP; MTCW

Eddison, E(ric) R(ucker)
1882-1945 ................. TCLC 15
See also CA 109

Edel, (Joseph) Leon 1907-...... CLC 29, 34
See also CA 1-4R; CANR 1, 22; DLB 103;
INT CANR-22

Eden, Emily 1797-1869 ......... NCLC 10

Edgar, David 1948-.............. CLC 42
See also CA 57-60; CANR 12;
DAM DRAM; DLB 13; MTCW

Edgerton, Clyde (Carlyle) 1944- .... CLC 39
See also AAYA 17; CA 118; 134; INT 134

Edgeworth, Maria 1768-1849... NCLC 1, 51
See also DLB 116, 159, 163; SATA 21

Edmonds, Paul
See Kuttner, Henry

**Edmonds, Walter D(umaux)** 1903- . . **CLC 35**
See also CA 5-8R; CANR 2; DLB 9;
MAICYA; SAAS 4; SATA 1, 27

**Edmondson, Wallace**
See Ellison, Harlan (Jay)

**Edson, Russell** . . . . . . . . . . . . . . . . . . . . **CLC 13**
See also CA 33-36R

**Edwards, Bronwen Elizabeth**
See Rose, Wendy

**Edwards, G(erald) B(asil)**
1899-1976 . . . . . . . . . . . . . . . . . . . **CLC 25**
See also CA 110

**Edwards, Gus** 1939- . . . . . . . . . . . . . . **CLC 43**
See also CA 108; INT 108

**Edwards, Jonathan**
1703-1758 . . . . . . . . . . . **LC 7; DA; DAC**
See also DAM MST; DLB 24

**Efron, Marina Ivanovna Tsvetaeva**
See Tsvetaeva (Efron), Marina (Ivanovna)

**Ehle, John (Marsden, Jr.)** 1925- . . . . **CLC 27**
See also CA 9-12R

**Ehrenbourg, Ilya (Grigoryevich)**
See Ehrenburg, Ilya (Grigoryevich)

**Ehrenburg, Ilya (Grigoryevich)**
1891-1967 . . . . . . . . . . . . **CLC 18, 34, 62**
See also CA 102; 25-28R

**Ehrenburg, Ilyo (Grigoryevich)**
See Ehrenburg, Ilya (Grigoryevich)

**Eich, Guenter** 1907-1972 . . . . . . . . . . **CLC 15**
See also CA 111; 93-96; DLB 69, 124

**Eichendorff, Joseph Freiherr von**
1788-1857 . . . . . . . . . . . . . . . . . **NCLC 8**
See also DLB 90

**Eigner, Larry** . . . . . . . . . . . . . . . . . . . . . **CLC 9**
See also Eigner, Laurence (Joel)
See also CAAS 23; DLB 5

**Eigner, Laurence (Joel)** 1927-1996
See Eigner, Larry
See also CA 9-12R; CANR 6

**Eiseley, Loren Corey** 1907-1977 . . . . . **CLC 7**
See also AAYA 5; CA 1-4R; 73-76;
CANR 6

**Eisenstadt, Jill** 1963- . . . . . . . . . . . . . **CLC 50**
See also CA 140

**Eisenstein, Sergei (Mikhailovich)**
1898-1948 . . . . . . . . . . . . . . . . . **TCLC 57**
See also CA 114; 149

**Eisner, Simon**
See Kornbluth, C(yril) M.

**Ekeloef, (Bengt) Gunnar**
1907-1968 . . . . . . . . . . . . . . . . . **CLC 27**
See also CA 123; 25-28R; DAM POET

**Ekelof, (Bengt) Gunnar**
See Ekeloef, (Bengt) Gunnar

**Ekwensi, C. O. D.**
See Ekwensi, Cyprian (Odiatu Duaka)

**Ekwensi, Cyprian (Odiatu Duaka)**
1921- . . . . . . . . . . . . . . . . . **CLC 4; BLC**
See also BW 2; CA 29-32R; CANR 18, 42;
DAM MULT; DLB 117; MTCW;
SATA 66

**Elaine** . . . . . . . . . . . . . . . . . . . . . . . . **TCLC 18**
See also Leverson, Ada

**El Crummo**
See Crumb, R(obert)

**Elia**
See Lamb, Charles

**Eliade, Mircea** 1907-1986 . . . . . . . . . **CLC 19**
See also CA 65-68; 119; CANR 30; MTCW

**Eliot, A. D.**
See Jewett, (Theodora) Sarah Orne

**Eliot, Alice**
See Jewett, (Theodora) Sarah Orne

**Eliot, Dan**
See Silverberg, Robert

**Eliot, George**
1819-1880 . . . . . **NCLC 4, 13, 23, 41, 49;
DA; DAB; DAC; WLC**
See also CDBLB 1832-1890; DAM MST,
NOV; DLB 21, 35, 55

**Eliot, John** 1604-1690 . . . . . . . . . . . . . . **LC 5**
See also DLB 24

**Eliot, T(homas) S(tearns)**
1888-1965 . . . . . **CLC 1, 2, 3, 6, 9, 10, 13,
15, 24, 34, 41, 55, 57; DA; DAB; DAC;
PC 5; WLC 2**
See also CA 5-8R; 25-28R; CANR 41;
CDALB 1929-1941; DAM DRAM, MST,
POET; DLB 7, 10, 45, 63; DLBY 88;
MTCW

**Elizabeth** 1866-1941 . . . . . . . . . . . . . **TCLC 41**

**Elkin, Stanley L(awrence)**
1930-1995 . . . . . . **CLC 4, 6, 9, 14, 27, 51,
91; SSC 12**
See also CA 9-12R; 148; CANR 8, 46;
DAM NOV, POP; DLB 2, 28; DLBY 80;
INT CANR-8; MTCW

**Elledge, Scott** . . . . . . . . . . . . . . . . . . . . **CLC 34**

**Elliott, Don**
See Silverberg, Robert

**Elliott, George P(aul)** 1918-1980 . . . . . **CLC 2**
See also CA 1-4R; 97-100; CANR 2

**Elliott, Janice** 1931- . . . . . . . . . . . . . . **CLC 47**
See also CA 13-16R; CANR 8, 29; DLB 14

**Elliott, Sumner Locke** 1917-1991 . . . **CLC 38**
See also CA 5-8R; 134; CANR 2, 21

**Elliott, William**
See Bradbury, Ray (Douglas)

**Ellis, A. E.** . . . . . . . . . . . . . . . . . . . . . . . . **CLC 7**

**Ellis, Alice Thomas** . . . . . . . . . . . . . . . **CLC 40**
See also Haycraft, Anna

**Ellis, Bret Easton** 1964- . . . . . . . . **CLC 39, 71**
See also AAYA 2; CA 118; 123; CANR 51;
DAM POP; INT 123

**Ellis, (Henry) Havelock**
1859-1939 . . . . . . . . . . . . . . . . . **TCLC 14**
See also CA 109

**Ellis, Landon**
See Ellison, Harlan (Jay)

**Ellis, Trey** 1962- . . . . . . . . . . . . . . . . . **CLC 55**
See also CA 146

**Ellison, Harlan (Jay)**
1934- . . . . . . . . . **CLC 1, 13, 42; SSC 14**
See also CA 5-8R; CANR 5, 46;
DAM POP; DLB 8; INT CANR-5;
MTCW

**Ellison, Ralph (Waldo)**
1914-1994 . . . . . . . **CLC 1, 3, 11, 54, 86;
BLC; DA; DAB; DAC; WLC**
See also BW 1; CA 9-12R; 145; CANR 24;
CDALB 1941-1968; DAM MST, MULT,
NOV; DLB 2, 76; DLBY 94; MTCW

**Ellmann, Lucy (Elizabeth)** 1956- . . . . **CLC 61**
See also CA 128

**Ellmann, Richard (David)**
1918-1987 . . . . . . . . . . . . . . . . . **CLC 50**
See also BEST 89:2; CA 1-4R; 122;
CANR 2, 28; DLB 103; DLBY 87;
MTCW

**Elman, Richard** 1934- . . . . . . . . . . . . . **CLC 19**
See also CA 17-20R; CAAS 3; CANR 47

**Elron**
See Hubbard, L(afayette) Ron(ald)

**Eluard, Paul** . . . . . . . . . . . . . . . . . . **TCLC 7, 41**
See also Grindel, Eugene

**Elyot, Sir Thomas** 1490(?)-1546 . . . . . **LC 11**

**Elytis, Odysseus** 1911- . . . . . . . . . **CLC 15, 49**
See also CA 102; DAM POET; MTCW

**Emecheta, (Florence Onye) Buchi**
1944- . . . . . . . . . . . . . . . **CLC 14, 48; BLC**
See also BW 2; CA 81-84; CANR 27;
DAM MULT; DLB 117; MTCW;
SATA 66

**Emerson, Ralph Waldo**
1803-1882 . . . . . **NCLC 1, 38; DA; DAB;
DAC; WLC**
See also CDALB 1640-1865; DAM MST,
POET; DLB 1, 59, 73

**Eminescu, Mihail** 1850-1889 . . . . . **NCLC 33**

**Empson, William**
1906-1984 . . . . . . . . **CLC 3, 8, 19, 33, 34**
See also CA 17-20R; 112; CANR 31;
DLB 20; MTCW

**Enchi Fumiko (Ueda)** 1905-1986 . . . . **CLC 31**
See also CA 129; 121

**Ende, Michael (Andreas Helmuth)**
1929-1995 . . . . . . . . . . . . . . . . . **CLC 31**
See also CA 118; 124; 149; CANR 36;
CLR 14; DLB 75; MAICYA; SATA 61;
SATA-Brief 42; SATA-Obit 86

**Endo, Shusaku** 1923- . . . . . **CLC 7, 14, 19, 54**
See also CA 29-32R; CANR 21;
DAM NOV; MTCW

**Engel, Marian** 1933-1985 . . . . . . . . . . **CLC 36**
See also CA 25-28R; CANR 12; DLB 53;
INT CANR-12

**Engelhardt, Frederick**
See Hubbard, L(afayette) Ron(ald)

**Enright, D(ennis) J(oseph)**
1920- . . . . . . . . . . . . . . . . . . **CLC 4, 8, 31**
See also CA 1-4R; CANR 1, 42; DLB 27;
SATA 25

**Enzensberger, Hans Magnus**
1929- . . . . . . . . . . . . . . . . . . . . . . . **CLC 43**
See also CA 116; 119

**Ephron, Nora** 1941- . . . . . . . . . . . **CLC 17, 31**
See also AITN 2; CA 65-68; CANR 12, 39

**Epsilon**
See Betjeman, John

**Epstein, Daniel Mark** 1948- . . . . . . . . **CLC 7**
See also CA 49-52; CANR 2

**Epstein, Jacob** 1956- ............. **CLC 19**
See also CA 114

**Epstein, Joseph** 1937-............. **CLC 39**
See also CA 112; 119; CANR 50

**Epstein, Leslie** 1938- ............. **CLC 27**
See also CA 73-76; CAAS 12; CANR 23

**Equiano, Olaudah**
1745(?)-1797 ............. **LC 16; BLC**
See also DAM MULT; DLB 37, 50

**Erasmus, Desiderius** 1469(?)-1536.... **LC 16**

**Erdman, Paul E(mil)** 1932- ........ **CLC 25**
See also AITN 1; CA 61-64; CANR 13, 43

**Erdrich, Louise** 1954-.......... **CLC 39, 54**
See also AAYA 10; BEST 89:1; CA 114;
CANR 41; DAM MULT, NOV, POP;
DLB 152; MTCW; NNAL

**Erenburg, Ilya (Grigoryevich)**
See Ehrenburg, Ilya (Grigoryevich)

**Erickson, Stephen Michael** 1950-
See Erickson, Steve
See also CA 129

**Erickson, Steve** ................... **CLC 64**
See also Erickson, Stephen Michael

**Ericson, Walter**
See Fast, Howard (Melvin)

**Eriksson, Buntel**
See Bergman, (Ernst) Ingmar

**Ernaux, Annie** 1940- ............. **CLC 88**
See also CA 147

**Eschenbach, Wolfram von**
See Wolfram von Eschenbach

**Eseki, Bruno**
See Mphahlele, Ezekiel

**Esenin, Sergei (Alexandrovich)**
1895-1925 ................... **TCLC 4**
See also CA 104

**Eshleman, Clayton** 1935-........... **CLC 7**
See also CA 33-36R; CAAS 6; DLB 5

**Espriella, Don Manuel Alvarez**
See Southey, Robert

**Espriu, Salvador** 1913-1985........ **CLC 9**
See also CA 115; DLB 134

**Espronceda, Jose de** 1808-1842... **NCLC 39**

**Esse, James**
See Stephens, James

**Esterbrook, Tom**
See Hubbard, L(afayette) Ron(ald)

**Estleman, Loren D.** 1952- ........ **CLC 48**
See also CA 85-88; CANR 27; DAM NOV,
POP; INT CANR-27; MTCW

**Eugenides, Jeffrey** 1960(?)- ........ **CLC 81**
See also CA 144

**Euripides** c. 485B.C.-406B.C. ........ **DC 4**
See also DA; DAB; DAC; DAM DRAM,
MST

**Evan, Evin**
See Faust, Frederick (Schiller)

**Evans, Evan**
See Faust, Frederick (Schiller)

**Evans, Marian**
See Eliot, George

**Evans, Mary Ann**
See Eliot, George

**Evarts, Esther**
See Benson, Sally

**Everett, Percival L.** 1956- ........ **CLC 57**
See also BW 2; CA 129

**Everson, R(onald) G(ilmour)**
1903- ....................... **CLC 27**
See also CA 17-20R; DLB 88

**Everson, William (Oliver)**
1912-1994 ............... **CLC 1, 5, 14**
See also CA 9-12R; 145; CANR 20; DLB 5,
16; MTCW

**Evtushenko, Evgenii Aleksandrovich**
See Yevtushenko, Yevgeny (Alexandrovich)

**Ewart, Gavin (Buchanan)**
1916-1995 ............... **CLC 13, 46**
See also CA 89-92; 150; CANR 17, 46;
DLB 40; MTCW

**Ewers, Hanns Heinz** 1871-1943 ... **TCLC 12**
See also CA 109; 149

**Ewing, Frederick R.**
See Sturgeon, Theodore (Hamilton)

**Exley, Frederick (Earl)**
1929-1992 ................. **CLC 6, 11**
See also AITN 2; CA 81-84; 138; DLB 143;
DLBY 81

**Eynhardt, Guillermo**
See Quiroga, Horacio (Sylvestre)

**Ezekiel, Nissim** 1924-............. **CLC 61**
See also CA 61-64

**Ezekiel, Tish O'Dowd** 1943-....... **CLC 34**
See also CA 129

**Fadeyev, A.**
See Bulgya, Alexander Alexandrovich

**Fadeyev, Alexander**.............. **TCLC 53**
See also Bulgya, Alexander Alexandrovich

**Fagen, Donald** 1948-............. **CLC 26**

**Fainzilberg, Ilya Arnoldovich** 1897-1937
See Ilf, Ilya
See also CA 120

**Fair, Ronald L.** 1932-............. **CLC 18**
See also BW 1; CA 69-72; CANR 25;
DLB 33

**Fairbairns, Zoe (Ann)** 1948- ....... **CLC 32**
See also CA 103; CANR 21

**Falco, Gian**
See Papini, Giovanni

**Falconer, James**
See Kirkup, James

**Falconer, Kenneth**
See Kornbluth, C(yril) M.

**Falkland, Samuel**
See Heijermans, Herman

**Fallaci, Oriana** 1930-............. **CLC 11**
See also CA 77-80; CANR 15; MTCW

**Faludy, George** 1913-............. **CLC 42**
See also CA 21-24R

**Faludy, Gyoergy**
See Faludy, George

**Fanon, Frantz** 1925-1961..... **CLC 74; BLC**
See also BW 1; CA 116; 89-92;
DAM MULT

**Fanshawe, Ann** 1625-1680.......... **LC 11**

**Fante, John (Thomas)** 1911-1983 ... **CLC 60**
See also CA 69-72; 109; CANR 23;
DLB 130; DLBY 83

**Farah, Nuruddin** 1945-....... **CLC 53; BLC**
See also BW 2; CA 106; DAM MULT;
DLB 125

**Fargue, Leon-Paul** 1876(?)-1947 ... **TCLC 11**
See also CA 109

**Farigoule, Louis**
See Romains, Jules

**Farina, Richard** 1936(?)-1966 ....... **CLC 9**
See also CA 81-84; 25-28R

**Farley, Walter (Lorimer)**
1915-1989 ................... **CLC 17**
See also CA 17-20R; CANR 8, 29; DLB 22;
JRDA; MAICYA; SATA 2, 43

**Farmer, Philip Jose** 1918-....... **CLC 1, 19**
See also CA 1-4R; CANR 4, 35; DLB 8;
MTCW

**Farquhar, George** 1677-1707........ **LC 21**
See also DAM DRAM; DLB 84

**Farrell, J(ames) G(ordon)**
1935-1979 ................... **CLC 6**
See also CA 73-76; 89-92; CANR 36;
DLB 14; MTCW

**Farrell, James T(homas)**
1904-1979 ........ **CLC 1, 4, 8, 11, 66**
See also CA 5-8R; 89-92; CANR 9; DLB 4,
9, 86; DLBD 2; MTCW

**Farren, Richard J.**
See Betjeman, John

**Farren, Richard M.**
See Betjeman, John

**Fassbinder, Rainer Werner**
1946-1982 ................... **CLC 20**
See also CA 93-96; 106; CANR 31

**Fast, Howard (Melvin)** 1914- ...... **CLC 23**
See also AAYA 16; CA 1-4R; CAAS 18;
CANR 1, 33; DAM NOV; DLB 9;
INT CANR-33; SATA 7

**Faulcon, Robert**
See Holdstock, Robert P.

**Faulkner, William (Cuthbert)**
1897-1962 ..... **CLC 1, 3, 6, 8, 9, 11, 14,
18, 28, 52, 68; DA; DAB; DAC; SSC 1;
WLC**
See also AAYA 7; CA 81-84; CANR 33;
CDALB 1929-1941; DAM MST, NOV;
DLB 9, 11, 44, 102; DLBD 2; DLBY 86;
MTCW

**Fauset, Jessie Redmon**
1884(?)-1961 ........ **CLC 19, 54; BLC**
See also BW 1; CA 109; DAM MULT;
DLB 51

**Faust, Frederick (Schiller)**
1892-1944(?) ............... **TCLC 49**
See also CA 108; DAM POP

**Faust, Irvin** 1924-.................. **CLC 8**
See also CA 33-36R; CANR 28; DLB 2, 28;
DLBY 80

**Fawkes, Guy**
See Benchley, Robert (Charles)

**Fearing, Kenneth (Flexner)**
1902-1961 ................... **CLC 51**
See also CA 93-96; DLB 9

Foote, Shelby 1916- .............. CLC 75
See also CA 5-8R; CANR 3, 45;
DAM NOV, POP; DLB 2, 17

Forbes, Esther 1891-1967.......... CLC 12
See also AAYA 17; CA 13-14; 25-28R;
CAP 1; CLR 27; DLB 22; JRDA;
MAICYA; SATA 2

Forche, Carolyn (Louise)
1950- .......... CLC 25, 83, 86; PC 10
See also CA 109; 117; CANR 50;
DAM POET; DLB 5; INT 117

Ford, Elbur
See Hibbert, Eleanor Alice Burford

Ford, Ford Madox
1873-1939 ......... TCLC 1, 15, 39, 57
See also CA 104; 132; CDBLB 1914-1945;
DAM NOV; DLB 162; MTCW

Ford, John 1895-1973............. CLC 16
See also CA 45-48

Ford, Richard 1944- .............. CLC 46
See also CA 69-72; CANR 11, 47

Ford, Webster
See Masters, Edgar Lee

Foreman, Richard 1937-........... CLC 50
See also CA 65-68; CANR 32

Forester, C(ecil) S(cott)
1899-1966 ................... CLC 35
See also CA 73-76; 25-28R; SATA 13

Forez
See Mauriac, Francois (Charles)

Forman, James Douglas 1932-...... CLC 21
See also AAYA 17; CA 9-12R; CANR 4,
19, 42; JRDA; MAICYA; SATA 8, 70

Fornes, Maria Irene 1930-...... CLC 39, 61
See also CA 25-28R; CANR 28; DLB 7;
HW; INT CANR-28; MTCW

Forrest, Leon 1937- .............. CLC 4
See also BW 2; CA 89-92; CAAS 7;
CANR 25; DLB 33

Forster, E(dward) M(organ)
1879-1970 ..... CLC 1, 2, 3, 4, 9, 10, 13,
15, 22, 45, 77; DA; DAB; DAC; WLC
See also AAYA 2; CA 13-14; 25-28R;
CANR 45; CAP 1; CDBLB 1914-1945;
DAM MST, NOV; DLB 34, 98, 162;
DLBD 10; MTCW; SATA 57

Forster, John 1812-1876 ........ NCLC 11
See also DLB 144

Forsyth, Frederick 1938-...... CLC 2, 5, 36
See also BEST 89:4; CA 85-88; CANR 38;
DAM NOV, POP; DLB 87; MTCW

Forten, Charlotte L. ........ TCLC 16; BLC
See also Grimke, Charlotte L(ottie) Forten
See also DLB 50

Foscolo, Ugo 1778-1827.......... NCLC 8

Fosse, Bob ..................... CLC 20
See also Fosse, Robert Louis

Fosse, Robert Louis 1927-1987
See Fosse, Bob
See also CA 110; 123

Foster, Stephen Collins
1826-1864 ................ NCLC 26

Foucault, Michel
1926-1984 ............ CLC 31, 34, 69
See also CA 105; 113; CANR 34; MTCW

Fouque, Friedrich (Heinrich Karl) de la Motte
1777-1843 .................. NCLC 2
See also DLB 90

Fourier, Charles 1772-1837 ...... NCLC 51

Fournier, Henri Alban 1886-1914
See Alain-Fournier
See also CA 104

Fournier, Pierre 1916- ............ CLC 11
See also Gascar, Pierre
See also CA 89-92; CANR 16, 40

Fowles, John
1926- ...... CLC 1, 2, 3, 4, 6, 9, 10, 15,
33, 87; DAB; DAC
See also CA 5-8R; CANR 25; CDBLB 1960
to Present; DAM MST; DLB 14, 139;
MTCW; SATA 22

Fox, Paula 1923-................ CLC 2, 8
See also AAYA 3; CA 73-76; CANR 20,
36; CLR 1; DLB 52; JRDA; MAICYA;
MTCW; SATA 17, 60

Fox, William Price (Jr.) 1926- ..... CLC 22
See also CA 17-20R; CAAS 19; CANR 11;
DLB 2; DLBY 81

Foxe, John 1516(?)-1587 ........... LC 14

Frame, Janet .......... CLC 2, 3, 6, 22, 66
See also Clutha, Janet Paterson Frame

France, Anatole ................... TCLC 9
See also Thibault, Jacques Anatole Francois
See also DLB 123

Francis, Claude 19(?)- ............ CLC 50

Francis, Dick 1920- ........ CLC 2, 22, 42
See also AAYA 5; BEST 89:3; CA 5-8R;
CANR 9, 42; CDBLB 1960 to Present;
DAM POP; DLB 87; INT CANR-9;
MTCW

Francis, Robert (Churchill)
1901-1987 ................... CLC 15
See also CA 1-4R; 123; CANR 1

Frank, Anne(lies Marie)
1929-1945 ....... TCLC 17; DA; DAB;
DAC; WLC
See also AAYA 12; CA 113; 133;
DAM MST; MTCW; SATA-Brief 42

Frank, Elizabeth 1945-............ CLC 39
See also CA 121; 126; INT 126

Franklin, Benjamin
See Hasek, Jaroslav (Matej Frantisek)

Franklin, Benjamin
1706-1790 ..... LC 25; DA; DAB; DAC
See also CDALB 1640-1865; DAM MST;
DLB 24, 43, 73

Franklin, (Stella Maraia Sarah) Miles
1879-1954 ................... TCLC 7
See also CA 104

Fraser, (Lady) Antonia (Pakenham)
1932-....................... CLC 32
See also CA 85-88; CANR 44; MTCW;
SATA-Brief 32

Fraser, George MacDonald 1925-.... CLC 7
See also CA 45-48; CANR 2, 48

Fraser, Sylvia 1935-.............. CLC 64
See also CA 45-48; CANR 1, 16

Frayn, Michael 1933-...... CLC 3, 7, 31, 47
See also CA 5-8R; CANR 30;
DAM DRAM, NOV; DLB 13, 14;
MTCW

Fraze, Candida (Merrill) 1945-..... CLC 50
See also CA 126

Frazer, J(ames) G(eorge)
1854-1941 ................... TCLC 32
See also CA 118

Frazer, Robert Caine
See Creasey, John

Frazer, Sir James George
See Frazer, J(ames) G(eorge)

Frazier, Ian 1951-................ CLC 46
See also CA 130

Frederic, Harold 1856-1898...... NCLC 10
See also DLB 12, 23; DLBD 13

Frederick, John
See Faust, Frederick (Schiller)

Frederick the Great 1712-1786 ...... LC 14

Fredro, Aleksander 1793-1876..... NCLC 8

Freeling, Nicolas 1927- ........... CLC 38
See also CA 49-52; CAAS 12; CANR 1, 17,
50; DLB 87

Freeman, Douglas Southall
1886-1953 ................. TCLC 11
See also CA 109; DLB 17

Freeman, Judith 1946-............ CLC 55
See also CA 148

Freeman, Mary Eleanor Wilkins
1852-1930 ............ TCLC 9; SSC 1
See also CA 106; DLB 12, 78

Freeman, R(ichard) Austin
1862-1943 ................. TCLC 21
See also CA 113; DLB 70

French, Albert 1943- ............. CLC 86

French, Marilyn 1929-...... CLC 10, 18, 60
See also CA 69-72; CANR 3, 31;
DAM DRAM, NOV, POP;
INT CANR-31; MTCW

French, Paul
See Asimov, Isaac

Freneau, Philip Morin 1752-1832 .. NCLC 1
See also DLB 37, 43

Freud, Sigmund 1856-1939 ....... TCLC 52
See also CA 115; 133; MTCW

Friedan, Betty (Naomi) 1921-...... CLC 74
See also CA 65-68; CANR 18, 45; MTCW

Friedlaender, Saul 1932- .......... CLC 90
See also CA 117; 130

Friedman, B(ernard) H(arper)
1926-....................... CLC 7
See also CA 1-4R; CANR 3, 48

Friedman, Bruce Jay 1930-.... CLC 3, 5, 56
See also CA 9-12R; CANR 25; DLB 2, 28;
INT CANR-25

Friel, Brian 1929-........... CLC 5, 42, 59
See also CA 21-24R; CANR 33; DLB 13;
MTCW

Friis-Baastad, Babbis Ellinor
1921-1970 ................... CLC 12
See also CA 17-20R; 134; SATA 7

**Garrigue, Jean** 1914-1972 . . . . . . . . **CLC 2, 8**
See also CA 5-8R; 37-40R; CANR 20

**Garrison, Frederick**
See Sinclair, Upton (Beall)

**Garth, Will**
See Hamilton, Edmond; Kuttner, Henry

**Garvey, Marcus (Moziah, Jr.)**
1887-1940 . . . . . . . . . . . . **TCLC 41; BLC**
See also BW 1; CA 120; 124; DAM MULT

**Gary, Romain** . . . . . . . . . . . . . . . . . . . . **CLC 25**
See also Kacew, Romain
See also DLB 83

**Gascar, Pierre** . . . . . . . . . . . . . . . . . . . . **CLC 11**
See also Fournier, Pierre

**Gascoyne, David (Emery)** 1916- . . . . **CLC 45**
See also CA 65-68; CANR 10, 28; DLB 20;
MTCW

**Gaskell, Elizabeth Cleghorn**
1810-1865 . . . . . . . . . . . **NCLC 5; DAB**
See also CDBLB 1832-1890; DAM MST;
DLB 21, 144, 159

**Gass, William H(oward)**
1924- . . . **CLC 1, 2, 8, 11, 15, 39; SSC 12**
See also CA 17-20R; CANR 30; DLB 2;
MTCW

**Gasset, Jose Ortega y**
See Ortega y Gasset, Jose

**Gates, Henry Louis, Jr.** 1950- . . . . . . **CLC 65**
See also BW 2; CA 109; CANR 25;
DAM MULT; DLB 67

**Gautier, Theophile**
1811-1872 . . . . . . . . . . **NCLC 1; SSC 20**
See also DAM POET; DLB 119

**Gawsworth, John**
See Bates, H(erbert) E(rnest)

**Gay, Oliver**
See Gogarty, Oliver St. John

**Gaye, Marvin (Penze)** 1939-1984 . . . **CLC 26**
See also CA 112

**Gebler, Carlo (Ernest)** 1954- . . . . . . . **CLC 39**
See also CA 119; 133

**Gee, Maggie (Mary)** 1948- . . . . . . . . **CLC 57**
See also CA 130

**Gee, Maurice (Gough)** 1931- . . . . . . . **CLC 29**
See also CA 97-100; SATA 46

**Gelbart, Larry (Simon)** 1923- . . . **CLC 21, 61**
See also CA 73-76; CANR 45

**Gelber, Jack** 1932- . . . . . . . . **CLC 1, 6, 14, 79**
See also CA 1-4R; CANR 2; DLB 7

**Gellhorn, Martha (Ellis)** 1908- . . **CLC 14, 60**
See also CA 77-80; CANR 44; DLBY 82

**Genet, Jean**
1910-1986 . . . **CLC 1, 2, 5, 10, 14, 44, 46**
See also CA 13-16R; CANR 18;
DAM DRAM; DLB 72; DLBY 86;
MTCW

**Gent, Peter** 1942- . . . . . . . . . . . . . . . . . **CLC 29**
See also AITN 1; CA 89-92; DLBY 82

**Gentlewoman in New England, A**
See Bradstreet, Anne

**Gentlewoman in Those Parts, A**
See Bradstreet, Anne

**George, Jean Craighead** 1919- . . . . . . **CLC 35**
See also AAYA 8; CA 5-8R; CANR 25;
CLR 1; DLB 52; JRDA; MAICYA;
SATA 2, 68

**George, Stefan (Anton)**
1868-1933 . . . . . . . . . . . . . . . **TCLC 2, 14**
See also CA 104

**Georges, Georges Martin**
See Simenon, Georges (Jacques Christian)

**Gerhardi, William Alexander**
See Gerhardie, William Alexander

**Gerhardie, William Alexander**
1895-1977 . . . . . . . . . . . . . . . . . . . **CLC 5**
See also CA 25-28R; 73-76; CANR 18;
DLB 36

**Gerstler, Amy** 1956- . . . . . . . . . . . . . . **CLC 70**
See also CA 146

**Gertler, T.** . . . . . . . . . . . . . . . . . . . . . . **CLC 34**
See also CA 116; 121; INT 121

**Ghalib** . . . . . . . . . . . . . . . . . . . . . . . . . **NCLC 39**
See also Ghalib, Hsadullah Khan

**Ghalib, Hsadullah Khan** 1797-1869
See Ghalib
See also DAM POET

**Ghelderode, Michel de**
1898-1962 . . . . . . . . . . . . . . . . **CLC 6, 11**
See also CA 85-88; CANR 40;
DAM DRAM

**Ghiselin, Brewster** 1903- . . . . . . . . . . **CLC 23**
See also CA 13-16R; CAAS 10; CANR 13

**Ghose, Zulfikar** 1935- . . . . . . . . . . . . . **CLC 42**
See also CA 65-68

**Ghosh, Amitav** 1956- . . . . . . . . . . . . . **CLC 44**
See also CA 147

**Giacosa, Giuseppe** 1847-1906 . . . . . . **TCLC 7**
See also CA 104

**Gibb, Lee**
See Waterhouse, Keith (Spencer)

**Gibbon, Lewis Grassic** . . . . . . . . . . . . **TCLC 4**
See also Mitchell, James Leslie

**Gibbons, Kaye** 1960- . . . . . . . . **CLC 50, 88**
See also DAM POP

**Gibran, Kahlil**
1883-1931 . . . . . . . . . . **TCLC 1, 9; PC 9**
See also CA 104; 150; DAM POET, POP

**Gibran, Khalil**
See Gibran, Kahlil

**Gibson, William**
1914- . . . . . . . . **CLC 23; DA; DAB; DAC**
See also CA 9-12R; CANR 9, 42;
DAM DRAM, MST; DLB 7; SATA 66

**Gibson, William (Ford)** 1948- . . . **CLC 39, 63**
See also AAYA 12; CA 126; 133;
DAM POP

**Gide, Andre (Paul Guillaume)**
1869-1951 . . . . . . . **TCLC 5, 12, 36; DA;
DAB; DAC; SSC 13; WLC**
See also CA 104; 124; DAM MST, NOV;
DLB 65; MTCW

**Gifford, Barry (Colby)** 1946- . . . . . . . **CLC 34**
See also CA 65-68; CANR 9, 30, 40

**Gilbert, W(illiam) S(chwenck)**
1836-1911 . . . . . . . . . . . . . . . . . . **TCLC 3**
See also CA 104; DAM DRAM, POET;
SATA 36

**Gilbreth, Frank B., Jr.** 1911- . . . . . . . **CLC 17**
See also CA 9-12R; SATA 2

**Gilchrist, Ellen** 1935- . . **CLC 34, 48; SSC 14**
See also CA 113; 116; CANR 41;
DAM POP; DLB 130; MTCW

**Giles, Molly** 1942- . . . . . . . . . . . . . . . **CLC 39**
See also CA 126

**Gill, Patrick**
See Creasey, John

**Gilliam, Terry (Vance)** 1940- . . . . . . . **CLC 21**
See also Monty Python
See also CA 108; 113; CANR 35; INT 113

**Gillian, Jerry**
See Gilliam, Terry (Vance)

**Gilliatt, Penelope (Ann Douglass)**
1932-1993 . . . . . . . . . . **CLC 2, 10, 13, 53**
See also AITN 2; CA 13-16R; 141;
CANR 49; DLB 14

**Gilman, Charlotte (Anna) Perkins (Stetson)**
1860-1935 . . . . . . . . **TCLC 9, 37; SSC 13**
See also CA 106; 150

**Gilmour, David** 1949- . . . . . . . . . . . . . **CLC 35**
See also CA 138, 147

**Gilpin, William** 1724-1804 . . . . . . . **NCLC 30**

**Gilray, J. D.**
See Mencken, H(enry) L(ouis)

**Gilroy, Frank D(aniel)** 1925- . . . . . . . . **CLC 2**
See also CA 81-84; CANR 32; DLB 7

**Ginsberg, Allen**
1926- . . . . . . **CLC 1, 2, 3, 4, 6, 13, 36, 69;
DA; DAB; DAC; PC 4; WLC 3**
See also AITN 1; CA 1-4R; CANR 2, 41;
CDALB 1941-1968; DAM MST, POET;
DLB 5, 16; MTCW

**Ginzburg, Natalia**
1916-1991 . . . . . . . . . . **CLC 5, 11, 54, 70**
See also CA 85-88; 135; CANR 33; MTCW

**Giono, Jean** 1895-1970 . . . . . . . . . . **CLC 4, 11**
See also CA 45-48; 29-32R; CANR 2, 35;
DLB 72; MTCW

**Giovanni, Nikki**
1943- . . . . . . **CLC 2, 4, 19, 64; BLC; DA;
DAB; DAC**
See also AITN 1; BW 2; CA 29-32R;
CAAS 6; CANR 18, 41; CLR 6;
DAM MST, MULT, POET; DLB 5, 41;
INT CANR-18; MAICYA; MTCW;
SATA 24

**Giovene, Andrea** 1904- . . . . . . . . . . . . . **CLC 7**
See also CA 85-88

**Gippius, Zinaida (Nikolayevna)** 1869-1945
See Hippius, Zinaida
See also CA 106

**Giraudoux, (Hippolyte) Jean**
1882-1944 . . . . . . . . . . . . . . . **TCLC 2, 7**
See also CA 104; DAM DRAM; DLB 65

**Gironella, Jose Maria** 1917- . . . . . . . **CLC 11**
See also CA 101

**Gissing, George (Robert)**
1857-1903 . . . . . . . . . . . **TCLC 3, 24, 47**
See also CA 105; DLB 18, 135

**Giurlani, Aldo**
See Palazzeschi, Aldo

**Gladkov, Fyodor (Vasilyevich)**
1883-1958 . . . . . . . . . . . . . . . . . **TCLC 27**

**Grade, Chaim** 1910-1982 . . . . . . . . . **CLC 10**
See also CA 93-96; 107

**Graduate of Oxford, A**
See Ruskin, John

**Graham, John**
See Phillips, David Graham

**Graham, Jorie** 1951- . . . . . . . . . . . . . **CLC 48**
See also CA 111; DLB 120

**Graham, R(obert) B(ontine) Cunninghame**
See Cunninghame Graham, R(obert)
B(ontine)
See also DLB 98, 135

**Graham, Robert**
See Haldeman, Joe (William)

**Graham, Tom**
See Lewis, (Harry) Sinclair

**Graham, W(illiam) S(ydney)**
1918-1986 . . . . . . . . . . . . . . . . . . **CLC 29**
See also CA 73-76; 118; DLB 20

**Graham, Winston (Mawdsley)**
1910- . . . . . . . . . . . . . . . . . . . . . . **CLC 23**
See also CA 49-52; CANR 2, 22, 45;
DLB 77

**Grant, Skeeter**
See Spiegelman, Art

**Granville-Barker, Harley**
1877-1946 . . . . . . . . . . . . . . . . . . **TCLC 2**
See also Barker, Harley Granville
See also CA 104; DAM DRAM

**Grass, Guenter (Wilhelm)**
1927- . . . . . CLC 1, 2, 4, 6, 11, 15, 22, 32,
**49, 88; DA; DAB; DAC; WLC**
See also CA 13-16R; CANR 20;
DAM MST, NOV; DLB 75, 124; MTCW

**Gratton, Thomas**
See Hulme, T(homas) E(rnest)

**Grau, Shirley Ann**
1929- . . . . . . . . . . . . . . **CLC 4, 9; SSC 15**
See also CA 89-92; CANR 22; DLB 2;
INT CANR-22; MTCW

**Gravel, Fern**
See Hall, James Norman

**Graver, Elizabeth** 1964- . . . . . . . . . . . **CLC 70**
See also CA 135

**Graves, Richard Perceval** 1945- . . . . **CLC 44**
See also CA 65-68; CANR 9, 26, 51

**Graves, Robert (von Ranke)**
1895-1985 . . . . . . CLC 1, 2, 6, 11, 39, 44,
**45; DAB; DAC; PC 6**
See also CA 5-8R; 117; CANR 5, 36;
CDBLB 1914-1945; DAM MST, POET;
DLB 20, 100; DLBY 85; MTCW;
SATA 45

**Gray, Alasdair (James)** 1934- . . . . . . **CLC 41**
See also CA 126; CANR 47; INT 126;
MTCW

**Gray, Amlin** 1946- . . . . . . . . . . . . . . **CLC 29**
See also CA 138

**Gray, Francine du Plessix** 1930- . . . . **CLC 22**
See also BEST 90:3; CA 61-64; CAAS 2;
CANR 11, 33; DAM NOV;
INT CANR-11; MTCW

**Gray, John (Henry)** 1866-1934 . . . . **TCLC 19**
See also CA 119

**Gray, Simon (James Holliday)**
1936- . . . . . . . . . . . . . . . . . . **CLC 9, 14, 36**
See also AITN 1; CA 21-24R; CAAS 3;
CANR 32; DLB 13; MTCW

**Gray, Spalding** 1941- . . . . . . . . . . . . . **CLC 49**
See also CA 128; DAM POP

**Gray, Thomas**
1716-1771 . . . . . . LC 4; DA; DAB; DAC;
**PC 2; WLC**
See also CDBLB 1660-1789; DAM MST;
DLB 109

**Grayson, David**
See Baker, Ray Stannard

**Grayson, Richard (A.)** 1951- . . . . . . . **CLC 38**
See also CA 85-88; CANR 14, 31

**Greeley, Andrew M(oran)** 1928- . . . . **CLC 28**
See also CA 5-8R; CAAS 7; CANR 7, 43;
DAM POP; MTCW

**Green, Anna Katharine**
1846-1935 . . . . . . . . . . . . . . . . . . **TCLC 63**
See also CA 112

**Green, Brian**
See Card, Orson Scott

**Green, Hannah**
See Greenberg, Joanne (Goldenberg)

**Green, Hannah** . . . . . . . . . . . . . . . . . . **CLC 3**
See also CA 73-76

**Green, Henry** . . . . . . . . . . . . . . . . **CLC 2, 13**
See also Yorke, Henry Vincent
See also DLB 15

**Green, Julian (Hartridge)** 1900-
See Green, Julien
See also CA 21-24R; CANR 33; DLB 4, 72;
MTCW

**Green, Julien** . . . . . . . . . . . . . . **CLC 3, 11, 77**
See also Green, Julian (Hartridge)

**Green, Paul (Eliot)** 1894-1981 . . . . . . **CLC 25**
See also AITN 1; CA 5-8R; 103; CANR 3;
DAM DRAM; DLB 7, 9; DLBY 81

**Greenberg, Ivan** 1908-1973
See Rahv, Philip
See also CA 85-88

**Greenberg, Joanne (Goldenberg)**
1932- . . . . . . . . . . . . . . . . . . . **CLC 7, 30**
See also AAYA 12; CA 5-8R; CANR 14,
32; SATA 25

**Greenberg, Richard** 1959(?)- . . . . . . . **CLC 57**
See also CA 138

**Greene, Bette** 1934- . . . . . . . . . . . . . . **CLC 30**
See also AAYA 7; CA 53-56; CANR 4;
CLR 2; JRDA; MAICYA; SAAS 16;
SATA 8

**Greene, Gael** . . . . . . . . . . . . . . . . . . . . **CLC 8**
See also CA 13-16R; CANR 10

**Greene, Graham**
1904-1991 . . . . CLC 1, 3, 6, 9, 14, 18, 27,
**37, 70, 72; DA; DAB; DAC; WLC**
See also AITN 2; CA 13-16R; 133;
CANR 35; CDBLB 1945-1960;
DAM MST, NOV; DLB 13, 15, 77, 100,
162; DLBY 91; MTCW; SATA 20

**Greer, Richard**
See Silverberg, Robert

**Gregor, Arthur** 1923- . . . . . . . . . . . . . . **CLC 9**
See also CA 25-28R; CAAS 10; CANR 11;
SATA 36

**Gregor, Lee**
See Pohl, Frederik

**Gregory, Isabella Augusta (Persse)**
1852-1932 . . . . . . . . . . . . . . . . . . **TCLC 1**
See also CA 104; DLB 10

**Gregory, J. Dennis**
See Williams, John A(lfred)

**Grendon, Stephen**
See Derleth, August (William)

**Grenville, Kate** 1950- . . . . . . . . . . . . . **CLC 61**
See also CA 118

**Grenville, Pelham**
See Wodehouse, P(elham) G(renville)

**Greve, Felix Paul (Berthold Friedrich)**
1879-1948
See Grove, Frederick Philip
See also CA 104; 141; DAC; DAM MST

**Grey, Zane** 1872-1939 . . . . . . . . . . . . **TCLC 6**
See also CA 104; 132; DAM POP; DLB 9;
MTCW

**Grieg, (Johan) Nordahl (Brun)**
1902-1943 . . . . . . . . . . . . . . . . . . **TCLC 10**
See also CA 107

**Grieve, C(hristopher) M(urray)**
1892-1978 . . . . . . . . . . . . . . . . **CLC 11, 19**
See also MacDiarmid, Hugh; Pteleon
See also CA 5-8R; 85-88; CANR 33;
DAM POET; MTCW

**Griffin, Gerald** 1803-1840 . . . . . . . . **NCLC 7**
See also DLB 159

**Griffin, John Howard** 1920-1980 . . . . **CLC 68**
See also AITN 1; CA 1-4R; 101; CANR 2

**Griffin, Peter** 1942- . . . . . . . . . . . . . . **CLC 39**
See also CA 136

**Griffiths, Trevor** 1935- . . . . . . . . . **CLC 13, 52**
See also CA 97-100; CANR 45; DLB 13

**Grigson, Geoffrey (Edward Harvey)**
1905-1985 . . . . . . . . . . . . . . . . . **CLC 7, 39**
See also CA 25-28R; 118; CANR 20, 33;
DLB 27; MTCW

**Grillparzer, Franz** 1791-1872 . . . . . . **NCLC 1**
See also DLB 133

**Grimble, Reverend Charles James**
See Eliot, T(homas) S(tearns)

**Grimke, Charlotte L(ottie) Forten**
1837(?)-1914
See Forten, Charlotte L.
See also BW 1; CA 117; 124; DAM MULT,
POET

**Grimm, Jacob Ludwig Karl**
1785-1863 . . . . . . . . . . . . . . . . . . **NCLC 3**
See also DLB 90; MAICYA; SATA 22

**Grimm, Wilhelm Karl** 1786-1859 . . **NCLC 3**
See also DLB 90; MAICYA; SATA 22

**Grimmelshausen, Johann Jakob Christoffel**
von 1621-1676 . . . . . . . . . . . . . . . **LC 6**

**Grindel, Eugene** 1895-1952
See Eluard, Paul
See also CA 104

**Grisham, John** 1955- . . . . . . . . . . . . . **CLC 84**
See also AAYA 14; CA 138; CANR 47;
DAM POP

**Grossman, David** 1954- . . . . . . . . . . CLC **67**
See also CA 138

**Grossman, Vasily (Semenovich)**
1905-1964 . . . . . . . . . . . . . . . . . . CLC **41**
See also CA 124; 130; MTCW

**Grove, Frederick Philip** . . . . . . . . . . . TCLC **4**
See also Greve, Felix Paul (Berthold Friedrich)
See also DLB 92

**Grubb**
See Crumb, R(obert)

**Grumbach, Doris (Isaac)**
1918- . . . . . . . . . . . . . . . . CLC **13, 22, 64**
See also CA 5-8R; CAAS 2; CANR 9, 42;
INT CANR-9

**Grundtvig, Nicolai Frederik Severin**
1783-1872 . . . . . . . . . . . . . . . . . NCLC **1**

**Grunge**
See Crumb, R(obert)

**Grunwald, Lisa** 1959- . . . . . . . . . . . . . CLC **44**
See also CA 120

**Guare, John** 1938- . . . . . . . CLC **8, 14, 29, 67**
See also CA 73-76; CANR 21;
DAM DRAM; DLB 7; MTCW

**Gudjonsson, Halldor Kiljan** 1902-
See Laxness, Halldor
See also CA 103

**Guenter, Erich**
See Eich, Guenter

**Guest, Barbara** 1920- . . . . . . . . . . . . . CLC **34**
See also CA 25-28R; CANR 11, 44; DLB 5

**Guest, Judith (Ann)** 1936- . . . . . . . CLC **8, 30**
See also AAYA 7; CA 77-80; CANR 15;
DAM NOV, POP; INT CANR-15;
MTCW

**Guevara, Che** . . . . . . . . . . . . . CLC **87**; HLC
See also Guevara (Serna), Ernesto

**Guevara (Serna), Ernesto** 1928-1967
See Guevara, Che
See also CA 127; 111; DAM MULT; HW

**Guild, Nicholas M.** 1944- . . . . . . . . . . CLC **33**
See also CA 93-96

**Guillemin, Jacques**
See Sartre, Jean-Paul

**Guillen, Jorge** 1893-1984 . . . . . . . . . CLC **11**
See also CA 89-92; 112; DAM MULT,
POET; DLB 108; HW

**Guillen (y Batista), Nicolas (Cristobal)**
1902-1989 . . . . . CLC **48, 79**; BLC; HLC
See also BW 2; CA 116; 125; 129;
DAM MST, MULT, POET; HW

**Guillevic, (Eugene)** 1907- . . . . . . . . . . CLC **33**
See also CA 93-96

**Guillois**
See Desnos, Robert

**Guiney, Louise Imogen**
1861-1920 . . . . . . . . . . . . . . . . . TCLC **41**
See also DLB 54

**Guiraldes, Ricardo (Guillermo)**
1886-1927 . . . . . . . . . . . . . . . . . TCLC **39**
See also CA 131; HW; MTCW

**Gumilev, Nikolai Stephanovich**
1886-1921 . . . . . . . . . . . . . . . . . TCLC **60**

**Gunesekera, Romesh** . . . . . . . . . . . . . CLC **91**

**Gunn, Bill** . . . . . . . . . . . . . . . . . . . . CLC **5**
See also Gunn, William Harrison
See also DLB 38

**Gunn, Thom(son William)**
1929- . . . . . . . . . . . . CLC **3, 6, 18, 32, 81**
See also CA 17-20R; CANR 9, 33;
CDBLB 1960 to Present; DAM POET;
DLB 27; INT CANR-33; MTCW

**Gunn, William Harrison** 1934(?)-1989
See Gunn, Bill
See also AITN 1; BW 1; CA 13-16R; 128;
CANR 12, 25

**Gunnars, Kristjana** 1948- . . . . . . . . . CLC **69**
See also CA 113; DLB 60

**Gurganus, Allan** 1947- . . . . . . . . . . . CLC **70**
See also BEST 90:1; CA 135; DAM POP

**Gurney, A(lbert) R(amsdell), Jr.**
1930- . . . . . . . . . . . . . . CLC **32, 50, 54**
See also CA 77-80; CANR 32;
DAM DRAM

**Gurney, Ivor (Bertie)** 1890-1937 . . . TCLC **33**

**Gurney, Peter**
See Gurney, A(lbert) R(amsdell), Jr.

**Guro, Elena** 1877-1913 . . . . . . . . . . TCLC **56**

**Gustafson, Ralph (Barker)** 1909- . . . . CLC **36**
See also CA 21-24R; CANR 8, 45; DLB 88

**Gut, Gom**
See Simenon, Georges (Jacques Christian)

**Guterson, David** 1956- . . . . . . . . . . . CLC **91**
See also CA 132

**Guthrie, A(lfred) B(ertram), Jr.**
1901-1991 . . . . . . . . . . . . . . . . CLC **23**
See also CA 57-60; 134; CANR 24; DLB 6;
SATA 62; SATA-Obit 67

**Guthrie, Isobel**
See Grieve, C(hristopher) M(urray)

**Guthrie, Woodrow Wilson** 1912-1967
See Guthrie, Woody
See also CA 113; 93-96

**Guthrie, Woody** . . . . . . . . . . . . . . . CLC **35**
See also Guthrie, Woodrow Wilson

**Guy, Rosa (Cuthbert)** 1928- . . . . . . . CLC **26**
See also AAYA 4; BW 2; CA 17-20R;
CANR 14, 34; CLR 13; DLB 33; JRDA;
MAICYA; SATA 14, 62

**Gwendolyn**
See Bennett, (Enoch) Arnold

**H. D.** . . . . . . . . CLC **3, 8, 14, 31, 34, 73**; PC **5**
See also Doolittle, Hilda

**H. de V.**
See Buchan, John

**Haavikko, Paavo Juhani**
1931- . . . . . . . . . . . . . . . . . CLC **18, 34**
See also CA 106

**Habbema, Koos**
See Heijermans, Herman

**Hacker, Marilyn**
1942- . . . . . . . . . . . CLC **5, 9, 23, 72, 91**
See also CA 77-80; DAM POET; DLB 120

**Haggard, H(enry) Rider**
1856-1925 . . . . . . . . . . . . . . . . TCLC **11**
See also CA 108; 148; DLB 70, 156;
SATA 16

**Hagiwara Sakutaro** 1886-1942 . . . . TCLC **60**

**Haig, Fenil**
See Ford, Ford Madox

**Haig-Brown, Roderick (Langmere)**
1908-1976 . . . . . . . . . . . . . . . . CLC **21**
See also CA 5-8R; 69-72; CANR 4, 38;
CLR 31; DLB 88; MAICYA; SATA 12

**Hailey, Arthur** 1920- . . . . . . . . . . . . . CLC **5**
See also AITN 2; BEST 90:3; CA 1-4R;
CANR 2, 36; DAM NOV, POP; DLB 88;
DLBY 82; MTCW

**Hailey, Elizabeth Forsythe** 1938- . . . CLC **40**
See also CA 93-96; CAAS 1; CANR 15, 48;
INT CANR-15

**Haines, John (Meade)** 1924- . . . . . . . CLC **58**
See also CA 17-20R; CANR 13, 34; DLB 5

**Hakluyt, Richard** 1552-1616 . . . . . . . LC **31**

**Haldeman, Joe (William)** 1943- . . . . . CLC **61**
See also CA 53-56; CANR 6; DLB 8;
INT CANR-6

**Haley, Alex(ander Murray Palmer)**
1921-1992 . . . . CLC **8, 12, 76**; BLC; DA;
                                           DAB; DAC
See also BW 2; CA 77-80; 136; DAM MST,
MULT, POP; DLB 38; MTCW

**Haliburton, Thomas Chandler**
1796-1865 . . . . . . . . . . . . . . . NCLC **15**
See also DLB 11, 99

**Hall, Donald (Andrew, Jr.)**
1928- . . . . . . . . . . . . . . CLC **1, 13, 37, 59**
See also CA 5-8R; CAAS 7; CANR 2, 44;
DAM POET; DLB 5; SATA 23

**Hall, Frederic Sauser**
See Sauser-Hall, Frederic

**Hall, James**
See Kuttner, Henry

**Hall, James Norman** 1887-1951 . . . TCLC **23**
See also CA 123; SATA 21

**Hall, (Marguerite) Radclyffe**
1886-1943 . . . . . . . . . . . . . . . . TCLC **12**
See also CA 110; 150

**Hall, Rodney** 1935- . . . . . . . . . . . . . CLC **51**
See also CA 109

**Halleck, Fitz-Greene** 1790-1867 . . NCLC **47**
See also DLB 3

**Halliday, Michael**
See Creasey, John

**Halpern, Daniel** 1945- . . . . . . . . . . . CLC **14**
See also CA 33-36R

**Hamburger, Michael (Peter Leopold)**
1924- . . . . . . . . . . . . . . . . . . CLC **5, 14**
See also CA 5-8R; CAAS 4; CANR 2, 47;
DLB 27

**Hamill, Pete** 1935- . . . . . . . . . . . . . . CLC **10**
See also CA 25-28R; CANR 18

**Hamilton, Alexander**
1755(?)-1804 . . . . . . . . . . . . . . NCLC **49**
See also DLB 37

**Hamilton, Clive**
See Lewis, C(live) S(taples)

**Hamilton, Edmond** 1904-1977 . . . . . . CLC **1**
See also CA 1-4R; CANR 3; DLB 8

**Hamilton, Eugene (Jacob) Lee**
See Lee-Hamilton, Eugene (Jacob)

**Hamilton, Franklin**
  See Silverberg, Robert

**Hamilton, Gail**
  See Corcoran, Barbara

**Hamilton, Mollie**
  See Kaye, M(ary) M(argaret)

**Hamilton, (Anthony Walter) Patrick**
  1904-1962 .................. **CLC 51**
  See also CA 113; DLB 10

**Hamilton, Virginia** 1936-......... **CLC 26**
  See also AAYA 2; BW 2; CA 25-28R;
  CANR 20, 37; CLR 1, 11, 40;
  DAM MULT; DLB 33, 52;
  INT CANR-20; JRDA; MAICYA;
  MTCW; SATA 4, 56, 79

**Hammett, (Samuel) Dashiell**
  1894-1961 ....... **CLC 3, 5, 10, 19, 47;**
                                              **SSC 17**
  See also AITN 1; CA 81-84; CANR 42;
  CDALB 1929-1941; DLBD 6; MTCW

**Hammon, Jupiter**
  1711(?)-1800(?) ......... **NCLC 5; BLC**
  See also DAM MULT, POET; DLB 31, 50

**Hammond, Keith**
  See Kuttner, Henry

**Hamner, Earl (Henry), Jr.** 1923- ... **CLC 12**
  See also AITN 2; CA 73-76; DLB 6

**Hampton, Christopher (James)**
  1946-....................... **CLC 4**
  See also CA 25-28R; DLB 13; MTCW

**Hamsun, Knut** ............. **TCLC 2, 14, 49**
  See also Pedersen, Knut

**Handke, Peter** 1942- .. **CLC 5, 8, 10, 15, 38**
  See also CA 77-80; CANR 33;
  DAM DRAM, NOV; DLB 85, 124;
  MTCW

**Hanley, James** 1901-1985 ... **CLC 3, 5, 8, 13**
  See also CA 73-76; 117; CANR 36; MTCW

**Hannah, Barry** 1942-....... **CLC 23, 38, 90**
  See also CA 108; 110; CANR 43; DLB 6;
  INT 110; MTCW

**Hannon, Ezra**
  See Hunter, Evan

**Hansberry, Lorraine (Vivian)**
  1930-1965 ...... **CLC 17, 62; BLC; DA;**
                                       **DAB; DAC; DC 2**
  See also BW 1; CA 109; 25-28R; CABS 3;
  CDALB 1941-1968; DAM DRAM, MST,
  MULT; DLB 7, 38; MTCW

**Hansen, Joseph** 1923-............ **CLC 38**
  See also CA 29-32R; CAAS 17; CANR 16,
  44; INT CANR-16

**Hansen, Martin A.** 1909-1955..... **TCLC 32**

**Hanson, Kenneth O(stlin)** 1922- .... **CLC 13**
  See also CA 53-56; CANR 7

**Hardwick, Elizabeth** 1916- ........ **CLC 13**
  See also CA 5-8R; CANR 3, 32;
  DAM NOV; DLB 6; MTCW

**Hardy, Thomas**
  1840-1928 ...... **TCLC 4, 10, 18, 32, 48,**
     **53; DA; DAB; DAC; PC 8; SSC 2; WLC**
  See also CA 104; 123; CDBLB 1890-1914;
  DAM MST, NOV, POET; DLB 18, 19,
  135; MTCW

**Hare, David** 1947- ........... **CLC 29, 58**
  See also CA 97-100; CANR 39; DLB 13;
  MTCW

**Harford, Henry**
  See Hudson, W(illiam) H(enry)

**Hargrave, Leonie**
  See Disch, Thomas M(ichael)

**Harjo, Joy** 1951- ............... **CLC 83**
  See also CA 114; CANR 35; DAM MULT;
  DLB 120; NNAL

**Harlan, Louis R(udolph)** 1922-..... **CLC 34**
  See also CA 21-24R; CANR 25

**Harling, Robert** 1951(?)- .......... **CLC 53**
  See also CA 147

**Harmon, William (Ruth)** 1938-..... **CLC 38**
  See also CA 33-36R; CANR 14, 32, 35;
  SATA 65

**Harper, F. E. W.**
  See Harper, Frances Ellen Watkins

**Harper, Frances E. W.**
  See Harper, Frances Ellen Watkins

**Harper, Frances E. Watkins**
  See Harper, Frances Ellen Watkins

**Harper, Frances Ellen**
  See Harper, Frances Ellen Watkins

**Harper, Frances Ellen Watkins**
  1825-1911 ............. **TCLC 14; BLC**
  See also BW 1; CA 111; 125; DAM MULT,
  POET; DLB 50

**Harper, Michael S(teven)** 1938- .. **CLC 7, 22**
  See also BW 1; CA 33-36R; CANR 24;
  DLB 41

**Harper, Mrs. F. E. W.**
  See Harper, Frances Ellen Watkins

**Harris, Christie (Lucy) Irwin**
  1907-....................... **CLC 12**
  See also CA 5-8R; CANR 6; DLB 88;
  JRDA; MAICYA; SAAS 10; SATA 6, 74

**Harris, Frank** 1856-1931........ **TCLC 24**
  See also CA 109; 150; DLB 156

**Harris, George Washington**
  1814-1869 ................. **NCLC 23**
  See also DLB 3, 11

**Harris, Joel Chandler**
  1848-1908 ........... **TCLC 2; SSC 19**
  See also CA 104; 137; DLB 11, 23, 42, 78,
  91; MAICYA; YABC 1

**Harris, John (Wyndham Parkes Lucas)
  Beynon** 1903-1969
  See Wyndham, John
  See also CA 102; 89-92

**Harris, MacDonald................. CLC 9**
  See also Heiney, Donald (William)

**Harris, Mark** 1922- ............. **CLC 19**
  See also CA 5-8R; CAAS 3; CANR 2;
  DLB 2; DLBY 80

**Harris, (Theodore) Wilson** 1921-.... **CLC 25**
  See also BW 2; CA 65-68; CAAS 16;
  CANR 11, 27; DLB 117; MTCW

**Harrison, Elizabeth Cavanna** 1909-
  See Cavanna, Betty
  See also CA 9-12R; CANR 6, 27

**Harrison, Harry (Max)** 1925-...... **CLC 42**
  See also CA 1-4R; CANR 5, 21; DLB 8;
  SATA 4

**Harrison, James (Thomas)**
  1937- ....... **CLC 6, 14, 33, 66; SSC 19**
  See also CA 13-16R; CANR 8, 51;
  DLBY 82; INT CANR-8

**Harrison, Jim**
  See Harrison, James (Thomas)

**Harrison, Kathryn** 1961-.......... **CLC 70**
  See also CA 144

**Harrison, Tony** 1937-............. **CLC 43**
  See also CA 65-68; CANR 44; DLB 40;
  MTCW

**Harriss, Will(ard Irvin)** 1922-...... **CLC 34**
  See also CA 111

**Harson, Sley**
  See Ellison, Harlan (Jay)

**Hart, Ellis**
  See Ellison, Harlan (Jay)

**Hart, Josephine** 1942(?)-.......... **CLC 70**
  See also CA 138; DAM POP

**Hart, Moss** 1904-1961............ **CLC 66**
  See also CA 109; 89-92; DAM DRAM;
  DLB 7

**Harte, (Francis) Bret(t)**
  1836(?)-1902 .... **TCLC 1, 25; DA; DAC;**
                                          **SSC 8; WLC**
  See also CA 104; 140; CDALB 1865-1917;
  DAM MST; DLB 12, 64, 74, 79;
  SATA 26

**Hartley, L(eslie) P(oles)**
  1895-1972 ................. **CLC 2, 22**
  See also CA 45-48; 37-40R; CANR 33;
  DLB 15, 139; MTCW

**Hartman, Geoffrey H.** 1929-....... **CLC 27**
  See also CA 117; 125; DLB 67

**Hartmann von Aue**
  c. 1160-c. 1205 ............. **CMLC 15**
  See also DLB 138

**Hartmann von Aue** 1170-1210.... **CMLC 15**

**Haruf, Kent** 1943- ............... **CLC 34**
  See also CA 149

**Harwood, Ronald** 1934-........... **CLC 32**
  See also CA 1-4R; CANR 4; DAM DRAM,
  MST; DLB 13

**Hasek, Jaroslav (Matej Frantisek)**
  1883-1923 ...................... **TCLC 4**
  See also CA 104; 129; MTCW

**Hass, Robert** 1941-............. **CLC 18, 39**
  See also CA 111; CANR 30, 50; DLB 105

**Hastings, Hudson**
  See Kuttner, Henry

**Hastings, Selina................. CLC 44**

**Hatteras, Amelia**
  See Mencken, H(enry) L(ouis)

**Hatteras, Owen................. TCLC 18**
  See also Mencken, H(enry) L(ouis); Nathan,
  George Jean

**Hauptmann, Gerhart (Johann Robert)**
  1862-1946 ...................... **TCLC 4**
  See also CA 104; DAM DRAM; DLB 66,
  118

**Havel, Vaclav**
  1936- .......... **CLC 25, 58, 65; DC 6**
  See also CA 104; CANR 36; DAM DRAM;
  MTCW

Haviaras, Stratis ................. **CLC 33**
See also Chaviaras, Strates

Hawes, Stephen 1475(?)-1523(?) ..... **LC 17**

Hawkes, John (Clendennin Burne, Jr.)
1925- ...... **CLC 1, 2, 3, 4, 7, 9, 14, 15,
27, 49**
See also CA 1-4R; CANR 2, 47; DLB 2, 7;
DLBY 80; MTCW

Hawking, S. W.
See Hawking, Stephen W(illiam)

Hawking, Stephen W(illiam)
1942- ..................... **CLC 63**
See also AAYA 13; BEST 89:1; CA 126;
129; CANR 48

Hawthorne, Julian 1846-1934 ..... **TCLC 25**

Hawthorne, Nathaniel
1804-1864 ....... **NCLC 39; DA; DAB;
DAC; SSC 3; WLC**
See also CDALB 1640-1865; DAM MST,
NOV; DLB 1, 74; YABC 2

Haxton, Josephine Ayres 1921-
See Douglas, Ellen
See also CA 115; CANR 41

Hayaseca y Eizaguirre, Jorge
See Echegaray (y Eizaguirre), Jose (Maria
Waldo)

Hayashi Fumiko 1904-1951 ....... **TCLC 27**

Haycraft, Anna
See Ellis, Alice Thomas
See also CA 122

Hayden, Robert E(arl)
1913-1980 ...... **CLC 5, 9, 14, 37; BLC;
DA; DAC; PC 6**
See also BW 1; CA 69-72; 97-100; CABS 2;
CANR 24; CDALB 1941-1968;
DAM MST, MULT, POET; DLB 5, 76;
MTCW; SATA 19; SATA-Obit 26

Hayford, J(oseph) E(phraim) Casely
See Casely-Hayford, J(oseph) E(phraim)

Hayman, Ronald 1932- ............ **CLC 44**
See also CA 25-28R; CANR 18, 50;
DLB 155

Haywood, Eliza (Fowler)
1693(?)-1756 ................... **LC 1**

Hazlitt, William 1778-1830 ...... **NCLC 29**
See also DLB 110, 158

Hazzard, Shirley 1931- ........... **CLC 18**
See also CA 9-12R; CANR 4; DLBY 82;
MTCW

Head, Bessie 1937-1986 ... **CLC 25, 67; BLC**
See also BW 2; CA 29-32R; 119; CANR 25;
DAM MULT; DLB 117; MTCW

Headon, (Nicky) Topper 1956(?)- ... **CLC 30**

Heaney, Seamus (Justin)
1939- ...... **CLC 5, 7, 14, 25, 37, 74, 91;
DAB**
See also CA 85-88; CANR 25, 48;
CDBLB 1960 to Present; DAM POET;
DLB 40; MTCW

Hearn, (Patricio) Lafcadio (Tessima Carlos)
1850-1904 ................... **TCLC 9**
See also CA 105; DLB 12, 78

Hearne, Vicki 1946- ............. **CLC 56**
See also CA 139

Hearon, Shelby 1931- ............ **CLC 63**
See also AITN 2; CA 25-28R; CANR 18,
48

Heat-Moon, William Least ......... **CLC 29**
See also Trogdon, William (Lewis)
See also AAYA 9

Hebbel, Friedrich 1813-1863 ..... **NCLC 43**
See also DAM DRAM; DLB 129

Hebert, Anne 1916- ... **CLC 4, 13, 29; DAC**
See also CA 85-88; DAM MST, POET;
DLB 68; MTCW

Hecht, Anthony (Evan)
1923- .................. **CLC 8, 13, 19**
See also CA 9-12R; CANR 6; DAM POET;
DLB 5

Hecht, Ben 1894-1964 ............. **CLC 8**
See also CA 85-88; DLB 7, 9, 25, 26, 28, 86

Hedayat, Sadeq 1903-1951 ....... **TCLC 21**
See also CA 120

Hegel, Georg Wilhelm Friedrich
1770-1831 ................ **NCLC 46**
See also DLB 90

Heidegger, Martin 1889-1976 ...... **CLC 24**
See also CA 81-84; 65-68; CANR 34;
MTCW

Heidenstam, (Carl Gustaf) Verner von
1859-1940 .................. **TCLC 5**
See also CA 104

Heifner, Jack 1946- .............. **CLC 11**
See also CA 105; CANR 47

Heijermans, Herman 1864-1924 ... **TCLC 24**
See also CA 123

Heilbrun, Carolyn G(old) 1926- ..... **CLC 25**
See also CA 45-48; CANR 1, 28

Heine, Heinrich 1797-1856 .... **NCLC 4, 54**
See also DLB 90

Heinemann, Larry (Curtiss) 1944- .. **CLC 50**
See also CA 110; CAAS 21; CANR 31;
DLBD 9; INT CANR-31

Heiney, Donald (William) 1921-1993
See Harris, MacDonald
See also CA 1-4R; 142; CANR 3

Heinlein, Robert A(nson)
1907-1988 ...... **CLC 1, 3, 8, 14, 26, 55**
See also AAYA 17; CA 1-4R; 125;
CANR 1, 20; DAM POP; DLB 8; JRDA;
MAICYA; MTCW; SATA 9, 69;
SATA-Obit 56

Helforth, John
See Doolittle, Hilda

Hellenhofferu, Vojtech Kapristian z
See Hasek, Jaroslav (Matej Frantisek)

Heller, Joseph
1923- .... **CLC 1, 3, 5, 8, 11, 36, 63; DA;
DAB; DAC; WLC**
See also AITN 1; CA 5-8R; CABS 1;
CANR 8, 42; DAM MST, NOV, POP;
DLB 2, 28; DLBY 80; INT CANR-8;
MTCW

Hellman, Lillian (Florence)
1906-1984 ...... **CLC 2, 4, 8, 14, 18, 34,
44, 52; DC 1**
See also AITN 1, 2; CA 13-16R; 112;
CANR 33; DAM DRAM; DLB 7;
DLBY 84; MTCW

Helprin, Mark 1947- ..... **CLC 7, 10, 22, 32**
See also CA 81-84; CANR 47; DAM NOV,
POP; DLBY 85; MTCW

Helvetius, Claude-Adrien
1715-1771 ................... **LC 26**

Helyar, Jane Penelope Josephine 1933-
See Poole, Josephine
See also CA 21-24R; CANR 10, 26;
SATA 82

Hemans, Felicia 1793-1835 ...... **NCLC 29**
See also DLB 96

Hemingway, Ernest (Miller)
1899-1961 .... **CLC 1, 3, 6, 8, 10, 13, 19,
30, 34, 39, 41, 44, 50, 61, 80; DA; DAB;
DAC; SSC 1; WLC**
See also CA 77-80; CANR 34;
CDALB 1917-1929; DAM MST, NOV;
DLB 4, 9, 102; DLBD 1; DLBY 81, 87;
MTCW

Hempel, Amy 1951- .............. **CLC 39**
See also CA 118; 137

Henderson, F. C.
See Mencken, H(enry) L(ouis)

Henderson, Sylvia
See Ashton-Warner, Sylvia (Constance)

Henley, Beth .............. **CLC 23; DC 6**
See also Henley, Elizabeth Becker
See also CABS 3; DLBY 86

Henley, Elizabeth Becker 1952-
See Henley, Beth
See also CA 107; CANR 32; DAM DRAM,
MST; MTCW

Henley, William Ernest
1849-1903 .................. **TCLC 8**
See also CA 105; DLB 19

Hennissart, Martha
See Lathen, Emma
See also CA 85-88

Henry, O. ........ **TCLC 1, 19; SSC 5; WLC**
See also Porter, William Sydney

Henry, Patrick 1736-1799 ......... **LC 25**

Henryson, Robert 1430(?)-1506(?) .... **LC 20**
See also DLB 146

Henry VIII 1491-1547 ............. **LC 10**

Henschke, Alfred
See Klabund

Hentoff, Nat(han Irving) 1925- ..... **CLC 26**
See also AAYA 4; CA 1-4R; CAAS 6;
CANR 5, 25; CLR 1; INT CANR-25;
JRDA; MAICYA; SATA 42, 69;
SATA-Brief 27

Heppenstall, (John) Rayner
1911-1981 ................... **CLC 10**
See also CA 1-4R; 103; CANR 29

Herbert, Frank (Patrick)
1920-1986 ...... **CLC 12, 23, 35, 44, 85**
See also CA 53-56; 118; CANR 5, 43;
DAM POP; DLB 8; INT CANR-5;
MTCW; SATA 9, 37; SATA-Obit 47

Herbert, George
1593-1633 ......... **LC 24; DAB; PC 4**
See also CDBLB Before 1660; DAM POET;
DLB 126

**Herbert, Zbigniew** 1924- ........ **CLC 9, 43**
See also CA 89-92; CANR 36;
DAM POET; MTCW

**Herbst, Josephine (Frey)**
1897-1969 ................... **CLC 34**
See also CA 5-8R; 25-28R; DLB 9

**Hergesheimer, Joseph**
1880-1954 ................. **TCLC 11**
See also CA 109; DLB 102, 9

**Herlihy, James Leo** 1927-1993 ..... **CLC 6**
See also CA 1-4R; 143; CANR 2

**Hermogenes** fl. c. 175- .......... **CMLC 6**

**Hernandez, Jose** 1834-1886...... **NCLC 17**

**Herodotus** c. 484B.C.-429B.C..... **CMLC 17**

**Herrick, Robert**
1591-1674 ..... **LC 13; DA; DAB; DAC;
PC 9**
See also DAM MST, POP; DLB 126

**Herring, Guilles**
See Somerville, Edith

**Herriot, James** 1916-1995 ........ **CLC 12**
See also Wight, James Alfred
See also AAYA 1; CA 148; CANR 40;
DAM POP; SATA 86

**Herrmann, Dorothy** 1941- ........ **CLC 44**
See also CA 107

**Herrmann, Taffy**
See Herrmann, Dorothy

**Hersey, John (Richard)**
1914-1993 ....... **CLC 1, 2, 7, 9, 40, 81**
See also CA 17-20R; 140; CANR 33;
DAM POP; DLB 6; MTCW; SATA 25;
SATA-Obit 76

**Herzen, Aleksandr Ivanovich**
1812-1870 ................ **NCLC 10**

**Herzl, Theodor** 1860-1904 ....... **TCLC 36**

**Herzog, Werner** 1942- ........... **CLC 16**
See also CA 89-92

**Hesiod** c. 8th cent. B.C.- ......... **CMLC 5**

**Hesse, Hermann**
1877-1962 .... **CLC 1, 2, 3, 6, 11, 17, 25,
69; DA; DAB; DAC; SSC 9; WLC**
See also CA 17-18; CAP 2; DAM MST,
NOV; DLB 66; MTCW; SATA 50

**Hewes, Cady**
See De Voto, Bernard (Augustine)

**Heyen, William** 1940- ........ **CLC 13, 18**
See also CA 33-36R; CAAS 9; DLB 5

**Heyerdahl, Thor** 1914- ........... **CLC 26**
See also CA 5-8R; CANR 5, 22; MTCW;
SATA 2, 52

**Heym, Georg (Theodor Franz Arthur)**
1887-1912 ................... **TCLC 9**
See also CA 106

**Heym, Stefan** 1913- .............. **CLC 41**
See also CA 9-12R; CANR 4; DLB 69

**Heyse, Paul (Johann Ludwig von)**
1830-1914 ................... **TCLC 8**
See also CA 104; DLB 129

**Heyward, (Edwin) DuBose**
1885-1940 ................. **TCLC 59**
See also CA 108; DLB 7, 9, 45; SATA 21

**Hibbert, Eleanor Alice Burford**
1906-1993 ................... **CLC 7**
See also BEST 90:4; CA 17-20R; 140;
CANR 9, 28; DAM POP; SATA 2;
SATA-Obit 74

**Higgins, George V(incent)**
1939- ................ **CLC 4, 7, 10, 18**
See also CA 77-80; CAAS 5; CANR 17, 51;
DLB 2; DLBY 81; INT CANR-17;
MTCW

**Higginson, Thomas Wentworth**
1823-1911 ................. **TCLC 36**
See also DLB 1, 64

**Highet, Helen**
See MacInnes, Helen (Clark)

**Highsmith, (Mary) Patricia**
1921-1995 ........... **CLC 2, 4, 14, 42**
See also CA 1-4R; 147; CANR 1, 20, 48;
DAM NOV, POP; MTCW

**Highwater, Jamake (Mamake)**
1942(?)- ..................... **CLC 12**
See also AAYA 7; CA 65-68; CAAS 7;
CANR 10, 34; CLR 17; DLB 52;
DLBY 85; JRDA; MAICYA; SATA 32,
69; SATA-Brief 30

**Highway, Tomson** 1951- ...... **CLC 92; DAC**
See also DAM MULT; NNAL

**Higuchi, Ichiyo** 1872-1896 ...... **NCLC 49**

**Hijuelos, Oscar** 1951- ...... **CLC 65; HLC**
See also BEST 90:1; CA 123; CANR 50;
DAM MULT, POP; DLB 145; HW

**Hikmet, Nazim** 1902(?)-1963 ....... **CLC 40**
See also CA 141; 93-96

**Hildesheimer, Wolfgang**
1916-1991 ................... **CLC 49**
See also CA 101; 135; DLB 69, 124

**Hill, Geoffrey (William)**
1932- ................ **CLC 5, 8, 18, 45**
See also CA 81-84; CANR 21;
CDBLB 1960 to Present; DAM POET;
DLB 40; MTCW

**Hill, George Roy** 1921- ........... **CLC 26**
See also CA 110; 122

**Hill, John**
See Koontz, Dean R(ay)

**Hill, Susan (Elizabeth)**
1942- ................. **CLC 4; DAB**
See also CA 33-36R; CANR 29;
DAM MST, NOV; DLB 14, 139; MTCW

**Hillerman, Tony** 1925- ............ **CLC 62**
See also AAYA 6; BEST 89:1; CA 29-32R;
CANR 21, 42; DAM POP; SATA 6

**Hillesum, Etty** 1914-1943 ........ **TCLC 49**
See also CA 137

**Hilliard, Noel (Harvey)** 1929- ...... **CLC 15**
See also CA 9-12R; CANR 7

**Hillis, Rick** 1956- ................. **CLC 66**
See also CA 134

**Hilton, James** 1900-1954 ........ **TCLC 21**
See also CA 108; DLB 34, 77; SATA 34

**Himes, Chester (Bomar)**
1909-1984 .... **CLC 2, 4, 7, 18, 58; BLC**
See also BW 2; CA 25-28R; 114; CANR 22;
DAM MULT; DLB 2, 76, 143; MTCW

**Hinde, Thomas** ................. **CLC 6, 11**
See also Chitty, Thomas Willes

**Hindin, Nathan**
See Bloch, Robert (Albert)

**Hine, (William) Daryl** 1936- ....... **CLC 15**
See also CA 1-4R; CAAS 15; CANR 1, 20;
DLB 60

**Hinkson, Katharine Tynan**
See Tynan, Katharine

**Hinton, S(usan) E(loise)**
1950- ........ **CLC 30; DA; DAB; DAC**
See also AAYA 2; CA 81-84; CANR 32;
CLR 3, 23; DAM MST, NOV; JRDA;
MAICYA; MTCW; SATA 19, 58

**Hippius, Zinaida** ................. **TCLC 9**
See also Gippius, Zinaida (Nikolayevna)

**Hiraoka, Kimitake** 1925-1970
See Mishima, Yukio
See also CA 97-100; 29-32R; DAM DRAM;
MTCW

**Hirsch, E(ric) D(onald), Jr.** 1928-... **CLC 79**
See also CA 25-28R; CANR 27, 51;
DLB 67; INT CANR-27; MTCW

**Hirsch, Edward** 1950- ......... **CLC 31, 50**
See also CA 104; CANR 20, 42; DLB 120

**Hitchcock, Alfred (Joseph)**
1899-1980 ................. **CLC 16**
See also CA 97-100; SATA 27;
SATA-Obit 24

**Hitler, Adolf** 1889-1945 .......... **TCLC 53**
See also CA 117; 147

**Hoagland, Edward** 1932- .......... **CLC 28**
See also CA 1-4R; CANR 2, 31; DLB 6;
SATA 51

**Hoban, Russell (Conwell)** 1925- .. **CLC 7, 25**
See also CA 5-8R; CANR 23, 37; CLR 3;
DAM NOV; DLB 52; MAICYA;
MTCW; SATA 1, 40, 78

**Hobbs, Perry**
See Blackmur, R(ichard) P(almer)

**Hobson, Laura Z(ametkin)**
1900-1986 ................. **CLC 7, 25**
See also CA 17-20R; 118; DLB 28;
SATA 52

**Hochhuth, Rolf** 1931- ........ **CLC 4, 11, 18**
See also CA 5-8R; CANR 33;
DAM DRAM; DLB 124; MTCW

**Hochman, Sandra** 1936- .......... **CLC 3, 8**
See also CA 5-8R; DLB 5

**Hochwaelder, Fritz** 1911-1986 ...... **CLC 36**
See also CA 29-32R; 120; CANR 42;
DAM DRAM; MTCW

**Hochwalder, Fritz**
See Hochwaelder, Fritz

**Hocking, Mary (Eunice)** 1921- ..... **CLC 13**
See also CA 101; CANR 18, 40

**Hodgins, Jack** 1938- .............. **CLC 23**
See also CA 93-96; DLB 60

**Hodgson, William Hope**
1877(?)-1918 ............... **TCLC 13**
See also CA 111; DLB 70, 153, 156

**Hoffman, Alice** 1952- ............. **CLC 51**
See also CA 77-80; CANR 34; DAM NOV;
MTCW

**Howes, Barbara** 1914- . . . . . . . . . . . **CLC 15**
See also CA 9-12R; CAAS 3; SATA 5

**Hrabal, Bohumil** 1914- . . . . . . . . **CLC 13, 67**
See also CA 106; CAAS 12

**Hsun, Lu**
See Lu Hsun

**Hubbard, L(afayette) Ron(ald)**
1911-1986 . . . . . . . . . . . . . **CLC 43**
See also CA 77-80; 118; CANR 22;
DAM POP

**Huch, Ricarda (Octavia)**
1864-1947 . . . . . . . . . . . . . . . **TCLC 13**
See also CA 111; DLB 66

**Huddle, David** 1942- . . . . . . . . . . . . **CLC 49**
See also CA 57-60; CAAS 20; DLB 130

**Hudson, Jeffrey**
See Crichton, (John) Michael

**Hudson, W(illiam) H(enry)**
1841-1922 . . . . . . . . . . . . . . . **TCLC 29**
See also CA 115; DLB 98, 153; SATA 35

**Hueffer, Ford Madox**
See Ford, Ford Madox

**Hughart, Barry** 1934- . . . . . . . . . . . . **CLC 39**
See also CA 137

**Hughes, Colin**
See Creasey, John

**Hughes, David (John)** 1930- . . . . . . . **CLC 48**
See also CA 116; 129; DLB 14

**Hughes, Edward James**
See Hughes, Ted
See also DAM MST, POET

**Hughes, (James) Langston**
1902-1967 . . . . . **CLC 1, 5, 10, 15, 35, 44;**
**BLC; DA; DAB; DAC; DC 3; PC 1;**
**SSC 6; WLC**
See also AAYA 12; BW 1; CA 1-4R;
25-28R; CANR 1, 34; CDALB 1929-1941;
CLR 17; DAM DRAM, MST, MULT,
POET; DLB 4, 7, 48, 51, 86; JRDA;
MAICYA; MTCW; SATA 4, 33

**Hughes, Richard (Arthur Warren)**
1900-1976 . . . . . . . . . . . . . . . **CLC 1, 11**
See also CA 5-8R; 65-68; CANR 4;
DAM NOV; DLB 15, 161; MTCW;
SATA 8; SATA-Obit 25

**Hughes, Ted**
1930- . . . . . . . **CLC 2, 4, 9, 14, 37; DAB;**
**DAC; PC 7**
See also Hughes, Edward James
See also CA 1-4R; CANR 1, 33; CLR 3;
DLB 40, 161; MAICYA; MTCW;
SATA 49; SATA-Brief 27

**Hugo, Richard F(ranklin)**
1923-1982 . . . . . . . . . . . . . **CLC 6, 18, 32**
See also CA 49-52; 108; CANR 3;
DAM POET; DLB 5

**Hugo, Victor (Marie)**
1802-1885 . . . . . . . . **NCLC 3, 10, 21; DA;**
**DAB; DAC; WLC**
See also DAM DRAM, MST, NOV, POET;
DLB 119; SATA 47

**Huidobro, Vicente**
See Huidobro Fernandez, Vicente Garcia

**Huidobro Fernandez, Vicente Garcia**
1893-1948 . . . . . . . . . . . . . . . **TCLC 31**
See also CA 131; HW

**Hulme, Keri** 1947- . . . . . . . . . . . . . . **CLC 39**
See also CA 125; INT 125

**Hulme, T(homas) E(rnest)**
1883-1917 . . . . . . . . . . . . . . . **TCLC 21**
See also CA 117; DLB 19

**Hume, David** 1711-1776 . . . . . . . . . . . **LC 7**
See also DLB 104

**Humphrey, William** 1924- . . . . . . . . **CLC 45**
See also CA 77-80; DLB 6

**Humphreys, Emyr Owen** 1919- . . . . . **CLC 47**
See also CA 5-8R; CANR 3, 24; DLB 15

**Humphreys, Josephine** 1945- . . . . **CLC 34, 57**
See also CA 121; 127; INT 127

**Hungerford, Pixie**
See Brinsmead, H(esba) F(ay)

**Hunt, E(verette) Howard, (Jr.)**
1918- . . . . . . . . . . . . . . . . . . . . . **CLC 3**
See also AITN 1; CA 45-48; CANR 2, 47

**Hunt, Kyle**
See Creasey, John

**Hunt, (James Henry) Leigh**
1784-1859 . . . . . . . . . . . . . . . . . **NCLC 1**
See also DAM POET

**Hunt, Marsha** 1946- . . . . . . . . . . . . . **CLC 70**
See also BW 2; CA 143

**Hunt, Violet** 1866-1942 . . . . . . . . . . **TCLC 53**
See also DLB 162

**Hunter, E. Waldo**
See Sturgeon, Theodore (Hamilton)

**Hunter, Evan** 1926- . . . . . . . . . . . **CLC 11, 31**
See also CA 5-8R; CANR 5, 38;
DAM POP; DLBY 82; INT CANR-5;
MTCW; SATA 25

**Hunter, Kristin (Eggleston)** 1931- . . . **CLC 35**
See also AITN 1; BW 1; CA 13-16R;
CANR 13; CLR 3; DLB 33;
INT CANR-13; MAICYA; SAAS 10;
SATA 12

**Hunter, Mollie** 1922- . . . . . . . . . . . . . **CLC 21**
See also McIlwraith, Maureen Mollie
Hunter
See also AAYA 13; CANR 37; CLR 25;
DLB 161; JRDA; MAICYA; SAAS 7;
SATA 54

**Hunter, Robert** (?)-1734 . . . . . . . . . . . **LC 7**

**Hurston, Zora Neale**
1903-1960 . . . . **CLC 7, 30, 61; BLC; DA;**
**DAC; SSC 4**
See also AAYA 15; BW 1; CA 85-88;
DAM MST, MULT, NOV; DLB 51, 86;
MTCW

**Huston, John (Marcellus)**
1906-1987 . . . . . . . . . . . . . . . . . **CLC 20**
See also CA 73-76; 123; CANR 34; DLB 26

**Hustvedt, Siri** 1955- . . . . . . . . . . . . . **CLC 76**
See also CA 137

**Hutten, Ulrich von** 1488-1523 . . . . . . . **LC 16**

**Huxley, Aldous (Leonard)**
1894-1963 . . . . . **CLC 1, 3, 4, 5, 8, 11, 18,**
**35, 79; DA; DAB; DAC; WLC**
See also AAYA 11; CA 85-88; CANR 44;
CDBLB 1914-1945; DAM MST, NOV;
DLB 36, 100, 162; MTCW; SATA 63

**Huysmans, Charles Marie Georges**
1848-1907
See Huysmans, Joris-Karl
See also CA 104

**Huysmans, Joris-Karl** . . . . . . . . . . . . . **TCLC 7**
See also Huysmans, Charles Marie Georges
See also DLB 123

**Hwang, David Henry**
1957- . . . . . . . . . . . . . . . . **CLC 55; DC 4**
See also CA 127; 132; DAM DRAM;
INT 132

**Hyde, Anthony** 1946- . . . . . . . . . . . . . **CLC 42**
See also CA 136

**Hyde, Margaret O(ldroyd)** 1917- . . . **CLC 21**
See also CA 1-4R; CANR 1, 36; CLR 23;
JRDA; MAICYA; SAAS 8; SATA 1, 42,
76

**Hynes, James** 1956(?)- . . . . . . . . . . . . **CLC 65**

**Ian, Janis** 1951- . . . . . . . . . . . . . . . . . **CLC 21**
See also CA 105

**Ibanez, Vicente Blasco**
See Blasco Ibanez, Vicente

**Ibarguengoitia, Jorge** 1928-1983 . . . . **CLC 37**
See also CA 124; 113; HW

**Ibsen, Henrik (Johan)**
1828-1906 . . . . . . . **TCLC 2, 8, 16, 37, 52;**
**DA; DAB; DAC; DC 2; WLC**
See also CA 104; 141; DAM DRAM, MST

**Ibuse Masuji** 1898-1993 . . . . . . . . . . . **CLC 22**
See also CA 127; 141

**Ichikawa, Kon** 1915- . . . . . . . . . . . . . **CLC 20**
See also CA 121

**Idle, Eric** 1943- . . . . . . . . . . . . . . . . . **CLC 21**
See also Monty Python
See also CA 116; CANR 35

**Ignatow, David** 1914- . . . . . . **CLC 4, 7, 14, 40**
See also CA 9-12R; CAAS 3; CANR 31;
DLB 5

**Ihimaera, Witi** 1944- . . . . . . . . . . . . . **CLC 46**
See also CA 77-80

**Ilf, Ilya** . . . . . . . . . . . . . . . . . . . . . . **TCLC 21**
See also Fainzilberg, Ilya Arnoldovich

**Immermann, Karl (Lebrecht)**
1796-1840 . . . . . . . . . . . . . . . . **NCLC 4, 49**
See also DLB 133

**Inclan, Ramon (Maria) del Valle**
See Valle-Inclan, Ramon (Maria) del

**Infante, G(uillermo) Cabrera**
See Cabrera Infante, G(uillermo)

**Ingalls, Rachel (Holmes)** 1940- . . . . . **CLC 42**
See also CA 123; 127

**Ingamells, Rex** 1913-1955 . . . . . . . . **TCLC 35**

**Inge, William Motter**
1913-1973 . . . . . . . . . . . . **CLC 1, 8, 19**
See also CA 9-12R; CDALB 1941-1968;
DAM DRAM; DLB 7; MTCW

**Ingelow, Jean** 1820-1897 . . . . . . . . **NCLC 39**
See also DLB 35, 163; SATA 33

**Ingram, Willis J.**
See Harris, Mark

**Innaurato, Albert (F.)** 1948(?)- . . **CLC 21, 60**
See also CA 115; 122; INT 122

**Innes, Michael**
See Stewart, J(ohn) I(nnes) M(ackintosh)

Ionesco, Eugene
   1909-1994 .... **CLC 1, 4, 6, 9, 11, 15, 41,
      86; DA; DAB; DAC; WLC**
   See also CA 9-12R; 144; DAM DRAM,
      MST; MTCW; SATA 7; SATA-Obit 79

Iqbal, Muhammad 1873-1938 ..... **TCLC 28**

Ireland, Patrick
   See O'Doherty, Brian

Iron, Ralph
   See Schreiner, Olive (Emilie Albertina)

Irving, John (Winslow)
   1942- ................ **CLC 13, 23, 38**
   See also AAYA 8; BEST 89:3; CA 25-28R;
      CANR 28; DAM NOV, POP; DLB 6;
      DLBY 82; MTCW

Irving, Washington
   1783-1859 ..... **NCLC 2, 19; DA; DAB;
      SSC 2; WLC**
   See also CDALB 1640-1865; DAM MST;
      DLB 3, 11, 30, 59, 73, 74; YABC 2

Irwin, P. K.
   See Page, P(atricia) K(athleen)

Isaacs, Susan 1943- .............. **CLC 32**
   See also BEST 89:1; CA 89-92; CANR 20,
      41; DAM POP; INT CANR-20; MTCW

Isherwood, Christopher (William Bradshaw)
   1904-1986 ....... **CLC 1, 9, 11, 14, 44**
   See also CA 13-16R; 117; CANR 35;
      DAM DRAM, NOV; DLB 15; DLBY 86;
      MTCW

Ishiguro, Kazuo 1954- ...... **CLC 27, 56, 59**
   See also BEST 90:2; CA 120; CANR 49;
      DAM NOV; MTCW

Ishikawa Takuboku
   1886(?)-1912 ......... **TCLC 15; PC 10**
   See also CA 113; DAM POET

Iskander, Fazil 1929- ............. **CLC 47**
   See also CA 102

Isler, Alan ........................ **CLC 91**

Ivan IV 1530-1584 ................ **LC 17**

Ivanov, Vyacheslav Ivanovich
   1866-1949 ................. **TCLC 33**
   See also CA 122

Ivask, Ivar Vidrik 1927-1992....... **CLC 14**
   See also CA 37-40R; 139; CANR 24

J. R. S.
   See Gogarty, Oliver St. John

Jabran, Kahlil
   See Gibran, Kahlil

Jabran, Khalil
   See Gibran, Kahlil

Jackson, Daniel
   See Wingrove, David (John)

Jackson, Jesse 1908-1983 ........ **CLC 12**
   See also BW 1; CA 25-28R; 109; CANR 27;
      CLR 28; MAICYA; SATA 2, 29;
      SATA-Obit 48

Jackson, Laura (Riding) 1901-1991
   See Riding, Laura
   See also CA 65-68; 135; CANR 28; DLB 48

Jackson, Sam
   See Trumbo, Dalton

Jackson, Sara
   See Wingrove, David (John)

Jackson, Shirley
   1919-1965 ....... **CLC 11, 60, 87; DA;
      DAC; SSC 9; WLC**
   See also AAYA 9; CA 1-4R; 25-28R;
      CANR 4; CDALB 1941-1968;
      DAM MST; DLB 6; SATA 2

Jacob, (Cyprien-)Max 1876-1944 ... **TCLC 6**
   See also CA 104

Jacobs, Jim 1942-................ **CLC 12**
   See also CA 97-100; INT 97-100

Jacobs, W(illiam) W(ymark)
   1863-1943 .................. **TCLC 22**
   See also CA 121; DLB 135

Jacobsen, Jens Peter 1847-1885 .. **NCLC 34**

Jacobsen, Josephine 1908-........ **CLC 48**
   See also CA 33-36R; CAAS 18; CANR 23,
      48

Jacobson, Dan 1929- ........... **CLC 4, 14**
   See also CA 1-4R; CANR 2, 25; DLB 14;
      MTCW

Jacqueline
   See Carpentier (y Valmont), Alejo

Jagger, Mick 1944-............... **CLC 17**

Jakes, John (William) 1932- ....... **CLC 29**
   See also BEST 89:4; CA 57-60; CANR 10,
      43; DAM NOV, POP; DLBY 83;
      INT CANR-10; MTCW; SATA 62

James, Andrew
   See Kirkup, James

James, C(yril) L(ionel) R(obert)
   1901-1989 ................... **CLC 33**
   See also BW 2; CA 117; 125; 128; DLB 125;
      MTCW

James, Daniel (Lewis) 1911-1988
   See Santiago, Danny
   See also CA 125

James, Dynely
   See Mayne, William (James Carter)

James, Henry Sr. 1811-1882..... **NCLC 53**

James, Henry
   1843-1916 ...... **TCLC 2, 11, 24, 40, 47;
      DA; DAB; DAC; SSC 8; WLC**
   See also CA 104; 132; CDALB 1865-1917;
      DAM MST, NOV; DLB 12, 71, 74;
      DLBD 13; MTCW

James, M. R.
   See James, Montague (Rhodes)
   See also DLB 156

James, Montague (Rhodes)
   1862-1936 .......... **TCLC 6; SSC 16**
   See also CA 104

James, P. D. ................. **CLC 18, 46**
   See also White, Phyllis Dorothy James
   See also BEST 90:2; CDBLB 1960 to
      Present; DLB 87

James, Philip
   See Moorcock, Michael (John)

James, William 1842-1910..... **TCLC 15, 32**
   See also CA 109

James I 1394-1437 ................ **LC 20**

Jameson, Anna 1794-1860....... **NCLC 43**
   See also DLB 99

Jami, Nur al-Din 'Abd al-Rahman
   1414-1492 ................... **LC 9**

Jandl, Ernst 1925- ............... **CLC 34**

Janowitz, Tama 1957- ............ **CLC 43**
   See also CA 106; DAM POP

Japrisot, Sebastien 1931-......... **CLC 90**

Jarrell, Randall
   1914-1965 ....... **CLC 1, 2, 6, 9, 13, 49**
   See also CA 5-8R; 25-28R; CABS 2;
      CANR 6, 34; CDALB 1941-1968; CLR 6;
      DAM POET; DLB 48, 52; MAICYA;
      MTCW; SATA 7

Jarry, Alfred
   1873-1907 ........ **TCLC 2, 14; SSC 20**
   See also CA 104; DAM DRAM

Jarvis, E. K.
   See Bloch, Robert (Albert); Ellison, Harlan
      (Jay); Silverberg, Robert

Jeake, Samuel, Jr.
   See Aiken, Conrad (Potter)

Jean Paul 1763-1825 ............. **NCLC 7**

Jefferies, (John) Richard
   1848-1887 ................. **NCLC 47**
   See also DLB 98, 141; SATA 16

Jeffers, (John) Robinson
   1887-1962 .... **CLC 2, 3, 11, 15, 54; DA;
      DAC; WLC**
   See also CA 85-88; CANR 35;
      CDALB 1917-1929; DAM MST, POET;
      DLB 45; MTCW

Jefferson, Janet
   See Mencken, H(enry) L(ouis)

Jefferson, Thomas 1743-1826 .... **NCLC 11**
   See also CDALB 1640-1865; DLB 31

Jeffrey, Francis 1773-1850....... **NCLC 33**
   See also DLB 107

Jelakowitch, Ivan
   See Heijermans, Herman

Jellicoe, (Patricia) Ann 1927-...... **CLC 27**
   See also CA 85-88; DLB 13

Jen, Gish ...................... **CLC 70**
   See also Jen, Lillian

Jen, Lillian 1956(?)-
   See Jen, Gish
   See also CA 135

Jenkins, (John) Robin 1912-....... **CLC 52**
   See also CA 1-4R; CANR 1; DLB 14

Jennings, Elizabeth (Joan)
   1926- .................... **CLC 5, 14**
   See also CA 61-64; CAAS 5; CANR 8, 39;
      DLB 27; MTCW; SATA 66

Jennings, Waylon 1937-........... **CLC 21**

Jensen, Johannes V. 1873-1950.... **TCLC 41**

Jensen, Laura (Linnea) 1948- ...... **CLC 37**
   See also CA 103

Jerome, Jerome K(lapka)
   1859-1927 ................. **TCLC 23**
   See also CA 119; DLB 10, 34, 135

Jerrold, Douglas William
   1803-1857 ................. **NCLC 2**
   See also DLB 158, 159

Jewett, (Theodora) Sarah Orne
   1849-1909 ........ **TCLC 1, 22; SSC 6**
   See also CA 108; 127; DLB 12, 74;
      SATA 15

**Jewsbury, Geraldine (Endsor)**
1812-1880 ................. NCLC 22
See also DLB 21

**Jhabvala, Ruth Prawer**
1927- ............. CLC 4, 8, 29; DAB
See also CA 1-4R; CANR 2, 29, 51;
DAM NOV; DLB 139; INT CANR-29;
MTCW

**Jibran, Kahlil**
See Gibran, Kahlil

**Jibran, Khalil**
See Gibran, Kahlil

**Jiles, Paulette**  1943- ........... CLC 13, 58
See also CA 101

**Jimenez (Mantecon), Juan Ramon**
1881-1958 ........ TCLC 4; HLC; PC 7
See also CA 104; 131; DAM MULT,
POET; DLB 134; HW; MTCW

**Jimenez, Ramon**
See Jimenez (Mantecon), Juan Ramon

**Jimenez Mantecon, Juan**
See Jimenez (Mantecon), Juan Ramon

**Joel, Billy** ....................... CLC 26
See also Joel, William Martin

**Joel, William Martin**  1949-
See Joel, Billy
See also CA 108

**John of the Cross, St.**  1542-1591 .... LC 18

**Johnson, B(ryan) S(tanley William)**
1933-1973 ................. CLC 6, 9
See also CA 9-12R; 53-56; CANR 9;
DLB 14, 40

**Johnson, Benj. F. of Boo**
See Riley, James Whitcomb

**Johnson, Benjamin F. of Boo**
See Riley, James Whitcomb

**Johnson, Charles (Richard)**
1948- ............. CLC 7, 51, 65; BLC
See also BW 2; CA 116; CAAS 18;
CANR 42; DAM MULT; DLB 33

**Johnson, Denis**  1949- ............ CLC 52
See also CA 117; 121; DLB 120

**Johnson, Diane**  1934- ....... CLC 5, 13, 48
See also CA 41-44R; CANR 17, 40;
DLBY 80; INT CANR-17; MTCW

**Johnson, Eyvind (Olof Verner)**
1900-1976 ................. CLC 14
See also CA 73-76; 69-72; CANR 34

**Johnson, J. R.**
See James, C(yril) L(ionel) R(obert)

**Johnson, James Weldon**
1871-1938 ......... TCLC 3, 19; BLC
See also BW 1; CA 104; 125;
CDALB 1917-1929; CLR 32;
DAM MULT, POET; DLB 51; MTCW;
SATA 31

**Johnson, Joyce**  1935- ........... CLC 58
See also CA 125; 129

**Johnson, Lionel (Pigot)**
1867-1902 ................. TCLC 19
See also CA 117; DLB 19

**Johnson, Mel**
See Malzberg, Barry N(athaniel)

**Johnson, Pamela Hansford**
1912-1981 ............... CLC 1, 7, 27
See also CA 1-4R; 104; CANR 2, 28;
DLB 15; MTCW

**Johnson, Samuel**
1709-1784 ..... LC 15; DA; DAB; DAC;
WLC
See also CDBLB 1660-1789; DAM MST;
DLB 39, 95, 104, 142

**Johnson, Uwe**
1934-1984 .......... CLC 5, 10, 15, 40
See also CA 1-4R; 112; CANR 1, 39;
DLB 75; MTCW

**Johnston, George (Benson)**  1913- ... CLC 51
See also CA 1-4R; CANR 5, 20; DLB 88

**Johnston, Jennifer**  1930- ........... CLC 7
See also CA 85-88; DLB 14

**Jolley, (Monica) Elizabeth**
1923- ............... CLC 46; SSC 19
See also CA 127; CAAS 13

**Jones, Arthur Llewellyn**  1863-1947
See Machen, Arthur
See also CA 104

**Jones, D(ouglas) G(ordon)**  1929- .... CLC 10
See also CA 29-32R; CANR 13; DLB 53

**Jones, David (Michael)**
1895-1974 ......... CLC 2, 4, 7, 13, 42
See also CA 9-12R; 53-56; CANR 28;
CDBLB 1945-1960; DLB 20, 100; MTCW

**Jones, David Robert**  1947-
See Bowie, David
See also CA 103

**Jones, Diana Wynne**  1934- ........ CLC 26
See also AAYA 12; CA 49-52; CANR 4,
26; CLR 23; DLB 161; JRDA; MAICYA;
SAAS 7; SATA 9, 70

**Jones, Edward P.**  1950- ........... CLC 76
See also BW 2; CA 142

**Jones, Gayl**  1949- ........... CLC 6, 9; BLC
See also BW 2; CA 77-80; CANR 27;
DAM MULT; DLB 33; MTCW

**Jones, James**  1921-1977.... CLC 1, 3, 10, 39
See also AITN 1, 2; CA 1-4R; 69-72;
CANR 6; DLB 2, 143; MTCW

**Jones, John J.**
See Lovecraft, H(oward) P(hillips)

**Jones, LeRoi** ......... CLC 1, 2, 3, 5, 10, 14
See also Baraka, Amiri

**Jones, Louis B.** ................... CLC 65
See also CA 141

**Jones, Madison (Percy, Jr.)**  1925- ... CLC 4
See also CA 13-16R; CAAS 11; CANR 7;
DLB 152

**Jones, Mervyn**  1922- .......... CLC 10, 52
See also CA 45-48; CAAS 5; CANR 1;
MTCW

**Jones, Mick**  1956(?)- ............. CLC 30

**Jones, Nettie (Pearl)**  1941- ........ CLC 34
See also BW 2; CA 137; CAAS 20

**Jones, Preston**  1936-1979 ........ CLC 10
See also CA 73-76; 89-92; DLB 7

**Jones, Robert F(rancis)**  1934- ....... CLC 7
See also CA 49-52; CANR 2

**Jones, Rod**  1953- ............... CLC 50
See also CA 128

**Jones, Terence Graham Parry**
1942- ....................... CLC 21
See also Jones, Terry; Monty Python
See also CA 112; 116; CANR 35; INT 116

**Jones, Terry**
See Jones, Terence Graham Parry
See also SATA 67; SATA-Brief 51

**Jones, Thom**  1945(?)- ............. CLC 81

**Jong, Erica**  1942- ...... CLC 4, 6, 8, 18, 83
See also AITN 1; BEST 90:2; CA 73-76;
CANR 26; DAM NOV, POP; DLB 2, 5,
28, 152; INT CANR-26; MTCW

**Jonson, Ben(jamin)**
1572(?)-1637 .... LC 6; DA; DAB; DAC;
DC 4; WLC
See also CDBLB Before 1660;
DAM DRAM, MST, POET; DLB 62,
121

**Jordan, June**  1936- .......... CLC 5, 11, 23
See also AAYA 2; BW 2; CA 33-36R;
CANR 25; CLR 10; DAM MULT,
POET; DLB 38; MAICYA; MTCW;
SATA 4

**Jordan, Pat(rick M.)**  1941- ........ CLC 37
See also CA 33-36R

**Jorgensen, Ivar**
See Ellison, Harlan (Jay)

**Jorgenson, Ivar**
See Silverberg, Robert

**Josephus, Flavius**  c. 37-100 ...... CMLC 13

**Josipovici, Gabriel**  1940- ........ CLC 6, 43
See also CA 37-40R; CAAS 8; CANR 47;
DLB 14

**Joubert, Joseph**  1754-1824 ....... NCLC 9

**Jouve, Pierre Jean**  1887-1976 ...... CLC 47
See also CA 65-68

**Joyce, James (Augustine Aloysius)**
1882-1941 ....... TCLC 3, 8, 16, 35, 52;
DA; DAB; DAC; SSC 3; WLC
See also CA 104; 126; CDBLB 1914-1945;
DAM MST, NOV, POET; DLB 10, 19,
36, 162; MTCW

**Jozsef, Attila**  1905-1937.......... TCLC 22
See also CA 116

**Juana Ines de la Cruz**  1651(?)-1695 ... LC 5

**Judd, Cyril**
See Kornbluth, C(yril) M.; Pohl, Frederik

**Julian of Norwich**  1342(?)-1416(?) .... LC 6
See also DLB 146

**Juniper, Alex**
See Hospital, Janette Turner

**Junius**
See Luxemburg, Rosa

**Just, Ward (Swift)**  1935- ........ CLC 4, 27
See also CA 25-28R; CANR 32;
INT CANR-32

**Justice, Donald (Rodney)**  1925- .. CLC 6, 19
See also CA 5-8R; CANR 26; DAM POET;
DLBY 83; INT CANR-26

**Juvenal**  c. 55-c. 127 ............. CMLC 8

**Juvenis**
See Bourne, Randolph S(illiman)

Kenyon, Robert O.
See Kuttner, Henry

Kerouac, Jack . . . . . CLC 1, 2, 3, 5, 14, 29, 61
See also Kerouac, Jean-Louis Lebris de
See also CDALB 1941-1968; DLB 2, 16;
DLBD 3

Kerouac, Jean-Louis Lebris de   1922-1969
See Kerouac, Jack
See also AITN 1; CA 5-8R; 25-28R;
CANR 26; DA; DAB; DAC; DAM MST,
NOV, POET, POP; MTCW; WLC

Kerr, Jean   1923-. . . . . . . . . . . . . . . . CLC 22
See also CA 5-8R; CANR 7; INT CANR-7

Kerr, M. E. . . . . . . . . . . . . . . . . . CLC 12, 35
See also Meaker, Marijane (Agnes)
See also AAYA 2; CLR 29; SAAS 1

Kerr, Robert . . . . . . . . . . . . . . . . . . . CLC 55

Kerrigan, (Thomas) Anthony
1918- . . . . . . . . . . . . . . . . . . . . CLC 4, 6
See also CA 49-52; CAAS 11; CANR 4

Kerry, Lois
See Duncan, Lois

Kesey, Ken (Elton)
1935- . . . . . . CLC 1, 3, 6, 11, 46, 64; DA;
DAB; DAC; WLC
See also CA 1-4R; CANR 22, 38;
CDALB 1968-1988; DAM MST, NOV,
POP; DLB 2, 16; MTCW; SATA 66

Kesselring, Joseph (Otto)
1902-1967 . . . . . . . . . . . . . . . . . . CLC 45
See also CA 150; DAM DRAM, MST

Kessler, Jascha (Frederick)   1929-. . . . CLC 4
See also CA 17-20R; CANR 8, 48

Kettelkamp, Larry (Dale)   1933- . . . . CLC 12
See also CA 29-32R; CANR 16; SAAS 3;
SATA 2

Keyber, Conny
See Fielding, Henry

Keyes, Daniel   1927-. . . . CLC 80; DA; DAC
See also CA 17-20R; CANR 10, 26;
DAM MST, NOV; SATA 37

Khanshendel, Chiron
See Rose, Wendy

Khayyam, Omar
1048-1131 . . . . . . . . . . . CMLC 11; PC 8
See also DAM POET

Kherdian, David   1931-. . . . . . . . . . CLC 6, 9
See also CA 21-24R; CAAS 2; CANR 39;
CLR 24; JRDA; MAICYA; SATA 16, 74

Khlebnikov, Velimir . . . . . . . . . . . . . TCLC 20
See also Khlebnikov, Viktor Vladimirovich

Khlebnikov, Viktor Vladimirovich   1885-1922
See Khlebnikov, Velimir
See also CA 117

Khodasevich, Vladislav (Felitsianovich)
1886-1939 . . . . . . . . . . . . . . . . TCLC 15
See also CA 115

Kielland, Alexander Lange
1849-1906 . . . . . . . . . . . . . . . . . TCLC 5
See also CA 104

Kiely, Benedict   1919-. . . . . . . . . CLC 23, 43
See also CA 1-4R; CANR 2; DLB 15

Kienzle, William X(avier)   1928- . . . . CLC 25
See also CA 93-96; CAAS 1; CANR 9, 31;
DAM POP; INT CANR-31; MTCW

Kierkegaard, Soren   1813-1855. . . . NCLC 34

Killens, John Oliver   1916-1987. . . . . CLC 10
See also BW 2; CA 77-80; 123; CAAS 2;
CANR 26; DLB 33

Killigrew, Anne   1660-1685. . . . . . . . . . LC 4
See also DLB 131

Kim
See Simenon, Georges (Jacques Christian)

Kincaid, Jamaica   1949-. . . CLC 43, 68; BLC
See also AAYA 13; BW 2; CA 125;
CANR 47; DAM MULT, NOV;
DLB 157

King, Francis (Henry)   1923-. . . . . CLC 8, 53
See also CA 1-4R; CANR 1, 33;
DAM NOV; DLB 15, 139; MTCW

King, Martin Luther, Jr.
1929-1968 . . . . CLC 83; BLC; DA; DAB;
DAC
See also BW 2; CA 25-28; CANR 27, 44;
CAP 2; DAM MST, MULT; MTCW;
SATA 14

King, Stephen (Edwin)
1947- . . . . . . CLC 12, 26, 37, 61; SSC 17
See also AAYA 1, 17; BEST 90:1;
CA 61-64; CANR 1, 30; DAM NOV,
POP; DLB 143; DLBY 80; JRDA;
MTCW; SATA 9, 55

King, Steve
See King, Stephen (Edwin)

King, Thomas   1943-. . . . . . . . . CLC 89; DAC
See also CA 144; DAM MULT; NNAL

Kingman, Lee. . . . . . . . . . . . . . . . . . . CLC 17
See also Natti, (Mary) Lee
See also SAAS 3; SATA 1, 67

Kingsley, Charles   1819-1875 . . . . . NCLC 35
See also DLB 21, 32, 163; YABC 2

Kingsley, Sidney   1906-1995. . . . . . . CLC 44
See also CA 85-88; 147; DLB 7

Kingsolver, Barbara   1955-. . . . . . CLC 55, 81
See also AAYA 15; CA 129; 134;
DAM POP; INT 134

Kingston, Maxine (Ting Ting) Hong
1940- . . . . . . . . . . . . . . . CLC 12, 19, 58
See also AAYA 8; CA 69-72; CANR 13,
38; DAM MULT, NOV; DLBY 80;
INT CANR-13; MTCW; SATA 53

Kinnell, Galway
1927-. . . . . . . . . . CLC 1, 2, 3, 5, 13, 29
See also CA 9-12R; CANR 10, 34; DLB 5;
DLBY 87; INT CANR-34; MTCW

Kinsella, Thomas   1928- . . . . . . . . CLC 4, 19
See also CA 17-20R; CANR 15; DLB 27;
MTCW

Kinsella, W(illiam) P(atrick)
1935- . . . . . . . . . . . . . . CLC 27, 43; DAC
See also AAYA 7; CA 97-100; CAAS 7;
CANR 21, 35; DAM NOV, POP;
INT CANR-21; MTCW

Kipling, (Joseph) Rudyard
1865-1936 . . . . . . TCLC 8, 17; DA; DAB;
DAC; PC 3; SSC 5; WLC
See also CA 105; 120; CANR 33;
CDBLB 1890-1914; CLR 39; DAM MST,
POET; DLB 19, 34, 141, 156; MAICYA;
MTCW; YABC 2

Kirkup, James   1918- . . . . . . . . . . . . . CLC 1
See also CA 1-4R; CAAS 4; CANR 2;
DLB 27; SATA 12

Kirkwood, James   1930(?)-1989 . . . . . . CLC 9
See also AITN 2; CA 1-4R; 128; CANR 6,
40

Kirshner, Sidney
See Kingsley, Sidney

Kis, Danilo   1935-1989 . . . . . . . . . . . CLC 57
See also CA 109; 118; 129; MTCW

Kivi, Aleksis   1834-1872. . . . . . . . NCLC 30

Kizer, Carolyn (Ashley)
1925-. . . . . . . . . . . . . . . CLC 15, 39, 80
See also CA 65-68; CAAS 5; CANR 24;
DAM POET; DLB 5

Klabund   1890-1928. . . . . . . . . . . . TCLC 44
See also DLB 66

Klappert, Peter   1942-. . . . . . . . . . . . CLC 57
See also CA 33-36R; DLB 5

Klein, A(braham) M(oses)
1909-1972 . . . . . . . . CLC 19; DAB; DAC
See also CA 101; 37-40R; DAM MST;
DLB 68

Klein, Norma   1938-1989 . . . . . . . . . . CLC 30
See also AAYA 2; CA 41-44R; 128;
CANR 15, 37; CLR 2, 19;
INT CANR-15; JRDA; MAICYA;
SAAS 1; SATA 7, 57

Klein, T(heodore) E(ibon) D(onald)
1947-. . . . . . . . . . . . . . . . . . . . . . CLC 34
See also CA 119; CANR 44

Kleist, Heinrich von
1777-1811 . . . . . . . . . . . . . NCLC 2, 37
See also DAM DRAM; DLB 90

Klima, Ivan   1931-. . . . . . . . . . . . . . CLC 56
See also CA 25-28R; CANR 17, 50;
DAM NOV

Klimentov, Andrei Platonovich   1899-1951
See Platonov, Andrei
See also CA 108

Klinger, Friedrich Maximilian von
1752-1831 . . . . . . . . . . . . . . . . . NCLC 1
See also DLB 94

Klopstock, Friedrich Gottlieb
1724-1803 . . . . . . . . . . . . . . . . NCLC 11
See also DLB 97

Knebel, Fletcher   1911-1993. . . . . . . CLC 14
See also AITN 1; CA 1-4R; 140; CAAS 3;
CANR 1, 36; SATA 36; SATA-Obit 75

Knickerbocker, Diedrich
See Irving, Washington

Knight, Etheridge
1931-1991 . . . . . . . CLC 40; BLC; PC 14
See also BW 1; CA 21-24R; 133; CANR 23;
DAM POET; DLB 41

Knight, Sarah Kemble   1666-1727 . . . . . LC 7
See also DLB 24

Knister, Raymond   1899-1932. . . . . . TCLC 56
See also DLB 68

Knowles, John
1926-. . . . . . CLC 1, 4, 10, 26; DA; DAC
See also AAYA 10; CA 17-20R; CANR 40;
CDALB 1968-1988; DAM MST, NOV;
DLB 6; MTCW; SATA 8

**Lermontov, Mikhail Yuryevich**
1814-1841 . . . . . . . . . . . . . . . . **NCLC 47**

**Leroux, Gaston** 1868-1927 . . . . . . . **TCLC 25**
See also CA 108; 136; SATA 65

**Lesage, Alain-Rene** 1668-1747 . . . . . . **LC 28**

**Leskov, Nikolai (Semyonovich)**
1831-1895 . . . . . . . . . . . . . . . . **NCLC 25**

**Lessing, Doris (May)**
1919- . . . . . **CLC 1, 2, 3, 6, 10, 15, 22, 40,
91; DA; DAB; DAC; SSC 6**
See also CA 9-12R; CAAS 14; CANR 33;
CDBLB 1960 to Present; DAM MST,
NOV; DLB 15, 139; DLBY 85; MTCW

**Lessing, Gotthold Ephraim**
1729-1781 . . . . . . . . . . . . . . . . . . . **LC 8**
See also DLB 97

**Lester, Richard** 1932- . . . . . . . . . . . . **CLC 20**

**Lever, Charles (James)**
1806-1872 . . . . . . . . . . . . . . . . **NCLC 23**
See also DLB 21

**Leverson, Ada** 1865(?)-1936(?) . . . . **TCLC 18**
See also Elaine
See also CA 117; DLB 153

**Levertov, Denise**
1923- . . . . . . **CLC 1, 2, 3, 5, 8, 15, 28, 66;
PC 11**
See also CA 1-4R; CAAS 19; CANR 3, 29,
50; DAM POET; DLB 5; INT CANR-29;
MTCW

**Levi, Jonathan** . . . . . . . . . . . . . . . . . . **CLC 76**

**Levi, Peter (Chad Tigar)** 1931- . . . . . **CLC 41**
See also CA 5-8R; CANR 34; DLB 40

**Levi, Primo**
1919-1987 . . . . . . . . **CLC 37, 50; SSC 12**
See also CA 13-16R; 122; CANR 12, 33;
MTCW

**Levin, Ira** 1929- . . . . . . . . . . . . . . . . **CLC 3, 6**
See also CA 21-24R; CANR 17, 44;
DAM POP; MTCW; SATA 66

**Levin, Meyer** 1905-1981 . . . . . . . . . . **CLC 7**
See also AITN 1; CA 9-12R; 104;
CANR 15; DAM POP; DLB 9, 28;
DLBY 81; SATA 21; SATA-Obit 27

**Levine, Norman** 1924- . . . . . . . . . . . **CLC 54**
See also CA 73-76; CAAS 23; CANR 14;
DLB 88

**Levine, Philip** 1928- . . **CLC 2, 4, 5, 9, 14, 33**
See also CA 9-12R; CANR 9, 37;
DAM POET; DLB 5

**Levinson, Deirdre** 1931- . . . . . . . . . . **CLC 49**
See also CA 73-76

**Levi-Strauss, Claude** 1908- . . . . . . . . **CLC 38**
See also CA 1-4R; CANR 6, 32; MTCW

**Levitin, Sonia (Wolff)** 1934- . . . . . . . **CLC 17**
See also AAYA 13; CA 29-32R; CANR 14,
32; JRDA; MAICYA; SAAS 2; SATA 4,
68

**Levon, O. U.**
See Kesey, Ken (Elton)

**Lewes, George Henry**
1817-1878 . . . . . . . . . . . . . . . . **NCLC 25**
See also DLB 55, 144

**Lewis, Alun** 1915-1944 . . . . . . . . . . . **TCLC 3**
See also CA 104; DLB 20, 162

**Lewis, C. Day**
See Day Lewis, C(ecil)

**Lewis, C(live) S(taples)**
1898-1963 . . . . . **CLC 1, 3, 6, 14, 27; DA;
DAB; DAC; WLC**
See also AAYA 3; CA 81-84; CANR 33;
CDBLB 1945-1960; CLR 3, 27;
DAM MST, NOV, POP; DLB 15, 100,
160; JRDA; MAICYA; MTCW;
SATA 13

**Lewis, Janet** 1899- . . . . . . . . . . . . . . **CLC 41**
See also Winters, Janet Lewis
See also CA 9-12R; CANR 29; CAP 1;
DLBY 87

**Lewis, Matthew Gregory**
1775-1818 . . . . . . . . . . . . . . . . **NCLC 11**
See also DLB 39, 158

**Lewis, (Harry) Sinclair**
1885-1951 . . . . . **TCLC 4, 13, 23, 39; DA;
DAB; DAC; WLC**
See also CA 104; 133; CDALB 1917-1929;
DAM MST, NOV; DLB 9, 102; DLBD 1;
MTCW

**Lewis, (Percy) Wyndham**
1884(?)-1957 . . . . . . . . . . . . . . **TCLC 2, 9**
See also CA 104; DLB 15

**Lewisohn, Ludwig** 1883-1955 . . . . . . **TCLC 19**
See also CA 107; DLB 4, 9, 28, 102

**Leyner, Mark** 1956- . . . . . . . . . . . . . **CLC 92**
See also CA 110; CANR 28

**Lezama Lima, Jose** 1910-1976 . . . **CLC 4, 10**
See also CA 77-80; DAM MULT;
DLB 113; HW

**L'Heureux, John (Clarke)** 1934- . . . . **CLC 52**
See also CA 13-16R; CANR 23, 45

**Liddell, C. H.**
See Kuttner, Henry

**Lie, Jonas (Lauritz Idemil)**
1833-1908(?) . . . . . . . . . . . . . . . . **TCLC 5**
See also CA 115

**Lieber, Joel** 1937-1971 . . . . . . . . . . . . **CLC 6**
See also CA 73-76; 29-32R

**Lieber, Stanley Martin**
See Lee, Stan

**Lieberman, Laurence (James)**
1935- . . . . . . . . . . . . . . . . . . . . **CLC 4, 36**
See also CA 17-20R; CANR 8, 36

**Lieksman, Anders**
See Haavikko, Paavo Juhani

**Li Fei-kan** 1904-
See Pa Chin
See also CA 105

**Lifton, Robert Jay** 1926- . . . . . . . . . . **CLC 67**
See also CA 17-20R; CANR 27;
INT CANR-27; SATA 66

**Lightfoot, Gordon** 1938- . . . . . . . . . . **CLC 26**
See also CA 109

**Lightman, Alan P.** 1948- . . . . . . . . . . **CLC 81**
See also CA 141

**Ligotti, Thomas (Robert)**
1953- . . . . . . . . . . . . . . . **CLC 44; SSC 16**
See also CA 123; CANR 49

**Li Ho** 791-817 . . . . . . . . . . . . . . . . . . **PC 13**

**Liliencron, (Friedrich Adolf Axel) Detlev von**
1844-1909 . . . . . . . . . . . . . . . . . **TCLC 18**
See also CA 117

**Lilly, William** 1602-1681 . . . . . . . . . . **LC 27**

**Lima, Jose Lezama**
See Lezama Lima, Jose

**Lima Barreto, Afonso Henrique de**
1881-1922 . . . . . . . . . . . . . . . . . **TCLC 23**
See also CA 117

**Limonov, Edward** 1944- . . . . . . . . . . **CLC 67**
See also CA 137

**Lin, Frank**
See Atherton, Gertrude (Franklin Horn)

**Lincoln, Abraham** 1809-1865 . . . . . **NCLC 18**

**Lind, Jakov** . . . . . . . . . . . . **CLC 1, 2, 4, 27, 82**
See also Landwirth, Heinz
See also CAAS 4

**Lindbergh, Anne (Spencer) Morrow**
1906- . . . . . . . . . . . . . . . . . . . . . . **CLC 82**
See also CA 17-20R; CANR 16;
DAM NOV; MTCW; SATA 33

**Lindsay, David** 1878-1945 . . . . . . . . **TCLC 15**
See also CA 113

**Lindsay, (Nicholas) Vachel**
1879-1931 . . . **TCLC 17; DA; DAC; WLC**
See also CA 114; 135; CDALB 1865-1917;
DAM MST, POET; DLB 54; SATA 40

**Linke-Poot**
See Doeblin, Alfred

**Linney, Romulus** 1930- . . . . . . . . . . . **CLC 51**
See also CA 1-4R; CANR 40, 44

**Linton, Eliza Lynn** 1822-1898 . . . . **NCLC 41**
See also DLB 18

**Li Po** 701-763 . . . . . . . . . . . . . . . . . . **CMLC 2**

**Lipsius, Justus** 1547-1606 . . . . . . . . . . **LC 16**

**Lipsyte, Robert (Michael)**
1938- . . . . . . . . . . . . . **CLC 21; DA; DAC**
See also AAYA 7; CA 17-20R; CANR 8;
CLR 23; DAM MST, NOV; JRDA;
MAICYA; SATA 5, 68

**Lish, Gordon (Jay)** 1934- . . **CLC 45; SSC 18**
See also CA 113; 117; DLB 130; INT 117

**Lispector, Clarice** 1925-1977 . . . . . . . **CLC 43**
See also CA 139; 116; DLB 113

**Littell, Robert** 1935(?)- . . . . . . . . . . . **CLC 42**
See also CA 109; 112

**Little, Malcolm** 1925-1965
See Malcolm X
See also BW 1; CA 125; 111; DA; DAB;
DAC; DAM MST, MULT; MTCW

**Littlewit, Humphrey Gent.**
See Lovecraft, H(oward) P(hillips)

**Litwos**
See Sienkiewicz, Henryk (Adam Alexander
Pius)

**Liu E** 1857-1909 . . . . . . . . . . . . . . . . **TCLC 15**
See also CA 115

**Lively, Penelope (Margaret)**
1933- . . . . . . . . . . . . . . . . . . **CLC 32, 50**
See also CA 41-44R; CANR 29; CLR 7;
DAM NOV; DLB 14, 161; JRDA;
MAICYA; MTCW; SATA 7, 60

**Luzi, Mario** 1914- ............... **CLC 13**
See also CA 61-64; CANR 9; DLB 128

**L'Ymagier**
See Gourmont, Remy (-Marie-Charles) de

**Lynch, B. Suarez**
See Bioy Casares, Adolfo; Borges, Jorge
Luis

**Lynch, David (K.)** 1946- .......... **CLC 66**
See also CA 124; 129

**Lynch, James**
See Andreyev, Leonid (Nikolaevich)

**Lynch Davis, B.**
See Bioy Casares, Adolfo; Borges, Jorge
Luis

**Lyndsay, Sir David** 1490-1555 ...... **LC 20**

**Lynn, Kenneth S(chuyler)** 1923- .... **CLC 50**
See also CA 1-4R; CANR 3, 27

**Lynx**
See West, Rebecca

**Lyons, Marcus**
See Blish, James (Benjamin)

**Lyre, Pinchbeck**
See Sassoon, Siegfried (Lorraine)

**Lytle, Andrew (Nelson)** 1902-1995 .. **CLC 22**
See also CA 9-12R; 150; DLB 6

**Lyttelton, George** 1709-1773 ........ **LC 10**

**Maas, Peter** 1929- .............. **CLC 29**
See also CA 93-96; INT 93-96

**Macaulay, Rose** 1881-1958 ..... **TCLC 7, 44**
See also CA 104; DLB 36

**Macaulay, Thomas Babington**
1800-1859 ................ **NCLC 42**
See also CDBLB 1832-1890; DLB 32, 55

**MacBeth, George (Mann)**
1932-1992 ............... **CLC 2, 5, 9**
See also CA 25-28R; 136; DLB 40; MTCW;
SATA 4; SATA-Obit 70

**MacCaig, Norman (Alexander)**
1910- ................. **CLC 36; DAB**
See also CA 9-12R; CANR 3, 34;
DAM POET; DLB 27

**MacCarthy, (Sir Charles Otto) Desmond**
1877-1952 ................ **TCLC 36**

**MacDiarmid, Hugh**
............ **CLC 2, 4, 11, 19, 63; PC 9**
See also Grieve, C(hristopher) M(urray)
See also CDBLB 1945-1960; DLB 20

**MacDonald, Anson**
See Heinlein, Robert A(nson)

**Macdonald, Cynthia** 1928- ...... **CLC 13, 19**
See also CA 49-52; CANR 4, 44; DLB 105

**MacDonald, George** 1824-1905 ..... **TCLC 9**
See also CA 106; 137; DLB 18, 163;
MAICYA; SATA 33

**Macdonald, John**
See Millar, Kenneth

**MacDonald, John D(ann)**
1916-1986 ............. **CLC 3, 27, 44**
See also CA 1-4R; 121; CANR 1, 19;
DAM NOV, POP; DLB 8; DLBY 86;
MTCW

**Macdonald, John Ross**
See Millar, Kenneth

**Macdonald, Ross..... CLC 1, 2, 3, 14, 34, 41**
See also Millar, Kenneth
See also DLBD 6

**MacDougal, John**
See Blish, James (Benjamin)

**MacEwen, Gwendolyn (Margaret)**
1941-1987 ................ **CLC 13, 55**
See also CA 9-12R; 124; CANR 7, 22;
DLB 53; SATA 50; SATA-Obit 55

**Macha, Karel Hynek** 1810-1846 .. **NCLC 46**

**Machado (y Ruiz), Antonio**
1875-1939 ................. **TCLC 3**
See also CA 104; DLB 108

**Machado de Assis, Joaquim Maria**
1839-1908 ............. **TCLC 10; BLC**
See also CA 107

**Machen, Arthur.......... TCLC 4; SSC 20**
See also Jones, Arthur Llewellyn
See also DLB 36, 156

**Machiavelli, Niccolo**
1469-1527 ...... **LC 8; DA; DAB; DAC**
See also DAM MST

**MacInnes, Colin** 1914-1976...... **CLC 4, 23**
See also CA 69-72; 65-68; CANR 21;
DLB 14; MTCW

**MacInnes, Helen (Clark)**
1907-1985 ............... **CLC 27, 39**
See also CA 1-4R; 117; CANR 1, 28;
DAM POP; DLB 87; MTCW; SATA 22;
SATA-Obit 44

**Mackay, Mary** 1855-1924
See Corelli, Marie
See also CA 118

**Mackenzie, Compton (Edward Montague)**
1883-1972 ................. **CLC 18**
See also CA 21-22; 37-40R; CAP 2;
DLB 34, 100

**Mackenzie, Henry** 1745-1831 .... **NCLC 41**
See also DLB 39

**Mackintosh, Elizabeth** 1896(?)-1952
See Tey, Josephine
See also CA 110

**MacLaren, James**
See Grieve, C(hristopher) M(urray)

**Mac Laverty, Bernard** 1942- ....... **CLC 31**
See also CA 116; 118; CANR 43; INT 118

**MacLean, Alistair (Stuart)**
1922-1987 .......... **CLC 3, 13, 50, 63**
See also CA 57-60; 121; CANR 28;
DAM POP; MTCW; SATA 23;
SATA-Obit 50

**Maclean, Norman (Fitzroy)**
1902-1990 .......... **CLC 78; SSC 13**
See also CA 102; 132; CANR 49;
DAM POP

**MacLeish, Archibald**
1892-1982 ........... **CLC 3, 8, 14, 68**
See also CA 9-12R; 106; CANR 33;
DAM POET; DLB 4, 7, 45; DLBY 82;
MTCW

**MacLennan, (John) Hugh**
1907-1990 ......... **CLC 2, 14, 92; DAC**
See also CA 5-8R; 142; CANR 33;
DAM MST; DLB 68; MTCW

**MacLeod, Alistair** 1936- ..... **CLC 56; DAC**
See also CA 123; DAM MST; DLB 60

**MacNeice, (Frederick) Louis**
1907-1963 ....... **CLC 1, 4, 10, 53; DAB**
See also CA 85-88; DAM POET; DLB 10,
20; MTCW

**MacNeill, Dand**
See Fraser, George MacDonald

**Macpherson, James** 1736-1796 ...... **LC 29**
See also DLB 109

**Macpherson, (Jean) Jay** 1931- ...... **CLC 14**
See also CA 5-8R; DLB 53

**MacShane, Frank** 1927- ........... **CLC 39**
See also CA 9-12R; CANR 3, 33; DLB 111

**Macumber, Mari**
See Sandoz, Mari(e Susette)

**Madach, Imre** 1823-1864 ........ **NCLC 19**

**Madden, (Jerry) David** 1933- .... **CLC 5, 15**
See also CA 1-4R; CAAS 3; CANR 4, 45;
DLB 6; MTCW

**Maddern, Al(an)**
See Ellison, Harlan (Jay)

**Madhubuti, Haki R.**
1942- .......... **CLC 6, 73; BLC; PC 5**
See also Lee, Don L.
See also BW 2; CA 73-76; CANR 24, 51;
DAM MULT, POET; DLB 5, 41;
DLBD 8

**Maepenn, Hugh**
See Kuttner, Henry

**Maepenn, K. H.**
See Kuttner, Henry

**Maeterlinck, Maurice** 1862-1949 ... **TCLC 3**
See also CA 104; 136; DAM DRAM;
SATA 66

**Maginn, William** 1794-1842 ...... **NCLC 8**
See also DLB 110, 159

**Mahapatra, Jayanta** 1928- ......... **CLC 33**
See also CA 73-76; CAAS 9; CANR 15, 33;
DAM MULT

**Mahfouz, Naguib (Abdel Aziz Al-Sabilgi)**
1911(?)-
See Mahfuz, Najib
See also BEST 89:2; CA 128; DAM NOV;
MTCW

**Mahfuz, Najib** ................. **CLC 52, 55**
See also Mahfouz, Naguib (Abdel Aziz
Al-Sabilgi)
See also DLBY 88

**Mahon, Derek** 1941- .............. **CLC 27**
See also CA 113; 128; DLB 40

**Mailer, Norman**
1923- ...... **CLC 1, 2, 3, 4, 5, 8, 11, 14,
28, 39, 74; DA; DAB; DAC**
See also AITN 2; CA 9-12R; CABS 1;
CANR 28; CDALB 1968-1988;
DAM MST, NOV, POP; DLB 2, 16, 28;
DLBD 3; DLBY 80, 83; MTCW

**Maillet, Antonine** 1929- ...... **CLC 54; DAC**
See also CA 115; 120; CANR 46; DLB 60;
INT 120

**Mais, Roger** 1905-1955 ........... **TCLC 8**
See also BW 1; CA 105; 124; DLB 125;
MTCW

**Maistre, Joseph de** 1753-1821 .... **NCLC 37**

**Maitland, Sara (Louise)** 1950- ...... **CLC 49**
See also CA 69-72; CANR 13

McCarthy, Charles, Jr.  1933-
See McCarthy, Cormac
See also CANR 42; DAM POP

McCarthy, Cormac  1933-..... CLC 4, 57, 59
See also McCarthy, Charles, Jr.
See also DLB 6, 143

McCarthy, Mary (Therese)
1912-1989 ... CLC 1, 3, 5, 14, 24, 39, 59
See also CA 5-8R; 129; CANR 16, 50;
DLB 2; DLBY 81; INT CANR-16;
MTCW

McCartney, (James) Paul
1942-.................... CLC 12, 35
See also CA 146

McCauley, Stephen (D.)  1955- ..... CLC 50
See also CA 141

McClure, Michael (Thomas)
1932-...................... CLC 6, 10
See also CA 21-24R; CANR 17, 46;
DLB 16

McCorkle, Jill (Collins)  1958-...... CLC 51
See also CA 121; DLBY 87

McCourt, James  1941-............. CLC 5
See also CA 57-60

McCoy, Horace (Stanley)
1897-1955 ................. TCLC 28
See also CA 108; DLB 9

McCrae, John  1872-1918........ TCLC 12
See also CA 109; DLB 92

McCreigh, James
See Pohl, Frederik

McCullers, (Lula) Carson (Smith)
1917-1967 .... CLC 1, 4, 10, 12, 48; DA;
DAB; DAC; SSC 9; WLC
See also CA 5-8R; 25-28R; CABS 1, 3;
CANR 18; CDALB 1941-1968;
DAM MST, NOV; DLB 2, 7; MTCW;
SATA 27

McCulloch, John Tyler
See Burroughs, Edgar Rice

McCullough, Colleen  1938(?)-...... CLC 27
See also CA 81-84; CANR 17, 46;
DAM NOV, POP; MTCW

McDermott, Alice  1953- .......... CLC 90
See also CA 109; CANR 40

McElroy, Joseph  1930- ......... CLC 5, 47
See also CA 17-20R

McEwan, Ian (Russell)  1948- ... CLC 13, 66
See also BEST 90:4; CA 61-64; CANR 14,
41; DAM NOV; DLB 14; MTCW

McFadden, David  1940-.......... CLC 48
See also CA 104; DLB 60; INT 104

McFarland, Dennis  1950- ........ CLC 65

McGahern, John
1934-.......... CLC 5, 9, 48; SSC 17
See also CA 17-20R; CANR 29; DLB 14;
MTCW

McGinley, Patrick (Anthony)
1937-...................... CLC 41
See also CA 120; 127; INT 127

McGinley, Phyllis  1905-1978 ...... CLC 14
See also CA 9-12R; 77-80; CANR 19;
DLB 11, 48; SATA 2, 44; SATA-Obit 24

McGinniss, Joe  1942-............. CLC 32
See also AITN 2; BEST 89:2; CA 25-28R;
CANR 26; INT CANR-26

McGivern, Maureen Daly
See Daly, Maureen

McGrath, Patrick  1950-.......... CLC 55
See also CA 136

McGrath, Thomas (Matthew)
1916-1990 ............... CLC 28, 59
See also CA 9-12R; 132; CANR 6, 33;
DAM POET; MTCW; SATA 41;
SATA-Obit 66

McGuane, Thomas (Francis III)
1939-................ CLC 3, 7, 18, 45
See also AITN 2; CA 49-52; CANR 5, 24,
49; DLB 2; DLBY 80; INT CANR-24;
MTCW

McGuckian, Medbh  1950-......... CLC 48
See also CA 143; DAM POET; DLB 40

McHale, Tom  1942(?)-1982....... CLC 3, 5
See also AITN 1; CA 77-80; 106

McIlvanney, William  1936-....... CLC 42
See also CA 25-28R; DLB 14

McIlwraith, Maureen Mollie Hunter
See Hunter, Mollie
See also SATA 2

McInerney, Jay  1955- ............ CLC 34
See also CA 116; 123; CANR 45;
DAM POP; INT 123

McIntyre, Vonda N(eel)  1948- ..... CLC 18
See also CA 81-84; CANR 17, 34; MTCW

McKay, Claude
........ TCLC 7, 41; BLC; DAB; PC 2
See also McKay, Festus Claudius
See also DLB 4, 45, 51, 117

McKay, Festus Claudius  1889-1948
See McKay, Claude
See also BW 1; CA 104; 124; DA; DAC;
DAM MST, MULT, NOV, POET;
MTCW; WLC

McKuen, Rod  1933-............. CLC 1, 3
See also AITN 1; CA 41-44R; CANR 40

McLoughlin, R. B.
See Mencken, H(enry) L(ouis)

McLuhan, (Herbert) Marshall
1911-1980 ............... CLC 37, 83
See also CA 9-12R; 102; CANR 12, 34;
DLB 88; INT CANR-12; MTCW

McMillan, Terry (L.)  1951-..... CLC 50, 61
See also BW 2; CA 140; DAM MULT,
NOV, POP

McMurtry, Larry (Jeff)
1936-.......... CLC 2, 3, 7, 11, 27, 44
See also AAYA 15; AITN 2; BEST 89:2;
CA 5-8R; CANR 19, 43;
CDALB 1968-1988; DAM NOV, POP;
DLB 2, 143; DLBY 80, 87; MTCW

McNally, T. M.  1961-............. CLC 82

McNally, Terrence  1939-...CLC 4, 7, 41, 91
See also CA 45-48; CANR 2;
DAM DRAM; DLB 7

McNamer, Deirdre  1950-......... CLC 70

McNeile, Herman Cyril  1888-1937
See Sapper
See also DLB 77

McNickle, (William) D'Arcy
1904-1977 .................. CLC 89
See also CA 9-12R; 85-88; CANR 5, 45;
DAM MULT; NNAL; SATA-Obit 22

McPhee, John (Angus)  1931- ...... CLC 36
See also BEST 90:1; CA 65-68; CANR 20,
46; MTCW

McPherson, James Alan
1943-..................... CLC 19, 77
See also BW 1; CA 25-28R; CAAS 17;
CANR 24; DLB 38; MTCW

McPherson, William (Alexander)
1933-...................... CLC 34
See also CA 69-72; CANR 28;
INT CANR-28

Mead, Margaret  1901-1978........ CLC 37
See also AITN 1; CA 1-4R; 81-84;
CANR 4; MTCW; SATA-Obit 20

Meaker, Marijane (Agnes)  1927-
See Kerr, M. E.
See also CA 107; CANR 37; INT 107;
JRDA; MAICYA; MTCW; SATA 20, 61

Medoff, Mark (Howard)  1940- ... CLC 6, 23
See also AITN 1; CA 53-56; CANR 5;
DAM DRAM; DLB 7; INT CANR-5

Medvedev, P. N.
See Bakhtin, Mikhail Mikhailovich

Meged, Aharon
See Megged, Aharon

Meged, Aron
See Megged, Aharon

Megged, Aharon  1920-............. CLC 9
See also CA 49-52; CAAS 13; CANR 1

Mehta, Ved (Parkash)  1934-....... CLC 37
See also CA 1-4R; CANR 2, 23; MTCW

Melanter
See Blackmore, R(ichard) D(oddridge)

Melikow, Loris
See Hofmannsthal, Hugo von

Melmoth, Sebastian
See Wilde, Oscar (Fingal O'Flahertie Wills)

Meltzer, Milton  1915-............. CLC 26
See also AAYA 8; CA 13-16R; CANR 38;
CLR 13; DLB 61; JRDA; MAICYA;
SAAS 1; SATA 1, 50, 80

Melville, Herman
1819-1891 ..... NCLC 3, 12, 29, 45, 49;
DA; DAB; DAC; SSC 1, 17; WLC
See also CDALB 1640-1865; DAM MST,
NOV; DLB 3, 74; SATA 59

Menander
c. 342B.C.-c. 292B.C. .... CMLC 9; DC 3
See also DAM DRAM

Mencken, H(enry) L(ouis)
1880-1956 .................. TCLC 13
See also CA 105; 125; CDALB 1917-1929;
DLB 11, 29, 63, 137; MTCW

Mercer, David  1928-1980.......... CLC 5
See also CA 9-12R; 102; CANR 23;
DAM DRAM; DLB 13; MTCW

Merchant, Paul
See Ellison, Harlan (Jay)

Meredith, George  1828-1909 ... TCLC 17, 43
See also CA 117; CDBLB 1832-1890;
DAM POET; DLB 18, 35, 57, 159

**Meredith, William (Morris)**
1919- ............. **CLC 4, 13, 22, 55**
See also CA 9-12R; CAAS 14; CANR 6, 40;
DAM POET; DLB 5

**Merezhkovsky, Dmitry Sergeyevich**
1865-1941 .................. **TCLC 29**

**Merimee, Prosper**
1803-1870 ........... **NCLC 6; SSC 7**
See also DLB 119

**Merkin, Daphne** 1954- ............ **CLC 44**
See also CA 123

**Merlin, Arthur**
See Blish, James (Benjamin)

**Merrill, James (Ingram)**
1926-1995 .... **CLC 2, 3, 6, 8, 13, 18, 34, 91**
See also CA 13-16R; 147; CANR 10, 49;
DAM POET; DLB 5; DLBY 85;
INT CANR-10; MTCW

**Merriman, Alex**
See Silverberg, Robert

**Merritt, E. B.**
See Waddington, Miriam

**Merton, Thomas**
1915-1968 .. **CLC 1, 3, 11, 34, 83; PC 10**
See also CA 5-8R; 25-28R; CANR 22;
DLB 48; DLBY 81; MTCW

**Merwin, W(illiam) S(tanley)**
1927- ... **CLC 1, 2, 3, 5, 8, 13, 18, 45, 88**
See also CA 13-16R; CANR 15, 51;
DAM POET; DLB 5; INT CANR-15;
MTCW

**Metcalf, John** 1938- ............. **CLC 37**
See also CA 113; DLB 60

**Metcalf, Suzanne**
See Baum, L(yman) Frank

**Mew, Charlotte (Mary)**
1870-1928 ................... **TCLC 8**
See also CA 105; DLB 19, 135

**Mewshaw, Michael** 1943- .......... **CLC 9**
See also CA 53-56; CANR 7, 47; DLBY 80

**Meyer, June**
See Jordan, June

**Meyer, Lynn**
See Slavitt, David R(ytman)

**Meyer-Meyrink, Gustav** 1868-1932
See Meyrink, Gustav
See also CA 117

**Meyers, Jeffrey** 1939- ............ **CLC 39**
See also CA 73-76; DLB 111

**Meynell, Alice (Christina Gertrude Thompson)**
1847-1922 ................... **TCLC 6**
See also CA 104; DLB 19, 98

**Meyrink, Gustav** ................ **TCLC 21**
See also Meyer-Meyrink, Gustav
See also DLB 81

**Michaels, Leonard**
1933- ............. **CLC 6, 25; SSC 16**
See also CA 61-64; CANR 21; DLB 130;
MTCW

**Michaux, Henri** 1899-1984 ...... **CLC 8, 19**
See also CA 85-88; 114

**Michelangelo** 1475-1564............ **LC 12**

**Michelet, Jules** 1798-1874 ....... **NCLC 31**

**Michener, James A(lbert)**
1907(?)- .......... **CLC 1, 5, 11, 29, 60**
See also AITN 1; BEST 90:1; CA 5-8R;
CANR 21, 45; DAM NOV, POP; DLB 6;
MTCW

**Mickiewicz, Adam** 1798-1855 ..... **NCLC 3**

**Middleton, Christopher** 1926- ...... **CLC 13**
See also CA 13-16R; CANR 29; DLB 40

**Middleton, Richard (Barham)**
1882-1911 .................. **TCLC 56**
See also DLB 156

**Middleton, Stanley** 1919-........ **CLC 7, 38**
See also CA 25-28R; CAAS 23; CANR 21,
46; DLB 14

**Middleton, Thomas** 1580-1627........ **DC 5**
See also DAM DRAM, MST; DLB 58

**Migueis, Jose Rodrigues** 1901- ..... **CLC 10**

**Mikszath, Kalman** 1847-1910 ..... **TCLC 31**

**Miles, Josephine**
1911-1985 ........ **CLC 1, 2, 14, 34, 39**
See also CA 1-4R; 116; CANR 2;
DAM POET; DLB 48

**Militant**
See Sandburg, Carl (August)

**Mill, John Stuart** 1806-1873..... **NCLC 11**
See also CDBLB 1832-1890; DLB 55

**Millar, Kenneth** 1915-1983 ........ **CLC 14**
See also Macdonald, Ross
See also CA 9-12R; 110; CANR 16;
DAM POP; DLB 2; DLBD 6; DLBY 83;
MTCW

**Millay, E. Vincent**
See Millay, Edna St. Vincent

**Millay, Edna St. Vincent**
1892-1950 ...... **TCLC 4, 49; DA; DAB; DAC; PC 6**
See also CA 104; 130; CDALB 1917-1929;
DAM MST, POET; DLB 45; MTCW

**Miller, Arthur**
1915- .... **CLC 1, 2, 6, 10, 15, 26, 47, 78; DA; DAB; DAC; DC 1; WLC**
See also AAYA 15; AITN 1; CA 1-4R;
CABS 3; CANR 2, 30;
CDALB 1941-1968; DAM DRAM, MST;
DLB 7; MTCW

**Miller, Henry (Valentine)**
1891-1980 .... **CLC 1, 2, 4, 9, 14, 43, 84; DA; DAB; DAC; WLC**
See also CA 9-12R; 97-100; CANR 33;
CDALB 1929-1941; DAM MST, NOV;
DLB 4, 9; DLBY 80; MTCW

**Miller, Jason** 1939(?)- ............. **CLC 2**
See also AITN 1; CA 73-76; DLB 7

**Miller, Sue** 1943- ................ **CLC 44**
See also BEST 90:3; CA 139; DAM POP;
DLB 143

**Miller, Walter M(ichael, Jr.)**
1923- ..................... **CLC 4, 30**
See also CA 85-88; DLB 8

**Millett, Kate** 1934-................ **CLC 67**
See also AITN 1; CA 73-76; CANR 32;
MTCW

**Millhauser, Steven** 1943-....... **CLC 21, 54**
See also CA 110; 111; DLB 2; INT 111

**Millin, Sarah Gertrude** 1889-1968 .. **CLC 49**
See also CA 102; 93-96

**Milne, A(lan) A(lexander)**
1882-1956 ........ **TCLC 6; DAB; DAC**
See also CA 104; 133; CLR 1, 26;
DAM MST; DLB 10, 77, 100, 160;
MAICYA; MTCW; YABC 1

**Milner, Ron(ald)** 1938-....... **CLC 56; BLC**
See also AITN 1; BW 1; CA 73-76;
CANR 24; DAM MULT; DLB 38;
MTCW

**Milosz, Czeslaw**
1911- ... **CLC 5, 11, 22, 31, 56, 82; PC 8**
See also CA 81-84; CANR 23, 51;
DAM MST, POET; MTCW

**Milton, John**
1608-1674 ...... **LC 9; DA; DAB; DAC; WLC**
See also CDBLB 1660-1789; DAM MST,
POET; DLB 131, 151

**Min, Anchee** 1957-................ **CLC 86**
See also CA 146

**Minehaha, Cornelius**
See Wedekind, (Benjamin) Frank(lin)

**Miner, Valerie** 1947- ............. **CLC 40**
See also CA 97-100

**Minimo, Duca**
See D'Annunzio, Gabriele

**Minot, Susan** 1956- .............. **CLC 44**
See also CA 134

**Minus, Ed** 1938-................. **CLC 39**

**Miranda, Javier**
See Bioy Casares, Adolfo

**Mirbeau, Octave** 1848-1917...... **TCLC 55**
See also DLB 123

**Miro (Ferrer), Gabriel (Francisco Victor)**
1879-1930 .................. **TCLC 5**
See also CA 104

**Mishima, Yukio**
....... **CLC 2, 4, 6, 9, 27; DC 1; SSC 4**
See also Hiraoka, Kimitake

**Mistral, Frederic** 1830-1914 ...... **TCLC 51**
See also CA 122

**Mistral, Gabriela**........... **TCLC 2; HLC**
See also Godoy Alcayaga, Lucila

**Mistry, Rohinton** 1952-...... **CLC 71; DAC**
See also CA 141

**Mitchell, Clyde**
See Ellison, Harlan (Jay); Silverberg, Robert

**Mitchell, James Leslie** 1901-1935
See Gibbon, Lewis Grassic
See also CA 104; DLB 15

**Mitchell, Joni** 1943-.............. **CLC 12**
See also CA 112

**Mitchell, Margaret (Munnerlyn)**
1900-1949 .................. **TCLC 11**
See also CA 109; 125; DAM NOV, POP;
DLB 9; MTCW

**Mitchell, Peggy**
See Mitchell, Margaret (Munnerlyn)

**Mitchell, S(ilas) Weir** 1829-1914 .. **TCLC 36**

**Morris, William** 1834-1896 . . . . . . . **NCLC 4**
See also CDBLB 1832-1890; DLB 18, 35, 57, 156

**Morris, Wright** 1910- . . . **CLC 1, 3, 7, 18, 37**
See also CA 9-12R; CANR 21; DLB 2; DLBY 81; MTCW

**Morrison, Chloe Anthony Wofford**
See Morrison, Toni

**Morrison, James Douglas** 1943-1971
See Morrison, Jim
See also CA 73-76; CANR 40

**Morrison, Jim** . . . . . . . . . . . . . . . . . . **CLC 17**
See also Morrison, James Douglas

**Morrison, Toni**
1931- . . . . . . . . **CLC 4, 10, 22, 55, 81, 87;**
**BLC; DA; DAB; DAC**
See also AAYA 1; BW 2; CA 29-32R; CANR 27, 42; CDALB 1968-1988; DAM MST, MULT, NOV, POP; DLB 6, 33, 143; DLBY 81; MTCW; SATA 57

**Morrison, Van** 1945- . . . . . . . . . . . . . **CLC 21**
See also CA 116

**Mortimer, John (Clifford)**
1923- . . . . . . . . . . . . . . . . . . . **CLC 28, 43**
See also CA 13-16R; CANR 21; CDBLB 1960 to Present; DAM DRAM, POP; DLB 13; INT CANR-21; MTCW

**Mortimer, Penelope (Ruth)** 1918- . . . . **CLC 5**
See also CA 57-60; CANR 45

**Morton, Anthony**
See Creasey, John

**Mosher, Howard Frank** 1943- . . . . . . **CLC 62**
See also CA 139

**Mosley, Nicholas** 1923- . . . . . . . . **CLC 43, 70**
See also CA 69-72; CANR 41; DLB 14

**Moss, Howard**
1922-1987 . . . . . . . . . . **CLC 7, 14, 45, 50**
See also CA 1-4R; 123; CANR 1, 44; DAM POET; DLB 5

**Mossgiel, Rab**
See Burns, Robert

**Motion, Andrew (Peter)** 1952- . . . . . . **CLC 47**
See also CA 146; DLB 40

**Motley, Willard (Francis)**
1909-1965 . . . . . . . . . . . . . . . . . . **CLC 18**
See also BW 1; CA 117; 106; DLB 76, 143

**Motoori, Norinaga** 1730-1801 . . . . **NCLC 45**

**Mott, Michael (Charles Alston)**
1930- . . . . . . . . . . . . . . . . . . . . **CLC 15, 34**
See also CA 5-8R; CAAS 7; CANR 7, 29

**Mountain Wolf Woman**
1884-1960 . . . . . . . . . . . . . . . . . . **CLC 92**
See also CA 144; NNAL

**Moure, Erin** 1955- . . . . . . . . . . . . . . **CLC 88**
See also CA 113; DLB 60

**Mowat, Farley (McGill)**
1921- . . . . . . . . . . . . . . . . . . **CLC 26; DAC**
See also AAYA 1; CA 1-4R; CANR 4, 24, 42; CLR 20; DAM MST; DLB 68; INT CANAR-24; JRDA; MAICYA; MTCW; SATA 3, 55

**Moyers, Bill** 1934- . . . . . . . . . . . . . . **CLC 74**
See also AITN 2; CA 61-64; CANR 31

**Mphahlele, Es'kia**
See Mphahlele, Ezekiel
See also DLB 125

**Mphahlele, Ezekiel** 1919- . . . . . **CLC 25; BLC**
See also Mphahlele, Es'kia
See also BW 2; CA 81-84; CANR 26; DAM MULT

**Mqhayi, S(amuel) E(dward) K(rune Loliwe)**
1875-1945 . . . . . . . . . . . . . **TCLC 25; BLC**
See also DAM MULT

**Mr. Martin**
See Burroughs, William S(eward)

**Mrozek, Slawomir** 1930- . . . . . . . . **CLC 3, 13**
See also CA 13-16R; CAAS 10; CANR 29; MTCW

**Mrs. Belloc-Lowndes**
See Lowndes, Marie Adelaide (Belloc)

**Mtwa, Percy** (?)- . . . . . . . . . . . . . . . **CLC 47**

**Mueller, Lisel** 1924- . . . . . . . . . . **CLC 13, 51**
See also CA 93-96; DLB 105

**Muir, Edwin** 1887-1959 . . . . . . . . . . **TCLC 2**
See also CA 104; DLB 20, 100

**Muir, John** 1838-1914 . . . . . . . . . . **TCLC 28**

**Mujica Lainez, Manuel**
1910-1984 . . . . . . . . . . . . . . . . . . **CLC 31**
See also Lainez, Manuel Mujica
See also CA 81-84; 112; CANR 32; HW

**Mukherjee, Bharati** 1940- . . . . . . . . **CLC 53**
See also BEST 89:2; CA 107; CANR 45; DAM NOV; DLB 60; MTCW

**Muldoon, Paul** 1951- . . . . . . . . . **CLC 32, 72**
See also CA 113; 129; DAM POET; DLB 40; INT 129

**Mulisch, Harry** 1927- . . . . . . . . . . . . **CLC 42**
See also CA 9-12R; CANR 6, 26

**Mull, Martin** 1943- . . . . . . . . . . . . . . **CLC 17**
See also CA 105

**Mulock, Dinah Maria**
See Craik, Dinah Maria (Mulock)

**Munford, Robert** 1737(?)-1783 . . . . . . . **LC 5**
See also DLB 31

**Mungo, Raymond** 1946- . . . . . . . . . . **CLC 72**
See also CA 49-52; CANR 2

**Munro, Alice**
1931- . . . **CLC 6, 10, 19, 50; DAC; SSC 3**
See also AITN 2; CA 33-36R; CANR 33; DAM MST, NOV; DLB 53; MTCW; SATA 29

**Munro, H(ector) H(ugh)** 1870-1916
See Saki
See also CA 104; 130; CDBLB 1890-1914; DA; DAB; DAC; DAM MST, NOV; DLB 34, 162; MTCW; WLC

**Murasaki, Lady** . . . . . . . . . . . . . . . . **CMLC 1**

**Murdoch, (Jean) Iris**
1919- . . . . . . **CLC 1, 2, 3, 4, 6, 8, 11, 15, 22, 31, 51; DAB; DAC**
See also CA 13-16R; CANR 8, 43; CDBLB 1960 to Present; DAM MST, NOV; DLB 14; INT CANR-8; MTCW

**Murnau, Friedrich Wilhelm**
See Plumpe, Friedrich Wilhelm

**Murphy, Richard** 1927- . . . . . . . . . . . **CLC 41**
See also CA 29-32R; DLB 40

**Murphy, Sylvia** 1937- . . . . . . . . . . . . **CLC 34**
See also CA 121

**Murphy, Thomas (Bernard)** 1935- . . . **CLC 51**
See also CA 101

**Murray, Albert L.** 1916- . . . . . . . . . . **CLC 73**
See also BW 2; CA 49-52; CANR 26; DLB 38

**Murray, Les(lie) A(llan)** 1938- . . . . . **CLC 40**
See also CA 21-24R; CANR 11, 27; DAM POET

**Murry, J. Middleton**
See Murry, John Middleton

**Murry, John Middleton**
1889-1957 . . . . . . . . . . . . . . . . . **TCLC 16**
See also CA 118; DLB 149

**Musgrave, Susan** 1951- . . . . . . . . **CLC 13, 54**
See also CA 69-72; CANR 45

**Musil, Robert (Edler von)**
1880-1942 . . . . . . . . **TCLC 12; SSC 18**
See also CA 109; DLB 81, 124

**Muske, Carol** 1945- . . . . . . . . . . . . . **CLC 90**
See also Muske-Dukes, Carol (Anne)

**Muske-Dukes, Carol (Anne)** 1945-
See Muske, Carol
See also CA 65-68; CANR 32

**Musset, (Louis Charles) Alfred de**
1810-1857 . . . . . . . . . . . . . . . . **NCLC 7**

**My Brother's Brother**
See Chekhov, Anton (Pavlovich)

**Myers, L. H.** 1881-1944 . . . . . . . . . **TCLC 59**
See also DLB 15

**Myers, Walter Dean** 1937- . . . **CLC 35; BLC**
See also AAYA 4; BW 2; CA 33-36R; CANR 20, 42; CLR 4, 16, 35; DAM MULT, NOV; DLB 33; INT CANR-20; JRDA; MAICYA; SAAS 2; SATA 41, 71; SATA-Brief 27

**Myers, Walter M.**
See Myers, Walter Dean

**Myles, Symon**
See Follett, Ken(neth Martin)

**Nabokov, Vladimir (Vladimirovich)**
1899-1977 . . . . . **CLC 1, 2, 3, 6, 8, 11, 15, 23, 44, 46, 64; DA; DAB; DAC; SSC 11; WLC**
See also CA 5-8R; 69-72; CANR 20; CDALB 1941-1968; DAM MST, NOV; DLB 2; DLBD 3; DLBY 80, 91; MTCW

**Nagai Kafu** . . . . . . . . . . . . . . . . . . . **TCLC 51**
See also Nagai Sokichi

**Nagai Sokichi** 1879-1959
See Nagai Kafu
See also CA 117

**Nagy, Laszlo** 1925-1978 . . . . . . . . . . . **CLC 7**
See also CA 129; 112

**Naipaul, Shiva(dhar Srinivasa)**
1945-1985 . . . . . . . . . . . . . . . **CLC 32, 39**
See also CA 110; 112; 116; CANR 33; DAM NOV; DLB 157; DLBY 85; MTCW

North Staffs
See Hulme, T(homas) E(rnest)

Norton, Alice Mary
See Norton, Andre
See also MAICYA; SATA 1, 43

Norton, Andre 1912- ............. CLC 12
See also Norton, Alice Mary
See also AAYA 14; CA 1-4R; CANR 2, 31;
DLB 8, 52; JRDA; MTCW

Norton, Caroline 1808-1877...... NCLC 47
See also DLB 21, 159

Norway, Nevil Shute 1899-1960
See Shute, Nevil
See also CA 102; 93-96

Norwid, Cyprian Kamil
1821-1883 ................. NCLC 17

Nosille, Nabrah
See Ellison, Harlan (Jay)

Nossack, Hans Erich 1901-1978..... CLC 6
See also CA 93-96; 85-88; DLB 69

Nostradamus 1503-1566............ LC 27

Nosu, Chuji
See Ozu, Yasujiro

Notenburg, Eleanora (Genrikhovna) von
See Guro, Elena

Nova, Craig 1945-............. CLC 7, 31
See also CA 45-48; CANR 2

Novak, Joseph
See Kosinski, Jerzy (Nikodem)

Novalis 1772-1801 ............. NCLC 13
See also DLB 90

Nowlan, Alden (Albert)
1933-1983 ............. CLC 15; DAC
See also CA 9-12R; CANR 5; DAM MST;
DLB 53

Noyes, Alfred 1880-1958 ......... TCLC 7
See also CA 104; DLB 20

Nunn, Kem 19(?)-................. CLC 34

Nye, Robert 1939- ............. CLC 13, 42
See also CA 33-36R; CANR 29;
DAM NOV; DLB 14; MTCW; SATA 6

Nyro, Laura 1947- ................ CLC 17

Oates, Joyce Carol
1938- ...... CLC 1, 2, 3, 6, 9, 11, 15, 19,
33, 52; DA; DAB; DAC; SSC 6; WLC
See also AAYA 15; AITN 1; BEST 89:2;
CA 5-8R; CANR 25, 45;
CDALB 1968-1988; DAM MST, NOV,
POP; DLB 2, 5, 130; DLBY 81;
INT CANR-25; MTCW

O'Brien, Darcy 1939-............. CLC 11
See also CA 21-24R; CANR 8

O'Brien, E. G.
See Clarke, Arthur C(harles)

O'Brien, Edna
1936- ... CLC 3, 5, 8, 13, 36, 65; SSC 10
See also CA 1-4R; CANR 6, 41;
CDBLB 1960 to Present; DAM NOV;
DLB 14; MTCW

O'Brien, Fitz-James 1828-1862... NCLC 21
See also DLB 74

O'Brien, Flann........ CLC 1, 4, 5, 7, 10, 47
See also O Nuallain, Brian

O'Brien, Richard 1942- .......... CLC 17
See also CA 124

O'Brien, Tim 1946-.......... CLC 7, 19, 40
See also AAYA 16; CA 85-88; CANR 40;
DAM POP; DLB 152; DLBD 9;
DLBY 80

Obstfelder, Sigbjoern 1866-1900... TCLC 23
See also CA 123

O'Casey, Sean
1880-1964 ...... CLC 1, 5, 9, 11, 15, 88;
DAB; DAC
See also CA 89-92; CDBLB 1914-1945;
DAM DRAM, MST; DLB 10; MTCW

O'Cathasaigh, Sean
See O'Casey, Sean

Ochs, Phil 1940-1976............ CLC 17
See also CA 65-68

O'Connor, Edwin (Greene)
1918-1968 ................. CLC 14
See also CA 93-96; 25-28R

O'Connor, (Mary) Flannery
1925-1964 .... CLC 1, 2, 3, 6, 10, 13, 15,
21, 66; DA; DAB; DAC; SSC 1; WLC
See also AAYA 7; CA 1-4R; CANR 3, 41;
CDALB 1941-1968; DAM MST, NOV;
DLB 2, 152; DLBD 12; DLBY 80;
MTCW

O'Connor, Frank........... CLC 23; SSC 5
See also O'Donovan, Michael John
See also DLB 162

O'Dell, Scott 1898-1989........... CLC 30
See also AAYA 3; CA 61-64; 129;
CANR 12, 30; CLR 1, 16; DLB 52;
JRDA; MAICYA; SATA 12, 60

Odets, Clifford
1906-1963 ........... CLC 2, 28; DC 6
See also CA 85-88; DAM DRAM; DLB 7,
26; MTCW

O'Doherty, Brian 1934-........... CLC 76
See also CA 105

O'Donnell, K. M.
See Malzberg, Barry N(athaniel)

O'Donnell, Lawrence
See Kuttner, Henry

O'Donovan, Michael John
1903-1966 ................. CLC 14
See also O'Connor, Frank
See also CA 93-96

Oe, Kenzaburo
1935- ......... CLC 10, 36, 86; SSC 20
See also CA 97-100; CANR 36, 50;
DAM NOV; DLBY 94; MTCW

O'Faolain, Julia 1932-....... CLC 6, 19, 47
See also CA 81-84; CAAS 2; CANR 12;
DLB 14; MTCW

O'Faolain, Sean
1900-1991 ....... CLC 1, 7, 14, 32, 70;
SSC 13
See also CA 61-64; 134; CANR 12;
DLB 15, 162; MTCW

O'Flaherty, Liam
1896-1984 ......... CLC 5, 34; SSC 6
See also CA 101; 113; CANR 35; DLB 36,
162; DLBY 84; MTCW

Ogilvy, Gavin
See Barrie, J(ames) M(atthew)

O'Grady, Standish James
1846-1928 ................. TCLC 5
See also CA 104

O'Grady, Timothy 1951-.......... CLC 59
See also CA 138

O'Hara, Frank
1926-1966 ........... CLC 2, 5, 13, 78
See also CA 9-12R; 25-28R; CANR 33;
DAM POET; DLB 5, 16; MTCW

O'Hara, John (Henry)
1905-1970 ....... CLC 1, 2, 3, 6, 11, 42;
SSC 15
See also CA 5-8R; 25-28R; CANR 31;
CDALB 1929-1941; DAM NOV; DLB 9,
86; DLBD 2; MTCW

O Hehir, Diana 1922- ............. CLC 41
See also CA 93-96

Okigbo, Christopher (Ifenayichukwu)
1932-1967 ..... CLC 25, 84; BLC; PC 7
See also BW 1; CA 77-80; DAM MULT,
POET; DLB 125; MTCW

Okri, Ben 1959- .................. CLC 87
See also BW 2; CA 130; 138; DLB 157;
INT 138

Olds, Sharon 1942-......... CLC 32, 39, 85
See also CA 101; CANR 18, 41;
DAM POET; DLB 120

Oldstyle, Jonathan
See Irving, Washington

Olesha, Yuri (Karlovich)
1899-1960 .................... CLC 8
See also CA 85-88

Oliphant, Laurence
1829(?)-1888 .............. NCLC 47
See also DLB 18

Oliphant, Margaret (Oliphant Wilson)
1828-1897 ................. NCLC 11
See also DLB 18, 159

Oliver, Mary 1935-............. CLC 19, 34
See also CA 21-24R; CANR 9, 43; DLB 5

Olivier, Laurence (Kerr)
1907-1989 .................... CLC 20
See also CA 111; 150; 129

Olsen, Tillie
1913- ..... CLC 4, 13; DA; DAB; DAC;
SSC 11
See also CA 1-4R; CANR 1, 43;
DAM MST; DLB 28; DLBY 80; MTCW

Olson, Charles (John)
1910-1970 ..... CLC 1, 2, 5, 6, 9, 11, 29
See also CA 13-16; 25-28R; CABS 2;
CANR 35; CAP 1; DAM POET; DLB 5,
16; MTCW

Olson, Toby 1937- ............... CLC 28
See also CA 65-68; CANR 9, 31

Olyesha, Yuri
See Olesha, Yuri (Karlovich)

Ondaatje, (Philip) Michael
1943- ... CLC 14, 29, 51, 76; DAB; DAC
See also CA 77-80; CANR 42; DAM MST;
DLB 60

Oneal, Elizabeth 1934-
See Oneal, Zibby
See also CA 106; CANR 28; MAICYA;
SATA 30, 82

**Parson Lot**
See Kingsley, Charles

**Partridge, Anthony**
See Oppenheim, E(dward) Phillips

**Pascoli, Giovanni** 1855-1912 ...... **TCLC 45**

**Pasolini, Pier Paolo**
1922-1975 ............... **CLC 20, 37**
See also CA 93-96; 61-64; DLB 128;
MTCW

**Pasquini**
See Silone, Ignazio

**Pastan, Linda (Olenik)** 1932- ...... **CLC 27**
See also CA 61-64; CANR 18, 40;
DAM POET; DLB 5

**Pasternak, Boris (Leonidovich)**
1890-1960 ...... **CLC 7, 10, 18, 63; DA;**
**DAB; DAC; PC 6; WLC**
See also CA 127; 116; DAM MST, NOV,
POET; MTCW

**Patchen, Kenneth** 1911-1972 ... **CLC 1, 2, 18**
See also CA 1-4R; 33-36R; CANR 3, 35;
DAM POET; DLB 16, 48; MTCW

**Pater, Walter (Horatio)**
1839-1894 ................. **NCLC 7**
See also CDBLB 1832-1890; DLB 57, 156

**Paterson, A(ndrew) B(arton)**
1864-1941 ................. **TCLC 32**

**Paterson, Katherine (Womeldorf)**
1932- .................... **CLC 12, 30**
See also AAYA 1; CA 21-24R; CANR 28;
CLR 7; DLB 52; JRDA; MAICYA;
MTCW; SATA 13, 53

**Patmore, Coventry Kersey Dighton**
1823-1896 ................. **NCLC 9**
See also DLB 35, 98

**Paton, Alan (Stewart)**
1903-1988 ...... **CLC 4, 10, 25, 55; DA;**
**DAB; DAC; WLC**
See also CA 13-16; 125; CANR 22; CAP 1;
DAM MST, NOV; MTCW; SATA 11;
SATA-Obit 56

**Paton Walsh, Gillian** 1937-
See Walsh, Jill Paton
See also CANR 38; JRDA; MAICYA;
SAAS 3; SATA 4, 72

**Paulding, James Kirke** 1778-1860.. **NCLC 2**
See also DLB 3, 59, 74

**Paulin, Thomas Neilson** 1949-
See Paulin, Tom
See also CA 123; 128

**Paulin, Tom** ....................... **CLC 37**
See also Paulin, Thomas Neilson
See also DLB 40

**Paustovsky, Konstantin (Georgievich)**
1892-1968 ................... **CLC 40**
See also CA 93-96; 25-28R

**Pavese, Cesare**
1908-1950 ..... **TCLC 3; PC 13; SSC 19**
See also CA 104; DLB 128

**Pavic, Milorad** 1929- ............. **CLC 60**
See also CA 136

**Payne, Alan**
See Jakes, John (William)

**Paz, Gil**
See Lugones, Leopoldo

**Paz, Octavio**
1914- ....... **CLC 3, 4, 6, 10, 19, 51, 65;**
**DA; DAB; DAC; HLC; PC 1; WLC**
See also CA 73-76; CANR 32; DAM MST,
MULT, POET; DLBY 90; HW; MTCW

**Peacock, Molly** 1947-............. **CLC 60**
See also CA 103; CAAS 21; DLB 120

**Peacock, Thomas Love**
1785-1866 ................. **NCLC 22**
See also DLB 96, 116

**Peake, Mervyn** 1911-1968 ...... **CLC 7, 54**
See also CA 5-8R; 25-28R; CANR 3;
DLB 15, 160; MTCW; SATA 23

**Pearce, Philippa** .................. **CLC 21**
See also Christie, (Ann) Philippa
See also CLR 9; DLB 161; MAICYA;
SATA 1, 67

**Pearl, Eric**
See Elman, Richard

**Pearson, T(homas) R(eid)** 1956- .... **CLC 39**
See also CA 120; 130; INT 130

**Peck, Dale** 1967- ................. **CLC 81**
See also CA 146

**Peck, John** 1941- ................. **CLC 3**
See also CA 49-52; CANR 3

**Peck, Richard (Wayne)** 1934- ...... **CLC 21**
See also AAYA 1; CA 85-88; CANR 19,
38; CLR 15; INT CANR-19; JRDA;
MAICYA; SAAS 2; SATA 18, 55

**Peck, Robert Newton**
1928- .............. **CLC 17; DA; DAC**
See also AAYA 3; CA 81-84; CANR 31;
DAM MST; JRDA; MAICYA; SAAS 1;
SATA 21, 62

**Peckinpah, (David) Sam(uel)**
1925-1984 ................... **CLC 20**
See also CA 109; 114

**Pedersen, Knut** 1859-1952
See Hamsun, Knut
See also CA 104; 119; MTCW

**Peeslake, Gaffer**
See Durrell, Lawrence (George)

**Peguy, Charles Pierre**
1873-1914 ................. **TCLC 10**
See also CA 107

**Pena, Ramon del Valle y**
See Valle-Inclan, Ramon (Maria) del

**Pendennis, Arthur Esquir**
See Thackeray, William Makepeace

**Penn, William** 1644-1718 .......... **LC 25**
See also DLB 24

**Pepys, Samuel**
1633-1703 ..... **LC 11; DA; DAB; DAC;**
**WLC**
See also CDBLB 1660-1789; DAM MST;
DLB 101

**Percy, Walker**
1916-1990 .... **CLC 2, 3, 6, 8, 14, 18, 47,**
**65**
See also CA 1-4R; 131; CANR 1, 23;
DAM NOV, POP; DLB 2; DLBY 80, 90;
MTCW

**Perec, Georges** 1936-1982 ........ **CLC 56**
See also CA 141; DLB 83

**Pereda (y Sanchez de Porrua), Jose Maria de**
1833-1906 ................. **TCLC 16**
See also CA 117

**Pereda y Porrua, Jose Maria de**
See Pereda (y Sanchez de Porrua), Jose
Maria de

**Peregoy, George Weems**
See Mencken, H(enry) L(ouis)

**Perelman, S(idney) J(oseph)**
1904-1979 ... **CLC 3, 5, 9, 15, 23, 44, 49**
See also AITN 1, 2; CA 73-76; 89-92;
CANR 18; DAM DRAM; DLB 11, 44;
MTCW

**Peret, Benjamin** 1899-1959 ...... **TCLC 20**
See also CA 117

**Peretz, Isaac Loeb** 1851(?)-1915... **TCLC 16**
See also CA 109

**Peretz, Yitzkhok Leibush**
See Peretz, Isaac Loeb

**Perez Galdos, Benito** 1843-1920 ... **TCLC 27**
See also CA 125; HW

**Perrault, Charles** 1628-1703 ......... **LC 2**
See also MAICYA; SATA 25

**Perry, Brighton**
See Sherwood, Robert E(mmet)

**Perse, St.-John** .............. **CLC 4, 11, 46**
See also Leger, (Marie-Rene Auguste) Alexis
Saint-Leger

**Perutz, Leo** 1882-1957.......... **TCLC 60**
See also DLB 81

**Peseenz, Tulio F.**
See Lopez y Fuentes, Gregorio

**Pesetsky, Bette** 1932-............. **CLC 28**
See also CA 133; DLB 130

**Peshkov, Alexei Maximovich** 1868-1936
See Gorky, Maxim
See also CA 105; 141; DA; DAC;
DAM DRAM, MST, NOV

**Pessoa, Fernando (Antonio Nogueira)**
1888-1935 ........... **TCLC 27; HLC**
See also CA 125

**Peterkin, Julia Mood** 1880-1961.... **CLC 31**
See also CA 102; DLB 9

**Peters, Joan K.** 1945-............. **CLC 39**

**Peters, Robert L(ouis)** 1924-........ **CLC 7**
See also CA 13-16R; CAAS 8; DLB 105

**Petofi, Sandor** 1823-1849........ **NCLC 21**

**Petrakis, Harry Mark** 1923-........ **CLC 3**
See also CA 9-12R; CANR 4, 30

**Petrarch** 1304-1374................ **PC 8**
See also DAM POET

**Petrov, Evgeny** ................. **TCLC 21**
See also Kataev, Evgeny Petrovich

**Petry, Ann (Lane)** 1908- ...... **CLC 1, 7, 18**
See also BW 1; CA 5-8R; CAAS 6;
CANR 4, 46; CLR 12; DLB 76; JRDA;
MAICYA; MTCW; SATA 5

**Petursson, Halligrimur** 1614-1674 .... **LC 8**

**Philips, Katherine** 1632-1664........ **LC 30**
See also DLB 131

**Philipson, Morris H.** 1926- ....... **CLC 53**
See also CA 1-4R; CANR 4

**Porter, Gene(va Grace) Stratton**
1863(?)-1924 . . . . . . . . . . . . . . . TCLC 21
See also CA 112

**Porter, Katherine Anne**
1890-1980 . . . . . . CLC 1, 3, 7, 10, 13, 15,
27; DA; DAB; DAC; SSC 4
See also AITN 2; CA 1-4R; 101; CANR 1;
DAM MST, NOV; DLB 4, 9, 102;
DLBD 12; DLBY 80; MTCW; SATA 39;
SATA-Obit 23

**Porter, Peter (Neville Frederick)**
1929- . . . . . . . . . . . . . . . . . . CLC 5, 13, 33
See also CA 85-88; DLB 40

**Porter, William Sydney** 1862-1910
See Henry, O.
See also CA 104; 131; CDALB 1865-1917;
DA; DAB; DAC; DAM MST; DLB 12,
78, 79; MTCW; YABC 2

**Portillo (y Pacheco), Jose Lopez**
See Lopez Portillo (y Pacheco), Jose

**Post, Melville Davisson**
1869-1930 . . . . . . . . . . . . . . . . . TCLC 39
See also CA 110

**Potok, Chaim** 1929- . . . . . . . CLC 2, 7, 14, 26
See also AAYA 15; AITN 1, 2; CA 17-20R;
CANR 19, 35; DAM NOV; DLB 28, 152;
INT CANR-19; MTCW; SATA 33

**Potter, Beatrice**
See Webb, (Martha) Beatrice (Potter)
See also MAICYA

**Potter, Dennis (Christopher George)**
1935-1994 . . . . . . . . . . . . . . . . CLC 58, 86
See also CA 107; 145; CANR 33; MTCW

**Pound, Ezra (Weston Loomis)**
1885-1972 . . . . . . CLC 1, 2, 3, 4, 5, 7, 10,
13, 18, 34, 48, 50; DA; DAB; DAC; PC 4;
WLC
See also CA 5-8R; 37-40R; CANR 40;
CDALB 1917-1929; DAM MST, POET;
DLB 4, 45, 63; MTCW

**Povod, Reinaldo** 1959-1994 . . . . . . . . CLC 44
See also CA 136; 146

**Powell, Adam Clayton, Jr.**
1908-1972 . . . . . . . . . . . . . . CLC 89; BLC
See also BW 1; CA 102; 33-36R;
DAM MULT

**Powell, Anthony (Dymoke)**
1905- . . . . . . . . . . CLC 1, 3, 7, 9, 10, 31
See also CA 1-4R; CANR 1, 32;
CDBLB 1945-1960; DLB 15; MTCW

**Powell, Dawn** 1897-1965 . . . . . . . . . CLC 66
See also CA 5-8R

**Powell, Padgett** 1952- . . . . . . . . . . . . CLC 34
See also CA 126

**Power, Susan** . . . . . . . . . . . . . . . . . . . CLC 91

**Powers, J(ames) F(arl)**
1917- . . . . . . . . . CLC 1, 4, 8, 57; SSC 4
See also CA 1-4R; CANR 2; DLB 130;
MTCW

**Powers, John J(ames)** 1945-
See Powers, John R.
See also CA 69-72

**Powers, John R.** . . . . . . . . . . . . . . . . . CLC 66
See also Powers, John J(ames)

**Pownall, David** 1938- . . . . . . . . . . . . . CLC 10
See also CA 89-92; CAAS 18; CANR 49;
DLB 14

**Powys, John Cowper**
1872-1963 . . . . . . . . . . . CLC 7, 9, 15, 46
See also CA 85-88; DLB 15; MTCW

**Powys, T(heodore) F(rancis)**
1875-1953 . . . . . . . . . . . . . . . . . . TCLC 9
See also CA 106; DLB 36, 162

**Prager, Emily** 1952- . . . . . . . . . . . . . CLC 56

**Pratt, E(dwin) J(ohn)**
1883(?)-1964 . . . . . . . . . . . CLC 19; DAC
See also CA 141; 93-96; DAM POET;
DLB 92

**Premchand** . . . . . . . . . . . . . . . . . . . . TCLC 21
See also Srivastava, Dhanpat Rai

**Preussler, Otfried** 1923- . . . . . . . . . . CLC 17
See also CA 77-80; SATA 24

**Prevert, Jacques (Henri Marie)**
1900-1977 . . . . . . . . . . . . . . . . . . CLC 15
See also CA 77-80; 69-72; CANR 29;
MTCW; SATA-Obit 30

**Prevost, Abbe (Antoine Francois)**
1697-1763 . . . . . . . . . . . . . . . . . . . . LC 1

**Price, (Edward) Reynolds**
1933- . . . . . . . . . CLC 3, 6, 13, 43, 50, 63
See also CA 1-4R; CANR 1, 37;
DAM NOV; DLB 2; INT CANR-37

**Price, Richard** 1949- . . . . . . . . . . . CLC 6, 12
See also CA 49-52; CANR 3; DLBY 81

**Prichard, Katharine Susannah**
1883-1969 . . . . . . . . . . . . . . . . . . CLC 46
See also CA 11-12; CANR 33; CAP 1;
MTCW; SATA 66

**Priestley, J(ohn) B(oynton)**
1894-1984 . . . . . . . . . . . . CLC 2, 5, 9, 34
See also CA 9-12R; 113; CANR 33;
CDBLB 1914-1945; DAM DRAM, NOV;
DLB 10, 34, 77, 100, 139; DLBY 84;
MTCW

**Prince** 1958(?)- . . . . . . . . . . . . . . . . . CLC 35

**Prince, F(rank) T(empleton)** 1912- . . CLC 22
See also CA 101; CANR 43; DLB 20

**Prince Kropotkin**
See Kropotkin, Peter (Aleksieevich)

**Prior, Matthew** 1664-1721 . . . . . . . . . . LC 4
See also DLB 95

**Pritchard, William H(arrison)**
1932- . . . . . . . . . . . . . . . . . . . . . CLC 34
See also CA 65-68; CANR 23; DLB 111

**Pritchett, V(ictor) S(awdon)**
1900- . . . . . . . CLC 5, 13, 15, 41; SSC 14
See also CA 61-64; CANR 31; DAM NOV;
DLB 15, 139; MTCW

**Private 19022**
See Manning, Frederic

**Probst, Mark** 1925- . . . . . . . . . . . . . . CLC 59
See also CA 130

**Prokosch, Frederic** 1908-1989 . . . . CLC 4, 48
See also CA 73-76; 128; DLB 48

**Prophet, The**
See Dreiser, Theodore (Herman Albert)

**Prose, Francine** 1947- . . . . . . . . . . . . CLC 45
See also CA 109; 112; CANR 46

**Proudhon**
See Cunha, Euclides (Rodrigues Pimenta) da

**Proulx, E. Annie** 1935- . . . . . . . . . . CLC 81

**Proust, (Valentin-Louis-George-Eugene-)**
**Marcel**
1871-1922 . . . . . . . . TCLC 7, 13, 33; DA;
DAB; DAC; WLC
See also CA 104; 120; DAM MST, NOV;
DLB 65; MTCW

**Prowler, Harley**
See Masters, Edgar Lee

**Prus, Boleslaw** 1845-1912 . . . . . . . TCLC 48

**Pryor, Richard (Franklin Lenox Thomas)**
1940- . . . . . . . . . . . . . . . . . . . . . CLC 26
See also CA 122

**Przybyszewski, Stanislaw**
1868-1927 . . . . . . . . . . . . . . . . . TCLC 36
See also DLB 66

**Pteleon**
See Grieve, C(hristopher) M(urray)
See also DAM POET

**Puckett, Lute**
See Masters, Edgar Lee

**Puig, Manuel**
1932-1990 . . . CLC 3, 5, 10, 28, 65; HLC
See also CA 45-48; CANR 2, 32;
DAM MULT; DLB 113; HW; MTCW

**Purdy, Al(fred Wellington)**
1918- . . . . . . . . . . CLC 3, 6, 14, 50; DAC
See also CA 81-84; CAAS 17; CANR 42;
DAM MST, POET; DLB 88

**Purdy, James (Amos)**
1923- . . . . . . . . . . . . CLC 2, 4, 10, 28, 52
See also CA 33-36R; CAAS 1; CANR 19,
51; DLB 2; INT CANR-19; MTCW

**Pure, Simon**
See Swinnerton, Frank Arthur

**Pushkin, Alexander (Sergeyevich)**
1799-1837 . . . . . NCLC 3, 27; DA; DAB;
DAC; PC 10; WLC
See also DAM DRAM, MST, POET;
SATA 61

**P'u Sung-ling** 1640-1715 . . . . . . . . . . . LC 3

**Putnam, Arthur Lee**
See Alger, Horatio, Jr.

**Puzo, Mario** 1920- . . . . . . . . . CLC 1, 2, 6, 36
See also CA 65-68; CANR 4, 42;
DAM NOV, POP; DLB 6; MTCW

**Pym, Barbara (Mary Crampton)**
1913-1980 . . . . . . . . . . . . CLC 13, 19, 37
See also CA 13-14; 97-100; CANR 13, 34;
CAP 1; DLB 14; DLBY 87; MTCW

**Pynchon, Thomas (Ruggles, Jr.)**
1937- . . . . . CLC 2, 3, 6, 9, 11, 18, 33, 62,
72; DA; DAB; DAC; SSC 14; WLC
See also BEST 90:2; CA 17-20R; CANR 22,
46; DAM MST, NOV, POP; DLB 2;
MTCW

**Qian Zhongshu**
See Ch'ien Chung-shu

**Qroll**
See Dagerman, Stig (Halvard)

**Quarrington, Paul (Lewis)** 1953- . . . . CLC 65
See also CA 129

**Reid, Desmond**
See Moorcock, Michael (John)

**Reid Banks, Lynne** 1929-
See Banks, Lynne Reid
See also CA 1-4R; CANR 6, 22, 38;
CLR 24; JRDA; MAICYA; SATA 22, 75

**Reilly, William K.**
See Creasey, John

**Reiner, Max**
See Caldwell, (Janet Miriam) Taylor
(Holland)

**Reis, Ricardo**
See Pessoa, Fernando (Antonio Nogueira)

**Remarque, Erich Maria**
1898-1970 . . . . CLC 21; DA; DAB; DAC
See also CA 77-80; 29-32R; DAM MST,
NOV; DLB 56; MTCW

**Remizov, A.**
See Remizov, Aleksei (Mikhailovich)

**Remizov, A. M.**
See Remizov, Aleksei (Mikhailovich)

**Remizov, Aleksei (Mikhailovich)**
1877-1957 . . . . . . . . . . . . . . . . . TCLC 27
See also CA 125; 133

**Renan, Joseph Ernest**
1823-1892 . . . . . . . . . . . . . . . . . NCLC 26

**Renard, Jules** 1864-1910 . . . . . . . . TCLC 17
See also CA 117

**Renault, Mary** . . . . . . . . . . . . . CLC 3, 11, 17
See also Challans, Mary
See also DLBY 83

**Rendell, Ruth (Barbara)** 1930- . . CLC 28, 48
See also Vine, Barbara
See also CA 109; CANR 32; DAM POP;
DLB 87; INT CANR-32; MTCW

**Renoir, Jean** 1894-1979 . . . . . . . . . . CLC 20
See also CA 129; 85-88

**Resnais, Alain** 1922- . . . . . . . . . . . . . CLC 16

**Reverdy, Pierre** 1889-1960 . . . . . . . . CLC 53
See also CA 97-100; 89-92

**Rexroth, Kenneth**
1905-1982 . . . . . . CLC 1, 2, 6, 11, 22, 49
See also CA 5-8R; 107; CANR 14, 34;
CDALB 1941-1968; DAM POET;
DLB 16, 48; DLBY 82; INT CANR-14;
MTCW

**Reyes, Alfonso** 1889-1959 . . . . . . . TCLC 33
See also CA 131; HW

**Reyes y Basoalto, Ricardo Eliecer Neftali**
See Neruda, Pablo

**Reymont, Wladyslaw (Stanislaw)**
1868(?)-1925 . . . . . . . . . . . . . . . . TCLC 5
See also CA 104

**Reynolds, Jonathan** 1942- . . . . . . . CLC 6, 38
See also CA 65-68; CANR 28

**Reynolds, Joshua** 1723-1792 . . . . . . . LC 15
See also DLB 104

**Reynolds, Michael Shane** 1937- . . . . CLC 44
See also CA 65-68; CANR 9

**Reznikoff, Charles** 1894-1976 . . . . . . . CLC 9
See also CA 33-36; 61-64; CAP 2; DLB 28,
45

**Rezzori (d'Arezzo), Gregor von**
1914- . . . . . . . . . . . . . . . . . . . . . CLC 25
See also CA 122; 136

**Rhine, Richard**
See Silverstein, Alvin

**Rhodes, Eugene Manlove**
1869-1934 . . . . . . . . . . . . . . . . . TCLC 53

**R'hoone**
See Balzac, Honore de

**Rhys, Jean**
1890(?)-1979 . . . . CLC 2, 4, 6, 14, 19, 51;
SSC 21
See also CA 25-28R; 85-88; CANR 35;
CDBLB 1945-1960; DAM NOV; DLB 36,
117, 162; MTCW

**Ribeiro, Darcy** 1922- . . . . . . . . . . . . . CLC 34
See also CA 33-36R

**Ribeiro, Joao Ubaldo (Osorio Pimentel)**
1941- . . . . . . . . . . . . . . . . . . CLC 10, 67
See also CA 81-84

**Ribman, Ronald (Burt)** 1932- . . . . . . . CLC 7
See also CA 21-24R; CANR 46

**Ricci, Nino** 1959- . . . . . . . . . . . . . . . CLC 70
See also CA 137

**Rice, Anne** 1941- . . . . . . . . . . . . . . . CLC 41
See also AAYA 9; BEST 89:2; CA 65-68;
CANR 12, 36; DAM POP

**Rice, Elmer (Leopold)**
1892-1967 . . . . . . . . . . . . . . . . CLC 7, 49
See also CA 21-22; 25-28R; CAP 2;
DAM DRAM; DLB 4, 7; MTCW

**Rice, Tim(othy Miles Bindon)**
1944- . . . . . . . . . . . . . . . . . . . . . CLC 21
See also CA 103; CANR 46

**Rich, Adrienne (Cecile)**
1929- . . . . CLC 3, 6, 7, 11, 18, 36, 73, 76;
PC 5
See also CA 9-12R; CANR 20;
DAM POET; DLB 5, 67; MTCW

**Rich, Barbara**
See Graves, Robert (von Ranke)

**Rich, Robert**
See Trumbo, Dalton

**Richard, Keith** . . . . . . . . . . . . . . . . . CLC 17
See also Richards, Keith

**Richards, David Adams**
1950- . . . . . . . . . . . . . . . . . CLC 59; DAC
See also CA 93-96; DLB 53

**Richards, I(vor) A(rmstrong)**
1893-1979 . . . . . . . . . . . . . . . CLC 14, 24
See also CA 41-44R; 89-92; CANR 34;
DLB 27

**Richards, Keith** 1943-
See Richard, Keith
See also CA 107

**Richardson, Anne**
See Roiphe, Anne (Richardson)

**Richardson, Dorothy Miller**
1873-1957 . . . . . . . . . . . . . . . . . TCLC 3
See also CA 104; DLB 36

**Richardson, Ethel Florence (Lindesay)**
1870-1946
See Richardson, Henry Handel
See also CA 105

**Richardson, Henry Handel** . . . . . . . . . TCLC 4
See also Richardson, Ethel Florence
(Lindesay)

**Richardson, Samuel**
1689-1761 . . . . . . LC 1; DA; DAB; DAC;
WLC
See also CDBLB 1660-1789; DAM MST,
NOV; DLB 39

**Richler, Mordecai**
1931- . . . . . . . CLC 3, 5, 9, 13, 18, 46, 70;
DAC
See also AITN 1; CA 65-68; CANR 31;
CLR 17; DAM MST, NOV; DLB 53;
MAICYA; MTCW; SATA 44;
SATA-Brief 27

**Richter, Conrad (Michael)**
1890-1968 . . . . . . . . . . . . . . . . . CLC 30
See also CA 5-8R; 25-28R; CANR 23;
DLB 9; MTCW; SATA 3

**Ricostranza, Tom**
See Ellis, Trey

**Riddell, J. H.** 1832-1906 . . . . . . . . TCLC 40

**Riding, Laura** . . . . . . . . . . . . . . . . CLC 3, 7
See also Jackson, Laura (Riding)

**Riefenstahl, Berta Helene Amalia** 1902-
See Riefenstahl, Leni
See also CA 108

**Riefenstahl, Leni** . . . . . . . . . . . . . . . CLC 16
See also Riefenstahl, Berta Helene Amalia

**Riffe, Ernest**
See Bergman, (Ernst) Ingmar

**Riggs, (Rolla) Lynn** 1899-1954 . . . . TCLC 56
See also CA 144; DAM MULT; NNAL

**Riley, James Whitcomb**
1849-1916 . . . . . . . . . . . . . . . . . TCLC 51
See also CA 118; 137; DAM POET;
MAICYA; SATA 17

**Riley, Tex**
See Creasey, John

**Rilke, Rainer Maria**
1875-1926 . . . . . . . . TCLC 1, 6, 19; PC 2
See also CA 104; 132; DAM POET;
DLB 81; MTCW

**Rimbaud, (Jean Nicolas) Arthur**
1854-1891 . . . . . NCLC 4, 35; DA; DAB;
DAC; PC 3; WLC
See also DAM MST, POET

**Rinehart, Mary Roberts**
1876-1958 . . . . . . . . . . . . . . . . . TCLC 52
See also CA 108

**Ringmaster, The**
See Mencken, H(enry) L(ouis)

**Ringwood, Gwen(dolyn Margaret) Pharis**
1910-1984 . . . . . . . . . . . . . . . . . CLC 48
See also CA 148; 112; DLB 88

**Rio, Michel** 19(?)- . . . . . . . . . . . . . . . CLC 43

**Ritsos, Giannes**
See Ritsos, Yannis

**Ritsos, Yannis** 1909-1990 . . . . . CLC 6, 13, 31
See also CA 77-80; 133; CANR 39; MTCW

**Ritter, Erika** 1948(?)- . . . . . . . . . . . . . CLC 52

**Rivera, Jose Eustasio** 1889-1928 . . . TCLC 35
See also HW

**Rivers, Conrad Kent** 1933-1968 . . . . . . CLC 1
See also BW 1; CA 85-88; DLB 41

**Rivers, Elfrida**
See Bradley, Marion Zimmer

**Riverside, John**
See Heinlein, Robert A(nson)

**Rizal, Jose** 1861-1896. . . . . . . . . . **NCLC 27**

**Roa Bastos, Augusto (Antonio)**
1917- . . . . . . . . . . . . . . . . . **CLC 45; HLC**
See also CA 131; DAM MULT; DLB 113;
HW

**Robbe-Grillet, Alain**
1922- . . . . . . **CLC 1, 2, 4, 6, 8, 10, 14, 43**
See also CA 9-12R; CANR 33; DLB 83;
MTCW

**Robbins, Harold** 1916- . . . . . . . . . . . . **CLC 5**
See also CA 73-76; CANR 26; DAM NOV;
MTCW

**Robbins, Thomas Eugene** 1936-
See Robbins, Tom
See also CA 81-84; CANR 29; DAM NOV,
POP; MTCW

**Robbins, Tom** . . . . . . . . . . . . . **CLC 9, 32, 64**
See also Robbins, Thomas Eugene
See also BEST 90:3; DLBY 80

**Robbins, Trina** 1938- . . . . . . . . . . . . . **CLC 21**
See also CA 128

**Roberts, Charles G(eorge) D(ouglas)**
1860-1943 . . . . . . . . . . . . . . . . **TCLC 8**
See also CA 105; CLR 33; DLB 92;
SATA-Brief 29

**Roberts, Kate** 1891-1985 . . . . . . . . . . **CLC 15**
See also CA 107; 116

**Roberts, Keith (John Kingston)**
1935- . . . . . . . . . . . . . . . . . . . . . . **CLC 14**
See also CA 25-28R; CANR 46

**Roberts, Kenneth (Lewis)**
1885-1957 . . . . . . . . . . . . . . . . . **TCLC 23**
See also CA 109; DLB 9

**Roberts, Michele (B.)** 1949- . . . . . . . . **CLC 48**
See also CA 115

**Robertson, Ellis**
See Ellison, Harlan (Jay); Silverberg, Robert

**Robertson, Thomas William**
1829-1871 . . . . . . . . . . . . . . . . . **NCLC 35**
See also DAM DRAM

**Robinson, Edwin Arlington**
1869-1935 . . . . **TCLC 5; DA; DAC; PC 1**
See also CA 104; 133; CDALB 1865-1917;
DAM MST, POET; DLB 54; MTCW

**Robinson, Henry Crabb**
1775-1867 . . . . . . . . . . . . . . . . . **NCLC 15**
See also DLB 107

**Robinson, Jill** 1936- . . . . . . . . . . . . . . **CLC 10**
See also CA 102; INT 102

**Robinson, Kim Stanley** 1952- . . . . . . **CLC 34**
See also CA 126

**Robinson, Lloyd**
See Silverberg, Robert

**Robinson, Marilynne** 1944- . . . . . . . . **CLC 25**
See also CA 116

**Robinson, Smokey** . . . . . . . . . . . . . . . **CLC 21**
See also Robinson, William, Jr.

**Robinson, William, Jr.** 1940-
See Robinson, Smokey
See also CA 116

**Robison, Mary** 1949- . . . . . . . . . . . . . **CLC 42**
See also CA 113; 116; DLB 130; INT 116

**Rod, Edouard** 1857-1910 . . . . . . . . **TCLC 52**

**Roddenberry, Eugene Wesley** 1921-1991
See Roddenberry, Gene
See also CA 110; 135; CANR 37; SATA 45;
SATA-Obit 69

**Roddenberry, Gene** . . . . . . . . . . . . . . . **CLC 17**
See also Roddenberry, Eugene Wesley
See also AAYA 5; SATA-Obit 69

**Rodgers, Mary** 1931- . . . . . . . . . . . . . . **CLC 12**
See also CA 49-52; CANR 8; CLR 20;
INT CANR-8; JRDA; MAICYA;
SATA 8

**Rodgers, W(illiam) R(obert)**
1909-1969 . . . . . . . . . . . . . . . . . . . **CLC 7**
See also CA 85-88; DLB 20

**Rodman, Eric**
See Silverberg, Robert

**Rodman, Howard** 1920(?)-1985 . . . . . **CLC 65**
See also CA 118

**Rodman, Maia**
See Wojciechowska, Maia (Teresa)

**Rodriguez, Claudio** 1934- . . . . . . . . . **CLC 10**
See also DLB 134

**Roelvaag, O(le) E(dvart)**
1876-1931 . . . . . . . . . . . . . . . . . **TCLC 17**
See also CA 117; DLB 9

**Roethke, Theodore (Huebner)**
1908-1963 . . . . . . **CLC 1, 3, 8, 11, 19, 46;**
**PC 15**
See also CA 81-84; CABS 2;
CDALB 1941-1968; DAM POET; DLB 5;
MTCW

**Rogers, Thomas Hunton** 1927- . . . . . **CLC 57**
See also CA 89-92; INT 89-92

**Rogers, Will(iam Penn Adair)**
1879-1935 . . . . . . . . . . . . . . . . . . **TCLC 8**
See also CA 105; 144; DAM MULT;
DLB 11; NNAL

**Rogin, Gilbert** 1929- . . . . . . . . . . . . . . **CLC 18**
See also CA 65-68; CANR 15

**Rohan, Koda** . . . . . . . . . . . . . . . . . . . **TCLC 22**
See also Koda Shigeyuki

**Rohmer, Eric** . . . . . . . . . . . . . . . . . . . **CLC 16**
See also Scherer, Jean-Marie Maurice

**Rohmer, Sax** . . . . . . . . . . . . . . . . . . . **TCLC 28**
See also Ward, Arthur Henry Sarsfield
See also DLB 70

**Roiphe, Anne (Richardson)**
1935- . . . . . . . . . . . . . . . . . . . . . **CLC 3, 9**
See also CA 89-92; CANR 45; DLBY 80;
INT 89-92

**Rojas, Fernando de** 1465-1541 . . . . . . **LC 23**

**Rolfe, Frederick (William Serafino Austin**
**Lewis Mary)** 1860-1913 . . . . . . **TCLC 12**
See also CA 107; DLB 34, 156

**Rolland, Romain** 1866-1944 . . . . . . . . **TCLC 23**
See also CA 118; DLB 65

**Rolvaag, O(le) E(dvart)**
See Roelvaag, O(le) E(dvart)

**Romain Arnaud, Saint**
See Aragon, Louis

**Romains, Jules** 1885-1972 . . . . . . . . . . **CLC 7**
See also CA 85-88; CANR 34; DLB 65;
MTCW

**Romero, Jose Ruben** 1890-1952 . . . **TCLC 14**
See also CA 114; 131; HW

**Ronsard, Pierre de**
1524-1585 . . . . . . . . . . . . . . **LC 6; PC 11**

**Rooke, Leon** 1934- . . . . . . . . . . . . **CLC 25, 34**
See also CA 25-28R; CANR 23; DAM POP

**Roper, William** 1498-1578 . . . . . . . . . . **LC 10**

**Roquelaure, A. N.**
See Rice, Anne

**Rosa, Joao Guimaraes** 1908-1967 . . . **CLC 23**
See also CA 89-92; DLB 113

**Rose, Wendy** 1948- . . . . . . . . . **CLC 85; PC 13**
See also CA 53-56; CANR 5, 51;
DAM MULT; NNAL; SATA 12

**Rosen, Richard (Dean)** 1949- . . . . . . . **CLC 39**
See also CA 77-80; INT CANR-30

**Rosenberg, Isaac** 1890-1918 . . . . . . . **TCLC 12**
See also CA 107; DLB 20

**Rosenblatt, Joe** . . . . . . . . . . . . . . . . . . **CLC 15**
See also Rosenblatt, Joseph

**Rosenblatt, Joseph** 1933-
See Rosenblatt, Joe
See also CA 89-92; INT 89-92

**Rosenfeld, Samuel** 1896-1963
See Tzara, Tristan
See also CA 89-92

**Rosenthal, M(acha) L(ouis)** 1917- . . . **CLC 28**
See also CA 1-4R; CAAS 6; CANR 4, 51;
DLB 5; SATA 59

**Ross, Barnaby**
See Dannay, Frederic

**Ross, Bernard L.**
See Follett, Ken(neth Martin)

**Ross, J. H.**
See Lawrence, T(homas) E(dward)

**Ross, Martin**
See Martin, Violet Florence
See also DLB 135

**Ross, (James) Sinclair**
1908- . . . . . . . . . . . . . . . . . **CLC 13; DAC**
See also CA 73-76; DAM MST; DLB 88

**Rossetti, Christina (Georgina)**
1830-1894 . . . . . **NCLC 2, 50; DA; DAB;**
**DAC; PC 7; WLC**
See also DAM MST, POET; DLB 35, 163;
MAICYA; SATA 20

**Rossetti, Dante Gabriel**
1828-1882 . . . . . . . **NCLC 4; DA; DAB;**
**DAC; WLC**
See also CDBLB 1832-1890; DAM MST,
POET; DLB 35

**Rossner, Judith (Perelman)**
1935- . . . . . . . . . . . . . . . . . . **CLC 6, 9, 29**
See also AITN 2; BEST 90:3; CA 17-20R;
CANR 18, 51; DLB 6; INT CANR-18;
MTCW

**Rostand, Edmond (Eugene Alexis)**
1868-1918 . . . . . . **TCLC 6, 37; DA; DAB;**
**DAC**
See also CA 104; 126; DAM DRAM, MST;
MTCW

**Schnitzler, Arthur**
1862-1931 . . . . . . . . . . **TCLC 4; SSC 15**
See also CA 104; DLB 81, 118

**Schopenhauer, Arthur**
1788-1860 . . . . . . . . . . . . . . . . **NCLC 51**
See also DLB 90

**Schor, Sandra (M.)**  1932(?)-1990 . . . **CLC 65**
See also CA 132

**Schorer, Mark**  1908-1977 . . . . . . . . . . **CLC 9**
See also CA 5-8R; 73-76; CANR 7;
DLB 103

**Schrader, Paul (Joseph)**  1946- . . . . . . **CLC 26**
See also CA 37-40R; CANR 41; DLB 44

**Schreiner, Olive (Emilie Albertina)**
1855-1920 . . . . . . . . . . . . . . . . . **TCLC 9**
See also CA 105; DLB 18, 156

**Schulberg, Budd (Wilson)**
1914- . . . . . . . . . . . . . . . . . . . **CLC 7, 48**
See also CA 25-28R; CANR 19; DLB 6, 26,
28; DLBY 81

**Schulz, Bruno**
1892-1942 . . . . . . . . **TCLC 5, 51; SSC 13**
See also CA 115; 123

**Schulz, Charles M(onroe)**  1922- . . . . **CLC 12**
See also CA 9-12R; CANR 6;
INT CANR-6; SATA 10

**Schumacher, E(rnst) F(riedrich)**
1911-1977 . . . . . . . . . . . . . . . . . **CLC 80**
See also CA 81-84; 73-76; CANR 34

**Schuyler, James Marcus**
1923-1991 . . . . . . . . . . . . . . . **CLC 5, 23**
See also CA 101; 134; DAM POET; DLB 5;
INT 101

**Schwartz, Delmore (David)**
1913-1966 . . . **CLC 2, 4, 10, 45, 87; PC 8**
See also CA 17-18; 25-28R; CANR 35;
CAP 2; DLB 28, 48; MTCW

**Schwartz, Ernst**
See Ozu, Yasujiro

**Schwartz, John Burnham**  1965- . . . . **CLC 59**
See also CA 132

**Schwartz, Lynne Sharon**  1939- . . . . . **CLC 31**
See also CA 103; CANR 44

**Schwartz, Muriel A.**
See Eliot, T(homas) S(tearns)

**Schwarz-Bart, Andre**  1928- . . . . . . . **CLC 2, 4**
See also CA 89-92

**Schwarz-Bart, Simone**  1938- . . . . . . . . **CLC 7**
See also BW 2; CA 97-100

**Schwob, (Mayer Andre) Marcel**
1867-1905 . . . . . . . . . . . . . . . . . **TCLC 20**
See also CA 117; DLB 123

**Sciascia, Leonardo**
1921-1989 . . . . . . . . . . . . . **CLC 8, 9, 41**
See also CA 85-88; 130; CANR 35; MTCW

**Scoppettone, Sandra**  1936- . . . . . . . . **CLC 26**
See also AAYA 11; CA 5-8R; CANR 41;
SATA 9

**Scorsese, Martin**  1942- . . . . . . . . **CLC 20, 89**
See also CA 110; 114; CANR 46

**Scotland, Jay**
See Jakes, John (William)

**Scott, Duncan Campbell**
1862-1947 . . . . . . . . . . . . . **TCLC 6; DAC**
See also CA 104; DLB 92

**Scott, Evelyn**  1893-1963 . . . . . . . . . . **CLC 43**
See also CA 104; 112; DLB 9, 48

**Scott, F(rancis) R(eginald)**
1899-1985 . . . . . . . . . . . . . . . . . **CLC 22**
See also CA 101; 114; DLB 88; INT 101

**Scott, Frank**
See Scott, F(rancis) R(eginald)

**Scott, Joanna**  1960- . . . . . . . . . . . . . **CLC 50**
See also CA 126

**Scott, Paul (Mark)**  1920-1978 . . . . **CLC 9, 60**
See also CA 81-84; 77-80; CANR 33;
DLB 14; MTCW

**Scott, Walter**
1771-1832 . . . . . . . **NCLC 15; DA; DAB;
DAC; PC 13; WLC**
See also CDBLB 1789-1832; DAM MST,
NOV, POET; DLB 93, 107, 116, 144, 159;
YABC 2

**Scribe, (Augustin) Eugene**
1791-1861 . . . . . . . . . . . **NCLC 16; DC 5**
See also DAM DRAM

**Scrum, R.**
See Crumb, R(obert)

**Scudery, Madeleine de**  1607-1701 . . . . . **LC 2**

**Scum**
See Crumb, R(obert)

**Scumbag, Little Bobby**
See Crumb, R(obert)

**Seabrook, John**
See Hubbard, L(afayette) Ron(ald)

**Sealy, I. Allan**  1951- . . . . . . . . . . . . . **CLC 55**

**Search, Alexander**
See Pessoa, Fernando (Antonio Nogueira)

**Sebastian, Lee**
See Silverberg, Robert

**Sebastian Owl**
See Thompson, Hunter S(tockton)

**Sebestyen, Ouida**  1924- . . . . . . . . . . . **CLC 30**
See also AAYA 8; CA 107; CANR 40;
CLR 17; JRDA; MAICYA; SAAS 10;
SATA 39

**Secundus, H. Scriblerus**
See Fielding, Henry

**Sedges, John**
See Buck, Pearl S(ydenstricker)

**Sedgwick, Catharine Maria**
1789-1867 . . . . . . . . . . . . . . . . . **NCLC 19**
See also DLB 1, 74

**Seelye, John**  1931- . . . . . . . . . . . . . . . . **CLC 7**

**Seferiades, Giorgos Stylianou**  1900-1971
See Seferis, George
See also CA 5-8R; 33-36R; CANR 5, 36;
MTCW

**Seferis, George** . . . . . . . . . . . . . . . . **CLC 5, 11**
See also Seferiades, Giorgos Stylianou

**Segal, Erich (Wolf)**  1937- . . . . . . . **CLC 3, 10**
See also BEST 89:1; CA 25-28R; CANR 20,
36; DAM POP; DLBY 86;
INT CANR-20; MTCW

**Seger, Bob**  1945- . . . . . . . . . . . . . . . . **CLC 35**

**Seghers, Anna** . . . . . . . . . . . . . . . . . . . **CLC 7**
See also Radvanyi, Netty
See also DLB 69

**Seidel, Frederick (Lewis)**  1936- . . . . . **CLC 18**
See also CA 13-16R; CANR 8; DLBY 84

**Seifert, Jaroslav**  1901-1986 . . . . . **CLC 34, 44**
See also CA 127; MTCW

**Sei Shonagon**  c. 966-1017(?) . . . . . . **CMLC 6**

**Selby, Hubert, Jr.**
1928- . . . . . . . . . . **CLC 1, 2, 4, 8; SSC 20**
See also CA 13-16R; CANR 33; DLB 2

**Selzer, Richard**  1928- . . . . . . . . . . . . . **CLC 74**
See also CA 65-68; CANR 14

**Sembene, Ousmane**
See Ousmane, Sembene

**Senancour, Etienne Pivert de**
1770-1846 . . . . . . . . . . . . . . . . . **NCLC 16**
See also DLB 119

**Sender, Ramon (Jose)**
1902-1982 . . . . . . . . . . . . . . **CLC 8; HLC**
See also CA 5-8R; 105; CANR 8;
DAM MULT; HW; MTCW

**Seneca, Lucius Annaeus**
4B.C.-65 . . . . . . . . . . . . . **CMLC 6; DC 5**
See also DAM DRAM

**Senghor, Leopold Sedar**
1906- . . . . . . . . . . . . . . . . . **CLC 54; BLC**
See also BW 2; CA 116; 125; CANR 47;
DAM MULT, POET; MTCW

**Serling, (Edward) Rod(man)**
1924-1975 . . . . . . . . . . . . . . . . . **CLC 30**
See also AAYA 14; AITN 1; CA 65-68;
57-60; DLB 26

**Serna, Ramon Gomez de la**
See Gomez de la Serna, Ramon

**Serpieres**
See Guillevic, (Eugene)

**Service, Robert**
See Service, Robert W(illiam)
See also DAB; DLB 92

**Service, Robert W(illiam)**
1874(?)-1958 . . . . . . **TCLC 15; DA; DAC;
WLC**
See also Service, Robert
See also CA 115; 140; DAM MST, POET;
SATA 20

**Seth, Vikram**  1952- . . . . . . . . . . . . **CLC 43, 90**
See also CA 121; 127; CANR 50;
DAM MULT; DLB 120; INT 127

**Seton, Cynthia Propper**
1926-1982 . . . . . . . . . . . . . . . . . **CLC 27**
See also CA 5-8R; 108; CANR 7

**Seton, Ernest (Evan) Thompson**
1860-1946 . . . . . . . . . . . . . . . . . **TCLC 31**
See also CA 109; DLB 92; DLBD 13;
JRDA; SATA 18

**Seton-Thompson, Ernest**
See Seton, Ernest (Evan) Thompson

**Settle, Mary Lee**  1918- . . . . . . . . **CLC 19, 61**
See also CA 89-92; CAAS 1; CANR 44;
DLB 6; INT 89-92

**Seuphor, Michel**
See Arp, Jean

**Sevigne, Marie (de Rabutin-Chantal) Marquise**
**de**  1626-1696 . . . . . . . . . . . . . . . **LC 11**

**Sexton, Anne (Harvey)**
1928-1974 .... **CLC 2, 4, 6, 8, 10, 15, 53;**
**DA; DAB; DAC; PC 2; WLC**
See also CA 1-4R; 53-56; CABS 2;
CANR 3, 36; CDALB 1941-1968;
DAM MST, POET; DLB 5; MTCW;
SATA 10

**Shaara, Michael (Joseph, Jr.)**
1929-1988 .................... **CLC 15**
See also AITN 1; CA 102; 125; DAM POP;
DLBY 83

**Shackleton, C. C.**
See Aldiss, Brian W(ilson)

**Shacochis, Bob** .................... **CLC 39**
See also Shacochis, Robert G.

**Shacochis, Robert G.** 1951-
See Shacochis, Bob
See also CA 119; 124; INT 124

**Shaffer, Anthony (Joshua)** 1926-.... **CLC 19**
See also CA 110; 116; DAM DRAM;
DLB 13

**Shaffer, Peter (Levin)**
1926- ...... **CLC 5, 14, 18, 37, 60; DAB**
See also CA 25-28R; CANR 25, 47;
CDBLB 1960 to Present; DAM DRAM,
MST; DLB 13; MTCW

**Shakey, Bernard**
See Young, Neil

**Shalamov, Varlam (Tikhonovich)**
1907(?)-1982 .................. **CLC 18**
See also CA 129; 105

**Shamlu, Ahmad** 1925- ............ **CLC 10**

**Shammas, Anton** 1951-............ **CLC 55**

**Shange, Ntozake**
1948- .... **CLC 8, 25, 38, 74; BLC; DC 3**
See also AAYA 9; BW 2; CA 85-88;
CABS 3; CANR 27, 48; DAM DRAM,
MULT; DLB 38; MTCW

**Shanley, John Patrick** 1950-....... **CLC 75**
See also CA 128; 133

**Shapcott, Thomas W(illiam)** 1935-.. **CLC 38**
See also CA 69-72; CANR 49

**Shapiro, Jane**..................... **CLC 76**

**Shapiro, Karl (Jay)** 1913- .. **CLC 4, 8, 15, 53**
See also CA 1-4R; CAAS 6; CANR 1, 36;
DLB 48; MTCW

**Sharp, William** 1855-1905 ....... **TCLC 39**
See also DLB 156

**Sharpe, Thomas Ridley** 1928-
See Sharpe, Tom
See also CA 114; 122; INT 122

**Sharpe, Tom**....................... **CLC 36**
See also Sharpe, Thomas Ridley
See also DLB 14

**Shaw, Bernard**................... **TCLC 45**
See also Shaw, George Bernard
See also BW 1

**Shaw, G. Bernard**
See Shaw, George Bernard

**Shaw, George Bernard**
1856-1950 ... **TCLC 3, 9, 21; DA; DAB;**
**DAC; WLC**
See also Shaw, Bernard
See also CA 104; 128; CDBLB 1914-1945;
DAM DRAM, MST; DLB 10, 57;
MTCW

**Shaw, Henry Wheeler**
1818-1885 ................. **NCLC 15**
See also DLB 11

**Shaw, Irwin** 1913-1984...... **CLC 7, 23, 34**
See also AITN 1; CA 13-16R; 112;
CANR 21; CDALB 1941-1968;
DAM DRAM, POP; DLB 6, 102;
DLBY 84; MTCW

**Shaw, Robert** 1927-1978 ........... **CLC 5**
See also AITN 1; CA 1-4R; 81-84;
CANR 4; DLB 13, 14

**Shaw, T. E.**
See Lawrence, T(homas) E(dward)

**Shawn, Wallace** 1943- ............ **CLC 41**
See also CA 112

**Shea, Lisa** 1953-................. **CLC 86**
See also CA 147

**Sheed, Wilfrid (John Joseph)**
1930- ................. **CLC 2, 4, 10, 53**
See also CA 65-68; CANR 30; DLB 6;
MTCW

**Sheldon, Alice Hastings Bradley**
1915(?)-1987
See Tiptree, James, Jr.
See also CA 108; 122; CANR 34; INT 108;
MTCW

**Sheldon, John**
See Bloch, Robert (Albert)

**Shelley, Mary Wollstonecraft (Godwin)**
1797-1851 ....... **NCLC 14; DA; DAB;**
**DAC; WLC**
See also CDBLB 1789-1832; DAM MST,
NOV; DLB 110, 116, 159; SATA 29

**Shelley, Percy Bysshe**
1792-1822 ....... **NCLC 18; DA; DAB;**
**DAC; PC 14; WLC**
See also CDBLB 1789-1832; DAM MST,
POET; DLB 96, 110, 158

**Shepard, Jim** 1956-.............. **CLC 36**
See also CA 137

**Shepard, Lucius** 1947- ............ **CLC 34**
See also CA 128; 141

**Shepard, Sam**
1943- .... **CLC 4, 6, 17, 34, 41, 44; DC 5**
See also AAYA 1; CA 69-72; CABS 3;
CANR 22; DAM DRAM; DLB 7;
MTCW

**Shepherd, Michael**
See Ludlum, Robert

**Sherburne, Zoa (Morin)** 1912-...... **CLC 30**
See also AAYA 13; CA 1-4R; CANR 3, 37;
MAICYA; SAAS 18; SATA 3

**Sheridan, Frances** 1724-1766........ **LC 7**
See also DLB 39, 84

**Sheridan, Richard Brinsley**
1751-1816 ....... **NCLC 5; DA; DAB;**
**DAC; DC 1; WLC**
See also CDBLB 1660-1789; DAM DRAM,
MST; DLB 89

**Sherman, Jonathan Marc**.......... **CLC 55**

**Sherman, Martin** 1941(?)- ......... **CLC 19**
See also CA 116; 123

**Sherwin, Judith Johnson** 1936-... **CLC 7, 15**
See also CA 25-28R; CANR 34

**Sherwood, Frances** 1940-......... **CLC 81**
See also CA 146

**Sherwood, Robert E(mmet)**
1896-1955 .................... **TCLC 3**
See also CA 104; DAM DRAM; DLB 7, 26

**Shestov, Lev** 1866-1938 ......... **TCLC 56**

**Shevchenko, Taras** 1814-1861 .... **NCLC 54**

**Shiel, M(atthew) P(hipps)**
1865-1947 .................. **TCLC 8**
See also CA 106; DLB 153

**Shields, Carol** 1935-......... **CLC 91; DAC**
See also CA 81-84; CANR 51

**Shiga, Naoya** 1883-1971........... **CLC 33**
See also CA 101; 33-36R

**Shilts, Randy** 1951-1994 ......... **CLC 85**
See also CA 115; 127; 144; CANR 45;
INT 127

**Shimazaki Haruki** 1872-1943
See Shimazaki Toson
See also CA 105; 134

**Shimazaki Toson**................. **TCLC 5**
See also Shimazaki Haruki

**Sholokhov, Mikhail (Aleksandrovich)**
1905-1984 ................. **CLC 7, 15**
See also CA 101; 112; MTCW;
SATA-Obit 36

**Shone, Patric**
See Hanley, James

**Shreve, Susan Richards** 1939-...... **CLC 23**
See also CA 49-52; CAAS 5; CANR 5, 38;
MAICYA; SATA 46; SATA-Brief 41

**Shue, Larry** 1946-1985............ **CLC 52**
See also CA 145; 117; DAM DRAM

**Shu-Jen, Chou** 1881-1936
See Lu Hsun
See also CA 104

**Shulman, Alix Kates** 1932- ...... **CLC 2, 10**
See also CA 29-32R; CANR 43; SATA 7

**Shuster, Joe** 1914- .............. **CLC 21**

**Shute, Nevil**..................... **CLC 30**
See also Norway, Nevil Shute

**Shuttle, Penelope (Diane)** 1947- ..... **CLC 7**
See also CA 93-96; CANR 39; DLB 14, 40

**Sidney, Mary** 1561-1621 ........... **LC 19**

**Sidney, Sir Philip**
1554-1586 ..... **LC 19; DA; DAB; DAC**
See also CDBLB Before 1660; DAM MST,
POET

**Siegel, Jerome** 1914- .............. **CLC 21**
See also CA 116

**Siegel, Jerry**
See Siegel, Jerome

**Sienkiewicz, Henryk (Adam Alexander Pius)**
1846-1916 .................. **TCLC 3**
See also CA 104; 134

**Sierra, Gregorio Martinez**
See Martinez Sierra, Gregorio

**Sierra, Maria (de la O'LeJarraga) Martinez**
See Martinez Sierra, Maria (de la O'LeJarraga)

**Sigal, Clancy** 1926-............... **CLC 7**
See also CA 1-4R

**Sigourney, Lydia Howard (Huntley)**
1791-1865 ................. **NCLC 21**
See also DLB 1, 42, 73

**Siguenza y Gongora, Carlos de**
1645-1700 .................... **LC 8**

**Sigurjonsson, Johann** 1880-1919... **TCLC 27**

**Sikelianos, Angelos** 1884-1951 .... **TCLC 39**

**Silkin, Jon** 1930- ........... **CLC 2, 6, 43**
See also CA 5-8R; CAAS 5; DLB 27

**Silko, Leslie (Marmon)**
1948- .......... **CLC 23, 74; DA; DAC**
See also AAYA 14; CA 115; 122;
CANR 45; DAM MST, MULT, POP;
DLB 143; NNAL

**Sillanpaa, Frans Eemil** 1888-1964... **CLC 19**
See also CA 129; 93-96; MTCW

**Sillitoe, Alan**
1928- .......... **CLC 1, 3, 6, 10, 19, 57**
See also AITN 1; CA 9-12R; CAAS 2;
CANR 8, 26; CDBLB 1960 to Present;
DLB 14, 139; MTCW; SATA 61

**Silone, Ignazio** 1900-1978 .......... **CLC 4**
See also CA 25-28; 81-84; CANR 34;
CAP 2; MTCW

**Silver, Joan Micklin** 1935- ........ **CLC 20**
See also CA 114; 121; INT 121

**Silver, Nicholas**
See Faust, Frederick (Schiller)

**Silverberg, Robert** 1935- ........... **CLC 7**
See also CA 1-4R; CAAS 3; CANR 1, 20,
36; DAM POP; DLB 8; INT CANR-20;
MAICYA; MTCW; SATA 13

**Silverstein, Alvin** 1933- ........... **CLC 17**
See also CA 49-52; CANR 2; CLR 25;
JRDA; MAICYA; SATA 8, 69

**Silverstein, Virginia B(arbara Opshelor)**
1937- ...................... **CLC 17**
See also CA 49-52; CANR 2; CLR 25;
JRDA; MAICYA; SATA 8, 69

**Sim, Georges**
See Simenon, Georges (Jacques Christian)

**Simak, Clifford D(onald)**
1904-1988 ................. **CLC 1, 55**
See also CA 1-4R; 125; CANR 1, 35;
DLB 8; MTCW; SATA-Obit 56

**Simenon, Georges (Jacques Christian)**
1903-1989 ...... **CLC 1, 2, 3, 8, 18, 47**
See also CA 85-88; 129; CANR 35;
DAM POP; DLB 72; DLBY 89; MTCW

**Simic, Charles** 1938-... **CLC 6, 9, 22, 49, 68**
See also CA 29-32R; CAAS 4; CANR 12,
33; DAM POET; DLB 105

**Simmons, Charles (Paul)** 1924-..... **CLC 57**
See also CA 89-92; INT 89-92

**Simmons, Dan** 1948-.............. **CLC 44**
See also AAYA 16; CA 138; DAM POP

**Simmons, James (Stewart Alexander)**
1933- ....................... **CLC 43**
See also CA 105; CAAS 21; DLB 40

**Simms, William Gilmore**
1806-1870 .................. **NCLC 3**
See also DLB 3, 30, 59, 73

**Simon, Carly** 1945-.............. **CLC 26**
See also CA 105

**Simon, Claude** 1913-...... **CLC 4, 9, 15, 39**
See also CA 89-92; CANR 33; DAM NOV;
DLB 83; MTCW

**Simon, (Marvin) Neil**
1927- ........... **CLC 6, 11, 31, 39, 70**
See also AITN 1; CA 21-24R; CANR 26;
DAM DRAM; DLB 7; MTCW

**Simon, Paul** 1942(?)- .............. **CLC 17**
See also CA 116

**Simonon, Paul** 1956(?)- ........... **CLC 30**

**Simpson, Harriette**
See Arnow, Harriette (Louisa) Simpson

**Simpson, Louis (Aston Marantz)**
1923- ................. **CLC 4, 7, 9, 32**
See also CA 1-4R; CAAS 4; CANR 1;
DAM POET; DLB 5; MTCW

**Simpson, Mona (Elizabeth)** 1957-... **CLC 44**
See also CA 122; 135

**Simpson, N(orman) F(rederick)**
1919- ....................... **CLC 29**
See also CA 13-16R; DLB 13

**Sinclair, Andrew (Annandale)**
1935- ...................... **CLC 2, 14**
See also CA 9-12R; CAAS 5; CANR 14, 38;
DLB 14; MTCW

**Sinclair, Emil**
See Hesse, Hermann

**Sinclair, Iain** 1943-.............. **CLC 76**
See also CA 132

**Sinclair, Iain MacGregor**
See Sinclair, Iain

**Sinclair, Mary Amelia St. Clair** 1865(?)-1946
See Sinclair, May
See also CA 104

**Sinclair, May**.................. **TCLC 3, 11**
See also Sinclair, Mary Amelia St. Clair
See also DLB 36, 135

**Sinclair, Upton (Beall)**
1878-1968 ...... **CLC 1, 11, 15, 63; DA;
DAB; DAC; WLC**
See also CA 5-8R; 25-28R; CANR 7;
CDALB 1929-1941; DAM MST, NOV;
DLB 9; INT CANR-7; MTCW; SATA 9

**Singer, Isaac**
See Singer, Isaac Bashevis

**Singer, Isaac Bashevis**
1904-1991 .... **CLC 1, 3, 6, 9, 11, 15, 23,
38, 69; DA; DAB; DAC; SSC 3; WLC**
See also AITN 1, 2; CA 1-4R; 134;
CANR 1, 39; CDALB 1941-1968; CLR 1;
DAM MST, NOV; DLB 6, 28, 52;
DLBY 91; JRDA; MAICYA; MTCW;
SATA 3, 27; SATA-Obit 68

**Singer, Israel Joshua** 1893-1944... **TCLC 33**

**Singh, Khushwant** 1915-........... **CLC 11**
See also CA 9-12R; CAAS 9; CANR 6

**Sinjohn, John**
See Galsworthy, John

**Sinyavsky, Andrei (Donatevich)**
1925- ...................... **CLC 8**
See also CA 85-88

**Sirin, V.**
See Nabokov, Vladimir (Vladimirovich)

**Sissman, L(ouis) E(dward)**
1928-1976 ................. **CLC 9, 18**
See also CA 21-24R; 65-68; CANR 13;
DLB 5

**Sisson, C(harles) H(ubert)** 1914-..... **CLC 8**
See also CA 1-4R; CAAS 3; CANR 3, 48;
DLB 27

**Sitwell, Dame Edith**
1887-1964 ........ **CLC 2, 9, 67; PC 3**
See also CA 9-12R; CANR 35;
CDBLB 1945-1960; DAM POET;
DLB 20; MTCW

**Sjoewall, Maj** 1935-.............. **CLC 7**
See also CA 65-68

**Sjowall, Maj**
See Sjoewall, Maj

**Skelton, Robin** 1925-............. **CLC 13**
See also AITN 2; CA 5-8R; CAAS 5;
CANR 28; DLB 27, 53

**Skolimowski, Jerzy** 1938- ......... **CLC 20**
See also CA 128

**Skram, Amalie (Bertha)**
1847-1905 ................... **TCLC 25**

**Skvorecky, Josef (Vaclav)**
1924- ........... **CLC 15, 39, 69; DAC**
See also CA 61-64; CAAS 1; CANR 10, 34;
DAM NOV; MTCW

**Slade, Bernard**................. **CLC 11, 46**
See also Newbound, Bernard Slade
See also CAAS 9; DLB 53

**Slaughter, Carolyn** 1946-.......... **CLC 56**
See also CA 85-88

**Slaughter, Frank G(ill)** 1908- ...... **CLC 29**
See also AITN 2; CA 5-8R; CANR 5;
INT CANR-5

**Slavitt, David R(ytman)** 1935-.... **CLC 5, 14**
See also CA 21-24R; CAAS 3; CANR 41;
DLB 5, 6

**Slesinger, Tess** 1905-1945 ........ **TCLC 10**
See also CA 107; DLB 102

**Slessor, Kenneth** 1901-1971........ **CLC 14**
See also CA 102; 89-92

**Slowacki, Juliusz** 1809-1849 ..... **NCLC 15**

**Smart, Christopher**
1722-1771 ............... **LC 3; PC 13**
See also DAM POET; DLB 109

**Smart, Elizabeth** 1913-1986........ **CLC 54**
See also CA 81-84; 118; DLB 88

**Smiley, Jane (Graves)** 1949- .... **CLC 53, 76**
See also CA 104; CANR 30, 50;
DAM POP; INT CANR-30

**Smith, A(rthur) J(ames) M(arshall)**
1902-1980 .............**CLC 15; DAC**
See also CA 1-4R; 102; CANR 4; DLB 88

**Smith, Anna Deavere** 1950-........ **CLC 86**
See also CA 133

**Smith, Betty (Wehner)** 1896-1972... **CLC 19**
See also CA 5-8R; 33-36R; DLBY 82;
SATA 6

Smith, Charlotte (Turner)
1749-1806 ................ NCLC 23
See also DLB 39, 109

Smith, Clark Ashton   1893-1961 .... CLC 43
See also CA 143

Smith, Dave .................. CLC 22, 42
See also Smith, David (Jeddie)
See also CAAS 7; DLB 5

Smith, David (Jeddie)   1942-
See Smith, Dave
See also CA 49-52; CANR 1; DAM POET

Smith, Florence Margaret   1902-1971
See Smith, Stevie
See also CA 17-18; 29-32R; CANR 35;
CAP 2; DAM POET; MTCW

Smith, Iain Crichton   1928- ........ CLC 64
See also CA 21-24R; DLB 40, 139

Smith, John   1580(?)-1631 .......... LC 9

Smith, Johnston
See Crane, Stephen (Townley)

Smith, Joseph, Jr.   1805-1844 .... NCLC 53

Smith, Lee   1944- ............. CLC 25, 73
See also CA 114; 119; CANR 46; DLB 143;
DLBY 83; INT 119

Smith, Martin
See Smith, Martin Cruz

Smith, Martin Cruz   1942- ........ CLC 25
See also BEST 89:4; CA 85-88; CANR 6,
23, 43; DAM MULT, POP;
INT CANR-23; NNAL

Smith, Mary-Ann Tirone   1944- ..... CLC 39
See also CA 118; 136

Smith, Patti   1946- ............. CLC 12
See also CA 93-96

Smith, Pauline (Urmson)
1882-1959 ................. TCLC 25

Smith, Rosamond
See Oates, Joyce Carol

Smith, Sheila Kaye
See Kaye-Smith, Sheila

Smith, Stevie ....... CLC 3, 8, 25, 44; PC 12
See also Smith, Florence Margaret
See also DLB 20

Smith, Wilbur (Addison)   1933- ..... CLC 33
See also CA 13-16R; CANR 7, 46; MTCW

Smith, William Jay   1918- .......... CLC 6
See also CA 5-8R; CANR 44; DLB 5;
MAICYA; SAAS 22; SATA 2, 68

Smith, Woodrow Wilson
See Kuttner, Henry

Smolenskin, Peretz   1842-1885 .... NCLC 30

Smollett, Tobias (George)   1721-1771 .. LC 2
See also CDBLB 1660-1789; DLB 39, 104

Snodgrass, W(illiam) D(e Witt)
1926- ............. CLC 2, 6, 10, 18, 68
See also CA 1-4R; CANR 6, 36;
DAM POET; DLB 5; MTCW

Snow, C(harles) P(ercy)
1905-1980 ....... CLC 1, 4, 6, 9, 13, 19
See also CA 5-8R; 101; CANR 28;
CDBLB 1945-1960; DAM NOV; DLB 15,
77; MTCW

Snow, Frances Compton
See Adams, Henry (Brooks)

Snyder, Gary (Sherman)
1930- ............. CLC 1, 2, 5, 9, 32
See also CA 17-20R; CANR 30;
DAM POET; DLB 5, 16

Snyder, Zilpha Keatley   1927- ...... CLC 17
See also AAYA 15; CA 9-12R; CANR 38;
CLR 31; JRDA; MAICYA; SAAS 2;
SATA 1, 28, 75

Soares, Bernardo
See Pessoa, Fernando (Antonio Nogueira)

Sobh, A.
See Shamlu, Ahmad

Sobol, Joshua ................... CLC 60

Soderberg, Hjalmar   1869-1941 .... TCLC 39

Sodergran, Edith (Irene)
See Soedergran, Edith (Irene)

Soedergran, Edith (Irene)
1892-1923 ................. TCLC 31

Softly, Edgar
See Lovecraft, H(oward) P(hillips)

Softly, Edward
See Lovecraft, H(oward) P(hillips)

Sokolov, Raymond   1941- .......... CLC 7
See also CA 85-88

Solo, Jay
See Ellison, Harlan (Jay)

Sologub, Fyodor ................. TCLC 9
See also Teternikov, Fyodor Kuzmich

Solomons, Ikey Esquir
See Thackeray, William Makepeace

Solomos, Dionysios   1798-1857 ... NCLC 15

Solwoska, Mara
See French, Marilyn

Solzhenitsyn, Aleksandr I(sayevich)
1918- ...... CLC 1, 2, 4, 7, 9, 10, 18, 26,
34, 78; DA; DAB; DAC; WLC
See also AITN 1; CA 69-72; CANR 40;
DAM MST, NOV; MTCW

Somers, Jane
See Lessing, Doris (May)

Somerville, Edith   1858-1949 ...... TCLC 51
See also DLB 135

Somerville & Ross
See Martin, Violet Florence; Somerville,
Edith

Sommer, Scott   1951- ............. CLC 25
See also CA 106

Sondheim, Stephen (Joshua)
1930- ................... CLC 30, 39
See also AAYA 11; CA 103; CANR 47;
DAM DRAM

Sontag, Susan   1933- ... CLC 1, 2, 10, 13, 31
See also CA 17-20R; CANR 25, 51;
DAM POP; DLB 2, 67; MTCW

Sophocles
496(?)B.C.-406(?)B.C. .... CMLC 2; DA;
DAB; DAC; DC 1
See also DAM DRAM, MST

Sordello   1189-1269 ............ CMLC 15

Sorel, Julia
See Drexler, Rosalyn

Sorrentino, Gilbert
1929- ............ CLC 3, 7, 14, 22, 40
See also CA 77-80; CANR 14, 33; DLB 5;
DLBY 80; INT CANR-14

Soto, Gary   1952- ........ CLC 32, 80; HLC
See also AAYA 10; CA 119; 125;
CANR 50; CLR 38; DAM MULT;
DLB 82; HW; INT 125; JRDA; SATA 80

Soupault, Philippe   1897-1990 ...... CLC 68
See also CA 116; 147; 131

Souster, (Holmes) Raymond
1921- ................ CLC 5, 14; DAC
See also CA 13-16R; CAAS 14; CANR 13,
29; DAM POET; DLB 88; SATA 63

Southern, Terry   1924(?)-1995 ....... CLC 7
See also CA 1-4R; 150; CANR 1; DLB 2

Southey, Robert   1774-1843 ....... NCLC 8
See also DLB 93, 107, 142; SATA 54

Southworth, Emma Dorothy Eliza Nevitte
1819-1899 ................ NCLC 26

Souza, Ernest
See Scott, Evelyn

Soyinka, Wole
1934- ....... CLC 3, 5, 14, 36, 44; BLC;
DA; DAB; DAC; DC 2; WLC
See also BW 2; CA 13-16R; CANR 27, 39;
DAM DRAM, MST, MULT; DLB 125;
MTCW

Spackman, W(illiam) M(ode)
1905-1990 .................. CLC 46
See also CA 81-84; 132

Spacks, Barry   1931- .............. CLC 14
See also CA 29-32R; CANR 33; DLB 105

Spanidou, Irini   1946- .............. CLC 44

Spark, Muriel (Sarah)
1918- ........ CLC 2, 3, 5, 8, 13, 18, 40;
DAB; DAC; SSC 10
See also CA 5-8R; CANR 12, 36;
CDBLB 1945-1960; DAM MST, NOV;
DLB 15, 139; INT CANR-12; MTCW

Spaulding, Douglas
See Bradbury, Ray (Douglas)

Spaulding, Leonard
See Bradbury, Ray (Douglas)

Spence, J. A. D.
See Eliot, T(homas) S(tearns)

Spencer, Elizabeth   1921- .......... CLC 22
See also CA 13-16R; CANR 32; DLB 6;
MTCW; SATA 14

Spencer, Leonard G.
See Silverberg, Robert

Spencer, Scott   1945- .............. CLC 30
See also CA 113; CANR 51; DLBY 86

Spender, Stephen (Harold)
1909-1995 ...... CLC 1, 2, 5, 10, 41, 91
See also CA 9-12R; 149; CANR 31;
CDBLB 1945-1960; DAM POET;
DLB 20; MTCW

Spengler, Oswald (Arnold Gottfried)
1880-1936 ................. TCLC 25
See also CA 118

**Spenser, Edmund**
1552(?)-1599 .... **LC 5; DA; DAB; DAC;**
**PC 8; WLC**
See also CDBLB Before 1660; DAM MST,
POET

**Spicer, Jack** 1925-1965 ...... **CLC 8, 18, 72**
See also CA 85-88; DAM POET; DLB 5, 16

**Spiegelman, Art** 1948- ............ **CLC 76**
See also AAYA 10; CA 125; CANR 41

**Spielberg, Peter** 1929- .............. **CLC 6**
See also CA 5-8R; CANR 4, 48; DLBY 81

**Spielberg, Steven** 1947- ........... **CLC 20**
See also AAYA 8; CA 77-80; CANR 32;
SATA 32

**Spillane, Frank Morrison** 1918-
See Spillane, Mickey
See also CA 25-28R; CANR 28; MTCW;
SATA 66

**Spillane, Mickey** ................ **CLC 3, 13**
See also Spillane, Frank Morrison

**Spinoza, Benedictus de** 1632-1677 .... **LC 9**

**Spinrad, Norman (Richard)** 1940-... **CLC 46**
See also CA 37-40R; CAAS 19; CANR 20;
DLB 8; INT CANR-20

**Spitteler, Carl (Friedrich Georg)**
1845-1924 .................. **TCLC 12**
See also CA 109; DLB 129

**Spivack, Kathleen (Romola Drucker)**
1938- ....................... **CLC 6**
See also CA 49-52

**Spoto, Donald** 1941- .............. **CLC 39**
See also CA 65-68; CANR 11

**Springsteen, Bruce (F.)** 1949- ...... **CLC 17**
See also CA 111

**Spurling, Hilary** 1940- ............ **CLC 34**
See also CA 104; CANR 25

**Spyker, John Howland**
See Elman, Richard

**Squires, (James) Radcliffe**
1917-1993 .................. **CLC 51**
See also CA 1-4R; 140; CANR 6, 21

**Srivastava, Dhanpat Rai** 1880(?)-1936
See Premchand
See also CA 118

**Stacy, Donald**
See Pohl, Frederik

**Stael, Germaine de**
See Stael-Holstein, Anne Louise Germaine
Necker Baronn
See also DLB 119

**Stael-Holstein, Anne Louise Germaine Necker**
**Baronn** 1766-1817 ......... **NCLC 3**
See also Stael, Germaine de

**Stafford, Jean** 1915-1979 ... **CLC 4, 7, 19, 68**
See also CA 1-4R; 85-88; CANR 3; DLB 2;
MTCW; SATA-Obit 22

**Stafford, William (Edgar)**
1914-1993 .............. **CLC 4, 7, 29**
See also CA 5-8R; 142; CAAS 3; CANR 5,
22; DAM POET; DLB 5; INT CANR-22

**Staines, Trevor**
See Brunner, John (Kilian Houston)

**Stairs, Gordon**
See Austin, Mary (Hunter)

**Stannard, Martin** 1947- ........... **CLC 44**
See also CA 142; DLB 155

**Stanton, Maura** 1946- ............. **CLC 9**
See also CA 89-92; CANR 15; DLB 120

**Stanton, Schuyler**
See Baum, L(yman) Frank

**Stapledon, (William) Olaf**
1886-1950 ................. **TCLC 22**
See also CA 111; DLB 15

**Starbuck, George (Edwin)** 1931-.... **CLC 53**
See also CA 21-24R; CANR 23;
DAM POET

**Stark, Richard**
See Westlake, Donald E(dwin)

**Staunton, Schuyler**
See Baum, L(yman) Frank

**Stead, Christina (Ellen)**
1902-1983 ........ **CLC 2, 5, 8, 32, 80**
See also CA 13-16R; 109; CANR 33, 40;
MTCW

**Stead, William Thomas**
1849-1912 ................. **TCLC 48**

**Steele, Richard** 1672-1729 .......... **LC 18**
See also CDBLB 1660-1789; DLB 84, 101

**Steele, Timothy (Reid)** 1948-....... **CLC 45**
See also CA 93-96; CANR 16, 50; DLB 120

**Steffens, (Joseph) Lincoln**
1866-1936 ................. **TCLC 20**
See also CA 117

**Stegner, Wallace (Earle)**
1909-1993 ............. **CLC 9, 49, 81**
See also AITN 1; BEST 90:3; CA 1-4R;
141; CAAS 9; CANR 1, 21, 46;
DAM NOV; DLB 9; DLBY 93; MTCW

**Stein, Gertrude**
1874-1946 ...... **TCLC 1, 6, 28, 48; DA;**
**DAB; DAC; WLC**
See also CA 104; 132; CDALB 1917-1929;
DAM MST, NOV, POET; DLB 4, 54, 86;
MTCW

**Steinbeck, John (Ernst)**
1902-1968 ...... **CLC 1, 5, 9, 13, 21, 34,**
**45, 75; DA; DAB; DAC; SSC 11; WLC**
See also AAYA 12; CA 1-4R; 25-28R;
CANR 1, 35; CDALB 1929-1941;
DAM DRAM, MST, NOV; DLB 7, 9;
DLBD 2; MTCW; SATA 9

**Steinem, Gloria** 1934-............. **CLC 63**
See also CA 53-56; CANR 28, 51; MTCW

**Steiner, George** 1929-............. **CLC 24**
See also CA 73-76; CANR 31; DAM NOV;
DLB 67; MTCW; SATA 62

**Steiner, K. Leslie**
See Delany, Samuel R(ay, Jr.)

**Steiner, Rudolf** 1861-1925 ....... **TCLC 13**
See also CA 107

**Stendhal**
1783-1842 .... **NCLC 23, 46; DA; DAB;**
**DAC; WLC**
See also DAM MST, NOV; DLB 119

**Stephen, Leslie** 1832-1904 ....... **TCLC 23**
See also CA 123; DLB 57, 144

**Stephen, Sir Leslie**
See Stephen, Leslie

**Stephen, Virginia**
See Woolf, (Adeline) Virginia

**Stephens, James** 1882(?)-1950 ...... **TCLC 4**
See also CA 104; DLB 19, 153, 162

**Stephens, Reed**
See Donaldson, Stephen R.

**Steptoe, Lydia**
See Barnes, Djuna

**Sterchi, Beat** 1949-............... **CLC 65**

**Sterling, Brett**
See Bradbury, Ray (Douglas); Hamilton,
Edmond

**Sterling, Bruce** 1954-............. **CLC 72**
See also CA 119; CANR 44

**Sterling, George** 1869-1926 ....... **TCLC 20**
See also CA 117; DLB 54

**Stern, Gerald** 1925- .............. **CLC 40**
See also CA 81-84; CANR 28; DLB 105

**Stern, Richard (Gustave)** 1928-... **CLC 4, 39**
See also CA 1-4R; CANR 1, 25; DLBY 87;
INT CANR-25

**Sternberg, Josef von** 1894-1969..... **CLC 20**
See also CA 81-84

**Sterne, Laurence**
1713-1768 ...... **LC 2; DA; DAB; DAC;**
**WLC**
See also CDBLB 1660-1789; DAM MST,
NOV; DLB 39

**Sternheim, (William Adolf) Carl**
1878-1942 .................. **TCLC 8**
See also CA 105; DLB 56, 118

**Stevens, Mark** 1951- ............. **CLC 34**
See also CA 122

**Stevens, Wallace**
1879-1955 ........ **TCLC 3, 12, 45; DA;**
**DAB; DAC; PC 6; WLC**
See also CA 104; 124; CDALB 1929-1941;
DAM MST, POET; DLB 54; MTCW

**Stevenson, Anne (Katharine)**
1933- .................... **CLC 7, 33**
See also CA 17-20R; CAAS 9; CANR 9, 33;
DLB 40; MTCW

**Stevenson, Robert Louis (Balfour)**
1850-1894 ..... **NCLC 5, 14; DA; DAB;**
**DAC; SSC 11; WLC**
See also CDBLB 1890-1914; CLR 10, 11;
DAM MST, NOV; DLB 18, 57, 141, 156;
DLBD 13; JRDA; MAICYA; YABC 2

**Stewart, J(ohn) I(nnes) M(ackintosh)**
1906-1994 .............. **CLC 7, 14, 32**
See also CA 85-88; 147; CAAS 3;
CANR 47; MTCW

**Stewart, Mary (Florence Elinor)**
1916- ............... **CLC 7, 35; DAB**
See also CA 1-4R; CANR 1; SATA 12

**Stewart, Mary Rainbow**
See Stewart, Mary (Florence Elinor)

**Stifle, June**
See Campbell, Maria

**Stifter, Adalbert** 1805-1868 ...... **NCLC 41**
See also DLB 133

**Still, James** 1906-................ **CLC 49**
See also CA 65-68; CAAS 17; CANR 10,
26; DLB 9; SATA 29

**Swarthout, Glendon (Fred)**
1918-1992 . . . . . . . . . . . . . . . . . . CLC 35
See also CA 1-4R; 139; CANR 1, 47;
SATA 26

**Sweet, Sarah C.**
See Jewett, (Theodora) Sarah Orne

**Swenson, May**
1919-1989 . . . . CLC 4, 14, 61; DA; DAB;
DAC; PC 14
See also CA 5-8R; 130; CANR 36;
DAM MST, POET; DLB 5; MTCW;
SATA 15

**Swift, Augustus**
See Lovecraft, H(oward) P(hillips)

**Swift, Graham (Colin)** 1949- . . . . CLC 41, 88
See also CA 117; 122; CANR 46

**Swift, Jonathan**
1667-1745 . . . . . . LC 1; DA; DAB; DAC;
PC 9; WLC
See also CDBLB 1660-1789; DAM MST,
NOV, POET; DLB 39, 95, 101; SATA 19

**Swinburne, Algernon Charles**
1837-1909 . . . . . . TCLC 8, 36; DA; DAB;
DAC; WLC
See also CA 105; 140; CDBLB 1832-1890;
DAM MST, POET; DLB 35, 57

**Swinfen, Ann** . . . . . . . . . . . . . . . . . . . . CLC 34

**Swinnerton, Frank Arthur**
1884-1982 . . . . . . . . . . . . . . . . . . . . CLC 31
See also CA 108; DLB 34

**Swithen, John**
See King, Stephen (Edwin)

**Sylvia**
See Ashton-Warner, Sylvia (Constance)

**Symmes, Robert Edward**
See Duncan, Robert (Edward)

**Symonds, John Addington**
1840-1893 . . . . . . . . . . . . . . . . . NCLC 34
See also DLB 57, 144

**Symons, Arthur** 1865-1945 . . . . . . . TCLC 11
See also CA 107; DLB 19, 57, 149

**Symons, Julian (Gustave)**
1912-1994 . . . . . . . . . . . . . . CLC 2, 14, 32
See also CA 49-52; 147; CAAS 3; CANR 3,
33; DLB 87, 155; DLBY 92; MTCW

**Synge, (Edmund) J(ohn) M(illington)**
1871-1909 . . . . . . . . . TCLC 6, 37; DC 2
See also CA 104; 141; CDBLB 1890-1914;
DAM DRAM; DLB 10, 19

**Syruc, J.**
See Milosz, Czeslaw

**Szirtes, George** 1948- . . . . . . . . . . . . CLC 46
See also CA 109; CANR 27

**Tabori, George** 1914- . . . . . . . . . . . . CLC 19
See also CA 49-52; CANR 4

**Tagore, Rabindranath**
1861-1941 . . . . . . . . . TCLC 3, 53; PC 8
See also CA 104; 120; DAM DRAM,
POET; MTCW

**Taine, Hippolyte Adolphe**
1828-1893 . . . . . . . . . . . . . . . . . NCLC 15

**Talese, Gay** 1932- . . . . . . . . . . . . . . . CLC 37
See also AITN 1; CA 1-4R; CANR 9;
INT CANR-9; MTCW

**Tallent, Elizabeth (Ann)** 1954- . . . . . CLC 45
See also CA 117; DLB 130

**Tally, Ted** 1952- . . . . . . . . . . . . . . . . CLC 42
See also CA 120; 124; INT 124

**Tamayo y Baus, Manuel**
1829-1898 . . . . . . . . . . . . . . . . . NCLC 1

**Tammsaare, A(nton) H(ansen)**
1878-1940 . . . . . . . . . . . . . . . . . TCLC 27

**Tan, Amy** 1952- . . . . . . . . . . . . . . . . CLC 59
See also AAYA 9; BEST 89:3; CA 136;
DAM MULT, NOV, POP; SATA 75

**Tandem, Felix**
See Spitteler, Carl (Friedrich Georg)

**Tanizaki, Jun'ichiro**
1886-1965 . . . . . . CLC 8, 14, 28; SSC 21
See also CA 93-96; 25-28R

**Tanner, William**
See Amis, Kingsley (William)

**Tao Lao**
See Storni, Alfonsina

**Tarassoff, Lev**
See Troyat, Henri

**Tarbell, Ida M(inerva)**
1857-1944 . . . . . . . . . . . . . . . . . TCLC 40
See also CA 122; DLB 47

**Tarkington, (Newton) Booth**
1869-1946 . . . . . . . . . . . . . . . . . TCLC 9
See also CA 110; 143; DLB 9, 102;
SATA 17

**Tarkovsky, Andrei (Arsenyevich)**
1932-1986 . . . . . . . . . . . . . . . . . CLC 75
See also CA 127

**Tartt, Donna** 1964(?)- . . . . . . . . . . . . CLC 76
See also CA 142

**Tasso, Torquato** 1544-1595 . . . . . . . . . . LC 5

**Tate, (John Orley) Allen**
1899-1979 . . . . CLC 2, 4, 6, 9, 11, 14, 24
See also CA 5-8R; 85-88; CANR 32;
DLB 4, 45, 63; MTCW

**Tate, Ellalice**
See Hibbert, Eleanor Alice Burford

**Tate, James (Vincent)** 1943- . . . CLC 2, 6, 25
See also CA 21-24R; CANR 29; DLB 5

**Tavel, Ronald** 1940- . . . . . . . . . . . . . . CLC 6
See also CA 21-24R; CANR 33

**Taylor, C(ecil) P(hilip)** 1929-1981 . . . CLC 27
See also CA 25-28R; 105; CANR 47

**Taylor, Edward**
1642(?)-1729 . . . LC 11; DA; DAB; DAC
See also DAM MST, POET; DLB 24

**Taylor, Eleanor Ross** 1920- . . . . . . . . CLC 5
See also CA 81-84

**Taylor, Elizabeth** 1912-1975 . . . CLC 2, 4, 29
See also CA 13-16R; CANR 9; DLB 139;
MTCW; SATA 13

**Taylor, Henry (Splawn)** 1942- . . . . . . CLC 44
See also CA 33-36R; CAAS 7; CANR 31;
DLB 5

**Taylor, Kamala (Purnaiya)** 1924-
See Markandaya, Kamala
See also CA 77-80

**Taylor, Mildred D.** . . . . . . . . . . . . . . . CLC 21
See also AAYA 10; BW 1; CA 85-88;
CANR 25; CLR 9; DLB 52; JRDA;
MAICYA; SAAS 5; SATA 15, 70

**Taylor, Peter (Hillsman)**
1917-1994 . . . . . CLC 1, 4, 18, 37, 44, 50,
71; SSC 10
See also CA 13-16R; 147; CANR 9, 50;
DLBY 81, 94; INT CANR-9; MTCW

**Taylor, Robert Lewis** 1912- . . . . . . . . CLC 14
See also CA 1-4R; CANR 3; SATA 10

**Tchekhov, Anton**
See Chekhov, Anton (Pavlovich)

**Teasdale, Sara** 1884-1933 . . . . . . . . . . TCLC 4
See also CA 104; DLB 45; SATA 32

**Tegner, Esaias** 1782-1846 . . . . . . . . . NCLC 2

**Teilhard de Chardin, (Marie Joseph) Pierre**
1881-1955 . . . . . . . . . . . . . . . . . TCLC 9
See also CA 105

**Temple, Ann**
See Mortimer, Penelope (Ruth)

**Tennant, Emma (Christina)**
1937- . . . . . . . . . . . . . . . . . . . CLC 13, 52
See also CA 65-68; CAAS 9; CANR 10, 38;
DLB 14

**Tenneshaw, S. M.**
See Silverberg, Robert

**Tennyson, Alfred**
1809-1892 . . . . . . . NCLC 30; DA; DAB;
DAC; PC 6; WLC
See also CDBLB 1832-1890; DAM MST,
POET; DLB 32

**Teran, Lisa St. Aubin de** . . . . . . . . . . CLC 36
See also St. Aubin de Teran, Lisa

**Terence** 195(?)B.C.-159B.C. . . . . . . CMLC 14

**Teresa de Jesus, St.** 1515-1582 . . . . . . LC 18

**Terkel, Louis** 1912-
See Terkel, Studs
See also CA 57-60; CANR 18, 45; MTCW

**Terkel, Studs** . . . . . . . . . . . . . . . . . . . . CLC 38
See also Terkel, Louis
See also AITN 1

**Terry, C. V.**
See Slaughter, Frank G(ill)

**Terry, Megan** 1932- . . . . . . . . . . . . . . CLC 19
See also CA 77-80; CABS 3; CANR 43;
DLB 7

**Tertz, Abram**
See Sinyavsky, Andrei (Donatevich)

**Tesich, Steve** 1943(?)- . . . . . . . . . . CLC 40, 69
See also CA 105; DLBY 83

**Teternikov, Fyodor Kuzmich** 1863-1927
See Sologub, Fyodor
See also CA 104

**Tevis, Walter** 1928-1984 . . . . . . . . . . CLC 42
See also CA 113

**Tey, Josephine** . . . . . . . . . . . . . . . . . . TCLC 14
See also Mackintosh, Elizabeth
See also DLB 77

**Thackeray, William Makepeace**
1811-1863 . . . . NCLC 5, 14, 22, 43; DA;
DAB; DAC; WLC
See also CDBLB 1832-1890; DAM MST,
NOV; DLB 21, 55, 159, 163; SATA 23

Thakura, Ravindranatha
  See Tagore, Rabindranath

Tharoor, Shashi 1956- ........... CLC 70
  See also CA 141

Thelwell, Michael Miles 1939- ..... CLC 22
  See also BW 2; CA 101

Theobald, Lewis, Jr.
  See Lovecraft, H(oward) P(hillips)

Theodorescu, Ion N. 1880-1967
  See Arghezi, Tudor
  See also CA 116

Theriault, Yves 1915-1983.... CLC 79; DAC
  See also CA 102; DAM MST; DLB 88

Theroux, Alexander (Louis)
  1939- ..................... CLC 2, 25
  See also CA 85-88; CANR 20

Theroux, Paul (Edward)
  1941- ........ CLC 5, 8, 11, 15, 28, 46
  See also BEST 89:4; CA 33-36R; CANR 20,
    45; DAM POP; DLB 2; MTCW;
    SATA 44

Thesen, Sharon 1946-............. CLC 56

Thevenin, Denis
  See Duhamel, Georges

Thibault, Jacques Anatole Francois
  1844-1924
  See France, Anatole
  See also CA 106; 127; DAM NOV; MTCW

Thiele, Colin (Milton) 1920- ....... CLC 17
  See also CA 29-32R; CANR 12, 28;
    CLR 27; MAICYA; SAAS 2; SATA 14,
    72

Thomas, Audrey (Callahan)
  1935- .......... CLC 7, 13, 37; SSC 20
  See also AITN 2; CA 21-24R; CAAS 19;
    CANR 36; DLB 60; MTCW

Thomas, D(onald) M(ichael)
  1935- ................. CLC 13, 22, 31
  See also CA 61-64; CAAS 11; CANR 17,
    45; CDBLB 1960 to Present; DLB 40;
    INT CANR-17; MTCW

Thomas, Dylan (Marlais)
  1914-1953 ... TCLC 1, 8, 45; DA; DAB;
               DAC; PC 2; SSC 3; WLC
  See also CA 104; 120; CDBLB 1945-1960;
    DAM DRAM, MST, POET; DLB 13, 20,
    139; MTCW; SATA 60

Thomas, (Philip) Edward
  1878-1917 .................. TCLC 10
  See also CA 106; DAM POET; DLB 19

Thomas, Joyce Carol 1938-........ CLC 35
  See also AAYA 12; BW 2; CA 113; 116;
    CANR 48; CLR 19; DLB 33; INT 116;
    JRDA; MAICYA; MTCW; SAAS 7;
    SATA 40, 78

Thomas, Lewis 1913-1993 ........ CLC 35
  See also CA 85-88; 143; CANR 38; MTCW

Thomas, Paul
  See Mann, (Paul) Thomas

Thomas, Piri 1928-............. CLC 17
  See also CA 73-76; HW

Thomas, R(onald) S(tuart)
  1913- ............ CLC 6, 13, 48; DAB
  See also CA 89-92; CAAS 4; CANR 30;
    CDBLB 1960 to Present; DAM POET;
    DLB 27; MTCW

Thomas, Ross (Elmore) 1926-1995 .. CLC 39
  See also CA 33-36R; 150; CANR 22

Thompson, Francis Clegg
  See Mencken, H(enry) L(ouis)

Thompson, Francis Joseph
  1859-1907 .................. TCLC 4
  See also CA 104; CDBLB 1890-1914;
    DLB 19

Thompson, Hunter S(tockton)
  1939- ................. CLC 9, 17, 40
  See also BEST 89:1; CA 17-20R; CANR 23,
    46; DAM POP; MTCW

Thompson, James Myers
  See Thompson, Jim (Myers)

Thompson, Jim (Myers)
  1906-1977(?) ................ CLC 69
  See also CA 140

Thompson, Judith ................ CLC 39

Thomson, James 1700-1748...... LC 16, 29
  See also DAM POET; DLB 95

Thomson, James 1834-1882...... NCLC 18
  See also DAM POET; DLB 35

Thoreau, Henry David
  1817-1862 ..... NCLC 7, 21; DA; DAB;
                                DAC; WLC
  See also CDALB 1640-1865; DAM MST;
    DLB 1

Thornton, Hall
  See Silverberg, Robert

Thucydides c. 455B.C.-399B.C.... CMLC 17

Thurber, James (Grover)
  1894-1961 .... CLC 5, 11, 25; DA; DAB;
                            DAC; SSC 1
  See also CA 73-76; CANR 17, 39;
    CDALB 1929-1941; DAM DRAM, MST,
    NOV; DLB 4, 11, 22, 102; MAICYA;
    MTCW; SATA 13

Thurman, Wallace (Henry)
  1902-1934 .............. TCLC 6; BLC
  See also BW 1; CA 104; 124; DAM MULT;
    DLB 51

Ticheburn, Cheviot
  See Ainsworth, William Harrison

Tieck, (Johann) Ludwig
  1773-1853 .............. NCLC 5, 46
  See also DLB 90

Tiger, Derry
  See Ellison, Harlan (Jay)

Tilghman, Christopher 1948(?)-..... CLC 65

Tillinghast, Richard (Williford)
  1940- ..................... CLC 29
  See also CA 29-32R; CAAS 23; CANR 26,
    51

Timrod, Henry 1828-1867 ....... NCLC 25
  See also DLB 3

Tindall, Gillian 1938-.............. CLC 7
  See also CA 21-24R; CANR 11

Tiptree, James, Jr. ............. CLC 48, 50
  See also Sheldon, Alice Hastings Bradley
  See also DLB 8

Titmarsh, Michael Angelo
  See Thackeray, William Makepeace

Tocqueville, Alexis (Charles Henri Maurice
  Clerel Comte) 1805-1859..... NCLC 7

Tolkien, J(ohn) R(onald) R(euel)
  1892-1973 ....... CLC 1, 2, 3, 8, 12, 38;
                            DA; DAB; DAC; WLC
  See also AAYA 10; AITN 1; CA 17-18;
    45-48; CANR 36; CAP 2;
    CDBLB 1914-1945; DAM MST, NOV,
    POP; DLB 15, 160; JRDA; MAICYA;
    MTCW; SATA 2, 32; SATA-Obit 24

Toller, Ernst 1893-1939......... TCLC 10
  See also CA 107; DLB 124

Tolson, M. B.
  See Tolson, Melvin B(eaunorus)

Tolson, Melvin B(eaunorus)
  1898(?)-1966 ........... CLC 36; BLC
  See also BW 1; CA 124; 89-92;
    DAM MULT, POET; DLB 48, 76

Tolstoi, Aleksei Nikolaevich
  See Tolstoy, Alexey Nikolaevich

Tolstoy, Alexey Nikolaevich
  1882-1945 ................ TCLC 18
  See also CA 107

Tolstoy, Count Leo
  See Tolstoy, Leo (Nikolaevich)

Tolstoy, Leo (Nikolaevich)
  1828-1910 ...... TCLC 4, 11, 17, 28, 44;
               DA; DAB; DAC; SSC 9; WLC
  See also CA 104; 123; DAM MST, NOV;
    SATA 26

Tomasi di Lampedusa, Giuseppe 1896-1957
  See Lampedusa, Giuseppe (Tomasi) di
  See also CA 111

Tomlin, Lily..................... CLC 17
  See also Tomlin, Mary Jean

Tomlin, Mary Jean 1939(?)-
  See Tomlin, Lily
  See also CA 117

Tomlinson, (Alfred) Charles
  1927- .......... CLC 2, 4, 6, 13, 45
  See also CA 5-8R; CANR 33; DAM POET;
    DLB 40

Tonson, Jacob
  See Bennett, (Enoch) Arnold

Toole, John Kennedy
  1937-1969 ............... CLC 19, 64
  See also CA 104; DLBY 81

Toomer, Jean
  1894-1967 ...... CLC 1, 4, 13, 22; BLC;
                            PC 7; SSC 1
  See also BW 1; CA 85-88;
    CDALB 1917-1929; DAM MULT;
    DLB 45, 51; MTCW

Torley, Luke
  See Blish, James (Benjamin)

Tornimparte, Alessandra
  See Ginzburg, Natalia

Torre, Raoul della
  See Mencken, H(enry) L(ouis)

Torrey, E(dwin) Fuller 1937-....... CLC 34
  See also CA 119

Torsvan, Ben Traven
  See Traven, B.

Torsvan, Benno Traven
  See Traven, B.

Torsvan, Berick Traven
  See Traven, B.

**Torsvan, Berwick Traven**
See Traven, B.

**Torsvan, Bruno Traven**
See Traven, B.

**Torsvan, Traven**
See Traven, B.

**Tournier, Michel (Edouard)**
1924- ................ CLC 6, 23, 36
See also CA 49-52; CANR 3, 36; DLB 83;
MTCW; SATA 23

**Tournimparte, Alessandra**
See Ginzburg, Natalia

**Towers, Ivar**
See Kornbluth, C(yril) M.

**Towne, Robert (Burton)**  1936(?)-.... CLC 87
See also CA 108; DLB 44

**Townsend, Sue**  1946-.. CLC 61; DAB; DAC
See also CA 119; 127; INT 127; MTCW;
SATA 55; SATA-Brief 48

**Townshend, Peter (Dennis Blandford)**
1945- .................... CLC 17, 42
See also CA 107

**Tozzi, Federigo**  1883-1920....... TCLC 31

**Traill, Catharine Parr**
1802-1899 ................. NCLC 31
See also DLB 99

**Trakl, Georg**  1887-1914........... TCLC 5
See also CA 104

**Transtroemer, Tomas (Goesta)**
1931- ................... CLC 52, 65
See also CA 117; 129; CAAS 17;
DAM POET

**Transtromer, Tomas Gosta**
See Transtroemer, Tomas (Goesta)

**Traven, B.**  (?)-1969............. CLC 8, 11
See also CA 19-20; 25-28R; CAP 2; DLB 9,
56; MTCW

**Treitel, Jonathan**  1959- ........... CLC 70

**Tremain, Rose**  1943-.............. CLC 42
See also CA 97-100; CANR 44; DLB 14

**Tremblay, Michel**  1942-...... CLC 29; DAC
See also CA 116; 128; DAM MST; DLB 60;
MTCW

**Trevanian**....................... CLC 29
See also Whitaker, Rod(ney)

**Trevor, Glen**
See Hilton, James

**Trevor, William**
1928- ..... CLC 7, 9, 14, 25, 71; SSC 21
See also Cox, William Trevor
See also DLB 14, 139

**Trifonov, Yuri (Valentinovich)**
1925-1981 ................... CLC 45
See also CA 126; 103; MTCW

**Trilling, Lionel**  1905-1975.... CLC 9, 11, 24
See also CA 9-12R; 61-64; CANR 10;
DLB 28, 63; INT CANR-10; MTCW

**Trimball, W. H.**
See Mencken, H(enry) L(ouis)

**Tristan**
See Gomez de la Serna, Ramon

**Tristram**
See Housman, A(lfred) E(dward)

**Trogdon, William (Lewis)**  1939-
See Heat-Moon, William Least
See also CA 115; 119; CANR 47; INT 119

**Trollope, Anthony**
1815-1882 ..... NCLC 6, 33; DA; DAB;
DAC; WLC
See also CDBLB 1832-1890; DAM MST,
NOV; DLB 21, 57, 159; SATA 22

**Trollope, Frances**  1779-1863 ..... NCLC 30
See also DLB 21

**Trotsky, Leon**  1879-1940........ TCLC 22
See also CA 118

**Trotter (Cockburn), Catharine**
1679-1749 .................... LC 8
See also DLB 84

**Trout, Kilgore**
See Farmer, Philip Jose

**Trow, George W. S.**  1943-........ CLC 52
See also CA 126

**Troyat, Henri**  1911-............. CLC 23
See also CA 45-48; CANR 2, 33; MTCW

**Trudeau, G(arretson) B(eekman)**  1948-
See Trudeau, Garry B.
See also CA 81-84; CANR 31; SATA 35

**Trudeau, Garry B.**.................. CLC 12
See also Trudeau, G(arretson) B(eekman)
See also AAYA 10; AITN 2

**Truffaut, Francois**  1932-1984....... CLC 20
See also CA 81-84; 113; CANR 34

**Trumbo, Dalton**  1905-1976 ....... CLC 19
See also CA 21-24R; 69-72; CANR 10;
DLB 26

**Trumbull, John**  1750-1831....... NCLC 30
See also DLB 31

**Trundlett, Helen B.**
See Eliot, T(homas) S(tearns)

**Tryon, Thomas**  1926-1991 ....... CLC 3, 11
See also AITN 1; CA 29-32R; 135;
CANR 32; DAM POP; MTCW

**Tryon, Tom**
See Tryon, Thomas

**Ts'ao Hsueh-ch'in**  1715(?)-1763....... LC 1

**Tsushima, Shuji**  1909-1948
See Dazai, Osamu
See also CA 107

**Tsvetaeva (Efron), Marina (Ivanovna)**
1892-1941 ........ TCLC 7, 35; PC 14
See also CA 104; 128; MTCW

**Tuck, Lily**  1938-................. CLC 70
See also CA 139

**Tu Fu**  712-770.................... PC 9
See also DAM MULT

**Tunis, John R(oberts)**  1889-1975 ... CLC 12
See also CA 61-64; DLB 22; JRDA;
MAICYA; SATA 37; SATA-Brief 30

**Tuohy, Frank**.................... CLC 37
See also Tuohy, John Francis
See also DLB 14, 139

**Tuohy, John Francis**  1925-
See Tuohy, Frank
See also CA 5-8R; CANR 3, 47

**Turco, Lewis (Putnam)**  1934- ... CLC 11, 63
See also CA 13-16R; CAAS 22; CANR 24,
51; DLBY 84

**Turgenev, Ivan**
1818-1883 ....... NCLC 21; DA; DAB;
DAC; SSC 7; WLC
See also DAM MST, NOV

**Turgot, Anne-Robert-Jacques**
1727-1781 .................... LC 26

**Turner, Frederick**  1943-........... CLC 48
See also CA 73-76; CAAS 10; CANR 12,
30; DLB 40

**Tutu, Desmond M(pilo)**
1931- .................. CLC 80; BLC
See also BW 1; CA 125; DAM MULT

**Tutuola, Amos**  1920- ... CLC 5, 14, 29; BLC
See also BW 2; CA 9-12R; CANR 27;
DAM MULT; DLB 125; MTCW

**Twain, Mark**
..... TCLC 6, 12, 19, 36, 48, 59; SSC 6;
WLC
See also Clemens, Samuel Langhorne
See also DLB 11, 12, 23, 64, 74

**Tyler, Anne**
1941- ........ CLC 7, 11, 18, 28, 44, 59
See also BEST 89:1; CA 9-12R; CANR 11,
33; DAM NOV, POP; DLB 6, 143;
DLBY 82; MTCW; SATA 7

**Tyler, Royall**  1757-1826.......... NCLC 3
See also DLB 37

**Tynan, Katharine**  1861-1931 ....... TCLC 3
See also CA 104; DLB 153

**Tyutchev, Fyodor**  1803-1873..... NCLC 34

**Tzara, Tristan** .................... CLC 47
See also Rosenfeld, Samuel
See also DAM POET

**Uhry, Alfred**  1936-............... CLC 55
See also CA 127; 133; DAM DRAM, POP;
INT 133

**Ulf, Haerved**
See Strindberg, (Johan) August

**Ulf, Harved**
See Strindberg, (Johan) August

**Ulibarri, Sabine R(eyes)**  1919- ..... CLC 83
See also CA 131; DAM MULT; DLB 82;
HW

**Unamuno (y Jugo), Miguel de**
1864-1936 .... TCLC 2, 9; HLC; SSC 11
See also CA 104; 131; DAM MULT, NOV;
DLB 108; HW; MTCW

**Undercliffe, Errol**
See Campbell, (John) Ramsey

**Underwood, Miles**
See Glassco, John

**Undset, Sigrid**
1882-1949 ......... TCLC 3; DA; DAB;
DAC; WLC
See also CA 104; 129; DAM MST, NOV;
MTCW

**Ungaretti, Giuseppe**
1888-1970 .............. CLC 7, 11, 15
See also CA 19-20; 25-28R; CAP 2;
DLB 114

**Unger, Douglas**  1952-............. CLC 34
See also CA 130

**Unsworth, Barry (Forster)**  1930-.... CLC 76
See also CA 25-28R; CANR 30

Vine, Barbara .................... CLC 50
See also Rendell, Ruth (Barbara)
See also BEST 90:4

Vinge, Joan D(ennison) 1948- ...... CLC 30
See also CA 93-96; SATA 36

Violis, G.
See Simenon, Georges (Jacques Christian)

Visconti, Luchino 1906-1976 ....... CLC 16
See also CA 81-84; 65-68; CANR 39

Vittorini, Elio 1908-1966 ...... CLC 6, 9, 14
See also CA 133; 25-28R

Vizinczey, Stephen 1933- .......... CLC 40
See also CA 128; INT 128

Vliet, R(ussell) G(ordon)
1929-1984 ................... CLC 22
See also CA 37-40R; 112; CANR 18

Vogau, Boris Andreyevich 1894-1937(?)
See Pilnyak, Boris
See also CA 123

Vogel, Paula A(nne) 1951- ......... CLC 76
See also CA 108

Voight, Ellen Bryant 1943- ....... CLC 54
See also CA 69-72; CANR 11, 29; DLB 120

Voigt, Cynthia 1942- ............. CLC 30
See also AAYA 3; CA 106; CANR 18, 37,
40; CLR 13; INT CANR-18; JRDA;
MAICYA; SATA 48, 79; SATA-Brief 33

Voinovich, Vladimir (Nikolaevich)
1932- .................... CLC 10, 49
See also CA 81-84; CAAS 12; CANR 33;
MTCW

Vollmann, William T. 1959- ........ CLC 89
See also CA 134; DAM NOV, POP

Voloshinov, V. N.
See Bakhtin, Mikhail Mikhailovich

Voltaire
1694-1778 ..... LC 14; DA; DAB; DAC;
SSC 12; WLC
See also DAM DRAM, MST

von Daeniken, Erich 1935- ........ CLC 30
See also AITN 1; CA 37-40R; CANR 17,
44

von Daniken, Erich
See von Daeniken, Erich

von Heidenstam, (Carl Gustaf) Verner
See Heidenstam, (Carl Gustaf) Verner von

von Heyse, Paul (Johann Ludwig)
See Heyse, Paul (Johann Ludwig von)

von Hofmannsthal, Hugo
See Hofmannsthal, Hugo von

von Horvath, Odon
See Horvath, Oedoen von

von Horvath, Oedoen
See Horvath, Oedoen von

von Liliencron, (Friedrich Adolf Axel) Detlev
See Liliencron, (Friedrich Adolf Axel)
Detlev von

Vonnegut, Kurt, Jr.
1922- ...... CLC 1, 2, 3, 4, 5, 8, 12, 22,
40, 60; DA; DAB; DAC; SSC 8; WLC
See also AAYA 6; AITN 1; BEST 90:4;
CA 1-4R; CANR 1, 25, 49;
CDALB 1968-1988; DAM MST, NOV,
POP; DLB 2, 8, 152; DLBD 3; DLBY 80;
MTCW

Von Rachen, Kurt
See Hubbard, L(afayette) Ron(ald)

von Rezzori (d'Arezzo), Gregor
See Rezzori (d'Arezzo), Gregor von

von Sternberg, Josef
See Sternberg, Josef von

Vorster, Gordon 1924- ............ CLC 34
See also CA 133

Vosce, Trudie
See Ozick, Cynthia

Voznesensky, Andrei (Andreievich)
1933- .................. CLC 1, 15, 57
See also CA 89-92; CANR 37;
DAM POET; MTCW

Waddington, Miriam 1917- ........ CLC 28
See also CA 21-24R; CANR 12, 30;
DLB 68

Wagman, Fredrica 1937- .......... CLC 7
See also CA 97-100; INT 97-100

Wagner, Richard 1813-1883 ....... NCLC 9
See also DLB 129

Wagner-Martin, Linda 1936- ...... CLC 50

Wagoner, David (Russell)
1926- .................. CLC 3, 5, 15
See also CA 1-4R; CAAS 3; CANR 2;
DLB 5; SATA 14

Wah, Fred(erick James) 1939- ...... CLC 44
See also CA 107; 141; DLB 60

Wahloo, Per 1926-1975 ........... CLC 7
See also CA 61-64

Wahloo, Peter
See Wahloo, Per

Wain, John (Barrington)
1925-1994 .......... CLC 2, 11, 15, 46
See also CA 5-8R; 145; CAAS 4; CANR 23;
CDBLB 1960 to Present; DLB 15, 27,
139, 155; MTCW

Wajda, Andrzej 1926- ............ CLC 16
See also CA 102

Wakefield, Dan 1932- ............ CLC 7
See also CA 21-24R; CAAS 7

Wakoski, Diane
1937- ..... CLC 2, 4, 7, 9, 11, 40; PC 15
See also CA 13-16R; CAAS 1; CANR 9;
DAM POET; DLB 5; INT CANR-9

Wakoski-Sherbell, Diane
See Wakoski, Diane

Walcott, Derek (Alton)
1930- .... CLC 2, 4, 9, 14, 25, 42, 67, 76;
BLC; DAB; DAC
See also BW 2; CA 89-92; CANR 26, 47;
DAM MST, MULT, POET; DLB 117;
DLBY 81; MTCW

Waldman, Anne 1945- ............ CLC 7
See also CA 37-40R; CAAS 17; CANR 34;
DLB 16

Waldo, E. Hunter
See Sturgeon, Theodore (Hamilton)

Waldo, Edward Hamilton
See Sturgeon, Theodore (Hamilton)

Walker, Alice (Malsenior)
1944- ....... CLC 5, 6, 9, 19, 27, 46, 58;
BLC; DA; DAB; DAC; SSC 5
See also AAYA 3; BEST 89:4; BW 2;
CA 37-40R; CANR 9, 27, 49;
CDALB 1968-1988; DAM MST, MULT,
NOV, POET, POP; DLB 6, 33, 143;
INT CANR-27; MTCW; SATA 31

Walker, David Harry 1911-1992 .... CLC 14
See also CA 1-4R; 137; CANR 1; SATA 8;
SATA-Obit 71

Walker, Edward Joseph 1934-
See Walker, Ted
See also CA 21-24R; CANR 12, 28

Walker, George F.
1947- ......... CLC 44, 61; DAB; DAC
See also CA 103; CANR 21, 43;
DAM MST; DLB 60

Walker, Joseph A. 1935- .......... CLC 19
See also BW 1; CA 89-92; CANR 26;
DAM DRAM, MST; DLB 38

Walker, Margaret (Abigail)
1915- .................. CLC 1, 6; BLC
See also BW 2; CA 73-76; CANR 26;
DAM MULT; DLB 76, 152; MTCW

Walker, Ted ................... CLC 13
See also Walker, Edward Joseph
See also DLB 40

Wallace, David Foster 1962- ....... CLC 50
See also CA 132

Wallace, Dexter
See Masters, Edgar Lee

Wallace, (Richard Horatio) Edgar
1875-1932 ................. TCLC 57
See also CA 115; DLB 70

Wallace, Irving 1916-1990 ....... CLC 7, 13
See also AITN 1; CA 1-4R; 132; CAAS 1;
CANR 1, 27; DAM NOV, POP;
INT CANR-27; MTCW

Wallant, Edward Lewis
1926-1962 ................. CLC 5, 10
See also CA 1-4R; CANR 22; DLB 2, 28,
143; MTCW

Walley, Byron
See Card, Orson Scott

Walpole, Horace 1717-1797 ......... LC 2
See also DLB 39, 104

Walpole, Hugh (Seymour)
1884-1941 ................... TCLC 5
See also CA 104; DLB 34

Walser, Martin 1927- ............ CLC 27
See also CA 57-60; CANR 8, 46; DLB 75,
124

Walser, Robert
1878-1956 .......... TCLC 18; SSC 20
See also CA 118; DLB 66

Walsh, Jill Paton ................ CLC 35
See also Paton Walsh, Gillian
See also AAYA 11; CLR 2; DLB 161;
SAAS 3

Walter, Villiam Christian
See Andersen, Hans Christian

**Wambaugh, Joseph (Aloysius, Jr.)**
1937- .................... CLC 3, 18
See also AITN 1; BEST 89:3; CA 33-36R;
CANR 42; DAM NOV, POP; DLB 6;
DLBY 83; MTCW

**Ward, Arthur Henry Sarsfield** 1883-1959
See Rohmer, Sax
See also CA 108

**Ward, Douglas Turner** 1930- ....... CLC 19
See also BW 1; CA 81-84; CANR 27;
DLB 7, 38

**Ward, Mary Augusta**
See Ward, Mrs. Humphry

**Ward, Mrs. Humphry**
1851-1920 ................. TCLC 55
See also DLB 18

**Ward, Peter**
See Faust, Frederick (Schiller)

**Warhol, Andy** 1928(?)-1987....... CLC 20
See also AAYA 12; BEST 89:4; CA 89-92;
121; CANR 34

**Warner, Francis (Robert le Plastrier)**
1937- ...................... CLC 14
See also CA 53-56; CANR 11

**Warner, Marina** 1946-........... CLC 59
See also CA 65-68; CANR 21

**Warner, Rex (Ernest)** 1905-1986.... CLC 45
See also CA 89-92; 119; DLB 15

**Warner, Susan (Bogert)**
1819-1885 ............... NCLC 31
See also DLB 3, 42

**Warner, Sylvia (Constance) Ashton**
See Ashton-Warner, Sylvia (Constance)

**Warner, Sylvia Townsend**
1893-1978 ................. CLC 7, 19
See also CA 61-64; 77-80; CANR 16;
DLB 34, 139; MTCW

**Warren, Mercy Otis** 1728-1814... NCLC 13
See also DLB 31

**Warren, Robert Penn**
1905-1989 .... CLC 1, 4, 6, 8, 10, 13, 18,
**39, 53, 59; DA; DAB; DAC; SSC 4; WLC**
See also AITN 1; CA 13-16R; 129;
CANR 10, 47; CDALB 1968-1988;
DAM MST, NOV, POET; DLB 2, 48,
152; DLBY 80, 89; INT CANR-10;
MTCW; SATA 46; SATA-Obit 63

**Warshofsky, Isaac**
See Singer, Isaac Bashevis

**Warton, Thomas** 1728-1790........ LC 15
See also DAM POET; DLB 104, 109

**Waruk, Kona**
See Harris, (Theodore) Wilson

**Warung, Price** 1855-1911........ TCLC 45

**Warwick, Jarvis**
See Garner, Hugh

**Washington, Alex**
See Harris, Mark

**Washington, Booker T(aliaferro)**
1856-1915 ............. TCLC 10; BLC
See also BW 1; CA 114; 125; DAM MULT;
SATA 28

**Washington, George** 1732-1799...... LC 25
See also DLB 31

**Wassermann, (Karl) Jakob**
1873-1934 ................. TCLC 6
See also CA 104; DLB 66

**Wasserstein, Wendy**
1950- .......... CLC 32, 59, 90; DC 4
See also CA 121; 129; CABS 3;
DAM DRAM; INT 129

**Waterhouse, Keith (Spencer)**
1929- ...................... CLC 47
See also CA 5-8R; CANR 38; DLB 13, 15;
MTCW

**Waters, Frank (Joseph)**
1902-1995 ................. CLC 88
See also CA 5-8R; 149; CAAS 13; CANR 3,
18; DLBY 86

**Waters, Roger** 1944-.............. CLC 35

**Watkins, Frances Ellen**
See Harper, Frances Ellen Watkins

**Watkins, Gerrold**
See Malzberg, Barry N(athaniel)

**Watkins, Paul** 1964-.............. CLC 55
See also CA 132

**Watkins, Vernon Phillips**
1906-1967 ................... CLC 43
See also CA 9-10; 25-28R; CAP 1; DLB 20

**Watson, Irving S.**
See Mencken, H(enry) L(ouis)

**Watson, John H.**
See Farmer, Philip Jose

**Watson, Richard F.**
See Silverberg, Robert

**Waugh, Auberon (Alexander)** 1939- .. CLC 7
See also CA 45-48; CANR 6, 22; DLB 14

**Waugh, Evelyn (Arthur St. John)**
1903-1966 ...... CLC 1, 3, 8, 13, 19, 27,
**44; DA; DAB; DAC; WLC**
See also CA 85-88; 25-28R; CANR 22;
CDBLB 1914-1945; DAM MST, NOV,
POP; DLB 15, 162; MTCW

**Waugh, Harriet** 1944- ............. CLC 6
See also CA 85-88; CANR 22

**Ways, C. R.**
See Blount, Roy (Alton), Jr.

**Waystaff, Simon**
See Swift, Jonathan

**Webb, (Martha) Beatrice (Potter)**
1858-1943 ................. TCLC 22
See also Potter, Beatrice
See also CA 117

**Webb, Charles (Richard)** 1939-...... CLC 7
See also CA 25-28R

**Webb, James H(enry), Jr.** 1946-.... CLC 22
See also CA 81-84

**Webb, Mary (Gladys Meredith)**
1881-1927 ................. TCLC 24
See also CA 123; DLB 34

**Webb, Mrs. Sidney**
See Webb, (Martha) Beatrice (Potter)

**Webb, Phyllis** 1927-.............. CLC 18
See also CA 104; CANR 23; DLB 53

**Webb, Sidney (James)**
1859-1947 ................. TCLC 22
See also CA 117

**Webber, Andrew Lloyd............. CLC 21
See also Lloyd Webber, Andrew

**Weber, Lenora Mattingly**
1895-1971 ................... CLC 12
See also CA 19-20; 29-32R; CAP 1;
SATA 2; SATA-Obit 26

**Webster, John** 1579(?)-1634(?) ....... DC 2
See also CDBLB Before 1660; DA; DAB;
DAC; DAM DRAM, MST; DLB 58;
WLC

**Webster, Noah** 1758-1843 ....... NCLC 30

**Wedekind, (Benjamin) Frank(lin)**
1864-1918 ................. TCLC 7
See also CA 104; DAM DRAM; DLB 118

**Weidman, Jerome** 1913-............ CLC 7
See also AITN 2; CA 1-4R; CANR 1;
DLB 28

**Weil, Simone (Adolphine)**
1909-1943 ................. TCLC 23
See also CA 117

**Weinstein, Nathan**
See West, Nathanael

**Weinstein, Nathan von Wallenstein**
See West, Nathanael

**Weir, Peter (Lindsay)** 1944- ....... CLC 20
See also CA 113; 123

**Weiss, Peter (Ulrich)**
1916-1982 ........... CLC 3, 15, 51
See also CA 45-48; 106; CANR 3;
DAM DRAM; DLB 69, 124

**Weiss, Theodore (Russell)**
1916- ................... CLC 3, 8, 14
See also CA 9-12R; CAAS 2; CANR 46;
DLB 5

**Welch, (Maurice) Denton**
1915-1948 ................. TCLC 22
See also CA 121; 148

**Welch, James** 1940-......... CLC 6, 14, 52
See also CA 85-88; CANR 42;
DAM MULT, POP; NNAL

**Weldon, Fay**
1933- ......... CLC 6, 9, 11, 19, 36, 59
See also CA 21-24R; CANR 16, 46;
CDBLB 1960 to Present; DAM POP;
DLB 14; INT CANR-16; MTCW

**Wellek, Rene** 1903-1995........... CLC 28
See also CA 5-8R; 150; CAAS 7; CANR 8;
DLB 63; INT CANR-8

**Weller, Michael** 1942-......... CLC 10, 53
See also CA 85-88

**Weller, Paul** 1958-.............. CLC 26

**Wellershoff, Dieter** 1925-......... CLC 46
See also CA 89-92; CANR 16, 37

**Welles, (George) Orson**
1915-1985 ............. CLC 20, 80
See also CA 93-96; 117

**Wellman, Mac** 1945- ............. CLC 65

**Wellman, Manly Wade** 1903-1986 .. CLC 49
See also CA 1-4R; 118; CANR 6, 16, 44;
SATA 6; SATA-Obit 47

**Wells, Carolyn** 1869(?)-1942 ...... TCLC 35
See also CA 113; DLB 11

**Wells, H(erbert) G(eorge)**
1866-1946 . . . . . . . TCLC 6, 12, 19; DA;
DAB; DAC; SSC 6; WLC
See also CA 110; 121; CDBLB 1914-1945;
DAM MST, NOV; DLB 34, 70, 156;
MTCW; SATA 20

**Wells, Rosemary** 1943- . . . . . . . . . . CLC 12
See also AAYA 13; CA 85-88; CANR 48;
CLR 16; MAICYA; SAAS 1; SATA 18,
69

**Welty, Eudora**
1909- . . . . . . CLC 1, 2, 5, 14, 22, 33; DA;
DAB; DAC; SSC 1; WLC
See also CA 9-12R; CABS 1; CANR 32;
CDALB 1941-1968; DAM MST, NOV;
DLB 2, 102, 143; DLBD 12; DLBY 87;
MTCW

**Wen I-to** 1899-1946 . . . . . . . . . . . TCLC 28

**Wentworth, Robert**
See Hamilton, Edmond

**Werfel, Franz (V.)** 1890-1945 . . . . . . TCLC 8
See also CA 104; DLB 81, 124

**Wergeland, Henrik Arnold**
1808-1845 . . . . . . . . . . . . . . . . NCLC 5

**Wersba, Barbara** 1932- . . . . . . . . . . . CLC 30
See also AAYA 2; CA 29-32R; CANR 16,
38; CLR 3; DLB 52; JRDA; MAICYA;
SAAS 2; SATA 1, 58

**Wertmueller, Lina** 1928- . . . . . . . . . . CLC 16
See also CA 97-100; CANR 39

**Wescott, Glenway** 1901-1987. . . . . . . CLC 13
See also CA 13-16R; 121; CANR 23;
DLB 4, 9, 102

**Wesker, Arnold** 1932- . . CLC 3, 5, 42; DAB
See also CA 1-4R; CAAS 7; CANR 1, 33;
CDBLB 1960 to Present; DAM DRAM;
DLB 13; MTCW

**Wesley, Richard (Errol)** 1945- . . . . . . CLC 7
See also BW 1; CA 57-60; CANR 27;
DLB 38

**Wessel, Johan Herman** 1742-1785 . . . . LC 7

**West, Anthony (Panther)**
1914-1987 . . . . . . . . . . . . . . . . . CLC 50
See also CA 45-48; 124; CANR 3, 19;
DLB 15

**West, C. P.**
See Wodehouse, P(elham) G(renville)

**West, (Mary) Jessamyn**
1902-1984 . . . . . . . . . . . . . . . . CLC 7, 17
See also CA 9-12R; 112; CANR 27; DLB 6;
DLBY 84; MTCW; SATA-Obit 37

**West, Morris L(anglo)** 1916- . . . . . CLC 6, 33
See also CA 5-8R; CANR 24, 49; MTCW

**West, Nathanael**
1903-1940 . . . . . TCLC 1, 14, 44; SSC 16
See also CA 104; 125; CDALB 1929-1941;
DLB 4, 9, 28; MTCW

**West, Owen**
See Koontz, Dean R(ay)

**West, Paul** 1930- . . . . . . . . . . . . . CLC 7, 14
See also CA 13-16R; CAAS 7; CANR 22;
DLB 14; INT CANR-22

**West, Rebecca** 1892-1983 . . CLC 7, 9, 31, 50
See also CA 5-8R; 109; CANR 19; DLB 36;
DLBY 83; MTCW

**Westall, Robert (Atkinson)**
1929-1993 . . . . . . . . . . . . . . . . . . CLC 17
See also AAYA 12; CA 69-72; 141;
CANR 18; CLR 13; JRDA; MAICYA;
SAAS 2; SATA 23, 69; SATA-Obit 75

**Westlake, Donald E(dwin)**
1933- . . . . . . . . . . . . . . . . . . . CLC 7, 33
See also CA 17-20R; CAAS 13; CANR 16,
44; DAM POP; INT CANR-16

**Westmacott, Mary**
See Christie, Agatha (Mary Clarissa)

**Weston, Allen**
See Norton, Andre

**Wetcheek, J. L.**
See Feuchtwanger, Lion

**Wetering, Janwillem van de**
See van de Wetering, Janwillem

**Wetherell, Elizabeth**
See Warner, Susan (Bogert)

**Whale, James** 1889-1957 . . . . . . . . TCLC 63

**Whalen, Philip** 1923- . . . . . . . . . . . CLC 6, 29
See also CA 9-12R; CANR 5, 39; DLB 16

**Wharton, Edith (Newbold Jones)**
1862-1937 . . . . . . TCLC 3, 9, 27, 53; DA;
DAB; DAC; SSC 6; WLC
See also CA 104; 132; CDALB 1865-1917;
DAM MST, NOV; DLB 4, 9, 12, 78;
DLBD 13; MTCW

**Wharton, James**
See Mencken, H(enry) L(ouis)

**Wharton, William (a pseudonym)**
. . . . . . . . . . . . . . . . . . . . . . CLC 18, 37
See also CA 93-96; DLBY 80; INT 93-96

**Wheatley (Peters), Phillis**
1754(?)-1784 . . . . LC 3; BLC; DA; DAC;
PC 3; WLC
See also CDALB 1640-1865; DAM MST,
MULT, POET; DLB 31, 50

**Wheelock, John Hall** 1886-1978 . . . . CLC 14
See also CA 13-16R; 77-80; CANR 14;
DLB 45

**White, E(lwyn) B(rooks)**
1899-1985 . . . . . . . . . . . . CLC 10, 34, 39
See also AITN 2; CA 13-16R; 116;
CANR 16, 37; CLR 1, 21; DAM POP;
DLB 11, 22; MAICYA; MTCW;
SATA 2, 29; SATA-Obit 44

**White, Edmund (Valentine III)**
1940- . . . . . . . . . . . . . . . . . . . . CLC 27
See also AAYA 7; CA 45-48; CANR 3, 19,
36; DAM POP; MTCW

**White, Patrick (Victor Martindale)**
1912-1990 . . CLC 3, 4, 5, 7, 9, 18, 65, 69
See also CA 81-84; 132; CANR 43; MTCW

**White, Phyllis Dorothy James** 1920-
See James, P. D.
See also CA 21-24R; CANR 17, 43;
DAM POP; MTCW

**White, T(erence) H(anbury)**
1906-1964 . . . . . . . . . . . . . . . . . . CLC 30
See also CA 73-76; CANR 37; DLB 160;
JRDA; MAICYA; SATA 12

**White, Terence de Vere**
1912-1994 . . . . . . . . . . . . . . . . . . CLC 49
See also CA 49-52; 145; CANR 3

**White, Walter F(rancis)**
1893-1955 . . . . . . . . . . . . . . . . TCLC 15
See also White, Walter
See also BW 1; CA 115; 124; DLB 51

**White, William Hale** 1831-1913
See Rutherford, Mark
See also CA 121

**Whitehead, E(dward) A(nthony)**
1933- . . . . . . . . . . . . . . . . . . . . . CLC 5
See also CA 65-68

**Whitemore, Hugh (John)** 1936- . . . . . CLC 37
See also CA 132; INT 132

**Whitman, Sarah Helen (Power)**
1803-1878 . . . . . . . . . . . . . . . . NCLC 19
See also DLB 1

**Whitman, Walt(er)**
1819-1892 . . . . . NCLC 4, 31; DA; DAB;
DAC; PC 3; WLC
See also CDALB 1640-1865; DAM MST,
POET; DLB 3, 64; SATA 20

**Whitney, Phyllis A(yame)** 1903- . . . . CLC 42
See also AITN 2; BEST 90:3; CA 1-4R;
CANR 3, 25, 38; DAM POP; JRDA;
MAICYA; SATA 1, 30

**Whittemore, (Edward) Reed (Jr.)**
1919- . . . . . . . . . . . . . . . . . . . . . CLC 4
See also CA 9-12R; CAAS 8; CANR 4;
DLB 5

**Whittier, John Greenleaf**
1807-1892 . . . . . . . . . . . . . . . . . NCLC 8
See also CDALB 1640-1865; DAM POET;
DLB 1

**Whittlebot, Hernia**
See Coward, Noel (Peirce)

**Wicker, Thomas Grey** 1926-
See Wicker, Tom
See also CA 65-68; CANR 21, 46

**Wicker, Tom** . . . . . . . . . . . . . . . . . . CLC 7
See also Wicker, Thomas Grey

**Wideman, John Edgar**
1941- . . . . . . . . . CLC 5, 34, 36, 67; BLC
See also BW 2; CA 85-88; CANR 14, 42;
DAM MULT; DLB 33, 143

**Wiebe, Rudy (Henry)**
1934- . . . . . . . . . . . . . CLC 6, 11, 14; DAC
See also CA 37-40R; CANR 42;
DAM MST; DLB 60

**Wieland, Christoph Martin**
1733-1813 . . . . . . . . . . . . . . . . NCLC 17
See also DLB 97

**Wiene, Robert** 1881-1938. . . . . . . . TCLC 56

**Wieners, John** 1934- . . . . . . . . . . . . . CLC 7
See also CA 13-16R; DLB 16

**Wiesel, Elie(zer)**
1928- . . . . . . CLC 3, 5, 11, 37; DA; DAB;
DAC
See also AAYA 7; AITN 1; CA 5-8R;
CAAS 4; CANR 8, 40; DAM MST,
NOV; DLB 83; DLBY 87; INT CANR-8;
MTCW; SATA 56

**Wiggins, Marianne** 1947- . . . . . . . . . CLC 57
See also BEST 89:3; CA 130

**Wight, James Alfred** 1916-
See Herriot, James
See also CA 77-80; SATA 55;
SATA-Brief 44

Wilbur, Richard (Purdy)
1921- . . . CLC 3, 6, 9, 14, 53; DA; DAB;
DAC
See also CA 1-4R; CABS 2; CANR 2, 29;
DAM MST, POET; DLB 5;
INT CANR-29; MTCW; SATA 9

Wild, Peter 1940- . . . . . . . . . . . . . . . CLC 14
See also CA 37-40R; DLB 5

Wilde, Oscar (Fingal O'Flahertie Wills)
1854(?)-1900 . . . . TCLC 1, 8, 23, 41; DA;
DAB; DAC; SSC 11; WLC
See also CA 104; 119; CDBLB 1890-1914;
DAM DRAM, MST, NOV; DLB 10, 19,
34, 57, 141, 156; SATA 24

Wilder, Billy . . . . . . . . . . . . . . . . . . . . CLC 20
See also Wilder, Samuel
See also DLB 26

Wilder, Samuel 1906-
See Wilder, Billy
See also CA 89-92

Wilder, Thornton (Niven)
1897-1975 . . . . . . CLC 1, 5, 6, 10, 15, 35,
82; DA; DAB; DAC; DC 1; WLC
See also AITN 2; CA 13-16R; 61-64;
CANR 40; DAM DRAM, MST, NOV;
DLB 4, 7, 9; MTCW

Wilding, Michael 1942- . . . . . . . . . . . CLC 73
See also CA 104; CANR 24, 49

Wiley, Richard 1944- . . . . . . . . . . . . . CLC 44
See also CA 121; 129

Wilhelm, Kate . . . . . . . . . . . . . . . . . . . CLC 7
See also Wilhelm, Katie Gertrude
See also CAAS 5; DLB 8; INT CANR-17

Wilhelm, Katie Gertrude 1928-
See Wilhelm, Kate
See also CA 37-40R; CANR 17, 36; MTCW

Wilkins, Mary
See Freeman, Mary Eleanor Wilkins

Willard, Nancy 1936- . . . . . . . . . . . CLC 7, 37
See also CA 89-92; CANR 10, 39; CLR 5;
DLB 5, 52; MAICYA; MTCW;
SATA 37, 71; SATA-Brief 30

Williams, C(harles) K(enneth)
1936- . . . . . . . . . . . . . . . . . . . CLC 33, 56
See also CA 37-40R; DAM POET; DLB 5

Williams, Charles
See Collier, James L(incoln)

Williams, Charles (Walter Stansby)
1886-1945 . . . . . . . . . . . . . . . TCLC 1, 11
See also CA 104; DLB 100, 153

Williams, (George) Emlyn
1905-1987 . . . . . . . . . . . . . . . . . . CLC 15
See also CA 104; 123; CANR 36;
DAM DRAM; DLB 10, 77; MTCW

Williams, Hugo 1942- . . . . . . . . . . . . CLC 42
See also CA 17-20R; CANR 45; DLB 40

Williams, J. Walker
See Wodehouse, P(elham) G(renville)

Williams, John A(lfred)
1925- . . . . . . . . . . . . . . . CLC 5, 13; BLC
See also BW 2; CA 53-56; CAAS 3;
CANR 6, 26, 51; DAM MULT; DLB 2,
33; INT CANR-6

Williams, Jonathan (Chamberlain)
1929- . . . . . . . . . . . . . . . . . . . . . CLC 13
See also CA 9-12R; CAAS 12; CANR 8;
DLB 5

Williams, Joy 1944- . . . . . . . . . . . . . CLC 31
See also CA 41-44R; CANR 22, 48

Williams, Norman 1952- . . . . . . . . . . CLC 39
See also CA 118

Williams, Sherley Anne
1944- . . . . . . . . . . . . . . . . . CLC 89; BLC
See also BW 2; CA 73-76; CANR 25;
DAM MULT, POET; DLB 41;
INT CANR-25; SATA 78

Williams, Shirley
See Williams, Sherley Anne

Williams, Tennessee
1911-1983 . . . . . CLC 1, 2, 5, 7, 8, 11, 15,
19, 30, 39, 45, 71; DA; DAB; DAC;
DC 4; WLC
See also AITN 1, 2; CA 5-8R; 108;
CABS 3; CANR 31; CDALB 1941-1968;
DAM DRAM, MST; DLB 7; DLBD 4;
DLBY 83; MTCW

Williams, Thomas (Alonzo)
1926-1990 . . . . . . . . . . . . . . . . . . CLC 14
See also CA 1-4R; 132; CANR 2

Williams, William C.
See Williams, William Carlos

Williams, William Carlos
1883-1963 . . . . CLC 1, 2, 5, 9, 13, 22, 42,
67; DA; DAB; DAC; PC 7
See also CA 89-92; CANR 34;
CDALB 1917-1929; DAM MST, POET;
DLB 4, 16, 54, 86; MTCW

Williamson, David (Keith) 1942- . . . . CLC 56
See also CA 103; CANR 41

Williamson, Ellen Douglas 1905-1984
See Douglas, Ellen
See also CA 17-20R; 114; CANR 39

Williamson, Jack . . . . . . . . . . . . . . . . CLC 29
See also Williamson, John Stewart
See also CAAS 8; DLB 8

Williamson, John Stewart 1908-
See Williamson, Jack
See also CA 17-20R; CANR 23

Willie, Frederick
See Lovecraft, H(oward) P(hillips)

Willingham, Calder (Baynard, Jr.)
1922-1995 . . . . . . . . . . . . . . . . CLC 5, 51
See also CA 5-8R; 147; CANR 3; DLB 2,
44; MTCW

Willis, Charles
See Clarke, Arthur C(harles)

Willy
See Colette, (Sidonie-Gabrielle)

Willy, Colette
See Colette, (Sidonie-Gabrielle)

Wilson, A(ndrew) N(orman) 1950- . . CLC 33
See also CA 112; 122; DLB 14, 155

Wilson, Angus (Frank Johnstone)
1913-1991 . . CLC 2, 3, 5, 25, 34; SSC 21
See also CA 5-8R; 134; CANR 21; DLB 15,
139, 155; MTCW

Wilson, August
1945- . . . . . . . CLC 39, 50, 63; BLC; DA;
DAB; DAC; DC 2
See also AAYA 16; BW 2; CA 115; 122;
CANR 42; DAM DRAM, MST, MULT;
MTCW

Wilson, Brian 1942- . . . . . . . . . . . . . . CLC 12

Wilson, Colin 1931- . . . . . . . . . . . . CLC 3, 14
See also CA 1-4R; CAAS 5; CANR 1, 22,
33; DLB 14; MTCW

Wilson, Dirk
See Pohl, Frederik

Wilson, Edmund
1895-1972 . . . . . . . . . . CLC 1, 2, 3, 8, 24
See also CA 1-4R; 37-40R; CANR 1, 46;
DLB 63; MTCW

Wilson, Ethel Davis (Bryant)
1888(?)-1980 . . . . . . . . . . . . CLC 13; DAC
See also CA 102; DAM POET; DLB 68;
MTCW

Wilson, John 1785-1854 . . . . . . . . . NCLC 5

Wilson, John (Anthony) Burgess 1917-1993
See Burgess, Anthony
See also CA 1-4R; 143; CANR 2, 46; DAC;
DAM NOV; MTCW

Wilson, Lanford 1937- . . . . . . . CLC 7, 14, 36
See also CA 17-20R; CABS 3; CANR 45;
DAM DRAM; DLB 7

Wilson, Robert M. 1944- . . . . . . . . . CLC 7, 9
See also CA 49-52; CANR 2, 41; MTCW

Wilson, Robert McLiam 1964- . . . . . CLC 59
See also CA 132

Wilson, Sloan 1920- . . . . . . . . . . . . . CLC 32
See also CA 1-4R; CANR 1, 44

Wilson, Snoo 1948- . . . . . . . . . . . . . . CLC 33
See also CA 69-72

Wilson, William S(mith) 1932- . . . . . CLC 49
See also CA 81-84

Winchilsea, Anne (Kingsmill) Finch Counte
1661-1720 . . . . . . . . . . . . . . . . . . . . LC 3

Windham, Basil
See Wodehouse, P(elham) G(renville)

Wingrove, David (John) 1954- . . . . . . CLC 68
See also CA 133

Winters, Janet Lewis . . . . . . . . . . . . . CLC 41
See also Lewis, Janet
See also DLBY 87

Winters, (Arthur) Yvor
1900-1968 . . . . . . . . . . . . . . CLC 4, 8, 32
See also CA 11-12; 25-28R; CAP 1;
DLB 48; MTCW

Winterson, Jeanette 1959- . . . . . . . . . CLC 64
See also CA 136; DAM POP

Winthrop, John 1588-1649 . . . . . . . . . LC 31
See also DLB 24, 30

Wiseman, Frederick 1930- . . . . . . . . . CLC 20

Wister, Owen 1860-1938 . . . . . . . . . TCLC 21
See also CA 108; DLB 9, 78; SATA 62

Witkacy
See Witkiewicz, Stanislaw Ignacy

Witkiewicz, Stanislaw Ignacy
1885-1939 . . . . . . . . . . . . . . . . . . TCLC 8
See also CA 105

**Wittgenstein, Ludwig (Josef Johann)**
1889-1951 . . . . . . . . . . . . . . . . . . **TCLC 59**
See also CA 113

**Wittig, Monique** 1935(?)- . . . . . . . . . **CLC 22**
See also CA 116; 135; DLB 83

**Wittlin, Jozef** 1896-1976 . . . . . . . . . . **CLC 25**
See also CA 49-52; 65-68; CANR 3

**Wodehouse, P(elham) G(renville)**
1881-1975 . . . **CLC 1, 2, 5, 10, 22; DAB;**
**DAC; SSC 2**
See also AITN 2; CA 45-48; 57-60;
CANR 3, 33; CDBLB 1914-1945;
DAM NOV; DLB 34, 162; MTCW;
SATA 22

**Woiwode, L.**
See Woiwode, Larry (Alfred)

**Woiwode, Larry (Alfred)** 1941- . . . **CLC 6, 10**
See also CA 73-76; CANR 16; DLB 6;
INT CANR-16

**Wojciechowska, Maia (Teresa)**
1927- . . . . . . . . . . . . . . . . . . . . . . . **CLC 26**
See also AAYA 8; CA 9-12R; CANR 4, 41;
CLR 1; JRDA; MAICYA; SAAS 1;
SATA 1, 28, 83

**Wolf, Christa** 1929- . . . . . . . . **CLC 14, 29, 58**
See also CA 85-88; CANR 45; DLB 75;
MTCW

**Wolfe, Gene (Rodman)** 1931- . . . . . . . **CLC 25**
See also CA 57-60; CAAS 9; CANR 6, 32;
DAM POP; DLB 8

**Wolfe, George C.** 1954- . . . . . . . . . . . **CLC 49**
See also CA 149

**Wolfe, Thomas (Clayton)**
1900-1938 . . . . . **TCLC 4, 13, 29, 61; DA;**
**DAB; DAC; WLC**
See also CA 104; 132; CDALB 1929-1941;
DAM MST, NOV; DLB 9, 102; DLBD 2;
DLBY 85; MTCW

**Wolfe, Thomas Kennerly, Jr.** 1931-
See Wolfe, Tom
See also CA 13-16R; CANR 9, 33;
DAM POP; INT CANR-9; MTCW

**Wolfe, Tom** . . . . . . . . . **CLC 1, 2, 9, 15, 35, 51**
See also Wolfe, Thomas Kennerly, Jr.
See also AAYA 8; AITN 2; BEST 89:1;
DLB 152

**Wolff, Geoffrey (Ansell)** 1937- . . . . . **CLC 41**
See also CA 29-32R; CANR 29, 43

**Wolff, Sonia**
See Levitin, Sonia (Wolff)

**Wolff, Tobias (Jonathan Ansell)**
1945- . . . . . . . . . . . . . . . . . . . . . **CLC 39, 64**
See also AAYA 16; BEST 90:2; CA 114;
117; CAAS 22; DLB 130; INT 117

**Wolfram von Eschenbach**
c. 1170-c. 1220 . . . . . . . . . . . . . . **CMLC 5**
See also DLB 138

**Wolitzer, Hilma** 1930- . . . . . . . . . . . . **CLC 17**
See also CA 65-68; CANR 18, 40;
INT CANR-18; SATA 31

**Wollstonecraft, Mary** 1759-1797 . . . . . . **LC 5**
See also CDBLB 1789-1832; DLB 39, 104,
158

**Wonder, Stevie** . . . . . . . . . . . . . . . . . . **CLC 12**
See also Morris, Steveland Judkins

**Wong, Jade Snow** 1922- . . . . . . . . . . . **CLC 17**
See also CA 109

**Woodcott, Keith**
See Brunner, John (Kilian Houston)

**Woodruff, Robert W.**
See Mencken, H(enry) L(ouis)

**Woolf, (Adeline) Virginia**
1882-1941 . . . . . . **TCLC 1, 5, 20, 43, 56;**
**DA; DAB; DAC; SSC 7; WLC**
See also CA 104; 130; CDBLB 1914-1945;
DAM MST, NOV; DLB 36, 100, 162;
DLBD 10; MTCW

**Woollcott, Alexander (Humphreys)**
1887-1943 . . . . . . . . . . . . . . . . . . **TCLC 5**
See also CA 105; DLB 29

**Woolrich, Cornell** 1903-1968 . . . . . . **CLC 77**
See also Hopley-Woolrich, Cornell George

**Wordsworth, Dorothy**
1771-1855 . . . . . . . . . . . . . . . . . **NCLC 25**
See also DLB 107

**Wordsworth, William**
1770-1850 . . . . **NCLC 12, 38; DA; DAB;**
**DAC; PC 4; WLC**
See also CDBLB 1789-1832; DAM MST,
POET; DLB 93, 107

**Wouk, Herman** 1915- . . . . . . . . . **CLC 1, 9, 38**
See also CA 5-8R; CANR 6, 33;
DAM NOV, POP; DLBY 82;
INT CANR-6; MTCW

**Wright, Charles (Penzel, Jr.)**
1935- . . . . . . . . . . . . . . . . . **CLC 6, 13, 28**
See also CA 29-32R; CAAS 7; CANR 23,
36; DLBY 82; MTCW

**Wright, Charles Stevenson**
1932- . . . . . . . . . . . . . . . . **CLC 49; BLC 3**
See also BW 1; CA 9-12R; CANR 26;
DAM MULT, POET; DLB 33

**Wright, Jack R.**
See Harris, Mark

**Wright, James (Arlington)**
1927-1980 . . . . . . . . . . . . **CLC 3, 5, 10, 28**
See also AITN 2; CA 49-52; 97-100;
CANR 4, 34; DAM POET; DLB 5;
MTCW

**Wright, Judith (Arandell)**
1915- . . . . . . . . . . . . . **CLC 11, 53; PC 14**
See also CA 13-16R; CANR 31; MTCW;
SATA 14

**Wright, L(aurali) R.** 1939- . . . . . . . . **CLC 44**
See also CA 138

**Wright, Richard (Nathaniel)**
1908-1960 . . . . **CLC 1, 3, 4, 9, 14, 21, 48,**
**74; BLC; DA; DAB; DAC; SSC 2; WLC**
See also AAYA 5; BW 1; CA 108;
CDALB 1929-1941; DAM MST, MULT,
NOV; DLB 76, 102; DLBD 2; MTCW

**Wright, Richard B(ruce)** 1937- . . . . . . **CLC 6**
See also CA 85-88; DLB 53

**Wright, Rick** 1945- . . . . . . . . . . . . . . . **CLC 35**

**Wright, Rowland**
See Wells, Carolyn

**Wright, Stephen Caldwell** 1946- . . . . **CLC 33**
See also BW 2

**Wright, Willard Huntington** 1888-1939
See Van Dine, S. S.
See also CA 115

**Wright, William** 1930- . . . . . . . . . . . . **CLC 44**
See also CA 53-56; CANR 7, 23

**Wroth, LadyMary** 1587-1653(?) . . . . . **LC 30**
See also DLB 121

**Wu Ch'eng-en** 1500(?)-1582(?) . . . . . . . **LC 7**

**Wu Ching-tzu** 1701-1754 . . . . . . . . . . . **LC 2**

**Wurlitzer, Rudolph** 1938(?)- . . . **CLC 2, 4, 15**
See also CA 85-88

**Wycherley, William** 1641-1715 . . . . **LC 8, 21**
See also CDBLB 1660-1789; DAM DRAM;
DLB 80

**Wylie, Elinor (Morton Hoyt)**
1885-1928 . . . . . . . . . . . . . . . . . . **TCLC 8**
See also CA 105; DLB 9, 45

**Wylie, Philip (Gordon)** 1902-1971 . . . **CLC 43**
See also CA 21-22; 33-36R; CAP 2; DLB 9

**Wyndham, John** . . . . . . . . . . . . . . . . . . **CLC 19**
See also Harris, John (Wyndham Parkes
Lucas) Beynon

**Wyss, Johann David Von**
1743-1818 . . . . . . . . . . . . . . . . . **NCLC 10**
See also JRDA; MAICYA; SATA 29;
SATA-Brief 27

**Xenophon**
c. 430B.C.-c. 354B.C. . . . . . . . . **CMLC 17**

**Yakumo Koizumi**
See Hearn, (Patricio) Lafcadio (Tessima
Carlos)

**Yanez, Jose Donoso**
See Donoso (Yanez), Jose

**Yanovsky, Basile S.**
See Yanovsky, V(assily) S(emenovich)

**Yanovsky, V(assily) S(emenovich)**
1906-1989 . . . . . . . . . . . . . . . . . **CLC 2, 18**
See also CA 97-100; 129

**Yates, Richard** 1926-1992 . . . . . **CLC 7, 8, 23**
See also CA 5-8R; 139; CANR 10, 43;
DLB 2; DLBY 81, 92; INT CANR-10

**Yeats, W. B.**
See Yeats, William Butler

**Yeats, William Butler**
1865-1939 . . . . . **TCLC 1, 11, 18, 31; DA;**
**DAB; DAC; WLC**
See also CA 104; 127; CANR 45;
CDBLB 1890-1914; DAM DRAM, MST,
POET; DLB 10, 19, 98, 156; MTCW

**Yehoshua, A(braham) B.**
1936- . . . . . . . . . . . . . . . . . . . **CLC 13, 31**
See also CA 33-36R; CANR 43

**Yep, Laurence Michael** 1948- . . . . . . **CLC 35**
See also AAYA 5; CA 49-52; CANR 1, 46;
CLR 3, 17; DLB 52; JRDA; MAICYA;
SATA 7, 69

**Yerby, Frank G(arvin)**
1916-1991 . . . . . . . . . . **CLC 1, 7, 22; BLC**
See also BW 1; CA 9-12R; 136; CANR 16;
DAM MULT; DLB 76; INT CANR-16;
MTCW

**Yesenin, Sergei Alexandrovich**
See Esenin, Sergei (Alexandrovich)

**Yevtushenko, Yevgeny (Alexandrovich)**
1933- . . . . . . . . . . . . **CLC 1, 3, 13, 26, 51**
See also CA 81-84; CANR 33;
DAM POET; MTCW

Yezierska, Anzia 1885(?)-1970 ..... CLC 46
See also CA 126; 89-92; DLB 28; MTCW

Yglesias, Helen 1915-.......... CLC 7, 22
See also CA 37-40R; CAAS 20; CANR 15;
INT CANR-15; MTCW

Yokomitsu Riichi 1898-1947 ...... TCLC 47

Yonge, Charlotte (Mary)
1823-1901 ................. TCLC 48
See also CA 109; DLB 18, 163; SATA 17

York, Jeremy
See Creasey, John

York, Simon
See Heinlein, Robert A(nson)

Yorke, Henry Vincent 1905-1974 ... CLC 13
See also Green, Henry
See also CA 85-88; 49-52

Yosano Akiko 1878-1942 .. TCLC 59; PC 11

Yoshimoto, Banana ................ CLC 84
See also Yoshimoto, Mahoko

Yoshimoto, Mahoko 1964-
See Yoshimoto, Banana
See also CA 144

Young, Al(bert James)
1939- ................. CLC 19; BLC
See also BW 2; CA 29-32R; CANR 26;
DAM MULT; DLB 33

Young, Andrew (John) 1885-1971 .... CLC 5
See also CA 5-8R; CANR 7, 29

Young, Collier
See Bloch, Robert (Albert)

Young, Edward 1683-1765 ........... LC 3
See also DLB 95

Young, Marguerite (Vivian)
1909-1995 ................. CLC 82
See also CA 13-16; 150; CAP 1

Young, Neil 1945-................ CLC 17
See also CA 110

Yourcenar, Marguerite
1903-1987 .......... CLC 19, 38, 50, 87
See also CA 69-72; CANR 23; DAM NOV;
DLB 72; DLBY 88; MTCW

Yurick, Sol 1925-................. CLC 6
See also CA 13-16R; CANR 25

Zabolotskii, Nikolai Alekseevich
1903-1958 ................. TCLC 52
See also CA 116

Zamiatin, Yevgenii
See Zamyatin, Evgeny Ivanovich

Zamora, Bernice (B. Ortiz)
1938- ................. CLC 89; HLC
See also DAM MULT; DLB 82; HW

Zamyatin, Evgeny Ivanovich
1884-1937 ............... TCLC 8, 37
See also CA 105

Zangwill, Israel 1864-1926 ....... TCLC 16
See also CA 109; DLB 10, 135

Zappa, Francis Vincent, Jr. 1940-1993
See Zappa, Frank
See also CA 108; 143

Zappa, Frank .................... CLC 17
See also Zappa, Francis Vincent, Jr.

Zaturenska, Marya 1902-1982 .... CLC 6, 11
See also CA 13-16R; 105; CANR 22

Zelazny, Roger (Joseph)
1937-1995 .................. CLC 21
See also AAYA 7; CA 21-24R; 148;
CANR 26; DLB 8; MTCW; SATA 57;
SATA-Brief 39

Zhdanov, Andrei A(lexandrovich)
1896-1948 ................ TCLC 18
See also CA 117

Zhukovsky, Vasily 1783-1852 .... NCLC 35

Ziegenhagen, Eric ................ CLC 55

Zimmer, Jill Schary
See Robinson, Jill

Zimmerman, Robert
See Dylan, Bob

Zindel, Paul
1936- ..... CLC 6, 26; DA; DAB; DAC;
DC 5
See also AAYA 2; CA 73-76; CANR 31;
CLR 3; DAM DRAM, MST, NOV;
DLB 7, 52; JRDA; MAICYA; MTCW;
SATA 16, 58

Zinov'Ev, A. A.
See Zinoviev, Alexander (Aleksandrovich)

Zinoviev, Alexander (Aleksandrovich)
1922- ...................... CLC 19
See also CA 116; 133; CAAS 10

Zoilus
See Lovecraft, H(oward) P(hillips)

Zola, Emile (Edouard Charles Antoine)
1840-1902 ...... TCLC 1, 6, 21, 41; DA;
DAB; DAC; WLC
See also CA 104; 138; DAM MST, NOV;
DLB 123

Zoline, Pamela 1941-............. CLC 62

Zorrilla y Moral, Jose 1817-1893 .. NCLC 6

Zoshchenko, Mikhail (Mikhailovich)
1895-1958 .......... TCLC 15; SSC 15
See also CA 115

Zuckmayer, Carl 1896-1977........ CLC 18
See also CA 69-72; DLB 56, 124

Zuk, Georges
See Skelton, Robin

Zukofsky, Louis
1904-1978 ....... CLC 1, 2, 4, 7, 11, 18;
PC 11
See also CA 9-12R; 77-80; CANR 39;
DAM POET; DLB 5; MTCW

Zweig, Paul 1935-1984........ CLC 34, 42
See also CA 85-88; 113

Zweig, Stefan 1881-1942 ......... TCLC 17
See also CA 112; DLB 81, 118

# Literary Criticism Series
# Cumulative Topic Index

This index lists all topic entries in Gale's *Classical and Medieval Literature Criticism, Contemporary Literary Criticism, Literature Criticism from 1400 to 1800, Nineteenth-Century Literature Criticism,* and *Twentieth-Century Literary Criticism.*

**Topic Index**

# *CLC* Cumulative Nationality Index

Nationality Index

Nationality Index

Nationality Index

**Nationality Index**

# CLC-92 Title Index

ISBN 0-8103-9270-4

90000

9 780810 392700